DATE DUE

9-12-11			

Demco

The Wages of Destruction

ADAM TOOZE

The Wages of Destruction

The Making and Breaking of the Nazi Economy

VIKING

VIKING
Published by the Penguin Group
Penguin Group (USA) Inc., 375 Hudson Street,
New York, New York 10014, U.S.A.
Penguin Group (Canada), 90 Eglinton Avenue East, Suite 700,
Toronto, Ontario, Canada M4P 2Y3
(a division of Pearson Penguin Canada Inc.)
Penguin Books Ltd, 80 Strand, London WC2R 0RL, England
Penguin Ireland, 25 St. Stephen's Green, Dublin 2, Ireland
(a division of Penguin Books Ltd)
Penguin Books Australia Ltd, 250 Camberwell Road, Camberwell,
Victoria 3124, Australia
(a division of Pearson Australia Group Pty Ltd)
Penguin Books India Pvt Ltd, 11 Community Centre, Panchsheel Park,
New Delhi – 110 017, India
Penguin Group (NZ), 67 Apollo Drive, Mairangi Bay,
Auckland 1311, New Zealand
(a division of Pearson New Zealand Ltd)
Penguin Books (South Africa) (Pty) Ltd, 24 Sturdee Avenue,
Rosebank, Johannesburg 2196, South Africa

Penguin Books Ltd, Registered Offices:
80 Strand, London WC2R 0RL, England

First American edition
Published in 2007 by Viking Penguin,
a member of Penguin Group (USA) Inc.

1 3 5 7 9 10 8 6 4 2

Copyright © Adam Tooze, 2006
All rights reserved

ISBN 978-0-670-03826-8

Printed in the United States of America

This book is dedicated to my grandparents
Peggy and Arthur Wynn
with thanks for the example they have always provided

Contents

Part III World War

List of Figures

List of Illustrations

Photographic acknowledgements are given in parentheses.

List of Tables

Acknowledgements

I would not have written this book but for four people. In the spring of 2000 Richard Overy alerted me to the fact that Penguin needed somebody to take on this project. Simon Winder took the time to come to Cambridge for an early discussion. John Cornwell placed me in contact with Clare Alexander and read an early draft of the proposal. Clare finalized the terms of the deal. To all of them I owe a great debt. Though Richard in particular may not agree with all of this book's conclusions, I nevertheless hope that the delivery of the finished manuscript goes some way towards justifying the faith they placed in me.

Since 1996 barely a day has gone by in which I have not felt profoundly fortunate to work at the University of Cambridge and Jesus College. This is one of the places in the world at which the academic life is still a virtually unalloyed pleasure. I wish to thank the University, the University Librarians, my Faculty, the master and my colleagues in the fellowship at Jesus for providing such a truly wonderful place to work and granting me two periods of leave in which to concentrate on the writing of this book. Without the collegial give and take of Faculty and College life, so much less would be possible.

In 2002 I was extremely fortunate to receive a Leverhulme Prize for modern history. I am deeply grateful to the trustees for providing me with this support and all the benefits that it brought. It was Martin Daunton who put my name into the ring and I am thankful for this and in general for his enthusiastic and collegial support.

Quite unexpectedly, I spent a large part of the academic year 2004–5 at the University of Illinois, accompanying my wife who held a fellowship there. At a critical stage in the writing of this manuscript I must admit that the thought of such a move filled me with something close to dread. Thankfully, due to Becky's sterling organizational efforts these fears turned out to be completely unfounded. It is hard to think of an academic environment more conducive to relaxed productivity. I wish to thank the History Faculty of the University of Illinois and the extraordinary University Library for its hospitality. Peter Fritzsche, as chair of the Faculty, facilitated my stay and ensured that I had office space to work in. Marc Micale and Tamara Matheson kindly lent me their offices. For companionship and intellectual stimulation, I am grateful to Max Edelson and Mark Leff. Kathy Cebula provided invaluable editorial assistance. Most of all, however, I want to thank our incomparable friends Craig Koslofsky and Dana Rabin and their wonderful children Jonah and Evie, without whom our stay in Urbana would have been both emotionally and practically impossible.

Thanks to email, our long sojourn in the Midwest meant no interruption in an ongoing process of discussion with friends and colleagues in Britain, France and Germany. Over the last years, I have worked closely with Bernhard Fulda, who was the first person to read the entire manuscript and to provide me with invaluable encouragement and feedback. His support was crucial in sustaining the evolution of my ideas through 2003 and 2004. In early 2005 I was enormously fortunate to gain David Reynolds as a reader. It is not too much to say that David is the ideal reader – fast, efficient, hugely knowledgeable and constructively critical. His comments have shaped this book quite dramatically. Martin Ivanov (Academy of Science, Sofia) is the third colleague to have read the entire manuscript. I am extremely grateful for his perceptive criticism and immensely glad of the collaboration that has emerged between us over the last two years. I want also to thank Matt Inniss for taking time in his busy working life at Her Majesty's Treasury to read the manuscript and for giving me exciting glimpses of the world beyond academia.

Other friends and colleagues who have read substantial sections of the manuscript include Francesca Carnevali, Chris Clark, Deborah Cohen, Becky Conekin, Joe Maiolo, Ralf Richter, Cristiano Ristuccia, Jonas Scherner and Zara Steiner. I am hugely grateful to all of them.

One of the great pleasures of completing this project is the opportunity it has provided for dialogue with colleagues in Germany. For conversation, feedback and assistance in obtaining material from Germany I am immensely grateful to Ralf Banken, Knut Borchardt, Christoph Buchheim, Michael Ebi, Emanuel Heisenberg, Ulrich Hensler, Jan Otmar Hesse, Rolf-Dieter Mueller, Werner Plumpe, Alfred Reckendrees,

Albrecht Ritschl, Michael Schneider, Mark Spoerer, Sybille Steinbacher and Jochen Streb. Dozens of endnotes suggest the debt I owe to these researchers. Personal contact at conferences, by mail or by email has only increased my debt.

For assistance in obtaining absolutely priceless material from the Library of Congress in Washington, I wish particularly to thank Deborah Cohen.

Over the last five years elements of the argument of this book have been patiently listened to and argued over by seminar audiences in Cambridge, Coventry, Frankfurt, Manchester, Mannheim, Munich, Oxford, Paris, Philadelphia, Sofia and Urbana-Champaign. I am particularly grateful for comments from Theo Balderston, Jeffrey Fear, Peter Fritzsche, Mark Harrison, Craig Koslofsky, Alan Milward, Avner Offer, Dan Raff, Nick Stargardt and Jonathan Steinberg.

Like every historian of Germany I owe a huge debt to the staff of the various branches of the Bundesarchiv. I would also like to thank the staff of the Public Record Office in Kew and the Imperial War Museum, and most particularly Stephen Walton, a historian's archivist if there ever was one.

For hospitality during archival visits, I would like to thank my old friend Jakob Vogel and friends old and new in the colourful patchwork of the Brigitte Vogel–Martin Janotta household. Amongst other old Berlin friends, I am almost particularly grateful to Daniel Haeufler for providing me with a sudden and quite unexpected burst of publicity in the Aly–Tooze exchange in the review pages of the *TAZ*.

Simon Winder has proved an unfailingly supportive editor, providing encouragement at precisely the right moments. I, like so many of my colleagues, owe him a huge debt. I would like to thank him and all the other people at Penguin, notably Chloe Campbell, for smoothing the passage of this book. I would also like to extend heartfelt thanks to Elizabeth Stratford, my meticulous and admirably patient copy editor. In responding to Elizabeth's numerous queries and comments I had the invaluable assistance of Rosanna Sharkey, without whose help, both at the computer and at home, it would have been difficult to survive Michaelmas term 2005.

Life would be unthinkable without my wife, Becky Conekin. I am immensely grateful to her for sustaining me for what is now a very long time. My sense of adult self is too deeply rooted in our relationship and

ACKNOWLEDGEMENTS

day-to-day partnership for me to be able to think of a book, even a book as large and personally significant as this, as more than a part of a much larger whole of which she is the sustaining centre. For this I am deeply grateful and I am pleased that this book does not stand alone, but is framed by so many other things in our lives – Becky's first book and many other projects, our new home and, most of all, the upbringing of our daughter Edith Elizabeth, the light of both our lives. As a marvellously opinionated pre-schooler, Edie is healthily sceptical about all of her daddy's obsessions. One can only hope that her generation will be freer of this awful history than those born within a few short decades of 1945. I am, however, given to looking backwards and this book is dedicated to my maternal grandparents, Peggy Wynn and the late Arthur Wynn, two people who lived through virtually all of the twentieth century with an extraordinary degree of sustained and passionate engagement. Their generosity, their hospitality, their curiosity and their vigorous intellectual and practical activity have inspired me all my life. This dedication is a small token of the admiration and gratitude I feel towards them.

List of Frequently Used Abbreviations

AEG	Allgemeine Elektrizitaets Gesellschaft
BAL	Bundesarchiv Lichterfelde
BDM	Bund deutscher Maedel
Brabag	Braunkohlenbenzin AG
DAF	Deutsche Arbeitsfront (German Labour Front)
DKE	Deutsche Kleinempfaenger
DNVP	Deutschnationale Volkspartei (Nationalist party)
DP	displaced person
DVP	Deutsche Volkspartei (National-Liberal party)
GBA	Generalbevollmaechtigter fuer den Arbeitseinsatz
GM	General Motors
IMT	International Military Tribunal
KdF	Kraft durch Freude (Strength through Joy)
NSDAP	National sozialistische deutsche Arbeiterpartei
OKW	Oberkommando Wehrmacht
PPP	Purchasing Power Parity
RFM	Reichsfinanzministerium (Finance Ministry)
RKF	Reichskommissar fuer die Festigung deutschen Volkstums
RLM	Reichsluftfahrtministerium (Air Ministry)
RNS	Reichsnaehrstand
RSHA	Reichssicherheitshauptamt
RVE	Reichsvereinigung Eisen
RWE	Rheinisch-Westfaelische Elektrizitaetswerke
RWM	Reichswirtschaftsministerium (Ministry of Economic Affairs)
SA	Sturmabteilungen
SD	Sicherheitsdienst
VE	Volksempfaenger
Vestag	Vereinigte Stahlwerke

Preface

How was this possible? In 1938 the Third Reich embarked on Germany's second campaign of conquest and destruction in less than a generation. At first, Hitler's Wehrmacht seemed unstoppable, better prepared and more aggressive than the Kaiser's armies. But as Hitler charged from victory to victory, his enemies multiplied. For the second time, a German bid to dominate the continent of Europe ran up against overwhelming opposition. By December 1941 the Third Reich was at war not only with the British Empire and the Soviet Union but with the United States as well. It took three years and five months, but in the end Hitler went down to a defeat far more cataclysmic than that which felled the Kaiser. Germany, along with large swathes of the rest of Eastern and Western Europe, was left in ruins. Poland and the western Soviet Union were practically eviscerated. France and Italy lurched perilously close to civil war. The overseas empires of Britain, France and the Netherlands were shaken beyond repair. And as the world learned of the extraordinary genocide committed by the National Socialist regime, the superiority once confidently claimed for European civilization was thrown for ever into question. How was this possible?

People make their own history. In the last instance, human will – both individual and collective – must be the starting point for any account of Nazi Germany. If we are to understand the awful deeds of the Third Reich we must seek to understand their perpetrators. We must treat Adolf Hitler and his followers seriously. We must seek to penetrate their mindset and to map the dark interstices of their ideology. It is not for nothing that biography – both individual and collective – is one of the most illuminating ways to study the Third Reich. But if it is true that 'people make their own history', it is also true, as Karl Marx put it, that 'they do not make it just as they please; they do not make it under circumstances chosen by themselves, but under circumstances directly encountered, given and transmitted from the past'.[1]

What, then, are these circumstances? Somewhat surprisingly for those who think of him as a simplistic economic determinist, Marx followed up his famous aphorism, not with a disquisition on the mode of production, but with a paragraph about the way in which 'the tradition of all the dead generations weighs like a nightmare on the brain of the living'. Historical actors, 'just when they seem engaged in revolutionizing themselves and things, anxiously conjure up the spirits of the past . . . and borrow from them names, battle cries and costumes' that allow the 'new scene of world history' to be dressed up in 'time-honoured disguise'. Hitler and his cronies certainly inhabited such a self-fashioned world. And it is with good reason therefore that recent writing on the Third Reich has been preoccupied with politics and ideology. The cultural crises of early twentieth-century Europe, the vacuum left by the secularizing tendencies of the late nineteenth century, the radicalizing horror of World War I, all demand attention from anyone seriously interested in plumbing the deeper motives of National Socialism. How else can we understand a regime that took as its central objective the destruction of European Jewry, an objective apparently devoid of all economic rationale, a project that, if it can be understood at all, seems to be intelligible only in terms of a violent theology of redemptive purification?[2]

The cultural and ideological turn in the study of Fascism has permanently remodelled our understanding of Hitler and his regime. It is hard to imagine now, but there was a time, not so long ago, when historians routinely dismissed *Mein Kampf* as a historical source and thought it reasonable to treat Hitler as just another opportunistic imperialist. Those days are gone. Thanks to the work of two generations of historians, we now have a far better understanding of the way in which Nazi ideology conditioned the thought and action of the Nazi leadership and wider German society. But whilst we have been busy unravelling the central ideological and political thread of Hitler's regime, other crucial strands of the story have been relatively neglected. Most notably, historians have tended to downplay or even ignore the importance of the economy. In part, this has been a deliberate act of rejection. In part, the marginalization of economic history has been self-inflicted. The statistical terminology in which much economic history is couched is inaccessible to readers trained in the humanities, and too little effort has been made by either side to bridge the gap. Perhaps most of all, the turn against socio-economic analysis has been motivated by a sense of ennui, the impression that there is simply nothing new to say, that all the major questions were answered by the first two generations of historians and social scientists writing after 1945, who seized on such topics as the Nazi economic recovery or the history of the war economy.

What we are left with is a historiography moving at two speeds. Whereas our understanding of the regime's racial policies and the inner workings of German society under National Socialism has been transformed over the last twenty years, the economic history of the regime has progressed very little. The aim of this book is to start a long overdue process of intellectual realignment. To do so, this book reassesses the archival and statistical evidence, much of which has gone unquestioned in sixty years, brings it into dialogue with the latest research, both by historians of the Third Reich and by economic historians exploring the dynamics of the inter-war economy, and asks what light this throws on some of the central questions in the history of Hitler's regime. How did the fissures in the global power structure created by the great depression of 1929–32 enable Hitler's government to have such a dramatic impact on the world scene? What was the relationship between the extraordinary imperial ambition of Hitler and his movement and the peculiar situation of the German economy and society in the 1920s and 1930s? How did domestic and international economic tensions contribute to Hitler's drive to war in 1939 and his restless drive to widen the war thereafter? When and how did the Third Reich develop the Blitzkrieg strategy that is widely seen as the hallmark of its spectacular success in World War II? When the Blitzkrieg failed outside Moscow in December 1941, how did the Third Reich continue the war for almost three and half years against overwhelming material odds? And what are we to make of Albert Speer? In recent years this singular figure has attracted an extraordinary amount of attention, yet, and it is surely a sign of the times, what has been in the foreground has not been Speer's primary function as Armaments Minister but questions relating to his role as Hitler's architect, Speer's personal knowledge of the Holocaust and his tortured efforts after 1945 to come to terms with the truth. This book is the first in sixty years to offer a truly critical account of the performance of the German war economy both under Speer and his predecessors and it casts stark new light on his role in sustaining the Third Reich to its bloody end. For it is only by re-examining the economic under-pinnings of the Third Reich, by focusing on questions of land, food and labour that we can fully get to grips with the breathtaking process of cumulative radicalization that found its most extraordinary manifes-tation in the Holocaust.

The first aim of this book, therefore, is to reposition economics at the centre of our understanding of Hitler's regime, by providing an economic narrative that helps to make sense of and underpin the political histories produced over the last generation. No less urgent, however, is the need to bring our understanding of the economic history of the Third Reich into line with the subtle but profound rewriting of the history of the European economy that has been ongoing since the late 1980s but has gone largely unnoticed in the mainstream historiography of Germany.

It is hardly an exaggeration to say that historians of twentieth-century Germany share at least one common starting point: the assumption of the peculiar strength of the German economy. Obviously, when Hitler took power Germany was in the midst of a deep economic crisis. But the common sense of twentieth-century European history is that Germany was an economic superpower in waiting, an economic force comparable only to that of the United States. For all the argument there has been over the backwardness or otherwise of German political culture, the assumption of Germany's peculiar economic modernity has gone largely unquestioned. This assumption frames the writing of much of German social history, as much as it also informs accounts of German imperialism in the foreign policy field. Indeed, so influential has been the assumption of Germany's economic superiority that it has influenced narratives, not only of German history, but those of other countries as well. For most of the twentieth century it was Germany with which Britain, France, Italy and even the United States were compared.

From the vantage point of the early twenty-first century, it is this assumption that we must start by challenging. Both the real-life experi-ence of Europeans since the early 1990s and a generation of technical work by economists and economic historians has shaken, if not demol-ished, the myth of Germany's peculiar economic superiority. The master-narrative of European economic history in the twentieth century, it turns out, was one of progressive convergence around a norm that was defined for most of the period, not by Germany, but by Britain, which in 1900 was already the world's first fully industrial and urban society. Furthermore, Britain up to 1945 was no mere European country; it was the largest global empire the world had ever seen. In 1939, as the war started, the combined GDP of the British and French empires exceeded that of Germany and Italy by 60 per cent. Of course, the idea of inherent German economic superiority was not simply a figment of the historical imagination. Germany from the late nineteenth century onwards was the home for a cluster of world-beating industrial companies. Brand names like Krupp, Siemens and IG Farben gave substance to the myth of German industrial invincibility. Viewed in wider terms, however, the German economy differed little from the European average: its national per capita income in the 1930s was middling; in present-day terms it was comparable to that of Iran or South Africa. The standard of consumption enjoyed by the majority of the German population was modest and lagged behind that of most of its Western European neighbours. Germany under Hitler was still only a partially modernized society, in which upwards of 15 million people depended for their living either on traditional handicrafts or on peasant agriculture.

What strikes one today as the defining feature of twentieth-century economic history is not the peculiar dominance of Germany or any other European country, but the eclipse of the 'old Continent' by a sequence of new economic powers, above all the United States. In 1870, at the time of German national unification, the population of the United States and Germany was roughly equal and the total output of America, despite its enormous abundance of land and resources, was only one-third larger than that of Germany. Just before the outbreak of World War I the American economy had expanded to roughly twice the size of that of Imperial Germany. By 1943, before the aerial bombardment had hit top gear, total American output was almost four times that of the Third Reich.

We start the twenty-first century, therefore, with an altered historical perception from that which framed narratives of German history for most of the last hundred years. On the one hand we have a sharpened appreciation of the truly exceptional position of the United States within the modern global economy. On the other hand the common European experience of 'convergence' provides us with a distinctly disenchanted perspective on Germany's economic history. The basic and possibly most radical contention of this book is that these interrelated shifts in our historical perception require a reframing of the history of the Third Reich, a reframing which has the disturbing effect both of rendering the history of Nazism more intelligible, indeed eerily contemporary, and at the same time bringing into even sharper relief its fundamental ideological irrationality. Economic history throws new light both on the motives for Hitler's aggression and on the reasons why it failed, why indeed it was bound to fail.

In both respects, America should provide the pivot for our understanding of the Third Reich. In seeking to explain the urgency of Hitler's aggression, historians have underestimated his acute awareness of the threat posed to Germany, along with the rest of the European powers, by the emergence of the United States as the dominant global superpower. On the basis of contemporary economic trends, Hitler predicted already in the 1920s that the European powers had only a few more years to organize themselves against this inevitability. Furthermore, Hitler understood the overwhelming attraction already exerted on Europeans by America's affluent consumer lifestyle, an attraction whose force we can appreciate more vividly, given our sharpened awareness of the more generally transitional status of the European economies in the inter-war period. As in many semi-peripheral economies today, the German population in the 1930s was already thoroughly immersed in the commodity world of Hollywood, but at the same time many millions of people lived three or four to a room, without indoor bathrooms or access to electricity. Motor vehicles, radios and other accoutrements of modern living such as electrical household appliances were the aspiration of the social elite. The originality of National Socialism was that, rather than meekly accepting a place for Germany within a global economic order dominated by the affluent English-speaking countries, Hitler sought to mobilize the pent-up frustrations of his population to mount an epic challenge to this order. Repeating what Europeans had done across the globe over the previous three centuries, Germany would carve out its own imperial hinterland; by one last great land grab in the East it would create the self-sufficient basis both for domestic affluence and the platform necessary to prevail in the coming superpower competition with the United States.

The aggression of Hitler's regime can thus be rationalized as an intelligible response to the tensions stirred up by the uneven development of global capitalism, tensions that are of course still with us today. But at the same time an understanding of the economic fundamentals also serves to sharpen our appreciation of the profound irrationality of Hitler's project. As this book will show, Hitler's regime after 1933 undertook a truly remarkable campaign of economic mobilization. The armaments programme of the Third Reich was the largest transfer of resources ever undertaken by a capitalist state in peacetime. Nevertheless, Hitler was powerless to alter the underlying balance of economic and military force. The German economy was simply not strong enough to create the military force necessary to overwhelm all its European neighbours, including both Britain and the Soviet Union, let alone the United States. Though Hitler scored brilliant short-term successes in 1936 and 1938, the diplomacy of the Third Reich failed to bring about the anti-Soviet alliance proposed in *Mein Kampf*. Faced with a war against Britain and France, Hitler was forced at the last moment to resort to an opportunistic arrangement with Stalin. The devastating effectiveness of the Panzer forces, the deus ex machina of the early years of the war, certainly did not form the basis for strategy in advance of the summer of 1940, since it came as a surprise even to the German leadership. And though the victories of the German army in 1940 and 1941 were undoubtedly spectacular they were inconclusive. We are thus left with the truly vertiginous conclusion that Hitler went to war in September 1939 without any coherent plan as to how actually to defeat the British Empire, his major antagonist.

Why did Hitler take this epic gamble? This surely is the fundamental question. Even if the conquest of living space can be rationalized as an act of imperialism, even if the Third Reich can be credited with a remarkable effort to muster its resources for combat, even if Germany's soldiers fought brilliantly, Hitler's conduct of the war involved risks so great that they defy rationalization in terms of pragmatic self-interest.[3] And it is with this question that we reconnect to mainstream historiography and its insistence on the importance of ideology. It was ideology which provided Hitler with the lens through which he understood the international balance of power and the unfolding of the increasingly globalized struggle that began in Europe with the Spanish Civil War in the summer of 1936. In Hitler's mind, the threat posed to the Third Reich by the United States was not just that of conventional superpower rivalry. The threat was existential and bound up with Hitler's abiding fear of the world Jewish conspiracy, manifested in the shape of 'Wall Street Jewry' and the 'Jewish media' of the United States. It was this fantastical interpretation of the real balance of power that gave Hitler's decision-making its volatile, risk-taking quality. Germany could not simply settle down to become an affluent satellite of the United States, as had seemed to be the destiny of the Weimar Republic in the 1920s, because this would result in enslavement to the world Jewish conspiracy, and ultimately race death. Given the pervasive influence of the Jews, as revealed by the mounting international tension of the late 1930s, a prosperous future of capitalist partnership with the Western powers was simply impossible. War was inevitable. The question was not if, but when.

This is a long book and, since it is written to be read from beginning to end, I don't want to deflate the tension by revealing the decisive punch lines in the first few pages. Suffice to say that, though the broad outline of the history of the Third Reich has been deeply engraved in decades of painstaking investigative labour, the story as it is told here is new. My goal is to provide the reader with a deeper and broader understanding of how Hitler established himself in power and mobilized his society for war. I provide a new account of the dynamic that launched Germany into war and explain both how this sustained a successful war effort up to 1941 and how it reached its inevitable limit in the Russian snow. Next, the book takes on what is surely still the fundamental interpretative challenge facing any historian of the Third Reich, and perhaps particularly an economic historian: explaining the Holocaust. Drawing both on archival material and a generation of brilliant historical research, I emphasize the connections between the war against the Jews and the regime's wider projects of imperialism, forced labour and deliberate starvation. In the minds of the Nazi leadership, there were, in fact, not one but a number of different economic rationales for genocide. Finally, building on these decisive chapters on 1939–42, I explain the extraordinary coercive effort through which the regime sustained Germany's war effort for three bitter years, at the heart of which stood Albert Speer.

Those who at this point are already impatient for more specific conclusions should turn to Chapter 20, which provides a brief summary of at least some of the key points. To avoid the book being even longer, I have not burdened it with a full bibliography. The titles of all works cited appear in full at their first appearance in each chapter. A full bibliography, as well as other resources on the economic history of the Third Reich, is available from the author's webpage www.hist.cam. ac.uk/academic_staff/further_details/tooze.html.

'Tons' means metric tons throughout.

I

Introduction

Reviewing the twentieth century, it is hard to escape the conclusion that two themes have dominated Germany's history. On the one hand there is the pursuit of economic and technological progress, which for much of the century made Germany, along with the United States and latterly Japan, China and India, one of the largest economies in the world. On the other hand there is the pursuit of warfare on a hitherto unimagined scale.[1]

Germany was chiefly responsible for unleashing the first shattering World War of the twentieth century. It was solely responsible for the second. Furthermore, in the course of World War II Hitler and his regime extended the boundaries of war to include a wholesale campaign of genocide that stands unrivalled in its intensity, scope and deliberateness. After the second catastrophe of 1945, the occupying powers made sure to leave Germany with no choice. Though sport, technology, science and culture were gradually readmitted as fields of national and individual self-expression, and though German politics became more multi-dimensional from the late 1960s onwards, it was the depoliticized pursuit of material welfare that dominated national life, certainly in West Germany after 1945.[2] By contrast, Germany's first surrender, in 1918, was far less complete and the conclusions drawn both by Germans and their former opponents were correspondingly more ambiguous. One of the many extraordinary features of German politics in the aftermath of World War I is that throughout the existence of the Weimar Republic the German electorate faced a choice between a politics centred on the peaceful pursuit of national prosperity and a militant nationalism that more or less openly demanded a resumption of hostilities with France, Britain and the United States. Since most of this book will be taken up with a dissection of the way in which Hitler harnessed the German economy in pursuit of this latter option, it seems important to begin by clearly establishing the alternative against which his vision was framed and how that alternative was pushed out of view by the disastrous events leading up to Hitler's seizure of power.

It would be wrong, of course, to deny that there are continuities that connect all sides in the strategic debate in Germany in the 1920s and 1930s to the imperialist legacy of the Wilhelmine era.[3] Hostility towards the French and Poles and imperial designs on Germany's neighbours both in the West and in the East were nothing new. However, an excessive stress on continuity obscures the transformative impact on German politics of the defeat of November 1918 and the traumatic crisis that followed. This agony reached its climax in 1923 when the French occupied the Ruhr, the industrial heart of the German economy. Over the following months, as Berlin sponsored a mass campaign of passive resistance, the country descended into hyperinflation and political disorder so severe that by the autumn of 1923 it called into question the survival of the German nation-state as such.[4] Strategic debate in Germany was never the same again. On the one hand, the crisis of 1918–23 gave rise to an ultra-nationalism – in the form of the radical wing of the DNVP and Hitler's Nazi party – that was more apocalyptic in its intensity than anything prior to 1914. On the other hand, it also produced a truly novel departure in German foreign and economic policy. This alternative to nationalist militancy also aimed to achieve a revision of the onerous terms of the Treaty of Versailles. But it aimed to do so not by gambling on military force. Instead, Weimar's foreign policy prioritized the economy as the main field within which Germany could still exercise influence in the world. Above all, it sought security and leverage for Germany by developing financial connections with the United States and closer industrial integration with France. In certain key respects, this clearly anticipated the strategy pursued by West Germany after 1945. It was a policy that enjoyed the backing of all of the parties of the Weimar coalition – the Social Democrats, the left liberal DDP and the Catholic Centre party. But it was personified by Gustav Stresemann, leader of the national liberals, the DVP, and Germany's Foreign Minister between 1923 and 1929.[5]

Four years after the stabilization of 1924, the general election of 20 May 1928 was the first occasion on which the entire electorate of Germany had the opportunity to give their verdict on the achievements of the Weimar Republic and Stresemann's foreign policy. Gustav Strese-mann chose to fight that general election in Bavaria. Munich, of course, was also one of the favourite stomping grounds of the NSDAP and as the leader of that fringe party, Hitler hoped to gain added attention by crossing swords with Stresemann. The voters of Bavaria were thus offered a dramatic choice between Stresemann's conception of Germany's future, based on four years of peaceful 'economic revisionism', and Hitler's sweeping rejection of the foundations of Weimar's foreign and economic policy. Both Hitler and Stresemann took the contest seriously. Though it was essential for Stresemann to present Hitler as little more than a crank, he admitted that he had taken time to read at least one of Hitler's published speeches to inform himself about the arguments he might face.[6] Hitler for his part used the argument with Stresemann to refine the ideas on foreign policy and economics that he had first formu-lated in *Mein Kampf*, his manifesto compiled in Landsberg prison in 1924.[7] The result was the manuscript known as Hitler's 'Second Book', which was completed in the summer of 1928 and contained substantial passages culled directly from stump speeches.[8]

I

Gustav Stresemann had first enunciated his view that 'politics ... [is] today first of all the politics of the world economy', as an ambitious young representative of the National Liberal party in the Wilhelmine Reichstag.[9] And this was no mere rhetoric, it was an experience in-grained in his biography.[10] Born in 1878 in Berlin, the son of a small independent bottler of flavoured Weiss Bier, one of the capital's favourite tipples, Stresemann had watched his father's business squeezed by the competition of the larger breweries. As the only one of seven siblings to attend university he had completed his studies with a dissertation in historical economics and started work in 1901 as a syndic for the light-manufacturing industries of Saxony, where it was his job to lobby for the interest of export-orientated manufacturing against the over-weening demands both of heavy industry and protectionist agriculture. Both by his reading of economic history and his practical experience of trade policy, Stresemann was convinced that the dominant forces in the twentieth-century world would be the three major industrial economies:

Britain, Germany and the United States. The economic great powers were rivalrous, certainly. But they were also functionally and inescapably interconnected. Germany needed raw materials and food from overseas export markets to provide its population with work and bread. The British Empire was better placed with regard to raw materials, but it needed Germany as an export market. Furthermore, Stresemann was convinced from an early stage that the emergence of the United States as the dominant force in the world economy permanently altered the dynamic of competition between the European powers.[11] In the twentieth century the future of the balance of power in Europe would be defined in large part by the relationship of the competing interests in Europe to the United States. Stresemann certainly did not underestimate either military force or the popular will as factors in power politics. In the dreadnought race, Stresemann was a consistent advocate of the Imperial fleet, in the hope that Germany might one day rival the British in backing its overseas trade with naval power. After 1914 he was amongst the Reichstag's most aggressive advocates of all-out U-boat war. But even in his most annexationist moment, Stresemann was above all motivated by an economic logic centred on the United States.[12] The expansion of German territory to include Belgium, the French coastline to Calais, Morocco and extensive territory in the East was 'necessary' to secure for Germany an adequate platform for competition with America. No economy without a secure market of at least 150 million customers could hope to compete with the economies of scale that Stresemann had witnessed first hand in the industrial heartlands of the United States.

There can be no doubt that Germany's sudden defeat in the autumn of 1918 shocked Stresemann deeply, leaving him close to both physical and psychological collapse. It permanently shook his confidence in military force as a means of power politics, certainly as far as Germany was concerned. More fundamentally, it raised doubts in his mind about the German social and political system, which had proved less resilient than that of either Britain or France. This, however, merely reinforced his belief in the determining force of economics. The world economy was the one sphere in which Germany was truly indispensable. Already in April 1919 Stresemann demanded that, given Germany's military weakness, the basis of its foreign policy should be the strength of its major corporations. 'Today we need credits from abroad. The Reich is no longer creditworthy ... but the private individual, individual large corporations still have credit. This is founded on the unlimited respect of the world for the achievements of German industry and of the German trader.'[13] Crucially, the economy was the one sphere through which Germany could build a connection to the United States, the only power that could help Germany in counterbalancing the aggression of the French and the disinterest of the British. And this vision of a trans-Atlantic partnership clearly impelled Stresemann's actions, both during his brief but decisive spell as Chancellor of the Republic in 1923 and then as Foreign Minister between 1924 and 1929. By facing down a storm of nationalist outrage and ending the ruinous campaign of passive resistance to the French occupation of the Ruhr, whilst at the same time signalling Germany's willingness to pay reparations, Stresemann opened the door to a special relationship with the United States.

This of course came at a price. Stresemann was vulnerable for ever afterwards to accusations from the right that he was a 'French candidate'.[14] And these accusations were further strengthened by Stresemann's decision to use cooperative tactics rather than confrontation, to achieve an accelerated withdrawal of the French forces that patrolled the Rhineland.[15] Of course, nothing could have been further from the truth. Stresemann was in every respect a full-blooded German nationalist. He never distanced himself from the annexationist positions he had adopted during World War I, because he saw no reason to regret them. Nor was he ever willing to accept as a long-term solution the eastern border with Poland as defined by the 1921 plebiscite and League of Nations decision. His strategy, which relied on manipulating the interlocking interests of the United States, Britain and France, was simply more complex than the confrontational mode favoured by the ultra-nationalists.

Stresemann's first success was the Dawes Committee, which met in Paris in 1924 to establish a workable system through which Germany could pay reparations without jeopardizing its financial stability.[16] The chairman of the Committee was General Charles G. Dawes, a Chicago banker and industrialist who had presided over the American and inter-Allied procurement in World War I. But the actual architect of the scheme was Owen Young, the chairman of General Electric and as such one of the leaders of American industry.[17] General Electric was furthermore closely allied with the Allgemeine Elektrizitaets Gesellschaft (AEG), Germany's second-largest electrical engineering conglomerate. Dawes and Young more than fulfilled the hopes that Stresemann placed in the United States. The immediate reparation demands on Germany were substantially reduced, with the full annuity of 2.5 billion pre-war Goldmarks not to come into effect until 1928/9. J. P. Morgan did their bit by mobilizing an enthusiastic vote of confidence from Wall Street, with an initial and massively over-subscribed loan of $100 million. Re-establishing the Reichsmark on gold at its pre-war parity against the dollar ended the instability of Germany's currency.[18] Further protection was provided by the so-called Reparations Agent. This office was occupied by a young Wall Street star, Parker Gilbert, who had the power to halt transfers of reparations payments if they would endanger the stability of the German currency. The demands of the European 'reparations creditors' were thus relegated to a second order claim on Germany's finances. American capital did not immediately crowd into Germany, as is sometimes suggested.[19] However, given the large interest rate differential between the United States and Germany, where savings had been evaporated in the heat of hyperinflation, the conditions for lending were clearly good. And between October 1925 and the end of 1928 the inflow of foreign capital was so large that Germany could make its reparations payments without even having to earn a surplus on its trade account. This was convenient for the British and French since it enabled them to insist on German payments without having to open their markets to billions of Goldmarks' worth of goods. At the same time it allowed Washington to insist that France and Britain should honour the debts they owed to America as a result of the war.

This merry-go-round in which Germans borrowed money from the Americans to pay the British and French who then paid the Americans raised anxiety on all sides.[20] However, it served its purpose. The US Congress insisted on the fullest possible repayment of the inter-Allied credits owing to America.[21] The new American lenders to Germany were making handsome profits. And the Weimar Republic enjoyed a standard of living considerably higher than would have been possible if it had been constrained to pay reparations out of an export surplus. Hjalmar Schacht, the president of the Reichsbank installed by Stresemann in November 1923, was deeply concerned about Germany's mounting international debt burden.[22] But he shared Stresemann's strategic vision. As America's stake in Germany grew, so would Washington's interest in ensuring that excessive reparations demands by Britain and France did not jeopardize American investments. Put at its most simple and

Table 1. Borrowing from abroad: Germany's foreign debt
position, spring 1931 (million RM)

	Long-term	Short-term	Total
United States	5,265	3,143	8,408
Britain	1,100	2,053	3,153
Netherlands	1,174	2,069	3,243
Switzerland	512	1,878	2,390
Other	1,494	2,826	4,320
Total	9,545	11,969	21,514

Source: C. R. S. Harris, *Germany's Foreign Indebtedness* (Oxford, 1935),
9, 95

most cynical, Germany's strategy consisted of exploiting the protection
provided by the Reparations Agent to borrow so much from America
that the service on this debt made it impossible to transfer reparations.[23]
More subtly, what Stresemann and Schacht aimed to do was to make
American financial interests into the main force pushing for the revision
of Germany's reparations, allowing Berlin to normalize its relations with
London and Paris. And in the late 1920s this strategy appeared to be
working. In 1928, rather than the Germans it was the Americans and
most notably the chairman of the US Federal Reserve, Benjamin Strong,
who began to push for the renegotiation of Germany's reparation obligations before the full annuities owing under the Dawes Plan came into
effect.[24] Strong did so not out of any love for Germany but in the interest
of securing America's huge stake in the German economy. A full-blown
crisis could easily have destabilized a number of America's largest banks.

II

If in Stresemann's case our problems of interpretation stem from the
fact that his policies seem uncannily similar to those on which the
stability of Germany has rested since 1945, the difficulty in getting to

grips with Hitler's vision is the reverse. Hitler inhabited a strange and embattled mental universe that we struggle to comprehend or even to take seriously.

It is tempting to deduce the very different world-views adopted by Hitler and Stresemann from their markedly different life histories. Hitler's difficulties in finding a place in the world are too familiar to need rehearsing here.[25] They certainly stand in marked contrast to Stresemann's story of upward social mobility. For both men, the war was a turning point. But whereas Stresemann's chronic ill health debarred him from active service in World War I, Hitler experienced the war from the trenches. It is hardly surprising in the light of this that Stresemann managed to retain his quintessential bourgeois optimism even during the nightmare of 1918–23, whereas Hitler's thinking had a far darker edge. Nevertheless, Hitler and Stresemann were both products of a shared political culture. They were both advocates of the widely held view that World War I was the result of Imperial competition.[26] Specifically, both blamed Great Britain for having initiated the war, in a deliberate attempt to cripple Germany as an economic and naval competitor. In Stresemann's case, however, this common-sense model of military-economic competition was softened by his understanding of the mutual interconnectedness of the world economy and above all by the importance he attached to the United States as a counter-weight to Britain and France. Hitler's outlook, by contrast, was far more embattled. He regarded the liberal ideology of progress through industry, hard work and free trade as nothing more than a lie spread by Jewish propagandists. In fact, any effort by the German people to seek salvation through industry and trade would eventually bring them into competition with Britain. Germany would again face the constellation of August 1914 – an overpowering Continental alliance masterminded and bankrolled by the Jewish bankers of the city. The international Jewish conspiracy, which ruled now not only in Washington and London but in the Bolshevik dictatorship as well, would again force Germany into defeat.

For Hitler, the decisive factors in world history were not labour and industry, but struggle for the limited means of sustenance.[27] Britain could sustain itself through free trade, but only because it had already conquered an empire by military force. What the German people needed to secure a decent standard of living was 'living space', Lebensraum, and this could be achieved only by warlike conquest. Colonies had been the great enthusiasm of Wilhelmine Germany, but that meant scattering Germany's precious blood all over the world. Instead, Hitler favoured the conquest of contiguous *Lebensraum* in the East. Here again one can certainly point to similarities with the thinking of wartime annexationists. After the Treaty of Brest-Litovsk, Stresemann too had dreamed of a German *Grossraum* in the East. But, as we have seen, his primary aim was to gain a market sufficient in scale to match the United States. Hitler, by contrast, wanted the land, not the native inhabitants. The purpose of conquest was not the addition of non-German people. The population of the conquered territories would have to be removed. The bourgeois regime of Imperial Germany had lacked the nerve for this kind of radical racial policy in relation to the large Polish minority that inhabited its eastern borders. But if Germany was to prevail, there was no alternative to a ruthless policy of conquest and depopulation. War was Germany's destiny. Concretely, Hitler seems to have envisioned a more or less systematic series of steps starting with the incorporation of Austria, then the subordination of the major Central European successor states, most notably Czechoslovakia, culminating in a settling of accounts with the French.[28] The path would then be clear for a drive to the east. Hitler did not of course wish to repeat the constellation of World War I and in this respect Britain was crucial. Hitler was firmly convinced that, unlike an export-directed strategy, which would lead inevitably into conflict with the global influence of the British Empire, his strategy of Continental expansion posed no fundamental threat to Britain, whose basic interests lay outside Europe. It was fundamental to his strategic conception in the 1920s and early 1930s that he would be able to secure a dominant position for Germany in Europe without coming into conflict with Britain. Indeed, reversing Stresemann's logic, Hitler believed that Britain would come to view Germany as an ally in the competition that it was bound to face from the United States.

In his childhood, like many millions of German-speaking boys, Hitler had been an enthusiastic reader of Karl May's Germanic Westerns.[29] In the immediate aftermath of World War I his fascination took on a darker hue, particularly in relation to President Wilson, who in the wake of Versailles became an object of near universal revulsion in Germany. In 1923 Hitler wrote that only a spasm of temporary imbecility brought on by the hunger pangs of the Anglo-Jewish blockade could explain how Germany had thrown itself on the mercy of a 'crook like Wilson, who had come to Paris with a staff of 117 Jewish bankers and financiers . . .'.[30] In *Mein Kampf*, drafted the following year, the United States barely figured in Hitler's strategic vision. Three years later, given the role played by the United States in German affairs, such parochialism was no longer possible. As Hitler could not fail to note, the United States – even if it was not a military factor in European affairs – was an economic force to be reckoned with. Indeed, the remarkable industrial advance of the United States had changed the parameters of everyday life on the 'old continent'. As Hitler himself put it, in what is surely one of the key passages in his 'Second Book':

The European today dreams of a standard of living, which he derives as much from Europe's possibilities as from the real conditions of America. Due to modern technology and the communication it makes possible, the international relations amongst peoples have become so close that the European, even without being fully conscious of it, applies as the yardstick for his life, the conditions of American life . . .[31]

And not surprisingly, what most caught Hitler's eye was the American domination of the motor vehicle industry. Hitler, of course, was a motor enthusiast. But what concerned him in his 'Second Book' were the strategic implications of America's leadership in this crucial new industry. In their imaginings of a future of American affluence Europeans were apt to forget 'that the relationship of surface area to the population of the American continent is vastly superior . . .'. America's enormous competitive advantage in industrial technology was above all a function of 'the size of' America's 'internal market' and its 'wealth in purchasing power but also in raw materials'. It was the huge volume of 'guarantee[d] . . . internal sales' that enabled the American motor vehicle industry to adopt 'methods of production that in Europe due to the lack of such internal sales would simply be impossible'.[32] Fordism, in other words, required *Lebensraum*.

Whereas Stresemann saw the rise of the United States as a stabilizing factor in European affairs, for Hitler it merely raised the stakes in the struggle for racial survival. Nor could this struggle remain limited to the economic sphere: 'The final decision in the struggle for the world market will lie with force . . .'[33] Even if its businessmen were successful, Germany would soon find itself back in the situation of 1914, forced to fight for its access to world markets on highly unfavourable terms. Indeed, Hitler believed that the emerging economic dominance of the United States placed in jeopardy the 'global significance' of all the European countries. Unless the political leaders of Europe could shake their populations out of their usual 'political thoughtlessness', the 'threatened global hegemony of the North American continent' would reduce all of them to the status of 'Switzerland and Holland'.[34] Not that Hitler was an adherent of pan-European ideas. He regarded any such suggestion as vapid, 'Jewish' nonsense. The European response to the United States had to be led by the most powerful European state, on the model of the Roman or British empires, or for that matter the unifying actions of Prussia in nineteenth-century Germany.

In future the only state that will be able to stand up to North America, will be the one which has understood how, through the essence of its inner life and the meaning of its foreign policy, to raise the value of its people in racial terms and to bring them into the state-form most appropriate for this purpose . . . It is the task of the national socialist movement to strengthen and to prepare its fatherland for this mission.[35]

Along with France and the Soviet Union, the United States thus entered the ranks of Hitler's enemies, to be confronted, after a period of internal consolidation, if possible in alliance with Great Britain. It is worth emphasizing this latter point. Hitler's insistent emphasis on the need for an alliance with Britain was driven not only by his focus on conquest in the East, the central strategic argument of *Mein Kampf*, but also by his awareness of the threat posed by the United States, the new theme of the 'Second Book'.

Hitler and Stresemann thus differed in their assessment of Germany's position in relation to the dawning 'American century' and they differed in their assessment of the relative importance of economics and politics. Underpinning these divergences, however, was a more fundamental difference in their understanding of history.[36] This is most clearly illustrated by their responses to the disaster of World War I. The essence of Stresemann's position was that the war did not change the fundamental direction of world history, which was dictated by the inevitable trajectory of economic development. Though Germany had been defeated, the war, by weakening Britain and France and promoting the United States, opened the door to a reassertion of German power, though limited to the economic sphere. Hitler regarded this kind of thinking as characteristic of the naïve optimism of the German bourgeois. Hitler was not a pessimist. He rejected the doom-laden prophecies of Spengler. For him, however, history offered no guarantees. The fundamental determining factor in history was not the predictable telos of economic development, but struggle between peoples for the means of life. In this battle for survival the outcome was always uncertain. Even in the short span of '2,000 years' of human history, Hitler declared,

world powers ruled cultures of which only legend now tells, enormous cities have fallen into ruins . . . Almost beyond all comprehension . . . are the concerns, the needs and suffering of millions upon millions of individual people, who were once, as living substance, the bearers and victims of these events . . . And how indifferent is . . . the present. How unfounded is its eternal optimism and how ruinous its wilful ignorance, its refusal to see and its refusal to learn.[37]

To shake the populace out of its optimistic stupor and to energize it with a sense of apocalyptic risk, this was the true task of political leadership. The idea that Germany could simply progress steadily towards a higher standard of living like that on show in the United States was a delusion. For Hitler, defeat in World War I heralded the starting point of a struggle no less definitive than that between Carthage and Rome. Unless Germans rose to the challenge, 1918 might well be the harbinger of an 'Untergang' as complete as that suffered by the great civilizations of antiquity. Such a prospect left no room for passivity and no room for patience. Faced with the utter ruthlessness of the Judaeo-Bolshevik enemy, even a strategy fraught with the most extreme risks could be justified. In the 1920s and early 1930s audiences could be forgiven for taking Hitler's extreme warlike language as a rhetorical affectation. How deadly serious he was in his apocalyptic world-view was not to become fully apparent until 1939.

III

The German electorate thus faced a stark choice and they gave a clear answer. In the general election of May 1928, Hitler's party gained a tiny 2.5 per cent of the vote giving it only 12 seats out of 491 in the Reichstag. By contrast, though the DVP's share of the vote declined, Stresemann's party still held a respectable 45 seats.[38] And whereas the DVP enjoyed the generous backing of big business, the Nazis were so cash-strapped by the autumn of 1928 that they were forced to call off their annual party rally. Sales of *Mein Kampf* had slumped so badly that Hitler's publishers decided to hold back his 'Second Book' for fear of spoiling the market. The DNVP, the other party on the extreme right, saw its share of seats cut from 103 to 73. These losses and the ensuing leadership crisis in the nationalist movement, leading to the election of the ultra-nationalist Alfred Hugenberg as head of the DNVP, were the headline news of the summer and autumn of 1928. By contrast, the Social Democrats, the founding party of the Weimar Republic, scored a major victory. Their representation in the Reichstag rose from 131 to 153 seats. Together with Stresemann's DVP, the DDP and the Centre party they had a workable majority with Hermann Mueller as Chancellor. Gustav Stresemann continued for a fifth year as Foreign Minister.

In 1928, therefore, despite the presence of elements such as Hitler and his party, the Weimar Republic had a functioning parliamentary system and a government committed to pursuing the revision of the Versailles Treaty under the good auspices of the United States. The potential for disaster was clearly there. But even the most pessimistic observers would have been hard pressed to predict that within ten years Germany would launch Europe back into a dreadful war and embark on the single most ruthless campaign of genocidal murder in human history. This book is not a history of the Weimar Republic. But to start our account of Hitler's regime, we must clearly first explain how Stresemann's strategy was overturned, opening the door to Hitler's far more radical vision.

One key factor contributing to the destabilization of the Weimar Republic after 1929 was the disappointment of the hopes invested in America's 'new order' by Germany's pro-Republican forces.[39] In 1923–4 the successful stabilization of the Weimar Republic had depended crucially on the involvement of the United States. Thereafter, the credibility of Stresemann and Schacht's 'Atlanticist strategy' hinged on the expectation that America's influence in Europe would continue to grow and would ultimately open the door to comprehensive revision of the Versailles Treaty terms. This depended on American recognition of the linkage between the war debts owed by Britain and France to America and the reparations demands made by those powers on Germany. Owen Young did return to Paris in the spring of 1929 to renegotiate the reparations settlement.[40] However, he came without any commitment from Herbert Hoover's incoming administration to allow an explicit linkage between inter-Allied war debts and reparations.[41] This in turn meant that the Young Plan was bound to disappoint.[42] Instead of a reduction in the reparations annuity from 2.5 billion to 1.5 billion pre-war Goldmarks hoped for by the Mueller government, the amount demanded of Germany was reduced only marginally to just over 2 billion Goldmarks. In addition, the Young Plan removed the protection provided by the Reparations Agent. This relieved Germany of intrusive and humiliating foreign oversight and was intended as a first step towards placing Germany's reparations bonds on a depoliticized, commercial footing. But it also meant that Germany was now permitted to postpone transfer on the majority of its reparations, for a maximum of only two years. And it was now the German government rather than a 'neutral' American agency that would have to make the decision.

The disappointment that followed in the wake of the Young Plan was devastating to the credibility of the Atlanticist strategy. The acrimony surrounding the negotiations negated any hope of a large-scale commercialization of Germany's political debts. From 1928 onwards long-term American lending to Germany began to fall, as rumours swirled about the future of reparations and interest rates in the United States rose.[43] Germany continued to borrow in 1929 and to sell shares in German firms to foreigners, but more than half the inflow was now short-term. And further damage to trans-Atlantic economic relations was to follow. In the course of the American election Herbert Hoover had won the Midwest with promises of agricultural protection. During its passage through Congress the trade bill which became notorious as the Smoot–Hawley tariff was festooned with a variety of demands, including significant protection against European manufactured imports. By the autumn of 1929 the Europeans knew that not only would Congress not permit any substantial reduction in the inter-Allied debt payments, and not only was there little prospect of any new long-term credit from America, but that the new tariff would in all likelihood make it harder for America's European debtors to earn the dollars they needed to service their obligations to Wall Street.[44]

How Stresemann would have responded to this disastrous chain of events we shall never know. His health had been collapsing since the spring of 1928 and the effort to hold the right wing of the DVP in line with the Grand Coalition government was too much. Within hours of securing the agreement of the German government to the Young Plan, Stresemann suffered a series of strokes and died. But even before his untimely death there were indications of a shift in direction. Some have argued that the intensified discussions between Stresemann and the French Foreign Minister, Aristide Briand, in the summer and autumn of 1929 were motivated at least in part by a sense of disappointment with the United States. And in the last week of June 1929 Stresemann had spoken in the Reichstag of Europe becoming 'a colony of those who have been more fortunate than us'. The time had come in which 'French, German and perhaps also other European economies must find a way together to counter a competition that weighs heavily on us all', an unusually antagonistic reference to the United States.[45]

A turn towards European integration was however only one possible reaction to the disappointment of hopes placed in America.[46] A diametrically opposed option was presented by the behaviour of Hjalmar Schacht, president of the Reichsbank. In evolutionary terms Schacht forms the 'missing link' between Stresemann's strategy of economic revisionism and the unilateral militarist aggression that replaced it after 1933. Born in 1877 into a German-American family, Horace Greeley Hjalmar Schacht, like Stresemann, was a Wilhelmine success story.[47] Whereas his father had had a troubled career, first as a journalist and then in a succession of failed businesses, Schacht made the best of his first-class education. Like Stresemann, he started his professional life as a lobbyist for liberal free trade interests, before rising rapidly through the ranks of the Dresdner Bank. In 1914 he became part of the financial administration of occupied Belgium but was forced to resign in 1915 amidst rumours of corruption. Soon afterwards he was hired by the Dresdner's rival, the Nationalbank. As a director of this rapidly expanding business, Schacht became one of the true profiteers of the hyperinflation. Like Stresemann, Schacht was a *Vernunftrepublikaner* (a republican by reason rather than by conviction). A founding member in 1918 of the left liberal DDP, he was Stresemann's candidate to take over the Reichsbank at the height of the Ruhr crisis.[48] Thereafter, Schacht was widely seen as a key ally in Stresemann's effort to restore Germany's international respectability. Widely credited with the stabilization of the Reichsmark in 1924, Schacht enjoyed close links both with banking circles in the United States and with Montagu Norman, governor of the

Bank of England. Indeed, during the chaos of 1923–4 Schacht had toyed with a British alternative to Stresemann's strategy, sounding out the possibility of tying the Reichsmark to the pound sterling rather than to the dollar.[49] But once the Dawes deal was done Schacht was if anything even more committed to the Atlanticist approach than was Stresemann.[50] Even more than in Stresemann's case, however, this rational conception of German strategy clashed in Schacht with a deep sense of wounded national pride. Far more persistently and far less tactfully than Stresemann, Schacht linked the question of a financial settlement with demands for territorial revision.[51] Schacht not only wanted to achieve an accelerated withdrawal of French troops from German soil. He also took every opportunity to reopen the territorial issue with Poland and even pressed for a restitution of German colonies. In April 1929, Schacht's revisionist demands came close to derailing the entire Young Plan discussions. The Plan itself was clearly a devastating blow to Schacht's faith in the American option. Immediately after Stresemann's death, Schacht adopted a position of outright opposition to the Mueller government. He used his contacts in Wall Street to sabotage an effort by the German government to raise a new American loan and on 6 December 1929 he published a report that was devastatingly critical of the Young Plan and indeed of the entire financial strategy pursued by the Weimar Republic since 1924.[52] Schacht's days as Reichsbank president were clearly numbered. By the spring of 1930 he had resigned and thrown in his lot with the forces now gathering on the extreme right of German politics, who were bitterly opposed to any further financial cooperation with Germany's former enemies.

The majority of the German political parties, however, remained committed to the basic principles of fulfilment. Indeed, the requirement to fulfil the Young Plan justified measures of domestic austerity that were extremely attractive to a large section of the right wing and business community. In the spring of 1930, therefore, the Grand Coalition was toppled over the question of budget cuts.[53] Hermann Mueller was to be Germany's last Social Democrat chancellor for almost forty years. He was ousted in favour of a minority government led by the staunchly nationalist Catholic Heinrich Bruening. At the Reichsbank, Schacht was replaced by Hans Luther. Ever since, there has been heated discussion about the economic policy choices made by Chancellor Bruening and Reichsbank president Luther between March 1930 and May 1932.[54]

Much of this, however, is beside the point. When one bears in mind the international constraints, it is clear that Bruening and Luther's hands were forced, certainly in 1930.[55] Under the rules of the gold standard, with the Young Plan demanding annual payments of 2 billion Reichsmarks and international capital markets increasingly nervous about German borrowing, deflation was the only option.[56] The political costs were huge. Between April and July 1930 Germany's parliamentary system tore itself apart in the struggle over Bruening's deflation package. It was to force through the highly controversial poll tax on 16 July 1930 that Bruening first resorted to the emergency powers provided under Article 48 of the Weimar constitution. More cuts and tax increases followed with the comprehensive emergency decree of 26 July. On top of the collapse in world trade and the gathering force of the business-cycle, the effect was to crash-land the economy. Between June 1930 and February 1931 unemployment rose by 2.1 million, twice the normal seasonal increase. In the general election of September 1930, Hitler's National Socialists achieved a stunning electoral breakthrough, raising their share of the vote from 2.5 to 18.3 per cent and gaining 107 seats, making them the second largest party in the Reichstag. The ensuing capital flight stripped the Reichsbank of one-third of its reserves and forced a further hike in interest rates.[57] But at the same time, the deflation strategy was having its intended effect. A trade deficit of 2.9 billion Reichsmarks in 1928 was, by 1931, turned into a trade surplus of 2.8 billion Reichsmarks (see Appendix, Table A1). This surplus, however, resulted not from rising exports but from the fact that due to the Depression, demand for foreign imports fell even more rapidly than German sales abroad. As factories shut down, and the blight of joblessness and poverty spread across German society, demand for foreign raw materials and consumer goods plummeted. It was a brutal process of adjustment, but Germany was following the normal prescriptions of the gold standard mechanism. And Bruening was rewarded in October 1930 with a bridging credit of $125 million brokered by Lee, Higginson and Co. of New York.[58]

If Bruening's government did have room for manoeuvre in 1930 and early 1931, it was with regard to foreign policy, not economics, and it used this freedom to dreadful effect.[59] Instead of following Stresemann's formula of the 1920s, which combined economic fulfilment with cautious diplomacy, Bruening and Julius Curtius coupled compliance with the financial provisions of the Young Plan with a foreign policy rhetoric borrowed from the nationalist right. The first element of the new German policy was the decision, despite the Reich's desperate financial situation, to build two new battle cruisers for the navy. The second and third elements were the proposal for Austro-German customs union and the increasingly proactive German policy in Central and South-eastern Europe, symbolized by the effort to conclude exclusive bilateral trade agreements with Hungary and Romania. All three prongs of this strategy were directed against France. This followed logically from Bruening's earlier rejection of Briand's proposal for closer Franco-German economic relations. But it was spectacularly ill-timed. Throughout the 1920s it had been a premise of German policy that though France posed the primary military threat to Germany, in financial terms it was a third-rate power, behind the United States and Britain.[60] By 1931, however, this was to seriously misunderstand the balance of power within the international financial system. Following the stabilization of the franc in 1926, the French central bank had set about systematically accumulating gold. By 1931 its gold holdings were substantially larger than those of the Bank of England and rivalled even those of the US Federal Reserve. Remarkably, in early 1931 Briand renewed his approach to Germany, suggesting that to assist Bruening in complying with the Young Plan, the Paris capital market might be opened to long-term German borrowing. Bruening's government replied on 21 March 1931 by publicly announcing the proposal for an Austro-German customs union, slamming shut the door to Franco-German economic cooperation.

Through aggressive foreign policy, Bruening thus further constrained his own room for economic manoeuvre.[61] Without the prospect of a foreign loan, Bruening had no option but to force through another painful round of deflation. And this, to make it palatable to the domestic electorate, required immediate action to accelerate the revision of the Young Plan. On 6 June 1931, therefore, in conjunction with his second emergency deflation decree, Bruening issued an aggressive demand for an end to reparations.[62] It was this, finally, which precipitated disaster. The financial markets had been troubled since March by the ominous resurgence of German nationalism. But despite the banking crisis in Austria there had not been a run either on the German banks or the German currency.[63] What triggered the crisis was Bruening's further

escalation of international tension. Within hours of the German government's aggressive communiqué, fear spread throughout the world's
financial markets that Bruening was about to announce a unilateral
moratorium, both on reparations and on Germany's obligations to its
private creditors. Over the next week the Reichsbank's reserves fell from
2.6 billion to 1.9 billion Reichsmarks. Despite a shocking rise in interest
rates, the reserves plunged inexorably towards the minimum level
required to provide 'gold-exchange backing' for the currency. By the
time the trouble at the DANAT and Dresdner banks hit the headlines
on 17 June, the Reichsbank was already facing a full-blown currency
crisis. Indeed, so severe was Germany's international financial situation
that on 20 June President Herbert Hoover was forced into a dramatic
and unprecedented intervention.

Even as the German situation became critical in the early summer of
1931, the fundamental logic of the Atlanticist strategy continued to
operate.[64] Misjudging the French reaction, Hoover's administration had
taken a remarkably weak line in response to the nationalist turn in
Bruening's foreign policy.[65] Instead of slapping down the customs union
proposal, Washington indicated its willingness to consider it as a first
step towards European economic integration. In the autumn of 1931,
the US State Department even expressed its impatience with France and
Poland for failing to address German concerns about its eastern borders.
Most critically of all, on 20 June 1931, in response to the talk of an
imminent debt moratorium, Washington finally conceded the linkage
between reparations and the inter-Allied war debts.[66] In the interests of
preserving America's loans to Germany, Hoover proposed a general
moratorium both on 'political payments' by Germany and on inter-
Allied war debts, opening the door to the formal cancellation of Ger-
many's reparations obligations a year later at the Lausanne conference.[67]
By June 1931, however, the French were in no mood for concessions.
Not having been consulted by Hoover and resenting the fact that the
United States was putting the interests of its long-term creditors above
French demands for reparations, Paris delayed its approval of the moratorium until 6 July, long enough for the German financial system to
haemorrhage hundreds of millions of Reichsmarks in foreign exchange.
It was in this crucial interval that the banking and currency crises became
fatally entangled. On Monday, 13 July the DANAT Bank collapsed,
precipitating a general bank run.[68] The cabinet and Reichsbank had no

option but to declare a general closure of the German financial system and on 15 July to announce a new system of exchange controls ending the operation of the free gold standard in Germany.[69] The value of the Reichsmark in terms of gold remained nominally the same. However, from the summer of 1931 onwards private holdings of foreign currency in Germany were nationalized. Any resident who received foreign currency in any form was required to exchange it for Reichsmarks provided by the Reichsbank. Anyone requiring foreign currency could obtain it only by application to the Reichsbank and all such applications were subject to severe rationing. Foreign currency was allocated to importers as a fixed percentage of the volume of their foreign transactions in the twelve months prior to the crisis. The Reichsbank thus acquired a direct means for regulating all imports to the German economy. In August, to complete the narrative of the crisis, the debt moratorium was extended by means of the so-called Standstill Agreement from German reparations to Germany's short-term credits, the most unstable element in Germany's debt mountain.[70]

But the storm had not yet passed. After Vienna and Berlin, London was the next casualty of the wave of financial instability sweeping across Europe. On 20 September, after weeks of severe speculation against the pound, Britain followed Germany in abandoning the gold standard.[71] Unlike the Reichsbank, however, the Bank of England chose to leave the gold standard not by suspending free convertibility, but by abandoning the fixed peg against gold. Sterling continued to be bought and sold freely, but its value was no longer guaranteed against gold. Within weeks the world's leading trading currency had plunged against the Reichsmark by 20 per cent. The anchor of the global financial system had torn loose. Britain's abandonment of gold turned a severe recession into a profound crisis of the international economy. By the end of September, twelve countries had followed Britain in allowing their currencies to float freely. Eleven more countries had devalued their exchange rates whilst retaining a gold peg; whilst those that stayed on gold at their old parities, like Germany, France and the Netherlands, had no option but to defend their balance of payments by adopting draconian restrictions on currency convertibility and trade. This took care of the import side of the current account. But German exporters now faced huge obstacles. With most of Germany's closest trade competitors having gained a major competitive advantage through devaluation, the volume of German exports fell between 1931 and 1932 by a further 30 per cent. The hard-won trade surplus of 2.8 billion Reichsmarks in 1931 was slashed within a year to no more than a few hundred million Reichsmarks, and even this precarious balance could only be maintained by further savage reductions in imports. By the spring of 1932, the allocation of hard currency to German importers was reduced to half the level that had been available prior to the crisis.[72]

One obvious way to alleviate Germany's predicament would have been to devalue the Reichsmark to bring it into line with sterling.[73] Indeed, the Bank of England had favoured devaluation of the Reichsmark already in the summer, as the most effective response to the banking and currency crisis.[74] Nor should one imagine that responsible officials in Germany had set themselves absolutely against such a measure. Bruening later claimed to have hoped to carry out a 20 per cent devaluation once the acute crisis had passed and Germany had obtained sufficient foreign exchange reserves to be sure of being able to maintain the new level of the Reichsmark.[75] In September 1931 Hjalmar Schacht hoped that Germany could take advantage of Britain's embarrassment to gain concessions on trade or credits, whilst pegging the Reichsmark to sterling. However, there were severe risks associated with such a strategy of which the Reichsbank was only too well aware. In the popular mind, devaluation was inseparably connected with the experience of hyperinflation. In 1922 and 1923 the plummeting value of the Reichsmark against the dollar had been the daily index of German misery. It was hardly surprising therefore that German commentators scared themselves with a scenario in which a large devaluation dramatically increased the price of imports, sparking an inflation. The Reichsbank was certainly concerned that its limited currency reserves would leave it defenceless if there were a speculative attack on a devalued German currency. What was ultimately decisive, however, was the effect of devaluation on the Reichsmark value of Germany's foreign debt. The vast bulk of Germany's foreign debt was denominated in foreign currency. The immediate effect of a reduction in the value of the Reichsmark would, therefore, have been to raise the burden in Reichsmark terms of Germany's foreign obligations. Though the Bank of England would have welcomed a German devaluation, the United States made it clear that it wanted to see Germany servicing its long-term loans whilst protecting its balance of payments by means of exchange controls.[76]

With President Hoover finally intervening decisively in the reparations question and even hinting that he might support German claims against Poland, Berlin opted one more time for the Atlantic strategy. Chancellor Bruening's government gambled that, sooner rather than later, American action on war debts would enable Britain and France to accept the end of reparations. This, Bruening confidently expected, would open the door to the normalization of both political and economic relations in Europe.[77] In the event, however, it took twelve disastrous months until the deal was finally done in Lausanne. Meanwhile, the outlook for the German economy was dire.

Pinned to gold by the American loans, but faced with devaluation of the majority of currencies in which Germany's trade was transacted, Bruening had no option but to push through another round of deflation and to do so by decree. The fourth Presidential emergency decree of 8 December 1931, apart from banning the wearing of party uniforms and political demonstrations, also ordered mandatory cuts in wages, salaries, prices and interest rates, followed by a further decrease in government spending and an increase in taxation.[78] It was, as *The Economist* put it, an intervention in 'economic liberty unparalleled outside the territory of the USSR'.[79] As his deflation Commissar, Bruening chose the severely conservative mayor of Leipzig, Carl Goerdeler, who immediately launched into a well-publicized austerity campaign.[80] This could not disguise, however, that Germany now faced ruin. Unemployment was rising to more than 6 million and large parts of the business community faced imminent collapse. Clearly inflation was a bugbear to the German public. But in its immediate impact on the economy, deflation was infinitely worse, principally because of its impact on balance sheets. Whilst incomes and revenues fell in line with the deflation of prices and wages, debts, mortgages and other financial obligations remained at their high pre-Depression levels. Over the winter of 1931–2, bankruptcies began to eat away at the fabric of German business. After the summer crisis of 1931, all the major banks were under state control. There were spectacular failures in the insurance and the engineering industries. AEG, one of Germany's premier electrical engineering firms, was ailing. A crisis was only averted at Vereinigte Stahlwerke, Europe's leading steel and coal conglomerate, through the Reich's acquisition of a large tranche of shares formerly owned by Friedrich Flick. As the Finance Minister, Hermann Dietrich, put it to a party colleague: 'I did not set out to nationalize half the Ruhr ... but the danger that foreign interests would buy up the shares and the fact that a collapse ... would have shaken ... the Stahlverein and that in turn would have rocked the painfully reconstructed structure of the German banks, have left me with no choice ...'[81]

Faced with this mounting economic disaster, the 'deflation consensus' that had sustained Bruening in his first eighteen months as Chancellor collapsed.[82] And Hjalmar Schacht again served as a bellwether. Throughout 1930 and early 1931 Schacht had abstained from overt criticism of the Bruening government, in the hope perhaps of returning to office as part of a conservative nationalist coalition. Following the disasters of the summer of 1931, Schacht abandoned this restraint to make a dramatic appearance at the rally of nationalist forces held at Bad Harzburg to denounce the spinelessness of Bruening's reparations policy.[83] A rejuvenation of Germany, he declared, was not a matter of party political programmes, or even of intelligence. It was a question of 'character'. And Schacht no longer made any secret of the source from which he expected this moral renewal. The main organizers of the event were Hugenberg and the DNVP. But the headline news was the appearance of Schacht on the Harzburg platform alongside Adolf Hitler.[84]

IV

Clearly, the nationalist turn in German foreign policy in 1930–31 was disastrously mistimed. Nevertheless, with the Hoover moratorium in place and with the Americans now pushing decisively towards an end to reparations, the Atlanticist programme had in a sense reached its logical conclusion. Under normal circumstances the continuation of a trans-Atlantic financial axis would of course have remained an attractive option for Germany. However, the collapse of the American economy and the British decision to abandon gold shattered the fundamental assumption on which Stresemann's conception had been based. Far from being a self-evident historical necessity, the unity and mutual interdependence of the world economy was now profoundly in question. There were, of course, voices both inside and outside Germany calling for a constructive effort to rebuild the fabric of the international order.[85] But, given the global economic disaster, it appeared to many that international economic dependence itself was actually the problem.[86] Nationalist visions, visions of a future in which global financial connections were not the determining influence in a nation's fate, now had far greater plausibility.[87] And even before Hitler took power four key elements in this nationalist agenda had already pushed well to the fore.

There is a deeply entrenched prejudice both in popular historical consciousness and the historical literature that the really important change in economic policy between the Weimar Republic and the Third Reich was the urgent implementation, after 1933, of programmes of national recovery and work creation.[88] To put it crudely, Heinrich Bruening made a fetish out of deflation. By contrast, work creation and the struggle against unemployment played a critical role in the propaganda of Hitler's regime. And in the light of the near contemporaneous 'Keynesian revolution' in economics, this contrast between before and after 1933 took on an even greater historical significance. For Keynesians, both in Germany and beyond, the disaster of the Weimar Republic will always stand as the most stark illustration of the consequences that follow from placing too much faith in the self-healing properties of the free market, a rhetorical connection that was put to extensive use in the long rearguard action that Keynesians fought against the intellectual forces of the New Right in the 1970s and 1980s.[89] Germany's history between 1929 and 1933 can certainly be made to serve this purpose. But if we seek to understand Hitler's regime outside this anachronistic frame of reference the emphasis on work creation as the key to understanding Nazi economic policy seems misplaced. Work creation in fact emerged as a subject for intense discussion on the right wing of German politics only in the second half of 1931. The Nazi party did not adopt work creation as a key part of its programme until the late spring of 1932, and it retained that status for only eighteen months, until December 1933, when civilian work creation spending was formally removed from the priority list of Hitler's government. Despite the claims of Goebbels's propaganda and despite the preoccupations of later commentators and historians, civilian work creation measures were clearly not a core agenda item for the nationalist coalition that seized power in January 1933. In fact, amongst the coalition partners of January 1933, work creation was highly divisive.[90] Credit-financed measures were fiercely opposed by Hugenberg, the leader of the DNVP, Hitler's indispensable coalition partner. Work creation was also viewed with suspicion by business and banking circles close to the Nazi party, who on this issue had a vocal spokesman in Hjalmar Schacht. All of which was in sharp contrast to the three issues that truly united the nationalist right and made possible the Hitler government of 30 January 1933: the triple priority of rearmament, repudiating Germany's foreign debts and saving German agriculture. These were the issues that had dominated the right-wing agenda since the 1920s. After 1933 they took priority, if necessary at the expense of work creation. It was Hitler's action on these three issues not work creation that truly marked the dividing line between the Weimar Republic and the Third Reich.

Disarmament and international finances had been linked ever since the 1920s. But in 1932, in a last desperate bid to fashion a peaceful solution to Europe's problems, President Hoover's administration forced them into an even tighter connection.[91] By the end of 1931 it was accepted by all sides that an end to reparations depended on American cancellation of French and British war debts. The emergency moratorium of 1931 had acknowledged this in practice. However, Hoover still had to sell debt reduction to Congress and to do so he needed to make progress on disarmament. It would be wholly unacceptable, if France and Britain used the financial relief they were asking for from the United States to engage in greater military spending. In early 1932 the Americans thus launched twin conference 'processes', in Geneva for disarmament and in Lausanne for political debts. A third track was provided by the long-winded preparations for an international conference on the global economy, which was to address the disorder in the world financial system and the damaging increase in international protectionism. In the 1920s, faced with an earlier American effort to reconstitute the international order, Stresemann's strategy had been to position Germany as a key ally of the United States. By contrast, from 1932 the governments of Franz von Papen, General Kurt von Schleicher and finally Adolf Hitler adopted a contrary position. Rather than seeking prosperity and security in multilateral arrangements guaranteed by the power of the United States, they sought to secure unilateral German advantage, if necessary even in opposition to America's efforts to restore the international order.[92]

Secret preparations for German rearmament had gone on throughout the 1920s but had never taken on truly threatening proportions.[93] Stresemann had always ensured that the clandestine activity of the military did not jeopardize his primary objectives of negotiating the removal of French troops from German soil and achieving a substantial reduction in reparations. The evacuation of the last foreign troops from the Rhineland in the summer of 1930 set the stage for more concrete discussions. Bruening apparently favoured a timetable under which the Reichswehr, the German Army, was to begin its rearmament as soon as the issue of reparations had been resolved. By December 1931, the Reichswehr had finalized the second so-called Ruestungsplan (Rearmament Plan), which called for spending of just over 480 million Reichsmarks over five years.[94] It was to provide Germany, in case of attack, with the capacity to supply a defensive force of twenty-one divisions, equipped with a small complement of artillery, tanks and aircraft. A more ambitious version of the plan, the so-called 'Milliardenprogram' (billion Reichsmark programme), set out the extra spending on industrial infrastructure required to keep this force permanently in the field. This planning, however, since it required no expansion of the peacetime strength of the Reichswehr, remained at least formally within the terms of Versailles. During 1932, General Schleicher's increasingly prominent role in German politics added a new urgency and boldness to the thinking of the Reichswehr. In the second half of 1932 the Reichswehr leadership began planning for an outright Treaty breach through a significant increase in peacetime military strength. The Umbau Plan, authorized by Schleicher on 7 November 1932, called for the creation of a standing army of 21 divisions based around a cadre of 147,000 professional soldiers and a substantial militia. In the autumn of 1932 the German delegation to the Geneva disarmament talks temporarily withdrew from the conference in a bid to force France and Britain to accept Germany's equality of status: whatever agreement was reached was to apply equally to all parties. But Schleicher, who succeeded to the Chancellorship in December 1932, still shrank from a complete breach with the international community. With the principle of equality conceded, the Germans returned to Geneva. Behind Schleicher, however, was a more aggressive cohort of generals, including Werner von Blomberg, who demanded an open resort to unilateral rearmament. Furthermore, the practical problem of rearmament imposed its own timetable. With the Depression taking its toll on the German engineering industry, it seemed that unless substantial government funds were soon forthcoming, the industrial capacity on which rearmament ultimately depended might soon cease to exist.[95] It was with this in mind that General Schleicher's government pioneered the use of work creation, both as a means of hiding military spending from foreign observers and as a way of uniting the German people behind rearmament.

In strictly economic terms, the defining agenda of German nationalism from the Dawes Plan of 1924 onwards was not work creation but the repudiation of Germany's international obligations, first reparations and then the international credits taken up since the early 1920s to pay them. Until 1932, as we have seen, logic dictated the need to stick to the United States. The Young Plan did at least offer a reduced annuity and only pressure from the United States offered any prospect of a final elimination of reparations. The ultra-nationalists thus remained in a minority and fulfilment remained the bedrock of respectable politics. By the autumn of 1932, however, the situation was quite different. In July 1932 at the reparations conference in Lausanne, Britain and France agreed to a deal that brought a de facto end to Germany's reparations payments.[96] Significantly, they did so, against the will of the Americans, by tying a final end to all German obligations to a cancellation of the war debts owed by them to the United States. Britain made one last payment on its American war debts in December 1932, but only under protest. France, Belgium, Poland, Estonia and Hungary simply defaulted. Prime Minister Édouard Herriot, who had advocated honouring France's obligations, suffered a crushing defeat in parliament. America was no longer able to hold the ring in Europe. And this in turn had dramatic implications for German strategy.

In January 1933, Germany still owed 19 billion Reichsmarks to foreign creditors, of which 10.3 billion were long-term bonds and 4.1 billion were short-term loans covered by the Standstill Agreement.[97] At least 8.3 billion Reichsmarks were owed to the United States, by far the largest creditor. This debt burden, contracted since 1924, threatened Germany's standard of living no less seriously than the reparations that had now been removed from the table. To service its debts Germany faced the need to transfer abroad interest and principal totalling something close to 1 billion Reichsmarks per annum, and, given the unavailability of new credit, in the 1930s unlike in the 1920s Germany faced the prospect of having to make 'real transfers'. It could not simply borrow afresh to repay its creditors. If Germany was to service its debts, exports would have to exceed German imports by at least 1 billion

Reichsmarks. This meant a substantial reduction in the standard of living. And with reparations gone, almost half of Germany's onerous debt service payments would go to one country, the United States. Whilst Germany still needed American assistance in forcing Britain and France to end reparations, it was in Berlin's interest to cooperate with Washington, even if the burden of American debts was heavy and the chance of new credits was slim. After the Lausanne agreement on reparations, with France and Britain bitterly at odds with the United States over their war debts, this imperative evaporated. Nor, in case of default, did Germany have much to fear from American trade sanctions. The balance of trans-Atlantic trade was hugely unfavourable to Germany. In this respect, American efforts to stabilize Europe had been fundamentally contradictory.[98] American tariffs in excess of 44 per cent, compounding America's competitive advantage in virtually every area of manufacturing, made it difficult, if not impossible, for America's debtors to repay their debts, even if they had wanted to. Once reparations were lifted, this contradiction at the heart of American foreign economic policy provided Germany's nationalists with a ready-made excuse for default.

Of course, this was not the only possible conclusion that could have been drawn from Germany's situation. Aggressive unilateralism and default were not foreordained. In the 1920s Stresemann had sought to make Germany into a leading advocate of multilateral free trade, a line that was enthusiastically backed by at least the export-orientated industries.[99] After all, Germany in times of prosperity had been one of the world's pre-eminent trading nations, with exports going to literally every corner of the globe. In 1932 and 1933 preliminary negotiations were already under way for the World Economic Conference to be held in London, at which tariffs would be a key issue.[100] There was still the opportunity for Germany to act as a positive force for liberalization rather than nationalist disintegration. By 1932, however, the voices of liberalism were drowned out by the deafening clamour of economic nationalism. Indeed, given the disintegration of the gold standard, even the Reich's industrial association found it difficult to sustain a consensus on multilateral free trade. And here again it was the ex-president of the Reichsbank, Hjalmar Schacht, who led the nationalist charge. At the end of 1931 he put before some of Germany's leading industrialists a new trade plan.[101] Using an organization reminiscent of that employed during World War I, all German imports would be subject to central control. They could then be used to force those countries supplying Germany with goods, to accept at least equal quantities of German exports. Given the damage that this would cause to Germany's complex multilateral trading relations, Schacht's plan found favour with only a minority of German industrialists. In the ranks of agriculture, however, the enemies of liberalism found more eager supporters.

In so far as economic interests were responsible for the collapse of the Weimar Republic and the installation on 30 January 1933 of Hitler's government, the group chiefly responsible was not big business or even heavy industry, but Germany's embattled farmers.[102] Ever since the 1870s, agriculture had been a lost cause to liberalism.[103] Bismarck had won over the agrarians in 1879 with the imposition of the first substantial grain tariff. This had not halted the decline of agriculture, but it had significantly slowed what might otherwise have been a very dramatic process of social displacement and internal migration. In the mid-nineteenth century the share of workers in agriculture had stood at a half. By 1925 that had fallen to 25 per cent, but this still meant that 13 million people depended directly on farming for a living. The farm lobby was thus a vital constituency for all political parties other than the Social Democrats and Communists, neither of whom managed to devise a credible agrarian programme. By the late 1920s, however, the respectable parties of the centre right were struggling to maintain their support in agrarian circles, as the German farming community became progressively radicalized by the worldwide collapse in commodity prices.[104] As a result, the farm lobby began demanding not only increased protection and relief from its debts, but a fundamental reorientation in German trade policy. Since tariffs had not proved effective in keeping out low-priced competition, the agrarians now demanded the introduction of specific quotas with which to restrict the import of key agricultural products to Germany from particular countries.[105] Agricultural tariffs had always been objectionable to liberal-minded Germans. The new proposals, by discriminating between individual trading partners, threatened to destroy the system of multilateral trade altogether. It could not be denied, however, that the emergency measures of July 1931 pointed in this direction. After all, the Reichsbank's new system of foreign exchange rationing provided precisely the instrument that was needed to control the composition of German imports.[106] On quotas, however, Bruening dug in his heels. His government was lavish in its support for agriculture in every other respect, but on quotas there could be no compromise.[107] On this point both Papen and Schleicher followed Bruening's lead. Papen though he approved quotas in principle, did so only within the limits 'permissible according to current trade treaties' and when Papen fell, there was no decisive action by Schleicher.[108] This, however, drove the farm lobby into outright opposition to the Republic.[109] In early 1933 key leaders of the agrarian lobby intervened decisively with President Paul von Hindenburg, himself the owner of a large estate, to push him towards accepting a coalition between Hugenberg's DNVP and Hitler's Nazi party. Like the advocates of debt default and rearmament, what the agrarians wanted was a government that would pursue their conception of Germany's national interest unilaterally, forcing Germany's neighbours and trading partners to accept its terms.

V

The enemies of liberalism were clearly on the march in Germany. By 1932 the damage done to the parliamentary system may well have been irreparable, making it more likely than not that the Weimar Republic would have been replaced by some kind of authoritarian, nationalist regime. After all, Germany ended 1932 with generals both as Chancellor and as President of the Republic. But the more we know about the back-door manoeuvring that led to Hitler's appointment on 30 January 1933 the less certain it seems that that particular outcome was in any sense predetermined. There seems every reason to believe that the world might have been spared the nightmare of a National Socialist dictatorship if only Hitler had been kept out of government for a few months longer. The Nazis had surged to their most spectacular electoral triumph in July 1932 in the general election that followed the ousting of Chancellor Bruening, garnering 37.2 per cent of the vote. However, thanks to the resistance of President Hindenburg and key members of Papen's cabinet, Hitler had not been offered the post of Reich Chancellor and he refused to accept any lesser position.[110] Despite its electoral triumph, the NSDAP remained in opposition and in the second general election of 1932, in November, it suffered the consequences. Though the poll yielded no workable parliamentary majority, precipitating the fall of Chancellor Papen, it also delivered a severe setback to Hitler's party, which saw its vote slump back to 33 per cent. The electorate were clearly disappointed with Hitler's failure to take office. The party activists were beginning to flag. The momentum that had carried the NSDAP from victory to victory since 1929 was exhausted. In the aftermath of the November setback, the divisions between left and right wings that had plagued National Socialism in the 1920s, suddenly re-emerged. In December 1932 General Schleicher, the real king-maker in German politics, finally took power himself and made a popular start by launching the first national work creation initiative. Gustav Stolper later recalled a jocular breakfast meeting in the Reich Chancellery in January 1933, at which Schleicher and his aides took turns to predict how many more votes the Nazis would lose in the election that Schleicher hoped to call in the spring.[111]

Meanwhile, the first hints of an economic recovery had made their appearance in America in June 1932.[112] After the lifting of reparations at Lausanne, demand for German bonds began to strengthen.[113] This was crucial, because it provided an opportunity for hard-pressed banks to offload illiquid assets and to rebuild their cash balances. In late summer there were signs of a revival in construction. Inevitably, once the harvest was in and building activity slowed for the winter, unemployment did begin to rise again, heading back towards the shock figure of 6 million. But the mere fact that this did not exceed the level reached the previous year was encouraging to the experts. The 'seasonally adjusted unemployment level', a novel concept made fashionable by the new-fangled science of business cycle analysis, had stabilized. By the end of 1932, Stolper's journal *Der Deutsche Volkswirt* was joined in its optimistic assessment of Germany's economic situation by the authoritative biannual report of the Reichskreditgesellschaft.[114] In December 1932, even the Berlin institute for business cycle research, the most influential economic commentator in inter-war Germany and also one of the most pessimistic, declared that at least the process of contraction was over.[115] *The Economist*'s Berlin correspondent reported that 'for the first time for three or four years', the German bourgeoisie could see 'a glimmer of economic light'.[116] This is a crucial point because it contradicts all subsequent portrayals of the German economy under National Socialism.[117] The German economy in 1933 was not a lifeless wreck. It was beginning what might well have become a vigorous cylical rebound. Certainly, on 1 January 1933 the New Year editorials of the Berlin press were optimistic. *Vorwaerts*, the social democratic daily, welcomed the New Year with the headline: 'Hitler's Rise and Fall'.[118]

In the event, what decided the fate of Germany and with it the world was the tragic miscalculation of a small coterie of ultra-nationalist conservatives. Ex-Chancellor Papen, embittered by his ousting in December 1932, conspired with the agrarian lobby and some of the most aggressive elements in the military to pressure the ailing Hindenburg into dismissing Schleicher and forming a new government founded on the popular platform of National Socialism. This was not possible without giving Hitler the Chancellorship. But the ultra-nationalist Hugenberg would take responsibility for both Agriculture and Economic Affairs. General Blomberg would take the Defence Ministry and Papen the Vice-Chancellorship. Nor should we assume that the balance of forces within the Hitler–Hugenberg–Papen–Blomberg government was fore-ordained. There were powerful forces in German society, most notably the military and the churches, but also the leadership of German business that could have done much to deflect Hitler and his followers from their path.[119] The policy of anti-Semitism, aggressive rearmament and unilateral diplomacy was clearly in no sense forced on Germany. Indeed, it may strike some readers as absurd to have to make this point. But doing so makes clear that this standard of counterfactual criticism is not always applied even-handedly to all aspects of Hitler's regime. The economic sphere, in fact, is often exempt from such critical scrutiny altogether. Too often it is assumed that real strategic choices in economic policy, choices in which National Socialist ideology really mattered, were faced by Hitler's regime only in 1936, four years after the seizure of power. Too often it is assumed that addressing the unemployment crisis must have been the first priority of the regime. But this is one more effect of giving excessive attention to work creation. In relation to the unemployment crisis it is possible to tell a story in which Hitler's regime simply pursued a long-overdue functional response to Germany's dire economic crisis. Indeed, in many accounts, even recent accounts, one detects a hint of admiration for the ability of Hitler's regime to break with the hidebound conservatism that supposedly constricted previous governments.[120] But, as has already been suggested and will be shown in detail in the next chapter, the 'Keynesian' issues of work creation and unemployment were never as prominent in the agenda of Hitler's government as is commonly supposed. The most crucial economic policy decisions taken in 1933–4 concerned not unemployment, but Germany's foreign debts, its currency and rearmament, and in relation to these questions there could never be any pretence of political innocence. These issues were at the very core of the nationalist programme of self-assertion that was the true agenda of Hitler's government. Furthermore, once we give due emphasis to the questions of foreign debt and foreign trade, it becomes clear that, for many millions of Germans, Hitler's economic miracle was in fact a highly ambiguous experience.

If we are to avoid a depoliticized economic history of the Nazi regime, at odds with our view of every other aspect of the regime's history, we must always bear in mind that even in 1933 there were alternatives to the economic strategy pursued by Hitler's government. And not only that: these alternatives might well have brought greater material benefits to the majority of the German population. However, whilst keeping the sense of alternatives and thus the possibility of critique firmly in view, we must also not underestimate the damage done both inside and outside Germany by the Great Depression. Even if Hitler had not been appointed Chancellor and Schleicher had remained in power, it is hard to imagine Germany pursuing a course that was anything other than disruptive to the last-ditch efforts to restore peace and stability to the world, at the disarmament talks in Geneva and at the World Economic Conference in London. Added to which, one would be falling into the solipsistic trap of nationalist strategy if one imagined that the question was ultimately Germany's to decide. Germany could pursue a policy more or less congenial to global stabilization, but the chance of achieving that elusive goal depended critically on the other major powers. And in 1933 the environment was far less congenial to a multilateral strategy than ten years earlier. Above all, the position of the United States had dramatically changed. In 1923 Stresemann had clearly been right to gamble on America as the dominant force in world affairs, both economically and as a future military superpower. Ten years later America's position was fatally weakened by the most severe crisis in recorded economic history. As Hitler took power, Hoover was replaced by Roosevelt, who in his first months in office was focused, to the exclusion of all else, on saving America from the final disastrous spasm of the Depression. It would be years before the United States re-emerged as the pivot in all strategic calculations, and by that time Hitler's ghastly regime had gathered too much momentum to be stopped by anything other than brute force.

PART I

Recovery

2

'Every Worker his Work'

On 1 February 1933, two days after his appointment as Chancellor, sweating with anticipation, Hitler recorded the first national radio address of his life.[1] The unifying thread of his speech was the determination of his government to overcome the disintegration that had resulted from Germany's surrender in November 1918 and the 'Communist' revolution that had followed.[2] The fact that Hitler chose even on this triumphant occasion to return to this moment, fourteen years earlier, provides a striking testament to the centrality of this trauma to his politics. By way of specific policies Hitler promised a four-year programme to rescue the German peasantry from poverty and to overcome the unemployment of German workers. He promised to reform the German state apparatus and to bring order to the ramshackle division of labour between the Reich, states and local authorities. By way of social policy, he offered the promise of an agrarian settlement programme, labour service and a guarantee to maintain health care and pensions. Promoting work and economy in the public services would in turn provide a guarantee against any 'danger to our currency'. All of this was clearly more or less what Hitler actually intended. On foreign policy, by contrast, one had to read between the lines. Hitler paid ritual lip-service to the Geneva disarmament negotiations, stressing his willingness even to accept the abolition of Germany's army, provided there was general disarmament. However, he also stated that the highest mission of the national government was the 'protection of the [national] right to life and thereby the restoration of the freedom of our *Volk*'.[3] This was nationalist code for the opposite. The freedom that Hitler had in mind was the freedom for Germany to pursue its national self-interest through unilateral action, if necessary by military means, regardless of international constraints or treaties.

Two days later, at the invitation of General Blomberg, the newly appointed Defence Minister, Hitler gave Germany's military leadership a more honest insight into his goals. On this occasion he restated the views he had developed in *Mein Kampf* and his 'Second Book'. What was remarkable was simply that he did so now as the newly appointed Chancellor of Germany. Nothing had changed his fundamental belief that struggle for *Lebensraum* was Germany's only salvation.[4] The task of domestic policy was to consolidate the foundations of rearmament. The destruction of Marxism, the reconstruction of the economy and the rescue of the peasantry were means to that end. And, as in 1928, Hitler made no secret of his long-term intentions. The first priority of German rearmament was to escape the overwhelming threat posed by France and its Allies, who might intervene at any time. The longer-term objective was 'possibly the struggle for new export possibilities [i.e. colonies], possibly – and probably better – conquest of new *Lebensraum* in the East and its ruthless Germanization. Certain that the current economic situation can be changed only with political power and struggle. Everything that can occur now . . . mere makeshift.'[5] Less than a week later, on 9 February, whilst chairing the cabinet committee on work creation, Hitler reiterated the same basic points. As far as Hitler was concerned there was only one priority: rearmament. 'The future of Germany depends exclusively and only on the reconstruction of the Wehrmacht. All other tasks must cede precedence to the task of rearmament . . . In any case, I [Hitler] take the view that in future in case of conflict between the demands of the Wehrmacht and demands for other purposes, the interests of the Wehrmacht must in every case have priority.'[6]

Within days of Hitler's accession to power, the direction was set. But the timing of the subsequent moves depended on a complex mesh of domestic and international constraints.

I

The general election scheduled for 5 March was a crucial test of Hitler's popularity. It was essential that the government parties should gain a large majority if they were to push through their dictatorial agenda under cover of legality. In three previous general elections, in 1930 and 1932, Germany's 19 million voters had been unable to agree on a programme for national economic recovery. Even in 1932, at the height of their popularity, with Strasser's work creation pledges emblazoned on their banners, the Nazis had attracted the support of only slightly more than a third of the electorate. If the Hitler government was to secure a solid majority, it was clearly essential to avoid alarming the public with dangerous foreign policy adventures. It was also crucial to preserve the façade of nationalist unity on which Hitler's government was based. In Hitler's cabinet the finance portfolio was retained by Schwerin von Krosigk, a conservative former civil servant, who was known to oppose credit-financed work creation. Hans Luther, the pope of monetary orthodoxy, remained as president of the Reichsbank. Alfred Hugenberg the leader of the DNVP, an essential element in the Hitler coalition, held the portfolios both for economic affairs and for agriculture. Though he was an economic nationalist in every sense of the word, Hugenberg too opposed work creation beyond that already approved by Chancellor Schleicher. Forcing through an immediate expansion in government spending against this kind of opposition would have been a distraction from Hitler's chief priority in February 1933, mobilizing the exhausted Nazi party for one last electoral effort.[7]

Both the 'gigantic and comprehensive' work creation package that Hitler had promised on his first night in office and the handsome promises made to the military would have to wait until after the votes were counted. In any case, there was little need for immediate action.[8] From his predecessor General Schleicher Hitler inherited a fully fledged, credit-financed work creation programme budgeted at a total of 600 million Reichsmarks. None of this money had been spent by the time Hitler took office. The initial rearmament and the initial work creation measures of Hitler's government therefore consisted of spending Schleicher's money. Two hundred million out of the 600 million were allocated for the purposes of the Reich, of which 190 million was claimed by the military; 200 million was spent by local government. The rest went on agricultural land amelioration.

The results of the March election were a disappointment to Hitler and Goebbels. The failure of the Nazis to achieve anywhere near an absolute majority, even when their electoral appeal was backed up by considerable intimidation, confirms the conclusion reached by most observers in the autumn of 1932. As a political movement, the Nazi party had reached its limit well short of a majority of the German electorate. Now, however, Hitler and his party no longer needed to rely exclusively on the electoral process.[9] After applying massive pressure to the Catholic Centre party, Hitler got the two-thirds majority he needed for the Enabling Law of 23 March 1933. This freed his government to rule by decree. The road was open to the decisive application of physical force. In stark contrast to the reluctant revolutionaries of November 1918, who had done their best to suppress the popular uprising against World War I and the Wilhelmine monarchy, the Nazis did not hesitate to combine the ballot box with physical force. Across Germany in the spring of 1933, the Nazi party and its nationalist allies unleashed a ferocious wave of violence directed above all against the Communists, Social Democrats and Germany's small Jewish minority. Inexplicably, the socialist trade unions lulled themselves into believing that they might be able to cooperate with Hitler's government. They even joined with Hitler and Goebbels in orchestrating 1 May 1933 as a celebration of national labour, the first time that May Day had been treated as a public holiday. On the day after, brownshirt squads stormed the offices of the trade unions and shut them down. Hundreds of millions of Reichsmarks in property and welfare funds were impounded. Robert Ley, a hard-drinking Hitler loyalist, established himself in command of the new German Labour Front (Deutsche Arbeitsfront, DAF). The dynamism of Nazi shopfloor activists (NSBO) had by this time reached proportions that were disturbing even to Ley. So, to restore order, the Reich appointed regional trustees of labour (Treuhaender der Arbeit) to set wages and to moderate conflicts between employers and rebellious Nazi shop stewards.

Meanwhile, the domestic obstacles to a more expansionary government spending policy were being cleared away. In April 1933, the Reich Labour Minister, Franz Seldte, a nationalist, had taken up the cause of work creation, urging Hitler to use the May Day parades as the launching pad for the long promised work creation programme. A credit-financed work creation package costed at between 1 billion and 1.6 billion Reichsmarks was to energize the labour markets.[10] In the midst of the violence of the Machtergreifung (seizure of power) Hans Luther was dispatched as the new German ambassador to Washington. He was replaced as president of the Reichsbank by Hjalmar Schacht, returning for his second stint at the helm of German monetary policy. Given Schacht's open affiliation with the Nazi party since the autumn of 1931, this came as no surprise. But it sent a clear signal as to Hitler's aggressive intentions. In April, the changes at the Reichsbank were followed by the appointment of Fritz Reinhardt (b. 1895) as Secretary of State at the Reich Finance Ministry. Since 1932 Reinhardt had made a name for himself, alongside the ill-fated Gregor Strasser, as the party's leading spokesman on work creation.[11] His appointment alongside the conservative Krosigk signalled the decisive shift in the balance of power.

Schacht's position on work creation and credit inflation was complex. He was no friend of public works schemes.[12] On the other hand, he clearly did believe in a creative role for monetary policy. Furthermore, his appointment in March 1933 may well have been conditional on his prior agreement to substantial spending on work creation. In any case, Schacht's real affinity with the nationalist right concerned not domestic policy but the international agenda. What is often overlooked in parochial discussions of the Nazi seizure of power is the tumultuous international context in which it took place. Hitler's Machtergreifung coincided both with the inauguration of a new American President and the final dramatic aftershocks of the Great Depression.[13] As Roosevelt took office the United States was swept by a financial panic which forced him to impose a nationwide bank closure and restrict the export of capital. On 19 April 1933 the United States unilaterally suspended gold convertibility and allowed the dollar to depreciate. Over the next four months the dollar fell by 30 per cent against the Reichsmark. Replicated across the world this delivered a devastating shock to what remained of the international system of fixed exchange rates.[14] The dollar devaluation again faced Germany with a choice, whether or not to devalue. If it did not follow the dollar off gold, Germany would be left completely uncompetitive in every export market in the world. On the other hand, the dollar's devaluation also brought a huge windfall, by reducing the Reichsmark value of the debts Germany owed to the United States. We shall have more to say about the question of devaluation in the next chapter. But in the spring of 1933, Schacht seconded Hitler in denouncing any currency experiments.[15] Pandering to popular sentiment, Hitler and Schacht made the defence of the official gold value of the Reichsmark into a symbol of the new regime's reliability and trustworthiness. Unlike in 1923, it was now the dollar not the Reichsmark that was plunging in value on the foreign exchanges.

At the same time Schacht clearly sensed the opportunity presented by the chaotic international situation and embarked on a trip to the United States, hoping to exploit the temporary enfeeblement of Germany's major creditor.[16] Schacht's absence from Berlin was the major reason why final agreement on the unemployment scheme was postponed until the end of May. On his return, he immediately agreed terms with the Finance Ministry (RFM) on a one-billion-Reichsmark work creation package.[17] The so-called 'Reinhardt programme' was finally approved by the cabinet on 28 May and announced to the German public on 1 June. A little more than a year after Gregor Strasser's famous address to the Reichstag demanding action to address the unemployment crisis, the Nazi party had delivered on its promise. The package was large. One billion Reichsmarks was a very substantial sum when compared to the Reich's regular expenditure on goods and services, which during the worst years of the crisis, 1932–3, had fallen to as little as 1.95 billion Reichsmarks. Reinhardt's funds were directed towards precisely the priorities outlined before 1932 by Strasser and other advocates of work creation. The money was to flow into ex-urban settlements, road works and housing, appealing to a wide spectrum of both social and national interests. Above all the package was to be credit-financed.

'Productive credit creation' was the nub of the debate that bitterly divided economic opinion across the world in the inter-war period.[18] The fundamental question was whether public expenditure, financed in the short term by newly minted money, could have any real impact on production and employment. All sides in the argument agreed that work creation spending financed by higher taxes could add nothing to the total volume of demand. Taxes simply transferred purchasing power from private hands to the state. If, as an alternative, the state raised funds by conventional borrowing on the capital market this did not involve an immediate reduction in private spending because the funds available for long-term borrowing came ultimately from household savings, that is, unspent household income. However, if the capital market was tight, the Reichsmark borrowed by the state could not be taken up by private borrowers. To this extent, state borrowing would 'crowd out' private investment. The only way to finance work creation that was guaranteed not to squeeze private economic activity was through the creation of 'new credit'. For the defenders of orthodoxy this was illogical. Writing cheques could not produce more real goods, more equipment or plant. Money was merely a token, a means of exchange. Printing more money could not create 'real' jobs, any more than talking about work creation would by itself create new employment opportunities. Credit-financed work creation would simply result in inflation. At first, there might be the illusion of a 'real' effect. Men would be set to work on government building sites. But as prices rose, the purchasing power of wages and profits would be eaten away. Private spending would fall. The inflation induced by government credit creation would act as a hidden tax. There would be no more real jobs created than if the government spending had been financed out of regular taxation. For the advocates of work creation, this orthodox argument was based on a misunderstanding. If the economy was fully employed – with every worker and every factory at full stretch – new credit creation might well lead to inflation. In that case it would indeed be true that additional government spending would be financed by 'involuntary saving'. But if labour and machinery were lying idle, the game need not be zero-sum. After all, with millions of workers desperate for work and with factories starved of orders, there was little reason to expect prices to rise. Under conditions of mass unemployment, government spending financed by new credit would result in greater real demand, greater production and employment rather than inflation. The art of economic policy was to provide the correct dose of credit-financed stimulation, sufficient to restore full employment, but not an excessive amount that would push the economy beyond the limit of full employment and unleash an inflationary free-for-all. In 1933, given that there were 6 million unemployed and most of German industry was running at less than 50 per cent capacity, this was not a hard balance to strike.

The initial experiment in credit-financed work creation was launched not by Hitler's government, but by General Schleicher in December 1932.[19] The first step was to arrange for companies that were carrying out government projects to be paid, not directly in cash, but in the form of interest-bearing IOUs (work creation bills) in the name of the state agency commissioning the work. To persuade contractors to accept this unusual form of payment, the work creation bills were guaranteed by a cluster of state-affiliated banks. The most important of these were the Deutsche Gesellschaft fuer oeffentliche Arbeiten and the Deutsche Bau- und Bodenbank, which had been established in 1930 with a view to financing Bruening's abortive plan for a work creation programme to counter the onset of the Depression.[20] Against a discount, a contractor could cash the work creation bills with any of the banks in the consortium. The banks were provided with the necessary cash, by themselves discounting the bills with the Reichsbank. The Reichsbank thus ended up holding the work creation bills, in exchange for new cash. To make this acceptable to the Reichsbank, the RFM promised to redeem the bills according to a fixed timetable. Once recovery had been achieved, the RFM would raise the necessary funds through the additional flow of tax revenue generated by economic revival, or by floating long-term government loans, once the financial markets had recovered and savings were buoyant.

The announcement of the Reinhardt programme certainly had its intended propagandistic effect. Across Germany it unleashed a wave of local activism.[21] The national champion in the Battle for Work (Arbeitsschlacht) was Erich Koch, the Gauleiter of East Prussia. When Hitler took power in January 1933, this backward rural enclave, separated from Germany by the Polish corridor, registered 130,000 unemployed. Within only six months, on 16 July 1933, the first East Prussian district was declared free of unemployment. A month later, Gauleiter Koch proudly reported to the Fuehrer the total 'cleansing' of his province. More than a hundred thousand men and women had been put to work in a spectacular display of National Socialist energy. Wasteland was ploughed up, fertilized and reseeded. Homesteads were created for a new generation of agricultural colonists. Goebbels saw to it that this feat attracted 'astonishment and admiration throughout the Reich and far beyond Germany's borders'. But, in fact, closer investigation reveals that the East Prussian 'Battle for Work' was, from start to finish, a carefully stage-managed media event. The agricultural economy of East Prussia was ideally suited for fast-acting but primitive work creation measures. And it was Walther Funk, the ex-business editor now acting as State Secretary in Goebbels's Propaganda Ministry, who chose Koch's provincial backwater as the launch pad for the national campaign. Goering, as Prime Minister of Prussia, pressured the Reich's Finance Ministry into concentrating a disproportionate share of the national work creation fund in a territory with only 1.89 per cent of the national unemployed.[22] And Koch did not disappoint. The jobless of East Prussia were ruthlessly conscripted. Thousands of married men were herded together into so-called 'Camps of Comradeship' (Kameradschaftslager), where they were subjected to a heavy programme of earth-moving and political education laid on by the German Labour Front. Koch even managed to get one of the early, improvised concentration camps accredited as a work creation venture.

The East Prussian triumph provided an example for party leaders across Germany. The 'Koch Plan' was followed by the 'Tapolski Plan' for the Rhineland, the 'Goering Plan' for Berlin, the 'Siebert Plan' for Bavaria and the 'Hellmuth Plan' for Franconia. However, Koch's primitive programme of 'generalized shovelling' was unsuitable for more developed regions of Germany.[23] Even within the construction sector, earth-moving was suitable employment only for the least skilled labourers. Bricklayers, carpenters, plumbers and electricians needed alternative employment. After construction workers, the second largest group of unemployed were metalworkers, who regarded road work with contempt. Construction was even less appropriate for the tens of thousands of clerks and secretaries who were desperately seeking work in the commercial districts of Hamburg or Berlin. No surprise, therefore, that the fall in unemployment during 1933 benefited mainly the rural areas. The actual hot spots of unemployment, Berlin, Hamburg, Bremen and the Ruhr, as well as the southern cities of Stuttgart and Munich, benefited relatively little in the early stages of the recovery. To make matters worse, municipalities found that when they applied for Reinhardt funds, their requests were often subject to minute and obstructive criticism. The construction of new buildings was discouraged in favour of road work. Cities that were in arrears with their repayment of work creation credits issued before 1933 were excluded from consideration. The reason for this niggardliness in the management of the Reinhardt programme becomes clearer when we consider the overall allocation of the funds. The majority of the moneys was reserved for local infrastructure work of various kinds. However, between 1933 and 1934 a steadily rising amount, finally to reach 230 million Reichmarks, was siphoned off for 'special measures' at the discretion of the Reich's authorities. 'Special measures' was a euphemism for military infrastructure – strategic roads, airfields, barracks and waterways.[24]

In the work creation mythology of the Nazi regime, the autobahns occupy a special place.[25] Ironically, however, the autobahns were never principally conceived as work creation measures and they did not contribute materially to the relief of unemployment.[26] They followed a logic, not of work creation, but of national reconstruction and rearmament, a logic indeed that was as much symbolic as it was practical. The idea of a long-distance road network to join together Germany's population centres had fascinated the pundits since the 1920s. As far back as 1925 a company had been set up to promote a new motorized Hansa, a network of commercial cities joined by superhighways. Hitler enthusiastically embraced this vision and, soon after he came to power, he nominated Fritz Todt to construct the network.[27] Todt was a competent civil engineer, but he was chosen principally for his political commitment. Todt (1891–1942) was an 'old fighter' of the Nazi party, a man of unquestioning personal loyalty to Hitler, who embraced racial *Weltanschauung* without hesitation. In his seminal memorandum on 'Road construction and road administration' of December 1932, Todt presented the programme of road modernization, not as an answer to the crisis of unemployment, but as a means of national reconstruction.[28] With an allocation of 5 billion Reichsmarks spread over five years, Todt promised to build an integrated network of 6,000 new kilometres of roadway. Finances would be provided, not by borrowing from 'Jewish banks', but from the savings of German workers themselves. As Todt himself made clear, the ultimate rationale for these gigantic roadways was military. Germany's fundamental strategic dilemma was its vulnerability to military attack from both east and west. The autobahns would serve as the 'lifeline' of a reconstructed national defence system. Within five years, Todt promised, he would be able to pull off a grandiose repeat of the French operation on the Marne, which had saved Paris from the Kaiser's armies. On Todt's motorways, 300,000 troops could be ferried from the eastern to the western border of the Reich in two nights of hard driving. From its inception, Todt's vision was thus intertwined with the dream of national rearmament. An army of 300,000 was three times the limit stipulated by the Treaty of Versailles. This did not preclude, of course, the opening of the roads in peacetime for 'economic usage by passenger and freight traffic'. Nor was Todt blind to the appeal of work creation. He estimated that an annual budget of 1 billion Reichsmarks would enable him to employ 600,000 workers, especially if the use of machinery was kept to a minimum.

Hitler was delighted. Overriding opposition from the Reichsbahn, the national railway company, he gave Todt backing for the establishment of a Reich motorway corporation. In the last days of June 1933,

Todt was appointed as general inspector for German roads, with authority over both the autobahns and major provincial roads. Todt's organization was to become a powerful institution in the Third Reich, a real counterpart to the Reichsbahn as an influence on national transport infrastructure and one of the seedbeds for the future system of economic control. On 23 September, on the Frankfurt–Darmstadt building site, Hitler and Goebbels put on a great show for the newsreel cameras. Hitler did more than just turn the first shovel, he filled an entire wheelbarrow.[29] In practice, however, the effect of the autobahn programme on unemployment was negligible. In 1933 no more than 1,000 labourers were employed on the first autobahn section. Twelve months after Todt's appointment, the autobahn workforce numbered only 38,000, a tiny fraction of the jobs created since Hitler took office. Given the other, more pressing financial commitments of Hitler's regime, Todt struggled even to obtain the funds necessary to maintain the existing roadways.

With Schleicher's funds fully allocated by the late summer of 1933 and the Reinhardt programme taking time to come into effect, the Reich Labour Ministry viewed the prospects of the winter with foreboding.[30] By September 1933, unemployment had fallen to well below 4 million. However, with the harvest drawing to a close and the building season almost over, an imminent setback was to be feared. Once before, in the summer of 1932, Chancellor Papen had made the disastrous mistake of promising an end to economic misery, only to face a renewed rise in unemployment over the winter of 1932–3. As Hitler declared to representatives of industry in late September 1933, it was vital to avoid a second psychological setback. The Germans had to be convinced that they were 'over the hump'.[31] To this end the Nazi party, in the autumn of 1933, redoubled its propagandistic drive against unemployment. At the same time the Reich Ministries began to prepare a new programme specifically designed to see the building trades in the urban areas through the difficult winter months. The second Reinhardt programme of September 1933 was a return to less ambitious ideas of work creation, relying not on the direct effect of credit-financed government spending, but on indirect subsidies to private activity. It was also more modest in scope. Five hundred million Reichsmarks were set aside for subsidies for repair work to buildings and a further 300 million were earmarked for an interest rate subsidy on mortgages taken out by the end of the 1933–4

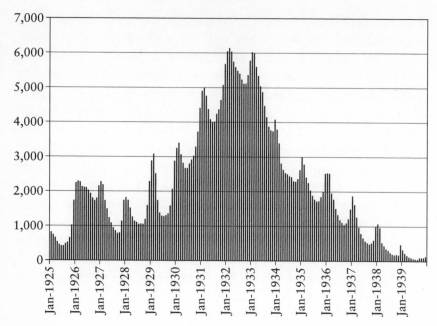

Figure 1. Unemployment in Germany, pre-1938 territory (1,000s)

tax year. Both these programmes had a measurable effect. During the first winter of the Third Reich, the number of unemployed did not increase significantly above the level of 4 million to which it had fallen in the autumn of 1933. In political terms the job was done.

Relief was now finally coming to the urban areas. In the Hanoverian town of Northeim, for instance, the Battle for Work did not begin in earnest until October 1933.[32] The new Nazi mayor put concerted pressure on local employers to take on new staff. In the following spring, exhortation was backed up by a substantial programme of public works. Displaying a new sense of social solidarity, the Nazi city authorities devoted tens of thousands of man-hours to the construction of apartments for the overcrowded population of the town. The medieval town centre was carefully restored. The ring-wall and moat became a public park. New attention was lavished on the surviving half-timbered buildings in the town centre. A large open-air theatre was carved out of the nearby forest. In keeping with the mood of the times, it was consecrated as an ancient Teutonic holy place or *Thingstaette*. But the intent behind this archaism was thoroughly modern. By 1936, the Northeim tourist office was attracting 60,000 visitors annually and the *Thingstaette* had established itself as a popular venue on the Nazi conference circuit.

Local government across Germany, encouraged by Goebbels's relentless propaganda, was eager to see a renewed effort against unemployment in the spring of 1934. The Hamburg city council, which continued to struggle with above-average unemployment rates, drew up a wish-list of projects running into the tens of millions of Reichsmarks.[33] And they did so in the expectation of a sympathetic hearing in Berlin. In August 1933, in an address to the Gauleiter, Hitler had set out the struggle against unemployment as a three-stage campaign. The first wave had come in the first half of 1933. The second, the Reinhardt programme, was a vigorous holding action aimed to consolidate the gains of the previous year. Nineteen thirty-four would see the third wave in the battle for work. But, as the Gauleiter were to discover twelve months after the Nazis took power, civilian work creation for its own sake was no longer the top priority of Hitler's regime. Rearmament, the central objective of nationalist politics, now dominated the agenda.

II

The rearmament measures taken by Hitler's government in its first few months were, like those taken in civilian work creation, built on money and planning inherited from the Weimar Republic. Any more radical move depended on the international situation. Expanding the peacetime size of the German armed forces implied a flagrant Treaty breach and an affront to the international disarmament conference in Geneva. This had to be carefully prepared and coordinated with other aspects of foreign policy, most notably in the financial arena.[34]

As we have seen, reparations payments had effectively been halted by the Hoover moratorium in July 1931. In the autumn there had followed the Standstill Agreement covering Germany's short-term debts. In July 1932 France and Britain had agreed to end their demand for reparations. In December 1932 France itself defaulted on its war debts to America. Following that precedent, Germany's default on the 10 billion Reichsmarks it owed to its long-term creditors, principally to the United States, was only a matter of time.[35] Even after the agreement on the end of reparations in Lausanne in 1932, servicing Germany's international debts required an annual sum of 1 billion Reichsmarks in foreign exchange.[36] The severity of this demand on the German economy can be appreciated when it is set against total exports valued in 1933 at 4.8 billion Reichsmarks and imports valued at 4.2 billion. Here too we see the devastating impact of the global deflation on the world's debtors. In 1929 German exports had run at in excess of 8 billion Reichsmarks. Germany's import bill had of course shrunk in line with world commodity prices. But in proportional terms the debt burden had dramatically increased.

The German economy could not live without imports. To feed its densely packed population, Germany needed imports of fats and animal feed. Nineteen million German households could not satisfy their immense appetite for meat, milk and butter from domestic sources. Germany's giant herds of pigs and cows could only be sustained through the import of huge quantities of high-energy animal feed. Huge industries such as textiles depended entirely on imported cotton and wool. The blast furnaces of the Ruhr were fed with iron ore from Scandinavia, a dependence made worse by the loss of Alsace-Lorraine in 1918. The one resource that Germany did have in abundance was coal. But Germany's growing fleet of cars, trucks and aircraft burned oil and they rolled on tyres manufactured from imported rubber. Given this dependence, the level of imports was the best indicator of the vigour of the German economic metabolism. In 1928, when the Weimar Republic had been close to full employment, the real volume of imports, allowing for the very sharp fall in global commodity prices, had been 50 per cent higher than that on which Germany survived in 1933. The German economy could not recover to anything like its normal level of economic activity without a substantial increase in the volume of foreign inputs. To make matters worse, as Germany recovered along with Britain and the United States, their combined demand would have the knock-on effect of raising prices on world commodity markets. Everything depended therefore on Germany's ability to sustain a healthy flow of exports with which to service debts and pay for imports.

Germany's export trade, however, had been hit hard by the wave of currency instability precipitated by the British abandonment of gold in 1931 and the ensuing upsurge in global protectionism. As Sir Frederick Phillips of His Majesty's Treasury admitted with disarming frankness: 'No country ever administered a more severe shock to international trade than we did when we both (1) depreciated the £. (2) almost simultaneously turned from free trade to protection.'[37] Roosevelt's devaluation of the dollar in April 1933 made things even worse. Though the dollar's devaluation reduced the Reichsmark burden of Germany's debts, it made it even harder for Germany's exporters to earn the necessary dollars. By 1933 the German trade balance began shifting inexorably into deficit and the Reichsbank's limited foreign exchange holdings drained rapidly away.[38] In January 1933 the national foreign exchange reserve had stood at over 800 million Reichsmarks. By the summer the Reichsbank's holdings had been reduced by debt repayments to only 400 million, enough to cover no more than one month of minimal imports. Quite apart from the political significance of the foreign debts, the moment was fast approaching at which Hitler's regime would have to face a difficult choice. On the one hand it could take desperate measures to increase exports, including a devaluation of the Reichsmark to make it more competitive with the pound and the dollar. If exports did not increase, they would face a stark choice between sustaining the bare minimum of imports necessary to the German recovery, or aborting the recovery to satisfy the demands of Germany's foreign creditors.

Faced with this same dilemma in 1930, Bruening's government had taken the latter option, deflating and slashing imports so as to enable Germany to honour its reparations obligations. In light of the position that Hitler and his colleagues had taken ever since the announcement of the Young Plan, there was no doubt how they would proceed. In April 1933 the cabinet gave Schacht carte blanche to instigate a moratorium on Germany's international debts, at a moment of his choosing.[39] At first, Schacht hoped to exploit the confused situation in the United States by announcing an immediate default.[40] He gambled that Roosevelt's administration, preoccupied with the agricultural depression at home, might be willing to sacrifice the interests of Wall Street in exchange for a German agreement to increase raw material imports. Schacht's first interview with the President seemed to confirm this hunch. But, before Schacht could take irrevocable action, the US State Department intervened, issuing a brusque communiqué stressing that the new administration expected Germany to honour its debts. At the last moment, Schacht was forced into an embarrassing retreat.[41] Unlike in the 1920s, however, pressure from the United States was no longer enough to force Germany into line. At the end of May 1933 Schacht convoked a conference of Germany's creditors in Berlin where he sought to persuade them of the need for at least a partial moratorium. The creditors, however, were not convinced that Schacht was acting in good faith and refused to make any concessions. The monthly returns of the Reichsbank suggested that Schacht was deliberately exacerbating the currency shortage by needlessly accelerating the repayment of short-term debts.[42] The failure to reach a compromise provided Schacht with the excuse he needed for unilateral action. On 8 June the cabinet gave its approval for a unilateral moratorium on Germany's long-term foreign debts, to begin as of 30 June. As a sign of 'good faith', German debtors would go on making payments in Reichsmarks into accounts administered by the Reichsbank. However, the Reichsmarks accumulated in the creditors' accounts would no longer be transferred into foreign currency. Payment in foreign currency would only resume once Germany's foreign trade position was restored to a healthy surplus. This ultimately depended on the creditor countries. If they wanted repayment of their debts, they would have to purchase German goods. If Germany could not achieve the required trade surplus, it could not be expected to engage in large-scale foreign debt service.

The suspension of debt repayments was the first overtly aggressive foreign policy move by Hitler's government. Though it had been widely anticipated, it nevertheless produced shock and outrage in the commercial capitals of the world.[43] After his first experience with Schacht, Roosevelt described him simply as a 'bastard'.[44] The World Economic Conference that opened in London on 12 June 1933 might have provided the stage for a concerted international response. But in the summer of 1933 there was little chance of that. The United States, Britain and France were deeply divided over all fundamental issues of economic policy.[45] Indeed, American policy was divided even against itself.[46] On the one hand Secretary of State Cordell Hull and President Roosevelt presented themselves as internationalists, urging that the World Economic Conference should be held as soon as possible and smoothing the way with a global tariff truce. After Hugenberg had rushed through a new system of quotas and import monopolies to meet the key demand of the agrarian community, Hitler's government thought it best to sign up to Hull's agenda, at least until the Conference was over. On the other hand, Roosevelt undermined his own pro-trade position, first by publicly postponing any reduction in American tariffs until 1934, and more immediately by allowing the dollar to go into free fall.[47] To limit the damage the British desperately tried to persuade Roosevelt to agree to a stabilization of the dollar–sterling rate, at a level close to that prevailing before 1931. But on 3 July President Roosevelt delivered his so-called 'bomb-shell telegram', letting it be known that a dollar stabilization was out of the question. The recovery of the United States had absolute priority, even if this meant beggaring America's major trading partners.

Against this backdrop, there was no hope of any substantial agreement at London and certainly no hope of a concerted official response to Germany. Reich Minister Hugenberg did manage to embarrass the rest of the German delegation with an unscripted outburst in which he demanded not only the return of Germany's colonies, but also a free hand for expansion towards the east. In the summer of 1933, however, Germany's problems were dwarfed by the more general dislocation of the global financial system. Nor was Berlin willing to back Hugenberg. Colonies were a preoccupation of the old school and were not an essential part of Hitler's foreign policy vision. By the end of the month Hugenberg had resigned from all his offices and his party the DNVP went with him into oblivion. Hugenberg was succeeded in Agriculture by the radical Nazi ideologue Walther Darré. At the Ministry for Economic Affairs Hugenberg was replaced by Kurt Schmitt, CEO of Allianz, Germany's leading insurance company. Schacht for his part left London with his conviction reinforced that the days of the multilateral world economy were over.

At precisely the same moment as Germany announced the moratorium on its long-term debts, Hitler's government also took the decisive steps towards rearmament. The terms of the financial package that under-pinned the first real phase of rearmament were documented retrospectively in a Wehrmacht memorandum dating from 1938. This source is unclear as to the precise date on which the agreement was reached, but the balance of probabilities points to the cabinet meeting on 8 June 1933, the same day on which Germany announced its debt moratorium.[48] The meeting was attended by Schacht, Defence Minister Blomberg, Goering and Erhard Milch, Secretary of State at the Air Ministry. And the scale of what was agreed marked a dramatic break with all previous conceptions of German rearmament. The figure approved by Schacht was 35 billion Reichsmarks, to be spent over eight years, at a rate of almost 4.4 billion Reichsmarks per annum. To put this in perspective, annual military spending by the Weimar Republic was counted not in billions but in hundreds of millions of Reichsmarks. Total national income in 1933 had slumped to as little as 43 billion Reichsmarks. Even allowing for a rapid recovery, Schacht's programme called for between 5 and 10 per cent of German GDP to be devoted to defence for the next eight years. By comparison with the present day, this is two or three times the defence burden of most Western countries, to be borne by a country with a much lower level of per capita income. The United States and Britain sustained peacetime military spending at this rate only during the most intense phases of the Cold War in the 1950s and they did so on the back of much higher levels of per capita income. The 35 billion Reichsmark programme of June 1933 thus implied, if not the wholesale militarization of German society, at the least the formation of a substantial military-industrial complex with serious ramifications for the rest of the economy.

Given the parlous state of the German economy in 1933 and the shell shock in the financial markets, raising even the first instalment of the 35 billion Reichsmarks through taxation or conventional borrowing was out of the question. So over the summer of 1933 Schacht initiated a military version of the off-budget financing system first used for civilian work creation.[49] Already in April 1933 the cabinet had agreed to release the military from the normal processes of budgetary oversight.[50] A few weeks after the meetings of early June, special account offices were set up to channel the off-budget funds that were now to flow to the military. As of April 1934, armaments contractors were to be paid in IOUs issued in the name of the Mefo GmbH. This shadowy company was formed with a capital of 1 million Reichsmarks, provided by the Vereinigte Stahlwerke, Krupp, Siemens, Deutsche Industrie Werke and Gutehoffnungshuette (GHH).[51] Krupp and Deutsche Industrie Werke were major armaments producers. The Deutsche Industrie Werke were Reich-owned. Siemens and the Vereinigte Stahlwerke, though they too would benefit on a grand scale from military spending, were most probably included because of their premium credit rating. Secured by these big names, the rearmament bills became acceptable collateral for the Reichsbank. For a small discount, contractors to the rearmament drive could cash in their Mefo bills at the central bank. In the event, since they paid good interest and were effectively guaranteed by the Reich, the majority of the Mefo bills in fact stayed in circulation. Small numbers of Mefo bills were issued in the autumn of 1933 to tide the early Luftwaffe contractors over a cash crisis.[52] Large-scale disbursement began in April 1934, conveniently timed to coincide with the renewed propaganda surrounding the second wave of work creation measures.

In every respect except propaganda, the civilian work creation measures of 1933 were dwarfed by the decisions taken in relation to rearmament and foreign debt. The military spending package vastly exceeded anything ever contemplated for work creation. According to the agreement of June 1933, military spending was to be almost three times larger than the combined total of all of the civilian work creation measures announced in 1932 and 1933. More important, however, was the strategic dimension. Work creation was a strictly domestic issue. By contrast, Germany's debt moratorium and the rearmament decisions had ramifications that were global in scale. It may have been no more than coincidence that the debt moratorium was announced on the same day as the cabinet reached its decision on rearmament, but the coincidence nevertheless points to a deeper logic. As we have seen, since the early 1920s the basis of Germany's security strategy had been to play off the economic influence of the United States against the military threat posed by Germany's European neighbours. Germany's debts to the United States were the financial embodiment of that trans-Atlantic gamble. And as we have seen, Bruening had continued to honour these obligations throughout the crises of 1931 and 1932. The decision in the summer of 1933 to initiate default marked a fundamental turning point.[53] In effect, Hitler's government was declaring its independence from the implicit security guarantee that America had provided to the Weimar Republic since 1923–4. The break was at first only partial. In the face of creditor indignation, Hitler and Schacht shrank from forcing through a total moratorium. After the initial announcement they agreed to continue at least partial repayment. Meanwhile, German propaganda continued to pay lip-service to the need to preserve good relations with America. The moratorium, however, was a decisive first step and it was only logical that it should be coupled with rearmament. Having thrown off both the burden of American debts and the protection that America offered, Hitler's government had announced its intention to re-enter the dangerous game of Continental military competition.

In his 'peace speech' of 17 May 1933, Hitler had still sought to calm nerves both at home and abroad.[54] But this was nothing more than tactical. In confidential discussions with Hungary's authoritarian Prime Minister Julius Goemboes on 17–18 June 1933, Hitler stated explicitly his intention to 'utterly crush France'.[55] And once the 35 billion Reichsmark programme was agreed, it was clear that the charade could not be maintained for long. Germany needed to find a way out of the Geneva disarmament talks. The opportunity presented itself in October 1933 when the British launched a new round of disarmament proposals. The French immediately rejected any suggestion that they should make the first move in reducing their substantial armed forces. The British refused to agree to a German counter-proposal that they should be allowed to rearm to the reduced level being proposed for the other European powers. Hitler's government chose to interpret this as a British retreat from the all-important principle of parity that had supposedly been conceded to Germany in December 1932. On 14 October 1933 Hitler announced that he was no longer willing to accept Germany's humiliating second-class status and withdrew both from the disarmament talks and from membership in the League of Nations.[56] Hitler made his move with the full backing of Blomberg and Foreign Minister Konstantin von Neurath and with the warm endorsement of Schacht and more politically minded representatives of German industry. Nor can there be any doubt that this bold rejection of the last humiliating relic of Versailles was hugely popular with the German public. However, behind the scenes the mood in Berlin was panicky. Blomberg and Goering apparently expected Poland and France to respond with military intervention. Desperate plans were prepared for a last-ditch defence of Berlin. In the event, the Third Reich benefited once more from the disunity of its enemies. Over the winter of 1933–4 the government of France was paralysed by a sudden upsurge of domestic fascist activity, which culminated in the extraordinary street-fighting of early 1934.[57] Poland was neutralized in early 1934 with economic concessions and a friendship treaty. Nevertheless, in a pattern that was to repeat itself, Berlin's aggression created a sense of menace that in turn provided the justification for an escalation of German rearmament planning.[58] In rapid succession, all three branches of the German armed forces prepared to take advantage of the 35 billion Reichsmarks promised by their benefactor at the Reichsbank.

Goering and the new Reich Air Ministry (RLM) were the first off the blocks. Plans prepared in 1932 had called for a secret air force of 200 aircraft. In mid-September Milch raised this to 2,000 front-line aircraft by 1935.[59] As we shall see, this marked the beginning of a gigantic programme of industrial construction controlled by Goering's Air Ministry. The army finalized its expanded armaments programme in December 1933.[60] The army's build-up was to be divided into two four-year phases. By the end of 1937 Germany was to have a standing army of 21 divisions, or 300,000 men, which in wartime could be inflated to 63 divisions. This would be enough, it was hoped, to mount an effective defence against a combined attack by Poland and France. Offensive striking capacity was to be added in the next four-year phase stretching from 1938 to 1941. The army programme of December 1933 is crucial because it pre-programmed the subsequent escalation of Hitler's foreign policy. To meet the army's new objective of creating a 300,000-man force, conscription would have to be introduced within the next two years, a fundamental breach of the Treaty of Versailles. Furthermore, the issue of the Rhineland had to be resolved. Under the provisions of the Treaty, the zone west of the Rhine had remained demilitarized. This meant that the Ruhr, the heavy industrial heartland of Germany, could not be defended. But without the industrial resources of the Ruhr, no realistic war-planning was possible. The Rhineland would therefore have to be brought fully under German control, at the latest by the end of 1937. From December 1933 onwards, the clock was ticking towards confrontation with France.

In light of this antagonism one might have expected Hitler's government to seek protection through a closer relationship with Britain. However, in December 1933, with the full backing of the cabinet, Schacht raised the pressure on the financial front in a way that was calculated to cause maximum offence to the British and the Americans. In June 1933 the protests against Schacht's moratorium had been such that Germany had been forced to backtrack and to carry on making payments of at least half of the principal and interest it owed to its foreign creditors. And even more favourable arrangements were reached with the Dutch and the Swiss.[61] Though small in size, these countries were amongst Germany's largest short-term creditors. As major customers for German exports they were also a vital source of hard currency. They thus had the whip hand in negotiations with the Reich. If Switzerland, for instance, had imposed a compulsory clearing agreement, asserting a prior claim on behalf of its creditors against all German export earnings, this would have deprived the Reichsbank of the hard currency it desperately needed to pay for imports of raw materials and food from the United States and the British Empire.[62] On the other hand, the Dutch and the Swiss had a strong interest in retaining their trading links with their much larger neighbour and every reason to fear that they might be disadvantaged in a debt settlement negotiated over their heads by Britain and the United States. The result was clearing agreements, under which the Dutch and Swiss agreed to take high levels of imports in exchange for German agreement to continue repayment on Dutch and Swiss debt. Representatives of both British and American creditors protested strongly against this unequal treatment, but in vain. On 18 December, at exactly the moment at which the German army finalized its new plan of expansion, Schacht announced a unilateral reduction in the rate of cash payment to foreign creditors from 50 to 30 per cent. What particularly incensed the British was that this moratorium included the Dawes and Young Plan loans, which were supposed to enjoy first claim on German resources.[63] The outrage in both London and Washington reached new heights. In January 1934 the British government delivered Germany a formal ultimatum that unless Schacht returned to the bargaining table, German export earnings in Britain would be subject to forced clearing. They would be subject to official British control with a levy being imposed to satisfy the claims of the City. The violence of the British reaction forced Schacht into a temporary retreat. A general meeting of creditors was called to Berlin for April 1934 and service on the Dawes and Young loans temporarily resumed.

At the same time as Schacht forced the debt issue back into the spotlight the German navy also began preparing a direct military challenge to Britain. Initially, Hitler's expressed preference for an alliance with Britain had raised fears in the navy that they might be excluded from the armaments bonanza. Hitler was keen to avoid conflict with Britain over colonies. However, Admiral Erich Raeder's skilful manipulation of the Fuehrer meant that by March 1934 the navy too had begun its expansion in the form of the 'Replacement Shipbuilding Programme'.[64] Like the Luftwaffe and the army, Raeder started from the premise that Germany should act unilaterally without regard to the international ramifications of its rearmament. So Raeder projected a substantial force in violation of Versailles restrictions: 8 battleships, instead of 6 permitted by Versailles; 3 aircraft carriers, not provided for by the Treaty; 8 cruisers, instead of the 6 permitted; 48 destroyers, instead of 12 permitted under the Treaty; and 72 submarines, which were completely illegal. Given the cost and complexity of naval construction, the time-horizon of Raeder's planning was expansive. The new fleet would be ready for action no earlier than 1949. However, spending had to start immediately and from the second half of 1934 onwards large orders began to be placed with the dockyards of north Germany.

In 1933 and 1934 all of this military activity took place under a veil of complete secrecy. In interviews with the international press Hitler continued to deny any actual steps towards rearmament. However, by the spring of 1934 the extent of German activity was such that it could no longer be effectively disguised from quizzical foreign observers.[65] In April 1934, in response to the publication of a Reich budget that brought an extraordinary increase in military spending, the French withdrew from any further bilateral discussions of military issues.[66] When asked to explain its rising military budget, the Reich stonewalled, claiming that Germany was engaged only in essential maintenance and renewal expenditure.

III

What the Reich government was anxious to spotlight in early 1934 was the next phase of the Battle for Work. Early in 1934 the Propaganda Ministry and the Ministry for Economic Affairs were in busy consultation preparing for the grand opening of the second wave of the Battle for Work timed for 21 March, the traditional date for spring celebrations. The national festivities were choreographed literally to the minute. An address by Hitler to the building workers assembled on the autobahn building site at Unterhaching outside Munich was to form the highlight of the national event. The draft programme circulated confidentially on 5 March read as follows:

10.45   The workers of the Reichsautobahn (c. 1,000) present themselves at the building site, the newly employed workers as a separate group. The construction site is closed off for a stretch of 500 metres, so that it cannot be crowded by spectators (security cordon to be provided by police and SS).

11.00   The Fuehrer arrives at the construction site (beginning of radio transmission on all German stations), introductory radio report. The Fuehrer is welcomed by Gauleiter (3 minutes). The General Inspector of German Roads, Dr Todt, reports on the workers of the Munich segment and all other Reich motorways and reports on progress on construction (3 minutes). He invites the Fuehrer to inspect the roadway.

11.10–11.25   The Fuehrer inspects the roadworks. He is accompanied by:

The Gauleiter

The Reich Labour Minister

State Secretary Funk of the Reich Ministry for Public Enlightenment and Propaganda

The General Inspector of German Roads, Dr Todt

The Leader of the Labour Front, Dr Ley

The chair of the Reichsautobahn board, General Director Dorpmueller

The head of the Bavarian branch of the Reich Ministry of Popular Enlightenment and Propaganda, Nippold

The head construction engineer for the Munich sector

2 construction workers

(The security cordon ensures that no one else joins the Fuehrer's group). Whilst Hitler inspects the roadway, the Reich Minister for Public Enlightenment and Propaganda makes his address. This speech is transmitted only by radio not on the loudspeakers of the construction site. As the Fuehrer's group reaches the end of the construction site, the Munich Nationalsozialistische Betriebszellenorganisation band plays one verse of the song: 'Brothers of the Mine' [Brueder in Zechen und Gruben].[67] The speech of the Propaganda Minister ends as the band starts.

11.25   The Fuehrer's group reaches the end of the construction site.

11.25–11.45   The Fuehrer's speech.

11.45   One verse of the 'Deutschlandlied' and 'Horst Wessel'.

11.50   End of transmission.[68]

Across the country, the radio transmission of Hitler's address was the highlight of a morning of events and rallies. So that everyone could hear the Fuehrer, the Propaganda Ministry decreed a nationwide workbreak starting at 10.45. To avoid unseemly disputes, Hitler decided that workers should suffer no loss of wages, but that employers were entitled to an hour of unpaid overtime in compensation. The Propaganda Ministry laid down precise guidelines for local events to be held on every construction site, factory, shop, farm and office. Instructions were also issued to schools. Head teachers were to introduce the radio broadcast explaining the purpose of the day and the 'national economic significance of the Battle for Work'. In practice, the Propaganda Ministry instructions were no more than a minimal guideline. Local party officials took things into their own hands. In the industrial city of Hanover, for instance, the celebrations began at 7 a.m., with the ceremonial 'call to work' of 1,000 unemployed before the municipal labour exchange.[69] In rank and file, the newly employed men marched through the centre of town to ten building sites, especially opened for the occasion. The day ended with public speeches and a rally that joined together those who had been found work since 1933 and those still waiting for employment. The message was clear: in the national struggle for economic recovery, nobody was to be left behind.

As a propaganda exercise, the battle for work entered a new phase in the spring of 1934. However, the remarkable fact was that not a single Reichsmark of new money was allocated to national work creation projects in 1934 or at any point thereafter, a formal decision to this effect having been taken by the Berlin Ministries on 6 December 1933.[70] Enough projects had already been authorized to maintain the momentum into 1934. New applicants were informed that the Reinhardt funds were now fully allocated and no new money was available. It was only with the greatest difficulty that unemployment hot spots such as Berlin and Hamburg were able to obtain special allocations. In both cases, political considerations were paramount. Goebbels and Goering regarded Berlin as their personal fiefdom.[71] Hamburg lived up to its reputation as a dangerous centre of revolution by returning the lowest support for Hitler, in the referendum following Hindenburg's death in November 1934. But, in general, the Reich held firm. There was to be no new money for work creation after December 1933. Indeed, from the spring of 1934 the Reich's subsidy for local work creation projects was cut by a sixth, much to the horror of local officials anxious to maintain the downward pressure on the unemployment statistics.[72] By May, the Reich Chancellery was being bombarded by anxious appeals from the champions of work creation, including Gauleiter Koch of East Prussia, who feared that their achievements of the previous year were now under threat.[73]

Their appeals were in vain. By the spring of 1934 the balance of priorities had shifted irrevocably. In the capital, it was now an open secret that civilian work creation was no longer a top priority. As

Hamburg's delegation in Berlin reported: 'In a certain sense, work creation is continuing into the summer [of 1934] on the basis of the military measures that are planned. But, for obvious reasons, there can be no public propaganda about this.'[74] In April 1934 the secret financing mechanism for rearmament was set in full swing. Mefo bills flowed in their billions. The bookkeeping was not precise. However, in 1934 military spending came to at least 4 billion Reichsmarks, of which less than half appeared in the official Reich budget. This meant that by the second year of Hitler's government, military spending already accounted for over 50 per cent of central government expenditure on goods and services. In 1935, the military's share rose to 73 per cent.[75] At the same time, the spectacular announcement of the Battle for Work in March 1934 coincided exactly with the peak of the work creation drive. According to official labour market figures, the number employed on all forms of work creation scheme rose, from 289,000 in February 1933 when Hitler took power, to 1,075,000 in March 1934, an increase of almost 800,000.[76] In the same period unemployment fell by more than 2.6 million. Make-work schemes at their peak thus directly accounted for 30 per cent of the reduction in registered unemployment. Even when they were at their most extensive, they accounted for a minority of the jobs created. From the spring of 1934 onwards, numbers involved in work creation schemes fell to an average of 700,000, tailing off into 1935. The conclusion is inescapable: despite the propaganda fanfare that accompanied the renewed Battle for Work in 1934, it in fact made little if any contribution to the ongoing reduction in unemployment.

By 1934 the general recovery in the German economy clearly went far beyond the muddy building sites of the work creation schemes. To understand the forces driving this upswing we have to draw more extensively on the available statistical material. Thanks to the many innovations in economic statistics sponsored by the Weimar Republic, it is possible to reconstruct from contemporary sources a fairly comprehensive picture of the major components of the German economy during the period of the recovery.[77] We can piece together series not only for government spending but also for business investment. Deducting these figures from national income, we can also infer an estimate of household consumption.

What is unmistakable is that in both 1933 and 1934 there was a powerful 'natural' recovery in the German business sector. In 1933

Table 2. Accounting for economic growth in Nazi Germany

	1932	1933	1934	1935
GDP prices 1913	43.1	46.3	51.5	57.8
of which:				
Reich military	0.3	0.5	2.9	5.5
Reich civilian	1.3	2.1	2.8	2
local government	4.7	5.5	5.7	5.2
private consumption	39	37.6	38.2	40.5
private investment	1.1	3.6	5.5	7
foreign account	−3.2	−2.9	−3.6	−2.4
Year on year changes in GDP and components of demand, billion Reichsmarks				
GDP		3.2	5.2	6.2
Reich military		0.1	2.5	2.6
Reich civilian		0.9	0.7	−0.8
local government		0.8	0.2	−0.5
private consumption		−1.5	0.6	2.3
private investment		2.5	2	1.5
foreign account		0.4	−0.7	1.1
Share of GDP growth due to (%)				
Reich military		4.2	47	41.6
Reich civilian		27	13.1	−13.1
local government		24.6	4.1	−7.4
private consumption		−45.9	11.7	37.1
private investment		79	37.4	23.6
foreign account		11.2	−13.4	18.2
Total public sector contribution		55.7	64.3	21.1
Total private sector contribution		44.3	35.7	78.9

Source: A. Ritschl, *Deutschlands Krise und Konjunktur 1924–1934* (Berlin, 2002), appendix. A. Ritschl, 'Deficit Spending in the Nazi Recovery, 1933–1938', Working Paper No. 68, Institute for Empirical Research in Economics, University of Zurich (December 2000).

investment expenditure – mainly in stock-building – was a major driver of recovery. The first signs of this upswing had underpinned the strange wave of optimism that befell the Weimar Republic shortly before its demise.[78] After 1933 government policy left such a deep imprint on the evolution of the economy that talking about the continuation of the 'natural recovery' is to a degree speculative. We cannot know with any certainty what might have happened if a different government had been in power. However, the signs of a continued upswing in German business are there in the statistics. And it is certainly reasonable, therefore, to speculate that even without government intervention there might well have been a strong recovery, as there had been from the first major recession of the Weimar Republic in 1925.[79] In 1933 private investment both in construction and stock-building was by far the largest single contributor to the recovery. In the labour market statistics this is mirrored in large increases in employment in iron and steel production, metalworking, construction materials and textiles. In the first six months of Hitler's government, however, this recovery in the business sector was offset by a severe contraction in the real value of household consumption. And even in 1934, when one might have expected the recovery in the labour market to have powerfully stimulated household consumption – the famous 'knock-on effect' from work creation expenditure predicted by Keynesians – it in fact made no more than a modest contribution to the progress of the overall economy.[80] Though our ability to measure consumption is limited, this pessimistic story is confirmed by other indicators, such as the indices for turnover in retailing.[81] Sales of food, clothing and other household necessities did not pick up significantly until six months after Hitler took power. This is hardly surprising, when we bear in mind that the real wages of many workers fell quite sharply in 1933, as wages stagnated and prices for food began to rise. Nor was the lagged development of consumption lost on contemporaries. There was much concern over the winter of 1933–4, particularly in the Reich Ministry of Economic Affairs, that the recovery to date had not translated into a genuine increase in household purchasing power.[82] Indeed, when they made their decision to cancel any further plans for government work creation spending at the end of 1933, the Reich Ministries did so in part because they wanted the recovery in 1934 to be carried forward less by government-financed earth-moving and more by a revival in private consumption.

Since falling consumption offset rising investment, private demand in total accounted for less than half the resurgence in aggregate demand in both 1933 and 1934. From the outset, therefore, Hitler's economic recovery was driven primarily by the public sector.[83] What is also clear, furthermore, is that between 1933 and 1934 the priorities of the German state changed radically. In 1933 civilian work creation expenditure clearly did make a major difference, with increased spending at both local and national levels. Civilian spending by the Reich continued to grow strongly into 1934. But what is often forgotten is that from 1934 onwards this was offset by a severe squeeze on local government. In large part, Reich work creation spending simply 'repackaged' funds that might otherwise have been spent by local government. This was the reality behind Hitler's promise on 1 February 1933 to rationalize relations between the Reich and local government. A state-driven economic recovery went hand in hand with an unprecedented centralization of public spending, of which the military were the prime beneficiaries.[84]

By 1935 German GDP in real terms had recovered to roughly the same level it had stood at in 1928. This was no doubt a rapid recovery. But it was not vastly superior to the recovery achieved in the United States under a very different policy mix. Nor, in terms of the rate of growth, was it superior to the rebound from the Weimar Republic's first severe recession over the winter of 1926–7, when the twelve-month growth rate was higher than at any time during the Third Reich.[85] It is possible therefore to imagine a similarly rapid recovery taking place even under a very different policy regime. In this strict counterfactual sense, Nazi economic policy cannot claim to have 'caused' the German economic recovery.[86] However, what is unarguable is that the recovery as it actually occurred bore the clear imprint of Hitler's government. In 1935 private consumption was still 7 per cent below its pre-Depression levels and private investment was 22 per cent down. By contrast, state spending was 70 per cent higher than it had been in 1928 and that increase was almost entirely due to military spending. As far as the Reich was concerned, there can be no doubt that rearmament was already the dominant priority by early 1934. Between 1933 and 1935, the share of military spending in German national income rose from less than 1 per cent to close to 10 per cent. A reallocation of total national production on this scale in such a short space of time had never before been seen in any capitalist state in peacetime. Concentrated within a tight-knit military-industrial complex, the impact of 10 billion Reichsmarks of spending squeezed into the first three years of Hitler's rule was dramatic. According to contemporary estimates, as much as a quarter of German industry was already occupied in 1935 with 'non-marketed production' of various kinds.[87] And in 1934 the consequences of this dramatic restructuring of the German economy were to make themselves felt in the first real crisis of the Nazi regime.

3

Breaking Away

The summer of 1934 was the moment at which it became apparent, to all but the most indulgent foreign observers, that Hitler's was not a 'normal' government. For months it had been clear that political pressure was building on the regime.[1] The massed ranks of the brownshirts (SA) were resentful at the failure of 'their' government to deliver a thoroughgoing populist, nationalist and anti-Semitic revolution. On the other flank of Hitler's coalition, ex-Chancellor Franz von Papen and his aristocratic bevy were alarmed by signs of what they took to be 'plebeian degeneration'. Most ominously of all, the SA and the army were engaged in a bitter struggle over the future of rearmament. Ernst Roehm, the leader of the SA, envisioned German rearmament as a popular, national mobilization, of a kind that was profoundly distasteful to the professional soldiers. Hitler had made his own position clear in February 1934, by imposing an 'agreement' limiting the activities of the brownshirts.[2] But the SA defiantly continued their paramilitary exercises. By May 1934 these had become so alarming that Hitler ordered the brownshirts to take a collective 'holiday' for the entire month of June. The leadership of the Nazi party itself was divided. Whilst Goering and Himmler plotted against Roehm, Goebbels idolized the SA and fantasized about a final reckoning with 'the reactionaries'. The decisive factor, however, was the army. On 21 June Hitler was confronted by President Hindenburg and Defence Minister Blomberg with the demand to bring the 'revolutionary trouble-makers . . . to reason'. Otherwise, the army would impose martial law and Hindenburg would declare an end to the 'Hitler experiment'. The final decision was taken amidst the celebrations of Gauleiter Josef Terboven's wedding in Essen, at the heart of the Ruhr, on 28 June. Hitler took personal charge of the purge. Early in the morning of 30 June 1934, in the Munich resort of Bad Wiessee, he ordered the arrest and later the execution of the most senior leaders of the SA. In Berlin, meanwhile, Goebbels and Goering dealt with the 'reactionaries'. SS men stormed the offices of Vice-Chancellor Papen and gunned down his secretary. The rest of Papen's staff were arrested. Papen himself was only spared because of the diplomatic embarrassment involved in liquidating an active member of the German government. Others were less fortunate. General Schleicher, the former Chancellor of the Republic and head of the Reichswehr, was murdered along with his wife. Gregor Strasser, the architect of the Nazi party's work creation policy, who had been expelled from the party in December 1932 after intriguing with Schleicher, was killed in Berlin. The confirmed victims of the Night of the Long Knives numbered 85. The actual figure may have been as high as 200.

Outside Germany, the news of these state-sanctioned murders was greeted with horrified disbelief. Clearly Hitler's regime lacked any commitment to the basic norms of legality. And within weeks of the Night of the Long Knives this impression was confirmed by another outrageous demonstration of Nazi violence.[3] Since early 1934, Hitler's followers in Austria had been carrying out a campaign of terrorism against the authoritarian government of Chancellor Engelbert Dollfuss. On 25 July, with the encouragement of the German party, the Austrian Nazis launched a coup. Hoping for a spectacular success, Hitler instructed his southern army command to stand ready to provide aid to the putschists. In the event, the Austrian army remained loyal and the uprising was easily put down. But Chancellor Dollfuss was dead, shot down in the Vienna Chancellery by men wearing swastikas. Abroad, the reaction was one of unanimous condemnation. Particularly alarming was the sudden increase in tension along Austria's borders. To forestall any attempt to carry out an immediate Anschluss, Mussolini mobilized several divisions. Italy had no interest in seeing German influence extended across the Alps. Troop movements were also detected along the border with Hungary, which in turn triggered alarm in Yugoslavia.[4] The stage seemed set for a Balkan chain reaction reminiscent of August 1914. According to the Gestapo, Germany in the summer of 1934 was in the grips of a veritable 'war pyschosis'. But unlike twenty years earlier this was one of fear not enthusiasm.[5]

Not surprisingly, these extraordinary events dominate the historical memory of the summer of 1934. And yet at precisely the same moment

Germany teetered on the brink of economic disaster. Between March and September 1934 the Nazi regime suffered the closest thing to a comprehensive socio-economic crisis in its entire twelve-year history.[6] From the beginning of 1934 the Reichsbank's reserves of foreign currency dwindled alarmingly. So desperate was the situation that Germans travelling abroad were restricted to a foreign exchange ration of no more than 50 Reichsmarks per month. To prevent a 'black market' for Reichsmarks developing outside Germany, travellers were forbidden from taking German banknotes outside the country.[7] Simultaneously, the Reichsbank and the Ministry of Economic Affairs (RWM) began the painful process of reducing the monthly allocations of foreign exchange to Germany's importers. By the summer they were cut to 5 per cent of the levels they had received before the crisis in July 1931. Since all the most important industries in Germany were dependent on raw materials from abroad, this savage restriction prompted fears of a new wave of lay-offs. Shortages of raw materials spelled not only unemployment; they also implied shortages of supply for consumers, fears that were compounded by the unusually bad harvest of 1934. Popular discontent with the rising price of imported food was widespread. And it was not just consumers who had little to cheer about. The mood in business circles in the second year of Hitler's regime was far from good. The stock market responded to Hitler's aggressive opening address for the new Battle for Work on 21 March 1934 with a sharp fall in share prices.[8] By May 1934 the groundswell of popular discontent was such that Goebbels felt compelled to launch a national campaign against malcontents: a two-month 'barrage of meetings, demonstrations and announcements' against 'rubbishers and critics'.[9] The main theme of this campaign was the need for ordinary Germans to show more fortitude in coping with the effects of the foreign exchange shortage: 'Helping to overcome the foreign exchange crisis [transfer crisis] was the duty of every German.' But, like Hitler, Goebbels did not hold back in his criticism of business: 'Sacrifices would have to be made by all sides.' Most of all, the Jews would have to learn how to behave as 'guests' in their German home.[10] The Minister for Economic Affairs, Kurt Schmitt, who struggled vainly to impose himself on the mounting crisis, was assailed from all sides. Wilhelm Keppler, Hitler's personal economic adviser, conspired with Heinrich Himmler to bring about a more ideological turn in economic policy.[11] The shopfloor radicals of the NSBO and Robert Ley's

German Labour Front demanded a new deal for German labour. Schacht at the Reichsbank sided with Goering and the army in arguing for ever greater rearmament and made himself into the chief public spokesman for an aggressive programme of unilateral debt default. By the second week of June 1934, the London *Evening Standard*, a newspaper that could not be accused of anti-Nazi leanings, worried openly that the days of Hitler's regime were numbered.

The economic crisis came to a head right on cue.[12] On 14 June 1934 Schacht declared a complete suspension of foreign currency payments on all Germany's international debt. At the same time he slashed the foreign currency allocated to German importers. On 23 June 1934 the Reichsbank abandoned altogether the orderly system of monthly foreign exchange rationing. Henceforth, foreign currency was doled out on a daily basis, according to whatever was available. From day to day, German importers could not be certain of obtaining the foreign exchange they needed to satisfy the claims of their foreign suppliers. Foreign trade threatened to grind to a complete halt. Meanwhile, the international response to Germany's pending default was more enraged than ever.[13] On 25–6 June the House of Commons in London held an extraordinary forty-eight-hour session rushing through legislation authorizing coercive action. The tone of the debate was hostile. Even Neville Chamberlain spoke in warlike terms. After only fifteen months of Hitler's aggressive unilateralism, London's patience was exhausted. With support from both sides of the House, Parliament ratified comprehensive powers allowing the Treasury to impound the earnings of German exporters for the benefit of Britain's creditors. These sanctions were to come into effect on 1 July. Germany responded with a law empowering the RWM to take any retaliatory action necessary to protect German economic interests.

As the SS did their dirty work, Britain and Germany, the two largest economies in Europe, moved perilously close to an all-out trade war. Such a confrontation would have had incalculable effects on Hitler's economic recovery. Britain was not only Germany's main export market and hence its main source of hard currency; the British Empire was also the chief source of many of Germany's imported raw materials. To make matters worse, the City of London was the chief provider of short-term finance for German foreign trade. Even if German imports were not British in origin, they were, more often than not, financed by British banks. A concerted effort by Britain to punish Germany for its default would have had a serious impact on Hitler's still fragile regime. Certainly, the Reich Minister for Economic Affairs was feeling the strain. Kurt Schmitt, who liked to cut a dashing figure in the uniform of an honorary SS colonel, knew he was widely despised in SA circles. In the pubs frequented by the stormtroopers they were now singing the 'Horst Wessel Song' with new words:

> Prices up, close up the ranks of the cartel
> Capital marches with a quiet tread
> The stockbrokers are party members
> And capital's protector is Herr Schmitt.[14]

If the rumours of an SA coup were true, the Minister's days were surely numbered. By the early summer, Schmitt's health was collapsing under the strain.[15] The end came on 28 June during a routine after-dinner speech to an audience of Berlin exporters. The Minister began by setting out the extremely serious situation facing the German economy and asked: 'What is to be done?' Before he could answer his own question, the blood drained from his face and he collapsed in mid-sentence. The water from his glass dribbled across the pages of his speech.[16] The next day the press were informed of the Minister's leave of absence. Twenty-four hours later the SS were unleashed on the leaders of the SA. The way was clear for Hjalmar Schacht and his friends in the military to assert their unchallenged position as Hitler's partners in power.

I

The immediate cause of the crisis was the dangerously low level of the Reichsbank's foreign currency reserves. As we have seen, reserves declined sharply in the first months of Hitler's government. They then stabilized over the summer of 1933 at around 400 million Reichsmarks, before beginning a renewed and precipitate decline in February 1934. By June 1934 the Reichsbank's currency holdings were reduced to less than 100 million Reichsmarks, sufficient to cover barely a week's imports, even at minimal levels.

Driving this disastrous haemorrhage was the increasing deficit on the current account. As we have seen, the increase in the import bill was a

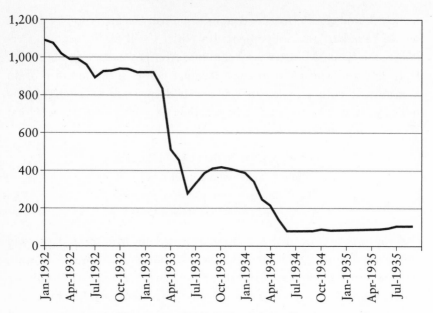

Figure 2. The declining gold and currency reserves of
the Reichsbank (million Reichsmarks)

predictable event and had been long anticipated.[17] Indeed, rising imports
were the clearest symptom of the vigour of Hitler's recovery. The truly
alarming problem was the trend in exports. Whilst the German domestic
economy rebounded, exports continued to decline. In every month of
1933 exports were lower than they had been in 1932 and the gap
widened as the year wore on. The trend continued into 1934, with
export earnings in the early summer of 1934 fully 20 per cent lower
than they had been a year earlier. Without exports, Germany could not
pay for its desperately needed imports, or service its foreign debts. And
this was not merely an abstract financial imperative. The livelihood of
thousands of firms and millions of workers depended on finding customers abroad. The light manufacturing districts of central and eastern
Germany, the great commercial cities of the Rhine valley, the port towns
of the Baltic and the North Sea all earned their living through foreign
trade. The fact that German export volumes remained 40 per cent below
their level in 1932 was one of the principal causes of unemployment
both in industry and commerce.[18]

The causes of the decline in German exports were hotly disputed both inside and outside the country.[19] Schacht and the officially inspired German press blamed 'unfair' restrictions of German trade. There is no doubt that the enormous hike in global protectionism that followed the currency crisis of 1931 made exporting very difficult.[20] But Germany was not simply a victim of other countries' protectionism. Other than Britain, Germany was Europe's largest market for exports and Germany's own turn towards protectionism since 1930 had played an important role in accelerating the cycle of tit-for-tat trade restriction. Furthermore, Germany's aggressive debt diplomacy added to its problems. One of the most alarming features of the Reich's trade statistics in 1934 was the serious fall in exports to France, the Netherlands and Switzerland. All three had responded to Germany's default in 1933 by negotiating clearing agreements, which ensured that they recouped at least some of Germany's export earnings in the form of debt service. Though initially these agreements were struck on the assumption that the trade balance would remain favourable to Germany, experience showed that bilateral clearing agreements actually had the effect of equalizing trade between the parties. German exports were impeded by the bureaucratic formalities of the clearing agreements. German importers on the other hand had every incentive to take full advantage of the open account offered under the terms of the treaties. From Germany's point of view this was a disastrous development, since it relied on the surpluses earned in trade with its European neighbours to pay for its imports of food and raw materials from overseas. Whilst the system of bilateral clearing deals was essential to expanding Germany's trade with its poorer Eastern and South-eastern European neighbours, the proliferation of such agreements in Western Europe was regarded by the Reichsbank as nothing short of a disaster.[21]

Furthermore, there can be no doubt that these obstacles to German exports were compounded after 1933 by widespread international antipathy towards the lawlessness and anti-Semitism of Hitler's regime. Outrages against Germany's Jewish population had begun immediately after the general election of 5 March and they had culminated in the official boycott of Jewish businesses proclaimed on 1 April 1933.[22] This in turn provoked Jewish organizations, most notably in the United States, into organizing a boycott of German goods. Though it is hard to assess the precise impact of this negative sentiment, it is clear that it was taken very seriously in Berlin. The boycott was the subject of anxious

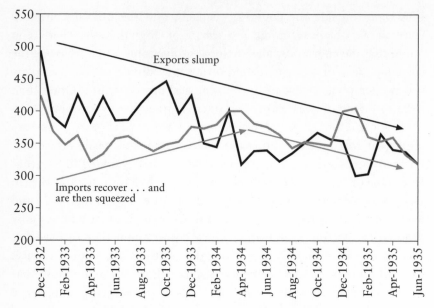

Figure 3. Pressure on the balance of trade:
monthly imports and exports (million Reichsmarks)

discussions between the Reichsbank and a number of Germany's largest corporations.[23] In July 1933 Hitler stated to a key meeting of leading Nazis that the first wave of revolutionary action against the Jews had had to be brought to a halt because of the front it created against Germany in international opinion.[24] Apart from the trade boycott, however, there was a far more direct contradiction between Nazi anti-Semitic policy and the constraints imposed by the balance of payments. In so far as the anti-Semitism of Hitler's regime had a coherent objective in the 1930s, it was the removal of Jews from German soil. In this respect it was fairly 'successful' in 1933, with 37,000 German Jews driven out of the country by the violence of the seizure of power. The 'problem' was that emigrants, unless they were very desperate, would move in large numbers only if they were permitted to take at least some of their possessions with them. German Jews were no different in this respect than any other migrant population. The Reichsbank was required by its statutes to provide migrants with the foreign currency needed to meet visa requirements abroad. But if prosperous Jewish families had emigrated en masse from Germany in 1933 and 1934, the effects on the

Reichsbank's foreign currency reserves would have been disastrous. At a conservative estimate German Jewish wealth in 1933 came to at least 8 billion Reichsmarks. Transferring even a modest fraction of this amount was clearly beyond the Reichsbank. As it was, the drain was serious enough. According to a detailed account compiled by the Reichsbank, the hard currency losses due to emigration between January 1933 and June 1935 came to a total of 132 million Reichsmarks, of which Jewish emigrants accounted for 124.8 million Reichsmarks.[25] Transfers had peaked in October 1933 at over 11 million Reichsmarks, but throughout the first half of 1934 they ran at around 6 million Reichsmarks per month. With total currency reserves standing at less than 100 million Reichsmarks, this was a drain that the Reichsbank could ill afford. In response, the Reichsbank therefore sharply raised the discount that was applied to holders of personal accounts wishing to transfer them abroad via the Golddiskontbank.[26] In addition, as of May 1934 the provisions of the so-called Reich flight tax were tightened up, with the lower threshold for liability being cut from 200,000 to 50,000 Reichsmarks and greater discretion given to the authorities in making the assessment.[27] These measures helped to reduce sharply the outflow of foreign exchange due to emigration. By the summer of 1935 the Reichsbank's monthly losses had fallen to 2 million Reichsmarks. However, the net effect was profoundly contradictory. Rather than encouraging emigration, the Third Reich was now imposing a severe tax on anyone seeking to leave the country. And the result was predictable. Once the initial violence of the seizure of power had passed, Jewish emigration dwindled to only 23,000 in 1934 and 21,000 in 1935. From 1934 onwards the lack of foreign exchange was to become the central obstacle to a coherent policy of forced emigration.

None of this, however, prevented paranoid anti-Semites such as Joseph Goebbels from placing the full blame for Germany's balance of payments problems on the machinations of world Jewry. Goebbels's opening speech in the campaign against 'critics and rubbishers' delivered to the Sportpalast on 11 May 1934 was laced with vicious anti-Semitic threats: 'If Germany was forced to declare to the world that it was no longer in a position to pay its debts and transfer interest, then the blame does not lie with us.' The ultimate cause of the problems was the Jewish boycott and it would be Germany's Jews who paid the price. To stormy applause Goebbels announced that in the event of an economic crisis, the 'hatred and anger and desperation of the German people would direct itself first of all against those we can get our hands on at home'.[28]

The basic reason for Germany's lack of competitiveness, however, was not political in this crude sense. The basic problem was the uncompetitive exchange rate of the Reichsmark. As we have seen, this fundamental misalignment had first emerged in the autumn of 1931 after the devaluation of sterling. The second shock had come in April 1933 with the devaluation of the dollar. By 1933 only 20 per cent of world trade was still conducted between countries with currencies fixed in terms of gold. Germany's failure to follow this trend meant that the prices of its exports, translated at the official exchange rate of the Reichsmark, were grossly uncompetitive. This was not a matter of particular industries or sectors. It was not a matter of high wages, or excessive taxes and social levies. At prevailing exchange rates, the entire system of prices and wages in Germany was out of line with that prevailing in most of the rest of the world economy.

In 1933 Hitler and Schacht had ruled out the most obvious solution to this problem, a devaluation. In Hitler's terms, a devaluation was tantamount to inflation and it was certainly true that by raising the cost of imported commodities any significant devaluation would have raised the German price level. The Reichsbank in the summer of 1934 estimated that a 40 per cent devaluation, sufficient to offset the British and American competitive lead, would have raised the working-class cost of living by 5.4–7.4 per cent, with the price of food going up by at least 10 per cent.[29] Whether or not this resulted in sustained inflation, of course, was another matter. In the Reichsbank's many assessments of the problem the question of German indebtedness was far more significant. Devaluing the Reichsmark would negate all the advantage that Germany had gained since 1931 through the devaluation of its creditors' currencies. This was clearly the clinching issue. As Schacht put it in a rare moment of candour in August 1934, 'He had never rejected a devaluation on principle. He had always said that so long as Germany had its large foreign indebtedness there was no point in doing a devaluation. As soon as we have got rid of the foreign debts the whole thing would look quite different.'[30]

The problem that now posed itself with ever greater urgency, however, was how to sustain German exports without a devaluation. A solution was found in the autumn of 1933 through a variety of schemes, all of which made use of the advantage that Germany had gained through the

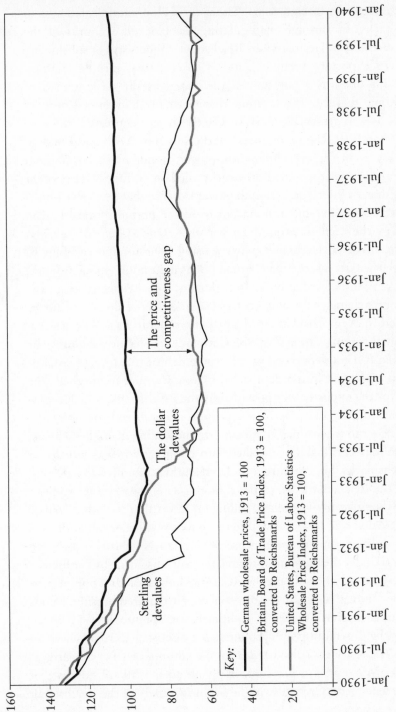

Figure 4. The competitiveness gap: the price of not devaluing

Note: To show the effect of the devaluation, this chart compares the German price level to the British and American price levels translated into Reichsmarks. As the value of the dollar and pound sterling fell against the Reichsmark, which remained fixed in terms of gold, a given level of the price index in the United States and Britain was lower relative to that prevailing in Germany.

moratorium on its foreign debts. Either through a complicated system of buy-backs, or through manipulating the blocked accounts of the foreign creditors in Germany, the Reichsbank found ways of subsidizing Germany's exporters at the expense of its creditors, earning Hjalmar Schacht his dubious reputation in the 1930s as the dark wizard of international finance. The leverage that Germany had gained over its creditors was represented most succinctly in the depressed value of German bonds (IOUs) on financial markets in New York and London. In January 1933, before Hitler took power, bonds owed by German municipalities and corporate borrowers traded on average at 62 per cent of face value.[31] Hitler's accession to power lowered that by twelve points to 50 per cent. After the announcement of the partial moratorium in June 1933 they fell to around 40 per cent. One system of subsidy, therefore, involved German exporters using their foreign earnings to buy up the heavily discounted German bonds in London and New York. A bond with a face value of $100 (valued at 350 Reichsmarks, at the prevailing exchange rate of 3.50 Reichsmarks to the dollar) could be purchased in New York in April 1934 for roughly $50 (175 Reichsmarks, at the going rate). With the German exporter now holding the discounted IOU, a debt owed by a German debtor to a foreign creditor had been converted into a debt owed by one German to another. The subsidy for the exporter was provided by the Reichsbank, which repurchased the bonds held by German exporters, either directly or indirectly, at rates closer to face value. To an exporter benefiting from this scheme, $50 in export earnings once cashed into dollar bonds was worth not 175 Reichsmarks, but closer to 350. In effect this amounted to a devaluation of the Reichsmark by 50 per cent, allowing the exporter to price his goods very keenly in dollars, selling on terms that would otherwise have implied severe losses. The difference to a regular devaluation was that this did not come at the expense of Germany's debtors or German importers. Under the buy-back scheme, the cost was borne by Germany's foreign creditors, who sold off their German bonds at a fraction of their face value.[32] Not all German exporters of course required subsidy. Goods sold through cartels, specialist equipment or commodities in which Germany held a monopoly accounted for almost a third of German exports. The rest were subsidized from the autumn of 1933 onwards at a rate of around 20–30 per cent, implying an overall subsidy rate of around 10 per cent. Certainly, in the position papers of the Reichsbank it was the success of the German authorities in devising these schemes for subsidizing exports that was the main reason offered against a move towards devaluation. Germany, it seemed, had found a way of boosting its exports without imposing the penalties of a devaluation – the high cost of imports and the onerous burden of foreign debt – on the rest of the economy.

However, by the spring of 1934, as the Reichsbank's reserves fell to crisis levels, this optimism began to wear rather thin.[33] Despite its promising beginnings the export subsidy system based on debt buy-backs was not working. Either Hitler's government would have to take drastic measures to boost exports, including perhaps devaluation, or it would have to impose severe restrictions on imports. This, however, would jeopardize the entire recovery. Germany could not produce, work or consume without imports. As we have seen, the basic priorities of the government had already been indicated in the first half of 1933. The quantity of spending envisioned for rearmament far outweighed anything that was ever contemplated for work creation, as did the diplomatic, financial and political risks that were taken. In the summer of 1933 it had been the interests of Germany's foreign creditors that had been sacrificed. From the beginning of 1934 onwards, the exhaustion of the Reichsbank's reserves forced Hitler's regime to choose again. To reiterate, it could either take radical measures to boost exports, or it could choose to prioritize selectively one type of import over another, either the import requirements of the industries catering to civilian consumer needs, or the requirements of state driven investment and rearmament. It could not have both. This stark choice throws new light on the remarkable decision, which was highlighted in the previous chapter, not to allocate any new funds towards civilian work creation after December 1933. If it had been possible to pursue a double-barrelled recovery based both on civilian work creation and rearmament, there seems little reason to doubt that Berlin would have embraced such an option. What ruled this out were the limitations of the balance of payments.

Within Germany, any public acknowledgement of the trade-off between civilian and military priorities was taboo. But foreign observers were not subject to the same restrictions. The connection between war debts and rearmament had been a staple of international discussion since the 1920s. The increase in Germany's military spending after 1933 was clear enough even in the published figures of the Reich's budget. By the spring of 1934 the foreign financial press was regularly highlighting the contradiction between the exuberant activity of Germany's military and Schacht's claim that the country was unable to service its foreign debt.[34] The conclusion was obvious. If Germany was serious about managing its foreign exchange crisis, if it wanted concessions from its creditors, then it would have to back away from unilateral rearmament. The point was made clearly to the German Foreign Minister by the American ambassador William Dodd in June 1934.[35] Indeed, so clear-cut was the choice facing Germany that debate could not be entirely suppressed, even within the Reich itself. Too much was at stake, for too many people.

Even in the minutes of the cabinet, there is evidence of severe differences of opinion over the future course of policy.[36] In February 1934 both Kurt Schmitt at the RWM and Krosigk at the Reich Finance Ministry prepared position papers, which suggested the possibility of an alternative course.[37] The RWM wanted to focus its efforts on raising the level of consumer demand, by cutting social insurance contributions and the levies of para-state organizations such as the German Labour Front. The RFM for its part hoped to clear the way for a 'natural' business-led recovery, by imposing a rigorous programme of fiscal discipline, not exempting the military. In this delicately balanced conjuncture it is conceivable that a determined intervention by Hjalmar Schacht, like that which he had made against the Young Plan in 1929, might have made a difference. Certainly, if he had thrown his weight behind Schmitt and Krosigk and had done so publicly, he could have forced Hitler to make a very painful choice between 'financial orthodoxy' and the demands of rearmament. But at this critical juncture Schacht was too preoccupied with his own position within the regime to take a principled stand. Rather than supporting Kurt Schmitt in his effort to limit military spending, Schacht deliberately outflanked him. The key moment appears to have come in March 1934, when Schmitt and Schacht were summoned by Hitler to a private meeting on the Obersalzberg at which they were to settle the future direction of economic policy. In advance of the meeting, Schmitt took care to reach an agreement with Schacht not to concede more than 15 billion Reichsmarks for rearmament. But when it came to the crucial meeting with Hitler, Schacht allowed Schmitt to break the unwelcome news before announcing that, as far he was concerned, 'no amount of money was too much for this vital national task'.[38] Indeed, Schmitt later recalled that Schacht declared himself willing to 'ruin the currency' in pursuit of rearmament.[39] At the cabinet meeting of 23 March 1934 Schacht sided with Defence Minister Blomberg to stave off any serious threat to the military budget. A few weeks later this was institutionalized by an agreement, which removed the military from detailed scrutiny by the Finance Ministry. Henceforth, Blomberg simply presented a grand total for military spending to a three-man committee consisting of Krosigk, Schacht and himself. As Krosigk described these meetings, he always attended in the full knowledge that if he opposed Blomberg's demands the General would call on Hitler, who would not hesitate to raise military spending to levels even higher than those originally requested. Not surprisingly, Krosigk rarely thought it wise to argue.

Having outmanoeuvred Schmitt over rearmament, Schacht in the spring of 1934 deliberately raised the tension on the international front. In a widely reported speech to the American Chamber of Commerce in Berlin he announced that unless German exports soon recovered, he would be forced to take drastic measures to reduce purchases of raw materials from both the United States and the British Empire. True to his word, in March 1934 the Reichsbank began progressively reducing the monthly foreign exchange quotas for Germany's importers. And in April the RWM agreed to the setting up of surveillance agencies (Ueberwachungsstellen), to ration the import of wool, cotton and packing material, thus providing the Reich with the administrative infrastructure needed for a selective import squeeze. By the summer, further organizations had been set up for leather, fur and nonferrous metals. Under the pressure of the balance of payments problem and the refusal to devalue, Schacht was imposing a system of ever more comprehensive bureaucratic control on the German economy and on German business.[40]

Given the cumbersome bureaucracy required both by the export subsidy system and the import restriction apparatus the option of devaluation refused to go away.[41] The subject remained something of a taboo. However, reading between the lines of the economic periodicals, it is clear that the possibility of devaluation was being widely discussed. And this is confirmed by the confidential internal reporting of the Reichsbank's economics department. One should not forget that as recently as

May 1932 Gregor Strasser had publicly committed the Nazi party to abandoning the gold standard. And though this promise had been quietly removed from the Nazi party electoral manifesto in the autumn of 1932 and Strasser himself had been expelled, there were still plenty of people within the party who saw a devaluation as a logical complement to a policy of work creation and national economic independence.[42] By 1934, they were joined by economic liberals and practical businessmen, who were deeply alarmed by the drift towards bureaucracy and state control. Whereas devaluation had once been a 'radical' cause, it now seemed the only way to preserve a degree of normality in the day-to-day business of that part of the German economy that depended on foreign trade. As we have seen, in commercial cities such as Hamburg, unemployment was still painfully high in 1934 and without a revival in foreign trade there was little prospect of any immediate improvement. It was the Hansa Bund, therefore, the organization of north German commercial circles, that was the strongest advocate of devaluation and it was the weekly Hamburg journal the *Wirtschaftsdienst* that provided the most open forum for debate.[43] In its editorials, the *Wirtschaftsdienst* toed the Schachtian line, rejecting devaluation as an immediate possibility. However, the journal was noticeably positive in its reports on the experience with devaluation in other countries. And after the spring meeting of the Hansa Bund in April 1934 it went a step further: 'In the light of the intensified private discussions about foreign trade . . .' the journal demanded that 'the question of devaluation' should no longer be 'skirted in a timid fashion'.[44]

The speculation about devaluation appears to have reached its peak in May 1934, in response to an ambiguous comment made by Finance Minister Krosigk, which was widely reported both inside and outside Germany.[45] Krosigk said in public what Schacht was quite willing to admit in private. The Third Reich rejected devaluation, not in principle, but because it was impractical and too risky for a country like Germany with enormous foreign debts and minimal foreign exchange reserves. The markets responded with a flurry of speculation.[46] Meanwhile, in the summer of 1934 business circles began to make their own preparations. Particularly in the textiles trade, which depended on large stocks of imported cotton and wool, contracts became popular that specified payment to be made in gold marks. In Hamburg, the association of raw rubber dealers distributed a model contract to its members specifying payment terms that would secure them against a possible devaluation. For speculators, the Reichsmark had become a 'one way bet'. Such was the mood that the party journal *Die Deutsche Volkswirtschaft* felt it necessary to denounce such activities as an act of national sabotage.[47]

By the end of May, the choices facing Germany had become starkly obvious. In a remarkably frank article, the *Wirtschaftsdienst* demanded that if the Reich government had decided definitively not to devalue, it should draw the necessary conclusions.[48] In the journal's view, the choice against devaluation marked a fundamental divide between the liberal economic policies of countries such as Britain and a newly emerging system of National Socialist economic management. If devaluation was ruled out, then there was no alternative but to begin as soon as possible with the establishment of a new and powerful system of economic controls. And the *Wirtschaftsdienst* did not hold back. If the German government meant to break definitively with the liberal economic order, then it was in a position much like that at the beginning of a war. It was dangerous to remain on the defensive. The Reich authorities needed to go over to the attack, adopting far more comprehensive measures to regulate imports and to promote exports regardless of the consequences for relations with its trading partners.

The *Wirtschaftsdienst* had correctly sensed the way the wind was blowing in Berlin. By the early summer of 1934, the media channels at Schacht's disposal, in particular the weekly *Der Deutsche Volkswirt*, were mobilized for an orchestrated campaign against Schmitt, the Minister of Economic Affairs, with the full backing of the military. Colonel Georg Thomas, the chief economic staff officer of the Defence Ministry, was a loyal Schachtian. In the early summer of 1934 he bombarded both his Minister, General Blomberg, and Wilhelm Keppler, Hitler's personal economic adviser, with memorandums calling for a new system of economic regulation. The parallel and uncoordinated system by which the Reichsbank allocated foreign exchange and the RWM sought to control trade directly through the surveillance agencies was not working. The system was leaky and the desperate efforts by German businessmen to exploit the loopholes in the system were having counterproductive effects. Since the surveillance agencies regulated only raw materials, traders imported increasing volumes of finished goods, which were more expensive. The restrictions did not apply to the clearing agreements covering trade with the Netherlands and Switzerland. So importers diverted trade through those countries. To lay their hands on foreign currency, German traders took to organizing new short-term loans with foreign banks, often at exorbitant interest rates. Meanwhile, the exchange reserves of the Reichsbank continued to dwindle from month to month and Schacht did little to resist the downward trend. Indeed, it is hard to escape the conclusion that rather than seeking to stabilize the situation Schacht was deliberately forcing the crisis, turning the screw on Schmitt.

The tension reached its climax in the second half of June, with Schacht's announcement on 14 June of a complete moratorium on foreign debt repayment and the imposition of a new regime of daily foreign exchange allocation. This not only plunged Germany's foreign relations into crisis. It also put Schacht in complete control. The hapless Schmitt was no match for Schacht. After his health let him down he gratefully retired from front-line politics, returning to an influential position in the insurance industry. The senior civil servants in the RWM, however, were made of sterner stuff. Under the leadership of Secretary of State Hans Posse, the Ministry made one last effort to change the course of events. Posse (1886–1965) had spent his career at the Ministry in trade policy and was formerly a supporter of Stresemann's DVP. But he made the best of the Machtergreifung, gaining appointment to the senior civil service position at the Reich Ministry following Hugenberg's resignation and joining the Nazi party in November 1933.[49] In the summer of 1934 Hitler even seems to have briefly considered him as a possible successor to Schmitt. Posse was certainly a conformist, but liberal habits died hard. In early July he and his staff drafted a plan for the management of Germany's foreign account based on a scheme devised by Vincent Krogmann, the Gauleiter of Hamburg, whose ideas reflected the commercial and free trading proclivities of his constituency. As a late convert to National Socialism, Krogmann (1889–1978) did not question his Fuehrer's decision to hold fast to the official value of the German currency. What Krogmann proposed instead was the creation of a 'pseudo-market' for foreign exchange, in which the price mechanism rather than bureaucratic regulation would be used to bring demand and supply into equilibrium. All exporters would continue to deliver their foreign exchange earnings to the Reichsbank. In return, they would be issued, not with Reichsmarks, but with foreign exchange vouchers.

These vouchers would entitle the holder to receive foreign exchange. The core of Krogmann's idea was to make these vouchers freely tradable. They would be exchanged for Reichsmarks, not at an arbitrary rate set by the officials of the Reichsbank, but in a competitive bidding process between the various contending interests seeking foreign currency for the import of scarce commodities, or the repayment of foreign debts. Their internal 'exchange rate' would therefore be set by market forces, resulting in a spontaneous 'internal' devaluation of the Reichsmark. Though its critics denounced the Krogmann Plan as just one more cranky currency scheme, a similar system was in fact adopted by Austria in early 1934 and this was widely cited as an example in German debates.[50]

By 19 July 1934 the RWM had finalized a draft version of the Krogmann Plan to put before cabinet.[51] However, just as the civil servants at the RWM were finishing their work, Colonel Thomas of the Defence Ministry contacted Wilhelm Keppler. Earlier in the summer, Thomas had reassured Keppler that the foreign exchange situation, though serious, did not pose an immediate threat to rearmament. Now he was more alarmist. Thomas stated bluntly that the desperate situation of the Reich's currency reserves posed an immediate threat to the continuation of rearmament. If, as seemed possible in the fraught summer of 1934, Germany were to be entangled in a war, the result would be a disaster. In making this dramatic declaration to Keppler, Thomas's intention was clearly to bring Hitler into play, and he was not disappointed. Within days, in the midst of the confusion surrounding the botched Austrian coup, Schacht was summoned to a personal audience at the Bayreuth festival. We have no reliable record of what transpired. However, the upshot was that Schacht was appointed as Acting Minister for Economic Affairs. He was not given the job in a permanent capacity, because for him to have held a cabinet position would have compromised his nominally independent position as head of the Reichsbank and his membership in the exclusive fraternity of central bankers at the Bank of International Settlements. As Acting Minister, however, Schacht had full authority over the RWM and he made this felt immediately upon his return to Berlin. Encountering Secretary of State Posse for the first time in his new offices, Schacht asked him: 'Are you interested in music?' To which Posse innocently replied: 'Yes, very.' Schacht's retort was typically sarcastic: 'I'm not at all musical, but I was in Bayreuth.'[52] With Hitler's personal approval and the strong backing of the military, Schacht's position was unassailable. The Krogmann Plan was dropped. The direction of German economic policy had been decided. Rather than attempting to manoeuvre its way out of the crisis through a combination of devaluation and rapprochement with the Western powers, the Third Reich would stay the course of nationalist self-assertion. The means to do so would be divisive bilateral diplomacy abroad and authoritarian organization at home.

II

The German balance of payments crisis of 1934 left a lasting impact on Germany's trade relations. It is commonplace to describe Germany's trade policy from the summer of 1934 onwards as autarchic – a generalized effort to restrict imports and achieve self-sufficiency. A close look at the trade statistics reveals that 'autarchy' in fact amounted to a selective policy of disengagement directed above all against the United States, the British Empire and, to a lesser degree, France.[53] This in turn was directly connected to the repudiation of Germany's foreign debts. Germany's balance of payments problems in the early 1930s were above all problems in relation to the world's largest economic blocs: the United States and the British Empire. The United States was overwhelmingly Germany's largest foreign lender. Service on American debts alone came to at least 600 million Reichsmarks in addition to the large bilateral trade deficit with the United States. In 1929 this had stood at close to 800 million Reichsmarks. By 1933–4 the deficit had been reduced to 230 million Reichsmarks. But, at 800 million Reichsmarks per annum, the combined American claims on the German balance of payments for debt service and net imports were clearly unsustainable. The leaders of the Weimar Republic accepted this situation so long as they needed American backing in the struggle against reparations. Once reparations were lifted at Lausanne in 1932, this consideration no longer applied.

The first step towards an outright default came with the partial moratorium of the summer of 1933. The American government could protest on behalf of its private creditors, as it did in early 1934. However, since there was no chance of any new loans to Germany in the foreseeable future, the United States had little real leverage. America could cut off supplies of key raw materials. But in an all-out trans-Atlantic trade war all that Germany stood to lose was a large trade deficit.[54] America's best defence against a default was to enrol Germany's other creditors, above all Britain, in a united front. But as the Germans clearly understood, their declaration of a general moratorium was more than likely to set the creditors against each other.[55] The Dutch and Swiss broke ranks in the autumn of 1933 to obtain favourable bilateral deals. In the spring of 1934 Anglo-American solidarity was still intact. The significance of the summer crisis of 1934 from Schacht's point of view was that it splintered the Anglo-American front. A trade war with Britain would undoubtedly have been a disaster for Germany, but it would also have had severe consequences for the British. Schacht's brinksmanship was clearly motivated by an acute sense of what was at stake for the City of London and for British exporters in Anglo-German economic relations. As he put it in August 1934 to a meeting of the Reichsbank and the RWM: 'I will take risks with England . . . we have to go through this valley. He was going to take it to the brink with England and with the Swiss.'[56]

In the end, Schacht's aggression paid off.[57] To avoid the imposition of compulsory clearing, the Germans agreed to resume service on the Dawes and Young loans, the most sensitive of Germany's debts. The British for their part allowed themselves to be enrolled in a bilateral commercial agreement in the form of the Anglo-German Payments Agreement of 1 November 1934. Remarkably, the Bank of England even went so far as to provide Schacht with a loan enabling Germany to settle an embarrassing volume of unpaid trade credits.[58] There can be no doubting the strategic importance of the Anglo-German agreement. Not only did it split the Anglo-American front and stabilize relations with Germany's most important trading partner, but the Anglo-German agreement also offered an escape from the impasse that had been reached in previous clearing agreements with Germany's Western European neighbours.[59] Unlike the earlier clearing deals with the Dutch and Swiss, the Anglo-German Payments Agreement guaranteed Germany a substantial margin of 'free foreign exchange' for use outside the sterling zone. Fifty-five per cent of Germany's sterling revenues were to be set aside for unrestricted import of British goods to Germany. A further 10 per cent were to be used to service Germany's short- and long-term obligations to British creditors. The rest, notionally at least, was available for use outside the sterling zone.

With the united front of the creditors broken, Schacht was free to complete the process of uncoupling the German economy from the United States. After 1934 Germany singled out its American creditors for particular discriminatory treatment. Even American holders of Dawes and Young loans, supposedly the most privileged form of debt, were repaid at a rate 30 per cent lower than that granted to British creditors. Meanwhile, at least $900 million worth of corporate and local government bonds were caught up in the complete moratorium on transfer payments.[60] Any improvement, Berlin made clear, would depend on securing more favourable terms for German exports to the United States. After 1934, however, American and German trade relations deteriorated sharply.[61] Schacht's strategy of bilateralism, crowned by the Anglo-German Payments Agreement, clashed with the strategy of multilateralism being pushed no less assertively by Secretary of State Hull in Washington. With the dollar having finally ended its precipitate collapse, Hull began a systematic campaign for trade liberalization with the Reciprocal Trade Agreements Act of June 1934.[62] This sought to use selective reductions in American tariffs as a way of prising open the log-jammed international trading system. Given the assertive mood in Washington, Germany's announcement in October 1934 that it was withdrawing from the Treaty of Trade and Friendship signed between the Weimar Republic and the United States in 1923, provoked a robust response. Secretary of State Hull denounced the German move as 'an act of aggression against the entire American system of trade treaties' and stripped Germany of its Most Favoured Nation status.[63] When Schacht requested tariff negotiations under the terms of the Reciprocal Trade Agreements Act, Hull refused, citing Germany's discriminatory trade practices.[64] Entering into bilateral trade agreements with Germany would have undermined the credibility of Hull's entire strategy, notably in the eyes of America's major trading partners in Latin America.[65] Meanwhile, trade between the United States and Germany dwindled rapidly. In 1928, American exports to Germany had been worth 2 billion Reichsmarks and exports from Germany to the United States were valued at 796 million Reichsmarks. By 1936, this trade had shrunk to derisory levels. American exports to Germany were worth no more than 232 million Reichsmarks and German exports amounted to less than 150 million Reichsmarks.

This extraordinary contraction in trade between Germany and the

United States, the two largest economies in the world, was the real substance of Schacht's 'autarchic' trade policy.[66] It was compensated by a concerted attempt by the Reich to cultivate links with producers in South-east Europe and Latin America who could supply substitutes for the raw materials no longer obtained from the United States and Britain.[67] Important trade deals were concluded with Hungary in February and with Yugoslavia in May 1934.[68] Arrangements were made with Chile to secure German access to saltpetre and copper. Brazil emerged as Germany's major supplier not only of coffee but also of cotton. By the late 1930s, the overall shift in the structure of German imports was very substantial. But the scope of Germany's new trading relationships was inherently limited by the imbalances in purchasing power between Germany and the less developed countries. As Schacht put it with characteristic charm: 'One can sell far less to coolies ... than one can to highly qualified ... factory workers.'[69] Furthermore, Germany's aggressive 'invasion' of Latin America did nothing to ease relations with the United States. Most notably in Brazil, Germany and America were in direct conflict. Germany's urgent drive to increase its imports of cotton and coffee allowed Rio to extricate itself from Cordell Hull's vision of a hemispheric free trade zone.[70] Indeed, such was American concern about the growing German influence in Brazil that Rio was able to follow Germany in defaulting on its large debts to the United States, without having to fear aggressive retaliation from Washington.

One of the more remarkable bilateral agreements, which began to work on a substantial scale after 1934, addressed itself directly to the conflict between Germany's limited foreign exchange reserves and the regime's urgent desire to encourage Jewish emigration.[71] Known as the Haavara Transfer, it involved a transaction between the Reich's authorities and a group of Zionist businesses based at the Hanotea orange plantation in Natania just outside Tel Aviv. Whereas the British mandate restricted immigration by applicants without financial means, anyone equipped with at least 1,000 Palestinian pounds (1 pound Palestine = 1 pound sterling) was granted free entry under a so-called 'capitalist visa'. The Haavara Transfer was designed to take advantage of this loophole. The scheme operated by allowing German Jews to make payments into a fund in Berlin in exchange for certificates crediting them with sufficient Palestinian pounds to allow them to obtain the coveted visa. Hanotea for its part used the funds deposited in Berlin to buy

German goods for export to Palestine. The emigrants were reimbursed in Palestinian pounds when the German goods were sold to Jewish or Arab customers. In effect, the arrangement ensured that every Reichsmark of capital exported by a German-Jewish emigrant was matched by a compensating export order. As the Reichsbank tightened its grip on its foreign exchange reserves, Haavara became, despite the tiny size of the Mandate economy, one of the most efficient means for Jews to export capital from Germany. In total, 50,000 people, one-tenth of the German-Jewish population in 1933, were able to use the scheme to make good their escape. They took with them 106 million Reichsmarks for which they obtained the remarkable total of 5.5 million Palestinian pounds. They thus paid a discount over the official exchange rate (12.50 Reichsmarks for one Palestinian pound) of only 35 per cent, at a time when the majority of Jewish emigrants were able to rescue only a tiny fraction of their wealth.

Structural rearrangements of this kind in Germany's trading relations, however, were a matter for long-term strategy. What was required in 1934 was an immediate solution to the looming foreign exchange crisis. Given the decision not to devalue, this could mean only one thing: more bureaucracy. The outline of a comprehensive new system of trade control was drafted by Schacht and his officials at the Reichsbank and the RWM during August 1934.[72] The Reichsbank would allocate the available foreign exchange on the basis of the export returns. It would reserve the funds required to make agreed debt repayments and to ensure that Germany could meet its short-term obligations. The remainder would then be handed to a group of supervisory agencies, twenty-five in total, one for each major class of commodities. The proposal that Schacht had originally drafted in 1932 for import monopolies modelled on those of World War I, was modified to provide for a greater degree of decentralization and private initiative. The supervisory agencies would not themselves engage in the import trade. Their job was to sift applications for foreign currency from private importers and to allocate the limited funds according to their national priority. Top priority, it was clear, was to be given to exporters and to suppliers to the armaments effort. Importers who had the approval of a surveillance agency were issued with so-called Exchange Certificates (Devisenbescheinigungen). Any importer in possession of such a certificate would be guaranteed foreign exchange from the Reichsbank. As of 1935, imports without Exchange Certificates were banned. Not surprisingly, this vision of a direct bureaucratic system of control met with the complete approval of the military. A draft plan was discussed between the Ministries in mid-August and Schacht presented it to Hitler on the Obersalzberg at the end of the month in the company of Defence Minister Blomberg and General Walter von Reichenau of the army. The composition of this group was a clear sign of where the power now lay in the Third Reich. The military had been Schacht's allies since 1933 and their relationship was even closer after the Night of the Long Knives. It is also significant, however, that the plan had to be cleared with Hitler. The Fuehrer may not have followed the day-to-day details of economic policy, but no important decisions could be taken without his approval.[73] Days later, Schacht announced the outline of the so-called New Plan to the crowd of businessmen attending the Leipzig trade fair. Characteristically, Schacht referred to his own design as a 'monstrosity' forced on Germany by the refusal of its creditors to accept more reasonable trade terms. Completely ignoring his own role in systematically exacerbating the crisis, Schacht blamed Germany's retreat into autarchy entirely on external circumstances.[74]

The system did its job in stopping the haemorrhage of foreign exchange. In the months following the announcement of the New Plan, imports were squeezed dramatically. By the third quarter of 1935, the volume of imports was almost exactly equal to that at the trough of the recession three years earlier. But, by comparison with 1932, industrial production was up almost 100 per cent.[75] Such a dramatic squeeze on foreign inputs to the German economy was clearly not sustainable. It was only possible in the short term because producers were able to draw on accumulated stocks of raw materials. Once these were exhausted, the economic recovery would be cut short. Any substantial increase in imports depended on achieving a recovery in exports. This, however, failed to arrive. By the summer of 1934, the optimism that had surrounded the export subsidy schemes a few months earlier was largely dispelled. The Reichsbank was so desperate for hard currency that it could no longer afford the bond repurchase mechanism as its main means of subsidy, since this left a substantial fraction of Germany's export earnings in foreign hands. And the other schemes that operated at the expense of Germany's foreign creditors were no longer sufficient to provide the necessary rate of support. The Reichsbank estimated that to offset Germany's crippling competitive disadvantage it needed to provide more than two-thirds of Germany's exports (240 million of 340 million Reichsmarks) with a subsidy of 25 per cent. This would cost 60 million Reichsmarks per month, of which at most 40 million could be raised from Germany's foreign creditors.[76] The rest would have to come more or less directly from the coffers of the Reich. Given the general stress on the Reich's finances and the likelihood of accusations of dumping, this was as Schacht acknowledged 'a measure of absolute desperation'.[77] Nor did he expect the system of generalized export subsidy to continue for more than a year: 'What we will do in the second year, is a different matter.' As we have seen, he did not rule out an eventual devaluation. On the other hand, 'If the dumping works and our import restrictions work, then we can reckon with a high inflow of foreign currency. Then we can go back on the offensive with respect to the bond repurchase mechanism.' The priority, as Schacht stressed in a meeting with party officials in November 1934, was to force through a final resolution of the debt problem whilst securing the necessary raw materials to sustain rearmament. For Schacht, the connection was obvious. Germany's trade problems could not ultimately be solved, 'until Germany again stands in the world as a power factor. So long as we have not regained this power it is pointless to get excited about theories.'[78]

With its tight regulation of imports and the proliferation of bilateral clearing agreements the New Plan could easily have become a corset restricting any further progress of Germany's economic recovery. What saved Schacht were three things: the continuing recovery of the global economy, which produced a resurgence in demand for German exports; the willingness of countries other than the United States, most notably Britain, to comply with Germany's new trading system; and the sheer determination and effectiveness with which the New Plan was imposed. The method used to fund the expanded export subsidy system was, as Schacht acknowledged, a measure of last resort. As of May 1935 a progressive tax was levied on the turnover of German industry to raise the tens of millions of Reichsmarks needed every month to maintain the competitiveness of German exports.[79] In effect, the profits of the domestic armaments boom were being recycled to assist the ailing export sector. For most industries the levy was assessed at rates between 2 and 4 per cent of turnover.[80] This may not seem draconian, but since it was levied on turnover not profit, the impact was very considerable. To take one example, the steel tube industry had monthly domestic sales in 1935 of 15.6 million Reichsmarks. The profit on this business was 1 million Reichsmarks per month. Of this amount, no less than 400,000 Reichsmarks, or 40 per cent, was taxed away in contributions towards the export subsidy.[81] On less profitable businesses the impact was more severe. Ford's ailing subsidiary in Cologne reported to corporate Head Office in Dearborn that the 3 per cent turnover levy would completely wipe out any profit it could expect to earn in 1935.[82] From German industry as a whole, the levy raised 700 million Reichsmarks in its first year. Not surprisingly, it was extremely unpopular. But protests from industry were rebuffed with reference to the 'special emergency of the state'.[83] And it could not be denied that the system was effective. By the end of 1935, the industrial levy was raising funds sufficient to provide the average German exporter with a subsidy of almost 30 per cent on every foreign order.

The measures taken in response to the foreign exchange crisis of 1934 laid the organizational foundations for the management of the Nazi economy for years to come. The surveillance agencies and the export subsidy scheme, together with the elaborate system of business organizations, cartels and price controls that underpinned them, were all still in operation ten years later at the heart of the war economy. The system survived because it worked. From 1935 onwards, as a result both of the recovery of the world economy and the effective new subsidy scheme, the disastrous decline of German exports was halted. From June 1935 until the spring of 1938, steady growth in exports was vital to sustaining the momentum of Hitler's economic recovery. Exports did not return to their pre-Depression levels. Nor were they enough to provide the Reichsbank with more than a bare minimum of comfort. But they did permit a steady increase in the volume of imports from the absolute trough reached in the summer of 1935. If we consider the extraordinarily small quantity of foreign exchange and gold at the Reichsbank's disposal and the difficulty of obtaining credit, the volume of import and export business that Nazi Germany was able to conduct under the New Plan was truly remarkable. Under modern conditions of uninhibited free trade and international lending, the IMF advises central banks to hold precautionary reserves equivalent to six months of imports. The elaborate apparatus of Schacht's New Plan allowed the Reichsbank to sustain the international trade of one of the world's largest and most sophisticated economies with foreign currency reserves amounting in the mid-1930s to little more than one week's cover. To say the least, this was a remarkable organizational achievement.

It was an achievement that depended, not surprisingly, on a great deal of bureaucratic effort. By the late 1930s it was estimated that the official organizations of the New Plan alone employed in excess of 18,000 officials, administrators and clerks working on currency control issues.[84] In private business there were many thousands more. But managing Germany's balance of payments also required a series of very painful political choices. From the spring of 1934 onwards, the Reichsbank and the RWM squeezed down hard on all aspects of household consumption that were dependent on imported raw materials. The result was to split the German economy in two. Whilst the investment goods industries and all sectors associated with the drive towards self-sufficiency continued their surging recovery, the upswing in the consumer sectors, above all textiles, was suddenly stopped in its tracks. For more than two years, starting in the spring of 1934, Hitler's Germany saw virtually no growth in the output of consumer goods.

The significance of this development should not be underestimated. The conventional image of the German economy as a powerhouse of industrial modernity, too often obscures the continued importance of 'traditional', consumer-orientated sectors such as food and textiles. The textile and clothing sectors did not boast the corporate champions of heavy industry, nor could they claim political connections at the highest level.[85] But in 1933 textiles and clothing were still amongst the largest industrial employers in Germany.[86] The census of that year counted 1.2 million people as employed in textiles – spinning and weaving – and in leather tanning. A further 1.477 million people earned their living in the production of shoes and clothing. In addition, half a million Germans were employed in the wholesale and retail trade connected with the textile industry. Altogether, textiles and clothing accounted for just under 20 per cent of industrial employment and a share of output that was not much smaller. In terms of sheer numbers employed, textiles and clothing were more important than mechanical engineering, electrical engineering, chemicals or coal mining. All the more serious were the implications of the decisions to dramatically squeeze the supply of imported cotton, leather and wool on which the sector depended for 80 per cent of its raw materials.

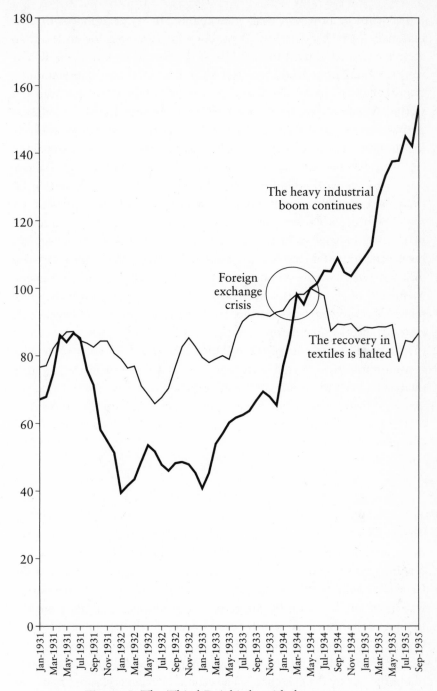

Figure 5. The Third Reich's lopsided recovery:
the production of textiles and investment goods (1929 = 100)

The choice, however, was inescapable. In 1934 imports of raw materials for textile and leather production accounted for no less than 26 per cent of the total import bill. If the Reichsbank and the RWM were serious about restricting Germany's imports whilst maintaining the rearmament drive, the textile industry was bound to be a principal victim. It was no surprise, therefore, that the first Reich surveillance agencies were established to monitor the import of cotton and wool. By the summer, the slowdown in textiles was so dramatic that Berlin agencies were beginning to worry about mass lay-offs. To prevent a major reverse to the work creation drive, the textile sector was restricted by decree to operating its mills no more than thirty-six hours per week. At the same time, a blanket ban was imposed on new investment in textile plant. Any expansion in the industry's capacity was made dependent on permission from the RWM. Not surprisingly, the impact of these measures was to cause panic buying by both merchants and consumers. Memories of the austerity of World War I were still fresh in people's minds. To calm fears of inflation, the RWM took its first steps towards systematic price regulation, in the textile sector. These dampened the immediate speculative wave. However, given the need to restrict consumption of imported cotton and wool it was not in the regime's interest to keep the price of clothing permanently low. After 1934, the textile industry stands out, even in the official statistics, as the sector of the German economy in which prices were allowed to rise most conspicuously.

III

There can be no doubt that the regime paid a serious political price for the economic difficulties of 1934. All the evidence we have on public opinion, mainly from confidential reports by the regional offices of the Gestapo, confirms that in the summer of 1934 the German population was unsettled far more by the economic problems resulting from the foreign exchange crisis than by the violence of the Night of the Long Knives. The simplistic cliché, which sees the Germans as having been won over to Hitler's regime by the triumphs of work creation, is simply not borne out by the evidence.[87] The economic recovery, rapid as it was, was incomplete, even in the first half of 1935. There were still millions of unemployed, many of whom had known nothing other than poverty for years. Their best hope in the first three winters of the Third Reich was the new National Socialist Winter Charity, which distributed hundreds of millions of Reichsmarks' worth of free food to the poorer *Volksgenossen*. Furthermore, after the crisis of 1934, the lopsidedness of Germany's economic recovery was acute. Millions of people who depended for their livelihoods on the consumer goods industries faced an outlook of short time and shortened wages. For entire regions of Germany, such as Saxony and Baden, that were disproportionately dependent on exports and consumer goods production, the recovery was partial at best.[88] Even those who did have jobs had to put up with price increases and deteriorating quality. The apparent inability of the regime to guarantee either stable prices or a regular supply of daily necessities, including food and clothing, was deeply disconcerting. According to Gestapo reports, the popular mood in the autumn of 1934 was apathetic and gloomy. Irritation with the many petty restrictions of everyday life was widespread and outright protest was not far beneath the surface. As one report commented: 'The housewives in the markets still hold their tongues. But if one of them protests – which happens quite often – nobody contradicts her.'[89] According to the Potsdam Gestapo office this was symptomatic of the repressed mood of frustration. Wherever crowds gathered in the autumn of 1934 – in the queues at the labour exchanges, at bus stops – there was more or less open agitation against the regime. The work camps on the autobahn building sites, where conditions were notoriously grim, were particularly worrying trouble spots. The records of the Berlin Gestapo reported 140 arrests in October 1934 following a 'mutiny' at a local construction site.[90] In Dortmund, workers took to replacing the official 'Hitler Gruss', with ironic expressions such as 'Heil 3.50 Reichsmarks!' to which the response was 'Kartoffeln 3.75 Reichmarks'. Even if the Nazi recovery did bring jobs and relief from dire poverty, it was still some way from the return to 'normality' for which Germans really yearned.

By the end of 1934, Joseph Goebbels, the Minister for Propaganda, who is commonly credited with an almost magical degree of control over the German population, was deeply frustrated by the public mood. The national campaign against 'critics and rubbishers', which he had launched with his anti-Semitic tirade of May 1934, had not gone well. In many parts of the country, meetings were so ill-attended that the whole programme had had to be quietly shelved. In other areas, local government complained that Goebbels's super-heated rhetoric actually served to agitate the population, alerting them to the full extent of the currency crisis. The dramas of June and July, reflected in the surges in the price of imported goods, only confirmed the public's fears about the insubstantial nature of the Nazi economic recovery.[91] In the first of a series of Reich Press Days on 18 November 1934, Goebbels gave a remarkably frank assessment of his strategy in response to this new mood of apathy and depression. The Minister was clearly fed up with the never-ending obsession with the petty inconveniences of everyday life. What was needed was not grumbling, but a resolute focus on the higher ambitions of the regime. It was the task of the press to cast the mundane difficulties of everyday life in the golden glow of the higher ideal. Goebbels himself wanted no more reports on the gloomy state of public opinion. 'I want to hear nothing, I want to see nothing, I want to know nothing . . . I know what is going on, but you don't need to tell me about it. Don't ruin my nerves. I need my confidence to be able to work.'[92]

4

Partners: The Regime and
German Business

On Monday, 20 February 1933, at 6.00 p.m., a group of about twenty-five businessmen were summoned to attend a private meeting in the villa of Hermann Goering, now acting as president of the Reichstag, at which Hitler, the Reich Chancellor, was to 'explain his policies'.[1] The guests were an oddly assorted bunch. The invitees included leaders of German industry, men such as Georg von Schnitzler, second in command at IG Farben, Krupp von Bohlen, who was both head-by-marriage of the Krupp empire and the current chairman of the Reich industrial association, and Dr Albert Voegler the CEO of the Vereinigte Stahlwerke, the world's second largest steel firm. But there were also a number of decidedly second-tier figures on the list. The businessmen were greeted first by Goering and Hjalmar Schacht. Hitler himself appeared only after a considerable wait. If the businessmen had expected a discussion of the specifics of economic policy they were to be disappointed. Hitler instead launched into a general survey of the political situation. As in his national address on 1 February, his central theme was the turning point in German history marked by the defeat and revolution of 1918. The experience of the last fourteen years had shown that 'private enterprise cannot be maintained in the age of democracy'. Business was founded above all on the principles of personality and individual leadership. Democracy and liberalism led inevitably to Social Democracy and Communism. After fourteen years of degeneration, the moment had now come to resolve the fatal divisions within the German body politic. Hitler would show no mercy towards his enemies on the left. It was time 'to crush the other side completely'. The next phase in the struggle would begin after the elections of 5 March. If the Nazis were able to gain another 33 seats in the Reichstag, then the actions against the Communists would be covered by 'constitutional means'. But, 'regardless of the outcome there will be no retreat . . . if the election does not decide . . . the decision must be brought about even by other means'.

Hitler did not take questions from his audience, nor did he spell out exactly what was expected of the business leaders. Hitler had not come to negotiate. He had come to inform them of his intentions. And his audience can have been left in no doubt. Germany's new Chancellor planned to put an end to parliamentary democracy. He planned to crush the German left and in the process he was more than willing to use physical force. At least according to the surviving record, the conflict between left and right was the central theme of the speeches by both Hitler and Goering on 20 February. There was no mention either of anti-Jewish policy or a campaign of foreign conquest.[2] Hitler left it to Goering to reveal the immediate purpose of the meeting. Since German business had a major stake in the struggle against the left, it should make an appropriate financial contribution. 'The sacrifice[s]', Goering pointed out, 'would be so much easier . . . to bear if it [industry] realized that the election of 5 March will surely be the last one for the next ten years, probably even for the next hundred years.' Krupp von Bohlen, the designated spokesman for the business side, had prepared extensive notes for a detailed discussion of economic policy, but confronted with this bald appeal, he thought better of introducing tedious details. Instead, he confined himself to stating that all present would surely agree on the need for the speediest possible resolution of the political situation. Business fully supported the goal of establishing a government in the interests of the German people. Only under a strong and independent state could the economy and business 'develop and flourish'.

After this exchange of nationalist platitudes, Hitler and Goering departed and Hjalmar Schacht got down to business. He proposed an election fund of 3 million Reichsmarks, to be shared between the Nazis and their nationalist coalition partners. Over the following three weeks Schacht received contributions from seventeen different business groups. The largest individual donations came from IG Farben (400,000 Reichsmarks) and the Deutsche Bank (200,000 Reichsmarks). The association of the mining industry also made a generous deposit of 400,000 Reichsmarks. Other large donors included the organizers of the Berlin Automobile Exhibition (100,000 Reichsmarks) and a cluster of electrical engineering corporations including Telefunken, AEG and the Accumulatoren Fabrik.[3] In the years that followed, the Adolf Hitler Spende was to become institutionalized as a regular contribution to the maintenance of Hitler's personal expenses. In practical terms, however, it was the donations in February and March 1933 that really made the difference. They provided a large cash injection at a moment when the party was severely short of funds and faced, as Goering had predicted, the last competitive election in its history.

I

The meeting of 20 February and its aftermath are the most notorious instances of the willingness of German big business to assist Hitler in establishing his dictatorial regime. The evidence cannot be dodged. Nothing suggests that the leaders of German big business were filled with ideological ardour for National Socialism, before or after February 1933. Nor did Hitler ask Krupp & Co. to sign up to an agenda of violent anti-Semitism or a war of conquest. The speech he gave to the businessmen in Goering's villa was not the speech he had given to the generals a few weeks earlier, in which he had spoken openly about rearmament and the need for territorial expansion. But what Hitler and his government did promise was an end to parliamentary democracy and the destruction of the German left and for this most of German big business was willing to make a substantial down-payment. In light of what Hitler said on the evening of 20 February, the violence of the Machtergreifung should not have come as any surprise. Krupp and his colleagues were willing partners in the destruction of political pluralism in Germany. And the net effect, by the end of 1934, was precisely as intended: a comprehensive popular demobilization. The contrast with the German political scene ten years before was stark. The labour movement was destroyed. But so too, after the Night of the Long Knives, was the autonomous paramilitary potential of the right. Power shifted decisively upwards. Of course, there was a large degree of ambiguity about who exactly could claim leadership of Hitler's National Revolution. And this ambiguity was compounded by the fact that the pacification of the 'masses' coincided with an enthusiastic rallying of a wide range of professional and other elite groups around the National Socialist cause.[4] This enthusiasm, which went far beyond mere *Gleichschaltung* (political 'coordination'), resulted in intense competition between various contenders for power and privilege. But what was clear was that legitimate authority in the Third Reich proceeded from the top down, ideally from the very top down. And what was also clear was that many leaders of German business thrived in this authoritarian atmosphere.[5] In the sphere of their own firms they were now the undisputed leaders, empowered as such by the national labour law of 1934.[6] Owners and managers alike bought enthusiastically into the rhetoric of *Fuehrertum*. It meshed all too neatly with the concept of *Unternehmertum* (entrepreneurial leadership) that had become increasingly fashionable in business circles, as an ideological counterpoint to the interventionist tendencies of trade unions and the Weimar welfare state.[7]

In material terms, the consequences of demobilization made themselves felt in a shift in bargaining power in the workplace.[8] In effect, the new regime froze wages and salaries at the level they had reached by the summer of 1933 and placed any future adjustment in the hands of regional trustees of labour (Treuhaender der Arbeit) whose powers were defined by the Law for the Regulation of National Labour (Gesetz zur Ordnung der nationalen Arbeit) issued on 20 January 1934. Often this is taken as an unambiguous expression of business power, since the nominal wage levels prevailing after 1933 were far lower than those in 1929. From the business point of view, however, the situation was rather more complex. Though wages had fallen relative to 1929, so had prices. In practice, the Depression brought very little relief to real wage costs.[9] In so far as wage bills had been reduced it was not by cutting real wages but by firing workers and placing the rest on short time. Nevertheless, when the wage freeze of 1933 was combined with the destruction of the trade unions and a highly permissive attitude towards business cartelization, a point to which we shall return, the outlook for profits was certainly very favourable. Though wages did begin to drift upwards as the labour market tightened, there was every prospect that they would lag behind prices and profits in the up-coming recovery. And, perhaps most importantly, Hitler's regime promised to free German firms to manage their own internal affairs, releasing them from the oversight of independent trade unions. In future, it seemed, wages would be determined by the productivity objectives of employers, not the dictates of collective bargaining.[10]

In this narrow sense, therefore, the establishment of Hitler's regime clearly accomplished what was promised on 20 February. And for those businessmen who operated in a small, national or local compass, the years after 1933 were clearly a golden age of authoritarian 'normality'. However, to stop the analysis at this point would result in a highly partial account. At the meeting of 20 February Krupp von Bohlen never got the chance to ventilate the full range of questions that concerned German industry.[11] To simplify for the sake of clarity, the peacetime agenda of the more politically minded elements in German business consisted of at least two distinct elements, the one domestic, the other international. The domestic agenda was one of authoritarian conservatism, with a pronounced distaste for parliamentary politics, high taxes, welfare spending and trade unions. The international outlook of German business, on the other hand, was far more 'liberal' in flavour. Though German industry was by no means averse to tariffs, the Reich industrial association strongly favoured a system of uninhibited capital movement and multilateralism underpinned by Most Favoured Nation principles.[12] In the case of heavy industry this advocacy of international trade was combined with visions of European trade blocs of varying dimensions.[13] In important industries including coal, steel and chemicals, international trade was organized within the framework of formal cartels, sometimes with global reach.[14] Siemens and AEG divided up the global market for electrical engineering through understandings with their main American competitors.[15] However, all of these were arrangements freely chosen by German businessmen and their foreign counterparts, independent of state interference. In this sense, though hardly liberal they were at least cases of voluntarist business self-administration. Meanwhile, large parts of German foreign commerce remained free of cartel regulation of any kind, most notably textiles, metalwares and engineering, with the machine-builders association, the VDMA, being a particularly aggressive exponent of free trade.

It was this contrast between domestic authoritarianism and international 'liberalism' that defined the ambiguous position in which German business found itself in 1933. On the one hand, Hitler's government brought German businessmen closer towards realizing their domestic agenda than ever before. By the end of 1934 the Third Reich had imposed a state of popular pacification that had not existed in Germany since the beginning of the industrial era in the nineteenth century. On the other hand, the disintegration of the world economy and the increasingly protectionist drift of German politics was profoundly at odds with the commercial interests of much of the German business community. In this sense one can draw what may be a helpful contrast between the positions of German business in 1933 and 1923. The traumatic birth crisis of the Weimar Republic had resulted in a domestic stabilization that was profoundly unsatisfying to a majority of the German business community. But this was accepted because the Dawes Plan brokered by the Americans offered such an attractive international settlement. Stresemann's strategy in practice amounted to resurrecting the German nation-state on the shoulders of Germany's banks and industrial corporations. As he repeatedly made clear, he counted on the export power and financial muscle of companies like Siemens, AEG, IG Farben and the Vereinigte Stahlwerke. It was their production potential and creditworthiness that would enable Germany to pacify its relations with France and to consolidate a new and powerful connection to the United States. Given the extraordinary arrogance, ambition and nationalism of some of Germany's most important heavy industrialists, Stresemann was taking serious risks.[16] In 1923 he had to fight off challenges from the Ruhr industrialist Hugo Stinnes who sought to pursue an independent foreign policy towards France.[17] In 1929 Albert Voegler of the Vereinigte Stahlwerke caused trouble over the ratification of the Young Plan. And to the right of Voegler there were men like Rudolf Blohm, the Hamburg ship-builder, or Ernst von Borsig, the heavy-engineering magnate from Berlin, who supported the DNVP and favoured an outright return to militarism and rearmament.[18] However, the Reich industrial association (Reichsverband der deutschen Industrie), the peak organization of German industry, on the whole justified the faith put in it by Stresemann. Though never completely silenced, the ultra-nationalists were in a minority and the Reichsverband used its influence to ensure that sufficient DNVP deputies voted with the government to pass first the Dawes Plan in 1924 and then the Young Plan in 1930.[19] Furthermore, it enthusiastically endorsed the international free trade agenda pursued by the Reich Ministry of Economic Affairs and the Foreign Ministry at the League of Nations. By contrast, though it paid lip-service to nationalism, the Reich industrial association was at best lukewarm in its support of the Reichswehr's efforts at clandestine rearmament.[20]

By the late 1920s, however, the limitations of Stresemann's fulfilment strategy were increasingly apparent also to Germany's businessmen. The influx of foreign capital and the lax fiscal policy of the Reich faced the

Reich industrial association with increasingly unbearable 'imbalances' in the domestic economy. Not surprisingly, therefore, it gave enthusiastic backing to Chancellor Bruening when, in the spring of 1930, he promised to satisfy both its domestic and its international agendas at one and the same time.[21] With the flow of new foreign capital temporarily halted, fulfilling the terms of the Young Plan required a severe programme of domestic deflation, which in turn enabled Bruening to move towards the domestic roll-back – the so-called 'domestic Young Plan' – that business had long hankered after. What the German business lobby, along with most other observers schooled in conventional economic experience, did not understand was the severity of the domestic and international crisis this would unleash. By 1932 many of the bastions of economic strength on which Stresemann had counted so confidently had been shaken to their foundations. The Deutsche, Dresdner and Commerz banks had been saved from collapse only by state intervention.[22] The engineering industry (Borsig and HANOMAG), brewing (Schultheiss-Patzenhofer) and insurance (Frankfurter Allgemeine Versicherungsgesellschaft, FAVAG) were hit by spectacular bankruptcies.[23] AEG, once one of Germany's major corporate champions, was ailing.[24] In 1932 Friedrich Flick only escaped financial disaster by persuading the Reich to purchase his stake in the coal wing of the Vereinigte Stahlwerke at a hugely inflated price.[25] As a result, the Reich came into possession of what was potentially a controlling stake not only in banking but in heavy industry as well. And the crisis was not limited to individual firms or sectors, it was systemic. The collapse of the gold standard and the disastrous proliferation of protectionism fractured the bedrock of economic liberalism.

Faced with this extraordinary chain of disaster, the Reich industrial association clung first to Chancellor Bruening and then to General Schleicher in the hope that they might salvage something from the wreckage.[26] Big business certainly did not wish to see a return to the domestic settlement of the 1920s. But what possible alternative could there be to an internationally orientated economic policy? With this in mind, big business had little good to expect from the government appointed by President Hindenburg on 30 January 1933. Hitler, Schacht and Hugenberg were all notorious enemies of economic liberalism. And despite the common ground of opposition to the Weimar constitution and hostility towards the parties of the left, this is the essential backdrop against which we must interpret the meeting on 20 February. Hitler was not addressing a constituency that he knew to be in full support of his government; on the contrary.[27] Some of Germany's leading businessmen, perhaps most notably Carl Friedrich von Siemens, had actually declined Goering's invitation.[28] And Krupp was naive if he expected that Hitler would allow himself to be drawn into a full discussion of economic policy. Hitler and Schacht knew that this would be counterproductive since there was no hope of agreeing on the key issues of international policy. Schacht had already had his views on trade policy and international debts roundly criticized by the Reichsverband.[29] But, more importantly, Hitler and Schacht knew that they did not need business to agree. In the aftermath of World War I, the business lobby had been strong enough to contain the revolutionary impulses of 1918–19. Now capitalism's deepest crisis left German business powerless to resist a state interventionism that came not from the left but the right.[30]

II

The first years of Hitler's regime saw the imposition of a series of controls on German business that were unprecedented in peacetime history. In large part these stemmed from the difficulty of managing the German balance of payments and in that sense they clearly had their origin in the great financial crisis of the summer and autumn of 1931. However, with the complete disintegration of the gold standard following the dollar devaluation, Germany's creeping default on its long-term debt, including hundreds of millions of Reichsmarks owed by German corporates, and the imposition of the New Plan, these regulations took on a new and more systematic character.[31] As we have already seen, the New Plan, which effectively regulated the access of each and every German firm to foreign raw materials, created a substantial new bureaucracy, which controlled the vital functions of a large slice of German industry. Though exports were of course to be encouraged, the government's refusal to devalue meant that most German exporters were only competitive if they first applied for a subsidy. This too required considerable paperwork and more bureaucracy. And the export subsidy in turn was financed by a severe redistributive tax levied on all of German industry. Managing this burdensome system of controls was the primary function of a new framework of compulsory business organizations imposed by Schacht between the autumn of 1934 and the spring of 1935.[32] In each sector, the existing multiplicity of voluntary associations was fused together into a hierarchy of Reich Groups (for industry, banking, insurance, and so on), Business Groups (Wirtschaftsgruppen, for mining, steel, engineering and so on) and Branch Groups (Fachgruppen, for anthracite as opposed to lignite mining, and so on). Every German firm was required to enrol. Each subdivision in each Business Group was headed by its own Fuehrer.[33] These men were nominated by the existing associations, vetted by the Reich Group and appointed by Schacht. The primary role of the Business Groups was to act as a channel between individual firms and the Reich Ministry of Economic Affairs. Decrees came down from the Ministry via the Business Group. Complaints, suggestions and information travelled upwards from the firms, via the Business Groups to Berlin. The organization was tireless in the production of publications, guidelines and recommendations for best practice. On the basis of emergency decrees first issued during the latter stages of World War I, the Business Groups were also empowered to collect compulsory reports from their members, establishing an unprecedented system of industrial statistics.[34] After 1936 they were authorized to penetrate even further into the internal workings of their members, with the introduction of standardized book-keeping systems. The really indispensable functions of the Business Groups, however, concerned the operation of the New Plan. On the import side, the supervisory agencies all had staff drawn from the Business Groups.[35] On the export side, from the summer of 1935 onwards it was the Business Groups that were charged with assessing the turnover of their members and administering the levy that funded the export subsidy.[36]

Since this entire apparatus of control was designed to limit German imports, it had the effect of virtually eliminating foreign competition from German markets. Nothing was imported that could be produced domestically and that meant virtually all manufactured goods. Combined with rising levels of domestic demand this enabled German producers to put an end to deflation and to push through a marked increase in prices. After years of deflation, the consumer price index rose by almost 6 per cent between the spring of 1933 and August 1934, enough to spark fears of inflation.[37] To prevent this getting out of hand, the RWM enacted a series of decrees on prices, culminating in November

1934 with the reappointment of Carl Goerdeler as Reich commissioner for price control.[38] As we have seen, Goerdeler had earned his austere reputation in the vain battle to counter the devaluation of sterling with the draconian measures of Bruening's fourth deflation. His role in the Third Reich was to purge all excessive price increases that had occurred since the summer of 1933. Ironically, given Goerdeler's liberal proclivities, the result by the end of 1935 was the creation of a comprehensive system of state supervised price-setting.

Fundamental to this system were the increased powers of oversight exercised by the Reich over Germany's ramified system of cartels.[39] In July 1933 the RWM equipped itself with the authority to impose compulsory cartels. The same decree also gave the RWM the right to oversee the actions of existing cartels, to issue regulations governing their members' activities and to regulate their price-setting. Altogether, in the three years between 1933 and 1936 the RWM oversaw the conclusion of no less than 1,600 voluntary cartels and imposed 120 compulsory agreements. Even large and highly fragmented industries such as printing, an industry with a turnover in excess of one billion Reichsmarks per annum divided between literally thousands of small firms, could now be formed into organized units with clearly established minimum prices. The compulsory cartels had the power to control investment in their sector and to rationalize the existing structure of the industry through systematic 'buyouts'. The second cartel law of the summer of 1933 removed the legal protection provided by the Weimar Republic for firms that were not members of cartels to carry on their business as they chose. Cartels could now use the courts to pursue outsiders who were charging 'unfair' prices, or prices that were 'detrimental to the welfare of the nation'. Voluntary cartels were thus transformed into compulsory organizations under state oversight. In 1936, day-to-day supervision of the cartels was delegated by the RWM to the Business Groups and Branch Groups.[40] And they in turn used their new standardized accounting systems to help reinforce and refine price-setting discipline.

The combination of rising domestic demand, an end to foreign competition, rising prices and relatively static wages created a context in which it was hard not to make healthy profits.[41] Indeed, by 1934 the bonuses being paid to the boards of some firms were so spectacular that they were causing acute embarrassment to Hitler's government.[42] In the light

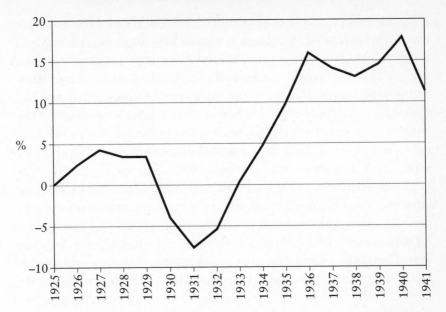

Figure 6. Rate of return on capital in German industry, 1925–1941

of the far more modest increase in workers' incomes, it seemed that the Communists and Social Democrats did indeed have a point. The Nazi regime was a 'dictatorship of the bosses'. Having regulated imports, exports and domestic price-setting, the RWM therefore moved in the spring of 1934 to control the use of business profits. The distribution of profits to shareholders was not to exceed a rate of 6 per cent of capital. This did not of course have any effect on underlying profitability. It simply meant that corporate accountants were encouraged to squirrel profits away in exaggerated depreciation and reserve bookings. Over the following years, German business built up gigantic financial reserves, which could be used for internally funded investment. And this, apart from the cosmetic aspects, was clearly the real purpose of the dividend decree. From the point of the Reich authorities the aim was to divide up the national resources available for investment and public spending. Industrial investment would be funded out of the profits not distributed to shareholders. Access by corporate borrowers to the long-term capital market – replenished out of household savings flowing through the banks, savings banks and insurance funds – would be restricted, reserving these funds for use by the state.[43]

Reichsbank control over the financial flows in the German economy was further enhanced by the new system of banking regulation imposed in 1934. The crisis of 1931 had left the Reich with a controlling stake in all three of the major national banks – Deutsche Bank, Dresdner Bank and Commerzbank. If some of the spokesmen of the Nazi left had had their way, there might even have been a wholesale nationalization of the banking system, followed by the breaking up of the national commercial banks and the creation of an integrated system of regional banks. Not surprisingly, this idea was also strongly backed by the regional savings banks (Sparkassen), in which local Nazi party activists had a strong interest.[44] But Hjalmar Schacht saw to it that this radicalism came to nothing. Instead, the moment of crisis was turned into an opportunity for managerial reform and tighter oversight by the central bank. Between September 1933 and October 1934 a committee of inquiry held a series of carefully stage-managed debates, in which radical positions were progressively sidelined. The end result was a draft law that gave the Reichsbank extensive powers of oversight. To prevent a repeat of the financial scandals of the early 1930s, limits were imposed on the level of loans that banks were permitted to provide to any one private borrower. For the first time, the Reichsbank was given the power to define basic reserve requirements and to fully regulate the deployment of private banking assets. The Great Banks of Berlin were thus saved from nationalization. The evidence suggests, however, that they never really recovered from the damage done to them by the financial crisis of 1931. In purely commercial terms the Berlin Great Banks were amongst the chief 'losers' of the Nazi economic recovery.[45] Between 1932 and 1939, in which period German output more than doubled, the total assets of the Berlin Great Banks rose by only 15 per cent. By contrast, the assets of the savings banks, the main vehicle for what one might call 'popular liquidity', rose by 102 per cent over the same period. At the same time, the international business of the Great Banks was sharply curtailed by the collapse in Germany's foreign trade. The funds accumulating in the accounts of bankers' industrial clients made them more independent than ever before of bank loans. And those that did need external funding for the regime's high priority projects could turn to new, state-backed lenders such as the Bank fuer Industrie-Obligationen or the Aero-Bank of the Luftwaffe.[46] This is not to say of course that all three of the surviving big banks did not make healthy profits. Nor can it be denied that the banks played an important role in determining the development of certain important companies. Most notably, perhaps, the Deutsche Bank was closely involved with Mannesmann, and its CEO Wilhelm Zangen, one of the most rapacious profiteers of the Nazi regime.[47] But, contrary to the view that the Great Banks were the ultimate string-pullers of National Socialism, it is in fact hard to think of any other period in modern German history in which these institutions had less influence than the period between 1933 and 1945.

A far more dynamic and no less essential part of the modern economic infrastructure was the electricity generating industry. And it too was given a new regulatory structure by National Socialism. As in the case of the banking system, Germany's electricity network was divided between a small group of gigantic oligopolists and a variety of local and municipal suppliers. The leading generators, with their huge power stations, vast transmission networks, coalfields and in-house construction companies, were amongst the largest industrial corporations in Germany. The dominant force in the industry was the Ruhr's own electricity generator, the mighty Rheinisch-Westfaelische Elektrizitaetswerke (RWE).[48] Nominally, a majority of its shares were controlled by the municipalities of the Ruhr, but de facto power within the RWE was exercised by a cadre of professional managers, lawyers and technicians and a key group of private shareholders, representing coal and steel interests. The leader of this business interest on the RWE's supervisory board was Albert Voegler, of the Vereinigte Stahlwerke, Germany's dominant steel producer. Albert's brother Eugen Voegler ran the RWE's construction associate, HOCHTIEF.[49] Outside the western regions of Germany, the main generators were the large electricity holding companies owned by the state of Prussia and the Reich, the VEBA, VIAG and BEWAG holdings, with whom the RWE had reached a market-sharing agreement, the so-called 'electro-peace' (*Elektrofrieden*), in 1929.[50] That left the small municipal and regional generators, set up in the early years of electrification, as the only real competitors. After 1933 many of these fell into the hands of the local Nazi party organizations and they, not surprisingly, raised a clamour against the overweening power of the major generators. But again they were outmanoeuvred by Schacht and the RWM, who acted both as a centralizing force and as a shield for corporate interests. Since his earliest days in banking Schacht had favoured a programme of centralization in electricity generation, as an imperative of efficient profitability. And this predilection was only too clear from the draft electricity law proposed by his Ministry to cabinet in the autumn of 1935. Schacht's officials justified the need for centralized control of new investment in electricity generation unabashedly in terms of the 'overarching interest of the German energy business' ('*uebergeordnetes Interesse der deutschen Energiewirtschaft*').[51] This was too much for the National Socialists, such as Reich Interior Minister Wilhelm Frick, who was so dissatisfied that he had the bill withdrawn and redrafted so that state intervention was now justified in terms of the need to secure 'unified leadership' ('*einheitliche Fuehrung*') in the 'interest of the common good' ('*interesse des Gemeinwohls*') and for the sake of 'securing national defence' ('*sicherstellung der Landesverteidigung*'). In content, however, the law remained the same. It solidified the position of the incumbent generators, whilst giving unprecedented powers of supervision to the Reich Ministry of Economic Affairs. The process of consolidation and concentration begun in the 1920s continued unabated by the ideological impulses of local Nazi activists.[52]

The tendency of the Reich's economic administration to develop in this more interventionist direction had been pronounced ever since the end of World War I. The reformed Reichsbank, the Reich Ministry of Economic Affairs, the Reich Labour Ministry and the Reich Ministry of Food and Agriculture were all products of World War I and its aftermath.[53] Many of the regulatory systems introduced after 1933 had been under discussion since the 1920s, including the electricity law and the new corporation law passed in 1937. However, the situation after 1933 was different, at least in the sense that the state acted with a far greater degree of authority and independence than ever before. For this purpose, the rhetoric of Hitler's National Revolution was a convenient cover. However, in practice the Reichsbank and the Reich Ministry of Economic Affairs had no intention of allowing the radical activists of the SA, the shopfloor militants of the Nazi party or Gauleiter commissioners to dictate the course of events. Under the slogan of the 'strong state', the ministerial bureaucracy fashioned a new national structure of economic regulation. Perhaps not surprisingly, in the reminiscences of bureaucrats in the RWM, the early years under Schacht were remembered in fond terms: 'We worked and governed with incredible elan. We really ruled. For the bureaucrats of the Ministry the contrast to the Weimar Republic was stark. Party chatter in the Reichstag was no longer heard. The language of the bureaucracy was rid of the paralysing formula: technically right but politically impossible.'[54]

It would be absurd to deny the reality of this shift. The crisis of corporate capitalism in the course of the Great Depression *did* permanently alter the balance of power. Never again was big business to influence the course of government in Germany as directly as it did between the outbreak of World War I in 1914 and the onset of the Depression in 1929. The Reich's economic administration, for its part, accumulated unprecedented powers of national economic control.[55] One might ask therefore why there was not more grumbling, protest, or even outright opposition to the new line being adopted in Berlin. As we have already discussed in the preceding chapter, it would not be right to say that there was no such dissent. There were those in the business community, whose views were reflected in periodicals such as the *Wirtschaftsdienst*, who did dare to contemplate the possibility of devaluation, a train of thought that called into question the necessity of adopting the restrictive corset of bureaucratic control. The day-to-day inconveniences of the New Plan, not to mention the export levy, were clearly extremely unpopular. But the scope for argument and debate was limited in a number of ways and not only through the regime's coercive control of the media.

A variety of argumentative obstacles overlapped. By staking their personal reputations on the stability of the Reichsmark already in the spring of 1933, Hitler and Schacht had done their best to render the topic of devaluation non-negotiable. Schacht, furthermore, in his arguments with Germany's creditors, played on habits of thought that had become deeply ingrained since the reparations debates of the 1920s. It had become a commonplace in German economic discussion to view the country's balance of payments problems as 'structural' and thus beyond Germany's own power to control.[56] The German economy, like any modern economy, could not do without imports of food and raw materials. To pay for these it needed to export. And if this flow of goods was obstructed by protectionism and beggar-my-neighbour devaluations, this left Germany no option but to resort to ever greater state control of imports and exports, which in turn necessitated a range of other interventions. In this sense, despite the questions about a possible devaluation, the dramatic increase in state control could be seen as an inevitable product of 'historic necessity' rather than conscious political choice.[57] In any case, given the limited recovery of world trade in 1934 and 1935, there was no reason for impatience. Businessmen had little to lose by concentrating on Germany's booming domestic markets. Anxieties only really became acute in 1936–7 when it seemed as though the rest of the world economy might finally be returning to prosperity.

Furthermore, though it is important to do justice to the shift in power relations between the state and business that undoubtedly occurred in the early 1930s, we must be careful to avoid falling into the trap of viewing German business merely as the passive object of the regime's draconian new system of regulation.[58] As we have seen, profits were rising rapidly after 1933 and this opened attractive future prospects for German corporate management. At first the profits were used to undo the damage done by the Depression. Then from the late 1930s onwards, they financed an extraordinary investment boom such as had never before been seen in German industrial history.[59] What Hitler's regime positively enabled German business to do was to recover from the disastrous recession, to accumulate capital and to engage in high-pressure development of certain key technologies: the technologies necessary to achieve the regime's twin objectives of increased self-sufficiency (autarchy) and rearmament. Technology, in fact, is one of the keys to understanding relations between Hitler's regime and the German business community. Whereas to Stresemann's strategy the importance of German business had been defined by economic factors – the international competitiveness and creditworthiness of German business – the Third Reich needed German industry above all for its productive resources, both technological and organizational. And if one of the definitions of 'power' is the capacity to get things done, then in this wider sense German industry continued to exercise power in the Third Reich. Despite the dramatic growth of state regulation, industrialists and their managerial and technical staffs were indispensable, if not in the conception then at least in the execution of national policy.

III

This intertwining of profit, politics and technology was nowhere more dramatic than in the case of Germany's great chemical giant, IG Farben. By the late 1930s IG Farben, with over two hundred thousand employees and assets totalling over 1.6 billion Reichsmarks, was one of the largest private companies not only in Germany, but in the world. At Nuremberg and after, its close relationship with the Nazi regime was taken as emblematic of the wider entanglement of German industry with the Third Reich.[60] In historical terms, however, the alliance between the German chemical industry and Hitler's regime was unique and developed out of a chain of decisions taken over the course of the preceding decades.[61] Before 1914 the German chemical industry, as a progressive leader of the second industrial revolution with a deep-seated stake in multilateral trade and a less than reactionary outlook in domestic politics, belonged in the liberal camp of German business, and to a degree this still held true in the 1920s. IG Farben was one of the most important industrial backers of Stresemann's policy of fulfilment and favoured a strategy of accommodation with the Republic. IG occupied a globally dominant position in a staggering array of chemical and pharmaceutical sectors. It maintained a relationship of equals with the mighty Standard Oil of the United States. Mere chemical companies such as Britain's ICI and America's DuPont were no match. Though the Depression hit IG hard, the firm would surely have prospered under virtually any regime imaginable in Germany in the 1930s. In no sense of the word did the German chemical industry 'need' Hitler. And yet, as a result of a series of technical decisions, the leaders of Germany's chemical industry moved into an ever-closer alliance with the German state.

Shortly after the turn of the century, scientists closely associated with IG embarked on the development of a new generation of synthetic chemicals, starting spectacularly with the synthetic production of ammonia, by the Haber–Bosch process.[62] By making possible the domestic production both of explosives and fertilizer, this made the German chemical industry and above all BASF into a mainstay of the German war effort in World War I. In the 1920s this path of technological development was pushed further by Carl Bosch, the real inspiration behind the merger that reshaped the Interessensgemeinschaft (IG)

Farben in 1925.[63] Indeed, Bosch's central objective in promoting the merger seems to have been to attain sufficient scale to be able to finance the progress of his immensely expensive synthetic technologies.[64] By September 1923 Bosch's research group had synthesized methane, and in 1926, at its Leuna facility near Merseburg, in the central German industrial belt, IG Farben embarked on the construction of the world's first facility for coal hydrogenation, the alchemical process through which coal was transformed into petrol. This programme followed a clear scientific logic. But it was also motivated by that most modern of fixations, the idea that one day the oil would run out. The 330 million Reichsmark investment in Leuna's coal-based technology would pay off when the oil wells ran dry and fuel prices rocketed.

It was this commitment to synthetic chemistry that made IG Farben into by far the closest and most important industrial collaborator of Hitler's regime. IG's technology offered Germany the chance of independence from imported oil. Indeed, in the near future, Bosch's research teams promised to go beyond hydrogenation to the efficient mass production of synthetic rubber, thus adding the second key ingredient of motorized warfare. Conversely, it was IG Farben's expensive investment in these technologies that gave the otherwise internationally minded corporation a powerful incentive to collaborate with Hitler and his nationalist programme. Bosch's gamble on the imminent exhaustion of oil backfired spectacularly. The prospect of an oil shortage fired a dramatic wave of prospecting success. By the late 1920s, after spectacular development in Venezuela, California, Oklahoma and the Permian Basin in west Texas, the world market for crude was glutted.[65] To make matters worse, in October 1930 wildcatters in east Texas found the famous 'Black Giant'. Within months the world oil price had collapsed, leaving IG Farben's investment at Leuna without economic rationale. For Carl Bosch this was clearly a severe setback. But IG could certainly have retreated from hydrogenation. Losses of a few hundred million Reichsmarks would not have broken the company. Such a retreat would, however, have run completely counter to Carl Bosch's vision of the firm, which now depended on the willingness of the German government to impose high taxes on imported oil.[66] It was this need for political assistance that impelled IG to make contact with Hitler's party. The Nazis were well-known advocates of national self-sufficiency. But Hitler was also a passionate motoring enthusiast and IG feared that this would make him an advocate of cheap, imported gasoline. In the autumn of 1932, after the Nazis' spectacular success in the July elections, two IG men with connections in far-right circles were dispatched to Munich to brief Hitler on the national importance of the synthetic fuel project.

In taking this action, IG was doing little more than hedging its bets. Its chief priority was to secure the future of Leuna and to continue its research programme, not to launch Germany into a large-scale programme of fuel self-sufficiency. The man who did push hardest in the early days of Hitler's government for a large-scale hydrogenation scheme, came not from chemistry but from coal. As CEO of Vestag, the giant steel and coal conglomerate, and as chair of the supervisory board at RWE, the huge electricity generator, Albert Voegler had a vital interest in expanding the market for coal and in forging new links to the chemical industry.[67] Playing on Hitler's interest in self-sufficiency, Voegler proposed a scheme to produce several million tons of synthetic fuel. Given the political turmoil in 1933, it took a few months. But on 10 August 1933 Voegler was able to inform Professor Dr Carl Krauch, the key technical man in IG's synthetics programme, that Secretary of State Erhard Milch at the Air Ministry was interested in consulting with IG about the future of Germany's fuel supplies. Two days later, IG Farben received reassurance from the Reich Ministry of Economic Affairs that IG need have no concern about the commercial future of the Leuna plant:

We National Socialists have the intention of generally expanding the German raw material base . . . from this position it is a matter of course that we desire an increase in the production of petrol from German raw materials. From a purely economic point of view it would be wrong to produce petrol domestically at a price of 19 Pfennigs, when the world market price is 5 Pfennigs. But I have declared to the importers, what guarantees can you give me for the maintenance of world peace? For us National Socialists, apart from economic criteria . . . military reasons are decisive. I am therefore determined to promote fuel production from German raw materials by all means and to provide the necessary price and sales guarantees.[68]

By the end of the year, with the urgent encouragement of both the Air Ministry and the army, the Reich Finance Ministry had finalized the terms of the so-called Benzinvertrag. The essentials of the contract were a commitment by IG to expand its facility at Leuna to a capacity of

350,000 tons per annum, in exchange for a guarantee by the Reich that IG would make a profit of at least 5 per cent on the capital invested. If market prices were forced down by cheap imports, then the Reich would provide a subsidy to secure Leuna's profitability. On the other hand, any profits in excess of 5 per cent would be handed over to the Reich. The Reich Finance Ministry was at first reluctant to provide this guarantee, fearing that Leuna would never pay for itself. But they need not have worried. From 1936 onwards Leuna generated large profits, the majority of which flowed to the Reich. It was IG Farben not the Reich that had cause to regret the terms of the Benzinvertrag.

The chief concern of Hitler and the advocates of rearmament was not the financial terms of the deal, but Leuna's inadequate scale of production: 350,000 tons per annum was a tiny step towards self-sufficiency. In early 1934 Hitler began to exert personal pressure for a more substantial programme and once Hjalmar Schacht took over at the RWM in August 1934, in the midst of the disastrous foreign exchange crisis, he got his wish. On 21 September Schacht convened a conference of the leading industrialists in the coal and mineral oil businesses in Berlin and informed them that Germany's foreign exchange situation required a very large expansion in domestic fuel production.[69] At the time, even with low world prices, imports of petrol and oil-related products were costing Germany 200 million Reichsmarks per annum. As Leuna had already demonstrated, hydrogenation plants were extremely expensive. Schacht estimated that between 250 and 300 million Reichsmarks would be needed for the first stage of the expansion. The state could, of course, have provided the funds. But the Reich had other pressing commitments. So Schacht made a direct appeal to the mining interests. They 'had earned good profits and gained great advantage from natural resources that actually belonged to the general public. Now they would be expected to make a contribution. It was widely known that a number of brown coal-mining corporations had substantial liquid means. Those companies that did not have the ready cash should take up loans.' Perhaps not surprisingly, the industrialists were completely taken aback. In their view, coal hydrogenation was uneconomic and the commitment of such large quantities of capital would prevent them from taking advantage of other opportunities in the course of the economic recovery. But Schacht would not back down. Having failed to obtain voluntary agreement, he had the Ministry draft a Decree for the Creation of Compulsory Economic Associations in the Brown Coal Industry (*Verordnung ueber die Errichtung wirtschaftlicher Pflichtgemein-schaften in der Braunkohlenwirtschaft*). Ten leading coal-mining corporations were conscripted on 25 October 1934 to form the Braunkohlenbenzin AG (Brabag). Each was instructed to make out a cheque for at least 1 million Reichsmarks for immediate use. When more coal companies were added in November, Schacht threatened both unlimited fines and imprisonment of anyone refusing to cooperate. To satisfy the demands of the military, three new synthetic fuel plants built under licence from IG Farben were to be brought into operation by 1936.

To ensure that this schedule was met, Brabag was to be run not by its reluctant owners, but by a hand-picked team of managers who could be counted on to bring the project in on time. Technical expertise was provided by IG's Carl Krauch.[70] The crash construction programme was overseen by Heinrich Koppenberg, an engineer recruited from the Flick conglomerate, who was proving himself at Junkers as one of the driving forces in the Luftwaffe's gigantic industrial expansion. The military interest was represented by the retired general Alfred von Vollard-Bockelberg, the former head of army procurement and a veteran of secret rearmament. Day-to-day operations at Brabag were to be overseen by Fritz Kranefuss (1900–1945?). Kranefuss came from a family of cigar manufacturers in Herford, Westphalia, and after a brief spell in the Imperial Navy and the Freikorps had undergone a normal commercial apprenticeship. However, his chief qualifications were his excellent political contacts. He was a nephew of Wilhelm Keppler, Hitler's personal economic adviser, and had been a member of the Nazi party since 1932. He was a close collaborator of Heinrich Himmler and was employed on the staff of Rudolf Hess, the deputy leader of the party. Kranefuss's appointment to head Brabag was approved by Hitler himself in a meeting with Schacht and Keppler in early November 1934. Keppler himself presided as chairman of Brabag's supervisory board. To calm the nerves of the foreign investors who held shares in the German coal industry, Schacht delegated his trusted collaborator Helmuth Wohlthat to the Brabag board. The commercial terms of Brabag's operations that were finalized in the spring of 1936 were no less favourable to the Reich than those agreed with IG Farben in 1933. The Reich guaranteed Brabag's shareholders against operational losses. It also provided them with a guarantee to cover the hundreds of millions of Reichsmarks that Brabag was forced to borrow to finance its breakneck expansion. But the rate of profit was fixed at 5 per cent and any amount in excess of the agreed rate was deducted for the benefit of the Reich. In practice, any profits were ploughed back ruthlessly into further expansion. By 1939 Brabag had assets on its books valued at 350 million Reichsmarks. The reluctant investors never saw a dividend, but the Third Reich was well on the way to achieving an important margin of self-sufficiency (see Appendix, Table A2).

IV

Like chemicals, the steel sector had also undergone dramatic consolidation in the 1920s. The result was the formation of the Vereinigte Stahlwerke (Vst or Vestag for short), a corporate giant that matched IG Farben for size and was second in the world steel rankings only to mighty US Steel.[71] Within the steel industry, however, the Vestag's position was nowhere near as dominant as that of IG Farben in chemistry. The Vestag competed with Krupp, Flick, GHH, Kloeckner, Mannesmann, Hoesch and Roechling. Each had areas of particular technical expertise; many of them had interests in engineering and other related industries. But all of them made iron and steel. And underlying this oligopolistic structure in steel-making was the no less tangled structure of the coal sector, which was closely interwoven with that of steel.[72] The result was a scene of bewildering complexity, which is still poorly understood.[73] Indeed, the difficulty of defining a single heavy industrial position towards Hitler's regime was evident from the very first months of the Third Reich.

Krupp, Fritz Thyssen and Albert Voegler were all closely involved in events after 30 January 1933. But all three pulled in different directions. Gustav Krupp (1870–1950) was not only head of Germany's fourth largest corporation, he was head of the Reichsverband der deutschen Industrie at the time of Hitler's seizure of power. If we are to believe the most recent account of his activities, Krupp was initially suspicious of Hitler's regime and was above all concerned to preserve the autonomy of the peak association of German business.[74] In so doing he appears to have been backed up by other members of the business old guard, most notably Paul Reusch, the general manager of GHH, and Carl Friedrich von Siemens.[75] It seems that Krupp even contemplated the possibility of reviving the strategy pursued by German industry in the face of the revolution in 1918. This involved an alliance with the German trade union movement, as a way of asserting the autonomous authority of private industry against the civil war threatening between Nazis and Communists. However, in the spring of 1933 this effort was even more short-lived than it had been after World War I. The decision by the Nazis to destroy the German trade union movement was irrevocable and Krupp, as chair of the Reich industrial association, found himself outmanoeuvred by Fritz Thyssen (1873–1951). The heir to one of the largest fortunes in the Ruhr, Thyssen was a key beneficiary of the merger that created the Vestag. Since the early 1930s he had been one of the few genuinely enthusiastic backers of Hitler in big business circles.[76] In this respect, however, Thyssen was to pursue a quixotic path. Thyssen's real inspiration was the corporatist model of industrial organization pioneered by Fascist Italy. The distinctive feature of this vision was that it included employers and workers in a single organiz-ation, imposing social unity by government fiat. Not surprisingly, this was not the sort of thing that appealed to old warhorses of reaction such as Krupp and Reusch. And Thyssen's social romanticism also found little favour with Kurt Schmitt at the Reich Ministry of Economic Affairs and Schacht at the Reichsbank. Both Krupp and Thyssen, therefore, found themselves excluded from the new structure of industrial organiz-ations set up by Schacht over the winter of 1934–5 to implement the New Plan.

At a corporate level, however, both Krupp and the Vestag found ways to arrange themselves more than comfortably with the new regime. Unsurprisingly, both of Germany's largest steel firms were founding members of the Mefo. By early 1936 military business already accounted for 20 per cent of Krupp's sales, with orders flowing both to the Gus-stahlfabrik in Essen but also to Krupp's Gruson works in Saxony, which was responsible for armoured plate and complex naval sub-assemblies.[77] By far the most troublesome part of the Krupp empire was the ship-building operation in Kiel, the Germaniawerft, which had been grossly unprofitable throughout the 1920s. The Germaniawerft was the home-base of German U-boat construction in World War I and it was only kept alive in the expectation of one day receiving new naval business.

As we have seen, naval rearmament initially lagged behind that of both the army and the Luftwaffe. But by the autumn of 1933, Essen had at least extracted a promise that the navy had a 'serious interest' (*ernstes Interesse*) in the survival of the Germaniawerft. And in August 1934 Krupp's patience was finally rewarded with the award of orders for 6 small U-boats, followed within a few months by a contract for 5 destroyers and the first series of U-VIIs, what was to become the standard U-boat of the German navy.[78] With Gruson also having received notification of major orders for armoured plate, by the end of 1934 all branches of the Krupp business were at least within sight of profit.

Vestag, like Krupp, had absorbed heavy losses during the Depression and was keen for military business. But it had even more urgent reasons than Krupp to reach an amicable modus vivendi with the new regime. As Hitler consolidated his power in 1933, the most pressing concern for the Vestag management was the smooth reprivatization of the shares taken into Reich ownership in early 1932. Seconding Thyssen in this effort was Albert Voegler (1877–1945), the chair of the Vestag board and a ubiquitous figure during the Machtergreifung.[79] Voegler had started his career as a humble apprentice and had risen to prominence as one of Hugo Stinnes's most able assistants. After Stinnes's death in April 1924, Voegler emerged as a dominant figure in German heavy industry and one of the architects of Vestag. In 1933 it was Voegler who approached Hitler with a grand proposal for a new coal-based fuel industry. This was clearly intended as part of a more general reorganization in the coal industry, which also included the notorious manoeuvre through which Paul Silverberg, Germany's leading Jewish industrialist, was stripped of his control of the lignite producer Rheinbraun and sent into exile in Switzerland.[80] In the spring of 1933, Voegler was rewarded for his cooperation with an appointment to the supervisory board of the Reich's industrial holding, the VIAG, and when Schacht was looking for an industrialist to sit on the banking inquiry, Voegler was an obvious choice.[81] Not only were Vestag's shares returned smoothly into private ownership, Germany's largest steel firm also assumed a controlling position in Schacht's new organizational structure for the steel industry.[82] The Business Groups for foundries and mining were both headed by Vestag associates and Schacht approved Ernst Poensgen to head the Business Group for the steel industry itself. Poensgen (1871–1949), born into a family of Ruhr industrialists, had been Voegler's deputy at Vestag since 1926 and was its leading cartel expert.[83] Since 1930 he had headed the German steel cartel and presided over the regional council of Ruhr heavy industry. Most distinctive, however, was Poensgen's role in negotiating the International Steel Cartel of 1926 and his extremely close connections to ARBED, the Luxembourg steel giant, and its director Aloyse Meyer. In 1935 Poensgen was the obvious choice to succeed Albert Voegler as chief of Vestag, when Voegler moved 'upstairs' to the supervisory board.

Whilst Voegler's diplomacy saw Vestag through the political turmoil of the Machtergreifung, the task of securing a generous slice of military business was delegated to subsidiaries, most notably the Bochumer Verein headed by Walter Borbet (1881–1942) and the Deutsche Edelstahlwerke, a specialist high quality steel producer, whose youthful chief Walter Rohland (1898–1981) was clearly marked for higher things. Borbet and Rohland represented successive generations of metallurgical militarism on the Ruhr. Borbet was a nationalist of the old school.[84] He was also a committed gun-maker, who harboured a lifelong envy of Krupp for the priority it claimed in armaments manufacture. During World War I Borbet had pioneered the introduction of low-cost gun steels requiring a minimum of imported alloys, and in the 1920s he made the Bochumer Verein into one of the centres for the development of centrifugal casting, a revolutionary process in which gun barrels, rather than being bored out of solid steel ingots, were spun out of molten metal. Walter Rohland's commitment to the project of rearmament was no less personal than that of Borbet.[85] In 1916 Rohland had joined the guards engineering corps as a teenage volunteer and had taken part in the latter stages of the Verdun battle. Walter Rohland survived, but his favourite brother Fritz was killed fighting alongside him in May 1917. Nor was 1918 the end of the war as far as Rohland was concerned. Some of the most vivid passages in his memoirs relate to the resistance to the French occupation of the Ruhr in 1923. When Hitler declared Germany's open rearmament in 1935, though Rohland had now risen to a responsible position within Vestag, he immediately seized the opportunity to resume his military career, joining the 11th Panzer regiment as a captain of the reserve and taking an enthusiastic part in manoeuvres. The future CEO of Vestag thus had first-hand knowledge of the vehicles, which were to earn him the nickname 'Panzer Rohland'.

Borbet for his part could barely contain his enthusiasm in 1933.

Within months of the seizure of power, he was actively discussing Mefo orders with both Erhard Milch of the Air Ministry and General Blomberg. In 1934 he gained his first personal interview with Hitler to discuss rearmament issues and in 1935 he played host in Bochum not only to General Blomberg (Defence Minister), but also to Goering (air force), Admiral Rader (navy), General Fritsch (Commander-in-Chief, army) and Hitler himself. In 1934, on the suggestion of the Wehrmacht, the Bochumer Verein acquired the bankrupt shell of the HANOMAG engineering firm, specifically for the purpose of artillery production.[86] And Borbet was rewarded for his enthusiasm with a steady stream of armaments business: 30 million Reichsmarks' worth of orders in 1934 rising to 50 million a year later, almost matching Krupp. Borbet and the Bochumer Verein may not have designed the Wehrmacht's cannons. But it was Borbet's success in developing the technique of centrifugal casting that allowed the famous 8.8 centimetre anti-aircraft gun developed jointly by Krupp and Rheinmetall to be put into low-cost mass-production. Walter Rohland, for his part, made the Deutsche Edelstahlwerke into the first choice for Panzer hulls. Not only did the Krefeld works provide top quality electrically smelted steel, it was also a world leader in the difficult technique of welding armoured plate, the fundamental breakthrough in modern tank production.

The common denominator in the metallurgical careers of both Borbet and Rohland was their preoccupation with the high-quality electrically smelted steels without which rearmament would have been impossible.[87] If one examines only the figures for the production of coal and raw steel one might gain the surprising impression that German heavy industry was a rather reluctant partner in rearmament (see Appendix, Table A2). The output of coal lagged well behind the growth of overall industrial output and the output of steel hardly increased at an exuberant rate. Nor would it be difficult to supply a rationale for this sluggishness. Ever since the early 1920s, the managers of the Ruhr had been struggling to cope with chronic over-capacity, the legacy of 'over-investment' during World War I and the hyperinflation that followed.[88] Faced with the armaments boom of the 1930s, they were not about to repeat their mistake. The aggregate figures, however, tell only part of the story. Though fears about over-capacity may have held back a general expansion in heavy industrial output in certain key areas, most notably specialist electrical smelting, there was no such conflict of interest between the needs of rearmament and the profit-seeking of industry. High-quality electrically smelted steel was both vital to rearmament and a major business of the future. Whereas German output of regular steel even at the height of production barely reached half the capacity of the United States, in electrically smelted steel Germany was level pegging by 1939.[89] With Borbet and Rohland leading the way, the Reich's output of specialist high-quality steel increased sevenfold between 1929 and 1939.

V

Unlike in chemicals and steel, where the regime was dealing with large and well-established producers, the most dramatic industrial inter-vention of the Third Reich concerned an industry which in 1933 was a sector of completely insignificant proportions. The story of aircraft production in the Third Reich deserves to stand at the centre of our understanding of the regime's entire industrial history.[90] In 1932 the German aircraft industry employed 3,200 people and had the capacity to produce no more than a hundred aircraft per year. Less than ten years later, the regime had created a multi-billion Reichsmark aircraft and aero-engine industry. It employed at least a quarter of a million people and was capable of turning out every year more than 10,000 of the most sophisticated combat aircraft in the world. Of all the industrial effects of rearmament this was by far the most significant. In the ranking of Germany's top one hundred firms, the Flick group, Deschimag, Henschel and Blohm & Voss were all directly involved in aircraft production.[91] Similarly, the elevated position in the ranking occupied by Daimler-Benz and BMW, best known for their cars and motorbikes, was owed largely to their rapidly expanding aero-engine sales. Specialist sub-components for the Luftwaffe boom were provided by Siemens and AEG, both directly and through their jointly owned Telefunken subsidiary. ITT-Lorenz, Bosch and the Vereinigte Deutsche Metallwerke (controlled by the Metallgesellschaft) were all major Luftwaffe suppliers. Aluminium and magnesium were supplied by the Vereinigte Aluminiumwerke owned by the state-holding VIAG and by IG Farben. Top quality steel castings came from Rohland's Deutsche Edelstahlwerke and Krupp. But alongside the contribution of these diversified industrial corporations, the really striking feature of the list of top corporations in Germany in the late 1930s is the presence of no less than six specialized aircraft producers, none of which, in 1933, would have ranked even in the top 500. By 1938 Junkers, even before it began its most dramatic period of expansion, already ranked alongside Daimler-Benz as Germany's twelfth largest private employer. Further down the list followed Arado, Heinkel, Dornier, Focke-Wulf and Bayerische Flugzeugwerke, better known as Messerschmitt.

What was distinctive about the aircraft producers was that, unlike ship-builders, gun- or tank-makers, the aircraft producers had no significant civilian production.[92] The military aircraft they were producing by the late 1930s had little or no value as commercial products. There was thus no alternative civilian employment for the vast specialist manufacturing capacity that the Air Ministry had brought into existence. Though all of the firms except Junkers were nominally in private ownership, they were all creatures of the Reich Air Ministry and its director, Secretary of State Erhard Milch. Fundamentally, therefore, Germany's largest new manufacturing sector was not merely state controlled. It was a product of state initiative, state funding and state direction. It was founded indeed on one of the most blatant acts of coercion applied to any non-Jewish business in the history of the Third Reich. Early in the morning of 17 October 1933 Dr Hugo Junkers was arrested at his vacation home in Bayrischzell on charges of treason.[93] Junkers was Germany's leading aviation pioneer, a celebrated engineer who at his plant at Dessau had constructed the world's first full-metal aircraft. Junkers's factory, though modest in size, was by far the largest aircraft factory in Germany. It has sometimes been suggested that Hugo Junkers's expropriation was due to his interest in internationalist politics and pacifism. But Junkers was in fact a conservative nationalist, who eagerly embraced the cause of rearmament. His difficulty was simply that he owned the largest aircraft plant in Germany and that Goering and his Secretary of State Erhard Milch were determined to have control of it. In the 1920s Junkers had squabbled with the German military about the future direction of aerial rearmament. The new holders of power were not willing to argue. After twenty-four hours in police detention, Junkers agreed to sign away his firm to the Reich. Managerial control was placed in the hands of Heinrich Koppenberg (1880–1960), a veteran of the Flick industrial conglomerate, who, like Krauch in chemicals and Voegler and Borbet in steel, had made his reputation in the armaments effort of World War I.[94] He was backed up on the Junkers supervisory board by Hellmuth Roehnert, soon to take charge of state-controlled Rheinmetall, Karl Rasche and Emil Meyer of the state-controlled Dresdner Bank and the ubiquitous Wilhelm Keppler. It was clearly no coincidence that the same combination of Keppler and Koppenberg was also to play a key role in the establishment of the Brabag synthetic fuel venture.

With Junkers as the core, Milch and the Air Ministry orchestrated a huge increase in the capacity for the production of aircraft and aero-engines. The new dispensation was spelled out to the German aircraft industry at a conference held in Berlin on 20 October 1933, two days after the Junkers expropriation.[95] Greeting the aircraft industrialists in solemn silence with arm raised in salute, Goering announced the Fuehrer's intention to re-establish Germany as an air power within the next twelve months. Every aircraft firm would have to accept its integration into the overall plan laid down by the RLM. The first programme was built around the existing designs, with Junkers and Dornier providing a makeshift bomber force, and Arado and Heinkel responsible for fighters, reconnaissance, ground attack and trainers. The new aircraft plants were to be 'trained up' by the established producers. Under tight supervision from the Ministry, the industry underwent a phenomenal expansion, from less than 4,000 workers in January 1933 to almost 54,000 two years later. At the same time the Air Ministry issued design contracts for an entire new generation of aircraft and aero-engines. It was after 1935, in the second phase of expansion, that Junkers, Dornier and Heinkel established themselves as the lead developers of bombers and Willy Messerschmitt's BfW gained its dominant position in fighter design and production. The other aircraft manufacturers were grouped around these main development firms in cooperative blocs, each assigned to a main plant that was responsible for organizing procurement, workforce training and the supply of jigs and fixtures required for the accurate production and assembly of aircraft parts. By the spring of 1938 almost 120,000 people worked in airframe manufacture and another 48,000 in aero-engine production, with 70,000 more employed in aircraft equipment and repair.

Building this industrial base was obviously a hugely expensive undertaking and the RLM appears to have hoped that it could mobilize significant amounts of private capital. The rush of firms that entered the industry in 1933 was certainly encouraging. The aspiring aircraft makers included Flick's heavy industrial conglomerate, Henschel, the locomotive builders, and the shipyards of Blohm and Deschimag. However, this initial wave of enthusiasm did not lead to a self-sustained increase in private investment. Though all the Luftwaffe firms other than Junkers remained in private hands, their expansion had to be financed almost entirely by the RLM. Given the general recovery of the German economy and the alternative investment opportunities this offered, it simply was not commercially justifiable to invest large quantities of money in an overcrowded industry that was entirely dependent on an unpredictable flow of government orders. In the mid-1930s, the RLM actually offered to sell Junkers, the crown jewel of the aircraft industry, to Vestag, the steel giant, only for the accountants of the Steel Trust to reject the offer as too risky. Siemens's decision to sell off its radial engine business to BMW was symptomatic.[96] Given Siemens's lucrative position in electronic components and communications, it was happy to leave the risky Luftwaffe business. In neither case did the refusal to become further entangled with the armaments boom have anything to do with political opposition. It simply reflected the precarious commercial logic of the Luftwaffe sector. Every parameter of the business was fixed by the state and could be altered by the Air Ministry at will. Engaging in this market exposed a firm to enormous risks, unless the finance for expansion was provided by the state itself. And this is what the Air Ministry did, through the mediation of the so-called Aerobank, which acted as the financier for the entire Luftwaffe sector.

The state also provided the other critical preconditions for the Luftwaffe expansion. On 10 June 1936 the Air Ministry signed a second major contract with IG Farben, this time to build a plant at Leuna capable of turning out 200,000 tons of air fuel per annum. The highly toxic tetraethyl lead additive required to boost the fuel's octane rating was supplied courtesy of IG's patent-sharing agreement with Standard Oil of New Jersey.[97] Standard transferred the technology to Leuna, regardless of protests from the State Department in Washington. In return, and with the full agreement of the German authorities, Standard received the secrets of IG's new synthetic rubber technology. Needless to say, air fuel expansion was entirely at the expense of the Air Ministry. The Reich also provided a second critical precondition for the Luftwaffe's precipitate expansion, by underwriting a huge increase in the production of aluminium, the aircraft industry's most indispensable raw material. Like steel, aluminium production in Germany depended on imports of bauxite ore. But unlike iron ore, bauxite could be obtained in sufficient quantity from Hungary and Yugoslavia, countries with which the RWM had negotiated efficient bilateral trading agreements. To process the ore, the state-owned Vereinigte Aluminiumwerke, part of the VIAG group, poured 180 million Reichsmarks into a tenfold expansion of smelting capacity.[98]

The aircraft industry was the Third Reich's model of successful state-directed industrial expansion. However, even here there was scope for entrepreneurial initiative. At times, indeed, the German aircraft industry was to become a byword for independent, competitive and often counterproductive entrepreneurship. Fundamentally this stemmed from the extreme difficulty of controlling a highly complex manufacturing industry which was subject to extreme technological uncertainty. In 1930 the majority of military aircraft were still wood and fabric biplanes. The Luftwaffe only tested its first generation of full metal monoplanes powered by high-performance piston engines in 1935. Less than five years later Ernst Heinkel launched the world's first prototype jet fighter, opening the prospect that military aircraft might soon be able to operate within striking distance of the sound barrier or beyond. Each of these transitions involved fundamental breakthroughs in aerodynamics, metallurgy, airframe and aero-engine design that were extremely hard to predict. Nor was designing the aircraft the only problem. The aircraft had to be manufactured efficiently and manufactured in bulk. And the Air Ministry was not, of course, buying aircraft for their own sake. What it needed was weapons to fight a future war, the shape of which was itself completely uncertain. Would the role of the air force be to support the army and the navy, or would it serve as an independent strategic weapon? If so, what kind of bombers did it need and how would they be protected? How would Germany protect itself against enemy air threats? Who indeed were Germany's enemies?

No other area of rearmament, indeed no other area of German industry was afflicted by such profound technological uncertainty. And it was this feature of the Luftwaffe boom that made it such a playground for entrepreneurial initiative, as rival aircraft manufacturers competed to offer the 'technical fix' that Goering needed. By 1936 Heinrich

Koppenberg was rapidly turning Junkers into a manufacturing complex capable of rivalling the very biggest firms in German industry. Henschel was pioneering a variety of new metal-pressing techniques and the highly complex jigs necessary for mass assembly. Daimler-Benz, BMW and Junkers were all competing fiercely in engine development. With the selection of Messerschmitt's (BfW) 109 fighter design in 1935–6 the Air Ministry solved at least one of its techno-strategic puzzles. Until the early 1940s, the Messerschmitt 109 would ensure that the German air force was equipped with a more than adequate fighter aircraft. The Luftwaffe, however, was still struggling to resolve the most basic question of modern air war: how to deliver bombs. Though Heinkel did begin development of a four-engined heavy bomber in the mid-1930s, the Air Ministry's main focus was on twin-engined medium bombers of which three designs were proposed in 1935 by Dornier (Do 17), Heinkel (He 111) and Junkers (Ju 86). To provide work for the new factories and to ensure that the newly trained air crews had something to fly, all three were pressed into immediate production. But it was clear that none of them was really a weapon of strategic air war. They lacked payload and speed. Furthermore, without protection it was unclear how they could break through enemy fighter defences. Despite its success, therefore, in building up production capacity, it was clear already in 1936 that the Luftwaffe needed to develop at least one more generation of aircraft and engines before it could become a truly effective fighting force. It was the search for this technical fix that was to keep the German aircraft industry in restless motion throughout the 1930s and early 1940s. Both the future of the Luftwaffe as a fighting force and billions of marks of investment hung on the outcome.

VI

What of the losers in the industrial politics of the 1930s? Nobody would ever describe the textile industry as a beneficiary of Hitler's regime. However, even here, through a bold exercise in industrial policy, the Nazi regime gathered around itself a cluster of collaborators with a stake in its programme of self-sufficiency and rearmament.[99] This did not involve the spectacular investments that characterized the Luftwaffe or the synthetic fuel programme. But the synthetic fibres programme was to be of crucial significance for a very large part of German industry and it was to be of vital importance in reshaping the clothing supply to the German population. On 20 June 1934 the RWM wrote to the two main producers of synthetic fibres – IG Farben and the Dutch-owned Vereinigte Glanzstofffabriken (VGF) – informing them that: 'The current state of the Reich's currency reserves necessitates a most extreme reduction in the import of cotton and wool . . .' More specifically, of course, this was required by Schacht's policy of selective uncoupling from the United States, Germany's traditional supplier of cotton. 'To strengthen the domestic raw material base as quickly as possible, it is the German rayon factories' peremptory duty not only to exploit their manufacturing capacity to the full, these must also be expanded with haste.' The Reich authorities wished to see a doubling in the production of viscose-rayon and a huge increase in the production of so-called staple fibres to at least 100,000 tons per annum.[100] The problem, as in the case of oil, was that world prices for wool and cotton were dramatically depressed. Certainly, as far as IG Farben was concerned, synthetic fibres were destined to remain a niche market. Any new capacity created in Germany would be entirely dependent on the state for its viability. In the summer of 1934, however, political involvement in the issue went to the very highest level. In August, Hitler personally inspected samples of fabric woven from IG Farben's Vistra staple fibre, and expressed 'extreme satisfaction' at the quality. In November 1934, as part of the reshuffle at the Reich Ministry of Economic Affairs, control over the synthetic textiles programme was handed to Hitler's personal representative for economic policy, Wilhelm Keppler, who in turn delegated the issue to Hans Kehrl (1900–1984).[101] Kehrl, the owner of a small textile plant in Cottbus, a party member since 1932 and Gauwirtschaftsberater (economic adviser) for the Kurmark Gau, had joined Keppler's team in early 1934. He had no sympathy for either IG Farben or VGF and was not to be stymied by their refusal. Keppler and Kehrl considered applying outright coercion of the kind that had been used against Junkers or in the construction of the Brabag oil corporation. But, as Keppler hastened to reassure IG, direct coercion was never a serious option in relation to Germany's largest corporation. Instead, Kehrl was authorized to outflank the incumbent producers. Exploiting his contacts in the regional party hierarchy, Kehrl set up four 'voluntary' syndicates, one for each of the major textile-producing regions of Germany: Silesia, Saxony,

Thuringia and the Rhineland. Each syndicate subscribed 4 million Reichsmarks of capital towards the construction of a new synthetic fibre plant, each with a minimum capacity of 7,000 tons per annum. There can be no doubt that political pressure played an important role in this subscription drive. Many firms saw their participation as a way of currying favour with the local Gauleitung. Another important motive was the hope of circumventing restrictions on imported natural fibres, by securing privileged access to the domestically produced synthetics. On the other hand, leading textile firms such as Dierig were genuinely enthusiastic participants, viewing rayon and the new staple fibres as long-term alternatives to the mature market for wool and cotton textiles. Marketed under the brand name Flox, the new artificial fibres enjoyed a considerable popularity in the 1930s. In any case, the Reich did its best to make the investment a low-risk gamble. Under the provisions of the 'Law on guarantees for expansion of the raw materials industry' (Gesetz ueber die Uebernahme von Garantien zum Ausbau der Roh-stoffwirtschaft), Keppler was empowered to provide all necessary sub-sidies to the new staple fibre plants. The Reich arranged to guarantee a syndicated loan under the auspices of the Dresdner Bank and provided the necessary technical expertise in the form of two leading experts, poached from IG Farben's fibres division. The most important of these was Walther Schieber, a member of the Thuringian Nazi party, who was installed as general manager of the Thuringian Zellwoll AG. Faced with a fait accompli, VGF, the weaker of the two incumbents, caved in and agreed to join in the state-financed expansion programme. IG Farben for its part maintained its independence and stuck to its limited expansion programme for rayon, raising its production to no more than 30,000 tons annually. By 1936, Kehrl could boast of additional production of 45,000 tons of staple fibres in addition to over 50,000 tons of synthetic silk. By 1937, the market share of German produced fibres had doubled to almost 40 per cent.

The example of VGF raises the more general question of how foreign owned companies fared in Hitler's Germany. Many sensationalist claims have been made on this score in recent years and a dose of realism is in order. It is true that there was substantial foreign direct investment in Germany both in the 1920s and before 1914. During World War II the Americans estimated that there were in the order of $450 million invested directly in businesses in Germany.[102] Standard Oil's investment of almost $65 million in the Deutsch-Amerikanische Petroleum Gesellschaft, combined with its close ties to IG Farben, made it the American industrial corporation with the greatest stake in Hitler's Germany. But it was closely followed by General Motors (GM) which had $54.8 million invested in Opel AG of Russelsheim, Germany's largest car-maker. By comparison, Ford's stake valued at only $8.5 million was relatively modest, as was the stake held by IBM in its German subsidiary Dehomag.[103] More significant American interests, with investments of roughly $20 million each, included Woolworths, the sewing-machine manufacturer Singer, and ITT, whose German interests included C. Lorenz AG, one of the Luftwaffe's most important suppliers of radio and electronic equipment. Nor were Americans the only foreigners with a stake in German industry. British and Dutch multinationals such as Anglo-Persian (BP) and Royal Dutch Shell (Anglo-Dutch) had major interests in German oil refining and distribution. The British tyre firm Dunlop had a considerable investment in the German rubber industry.[104] ARBED, the quintessentially European heavy industrial conglomerate, with its main base in Luxembourg, had significant cross-border interests both in coal and the Felten and Guilleaume cable works. All of these industrial investments in various ways profited from Hitler's economic recovery. The more they detached themselves from their foreign parents and the more closely they collaborated with the regime, the better they did. The regime for its part, particularly in its early years, went out of its way to reassure representatives from Ford, GM and ITT of their position in Germany. Wilhelm Keppler advised ITT to appoint the banker Baron von Schroeder, one of the men who had brokered Hitler's appointment to power in January 1933, to its board.[105] Ford had extremely pro-Nazi management at its plant in Cologne. And Opel probably profited more than any single car-maker from Hitler's motorization boom.

At the same time as acknowledging this important foreign involvement in the Nazi boom, one cannot ignore the fact that the cumulative total of direct investment in Germany was dwarfed by the billions that were in default to American and European banks and bond holders. And on the crucial question of repatriating the capital they had invested or the profits they earned, direct investors were treated no better than the holders of Germany's other foreign debts. They were all subject to the same exchange controls that made it possible to exchange Reichsmarks for foreign currency only at punitive discounts. At one point, in a desperate effort to liquidate its investment in IG Farben, DuPont of the United States offered to sell shares valued at $3 million in 1929 for less than $300,000.[106] Britain's ICI did finally manage to sell its shares in IG Farben, but only after protracted negotiation and only after accepting a complicated swap involving shares in IG's Swiss affiliate. Not surprisingly, once the initial panic was over, most of Germany's trapped investors chose to stay put and to plough back the profits they earned. In this sense they were subject to the same logic as the rest of German business. Even if they could not distribute profits in the ordinary way, they could at least achieve vigorous capital accumulation.

VII

By the mid-1930s the result of this multitude of negotiations and compromises was highly satisfactory to Hitler's regime. Rather than obstructing political change as it had done in Germany's first revolution in 1918–19, big business was an active partner in many key facets of Hitler's National Revolution. The initiative certainly lay with the political authorities. At times it came from Schacht, the Reich Ministry of Economic Affairs, or from the Reichsbank. At times it came from Goering's Air Ministry, or other branches of the military. At times it came from Wilhelm Keppler and his special staff for raw materials questions. However, in virtually every context, even settings in which one might have expected some resistance, the regime's political representatives found active collaborators in German business. The autarchy programme, rearmament, even the mass of new regulatory authorities were all backed up and energized by managerial expertise supplied courtesy of German industry. Hitler is famous for having said that there was no need to nationalize German businesses, if the population itself could be nationalized. Certainly in relation to Germany's managerial elite, one of the more important segments of that population, the regime found willing partners.

5

Volksgemeinschaft on a Budget

If Hitler was ultimately motivated by an apocalyptic vision of national destruction, he also harboured a more conventional vision of national progress and affluence.[1] Asked by a journalist to describe his ultimate political objectives, Hitler stated simply: 'I have the ambition to make the German people rich and Germany beautiful. I want to see the living standard of the individual raised.'[2] And Hitler clearly meant this to be an embracing vision of national prosperity for all the *Volksgenossen* (racial comrades). The Third Reich celebrated the German workers and their contribution to the racial community like no previous political regime. In this respect the official language of Nazi Germany set standards quite different from those of the Weimar Republic, let alone the Wilhelmine monarchy. Hitler's dream was undoubtedly collectivist at its core. But he derided the 'ideology of frugality' and 'the cult of primitivism' propagated by Bolsheviks. The German people deserved better. They needed to be raised to a higher level of life, more appropriate to the vision of the racial *Volksgemeinschaft* (racial community) as a community of superior racial worth. In the words of the German Labour Front, 'the political endgoal' of National Socialism was to ensure that 'the Volk is to be given a style of life that corresponds to its abilities and the level of its culture'. The fundamental problem was the enormous gap between these high-flown aspirations and German reality. By the standards of the day, let alone by the standards of the later twentieth century, Germany in the 1920s and 1930s was not an affluent society. And to avoid confusion, it is perhaps worth stressing that this was not a short-term effect of the Great Depression. The problem of international economic inequality was deep-seated.

Table 3. Germany in the world economy in the 1930s (averages 1924–1935)

	As seen from the 1930s (Colin Clark)				As seen from 2001 (Angus Maddison)			
	Total National Income, million International Units ($)	Per capita International Units	Total National Income relative to US = 100	Per capita income relative to US = 100	Total GDP, million 1990 International Geary-Khamis	GDP per capita	Total GDP relative to United States	Per capita GDP relative to United States
United States	66,203	542	100	100	727,803	5,963	100	100
Canada	5,084	494	8	91	44,787	4,347	6	73
Britain	21,854	477	33	88	242,385	5,287	33	89
Switzerland	1,917	476	3	88	23,877	5,922	3	99
New Zealand	691	468	1	86	7,142	4,839	1	81
Australia	2,543	399	4	74	32,395	5,091	4	85
Netherlands	2,624	335	4	62	41,443	5,289	6	89
France	12,480	302	19	56	177,404	4,287	24	72

Denmark	1,008	285	2	53	17,734	5,006	2	84
Germany	17,580	271	27	50	243,983	3,762	34	63
Belgium	2,033	253	3	47	38,842	4,832	5	81
Austria	1,613	242	2	45	22,103	3,314	3	56
Czechoslovakia	2,680	193	4	36	38,091	2,318	5	39
Hungary	1,205	177	2	33	19,975	1,796	3	30
Greece	922	145	1	27	14,304	2,261	2	38
Italy	5,320	131	8	24	119,207	2,934	16	49
Poland	3,428	122	5	23	51,620	1,204	7	20
Romania	1,471	104	2	19	17,027	1,239	2	21
Bulgaria	524	87	1	16	7,623	2,736	1	46
Soviet Union	14,710	87	22	16	255,719	1,461	35	25

Sources: A. Maddison, 'Quantifying and Interpreting World Development: Macromeasurement before and after Colin Clark', *Australian Economic History Review*, 44 (2004), 1–34; Maddison, *The World Economy: A Millennial Perspective* (Paris, 2001).

I

In 1938, the prestigious Hamburg journal the *Weltwirtschaftliches Archiv* published an article by Colin Clark, a young Australian who was making his reputation as one of the world's foremost economic statisticians.[3] The title of Clark's piece was 'The International Comparison of National Income' and its importance was that Clark made the first systematic effort to go beyond a simple translation of national income estimates using current exchange rates, to consider the complex question of purchasing power parities.[4] Clark's pioneering work established a picture, which has been expanded upon and refined, but not substantially modified in seventy years of subsequent research. In terms of per capita income, Clark estimated that Germany enjoyed a standard of living that was half that of the United States and at least a third lower than that prevailing in Britain. Drawing on work done in the last thirty years we can make these figures comparable not only across space but also across time.[5] In late-twentieth-century terms, German per capita national income in 1935 came to roughly $4,500, as compared to the current per capita income of Germany of around $20,000. In today's league table of economic development, the Third Reich would rank alongside South Africa, Iran and Tunisia. Of course, this comparison is strained because early twenty-first-century Iran and South Africa can import the high technology of more advanced societies, whether it be nuclear reactors, computers or jet aircraft, on terms that were not available to Hitler's Germany. The comparison is therefore flattering to Germany's situation. But it is nevertheless suggestive in pointing to the highly uneven nature of German economic development in the 1930s.

The gulf between Germany and the United States was the least surprising of Clark's findings. By the 1920s the standard accoutrements of twentieth-century mass consumption – the car, the refrigerator, the radio – were already establishing themselves as the norm in the United States, at a time when the enjoyment of these same commodities was limited to a restricted circle of the European upper middle class.[6] As Hitler noted in his 'Second Book', this large differential in the standard of living could not be understood without reference to the abundance of natural resources and to the vast scale of consumer markets in the United States. These conditions encouraged dramatic advances in manufacturing technology, which enabled average Americans to achieve a material standard of living of which ordinary people in Europe could only dream. The origins of the 'American system' date back at least to the mid-nineteenth century and the early mass-production of rifles in United States government arsenals.[7] But as the new century dawned the idea of mass manufacture was progressively extended to ever more complex machines: from rifles to sewing machines, from sewing machines to bicycles and from bicycles to cars. In the early 1920s it was above all the Ford Model T that embodied the triumphant breakthrough to a new era of industrial production. At his car factories at Highland Park and then on the River Rouge in Detroit, Henry Ford pioneered the essential elements of what was soon to become known as 'Fordism': high-speed assembly driven by conveyor belts; the use of new kinds of high-volume production tools, most notably grinders and automatic lathes; the deployment, wherever possible, of special-purpose machinery, designed specifically to optimize production of particular standardized products; a ruthless effort to force down the cost of raw materials and components through vertical integration from raw materials to final assembly; the employment of large volumes of semi-skilled and unskilled labour; and a shopfloor bargain in which extreme effort levels were traded against astonishing wages. The end result was a standardized product, mass-produced at remarkably low cost. So cheap were Ford's cars and so high were his rates of pay that Ford's workforce provided a major market for the cars they were making, a situation virtually unthinkable in Europe.

It would be naive, of course, to take the Ford myth at face value. Henry Ford was nothing if not a propagandist.[8] European industry by the early twentieth century was by no means ignorant of the techniques of mass production.[9] IG Farben, the Vereinigte Stahlwerke, Siemens and AEG were vertically integrated corporations to rival their American counterparts that profited from the bulk production of commodities ranging from textile dyes to pharmaceuticals, sheet metal and light bulbs.[10] One step down from these corporate giants, there were literally hundreds of smaller mass-producers in Germany, making everything from screws to gas lamps and harmonicas.[11] The ghastly slaughter of World War I would have been impossible but for the fact that all the combatants were capable of mass-producing the means of destruction on an enormous scale. Perhaps most remarkably, by 1918 Britain, France,

Germany and Italy were outbidding each other in the production of combat aircraft, surely the most spectacular mechanical invention of the early twentieth century.[12] Between 1914 and 1918 Germany alone turned out 47,000 aircraft of all types, a record which was in no way inferior to American production, which peaked in 1918 at 14,000 aircraft. These flying machines were fragile contraptions strung together from wood, wire and impregnated canvas. But they were complex machines by any standard, and they were driven by aero-engines that only fifteen years after the Wright brothers' first flight were already twenty to thirty times more powerful than their puny 12-horsepower power plant. None of this would have been possible without dramatic advances in metallurgy and machining that were by no means the exclusive preserve of Detroit. At the cutting edge of modern metalworking the Europeans held their own. But what was undeniable was the huge American advantage in mass-manufacturing. According to contemporary comparisons, in the mid-1930s America's productivity advantage over its European rivals was in excess of 2 : 1 in most branches of manufacturing, widening to as much as 4 : 1 or even 5 : 1 in the production of motor vehicles and radios.[13]

What is more surprising, from our early twenty-first-century perspective, is Germany's marked inferiority relative to Britain. According to Clark, Britain not only had a higher per capita income than Germany; he believed that despite the much smaller size of the British population, the British economy was still somewhat larger than that of Germany. This conclusion has been modified by more recent calculations. We now believe that the German economy in the 1930s was slightly larger. However, the claim that per capita incomes in Germany were substantially lower than in Britain has proved robust. This difference was clearly not attributable to any qualitative difference in the productivity of British and German manufacturing.[14] In virtually every industrial sector, German and British firms were closely matched. What dragged Germany down was its large and highly inefficient agricultural sector and the substantial tail of small shops and workshops in the craft and service sectors. In the 1930s productivity per head in German agriculture was only half that in German industry, at a time when more than 9 million people were still employed in farming.[15]

Of course, ordinary Germans would not have been acquainted with the latest statistical estimates. But Clark's figures merely confirmed the common sense of the time. In the 1890s and 1900s Wilhelmine Germany had cheered itself with the belief that it was rapidly catching up with Britain.[16] Though this was clearly good news, it also carried with it an acknowledgement of Germany's relative backwardness. In the aftermath of World War I, hyperinflation and the imposition of a punitive reparations regime, it was merely common sense that Germany's economic development had been thrown back by decades. So firm was this conviction that statistical evidence to the contrary was greeted with howls of anger and disbelief.[17] It was widely believed that British workers enjoyed a higher standard of living than their German counterparts, a fact to which many attributed the chronic underemployment of British industry in the 1920s. The remarkable affluence of the British middle classes in the inter-war period had no counterpart in Germany. Added to this, the impression of British economic power was multiplied by its Imperial possessions. To Germans it seemed that Britain and the other colonial powers, along with America, exercised a stranglehold over the raw materials of the world.[18] Though Germany, of course, had its own corporate giants, it was the multinationals of the City of London, the oil firms and rubber corporations that epitomized the uncanny global influence of modern capitalism. Given Germany's position today as one of the richest and most economically powerful countries in the world, this deeply ingrained sense of inferiority is hard to comprehend. But without it, it is impossible to understand the sense of beleaguered poverty that afflicted German public debate throughout the inter-war period. And it is against this backdrop that we must view Hitler's material aspirations for the *Volksgemeinschaft*.

If we are to engage with the everyday lives of ordinary Germans, we need to descend from the abstract heights of comparative national accounting. In the 1930s hourly wages for the majority of Germans were counted not in Reichsmarks, let alone PPP-adjusted dollars of 1990, but in Pfennigs. Only the most highly paid workers such as skilled machinists or typesetters earned more than one Reichsmark per hour. At the other end of the scale, the lowest-paid male workers in sawmills and textile factories were on hourly rates of 59 Pfennigs.[19] Unskilled women workers in textiles or the food industries could expect no more than 42–5 Pfennigs. In 1936, with the German economy at full employment, 14.5 million people, 62 per cent of all German taxpayers, reported annual incomes of less than 1,500 Reichsmarks, corresponding to weekly earnings of just over 30 Reichsmarks and hourly rates of about

60 Pfennigs.[20] A further 21 per cent, or 5 million white-collar and blue-collar workers, reported annual incomes of between 1,500 and 2,400 Reichsmarks (weekly earnings of between 30 and 50 Reichsmarks). Only 17 per cent of all taxpayers recorded incomes of more than 2,400 Reichsmarks, or 50 Reichsmarks per week. This income pyramid was sharply divided by class and gender. Male blue-collar workers on average took home 1,761 Reichsmarks in 1936, whilst working-class women earned only 952 Reichsmarks. The average white-collar male earned 3,000 Reichsmarks, almost twice the figure for his female counterpart. Moving from the incomes of individuals to combined household incomes is tricky. However, the figures quoted give some indication of the possible range of variation. A blue-collar household with a man and woman both in employment would be lucky to achieve a combined income of much more than 2,700 Reichsmarks per annum. A white-collar household, by contrast, could push its combined income above 4,000 Reichsmarks, by combining an average male salary with a second income, perhaps from an unmarried daughter.

The true significance of these modest figures becomes apparent when they are compared with the prices paid by German households for basic needs.[21] A 1 kilogram loaf of brown bread in the 1930s cost 31 Pfennigs, the equivalent of half an hour's work for many low-paid German workers. Potatoes were the staple diet of the German working class. Five kilos could be bought for only 50 Pfennigs. A kilogram of bacon cost half a day's work at 2 Reichsmarks and 14 Pfennigs. Butter was extraordinarily expensive. In 1936 the price per kilo of butter stood at 3 Reichsmarks and 10 Pfennigs. A 250-gram lump of butter cost more than an hour's wage. The phrase 'crying over spilt milk' takes on a new significance when we appreciate that a litre of the precious fluid cost 23 Pfennigs. Eggs at 1.44 Reichsmarks per dozen were hardly cheap. And even beer, retailing at 88 Pfennigs per litre, was a considerable drain on the working-class food budget. Not surprisingly, the majority of Germans lived on a modest and monotonous diet of bread and jam, potatoes, cabbage and pork, washed down with water and small amounts of milk and beer. Hence the derogatory term 'Kraut', popular both in France and Britain. Germans were also avid drinkers of coffee and coffee substitutes, consuming a total of almost 5 kilos per annum. And they were steady smokers, consuming two cigarettes per head per day. At only 3 Pfennigs apiece, cigarettes were a luxury even the poorest could afford. All in all, expenditure on food, drink and tobacco accounted in working-class households for between 43 and 50 per cent of average household budgets.[22] Rent accounted for another 12 per cent, implying average housing expenses for German working-class households of only 24 Reichsmarks per month. A further 5 per cent went on utility bills. That left a monthly total of only 67 Reichsmarks for a household of four people for all other forms of expenditure, on clothing, household equipment, transport, health care, insurance and social and educational expenditure. A pair of men's shoes would cost 10 Reichsmarks. Having them resoled cost 4 Reichsmarks. Children's shoes were not to be had for much less than 6 Reichsmarks, the daily wage for most workers. If the man of the house needed a new suit this consumed virtually the family's entire disposable income.

Clearly, in Hitler's Germany only a small minority of the population lived in circumstances which we today would describe as comfortable.[23] And this was further confirmed by international comparative study. In 1929, the Ford Motor Company commissioned an investigation of the wages that would be required in each of its fourteen European locations to enable its workers there to match the standard of living of those on the lowest rung of the Dearborn wage scale.[24] The inquiry was carried out by the International Labour Office in Geneva with financial assistance from the United States and yielded a startling impression of the gap that divided America from Europe. Perhaps not surprisingly, in a comparison of the spacious Midwest with crowded European cities the gap was most stark in relation to housing. Even the worst paid workers in Detroit took for granted an apartment of four and a half rooms. This caused the investigators in Frankfurt and Berlin some embarrassment since such spacious accommodation was 'not usually occupied by working men'. Annual rent for a basic four-and-a-half-room apartment would come to at least 1,020 Reichsmarks. If it were provided with the facilities taken for granted in the United States, such as separate bathroom and kitchen, indoor toilet and running water, the rent might be as much as 1,380 Reichsmarks. That was roughly four times the amount that the equivalent working-class family in Germany actually spent on housing. In total, to have matched the standard of living of Detroit in either Frankfurt or Berlin in the early 1930s would have required an income of between 5,380 and 6,055 Reichsmarks, sums that were beyond the wildest dreams of the majority of the German workforce.

To anyone with a conventional training in modern economics, the solution to Germany's problems is obvious. To escape its relative poverty what Germany needed was broad-based economic growth driven by technological change and the accumulation of both physical and human capital. This would enable increased labour productivity, better wages and lower prices for high-quality goods, permitting a general increase in the standard of living. On the basis of Germany's long-run growth trend, to put it at its most mechanistic, Germany was 25–30 years behind the United States. And there were certainly voices inside and outside the Third Reich that took this kind of approach.[25] By the 1920s the discourses of 'productivism' and 'rationalization' were already well established.[26] German industry, once it had recovered from the recession and once labour markets began to tighten in the mid-1930s, engaged actively in rationalization and investment in new capital equipment. By the early 1940s, as we shall see, German industry was benefiting from an investment boom like no other in its history. The Nazi regime also paid concerted attention to its 'human capital'. Improvements to the system of industrial training had been discussed intensively in the 1920s. And from 1933 onwards apprenticeships and on-the-job training were given massive state support. Amongst other requirements, an entirely new workforce of skilled metalworkers had to be created for the factories serving the Luftwaffe. In line with its rhetorical revalorization of German labour, the Third Reich established the norm that every German youth should aspire, at the very least, to the status of a semi-skilled worker.[27] And these were not mere words. In 1939 only 30,000 male school leavers entered the workforce as unskilled labourers, as compared to 200,000 in 1934. For many working-class families, the 1930s and 1940s were a period of real social mobility, not in the sense of an ascent into the middle class, but within the blue-collar skill hierarchy, prompting one author to speak of the 'deproletarianization' of the German working class.[28]

But whilst the Third Reich did not reject productivism and rationaliz-ation, one cannot grasp the specificity of Nazi thinking about economics if one focuses on this aspect alone. Nor indeed can one understand the broader intellectual milieu of the inter-war period. It cannot be stressed too strongly, that in the early 1930s Germany looked back on almost twenty years in which economic decline and insecurity massively out-weighed the experience of prosperity and economic advancement. Over the previous decade, international economic integration had brought crisis. Investment had led to bankruptcy. Hundreds of thousands of young people who had embarked optimistically on apprenticeships and university degrees found themselves stranded in unemployment. In light of this experience, one did not have to be a radical right-wing ideologue or paranoid anti-Semite to doubt the efficacy of the liberal doctrine of progress.[29] Germans had always worked hard. They had saved and invested diligently. Their industrial technology was second to none, certainly in Europe. Yet Germany was not a rich country. In light of this experience, what reason was there to believe that Germany could soon return to the path of steady progress that it had appeared to be on in the happy years before 1914? Nor did professional economists offer much comfort.[30] There were those of course who held fast to the liberal optimism of the nineteenth century. However, in the 1930s they were by no means the loudest voices. Those economists in Germany who did think about issues of long-term economic growth tended to agree with Rosa Luxemburg in arguing that the search for industrial expansion would lead to ever more fierce competition for export markets, a rivalry which provided both Stresemann and Hitler with their prime explanations for the disaster of World War I.[31] The advocates of the 'new economics' in the 1930s were no more optimistic. Contrary to the post-war popularization of his work, the Keynes of the 1930s was no apostle of growth. Keynes's *General Theory* of 1936 showed ways in which economies stuck in deflationary depressions could be helped to recover by government fiscal policy. It was not a magic formula for economic growth. Indeed, Keynes and many of his leading acolytes in the United States were sceptical about the possibility of sustained long-run economic expansion.[32]

This backdrop is essential if we are to understand Hitler's refusal to accept the liberal gospel of economic progress. Economic growth could not be taken for granted and Hitler was by no means the only person to say so. As we have seen, the doctrine of economic life as a field of struggle was already fully formed in *Mein Kampf* and Hitler's 'Second Book'. And this Darwinian outlook was only encouraged by the subsequent Depression. Given the density of Germany's population and Hitler's insistence on the inevitability of conflict arising from export-led growth, the conquest of new *Lebensraum* was certainly one means of raising Germany's per capita income level. Hitler could hardly have been

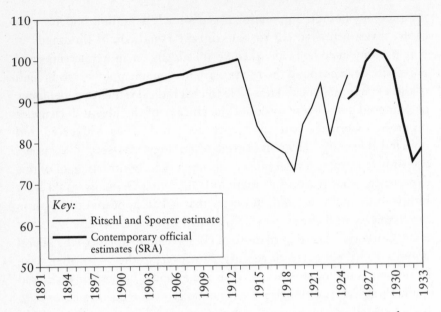

Figure 7. Forty-two years of German economic progress as seen from 1933 (national income per capita, 1913 = 100)

more emphatic or consistent in his advocacy of this position. As we have seen, he made a point of reiterating this belief in the very first days of his new government in 1933. An aggressive foreign policy based on military strength was the only real foundation of economic prosperity.

In the short term, however, there were specific political interventions that could be made to remedy the damage done to the German standard of living by years of prejudice and neglect. Hitler and his acolytes were firmly convinced that the development of the German standard of living had been held back since 1918 by an unholy alliance formed between selfish bourgeois liberals and primitivist socialists.[33] This conspiracy of low expectations had benefited only the German bourgeoisie, whilst robbing the majority of the German population of the full benefits of the new technologies of mass-production. Ford had had the entrepreneurial vision to break with the past and to turn what had once been a luxury product into a popular commodity. In Germany, what was required to break the deadlock was an act of decisive political will. The Third Reich made it its mission to use the authority of the state to coordinate efforts within industry to devise standardized and simplified versions of key consumer commodities. These would then be produced at the lowest possible price, enabling the German population to achieve an immediate breakthrough to a higher standard of living. The epithet which was generally attached to these products was *Volk*: the Volksempfaenger (radio), Volkswohnung (apartments), Volkswagen, Volkskuehlschrank (refrigerator), Volkstraktor (tractor).[34] This list contains only those products that enjoyed the official backing of one or more agencies in the Third Reich. Private producers, however, had long appreciated that the term '*Volk*' had good marketing potential, and they, too, joined the bandwagon. Amongst the various products they touted were Volks-gramophone (people's gramophone), Volksmotorraeder (people's motorbikes) and Volksnaehmaschinen (people's sewing machines). In fact, by 1933 the use of the term '*Volk*' had become so inflationary that the newly established German advertising council was forced to ban the unlicensed use of the term.

As we shall see, the majority of the Volksprodukte met with failure. And given the general lack of purchasing power in Germany it is not hard to see why. However, we should not be too hasty in dismissing this effort simply as an outgrowth of the irrationality of Hitler's regime.[35] If we are to do justice to the Third Reich we must seek to understand it in its own terms. We cannot hope to do so if we start from today's conception of economic progress as one of broad based and eventually limitless expansion. Knowing what we do about Germany's economic development after 1945, we can plausibly argue for the continuity and irresistible momentum of long-run economic growth. But why should that have been a plausible vision to Germans in 1933? Given that decisive political intervention was widely credited with bringing about a spectacular recovery in employment, why should it not have the same dramatic effect on consumption?

II

The first Volksprodukt announced by Hitler's regime, the people's radio, was both the most transparently politically motivated and also by far the most successful. As we have seen, Hitler made his first radio address as Chancellor on 1 February 1933 within days of taking power. At that point, however, there were only 4.3 million licensed radio receivers in

Germany for a population of 66 million. Only a quarter of German households could hear the Fuehrer speak.[36] If radio was to fulfil its promise as a propaganda tool, this clearly had to change. The chief obstacle to the wider diffusion of radios was their price. The cheapest radios on the market in the early 1930s were priced at over 100 Reichsmarks, which in light of the income figures we have just discussed was clearly excessive. If radio was ever to reach the mass of the population, something had to be done to design and produce a cheaper receiver. In May 1933 the Propaganda Ministry took the initiative by coming to an agreement with a group of radio manufacturers to push through the large-scale production of a new standard radio.[37] This was to be cheaper than any radio previously on the market, but would be of sufficient quality to enable listeners to receive regional radio stations as well as high-powered national transmissions. To secure a market niche, the members of the radio cartel agreed to offer no competitor products in this price range. The set was proudly entitled Volksempfaenger (VE) 301 after the date of Hitler's appointment as Chancellor (30 January 1933). It was priced at only 76 Reichsmarks. Clearly, for the average German household purchasing a VE 301 was still a serious financial commitment. So to increase the attractiveness of the sets a number of utility companies offered part-payment deals whereby a customer could acquire a set for an initial payment of as little as 7.25 Reichsmarks, followed by eighteen monthly instalments of 4.40 Reichsmarks.[38] Goebbels launched the VE 301 at the radio exhibition in Berlin in August 1933. Reportedly, the entire initial consignment was sold by the end of the first day. A huge additional order was placed immediately, with more than 650,000 Volksempfaenger being sold in the next twelve months and a further 852,000 in 1934–5.[39] Radios became one of the genuine boom industries of the 1930s, stimulating not only electronics production, but also the manufacture of Bakelite and wood cases. By 1935 the radio industry was showing all the symptoms of a speculative bubble. Production had outrun demand, inventories had risen to unhealthy levels and three of the smaller producers, including Seibt, whose chief designer had been responsible for the Volksempfaenger, went into liquidation.[40] Thereafter, with leadership from Telefunken, the dominant producer, progress was more steady and by 1937 economies of scale were such that the price for the standard VE 301 could be reduced to as little as 59 Reichsmarks. By 1938, the penetration of radios in the big cities of

Germany had reached 70 per cent. In the countryside, however, radios remained a luxury. And Germany's relative poverty was still starkly evident from the comparative statistics. In the second half of 1938 only half of German families afforded themselves a radio, as compared to 68 per cent in Britain and 84 per cent in the United States.[41] A year later a major breakthrough was achieved with the introduction of a new entry-level model, the Deutscher Kleinempfaenger (DKE), priced at as little as 35 Reichsmarks. Colloquially known as 'Goebbels' gob' ('Goebbels Schnautze'), the DKE could claim credit for having brought radio within the reach of virtually every German family. A million were sold in twelve months and business was buoyant even during the war. In the eight years between 1934 and 1942 radio penetration in Germany almost doubled. On the other hand it would be naive to attribute this simply to the Volksempfaenger programme. It did not escape notice that outside Germany, for the same price as the utilitarian Volksempfaenger one could buy a far superior superhet. receiver of American manufacture.[42] The Volksempfaenger, by contrast, was completely uncompetitive on world markets with only tiny numbers finding buyers abroad. It is entirely conceivable, therefore, that in a Germany freed from the corset of Schacht's exchange controls and open to the full benefits of international trade, the diffusion of radios might have been even more rapid. Nevertheless, the association of the Volksempfaenger with the radio boom made it the model for subsequent *Volk* products.

For Hitler, there can be no doubt, the car was the great symbol of a modern consumer lifestyle.[43] But in the early 1930s the car was still a luxury reserved for a tiny minority of the German population.[44] In 1932 there were only 486,001 licensed cars in all of Germany. In Berlin, a city of 4 million inhabitants, there were fewer than 51,000 cars. By comparison, Berlin's streets today are crowded with 1.2 million automobiles. If one imagines a modern city street with 29 out of every 30 cars removed from the scene, one gets an impression of how exclusive motor vehicles were in Nazi Germany.[45] Placed in relation to the number of households, there was one car for every 37 households in 1933. This, however, is misleading since it conveys the false impression that cars in 1930s Germany were primarily objects of household consumption. In fact, only a tiny minority of licensed vehicles were primarily for personal use. The overwhelming majority of cars in Hitler's Germany were owned for business purposes.

Even before the announcement of the Volkswagen, Hitler made no secret of his desire to see car ownership multiplied. Hitler was the first Chancellor of Germany to open the International Motor Show in Berlin and he made time for this appearance even during the frantic campaigning of February 1933. The significance he attached to motorization was made clear by his declaration that 'If one formerly attempted to measure the standard of living of a population by the number of kilometres of railway line, in future one will apply the kilometres of roads suitable for motor traffic'.[46] As Hitler was fully aware, Germany in 1933 did not measure up to this standard. In 1933 only 25 per cent of Germany's major roads had hardened surfaces suitable for high-volume motor traffic. To remedy this deficit, the autobahn project was announced in the summer and by early 1934 responsibility for national road construction and repair had been consolidated in the hands of Fritz Todt. In April 1933, the regime also announced the elimination of car tax on all newly acquired vehicles. Prior to 1933 these taxes were amongst the highest in Europe and at least ten times higher than those prevailing in the average State in the United States.[47] Not surprisingly, the result was a considerable surge in car production and ownership. From a total of 486,001 in 1932 the number of registered cars more than doubled to reach 1.271 million by 1938. As these figures suggest, however, the expansion in motorization had clear limits. Germany in the late 1930s was still a society in which car ownership was the preserve of a small minority.

Compared to average family incomes, cars were simply too expensive. In 1938 a comprehensive study by the Institut fuer Konjunkturforschung found that the minimum cost of purchasing a car and running it for 10,000 kilometres per year was 67.65 Reichsmarks per month.[48] A working-class family of four on an income of 2,300 Reichsmarks per annum would have found that, after allowing for food, housing and utility bills, running a car consumed their entire disposable income. According to the Reich Statistical Office, the amount that such an 'average' family actually spent on transport in the mid-1930s was 27 Reichsmarks per annum, allowing for fares on public transport and maintenance costs for bicycles. This was one-thirtieth of the outlay required for even the most inexpensive car. The Institut's study also revealed the two principal obstacles to cheaper motor travel. The capital cost of purchasing the vehicle accounted for 30 to 35 per cent of the monthly cost. The price of petrol was the other main factor.

By the late 1930s the price of a litre of petrol in the Third Reich stood at 39 Pfennigs (roughly $1.70 in dollars of 1990). At this price, a family outing of 160 kilometres in a fuel-efficient car cost an entire day's work for the average German worker.[49] Only a small fraction of this exorbitant price, however, was due to the market price for oil. Throughout the 1930s, given the worldwide glut of oil, the price of a litre of petrol in the Gulf of Mexico varied between 2 and 3 Pfennigs, around 10 per cent of the price charged to German motorists. Allowing for shipping, petrol could be had at Hamburg port for as little as 5.13 Pfennigs per litre. The costs of distribution and marketing added another 13 Pfennigs. The cost price for petrol, in other words, was probably around 20 Pfennigs per litre, the price paid by consumers in the United States.[50] What determined the actual cost of petrol in the Third Reich was politics. In this respect the Third Reich was no different from the Weimar Republic or most European societies today. And this must be borne in mind in any serious analysis of Nazi policy towards motorization. Taxes and the legal requirement to add domestically produced alcohol doubled the price of petrol. If promoting motorization had been the chief priority of Hitler's regime, it could have cut the operating cost for a small family car by as much as 15 per cent, by forgoing these taxes. This, however, was an impossibility. IG Farben had won its argument. Of far greater strategic importance to Hitler's regime than popular motorization were the problems of the balance of payments and the related project of fuel autarchy, which required that the price of petrol in Germany be raised to far in excess of world market levels. In the 1930s the cost of petrol produced at IG Farben's Leuna plant was 15–17 Pfennigs per litre, implying a price of at least 30 Pfennigs per litre at the petrol pump. A tax on imported fuel was therefore indispensable to sustaining the momentum of the synthetic fuel programme. But, as the pressure on the Reich's finances mounted in the course of the 1930s, this strategic imperative was combined with the more obvious needs of the Reich Finance Ministry. Taxes on imported oil were a significant source of revenue, bringing in 421 million Reichsmarks in 1936, a third of the total customs revenue of the German state. And, as of December 1936, as pressure on the Reich's finances mounted, even domestically produced fuel was subject to a tax of at least 4 Pfennigs per litre.

It was the non-negotiability of fuel tax that forced the advocates of mass-motorization in Hitler's regime to focus with even greater intensity on the cost of the car itself. The industry that had developed to serve Germany's cramped car market was far from the dominant industrial force which the German motor vehicle industry was to become in the later twentieth century.[51] A multitude of small, high-cost producers was sustained by hefty tariffs levied on imported vehicles. Though Fordism was widely discussed in management circles, the small size of Germany's producers meant that most of them were able to achieve few if any economies of scale. The major exception to this rule was Opel, which since 1929 had been wholly owned by General Motors. Ironically, it was not Ford, but Ford's great rival that introduced Fordist mass-production to German metalworking.[52] And the substantial increase in car ownership over which Hitler's regime presided after 1933 was in large part driven by investment decisions taken by GM in Detroit. Exploiting the efficiency of its state-of-the-art manufacturing plant in Ruesselsheim, it was Opel that took the lead in introducing a new generation of small family saloons, offering a good compromise of performance, reliability and comfort. And it was Opel that took the lead on costs, driving down the price of its P4 model to the headline-grabbing figure of only 1,450 Reichsmarks from the factory gate. In 1936, cars in the sub-1.5 litre class accounted for 70 per cent of the new registrations in Hitler's Germany, and, of the 150,000 cars sold in this class, almost half were made by GM's German affiliate. For Opel, however, 1,450 Reichsmarks was the sticking point. And since at this price cars were unaffordable to more than a small minority of the German population, it was hard to see, in the mid-1930s, how the German car industry could soon break into a truly mass market. The complete motorization of German society would have to wait for economic growth to take its course, allowing a gradual diffusion of ever-greater purchasing power to ever-wider groups in the community.

Hitler, however, was impatient. On 7 March 1934, on the occasion of the second International Motor Show of the Third Reich in Berlin, he seized the opportunity not only to announce the national fuel programme, but also to declare his intention of launching a people's car.[53] What Hitler had specifically in mind was a family saloon of 30 horsepower, capable of carrying four people in moderate comfort, priced at the extraordinarily low figure of only 1,000 Reichsmarks. Not surprisingly, the media reacted excitedly to this bold new project. The motor vehicle industry, however, was far less enthusiastic. Given the current state of manufacturing technology and the cost of raw materials, no one could see how it would be possible to produce an adequate vehicle for less than 1,000 Reichsmarks. Nor was it clear how the Reich would afford the necessary petrol and rubber for mass-motorization, given its chronic balance of payments problems. Nevertheless, in light of the huge excitement in the press, Daimler-Benz and Auto Union felt compelled at least to open negotiations on the Volkswagen project. The two main German-owned producers feared that otherwise the regime might resort to compulsion, or even that a deal might be struck with Detroit. Daimler-Benz and Auto Union therefore agreed with the Association of the German Motor Car Industry to jointly fund a research team, headed by Ferdinand Porsche, to explore the possibility of meeting Hitler's demands.

Porsche was undoubtedly an inspired engineer and he enjoyed an excellent relationship with Hitler based on their shared enthusiasm for motor sport. But what particularly recommended Porsche to the car industry was the fact that he appeared to agree with their basic attitude towards the Volkswagen project. To expect to produce a high-quality family car for less than 1,200 Reichsmarks was simply unrealistic. Industry gambled that Porsche was the man to persuade Hitler of this inescapable economic limit. The car-makers, however, underestimated both Hitler's bloody-minded determination and the ruthlessness of Porsche's ambition. Rather than backing away from the Volkswagen, Hitler renewed his commitment in his opening speech at the International Motor Show in February 1935. Later in the year Porsche began road-testing the first Beetle prototype. Predictably, however, Porsche had failed to solve the problem of cost. In confidential correspondence he put the price tag for the VW at between 1,400 and 1,450 Reichsmarks, no cheaper, in other words, than Opel's latest offering. Porsche, however, was not to be put off so easily. With work progressing fast on the prototypes and Opel adding pressure by announcing a new round of price cuts for its entry-level models, he began to intrigue actively against his employers in the motor vehicle industry. In January 1936 Porsche invited Hitler to the first official trial run of the VW Beetle, without even notifying the Automobile Association. When the Association responded with a report that criticized Porsche's design and revealed the fact that it was currently priced at 1,600 Reichsmarks per car, Hitler vented his fury not on Porsche but on the industry in a speech he delivered at the opening of the International Motor Show in February 1936. After reiterating his belief that only technical genius could lead the way to mass-mobilization, Hitler turned on the German car industry. He accused them of having unconsciously succumbed to an elitist view of the motor car as a costly luxury good. It was simply not acceptable that Germany, with half the population of America, should have one-fiftieth as many motor vehicles. No one should doubt the determination of the National Socialist government to bring the VW project to a successful conclusion.[54] As Hitler had assured Porsche, if necessary the VW project would be pushed through by decree even against the resistance of the industry. The price target would be met by imposing a compulsory cut in the price that Porsche paid for his steel and aluminium.

In July 1936, the project began to slip definitively out of the hands of German industry. After a successful demonstration on the Obersalzberg on 11 July 1936 Hitler decided that Porsche's car was to be built, not in any of the existing car factories in Germany, but in a new special-purpose plant. Hitler claimed that this could be constructed for 80–90 million Reichsmarks. The factory was to have a capacity of 300,000 cars per annum and deliveries were to begin in time for the International Motor Show in early 1938. Faced with the impossibility of meeting the 1,000 Reichsmarks target on commercial terms, it seems that Germany's private car industry was on the whole content to see Porsche and his troublesome project transferred to the state sector. As a commercial project the VW was not viable. A factory built through the compulsory conscription of private business, along Brabag lines, would damage the entire industry. Far better to use public funds, or rather the funds of the German Labour Front (DAF). This suggestion seems to have come from Franz Joseph Popp, the (CEO) of BMW, who also sat on the supervisory board at Daimler-Benz. Popp suggested that the DAF should take on the Volkswagen as a not-for-profit project. Non-profit status would qualify the factory for tax concessions that would help to cut the final price of the car. More importantly, from the point of view of industry, it would allow the sale of Volkswagens to be limited exclusively to the blue-collar membership of the DAF, thus reserving the profitable middle-class car market for the private manufacturers. The leadership of the DAF jumped at the chance. As Robert Ley, the leader of the DAF, later put it, the party in 1937 took over where private industry on account of its 'short sightedness, malevolence, profiteering and stupidity' had 'completely failed'.[55] In May 1937, with payments to Porsche and his design team totalling 1.8 million Reichsmarks, the industry cut its losses and ended its association with the VW project. On 28 May 1937 Porsche and his associates founded the Gesellschaft zur Vorbereitung des Deutschen Volkswagens mbH (Gezuvor). A year later, construction began on Porsche's factory at Fallersleben in central Germany. In October 1938, along with Fritz Todt and the aircraft designers Willy Messerschmitt and Ernst Heinkel, Porsche was awarded Hitler's alternative to the Nobel Prize, the German National Prize.

The basic question, however, remained unsolved. How could the Volkswagen be produced at a price affordable to the majority of Germans? The DAF claimed that the Volkswagen was now to be promoted in conformity with Nazi ideology as a tool of social policy rather than profit. However, it too lacked any coherent system for financing the project. From the outset it was clear that the capital costs of building the plant would never be paid off by the sale of cars priced at 990 Reichsmarks per vehicle. The construction of the plant would therefore have to be financed through other than commercial means. The DAF, which had inherited the substantial business operations of Germany's trade unions, had assets in 1937 estimated to be as much as 500 million Reichsmarks. It also commanded a huge annual flow of contributions from its 20 million members. However, the demands of constructing the VW plant were enormous. Rather than the 80–90 million Reichsmarks originally mooted by Hitler, Porsche's planning now envisioned the construction of the largest motor vehicle factory in the world. The first phase, to reach a capacity of 450,000 cars per annum, was costed at 200 million Reichsmarks. In its third and final phase the plant was to reach an annual output of 1.5 million cars, enough to out-produce even Henry Ford's River Rouge facility. Investment on this scale placed huge demands on the DAF. The initial tranche of 50 million Reichsmarks to start work on the factory could only be raised by a fire sale of office buildings and other trade union assets seized after May Day 1933. Another 100 million were raised by over-committing the funds of the DAF's house bank and the DAF's insurance society. The cars themselves were to be paid for by the so-called 'VW saving scheme'. Rather than providing its customers with loans to purchase their cars, the DAF conscripted the savings of future Volkswagen owners.

To purchase a Volkswagen, customers were required to make a weekly deposit of at least 5 Reichsmarks into a DAF account on which they received no interest. Once the account balance had reached 750 Reichsmarks, the customer was entitled to delivery of a VW. The DAF meanwhile achieved an interest saving of 130 Reichsmarks per car. In addition, purchasers of the VW were required to take out a two-year insurance contract priced at 200 Reichsmarks. The VW savings contract was non-transferable, except in case of death, and withdrawal from the contract normally meant the forfeit of the entire sum deposited. Remarkably, 270,000 people signed up to these contracts by the end of 1939 and by the end of the war the number of VW-savers had risen to 340,000. In total, the DAF netted 275 million Reichsmarks in deposits. But not a single Volkswagen was ever delivered to a civilian customer in the Third Reich. After 1939, the entire output was reserved for official uses of various kinds. Most of Porsche's half-finished factory was turned over to military production. The 275 million Reichsmarks deposited by the VW savers were lost in the post-war inflation. After a long legal battle, VW's first customers received partial compensation only in the 1960s. But even if the war had not intervened, developments up to 1939 made clear that the entire conception of the 'people's car' was a disastrous flop. To come even remotely close to achieving the fabled target of 990 Reichsmarks per car, the enormous VW plant had to produce vehicles at the rate of at least 450,000 per annum. This, however, was more than twice the entire current output of the German car industry and was vastly in excess of all the customers under contract by the end of 1939. Assuming a production of 'only' 250,000 vehicles per annum – which was significantly more than the German market could bear – the average cost per car was in excess of 2,000 Reichsmarks, resulting in a loss of more than 1,000 Reichsmarks per car at the official price. Furthermore, even priced at 990 Reichsmarks the VW was out of reach of the vast majority of Germans. A survey of the 300,000 people saving towards a VW in 1942 revealed that on average VW savers had an annual income of *c.* 4,000 Reichsmarks, placing them comfortably in the top tier of the German income distribution. Blue-collar workers, the true target of *Volksgemeinschaft* rhetoric, accounted for no more than 5 per cent of VW's prospective customers.

III

The Volksempfaenger and the Volkswagen were both desirable consumer goods and attractive symbols of modernity. But they were strictly items of discretionary expenditure. They impacted only marginally on the day-to-day material preoccupations of the vast majority of Germans. These centred around food, clothing and housing. The restrictions imposed on the German textile and clothing industry we have discussed in previous chapters; suffice to say that clothing was a key area of the consumer's budget, which increased very substantially in price after 1933. The issue of food will be addressed in connection with agriculture in the next chapter. Housing, however, deserves special attention, because it was a field of policy that went to the very heart of the kind of *Volksgemeinschaft* that National Socialism wanted to create. And unlike cars and radios, housing was an issue on which any German government had to take a stand. It was a field of consumption that had become progressively more and more politicized since the beginning of the century and it was to prove utterly unamenable to any kind of quick fix.

The most common way of describing the housing situation in Germany in the inter-war period was one of 'housing shortage'. Rival interest groups competed to define this deficit, with estimates varying between 1 and 2 million apartments depending on the author of the estimate.[56] The concept of shortage, however, is a problematic one. In a 'free', self-equilibrating market there are no shortages. An excess of demand over supply would tend to drive up the price, resulting in a reduction in effective demand and an increase in supply, eliminating the deficit. The symptoms of shortage in the housing market of inter-war Germany were, therefore, first and foremost a reflection of the 'distortions' introduced by the imposition of rent controls after the end of World War I.[57] These controls had been necessary during the inflationary period to prevent an epidemic of evictions and mass homelessness. In this respect they were highly effective. Rent controls were one of the key elements of the Weimar welfare state. They were not, however, without cost. With rents fixed for the majority of the housing stock at levels which in real terms were substantially below those prevailing in 1913, the construction of new apartments became extremely unattractive to private investors. The Weimar authorities attempted to alleviate the situation through a large-scale programme of publicly subsidized construction. This was funded by a tax levied on owners of existing property – the Hauszinssteuer – which was justified by the windfall they had received when their mortgages were wiped out by the hyperinflation.[58] This public funding undoubtedly made a considerable contribution to the housing stock. And the new estates often incorporated a pleasing version of modernist design. However, they were of only indirect benefit to the mass of the population since, given prevailing construction costs, the minimum monthly rent even allowing for subsidy was 40 Reichsmarks per month, greatly in excess of the sums that working-class families considered affordable. Meanwhile, a nationwide census conducted at the height of Weimar's public construction boom revealed symptoms, if not of housing shortage, then of serious housing poverty. In 1927, in the cities of Germany, as many as one in six apartments accommodated lodgers and sub-tenants along with their primary occupants. And these lodgers included at least 377,000 families of three or more people, who lived as sub-tenants in other people's apartments. In addition, the statisticians estimated that there were at least three-quarters of a million apartments in Germany that qualified as overcrowded. Hundreds of thousands of working-class families were forced to share, two or more to a room. Many huddled into one- or two-room apartments with neither bathroom nor separate kitchen. Contemporary accounts describe families living in windy attics and damp cellars. When mass unemployment threw thousands into homelessness, makeshift squatter camps housing tens of thousands of people sprang up on the outskirts of Germany's major cities.

The Depression fatally undercut Weimar's system of publicly subsidized construction. As tax revenue plunged and expenditure on welfare increased, the flow of public funds towards new construction collapsed. From a peak of 1.34 billion in 1928 the public subsidy to housing fell to as little as 150 million Reichsmarks in 1932 with devastating consequences for the building trades.[59] In Berlin, a city of more than 4 million people, construction was begun in the last six months of 1931 on only 2,606 new apartments. In this extreme situation, the Reich took the extraordinary step of announcing a subsidy for the self-built settlements of the unemployed and their families on the margins of Germany's cities. Each settlement was to be provided with enough land for the families to secure a high degree of self-sufficiency in their food supply.[60] The Reich would provide a subsidized loan of 2,500 Reichs-marks towards construction, the rest would come from the self-help of the settlers themselves.

Hitler's accession to power permanently ended Weimar's system of direct subsidy for housing construction. In the Third Reich, there were more important uses for the revenue of the Hauszinssteuer than the funding of social housing. The deflation had gone some way towards bringing rents back into alignment with the rest of wages and prices, improving the profitability of privately owned housing. However, any substantial degree of construction continued to rely on one form or another of subsidy. The largest single allocation to housing in Hitler's Germany came from the work creation programmes of 1932 and 1933 that provided a total of 667 million Reichsmarks to subsidize the repair and conversion of existing apartments. In addition, 45 million Reichs-marks were provided as a subsidy towards the construction of private homes. The results of this programme were substantial, but concentrated mainly on the conversion of existing large apartments into smaller and more lettable units. In general, the housing policy of the Third Reich in its early years consisted of shifting responsibility back towards private sources of funding. Whereas under the Weimar Republic 42.4 per cent of all housing finance had been provided by the public authorities, by 1936 this had fallen to 8 per cent. The most effective new mechanism of housing policy devised by Hitler's regime was the Reichsbuergschaft, a public guarantee for mortgages raised by private landlords. Though this required the Reich to provide no funds, the willingness of the Reich to guarantee lenders against default helped to reduce the cost of borrowing.[61]

In so far as Hitler's regime had an ideological housing policy, it consisted in the early years in accelerating the construction of the offici-ally sponsored settlement programme, first launched in 1931. Rather than being seen as a refuge from the industrial economy for unemployed workers, ex-urban settlements were now trumpeted as the future of German housing. The Nazi ideologue Gottfried Feder, who in 1934 briefly served as the chief commissioner for settlement (Reichskommissar fuer das Siedlungswesen), envisioned a gigantic programme of popu-lation redistribution to span the period up to the 1980s. Ten to fifteen million Germans were to find new homes in small towns, with fetching names such as Hitlerburg and Goeringen.[62] The reality, however, was completely at odds with this vision. Compared to the billions spent by the Weimar Republic on its vision of social housing, Hitler's regime provided a total of only 180 million Reichsmarks to subsidize its settlement programme. Even allowing the most modest sum for the construction of the settlements, and assuming that the settlers themselves would provide the bulk of the labour, this was enough to build only 35,000 units. These settlement homesteads were surrounded by an ample plot of land, but they were rudimentary even by contemporary standards in the quality of life they offered to their inhabitants. The materials used in construction were of such poor quality that in some cases mortgage lenders considered the buildings insufficiently durable to provide the necessary security. The settlements provided neither electricity nor running water. No sewerage connections were provided because it was assumed that the settlers would want to use their wastewater for manuring their allotments.[63] Perhaps not surprisingly, the uptake was far from enthusiastic. Though the ideology of settlement continued to be promoted by party agencies, the Third Reich clearly needed a new housing policy.

Facing a continuing problem of overcrowding in the cities, in 1935 the Reich Labour Ministry launched an alternative vision of National Socialist housing in the form of so-called Volkswohnungen.[64] Stripped of any conception of settlement or any wider ambition of connecting the German population to the soil, the Volkswohnungen were to provide no-frills urban housing for the working class, built according to the first projections for as little as 3,000–3,500 Reichsmarks. Hot running water, central heating and a proper bathroom were all ruled out as excessively expensive. Electricity was to be provided but only for lighting. Each housing unit was to be subsidized by Reich loans of a maximum of 1,300 Reichsmarks. Rent was to be set at a level which did not exceed 20 per cent of the incomes of those at the bottom of the blue-collar hierarchy, or between 25 and 28 Reichsmarks per month.[65] To achieve this low cost, however, the Volkswohnungen were to be no larger than 34 to 42 square metres. Though this was practical it was far from satisfying the propagandists of *Volksgemeinschaft*. The Goebbels Ministry refused to accept that accommodation of such a poor standard deserved the epithet 'Volkswohnung' and the DAF insisted that the minimal dimensions for a working-class apartment should be 50 to 70 square metres, sufficient to allow a family to be accommodated in three or four rooms.[66] But, as experience showed, the Labour Ministry's costings were in fact grossly over-optimistic. By 1939 the permissible cost of construction even for small Volkswohnungen had had to be raised to 6,000 Reichsmarks, driving rents to 60 Reichsmarks per month and thus pricing even this basic accommodation out of the popular rental market. The very most that working-class families were willing to pay was 35 Reichsmarks per month. Instead of the 300,000 per year that the Labour Ministry had intended, construction on only 117,000 Volkswohnungen was started between 1935 and 1939.

As in the case of the Volkswagen, what Hitler's regime could not resolve was the contradiction between its aspirations for the German standard of living and the actual purchasing power of the population. But as in the case of the Volkswagen this did not prevent the DAF from espousing a utopian programme of future construction.[67] By the late 1930s, the official ideal of 'people's housing' was a large family apartment of at least 74 square metres, fully electrified, with three bedrooms, one each for parents, male and female children. At the same time it was estimated that an apartment built to the DAF specification would cost in the order of 14,000 Reichsmarks, 40 per cent more even than those constructed by the Weimar Republic. The limitations of German family budgets, however, demanded that these generous apartments were to be provided to the *Volksgenossen* at monthly rents of no more than 30 Reichsmarks. In part, the costs would simply have to be borne by the Reich. But, as in the case of the Volkswagen, the DAF also hoped that mass-production might provide the answer. In 1938 the DAF's rationalization experts estimated that only 5 per cent of the content of a normal building was made up of mass-produced components; in the case of the VW it was to be 100 per cent. With efficient bulk production, the DAF hoped to be able to lower the cost for its generous Volkswohnungen to as little as 7,000 Reichsmarks.[68] As in the case of the VW, the seductive logic of scale economies combined with uninhibited state subsidy would make a reality of the National Socialist vision of an affluent *Volksgemeinschaft*.

IV

Clearly, by the late 1930s, the realization of this National Socialist vision was incomplete to say the least. Measured against their own ambitions, the Volksprodukte failed. But it is not enough to stop there. We must follow up this conclusion by asking what meaning the regime may have attached to these failures. And, as soon as we pose this question, it is clear that the frustration experienced with the Volksprodukte called into question none of the basic ideological tenets of National Socialism. This was not because the achievement of a higher standard of living was a secondary objective; it was not. As Hitler repeatedly stressed, raising the German people out of their state of relative poverty to a standard of living appropriate to their status as Aryans was a central objective of his politics. It was simply that the limitations of German purchasing power came as no surprise to Hitler and other true believers. Whilst Germans were constrained to inhabit an inadequate *Lebensraum* hedged around by hostile powers, egged on in their antagonism towards Germany by the global Jewish conspiracy, it was no surprise that Germans could not afford cars. It was no surprise that German working families struggled to pay the rent for as little as 40 square metres of inadequate housing. The Volksprodukt projects were harbingers of a new future. But it would be the utmost naivety to think that they could by themselves make it real. As Hitler himself had put it in his 'Second Book', if the German state could not secure sufficient *Lebensraum* for the German people, 'all social hopes' were 'utopian promises without the least real value'.[69] The real instrument for the attainment of American-style consumer affluence was the newly assembled Wehrmacht, the instrument through which Germany would achieve American-style living space.

It is conventional in histories of the Third Reich to counterpose rearmament to the 'civilian' objectives of the regime as though they were mutually exclusive alternatives, a view often summarized as a choice between 'guns or butter'. And there is an undeniable truth in this. As we have seen, from 1934 onwards Schacht's New Plan prioritized the import of industrial raw materials ultimately destined for rearmament over the import of raw materials required for civilian consumption. At the same time the Reich, to pay for rearmament, siphoned off taxes and private savings to a total of almost 60 billion Reichsmarks. Without this expenditure, household consumption and private investment could clearly have been substantially higher. As a share of national income, military spending by 1938 had climbed to 20 per cent, enough to pay for even the most gigantic housing programme. At the same time, however, the formula of 'guns or butter' is misleading. At a strategic level, guns were ultimately viewed as a means to obtaining more butter, quite literally through the conquest of Denmark, France and the rich agricultural territories of Eastern Europe. In this sense, rearmament was an investment in future prosperity. But though this may accurately summarize the thinking of Hitler, Goering and others in the German political-military leadership, it implies a degree of insight into the ultimate purposes of rearmament that was surely not shared by the average German in the 1930s.[70] This, however, begs the question of what rearmament did mean to Germans in the 1930s. Is it really right to see rearmament simply as a drag on the standard of living, as one more obstacle to the realization of dreams of mass-consumption? Or might it in fact be more appropriate to reverse this train of logic and to think of rearmament as a particular form of collective mass-consumption?

Certainly this is the way that conventional economic analysis views military expenditure, not as a form of productive investment, but as a form of unproductive public consumption. At this analytical level there is no difference between the purchasing of tanks and military aircraft and expenditure on the construction of public buildings, arenas, or gigantic vacation resorts on the Baltic. From an economic point of view again, the reintroduction of conscription in 1935 amounted to an enormous collective holiday for millions of young men, who were fed and clothed at public expense whilst not engaged in productive labour. It is hard to deny, furthermore, that there is a degree of parallelism between the various mass youth organizations of the Nazi party, the organized collective activity of the military and the organized mass leisure activities of the KdF (Kraft durch Freude). In the experience of young men, these organizations formed a succession through which one moved from the Hitler Youth via the Wehrmacht into the ranks of the DAF and its KdF. At a symbolic level, furthermore, the Wehrmacht formed the centrepiece for many of the ritualized mass events of the regime. From 1934, the 'Day of the Wehrmacht' was to become a popular fixture at the Nuremberg party rallies, featuring tens of thousands of troops, thousands of horses and vehicles including entire regiments of tanks and elaborately choreographed mock battles.[71] The Wehrmacht also appeared to great acclaim at the mass rallies of the peasantry.[72] On one occasion the Wehrmacht even dropped parachutists on a gaping mass of country folk. Though the subject has not been properly researched, there can be very little doubt that rearmament in the 1930s was as much a popular spectacle as it was a drain on the German standard of living, a form in other words of spectacular public consumption.

Contemporaries were struck by the enthusiasm that greeted the reintroduction of conscription in the spring of 1935.[73] And remarkable evidence collected by labour historians demonstrates the passionate identification that many German workers in the 1930s clearly felt with the weapons they were producing. This was no doubt in part due to the high status attached to the skilled work involved in armaments production.[74] But it also had something to do with the weapons themselves. These were not ordinary commodities. They were assertions of national strength, the common property of the German nation, to be handled by the pick of German manhood. A tank manual issued during the war brought this connection forcefully to the attention of its youthful crew:

For every shell you fire, your father has paid 100 Reichsmarks in taxes, your mother has worked for a week in the factory . . . The Tiger costs all told 800,000 Reichsmarks and 300,000 hours of labour. Thirty thousand people had to give an entire week's wages, 6,000 people worked for a week so that you can have a Tiger. Men of the Tiger, they all work for you. Think what you have in your hands![75]

Whatever the limitations on the supply of sophisticated consumer goods to civilian society, the Wehrmacht enrolled especially the male population in the collective consumption of the full fruits of industrial modernity.[76] Not that the Wehrmacht escaped the limitations of the German economy. It was a precise reflection of the incomplete modernization of German society. The majority of Hitler's soldiers marched into battle on foot and relied on horses for a large part of their transport. In this sense the German army of the 1930s and 1940s was destined to remain, as one military historian has put it, a 'poor army'. But as members of the Wehrmacht, young men were enrolled in an organization that was undeniably a vehicle for industrial modernization. As in World

War I, enrolment in the military provided many young men with their first hands-on experience of trucks and motor cars.[77] Whatever the limitations of the Volksempfaenger, hundreds of millions of Reichsmarks were invested in the 1930s in the radio equipment and electronic infrastructure of the Wehrmacht. And every German soldier was familiar with the basic workings of the radio system. Most spectacular of all was the Luftwaffe. If the German army was in many respects still rooted in the nineteenth century, the idea of a 'poor air force' is a contradiction in terms. By the late 1930s the Luftwaffe and its associated industries had enrolled the labour power of hundreds of thousands of men. Even if only a few thousand were trained as aircrew, hundreds of thousands more were engaged in the infrastructure necessary to sustain the fliers, and for millions more the Luftwaffe provided a point of imaginary identification, making a reality of a decade-old dream of national air power.[78] In this sense at least, the idea of an affluent *Volksgemeinschaft* was more than mere rhetoric. If Germany could not match the United States in terms of private consumption, in the number of cars, radios or refrigerators per household, it did at least boast a vastly greater national stock of combat aircraft and tanks.

6

Saving the Peasants

To the naked eye, by far the most striking difference between the economic situation of Germany, Britain and the United States was the huge command over raw materials and land provided by the continental expanse of North America and the vast reach of the British Empire. Land hunger was one, if not *the* most important impulse behind the European explosion into the world that had profoundly reshaped the structure of global power since the seventeenth century.[1] If the European Renaissance and Enlightenment with their rationalist legacy of science and technology were fundamental components of modernization, so was the insatiable European urge to overcome scarcity through the conquest and settlement of vast 'empty' tracts of land, whether in Eurasia, the Americas or Australasia. The result by the late nineteenth century was a dramatic transformation in the distribution of land and population. Meanwhile, native populations in North America, much of Latin America and Australasia were subject to more or less deliberate genocide. Thirty million African slaves were shipped across the Atlantic to work the rice paddies, sugar cane and cotton plantations. Forty million European settlers went overseas in search of a higher standard of living. In the opposite direction flowed the commodities produced in the new areas of conquest and settlement, a flow that accelerated to a flood in the late nineteenth century as the cost of transportation plunged. The result was a spectacular revolution in the global system of food supply, which in turn rebounded on the huge peasant populations of Europe.[2]

It is this epic of globalization that we should have in mind when we turn to the analysis of National Socialism and in particular its agrarian politics. Too often the preoccupation of Hitler and his followers with problems of *Lebensraum*, food and agriculture is seen as prima facie evidence of their atavism and backwardness. This could not be more wrong. The search for greater territory and natural resources was not the outlandish obsession of racist ideologues. These had been common European preoccupations for at least the last two hundred years. Of course, the European process of expansion had largely come to a halt by 1914. But the important exception to this rule was in Eurasia, with the ongoing Russian effort to populate and develop the vast territory east of the Urals. And it was to the east that Hitler looked to direct the expansive drive of the German people. The question of how European societies and their rural populations should respond to the new global economy in food was not a marginal issue. It was one of the fundamental questions facing European societies in the twentieth century.

Though Britain was the great exception, everywhere else in Europe large fractions of the population still continued to be employed in agriculture well into the second half of the twentieth century.[3] In Germany in the 1930s, the peasant life glorified by Nazi agrarians was not an archaic fantasy. Agrarian ideologues addressed a massive social reality. Though it is common to regard the German economy in the early twentieth century as a modern, dynamic, cutting-edge global competitor, in fact until the 1950s a substantial minority of the German population continued to eke out a living from the soil, under conditions, in many cases, of extraordinary backwardness.[4] The census of 1933 counted no less than 9.342 million people as working in agriculture, almost 29 per cent of the total workforce. And apart from full-time farmers, many millions of other Germans produced at least some of their own food from small allotments or from home-reared pigs and chickens.[5] According to the census of 1933, 32.7 per cent of the population lived in rural communities of less than 2,000 inhabitants. If we add to that the number living in small market towns of between 2,000 and 20,000, the share comes to 56.8 per cent. And what these statistics cannot convey is the sheer backwardness of much of German rural life even as late as the 1930s. In this respect, the photographic record is a better guide. In the inter-war period, class photographs from rural elementary schools routinely captured images of row upon row of barefoot children, whose parents were too poor to afford shoes, at least for the summer months.[6] Images of fieldwork show broken old people bent double over primitive ploughs pulled by worn-out cattle.[7] Hay mowing, reaping, threshing and the muddy ordeal of the potato and beet harvest were all performed by hand. And whilst half the German population lived in immediate proximity to the countryside, many more would carry with them the recent memory of rural–urban migration. Hitler himself chose to begin *Mein Kampf* with an account of how his father, 'the son of a poor cottager', made his way to the city from the mountainous provinces of Lower Austria to Vienna, only to retire after a career in the civil service to a farm 'near the market village of Lambach . . . thus in the circuit of a long and industrious life, returned to the origins of his forefathers'.[8] Nazi agrarianism, with its florid and racist rhetoric of blood and soil and its high-flown ideas about the future of the German peasant, was not an atavistic gloss on a modern industrial regime. Nazism, both as an ideology and as a mass political movement, was the product of a society still in transition.

Similarly, Hitler's obsessive preoccupation with food was rooted in contemporary reality. Though famine had been banished from Western Europe in the second half of the nineteenth century, in large part due to Europe's ability to tap huge new sources of overseas supply, World War I had forced the question of food supply back onto the agenda of European politics.[9] The British and French blockade, though it failed to produce outright famine, did succeed in producing an epidemic of chronic malnutrition in Germany and Austria that was widely blamed for killing at least 600,000 people.[10] Depression and mass unemployment brought a return of serious deprivation.[11] And even in good times, at the bottom of the social scale chronic malnutrition was widespread in Germany as it was in every other European society in the early twentieth century. One way or another, virtually everyone alive in Germany in the 1930s had an acute personal experience of prolonged and insatiable hunger. Nor was mass starvation a distant threat confined to Africa and Asia. On Germany's eastern borders in the early 1920s, the turmoil of war, revolution and civil war in Russia, Poland and the Ukraine had precipitated an agricultural disaster, which by 1923 had claimed the lives of perhaps as many as 5 million people.[12]

In a sense one might say that the originality and radicalism of National Socialism lay in its refusal to allow these basic questions of modernization to be removed from the twentieth-century agenda. Of course, it suited the satiated victors of World War I all too well to declare the issue of *Lebensraum* closed. By comparison with densely packed Germany, France had a vastly favourable ratio of population to land as well as its own considerable Empire. Britain and the United States controlled the agricultural heartlands of both halves of the American continent as well as Australasia. With their complete domination of the sea-lanes it was hardly surprising that they were happy to see German agriculture declining and its urban population slipping into dependence on imported food. By refusing to accept this state of affairs as inevitable, Nazi Germany was not seeking to turn back the clock. It was simply refusing to accept that the distribution of land, resources and population, which had resulted from the Imperial wars of the eighteenth and nineteenth centuries, should be accepted as final. It was refusing to accept that Germany's place in the world was that of a medium-sized workshop economy, entirely dependent on imported food. This, as Hitler saw it, was a recipe for 'race death'. Faced with overcrowding and low wages in the cities, urban families would do their best to reduce the birth rate. The best and the brightest would emigrate to new territories that offered more scope for advancement. For lack of natural resources, the German economy would never be able to match the affluence on show in the United States. And if Germany were ever to emerge as a serious trade competitor, it would be at the mercy of the British and the Jewish propagandists of global liberalism, who would not hesitate to unleash a second, ruinous world war, whilst crippling the German home front by means of blockade.

I

Agriculture, in fact, was a key issue for the entire nationalist right wing. And it was no coincidence that in the cabinet formed on 30 January 1933, the post of Agriculture Minister was initially assigned to Alfred Hugenberg. Whilst Hugenberg dragged his feet over work creation, he set to work diligently, reinforcing the protectionist walls that insulated German agriculture from the world market.[13] To consolidate the protection of the grain-growing interest he established a central purchasing agency that would guarantee minimum prices to all producers. In June 1933 German farm debtors were effectively removed from the ordinary credit system, being provided with complete protection against their creditors. Imports were subject to quotas, as the agricultural lobby had long demanded. It was Hugenberg's no-holds-barred approach to agricultural protection that gave the international community its first taste of the open aggression that was to be expected from Hitler's government. Compared to Hugenberg, even Hjalmar Schacht appeared a liberal. And worse was to come. When, following the scandal at the World Economic Conference, Hugenberg resigned from all his offices, the Ministry for Food and Agriculture was given to Richard Walther Darré, the head of the Nazi party's agricultural organization. The Agriculture Ministry thus became the only Ministry dealing with economics to be headed by a card-carrying Nazi. To back him up at the Ministry, Darré chose Herbert Backe, a close collaborator and party member of long standing. Together, Darré and Backe were to shape a programme of agrarian policy that was to reshape a large part of the German economy.

Richard Walther Darré was born in 1895 to a German emigrant family in Argentina. He was, like Hitler, a man saved by World War I.[14] His school career had ended disastrously without the Abitur, the passport to middle-class respectability. The war provided Darré with a second chance. Through contacts made in the trenches he was able to restart his education, securing a place at the Agricultural College in Halle, from which he graduated in 1925 with a Master's thesis on pig breeding. Over the following years, he combined this specialist knowledge of animal genetics with a close reading of the classic texts of nineteenth-century anti-Semitism to fashion a particularly extreme version of agrarian racism. Two books later he had established himself as a leading, young ideologue of the right, with close links to the nationalist coven known as the Artamanen.[15] Darré was introduced to Hitler in 1930, through mutual friends in Thuringia, and joined the Nazi party soon afterwards, charged with the special task of building an agrarian organization. Within the space of three years, Darré's agricultural organization conquered the German countryside. The farmers' organizations, which had always been dominated by the Junker interests, were entirely subverted. In the election of March 1933, the agricultural constituencies of northern and eastern Germany were amongst the few regions of Germany to give Hitler the absolute majority he craved. Apart from the inherent importance of the issue, the significance of the peasantry as a political constituency gave Darré, their undisputed leader, considerable political clout in the early years of the Nazi regime. In the sham elections to the all-Nazi Reichstag of November 1933, Darré appeared seventh in line on the electoral ticket after Hitler, Rudolf Hess (Hitler's deputy), Wilhelm Frick (Nazi Minister of the Interior), Goering, Goebbels and Roehm (SA leader). The annual harvest festival celebrations, first staged in October 1933 on the Bueckeberg in Lower Saxony, were awesome displays of Darré's political power. Larger than the annual party rallies in Nuremberg, they were unmissable events for the new regime's political elite.

But Darré was not only a highly successful political organizer. He also exercised a profound influence over Heinrich Himmler and his SS organization. Himmler had been acquainted with Darré, even before 1930, through the Artamenen. Himmler and Darré had both been to agricultural college and they shared a genuine interest in archaeology and the mystical early history of the Germanic tribes.[16] It was on Darré's instigation that the SS began the process of transforming itself from a sworn fraternal brotherhood into a self-perpetuating and expanding community of families of certified racial purity – a Sippengemeinschaft (clan community). It was Darré's SS-Sippenamt (clan office) to which SS men wishing to marry had to apply for permission. Thereafter, the SS and the leadership elite of the Nazi agrarian wing developed as an interconnected milieu. Darré expected all of his leading collaborators in the Agriculture Ministry to join the SS. Backe, most notably, was later to occupy a senior rank in the SS and enjoyed close relations with Himmler. There was rivalry, of course.[17] In the late 1930s personal relations between Darré and Himmler deteriorated badly. However, collaboration between Himmler's SS and Herbert Backe as acting head of the Agriculture Ministry was extremely close. Bearing in mind this intimate connection between the agrarians and the SS is crucial if we are to understand how the twin problems of fostering the German peasantry and managing the national food supply were capable of generating some of the most extreme and murderous policies of the Third Reich.

For Walther Darré and for the majority of ultra-nationalists what was at stake was not simply the economic health of farming, but the long-term future of the German race. Darré's particularly extreme version of peasant ideology was rooted in a selective reading of turn-of-the-century archaeology, linguistics and socio-biology. For Darré, the historic character of the Germanic tribes was defined by their history as rooted peasant farmers. The great enemies of the Germanic peasantry had always been rootless nomadic elements and the most dangerous of these were the Jews. The modern form of nomadism was the rootless population of the cities. The crisis afflicting the German peasantry by the early twentieth century was the result of long-term attack and erosion by rootless Jewish influences. The process of uprooting had begun across Europe in the sixteenth century. It had gathered pace over the following centuries, taking on spectacular political form in the aftermath of the French Revolution. In the name of freedom, nineteenth-century liberals had broken the fundamental bond that connected the German people to the soil. They had uprooted millions of peasants and turned land itself into a commodity, to be freely bought and sold. It was this capitalistic expropriation that had set in motion the disastrous process of migration and degeneration that had depleted the German countryside. Since unification in 1871, each national census had recorded a lower share of the population employed in farming. For Darré, the dire consequences of this development were most starkly evident in the birth rate. Starting from the 1870s, when fertility rates had been identical in town and country at 40 per thousand inhabitants, the birth rate in Germany's cities had fallen sharply. By the 1920s births were down to no more than 17 per thousand population. And since the war, the countryside as well had begun to follow this disastrous trend. By 1930 the birth rate in the countryside was as low as 20 per thousand. For Darré this confirmed the most basic tenets of his theory. The German race, born out of a deeply rooted connection to the soil, was simply not capable of sustaining itself in a society dominated by an urban culture propagated by the Jewish agents of commerce and free trade. Confined to the cities, the German race was doomed to extinction.

The archaeological and anthropological settings, which Darré liked to give to his musings, condemn them to appear to our eyes as manifestations of a bizarre atavism. But, rather than thinking of Darré as a backward-looking ideologue, it is more illuminating to view him as an agrarian fundamentalist, a man deeply critical of the present but one who aspired not to bringing about a wholesale regression to the backward conditions before 1800, but towards a vision of rebirth, of renaissance.[18] The *voelkisch* thinkers of the inter-war period consciously marked themselves off both from nineteenth-century romanticism on the one hand and the fatalistic pessimism made popular by Spengler's best-selling *Decline of the West*. No one who has actually tried to read Darré's books can escape the impression that their author was convinced that the principles of *Blut und Boden* were firmly rooted in the latest results of historical, anthropological and biological research. In its 'methodology' at least, Darré's racism was founded not on blind prejudice, but on a supposedly systematic understanding of the eternal, transhistorical characteristics of distinct races and cultures.[19] What gave Darré's thinking its particularly impractical, archaic feel was his inability to articulate a clearer vision of how the 'eternal characteristics of the German race', defined by their archaeological and biological origins, were related to the historical process of modernization that had had such a transformative impact on German society since the early nineteenth century. It was this inability to provide a convincing historical narrative of modernization that created the impression that Darré intended to bring about a wholesale return to the past. But in fact this characteristic lacuna in his thought had few if any practical implications for policy. Darré's ahistorical or transhistorical vision was only one strand in Nazi agrarianism. Where Darré left off, his right-hand man, the trained agronomist and Secretary of State in the Agriculture Ministry, Herbert Backe took over.

Backe (1896–1947) has often been characterized simply as an 'efficient', 'apolitical' technocrat in the image of Albert Speer.[20] As such he serves as a foil against which to compare Walther Darré. In fact, Backe was no less a Nazi ideologue than Darré or for that matter Heinrich Himmler.[21] Born in Batumi, Georgia, to a German businessman and the daughter of a Wuerttemberg peasant family that had resettled in Russia in the early nineteenth century, the 'drive to the East' (*Drang nach Osten*) was part of Backe's biography. Having been unsettled first by the revolution of 1905, Backe found himself in 1914 as an internee in the Urals. Profoundly disillusioned, he escaped to Germany in 1918, where he struggled to complete his education and support his family in extremely difficult circumstances. He joined the Nazi party in 1922, with the membership number of 22766, and distinguished himself even at this early stage by his fixation on the race question. After a lull in the 1920s Backe reactivated his party membership in 1931 and was elected to the Prussian parliament in 1932 with Darré's encouragement. As we shall see, in the 1940s Backe was to cooperate with Himmler in the execution of genocide on an epic scale. The difference between Darré and Backe does not lie in their different degrees of ideological commitment, but in the way in which they conceived the historic mission of National Socialism. Backe bridged the gap between Darré's eternal truths and the historical reality of the early twentieth century, with a conventional, stage view of history.[22] Much like Hitler, Backe saw National Socialism as having been assigned the role of overcoming the contradictions of nineteenth-century capitalism and achieving a reconciliation between the German people and the economy that sustained them. For all its ills, Backe saw the modernization of the German economy and German society in the nineteenth century as an inevitable and necessary preliminary to the possibilities of the twentieth century. As Hitler put it in February 1933, the new Reich would be built not only on the eternal foundations of Germany's *voelkisch* existence. It would also make use of all the 'accomplishments and traditions developed in the course of recent history'.[23]

Backe was well versed in economic history and the starting point for his analysis was precisely the story of globalization with which we began. He was under no illusion that there was any possibility of returning to the state of affairs before the advent of global free trade in the early nineteenth century. But at the same time, the last century had also demonstrated the pernicious consequences of pushing the revolutionary 'Jewish' doctrine of free trade to its limits. Free trade was simply the smokescreen behind which imperialist Britain, the favoured vehicle of Jewish parliamentarianism and liberalism, attempted to monopolize the riches of the entire world. Self-sufficient peasant production had been displaced by the dramatic emergence of a global market, first for wool and cotton raised on plantations in the American South and giant ranches in Latin America, South Africa and Australia. Then after 1870, with the advent of cheap long-distance transport, the staples of European agriculture – grain, meat and dairy produce – were sucked into the global division of labour. Across the world, diversified peasant production was displaced by plantation monocultures. The new global market in food may have banished famine in the industrial metropole. But, as Backe pointed out, the monocultures of capitalist agriculture had spread food insecurity to vast tracts of the globe. In recorded history there had never been famines so severe or so frequent as in the nineteenth century.[24] The agricultural crises of the 1920s and 1930s were simply the latest phase in liberalism's disastrous campaign of conquest.

In Backe's vision, Darré's racial agrarianism melded with a more conventional critique of capitalism as a transformative historical force. Drawing on a populist anti-capitalist canon, beloved of both right and left, Nazi ideologists conjured up images of grain being burned and tipped into the sea, thousands of hectares of land lying uncultivated, whilst at the same time armies of unemployed Europeans and Americans went hungry. Like Hitler, Backe saw the mission of National Socialism as being the supersession of the rotten rule of the bourgeoisie. Far from being impractical, Backe's ideology provided a grand historical rationale for the extreme protectionism already implemented by the nationalist agrarians. Far from being backward looking, Backe's vision assigned to National Socialism the mission of achieving a reconciliation of the unresolved contradictions of nineteenth-century liberalism. It was not National Socialism but the Victorian ideology of the free market that was the outdated relic of a bygone era.[25] After the economic disasters of the early 1930s there was no good reason to cling to such a dangerous, archaic doctrine. The future belonged to a new system of economic organization capable of ensuring both the security of the national food supply and the maintenance of a healthy farming community as the source of racial vitality.

II

As the Nazi leadership never tired of informing the population and the wider world, the fundamental problem of German politics was the shortage of land. Germany was far more densely populated than France and lacked the colonial outlets available to Britain. For readers today, living as we do in post-agricultural societies, this rhetoric has a somewhat empty ring. It is hard to believe that by *Lebensraum* Hitler really meant mere land, rather than something more valuable such as industrial raw materials. But in making such assumptions we are in danger of ignoring the fact that 'land shortage' was in the 1930s still one of the chief afflictions of German society. When compared to the richer Western European countries, let alone the fabulously well-endowed North American settlements, Germany was indeed land-poor. Compared to Britain, Germany had more land to devote to agriculture, but its rural population was disproportionately larger. Compared to France, the German agricultural population was smaller in relative terms, but France was far more favourably endowed with land. Though comparing itself in terms of per capita GDP to countries like Britain and the United

States, in terms of land per farmer Germany had far more in common with backward 'peasant nations' such as Ireland, Bulgaria or Romania. Amongst the large Western European states only Italy had a higher ratio of rural population to land endowment.

Table 4. Farm labour and land

	Farming population 000s	Arable land 000 ha	Arable ha per farmer	Arable ha per farmer, Germany = 100
Canada	1,107	23,120	20.9	1009.5
United States	10,752	137,333	12.8	617.4
Denmark	561	2,663	4.7	229.4
Britain	1,413	5,329	3.8	182.3
Soviet Union	71,734	223,916	3.1	150.9
France	7,709	21,386	2.8	134.1
Irish Free State	678	1,484	2.2	105.8
Germany	9,388	**19,422**	2.1	100.0
Poland	10,269	18,557	1.8	87.3
Italy	8,008	12,753	1.6	77.0
Romania	9,207	13,866	1.5	72.8
Bulgaria	2,464	3,711	1.5	72.8
British India	179,947	125,397	0.7	33.7

Source: SRA, *Statistisches Jahrbuch fuer das Deutsche Reich 1937* (Berlin, 1937), 38* and 41*

The shortage of land facing German peasant farmers was further compounded by issues of distribution. In the aftermath of World War I peasant uprisings across Eastern Europe were forestalled by a dramatic land reform movement that left most of the land, most notably in the Danubian plain, in the hands of peasant smallholders.[26] No such dramatic redistribution was carried out in Germany. In 1933, 7,000 estates of more than 500 hectares, just over 0.2 per cent of all farms, controlled almost 25 per cent of German farmland. By contrast, 74 per cent of all farms in Germany – 2.26 million in total – farmed only 19 per cent of the land, in often widely dispersed holdings of between 0.5 and 10 hectares. In the middle were the substantial peasant farms of between 10 and 100 hectares, accounting for 25 per cent of all farms and 43 per cent of farmland. This stratified farm population, consisting of a tiny number of large estates, a solid body of viable peasant farms and a teeming mass of struggling marginal units, produced a similarly differentiated rural population. Between 2 and 20 hectares, German farms were overwhelmingly reliant on full-time family labour, provided by the farm owners, both male and female, and their dependants. Below 2 hectares, part-timers predominated. Above 20 hectares, the work burden became too heavy for a single family. However, farms between 20 and 100 hectares were legitimately regarded as peasant farms in that they employed mainly 'farm servants' (*Knechte*) and maids, who lived in, remained unmarried and received a significant fraction of their compensation in kind, rather than in the form of wages.[27] Above 100 hectares, conventional wage labour dominated the agricultural labour force, with an important sprinkling of supervisory personnel, administrators and farm craftsmen.

For all but the most privileged members of the rural community, farm life was hard. On peasant farms in particular, survival depended on extraordinarily long hours, in excess of twelve hours, six days per week, for both men and women.[28] The work was dirty and often dangerous. Housing was far behind the modest standards of Germany's cities and rural communities lacked the amenities of the town. The rate of return per unit of farm labour was depressingly low. Farms above 20 hectares at least offered the prospect of a decent living for the farmer and his family.[29] In some areas, with good soils and proximity to urban markets, 10 hectare farms were still viable. But any family dependent on a unit smaller than that, unless they were in an unusually good location or possessed soil of exceptional quality, faced a dispiriting grind of poverty and overwork. The censuses provide at least a rough guide to the numbers in this situation. The critical threshold between full- and part-time farming came at 2 hectares.[30] Seventy per cent or more of farms below 2 hectares were part time. By contrast, of farms between 2 and 5 hectares two-thirds were farmed full time by their owners. In total, the German census of 1933 counted 1.1 million heads of household, with 3.9 million dependants, as full-time farmers of holdings between 2 and 10 hectares. Not all these families were entirely dependent on their farms alone. Of the 3.9 million dependants, 450,000 were listed as having an independent occupation. Assuming these earners were distributed evenly across the farm population, almost half of farming families in the marginal group between 2 and 10 hectares will have benefited from a significant source of additional income. But that left at least 2.3 million people entirely dependent on farms of between 2 and 10 hectares, 2.6 million if we count those subsisting on even smaller plots. For these families, land-hunger was a desperate and ever pressing reality. And if we adopt a more expansive definition, the true dimensions of the problem become even more evident. If we take 20 hectares as a satisfactory standard, then no less than 88 per cent of the farm population, cultivating 0.5 hectares or more, were land-poor – 12 million people or 18 per cent of the entire German population. For this huge group, many of whom were far from reconciled to abandoning the countryside, the shortage of space constantly invoked in nationalist propaganda had a very concrete meaning.

Dividing up the great eastern estates of more than 500 hectares into numerous more modest homesteads was an obvious solution to the problems of overcrowding that afflicted above all the southern and south-western provinces. Since the late nineteenth century land reform had been advocated by a wide spectrum of German opinion from national liberals in the centre – including the sainted Max Weber – to agrarian radicals on the far right.[31] Mass settlement of peasant farmers on the latifundia of East Prussia, they hoped, would consolidate the farming population of Germany. Intensive peasant cultivation of the eastern provinces would help to raise yields and contribute to national self-sufficiency. But most importantly, the creation of a new class of German peasants in the sparsely settled eastern marches would create an ethnic bulwark against the influx of Polish migrants. In 1919 the Weimar Republic explicitly endorsed this nationalist brand of social reform. The new constitution placed agricultural land ownership under a social obligation. Nowhere in the Reich was the share of land held by great estates to exceed 10 per cent. In provinces where this balance was not yet achieved, land purchase committees were progressively to buy up large estates and transfer land into the hands of peasant settlers. In practice, making land allotments suitable for peasant settlement was an extremely expensive business and the Junker interest was hostile. The Weimar Republic's grand programme of settlement therefore made only modest practical progress. Between 1919 and 1933 only 939,000 hectares were transferred to new settlement, less than 10 per cent of the land held by estates of more than 100 hectares. But it was not only the influence of the Junkers that limited the impact of settlement. Simple arithmetic suggested that even a wholesale programme of land reform could not satisfy the ambition of the German agrarians, to bring about a fundamental change in the balance between rural and urban society. If all the land held by farms over 500 hectares in 1933 had been comprehensively expropriated and used to create family farms of 20 hectares, the total number of new homesteads created would have been no more than 500,000. This would have enabled the consolidation of the most precarious peasant population on holdings of below 10 hectares. However, it would not have halted the long-term decline of the agricultural population. Indeed, even if the entire farmland of Germany had been available for redistribution, it would have been sufficient to provide each of Germany's 3 million farming families with an average of only 13 hectares. The conclusion was inescapable. Even under the most favourable assumptions, the territory of Germany was not sufficient to support an agricultural population substantially larger than that to which Germany had been reduced by 1933, at standards of living that were acceptable in relation to those prevailing in the cities.

This conclusion was not lost on the Nazi ideologues. In fact, it was precisely their scepticism about settlement as a remedy for Germany's problems that set the Nazi agrarians apart. As Hitler set out in chapter 4 of *Mein Kampf*, the idea of settlement in Germany's eastern territories was a worthy objective.[32] But to see it as a fundamental solution to Germany's problems was a dangerous illusion. It was one more instance of the liberal fallacy that Germany could prosper through an ever more intensive utilization of its national resources. Only through the conquest of new *Lebensraum* could Germany really prosper and the direction of this settlement drive was obvious. The Third Reich would start where the Germanic tribes had left off '. . . six hundred years ago. We will stop the eternal Germanic migration to the south and west and direct our vision towards the land in the east.'[33] At the Nuremberg trials Darré tried to present himself as a harmless advocate of the peasantry.[34] But there can in fact be no serious doubt that he and Backe were from the start fully complicit in Hitler's dreams of conquest. Backe's ill-fated Ph.D. dissertation of 1926 bore the title 'The Russian Grain Economy as the Basis for the People and Economy of Russia'.[35] But this was no ordinary study of Russian agriculture. Backe's thesis was in fact a manifesto for racial imperialism. For Backe, any constructive development in Russia could only occur through 'the infiltration of foreign ethnic elements of higher quality that will form themselves into an upper class and do battle with the mass of the population. The reservoir [for this infiltration] will be "The People without Space" [The Germans] . . .'[36] To their credit, Backe's examiners failed his thesis. In *voelkisch* circles, however, such racially inspired visions of conquest were commonplace. As the Nazi party prepared for power in the euphoric summer of 1932, Darré elaborated in very specific terms on the future mission of the SS in a report delivered to a secret leadership conference on the future eastern policy of the Third Reich.[37] As Hitler had made clear both in *Mein Kampf* and his 'Second Book', there could be no talk of incorporating the local population of Eastern Europe. The prelude to a massive programme of German settlement would therefore have to be a wholesale demographic 'rearrangement'. Those left in place were to serve as slave labour on German settler farms (*Adelhoefe*). The SS was to be the sword and shield of this settler movement. Himmler and Darré's carefully nurtured clan community would find its ultimate home as a solid racial wall, a close-knit belt of settler farms stretched across the eastern marches of the Reich, behind which the German peasantry could carry out their mission of colonization. Needless to say, such visions were not intended for public consumption. But there is no reason to doubt that they were taken seriously by the Nazi leadership. As hard as it may be for us to credit, agrarian ideology is crucial if we are to understand, not the archaism of Hitler's regime, but its extraordinary militancy.

III

There can certainly be no doubt about the popular energy behind Darré's peasant programme in the early years of the regime. On 1 October 1933 half a million people made their way to the sloping hillside of the Bueckeberg just outside Hameln (Hamelin) to attend the first celebration of the Reich harvest festival, a new national holiday in honour of Germany's peasantry.[38] Hundreds of trains from every farming community in the North German plain converged throughout the day carrying peasant delegations by the thousand, many of them kitted out in traditional garb. The majority of the audience came of their own accord, tempted by the prospect of a day out and the chance to see their Fuehrer in the flesh. But zealous party bureaucrats did their best to ensure that the event was a success. According to one regional coordinator from the Hanover area: 'Only the lame, feeble, lazy and listless should stay at home, as well as those elements hostile to the state.' The gigantic mass of people pouring out of the train stations around Hamelin marched six abreast down gangways secured on either side by uniformed SA, Reichswehr and Labour Service men. Instructions from above were delivered by loudspeakers mounted on Reichswehr observation balloons tethered at strategic points on the itinerary. One can only imagine the impression the gathering must have made on peasants from the provincial backwoods. The intention was clearly to orchestrate an overwhelming spectacle of strength and authoritative political direction. In 1933 this was not helped by the chaos on the slopes of the Bueckeberg itself. For hours the early arrivals waited on the hillside watching the endless columns snaking up from the valley, waiting for Hitler. His aeroplane did not finally descend on Hamelin until the early evening after a busy day receiving dozens of peasant delegations in the capital. As Hitler marched triumphantly to the summit of the Bueckeberg the crowd surged madly around him. Photographs suggest that, unlike at the Nuremberg rallies of later years, the peasants were allowed to get close enough to Hitler to touch him. Dozens of children broke out in front of his entourage clutching garlands of flowers. The last 600 metres of Hitler's approach to the speakers' platform took almost an hour. All the while the massed bands of the Reichswehr blared out the 'Badenweiler Marsch' interspersed by ecstatic 'Sieg Heils' from the crowd. Along with the Fuehrerkult, agrarianism and cod religion, popular militarism was a vital ingredient in the Bueckeberg formula. In later years elaborate mock battles were to become one of the main attractions of the harvest festival, but even in 1933 the soldiers were an essential element of the spectacle. When Hitler finally reached the platform, the tone was set by a fivefold fanfare followed by a 21-shot salute from a battery of field howitzers. Across the Weser valley, shrouded in mist, one could see the 13th Cavalry regiment at full gallop, forming up into a swastika revolving on its axis.

Mass rallies on the Bueckeberg scale were not the place for policy discussion. But they were key dates in the political calendar that dictated the timetable for policy-making in Berlin. They provided the faithful with a chance to celebrate the regime's achievements and they also served as a platform from which to give hints as to the future direction that policy might take. The Bueckeberg on 1 October 1933 served in both capacities. By early October, Hitler had already decided to make his most dramatic and public break with the international community, by leaving the League of Nations and abandoning the international disarmament discussions in Geneva. This was foreshadowed in his speech in characteristically ominous lines.[39] Furthermore, in light of subsequent events, the deliberate display of revived military prowess at the Bueckeberg took on a rather ominous meaning, even if the Reichswehr could manage no more than a cavalry charge. The buzz amongst Darré's faithful, however, did not concern foreign policy. The peasants on the Bueckeberg were fêting the bumper harvest of 1933. They were also there to celebrate a government which, in the last month, had enacted two of the most far-reaching acts of agricultural policy in modern history, measures on a par with the liberal reforms of the early nineteenth century but with the opposite intent.

On 26 September 1933 Darré and Backe had submitted to the surprised cabinet a radical proposal to secure for ever the landholding of the German peasantry. The Draft Reichserbhofgesetz enshrined Darré's *Blut und Boden* ideology in German law.[40] For the purpose of protecting the peasantry as the 'Blood Source of the German People', the law proposed to create a new category of farm, the Erbhof (hereditary farm), protected against debt, insulated from market forces and passed down from generation to generation within racially pure peasant families. The law applied to all farms that were sufficient in size to provide a German family with an adequate standard of living (an Ackernahrung, later defined as a minimum of *c.* 7.5 hectares), but did not exceed 125 hectares in extent. All owners of such farms were required to apply for entry in an Erbhofrolle. The term 'peasant' (*Bauer*) was henceforth defined as an honorary title, reserved for those registered on the Role. Those not entered in the Erbhofrolle were henceforth to be referred to merely as 'farmers' (*Landwirte*). Entry in the *Rolle* protected the Erbhof for ever against the nightmare of repossession. By the same token, it also imposed constraints. Erbhoefe could not be sold. Nor could they be used as security against mortgages. Farms registered as Erbhoefe were thus removed from the free disposal of their immediate owners. Regardless of existing arrangements between spouses, Erbhoefe were to have a single, preferably male, owner who was required to document his line of descent, at least as far back as 1800, the same requirement as for civil servants. 'Peasants' were to be of German or 'similar stock' (*Stammesgleich*), a provision that excluded Jews, or anyone of partial Jewish descent. Furthermore, Erbhof peasants were to be honourable and physically capable, a catch-all provision which excluded those married to Jews, but also the physically disabled or the infertile. In practice, of course, the number of Jews owning farmland, let alone peasant farms, was small and the number of German peasants with Jewish ancestors was also unlikely to be very large. But the symbolic importance of enshrining racial doctrine in property law was nevertheless considerable. Far more important for the average peasant was the fact that the Erbhof law removed his discretion in choosing his heirs. The line of inheritance was now fixed in law. The entire Hof was to be inherited by a single male heir (by Anerbenrecht), normally the oldest or youngest son, otherwise the father or brothers of the deceased. As far as possible, women were deprived of inheritance rights. Surviving widows were entitled to nothing more than maintenance. Other potential claimants to the inheritance were excluded altogether. Siblings who were not to inherit the farm were entitled only to receive vocational training appropriate to the social position of the household. In case of hardship in later life they were entitled to claim the protection of the family farm.

Coupled to this extraordinary intervention in the property rights of German peasants was an equally drastic programme of debt reduction. Backe and Darré proposed that the Erbhof farmers should assume collective responsibility for each other's debts. The debts of all Erbhoefe, variously estimated at between 6 and 9 billion Reichsmarks, were to be transferred to the Rentenbank Kreditanstalt, a state-sponsored mortgage bank. The Rentenbank would repay the original creditors at interest ranging between 2 and 4 per cent depending on the security of the original loan. For their part, all Erbhoefe, whether indebted or not, would in future make an annual payment to the Rentenbank, assessed at 1.5 per cent of the value of their farm (Einheitswert). For those Erbhoefe that were not burdened with debt this clearly constituted a significant imposition. By way of compensation, therefore, those Erbhoefe that were only lightly indebted would receive vouchers, which entitled their sons to privileged treatment in the settlement drive in East Prussia. Backe thereby hoped not only to create solidarity amongst the Erbhoefe but also to couple debt reduction to an accelerated programme of settlement.

The Erbhof law was targeted at the solid middle ground of German farming, approximately 1 million farms in total. It was not intended to cover marginal peasant holdings, let alone the tiny plots of the worker-peasants. Nor, significantly, was it addressed to the traditional benefici-aries of agricultural protectionism, the great estates. Darré was not a popular figure amongst the Junkers. Whereas Hugenberg and the nationalists were loyal to the landowner interest, the 'agrarian bolshev-ists' who were now in control of the Ministry were rumoured to be planning a massive programme of land reform to break the stranglehold of the aristocracy on the east. Of all the economic measures taken by Hitler's government in its first years, the Erbhof law was the measure marked most distinctively by specifically Nazi ideology. Agricultural protectionism, debt default, bilateralism in foreign trade and rearma-ment were all policies that united the competing factions of the Nazi party, Hjalmar Schacht, the nationalists and the military. The Erbhof law did not. It was a measure dictated first and foremost by the specifi-cally Nazi brand of agrarianism formulated by Darré and Backe. Fully aware of his exposed position, Darré had taken care to obtain Hitler's consent for the proposed law during a visit to the Obersalzberg in early September 1933.[41] In agriculture, as in other areas of policy, no major move was made without Hitler's approval. However, in cabinet Darré and Backe faced serious opposition. The Prussian Justice Ministry was indignant at the short notice at which such a 'step of extraordinary and fundamental importance' ('Schritt von ungeheurer grundsaetzlicher Bedeutung') was being brought before cabinet. Schmitt as Reich Minister for Economic Affairs was concerned that the protection offered by the Erbhof law would create a new breed of indolent, 'state peasants' with no interest in efficiency. Reichsbank president Schacht denounced the Erbhof proposal for undermining the entire basis of agricultural mort-gage credit.

Despite these heavyweight objections, Hitler's approval was decisive. Once Hitler had declared the Erbhof principle as unalterable, the law could not be stopped. At the same time, however, he suggested that the main parties continue negotiation over the details of implementation.

The result over the following months was a running battle between the Reichsbank, the RWM and the agrarians, which resulted in a significant compromise. The proposed programme of collective debt relief, the key economic element in the Erbhof project, was shelved. The unburdened Erbhoefe were preserved from the imposition of repaying other farmers' debts. And in his feud with Darré, Schacht went further than this. Since the Erbhoefe were unable to offer their land as security, Schacht issued instructions that they should be denied all forms of long-term credit. Schacht, of course, hoped that by so doing he would force Darré into retreat. However, Darré's position in the early years of the regime was too strong to succumb to such blackmail. Darré's own Ministry saw to it that hard-pressed Erbhof peasants were provided either with direct grants, or with loans guaranteed by the Ministry.[42] In many cases the Erbhof courts were persuaded to relax the highly restrictive rules on using Erbhof land as collateral. And the statistics certainly suggest that this was enough to prevent any serious setback to agricultural investment over the following years.[43]

A more serious problem, in fact, was to sell the Erbhof law to the peasants themselves. In the southern and western regions, where partible inheritance was the rule, the new law was met with blank hostility. But even in the North German plain where Anerbenrecht had long prevailed, the initial excitement about the Reichserbhofgesetz soon turned to discontent. The general principle of undivided inheritance of the family farm was popular enough. But it had never previously overridden the right of the farmer, in the last instance, to decide over the distribution of his property. Everywhere, it was normal to compensate the siblings who did not inherit the family farm. Never had farmers' wives and daughters, who often brought substantial assets into a marriage, been treated so inequitably. And how was a farmer to carry out investment and arrange his finances without access to mortgage credit? In early 1934, the Gestapo office in Hanover, an area of large and prosperous peasant farms, reported widespread anger at the new rules. If Darré and his men were interested in large families, they should think again, since the inheritance rules of the Erbhof law would export the one- or two-child family to the countryside. There was much resentment towards the large farms that were ineligible for inclusion in the Erbhof rules. In an area of Lower Saxony that might have been thought amenable to the Erbhof system, local officials reported simply: 'A large part of the peasantry does not believe that they will be able to live with the Erbhof law.'[44] In practice, what defused the initial headsteam of peasant resistance were a series of amendments to the inflexible framework of the original law and a continuous process of haggling through the new system of Erbhof courts. On the crucial issue of ownership, allowances were made to permit joint ownership of Erbhoefe in the first generation. The courts were also lenient in their handling of requests to take up new credits secured on property. Similarly, there was flexibility over land sales. In the south, one of the main bones of contention was the definition of the lower limit for inclusion in the Erbhof roll. This too was handled flexibly. On one principle, however, the authorities held firm. Whatever concessions were made to the current generation of farmers, the application of the law at the moment of inheritance was strict. Sole inheritance by a single owner was rigorously enforced across the Reich for all Erbhoefe, regardless of local sensibilities.

Given these objections, it is not surprising perhaps that the Erbhof rolls filled rather less quickly than had been hoped in the heady days of the first Reich harvest festival. The Erbhof law did not transform the structure of land ownership in Germany. There were simply not enough farms of the appropriate size. Nevertheless, in the size classes that fell squarely within the Erbhof range, between 10 and 100 hectares, the rate of enrolment was high. The vast majority of medium and large peasant farms were subject to the new regulations. And in those regions where such farms predominated, the Erbhof soon became the norm. In this sense the law accomplished its goal. It consolidated a group of farms whose average size nationally was just less than 20 hectares, a figure that was soon to be defined as the ideal size for efficient family farming in the new order of German agriculture.

IV

The second fundamental step taken by Darré and Backe in the autumn of 1933 was the organization of the Reichsnaehrstand (RNS).[45] It is not too much to say that the setting up of this organization and its associated system of price and production controls marked the end of the free market for agricultural produce in Germany. Agriculture and food production, which until the mid-nineteenth century had been overwhelmingly the most important part of the German economy and which still in the 1930s constituted a very significant element of national product, were removed from the influence of market forces. As Backe clearly articulated even before 1933, the mechanism of price-setting was the key.[46] The RNS made use of prices to regulate production. Higher prices were used to encourage production. Lowering a price in relative terms served to divert production into other lines. But the prices themselves were no longer freely determined by the balance of supply and demand. They were set centrally by the officers of the RNS. Furthermore, to ensure that production developed as efficiently as possible, the RNS extended its control and supervision into every field, barnyard and milking shed in the country. By contrast with the Erbhof law which singled out only a minority of farms, the RNS inserted itself into every nook and cranny of the food chain.[47] In every one of Germany's 55,000 villages, an Ortsbauernfuehrer was responsible for overseeing day-to-day activities. The Ortsbauernfuehrer reported to 500 Kreisbauernfuehrer who in turn reported to one of nineteen Landesbauernfuehrer. From the Reich down to the Kreis level, the organization was split into three functional divisions responsible for general ideology, farmyard and market issues. The political authority for this organization emanated from Berlin, where Darré and Backe directed policy, but the spiritual heart of the new regime was Lower Saxony, the heartland of North German peasant agriculture. Darré himself owned a farm in the region. The town of Goslar hosted both the annual meetings of the German Bauernstand and the ideological department of the RNS. The Nordic peasant association and the newly created international office for peasant affairs were all located there. Goslar was also the location for the Peasant University (Bauernhochschule) and two agricultural high schools. The Bueckeberg, the emotional centre of Darré's peasant empire, was only a few miles away.

The RNS, like Robert Ley's German Labour Front, was a self-supporting organization, operating in close cooperation with the Reich Ministry of Food and Agriculture. Funding for the RNS was provided by a levy on every farm in the country, to the tune of 2 Reichsmarks for every 1,000 Reichsmarks of estate value (Einheitswert). This gave the RNS the means, by the late 1930s, to employ a permanent staff from the Kreis level upwards of over 20,000 people and an annual budget in excess of 100 million Reichsmarks. Not surprisingly, this empire-building gave rise to a constant undercurrent of discontent, both amongst the peasantry for whom the intensive regulation of the RNS brought back memories of World War I, and from the business lobby who mistrusted the regulatory ambition of the RNS.[48] Hjalmar Schacht, in particular, was unrelenting in his criticism. However, when one bears in mind the sheer size of agricultural production in Germany in the 1930s, the RNS organization was hardly disproportionate.[49] In any given year, the value of the grain harvest alone was equal to the annual output of German heavy industry – coal mining, iron and steel. And yet the difference in the organizational effort devoted to the two operations was spectacular. The backwardness of much of German agriculture betokened a chronic lack of expert management and supervision, a deficit which the RNS sought to put right with an endless stream of lectures, educational material and courses as well as more direct interventions into peasant farming practice.

From an economic point of view, one of the most significant innovations of the RNS was that it extended not only to the farms but to all associated industries. The RNS included in its remit the credit cooperatives from which the farmers obtained funds to buy their annual stock of seed grain, the cooperatives and merchants to whom the farmers delivered their produce. It also included the dairies, mills and factories that processed food for consumption in the cities. The RNS did not claim exclusive organizational control over the food industry. It shared control with Schacht's Business Groups and with the relevant organizations of the craft industries. However, the RNS's influence was enormous, since it controlled the prices that the processers paid for their raw materials. Taking agriculture and the food industry together, the RNS was a truly formidable organization. Exercising more or less direct control over more than 25 per cent of German GDP, it was, Darré boasted, the largest single economic unit in the world, with sales of more than 30 billion Reichsmarks.[50] As well as a total of 6 million independent producers, it controlled more than 40 per cent of the total German workforce. The RNS had an even more direct impact on German households, since it controlled the prices at which they purchased their food and drink, which on average accounted for almost 50 per cent of family budgets. Viewed as a unit, the RNS was the largest single building block of the German economy and the ambitions harboured by Darré and Backe in the early 1930s were very far-reaching. At every opportunity in 1933 and 1934 they pushed the model of the RNS as a template of economic organization. Whilst the structure of Schacht's new industrial organization was undecided in 1934, Darré lobbied to have the producers of agricultural equipment, one of the largest elements of the German engineering industry, subordinated to the RNS. In 1933, after the fall of Hugenberg, and again in 1934, after Kurt Schmitt resigned, Darré was rumoured to be bidding to take over the Ministry of Economic Affairs. During the foreign exchange crisis of 1934, Ferdinand Fried, one of the leading propagandists of autarchy, published a blueprint for an organization of the entire industrial economy along RNS lines.[51] Instead of the loosely articulated system of cartels and business groups there would be a single coherent organization with prices and production targets directly controlled by the central authorities. Any such extension of the RNS model, however, was blocked by the opposition of both Schacht and industrial interest groups. In this arena as well, the events of the summer and autumn of 1934 were decisive. By the autumn, it was Darré who found himself fighting a rearguard action against the dominating influence of Schacht's system of exchange and trade controls, a struggle dictated by the fact that German agriculture no less than German industry depended on imported inputs.

In 1933 the mood in farming had been buoyed not only by the activism of the new government, but by perfect weather and a bumper harvest. The RNS started life with the happy task of buying up substantial grain stocks at subsidized minimum prices. The result, by May 1934, was a large reserve of grain both for human and animal consumption that was to provide the RNS with an important cushion in its early years. The generous prices paid to farmers were passed on directly to consumers, who were faced with a sharp increase in the cost of living. After years of falling prices, the official food-price index rose between 1933 and 1934 from 113.3 to 118.3. At the end of 1933, milk prices were raised by the direct intervention of the RNS to 22 Pfennigs per litre. These may seem like small changes, but one can gauge their significance when they are set against the modest budgets on which most German households coped from week to week. Furthermore, the inflation was highly unevenly distributed. One labour office in Hamburg in early 1934 reported panic buying, as consumers were faced with a 10 per cent increase in food prices in a single month. As we have seen, popular unrest about the inflation in food prices was one of the most worrying signs reported by the Gestapo in 1934. So severe were these anxieties that they seem largely to have outweighed any propaganda advantage gained in the struggle against unemployment. This extremely negative response to price increases during the economic and political crisis of 1934 had a remarkably long-lasting impact on the politics of agricultural production in the Third Reich. Thereafter the RNS faced enormous political pressure to refrain from any further price increases even if these were needed to stimulate production.

To make matters worse, by the early summer of 1934 it was clear that there would be no repetition of the record harvest of 1933. Grain yields were sharply down. As a result, on 21 July 1934 Darré was forced to appear before his political rivals in the cabinet to request a daily allocation of foreign exchange to the tune of 1.6 million Reichsmarks for the purchase of imports of food and feed.[52] Without these funds, Darré feared that he would have to contemplate drastic action to curtail household consumption. Given the precarious state of public opinion, this was a highly unattractive option. But in light of the crisis in Germany's balance of payments, no further increase in agricultural imports could be contemplated. In the summer of 1934 Schacht was allocating foreign exchange on a daily basis for only the most essential imports and had taken huge diplomatic risks in defaulting on a large part of Germany's foreign debt. As he had in his struggle with Schmitt, Schacht used the issue of foreign exchange allocation as a weapon against Darré. He demanded that the RNS sell off the stocks of grain accumulated the previous year and accused Darré of having created a bloated bureaucratic monster.[53] Darré responded by spreading the rumour that Schacht, the leading non-Nazi member of the cabinet, was, in fact, an agent of international freemasonry.[54] But beneath the bitter rhetoric the dilemma was real. Since the last decades of the nineteenth century, the German diet had become progressively richer in animal fats and protein. The meat and milk came largely from German animals, but they in turn depended on an abundant supply of imported, high-energy, high-protein animal feeds. Since the 1920s, oilseeds such as soya or peanuts had become a vital underpinning of German dairy farming. With the help of this highly proteinous and fatty diet it had been possible to push the average milk yield of the cows in the German dairy herd to 2,200 litres per year, with the best herds exceeding 4,000 litres per year.[55] Given the relative price of milk and oilseed, this was profitable from the point of view of farmers, but it imposed a serious burden on Germany's foreign exchange balance. In 1928 and 1929 oilseed imports ran at more than 850 million Reichsmarks per annum.[56] During the recession the collapse in world commodity prices did much to reduce this bill, but it remained an outlay of foreign currency that the Reichsbank could ill afford.

Following the disappointment of the 1934 harvest and the desperate foreign exchange crisis, the new challenge for Darré and Backe's organization was to prove itself, not just as a system of income support for the farmers, but as a vehicle for national self-sufficiency. Borrowing a catchphrase from Mussolini, the harvest festival for 1934 had as its slogan: 'The Battle for Production' ('Die Erzeugungsschlacht'). Everything had to be done to ensure a better harvest in 1935. The entire RNS organization was mobilized. More than 400,000 meetings were held and millions of leaflets and booklets on productive efficiency were distributed in every village up and down the country.[57] A separate propaganda budget was established by the RNS to fund the enormous publicity drive. In the rhetoric of the RNS, popular militarism increasingly displaced the language of blood and soil. The Erbhof peasants were now declared the 'shock troops' in the battle for grain. The new slogan of the RNS was: 'Erbhof peasants to the front!' ('Die Erbhofbauern vor die Front!').[58] The Battle for Production is commonly dismissed as little more than a propaganda exercise.[59] But this does no justice to the work of the RNS or to the constraints they faced. Once we allow for the reduction in imported inputs, farm production from domestic sources went up by 28 per cent between 1927 and 1936.[60] Given the structure of German agriculture and dietary patterns in the 1930s, it is hardly surprising that the RNS never achieved self-sufficiency. Maintaining, let alone raising production, with much reduced imports of energy and protein, without being able to substantially raise prices paid to farmers, was a tall order. What the RNS was able to achieve was not only a substantial increase in domestic food production, but also a substantial improvement in the resilience of German agriculture in the face of shocks.[61]

The key to the RNS's activities in the 1930s was the management of the national grain stock on the one hand and a determined effort to reduce the import dependence of the animal food chain. Behind the scenes, the RNS oversaw a significant shift in the nutritional basis of pig and dairy farming.[62] After 1933 the Reichsbank never allocated more than 260 million Reichsmarks to the importation of oilseeds, less than half the level of the Weimar Republic. Though feed was much cheaper in the 1930s, in volume terms the import of oilcake was cut between 1932 and 1936 from 2.3 million tons to less than 1.1 million tons per annum. Imported carbohydrate feeds such as maize, which could be more easily substituted by domestic production, were reduced by an even larger margin. By 1936 German farm animals were consuming only half the imported protein and 30 per cent of the imported carbohydrates that had been available in 1928–9.[63] To cover the gap, farmers were encouraged to substitute hay, turnips and the nutritious by-products of sugar beet farming – sugar beet leaves and heads. To make this feed palatable for the dairy herd, the RNS pushed through the near universal adoption of fermentation silos (Gaerfutterbehaelter). In the 1920s feed fermentation had been rare on German farms. By 1939 the RNS had overseen the installation of more than 8 million cubic metres of capacity. Similarly, the RNS redirected the feed bases of the pig herd.[64] The pig population, which was overwhelmingly the main source of meat for human consumption, served as a vital buffer in the food chain, with the swine herd fluctuating between 23 and 25 million animals, depending on the price of pig meat and the availability and cost of feed. From the point of view of the RNS, the fundamental consideration was the trade-off between using potatoes and bread grain as animal feed, or directly for human consumption. It was normal, prior to the advent of the RNS, for anywhere upwards of 2 million tons of rye to enter the food chain as pork rather than as bread grain. After 1935, given the difficulty of ensuring the grain supply for human consumption, this was no longer sustainable. The price of rye was raised and Germany's pigs were fed overwhelmingly on potatoes and other domestically produced feeds.

What the RNS could not do was to manipulate the weather. After the spectacular harvest summer of 1933, the next few years brought dismal yields. Between 1934 and 1937 the yields of wheat and rye were consistently disappointing. The potato harvest in 1935 was disastrous. In managing these setbacks the RNS's most important resource was the large grain reserve accumulated during the bumper harvest of 1933. Shortfalls in 1934 and 1935 were covered by running down the stock accumulated in the first good year of the Third Reich. This, however, was by its nature a short-term solution. By the summer of 1936 the grain stock, which in early 1934 had stood at 3.5 million tons, had been drawn down to the dangerous level of less than 700,000 tons. This was barely enough to ensure continuity to the new harvest. Already in the summer of 1935 there had been talk of the need to introduce ration cards for bread. For obvious reasons, this was deemed to be politically unacceptable. Instead, the RNS resorted to an organized programme of substitution through which bread flour was diluted with maize meal and even potato starch.[65] In relation to meat and butter the regime was more forceful. To dole out the scarce supply of butter, a discreet system of rationing was introduced in the autumn of 1935, in the form of customer lists kept by the retail outlets. Similarly, the meat supply could not be completely insulated from the impact of the disastrous potato failure in 1935. To ensure that there were sufficient potatoes for human consumption, the RNS culled the pig population and pushed through a sharp increase in the price of pork products. In Berlin, the price of cooked ham was raised by almost 30 per cent between 1934 and 1936. From 1936 onwards the RNS also supplemented the German food balance through imports. More than a million tons of grain were imported in 1936. In 1937 imports rose to in excess of 1.6 million tons. In 1936 there can be no doubt that this was a measure of last resort dictated by the two years of poor harvests and the exhaustion of stocks.[66] But this marked no fundamental turning point in the RNS's strategy and it certainly did not indicate a retreat from the Battle for Production.[67] From 1937 onwards German production was more than adequate to meet domestic demand. Imports were used, not to support current consumption, but to rebuild national grain stocks, which by 1939 were sufficient to cover the population's bread supply for an entire year.[68]

It is easy to misunderstand the constant talk of crisis that afflicted the RNS. At no point was the German population threatened with real food shortages.[69] The 'shortages' of meat and butter were due not to a collapse in supply, but to a huge surge in demand, especially from working-class consumers. Newly re-employed Germans with money in their pockets simply did not want to eat the austere vegetarian diet publicly espoused by the Nazi leadership with their Sunday lunches of vegetable stew. Under normal market conditions, of course, the gap between supply and demand would have been closed by rising prices. Higher prices would have discouraged demand whilst at the same time stimulating greater productive effort on the part of German farmers and attracting a wave of imports from abroad. And the RNS certainly adopted this option in relation to particularly scarce commodities. In general, however, a wholesale increase in food prices was ruled out by fear of provoking the kind of public outrage that had shown itself in 1934. It was this political freezing of the price system that created the appearance of shortages, forcing the RNS to resort to more or less overt forms of rationing. It was not until 1938, with the appearance of real supply problems in dairy farming, that the regime finally raised the prices paid to German farmers for milk. But even then the increase was not passed on to consumers. The price increase thus helped to stimulate production but did nothing to restrain demand.

And the RNS faced complaints not only about food shortages. The secret police who anxiously monitored the mood of the peasantry also found much evidence of dissatisfaction. There was incessant grumbling about low prices and administrative interference.[70] The farmers certainly found themselves more constrained than ever before in peacetime. In the first two years of Nazi rule, 250 new regulations were issued for agriculture: one every three days.[71] Probably the most onerous restrictions imposed by the RNS were those requiring farmers to deliver quotas of milk to licensed RNS dairies. This was a crucial intrusion, because the daily delivery of milk and butter to town was the most important source of ready cash for most peasant farms. The RNS dairies paid cash, of course, but farmers now had to accept a centrally determined price and a delivery schedule not of their own choosing. For those farms located within easy reach of urban markets this was a severe blow. In the Hamelin area, it was estimated that farmers suffered an annual loss in revenue of as much as 2,000 Reichsmarks per farm. Stiff fines had to be levied to force compliance with the delivery quotas. In September 1935, with hundreds of farms delivering suspiciously small amounts of milk to the local dairy, the Gestapo reported what amounted to a 'milk strike' in the Wesermuende area. At the same time, checkpoints on the road to Bremen caught six farmers smuggling 88 pounds of butter for illicit sale in town.[72]

Such examples are certainly picaresque. But the grumblings of the peasantry are rarely a good guide to the economics of agricultural support. German peasants had long memories and a well-cultivated sense of entitlement. They harked back to the golden days of the early twentieth century, when North American competition had been manageable with modest tariffs and minimal government interference. Those days were long gone. When we bear in mind the disastrous situation of world agriculture in the 1930s it is clear that German farmers, in fact, enjoyed a historically unprecedented level of protection and it is hardly surprising that this came at a price. In return for the exclusion of foreign competition from home markets, peasant smallholders had to accept comprehensive regulation and control. Farming in Germany, as in Europe generally, from the 1930s onwards resembled less and less a market-driven industry and more and more a strange hybrid of private ownership and state planning. The true story is told by the level of prices paid to German farmers compared to those that German farmers would have received if they had been exposed to the full force of foreign competition. On this basis the record is completely unambiguous. Though it is true that grain producers clearly enjoyed a larger margin of protection than dairy farmers, for all major types of farm produce the prices paid to German farmers under National Socialism were at least twice those prevailing on world markets. Of course, under Schacht's New Plan, German industry enjoyed blanket protection as well. So the really telling development after 1933 was the sharp improvement in the terms of trade between agriculture and industry. During the Depression, agricultural prices had fallen more than industrial prices. After 1933, the 'scissors' between industrial and agricultural prices shut abruptly. Agricultural prices rose more rapidly than industrial prices and, again, this was out of line with developments in global markets, where agriculture continued to lag behind.

The promise Hitler made on the night of 30 January 1933 was to restore the economic fortunes of the German peasantry within four years and the RNS certainly made good on that pledge. According to figures calculated by Germany's most authoritative economic research agency, total farm income, of which animal products accounted for more than 60 per cent, rose by almost 14 per cent in 1933–4 and by another 11.5 per cent in 1934–5. At the same time the burden of taxes and interest payments on agriculture fell significantly.[73] When we allow for the general deflation in prices, increases in money incomes on this scale more than made up for the Depression. The situation would have been even better if it had not been for the bad weather and poor harvest in 1934.

In its inability to satisfy any of the major constituencies in the Third

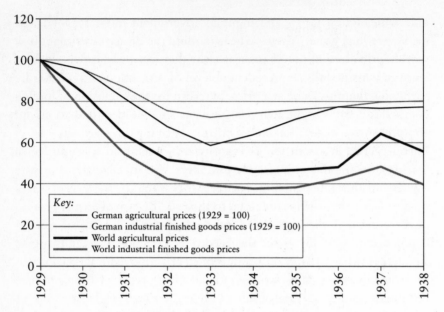

Figure 8. Industrial and agricultural prices,
Germany and the world, 1929–1938 (1929=100)

Reich, the RNS became a victim of its own effort to extend control to every aspect of food production. The creation of the RNS undoubtedly gave the Nazi regime an unprecedented degree of control over a vital part of the economy. But by the same token it politicized a vast swathe of everyday life. The organizational influence of the RNS extended into every home in the land. For the peasantry, there was virtually nothing, except the weather, that could not with some reason be blamed on the RNS and its intrusive regulation. Similarly, consumers found that their everyday tasks of shopping for food and even of preparing family meals were now the subject of political intervention and propagandistic comment.[74] In the final analysis, however, the difficulties faced by the RNS were not attributable to Darré's ideological whimsy or the lumbering incompetence of his organization. The problems facing the RNS were effects of Germany's struggle to manage its rapid economic recovery and its massive programme of industrial restructuring in the face of a binding balance of payments constraint. Since 1934, increases in industrial prices and wages had been held back in an attempt to prevent the industrial boom spilling over into inflation and a further deterioration in German competitiveness. This in turn meant that agricultural prices could not be substantially increased without hurting urban standards of living. At the same time the shortage of foreign exchange dramatically impeded progress in protein and fat production, by restricting the quantity and quality of feed available for the animal herd. All this meant that a gap between the consumer aspirations of Germany's urban population and the productive capacities of German agriculture was bound to make itself painfully felt. Straddling this gap were Darré and the Reichsnaehrstand.

V

By 1936 at the latest it was abundantly clear that even with the most concerted management, it was simply impossible for Germany within the confines of its present territory to achieve anything like self-sufficiency, certainly if the regime was determined to maintain the current standard of living and the current structure of German agriculture. One might speculate, of course, about the possibilities that might have been opened up if the Third Reich had been determined enough to force through the kind of wrenching structural changes being imposed by Stalin on the Soviet Union. Not of course that collectivization was on the cards, not at least until 1945 when the victorious Red Army finally made real the long-standing ambition of reorganizing the great eastern estates.[75] However, by the late 1930s there were German agronomists who were beginning to contemplate the possibility of overcoming Germany's agricultural problems by carrying out a radical concentration of all available land on farms of an efficient size, enabling the RNS to carry out a dramatic programme of rationalization and mechanization.[76] But none of this was practical politics in the 1930s. Instead, the problems facing Germany merely confirmed the belief on the part of the Nazi agrarians, including Hitler, that the ultimate solution to Germany's problems lay in conquest in the East. The calculations of RNS agronomists suggested that to achieve full self-sufficiency with current technology and at the current standard of living, the Third Reich would need to add 7–8 million empty hectares of farmland to the 34 million hectares currently within its borders.[77] It may seem far-fetched to suggest that it was the difficulties of German agriculture that drove the progressive radicalization of Hitler's regime. But when Hitler did attempt to give concrete meaning to his concept of *Lebensraum* it was to agriculture that he turned.

Documented statements of the full imperialist ambitions of the Nazi leadership after 1933 are rare, for obvious reasons. If blurted out publicly by a senior figure in Hitler's regime, they would have caused an international furore.[78] But though they remained largely unspoken there can be little doubt that the ultimate goal of eastern expansion provided an important point of reference for all the senior figures in the Nazi leadership. As we have mentioned, Darré invoked this prospect in the autumn of 1932, months prior to the seizure of power. Hitler did so in February 1933 in his first address to the German military leadership and again in early 1934 to the same audience. Early in 1936, in a speech which has only recently come to light in the archives, Darré sketched out a remarkably concrete vision of German conquest to an audience of RNS officials.[79] The regional expert advisers that Darré addressed were important figures in the RNS. They were all party members. However, they certainly did not belong to the inner circle of the Nazi leadership. All the more significant was Darré's willingness to concretize the long-term ambitions of the regime.

After expatiating at some length on the centrality of the category of race to Nazi ideology and the difference in this respect between National Socialism and Italian Fascism, Darré came to the nub of his remarks. The future of the German *Volk* depended above all on the conquest of new land for agrarian settlement. In complete agreement with Hitler, Darré rejected any possibility of overseas colonial settlement. The only possible area for this expansion was towards the east. So much was familiar to any conscientious reader of *Mein Kampf*. What Darré said next was rather more specific and rather more startling:

The natural area for settlement by the German people is the territory to the east of the Reich's boundaries up to the Urals, bordered in the south by the Caucasus, Caspian Sea, Black Sea and the watershed which divides the Mediterranean basin from the Baltic and the North Sea. We will settle this space, according to the law that a superior people always has the right to conquer and to own the land of an inferior people.

Issues of morality were beside the point. The German *Volk* had the right to claim this enormous territory and to displace those living on it. On earth there was only one law, that the weak should give way to the strong. Darré conceded that some of his audience might find these ideas fantastic or exaggerated. But he invited them to consider the fact that the entire territory from the Rhine to the Urals was in fact no larger than Australia or Canada. The extent of this future German Empire, therefore, would match the territory of just one British Dominion. For the Germans, as masters of all the most modern technologies of transportation, such dimensions were far from excessive. Clearly, Darré had no medieval fantasy in mind, when he reminded his audience that

we Germans are leaders in the field of airships and the most modern commercial aircraft. We Germans build the most modern roads in the world and have high-speed, streamlined railcars running on our railtracks, which vastly exceed in speed any ordinary train.

He was fully aware, of course, that Germany did not currently have the means to settle such a territory, but that was not the point.

It is necessary first of all to have the goal in view and to concern oneself with it. A political goal like this has to be passed by word of mouth from one German farm to another, it must become the foundation of teaching in our peasant schools. Then one day our people will follow the statesman, who seizes the chance open to him, to open up for the People Without Space, the land in the East.

And, Darré warned his audience, this was not a matter of the distant future:

Europe has been released from the paralysis of the Peace of Versailles and is in movement. Ten years will not pass before the political landscape of Europe will again look quite different from today. By then the German people must be ready to master the challenges posed to their race.

PART II

War in Europe

7
1936: Four Years to War

In retrospect it seems obvious that the world began its descent into war, not in 1939, but four years earlier.[1] In October 1935 Mussolini launched his unprovoked attack on Abyssinia. By May 1936, Emperor Haile Selassie was in exile and the Italians had installed a genocidal regime that was to claim the lives of hundreds of thousands of Ethiopians. Two months later, in July 1936, right-wing officers launched their rebellion against the newly elected Popular Front government of Spain. Within weeks, the country was engulfed in a bloody civil war. On the other side of the world, the uneasy balance was destabilized on 6 March 1936 by the overthrow of the liberal Japanese Prime Minister Okada Keisuke and his replacement by the pro-war Foreign Minister Hirota Koki. By the summer of 1937 open warfare had resumed in China. Nazi Germany left no one in doubt as to where it stood in this growing polarization of world politics. Hitler backed Mussolini in Africa and exploited the ensuing Anglo-French distraction to send German troops into the Rhineland, in a flagrant breach of the Treaty of Versailles. In the summer of 1936, Luftwaffe Ju 52 transports ferried Franco and his rebel troops to the Spanish mainland from Morocco. A few months later, the Luftwaffe's Condor Legion went into action over Madrid. Shortly afterwards, in November 1936, Germany allied itself with Japan, the chief aggressor in Asia, in the anti-Comintern pact.

The threat of war was obvious, so obvious in fact that the main global insurance market – Lloyds of London – ceased trading in war cover on property by the end of 1936.[2] The question was whether war was inevitable. The governments of both France and Britain were desperate to avoid a major conflict, not because they expected to lose, but because they believed that only the flanking powers – the United States, the Soviet Union and Japan would benefit. To simplify dramatically, their response to Germany consisted of three elements.[3] For both France and Britain the first priority was to ensure that they could negotiate from a position of defensive military strength. Both countries, therefore, began in 1936 to make serious efforts to respond to Germany's rearmament.[4] The second key element was to undo some of the damage done by the Great Depression in restoring a degree of economic coherence between the three major Western powers – France, Britain and the United States.[5] Since 1933 both Britain and the United States had experienced recovery from the recession, but they were still at loggerheads over America's new agenda of trade liberalization. France for its part languished in the tightening corset of the gold standard. The third and most familiar facet of appeasement, finally, was the effort to construct a package of concessions sufficient to tie Hitler into a lasting peace settlement in Europe. After his re-election in November 1936, Roosevelt revived the multi-sided American agenda that had foundered during the turmoil of 1932–3, floating the idea of a second European peace conference to discuss disarmament, trade and the reapportionment of colonial pos-sessions and the raw materials that went with them.[6] The British, how-ever, were cautious. Opinion in London was divided as to the reliance that could be placed on the United States. More importantly, the British were willing to discuss disarmament, Roosevelt's top priority, only from a position of defensive strength. A general conference would therefore have to wait until Britain's air defences were sufficiently reinforced. In the mean time, Chamberlain preferred a piecemeal approach, offering concessions on colonies, trade and credit in the hope that this would open the way to an agreement on peace and security.

The case for appeasement was powerfully reinforced by the fact that Hitler's regime, after weathering the storm of indignation that followed the Rhineland Aktion in March 1936, seemed to be entering a phase of comparative 'respectability'. In the summer of 1936, Germany hosted the athletes of the world at the Berlin Olympics, accompanied by a mob of international journalists. Goebbels bit his lip as the German press was instructed to give ample coverage to the triumphs of Jesse Owens and other African American athletes.[7] In 1937, at the Paris world's fair, the German pavilion was one of the star attractions.[8] In its fifth year, Hitler's regime could present itself as the model dictatorship. Unemploy-ment had fallen to negligible levels. The economy was booming. Life for millions of German households was returning to something like normal.[9]

The savage wave of repression in 1933–4 had done its job. Inmate numbers in Himmler's concentration camps dwindled to a few thousand. For a time, even the regime's anti-Semitism was toned down. When compared to the warlike aggression of Fascist Italy in Africa and Imperial Japan in China, not to mention the well-publicized excesses of Stalin's show trials, Hitler's government appeared positively reasonable. There were of course those who never wavered from the belief that no peace was possible so long as Hitler remained in power. But they were a minority. The majority in Britain and France, however distasteful they may have found Hitler's regime, were clearly willing to make space in Europe for an authoritarian Germany. An arrangement with the Western powers was on offer after 1936 that would have posed little or no challenge to the internal power structure of Hitler's regime and that would have allowed the Third Reich to be accommodated within a reconstructed international framework of finance and trade.

Furthermore, the majority of Germans would probably have accepted such an arrangement as a highly satisfactory outcome to the 'National Revolution' begun in 1933. All evidence of public opinion suggests that whatever their resentment at the outcome of World War I, the German population was deeply afraid of a European war and would have welcomed a settlement on the basis of the status quo as of 1936.[10] Evidence on attitudes within the business community is frustratingly scant. However, by 1936 there can be no doubt that the balance of the argument had shifted away from an exclusive focus on domestic markets, towards a return to international trade. As the authoritative Berlin Institute for Business Cycle Research pointed out in its report for early May 1936, the principal problem facing the German economy was access to raw materials.[11] This depended on increasing exports. And by the spring of 1936, there were at least some grounds for optimism on this score. The Institute counted the United States, Great Britain, Japan, Sweden, Argentina, Chile, Brazil, Norway, Austria and Belgium amongst the important economies that were now in full recovery. Only the gold-bloc states, led by France, remained in recession.

The opportunities for a major recovery in world trade were clearly there. And, as we shall see, France attempted to take advantage, undertaking a dramatic turn around in economic policy from the summer of 1936. But Hitler and his collaborators in the German leadership systematically refused any rapprochement with the Western powers.

Anti-Communism was one of the constant themes in Hitler's political life, but in 1936 it reached a high pitch. Whereas more conventional minds saw an opportunity in 1936 to reconnect with the world economy, Hitler and his entourage read the formation of Popular Front governments in France and Spain as symptomatic of an upsurge in international Communist activity. And given Hitler's ideological world-view this had wider implications. 'After a period of relative rhetorical prudence' in which Hitler, Goebbels and the rest had refrained from expounding publicly on the wider ramifications of their anti-Semitic cosmology, in 1936 'the basic themes of the Jewish world conspiracy' returned to the fore.[12] Faced with this existential threat, Hitler was in no mood for compromise. Backed by Goering and the army, Hitler evaded the efforts of the British, French and Americans to lure him into a negotiated settlement, in which economic concessions would be traded against a moderation of Germany's rearmament. In private, from the summer of 1936 onwards Hitler was frank. Having consolidated his regime and begun the process of rearmament, he now wanted Germany prepared for war. Hitler had not wavered from his central idea. Though he had yet to clarify the concrete steps, he was determined to realize his dream of expanding the *Lebensraum* of the German people. He knew that this must lead to military conflict, certainly by the early 1940s. He knew that it involved huge risks and he was determined to maximize Germany's chances of success both through systematic military-economic preparation and through opportunistic diplomacy.

This story has of course been told innumerable times and the documents have been raked over by at least four generations of scholars. However, the specific question that concerns us in this book still remains remarkably unclear. Up to now we have not had a full and coherent account of the role played by economic factors in Hitler's drive to war.[13] At the heart of any such discussion must be the dynamic of the armaments economy.[14] On the one hand, armaments were one aspect of industrial and economic activity in which Hitler displayed a lasting and persistent interest. On the other, it was military spending that increasingly dominated the behaviour of the German economy. Of the growth in total national output in Germany between 1935 and 1938 almost half (47 per cent) was accounted for directly by the increase in the Reich's military spending.[15] If we add investment, of which a very large part was dictated either by the priorities of autarchy or rearmament, the share rises to two-thirds (67 per cent). Private consumption, by contrast, was responsible for only 25 per cent of the growth over this same period, even though in 1935 it had accounted for 70 per cent of total economic activity. If we consider only that part of economic activity that was directly under the control of the state, the dominance of military spending is even more dramatic. Of the goods and services purchased by the Reich, the Wehrmacht accounted for 70 per cent in 1935 and 80 per cent three years later. Not surprisingly, therefore, discussion of every aspect of economic policy was increasingly dominated by rearmament. And it was through rearmament in turn that the future of the German economy was coupled to the ultimate question now facing Hitler's government, the question of peace or war.

I

Hjalmar Schacht was, as we have seen, one of the key architects of the new German Wehrmacht. And he was given due credit when the full array of German weaponry was put on public display for the first time at the Nuremberg rally of 1935.[16] But rearmament as it had been planned by Schacht in the summer of 1933 was rearmament within limits: 35 billion Reichsmarks over eight years at an average rate of 4.3 billion Reichsmarks per annum. This was an amount calculated to provide for the two-stage rearmament plan of 1933: four years to build a basic defensive capacity, four more years to build a significant offensive strike force. In 1934, military spending came to 4.2 billion Reichsmarks. In 1935, it rose to between 5 and 6 billion Reichsmarks. Broadly speaking, however, it remained within Schacht's guidelines. It is tempting, therefore, to describe this period as one of 'moderate' rearmament.[17] But, as we have seen, this would be misleading with regard to policy priorities in 1934. And the overshoot in military spending in 1935 was more than mere budgetary indiscipline. It was indicative of a powerful dynamic of acceleration. Increasingly, the Third Reich's rearmament was propelled by the pressures of an international arms race that Germany itself had unleashed. As Germany rearmed, it stirred its potential enemies into action of their own. In the spring of 1935 France lengthened its period of conscription to two years and the British government announced a major reconsideration of its defence policy.[18] France further secured itself in May 1935 with a mutual assistance treaty with the Soviets, which was reinforced by a similar agreement between the Soviets and the Czechs on Germany's eastern border. By 1936 France, Britain, the United States and the Soviet Union were all raising their military spending. And rather than responding with moderation, the German military leadership reacted to each new threat by heightening the pace of the build-up.[19] In December 1933, the army had envisioned a peacetime strength of 21 divisions. By the end of 1934 this was no longer enough. In March 1935 Hitler announced to the world the creation of a German peacetime army of no less than 36 divisions. This escalation by itself was enough to break Schacht's spending guidelines. But by the autumn of 1935, General Ludwig Beck, the new chief of staff, had convinced himself that even if Germany retained its defensive posture, it needed a force capable of responding aggressively to any threat facing its borders. This required a revision of the two-phase scheme that had underpinned rearmament planning since 1931. It also required a dramatic qualitative improvement. The only weapon that seemed to offer any chance of success against Germany's heavily fortified neighbours was the tank. So, in December 1935 Beck added 48 tank battalions to the projected 36 divisions, bringing forward by at least a year the creation of an offensive striking force that had originally been planned for the second phase of rearmament.[20] At the same time, the Luftwaffe began its latest phase of multiplication, with an expansion scheduled to raise its strength from 48 squadrons in August 1935 to over 200 by October 1938.[21] In March 1936, Hitler accelerated further by authorizing the Luftwaffe to begin the immediate introduction of the latest generation of streamlined, all-metal aircraft.[22]

The economic consequences were dramatic. For 1936, the armed forces envisioned budgets well in excess of the annual figure agreed by Schacht in 1933.[23] The balance of payments implications were no less serious. For 1936, the Wehrmacht demanded twice as much imported metal and iron ores, rubber and oil as it had received in 1935. Furthermore, rearmament on this scale had serious long-term implications for the structure of the German economy. Hundreds of thousands of jobs would become dependent on military business, which had an uncertain future beyond the immediate period of rearmament. The Wehrmacht, however, was no longer willing to exercise self-restraint. On 18 November 1935, Defence Minister Blomberg instructed the branches of the armed forces to ignore all financial limitations.[24] In 1934, as we have seen, Schacht had outmanoeuvred his rival at the RWM, Kurt Schmitt, by promising the Wehrmacht anything it needed. Now he was presented with the bill. In December 1935, when confronted with Blomberg's raw material demands, Schacht's response was categorical:

You expect from me that I should procure the necessary foreign exchange for your needs. I must respond that under current conditions I can see no possibility of doing so . . . if the demand is now . . . for increased rearmament, it is of course far from my mind to modify the support I have given for years to the greatest possible rearmament, both before and after the seizure of power. It is my duty, however, to point out the economic limits that constrain any such policy.[25]

The clash with the military came as such a shock to Schacht that he began to reconsider the entire basis of the policy he had pursued since 1933. In November 1935, the British embassy in Berlin was believed to have reliable information that Schacht 'would seize a favourable opportunity to devalue the Mark to sterling level'.[26] Whatever credence one attaches to such rumours, it is certain that Schacht believed himself to be facing a renewed balance of payments crisis. In the autumn of 1935, the Reichsbank predicted that in the coming year Germany would face a net foreign currency shortfall of at least 400 million Reichsmarks. To cover this deficit the Reichsbank held reserves of only 88 million Reichsmarks. By March 1936, after two years of reduced imports, Germany's stocks of foreign raw materials were at a desperately low ebb and there was a real threat that industrial production would be severely interrupted.[27] As we have seen, the same was true for grain. Most importantly, the steel industry, led by Ernst Poensgen of the Vereinigte Stahlwerke, was seriously alarmed about its dwindling stocks of iron ore and scrap metal. To conserve these reserves and to avoid a sudden interruption to supply, the Ruhr advocated a general slowdown in steel production. The industrialists held off from implementing this emergency measure only because the Reich Ministry of Economic Affairs feared that it would precipitate a nationwide panic.[28] The military for their part were more worried about rubber and oil. In 1936, Germany's rubber plants were operating with stocks of raw material sufficient to cover less than two months of normal production.[29] Even more threatening was the situation with regard to oil, where Germany remained dependent on deliveries from Romania. Though Schacht had been instrumental in setting in motion the expanded synthetic fuel programme in 1934, he was now accused of dragging his feet. And oil was not the only point of contention. In early 1936, Schacht made an enemy of Wilhelm Keppler, Hitler's personal economic adviser, by vetoing a proposal from Keppler's staff to alleviate the constraints on the steel industry by increasing the extraction and smelting of low-grade German iron ore.[30] In 1934 Keppler and Schacht had been allies. Now they were bitterly at odds.

As a direct result of the arms acceleration, a fault line had opened within the leadership of the Third Reich. Schacht was at loggerheads not only with Darré and the agrarians but also with the military and Keppler and his staff. Only Hitler could resolve a dispute of this seriousness. But Hitler's attention was consumed in early 1936 by the imminent remilitarization of the Rhineland – by far his boldest and most dangerous foreign policy move to date. Only after this had been brought to a triumphant conclusion on 7 March did he resolve the question of economic priorities. On 4 April 1936 Hitler appointed Hermann Goering as special commissioner for foreign exchange and raw materials.[31] Goering had previously played only a marginal role in economic policy. Amongst the Nazi elite, however, he enjoyed the reputation of being a pro-business conservative. Indeed, Schacht at first supported Goering's appointment, in the belief that he would shield the Reichsbank and Ministry for Economic Affairs against criticism from the Nazi party. But this was a severe miscalculation. Goering was hugely ambitious. He was ruthless. And, more importantly, as head of the Luftwaffe he was absolutely committed to the priority of rearmament. Moreover, Hitler's instructions to Goering were absolutely clear. His mission was not to strike a balance between military and civilian needs. The purpose of his commission was to ensure 'continued military preparation'.

By the end of April 1936 Goering had assembled his own expert staff and begun a series of meetings to discuss the future of Schacht's New Plan.[32] The results were not encouraging. The New Plan export subsidies were having some effect. However, their effectiveness depended largely on the state of demand abroad, over which Germany had no control. Meanwhile, the Wehrmacht's requirement for raw materials was increasing month by month and, due to the recovery in the international economy, the price of imported raw materials had risen by at least 10 per cent since 1935. Furthermore, by the early summer of 1936 the talk was no longer simply of rearmament. On 12 May 1936 Goering asked the committee on export questions to consider where Germany would get its raw materials 'if we are at war tomorrow'. On other occasions there was ominous talk of an 'emergency' or the 'A scenario'.[33] Faced with this possibility, the Wehrmacht launched into another round of expansion planning. In June 1936, Secretary of State Milch at the Air Ministry issued the order that the German air force should reach full strength by the spring of 1937, rather than in 1938. The army, for its part, raised its targeted peacetime strength from 36 divisions to 43, including 3 Panzer divisions and 4 of motorized infantry. Furthermore, a new plan was prepared in June 1936 which called for the provision by October 1940 of the infrastructure and equipment needed for a field army of 102 divisions and more than 3.6 million men.[34] This was a force larger even than that commanded by the Kaiser in 1914. The implications of this extraordinary expansion programme were spelled out in detail by Major General Friedrich Fromm, head of the central administrative office of the German army (Allgemeines Heeresamt), in a memorandum which marks a turning point in the history of the Third Reich.[35] Not only did it give the clearest statement of the kind of army that the Third Reich was trying to construct. Fromm also described with stark clarity the consequences of any such armaments programme for the German economy.

The offensive force that Ludwig Beck had first envisioned in December 1935 certainly had a sharp armoured tip.[36] Fromm budgeted for 3 full Panzer divisions, each with more than 500 tanks.[37] He also provided for 4 fully motorized infantry divisions and 3 so-called light divisions, which by the late 1930s were to be equipped with more than 200 armoured fighting vehicles. In addition, the war army of 1939 was to include 7 independent Panzer brigades, each capable of forming the nucleus of a Panzer division. All of these units were to form part of the standing army, so that they would be ready for immediate action at the outbreak of war. The precise number of tanks envisioned by Beck and Fromm is not easy to estimate, given the fluctuating establishment of these novel formations, but the total number cannot have been less than 5,000 vehicles. In 1936, however, the only tanks in series production in Germany were the Mark I and Mark II light tanks, both of which were armed only with machine guns. For the offensive purposes that Beck had in mind they were clearly inadequate. The hard core of Germany's armoured fighting force, as envisioned in 1936, was to consist of 1,812 medium tanks – Mark III and Mark IV models. These, however, were still in development in 1936 and were not expected to enter production until 1938. Fromm did not expect Germany's actual strength in battleworthy medium tanks in 1939 to exceed much more than 870 vehicles. This was clearly a considerable force. But one should not imagine that the German army plan of 1936 was sufficient to give the Wehrmacht overwhelming advantage in the international arms race. Scheduled production of French medium and heavy tanks significantly outstripped that of Germany in the late 1930s.[38]

More impressive than the armoured strength of Hitler's new army was its sheer size. Fromm's plan provided for 68 infantry divisions backed up by 21 second-string Landwehr divisions. The best-equipped infantry divisions, numbering 17,700 men, were provided with between 500 and 600 trucks, 390 cars and a similar number of motorcycles. But for the bulk of its transport the German army relied on horses.[39] As compared to a wartime complement of 120,000 trucks, mainly drafted from private business, Fromm allowed for 630,700 horses, one animal for every four men in the active field army. In the average Wehrmacht infantry division, cars and trucks were outnumbered by carts and wagons. A large part even of the heavy artillery was to be horse-drawn.[40] And it is also instructive to examine the distribution of expenditure foreseen by Fromm's budget. Of the 35.6 billion Reichsmarks to be spent between 1937 and 1941, less than 5 per cent (4.7 percent) was earmarked for tanks and motor vehicles. By contrast, guns, artillery and ammunition were allocated 32 per cent of the budget. Fortifications, mainly on Germany's western borders, claimed no less than 8.7 per cent, almost twice the amount to be spent on the motorized toops. None of this calls into question the qualitative leap marked by the army's planning of 1936. The German military was now embarked on the accelerated construction of a gigantic force, of which a significant element was explicitly intended for mobile, offensive operations. But we must clearly set aside any idea that the armaments effort of the Third Reich was carefully tailored towards the construction of a motorized 'Blitzkrieg' juggernaut. In quantitative terms the German army's expansion undoubtedly set new standards. But in qualitative terms, even in its moments of most florid fantasy, the German army remained rooted in a society characterized by very uneven development.

Fromm's report left no doubt that constructing this enormous fighting force would stretch the German economy to its limit. Stockpiling the equipment for a wartime army of 102 divisions in the space of only four years would require a huge acceleration in military spending. Over the next three years, the army alone would need to spend 9 billion Reichsmarks per annum, twice the figure agreed for the entire Wehrmacht in the summer of 1933. Setting aside the question of whether sufficient foreign exchange could be provided, the implications for the German economy and the Reich's finances were drastic. To produce the wartime equipment for a force of more than 4 million men in the space of only four years, large parts of German industry would have to be retooled. New factories would need to be brought into production in the shortest possible time. And the question would have to be faced of what was to be done with this capacity, once the targets for the accelerated build-up had been met. If the plants were to be maintained at war readiness, the ordnance office would need to issue huge follow-on orders for equipment that went far beyond the peacetime needs of the armed forces. If the Reich wished to escape these costs, it would have to undertake an extremely difficult process of conversion to civilian activity. It would be surprising if this could be accomplished without serious unemployment. And even if it were successful, a conversion to civilian production would leave Germany unready to actually resupply its enormous army in the case of war. As Fromm put it: 'Shortly after completion of the rearmament phase the Wehrmacht must be employed, otherwise there must be a reduction in demands or in the level of war readiness.' Before the army therefore embarked on this breakneck expansion, the political leadership needed to answer the question: was there 'a firm intention of employing the Wehrmacht at a date already fixed'?

The question of war and peace was now unavoidable. The gigantic machinery of mobilization could not be kept spinning indefinitely. If there was no intention to use the army at a predetermined point, then the whole rationale for rearmament at the pace being envisioned in the summer of 1936 had to be questioned. Given the scale of the resources required, means and ends could no longer be separated. War now had to be contemplated not as an option, but as the logical consequence of the preparations being made.

II

Not surprisingly, Fromm's top secret memorandum did not circulate widely. But in the summer of 1936 it must have been obvious to anyone closely involved in Berlin politics that the Third Reich had once more reached a crossroads. As in 1934, the foreign exchange situation was bad enough in its own right to force drastic action.[41] To stave off immediate disaster, Goering ordered a draconian intrusion into private property. Every dollar, franc or pound, every ounce of gold and all Germany's remaining foreign assets were to be put at the disposal of the Reich. Significantly, the man Goering charged with responsibility for setting up the special investigative service for foreign currency assets was Reinhard Heydrich of the SS.[42] Schacht opposed these measures, fearing that signs of desperation would shake confidence in the Reichsmark. But over the next twelve months Goering's teams bagged 473 million Reichsmarks in foreign currency, enough to see Germany through at least the next eighteen months.[43] And, in preparation for a showdown, Goering began consolidating his position against Schacht. On 6 July, a day before Heydrich's appointment, Goering called a meeting with Keppler and Herbert Backe, of the Agriculture Ministry. On the agenda was the creation of a new organization, under Goering's control, charged with an all-out drive to make Germany ready for war by expanding its domestic sources of food and raw materials. Goering guaranteed both the necessary funds and the necessary political protection against Schacht. He also announced that he was due to discuss the entire matter with Hitler during the Fuehrer's summer retreat in Berchtesgaden.[44] At the same time, Goering commissioned one final round of expert reports on the problem of the German balance of payments. This time they were to address the great taboo of Nazi economic policy, the question of devaluation. Could the pressure on the balance of payments be alleviated by reducing the exchange rate of the Reichsmark to a more competitive level?

Dr Trendelenburg, a veteran civil servant, who now occupied a key position in the state industrial holding, VIAG, was asked to analyse the devaluation from a technical point of view.[45] His report was considered so sensitive that the Reich printers produced a print run of only ten copies. The copies were numbered, the formes of type at the Reichsdruckerei were destroyed and all the paperwork of the committee was shredded. On the basis of the data compiled by Trendelenburg, Goering then commissioned Carl Goerdeler, the Oberbuergermeister of Leipzig and former Reich price commissioner, to make a general assessment of the policy options facing Germany. The resulting memorandum was a remarkably frank statement of the gravity of the choices facing Germany.

Goerdeler began by rejecting Schacht's existing system of export promotion. The New Plan had succeeded in offsetting much of Germany's competitive disadvantage in price terms. However, Goerdeler did not believe that Germany's trading partners would long tolerate a system that was tantamount to state-subsidized dumping. Instead of promoting trade, Germany's efforts to increase its exports would result only in hostility and aggressive countermeasures. Clear evidence of this was provided by the further deterioration in Germany's already strained commercial relations with the United States.[46] On 11 June 1936 the United States threatened Germany with the imposition of a punitive tariff unless it discontinued the subsidy system. Diplomatic efforts to resolve the crisis were rebuffed by Secretary of State Cordell Hull and in early August Germany was forced to give way. Given the critical state of Germany's currency reserves, Schacht could not afford an all-out trade war with America that might set an example for Canada and the rest of the British Empire to follow.[47] A full-scale confrontation was avoided, but at the expense of German exports to the United States, which now dwindled to complete insignificance. As far as Goerdeler could see, the only way to avoid a steady deterioration in Germany's international economic position was devaluation accompanied by a liberalization of foreign exchange movements. Goerdeler acknowledged the risks involved, but also pointed out the enormous advantages. By bringing the German price level into line with that of its competitors, devaluation would render redundant the entire cumbersome apparatus of trade promotion. German firms would at last be able to compete on level terms. Such an adjustment, however, could only be successful if it gained the acceptance of Germany's trading partners. If they responded by allowing their own currencies to devalue or by imposing trade restrictions, German exporters would gain no advantage. Devaluation, if it was to bring its full benefits, would have to be accompanied by a diplomatic rapprochement with Britain and America.

In the summer of 1936, Léon Blum's Popular Front government in

Paris was pursuing precisely this option.[48] Whilst Roosevelt and Hull were taking Germany to the brink of a trade war, a secret French delegation was welcomed in Washington to discuss a joint effort to realign the world's currencies. As Spain descended into civil war, both the French and American governments seized on the currency issue as an opportunity to cement the solidarity of 'the three great democracies' and to secure the basis for a future of 'liberal peace and prosperity'. The British, the third 'great democracy', did not like the high-flown rhetoric but the Treasury and Bank of England gave their full backing to the French desire to go off gold, promising to abstain from any retaliatory action. Nor was it a coincidence that Britain finally entered into discussions of a possible trade agreement with the United States in June 1936. As the British Foreign Secretary, Anthony Eden, put it, 'If peace is the aim of diplomacy' then 'no greater tasks lies before us than to retain the goodwill of the United States'.[49]

There are clear parallels in the arguments being offered at the same time in Berlin. In his memorandum for Goering, Goerdeler emphatically stressed the 'grandiose possibility' that a German return to the world economy would herald the beginning of a new era of international economic cooperation.[50] The precondition for cooperation, however, was an end to unilateralism. Germany would need the support of the British and French. It would need to bring its military spending under control. And Goerdeler went further than that. He believed that concessions would also have to be made on the 'Jewish question, free-masonry question, question of the rule of law, Church question': 'I can well imagine that we will have to bring certain issues ... into a greater degree of alignment with the imponderable attitudes of other peoples, not in substance, but in the manner of dealing with them.'[51] One is tempted to say that, given the mood prevailing in London and Paris, Goerdeler exaggerated the price that Germany would have had to pay for an economic accord. Moderation of rearmament certainly was a sine qua non. But the idea that the British and French would have made the anti-Jewish laws of 1935, or the treatment of the Churches, into a sticking point seems far-fetched. Goerdeler was pursuing an agenda that was as much domestic as international. What he wanted for Germany was a return to conservative respectability. He clearly saw a realignment with world opinion as a form of insurance against any further radicalization of Hitler's regime. And this same logic carried over into economic policy. One of the principal attractions of a policy of devaluation and exchange liberalization for Goerdeler was precisely that it would have a bracing effect on German public finances. To maintain the confidence of the currency markets following a devaluation, Germany would need to return to fiscal discipline. In the short run, the effects on the German economy might be severe. Goerdeler calculated that there might be as many as 2 to 2.5 million unemployed. But, as a veteran of Bruening's deflation, Goerdeler did not shrink from such hardships. A liberal policy demanded a long view. In due course, Germany's export industries would revive. And if Germany could lead the world back to harmonious commercial peace, the longer-term prospects were limitless. In any case, Germany had little choice. In 1936 it could still take the initiative. But from this point onwards, as Germany's situation became ever more strained, the 'enemy' would increasingly have the power to dictate terms. The longer Germany hesitated, the worse would be its bargaining position.

Goerdeler's memorandum was a rare act of individual courage, as was his decision, soon after 1936, to become a leading figure in the conspiratorial opposition to Hitler's regime.[52] For Goerdeler, there was a straight path that led from 1936 to the failed bomb plot of July 1944 and to Ploetzensee jail, where he was executed on 2 February 1945. Very few members of Germany's establishment were willing to follow him down that hard road. But there can be little doubt that his sentiments on economic policy were widely shared. Prominent business figures expressed their sympathy, including Voegeler of the Vereinigte Stahlwerke, Robert Bosch and Hermann Buecher of AEG.[53] They shared Goerdeler's contempt for the parvenu corruption of the Nazi party. And they shared his anxiety that the recovery driven by ever increasing state spending was unsustainable. In 1934, as we have seen, Schacht and Hitler had foreclosed any debate on devaluation, and conservatives like Goerdeler had sided with him.[54] Now even men like Goerdeler and Trendelenburg could see that devaluation was the only way for Germany to return to something like economic normality. According to widely disseminated rumours, business interests had lobbied Schacht hard in the spring of 1936 to abandon the system of export levies in favour of a currency adjustment.[55] And it was more than coincidental that, across the Rhine, French conservatives were undergoing exactly the same conversion at exactly the same moment. Faced with the prospect that Léon

Blum's Popular Front government, which depended on Communist support, might complement its policy of domestic work creation with the imposition of exchange controls – Schacht's formula since 1933 – the French right wing abruptly abandoned its dogged attachment to the gold standard. If the choice was between devaluing the franc in cooperation with Britain and America, or following Germany into 'economic fascism', the decision was easy.[56]

In Hitler's Germany, however, there could be no such open discussion.[57] Throughout the summer, various members of the Reichsbank board commissioned reports from their economic staff on the pros and cons of devaluation and the implications for Germany of a French departure from gold. Unlike in 1934, when even the Reichsbank's confidential memoranda had steered clear of any mention of rearmament, the connection was now too obvious to be ignored. Perhaps the most comprehensive of these papers was compiled by three Reichsbank department heads under the title 'The German Currency in Case of a Devaluation of the Goldbloc'.[58] It was far from optimistic. The consequences for Germany of a French devaluation would certainly be serious. But determining the appropriate response raised fundamental strategic questions. A successful devaluation, the Reichsbank officials concurred with Goerdeler, had to be flanked by fiscal consolidation.

The choice of whether we should in this case maintain our parity [with gold] will in the first instance have to be judged in relation to the question of rearmament. Maintaining the parity will make rearmament more difficult but not impossible. Devaluation and rearmament, by contrast, are mutually exclusive; one has to choose one or the other. If not, devaluation will slide into inflation, a second definitive devaluation would follow and rearmament would in any case be brought to a halt.[59]

Since the report was gloomy about the prospects for Germany, whether it chose to devalue or not, it is hard to avoid the conclusion that the real preoccupation of the Reichsbank economists was less the question of devaluation than the extraordinary financial demands of rearmament. As we have seen, Schacht had raised this concern already in December 1935. And his increasing criticism of excessive military spending was backed up in early 1936 by a series of internal Reichsbank reports stressing the severity of Germany's fiscal and monetary imbalance.[60] By the summer of 1936, however, Schacht was no longer the political force he had been in the first eighteen months of the regime. Hitler's dictatorship was now too firmly established. There was no general démarche by the Reichsbank leadership. Instead, the Reichsbank clung to the elaborate system of exchange and trade controls that had been built up since 1931 and colluded in the secrecy surrounding the Trendelenburg and Goerdeler reports. There was no coherent opposition to the course being pushed by Goering and he made easy meat of Goerdeler. In formal conversation, Goering dismissed Goerdeler's arguments as 'completely unusable'.[61] In private, he was less complimentary. Goering's personal copy of the Goerdeler memorandum is dotted with indignant marginalia – 'Oho!', 'What cheek', 'Nonsense'. Goering forwarded Goerdeler's report to Berchtesgaden, where the Fuehrer was himself drafting a memorandum on German economic policy, with the following comment: 'This may be quite important, my Fuehrer, for your memorandum, since it reveals the complete confusion and incomprehension of our bourgeois businessmen. Limitation of armaments, defeatism, incomprehension of the foreign policy situation alternate. His [Goerdeler's] recommendations are adequate for a mayor, but not for the state leadership.'[62]

In the end, everything hung on Hitler. And Hitler clearly appreciated the importance of the moment. He was not in the habit of drafting policy statements and did so only at decisive moments in the history of his regime. The memorandum of August–September 1936 is remembered above all as an economic policy statement.[63] Indeed, it is universally referred to as the 'Four Year Plan memorandum', providing Goering with the warrant for his new economic programme. But Hitler's statement has as much to say about grand strategy and armaments as it does about economics. This was typical of Hitler's rambling style. But given the questions facing Germany in 1936, a wide-ranging response was clearly called for. The argument was no longer about the balance of payments. What was at stake was the future of the Third Reich.

True to form, Hitler started his memo with a restatement of the basic themes of *Mein Kampf*. The essence of politics was 'the historical struggle of nations for life'. This had manifested itself in a succession of major clashes: Christianity and the barbarian invasion, the rise of Islam, the Reformation. The French Revolution marked the beginning of the modern era. Ever since, the world had been moving 'with ever-increasing speed towards a new conflict, the most extreme solution of which is

Bolshevism; and the essence and goal of Bolshevism is the elimination of those strata of mankind which have hitherto provided the leadership and their replacement by worldwide Jewry'. Compromise was impossible: 'A victory of Bolshevism over Germany would lead not to a Versailles Treaty, but to the final destruction, indeed to the annihilation, of the German people . . .' Given the apocalyptic nature of the threat, rearmament could not be 'too large, nor its pace too swift'. 'However well balanced the general pattern of a nation's life ought to be, there must at particular times be certain disturbances of the balance at the expense of other less vital tasks. If we do not succeed in bringing the German army as rapidly as possible to the rank of premier army in the world . . . then Germany will be lost!' Economic policy was entirely subordinate to this overriding priority: 'The nation does not live for the economy, for economic leaders, or for economic or financial theories; on the contrary, it is finance and the economy, economic leaders and theories, which all owe unqualified service in this struggle for the self-assertion of our nation.'

Germany's problems in this struggle for survival were all too familiar. 'We are overpopulated and cannot feed ourselves from our own resources.' But after four years of government, Hitler was tired of being brought up against these age-old problems. He was now impatient for action. 'There is . . . no point in endless repetition of the fact that we lack foodstuffs and raw materials; what matters is the taking of those measures that can bring about a final solution for the future and a temporary easing of conditions during the transition period.' Hitler did not expand on this 'final solution', beyond reiterating the euphemisms of *Mein Kampf*: 'The final solution lies in extending our living space . . .' It was only in the final lines of the memorandum that he returned to this point. The bulk of the paper was taken up with spelling out the measures necessary in the interim. Hitler rejected point blank any idea that Germany could save itself by raising exports. Given the competition on foreign markets there was little prospect of any relief from this side. He wasted no words on the subject of devaluation. Instead, he insisted that Germany's economic preparations should be approached with the same 'tempo', 'determination' and 'ruthlessness' that was applied in military affairs. Specifically, Germany needed to intensify its efforts to replace imported raw materials with domestic substitutes. Three areas were of immediate importance: petrol, rubber and iron ore. Questions of economic viability, technical feasibility 'and other such excuses' had to be set aside.

It is not a matter of discussing whether we are to wait any longer . . . it is not the job of . . . government to rack . . . [its] brains over methods of production . . . Either we possess today a private industry, in which case its job is to rack its brains about methods of production; or we believe that it is the government's job to determine methods of production, and in that case we have no further need of private industry.

Agencies of the state had no business siding with private management, as Schacht had done a few months earlier in backing the Vestag against Keppler over German iron ore.

The job of the Ministry of Economic Affairs is simply to set the national economic tasks; private industry has to fulfil them . . . Either German industry will grasp the new economic tasks, or else it will show itself incapable of surviving any longer in this modern age in which a Soviet state is setting up a gigantic plan. But in that case it will not be Germany that will go under, but at most a few industrialists.

Characteristically, Hitler's threats reached their climax in the final section of his memorandum dealing with business evasion of foreign currency controls. Fully in tune with Goering and Heydrich's requisitioning drive, Hitler railed against those who hoarded precious foreign assets:

Behind this in some cases there lies concealed the contemptible desire to possess, for any eventuality, certain reserves abroad, which are thus withheld from the grasp of the domestic economy. I regard this as a deliberate sabotage . . . of the defence of the Reich, and I therefore consider it necessary for the Reichstag to pass the following two laws:
1. a law providing the death penalty for economic sabotage, and
2. a law making the whole of Jewry liable for all damage inflicted upon the German economy by individual specimens of this community of criminals . . .

Apart from these specific measures, Hitler called for a 'multi-year plan' to tackle the various challenges he had outlined. The point here was political. Only when the National Socialist state had displayed the kind of ruthless leadership that the situation demanded would it be possible to ask the German people to make the kind of sacrifices that might well be needed. In particular, Hitler seems to have had in mind the dire predictions of the summer, which suggested that an acute shortage of foreign currency might necessitate the introduction of rationing for clothing and animal fats. Such burdens could only be borne if the German people knew that the party was providing firm leadership. Hitler's memorandum therefore concluded with a twofold mission for the new economic plan:

I. The German army must be operational within four years.
II. The German economy must be fit for war within four years.

Hitler thus answered the questions posed by Goerdeler and Fromm in a manner entirely consistent with the general position he had adopted since the 1920s. Germany's ultimate salvation could come only through conquest not trade. And the time-horizon for opening this campaign was four years, fully in line with the army's expansion plan.

The significance of these instructions is indicated by the way in which the 'Four Year Plan memorandum' was subsequently treated. In September 1936, only Goering and the War Minister, Blomberg, were given the complete text. Albert Speer inherited a copy from Fritz Todt in 1942. Hjalmar Schacht, against whom much of Hitler's argument was clearly directed, never saw the full text. But when he got wind of Hitler's intentions he panicked. Early in the afternoon of 2 September, he telephoned Colonel Thomas of the Wehrmacht's military-economic office, one of his closest allies in the military, begging him to intercede with Blomberg. The synthetic technologies on which Hitler placed so much faith were not yet ready. By announcing Germany's intention to break with the world market, Hitler was 'tightening the rope around our own neck'.[64] Germany's trading partners would react angrily, negating all Schacht's efforts to raise exports. Indeed, Britain and other European countries might be prodded into following the American lead, closing their markets to subsidized imports from Germany. But Schacht's former friends in the military had now deserted him. Blomberg refused to intercede and Thomas undertook no initiative of his own.[65] At a secret meeting of the Prussian ministerial council on 4 September 1936, Goering read out key passages from Hitler's memorandum.[66] In the stenographic notes of the minutes, his message was reduced to the following prophetic lines: 'Starts from the assumption that clash with Russia is unavoidable. What the Russians are able to do, we can do as well.' In future, all economic measures were to be taken 'as if we were in a state of imminent war!' Five days later the Fuehrer's Four Year Plan was announced to the cheering crowds at the annual party rally at Nuremberg, flanked by vicious anti-Semitic tirades both by Goebbels and Hitler.[67] This version, however, made no mention of war. The purpose of the Four Year Plan was merely to secure the German standard of living and to provide employment for German workers beyond the end of the rearmament boom.

The weeks that followed were filled with considerable uncertainty. Though Goering had publicly identified himself as the figurehead of the new 'multi-year plan', he had no official mandate from Hitler. Populist elements in the party were incensed at the prominence claimed by Goering, who was widely thought of as an establishment figure.[68] Nor had Schacht been completely outmanoeuvred. In late August he had been in Paris to hold discussions on improving Franco-German economic relations. He apparently raised the issue of colonial concessions and the immediate problem of securing sufficient raw materials to allow the German industrial economy to continue functioning normally.[69] One report even had him seeking a 'currency regulation' with the French, that is, a coordinated devaluation of the Reichsmark and the franc. It seems, in fact, that Schacht may have wanted to hitch the Reichsmark to the tripartite currency agreement that was finally announced to the world's press early on 26 September 1936. The Swiss, Dutch, Czechs and Italians all followed the French in devaluing over the following weeks. The ensuing struggle in Berlin was recorded in the diary of Joseph Goebbels, which for 30 September has the following brief entry: 'Schacht wanted to devalue . . .' He was prevented only by the prompt intervention of Walther Funk, former business editor and since 1933 Secretary of State in Goebbels's Propaganda Ministry. Hearing of Schacht's intention, Goebbels wrote: 'Funk went straight to Fuehrer . . . he intervened.' Only by this timely intervention, Goebbels boasted, had Funk 'prevent[ed] a German inflation'.[70]

The position Hitler had formulated in the Four Year Plan memorandum was final. There would be no devaluation and no backing away from the priority of rearmament. On 18 October Goering was given Hitler's formal authorization as general plenipotentiary for the Four Year Plan. Over the following days he presented decrees empowering him to take responsibility for virtually every aspect of economic policy, including control of the business media.[71] Schacht remained both as Minister for Economic Affairs and as president of the Reichsbank. But insiders noted that Goering had dropped the qualifier from his official title as 'Prime Minister of Prussia' and was now commonly referred to simply as 'Prime Minister'. Goering was now established as the second man in the Reich, not only as head of the Luftwaffe and the entire Prussian administration, but also as the new supremo of economic policy. In any case, the substance of the decisions taken in the autumn of 1936 concerned not Goering's political position, but rearmament, and this was driven home decisively in the weeks that followed. In early December, the Air Ministry set about preparing for the introduction of the full range of new combat aircraft, regardless of protests voiced by Schacht and the Finance Ministry.[72] On 5 December Goering chaired a meeting of the armed forces at which he announced that, in future, he would be in charge of military finances. Raw materials and labour, not money, would dictate the pace of Germany's military expansion.[73] A day later, General Fritsch as commander-in-chief of the army formally approved Fromm's monumental expansion plan as the basis for all further action.[74] On 17 December 1936 at the Preussenhaus in Berlin Goering addressed leading industrialists in positively apocalyptic tones.[75] He reminded his audience of the devastating impact of the blockade in World War I and of the enormous mobilization of which Germany had proved capable in that war. Whereas before the war men had talked anxiously about spending a few billion on defence, the war had cost 160 billion Marks. Now businessmen again hesitated to expand their factories, for fear of being burdened with surplus capacity. This was absurd. Goering assured his audience:

No end of the rearmament is in sight. The struggle which we are approaching demands a colossal measure of productive ability . . . The only deciding point in this case is victory or destruction. If we win, then business will be sufficiently compensated . . . It is entirely immaterial whether in every case new investment can be amortized. We are now playing for the highest stakes . . . All selfish interests must be put aside. Our whole nation is at stake. We live in a time when the final battles are in sight. We are already on the threshold of mobilization and are at war, only the guns are not yet firing.

A week later, on Christmas Day 1936, Goering decreed that the Luft-waffe industries were to go onto a mobilization footing. Procurement was to be carried out without regard to the budget of the Air Ministry. Workers from across German industry, who had received training in aircraft production, were to take up the places pre-assigned to them in case of war.[76]

Whilst the civilian economic administration still remained largely under Schacht's control, Goering created a new organization to realize the objectives of the Four Year Plan.[77] Key personnel were recruited from the military, such as Colonel Fritz Loeb, one of the architects of the Luftwaffe expansion. There were also party men, such as Herbert Backe, who added responsibility for agriculture in the Four Year Plan to his role at the Ministry of Agriculture, and Gauleiter Josef Wagner, who was to be responsible for price and wage controls. Then there were close personal associates of Goering such as Erich Neumann, a Prussian career civil servant, who in the Four Year Plan took responsibility for handling foreign exchange issues. Goering could also draw on a considerable number of technicians, who had been active in autarchy programmes since 1934. Within Loeb's raw material department, Carl Krauch, the leading IG Farben specialist for synthetic fuels, was made responsible for research and development. Paul Pleiger and Hans Kehrl, both committed party members, were coopted from Wilhelm Keppler's staff to take responsibility for metals and synthetic textiles respectively. These were men who had proved themselves in the first years of the regime and many of them were on close personal terms.[78] Though the budget of the Four Year Plan did not compare with the spending being contemplated by the army and the Luftwaffe, the investment planned by Goering's new organization was nevertheless enormous. By the end of 1937 the prospective investment budget for the Four Year Plan had risen to close to 10 billion Reichsmarks.[79] In total, the Plan was to account for somewhere between 20 and 25 per cent of all investment in the German economy between 1936 and 1940. The purpose of this spending was to halve Germany's import bill by creating the capacity to produce raw materials to the tune of 2.3 billion Reichsmarks, or roughly 5 per cent of total German industrial production.

The Four Year Plan was not starting from scratch, of course. Between 1934 and 1936 Hans Kehrl had already established a new industry for staple fibres (*Zellwolle*) with an annual capacity of 45,000 tons. Having been incorporated unceremoniously into the Four Year Plan, Kehrl set himself the new target of reaching 160,000 tons by 1940.[80] Carl Krauch,

Table 5. Four Year Plan: proposed levels of spending

	Plan II (January 1937)		Plan III (May 1937)		Plan IV (December 1937)	
	million RM	%	million RM	%	million RM	%
Mineral oil	1,438	16.7	1,989	22.6	2,684	28.3
Buna	517	6	687	7.8	654	6.9
Other chemistry	2,351	27.3	1,100	12.5	778	8.2
Waterways	1,826	21.2	1,567	17.8	1,518	16
Nonferrous metals	353	4.1	317	3.6	351	3.7
Iron and steel	232	2.7	449	5.1	360	3.8
Textiles	344	4	449	5.1	484	5.1
Food	267	3.1	643	7.3	1,518	16
Coal	43	0.5	194	2.2	199	2.1
Energy	947	11	1,171	13.3	721	7.6
Wood	86	1	26	0.3	66	0.7
Machines and equipment	198	2.3	194	2.2	76	0.8
Leather	9	0.1	18	0.2	9	0.1
Housing	0		0		66	0.7
Total planned investment billion Reichsmarks	8,611	100	8,802	100	9,485	100

Source: D. Petzina, *Autarkiepolitik im Dritten Reich* (Stuttgart, 1968), 83

for his part, had overseen expansion in synthetic fuel production that had already reached 1.78 million tons by 1936. But, due to the simultaneous increase in German fuel consumption, this covered only 34 per cent of domestic requirement.[81] Hitler now demanded that Germany should achieve self-sufficiency in motor fuel within eighteen months. This required a crash programme to add another 1 million tons of capacity.

Within four years, Germany was to achieve independence from all oil imports, with a domestic capacity of 5.4 million tons. Achieving the goal of fuel self-sufficiency consumed the lion's share of all resources invested in the Four Year Plan. But Krauch at least could build on technologies that had been in operation since the late 1920s. The one area where a truly dramatic technological step was envisioned in 1936 was the synthetic production of rubber.[82] In September 1936, when Hitler made his address to the Nuremberg rally, no one anywhere in the world had the technology to produce high-quality synthetic rubber in industrial quantities. In 1936, IG Farben's total production of Buna came to no more than a few hundred tons, the experimental production facility at Schkopau, rated at only 2,500 tons per annum, was still under construction, the German military had not yet approved Buna as an acceptable material for tyres, and the tyre manufacturers had not yet worked out how to process the material. Once this daunting list of problems had been overcome, the initial target was to raise production at Schkopau to 24,000 tons per annum, before embarking on the construction of three more Buna plants within the next four years.

As we have seen, the burden of financing and building the first generation of synthetic fuel plants had been spread across the entire German energy industry, by conscripting the coal mines. IG Farben's truly indispensable role was as a supplier of technology. But with the announcement of the Four Year Plan, the partnership between IG and the Nazi regime took on a new intensity. Carl Krauch's appointment as head of research and development in the raw materials office of the Plan cemented an involvement that dated back at least to 1933–4. Soon afterwards Krauch withdrew from his responsibilities on IG's managerial board, taking a position instead on the supervisory board, of which he was made the chairman in 1940.[83] Where exactly the balance of power and interest lay in this relationship remains a matter for argument. In his role in the Four Year Plan, Krauch clearly acted first and foremost in what he perceived to be the interests of the autarchy programme. But given his intimate knowledge of IG's enormous technical resources, it is hardly surprising that as far as Krauch was concerned the best solution was usually an 'IG solution'. All Krauch's senior advisers on fuel, rubber, explosives and other chemicals were colleagues from IG. Furthermore, Krauch lobbied overtly to ensure that leadership in all chemicals programmes lay in the hands not of the military

Table 6. Rubber and iron ore: twin priorities of the
Four Year Plan

000 tons	Rubber		Iron ore (fe content)	
	Natural rubber imports	Buna	Iron ore imports	Ore production pre-1938 Germany
1929	59		10,670	2,080
1930	51		7,271	1,845
1931	45		4,856	841
1932	50		3,254	442
1933	61		4,104	828
1934	72		6,822	1,372
1935	74	0	9,995	1,849
1936	83	1	8,430	2,259
1937	100	4	9,690	2,759
1938	92	6	10,470	3,360
1939	77	22	10,043	3,928
1940	19	41	6,874	5,019
1941	27	71	12,513	4,755
1942	24	101	13,581	4,137
1943	8	120	15,150	4,080

Sources: G. Plumpe, *Die IG Farbenindustrie AG* (Berlin, 1990), 385;
Statistisches Handbuch, 281

establishment but of private industry. At the same time, however, it must also be recognized that the entanglement with the Four Year Plan changed IG Farben. Despite IG's enormous size and technological muscle, the huge quantity of resources channelled through it by the German state could not but have a dramatic effect.

This point emerges very clearly from the soul-searching that went on after the war on the part of Dr Georg von Schnitzler, second in command at IG until 1945.[84] In an affidavit he composed in the desperate months prior to his trial at Nuremberg, Schnitzler described a Faustian pact between Hitler's regime and the younger generation of technologists within IG.[85] 'The ... possibilities' opened up by the autarchy programme 'undoubtedly exercised a great fascination upon our technical people,' Schnitzler wrote. 'Plans for which they could not see any practical realization as long as a normal economy existed became realizable, and the most fascinating prospects seemed to lie ahead.' Normally, of course, the huge funds required to build synthetic fuel or synthetic rubber plants would have been tightly controlled by the financial committees of IG's board. But from the early 1930s, IG's annual investment rose at an almost uncontrollable rate, from as little as 10–12 million Reichsmarks per annum at the trough of the recession to 500 million Reichsmarks per annum in the early 1940s. This extraordinary growth was driven not by coercion but by a financial environment of unprecedented generosity. As Schnitzler admitted: 'A high percentage of our turnover ... was more or less guaranteed by the Wehrmacht. Agreements of the most different kinds were being concluded, but nearly all were based on solid financial ground in so far as the Reich guaranteed the amortization or had arranged for a protective duty or prescribed the use for the consuming industry ...' This removal of financial constraints had a profoundly corrosive effect on IG's fragile system of corporate decision-making. 'The apparently splendid situation of IG's balance weakened the central administration. Young and active technicians like Ambros [synthetic rubber], Buetefisch [synthetic petrol]', both of whom worked on Krauch's Four Year Plan programmes, '... had independent responsibility for problems of the greatest importance, and engaged in ever greater commitments. When asked to justify their actions they were in the habit of referring to "instruction [Auflage] from Wehrmacht agency X".' But, as Schnitzler acknowledged, it was 'sometimes ... not quite clear, if our technical men themselves had not deliberately induced the Wehrmacht to issue the instruction. The central administration of IG Farben registered the facts, when it came to the settlement of the expenses, but had very little to say in the matter.'

Whatever else may be said about it, the functional nature of the relationship between IG and the Four Year Plan is betokened by its extraordinary stability. Carl Krauch was a fixture in the industrial politics of Nazi Germany from 1933 to 1945. Having played a key role in negotiating the Benzinvertrag in December 1933, he was still an important part of the industrial war effort twelve years later in the dark days of 1944–5. This gave IG Farben an absolutely unique place in the Third Reich, and one which contrasts sharply with the far more troubled relationship between the regime and German heavy industry.

III

Hitler's Four Year Plan speech answered the strategic question posed in the summer of 1936. But it in no way addressed the immediate practical question of how to conduct an enormous rearmament drive in the face of a severe balance of payments problem. In the short run, by adding to booming domestic demand Goering's investment programme could only make matters worse, diverting exportable goods for domestic uses, whilst sucking in more foreign raw materials for the production of large industrial facilities. What Germany needed was the precise opposite. To ensure an adequate inflow of hard currency and thus of food and raw materials, Schacht wanted to repress domestic demand, whilst boosting exports. Rearmament in the widest sense would have to accommodate itself to this wider reallocation, since without imported materials and food the German economy would simply grind to a halt. A devaluation would have provided a market mechanism for achieving this goal, reducing the foreign prices of German exports and raising the cost of imported goods. But, having rejected devaluation, the regime was forced, as in 1934, to resort to increased bureaucratic regulation.

In the months that followed the announcement of the Four Year Plan, the problem of securing sufficient steel overshadowed every other issue in German industrial politics. Though Goering and his staff were dedicating themselves to remedying the shortage by expanding production from German iron ore, this long-term programme in no way answered the questions facing German economic policy in 1936. The Four Year Plan could substantially alleviate the steel bottleneck at the earliest within two years. As we have seen, Ernst Poensgen and the Business Group for steel had been warning of an impending crisis in steel supply since at least the beginning of 1936. In November 1936 they finally got what they wanted: a government-ordered production cut of 15 per cent, in the interests of preserving Germany's dangerously low stocks of iron ore and scrap.[86] This might not seem draconian, but since exports had to be preserved at all costs, the entire cut fell on domestic demand. Out of total monthly production of roughly 1.725 million tons in early 1936, only 1.325 million tons were used domestically. The rest was exported, either directly or indirectly. As of November 1936 this supply of domestic steel was cut by 25 per cent to only 1.070 million tons, out of which had to be covered all the needs of the Wehrmacht, the Four Year Plan, investment and consumption.[87] This was of course precisely the kind of reallocation that would also have been induced by a devaluation. Now, however, it was imposed by government fiat. As the Reich Ministry had predicted, panic buying ensued. At the rolling mills, orders for hundreds of thousands of tons piled up that could not be met for the foreseeable future. Under normal conditions the response would have been to raise prices.[88] The Reich authorities, however, were desperate to avoid the scarcity of imported raw materials spilling over into general inflation. So, Gauleiter Wagner, who had responsibility for price control in the Four Year Plan, issued a blanket ban on 26 November 1936 prohibiting any price increases.[89] Formalizing a development begun in the early 1930s, this effectively eliminated the market mechanism as a means of regulating scarcity in the German economy. The logical next step, as had already been acknowledged by the RNS in agriculture at least a year earlier, was the introduction of rationing, managing scarcity by bureaucratic allocation rather than the market process. Rationing of nonferrous metals was adopted in January 1937; steel rationing was imposed as of 23 February 1937.[90] To clear the backlog with the rolling mills, all outstanding steel orders that could not be met by the end of April 1937 were cancelled. From the end of February, new orders for steel could only be placed on the basis of steel entitlements issued according to national priority as defined by the Reich Ministry for Economic Affairs.

For the actual operation of the German economy, the introduction of steel rationing was far more important than the announcement of the Four Year Plan six months earlier.[91] The fate of every industrial undertaking in the Nazi economy, the Four Year Plan and the entire rearmament programme, now depended on how much steel could be produced and how much was allocated under the steel rationing system. Ironically, though the introduction of a steel rationing system in peacetime was an extraordinary step which changed the day-to-day functioning of German industry, the system in its first fifteen months of operation was conservative in its effects. Much to its frustration, the Wehrmacht, instead of being allocated huge additional quantities of steel, found itself with a steel quota no larger than that purchased through normal channels a year earlier.[92] In effect, procurement and military construction was frozen at the rate already reached in 1936. This was significant by any standard, but in light of the goals set by Fromm, the implications were nevertheless serious. To meet the target, approved in December 1936, of creating a wartime army of 3.6 million men by 1940, the army had requested 270,500 tons of steel per month. The actual monthly allocation as of February 1937 was only 195,000 tons.[93] As a result, Fromm's department estimated that army ammunition stocks would not reach their intended levels before the autumn of 1942. The system of fortifications included in the 1936 Plan would not be completed until 1948.[94] The Luftwaffe and the Four Year Plan both suffered painful restrictions. The bold plan of the autumn of 1936 – to ready the German economy and the Wehrmacht for war within four years – was slipping away, only weeks after its announcement. By the end of May 1937, the army leadership felt compelled to inform the War Ministry that the raw material shortages were now so severe that the fighting strength projected for 1940 would not in fact be available for years to come, a problem 'which the political leadership must take into consideration'.[95] The army would expand as planned. Men would be recruited and trained. But the inadequate equipment of the German army would make it unready for war.[96] For the Luftwaffe, meanwhile, Goering approved a revised programme that implied an immediate 10 per cent cut in the aircraft industry workforce.[97] By the autumn of 1937, the Luftwaffe was talking about cutting its production plans by 25 per cent and the plant expansion programme by 66 per cent.[98] And the results are evident in the statistics. Rather than expanding, as had been demanded in 1936, aircraft output was actually on a downward trend between April 1937 and the summer of 1938.[99] The Luftwaffe carried through its re-equipment with modern combat aircraft, but only at the expense of a drastic reduction in the output of all other types of aircraft, especially of trainers.

What dictated this lull in the armaments drive was the absolute priority of the balance of payments. Schacht and the Nazi political leadership were clearly agreed on the need to avoid an acute crisis like that which had come close to halting the recovery in 1934. The first priority therefore was to restrict imports and to raise hard currency earnings by boosting exports. After averaging between 330 million and 340 million Reichsmarks per month in 1934 and 1935, Germany's monthly export earnings rose above 400 million Reichsmarks in August 1936 and scaled 530 million Reichsmarks in the summer of 1937. This would not have been possible without Schacht's much maligned system of export subsidies, which in early 1937 allowed every Reichsmark of German exports to be supported to the tune of approximately 30 Pfennigs.[100] But the export subsidy system had of course been in operation since 1935. What explains the sudden turnaround in German exports was the upsurge in world trade. In 1937 alone, global trade volumes grew by 25 per cent. For the first time since the 1920s there was rising demand for German goods and Germany's exporters were clearly determined to take advantage. Even if Schacht and Goerdeler had lost the political argument with the advocates of autarchy, IG Farben, Vereinigte Stahlwerke and Siemens, along with thousands of other smaller exporters, were not about to retreat into sole reliance on the domestic market. If there was a profitable world market to be serviced, then German businesses wanted to be present in it.

As Schacht well understood, however, this opportunity could not be taken for granted. Given Germany's record of debt default and its highly manipulative system of trade promotion, the mere fact that world demand was expanding did not imply that German firms would actually be allowed to benefit. As we have seen, the United States had already taken steps to block subsidized imports from Germany. If they had wanted to, Germany's other major trading partners could have followed this lead in shutting the Third Reich out of their markets. There were voices in Britain calling for precisely such a move.[101] At the end of 1936, the Anglo-German standstill agreement came up again for renewal. This was the arrangement that had been first put in place in 1931, on American urging, to limit Germany's obligations to its short-term creditors. In 1936, the British clearing banks, led by Reginald McKenna, the forceful chairman of Midland Bank and an Asquith-liberal, mounted an aggressive campaign against any further concessions to Germany. As McKenna saw it, the failure of the City to demand full repayment had done nothing but facilitate German rearmament. With the announcement of the Four Year Plan, this had clearly entered a new and dangerous phase. McKenna called for Britain to respond as in 1934 with the threat of trade war and compulsory clearing, unless Berlin honoured its full financial obligations. Schacht, however, held firm, refusing to make any concession to London. He could not afford to allow Britain to unpick the complex structure of bilateral agreements he had established since 1934, of which the Anglo-German Payments Agreement was the cornerstone. And he also knew that he could count on influential friends on the British side. As the British embassy in Berlin opined, a collapse in the Anglo-German Payments Agreement would have 'shake[n] confidence on both sides and also weaken[ed] Schacht's position'. Following Goering's appointment, Schacht was now seen as a vital moderating influence on Hitler's regime. To bolster his position, London felt it best to hold open the door to Germany's international trade.[102] Indeed, it is tempting to infer that it was precisely for this reason that Hitler had kept Schacht in office, as bait for the British. We should not, however, ignore the evidence, which suggests that at least in one sense the British strategy actually worked. Economic concessions to Germany may not have altered the political power balance in Berlin. However, in the light of Germany's desperate need for foreign currency, Schacht was able to insist that in early 1937 top priority should be given, not to armaments and the Four Year Plan, but to exports. In the first months of 1937 the steel allocation to the export sector was set at 505,000 monthly tons – as much as the Wehrmacht and the Four Year Plan combined.[103] A special committee was established with the task of ensuring that the needs of the Wehrmacht and the Four Year Plan were 'coordinated' with the absolute priority of exports.[104] And Ernst Poensgen, CEO of the Vestag, was charged with the task of finding markets abroad for an extra 100,000 monthly tons of German steel.[105]

Since the source of the steel shortage was the decision to restrict steel production, a decision forced on Germany by the acute shortage of foreign exchange, the top priority was clearly to find a way of expanding steel production without imposing an intolerable burden on the foreign exchange account. And the obvious way to do this was to intensify the exploitation of Germany's extensive deposits of iron ore. As we have already noted, an argument about this issue had been simmering since early 1936.[106] In one corner there was the Ruhr steel region led by Ernst Poensgen. The Ruhr firms were the legal owners of the German ore fields. But at least until 1937 they determinedly opposed the development of these low-grade ores. On economic grounds, the Ruhr much preferred to import high-quality Scandinavian ore, a position that found strong support from Schacht and the RWM. In the other corner there was Paul Pleiger, the steel expert on Keppler's raw-material staff, who insisted that the vast ore deposit at Salzgitter could be made to yield millions of tons of ore per annum. This would be sufficient to triple the iron content that German industry derived from domestic sources from around 2 million to around 6 million tons per annum, giving steel production a substantial base of self-sufficiency. In the course of 1936, Pleiger, along with the rest of Keppler's team, drifted into Goering's orbit and so too, in a sense, did the steel industry. In light of the acute steel shortage it was clearly untenable for the Ruhr firms to resist development of this national asset. By June 1937 the steel industry, in collaboration with the offices of the Four Year Plan, had worked out a programme to raise German steel production from its current maximum of 19.3 million tons to a 'final capacity' of 24 million tons, a figure which they believed would be sufficient to exhaust the capacity of the metal-processing industries.[107] This increase was to be based entirely on the increased utilization of German iron ore, precisely as had been demanded by Pleiger. The 24 million ton programme was, however, not a scheme for the creation of a new industry. It was a modestly costed programme of organic growth, calling for a 10 per cent increase in the number of blast furnaces and a proportional increase in the number of coke ovens, sufficient to ensure the full employment of Germany's existing steel converters and rolling mills.

If this proposal had been forthcoming six months earlier, there can be little doubt that it would have settled the argument. By the summer of 1937, however, it was too late.[108] After months of obstinate resistance from Poensgen and his colleagues, Pleiger was determined not simply to expand German iron ore mining, but to break the heavy industrial power bloc of the Ruhr. His goal was to establish an independent, state-controlled, vertically integrated steel conglomerate in central Germany large enough to challenge even the Vereinigte Stahlwerke.[109] The key was Hermann Roechling, the leading heavy industrialist of the Saar. Roechling (1872–1955) was a metallurgist of genius and a man given to dramatic visions. He was also a German nationalist of the old school who following the loss of Alsace-Lorraine was in the uncomfortable position of sourcing all his iron ore from France. He thus had an urgent interest in developing the new technologies required to smelt Germany's acidic ores. Roechling and Pleiger's relationship was soon to deteriorate. But it was through Roechling that Pleiger gained access to Hermann Brassert, a globetrotting German-American engineer, who was reputed to have been personally involved in the construction of at least 20 per cent of the world's modern blast furnaces.[110] Earlier in the 1930s, Brassert had built a plant at Corby, England, that used acidic iron ore of an even lower grade than that available in Salzgitter. The problem for Pleiger was that Brassert was also well known to the Vereinigte Stahlwerke, since in the 1920s he had acted as an expert adviser during the issue of over $40 million worth of steel bonds on the American financial markets.[111] It was crucial that Pleiger should get to Brassert before the Vereinigte Stahlwerke did. With Goering breathing down his neck, Pleiger acted fast. In the early summer of 1937, he contacted Brassert in mid-Atlantic by radio telephone and persuaded him to catch the next liner back to London. To prevent Brassert from being nobbled by the Vestag, Pleiger provided him with a round-the-clock escort and flew him back to Germany in Goering's personal Ju 52, an aeroplane known all over the country because it carried the famous red livery of the Richthofen squadron. After this adventure, Pleiger and Goering were ready to launch an all-out attack on the Vestag. The opening shot was fired on 16 June 1937, at a meeting held to discuss the inadequate situation of Germany's steel capacity at which Goering ignored the new proposal for the expansion of blast furnace capacity and berated the steel industrialists for failing to develop Germany's ore reserves. A month later, on 15 July 1937, Pleiger formally signed the articles of the Reichswerke Hermann Goering, a public company with an initial share capital of 5 million Reichsmarks subscribed by the Reich. At Salzgitter, Brassert was to build a fully integrated, state-of-the-art steelworks with an initial capacity of 1 million tons per annum, later to rise to 4 million tons. At that point, its output would rival that of the Vestag itself. A week later, on 23 July, Goering invited 300 representatives of the German steel industry to an after-dinner address at the Air Ministry. Earlier in the evening, representatives of the six leading firms were summoned to a private meeting. After keeping his distinguished guests waiting for some time, Goering swept into the room in full regalia surrounded by a large retinue of officials and military men. Unlike in February 1933, Goering had not come to ask for favours. In a loud and aggressive tone he read out a prepared statement. German heavy industry had failed to develop one of the nation's prize assets. Hitler had given them four years, but they had wasted that time. Now, Goering had lost patience. His job was 'to throw down the saboteurs of rearmament and the Four Year Plan and to send them where they belonged [to hell]'.[112] The state had shown itself capable of achieving dramatic expansion in the aluminium industry and the Luftwaffe sector. Now the same methods would be applied to steel. All private holdings of German iron ore deposits would be merged into a single state company. Three giant steelworks would be built on the ore fields. Salzgitter was to be the largest steel plant in the world. The shocked industrialists were then each handed a map showing the ore fields of their firms that were to be expropriated in the name of the new Reichswerke. Goering then read out a decree personally approved by Hitler, which authorized the forced sale.

Remarkably, Poensgen and the Vestag leadership did not yield immediately to this blatant attempt at intimidation. Instead, they sought to mobilize a united front in opposition to the Reichswerke project. And in doing so they had the full backing of Hjalmar Schacht, who remained both as president of the Reichsbank and Minister for Economic Affairs. The industry had agreed to the development of Germany's iron ore resources as part of the 24-million-ton expansion programme. It did not even oppose the idea of constructing an ironworks close to the iron ore deposits. The Ruhr could make good use of an additional source of pig iron. But what Germany did not need was to spend 200 million Reichsmarks on a new steelworks complete with foundries and rolling mills. It would lumber Germany with excess capacity, drive up costs and cause chaos in the complex network of international cartels that regulated the European steel trade.[113] Pleiger and Goering, however, were now deploying the full apparatus of the police state. They had informants both inside the Reich Ministry of Economic Affairs and the steel cartel and this, together with Goering's personal wire-tapping service, gave them advanced warning of Poensgen and Schacht's strategy. The critical meeting took place at the Stahlhof, the headquarters of the steel association in Duesseldorf, on 24 August 1937. In the middle of the meeting all the steel firms except the Vestag received a telegram from Goering that read as follows: 'I ask you urgently not to participate in the Duesseldorf memorandum of the steel association. The activities of the latter towards the Reichswerke take on more and more the form of sabotage. Heil Hitler! Goering.'[114] Goering's secretary Paul Koerner later confirmed to Flick's office 'that the telegram was the mildest expression of the mood prevailing' at Hitler's residence on the Obersalzberg.[115]

Even without this open threat, however, the Stahlhof meeting revealed deep divisions within the German steel industry. The ruthlessly ambitious CEO of Mannesmann, Wilhelm Zangen, refused from the outset to oppose the Reichswerke project.[116] Roechling also wanted to give it his full support. For Roechling, the warhorse of World War I annexationism, basic issues were at stake. Given the growth of Germany's population and the expansion of new metalworking industries he could see virtually no limit to the future need for steel. He also had personal memories of the short-sightedness of 1914, when General Falkenhayn had declared that he would not need even the full production of Germany's three state arsenals. As Roechling saw it, 'we have no chance in this crazy Europe. One day we will face a really big confrontation . . . You read the war reports from Spain. What conclusions should one draw?' If the German steel industry did not do everything 'to provide Germany with the foundation to be able to survive such a confrontation at least to some degree', who would be responsible? As a veteran of Wilhelmine industrial politics and the post-war reparations discussions, Roechling spoke with some authority. 'I knew virtually all of the statesmen of Europe up to 1934, personally . . . You, gentlemen, should have no illusion about what can happen to us.'[117] Faced with such opposition, Poensgen's effort to construct a united front collapsed. On 27 August the Vereinigte Stahlwerke, Hoesch and Krupp opened negotiations to sell their mining rights to Paul Pleiger and the Reichswerke. In the first week of September Schacht took leave of absence from the RWM, formally handing in his resignation in November.

Over the following years, not only did Pleiger and Brassert complete at least the first phase of the giant steelworks in Salzgitter, which entered production in October 1939, but the Reichswerke also provided the vehicle for an extraordinary campaign of corporate imperialism.[118] By the early 1940s the Reichswerke Hermann Goering had metastasized into what may have been the largest industrial conglomerate in the world.[119] In 1938 Pleiger took control of Rheinmetall, the leading armaments manufacturer, from the state holding company VIAG. After the Anschluss of Austria the Reichswerke bought up considerable industrial interests, largely at the expense of the Vereinigte Stahlwerke. In 1939, after the occupation of Prague, the Reichswerke added the giant Skoda works to its engineering division and the expansion continued following the occupation of Poland. In 1940 and 1941 there were further acquisitions in the occupied and annexed territories of Western Europe. However, this extraordinary empire-building can give a false impression of the significance of the Reichswerke to the wider economic history of the Nazi regime. The many affiliates added in the process of the expansion were only loosely controlled by corporate headquarters and many of them were divested after 1941. Since the expansion of the Reichswerke was mainly due to acquisitions rather than internal investment, it added little to the overall dynamic of the armaments driven economy. Though Pleiger's technological gamble paid off and the Salzgitter steelworks produced perfectly acceptable steel, it never acquired the dominant position in the steel industry that Goering and Pleiger had aimed for. The one crucial sector in which the Reichswerke did establish a leading position was in coal. Here Pleiger profited both from a series of ruthless Aryanization deals orchestrated by Friedrich Flick and from the seizure after 1939 of extensive Silesian mining interests.[120] In the 1940s it was coal not steel that was to make Paul Pleiger into a pivotal figure in the organization of the German war economy.

IV

Just as the Four Year Plan did little or nothing to alleviate Germany's immediate shortage of foreign currency, the Reichswerke project did nothing to resolve the immediate shortage of steel. The steel squeeze continued unabated and Hitler himself was forced to become involved. In the summer of 1937 a strongly worded memorandum from the military-economic department of the War Ministry headed by Colonel Thomas brought the derailment of the rearmament programmes directly to his attention.[121] As Thomas put it in his memo: 'The troops do not understand why the state, the [Nazi] party and business are permitted to undertake large construction projects, when for lack of barracks they are spending the winter [under canvas] on the training ground.'[122] One obvious way to deflect military criticism was to put a soldier in charge of steel rationing, and in early July 1937 Goering appointed Colonel Hermann von Hanneken, chief of staff at the army procurement office (Heereswaffenamt) to this thankless task. Hanneken did his best to reorganize the system and to ensure that the military received their rations on time. But he was unable to provide a substantial increase in steel allocations.[123] By September, War Minister Blomberg saw no option but to demand a decision from Hitler.[124] The accelerated rearmament programmes of 1936 could only be completed if the Wehrmacht was given at least 507,220 tons per month, 70 per cent more than it was currently receiving. As things stood, all programmes were falling dangerously behind schedule. The result, Blomberg announced ominously, would be 'such a serious reduction in offensive readiness . . . that it could not but have implications for the freedom of action of the political leadership of the Reich'.[125]

For the second time in two years, Hitler was forced to respond to economic difficulties with a fundamental restatement of strategic priorities, this time at a meeting with the senior leadership of the German armed forces on 5 November 1937. According to the surviving notes made by Colonel Friedrich Hossbach, Hitler demanded that in the event of his death his pronouncements on this occasion should be treated as 'his last will and testament'.[126] As usual, Hitler started with a strategic *tour d'horizon*, which differed little from that which prefaced the Four Year Plan.[127] What was new and hugely explosive was the indication that Hitler was now beginning to think in concrete terms about the territorial expansion of the Reich. Specifically, he announced his determination to take military action against Czechoslovakia. Czechoslovakia was not discussed in the grand design set out in *Mein Kampf* or the 'Second Book'. But apart from the deep-seated anti-Czech prejudice harboured by many members of the German leadership, a glance at a map of inter-war Europe was enough to explain why Czechoslovakia, along with Austria, had logically to be the first target of Hitler's aggression. The 'artificial' nation-state of Czechoslovakia had been created at Versailles as an integral part of the anti-German security system. It was bound by military alliance both to France and since 1935 to the Soviet Union. Protruding deep into southern Germany, it was regarded by the German military as an obvious base for air attacks on Berlin and southern Germany.

For Hitler, the central issue was one of timing. It was crucial to resolve the issue of *Lebensraum* before 1943–5, because after that point he expected Germany's relative advantage in the arms race to decrease. Hitler's reference to 1943–5 is significant because it suggests a modification of the timescale suggested in his Four Year Plan memorandum. Hitler was showing his awareness of the deceleration in the pace of rearmament over the last twelve months. The statement also indicates an awareness of the threat posed by the rearmament of the other European powers. And Hitler went further than this. If, prior to 1943, France were to be disarmed by a sudden escalation of internal social strife, as had occurred in early 1934, or if Britain and France were to be distracted by a conflict in the Mediterranean, then it might be profitable for Germany to act, even though its own military preparations were not yet fully completed. What this indicates is that though Hitler clearly understood the complexities of the armaments timetable, his decision for war would ultimately depend on the unpredictable evolution of the international scene.

With regard to the steel issue, Hitler reaffirmed his commitment to the rearmament decisions taken in 1936. And over the following weeks this was backed up by decisive action. The 'Hossbach' meeting did not yield an immediate or dramatic improvement in the Wehrmacht's steel rations.[128] The army remained well short of the targets set in 1936 and received far less steel than would have been needed to make good the shortfalls the Wehrmacht had suffered in 1937.[129] To break the deadlock, what was needed was a significant increase in steel production, not from the Reichswerke Hermann Goering – that would take years – but from Germany's existing blast furnaces and steel mills. And that is exactly what was set in motion in the weeks following the Hossbach conference. On 22 November 1937 Colonel Hanneken informed the Business Group for iron and steel that the restrictions that had constrained steel production since the autumn of 1936 were to be lifted. 'By means of increased domestic ore extraction and increased import', Germany's production of raw iron was to be raised to 'the limit of capacity'.[130] Providing that the existing restrictions on consumption remained in force, Hanneken believed that this would be sufficient to meet at least the most important needs of German industry. And by early February 1938 the Wehrmacht bureaucracy was beginning to respond, with renewed discussion of armaments acceleration.[131]

In 1937, however, the damage had been done. Rather than undergoing a dramatic expansion, as had clearly been intended in 1936, armaments procurement had stagnated. Indeed, in the entire pre-war history of Hitler's regime, 1937 was the only year in which military spending did not significantly increase.[132] As Blomberg had predicted this had serious strategic ramifications. As of December 1937, the German army high command did not expect Germany's wartime army to be fully equipped and ready for combat until the spring of 1943.[133] For the army leadership this had clear consequences. As we shall discuss in the next chapter, Colonel Beck, the army chief of staff, responded to Hitler's remarks at the Hossbach conference with an alarming strategic assessment, counselling Hitler against any aggressive action towards the Czechs. Hitler, however, had other plans. In 1936 he had outlined a timetable in which the road to war was prepared for by four years of all-out domestic mobilization. He had not got it. He was realistic enough, as he demonstrated at the Hossbach conference, to register the technical complaints from the Wehrmacht. But unlike the generals, Hitler did not have to accept as given either Germany's relations with its neighbours or the current level of economic mobilization. The generals responded by adjusting their time-horizons. Hitler responded by shifting the parameters. Whilst doing everything possible to raise steel production and reallocate it to the military, he now ceaselessly raised the level of international tension. Rather than domestic mobilization creating the conditions for war, international tension was to become the principal lever through which the leadership of the Third Reich – ably assisted both by key industrialists and careerist soldiers – catapulted the German economy into a dramatically higher level of mobilization. International escalation opened the door to domestic mobilization, not the other way around.[134]

In so far as any single individual was the driver of this process, it was Hitler. The consolidation of the Nazi regime around the person of the Fuehrer over the winter of 1937–8 was a decisive moment in the evolution of the Third Reich.[135] Most dramatically, the first week of February 1938 saw an abrupt restructuring at the top of the military hierarchy, necessitated by the scandals surrounding Defence Minister Blomberg and the Commander-in-Chief of the army, Colonel-General Werner von Fritsch.[136] The War Minister had rashly married a women 'with a past'. Fritsch's police file turned out to contain unresolved accusations of homosexuality. Hitler summarily dismissed both men and resolved the crisis by establishing the Wehrmacht as a separate organizational entity, independent of the three branches of the armed forces, with Hitler himself as Commander-in-Chief. Goering, who had wanted Blomberg's job as Defence Minister, was instead promoted to the rank of Field Marshal. Wilhelm Keitel, a previously innocuous officer, was promoted to the role of Hitler's principal military adviser at the head of the Wehrmacht. Meanwhile, Colonel Thomas, the Wehrmacht's chief economic expert, was put in charge of a new military-economic office. Command of the army was given to Walther von Brauchitsch, a respectable professional officer, but a man of weak character who showed no ability to stand up to Hitler. At the same time Hitler also instigated a major reshuffle at the Foreign Ministry. The conservative Neurath, who had been Minister since 1932, was moved aside. His place was taken by the former ambassador to London, Joachim von Ribbentrop, a man much more in tune with Hitler's new aggressive agenda.

The fate of the Reich Ministry of Economic Affairs was decided at the same time. To replace Schacht as RWM (he remained as president of the Reichsbank), Hitler chose Goebbels's close collaborator Walther Funk. Though Goering was also disappointed not to get this job, he had at least used the hiatus left by Schacht's departure to merge the administration of the Four Year Plan with the Ministerial apparatus.[137] All of the key Ministerial departments were now in the hands of politically reliable men. The new mood in the Ministry is well summed up by a quip circulating amongst the established civil servants, who described Goering's newcomers as the 'council of workers and soldiers', a throwback to the revolutionary days of 1918.[138] Hans Kehrl, a key figure from Wilhelm Keppler's raw-materials staff, was appointed to a free-roving assignment to ensure compliance with the new agenda of autarchy and rationing.

Even more important was the new role assumed by Hitler himself in relation to economic policy. Of course, neither Goering nor Hitler had the stomach for the excruciating technical details of industrial policy, but both were acutely interested in the armament programme and this meant that they had to take a serious interest in the problem of raw-material rationing. From November 1937 until the end of the Third Reich, there was not a single occasion on which the allocation of steel, the basic raw material of the industrial economy, was significantly altered without Hitler's personal approval. This assertion of Hitler's authority over economic policy deserves to rank alongside the more familiar aspects of the 'second seizure of power'. It constituted a central and much underrated feature of Hitler's exercise of power.[139] It is only if we couple together all three aspects of the Fuehrer's rule – diplomatic, military and industrial – that we can truly grasp the way in which he set about unhinging the European balance of power.

8

Into the Danger Zone

On 11 March 1938, at a morning meeting of IG Farben's corporate commercial committee, a routine discussion of the precautions to be taken in the event of a military emergency, the so-called 'M question', suddenly took on a shockingly real quality.[1]

Already at 9.30 the first alarming messages had reached us. Dr Fischer returned excitedly from a telephone conversation and reported that the Deutsche Gasoline AG [an IG affiliate] had received instructions to refuel all petrol stations in Bavaria and in other parts of southern Germany towards the Czech border. A quarter of an hour later, there came a telephone call from Burghausen, according to which quite a number of workers had already been called to arms. Mobilization in Bavaria was in full swing. In the absence of official information, which came only in the evening, we were uncertain whether, simultaneously with the march into Austria, which to us was already an established fact, there would not also take place the 'short thrust' into Czechoslovakia with all the international complications that would be kindled by it.

Executives scrambled to the phones to call back the senior IG delegation that was on its way to Cannes for the negotiation of an international molybdenum cartel. 'Under these circumstances,' the minute-taker noted, 'the conference on M matters took on highly significant features. We realized suddenly – like a stroke of lightning from a clear sky – that a matter, which one had once treated more or less theoretically, could become deadly serious . . .'

I

The annexation of Austria to Germany was set in motion on 11 March and completed two days later.[2] The Anschluss was a classic foreign policy coup, in the style of the Rhineland remilitarization of March 1936. As we have seen, German aggression against Czechoslovakia had been under discussion since November 1937. Annexing Austria was an obvious first step towards unhinging the balance of power in Central Europe. Given the mounting public and private pressure applied to Austria from the beginning of 1938 onwards, the Anschluss when it came was no surprise. Hitler's timing was good and depended on a clear-headed reading of the wider diplomatic scene.[3] Crucially, Italy had signalled its preoccupation with the Mediterranean and its lack of interest in Austrian affairs. In early 1938, Hitler first faced Austrian Chancellor Kurt Schuschnigg with a series of ultimatums and then allowed him to make the first wrong move by calling a referendum on Austrian national independence for 13 March. To forestall this event, the outcome of which would probably have favoured independence, the Wehrmacht carried out a hasty and partial mobilization and occupied Austria with help from the local Nazi party and its supporters. The other European powers were left with no time to react.

For the German economy, Austria provided a useful fillip.[4] The Anschluss added somewhat less than 8 per cent to Germany's existing industrial output. Austria's heavy industrial resources, however, were relatively scanty. In 1937, Austria produced only 600,000 tons of steel, of which more than half went to exports. That was just under 4 per cent of German production. Two-thirds of this was accounted for by the Oesterreichisch-Alpine Montangesellschaft, or Alpine, the owner of the Erzberg, a fabled 200-million-ton mountain of the highest grade iron ore.[5] Alpine was a key supplier not only to the Austrian economy, but to Czech and Italian industry as well. It was clearly the prize industrial asset in Austria. By rights it should have fallen to the Vereinigte Stahlwerke with which it had a long-standing connection. Instead, it was seized by the Reichswerke Hermann Goering, which thus acquired considerable economic influence throughout South-eastern Europe. For the German economy as a whole, the main benefit of the Anschluss was the addition of the underemployed Austrian workforce. According to the official figures, the Anschluss added 401,000 unemployed to the German roll, increasing the labour reserve available to Germany by between 30 and 40 per cent.

By contrast, the impact of the Anschluss on the all-important balance of payments was ambiguous. In the longer term, the effects were clearly negative. Like Germany, Austria depended on imports both for its food and industrial raw materials and it struggled to sustain exports at a sufficiently high level.[6] A large-scale revival of the Austrian economy could, therefore, be expected to add to Germany's balance of payments problems. In the short term, however, these problems were offset by the enormous haul of foreign exchange yielded by the imposition of Germany's draconian foreign exchange regulations on the much more liberal Austrian economy. The gold and foreign exchange reserves of the Austrian national bank alone totalled 345 million Reichsmarks.[7] Altogether, the Austrian foreign exchange dowry came to at least 782 million Reichsmarks, more than doubling Germany's reserves. These funds were crucial, because in the first weeks of 1938 Germany's balance of payments situation looked extremely bleak. The private holdings of foreign exchange conscripted since 1936 had largely been spent. And the revival in exports that had sustained the balance of payments throughout 1937 was clearly over. As the world economy slumped in the first half of 1938 global trade fell by 20 per cent.[8] As of January 1938, the Reichsbank faced a substantial monthly trade deficit.[9] Under normal circumstances this would have forced an immediate retrenchment. In a meeting of the Four Year Plan on 10 February 1938 there was talk of cuts not only to private consumption but also to the regime's highest priority projects.[10] Instead, thanks to the Austrian booty, Germany in 1938 was able to run a trade deficit of almost 450 million Reichsmarks, larger than at any time since 1929. For a brief moment at least, the Anschluss freed Hitler's regime from the balance of payments constraint.

But the motivation for the Anschluss was not booty. The real imperative was strategic. The joining together of Germany and Austria dramatically increased the Reich's power in relation to the smaller countries of Central and South-eastern Europe. From time immemorial, Vienna had been the hub around which the trade of Eastern and South-eastern Europe had flowed. The breaking apart of the Austro-Hungarian Empire and the ravages of the Depression had weakened that position. Now, following the Anschluss, the compensation offered to the Viennese for their relegation to second city of the Reich was their installation as the capital of Germany's 'Empire' in South-eastern Europe. Annexing Austrian trade to the share already going to Germany, raised Hungary's import-dependence on Germany from 26 to 44 per cent. Germany's share of Yugoslavia's imports rose from 32 to 43 per cent.[11] Over the months that followed, Germany was able to use its enhanced leverage to conclude new trade treaties with both Hungary and Poland.[12] For Czechoslovakia on the other hand, the Anschluss came as a devastating blow. The deployment of German troops into the eastern provinces of Austria meant that Bohemia was now encircled on three sides. Though the military occupation of Austria proceeded peacefully, and though the reaction from the Western powers was muted, the Anschluss marked the point at which fear of war in Europe began to take on concrete form. In Prague, the mood was one of panic. Throughout the spring of 1938 there were rumours of an imminent German attack, which reached their height during the 'weekend crisis' of 20–21 May. Alarmed by false reports of German troops massing along its borders, the Czech government mobilized not only its own armed forces, but also its allies in Paris and London. The British conducted an emergency evacuation of all non-essential staff from their Berlin embassy and issued a warning that if Germany attacked, the French would be bound to defend their Czech allies and Britain would not stand aside.[13]

In the event, this exaggerated Germany's readiness for war. Plans for an attack on Czechoslovakia were being prepared, but Hitler had no intention of launching the assault as early as 20 May. He was furious, however, that the 'weekend crisis' created the impression that he had been forced to climb down by threats of international action.[14] Hitler's response was characteristic. On 28 May, one week after the mobilization crisis, he convoked a meeting of the senior military leadership and announced his determination to deal with the Czechs at the earliest possible opportunity.[15] He expected to use military means. The Wehrmacht was ordered to stand ready for action any time after 1 October 1938. Hitler hoped that he would be able to isolate the Czechs and avoid Britain and France being drawn in. He still hoped that the British would see reason and that the confrontation with France could be delayed until 1943–4, by which time the German army would have completed its build-up. But if the Western powers were determined to oppose his first steps towards eastward expansion, Hitler would not shrink from war. From the spring of 1938 onwards, Hitler began seriously to contemplate the need for a major war in the West, as a prelude to his drive against the Soviet Union. As hard as it may be to credit, given the subsequent fate of Czechoslovakia, this was the essential lesson that was learned in Berlin by the early summer of 1938. The Third Reich had to regard the British Empire as a force opposed to Hitler's dream of conquest in the East.[16]

It would be hard to overestimate the importance of this shift in strategic posture in the months following the Anschluss. To anyone thinking clearly, it should not have come as any surprise.[17] No progress had been made towards an agreement with Britain since the naval treaty of 1935. The events of 1936 had only heightened public awareness of the profound fissure between 'the democracies' and the aggressive 'dictatorships'. Beck, the army's chief of staff, had made British hostility an axiom of his planning since 1937 at the latest. From April 1938 onwards, both the Luftwaffe and the navy were making the same assumption. But for Hitler it clearly came as a terrible frustration. In so far as there had been a rational core to the strategic vision first expounded in *Mein Kampf*, it was the assumption that Germany could not wage a war of conquest in the East if it was also fighting a Western coalition. The hostility of France had always been taken for granted. But France considered in isolation was not an insurmountable obstacle. The crucial factor was Britain. Germany's drive to the east needed to have at least the acquiescence of the British. If Germany had to force both France and Britain into submission, then by any reasonable reckoning, the prospect of a campaign of conquest in the East receded into the distant future. Our knowledge of the Wehrmacht's sweeping Blitzkrieg victory in 1940 tends to cloud our thinking on this point. In 1938 no one – neither the Germans nor their opponents – anticipated the Blitzkrieg. To reasonable German strategic planners, the French and British empires with friends in Eastern Europe and backing from across the Atlantic looked like truly formidable opponents. It was this coalition, after all, that had defeated Germany in 1918. As we have seen, the army that was planned in 1936 was vast, but it was not enough to give the Germans a convincing margin of superiority in offensive weaponry, notably in tanks. German generals did not underestimate the French and they were fully aware of the severe setback that their own expansion programme had suffered in 1937. Furthermore, whatever the size of the army, a land-based offensive would never be enough to defeat the British Empire. The British and French fleets patrolling the Atlantic and the Mediterranean ensured their access to the raw materials of the world. Only if Germany was able to combine its puny naval forces with those of Italy and Japan could it even contemplate an open battle with the Royal Navy.[18] In the air race, Goering's Luftwaffe definitely had the lead. But there was no reason to doubt that the British and French aircraft industries had the potential to catch and overtake Germany's. Above all, a confrontation with the Western powers forced the Nazi regime to reckon with the enormous economic power of the United States. If America provided support to Britain and France, even if the Americans did not enter the war as combatants, one did not need to engage in detailed statistical comparison to realize that the odds were stacked hugely against Germany.

II

By the spring of 1938, the arms race unleashed by German, Italian and Japanese aggression was of such proportions that it threatened to unhinge Hitler's economic miracle altogether. By the time of the May crisis in 1938, France, Britain and the United States were all engaged in substantial rearmament.[19] The advantage that these powers already enjoyed in the naval arena was enormous. To those with access to Germany's confidential military budget, the best contemporary data suggested that the Royal Navy had outspent the Kriegsmarine by 30 per cent since 1933. Rather than narrowing the gap, Britain's already over-whelming advantage in warships had actually increased over the first eight years of Hitler's rule.[20] And Germany's disadvantage was further emphasized on 17 May 1938, a few days before the 'weekend crisis', when President Roosevelt signed into law the Naval Expansion Bill. At $1.15 billion this was the largest peacetime military appropriation in American history, and it ensured that the United States outspent any of its rivals in the worldwide naval arms race.[21] Of even greater concern was Britain's clear intention of matching Germany in the air. At the end of April 1938, sweeping aside the Treasury's financial concerns and the principle that British industry ought to be permitted to continue with 'business as usual', London adopted an ambitious new air programme (Scheme L), which called for the production of 12,000 modern combat aircraft over the next two years.[22] Meanwhile, in France the decision was taken both to step up naval construction, enhance the army and carry out a complete re-equipment of the air force under the so-called Plan V.[23] By May 1938 Edouard Daladier's new right-wing government was arguing over a doubling of the military budget.

If Germany was to make up its huge deficit in naval armaments, if the Luftwaffe was to be developed into a truly effective strategic weapon, whilst the army completed its build-up on the ground, the Reich's military spending would need to be quite unprecedented. We have already seen the difficulties that had prevented the Third Reich from making good on the army's expansion programme of 1936. Nevertheless, in the days following the May crisis of 1938, Hitler gave the order.[24] Germany was now heading towards war. All consideration for the civilian economy was to be set aside. The full, wartime army was now to be completed by April 1939, sooner even than the original target date of April 1940. Furthermore, the army was ordered to build up stocks of ammunition sufficient for at least three months of fighting. In addition, as a direct consequence of threats from Paris and London, Hitler embarked on the accelerated completion of his own version of the Maginot Line, the Westwall. Its purpose was to provide cover for the Western frontier, whilst the bulk of the German army dealt with the Czechs. And, as we have seen, it was to cost at least twice the amount budgeted for the armoured forces. In the space of a week between 25 and 31 May 1938, the German army tripled its request for steel from 400,000 extra tons to more than 1.2 million.[25] And this was only the beginning. In the immediate aftermath of the May crisis, the Luftwaffe's planning also underwent a quantum leap as Goering placed an order for a fleet of no less than 7,000 Ju 88 twin-engined bombers.[26] In so doing, he committed over half the Luftwaffe's workforce to the production of a medium-range bomber, whose only strategic rationale was offensive operations against France and Britain. More particularly, he gambled on Heinrich Koppenberg, the CEO of Junkers, and his expansive dream of Fordist mass production. All firms currently involved in bomber production were to be reorganized around the Junkers head office in Dessau. Each factory would concentrate on producing one major component: engines, fuselage, wings or final assembly. Through 'American' economies of scale,

Table 7. The democratic oceans: worldwide naval spending

million RM, PPP	Britain	United States	France	Germany	Italy	Japan	'Democracies'	'Dictatorships'	Ratio
1929	1,142	1,558	409	201	262	525	3,109	988	3.1
1930	1,072	1,571	448	198	309	501	3,091	1,008	3.1
1931	1,009	1,560	462	192	352	590	3,031	1,134	2.7
1932	872	1,457	399	187	346	593	2,728	1,126	2.4
1933	877	1,268	469	312	326	827	2,614	1,465	1.8
1934	938	1,376	485	497	278	859	2,799	1,634	1.7
1935	1,108	1,798	476	695	256	928	3,382	1,879	1.8
1936	1,388	2,072	517	1,161	300	938	3,977	2,399	1.7
1937	1,595	1,866	444	1,479	313	1,056	3,905	2,848	1.4
1938	1,878	2,026	462	1,756	339	1,049	4,366	3,144	1.4
1939	2,277	2,872	724	2,390	424	1,256	5,873	4,070	1.4
Total 1929–39	14,156	19,424	5,295	9,067	3,505	9,122	38,875	21,694	1.8
Total 1933–39	10,061	13,278	3,577	8,289	2,236	6,913	26,916	17,438	1.5

Sources: Institut fuer Konjunkturforschung, *Wochenbericht*, 12 July 1939, 169–72; J. Duelffer, *Weimar, Hitler und die Marine: Reichspolitik und Flottenbau, 1920–1939* (Duesseldorf, 1973), 563

Germany would secure its dominance over its European enemies. Within less than two years, Koppenberg promised to deliver state-of-the-art bombers, at the rate of 250 per month. Naval planning proceeded at a more leisurely pace, but it too was caught up in the drama of escalation.[27] On 24 May Hitler ordered the accelerated completion of battleships F and G (*Bismarck* and *Tirpitz*). He also ordered an expanded U-boat programme, in case of war with Britain.

All this posed huge new demands on the Four Year Plan.[28] And here, too, Goering could rely on initiative from within the military-industrial complex. Predictably enough, it was Carl Krauch and his close collaborator Otto Ambros – one of IG's up and coming synthetics experts – who took the lead.[29] After the completion of the Reich's new armaments schemes in 1942–3 they estimated that the Reich's annual requirement for fuel and oil would rise to no less than 13.8 million tons. Thanks to the steel shortages, the Four Year Plan was behind schedule. In 1938 synthetic production would not exceed 2.4 million tons and the supply of air fuel was even more inadequate. Deficiencies in explosives and gunpowder were no less glaring. In 1918, Imperial Germany had produced 13,600 tons of high explosives and 13,250 tons of gunpowder per month. In the summer of 1938 the Third Reich's capacity was no more than 5,400 tons of either. To make up the gap, on 12 July 1938 Goering approved a new version of the Four Year Plan known as the New Military-Economic Production Plan (Wehrwirtschaftliche Neuer Erzeugungsplan).[30] By the middle of 1941 Krauch aimed to reach monthly production of 17,100 tons of high explosives and 18,100 tons of powder. Synthetic fuel output was programmed for 8.3 million tons by 1942–3 and 11 million tons by 1944. And in August 1938, with war over the Sudetenland perhaps only weeks away, even this was not enough. To reach World War I levels by the end of 1939, Krauch launched the Schnellplan, a short-range emergency programme with absolutely top priority amongst all the Wehrmacht's many programmes. To ensure that Krauch got the resources he needed, Goering promoted him to the special status of general plenipotentiary for special questions of chemical production (GB Chem), a position from which he dominated the German chemicals industry until the end of the war.[31]

Krauch in chemicals and Koppenberg at Junkers were two of the foremost exponents of the new, freewheeling military industrialism. Their technological vision was beguiling, as was their can-do rhetoric of entrepreneurial leadership. And they found a willing audience in Goering. But despite their voluntarist rhetoric the realization of their promises depended on the allocation of resources. Since November 1937, Hitler had been promising more generous steel rations. Now, after months of frustrated waiting, he made good. On 17 June 1938, in conference with Goering, Hitler raised the Wehrmacht's steel quota from 325,000 to 500,000 tons.[32] Over the following months this was further supplemented to 658,333 tons. By August 1938, 35–6 per cent of Germany's steel production was going to the Wehrmacht. When one added in the allocations to the Four Year Plan and the military road building programme, the military's share of German steel production was more than 40 per cent. For scarcer imported metals, such as copper, the share was even larger. In the summer of 1938, though nominally still at peace, the Nazi regime was pushing the German economy onto a war footing.

The financial consequences were dramatic. Prior to the Anschluss, in early 1938 Reich Finance Minister Schwerin von Krosigk and Reichsbank president Schacht had agreed to apply a dose of fiscal conservatism to the overheating Germany economy.[33] As of March 1938, there was to be no more issuing of the Mefo bonds.[34] Henceforth, they agreed, the Reich would be required to respect the conventional rules of public finance. Current expenditure would be limited to the amount that could be paid for out of taxes. One-off expenses and long-term investments would be financed out of national savings, through the normal, non-inflationary channel of long-term borrowing. The dramatic escalation in international tension following the Anschluss put paid to this retrenchment programme. Rather than contracting, as Schacht and Krosigk had hoped, military spending surged. On 30 May Goering informed the army that 'in relation to money . . . we would no longer need to worry in future . . . dealing with this issue was a question for the political leadership'.[35] Though the Reichsbank held the line on Mefo bonds, short-term Treasury bills (Schatzanweisungen), which were originally intended to provide the Reich with a limited means of flexible finance, were used to fund a massive military spending spree. Between April and October 1938, the German army alone spent no less than 4.9 billion Reichsmarks, more than 5 per cent of total national income.[36] For the calendar year the share of military spending in national income topped 19 per cent.

This huge increase in military spending marked a decisive turning point. Up to 1938, though the expansion of the armaments sector had been dramatic and had forced trade-offs at the margin, especially in relation to import priorities, it had nevertheless proceeded side by side with growth in other parts of the economy. Compared to the trough of the recession in 1932, there had been, by 1937, a modest recovery both in business investment and household consumption. This had been possible, largely because the margin of unemployed resources was so large. With 6 million unemployed in 1933, both Wehrmacht expenditure and civilian economic activity could be expanded side by side. The main constraint on the German economy was the external limitation imposed by the balance of payments. In 1938 the German economy reached the limit of this type of extensive economic growth. It was impossible to reconcile a 70 per cent increase in military spending and the heavy investment programmes of the Four Year Plan with any further increase in consumption. In an economy in which output was expanding at 8 per cent per annum, household consumption stagnated.[37] And this understates the drama of the adjustment process going on within the German economy. Steel is more indicative. Measured in terms of steel, the quantity of materials available for non-Wehrmacht purposes was cut by 25 per cent between March and July 1938, from a high point of 1.345 million tons to 1.041 million tons.[38] The cutback would have been even more serious, but for the decision taken in late 1937 to raise German steel production to the limit of capacity. By mobilizing all available labour, scrap and a special consignment of top-quality Swedish iron ore, Germany's steelmills in 1938 achieved a record annual output of almost 21.5 million tons.[39] With the American economy slumping back into recession, Germany could claim, briefly at least, to be the world's leading steel producer.

The consequences of this reallocation of resources for the rest of the German economy were obviously drastic. But with war seemingly imminent, the Nazi leadership did not hesitate. To representatives of the army in the summer of 1938, Goering remarked: 'The armed forces should not concern themselves with the fate of the economy. The Field Marshal [i.e. Goering] had sole responsibility: the collapse of parts of the economy was irrelevant. Ways will be found. The Reich will provide supportive intervention.'[40] On 8 July during a major address to leading industrial representatives of the air industry Goering spelt out the implications for individual businessmen. With linguisitic coherence straining under the weight of his emphasis, he thumped the table. Germany was facing the possibility of a 'world war, in which' its enemies would include 'France and England, Russia, [and] America as the main forces'.[41] Whether or not America entered the war as a combatant, Goering was in no doubt that Britain and France would be able to draw on its 'immense reservoir of raw materials'.[42] Given the power of this enormous coalition, they faced the 'greatest hour of destiny ever since there has been a German history'. Everything had to be staked on a massive armaments effort. 'I am truly of the opinion – we shall not be able to save our fatherland unless we stake all our passions.' German industry should put aside all worries about excess capacity and long-term profitability. All that mattered was winning the war.

For this goal, however, we must take risks. We have to stake our best . . . nobody here exists by himself . . . everybody stands and falls with Germany's existence . . . It does not matter if someone says – I disapprove entirely of the national socialist system. I don't care. Let him disapprove, it is still the system which at this moment decides Germany's fate. This is why he has willy-nilly to cooperate . . . Gentlemen . . . not for a second and I mean a second, would I hesitate – as I proved with regard to another matter [the Reichswerke] – to intervene at once to confiscate . . . the whole business, if I should come to the conclusion that he does not understand, that he can see the world only from the toilet seat perspective of his own enterprise [Klosetedeckelhorizont], and cannot look further . . . that fellow must go. By a stroke of my pen he would lose his business and his property.

Goering's crass bullying aside, it is clear that the Reich's economic administration fully understood the problem of macroeconomic management facing them in 1938.[43] The Reichsbank economics department had been analysing the problem of excess demand and the dangers it posed at least since 1936. In late June 1938, the Reich Ministry of Economic Affairs had set up a specialist section dedicated to national investment management.[44] Drawing on the most sophisticated system of macroeconomic statistics available anywhere in the Western world, this section set itself to monitoring the competing demands being made on the German economy.[45] No peacetime capitalist economy had ever operated with military expenditure at the level now being contemplated in Nazi Germany. Assuming that the Reich's authorities were determined to force through the priorities of the Wehrmacht and the Four Year Plan, well in excess of 20 per cent of national income was now to be devoted to rearmament. The question was how this huge transfer of resources would be effected. Reallocating raw materials such as steel and copper was the most immediate means available. Notionally at least, shutting down a low priority building site by cutting its steel quota also had the effect of releasing other scarce resources such as labour and machinery. But this was, at best, a rough-and-ready mechanism, as evidenced by the half-finished construction projects dotted across Germany, populated by underemployed workers and idle machinery waiting for steel priorities to shift back in their favour. But quantitative rationing was not the only means of directing the economy. Despite Goering's blustering rhetoric, money and prices still mattered in the Third Reich. Even in the case of the steel industry, which was now subject to comprehensive command and control systems, transactions were completed by money payment. With private ownership still the norm, the profit motive remained the ultimate inducement to production. And from this point of view the problem facing the Reich authorities was a classic problem of macro-economic management: how to regulate the total volume of demand so that the key priorities of armament and autarchy were met, whilst at the same time ensuring that Germany did not slide into inflation?

The problem facing the Reich Ministries was a problem of excess demand. After allowing for consumer expenditure, financed directly out of household income, the total volume of planned government spending and business investment on the one side of the equation substantially exceeded the available sources of financing, namely tax revenues, retained business profits and household savings. For 1938, the RWM expected this gap to come to at least 8.1 billion Reichsmarks.[46] To put this in perspective, the tax and customs revenue of the Reich and local authorities came to 22.2 billion Reichsmarks. By 1938 German households were already saving an unusually high margin of their income, so there was little prospect of increased 'funding' from that direction. The main alternatives were therefore to raise taxes or to repress private investment. It has often been remarked that the Third Reich could have done more to raise taxes.[47] But this ignores the fact that Germany in the late 1930s was already the most heavily taxed society in Europe.[48] Given the modest standard of living of the German population there was little scope for raising broad-based income or consumption taxes. So the Finance Ministry proceeded selectively. Corporation tax was lifted in the autumn of 1938.[49] At the same time the Reich plundered the coffers

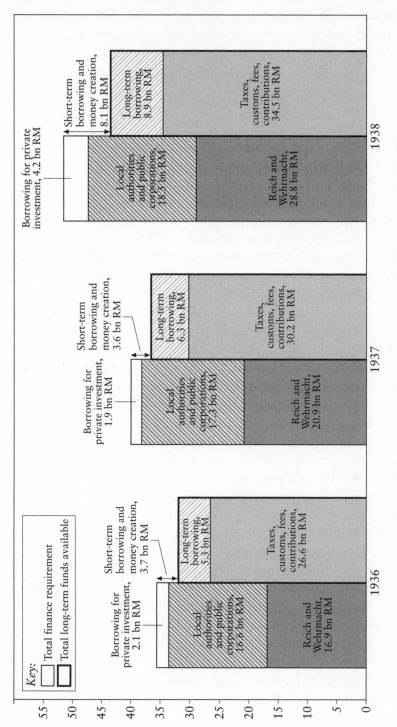

Figure 9. Inflationary imbalance between financing requirements and available funds, a contemporary view (billion Reichsmarks)

of local government, redirecting hundreds of millions of Reichsmarks towards national priorities. And the Reich Finance Ministry issued strict injunctions curbing all public construction not explicitly authorized by Berlin.[50] To ensure that it was the Reich not the private sector that secured the lion's share of German private saving, the Reichsbank exerted systematic pressure on savings banks and insurance offices to invest their funds in government bonds and short-term paper.[51] Most dramatically, the Reich made a determined effort to curb private construction, the most important form of private investment. As of the autumn of 1938 the Reichsbank banned all new mortgage borrowing.[52] Given the importance of both public and private construction contracts to tens of thousands of small businesses across the country and the importance of the housing shortage as a social issue, the significance of these restrictions can hardly be exaggerated. At a time when Germany was facing the worst housing shortage in its history, the decrees of the summer of 1938 meant an end to publicly funded housing construction. Under such circumstances, a despairing housing official in the Reich Labour Office commented: 'A severe crisis of [public] confidence and bitterness' were inevitable.[53]

The frustrations of the housing shortage were no doubt acute. But, more worrying for the Reich authorities was the impact of underinvestment on the German railway system. By 1938 the Reichsbahn was increasingly unable to cope with the combined demands of the Wehrmacht and a booming economy. Rail investment had been badly squeezed by the steel shortage. In 1938 the Reichsbahn was not able to obtain even half the steel it needed to maintain its current rail infrastructure and rolling stock.[54] From the summer onwards severe delays affected the entire system. Huge pressure was exerted on freight workers to speed up loading and unloading. But by the last days of September, as the Munich crisis reached its climax, the Reichsbahn was nearing the point of collapse. Less than half the requests for freight cars were being met on time. There was no option but to go over to an overt system of rationing in which priority was given first of all to the Wehrmacht and then perishable foods, coal, sugar beet and high-priority export orders.[55] The authorities did their best to suppress technical reports on the deterioration in the system.[56] But the symptoms of strain and disorganization were too obvious to be hidden from public view. In the autumn of 1938 freight trains regularly left stations festooned with red repair slips indicating faulty brakes, and the deterioration in Germany's once proud railway network had become so severe that it had begun to attract international comment.[57]

Behind the apparatus of price controls and rationing it was clear by the summer of 1938 that the wrenching acceleration of military expenditure since 1933 had created a situation of severe disequilibrium in German economic life. This at least was the conclusion that emerged from a day-long conference on 2 June 1938 attended by a roster of Germany's most prestigious economics professors and hosted by the Reichsbank together with the Wehrmacht's military-economic office.[58] The meeting opened with an address by Schacht on issues of money and credit followed by an extended discussion. After the meeting the Reichsbank compiled a list of the key points, which give a good indication of the questions preoccupying the policy-making elite in Nazi Germany in the summer of the Sudeten crisis. The list included:

The techniques of financial makeshift (Mefo *et al.*);

The dangers of the unconsolidated Reich debt;

The limits of public indebtedness;

The possibilities for a further restriction of consumption;

The Reichsbank's control over money and credit creation; . . .

The possibilities for satisfying an eventual increase in the demand for credit from the business sector;

The danger of deflationary symptoms in the event of a lull in government orders;

The dangers of a bubble economy outside the public sector (hire purchase credit . . .);

The dangers posed by the widespread false appearance of liquidity;

The dangers posed by [business] self-financing.

The minute concluded that the meeting had served its purpose in that it had achieved 'on the most important points a wide-ranging consensus between the views of the Reichsbank and the Wehrmacht's military-economic staff on the one hand, and the professors on the other'. There was unanimity that the chief problem was how to balance the demands of the state, in other words rearmament, against the limitations of the German economy. The economists also agreed with their hosts 'that we are already . . . in the danger zone and that an inflation in a peacetime economy would be as fruitless as it would be psychologically unacceptable'.

III

The two areas that were of greatest concern in the summer of 1938, were the labour market and the increasingly disorderly state of the German price system.[59] The two were closely interconnected. By any conventional standard, the German economy in 1938 was fully employed. Indeed, Germany was suffering from an acute shortage of labour.[60] In many industries both labour and plant were being 'over-worked'. On 14 July 1938 the Labour Ministry reported to the Reich Chancellery that there were only 292,327 unemployed in all of the Altreich (pre-Anschluss Germany), barely more than 1 per cent of the workforce. And of this total only 28,000 were fully fit for work.[61] In the last quarter of 1938, in Berlin, one of Germany's most important centres of industrial production, the labour exchanges recorded only 35,170 unemployed, of whom at most 6,000 were fully fit. Of these, at least a third were 'artistic professionals', would-be actors and musicians, who as paid-up members of the Reich's corporation of artistic workers enjoyed a protected status. Dealing with this bohemian residuum posed special problems for the officials of the Berlin labour exchanges, who faced 'fits of temper' and 'time-consuming complaints', if a change of profession was 'even suggested'. At a time of national emergency, the Berlin trustee of labour was moved to the philistine observation that it was surely unacceptable that 'such a large number of fully fit *Volksgenossen* should be exempt from ... radical occupational redirection'.[62]

The situation of the Labour Ministry officials might have been easier but for the effects of the wage stop that had been reinforced in November 1936 along with the price stop. This helped to prevent excess demand from spilling over into general wage inflation. But it also meant that there was no market mechanism to guide a 'spontaneous' redeployment of workers into the highest priority sectors. Here too Hitler's regime had robbed itself of one of the most effective, flexible and unobtrusive mechanisms for managing shortages. Indeed, by 1938 the fear of the inflationary pressure that everyone knew to be hanging over the German economy was such that any flexibility in wage setting was liable to be interpreted as indiscipline or even sabotage.[63] If the market was not allowed to function, the logical alternative was to allocate labour by administrative means, as in the rationing of steel. And by 1938, the Third Reich was clearly moving in that direction. Since the unemployment crisis of the early 1930s the Reich's labour exchanges had begun to monitor an ever-larger percentage of the German workforce with detailed card files covering individual career histories.[64] In 1935 this information system was made fully comprehensive with the introduction of compulsory workbooks. These identified every individual employed in the German economy and provided full details on education, skill level and job history.[65] One copy was kept by the local labour exchange, a second by the employer. Furthermore, in the early 1930s, as part of the effort to manage the most serious unemployment black spots, the labour administration adopted measures to limit regional migration. At one point, in an effort to retain workers in the countryside, the labour exchanges even banned people who had previously worked in agriculture from entering into non-agricultural employment. In February 1937, the demands of the Four Year Plan and rearmament made necessary a special decree covering metalworkers. This required them to seek prior permission before changing jobs.[66] And with the armaments effort reaching new heights, Goering's Decree for Securing Labour for Tasks of Special State Importance (Verordnung zur Sicherstellung des Kraeftebedarfs fuer Aufgaben von besonderer staatspolitischer Bedeutung) of 22 June 1938 provided the Reich with general powers of conscription.[67] Workers could be redeployed for any period required by the Reich, whilst their former employers were required to keep them on their rolls. By the end of 1939, no less than 1.3 million workers had been subject to such compulsory work orders.[68]

Though compulsion was not the norm in relation to German workers, any more than it was in the regime's dealings with German business, the possibility was now established that if rearmament demanded, the state could intervene in the working life of every single individual. In this respect as well, Hitler's regime clearly crossed a bridge in the summer of 1938. Perhaps not surprisingly, however, the rationing of labour functioned even less smoothly than the rationing of steel. The decree debarring rural workers from taking industrial jobs had to be abandoned, since, to avoid their children falling under the terms of the decree, rural families had taken to preventing them from entering farm work in the first place.[69] Meanwhile, in the inflation hot spots of urban Germany, the attempt to repress the market mechanism had only limited success.

It was, after all, in the interests of neither employers nor workers to abide by the official wage restrictions. Workers wanted better wages and employers – keen to take advantage of the boom – were willing to pay for their labour. Given the formal ban on wage increases, the resulting upward adjustment of earnings was a covert process, hidden in accelerated promotion, high-status apprenticeships, retraining schemes, hiring bonuses, improved working conditions and a variety of supplementary social benefits. The extent of this 'wage creep' depended on the degree to which employers were subject to direct official oversight. Ironically, the immediate producers of armaments, who came under the scrutiny of military inspectors, were often at a disadvantage relative to their sub-contractors and suppliers, who attracted less attention. But by 1938 the on-going distortion of pay scales could no longer be denied.[70] Furthermore, though they were decried as symptoms of inflationary indiscipline and though the emerging system of wage differentials did suffer from a degree of arbitrariness, these illicit monetary incentives were highly functional in sucking workers into those sectors where they were needed most. Whilst the number of people employed in consumer industries such as textiles and clothing remained lower than it had been before 1929, the number working in industries such as machine-building and electrical engineering increased dramatically and the shift was far larger than could be accounted for by administrative measures.

Whilst metalworking, chemicals and construction boomed, the inflationary battle for resources took a severe toll on the weakest sector of the German economy, agriculture.[71] The majority of German farms relied principally on family members, but paid farm labour was indispensable to the operation of all farms over 20 hectares. At the Bauerntag held on 27 November 1938, Walther Darré was forced to announce that the latest workbook survey compiled by the labour administration revealed that the population of paid farm labourers had fallen by 400,000 since 1933, a reduction of almost 20 per cent in the space of only five years. Allowing for the natural increase which Darré believed should have been expected, he arrived at the shock figure of 700,000 for the number of workers lost to agriculture since 1933.[72] Of course, agricultural labour had long been at the bottom of the occupational hierarchy. But the racist ideologues of Nazi agrarianism now feared that farm labour was becoming a sink for the least valuable elements in German society.[73] RNS experts scared themselves with surveys such as

Table 8. Blue-and-white collar occupations, 1938 v. 1933 (ooo workers)

	Census 1933	Workbook census 1938	Change	% Change
Farm labourers	2,494	1,981	−513	−21
Textiles and clothing	2,030	1,701	−329	−16
Food	1,207	953	−254	−21
Commerce	2,686	2,494	−192	−7
Health and social work	595	494	−101	−17
Woodworking	689	623	−66	−10
Mining	756	713	−43	−6
Entertainment	124	84	−40	−32
Transport	983	975	−8	−1
Total	11,564	10,018	−1,546	−13
Water, gas, electricity	188	195	7	4
Paper and printing	499	521	22	4
Building materials	587	632	45	8
Chemicals	353	453	100	28
Domestic service	1,280	1,438	158	12
Iron and steel	1,314	1,533	219	17
Construction and allied	1,745	2,071	326	19
Public service	725	1,226	501	69
Engineering, etc.	1,561	2,307	746	48
Total	8,252	10,376	2,124	26

Source: T. W. Mason, *Arbeiterklasse und Volksgemeinschaft* (Opladen, 1975), 1247–8

one conducted in the vicinity of Goettingen that counted four cases of 'subnormality' and two forced sterilizations in a sample of only twenty-six unmarried maids. In Marienburg the situation was no better with six cases of 'subnormality' and one forced sterilization in a sample of thirty-eight. This, needless to say, was not how Darré and his cohorts had imagined the future of the new countryside.

It may seem odd, at a moment of high international drama, to return to the placid fields of rural Germany. But there can be no doubt that in the summer of 1938 the leadership of the Third Reich believed itself to be threatened by a crisis in the national food supply. For the agrarians, a significant lobby in their own right with vital connections to the ideological heart of the Nazi party, the problems of agriculture called into question the entire achievement of Hitler's government. Above all, there was alarm in RNS circles about the way in which farming families were responding to the labour shortage. Farm women were the most overworked group in the rural population, and reducing the number of children was the most obvious way to cut their work burden.[74] In Niedersachsen, the very heartland of the German peasantry, the number of children per couple had fallen by as much as 33 per cent in a single generation.[75] At the same time the labour shortage was also threatening the efforts of the RNS to raise domestic production. Already in 1937 the harvest had borne all the hallmarks of an emergency 'Aktion'.[76] The regular farm workforce had had to be supported by Labour Front draftees, soldiers, convicts and schoolchildren. More worrying still were the signs that persistent labour shortages were inducing German commercial farms to cut back the more labour-intensive forms of production. Following the cattle census of 1938, there was extreme concern in the Reichsnaehrstand about the future of the dairy herd.[77] Though to a detached observer the small shifts in production visible in the German agricultural statistics hardly seem to warrant an acute state of alarm, there is no doubt that they were taken extremely seriously in Berlin. The prevailing school of thought in the Third Reich blamed the collapse of the German home front in World War I on the failure to maintain the food supply. And no less a figure than Ludwig Beck, chief of army general staff, repeatedly stressed a satisfactory harvest in 1938 as a key precondition for war readiness.[78] There was real concern that the full mobilization of the army with its demands both for manpower and horses would bring the agricultural labour situation to breaking point. And it was in part for this reason that Hitler set the date for a blow against Czechoslovakia in October, well after the harvest was in.

What caused labour to drain out of agriculture was the huge differential in wages and standard of living between town and country. This imbalance had been the driver of labour migration in Germany at least since the mid-nineteenth century. The acute labour shortage of the late

1930s merely accelerated the flow. The booming market for construction workers was particularly attractive for unskilled farm labour. The crash effort to construct the Westwall along the border with France was widely blamed for having thrown the west German labour market into utter confusion.[79] In the second half of 1938, country pubs buzzed with rumours of the fabulous sums that were to be earned on the Fuehrer's giant new building site. And the Reich Labour Ministry gave special mention to one lucky individual who, having laid some concrete on his farm, was signed up as a supervisor on the Westwall, at the extraordinary rate of 350 Reichsmarks per month. As the Ministerial officials commented disapprovingly: 'Shortly afterwards the farmer returned to his home village for a visit, fully kitted out with new clothes, and got all the attention one would expect in the local hostelry.'[80] Some skilled construction workers were rumoured to earn better wages than senior army officers. And this was no accident. In May 1938, Hitler had removed control of the Westwall from the army's engineering department and handed it to Fritz Todt, the man idolized as the master-builder of the autobahns. Todt's mission was to complete the fortifications before the outbreak of hostilities and he was to do so regardless of cost. Goering's decree on labour conscription provided Todt with all necessary legal powers to secure the quarter of a million workers he needed.[81] But typically for the situation of the German economy in the late 1930s he chose to supplement conscription with monetary incentives. The contractors on the Westwall were freed from standard military procurement rules, allowing them to inflate both their profits and their wage bills. By the summer of 1939, Todt had completed his mission. The most vulnerable sections of Germany's western frontier were reinforced with thousands of bunkers and gun emplacements. The price, however, was a huge inflationary shock to the labour market.

Agriculture thus exemplified the most basic problem afflicting the management of the German economy by the summer of 1938: the disorientation of decision-making induced by the politicization of every aspect of economic life. Who was to say what the appropriate level of income was for farm labourers? As far as the RNS was concerned, the low incomes of German farmers were the reflection of the continuing 'undervaluation' of agricultural labour, a bitter ideological legacy inherited by the Third Reich from its corrupt predecessors. To bolster this thesis, RNS agronomists compared the per capita share of national income accrued by workers in industry and agriculture and arrived at the conclusion that farm work was undervalued by at least 25 per cent.[82] What was required was a 'rebalancing' of agricultural and industrial incomes, for which the RNS suggested various solutions.[83] One option was to charge the urban population at least 10 per cent more for their food, choking off 'excess' urban demand and allowing farmers to pay better wages. If this was ruled out as inflationary, the RNS proposed a lengthening of the industrial working day by an hour, with the proceeds going to agriculture; what amounted, in effect, to a 10 per cent tax on urban incomes. Alternatively, the RNS suggested a general deflation of all urban prices and wages, to bring them into line with the prices and wages being paid to farmers.

Setting aside the shock to the urban economy that any of these proposals would have inflicted, it is the assumptions on which the arguments rested that are worthy of note. The RNS started from the premiss that all forms of labour were equal in worth and that one would, therefore, expect to see an equal distribution of per capita incomes across the economy. This assumption is alien to any kind of conventional economic reasoning, which assumes that relative incomes ultimately reflect productive contribution as valued at prices determined by supply and demand. From this point of view the fundamental explanation for the poverty of German agriculture was simple: low labour productivity. According to conventional measures, the productivity of the more than 9 million people employed on Germany's farms was roughly half that of the typical non-agricultural worker.[84] What was really scarce in the countryside was not labour but the necessary capital and technology to use labour efficiently. Such productivity comparisons of course depended on the relative prices paid for agricultural and industrial products. And the RNS demanded higher farm prices, but this ignored the enormous gulf between the prices paid by German consumers for their food and the prices prevailing on world markets.[85] By the late 1930s, however, the 'world market' as far as Germany was concerned was an increasingly irrelevant abstraction. Given the politicization of its foreign trade, Germany no longer purchased at 'world' prices. Instead, agricultural imports were bargaining items in a complex web of bilateral deals, in which Germany often paid substantial premiums for the willingness of its trading partners to remain loyal to the Third Reich.[86]

Indeed, by the late 1930s the politicization of Germany's economic system was so far-reaching that it was virtually impossible to find reliable standards of valuation, whether for agricultural labour or any other commodity. This was the distressing conclusion reached in a series of confidental reports on the 'true' external value of the Reichsmark compiled by the Reichsbank.[87] By 1938 the overvaluation of the Reichsmark, which had dominated the debate a few years earlier, was superseded by a more fundamental problem. The argument in favour of devaluation rested on the assumption that there was a coherent system of German prices that was out of alignment with that prevailing in other countries, a problem that could be resolved by an adjustment in the external value of the Reichsmark. According to the Reichsbank, this was no longer realistic. For years the rates at which goods were exchanged with each other had not been determined by the anonymous and continuous workings of the market system, but by a series of ad hoc and inconsistent political decisions. The consequence was that for foreign trade purposes the Reichsmark now lacked any well-defined value. The purchasing power of the Reichsmark in foreign transactions depended entirely on which commodity it was measured in terms of and from where those goods were sourced. To take raw cotton, one particularly important item: Germany paid close to world-market prices for imports from Egypt, a premium of only 15 per cent to British India, 28 per cent to its American suppliers, but no less than 47 per cent and 72 per cent to its new sources of supply in Brazil and Peru respectively. In the case of butter, Danish imports were at world prices, whereas the Dutch extracted a premium of 63 per cent. Nor was there a coherent pattern of 'country premiums'. By contrast with the enormous mark-up on Peruvian cotton, the premium for refined petrol from the same source was only 10 per cent. Similarly, the premiums paid to Romania varied between 27 per cent for wheat and 48 per cent for maize. Nor was there any corresponding discrepancy in the trade deals arranged with either Yugoslavia or Hungary; they received less than 30 per cent for both wheat and maize. As the Reichsbank concluded, it was increasingly idle to discuss the 'correct' devaluation necessary to bring the German and international price systems into alignment, since 'the entire price structure of foreign trade both in commodity and country terms has been confused to a barely credible degree'.[88]

When Walther Darré addressed the general assembly of the German peasantry (Bauerntag) in the autumn of 1938 and stated bluntly that the problem of agricultural labour could only be solved 'if the NSDAP ... took the unalterable decision, to overcome it whatever the circumstances',[89] this was not an expression of economic ignorance. It was an accurate statement about the basic determinant of resource allocation in Nazi Germany.[90] In the event, Darré's appeal was in vain. The Nazi leadership had other things on its mind. As serious as the situation appeared to be in agriculture, it was not the issue of milkmaids and dairy prices that really troubled Hitler's regime in the summer of 1938. After months of bitter argument, the problem of dairy farming was given a political 'fix' by raising the farm-price of milk by 2 Pfennigs. Since Rudolf Hess had made clear that an increase in the prices paid by consumers was out of the question, the conflict was resolved at the expense of the dairies, by squeezing their profit margins. This did not curb demand for milk. Nor was it enough to resolve the income deficit of German dairy farmers. But it did at least send a political signal that the regime was not oblivious to the interests of its agrarian constituency.[91] The real issue facing the Third Reich in the summer of 1938 was not the question of how to deal with the bothersome social side effects of breakneck rearmament. What had to be faced was the question of peace or war. And it was over this existential decision that a dangerous fissure threatened to open between various factions within the leadership of Hitler's regime.

IV

There was never much coherence amongst the opponents of war in 1938. They included marginal conservative figures such as Ulrich von Hassell and Carl Goerdeler, but also men with more influence such as Hjalmar Schacht, Schwerin von Krosigk at the Finance Ministry and the newly appointed Secretary of State at the Foreign Ministry, Ernst von Weizsaecker.[92] The majority of the army's generals also opposed a war with Britain and France. Most of them did so on purely military grounds, but some drew broader conclusions, most notably Ludwig Beck, and his successor as army chief of staff Franz Halder. Even Hermann Goering, despite the role he played in escalating the demands of the armaments effort, must be counted amongst the opponents of a premature war in 1938.[93] Obviously, what these men had in common was not principled opposition to Hitler's regime. Nor were they opposed to war per se. What they had in common was the view that, given the state of the Wehrmacht's armaments and the German economy, the Third Reich in the summer of 1938 was in no position to risk a major war with Britain and France, especially if those countries were backed by the United States.

General Beck first made the case against war in a memorandum drafted in direct response to Hitler's comments at the 'Hossbach' conference of 5 November 1937, and he repeated the same basic arguments in a series of reports and speeches up to the beginning of August 1938.[94] In Beck's view, the British and French response to the May crisis had to be taken seriously. Military action by Germany against the Czechs was bound to trigger intervention by the Western powers. Germany would then find itself facing the largest land army in Europe, fielded by the French, combined with the enormous economic resources of the British Empire, securely protected by the Royal Navy. Furthermore, it was a fallacy to consider France and Britain in isolation. Beck considered it axiomatic that both powers, in case of a conflict with Germany, would be able to draw on the economic resources of the United States. 'In this respect,' he wrote on 5 May 1938, 'the measures taken by both states to use America as a supplier of military material are highly significant, since they are far more advanced than was the case in 1914.' Germany in 1938, he wrote, faced a 'Czech, French, British and American coalition whose cooperation in case of war [was] already more closely coordinated than in 1914'.[95] Beck did not engage in a detailed comparison of forces. He did not need to. It was obvious to all concerned that this Western grouping had an overwhelming material advantage. Their naval superiority was already enormous. Any deficits in the air could easily be made good with American assistance. Rather than risking an immediate offensive, Britain and France would seek to draw Germany into a long war of attrition. The Wehrmacht's only hope was to strike decisive blows against both the Czechs and the French in quick succession. This, however, depended on the German army and the air force being ready for battle from the beginning. Beck did not comment on the Luftwaffe, but internal sources make it clear that it was far from ready for war in the autumn of 1938.[96] The German army would certainly have defeated the Czechs. What concerned Beck was the possibility that France might intervene in the West whilst the majority of the German armed forces were tied down in Bohemia. Furthermore, even if Germany did manage to survive this initial period of risk, the German army in 1938 was clearly not in a position to inflict a decisive battlefield defeat on the French. Even to make good the plans of 1936 would require a huge increase in the armaments effort. And Beck, for one, had learned his lesson from the setback of 1937. Whether or not a sustained 'acceleration of armaments is possible,' he wrote in the early summer of 1938, 'requires investigation. Many years of experience suggest that such attempts have always been frustrated by the limitations imposed by reality.'[97]

There were reasons to quibble with Beck's analysis of the risks involved in the Czech operation and in particular his judgement on the likelihood of an immediate French attack on Germany's western frontier.[98] But it was in any case a mistake on Beck's part to mix such operational concerns with his more important and accurate strategic assessment. As was demonstrated in the last week of September 1938, if Hitler had insisted on using military force to liquidate Czechoslovakia the French and the British governments would not have pulled back. On 28 September 1938 Europe teetered on the edge of war.[99] And for Germany the result would surely have been disaster. As Beck clearly understood, given the underlying balance in population, raw materials and financial power, it was the Germans not the British and French who needed to force a rapid military decision. Following the logic of Beck's own analysis it was most unlikely that the French would take the risk of a major offensive in the West. Instead, they would settle for a long war of attrition. The behaviour of Roosevelt's administration gave them every reason to expect American assistance.[100] Furthermore, Beck was clearly correct in his assessment of the state of the German army. Whatever the precise timetable for the conquest of Bohemia, Germany in 1938 certainly did not have the military means to follow up an invasion of Czechoslovakia with a swift and decisive blow against France. The Third Reich would therefore have been forced into a defensive posture, encircled in both East and West by potentially or actively hostile powers.

Interestingly, when Beck considered who else to enrol in his efforts to oppose the war, his list did not include Hjalmar Schacht, but it did include Goering – both as the Commander-in-Chief of the Luftwaffe and as the man Beck held responsible for the removal of Blomberg and Fritsch, who might therefore be tempted, 'at the right moment also to get rid of the Fuehrer'.[101] To make the economic case against war, Beck hoped to enrol Schwerin von Krosigk, the Reich Finance Minister. Tellingly, Beck thought that he could count on Krosigk to intervene with Hitler no later than the second half of September, 'since the state of the exchequer by that point will force him to'.[102] And Beck's judgement was accurate. By August 1938, apparently on his own initiative, Krosigk had contacted Secretary of State Weiszaecker at the Foreign Office to gain an insider's view of the diplomatic situation. Weizsaecker for his part had already concluded in early June 1938 that in the event of a war with Britain and France, Germany would find itself facing a 'world coalition' (*Weltkoalition*) including both the United States and the Soviet Union. Even if it could count on the assistance of Italy and Japan, the outcome of such a conflict could not be in doubt. Germany would suffer 'exhaustion and defeat' (*Erschoepfung und Niederlage*).[103] Soon afterwards, Krosigk asked Hitler for an interview and when the Fuehrer refused him this privilege Krosigk drafted a memorandum setting out the situation of the Reich's finances and their implications for German diplomacy.[104]

In making his case, Krosigk could not simply confront Hitler with an open declaration of bankruptcy. That would have been to fatally undermine his own credibility.[105] On the other hand, he was desperate to bring home to Hitler the seriousness of the Reich's financial situation. To start on a positive note, Krosigk began his memorandum by recounting how the Reich Finance Ministry had played its part in the programmes of work creation and rearmament. Up to 1938, Krosigk insisted, these had been financed in large part from tax revenues and secure long-term borrowing. This first phase of expansion had been brought to a conclusion with the end of the new issue of Mefo bills in the spring of 1938. To accommodate the sudden increase in military spending following the Anschluss, Krosigk had been forced to resort to the expedient of raising taxes and issuing short-term notes. This had sufficed in May and June. Now, however, due to the extraordinary acceleration of rearmament, the Reich was facing a serious cash-flow crisis. In August the army had spent 900 million Reichsmarks. In September this had risen to 1.2 billion Reichsmarks. By the end of the month, the Reich's cash resources would be 'exhausted'. To secure the necessary funds by 'printing of currency' was 'out of the question'. So Krosigk desperately needed to float a new loan. However, as Europe appeared to be sliding towards war, a wave of negative sentiment was sweeping the financial markets. Between April 1938 and the end of

August, the German stock market had fallen by 13 per cent.[106] The Reich, Krosigk claimed, was in the grip of a mounting wave of 'war- and inflation psychosis'. This 'psychosis' was strengthened by the signs of incipient inflation visible throughout the German economy. But above all the state of the markets was a reflection of the fact that the Reich was 'steering towards a serious financial crisis . . .', precipitated by a drive to war. 'Gossip by all circles of the people' expected war to break out on 1 October, which, as we have seen, was the date set by Hitler for possible action against the Czechs.[107] In the bond market, the veneer of confidence had been preserved only by official intervention. The Finance Ministry was repurchasing its own IOUs, at prices better than those on offer from private investors. Thanks to the cautious approach pursued at least up to the spring of 1938, all was not lost. Krosigk was keen to insist that financial stabilization was still possible. The great inflation of the 1920s had wiped out the majority of the Reich's financial obligations, so the total volume of debt weighing on the Reich was far from overwhelming. So long as the authorities took drastic measures to manage the capital market and to put their own house in order, the regime's borrowing requirement could be managed. However, if this was to happen in the normal fashion by means of long-term loans, Germany needed to restore market confidence, by 'clarifying' its foreign policy. Here Krosigk came to the real point of his memorandum. 'As every war in the future will be fought not only with military means but also will be an economic war of greatest scope', he considered it his 'unavoidable duty' to present 'in fullest truthfulness and sincerity my deep anxiety for the future of Germany . . .'. Whether or not the war stayed localized in the event of a showdown with the Czechs depended mainly on Britain. As a former Rhodes Scholar, Krosigk considered himself something of an expert on the English and as such he felt it necessary to warn Hitler against underestimating their determination. 'The fact that England is not ready for war militarily does not prevent England fomenting it. For she possesses two great trump cards. One is the soon-expected active participation of the United States of America in the war.' For Krosigk, no less than for Goering, Weizsaecker and Beck, American backing for the enemies of the Third Reich was axiomatic.[108] The second British 'trump card' was their knowledge of Germany's 'financial and economic weaknesses'. With this in mind, Britain and France would fight a war of attrition. 'The Western powers would not run against the Westwall but would let Germany's economic weakness take effect until we, after early military successes, become weaker and weaker and finally will lose our military advantage due to deliveries of armaments and aeroplanes from the United States.' Everything, to Krosigk's mind, spoke in favour of postponing a war. Germany could 'only gain by waiting' and it was precisely for this reason that 'Communists, Jews and Czechs' were displaying such a 'fanatical desire' to involve Hitler in a disastrously premature conflict. This was their 'last possibility to cause a world war' and to 'destroy the hated Third Reich'. Rather than responding to their provocations, Germany should 'await her hour', complete her armaments and create a 'balance between military and economic preparations . . .'. Then the day would soon come when Germany could deliver the 'final *coup de grâce*' to the Czechs without entangling itself in a disastrous confrontation with Britain and France.

In the final analysis it is hard to know how seriously to take the internal 'opposition' to Hitler in the summer of 1938.[109] The sources are simply too scanty and unreliable. By the time Krosigk finished his memorandum, Ludwig Beck had already resigned as army chief of staff, having failed in his effort to mobilize the military leadership for a collective stand against Hitler. Astonishingly, Beck even agreed to keep news of his resignation secret until the crisis had passed. It seems, however, that Beck's resignation was not the end of military plotting. Franz Halder, Beck's successor as chief of staff, shared his analysis of the strategic situation and was willing to go a step further towards organizing an outright military coup. In the fateful last week in September, with Europe poised on the brink of war, a snatch squad apparently stood ready in Berlin to storm the Reich Chancellery and to arrest Hitler and the Nazi leadership.[110] It has sometimes been said that it was the last-ditch effort at conciliation undertaken by Chamberlain which undermined the resolve of this group. But in fact Chamberlain's efforts ended in failure. If Hitler had wanted war on 1 October 1938, he could have had it. The French and British had reached the point at which they could make no further concessions.[111] The armies of France and the Soviet Union had mobilized. The Royal Navy stood at full alert. On 29 September 1938 it was Hitler who stepped back not his opponents, and there is no better explanation for this abrupt change of course than the sheer weight of evidence, argument and pressure that had been brought to bear on him over the previous weeks. Hitler was hearing expressions of concern not only from Beck and Krosigk, but also from Goering and most importantly perhaps from Mussolini, who intervened personally on 28 September.[112] Nobody could accuse either Goering or Mussolini of opposing war on principle. But neither wanted to risk a war against Britain and France in 1938. Furthermore, if Hitler abstained from open military aggression, the British and French were clearly willing to give him virtually everything he might ask for. Reluctantly, Hitler backed down and accepted the extraordinarily generous settlement on offer at the hastily convened conference in Munich. In so doing, he almost certainly saved his regime from disaster.

V

The violent energy pent up within the Nazi movement during the summer of 1938 unloaded itself not in war, but in an unprecedented assault on the Jewish population. Beginning already in the summer of 1938, the Nazi party orchestrated a wave of anti-Semitic outrages that culminated in a nationwide pogrom on 9 November 1938, an event without parallel in the modern history of Western Europe.[113] To make this connection between the Sudeten crisis and Kristallnacht is more than mere socio-psychological inference. In their reports on the pogrom in November 1938, the local branches of the SS intelligence service (SD) uniformly offered as their explanation that it was the behaviour of the Jewish minority during the crisis that had driven the German population to take violent reprisals against them. The SS leadership were clearly haunted by the fear that Germany might find itself engaged in a major war with hundreds of thousands of Jews still in the country. It was the fear of 'Jewish subversion' that led the SS in late October to carry out the brutal expulsion from Germany of 70,000 Polish Jews, including the parents of Herschel Grynzspan, the young man whose botched assassination attempt on the German ambassador in Paris provided the immediate trigger for the November pogrom.

But another longer-term motive for the drastic escalation in anti-Semitic violence in 1938 is revealed by the chronology of Jewish emigration from Germany and Austria. The key point is simply that, since the initial surge of 1933, Jewish emigration from Germany had stagnated at 'only' 20,000 people per annum. At this rate, allowing also for the natural rate of decline in the ageing Jewish population, it would have taken until the late 1940s for the SS to have achieved their objective of ridding Germany of its Jewish minority. One could cite many factors to explain the relatively slow rate of Jewish emigration. However, the most important single obstacle was clearly the extremely high cost of leaving Germany. This in turn was dictated by the same problem that afflicted virtually every other aspect of Nazi policy, the shortage of foreign exchange. In April 1938, prompted by party officials in Austria, the economics department of the Reichsbank conducted a brief study of the question: 'How much foreign currency would be required for the transfer of the entire stock of Jewish wealth invested in Germany?' For the German Jews alone, not including the Austrian population, it came to an estimate of between 2.2 and 5.15 billion Reichsmarks. Barring a large external loan, this was many times the hard currency reserves of the Reichsbank.[114] In light of this disparity, it is hardly surprising that the Reich imposed punitive taxes on would-be emigrants. And as the Reich's foreign exchange situation deteriorated after 1936, these financial penalties escalated.[115] Perversely, the very fact that Jews were being encouraged to emigrate made them prima facie suspects of wishing to smuggle capital out of the country. Rather than facilitating emigration, the bureaucracy of foreign exchange and emigration became an additional means of harassment and discrimination.[116] Having been closely involved in questions of foreign exchange since 1936, Reinhard Heydrich and the SD were in no way naive about the financial obstacles to 'voluntary emigration'. In the summer of 1938, the SD was in direct negotiations with the RWM in the hope of procuring more hard currency for this purpose.[117] But, not surprisingly given the Reichsbank's situation, they were disappointed. The SD's anti-Jewish policy thus faced a logjam. And it was against this backdrop that the mounting wave of anti-Semitic violence and discrimination in 1938 took on its real functional significance. If the SS could not make emigrating easier, it could at least increase the incentive, through a wave of physical terror and discrimination that rendered Jewish life in Germany impossible.

Only hours after the managers of IG Farben had discussed the exciting new vistas opened up by the Anschluss, a nightmarish wave of violence broke over the Jews of Austria. One witness remembered the evening of 11 March 1938 as an 'opening of hell's gates', a storm of 'envy, malevolence, hatred, a blind malevolent desire for revenge'.[118] Even the Germans were concerned about the torrent of popular anti-Semitism they had unleashed in Austria. Within weeks, virtually every Jewish business in Austria was under the control of a self-appointed Nazi commissioner. On 26 April 1938 Berlin stepped in. All German and Austrian Jews with assets of more than 5,000 Reichsmarks were required to report them to an official register. Henceforth, the Four Year Plan organization was to ensure the 'utilization' of Jewish assets 'in the interests of the German economy'. As of the same date, all sales of Jewish businesses were made conditional on the official approval of the Nazi party's regional economic advisers. In practice, this merely formalized a role which these officials had been playing since 1933. To increase the pressure for sale, the Reich Ministry of Economic Affairs, the Finance Ministry and the Reichsbank systematically victimized the remaining non-Aryan firms. Jewish-owned firms received the lowest priority in the allocation of raw materials. The Reichsbank instructed its branches to stop providing loans to non-Aryan businessmen. Tax and foreign exchange regulations were applied with punitive zeal. The remaining bastions of the Jewish business community soon succumbed. Aryanization sales in 1938 included 340 major factories, almost all of which were in textiles and clothing, 370 wholesale trading firms and no less than 22 private banks, including such prestigious names as Warburg and Bleichroeder.[119]

Both 'ordinary' Germans and leading representatives of German corporate capitalism seized the chance to buy businesses, property and other assets at knock-down prices. The major banks, led by the Deutsche and Dresdner, competed fiercely for Aryanization business.[120] Acquisitive heavy industrial groupings such as Flick and Mannesmann took full advantage.[121] However, the focus in recent years on the looting of Jewish businesses has obscured what was probably the most significant finding of the official registration of Jewish wealth. In total, German and Austrian Jews reported 8.5 billion Reichsmarks in gross assets – 7 billion net of outstanding liabilities. Of this considerable sum, only 1.19 billion Reichsmarks were active business assets. Allowing for the fact that the net wealth of Austrian Jewry was reported as just over 2 billion Reichsmarks, it is unlikely that Jewish business capital in Germany far exceeded 850 million Reichsmarks. This was, by any count, a small proportion of the total assets at work in the German economy. Aryanization undoubtedly changed the complexion of major shopping streets in cities like Berlin and Hamburg, and it also changed the structure of property ownership in some highly visible residential neighbourhoods. But its wider impact was limited. Only in a handful of sectors did it cause a major shift in ownership, most notably in retail, particularly in department stores, textiles, clothing and private banking. In general, the idea that the tiny Jewish minority had ever occupied a 'dominant position' in the economy and that Aryanization could therefore constitute a major turning point in national economic life, should be seen for what it always was – an absurd anti-Semitic myth.

By far the biggest beneficiary of the economic persecution of German Jewry was not German business, but the German state and thus indirectly the German taxpayer in general.[122] Since 1933 the Reich had led the way in stripping the Jewish population of its wealth through the flight tax and the discounts charged by the Reichsbank. To go further than this would have required an act of outright fiscal persecution. As we have seen, the idea of a 'Jew tax' had been repeatedly discussed since Hitler had issued his instruction in the Four Year Plan memorandum for the Jews to be made liable for any damage to the German economy. But the Ministries hesitated.[123] It took the mounting tension of the Sudeten crisis to overcome their inhibitions. As the expectation of war built to a climax in September 1938, so did the climate of violence against the Jews. The municipal authorities of Munich and Nuremberg set an important precedent with the demolition of their synagogues over the summer. This was followed by a rash of anti-Semitic attacks and demonstrations across south and south-western Germany, which according to the SD took on 'in part the character of pogroms'.[124] In Vienna, the hostility was unrelenting. By the autumn, entire Jewish neighbourhoods were being forcibly removed to temporary accommodation, pending 'voluntary' emigration. The nationwide pogrom ordered by Hitler on the night of 9 November thus came as the ghastly finale to a period of prolonged escalation. According to the meticulous records compiled by German loss adjusters, the material damage came to more than 220 million Reichsmarks. At least ninety-one Jewish citizens were murdered and hundreds more committed suicide. The extension of the concentration camp system, begun systematically in 1936, enabled the SS to incarcerate no less than 30,000 Jewish men in a single night.[125] They were released only after they had agreed to apply for emigration.

Three days after the pogrom, on 12 November, Goering asserted his authority with a major conference on the Jewish question. As head of the Four Year Plan, Goering was indignant at the wanton damage to property done over the previous days. 'I have had enough of these demonstrations! They don't harm the Jew, but me, who am the last authority for coordinating the German economy.' Goering was particularly incensed by the furs and jewels looted in Berlin and issued special orders for the arrest of the persons responsible. More seriously, Germany's streets were littered with the debris of thousands of smashed shop windows. The Jews would pay the bill for clearing up the mess, but replacing the high-quality Belgian plate glass would cost the Reichsbank 3 million Reichsmarks in precious foreign exchange.[126] As Goering put it: 'I wish you had killed 200 Jews, and not destroyed such values.' The Jewish question was now 'once and for all' to be 'coordinated and solved one way or another'. What this meant, in the first instance, was the imposition of a punitive tax. In the words of the decree formally announced on 12 November: 'The hostile attitude of Jewry towards the German people and Reich . . . makes necessary a decisive defence and harsh expiation.' The Jewish community was ordered to pay a fine of 1 billion Reichsmarks. In addition, Germany's Jews were required to repair all damage done on 9 November whilst forfeiting their insurance claims to the Reich. So anxious was the Reich Finance Ministry to get its hands on the funds that it persuaded a consortium of the major Berlin banks to provide it with an advance against the revenue from the 'Jew tax'.[127] At the same time the First Decree for the Removal of Jews from Economic Life (Erste Verordnung zur Ausschaltung der Juden aus dem Wirtschaftsleben) did exactly as its title promised. It banned all Jews from retail and crafts. It banned them from selling goods at trade fairs and debarred them from holding any position of authority in any firm.[128]

Taken together, the various measures adopted in 1938 amounted to a comprehensive expropriation of the Jewish population. The vast majority of the 1.1 billion Reichsmarks in business assets registered in the summer of 1938 had been sold by the end of the year. Benefits to the tune of several hundred million Reichsmarks had accrued to a cross-section of the most rapacious entrepreneurial interests in Germany. Over three years, the capital levy of 12 November garnered a total of 1.127 billion Reichsmarks for the Reich. In addition, hundreds of millions of marks were taken in 'flight tax' from the tens of thousands of

Jewish families now fleeing the country. Billions more were left behind in the accounts of the financial institutions that managed the transfer process. On 3 December, all unsold Jewish assets, including personal valuables such as jewellery or art, were placed under the supervision of German trustees, pending their future sale.[129] The proceeds nominally still held in the name of the Jewish community were invested in government bonds, thus easing the financial situation of the Reich.[130] By the end of the year, with regulations concerning the sale of real estate firmly in place, virtually all Jewish wealth remaining within the Reich was accounted for and the Reich's exchequer was several billion Reichsmarks to the good. To avoid confusion, it is worth stressing that this was a purely financial transfer. These acts of persecution in no way improved the overall position of the German economy. Of course, some gains in efficiency were to be expected from closing down the many small and inefficient craft businesses belonging to Jews.[131] But too much should not be made of this rationalization effect. Given the small scale of such businesses, the amount of labour and other resources released by these means cannot have been more than trivial. Nor should we exaggerate the fiscal benefits reaped by the Reich. According to the records of the Finance Ministry, revenue from the two main taxes levied on the Jews, the wealth tax and the flight tax, in the 1938–9 fiscal year came to 498.5 million and 342.6 million Reichsmarks respectively.[132] This was just 5 per cent of total Reich revenue from taxes and customs.[133] In 1939 the percentage was less. The billion or so Reichsmarks extracted in both 1938 and 1939 were devastating for the German Jewish community. And for the Reich's finances they provided welcome relief at a moment of severe fiscal embarrassment. But it is simply unrealistic to imagine that the financial persecution of a tiny and increasingly impoverished minority could make a significant and lasting contribution towards the enormous costs of German rearmament.

Furthermore, though the escalation of persecution and violence gave the German Jewish community every incentive to leave, the problem of securing sufficient foreign exchange had not been resolved. On 25 March 1938, within weeks of the Anschluss, President Roosevelt had proposed the formation of an international committee to address the problem of 'political refugees' from Germany and newly annexed Austria.[134] On 6 July delegates from thirty-two nations, led by the United States, Britain and France, met at the Hôtel Royal in the French spa town of Évian. The conference was also attended by representatives of thirty-nine NGOs and a mob of at least two hundred journalists. Over the following nine days they were treated to a dispiriting spectacle. The obvious precondition for a 'solution' to the refugee problem was a willingness to admit more refugees. Apart from more or less explicit anti-Semitic prejudice, the open expressions of which provided a field day for the Nazi press, the main obstacle to any such relaxation of immigration quotas was the question of finance. How would the refugees support themselves in countries all of which were still suffering substantial unemployment? The answer to that question, it was commonly agreed, depended on the willingness of Germany to allow would-be emigrants to take with them at least some of their personal assets. The German government, however, refused to have anything to do with the Évian Conference, denouncing it as a concerted international effort to strip Germany of its last remaining foreign currency reserves. This deadlock continued throughout the autumn, with the German Foreign Office and the SS shunning any contact with the newly established Intergovernmental Committee on Refugees and its director, George Rublee. It was not until after the conference with Goering on 12 November 1938 that Reichsbank president Hjalmar Schacht was authorized to attempt one last act of cynical financial wizardry.[135]

In collaboration with the Austrian Economic Minister Hans Fischboeck, Schacht devised a scheme that would enable Germany to 'export' its Jewish population without doing damage to its foreign exchange holdings. The idea was to use the wealth of Austrian and German Jewry, which was now effectively under the control of the Reich, to secure a foreign currency loan to the sum of at least 1.5 billion Reichsmarks. This fund, to be subscribed by 'international Jewry', would permit all those physically capable of emigration to start a new life abroad. In December 1938 Schacht travelled to London to broach the scheme with Rublee. Hitler clearly approved of Schacht's plan and Goering too seems to have taken it seriously.[136] At the end of January Goering placed Reinhard Heydrich in charge of a central agency for Jewish emigration (Zentralstelle fuer juedische Auswanderung), to expedite emigration along Schacht's lines. There seems little reason to doubt that if the Third Reich had been able to expel hundreds of thousands of Jews, whilst raising a substantial volume of foreign currency through an international loan, it would have jumped at the chance. The fact was, however, that the 'global network of Jewish high finance' on which Schacht counted to raise the funds was a figment of the anti-Semitic imagination. All existing schemes for buying Jews out of Germany had struggled against considerable opposition from Jewish communities both inside and outside the country. And with the exception of the Zionist Haavara programme, no significant funding was ever forthcoming.[137] Rather than a well-ordered retreat, what ensued was a rout. Between March 1938 and September 1939, more than 200,000 Jewish people flooded out of Germany and Austria.[138] They did so despite the perfection of a rapacious German bureaucracy that stripped them of virtually all their material assets.[139] They subjected themselves to this ordeal because the threat of what now awaited them in Germany made it seem worth paying virtually any price to leave.

VI

In the second half of 1938, the international outrage caused by Germany's mistreatment of its Jewish population, the anti-Semitic fantasies of the National Socialist leadership, the mounting confrontation between Germany and the Western powers and Germany's domestic social and economic tensions were mixed together into an explosive cocktail.[140] Ever more emphatically, Hitler and other key figures in the Nazi leadership interpreted the mounting confrontation between the Third Reich and the 'Western powers' not merely in the conventional terms of great power competition, but through the lens of their anti-Semitic cosmology. For the Nazi leadership, the gathering international coalition against Hitler's aggression was clear evidence of the worldwide reach of the Jewish conspiracy. Perversely, Goering, Heydrich and others appear to have believed that their success in expediting emigration would actually increase Jewish agitation against Germany, since this was the best way for Jews to defuse the anti-Semitic feelings aroused in those countries receiving the refugees. This was a point that Goering made at the beginning of his tub-thumping address to the aircraft industrialists on 8 July 1938: 'The Jew . . . agitates for war all over the world. So much is clear – anti-Semitism has risen now in every country as a logical consequence of the excessive increase of the number of Jews in these countries, and the Jew can expect salvation only if he succeeds in letting loose a general world war.' Clearly, in the company of aircraft industrialists Goering felt some need to justify this outburst, so he added: 'If I mention the Jewish agitation for war, I have a good reason to do so, since the Jew who dominates the bulk of the world press is in a position to use it for psychological propaganda.'[141] As we have seen, Krosigk used a similar argument in his appeal to Hitler in September to avoid a war over Czechoslovakia. And, in fact, Goering and Krosigk were not entirely wrong. There was a connection in 1938 between Nazi anti-Semitism and the escalation in international tension. But it was international abhorrence at the outrages committed by Nazism, not Jewish agitation, that did the damage.[142] In this respect, Kristallnacht was a decisive turning point. In its aftermath, Lord Halifax, Britain's Foreign Secretary, abandoned his earlier advocacy of appeasement in favour of a more aggressive form of containment.[143] Of even greater long-term significance, however, was the reaction in the United States.

It has been remarked that the United States barely figured in Hitler's various strategic musings in the eighteen months leading up to the outbreak of war in September 1939.[144] Though this is true with regard to Hitler's statements on grand strategy, and particularly those he made to the military leadership in May and August 1939, it must be qualified in a number of vital respects.[145] As we have seen, Beck, Goering and Krosigk all considered the industrial potential of the United States to be a key strategic consideration and, as we shall see, this point was to be forcefully restated by voices both within the Wehrmacht high command and the Four Year Plan in the first half of 1939. It is possible, of course, that Hitler waved all this aside, though this is contradicted by later evidence which shows him to have been entirely realistic about the threat posed to Germany by America's economic might. What cannot be denied, however, is the centrality of the United States to at least one of Hitler's key preoccupations, the Jewish question. From 1938 onwards, the 'international Jewish question' came to be understood in the Third Reich as synonymous with America.[146] The anti-German boycott movement of the early 1930s had set the stage. Roosevelt's role in setting in motion the Évian conference and intervening in the question of a Jewish state in Palestine further reinforced the conspiratorial worldview. But Kristallnacht was the key turning point.[147] America responded to 9 November with a 'hurricane' of public outrage.[148] As the Reich's hapless ambassador remarked, he faced a wave of public emotion so intense that it made any 'steady work' on behalf of German interests 'impossible'.[149] Shortly afterwards, following America's decision to withdraw its ambassador from Germany, he was recalled to Berlin. In the weeks that followed, only intervention by Secretary of State Cordell Hull prevented the US Treasury from imposing severe punitive tariffs on German exports. In his State of the Union Address on 4 January 1939 Roosevelt drew stark conclusions.[150] Linking ideological questions directly to foreign policy he emphasized the threat both to the security and to the core values of the United States posed by states 'where religion and democracy have vanished' and where 'good faith and reason in international affairs have given way to strident ambition and brute force'. After Sudetenland and Kristallnacht, nobody needed to name names. The Nazi press replied with a vicious campaign of anti-Semitic and anti-American propaganda, in which Roosevelt was depicted as the tool of Jewish capital.[151] On 25 January the German Foreign Ministry circulated its officials with an analysis of 'the Jewish question as a factor in foreign policy in 1938' in which the United States was explicitly identified as the 'headquarters of world Jewry'.[152] And Hitler himself responded to Roosevelt in his address to the Reichstag on 30 January 1939, the anniversary of the seizure of power.

Hitler's '30 January speech' is commonly cited as a harbinger of the Holocaust. But what concerns us here is its significance as a gauge of Hitler's wider economic and military assessment at the start of 1939. The dire threats that Hitler uttered against European Jewry were set within a wider rhetorical context that is crucial to understanding the embattled mood in the leadership of the Third Reich in the aftermath of Munich and Kristallnacht. The anti-Semitic theme ran throughout Hitler's speech. But it was intertwined, on the one hand with the old theme of *Lebensraum*, and on the other with a new and overt challenge to Britain and America. As usual, Hitler posed the alternative between a future for Germany based on exports, or an extension of its *Lebensraum*. The blind resistance of the warmongering Western powers was blocking Germany's route to expansion in the East. So Germany had no option in the short run but to 'export, or die'.[153] Should the democratic powers continue to stand in Germany's way, should the United States raise obstacles to Germany's efforts to increase trade with Latin America, then Germany would be forced into a life-and-death struggle for which it was now, thanks to National Socialism, well prepared. All of this was of course wholly unnecessary since Germany wanted only to live in peace with its great European neighbours. But if the warmongering 'Jewish media' in America and their allies in British and American politics got their way then National Socialism stood ready for battle. It was this specific context of post-Munich and post-Kristallnacht frustration that led Hitler to utter his famous 'prophecy': 'If international finance-Jewry inside and outside Europe should succeed in plunging the nations once more into a world war, the result will be not the Bolshevization of the earth and thereby the victory of Jewry, but the annihilation of the Jewish race in Europe!'

As Hitler's aggression ran up against ever more concerted opposition and the threat of a European war became more real, Hitler and the Nazi leadership were ever more convinced that the hands of the Jews were at work. America, the global hegemon in the making, thus returned to the centre of Hitler's worldview, as the fulcrum of a world Jewish conspiracy for the ruination of Germany and the rest of Europe.

9

1939: Nothing to Gain by Waiting

Within days of the Munich agreement, the Reichsbank economics department drafted a memorandum, which, though it was never circulated outside the offices of the central bank, nevertheless deserves to stand as the final monument to Hjalmar Schacht's career in the Third Reich: 'With the incorporation of the Sudetenland into the Reich,' the Reichsbank declared, 'the Fuehrer has completed a task that is without parallel in history. In barely five years of National Socialist rule, Germany has achieved military freedom, sovereign control of its territory and the incorporation of the Saarland, Austria and the Sudetenland. It has thereby turned itself from a political *non-valeur* into the pre-eminent power in continental Europe.'[1] Hitler had achieved the ultimate goal of German nationalism, the establishment of Grossdeutschland, something which had eluded even Bismarck, and he had done so without provoking war. This extraordinary national resurrection was above all based on a gigantic armaments effort, which had been managed in such a way as to give full employment to the German people whilst avoiding the curse of inflation. This too was a unique historical accomplishment. But, in the autumn of 1938, at the moment of Hitler's greatest triumph, the economic foundations of his success were in question. The Reichsbank was forced to acknowledge that despite its best efforts, there was 'no longer . . . complete stability of the German currency'. 'An inflation of the Reichsmark' had begun, even if this was 'not yet fully apparent'. This was an admission that Schacht repeated a few weeks later in a report to the Capital Market Committee (Kapitalmarktauschuss) – the committee of the RFM, RWM and Reichsbank which oversaw the raising of funds on the German financial markets.[2] In front of his colleagues, Schacht openly stated: 'It cannot be denied . . . that we are already on the threshold of inflation.' To restore the Reichsmark to a state worthy of a great power, Germany needed a restoration of monetary and fiscal stability. Since the spring of 1938, the Reich's finances had been spiralling towards disaster. For months the Finance Ministry had been living 'from hand to mouth' and the Reichsbank had been forced into an 'inflationary creation of money'.[3] Like Krosigk a few weeks earlier, the Reichsbank tied its assessment of the Reich's fiscal situation to a grander strategic panorama. 'German history has today obviously reached a turning point. In terms of active political tasks there remains only the regaining of colonies and the elimination of Bolshevism. The former is best achieved through negotiation, the latter through internal disintegration of the current Soviet regime.' In Europe, Germany no longer had any territorial claims to contest. After Munich Hitler had declared himself 'satisfied'. This political turning point now needed to be followed by a parallel transformation in the monetary sphere. As the Reichsbank put it: 'The currency must now underpin not an expansive power politics, but a policy of peaceful construction. Historically we have before us the same task of conversion as Frederick the Great after the Seven Years War, Prime Minister Peel after the Napoleonic War and Mussolini after the war in Abyssinia. The main task is to manage the transition from the current war economy to a peacetime economy.'

This transition would not be painless or free of risk. But there was no alternative. Any further government spending financed by monetary expansion would simply add to the overhang of excessive purchasing power, which could only be contained by a further elaboration of the already cumbersome and unmanageable apparatus of surveillance and control. That, in turn, would result in a chronic deterioration in the standard of living, 'the political and social consequence of which need not be further discussed'. 'One should not therefore reinforce the dykes, but reduce the weight that is pressing against them.' In doing so the Reichsbank knew that it had to proceed carefully. Though the inflationary spike could still be broken, this involved risks. An excessively sharp reduction in the volume of credit could easily turn the difficult transition into a disastrous 'deflationary crisis'. Instead, the Reichsbank proposed to drain off excess purchasing power by issuing long-term bonds, enabling the Finance Ministry to consolidate its precarious budgetary situation. More importantly, however, there was an urgent need to ensure a rapid increase in the production of consumer goods. Only a supply of real goods to absorb at least some of the excess purchasing power could stem the inflationary threat. What the Reichsbank was calling for, in short, was a dramatic shift in priorities: a sharp reduction in 'non-marketed output' for the purposes of the state, which according to contemporary estimates accounted for 30 per cent of industrial production in 1938, in favour of the production of household consumer goods.[4] A precondition, however, for all further action was the need to raise exports. The most serious threat to the German economy was the possibility of an acute balance of payments crisis. A sudden interruption of the import of essential raw materials and foodstuffs as in 1934 would be fatal for public confidence and might well jeopardize the delicate process of adjustment that the Reichsbank was trying to manage.

The draft memorandum of 3 October 1938 concluded with a dramatic warning:

The National Socialist state leadership has managed, despite the critical situation of recent times, to avoid a war that would have jeopardized its earlier successes. It now faces, after the political turning point has been reached, the further task of avoiding an inflation whose consequences would be almost as dangerous. This task is difficult, because despite every effort having been made, inflationary pressure has built up and because further financial tasks are on the agenda. However, it is possible, because the political preconditions are excellent and it will be all the easier, the sooner and the more determinedly the problem is tackled.

I

The Reichsbank officials, however, were engaged in wishful thinking if they believed that the peaceful achievement of Grossdeutschland was Hitler's final aim. As Schacht had himself predicted, Hitler could barely contain his frustration at the outcome of the Munich conference.[5] He had the Sudetenland. But that was not the point. The rump of Czechoslovakia remained to be liquidated and the Western powers had now shown their true colours. As Hitler and his military leadership had been forced to realize, Germany would have to fight in the West before it could pursue any large-scale campaign of military conquest in the East. It was only after the Czech crisis, therefore, that the full military-industrial implications of the anti-Western turn in German strategy became apparent. In his diary in late September, Major-General Thomas of the military-economic office of the Oberkommando Wehrmacht (OKW) noted: 'The day of Munich. By telephone I receive instructions: all preparations now for war against England, target 1942!'[6] Two weeks later, on 14 October 1938, Goering announced the new programme in a major address in the conference hall of the Air Ministry. Given the 'world situation', the 'Fuehrer has issued an order ... to carry out a gigantic programme compared to which previous achievements are insignificant'.[7] Within the shortest time the Luftwaffe was to be increased fivefold. The navy was to accelerate its armaments effort and the army was to procure large amounts of offensive weapons, particularly heavy artillery pieces and heavy tanks. In addition, fuel, rubber, gunpowder and explosives were to be 'moved into the foreground'. On top of all this, Goering also called for accelerated investment in railways, highways and canals to make up for the obvious deficiencies in Germany's transport infrastructure.

Over the following weeks, all three branches of the Wehrmacht responded to the new challenge. For the army, the first priority was simply to complete the enormous build-up begun in 1936. On 20 October 1938 it announced that it would need to claim no less than 4.5 million tons of steel in 1939, almost a quarter of Germany's total production, a figure not reached until the height of the Stalingrad battle in 1942.[8] The fivefold expansion of the Luftwaffe, announced by Goering on 14 October, was even more dramatic in its implications.[9] Within four years the Luftwaffe was to reach a peacetime strength of 21,750 aircraft. This was the logical extension of the decision taken five months earlier to base Germany's airfleet around a force of as many as 7,000 Ju 88 medium bombers. These were now to be flanked by over 800 heavy four-engined bombers (He 177) and swarms of long-range fighter escorts and Messerschmitt interceptors.[10] The navy, for its part, launched a new fleet-building programme, designed to put Germany in a position to compete with the Royal Navy within six years.[11] In December 1939, Hitler and Admiral Raeder agreed on a programme that gave first priority to the construction of 6 giant battleships, followed by a fleet of 249 U-boats and 8 cruisers for long-range operations. By 1948 the German navy was to include 797 vessels, at a total cost of 33 billion Reichsmarks over nine years. As in the case of the Luftwaffe's programme, the infrastructural costs of this giant fleet were enormous. Cavernous new dry docks were required at Wilhelmshaven and Hamburg. The island of Ruegen was to be hollowed out to provide shelter for a gigantic naval base. The navy's Z Plan, the last of the major pre-war armaments programmes, was signed into force on 27 January 1939, giving the Reichsmarine absolute priority over all other industrial projects of the Third Reich.

Given the concerns already expressed by the Reichsbank and Finance Minister Krosigk, it was apparent that rearmament on this scale must have drastic implications for the rest of economic policy. As we have seen, Major General Friedrich Fromm had already reached this conclusion in the summer of 1936. The demands of the spring and early summer 1938 had been unprecedented. The plans formulated in October 1938 were of an even larger magnitude. If the Third Reich was to have any hope of actually realizing them, the existing ramshackle system of planning and control would have to be coherently directed towards repressing civilian economic activity in favour of the Wehrmacht. Already in August 1938 the Reichsbank had reached the conclusion that, in managing the Wehrmacht's demand, 'the means of a peacetime economy are no longer sufficient, one must instead begin to reach for the tougher measures of the war economy'.[12] And everything suggests that this transition was agreed between Goering, the military and the civilian economic administration in the autumn of 1938. To provide the necessary political authority Goering appointed a new Reich defence council (Reichsverteidigungsrat) and he was backed by Major-General Georg Thomas and his military-economic office in Hitler's newly created OKW.

Thomas is one of the most ambiguous figures of the German war effort.[13] Born in 1890 into a family of industrialists, he embarked on a career in the army in 1908, which spanned both front-line service in World War I, for which he was awarded the Iron Cross, and a spell in the General Staff. After the war he remained in the Reichswehr and served in the same Koenigsberg Wehrkreis as Ludwig Beck, the future chief of staff. In 1928 Thomas moved to the centre of German military-politics in Berlin and by 1933 he had risen to be chief of staff in the army's procurement office (Heereswaffenamt). By 1934, as we have seen, he was collaborating actively with Schacht in promoting the interests of rearmament in the context of the currency crisis. It was no coincidence that in September 1934 he was promoted to the rank of Colonel to take charge of the Dienststelle Wehrwirtschafts und Waffenwesen im Wehrmachtsamt des Reichswehrministeriums (office for military economics and armaments in the Reichswehr Ministry). From this office he directed the creation of a national organization of military-economic inspectorates and an elaborate system of mobilization preparations.[14] As Thomas's bureaucratic ambition expanded, however, the coherence of his vision of military-economic organization was increasingly stretched.[15] Thomas was a fierce proponent of the absolute priority of rearmament over all other national concerns. At the same time, however, he supported Schacht in insisting on the need to promote exports and secure Germany's financial stability. That these priorities – armaments on the one hand, conventional economic stability on the other – were in fact contradictory was abundantly apparent by 1937 at the latest. To provide at least a partial reconciliation between them, Thomas made himself into the principal advocate of a draconian system of economic organization, through which the interests of every other aspect of the civilian economy would be systematically subordinated to the double priority of arms and exports. It was precisely this drastic reorganization of the economy that seemed to be within reach in the autumn of 1938.

Compiling statistics from within both the Wehrmacht and the Reichsbank, it was Thomas's office that drafted the speech that Goering delivered to the first meeting of the Reich Defence Council on 18 November 1938.[16] This made no bones about the severity of Germany's situation, the need to balance the needs of rearmament and export, the threat of inflation and the damage done to the public finances by the profligacy of the summer. Goering echoed Krosigk and Schacht in describing the state of the Reich's finances as 'very critical' and the exchange reserves as 'non-existent'. All the same, the Fuehrer had given his order. The total volume of German armaments production was to be tripled. To make this possible, Goering outlined a programme of drastic mobilization and rationalization. The convulsive acceleration of armaments activity in 1938 was the catalyst for the intimate coupling of these two key concepts in the politics of Hitler's regime: mobilization and rationalization.[17] Men like Koppenberg and Porsche had pointed the way with their grandiose schemes for the mass-production of bombers and family cars. And the language of modernist mass-production continued to serve its purpose as a legitimating device for entrepreneurial expansionism until the very end of Hitler's regime.

But, given the more general disparity that gaped from 1938 onwards between the goals of the Nazi leadership and the means provided by the German economy, rationalization also took on a wider societal dimension. To the Defence Council Goering announced that the entire population was to be registered in a national card index administered by SS police chief General Kurt Daluege. This was to allow the labour offices to allocate every man and woman to their most productive location in the national economy.[18] The state's legal and tax administration was to be simplified to release manpower. The civilian labour service introduced in 1933 was to be trimmed back. 'The great building projects of the Fuehrer would be carried through because of their importance for morale and psychology.' But all other construction projects would be shut down. All manufacturing plants would be subject to inspection to establish whether they were using labour efficiently. The automotive industry was to be taken in hand by a special plenipotentiary, who was to find savings of hundreds of millions of Reichsmarks. The national railway system, creaking under the strain of Germany's fully employed economy, was to benefit from a multi-billion-Reichsmark investment programme.[19] In an economy stretched as tightly as that of Germany, Goering reiterated that there was no room for acts of wanton destruction such as Kristallnacht. Germany's Jews would make their contribution through the huge new wealth tax. But it was not only the Jews that might be called upon. Goering raised the possibility that the entire German population would be asked to make a 'national thanksgiving sacrifice' (*Dankesopfer der Nation*) in the form of a single surrender of wealth.[20] Its task would be to 'secure armament production, on a large scale'. Faced with the challenge of raising armaments output by a factor of 3, Goering told the newly appointed defence council: 'One might even arrive at the conclusion: *non possumus*. This attitude had been expressed to him often enough.' But Goering 'had never given up and in the end he had always found a way through'.[21]

And actions followed from Goering's words. On 24 November the pricing guidelines that had been used to control the cost of military procurement since 1936 were extended to all public contracts. A month earlier German business had begun introducing standard cost accounts, which in future would form the basis for price control. On 15 November Colonel Adolf von Schell was appointed general plenipotentiary for motor vehicles (Generalbevollmaechtigter fuer das Kraftfahrzeugwesen) with the task of concentrating all available capacity on the efficient production of those models which were of greatest interest to the military.[22] Less than a month later, Goering appointed Fritz Todt, Hitler's new darling of the Westwall, to take overall responsibility for the entire construction sector. Though Todt hardly had a reputation for economy, he could at least be counted upon to ensure the absolute priority of the armaments effort. By the spring of 1939 Todt was able to report that, of the total construction volume of just over 12 billion Reichsmarks, 50 per cent was reserved for the Wehrmacht, 20 per cent was allocated to German industry and another 10 per cent was reserved for public construction projects. That left only 20 per cent to satisfy the housing needs of the population, with priority being given to accommodation for Four Year Plan workers.[23] Similarly drastic measures were taken to force through the navy's gigantic new construction programme. Immediately following approval of the Z Plan, privately owned shipyards were informed that the Kriegsmarine now had a veto over any non-naval work.[24] And it also seemed that rationalization and prioritization were to be applied to the Wehrmacht itself. On 11 November 1938, Keitel, the chief of the OKW, noted: 'After having been put in the picture about the armaments programmes by the Commanders-in-Chief, the Fuehrer intends to prioritize the entire armaments programme of the Wehrmacht according to uniform criteria and to distribute it organically over a number of years, bringing it into concordance with the available labour, raw materials and funds.'[25] In practice, this meant that Germany's armaments programme was to be organized around a four-year time-horizon, in line with the timescale that had been communicated to Colonel Thomas on the day of the Munich conference.

It seems, in short, that in the aftermath of the Sudeten crisis a real effort was made to impose a new discipline and coordination on the management of the German economy.[26] Furthermore, since both Goering and the OKW had dual responsibilities in the formulation of economic and foreign policy there is good reason to believe that the new, more concerted armaments programme may have been coordinated, at least notionally, with the foreign policy line adopted in the aftermath of Munich.[27] With the focus now firmly on the confrontation with France and Britain, the OKW and Ribbentrop's Foreign Ministry embarked on a strategy of alliance building. Apart from the elimination of the rump of Czechoslovakia, the first key element in this strategy was the incorporation of Poland alongside Italy into an offensive alliance against Britain and France. Ribbentrop contacted the Poles on 24 October to suggest an anti-Soviet alliance that would guarantee the Polish-German border for twenty-five years. The OKW for its part drew up sketch plans for coordinated action by Germany and Italy against France.[28] The Japanese were to be added to the combination, both as a counter-weight to the Royal Navy and as a deterrent to the Soviet Union.

Given the usual presumptions about the internal politics of the Third Reich, this suggestion of concerted and long-term preparations may strike some readers as far-fetched. However, the evidence is there in October and November 1938. And the best reason for thinking that in the last months of 1938 a degree of overall strategic coherence was reached by Hitler's regime was the shock therapy provided by the Sudeten crisis. In September 1938 the German leadership had confronted the real possibility that they would soon be involved in a general European war. It is perhaps not surprising that in the aftermath, having been given a 'second chance', Goering, Keitel, Thomas and Ribbentrop were able to achieve at least some degree of unity. If Germany was to avoid disaster, a strategy clearly needed to be worked out. If the Third Reich really was to fight Britain and France, then the preparations needed to be enormous in scale. If they were to seem even mildly realistic, they therefore needed to be stretched over a time-horizon extending at least into the early 1940s. And in such a war Germany would clearly need all the allies it could get. Since an offensive alliance with Britain was off the agenda, Italy and Japan were Germany's obvious partners. So much was simply common sense. How far Goering, Ribbentrop and Keitel had arrived at a true strategic synthesis remains open to question. But setting this scepticism aside for a moment, if there ever was a period in the 1930s when Hitler's Germany had the makings of a coherent, medium-term strategy this was it – the few weeks of calm that followed the Sudeten crisis. It was not to last.

II

If we go beyond the superficial efforts at organizational coordination it is clear that the armaments plans of October 1938 never had any chance of being realized, certainly not in peacetime. The aim of tripling the total armaments effort from its already high level in 1938 was simply unrealistic. For a middle-income country such as Germany in the 1930s, military spending on the scale being contemplated in November 1938 was incompatible with maintaining even the semblance of a normal standard of living. More immediately, it was incompatible with preserving either price stability or balance of payments equilibrium.

By far the most excessive in its implications was the programme of the Luftwaffe. Its real absurdity lay, not in the targets set for the annual production of aircraft, but in the goal of starting the war with an air fleet of 21,000 planes. During World War II, the Luftwaffe's maximum strength barely exceeded 5,000 aircraft in December 1944. Britain, which devoted a larger share of its armaments effort to the air war, managed to accumulate just over 8,300 aircraft for the final phase of its bomber offensive in 1944. The Soviet Union peaked at 17,000 front-line aircraft in April 1945, of which only a small number were heavy bombers. Even the mighty US Army Air Force deployed no more than 21,000 front-line combat aircraft.[29] For medium-sized European states like Britain or Germany, the infrastructural costs of an airfleet of 21,000 planes were simply outlandish. A first estimate of the full cost of quintupling the Luftwaffe came to 60 billion Reichsmarks.[30] This would have meant spending 50 per cent more on the Luftwaffe between 1938 and 1942 than had been spent on the entire Wehrmacht between 1933 and 1938. Even more daunting were the fuel requirements. To keep an airfleet of 21,000 aircraft airborne, the Luftwaffe would need to start the war with stocks of at least 10.7 million cubic metres of fuel. To build this gigantic reservoir Germany would have needed to purchase fuel in the early 1940s at the rate of 3 million cubic metres per annum, twice the current level of global production.[31] The Luftwaffe's own technical office described the requirements as 'superhuman' (uebermenschlich).[32] And similar problems haunted the navy's Z Plan. Given time, labour and steel, the German dockyards could probably have built Hitler's battleships. The truly prohibitive obstacle was ensuring their fuel supply. Under the Z Plan the navy's heating-oil needs were expected to rise from the 1.4 million tons per annum originally envisioned in 1936 to 6 million tons by 1947–8, and its requirements for diesel fuel to rise from 400,000 tons to 2 million tons. Even on the most optimistic assumptions, domestic production was not expected to exceed 2 million tons of oil and 1.34 million tons of diesel fuel by 1947–8. The German navy would therefore have to rely on accumulated stocks, which in 1939 amounted to less than 1 million tons for fuel oil and diesel combined. To provide even twelve months of unlimited operations it was calculated that the Kriegsmarine would need to construct no less than 9.6 million cubic metres of protected storage capacity.[33]

In the event, the gigantic rearmament plans of late 1938 never had the chance to unfold their inherent absurdity. The entire effort to construct a coherent framework for Germany's ongoing rearmament was interrupted within weeks by the financial after-effects of the Sudeten emergency. By the end of the year, the Reich found itself facing both a cash flow crisis and a severe squeeze on its foreign exchange account, blocking any substantial progress towards Hitler's target of tripling armaments production.

As we have seen, the financial markets were a sensitive indicator of the general mood in the German economy. In August 1938, despite the desperate need for cash, the Finance Ministry had been forced to do without a new loan due to the uncertainty provoked by the Sudeten crisis. The sharp drop in market sentiment made it unsafe for the government to launch a new bond issue. In early October the markets were buoyed, as was the Reichsbank, by the hope that Germany could now look forward to an era of peaceful prosperity. In a surge of optimism, savers, insurance funds and other financial institutions swallowed not only an offering of 1.5 billion Reichsmarks in government bonds, but also a further 350 million added at short notice by the cash-starved Finance Ministry.[34] As one expert has put it: 'After Munich . . . there appeared to be no end to the willingness of Germans to hold public debt . . .'[35] But this was to prove short-lived. At the end of November, the Reichsbank's efforts to float a fourth loan of 1.5 billion Reichsmarks suffered a spectacular failure. Almost a third of the new bonds failed to find a buyer.[36] The market was on strike. This was a critical development because it dramatically reduced the Reich's room for manoeuvre in balancing the competing needs of public spending and private investment. If the Reich could no longer raise funds through safe long-term borrowing, then there was no alternative but to engage either in more or less open inflation or to make painful cuts to government spending and to further raise taxes. This choice emerged with stark clarity from a bitter exchange in November 1938 between the RWM and the Reichsbank.

Following the disastrous failure of the Reich bond issue, the RWM, which since Schacht's resignation in November 1937 had been under the influence of the Four Year Plan, was highly critical of the Reichsbank's decision to launch a new tranche of bonds with such unseemly haste.[37] Only three weeks after the successful issue of October, the market was simply not ready to absorb more government debt. The effect of such a sudden and large-scale call on the bond market had been to suck money out of the stock market. 'The anxiety that Reich loans would now be floated every four weeks has paralysed all demand on the stock market . . .' This in turn had made it impossible for a number of important industrial companies to issue the shares and bonds they needed to finance investment projects required by the Four Year Plan. Rather than issuing a new loan, the RWM argued that the Reich should have tided itself over until January with short-term bank credits, freeing the capital market to satisfy the needs of the Four Year Plan. Characteristically, the solution proposed by the Ministerial officials was organizational. Henceforth, the RWM demanded an equal say with the Finance Ministry and the Reichsbank in deciding the timing of new loan issues. This would ensure that the wider interests of the Four Year Plan were properly considered. The rebuttal from the Reichsbank came within days. As the bank's economists explained, the problem was not organizational and it was not amenable to technical expedients. What the failure of the November loan revealed was simply the overburdening of the German economy. The Reichsbank had been fully aware of the dangers. But given the financial needs of the Reich they had had no choice. 'The financial situation of the Reich presented itself in mid-November of this year . . . as exceptionally difficult; there was a cash flow deficit of 2 billion Reichsmarks; we were faced with the imminent possibility that the Reich would have to cease payments.' Since all parties were agreed in rejecting a resort to the printing press, the Reich had consulted intensively with the banks about the possibility of a short-term bridging loan. This too had had to be rejected, since it would have been impossible to keep it completely secret and 'the public both at home and abroad, if it had become aware of these emergency measures, would have with reason arrived at the conclusion that the financing of the Reich's projects along present lines was no longer possible . . . this seemed unacceptable . . . for reasons of prestige alone'. In any case, given the fact that the Reich needed to borrow in excess of 1 billion Reichsmarks simply to pay its bills until Christmas, the effect on the market was bound to be severe, however the money was raised. If the Reich had taken up a huge overdraft, the banks would have been unable to discount commercial bills, squeezing industrial liquidity and forcing a sell-off of share holdings. Furthermore, with the end-of-year balance sheets upcoming it would have done serious damage to the international standing of Germany's banks if their accounts had been burdened with huge short-term loans to the Reich. As things stood, with the November loan having brought in only 1.138 billion Reichsmarks, the Reich had been tided over only by the desperate expedient of selling its reserve portfolio of bills and by drawing on the overdraft facilities of both the Reich Postal Service and the Reichsbahn. The remaining deficit of 300–400 million Reichsmarks had been filled by printing new banknotes. Given the situation of the Reich and the mood of the financial markets, the Ministry would have to accept that 'the execution of those tasks for which it has special responsibility in the area of general economic rearmament and the Four Year Plan would not be possible on the scale intended'. If an attempt was made to force more loans onto the market, the Reichsbank feared that the effect could well be disastrous. 'A reduction in bond prices that would be the natural outcome of any such measure would automatically conjure up the danger that the entire block of Reich debt could be set in motion. Such a development would mean the end of any Reich financing by means of loans.' So long as the huge deficits of the Reich continued, the lack of confidence in the capital markets meant that there was a constant threat that the Reich would be forced 'to halt payments'. The only real alternative was a decision 'ruthlessly to cut expenditure in the civilian and military sector . . .'.

And the Reichsbank directorate did not content itself with rebutting the RWM. Some time in December, Schacht made an appointment with Hitler to discuss Germany's financial situation early in the New Year.[38] In anticipation of this meeting, the Reichsbank directorate prepared a new document on Germany's economic situation, which was submitted to Hitler's office on 7 January 1939. In light of the collapse of confidence in the bond market, the Reichsbank returned with renewed urgency to the demands first formulated in early October, in the immediate aftermath of Munich. Germany was now facing the acute risk of an outbreak of inflation resulting from the 'overstraining of public expenditures and of short-term credits'.[39] The Reichsbank had been glad to play its part in Hitler's programme of national reconstruction. This included the 'two great actions in Austria and Sudetenland'. But it was deeply concerned that though the programme of national reintegration had been brought to a triumphant conclusion there was still no sign of any let-up in the pace of spending. Instead, 'all indications' suggested that a further 'extension of expenditures' was planned. Whilst the Reichsbank directorate had 'gladly cooperated to attain the great goal' of national rearmament it was 'now time to put a stop to it'. The damage done to the currency during the last ten months could be remedied, but only by the strict maintenance of a balanced budget. Since February 1938, the German money supply had increased 'more than during the preceding five years'. This sudden burst of monetary expansion, driven as it was by a lopsided programme of public works and rearmament, had opened up glaring disparities between the wages of different groups of workers. In the words of the Reichsbank, the 'wage- and price-structure' had 'totally fallen apart'. Reciting the concerns that had been repeatedly voiced over the last six to nine months, the Reichsbank pointed to the huge discrepancies in wage and price levels between different sectors. Furthermore, though average prices had been maintained at a relatively constant level, there had been a marked deterioration in the quality and quantity of daily necessities. 'Children's clothes and workwear, which formerly lasted for years, last now only for months, but cost the same or even more.' And the basic cause of this disorder was clear. 'There is no "recipe" or system of financial or money technique, regardless how ingenious or well thought out it may be, there are no organization or control measures that would be effective enough, to prevent a policy of unlimited expenditures having a disastrous effect on the currency.'

It is important to be clear about the nature of the Reichsbank's warning. The Reichsbank believed that the existing level of inflationary pressure could be contained, though at the cost of mounting bureaucratic regulation and inefficiency. If, however, the Reich embarked on the spending required to make good Hitler's demand of a tripling in armaments output, there was the real risk of an inflationary disaster. On Fromm's original forecast of 1936, the army had planned to spend 49 billion Reichsmarks by the end of budget year 1942. The Luftwaffe's fivefold expansion plan of 1938 was costed at 60 billion Reichsmarks over four years. The naval expansion plan that reached its final draft in early January 1939 came in at 33 billion Reichsmarks over ten years.[40]

Taking rough annual averages, these plans implied total Wehrmacht spending of 30 billion Reichsmarks per annum between 1939 and 1942 – 30 per cent of German national income in 1938, making no allowances for the Four Year Plan or any other state projects. In fact, the distribution of planned expenditure was more uneven than is implied by this average. For 1939–40, the total budgetary request from the Wehrmacht came to 'only' 24–25 billion Reichsmarks.[41] But, having seen the effects of military spending running at 18 billion Reichsmarks in 1938, the Reichsbank had every reason to fear the consequences of such expenditure.

The Reichsbank's interventions during the winter of 1938–9 represented a last attempt by Schacht and his colleagues to use economic argument as a lever with which to divert Hitler from his chosen course. As on previous occasions, however, Hitler brooked no such diversion. Within a fortnight of receiving the Reichsbank's petition, Schacht, Vice-President Friedrich Dreyse and Director Ernst Huelse had been relieved of their posts. Two other signatories of the letter resigned in solidarity. Schacht was replaced as Reichsbank president by the ever-pliant Walther Funk. In June 1939, the statutes of the Reichsbank were revised to abolish any formal limitation on the expansion of the money supply. Though the external value of the Reichsmark remained officially at gold parity, the abandonment of the gold standard demanded by Nazi monetary theorists since the 1920s was now finally acknowledged as a reality. Hitler as Fuehrer of the German people was given the power to determine the money supply at will. The path was cleared for unfettered military spending. The Wehrmacht did not get all it had wanted. But the enormous spending of 1938 was maintained. The secret budget of the Reich for 1939 provided a total of 20.86 billion Reichsmarks for the Wehrmacht, of which 11.6 billion was to be devoted to recurring expenditure and 9.199 billion to one-off expansion measures.[42] The navy and Luftwaffe did well, with allocations of 2.744 billion and 7.018 billion Reichsmarks respectively. The army had to make do with 'only' 10.449 billion Reichsmarks, which was somewhat less than it had spent in 1938. To ease its cash flow problems the Reich adopted a new expedient in the form of the New Finance Plan (Neuer Finanzplan) of 20 March 1939.[43] Under its provisions, the Reich's suppliers of goods and services were required to accept payment for at least 40 per cent of contract value not in cash but in the form of tax credits. These could be offset in future years against tax liability and provided their holders with significant tax exemptions, but they bore no interest. They amounted in effect to a compulsory low-interest loan to the Reich, which by October 1939 had already risen to a total of 4.831 billion Reichsmarks.[44] The idea behind the New Finance Plan was that if the Reich's demand for credit could be met by paying its contractors in tax certificates, then the capital markets would be able to provide at least 1 billion Reichsmarks in loans to serve the needs of the Four Year Plan. From the outset, however, this emergency measure did little to hide the regime's financial embarrassment.[45] Technical expedients could not remedy the underlying problem of excess demand.[46] By reducing the share of cash payments, the New Finance Plan simply imposed a serious squeeze on the liquidity of government contractors. Nor was it ever substantial enough in scale to fill the Reich's financing gap. The 1938 Reich budget closed with an excess of spending over tax revenue and safe long-term borrowing of 5.7 billion Reichsmarks.[47] The additional shortfall allowed for in the 1939 budget came to 6 billion Reichsmarks. For this deficit, the only possible source of 'finance' was short-term credit from the Reichsbank, which amounted, in effect, to printing money. In the first eight months of 1939 the floating debt of the Reich increased by no less than 80 per cent. By the outbreak of war, the volume of money in circulation had doubled relative to the level prevailing only two years earlier.

The effort to impose financial restraint on armaments spending thus failed. As in 1934 and in 1936–7, the factor that ultimately dictated the pace of rearmament in 1939 was the balance of payments and the scarcity of foreign currency. This was entirely predictable. As we have seen, at the beginning of 1938, in the weeks prior to the Anschluss, the experts of the Four Year Plan had anticipated a bad year. In the event, Austria's foreign currency holdings provided temporary relief. In total in 1938 the Reichsbank disbursed 546 million Reichsmarks in foreign currency, acquired either in Austria or through the ongoing liquidation of privately owned foreign assets. One-third of Germany's requirement for 'cash foreign exchange' – as opposed to imports that could be financed by clearing credits – was financed from 'non-renewable' sources.[48] As Goering himself put it to the council of the Four Year Plan on 14 October 1938: 'In recent months, to attain our political goals we have had to engage in a *conscious* policy of stripping foreign exchange holdings and neglecting . . . exports.'[49] As Germany's foreign exchange reserves once again neared exhaustion, export revenues were plunging. In August 1938 export deliveries were 20 per cent lower than a year earlier, and the volume of fresh export orders was lower still.[50] By January 1939, the Reichsbank directorate in its report to Hitler stated bluntly: 'Gold or foreign exchange reserves of the Reichsbank are no more in existence.'[51] The balance of trade was deteriorating fast. 'The receipts for foreign exchange, which were issued by the control office at the time of importation, are today ... not covered by actual foreign exchange and therefore run the risk that some day they cannot be paid ... the last foreign credit to cover our imports of goods would then be ruined.'[52] By November 1938, given the prospective depletion of the foreign exchange reserves, it was already clear that Germany would soon have to abandon its all-out rearmament drive, in favour of a renewed concentration on exports.[53] In fact, Goering had already called for a renewed export drive in mid-October 1938.[54] In early November the Wehrmacht was informed that export orders would now have priority over all other contracts, including military orders.[55] And, as we have seen, the new line received the most public endorsement possible in Hitler's fateful speech to the Reichstag of 30 January 1939.[56]

The speech is famous above all for the threats that Hitler made against European Jewry. But what is often ignored is that these ominous threats against 'Germany's enemies' were coupled with an appeal to the German population for a new discipline and resolve in the face of their nation's persistent economic difficulties. No 'decaying social strata' or 'social prejudice' would be allowed to stand in the way of the new mobilization. Given the refusal of the Western powers to allow Germany the expansion of its *Lebensraum*, the German population faced a simple choice: 'export, or die'.[57] To meet this existential threat, Hitler proclaimed a new era in National Socialist economic policy. The Four Year Plan would have to be intensified and the German labour force mustered in the most efficient way possible. Through 'rationalization' and technical improvement the German economy would be brought to a new pitch of performance, enabling it to meet the competing demands of domestic investment, export and rearmament. The technical means would be provided by the capital market mechanisms of the New Finance Plan. But above all what was required was unified National Socialist leadership and the enthusiastic cooperation of every German man and every German woman. It was this state of national emergency therefore that required the removal of Schacht and the placing of the Reichsbank under firm National Socialist leadership. And it was this national emergency that required the new concerted approach to economic policy which we have seen as emerging since October 1938.

The dilemma, however, could not be escaped. Something had to be done to revive Germany's faltering exports and this was bound to come at the expense of the armaments programmes. Already on 24 November 1938, the armed forces received the news that in the coming year their overall steel ration was to be cut back from 530,000 to only 300,000 tons.[58] This came as a complete shock to both the army and air force, which only a few weeks earlier had been basking in a sense of unlimited possibility. The army, the most steel-dependent of the armed forces, was told to expect an allocation barely in excess of the rations of 1937, with special caps being applied to the types of steel in heaviest demand.[59] The top priority given to the navy in January 1939 added to the army's woes. The navy's steel requirements were not huge, but, given the overall reduction in the Wehrmacht's quota, the shift in priorities was painful. Even allowing for the professional pessimism of military planners, the situation was clearly serious. By the spring of 1939, army procurement was in full retreat. As usual, the cuts fell most heavily on the big steel users. Orders for the mass-production of ammunition were slashed, to the consternation of the army's industrial suppliers.[60] As Brauchitsch, Commander-in-Chief of the army, noted in a letter of protest to Wehrmacht high command, the abrupt and apparently arbitrary cancellation of orders 'seriously endangers the confidence of the business community in the state's planning of the economy. The frequent enquiries from businessmen in recent days ... make this quite clear.'[61] Production of infantry ammunition plummeted. The manufacture of mortar bombs ceased altogether in the spring of 1939. Artillery shells continued to be produced, but without copper driving bands. And it was not only ammunition production that was affected. The shortage of building steel was such that by the end of 1939, 300 infantry battalions were without proper barracks or garages. Germany's army had grown so large that it could be accommodated only under canvas. By July 1939 there were cuts even to the army's weapons programmes. The original plans for 1939–40 had called for the production of 61,000 Model 34 machine guns, the new light machine gun that was to provide the infantry squads with their basic firepower. After the reduction in the army's steel contin-

gent this target was reduced to only 13,000. Similarly, targets for the
10.5 centimetre light field howitzer, the workhorse of the German artillery, were cut from 840 to 460.[62] Production of the standard infantry
carbine 98k was to cease altogether from the autumn of 1939. Perhaps
most dramatically in light of later events, the tank programme, which
aimed for the production of 1,200 medium battle tanks and command
vehicles between October 1939 and October 1940, was now to be cut
in half.[63] In total, 34 of Germany's wartime force of 105 divisions would
be seriously under-equipped. Of the replacement units responsible for
training new recruits, only 10 per cent would have any weapons at all.
Furthermore, specialist armaments manufacturers would be forced to
cut more than 100,000 skilled workers from their rolls.[64] Since they
would be immediately snapped up by other employers, this would make
it far harder to start up mass-production when war began. The army
administrators now estimated that it would take six months after the
outbreak of war for the ammunition factories to achieve peak production. The ammunition stockpiles of the Wehrmacht were sufficient
to cover only fourteen days of heavy fighting.

The Luftwaffe was hit in the same way. By contrast with the expansive
visions of 1938, planning in 1939 went into reverse.[65] The production
totals envisioned by successive plans between the summer of 1938 and
the summer of 1939 remained broadly speaking within the framework
set by Goering's Ideal Programme No. 9 of December 1938, calling for
21,000 aircraft by 1942. But this framework was maintained only by
shifting more and more output into the later years of the plans. The
targets for 1939 and 1940 were progressively reduced, as was the range
of aircraft that were included in the plans. Plans 8 and 9, drafted in
August and December 1938, each envisioned production of 10,000 or
more aircraft in 1939. As of January 1939, Plan 10 cut the target to
8,299 aircraft. Plan 12, drafted in July 1939, reduced this by a further
20 per cent for all aircraft other than the Ju 88. To preserve the Ju 88
programme, Plan 12 envisioned the accelerated phasing out of older
models such as the Ju 87 Stuka.[66] Though this dive-bomber had already
proved its worth in Spain, it had to be cut to make way for a new
generation of aircraft, most of which were untested. To cope with its
straitened supply of raw materials, the Luftwaffe was thus adopting an
increasingly risky strategy of weapons procurement. For aluminium, the
all-important material in airframe production, the Luftwaffe's ration as

of January 1939 was a third lower than that required to meet the modest procurement targets of Plan 11. For copper, the initial ration was set at 50 per cent of requirement. As of July 1939 this was cut to a derisory 20 per cent.[67]

Figure 10 shows the impact on both the Luftwaffe and army procurement first of the armaments recession of 1937 and then the even more dramatic slump in production caused by the raw material shortages of 1939. In both cases the response in final output of armaments was lagging by a few months. But, given that raw materials took up to nine months to work their way completely through the industrial metabolism, this was only to be expected. The overall pattern of boom and bust could hardly have been more pronounced. The only arm of the Wehrmacht exempt from this sudden contraction was the navy. Its relatively small allocations of steel continued to rise after January 1939 and there is no indication that its construction programmes were in any way hampered by shortages of materials. Ironically, however, this resulted in no increase in fighting strength since the navy's Z Plan gave priority to a new generation of giant battleships and the dockyards necessary to build them. This would take years.

III

Nor was armaments planning the only element of Hitler's anti-Western strategy that was derailed in the first months of 1939. Germany's foreign policy came unstuck as well.[68] Ribbentrop's ambition had been to combine the liquidation of the rump of Czechoslovakia with an effort to enrol Poland as Germany's ally. At the same time the German Foreign Ministry hoped to win the support of Japan and Italy against Britain and France. By the spring of 1939, Ribbentrop had been able to achieve none of these objectives. Poland warded off Germany's initial advances and even had the temerity to improve its relations with the Soviet Union. Japan was preoccupied with its war in northern China and had no interest in adding to its enemies. Italy was bent on a course of aggression that took it eastward into the Balkans, rather than westwards against France. When Hitler sent German troops into Prague on 15 March 1939 to establish a protectorate over the Czechs, the result was a diplomatic disaster.[69] Though the occupation of Bohemia outflanked Poland's

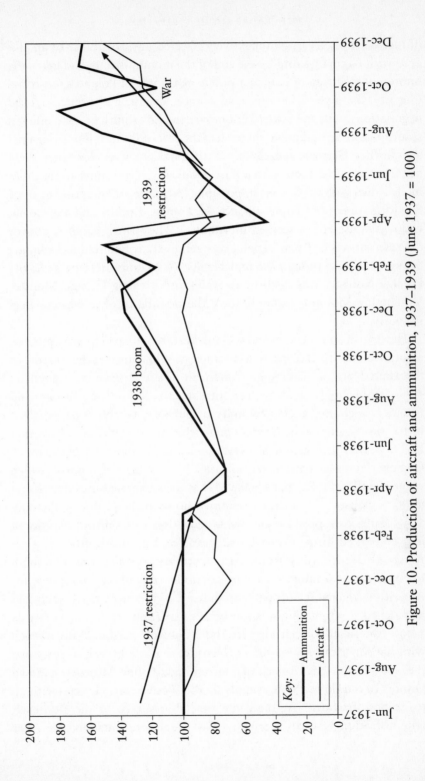

Figure 10. Production of aircraft and ammunition, 1937–1939 (June 1937 = 100)

border defences, Warsaw definitively rejected any possibility of an alliance with Germany. And by the end of the month, Britain had taken the unprecedented step of issuing a public guarantee of Poland's territorial integrity. To give this promise substance, Britain and France opened negotiations with the Soviet Union over the possibility of concluding a security agreement that would protect the rest of Eastern Europe against any further German aggression. With hindsight it is clear that these negotiations were doomed to failure. Ironically, a guarantee to the Poles made a deal with the Soviets impossible. However, in the spring of 1939 the formation of a triple alliance of France, Britain and the Soviet Union against Hitler seemed inevitable.[70] The British cabinet, despite the reservations of Chamberlain, was genuinely committed to seeking a Soviet deal. And though the replacement of Maxim Litvinov as Soviet Foreign Minister was disturbing, Stalin and his new Foreign Minister Vyacheslav Molotov certainly took the possibility of a Western deal seriously.

The British and French hand was further strengthened by the apparent assurance that the European democracies could count on the support of the United States. The Anglo-American Trade Agreement signed on 2 November 1938 sent a clear message to Berlin.[71] As Britain and America celebrated their new unity of purpose, Goebbels issued strict instructions banning the German press from any comment implying that Berlin viewed the agreement as a significant 'victory for democracy'.[72] Chamberlain was particularly pleased by intelligence reports, which suggested that the Germans believed that the agreement included 'secret military clauses'.[73] In fact, it contained no such thing. But by October 1938 America's position on arms deliveries was shifting. Roosevelt had embarked on a 'major bureaucratic and political effort' to shift America's stance away from strict neutrality, opening the door both to American rearmament and the possibility of military assistance for America's friends in Europe.[74] By the end of the year, the French had dispatched a purchasing mission with instructions to buy as many as 1,000 American combat aircraft and Roosevelt personally intervened with the American armed forces to ensure that the French were shown the best weapons that American industry had to offer.[75] Roosevelt talked grandly of the United States supplying the Western democracies with up to 20,000 aircraft.[76] At the same time, the stance of the Roosevelt administration towards Germany was ever more antagonistic. After the horror of Kristallnacht, only the intervention of Cordell Hull had prevented Treasury Secretary Henry Morgenthau from taking severe action. Following the occupation of Czechoslovakia in March 1939, there was no longer any restraint. Roosevelt imposed a 25 per cent punitive tariff on German imports, a measure viewed in Berlin as tantamount to a declaration of economic war.[77]

Though the occupation of Prague was fêted in Berlin as a huge triumph, it had conjured up against the Third Reich the nightmare of German strategy, an encirclement from both East and West, to which Hitler really had no answer.[78] Nevertheless, as in May 1938, his immediate response was aggression. He instructed the Wehrmacht to begin preparing for military action against Poland, to be taken in the event that he was able to isolate that country diplomatically. The new OKW plans were presented to Hitler on 1 April in Wilhelmshaven during the ceremonies attendant upon the launching of the giant new battleship, the *Tirpitz*.[79] This was an obvious occasion for an anti-British broadside and Hitler made the most of it. In an evening speech, he roused his audience with the memory of Britain's brutal blockade and savagely attacked the hypocrisy with which Britons habitually assumed the moral high ground, whilst they themselves presided with force over a quarter of the globe. The recent efforts by the British to ally themselves with the Soviet Union were indicative of the true forces at work behind the scenes. 'State after state will either fall under the Jewish Bolshevist plague or it will defend itself.' Only when the 'Jewish fission-fungus' was finally removed from world affairs would peace really be possible. Over the following weeks, this anti-British and anti-Semitic rhetoric proved a popular propaganda line, but it did nothing to alleviate the real threat of isolation which Germany was now facing.

In the offices of the Four Year Plan, Carl Krauch registered the true seriousness of the situation in a series of memorandums on Germany's raw material situation in the event of war. His starting point was the realization that Germany was increasingly losing its ability to dictate the pace of events.

When on 30 June 1938 the targets for a production increase . . . were set by the Field Marshal [Goering's Wehrwirtschaftlicher Neuer Erzeugungsplan], it seemed as if the [German] political leadership would have the possibility of solely determining the timing and scale of the political transformation in Europe –

whilst avoiding a confrontation with the power group led by England. Since March of this year [1939] there can no longer be any doubt that this possibility no longer exists. The economic war against the anti-Comintern powers that has already secretly begun under the leadership of England, France and the United States has now been openly declared and with time it will take on ever more severe forms.[80]

Taking his cue from Hitler's speech at Wilhelmshaven, Krauch demanded that the Four Year Plan should not watch passively as the Western powers completed their crippling encirclement. Germany's anti-Comintern alliance with Italy, Hungary and Franco's Spain must be consolidated to form a unified economic bloc capable of waging a prolonged 'defensive war' (*Verteidigungskrieg*) against the forces of 'almost the entire rest of the world' (*fast der ganzen uebrigen Welt*). What Krauch wanted was a gigantic new effort to construct synthetic fuel, rubber and light metal plants for each of Germany's allies. Leadership in this programme was to lie with industry, that is, IG Farben, and it was of course to be backed by generous new allocations of steel. But, as Krauch clearly recognized, given the scale of the threat facing Germany, autarchy was no longer enough. If the Third Reich was to survive a truly global war, it would need to extend its influence systematically to the oil fields of Romania and Iran. Turkey thus took on a strategic importance as the gateway to the Middle East. In addition, Germany urgently needed to cultivate its trade relations with the Soviet Union. 'Through the overt policy of encirclement pursued by our enemies a new situation has been created ... If these ideas are not translated immediately into action, then every sacrifice of blood in the next war will not protect us against the bitter end, to which a lack of foresight and decisiveness has already condemned us once before.'

A step in the right direction was the German-Romanian trade treaty of 23 March 1939.[81] This provoked great alarm in London and Paris, because Romania was Eastern Europe's only major oil producer and because the treaty was clearly the result of coercion as much as bribery.[82] In Berlin, the deal was heralded as a major breakthrough, which would secure Germany's oil and grain supplies for the foreseeable future. For the Romanians, however, it seems to have been little more than a means of warding off German and Hungarian pressure. A few weeks after concluding the deal, Romania inveigled the French into guaranteeing its security along with that of Poland. The British were forced to follow suit. Following the occupation of Prague, the balance of power in South-east Europe was delicately poised.[83] Whereas Germany attempted to suck Romania into its orbit, Turkey opted for the Western powers, securing the right flank of the British Empire in the Middle East.[84] Turkey's decision was premised on the common understanding in the spring of 1939 that there would soon be the announcement of a triple alliance binding the Western powers to the Soviet Union. Driven by the same assumption, the Yugoslavs, Greeks and even the Bulgarians drifted towards London and Paris in the summer of 1939, not towards Berlin. Even the Romanian trade deal failed to live up to German expectations. Once the threat of Hungarian military action had been lifted, the willingness of Bucharest to supply Germany with oil depended on Germany's ability to provide reciprocal deliveries, in particular of arms.[85] In June Romania interrupted oil deliveries for the first time, forcing Germany's trade negotiators to agree to a consignment of late-model Messerschmitts. On 22 July Hitler personally intervened to veto the deal. In his view, it was too uncertain whether the Romanians could be counted on to side with Germany in case of war. This, however, left the Four Year Plan worrying that Germany would soon have to introduce peacetime petrol rationing. Without Romanian oil imports, so much was already clear, Germany could not survive for long. Only weeks later, Goering therefore countermanded Hitler's order. Romania got its fighters. The conclusion, however, was inescapable. The effort to establish German economic dominance over South-eastern Europe by peaceful means was reaching its limit. In fact, the Wehrmacht's military-economic office had already concluded in April 1939 that oil supplies from Romania would be sufficient to cover Germany's needs only if the country was occupied by German troops, and if the entire Romanian oil industry, in which France and Britain currently held the dominant share, was turned over to production for Germany.[86]

The fundamental problem for Berlin was that in the aftermath of Prague, with Britain and France united and apparently able to count on the support of the United States, any conventional strategic analysis suggested that Germany was outmatched. Only if Germany could obtain the agreement of the Japanese and the Italians to combined action would the French and British empires be seriously stretched. Precisely this grand alliance, however, was eluding Ribbentrop's diplomacy in 1939. Neither

Japan nor Italy wanted to attach themselves too firmly to Hitler's dangerous course. Nor was there any lack of clarity in Berlin about the scale
of the military-economic challenge that Germany faced. On 24 May
1939 the Wehrmacht's chief economist, Major-General Thomas, presented members of the German Foreign Office with a lucid and highly
pessimistic analysis of the balance of forces.[87] Thomas presented his
audience with the latest comparisons of the defence expenditure planned
by the 'three democracies' in 1939–40, compared to the spending plans
of Italy and Germany. He concluded that, once differences in purchasing
power were allowed for, Britain, France and the United States would
outspend Germany and Italy by a margin of at least 2 billion Reichsmarks in the coming year. Even more strikingly, Thomas went on to
compare the burden of rearmament in macroeconomic terms, by placing
military spending in relation to national income. In this respect, the Axis
disadvantage was even starker. Whereas Germany in 1939 was already
planning to devote 23 per cent of its national income to the Wehrmacht,
the figure for France was 17 per cent, 12 per cent for Britain and only
2 per cent for the United States. The last two figures were crucial. Given
the fact that the British and German economies were relatively evenly
matched, a Franco-British alliance always enjoyed a significant advantage in a European arms race. And as Thomas fully realized, British
strategic planning was not confined to Europe. Britain counted 'the
entire Empire and the United States as an armoury and reservoir of raw
materials'. If the vast industrial capacity of the United States came in on
the side of Britain and France, the German disadvantage would be
overwhelming.

In making these comparisons, Thomas may well have intended to
restart the strategic debate that Ludwig Beck had abandoned the previous August. We know that Thomas was opposed to a premature war
with Britain and France and he may have been looking for allies amongst
the senior civil servants in the Foreign Office. On the other hand, if one
was bent on war, as Hitler and Ribbentrop appear increasingly to have
been, the data that Thomas presented could also be made to yield an
alternative conclusion. In an all-out arms race with the 'democracies',
time was clearly not on Germany's side.[88] If one gave credence to
Thomas's figures, if the democracies were already outspending Germany
by 2 billion Reichsmarks in 1939, with the United States making a
minimal contribution, how large might their advantage be in a few years'

time? This argument applied with most force to the Luftwaffe, where the extraordinarily rapid development of aviation technology in the 1930s had the effect of levelling the international playing field. Despite Goering's periodic outbursts, it was clear that the British were concentrating all available resources on the Royal Air Force, first as a defensive, but ultimately also as an offensive threat. There was no reason to believe that the German aircraft industry enjoyed any pronounced technical superiority over the British. Though intelligence was faulty on both sides, as of the spring of 1939, British aircraft production matched that of the Third Reich. In the short term, on the other hand, due to the rapid pace of expansion since 1933, the German air force still enjoyed a clear margin of superiority both in terms of the number of combat-worthy aircraft and in terms of overall war readiness.[89] When Goering spoke to the Italian Foreign Minister Galeazzo Ciano on 15 April 1939, the point he stressed was that the situation for the Axis, from the point of view of the air balance, would be most 'favourable' in nine to twelve months' time.[90]

What nobody who was in any way acquainted with Germany's economic situation could expect was a further acceleration of the armaments effort, certainly not under prevailing conditions. As we have seen, the army's efforts to stockpile enough ammunition and weapons to equip its millions of troops were in disarray. The Luftwaffe's programmes were shrinking, not expanding. We know, furthermore, that Hitler was fully informed of this situation. In February 1939, when the cuts first made themselves felt, Brauchitsch took the step of writing directly to Hitler.[91] This was a bold move because it was in defiance of an order, recently issued, banning members of army staff from attempting to sway Hitler by means of pessimistic reports on the armaments situation. Though it took weeks for Hitler to reply formally to Brauchitsch, he was clearly concerned. In February 1939 a senior official in the Heereswaffenamt received the following instruction:

As I have been informed confidentially by Captain Engel, the Fuehrer's Adjutant, the Fuehrer wishes, if possible by the end of the first week of March, to have the following facts:
1. the quantity of available weapons and ammunition
2. divided into those with the troops and those in quartermaster stores
3. what quantities are to be expected as additions.[92]

It seems only reasonable to assume that Hitler was trying to inform himself about the situation of the German army at the moment that he was planning to occupy Prague. One month later, on 15 April 1939, Brauchitsch prepared a report for Hitler which described in excruciating detail the impact not only of the overall steel cuts, but more particularly the acute shortage of rod iron. Backed up by thirty pages of statistics and charts, Brauchitsch delivered the punchline:

The situation created today by the shortage of rod iron in some ways corresponds to the situation before the Great War. Then the establishment of the three army corps that would have been necessary in the first year of the war to achieve a rapid decision was frustrated by the refusal of the necessary funds by parliament. Today, the army is being deprived of the rod iron necessary for its equipment with modern offensive weaponry. The consequences may be the same as in 1914.[93]

A few months later, it was no longer steel but nonferrous metals and in particular copper that forced Brauchitsch to appeal both to Hitler and to Keitel as chief of the Wehrmacht high command. Copper was the more sensitive indicator of the foreign exchange situation, because Germany was entirely dependent on foreign ores. Following in the wake of six months of reduced steel allocations, Brauchitsch described the new rations for nonferrous metals as tantamount, 'in their totality ... to the liquidation of the army's rearmament effort'.[94] Despite the ban on drawing political conclusions from such problems, Brauchitsch insisted to Keitel that 'under all circumstances means and ways must be found, to prevent this abrupt end of the army's build-up, particularly in a time of such political tensions'. As war over Poland approached, the German army's armaments programme was threatening to grind to a virtual standstill. Hitler's office again responded with a note to the armaments bureaucrats: 'The Fuehrer wishes to have the prospective level of armaments as of 1 April 1940 and 1 October 1940 following the same format as the documents recently provided for 1939 ... Please ensure that the deadlines are met.'[95] It would seem that Hitler was closely following the impact of declining raw material allocations on army production and was attempting to form an opinion as to the likely military strength at his disposal in the next twelve to eighteen months. Not surprisingly in light of Brauchitsch's comments, the army's procurement office replied to Hitler's request for information with a highly pessimistic outlook. Instead of an 'ideal' maximum of 375 million rounds of infantry ammunition per month, the allocation of raw materials as of July 1939 would permit production of less than 37 million. Instead of 650,000 3.7 centimetre anti-tank rounds per month, German industry would produce 39,000. Instead of 450,000 shells per month for light howitzers, German industry would produce 56,300. Figure 11 summarizes the future of German ammunition production, as it was presented to Hitler by the army staff in the summer of 1939.

Hitler's demand for information was so urgent that the head of army weapons procurement had no time to check the data compiled by his subordinates.[96] He was clearly worried about Hitler's reaction. If the Fuehrer felt that the army was attempting to influence his decision-making through the presentation of downbeat statistics, he was likely to react badly. So, after the data was dispatched to the Fuehrer's adjutant, the officer in charge made sure to double-check the exceedingly low forecasts that had been presented for infantry ammunition. The procurement staff responded immediately with a thorough explanation of their calculations. To arrive at their figures, the army procurement office had projected forward the steel rations as expected from the third quarter of 1939. Even more important as a limiting factor was the reduced copper allocation, which from July 1939 was expected to be no more than 415 tons per month. In addition, they had had to make allowance for the special priority that Hitler had ordered for tank guns, mortars, heavy infantry artillery and landmines. Assuming that 60 per cent of the available steel was allocated to these top priority weapons, their estimates for the output of standard 7.92 millimetre infantry ammunition were in fact on the high side.

How exactly Hitler responded to these forecasts the sources do not reveal. One thing we can rule out, however, is that Hitler in the autumn of 1939 was under any illusion about the viability of the long-term armaments programmes drawn up in the aftermath of Munich. Given the problems of finance and raw materials encountered since October 1938, the realization of those enormous goals was no longer realistic. Hitler had sacked Schacht in January 1939, clearing the last serious political obstacle to openly inflationary financing. But the balance of payments constraint could not be waved aside so easily. Though the strategic situation clearly demanded an acceleration of German rearmament, and though such an acceleration had clearly been planned in the autumn of 1938, the shortage of imported raw materials made it

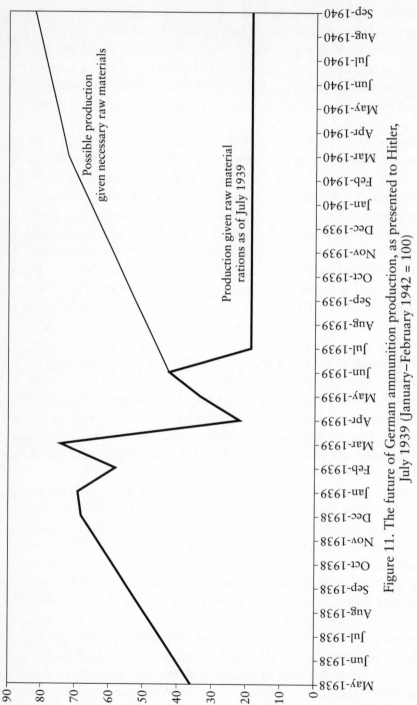

Figure 11. The future of German ammunition production, as presented to Hitler, July 1939 (January–February 1942 = 100)

Note: The chart is constructed on the basis of figures for actual production up to May 1939. The data beyond May 1939 are the predicted levels of production translated into an index using the appropriate weights for each type of ammunition. The 'ideal' figures refer to the manufacturing capacity available for ammunition production, allowing sufficient capacity for export orders and civilian needs, but assuming an unlimited allocation of raw materials.

impossible. The German armaments economy had once more reached the impasse that, since 1934, had repeatedly interrupted its expansion. Of course, by extreme measures it would have been possible to raise the share of national income going to the military to above the 20 per cent level already reached in 1938, but only at the expense of abandoning any pretence to a normal peacetime economic policy. Alternatively, Germany could have done what it had done in 1936–8. It could have held off from accelerating rearmament for a period of twelve to eighteen months, accumulating enough foreign exchange for one last burst of military expenditure. But this was hardly an attractive outlook when one considers Thomas's statistics on the global arms race. With close to 20 per cent of its national economy already dedicated to military spending and the Wehrmacht's share of critical raw materials hovering between 20 and 30 per cent, Germany's 'wartime economy at peace' had reached a critical threshold.

If on the one hand Hitler knew that the outlook for the immediate future of the German armaments effort was not good, he also knew in the summer of 1939 that the Third Reich had assembled both the largest and most combat-ready army in Europe, as well as the best air force. Already in March 1939, in conversation with the Italian ambassador, he stated that 'as regards her armed forces, Germany was now in a position to face all eventualities'.[97] Since 1933, the German army had recruited and trained 4 million men. It had never been able to sustain the rate of expansion that it had wanted. The setbacks both in 1937 and 1939 had been severe. The re-equipment of the front-line units with the latest generation of tanks and machine guns was incomplete. Ammunition stocks were sufficient to cover only a few weeks of fighting. But the progress since 1938, when the thought of a war over Czechoslovakia had been enough to drive the German army to near mutiny, was undeniable. By the summer of 1939, despite the protests from the procurement office, the German army was ready for a short war. There was no doubt at all that it could handle Poland. When Hitler gave the order to prepare for an attack in the spring of 1939 there was not a murmur of opposition from the generals.[98] To overwhelm Poland's 30 infantry and 7 cavalry divisions, the Germans could deploy 54 divisions, including 6 Panzer divisions equipped with at least a smattering of medium to heavy tanks.[99] Furthermore, the encircling position that Germany occupied in East Prussia and the former Czech lands meant that success was virtually guaranteed. The thought of a war against Britain and France was still daunting. And there was little or no conception as to how Germany would actually win a war in the West. If the French had pressed home a determined assault against western Germany whilst the bulk of the Wehrmacht and Luftwaffe were in Poland, the effects might well have been catastrophic. However, at least Germany was no longer defenceless. Whilst concentrating the bulk of its forces in the East, the Wehrmacht would be able to defend its western border with at least 11 first-line divisions, as opposed to only 5 in 1938. Furthermore, thanks to Todt's efforts, the gateway to the Rhineland between the Rhine and the Moselle was now heavily fortified.[100] The Westwall, which in September 1938 had been little more than a building site, now formed a deep defensive system, studded with 11,283 bunkers and gun emplacements. Air strength had increased to close to 4,000 front-line aircraft. And since the Luftwaffe had begun its re-equipment in 1936, all its planes were of modern design. Furthermore, since the summer of 1938 Krauch's Schnellplan had put Germany in a position to supply itself with more than enough explosives, gunpowder and poison gas, if required.

It was possible, in short, to construct a rationale for war in the autumn of 1939, considering only the dynamics of the armaments effort. If war was inevitable, as Hitler clearly believed it was, then the Wehrmacht had little to gain from waiting.[101] And Hitler certainly did espouse precisely this logic on a number of occasions. In justifying his decision to strike against Poland regardless of the dangers, Hitler referred explicitly to economic pressures. Most famously, on 22 August 1939, in an address to the German military leadership at Berchtesgaden he stated emphatically: 'We have nothing to lose; we have everything to gain. Because of our restrictions our economic situation is such that we can only hold out for a few more years. Goering can confirm this. We must act . . .' According to another rendition of the same speech, he was less flattering to Goering. 'The Four Year Plan has failed and we are finished if we do not achieve victory in the coming war.'[102] Albert Speer, who was with Hitler on a daily basis in 1939, recalled him making an argument for war that was directly based on the dynamic of the arms race. From 1940 onwards Hitler apparently believed that Germany's 'proportional superiority' would 'constantly diminish'. 'Right now, on the other hand, we have new weapons in all fields, the other side obsolete types.'[103] As we shall see, once war broke out Hitler became even more explicit about the time-pressure that he believed he was acting under, presenting his decision for action as a conscious choice to take the offensive against a gathering enemy coalition. In early March 1940 he wrote to Mussolini in remarkably explicit terms: 'Since the introduction of conscription in England [in the spring of 1939] it was perfectly clear that the decisive circles in British government had already decided on the next war against the totalitarian states.' The aims of these shadowy 'circles' were all encompassing, 'total' in Hitler's words. 'Nothing less', in fact, 'than the *elimination* [*Beseitigung*] of those regimes', Germany and Italy most notably, 'which in their essence constitute a threat to the feudal-reactionary plutocracies.' Faced with this threat of annihilation, Hitler's time-horizon had shortened.

In the light of Britain's intended armaments effort, as well as considering England's intention of mobilizing all conceivable auxiliaries . . . it appeared to me after all to be right . . . to begin immediately with the counterattack [Abwehr], even at the risk of thereby precipitating the war intended by the Western powers two or three years earlier. After all Duce, what could have been the improvement in our armaments in two or three years? As far as the Wehrmacht was concerned, in light of England's forced rearmament, a significant shift in the balance of forces in our favour was barely conceivable. And towards the east the situation could only deteriorate.[104]

In the light of the severe setback to Germany's armaments effort in the summer of 1939, fully revealed for the first time in this chapter, these justifications offered by Hitler for his decision to go to war deserve to be taken seriously and not waved aside as mere 'half-truths' and ex post facto rationalizations.[105] Hitler was well informed about the state of German armaments production. And he was essentially correct in his assessment that Germany had reached the point at which it had very little to gain from a continuation of the peacetime arms race. This is evident both from Thomas's broad-brush analysis of the macroeconomics of the arms race and from comparison of production figures for military aircraft. In the course of 1939 Britain and France were finally catching up with the Luftwaffe. If, as Hitler believed, war was inevitable, then in terms of his own 'mad logic' he did have an interest in taking the offensive at the earliest favourable opportunity. And the necessary opportunity was provided over the summer of 1939 by the extraordinary reversal in Germany's diplomatic fortunes.

IV

With the situation in Central and Western Europe increasingly polarized, it was the flanking powers that were of decisive strategic importance. Germany did not manage to gain Poland as an ally. Nor did Hitler manage to dislodge the British and French guarantees. On the other hand, by the end of August 1939 Hitler and Ribbentrop had prised apart the trans-Continental coalition that had seemed to threaten the Third Reich after the occupation of Prague.

The first to waver was the United States. Since Munich, Roosevelt had been lining up ever more unambiguously against Hitler's expansionism. The fundamental question, however, was whether the President could build the necessary domestic coalition in the United States to back his increasingly bellicose stance. As Europe moved ever closer towards war, the highly restrictive Neutrality Act of 1937 remained in force. Following the occupation of Prague efforts had begun in Congress to loosen the restrictions so as to permit belligerents to purchase arms on a 'cash and carry' basis.[106] But by the early summer these attempts at revision had been fought to a standstill by the isolationist minority both in the House and the Senate. On 18 July Roosevelt was forced to abandon the attempt until the next session. In Paris and London there was consternation. In the Fascist camp, the media rejoiced. America's promises were empty.[107] As the pro-Fascist *L'Action française* sneered with bitter sarcasm: 'America is with us! One hundred and twenty million free citizens of the United States burn to help our soldiers!'[108] As things stood in the summer of 1939, the United States was in no position to supply either Britain or France with arms or ammunition in case of war. It is hard to imagine that serious opinion in either Rome or Berlin was in any real doubt as to what would happen if war actually broke out. Nor did the isolationists oppose Roosevelt's efforts to raise the level of America's own armaments. But what was clear in the summer of 1939 was that, in case of a war in Europe, it would take months, if not years, before America's military and industrial might could be fully brought to bear.[109]

Whereas the engagement of the United States on the side of Britain and France merely wavered, the position of the Soviet Union shifted far more dramatically. Following the German occupation of Prague on 15 March, it was, as we have seen, generally assumed that a Triple

Alliance would soon bind France, Britain and the Soviet Union into a defensive system against Germany. So great was the threat posed to all three countries by Germany's relentless aggression that ideological objections would surely be set aside. Chamberlain, a committed anti-Communist if there ever was one, said as much to the British Parliament at the end of May.[110] Diplomatic and military discussions between France, Britain and the Soviet Union continued throughout the summer.[111] Hitler for his part continued to push for a binding global alliance with Japan and Italy, Germany's only hope of countering Britain and France's overwhelming naval superiority. Nor was this lost on the British. A 'triple threat' from an Axis coalition in the Atlantic, Mediterranean and Pacific was the real nightmare of Royal Navy strategists.[112] The pursuit of a global answer to Britain dictated that Germany not push for closer relations with the Soviet Union, since Japan and the Soviets were involved in a tense stand-off of their own in Manchuria. In Moscow, however, the signs of a new approach to European security were unmistakable.[113] At the same time as the Japanese increasingly pulled back from a firm military commitment to Germany and Italy, the Soviets drifted towards Hitler.

As Germany's diplomats clearly understood, Stalin's increasing emphasis from the spring of 1939 onwards on the classic Leninist doctrine of the inevitability of inter-capitalist war opened distinct possibilities for Germany.[114] After all, an alliance with Germany offered the Soviet Union the best chance of profiting from a war between the major capitalist powers. The Germans for their part, if they were serious about a war with Poland and still hoped to deter Britain and France, desperately needed an alliance with someone, if not with Japan then with Moscow. As early as 26 May Ribbentrop drafted a full set of instructions for the German embassy in Moscow, in which he firmly underlined the essentially anti-British emphasis of Germany's policy both in Europe and in its relations with Japan.[115] But these were never dispatched, since negotiations with the Japanese had reached a critical point.[116] It was only when the hope of a military pact with Japan was finally disappointed in early July that the German diplomatic corps was free to overtake Britain and France in the race for a deal with Moscow.[117] An added incentive was provided by the fact that on 31 May the Italians informed Berlin that, despite their recent recommitment to the Axis, they would not be ready for war before 1943.[118] At times, Goering and Hitler had talked to their Italian partners about such a drawn-out timetable for aggression.[119] But that was when they were considering a three-pronged assault on the British in cooperation with the Japanese. Of the three arms of the Wehrmacht, it was only the German navy that was not ready for any kind of war in 1939. By the summer of 1939 the naval alliance with Japan was off the table. British aerial rearmament was accelerating fast and the German army had reached an impasse. Hitler's timetable had shortened and his preferred alliance partner had changed. For an immediate air and land war against Poland and its Western allies, the ideal partner was not Japan, but the Soviet Union.

German-Soviet contacts became ever closer in June and moved quickly from narrowly economic issues to broader strategic concerns. In early July the German ambassador met with Foreign Minister Molotov for the first time.[120] By August, negotiations were progressing quickly. The framework for a credit and trade deal was agreed on 19 August. In the early hours of 24 August 1939, Hitler's Foreign Minister Ribbentrop signed a non-aggression pact with the Soviet Union, which included secret provisions for the division of Eastern Europe into separate spheres of influence. Poland was to be partitioned. Stalin and Hitler, sworn ideological enemies, were bound together in a pact of non-aggression and mutual assistance. The shock and disillusionment in the Communist movement following the announcement of the Hitler–Stalin pact is well attested. On the German side, there was bewilderment as well, but principally amongst men who now counted themselves as enemies of the regime. The fascist industrialist Fritz Thyssen was so appalled that he went into exile in Switzerland, allowing Goering to confiscate his large stake in the Vereinigte Stahlwerke.[121] Amongst the ideological followers of Nazism, however, the deal never seems to have been regarded as anything more than a convenient ceasefire. Hitler's anti-Communism was not in doubt. The absolute imperative was to avoid a two-front war. Hitler still hoped to deter Britain from making good on its commitment to Poland.[122] But if Britain could not be made to understand that all Germany's efforts were ultimately directed against the Jewish-Bolshevik threat in the East, and if Britain forced Germany into a war in the West, then a temporary arrangement with Russia was a strategic necessity.[123]

On the evening of 23 August, as Ribbentrop moved to clinch the deal, the mood of relief in Berlin was palpable. Hitler could hardly wait to announce the news from Moscow, boasting to his anxious generals that Germany now had nothing to fear from a blockade.[124] Negotiations began immediately for a gigantic trade deal, the precise terms of which were finally hammered out in February 1940. Over the coming year, the trade volume was set at between 600 and 700 million Reichsmarks. This was less than the Germans had hoped for, but it was the composition, not the absolute volume of Soviet supplies to Germany that was critical.[125] The Soviet Union rapidly became Germany's main source of imported animal feed. In 1940 the Soviet Union also supplied Germany with 74 per cent of its phosphates needs, 67 per cent of its asbestos imports, 65 per cent of its chrome ore supplies, 55 per cent of its manganese, 40 per cent of its nickel imports and 34 per cent of its imported oil.[126] As the Quartermaster General of the German army, Colonel Eduard Wagner, put it, 'the conclusion of this treaty has saved us'.[127]

V

Hitler chose war in September 1939 and he did so even though he knew that an attack on Poland would most likely provoke a declaration of war by Britain and France.[128] Hitler gave his first order for the attack on Poland as soon as he knew that the pact would definitely be signed in Moscow. He was ready for war on 26 August, but postponed because the flexibility of the German mobilization timetable allowed him three more days of diplomacy, designed not to avoid war, but to split up the Allied coalition and to shift the burden of 'war guilt' to Britain and France. As of 28 August, Hitler was driving towards war, fully aware of the likely involvement of the British. Both at the time and after the event there were those in and around the leadership of the Third Reich who refused to believe that Hitler could be deliberately courting such an enormous risk.[129] We, however, should not flinch from this enormity. To talk of 'miscalculations' and 'mistakes' in relation to the outbreak of World War II is to underestimate the deliberateness of Hitler's intent.[130]

As we have argued in this chapter, Hitler was encouraged to pursue this course of quick-fire aggression by interlocking economic and strategic pressures. We have deliberately avoided here any talk of 'crisis'. In 1939 there was no crisis in the Third Reich, either political or economic.[131] The means of coercion and control developed since the near-crisis of 1934 were too effective for that. But what could not be obscured by May 1939 was the complete frustration of the medium-term strategic vision that had taken shape in the aftermath of Munich.[132] The effort to construct a global alliance with which to support Germany's enormous new armaments drive had failed. Ribbentrop's inability to bind either the Italians or the Japanese into a firm military alliance against Britain rendered the longer-term planning horizons of the navy's Z Plan academic. And due to the renewed onset of severe balance of payments problems, Germany now faced losing its head start in the arms race much more quickly than Hitler had anticipated in November 1937. Hitler's time-horizon therefore shortened. If the future outlook was bleak, then in 1939 at least Germany was in a position to mount a limited offensive war with some prospect of success. On the ground and in the air, the Wehrmacht could expect to enjoy at least a temporary advantage. Meanwhile, over the summer of 1939 Germany's strategic situation suddenly took a turn for the better. Czechoslovakia was eliminated as a threat. Roosevelt was frustrated by a resurgence of isolationism. And through a few hectic weeks of diplomacy, Ribbentrop broke the encirclement that had seemed to threaten after the occupation of Prague. Rather than backing Britain and France, the Soviet Union committed itself to supporting Hitler's aggression. This in turn enormously strengthened Hitler's hand in relation to the smaller South-eastern European countries who would now, surely, be roped into the Axis corral. In the final analysis, there seems little reason to quibble with Hitler's own assessment, which was that he chose war in September 1939 because he had nothing to gain by further delay.[133]

But if there was thus a certain 'mad logic' to Hitler's decision to unleash a general European war, it nevertheless remained an enormous gamble. The Hitler–Stalin pact was an act of inspired opportunism. But it was also a measure of Germany's desperation. It signalled the abandonment, not only of the strategic blueprint of *Mein Kampf*, but also of the revised anti-Western strategy of the post-Munich period. The Nazi–Soviet pact, whilst it shifted the balance of power in Europe in Germany's favour, negated any chance of a deal with Japan. Immediately following the announcement, the pro-German cabinet in Tokyo resigned. Power passed to the Japanese army, which was preoccupied with keeping the Soviets out of Manchuria. At the same time Mussolini made clear his inability to join Germany in a premature war against the

Western powers.[134] The British for their part could heave a huge sigh of relief, safe in the knowledge that for the foreseeable future they would not have to deal with the triple threat of the German, Italian and Japanese navies. Nor had the Soviets concluded the deal out of any particular friendship towards the Third Reich. Stalin was buying time, assuming that Germany would soon embroil itself in a prolonged and bloody war with Britain and France.[135] Barring a military upset of historic proportions, only the Soviet Union and the United States could benefit from the exhaustion of the 'old' powers of Western Europe. This, after all, was the principal reason why both French and British politicians had been willing to go so far in their appeasement of Germany. Britain and France did not appease Germany because they expected to be defeated by the Wehrmacht, but because, in the words of France's right-wing Prime Minister Daladier, another European war would mean the 'utter destruction of European civilization', creating a vacuum that could only be filled by 'Cossack and Mongol hordes' and their 'culture' of Soviet Communism.[136] In less apocalyptic language, the same logic was neatly expressed by one of the Mongol hordes' diplomatic representatives in London. According to conventional bookkeeping, the Soviet diplomat remarked, the losses of the RAF were placed on one side of the balance sheet and the losses of the Luftwaffe on the other. The Soviet Union 'placed both in one column and added them up'.[137]

The truth was that in the late summer and autumn of 1939 no one in Europe, with the possible exception of Hitler, anticipated the remarkable military events that would unfold over the coming months. The mood in Paris and London was one of resigned optimism. Certainly no one anticipated an immediate German victory.[138] Though the German army and air force were ready for war in September 1939, the Wehrmacht did not have an overwhelming material advantage over its opponents. To conventional strategic minds, Germany's prospects seemed bleak. The 'rational' choice was clearly to step back from war over Poland, apart from anything else to allow time for the consequences of the Hitler–Stalin pact to make themselves fully felt across Central and Eastern Europe. Why then did Hitler press towards war with such furious intensity? Why did Hitler gamble?[139] The pressures of the arms race and the need to exploit diplomatic opportunity go only so far in explaining his actions. An argument in terms of 'windows of opportunity', after all, begs the question of why Hitler had come to see war with the Western powers as inevitable, such that it made sense to opt for battle 'sooner' rather than 'later'.

At this point in our argument we must point to the role of ideology. This might seem a strange suggestion in light of the fact that Hitler went to war in September 1939 in alliance with the Soviet Union against the British Empire, when *Mein Kampf* had called for the exact opposite. But to confront 'ideology' with reality in this way is too crude. The real bedrock of Hitlerine ideology was not the strategic schema of *Mein Kampf*. The truly central idea was the inevitability of race struggle. In a general sense this was always in the back of Hitler's mind. But from 1938 onwards, this apocalyptic vision motivating the leadership of the Third Reich increased dramatically in intensity. Specifically, Hitler comprehended the emerging Western coalition against Germany through the lens of anti-Semitism. After Kristallnacht, it was President Roosevelt who increasingly positioned himself as the most public opponent of the Third Reich and he did so in overtly ideological terms. As we have seen, the Third Reich responded in kind. For conventional strategic minds such as Ludwig Beck or General Thomas the convergence between Britain, France and the United States was in no way surprising. In light of their experience in World War I, the trans-Atlantic alliance seemed a natural counter-weight to German power in Europe. For Hitler, by contrast, it was profoundly counter-intuitive. In particular, it ran counter to his deeply held belief, expressed clearly in his 'Second Book', that British and American interests were fundamentally antagonistic.[140] What, therefore, explained the emerging Anglo-American alliance was the malevolent force of world Jewry personified by its 'chosen one', President Roosevelt.[141] Though Hitler barely mentioned the United States in the context of strategic discussions with the military leadership in May and August 1939, during the same period there was a dramatic escalation in anti-Semitic rhetoric and propaganda directed explicitly against the United States. And the central theme of this anti-Semitism was the supposed role of Roosevelt and American Jewry in inciting war by means of promises of arms deliveries and diplomatic assistance for Britain, France and Poland. The hook-nosed caricature of Bernard Baruch, architect of America's war effort in World War I and arch-representative of warmongering Wall Street Jewry, was the real menace behind the encirclement threatening Germany. It was the spokesman of international Jewry, President Roosevelt, who was coaxing the British and the Poles into obstinate resistance and raising a clamour for war.[142] It was the Roosevelt administration that was doing its best to shut Germany out of vital export markets. And it was the quantity and timing of American arms deliveries to Britain and France that would decide the balance of forces in Europe.[143]

This ominous constellation of forces was not as Hitler had predicted or as he had wished. But since the enemies of the Third Reich were improvising, Germany would have to do the same. What Hitler could not do, in light of the 'will to annihilation' (*Vernichtungswillen*) that Nazi conspiracy theory attributed to the enemies of Germany, was to back down or to hesitate.[144] War with the Western powers involved huge risk. But given the increasingly unmanageable dynamic of the global arms race and the existential threat supposedly posed to Germany by the gathering forces of the 'world Jewish conspiracy', Hitler could see no alternative but to take the offensive.

10

Going for Broke: The First Winter of War

In the last days of August 1939 Major-General Thomas made a last-ditch attempt to force Hitler to face facts.[1] Terrified by the prospect that Hitler's aggression towards Poland would lead to war with Britain and France, Thomas bombarded both his immediate boss, General Keitel, and Hitler, with tables and charts. These were intended to dramatize the inferiority of Germany's industrial resources when compared to those of Britain and France, assuming that the United States backed them.[2] Thomas's diary records the response he received:

Saturday 26 August prior to Polish campaign: Again with Generaloberst Keitel. Explained situation on basis of charts and tables. Was not well received, but K. agreed to speak with the Fuehrer again.

27 August Sunday prior to Polish war, when the telegram came in from England: make representations again! Point out that ammunition crisis to be expected, especially in relation to powder and explosives: Again sharp rebuke. Answer: I was thrown out. Fuehrer: stop bothering me with the bloody Western situation.[3]

In August 1914, the young Adolf Hitler had been amongst the ecstatic crowds that thronged the streets of Munich. He could not but have been struck by the starkly different mood that greeted his war in September 1939. There were no cheering mobs, no garlands for the troop trains and with good reason. In military terms Germany was not ready for a confrontation with the Western powers. Thomas of the Wehrmacht was not the only military man who was in a desperate mood. Admiral Raeder, Commander-in-Chief of the German navy, noted despairingly on 3 September: 'As far as the navy is concerned, it is . . . not at all adequately armed for the great struggle . . .' Germany's fleet was so heavily outnumbered by the Royal Navy that 'assuming it is fully com-

326

mitted in action – it can only demonstrate that it knows how to go down with dignity . . .'. Through a heroic gesture of self-sacrifice the German navy might lay the moral foundations for a 'later reconstruction'. It could certainly not be expected to win the war against Britain.[4] The German air force was in better shape. It was the largest and the most modern in Europe. However, studies done by the Luftwaffe staff in 1938 had concluded that a strategic air war against Britain was out of the question unless Germany could somehow gain control of airbases along the channel coastline.[5]

Given the pessimism of the Wehrmacht's chief economics expert, as well as the commanders of both the navy and the Luftwaffe, everything depended on the army. The army had been the decisive factor in the development of Hitler's regime since its inception. Unlike in 1938, there is no evidence that the escalating tension with Poland aroused any fundamental concerns amongst the generals.[6] In military terms the outcome was a foregone conclusion. Politically, Poland ranked even higher in the demonology of German nationalism than Britain. The destruction of the Polish state and the 'liberation' of the German minority were as popular with the generals as they were with the public at large. And the army's optimism was confirmed by events. The Polish campaign was a dramatic success. After only three weeks Warsaw surrendered and the Polish army was destroyed. The photogenic Commander-in-Chief of the German army, General Walther von Brauchitsch, was on the front cover of *Time Magazine* and the cloud of gloom that had overshadowed the declaration of war had begun to lift.[7] On their return home, the victorious troops were treated to wild celebrations.[8] Following the Polish campaign, large parts of the population now expected France and Britain to be crushed by Christmas, an expectation encouraged by the well-publicized success of Guenther Prien and the crew of U-47 in penetrating the home-base of the British fleet at Scapa Flow and sinking the battleship *Royal Oak*.[9] Over the weeks that followed, SS informants overheard children throughout the Reich reciting a blasphemous new version of the Lord's Prayer addressed to 'Our Father Chamberlain who art in London, erased be your name, your kingdom soon will be gone . . .'[10] The priggish commentators of the SD were appalled, but Goebbels was only too happy to capitalize on the boisterous new anti-British mood.[11] Hitler, too, demanded immediate action on the Western Front.

If the military-industrial logic of acceleration was only semi-explicit in his statements before September 1939, it was now absolutely clear-cut. To Brauchitsch, and his chief of staff, Franz Halder, Hitler remarked on 27 September: 'The "time factor" is in general not on our side, unless we exploit it to the utmost. Economic means of the other side are stronger. [Enemies] able to cash and carry.'[12] The latter point clearly referred to the imminent revision of American neutrality legislation and the opening of America's vast industrial capacity to British and French procurement. And Hitler reiterated the same strategic assessment on 9 October, when he took the highly unusual step of drafting a comprehensive memo on the conduct of the Western war. An immediate attack on the West was necessary, he argued, because in a protracted war the United States would be able to intervene.[13] A few weeks later he was to make the point even more explicitly: 'Because of its neutrality laws, America is *not yet* dangerous to us. The reinforcement of our enemies by America is *not yet* significant. The posture of Japan is *not yet* certain . . . Everything points to the fact that the moment now is propitious, in six months, however, it may perhaps not be.'[14] Meanwhile, Hitler was far from certain of his new ally in the East. In a long war, Hitler felt the Soviet Union could not be relied upon. He therefore demanded an immediate attack in the West, setting 12 November 1939 as the date for the Wehrmacht's assault across the French border.

The army leadership, however, were in quite a different state of mind. What had stirred the army to near mutiny in 1938 was not the prospect of a war with the Czechs, but the fact that this aggression was thought likely to trigger a war with Britain and France. This was precisely the situation that they now faced. Furthermore, despite the worldwide sensation caused by Germany's swift victory over Poland, a few weeks of sharp fighting had exposed severe shortcomings in Hitler's hastily assembled war machine. The raw material shortages that had restricted armaments production in 1937 and 1939 meant that Germany had gone to war without adequate stocks of equipment. Thomas's prediction of an ammunition crisis was immediately confirmed.[15] In only a few weeks of operations, the Luftwaffe had seriously depleted its stock of bombs. Monthly consumption in Poland exceeded production in September 1939 by a factor of 7.[16] For lack of training, the infantry had not performed to the high standards expected of the German army.[17] There had been incidents of panic amongst the third-string reserve formations that made up a large part of the wartime strength. And even the much vaunted new Panzer divisions had shown alarming weaknesses. The rate of attrition amongst their motley collection of vehicles had been high. In less than a month of fighting a quarter of the initial force of tanks had either been knocked out or broken down.[18] The antiquated Mark I and Mark II tanks, with which most of the Panzer divisions were still equipped, were clearly inadequate for an attack in the West. In France waited the fearsome Char B, at 32 tons the world's heaviest and most powerful fighting vehicle. On paper at least, the armies of France, Britain, Holland and Belgium matched the Wehrmacht both in manpower and equipment. Furthermore, the plan for an attack on France, hastily drafted by the army high command in the autumn of 1939, convinced no one.[19] It was an unimaginative revision of the Schlieffen Plan calling for the German army to punch its way to the Channel coastline so as to provide the Luftwaffe and the navy with bases for a close-range attack on Britain. Even if the Wehrmacht did manage to get to the Channel, the plan offered no prospect of knocking out the French army. Germany would find itself facing a prolonged war of attrition against two potent enemies, backed by the economic resources of the United States.

What Brauchitsch, Commander-in-Chief of the army, and General Franz Halder, his chief of staff, demanded was a breathing space.[20] They were willing to fight a war against France, but they needed time to re-equip their battered units and to put a million more draftees through intensified training. They may also have succumbed to the wishful hope that, with the Polish question settled to Germany's satisfaction, the Western powers might be brought back to the negotiating table before the real fighting started. Hitler, however, refused any delay. As the army struggled to redeploy its divisions to the west, the Fuehrer remained adamant that the offensive should be launched in early November. Faced with this extraordinary demand, the mood in army high command in Zossen turned mutinous.[21] The plotters who had come close to launching a *coup d'état* against Hitler in September 1938 resumed their preparations. General Halder contacted the commanders of Germany's three army groups to sound out their views on an immediate attack against France and their attitude towards a possible military overthrow of the Nazi regime. Hitler for his part worked himself into a state of increasing rage. His long-held antipathy towards the hereditary officer class spilled over into open contempt. As the clock ticked towards the date set for the Western assault, tension rose to an extraordinary peak. On 5 November Brauchitsch secured a personal meeting with Hitler with the aim of convincing him of the impossibility of a successful offensive. By way of evidence Brauchitsch took with him statistics supplied by the Quartermaster General, General Eduard Wagner, which highlighted the inadequate state of the army's equipment.[22] The result was an explosion. After listening impatiently to Brauchitsch's report, Hitler subjected him to a devastating tirade.[23] For hours afterwards, Hitler remained in a state of high agitation fuming at the 'sabotage of the army command'. Brauchitsch, for his part, left the meeting quaking with shock. Though he was not personally involved in the plotting, he immediately passed on Hitler's accusations to his chief of staff, including the remark that Hitler 'knew the spirit of Zossen and was determined to crush it'. Halder panicked. Fearing that the Gestapo had penetrated his conspiracy, he had all the incriminating plans destroyed. Without the support of the army's chief of staff, the more junior plotters had lost their linchpin. The coup was off and the military conspirators were thrown into disarray. Hitler for his part was clearly fully aware of the extreme tensions that his decision for war had provoked, not just in the military. Speaking to an audience of party apparatchiks on 27 August 1939, he had granted anyone who did not believe that his decision for war was motivated by love of Germany the right to shoot him dead.[24] Halder later confessed to one of his closest colleagues that he had attended his almost daily meeting with Hitler in the autumn of 1939 with the firm intention of 'shooting Emil down' (Emil was the plotters' code-name for Hitler). For this purpose he carried a loaded pistol in his pocket. What saved the Fuehrer were the centuries of soldier's blood that ran through Halder's veins. The General could not bring himself to assassinate the man to whom he had taken an oath of personal loyalty.

In the event, bad weather forced the cancellation of the attack planned for 12 November. Without the Luftwaffe in support, even Hitler had to concede that the offensive stood little chance of success. In so doing, Hitler almost certainly saved his regime from catastrophe. Too often our knowledge of the extraordinary victories achieved by the Wehrmacht in the summer of 1940 obscures the precariousness of Hitler's situation over the winter of 1939–40. At this critical moment he could count neither on the unquestioning loyalty of the army, nor on the unambiguous support of the German people. The dynamic of total war that was soon to cement German society firmly in support of the regime had only begun to take hold. Public opinion was jittery and could hardly be counted upon in case of a long and arduous war. Once the possibility of a negotiated peace with the Western powers had been ruled out, Hitler had only one option, to deliver military victory as quickly as possible. War against Britain and France was the worst-case scenario of German strategy. Only hindsight leads us to underestimate this fact. The leadership of Hitler's regime had only faced up to this possibility in the spring of 1938 and, as we have seen, they had failed to devise a coherent strategic response. The army had not even begun planning for an attack in the West until after war broke out. It is hardly surprising, therefore, that in the autumn of 1939 there was a degree of chaos and confusion in Berlin. On the other hand, the widely held view that the first year of the war was characterized by complacency is very wide of the mark.[25] The outbreak of war actually had the effect of removing many of the constraints that had hampered German rearmament in the previous years. And Hitler's regime responded to the existential challenge facing it with a combination of opportunism, technocratic radicalism and ideologically inspired violence.

I

On the other side of the Atlantic, Hitler's aggression against Poland sent shock waves through American public opinion. Within weeks of the outbreak of war, the isolationists lost the argument in Congress.[26] On 3 November 1939 President Roosevelt signed into law the 'cash and carry' bill that lifted the strict American neutrality provisions banning the sale of weapons to foreigners. So long as France and Britain paid in cash and shipped their American cargo in their own vessels, they could take their pick amongst the immense industrial capacity of the United States. Technically, Germany was free to do the same. But in practice it had neither the hard currency nor the means to protect its shipments on the long haul across the Atlantic. Whereas the Wehrmacht's economic staff estimated the dollar assets of Britain and France to be in the region of $7.37 billion, the German total, even on optimistic assumptions, came to no more than $700 million.[27] Goebbels did everything he could to dampen speculation about American involvement in the war, but in early 1940 a German military journal reported that British and French aircraft orders in the United States already came to between 5,000 and 8,000 planes.[28] This, in fact, exaggerated the extent of Allied procurement in the first months of the war. But serious negotiations were under way with representatives of America's mighty motor vehicles industry to arrange for a dramatic increase in aircraft and aero-engine capacity and, as of March 1940, Britain and France had agreed a joint programme of orders.[29] This was deliberately designed to permit the Europeans to stretch their foreign reserves over many years if necessary. But by the summer of 1940 they had orders in hand for more than 10,000 military aircraft to be delivered by the end of 1941, the equivalent of an entire year of German production.

At the same time as America was opening its gates to the Western Allies, Germany faced economic isolation. At the outset of World War II, thanks to French and British economic warfare, transport problems and its limited ability to pay, Germany found itself largely cut off from its overseas supplies of raw materials.[30] The monthly figures for the volume of imported raw materials, circulated in confidential reports by the Reich Statistical Office, showed an astonishing collapse.[31]

Within months of the outbreak of war, Germany's imports were reduced to a fraction of the level necessary to sustain a large-scale armaments effort. Ore supplies from Narvik were cut off.[32] Imports of copper and oil fell virtually to zero. Germany in the first months of World War II was more isolated in economic terms than at any time before 1944–5. The trade agreement with the Soviet Union promised some relief. But the significance of Germany's sudden exclusion from world markets cannot be overestimated. It overshadowed every aspect of German military strategy and economic policy in the first decisive months of the war.[33] In light of the huge shock to the balance of trade, it is simply incredible to suggest that the German economy continued as a 'peacelike war economy'. An economy like that of Germany, which despite the best efforts of the Four Year Plan continued to depend heavily on imported raw materials, could not function 'normally' in the face of an abrupt 80 per cent reduction in its import volumes. Within six months of the outbreak of war, Germany was importing in real terms less than a third of the raw materials it had consumed in 1932, at the trough of the Great Depression. At that time, more than half Germany's heavy industrial capacity had lain idle and the majority of its industrial work-

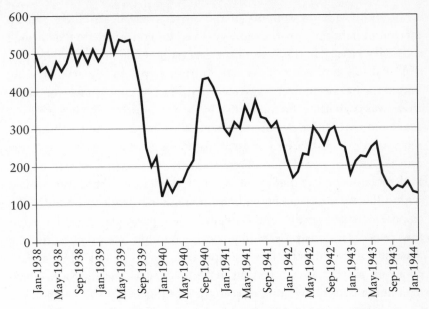

Figure 12. Volume of industrial inputs imported to Germany
(million Reichsmarks, 1928 prices)

force was unemployed or working short time. The fact that following
the outbreak of war, Hitler's regime was able not only to avoid an
industrial disaster but actually to increase its output of armaments
betokens not 'business as usual', but a series of draconian interventions
in the functioning of the economy.[34]

Since the spring of 1939, at the latest, Hitler had been driven forward
by the sense that time was not on Germany's side. Once war was
declared, the gathering strength of the Western coalition, reinforced by
the United States, contrasted with Germany's economic vulnerability
and its new dependence on the Soviet Union only reinforced this motive.
In pursuit of a swift and decisive victory in the West, Hitler was willing
to risk everything. And this was true not only in relation to the military
planning of the assault on France. Hitler followed the same line in
relation to the war economy. Through his closest confidants – Hermann
Goering, Fritz Todt and General Keitel of Wehrmacht high command –
Hitler repeatedly stressed his desire for an all-out production drive,
regardless of the consequences either for the civilian population or the
long-run viability of the German war effort. Given the constellation of

1939, even with the support of the Soviet trade deal, Hitler had no interest in fighting a protracted war. Everything depended on achieving a decisive victory in the West at the earliest possible opportunity.

The absolute priority of the war effort in 1939–40 is worth stressing because it has often been suggested that Hitler's concern for the home front was a limiting factor in the Nazi war effort.[35] Some have even suggested that Hitler's desire to achieve a swift victory in the West was motivated principally by his desire to minimize the impact of the war on the German population. This, however, is a serious misreading of Hitler's strategic calculation in 1939. It is true that there were voices within the Nazi movement calling for the home front to be protected against excessive strain. The Gauleiters were particularly vociferous in this respect, jealously defending local economic interests against the demands of the military. It is also true that the Gauleiters could always count on a sympathetic hearing in Berlin. It was part of their job to maintain a live connection between the Fuehrer and the grass roots. In October 1939 Gauleiter protests were successful in deflecting Walther Funk, the ineffectual Minister of Economic Affairs, from implementing the draconian package of mobilization decrees that his staff had prepared.[36] In the wake of this embarrassing setback, Funk sought to present his retreat as a principled decision in favour of a moderated mobilization. However, there is no evidence that this ever had Hitler's endorsement. To Hitler, all that mattered was winning the war. If the Wehrmacht could defeat France and Britain then public opinion would take care of itself. In his eagerness to please the Gauleiters, Walther Funk had radically misjudged the direction in which the political wind was blowing and he paid the price.[37] By December, the Reich Minister for Economic Affairs had been stripped of his special responsibility for the wartime organization of the civilian economy.[38] As the only figure in the top ranks of the German government fully to espouse the call for moderation, Funk was also the war's first political casualty. The reason why Hitler gambled everything on a massive attack in 1940 was not because he was worried about making excessive demands on the German population, but simply because he thought that this was the only way that Germany could win the war. Regardless of how intensively its home front was mobilized, Germany would lose a protracted war, because the combined economic might of its enemies was simply overwhelming. Germany therefore needed to concentrate all its resources on striking a single decisive blow at the earliest possible opportunity. If this meant temporarily sacrificing the needs of civilian consumption, so be it. As Hitler commented to the chief of army procurement, General Karl Becker, in early November 1939: 'One cannot win the war against England with cookers and washing-machines.'[39]

In pursuit of victory, the question that preoccupied the key players in Berlin was not how to balance the needs of the war effort and the civilian economy. The question was how best to organize the economy for total war. The military-economic staffs of the OKW, the Ministry of Economic Affairs and the Reichsnaehrstand (the national agricultural organization) were all haunted by memories of 1914–1918. In the light of that experience it seemed irresponsible to gamble everything on achieving decisive battlefield success in the first year of the war.[40] In their view, the only safe course was for Germany to harden its economy to sustain a long and drawn-out struggle. Top priority, of course, had to be given to producing armaments. But in a long war, the immediate needs of the fighting troops had to be balanced against the need to invest in infrastructure to allow Germany to survive the blockade. In a long war, priority also had to be given to sustaining exports, so as to be able to maintain imports of crucial raw materials from Germany's remaining trading partners. High priority had also to be given to agriculture, because without food, the home front would collapse, as it had done in Russia in 1917 and in Germany in 1918. This might look like a strategy that favoured the civilian economy. But this was deceptive. It was a strategy motivated first and foremost by the long-term sustainability of the war effort. Nobody in 1939 expected Germany to be able to last as long as in World War I. The Third Reich's deficiencies of foreign exchange and raw material stocks were too severe. But under the direction of State Secretary Backe, the Reichsnaehrstand was preparing for a three-year war.[41] General Thomas of the OKW and his collaborators in the Ministry of Economic Affairs believed that with careful husbanding, Germany's stocks of industrial raw materials could be stretched over a similar period of time.[42]

Superficially at least, the strategy of the military-economic experts had an appealing logic. If no swift military decision was to be expected, then it was clearly necessary to direct every effort towards ensuring that Germany could outlast its enemies.[43] But, given Germany's situation in 1939, this train of logic hid some drastic implications for the conduct of the war. To make Germany's stocks stretch over three years, the Wehrmacht would have to abstain from all serious offensive action.[44] Under the three-year raw material plans prepared by Thomas's office in the OKW, the rations allocated to armaments production were far lower than those required for an all-out armaments drive. The OKW's military-economic staff therefore proposed that after the swift victory in Poland the Wehrmacht should fight the rest of the war from a defensive posture. The army, in particular, should abstain from any offensive operations. A major effort to achieve a battlefield victory would involve running down stocks of raw materials and fuel to such critical levels that it would be impossible to recover to a sustainable defensive posture. Consistent implementation of the 'long war strategy' therefore meant abandoning, from the outset, any chance of achieving decisive military victory. What started as no more than a sensible precaution against the possibility that battlefield success might prove elusive turned out to be a strategy that precluded the possibility of such a victory. And this in turn begged the question of whether Germany, in fact, had any chance of winning the 'long war' for which Thomas and Backe were so urgently preparing. Did the 'long war' strategy not play directly into the hands of Britain and France? As the first months of the phoney war amply demonstrated, they were in no hurry to launch an attack on Germany, even when the vast bulk of the Wehrmacht was committed to Poland. They preferred to bide their time, confident in the belief that in a long war, the advantages conferred by American support would be decisive. Meanwhile, Germany would be subject to slow strangulation by naval blockade. If Germany sought to redress the balance by sending its U-boats against the Atlantic shipping lanes, as it had done in 1916, this would bring down upon the Wehrmacht the full force of American power. The military outcome would then no longer be in doubt. In fact, if one followed the 'long war strategy' favoured by Major-General Thomas, Germany's best hope was to settle the conflict by diplomatic means before the material superiority of its enemies made itself decisively felt. And the sooner it did so the better. Drawing out the struggle would simply make the peace more costly for Germany. The superficial rationality of the 'long war strategy' thus turned out to be self-defeating.

Hitler would have no truck with this kind of logic.[45] He had launched the attack on Poland, accepting the risk of British and French involvement. Now that Germany was at war with the Western powers and they were unwilling to come to terms, there was no alternative but to gamble again, this time in launching a spectacular assault on France. And Hitler was fully clear about the economic consequences that followed. He needed to force the Wehrmacht's economic experts to abandon their caution and to press immediately for the expenditure of all available resources in preparation for the 1940 offensive, regardless of the long-term consequences for the viability of the German war effort.[46] The files left by General Thomas record a series of interventions in which Keitel, Goering and Todt acted as mouthpieces for the Fuehrer, all with the same message. One telling exchange came in the first days of December 1939 when Thomas was attempting to persuade Keitel of the need to allocate raw materials to the production of exports.[47] Following his 'long war' line, Thomas demanded that the Wehrmacht should permit an increase in the steel ration allocated to exports since 'we cannot last out a war of long duration, if we already live today at the expense of future periods'. Keitel's reply was prompt and categorical: 'The Fuehrer himself has recognized that we cannot last out a war of long duration. The war must be finished rapidly. Therefore, the great blow was to be launched if possible even before Christmas. Everything had to be wagered on this card, including the use of stocks as well as raw materials [sic]. The necessary requirements were to be taken out of the export sector ruthlessly.' And Keitel went on to add a further consideration: 'Everything had to be concentrated so as to finish with the Western powers as soon as possible, since it was not clear how long the Russians would hold to us.' Exactly the same line was reiterated over the coming months, first by Goering at the end of January 1940 and then in early March by Fritz Todt. On 24 March, General Thomas noted the follow-ing conversation with Fritz Todt: 'Fuehrer has again emphasized ener-getically that everything is to be done so that the war can be ended in 1940 with a great military victory. From 1941 onwards, time works against us (USA-potential).'[48]

Of course, there were practicalities to consider. Despite the need to concentrate every effort on 1940, economic mobilization could not be achieved overnight. For major industrial projects a twelve-month time-horizon was simply too short. Much to the frustration of Thomas, the grand expansion plans of 1938 – Krauch's chemical plans and the plans of the Luftwaffe – continued to exert a formative influence on the

German armaments effort, even after the outbreak of the war. They were timed to reach their peak in 1941–2. When pressed into practical form, Germany's armaments programmes therefore continued to extend over a two-year period. After all, even if the French army could be defeated in the first year of the war with one great blow, the aerial and naval war against Britain was likely to stretch into a second year, and after the war in the West Hitler had other goals for German expansion. Fundamentally, however, there could be no compromise between the 'short war' and the 'long war' strategies. Whether or not the plans were geared towards a twelve- or eighteen-month time-horizon was not the key issue. The real question was what kind of war to fight in 1940 – offensive or defensive. And on this question Hitler never wavered. He had reluctantly agreed to the postponement of the attack he had ordered for 12 November 1939. But abstaining from offensive operations altogether, in an effort to drag out the war, was simply not an option. The Western offensive of 1940 would be an all-out assault.

I I

The basic priorities of the German armaments effort were dictated by Hitler in a series of decisions taken between September and November 1939. Within hours of the beginning of the war, he sacrificed the navy's Z Plan – the programme to construct a gigantic high seas fleet capable of taking on the Royal Navy – to which he had assigned absolute priority as recently as January 1939.[49] Work on capital ships that could not be completed in 1940 was halted with immediate effect. The dockyards of Hamburg, Bremen and Kiel scrambled to redeploy labour to the production of standard, Mark VII U-boats.[50] With this decision Hitler abandoned his ambition to establish Germany as a major naval power. But this was a precondition for restoring a semblance of order to the Wehrmacht's armaments programme. Henceforth, the navy would never again challenge the pre-eminence of the army and the Luftwaffe. At no point in the war did its share of armaments expenditure rise above 15 per cent. The most the navy's planners could realistically hope for was an intensive Atlantic trade war. The 'U-boat programme' that replaced the Z Plan called for the production of 25 submarines per month. Nominally, this was to enjoy high priority in the allocation of raw materials and labour. But actual production of U-boats in the first twelve months of the war was derisory.[51]

The main burden of the war against Britain would be carried not by the navy but by the Luftwaffe, and specifically by the fleet of Ju 88 bombers that had formed the core of Air Ministry planning since the spring of 1938. As we have seen, by July 1939 Air Ministry planning was in full retreat, under the impact of the progressive restriction of raw material allocations. Over the summer of 1939 it had been necessary to contemplate the cancellation of any further production of Stuka dive-bombers and reconnaissance aircraft, to preserve the Ju 88 programme. To gain a higher priority allocation for the Luftwaffe, the Air Ministry, backed up by Junkers CEO Heinrich Koppenberg, engaged in a frantic bout of lobbying.[52] On 3 July 1939 Hitler was treated to the infamous 'magic show' at the Rechlin air proving ground, featuring a stunning display of aerial wonder weapons – including jet fighters, rocket planes and large airborne cannon – all, supposedly, within months of entering production. Then, in the third week of August, when Hitler was preoccupied with the coming war, Koppenberg and Ernst Udet, chief of the technical office at the RLM, coaxed him into signing a Fuehrer Order restoring the Ju 88 programme to top priority. The consequences were dramatic. For the rest of the war, the Luftwaffe was to claim at least 40 per cent of the German armaments effort.

The real flashpoint of armaments politics in the first months of the war was ammunition. First of all, for political reasons. The ammunition crisis of twenty-five years earlier, at the beginning of World War I, lived long in the memory.[53] As an infantry veteran of the Great War, Hitler was a man with strong views about big guns and shells.[54] Furthermore, ammunition production for both the Luftwaffe and the army was handled by the army procurement office, a large, military organization that made an ideal scapegoat for ideologues in the Nazi party who disdained all forms of state bureaucracy.[55] The thought that the army's paper-pushers might be about to strangle the all-out offensive he was planning for 1940 was enough to drive Hitler into a rage. His Wehrmacht would be provided with all the firepower it needed to achieve the decision that had so cruelly eluded the Kaiser's army in 1914. But it was not office politics alone that made ammunition the truly divisive issue in the first year of the Nazi war effort. The fundamental question was one of resources. After aircraft production, supplying the enormous volumes of ammunition demanded by modern warfare was by far the largest industrial challenge facing the German economy in World War II. Not for nothing were shell factories amongst the iconic images of 1914–18. Though less prominent in the visual repertoire twenty-five years later, in industrial terms they were hardly less significant. Ammunition was voracious in its appetite for raw materials. In the final year of World War I, no less than 400,000 tons of steel per month was consumed by the ammunition factories. That was a quarter of Germany's total output of steel in the autumn of 1939. Shell cases and cartridges also consumed critical quantities of copper, which was in particularly short supply. With Hitler insisting on a major offensive in the West at the earliest possible opportunity, urgent action was clearly needed to make good Germany's inadequate stockpiles. To further complicate matters, the army procurement office, in managing ammunition production, was not dealing with the kind of dependent producers clustered around the Reich Air Ministry. The main suppliers of ammunition were the giants of German heavy industry, firms such as the Vereinigte Stahlwerke, Krupp, Kloeckner or the Reichswerke Hermann Goering. By the autumn of 1939, after three years under the haphazard steel rationing system, these firms had built up a head-steam of frustration that now vented itself on the army procurement office.[56]

Hitler made his first intervention in the ammunition question in October, to insist on the priority of artillery and artillery ammunition.[57] In mid-November, as the struggle with Brauchitsch and Halder neared its climax, he demanded ammunition production at three times the level previously envisaged by army procurement.[58] By the end of the month this so-called 'Fuehrerforderung' (Fuehrer's Challenge) had begun to take on more concrete form. Based on figures that Hitler had cribbed from the standard history of the Great War, it gave priority above all to howitzers and heavy mortars – the decisive weapons of trench warfare.[59] On 12 December 1939 Hitler personally approved the final version of the Fuehrerforderung, the most dramatic headline of which was the demand to raise monthly production by the autumn of 1940 to 3 million light howitzer shells, 650,000 rounds of heavy howitzer ammunition and no less than 150,000 21 centimetre mortar bombs.[60] For the standard 10.5 centimetre howitzer shells of the Wehrmacht, Hitler demanded an almost eightfold increase in production.[61] Relative to actual production in the autumn of 1939 measured in terms of weight of shot, the Fuehrerforderung implied a three-and-a-half-fold increase in the next twelve months and a fivefold increase by the autumn of 1941. These figures are important testimony to the kind of war that Hitler expected to have to fight in the coming year. In November and December 1939, Hitler appears to have been conceiving his armament programme, not around a brilliant vision of Blitzkrieg, but in relation to the army's first draft plan for the invasion of France. As we have seen, this foresaw not a sweeping war of manoeuvre, but a bludgeoning drive to the Channel, followed by an aerial bombardment of Britain. If there was to be a lightning blow, it would be delivered by the Luftwaffe against the British home front, not on the battlefields of Flanders.

With his twin decisions in favour of the Luftwaffe's Ju 88 and the army's ammunition programme Hitler determined the basic structure of the German armaments effort. In the welter of historical commentary on the politics of German war production, much of which is heavily indebted to the memoirs of the embittered General Thomas, this has tended to be obscured.[62] Far from lacking clear priorities, the German industrial war effort was dominated by only two components: aircraft and ammunition. Between them, these two items claimed more than two-thirds of the resources committed to all armaments production in the first ten months of the war. In June 1940, when Hitler's ammunition programme reached its peak, their combined share topped 70 per cent. Whatever else may be said about the organization of the German war economy, it can hardly be accused of a lack of focus. Tanks, vehicles, weapons and all the needs of the navy had to make do with one-third of the resources committed to the armaments effort. The real problem was not the lack of clear priorities, but the difficulty of translating Hitler's orders into productive results. Between September 1939 and January 1940, after an initial surge from the trough reached in the summer of 1939, German ammunition output stagnated.[63] The situation in the Luftwaffe sectors, where the cuts of the summer of 1939 took longer to show their full effect, was even worse.[64] The struggle to assign blame for this contradictory development defined the politics of the armaments effort. Shielded both by the self-sufficiency of the Luftwaffe–industry bloc and the political weight of Goering, the Air Ministry washed its dirty laundry in private. The army was not so fortunate. The party leadership and the Wehrmacht high command, backed up by key industrial interests, made the army procurement office into their scapegoat for the teething problems of the war effort.[65]

For a country that since 1933 had engaged in a crash programme of rearmament, the lacklustre performance of Germany's armaments industries in the first months of World War II was certainly anti-climactic. But it is less puzzling when we call to mind the course of events since early 1939. In the first half of the year, the armaments economy had been in full retreat. The effects of the drastic cuts in raw material rations from January 1939 onwards were still being felt nine months later.[66] As war loomed in the summer, the raw-material situation of the Wehrmacht had improved. The new priority secured by the Luftwaffe gave it a major boost. The long-awaited mass-production of the Ju 88 finally began in the autumn of 1939. However, it took months to reverse the deceleration of the first half of the year. In the case of the Luftwaffe, six months was the fastest that increased consignments of raw materials could work their way through the industrial metabolism. It also took time to identify new armaments plants, to distribute the necessary jigs and blueprints and to bring production up to full speed. These inevitable lags were compounded by the full mobilization of the armed forces in August 1939, weeks before the order was given for a general mobilization of the economy. This did not affect those firms that worked directly under the supervision of the armed forces, whose workers were protected from the draft.[67] But the removal of 4 million men from the rest of the economy inevitably caused disruption. Amongst those affected were many important sub-contractors and raw-material suppliers to the war effort. Then, in the autumn of 1939, the German economy was struck by a recurrence of the transport problems that had first appeared over the winter of 1937–8.[68]

In the mid-twentieth-century, the German economy, like all its European counterparts, was still overwhelmingly dependent on coal. Ninety per cent of Germany's energy needs were supplied, in one form or another, by either lignite (brown) or anthracite (black) coal. In addition, coal and coal derivatives such as coal dust and coal gas were vital raw materials in the production of steel and many chemicals. Coal was the only important industrial raw material with which Germany was richly endowed. Germany's coal mines, however, were heavily concentrated along the western and eastern fringes of the Reich, in the Ruhr and in Silesia respectively. Hundreds of thousands of tons of coal, therefore, had to be shipped every day from the borders of the Reich to the industrial and urban concentrations of north, south and central Germany. On any given day, at least a third of the tonnage shipped on the German railway system consisted of coal and coal derivatives.[69] The functioning of the entire economy depended on the capacity of the railway system to maintain these deliveries. Between 1929 and 1938, the Reichsbahn had suffered almost a decade of systematic neglect.[70] Whilst money from the railways was diverted to build the autobahns and to fund investment in an expansion of bus and truck transport, the Reichsbahn's rolling stock was allowed to deteriorate. Between 1933 and 1937, the railway purchased less than 2,000 new goods trucks per annum, a fraction of what would have been needed to offset wear and tear. As a result, the number of serviceable freight cars declined from an average of over 670,000 cars in the late 1920s to less than 575,000 in 1937. The Reichsbahn did its best to compensate by making more efficient use of its shrinking fleet, but from 1937 onwards the gap between the volume of traffic and the capacity of the railway system widened inexorably.

In 1939 the normal seasonal problems were compounded by the mass movement of troops, first to their jumping off positions along the eastern border and then to the western frontier. Bottlenecks and jams radiated across the system. Crashes multiplied, with two major disasters just before Christmas claiming the lives of 230 people and shaking public confidence.[71] Over the winter of 1939–40, Gestapo informants on platforms across the country reported public outrage at delays and arbitrary cancellations.[72] The rail administrators struggled to ease the problems of freight traffic by cutting passenger services wholesale. But even drastic measures could not prevent a crisis. By early 1940, tens of thousands of freight cars were frozen in kilometres of traffic jams. By January, turn-around times had risen to more than a week. The effective carrying capacity of the Reichsbahn's rolling stock plummeted and the immediate result was an interruption to coal supplies. By December, the mines were warning of an impending 'transportation calamity'. In the freezing city of Berlin, coal ran so short that even a leading armaments firm such as Rheinmetall could not protect its deliveries from requisitioning by the desperate municipal authorities.[73] Meanwhile, at the pitheads in the Ruhr, the mountains of undelivered coal reached dangerous levels, forcing the mines to slow down production. In total, in the early months of

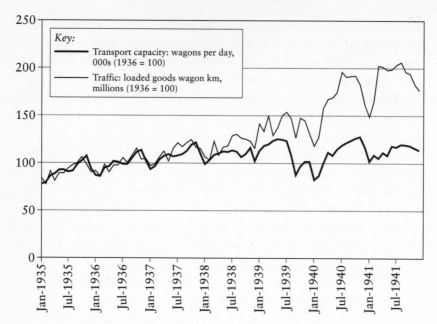

Figure 13. The Reichsbahn under pressure

1940 almost 10 per cent of German armaments plants were affected by the coal shortages.[74] In the central industrial district around Kassel the figure was as high as 27 per cent. In January 1940 Goering described transport as *the* problem of the German war economy.[75]

It was against this backdrop of disappointments, setbacks and crises that the army procurement office faced Hitler's demand for a drastic increase in ammunition production. It might seem odd that the army should object to Hitler's demands. The army was, after all, intended to be the prime beneficiary of the programme. However, the army had other priorities besides ammunition. And it was also the largest single recipient of steel and other metals. Unless there was a large increase in steel rations, the main victim of the gargantuan Fuehrerforderung would be the army's own programmes for weapons, tanks and vehicles. The steel and metal required by Hitler's ammunition plan were daunting. In the first quarter of 1940, the army estimated that it would need 566,000 tons of steel and more than 8,000 tons of copper, as compared to a current allocation of only 300,000 tons of steel and 3,800 tons of copper.[76] If history repeated itself, if expansive plans were not backed up by adequate allocations of materials, then the Fuehrerforderung would become just the latest in a series of armaments bubbles. The army bureaucrats had learned their lesson. They now feared that if their local armaments inspectorates did manage to identify and to 'clear out' sufficient metalworking capacity, the plants they had reserved for military uses would find themselves starved of either iron, copper or some other essential material. After a series of such disappointments, the army's reputation in industrial circles was already severely tarnished. Furthermore, on past performance, the army doubted whether Carl Krauch and the chemical organization of the Four Year Plan could achieve the fourfold increase in the production of powder and explosives that was necessary to fill Hitler's shells. After all, to meet these targets Krauch would need both increased allocations of steel and manpower and where were they to come from? If Krauch fell short, millions of rounds of ammunition would pile up in useless stockpiles without explosives to fill them. Three million tons of steel, 40,600 tons of aluminium and 10,000 tons of copper would be removed from circulation, whilst the rest of the war effort was starved of essential metal.[77] In the end, it would be the 'incompetent military bureaucrats' who took the blame.

In the first months of 1940, the ammunition problem moved to the centre of the ongoing battle between Hitler and the army leadership. On 27 January, Brauchitsch announced to Thomas of the OKW that given the current raw material allocation, the Fuehrer's ammunition demands could not be met.[78] Furthermore, General von Brauchitsch expostulated that the OKW had no right to dictate to the army the details of its armaments planning. In future, the army high command would accept only those orders from the Wehrmacht, and by implication from Hitler, that were backed up with sufficient allocations of raw materials. Keitel's response to this protest was uncompromising. He refused point-blank to reopen the issue of priorities. The Fuehrer had decided on his ammunition programme and his demands would be met, with or without the collaboration of the army procurement office. As Thomas noted in his office diary: 'The programme must be met and if the [army] procurement office cannot do it, then the Fuehrer will give the job to another agency.' And this was clearly no empty threat. Ever since the raw materials crisis began in early 1939, Brauchitsch had been fretting that a non-military 'plenipotentiary' might be appointed to 'sort out' the ammunition sector.[79]

The language was highly charged and the political stakes could not have been higher. The future of the German war effort hung in the balance. But in terms of the practical management of the armaments effort, the solution was clear from the outset. The moment for outright mutiny had passed months ago. In February 1940 Franz Halder and his operational planners were in the process of working out a daring new scheme for the attack on France. With the assault only months away, the army could not seriously object to giving immediate priority to ammunition. Further down the chain of command, the records of the regional armaments inspectorates clearly show that the much-maligned military bureaucrats were doing everything in their power to meet Hitler's challenge.[80] They even took seriously the idea that they should stockpile empty shells, which would then be filled according to the dictates of the military situation and the availability of the chemical ingredients. Nor did Keitel and Hitler simply override the professional judgement of the procurement authorities. Over the course of February, Keitel agreed to allow the army to decide which categories of ammunition should be produced, given the raw materials available. In any case, what really mattered was the ammunition produced over the next nine months. Given the 'fog of war', planning for two years hence could not be more than notional. As Major-General Thomas repeatedly reminded his superiors, if ammunition production was run up to the levels demanded by Hitler, Germany would soon have exhausted its stocks of copper and other nonferrous metals. After that, it would be neither Hitler nor the army, but the trickle of imported foreign raw materials that would dictate the make-up of the armaments programme. In the mean time, the objective was simply to produce as much ammunition as possible, as quickly as possible. As Keitel put it to Thomas in January 1940: 'The main thing is that one has the impression that the ammunition programme has now started up on a large scale and one would then have to consider in the summer whether, given our raw material situation, one should continue on the large scale proposed by the Fuehrer. But he could only decide that in the summer.'[81]

And despite the political bickering, the statistics show that once the transitional problems and the transport crisis had been overcome, Hitler got exactly what he had asked for: a dramatic acceleration in armaments production dominated by a huge surge in the production of ammunition and combat aircraft, timed to coincide with the assault on France. In only seven months, between January and July 1940, German armaments production doubled. This was to be the most sustained and most dramatic increase in armaments production in the entire war. In rate of increase it exceeded anything achieved in any equivalent period, even under Albert Speer's famous leadership. It was an increase made possible only by the ruthless mobilization of resources, without regard either for the needs of the civilian population or the future prospects of the war economy. In economic as well as military terms, Nazi Germany was going for broke.

Furthermore, there can be no serious doubt that credit for this surge in ammunition output was owed to the bureaucrats of the army procurement offices and the regional armaments inspectorates of the Wehrmacht.[82] The increase in output started in February, months before there was any major change to the Wehrmacht's procurement system. Politically, however, the turnaround in armaments production came too late to save the army procurement office. When in February 1940 the full extent of the winter crisis became visible in the freshly released statistical returns, Hitler was incandescent. First Brauchitsch and Halder had sabotaged his plan for an immediate attack on France in November 1939. Now the arrogance and incompetence of the army procurement office threatened the entire war effort. And it was clear where a solution had to come from. In late February, Hitler was removed from his usual wartime routine by the twentieth anniversary celebrations for the manifesto of the Nazi party. To mark this occasion, he attended a grand meeting of the 'Old fighters' in Munich and hosted a reception for the Gauleiters in Berlin. Immersion in this ideological atmosphere appears to have hardened his resolve. The 'bureaucratic lethargy' of the army would be overcome by the dynamism of the 'battle-hardened' National Socialist movement. By the end of the month, Keitel was instructed to write to Brauchitsch:

The Fuehrer and supreme commander of the Wehrmacht, after taking note of the last reported monthly production of weapons and ammunition [i.e. January 1940] has expressed to me his dissatisfaction with the low level of performance achieved since the beginning of the war . . . The modest production of ammunition in January in the most important calibres leaves little hope that the Fuehrer-forderung will be satisfied as of 1 April 1940. The Fuehrer stated that it is necessary to reorganize the procurement system.[83]

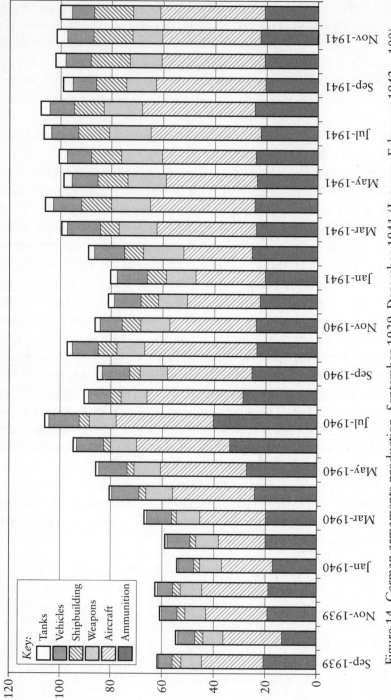

Figure 14. German armaments production, September 1939–December 1941 (January–February 1942 = 100)

Key:
Tanks
Vehicles
Shipbuilding
Weapons
Aircraft
Ammunition

The man who was to replace the army bureaucrats in charge of ammunition production – the most important aspect of armaments production other than aircraft – was Hitler's favourite miracle worker, Fritz Todt.[84] It was Todt who had made real the Fuehrer's vision of a national system of autobahns. In 1938, it was Todt who on the Westwall had demonstrated that the initiative of the politically committed engineer, harnessing the energies of private business, could deliver what the lumbering military bureaucracy apparently could not. And it was Todt who was duly appointed by Hitler on 17 March 1940 to head a new Ministry for Ammunition. This was a calculated snub to the officers of the army procurement office and it was bitterly felt. In early April 1940, General Becker, the head of the army procurement office, made one last attempt to placate Hitler by offering to integrate the army's procurement staff within a single central procurement agency for the entire Wehrmacht. The procurement office also made an attempt to placate the industrial interest by coopting Walter Borbet, the head of the Bochumer Verein, as its industrial adviser on ammunition matters. At first, Hitler seemed taken with this new approach. But at the last moment, on the night of 8 April, Becker's efforts to salvage the army's position were sabotaged by Erich Mueller, aka 'Cannon Mueller' (Kanonen-Mueller), the chief weapons designer of Krupp, a man who made a career out of indulging Hitler's whimsical ideas for oversized artillery pieces. Seizing the opportunity for an impromptu interview on the Fuehrer's private train, Mueller impressed upon Hitler that German industry wanted to see the new Ammunition Ministry headed not by a soldier, but by Todt. For good measure, he added a few insinuations about General Becker's private life. Soon afterwards, Becker was informed that his plan to preserve military control over procurement was a non-starter. Within hours, Germany's leading ballistics expert had shot himself.

It has sometimes been suggested that Todt's appointment was the direct result of intrigue by German capitalists, and it can hardly be denied that big business was one of the principal beneficiaries.[85] However, as usual, it is not easy to prove that business interests were really the prime movers. It is true that industrialists complained over the winter of 1939–40 about what they regarded as the army's excessive bureaucracy. And this may have been motivated by a singularly ill-judged announcement by Major-General Thomas that he expected the profit motive to play no part in the organization of the German war effort, an announcement which can hardly have endeared the soldiers to German industry. The disappointments over the cancelled ammunition programmes of 1937 and 1939 were certainly not forgotten. It is also true that a number of industrialists including 'Cannon Mueller', but also Walter Borbet, had privileged access to Hitler. However, given the tension between Hitler and the army leadership and the disappointing performance of armaments production in the first months of the war, Hitler hardly needed encouragement to take drastic action. And the man he chose for the job was not an industrialist, but a party loyalist.

But if Todt did not owe his appointment to a business conspiracy it cannot be denied that once in office he actively sought an alliance with German industry and that the Reich Group for industry responded with enthusiasm.[86] In the days following his appointment, Todt kept General Thomas of the OKW waiting whilst he conferred with Albert Pietzsch of the RwK (Reich economic chamber) and Wilhelm Zangen of the RgI (Reich Group for industry). He also had meetings with Philipp Kessler of the Fachgemeinschaft Eisen und Metallindustrie, Borbet of the Bochumer Verein, Karl Lange of Business Group engineering and Rudolf Bingel of Siemens.[87] By the end of his first week in office Todt had promised to set up a permanent industrial council and the RgI had supplied him with a list of its key priorities.[88] These included: a modification of the rigorous system of price controls, 'to stimulate the appetites' of businessmen; greater self-regulation by the largest corporations in the distribution of procurement contracts; and the reorganization of the raw materials rationing system, which was not providing the biggest firms with the raw materials they believed they were entitled to. Todt accepted all of these suggestions and did his best to implement them over the following months. Most importantly, he forced the army procurement offices to accept a modified system of pricing for ammunition orders – the lowest-cost producers were to be offered standard prices, rather than being subject to repeated price controls – and he set about decentralizing the distribution of ammunition orders. In each of the regions defined by the Wehrmacht's armaments inspectorates, the business organizations were to form working groups of producers interested in each calibre of ammunition.[89] These working groups were coordinated by a regional ammunition committee. Henceforth, the army procurement offices were to issue their orders to these committees. The industrialists themselves would then take responsibility for assigning the contracts to the most suitable producers. In the most important armaments inspectorate, the Ruhr, Walter Borbet was unsurprisingly given the job of chairing the regional ammunition committee.[90] To secure coordination across regions, an ammunition council was established in Berlin, which liaised between Todt's Ministry and the national business organizations of the metalworking industries. In due course, the role of the ammunition committees was expanded to include not just the distribution of orders, but also overseeing the productive capacity of all plants in their area. The committees were empowered by Todt to issue all orders necessary to secure the fulfilment of his production targets and to deny orders to firms if they lacked the necessary labour and raw materials. By May 1940 Todt had moved from a strictly regional system to set up national sub-committees (*Fachausschuesse*) in Berlin for all major types of ammunition. In the summer he followed this up by announcing the formation of a national committee for tank production, which began to meet from the autumn of 1940 under the chairmanship of Walter Rohland of the Deutsche Edelstahlwerke. Finally, in November 1940 the Todt Ministry established a national committee to oversee the production of guns and artillery, headed predictably enough by 'Cannon Mueller' from Krupp.

The war thus began with a convulsive rearrangement of power and influence within the army's segment of the armaments economy. The soldiers were the losers. After Becker's suicide, the army procurement office never recovered its authority. In addition, the ambition of the Wehrmacht military-economic organization to exercise overarching control over the entire armaments economy was dealt a fatal blow by Fritz Todt's emergence as an independent force in armaments politics. The winners in this power struggle, apart from Fritz Todt and the Nazi party, were the leaders of German industry who had rallied around the new Ammunition Minister in April 1940. In political terms, their victory was all the more decisive because it coincided with the extraordinary upsurge in armaments output in the first half of 1940 and the subsequent triumph of the Wehrmacht in France. The combination of military victory and surging production statistics was an intoxicating propaganda cocktail, which Fritz Todt and his backers in the Nazi party exploited to full effect. In his victory speech of the summer of 1940, Hitler gave credit for the armaments effort entirely to Fritz Todt, pointedly ignoring both the army's own procurement officers and General Thomas of the OKW.[91] This rhetoric accurately reflected the outcome of the political battle, but it had little to do with the realities of production.

The huge surge in the output of ammunition for which Todt and his collaborators claimed credit was in fact a function of raw material inputs. It was the huge increase in steel and copper allocated to the army after September 1939, not Todt's last minute efforts at rationalization, that drove the remarkable upsurge in the first half of 1940. As General Fromm, the overall head of army supplies, commented sarcastically: Todt's 'bed had been made for him'.[92] Monthly figures for ammunition production show quite unambiguously that take-off was achieved in February 1940, at least a month and a half before Todt's Ministry had even begun to operate.[93] Given the lead times in ammunition production, the measures taken by Todt from April onwards can have had no more than a marginal impact on a production boom that crested in July. In so far as organizational measures had any part in explaining this dramatic upsurge, it was the efforts of the regional inspectorates of the Wehrmacht that were the key. As early as December 1939, in an effort to accelerate the identification and 'booking' of plants suitable for ammunition contracts, Berlin head office had delegated responsibility for allocating contracts downwards to the local armaments inspectorates.[94] And contrary to the Todt myth, the soldiers were by no means blind to the importance of cultivating strong relationships with industry. By the spring of 1940, regional consultative arrangements had been set up by all the armaments inspectorates. Indeed, it was the armaments inspectorate of the Ruhr that established the model for Todt's national system of committees, in the form of the Gelsenkirchen Accord.[95] Under this arrangement a joint committee of industrialists and procurement officers, chaired by Ernst Poensgen, the head of the mighty Vereinigte Stahlwerke, was charged with responsibility for identifying those firms that could be enrolled in ammunition production. Not surprisingly, given this powerful backing, the Gelsenkirchen Accord was approved as a model for nationwide cooperation by Wilhelm Zangen, the chair of the Reich Group for industry only weeks before Todt's appointment as Ammunition Minister.[96] It is symptomatic of the politics of the 'ammunition crisis' that both Todt and the representatives of industry chose to ignore these early experiments and to announce Todt's ammunition committees as a fundamental break with all previous practice. It suited German business leaders only too well to assist Fritz Todt in mixing the ugly cocktail of Nazi leadership doctrine (*Fuehrertum*) and the self-serving rhetoric of entrepreneurial dynamism (*Unternehmertum*) that was soon to become the guiding ideology of the German war economy.

III

If, on the other hand, we want to understand the real workings of the German war effort we need to keep our eyes firmly fixed on the inputs and outputs of the industrial machine. In the first year of the war the Nazi regime raised the share of national output that was going to the military from 20 per cent to more than a third, a 60 per cent increase from an already high pre-war level. As one would expect, this redistribution of resources was accompanied by political wrangling. Some of the more spectacular measures that had been originally planned for the declaration of war were revised in favour of mobilization by 'stealth'. Most notably, the plan conceived by Reich Economic Minister Funk to finance the war through a sharp increase in taxation was dropped in favour of a comprehensive programme of rationing and national saving. And this apparent hesitancy has given rise to the impression that the Nazi political leadership was doing all it could to cushion the civilian standard of living. But this is a misapprehension. It is certainly true, of course, that a hefty increase in tax rates in the first months of the war would have sent a clearer signal as to the regime's intentions. Financing the war through tax increases would also have minimized the inflationary risk. But, in the short run, it made little difference whether civilian consumption was curtailed through taxation or through severe rationing leading to an increase in saving. In either case, consumption was reduced and resources – labour, industrial capacity and raw materials – were 'freed up' for war production. Viewed in these terms, the measures adopted by Nazi Germany were extremely effective.[97]

Within the pre-war territory of the Reich, the already constrained levels of civilian consumption fell by 11 per cent (on a per capita basis) in the first year of the war. By 1941, consumption spending was down by 18 per cent relative to 1938. As household expenditure dried up, unspent cash poured into the coffers of the German financial system. The most vivid indicator of this wave of war-induced saving is provided by the monthly returns of the German savings banks.[98] Unlike better known institutions such as the Deutsche Bank or the Dresdner, which catered for a relatively exclusive clientele, the Sparkassen were the banks of the common people. By the late 1930s, virtually every family in Germany held at least one 'savings book' (Sparbuch). The accounts of the Sparkassen thus provide a direct insight into the everyday financial dispositions of German households. In the months immediately preceding the war, they showed an unusually large net withdrawal, as millions of families did their best to stockpile necessities. Then, from the first months of 1940 onwards, as rationing began to bite and the shelves of the German shops emptied, the accounts of the savings banks swelled with a completely unprecedented volume of deposits. By 1941, the inflow was running at the rate of more than a billion Reichsmarks per month.

Under normal circumstances, these funds would have been put to work as loans to local government, or mortgages for small businesses. But wartime restrictions not only hit civilian consumption, they also bottled up civilian investment. Whilst construction of new armaments capacity accelerated after September 1939, investment in housing was cut to the bone. In 1937, the peak year for civilian construction in the Third Reich, a total of 320,057 apartments were added to the housing stock. By 1939, annual net additions had already fallen to just over 206,000, under the pressure of military construction demands. The year 1940 saw only 105,458 apartments added to the housing stock and by 1942 the annual total came to less than 40,000, a reduction relative to 1937 of 85 per cent.[99] With civilian investment at a standstill, the funds circulating through the German financial system were free for redirection into the Reichsbank's 'silent system' of war financing (*geraeuschlose Kriegsfinanzierung*).[100] After their embarrassing experiences with public offerings at the end of 1938, the Reichsbank and the Reich Finance Ministry had no intention of relying on the patriotic appeal of war bonds. Instead, they borrowed indirectly, by siphoning off the money accumulating in the coffers of local government, the insurance funds and local savings banks.[101] In 1940 the Sparkassen alone channelled 8 billion Reichsmarks into the war effort. In 1941 they contributed 12.8 billion Reichsmarks. Private investors who held their funds beyond the Reichsbank's immediate reach were directed into government debt through the simple expedient of restricting the issue of any other forms

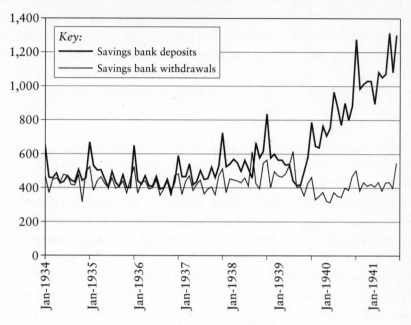

Figure 15. Silent financing at work (million Reichsmarks)

of interest-bearing asset and putting a tight cap on stock exchange speculation.[102] No compulsion was necessary. There was simply nothing other than government debt to invest in.

For the first four years of the war, this inconspicuous but highly effective system allowed the burden of Germany's war expenditure to be distributed relatively safely across the financial system. It also had political advantages in that it did not involve a direct attack on household incomes or business profits. Throughout the war, though a large part of German private income could not be spent, wages and salaries continued to rise, promising a higher post-war standard of living. But, by the same token, the silent system of war finance provided no direct pressure for the reallocation of resources. The onus fell entirely on the rationing system. It was by directly restricting consumption and redirecting the flow of raw materials and labour that the German authorities ensured that rising incomes were not translated into civilian consumption and investment. Rationing of consumer goods was the first line of defence. Within the first weeks of the war, comprehensive rationing was introduced for the two most basic items of household expenditure: food and clothing.[103] Some cash that could not be spent on the official rations, of course, leaked out into the black market. But at the start of the war this was a negligible phenomenon. A few households will have preferred to hoard their unspent cash rather than entrusting it to a bank. But the vast majority of unspent income flowed into savings accounts and thus into the 'silent system' of war finance.[104] Rationing thus operated to restrict civilian economic activity from the demand side. But this would not have been effective if it had not been backed up by the regulation of production and supply through the systematic redirection of raw materials and labour. The point is commonly made that the operation of the German raw material rationing system was haphazard. But given the pressure that the system was put under by the politically expedient system of war finance, the more surprising thing is that it functioned at all. The coordinating centres for the rationing process were the OKW, which collated military demands, and the RWM, which oversaw the overall allocation. The results were rough and ready at best. However, the system was also undeniably effective in shifting huge volumes of raw materials into armaments production.

As before the war, the central issue in the allocation of raw materials was steel. This was made worse at the outbreak of war by the sudden shortfall in imported iron ore and the closure of the steelworks in the exposed western border areas, notably the Saar. However, in the interests of satisfying the demands of the Wehrmacht, steel production was maintained at 1.6 million tons per month, even if this meant eating into Germany's limited stockpile of iron ore.[105] Of this monthly production, by the first quarter of 1940 the Wehrmacht was already receiving a share of 55 per cent, or 885,000 tons. This compared to only 620,000 tons which had been available for armaments production at the high point of World War I and a similar figure provided during the Munich crisis in 1938.[106] This enormous Wehrmacht contingent was 'funded' by making painful cuts to all other forms of steel consumption. The prestige projects of the regime, including party buildings and autobahns, were slashed almost completely, being reduced to only 6 per cent of their pre-war allocation. Iron for household consumption was reduced to 25 per cent of its pre-war level. As a result, there were already severe shortages of essential furnishings such as ovens and stoves during the first winter of the war.[107] Similarly, swingeing cuts were made to the allocation of steel to essential primary industries such as the electricity grid, coal mining and the steel industry. The engineering sector, which amongst other things produced spare parts for Germany's overstretched factories, saw its steel ration for non-Wehrmacht projects cut to 29 per cent of the pre-war level. And the steel allocated to the export industries was similarly reduced, despite the protests of the advocates of a long war. Already by January 1940, therefore, the German steel rationing system was prioritizing the immediate needs of the Wehrmacht, over all other considerations, including the long-run sustainability of the industrial war effort.

The Fuehrer's ammunition demands in December 1939 put the system under even greater strain. As we have seen, the army alone now demanded at least 560,000 monthly tons of steel. At first, Colonel Hermann von Hanneken, who since 1937 had been responsible for steel rationing at the Reich Ministry of Economic Affairs, resisted calls for a further increase in the Wehrmacht share. Further reductions in the allocation to other steel users were not an option, given the dangerously low rations to which they had already been cut. Issuing new quota entitlements in excess of actual production would simply lead to an 'inflation' of iron certificates and logjams of excess orders at the steelworks. The only way to provide the Wehrmacht with a real increase in steel was to increase overall steel production. This, however, would accelerate the rate at which Germany exhausted its stocks of iron ore. Given the uncertainty of Scandinavian supplies, this was potentially a fatal decision, but to fulfil the Fuehrerforderung it was a decision that had to be taken. Goering instructed Hanneken to raise the Wehrmacht's steel quota to 1.1 million tons, to be 'paid for' by raising overall production.[108] Goering was fully aware of the consequences of this decision, but, as he explained to Thomas on 30 January 1940, long-run considerations were irrelevant.

The Fuehrer is firmly convinced that the major attack in the West will give him decisive victory in the war in 1940. He assumes that Belgium, Holland and northern France will come into our possession, and he has worked out for himself [sic] that the industrial areas of Douai and Lens and those of Luxembourg, Longwy and Briey can replace raw material deliveries from Sweden. In consequence, the Fuehrer has decided to fully deploy our raw material reserves without regard to the future and at the expense of later war years.[109]

IV

Apart from raw materials, the other indispensable input to production was labour. Over the course of the war, labour was to emerge as a critical constraint in the German war economy.[110] The initial shock was sharp enough. On 31 May 1939, according to the Reich Statistical Office, the German workforce consisted of 24.5 million working men, 14.6 million working women and 300,000 people labelled as 'foreigners and Jews'; 39.4 million in total. A year later, the number of German men had been cut by 4 million to 20.5 million. The number of German women in work had also fallen slightly to 14.4 million. These reductions were offset to some degree by the addition of 350,000 prisoners of war and an increase in the number of foreigners working in Germany to 800,000. But the total workforce had fallen to just over 36 million people. This basic pattern continued for the rest of the war. The number of German men fell. The number of German women held steady. The share of prisoners of war and foreigners in the workforce rose from year to year.

The fact that more women were not mobilized for war work is sometimes taken as one more symptom of the inability of the Nazi regime to demand sacrifices from the German population. In this respect it has often been contrasted to Britain, where an increase in female participation in the workforce was the key to sustaining the war effort. Such comparisons, however, are completely misleading, since they ignore the fact that the labour market participation of German women in 1939 was higher than that reached by Britain and the United States even at the end of the war.[111] In 1939, a third of all married women in Germany were economically active and more than half of all women between the ages of 15 and 60 were in work. As a result, women made up more than a third of the German workforce before the war started, compared to a female share of only a quarter in Britain. A year later, the share of German women in the native workforce stood at 41 per cent, compared to less than 30 per cent in Britain. Not surprisingly, over the following years Britain caught up. But even in 1944 the participation rate for British women between the ages of 15 to 65 was only 41 per cent, as against a minimum of 51 per cent in Germany already in 1939. In large part, this difference was accounted for by the structural differences in the British and German economies. Of Germany's 14 million women workers in 1939, only 2.7 million worked in industry. By far the largest sector of women's work was peasant agriculture, which in 1939 employed almost 6 million women. By contrast, of Britain's 6 million working women fewer than 100,000 were employed on farms. As we have seen, the burden of maintaining the small peasant farms that dominated German agriculture fell disproportionately on women's shoulders. And as farm men were recruited away for the war, this burden grew ever more arduous. In areas such as Wuerttemberg and Bavaria, with dense populations of peasant farms, female workforce participation rates already exceeded 60 per cent in 1939. It goes without saying that by sustaining the food supply, Germany's farm women provided an indispensable service to the Nazi war effort. But, even allowing for this difference in economic structure, the German level of mobilization was greater than that in Britain. In Berlin, a major centre of both industrial and service sector employment, with virtually no farm workers, 53 per cent of women were at work in 1939.[112] The same was true of the eastern industrial hub of Saxony. Even in the port towns of Hamburg and Bremen or the heavy industrial centres of the Ruhr, where the occupational structure was particularly unfavourable to female employment, 40 per cent of women of working age had jobs, matching the national average for Britain at the end of the war.

Since the native workforce was already highly mobilized in 1939, the German war effort, in the early years of the war, was sustained above all by reallocating workers. The Nazi regime showed little hesitancy in forcing through this shift. In 1939, 22 per cent of the German industrial workforce was reported as working on Wehrmacht contracts. A year later, this figure had supposedly increased to 50.2 per cent. These statistics, which were produced by the Reich Group for industry, almost certainly overstate the degree of 'conversion' to war work. However, they do give at least some indication of the scale and direction of the shift. Hundreds of thousands of workers, particularly new entrants into the labour market, flowed 'naturally' into the war industries, attracted by high wages. In addition, in the late 1930s the regime had equipped itself with extensive powers of coercion permitting the labour market authorities to forcibly conscript German men and women into essential work. By early 1940 almost a million German workers were tied to their workplaces by the provisions of compulsory service (*Dienstverpflichtung*).

During the first twelve months of the war there was, in addition, an attempt to forcibly close down small businesses that were unsuitable for war work, releasing their workforce and machinery for employment elsewhere. Not surprisingly, this closure programme was hugely unpopular and it was soon abandoned as a waste of administrative effort. By far the largest process of conversion was achieved either through the issuing of Wehrmacht contracts to firms previously engaged on civilian work, or by the reallocation of labour within firms that already had Wehrmacht experience. In the first year of the war the number of men working in the 'consumer industries' on civilian contracts fell from 1.3 million in May 1939 to just over 750,000 in the summer of 1940.

The priority of the war effort was clear. The real dilemma was not the choice between the war effort and the 'civilian sector'. The choice was between recruiting a man into the armed forces, or leaving him in a factory to produce for the war effort. After raising its strength from 1.131 million in the summer of 1939 to 4.548 million by September 1939, the Wehrmacht drafted a further million men over the Christmas of 1939–40.[113] Altogether, the Wehrmacht between May 1939 and May 1940 called up three-quarters of a million farmers and farmhands, 1.3 million industrial workers, 930,000 men from the craft sector, 220,000 transport workers, 600,000 shopworkers and 600,000 clerks and civil servants. The intention of the German mobilization planners had always been to manage this huge withdrawal of labour by identifying those workers who were essential to wartime production and protecting them from the draft. This system worked satisfactorily for the hard core of armaments firms directly overseen by the Wehrmacht's armaments inspectorates. Not surprisingly, perhaps, the same could not be said for the vast tail of industrial firms that supplied sub-components and semi-finished materials to final armaments production. Here there were many skilled metalworkers who were snatched up by the Wehrmacht. As a result, a number of important suppliers to the war effort threatened to grind completely to a halt in the autumn of 1939. Clearly, better organization would have helped. But there was no escaping the dilemma. The Wehrmacht had no intention of using skilled metalworkers as cannon fodder. Mechanics, fitters and electricians were needed by the military for the same reasons that they were needed by industry. They were employed in the engineering corps, in army repair shops, as Luftwaffe ground crew and in naval engine rooms.[114] They were needed in increasing numbers to maintain the sophisticated electronic networks on which military communications depended. For the Wehrmacht, the problem was made worse by the fact that breakneck rearmament in the 1930s had coincided with the reintroduction of conscription. The same young men who had been the first to receive basic military training were also those who had been disproportionately drawn into Germany's new armaments industries.[115] From the outset, therefore, Germany faced a stark choice between manning its armed forces to full strength and depleting the workforce of its armaments industries.

V

The sector, however, where the draft for World War II produced most severe and immediate problems was agriculture. As we have seen, German farms had been struggling with a pressing problem of labour shortage since the late 1930s. Perhaps with this in mind, the Wehrmacht did not draw disproportionately on agriculture in the first round of call-ups. The recruitment of almost 800,000 men of prime working age was nevertheless sufficient to cause panic in the Ministry of Food and Agriculture. State Secretary Herbert Backe started the war in a grim mood. It was far from clear how well the RNS would respond to the challenge of a prolonged war. The rations set on 25 September 1939 were adequate: 2,570 calories for 'normal' civilians, rising to almost 4,000 calories per day for the troops. Given the prevailing class inequality in German society, rationing, as in wartime Britain, actually improved the diets of at least 40 per cent of working-class households.[116] Nevertheless, the authorities in Berlin were jumpy. Chief medical officer Dr Leonardo Conti declared as early as October 1939 that long hours and the restricted wartime diet were pushing the civilian population to the limit. Backe's goal was to stretch his stocks to cover at least three years of fighting. But the harvest of 1939 was clearly far less good than the bumper crop of 1938 and the sudden reduction in the workforce threatened to set off a disastrous chain reaction. Farms would cut back the labour-intensive production of potatoes and root crops. That would reduce the amount of animal feed. Supplies of meat and milk would plummet. What haunted everybody was the experience of World War I.[117]

Faced with this possibility, Backe demanded that every effort should be made to draft additional labour from outside Germany.[118] In 1938 the acute labour shortage in farming had already forced Berlin to negotiate an agreement with the Polish government, to admit 60,000 harvest helpers. Now, with the majority of Poland under German control, Backe envisioned a far larger programme. The first group to be conscripted were 300,000 Polish prisoners of war. But this was not enough to satisfy Germany's hunger for labour. In early 1940, Hans Frank, the new ruler of the General Government, the rump of Poland not annexed by Germany, initiated a programme to draw unemployed Poles into the Reich as temporary labourers. And on 25 January 1940 Goering rushed out a fundamental decree clarifying the role of the General Government in relation to the German economy. Rather than treating the General Government as a dumping ground, it was to be placed on a viable footing as a permanent labour reservoir for the Reich. From the General Government alone, a million Poles were to be recruited for work in Germany, 750,000 for agriculture, half of them women. In relation to Polish seasonal migration to Germany in the 1920s these figures were not extraordinary. But they applied to a territory which contained only slightly more than one-third of the pre-war Polish population and which was made up of regions that had no tradition of migrant labour. The demand for a supply of a million 'guest workers' out of a non-Jewish population in the General Government of just over 11 million people was therefore extremely severe. And Backe wanted the labour urgently. In the early months of 1940 he was expecting ten trains a day, each filled with 1,000 workers.

Ethnic tensions between Germans and Poles were, of course, of long standing. More or less severe discrimination in everyday life had been commonplace in the border regions, particularly since the formation of a Polish nation-state in the aftermath of World War I.[119] However, the system of coercive discrimination imposed on the Polish foreign workers in Nazi Germany was completely unprecedented. It was designed above all by officials acting on behalf of Heinrich Himmler, the chief of German police. In relation to Poland, the SS was pursuing an ambitious agenda of its own.[120] Shortly after the outbreak of the war, Himmler had been appointed Reich Commissioner for Securing the German Race (RKF). In this role, his mission was to remove all Jews and as many Poles as possible from the formerly Polish territories now annexed to the

Reich. At the same time he had set in motion a gigantic redistribution of population by repatriating ethnic Germans from the Baltic states annexed by Stalin and from the northern Italian region of Tyrol and settling them in the territory emptied of Poles and Jews. In one sense, Backe's demand for a huge influx of foreign labour was complementary to this programme, since it provided Himmler with an immediate excuse to uproot hundreds of thousands of Poles from the territories annexed to the Reich. More fundamentally, however, the incorporation of Poles into the German workforce was completely at odds with Himmler's vision of a racial state. It is indicative, therefore, of the mood of emergency prevailing in Berlin in early 1940 that Himmler was forced to compromise. Not only was he obliged to slow down the process of deporting Jews and Poles en masse across the border into the General Government. He was also forced to draft a set of guidelines specifying the conditions under which more than a million Poles would be permitted to take up at least temporary residence in the Reich.

The result was a system of penal apartheid. Polish workers in Germany were confined to the workplace and their allocated billets. They were to wear at all times an identifying tag bearing a large letter 'P'. To ensure that their status was always below that of their German co-workers, their wages were arbitrarily slashed to a maximum of 25 Reichsmarks per month. Polish workers were barred from all public conveyances and all social contacts with Germans. The prudishness of Himmler's elite revealed itself in the prohibition of visits to German cinemas, dances, bars, theatres and churches. Sexual intercourse with Germans was punishable by death. Any other transgression, including shirking at work, would result in committal to a concentration camp. Under no circumstances were shirkers to be sent back to Poland. The Germans were in no doubt that these measures constituted a breach of international law.[121] It was clear, in particular, that the SS code could not be applied to the hundreds of thousands of Polish prisoners of war who enjoyed the protection of the Geneva Convention. The solution was simple. With the extinction of the Polish state, the former members of the Polish army were 'released' from their status as prisoners of war. As civilians they could then be 'converted' to the normal status of Polish labourers in Nazi Germany. Special treatment was reserved for the 60,000 Polish prisoners identified as Jews. They were subject to a murderous regime of starvation and overwork, which by the spring of 1940 had already killed 25,000.

Not surprisingly, given the vicious attitude of the German authorities, the effort to recruit Polish workers by voluntary means was not a success. Only 200,000 Polish civilians had arrived in Germany by the spring of 1940, nowhere near Backe's target. In the General Government, Governor Hans Frank interpreted the refusal of Poles to volunteer themselves for work in Germany as 'malevolence'. By refusing to place themselves at the Reich's 'disposal' they were engaged in a deliberate act of sabotage against the German war effort.[122] Since February 1940, at least, Frank sensed a groundswell of Polish resistance that needed urgently to be quashed. This was a precondition not only for the mass recruitment of workers, but also for the execution of the SS plans for population displacement, which under current circumstances would constitute a threat to public order in the General Government. Backe for his part prophesied disaster unless Germany's farms were provided with the workforce they needed. In the council of the Four Year Plan, he explicitly invoked the nightmare of the Nazi regime, a collapse in the food supply like that which had unleashed revolution in 1918. Faced with this prospect, Backe shrank from nothing. A minimum of 400,000 workers were required as soon as possible to ensure the supply of grain and potatoes for the following year. If the Poles would not volunteer, then Backe demanded that the Wehrmacht be issued with the authority 'to cause, by force, the necessary number of workers to be transported to Germany'.[123] In April the administrators of the General Government agreed. Over the objection of the Foreign Ministry, Frank introduced conscription for all inhabitants of the General Government between the ages of 14 and 25. The youth of Poland would solve the labour shortage of German agriculture.[124]

It was clear within hours of the new decree's announcement that forced deportation would produce precisely the upsurge of Polish resistance that Frank had predicted. Rumours immediately began to circulate that young people were being arrested on the street and rounded up in cinemas and church services. In fact, the German approach to 'breaking the backbone' of the Polish people was more targeted than this. As Frank and his police chief SS Obergruppenfuehrer Friedrich-Wilhelm Krueger were well aware, they did not have sufficient manpower in the General Government to round up hundreds of thousands of Poles by force.[125] Instead, the Germans backed up their conscription drive with a surgical strike against what they believed to be the leadership of the nascent Polish resistance.[126] The necessary cover for this well-planned escalation of violence was provided by the long-awaited assault in the West. Up to this point, Frank clearly felt constrained by the international media attention directed towards the General Government. The dramatic battles in the West provided precisely the distraction they needed. Within days of the opening of the Western campaign, the German police in the General Government began a systematic programme of political murders, thinly disguised as routine courts martial. Two thousand prominent Poles already in German detention were killed; 2,000 more were targeted for arrest and immediate liquidation, in addition to 3,000 so-called 'professional criminals'.[127] Within less than a year of the outbreak of hostilities, murderous violence had thus became an officially sanctioned element in the management of the German war effort. Indeed, in the management of the food supply of the General Government, Frank and his collaborators went beyond selective purges to adopt a more comprehensive policy of genocide.

The General Government as it was constituted in 1939 was a territory of severe food deficit, Poland's best farming areas having been annexed to the Reich. In early 1940, to prevent the outbreak of famine in the major cities, State Secretary Backe agreed to provide Frank with at least 10,000 tons of bread grain per month, enough to provide the inhabitants of Warsaw with a half a pound of bread per day.[128] In April, in the days immediately following the decision to impose the conscription of labour, Backe visited Frank to discuss the food situation. To assist Frank in securing his grip on the General Government, and to enable him to effectively implement the policy of conscription which German agriculture so badly needed, Backe agreed to provide one further allocation of 135,000 tons of grain from German stocks. This would be sufficient to see the major cities through to the new harvest. After that, the General Government was expected to achieve self-sufficiency. As Frank and Backe agreed the grain available in the General Government was to be distributed strictly according to the needs of the German occupation. At the bottom of this racial and functional hierarchy were the Jews. In relation to the population of at least two and half million Jews in the General Government, Frank commented simply:

I am not interested in the Jews. Whether or not they get any fodder to eat [*fuettern*] is the last thing I'm concerned about . . .

The second category is made up of the Poles [perhaps as many as 10 million people] in so far as I can make use of them. I shall feed these Poles with what is left over and what we can spare. Otherwise, I will tell the Poles to look after themselves . . . I am only interested in the Poles in so far as I see in them a reservoir of labour, but not to the extent that I feel it is a governmental responsibility to give them a guarantee that they will get a specific amount to eat. We are not talking of rations for Poles but only of the possibilities of feeding them.[129]

Above the Poles came the Ukrainian minority in the General Government, who would be better treated. Above them Frank placed a few tens of thousands of privileged Poles who worked in important public services, such as the railways, or in factories producing for the German war effort. Finally, at the top of the hierarchy came the German occupation authorities themselves, numbered in the thousands, who would be provided with rations as in the Reich. What this meant in practice was that, by comparison with a German ration of more than 2,600 calories in early 1940, the 'ration' for the inhabitants of Poland's major cities was set at 609 calories. Jews were provided with 503 calories per day. By the end of the year the Polish ration had improved to 938 daily calories whereas that for Jews had fallen to 369. In 1940, according to the League of Nations, rations in the General Government were sufficient, on average, to cover 20 per cent of the recommended daily allowance of protein and less than 5 per cent of the necessary fats for the Polish urban population. By the spring of 1940 the Wehrmacht armaments inspectorates operating in the occupied territories were already reporting incidents of skilled factory workers collapsing at their workbenches for lack of food. In the regular meetings of the Wehrmacht's military-economic staff in Berlin, chaired by General Thomas, the prospect of famine was quite openly discussed.[130]

VI

The war that Hitler unleashed in September 1939 was not the war that he had wanted to fight. Nor was it a war for which Germany was adequately prepared. Once we undo the effects of hindsight, there can be no serious doubt that the declaration of war by Britain and France faced Hitler with the most serious challenge since his accession to power.

In military terms, it was far from obvious that Germany enjoyed any substantial margin of superiority, certainly if one considered the navy, along with the air force and the ground forces. In economic terms, everyone agreed that Britain and France held the advantage. The alliance with Moscow provided the Third Reich with some relief from the crushing effect of the blockade. However, this was far outweighed by the ability of the Western powers to draw on the resources of the United States. In domestic political terms, Hitler's position was highly exposed. The war was a direct result of his foreign policy. The Wehrmacht leadership had gone along, of course, and Ribbentrop had done his bit, but it was Hitler who had precipitated the war. And if Germany suffered any significant setback, it would be Hitler who would be blamed, if not by the population at large, then certainly by the army leadership. It was a war, therefore, that Hitler needed to win and to win quickly. And after a brief moment of hesitancy in the autumn of 1939, his regime responded not with indolence and complacency but with a radical effort to mobilize the resources both of Germany and of the newly acquired territory of Poland. Hitler was staking everything on achieving victory in the West and in pursuit of this goal he was willing to stop at nothing. But as a detailed discussion of armaments policy makes clear, even as late as the spring of 1940 Hitler did not have a coherent strategy for achieving this victory. Hitler's armament plans were certainly orientated in a general sense towards maximizing the Wehrmacht's firepower in the short term. But the operational design towards which these armaments programmes appear to have been directed did not promise an immediate military decision. Hitler's ammunition programme may have been designed to allow the Wehrmacht to fight its way to the coast, backed up by ample artillery firepower. But this would leave both France and Britain still in the war by the end of 1940. The military plan that was ultimately to allow Hitler to escape from his strategic impasse emerged belatedly and largely by accident over the winter months of 1939–40. It was not finally adopted until February 1940, by which time the great ammunition drive was already in full swing. And even after the German army leadership had finally approved the bold new plan, many remained profoundly sceptical. Hitler wagered everything in September 1939. And until the last weeks of May 1940, the outcome hung in the balance.

11

Victory in the West – *Sieg im Westen*

At 5.35 on the morning of 10 May 1940, after months of 'phoney war', the Western front roared into life.[1] Thousands of German guns began drubbing the opposing French, Dutch and Belgian positions. Company commanders sounded their whistles for the infantry assault. Tanks and trucks revved their engines. Overhead, streams of bombers and fighters droned westwards. The most dramatic action was to the north of the line. The famous Belgian fortifications on the river Maas were seized in audacious assaults by commandos and glider-born Special Forces. Meanwhile, in a military first, German parachutists descended on the outskirts of The Hague, Rotterdam and the bridges at Dordrecht and Moerdijk. These spectacular actions combined with the determined assault by German army Group B towards the Maas river line had their intended effect. The bulk of the French army, backed up by the British Expeditionary Force, marched rapidly northwards. This well-rehearsed manoeuvre was intended to stop the German army short of the Channel coast, on a line running north–south from Breda in the Netherlands to Dinant in Belgium, along the river Dyle. If the British and the French had been facing the original German plan of October 1939, or indeed the German Imperial army of 1914, this would have been a highly effective response. In the event, their prompt reaction was a prelude to disaster. The German attack on the Netherlands and northern Belgium was a feint. The main thrust of the German assault was directed not at Holland, but one hundred kilometres to the south, through the Ardennes forest. Undetected by Allied intelligence, 7 of Germany's 9 tank divisions, grouped under the command of Army Group A, pushed hurriedly along the twisted forest roads that led westwards through Belgium and Luxembourg towards the French border. Their objectives were the Maas bridges between Dinant and Sedan. If Army Group A could seize these crossing points, it would then be free to race westwards into the vacuum created by the northward deployment of the British and French. The two opposing armies would pivot, as if in a rotating door, leaving the British and French armies encircled, between German Army Group B in the Netherlands and Belgium and the tanks of Army Group A picketed across northern France.

By any conventional military standard, the German plan was astonishingly audacious. If the French and British had held back substantial reserves, Army Group A's pincer movement would have been vulnerable to counterattack, or even counter-encirclement. In the event, it worked to perfection. The Sedan and Dinant bridges fell on 13 May before the French and British realized the danger. The Panzer generals exploited their breakthrough brilliantly. Following closely behind the forward units in specially adapted radio vehicles, they drove their forces westwards into the rear of the French army, throwing the Allies completely off balance and preventing them from establishing any coherent line of defence. The much-feared counterattack against the exposed flanks of the Panzer divisions never came. In a disastrous miscalculation, the French had deployed their entire reserve towards the western end of the Dyle–Breda movement and the laborious command and control procedures of the Allied armies were overwhelmed by the pace of events. The bulk of the Anglo-French forces continued to move in a northerly direction, even as they were encircled by the tanks of Army Group A to the south. At 8.30 on the evening of 20 May, ten days after the start of the campaign, the advanced guard of the 2nd Panzer division reached Abbeville, where the river Somme flows into the sea. The trap had shut. In a gigantic scything blow Army Group A had carved out a pocket measuring 200 kilometres in length by 140 kilometres in breadth. It was the largest encirclement in military history and the yield was extraordinary. Caught between the hammer and anvil of the German attack were no less than 1.7 million Allied soldiers, including the entire Dutch and Belgian armies, the entire British Expeditionary Force and the pick of the French army. By 24 May, only the harbours of Dunkirk and Ostend were left as escape routes. Benefiting from the first lull in the German offensive in a fortnight, the British extracted 370,000 men by boat. Another 100,000 French soldiers slipped out of the pocket towards the south. But they left all their artillery, tanks and trucks behind. The rout was complete. The Germans took 1.2 million prisoners of war. Even in the East, no single disaster of the Red Army can compare to the Anglo-French debacle of May 1940.[2] Bitter fighting continued across the French heartland for another month, but the battle was over. On 17 June the French sued for peace and the Germans spared them no humiliation. The Armistice was signed in the same railway car in the forest of Compiègne in which, twenty-two years earlier, the Germans themselves had been forced to accept defeat. The Wehrmacht had completed its greatest victory of World War II at astonishingly low cost. The conquest of France cost the Germans 49,000 dead and missing. The French casualties give a truer indication of the intensity of the fighting: in only six weeks, the French suffered 120,000 killed.

I

The extraordinary train of events that began early in the morning on 10 May was, for most Germans, a vindication in every respect of Hitler and his regime.[3] The Fuehrer had pushed ceaselessly towards war. When war started he had pushed for an offensive at the earliest possible opportunity. He had argued doggedly against allowing Germany to be sucked into a war of attrition. Hitler had gambled and he had won. In a single blow the Wehrmacht had knocked France, Belgium and the Netherlands out of the war. Britain had been driven off the Continent. In economic terms, Germany now controlled the resources and productive potential of all of the western continent of Europe. World War I had been a futile slogging match, decided ultimately by the ability of the Western Allies to expend greater manpower and material than Imperial Germany. In the summer of 1940 it seemed that Hitler's Germany had found an escape from this dreadful materialist logic. The Wehrmacht had restored militarism to its proud place as the really decisive factor in world affairs. With sufficient expertise and élan, huge effects could be achieved with a comparatively modest expenditure of effort. If this is a correct interpretation of the events of 1940, it clearly poses a major challenge to any economic analysis of World War II.[4] We must therefore devote some space to anatomizing the military events in May and June 1940, before moving on to an assessment of their economic consequences.

One way, retrospectively, of rationalizing Germany's victories in 1940 was to attribute them to a conscious military-economic strategy of 'Blitz-krieg'.[5] We have seen how the prospect of a prolonged war of attrition haunted the German leadership in the 1930s. The conclusion seemed inescapable that the Third Reich had deliberately set out to create a new kind of military organization, all clanking tanks and screaming Stukas, designed to deliver battlefield victory at a single lightning stroke. In this view, the events of 1940 were extraordinary, but they were explicable in terms of the success of Hitler's regime in devising a 'strategic synthesis': a coherent response to Germany's strategic dilemma, in which battlefield technology, military planning, diplomacy and military-economic prep-aration were welded together into a devastatingly effective unit.[6] This interpretation is appealing, since it appears to provide a rational expla-nation for otherwise inexplicable events. It gives an important role to economic policy, as part of a coherent strategic synthesis, and it con-forms to the newsreel image of the Blitzkrieg, as a battle dominated by the new technologies of the tank and the dive-bomber. In support of this view one can point to the fact that Hitler had been arguing at least since 1936 that time was not on Germany's side. When he talked about a war in the West he liked to talk in terms of 'surprise attacks'. It is also true that over the winter of 1939–40 he intervened decisively to force the German military to concentrate exclusively on the battle to be fought in the coming summer. But to infer from this that he had been consist-ently pursuing a strategy of Blitzkrieg is at odds both with what we know about the inner workings of the Nazi regime and the battlefield of 1940.

The German army that invaded France in May 1940 was far from being a carefully honed weapon of modern armoured warfare.[7] Of Germany's 93 combat-ready divisions on 10 May 1940, only 9 were Panzer divisions, with a total of 2,439 tanks between them. These units faced a French army that was more heavily motorized, with 3,254 tanks in total. Altogether, the Belgian, Dutch, British and French tank forces numbered no less than 4,200 vehicles, heavily outnumbering the Wehr-macht. And Germany's quantitative inferiority was not compensated for in qualitative terms. Whether we compare armaments or armour, the majority of the German tanks sent into battle in 1940 were inferior to their French, British or even their Belgian counterparts. Nor should one accept unquestioningly the popular idea that the concentration of the German tanks in specialized tank divisions gave them a decisive advantage. Many French tanks were scattered amongst the infantry units, but with their ample stock of vehicles the French could afford to do this. The bulk of France's best tanks were concentrated in armoured units that, on paper at least, were every bit a match for the Panzer divisions. Nor did the Luftwaffe, despite its fearsome reputation, have any numerical superiority. The Luftwaffe was rated at 3,578 combat aircraft in May 1940, compared to a total Allied air strength of 4,469 combat aircraft. French strength had been substantially bolstered by May 1940 through the delivery of more than 500 American aircraft, including high-quality fighters quite capable of scoring successes against complacent Luftwaffe intruders.[8]

In the light of these figures, German success clearly cannot be attributed to overwhelming superiority in the industrial equipment of modern warfare. It still might be true, of course, that Germany had been pursuing a concerted strategy of Blitzkrieg but had simply lacked the time to make good the substantial lead enjoyed by Britain and France in 1933. But if we review the haphazard development of German rearmament, discussed in detailed in previous chapters, it seems hard to find evidence for the 'strategic synthesis' claimed by proponents of the Blitzkrieg thesis. Though the acceleration and scale of armaments spending after 1933 was certainly impressive, what is most characteristic of Hitler's rearmament drive is the lack of any clear strategic rationale, the lack of a realistic vision of the war that Germany might actually expect to fight. The gigantic armaments plans of 1936 and 1938 were certainly not premised on any clear-sighted anticipation of the Blitzkrieg. They gave priority to equipping and training a large but only partially mechanized army, a strategic air force and a high seas fleet. As we have seen, in the first half of 1939 these programmes were thrown into disarray by the Reich's acute balance of payments problems. Amidst the procurement crisis of the summer of 1939, it is hard to discern any coherent strategy at all. The outbreak of war helped to concentrate minds and to put military expansion back into top gear. But, as the last chapter showed, even at this late date there is no evidence of a coherent Blitzkrieg conception animating the German armaments programme. As far as the army was concerned the top priority was claimed by ammunition, a decision which seemed to be inspired more by memories of 1914 than the anticipation of what happened in 1940. The huge investment made in the Ju 88 medium bomber was certainly motivated by contemporary faith in the effectiveness of bombing as a way of achieving lightning victory. But that was one aspect of the Blitzkrieg idea that was soon proved to be entirely illusory.

The lack of connection between Germany's military-industrial preparations and the battle that the Wehrmacht actually fought is even more apparent when we retrace the tortuous path of military decision-making.[9] Before September 1939, the German army had not actually drafted a plan for an offensive operation in France. Given the strength of the French army and its allies, this was not a military contingency that the German army liked to contemplate. The first plan, hurriedly drafted in October 1939, satisfied no one. But it was towards that scheme, with its short, northerly stab towards the Channel coastline followed by an aerial campaign against Britain, that German armaments production appears to have been directed as of December 1939. The plan's limited objectives were at odds with Hitler's repeatedly stated goal of finishing the war in the West with a single decisive blow. But it remained in force until the middle of February 1940, when two careless officers were shot down over French territory, carrying a briefcase of staff maps. It was this accident that opened the door to the bold alternative vision of an encircling move through the Ardennes forest, first developed by General Erich von Manstein, the brilliant Chief of Staff of Army Group A. In December 1939, Brauchitsch and Halder in army high command had rejected Manstein's suggestion as absurdly risky. It was not until the last week of February, after much cajoling by Hitler, that they finally agreed to commit the bulk of the German army to Manstein's 'sickel cut', the operation that was ultimately to bring them such stunning success. By that time, however, it was far too late for a further modification of the armaments programme. The lightning victory in France thus emerged not as the logical endpoint of a carefully devised strategic synthesis, but as an inspired, high-risk improvisation, a 'quick, military fix' to the strategic dilemmas, which Hitler and the German military leadership had *failed* to resolve up to February 1940.[10]

In retrospect, it suited neither the Allies nor the Germans to expose the amazingly haphazard course through which the Wehrmacht had arrived at its most brilliant military success. The myth of the Blitzkrieg suited the British and French because it provided an explanation other than military incompetence for their pitiful defeat. But whereas it suited the Allies to stress the alleged superiority of German equipment, Germany's own propaganda viewed the Blitzkrieg in less materialistic terms. Technological determinism, after all, would have been fundamentally at odds with the voluntarist and anti-materialist axioms of Nazi ideology. This was clearly on the minds of the Swiss censors in the summer of 1940, when they instructed their newspapers, one of the most important sources of neutral information in continental Europe, to give due credit to the 'stupendous *military* performance of the German army'.[11] A sense of even-handedness and balance could only be preserved if Germany's success were not attributed in a 'demeaning' manner 'to "the machine" and the "deployment of technology"'. To celebrate its triumph, the German army commissioned a film entitled *Sieg im Westen*.[12] As one would expect, the film presents a collage of newsreel footage, in which ample space is given to the dramatic advance of Germany's Panzer divisions. The war was certainly depicted as a war of movement, a war of machines. But in this respect the film does not discriminate. Whenever the French and British appear in the film, they too are represented first and foremost by their machinery. Tanks and aircraft were a common denominator in modern warfare. At no point does the film suggest that technical superiority was the cause of German victory. In so far as the film offers an explanation, it is precisely the opposite. By far the most dramatic sequence in the entire film captures a lone German engineer as he single-handedly demolishes a gigantic Belgian bunker. At a pivotal point towards the end, *Sieg im Westen* gives extended coverage to the German destruction of the Maginot Line. In a series of dramatic cuts it juxtaposes pre-war footage of the inside of the Maginot Line, which is designed to highlight the extraordinary industrial modernity of the fortifications with the heroic action of individual German soldiers in reducing them. Over the top of the action a voice-over intones: 'Young German men, filled with ideological fervour, overcome technology and material.' For Hitler, and not only for him, the victory of the Wehrmacht was the vindication of the superiority of the German race and the genius of his personal leadership. This was the victory that the glorious German army was always supposed to achieve, living proof of the connection between the Third Reich and the mythic moment of national creation in September 1870 on precisely the same battlefield, at Sedan.[13] It was in the wake of the French surrender that Field Marshal Keitel solemnly announced Hitler as the Greatest Military Leader of All Time (*Groesster Feldheer Aller Zeiten*, shortened in contemporary slang to Groefaz). In official statements, Oberkommando Wehrmacht attributed its victory to the 'revolutionary dynamic of the Third Reich and its National Socialist leadership'.[14] It was the victory in France which cemented the view that the Wehrmacht was invincible, that it could overcome any odds, a superiority complex that was to become a taken-for-granted assumption in German military planning. Ironically, in debunking the technological version of the Blitzkrieg myth, recent historical research has tended to side with the regime's own account of its victory.[15] One of the greatest victories in European military history was achieved against the odds, through the genius of General Manstein and the superior fighting power of the German troops. From there it is a short step to asserting that at this crucial juncture the balance of material forces made little or no difference to the outcome of the war, which in turn raises questions about the significance of the material balance in general. One is then left wondering why the Allies won at all.[16]

It is at this point that we must sound a note of caution. If it is true that Blitzkrieg was not the result of a carefully calculated strategic synthesis, there are also grounds for scepticism about an overly voluntarist reading of events in 1940. What we need to appreciate are the very precise conditions under which the talents and training of Germany's soldiers could achieve such dramatic effects.[17] Though there was no grand strategic synthesis, the success of Manstein's plan did depend to a significant degree on the mobilization of the German economy in 1939. And its success was even more dependent on the very specific geographic configuration of the Western European battlefield. To start with the most obvious point: though it is true that the overall figures for tank strength in May 1940 clearly show that Germany had not been single-mindedly building tanks since 1933, this should not lead us to ignore the significant contribution made by the rapid mobilization of German industry in 1939–40. Though Germany's overall tank strength in May 1940 was certainly not overwhelming, matters would have been far worse but for the tank production drive that began in the autumn of 1939. After the successful completion of the Polish campaign in October 1939, the tank forces of the German army were at a shockingly low ebb. The Wehrmacht had only 2,701 serviceable vehicles of which the vast majority were obsolete Mark I and Mark II models.[18] There were only 541 battleworthy medium tanks, suitable for use against France.[19] If this inadequate equipment had been thrown against the Allied defences on the Breda–Dyle line, as was intended by the original German plan of October 1939, the Wehrmacht would have been lucky to have come away with a draw.[20] Over the winter of 1939–40, tanks were never given the attention accorded to the Ju 88 or the ammunition programme, but the seven months between the end of the Polish campaign and the beginning of the battle for France nevertheless saw a radical improvement in the quality of the German armoured forces. By 10 May 1940, Germany's equipment with medium-heavy battle-tanks had almost tripled relative to the position at the end of the Polish campaign. Germany now had 785 Mark IIIs, 290 Mark IVs and 381 Czech medium tanks, 1,456 vehicles in total. None of these was a match for the heaviest French armour. Nor did the Germans have any anti-tank guns capable of stopping the Char B, as became evident in a number of shocking incidents when individual French tanks massacred entire columns of German infantry.[21] Nevertheless, with their well-designed fighting compartments and excellent radio equipment, Germany's Panzers by the spring of 1940 had the makings of a highly effective armoured force.

Everything depended on the way in which this force was deployed. In so far as there is a single explanation for Germany's stunning victory in France, it is the brilliant conception of Manstein's plan of attack. But, contrary to legend, this plan was governed neither by revolutionary new doctrines of mechanized warfare, nor by a mystical faith in the superiority of the German soldier.[22] Manstein's touchstone was the classic Napoleonic equation: achieve success by concentrating a greater weight of force than the enemy at a single point. It was a synthesis, in other words, of crude materialism and military art. Since Germany had no overall material superiority (it had a total of 135 divisions to the Allies' 151), local superiority could only be achieved through the greatest possible concentration and by the greatest possible surprise. It was the exquisite realization of these classic principles of operational doctrine, not superior equipment or morale, that explains the success of the Blitzkrieg. The crucial diversion was created by Army Group B with its attack into Holland and northern Belgium. This part of the operation involved only 29 German divisions. But it attracted the attention of no fewer than 57 Allied divisions, amongst them the cream of the French and British armies. To the south, along the whole exposed length of the Rhine valley, the Germans deployed only 19 second-rate units, whilst the French kept 36 divisions entombed in the massive concrete defences of the Maginot Line. On the flanks, therefore, the Germans stretched the odds against themselves, to nearly 2:1. In the Ardennes, this enabled them to concentrate no less than 45 crack divisions, against a Franco-Belgian defensive screen of only 18 second-rate units. Though they were inferior across the entire length of the line, consistent planning allowed the Germans at the point of attack to achieve a ratio in their favour of almost 3:1. In this sense, the German victory does not overturn the principle that numbers are decisive. It simply confirms the point that, in an evenly balanced situation, the material superiority necessary to achieving a decisive breakthrough can only be attained by maximum concentration of force. Furthermore, since the enemy cannot be assumed to be passive, this advantage can only be sustained by strategic deception and maximum speed of manoeuvre.

This in turn involved a substantial element of risk. Most fundamentally, the Germans started their attack on France without a single Panzer formation in reserve. To achieve massive numerical superiority at the crucial point, every single unit was committed to the fight from the first day. If the attack had failed, Germany would have had no mobile units with which to respond to a possible Allied counter-offensive. As far as the German army was concerned, this strategy succeeded brilliantly. The fighting was intense. The daily rate of losses was high, but since the battle was over in a matter of weeks, the total cost was more than acceptable. But what is often omitted from accounts of the German victory in May 1940 is the fact that the equation for the Luftwaffe was far less favourable.[23] The German air force was committed even more intensively to the initial assault than was the army. The Allies, by contrast, anticipating a long-drawn-out defensive campaign, kept a large part of their air forces in reserve. The result was to tilt the odds decisively in Germany's favour. But the price that Germany paid for its command of the skies was far higher than the price paid for victory on the ground. On 10 May alone, to establish air superiority on the first day of the operation, the Luftwaffe sacrificed no less than 347 aircraft, including virtually all of the transports used in the air landing operations in Holland and Belgium.[24] By the end of May, 30 per cent of the aircraft with which the Luftwaffe started the campaign were written off. Another 13 per cent had been seriously damaged.

The Germans not only committed all their tanks and planes. In strictest conformity with the Schwerpunkt principle, they committed them on an astonishingly narrow front. Within Army Group A's sector, the bulk of the armour was grouped together in a single giant formation, Panzer Group Kleist, consisting of 1,222 tanks, 545 half-tracks and 39,373 trucks and cars, as well as numerous ancillary engineering and anti-aircraft units.[25] If this mass had been deployed on a single road, starting on the border with Luxembourg, its tail would have stretched to Koenigsberg, 1,540 kilometres to the east. The reality was only a little less outlandish. In the first days of the campaign, Panzer Group Kleist forced its way towards the upper reaches of the Maas along only four narrow roads. Each of the four columns approaching the vital river crossings was nearly 400 kilometres long. And they were required to fight their way forward under extreme time-pressure. It was essential that the advance guard should reach the Maas river line, with sufficient strength to take the bridges, by the evening of 13 May. Otherwise, the Allies would have time to react to the Schwerpunkt and to re-establish their overall superiority. This extraordinary concentration of force involved huge risks. If Allied bombers had penetrated the German fighter screen over the Ardennes they could have wreaked havoc amongst the slow-moving traffic. Never before had so many motor vehicles been concentrated on such a small segment of the European road network, and the potential for gridlock loomed far larger amongst German worries than the supposedly impassable terrain of the Ardennes. On both 11 and 12 May 1940 the advance of Panzer Group Kleist threatened to degenerate into the world's worst traffic jam. A disaster was only prevented by energetic traffic management directed by staff officers shuttling back and forth on motorbikes and flying overhead in light aircraft. The success of the advance also depended critically on a precisely calculated logistical plan. Germany's stocks of petrol, which in May 1940 were sufficient to cover no more than five months of mobile warfare, were completely committed to ensuring the smoothest possible advance. Highly inflammable fuel tankers were interspersed with the fighting vehicles at the very front of the German armoured columns. All along the march routes there were pre-planned fuel dumps at which tank crews could grab jerrycans and dump empty containers for recycling. The crews refuelled on the road, whenever there was a stop in the traffic. And it was not just the vehicles that had to be kept going. The plan called for the German armoured columns to drive for three days and three nights without interruption. To ensure that the drivers could go without sleep, the quartermasters of the advanced units stocked up with tens of thousands of doses of Pervitin, the original formulation of the amphetamine now known as 'speed', but more familiar in the 1940s as 'tank chocolate' (*Panzerschokolade*).[26]

The assault by Army Group A was a manoeuvre of astonishing audacity, which continues to set the standard even for the high-tech military operations of the twenty-first century. But the impression of modernity and mobility that surrounded this entire operation was to a degree illusory. The petrol and amphetamines were reserved for a dozen or so assault divisions. The vast majority of German troops invaded France, Belgium and the Netherlands on foot, with their supplies moved forward from the railheads in the classic nineteenth-century manner, by horse and cart. Despite the quality of the logistical planning and the truly remarkable marching performance of the German infantry, success would not have been possible had it not been for the particular nature of the battlefield. The Channel coastline provided the German army with a natural obstacle against which to pin their enemies, an obstacle which could be reached within only a few hundred kilometres of the German border. At this range, a well-organized system of motorized re-supply could still function efficiently and the difference in the rate of advance between the Panzer units and the rest of the German army was not too glaring. In addition, the Germans benefited from a dense network of well-made roads and the ample resources of the rich Western European countryside to feed off as they marched. In Poland, in September 1939, the Wehrmacht had struggled to maintain the momentum of its motorized troops, when faced with far more difficult conditions. They would struggle again in the future.

The success of the German attack on France in May 1940 may, therefore, defy explanation in terms of a simple logic of 'brute force'. But to imagine that the balance of material forces was irrelevant to the outcome is to fall prey to voluntarism. The Wehrmacht did not overturn the basic rules of war. The victory of May 1940 is not a mysterious event explicable only in terms of the uncanny élan of the German army and the unwillingness of the French to fight. The odds facing Germany were not good. But they were not so bad that they could not be overcome by superior planning and manoeuvre. A close analysis of the mechanics of the Blitzkrieg reveals the astonishing degree of concentration achieved, but also the enormous gamble that Hitler and the Wehrmacht leadership were taking on 10 May. Precisely because it involved such a concentrated use of force, Manstein's plan was a 'one-shot affair'.[27] If the initial assault had failed, and it could have failed in many ways, the Wehrmacht as an offensive force would have been spent. The gamble paid off. But contrary to appearances, the Germans had not discovered a patent recipe for military miracles. The overwhelming success of May 1940, resulting in the defeat of a major European power in a matter of weeks, was not a repeatable outcome. In fact, when we appreciate the huge risks involved in Manstein's plan, the attack on France appears more similar to the Wehrmacht's other great gamble, the attack on the Soviet Union in June 1941, than is commonly supposed. On both occasions, the Wehrmacht held no significant forces in reserve. In both campaigns, the Germans gambled on achieving decisive success in the opening phase of the assault. Anything less spelled disaster. The very different outcomes are fully explicable in terms of conventional military logic. Against an opponent with a greater margin of material superiority, with better leadership and with more space in which to manoeuvre, the basic Napoleonic criterion for military success – superior force at the decisive point – would be far harder, if not impossible to achieve. Inspired soldiering could only do so much.

II

In the summer of 1940, however, unlike after the victory over Poland, the Wehrmacht was not much concerned with self-critical, after-the-battle analysis. The defeat of France had shifted the balance of power in Western Europe dramatically.[28] France, for so long the pre-eminent nation-state of continental Europe, was at a stroke reduced to the status of a second-class power. The Netherlands and Belgium, small European countries but holders of large colonial empires, were under German occupation. Britain was driven off the Continent. Across Europe, occupied and neutral countries alike began to gravitate around the new centre of power. For a brief period at least, Germany's hegemony was undisputed across the entirety of Europe, from the North Sea to the Black Sea, from the Baltic to the Strait of Gibraltar.

Even before the attack on France, Germany had diverted considerable military forces to secure its northern flank.[29] Swedish iron ore was simply too important to the German war economy for Scandinavia to be allowed to remain comfortably neutral. In 1940 more than half of Germany's iron ore needs were supplied by imports and 83 per cent of these imports came from Sweden. If Swedish ore deliveries had stopped in September 1939, German armaments production would have been subject to a drastic squeeze from the autumn of 1940, at the latest. Not that Hitler's regime had anything to fear from the Swedes.[30] Germany held the whip hand over Sweden, as over Switzerland, since both depended on Germany for their supplies of coal. As early as April 1939, the Social Democratic government in Stockholm had assured Berlin of its willingness to continue iron ore deliveries in the event of war. Sweden was not the problem. The problem was Norway, with its exposed North Sea coastline and in particular the port of Narvik, through which Swedish ore was shipped to Germany during the winter months. If the British seized control of Narvik, they could strangle the Ruhr before the real war had even started and this was clearly Churchill's intention. On 1 March Hitler therefore gave orders for the so-called 'Weser Exercise', the military occupation of Denmark to be combined with landings in Norway. Simultaneously, the British readied an expeditionary force to respond to any German intervention. Battle was joined in the approaches to Narvik on 9 April. After three months of confused fighting, the British were driven out and Germany's access to Swedish iron ore was secured for the duration of the war.

Germany acted with equal decisiveness in South-east Europe to secure its oil supplies from Romania.[31] In the first months of the war Britain and France had applied sustained pressure to Bucharest to reduce its exports to Germany.[32] By February, alarm bells were ringing in Berlin. Unless drastic measures were taken, Germany's petroleum stocks would fall to critical levels by the end of the summer.[33] From the beginning of 1940 onwards, therefore, the German Foreign Office and Admiral Wilhelm Canaris's Abwehr, the Wehrmacht intelligence service, threw themselves into a major counter-offensive. Playing cynically on Romania's fear of the Soviet Union, Hitler offered King Carol of Romania protection against Germany's own principal ally. In March 1940, the German Foreign Office began the process of rolling back Anglo-French dominance in the Ploesti oilfield, by concluding an unprecedented arms-for-oil deal.[34] Romania guaranteed Germany an increased supply of oil at preferential prices, in exchange for German protection and substantial deliveries of weapons, most of them taken from the Poles. This deal, however, was only provisional and was set to expire after only two months. Conveniently for the Germans, the negotiations for a more permanent arrangement started in early May. As news of the Panzer advance in France swept across the world's media, the attitude of the Romanian government became ever friendlier. Finally, on 27 May Bucharest hastily agreed to the oil pact (*Oelpakt*), which monopolized Romanian oil supplies for Germany. From July 1940 Romanian oil deliveries to Britain, which only a few months earlier had accounted for almost 40 per cent of Ploesti's production, came to a complete standstill. Germany, by contrast, could now count on steady deliveries of 200,000–300,000 tons of Romanian oil per month, which in the years to come were to form a mainstay of the German fuel supply.

The non-combatants and neutrals of Southern Europe moved in a similar fashion.[35] Most spectacularly, Mussolini reversed his position of the autumn of 1939 and declared war on France and Britain on 10 June 1940. More cautiously, General Franco shifted Spain's position from that of strict neutrality to a position of 'non-combatant'.[36] With the U-boats now free to operate from naval bases on the French Atlantic, even Portugal, Britain's oldest ally, felt the need to distance itself from London. A further telling symptom of the shifting balance of power was the new mood in Switzerland.[37] In the months following France's capitulation, voices were raised both in business circles and across a wide spectrum of right-wing politics arguing for a reassessment of Switzerland's neutrality. At a meeting of business interests in Berne in July 1940, one of the Generaldirektoren of the Schweizerischen Nationalbank put the case clearly: 'The events of the last week have thrown the order of things in Europe completely out of balance, and this, it appears to me, will not be a transient aberration. The world, and with it our country as well, is confronted with new circumstances, to which one will have to accommodate oneself.'[38] If Switzerland remained passive in relation to Germany's new power, it risked being marginalized: 'Our country will have to consciously seek out its place in this new world and must aim to play an active role in it.' In the summer of 1940, collaboration with Hitler's Germany was simply common sense. Swiss trade policy was significantly modified to grant more generous export credits to Berlin, whilst severely restricting 'strategic exports' to Britain. Under German pressure, the list of goods that Swiss businesses were free to export without official licences was reduced to only twenty-eight innocuous categories, including fresh and preserved fruit, embroidery and lace, straw products of all kinds, hats, stoves, ovens, washing-machines and white goods. Switzerland's high-precision machine tools and 20 millimetre anti-aircraft guns were reserved for Germany.[39]

Taken together, Greater Germany, the occupied territories and the neutrals aligned with Germany constituted a formidable bloc. France, Belgium, Luxembourg and the Netherlands all had important steel industries. They were sophisticated manufacturers of motor vehicles, weapons, aircraft, electronics and consumer goods of all kinds. France and Norway were also major producers of aluminium and chemicals. Added to the formidable industrial capacity of Germany, Austria, Polish Silesia, the Czech Protectorate and northern Italy, they had the potential to form a mighty economic bloc. If it had been possible to preserve activity at pre-war levels, the German European bloc would have comprised an economy with a combined GDP greater than that of either the United States or the British Empire.[40] It was a sphere of influence with a population of 290 million people, covering a territory only slightly smaller than the United States. If the French, Belgian, Dutch and Italian empires were included in the calculation, the proportions of the German domain could be made to seem even more impressive. Potentially at least, the German sphere of influence after the conquest of Western Europe extended to roughly a fifth of the world's population, approximately the same proportion of the inhabited territory of the Earth and 30 per cent of global GDP. For sheer size its only rival was the British Empire. And these comparisons do not include the Soviet Union or Imperial Japan, both of which were prospective allies of Nazi Germany. In the summer of 1940, of course, this bloc was not a consolidated entity. The future of the French, Belgian and Dutch empires was in question. Would they go over to the German side, would other predators such as Japan swallow them up, or might they choose to side with Britain? Furthermore, it was far from obvious that it would be possible to maintain the economic activity of the German power bloc at its pre-war level. However, these figures do give some sense of the massive shift in the global power balance threatened by Germany's Blitzkrieg victories.

In the summer of 1940 the profit from Germany's conquests was enough to make heads spin. Looting, even when done by Germans, is

Table 9. The new world order?

	Population (millions)	Territory (000 square kilometres)	GDP 1938 (million PPP dollars, 1990 prices)
Britain	48	245	284
British dominions	30	19,185	115
British colonies	454	14,994	285
British Empire Total	531	34,424	683
United States	131	7,856	800
Germany	69	470	351
Austria	7	84	24
Czechoslovakia	11	140	30
Poland	35	389	77
France	42	551	186
Netherlands	9	33	45
Belgium	8	30	40
Denmark	4	43	21
Norway	3	323	12
Finland	4	383	13
Hungary	9	117	24
Bulgaria	7	103	11
Yugoslavia	16	248	22
Romania	16	295	19
Switzerland	4	41	26
Sweden	6	449	30
Italy	43	310	141
European *Grossraum*	292	4,009	1,071
Italian colonies	9	3,488	3
French colonies	71	12,099	49
Dutch colonies	68	1,904	77
Belgian colonies	11	2,337	6
Possible Axis empire	159	19,828	134
Japan	72	382	169
Japanese colonies	60	1,602	63
USSR	167	21,176	359

Sources: M. Harrison (ed.), *The Economics of World War II* (Cambridge, 1998), 7–8; A. Maddison, *The World Economy: Historical Statistics* (Paris, 2003); SRA, *Statistisches Jahrbuch fuer das Deutsche Reich (1941/42)* (Berlin, 1942)

not an activity that lends itself to precise statistical enumeration. However, the value of goods seized by the victorious Wehrmacht was clearly enormous.[41] A French enumeration of goods taken by the Germans between 1940 and 1944 came to no less than 154 billion francs or 7.7 billion Reichsmarks, at official exchange rates.[42] Of this vast sum, a third was accounted for by French military equipment. Amongst army weapons this included 314,878 rifles, 5,017 artillery pieces, 3.9 million shells and 2,170 tanks.[43] Of the tanks, hundreds were still in use with the Wehrmacht in France and in the Balkans years later. Captured French artillery made an even more important contribution to the defence of the Nazi Empire. In March 1944, of the total German artillery park of 17,589 guns, no less than 47 per cent were of foreign origin and of these the largest number was French.[44] Another third of the German booty was accounted for by transport and communications equipment and services provided by the French railway. The largest items here were the thousands of locomotives and tens of thousands of freight cars 'borrowed' by the Reichsbahn. All in all, the French, Dutch and Belgian railways provided Germany with 4,260 locomotives and 140,000 wagons, figures that dwarfed the Reich's own investment in rolling stock in the 1930s. Next in the French list came raw materials valued at 13 billion francs, whose strategic importance to the Germans vastly exceeded their monetary value to their French owners. In France, Belgium and the Netherlands, the Wehrmacht took 81,000 tons of copper, enough to extend the Reich's stocks to eight months. The Germans also found enough tin and nickel to cover their needs for a full year. Crucially, the Germans captured substantial stocks of petrol and oil. By the end of 1940, thanks to ample deliveries from Romania, the booty taken in France and the low level of military activity in the second half of the year, the alarming decline in Germany's fuel stocks had been repaired. The main worry over the winter of 1940–41 was the problem of finding sufficient storage facilities.

III

Even before the shooting finished, the German Foreign Ministry, Goering's Four Year Plan, the Ministry of Economic Affairs and the Reichsbank began an urgent discussion about the future organization of the European economy.[45] The promptness with which this debate started clearly reflected the thinking that had been going on in Germany since the 1920s.[46] The guiding idea of this debate was the need to create a large, unified economic space comparable in size, population and resources to the British Empire and the United States. In the 1930s this had narrowed into a discussion focused above all on Germany's 'informal economic empire' in South-east Europe. This offered important raw materials and abundant supplies of agricultural produce. However, from a business point of view the Balkans were clearly a second best. The purchasing power of these poor states was simply too limited. Not surprisingly, therefore, once the Wehrmacht had cleared the way, Germany's economic think tanks rapidly shifted their attention towards the far more promising vistas of Western Europe. The severing of strong commercial and financial connections to France had been one of the principal costs of Germany's unilateralism since 1931. Reconnecting the French and German economies and combining them with the economic potential of Italy, Benelux and Scandinavia offered a far more alluring vision of economic *Grossraum* than anything that had seemed possible in the 1930s.

More generally, the feverish debate in the summer of 1940 also indicates the extreme tension that German economic policy had been under since the early 1930s.[47] In the wake of the Wehrmacht's stupendous victories, it now seemed possible that Germany might be in a position to cast off many of the burdensome regulations that had been plaguing German business since the banking and currency crisis of 1931. There was general agreement in Berlin that the corset of Schacht's New Plan was unbecoming for the future hegemon of Europe.[48] Reparations imposed on the defeated powers would alleviate Germany's acute shortage of foreign exchange. The Reichsbank would be equipped, at the expense of the other central banks of Europe, with a strategic currency reserve of at least 10 billion Reichsmarks. Britain would be required to shoulder responsibility for the odious 'political debts' of the 1920s. The Reich would even be in a position to reopen negotiations about the repayment of the American loans, frozen six years earlier. And having demonstrated its ability to live without the United States, Germany would negotiate from a position of strength. Perhaps most remarkably, the Reich Finance Ministry, which was concerned about the spiralling cost of the export subsidy system, even suggested that Germany ought to seize this moment of maximum strength and prestige to devalue the Reichsmark, thus rectifying the long-standing misalignment with the rest of the world's currencies.[49] Not surprisingly, this suggestion did not go far. The hour of victory was not the moment for a downward adjustment in the external value of the German currency. From now on it was the Reichsmark that would set the standard. A degree of overvaluation in relation to the European satellite economies was quite welcome, since it would facilitate cheap imports.[50] If the exchange rate of the Reichsmark and the dollar needed realigning, it was the dollar that would have to adjust.

The German Foreign Office was the most ambitious in its objectives. It wanted to take advantage of the unique moment offered by military victory to move rapidly towards customs and currency union with as many European countries as possible. But Denmark, the first country on which this approach was tried, evaded Germany's offer, and the Reichsbank, the RWM and the Four Year Plan were averse to any over-hasty extension of Germany's economic frontier. They preferred a gradualist approach with the first step being the incorporation of all of Western Europe into a centralized clearing system, which would enable multilateral settlement of debts whenever it suited Germany. This was imposed in August 1940 and became the basis for an ever more intensified incorporation of the European economies into Germany's sphere of influence. Though there were those who saw in the centralized clearing system a vision of the economic future, its immediate practical purpose was to provide Germany with a virtually unlimited trade deficit. The brutal logic of the wartime clearing system was spelled out with remarkable frankness by Dr Gustav Schlotterer, the young National Socialist civil servant, who was its principal architect.[51] Speaking in July 1940 to an audience of German businessmen, Schlotterer explained:

It is a matter of fact that we have a number of countries so firmly in our grip that we can face them with a very serious problem in relation to settlement [of the clearing deficits]. In Denmark and Norway, we have adopted the position that the balances in clearing trade [i.e. German deficits] are no longer an issue . . . Our tendency is to use sleight of hand, guile and possibly violence to get the European states to sell their goods to Germany, but to leave their credits, when they build up, in Berlin . . . We don't know how far we are going to be able to go with these ideas. But we reckon it should work in the case of the occupied countries.[52]

The best measure of the success of Schlotterer's cynical system was the gigantic deficit that Germany was able to accumulate by the end of the war. Normally, of course, private suppliers in France, Belgium or the Netherlands would not have been willing to go on delivering goods to a foreign customer that had tens of billions of Reichsmarks in unpaid bills. But since the 1930s the Reichsbank's clearing systems had been designed to remove any such obstacles. Exporters in each country were paid, not by their customers in Germany, but by their own central banks, in their own currency. The foreign central bank then chalked up the deficit to Germany's clearing account in Berlin. The Germans received their goods, the foreign suppliers received prompt payment, but the account was never settled. At the end of 1944, the Reichsbank recorded almost 30 billion Reichsmarks owing to members of the clearing system. France, Germany's largest trade creditor, was owed 8.5 billion Reichsmarks. Almost 6 billion Reichsmarks were outstanding to the Dutch. Five billion Reichsmarks were owed to Belgium and Luxembourg and 4.7 billion were outstanding on the Polish account.[53]

Though this system provided Germany with a large net trade deficit – in other words, a flow of goods and services unrequited by German exports – it would be misleading to suggest that trade within the Nazi Empire was all one way. In fact, German exports continued at an uncomfortably high level throughout the war. In this respect, Germany's experience was very different from that of Britain. Over the entire period of the war, the net foreign contribution to the British and German war economies was comparable, but Germany throughout the war maintained a far higher volume of exports than Britain. Relative to their level in 1938, Germany's exports in 1942 were twice as high as Britain's. In 1943 they were three times as high.[54] For German business this was no burden. On the contrary, Germany's exporters were keen to maintain their European customers and enjoyed the excellent profit margins provided by foreign trade. But for the German war effort, every ton of goods exported was a net loss. Exports were sustained because they were functionally and politically necessary. Germany exported to its allies, to prop up their war economies and their standards of living. With allies such as Romania, Italy, Finland and Croatia, and with important neutrals such as Sweden and Turkey, Germany maintained a balanced trade account.[55] In this respect, 1940 marked a sharp reversal of Germany's trading position. Whereas Germany's deficits in the 1930s had been disproportionately with its South-eastern European satellites, it now paid for their military loyalty with proportionally greater exports. Germany's largest clearing deficits were with the newly occupied Western territories. Norway and the General Government were the exceptional cases of occupied territories with which Germany ran a net trade surplus, an indication of the extreme vulnerability of these small economies to the effects of blockade and occupation. But even in those cases where Germany did build up large net deficits, it continued to reciprocate to at least some extent with exports, most importantly in relation to France. It did so, not for political reasons, but because the French economy, having lost its connections to Britain, was simply not capable of functioning without a flow of imports from Germany, a point to which we shall return.[56]

Apart from the reorganization of European trade by means of the clearing system, the other key element in the German programme for the subordination of the European economy was the penetration of German capital into the businesses of Western Europe. Unsurprisingly, IG Farben, as Germany's largest firm and a key player in the world's chemical industry, was an active participant. IG used its long-standing contacts in the international dye cartel, to assume control of the French industry by means of the Francolor dye trust.[57] No less significant was the wholesale reappropriation of the heavy industry of Alsace and Lorraine by German corporations. The German firms that had lost plants in Lorraine when the territory was transferred to France by the Treaty of Versailles reclaimed control of their historic interests.[58] But it was not just formerly German steel mills and mines that were at stake. After 1940, no French firm was to be allowed to hold a controlling stake in any part of German industry, including businesses in those areas recently annexed to the Reich. Though the final legal settlement was postponed until after the war, the race was opened for the substantial French industrial interests in Lothringen.[59] Not surprisingly, the Reichswerke Hermann Goering was awarded the biggest prize, the de Wendel mining and steel conglomerate, and Flick was rewarded for his services to Goering with the award of the Rombacher Huette. But other bidders for French assets, most notably Roechling, the bastion of Germanism of the Saar, were disappointed. Outside Lothringen, the Germans did not engage in wholesale expropriation of private assets, with the sole exception of Jewish property, which was rapidly Aryanized across all the occupied territories. Particularly in the Netherlands this involved the transfer of a large part of the retail and banking sector into German hands.[60] But nowhere did Jewish shares account for a significant fraction of industrial capital. The major industrial firms that the Germans were able to seize were those which had been state controlled before the occupation, or which had previously been foreign-owned, such as the electrical engineering firm Thomson's in France.[61] It was by taking 'trusteeship' of foreign interests that Germany was able to dominate Norway's aluminium and electricity generating industry.[62] In the Netherlands, Rheinmetall was able to get its hands on the two largest engineering firms, NV Werkspoor and the Staatlichen Artillerie Inrichtingen, by taking over state holdings. Algemene Kunztzide Unie (AKU), the Dutch synthetic fibres firm, also came under German influence.[63] By contrast, Holland's great multinationals – Phillips, Unilever and Shell – all evaded German penetration, by transferring ownership to offshore offices. Neither in Belgium nor in unoccupied France did German capital make significant inroads. Most notably, perhaps, the great cross-border steel giant, Arbed, third only to the Vereinigte Stahlwerke and the Reichswerke amongst the giants of European heavy industry, evaded a swarm of German suitors.[64] The firm dominated the economy of Luxembourg but was controlled by Belgian interests led by the mighty Société Générale of Brussels. In the end, the Reichswerke, Vereinigte Stahlwerke, Mannesmann, the Dresdner and Deutsche banks were all outmanoeuvred by Alexandre Galopin, the supremely self-confident boss of the Société. After 1941, Arbed operated under close German supervision, but it remained an independent force in the politics of European heavy industry.

This frustration of German capital penetration was the result of local obstruction and the reluctance of the Germans to impose 'colonial-style' expropriations on their West European neighbours. But one must also bear in mind the macroeconomic context. As Hermann Abs, a leading director of the Deutsche Bank, reminded a meeting of German bankers in October 1940, buying large slices of foreign assets involves the export of capital.[65] Under normal circumstances, a country can only maintain a significant net export of capital if it is running a current account surplus. To have mounted a bid for ownership of a significant slice of the Western European economy, Germany would have needed to mount an export offensive. In the autumn of 1940, Abs could see the possibility of this, but only if there was a significant reduction in the demands of the war effort. In other words, the financial precondition for a truly significant capital offensive was a victorious peace. In the autumn of 1940, however, spending on the Wehrmacht and military-economic projects was accelerating and Germany's current account was being deliberately run deep into the red. Germany was not acquiring claims on the Western European economies. Western European countries, through their clearing credits to Germany, were acquiring ever larger claims on Germany. The only reason why this multi-billion-Reichsmark deficit did not manifest itself in private debts and transfers of German assets into foreign hands, as had happened under the Weimar Republic, was the peculiar structure of the clearing system. Germany's clearing debts were owed not by private German firms, but by the Reich. The debt was accumulating nevertheless and by the later stages of the war the Reichsbank was so concerned about its mountain of external liabilities that it even gave serious consideration to the proposal that Germany should settle at least part of its clearing debts by offering its Western European trading partners large packages of German shares.[66] In other words, the conquered territories would acquire stakes in German business, not the other way round. Not surprisingly, this idea was rejected. But it indicates the futility of trying to mount a bid for ownership of the European economy, whilst at the same time running a mammoth current account deficit.

Of course, Germany did have a way of squaring the circle. To provide itself with the necessary funds both to run a large trade deficit and buy foreign shares it needed only to impose 'reparations' on the occupied territories. In the final account, it was 'reparations' rather than the clearing debts that dominated the transfer of resources from the occupied territories to Germany. Since reparations were in bad odour following Versailles, and since Germany was not interested in concluding formal peace treaties until it had achieved total victory, payments to Germany took the form of 'occupation costs', credited to Germany on a regular basis from the summer of 1940 onwards by Poland and all the Western European states.[67] Clearly Germany did incur substantial costs in maintaining hundreds of thousands of soldiers in garrisons stationed across its new empire. And these costs escalated rapidly once the Luftwaffe began building air bases and the navy began constructing giant U-boat pens all along the coastline of the Atlantic and the North Sea. In 1943 and 1944, the construction of the monstrous Atlantikwall against Allied invasion added further to the bill.[68] However, it was clear from the outset that the sums demanded by Germany were far in excess of anything that could be immediately consumed by the military. The French estimated that the 20 million Reichsmarks per day demanded from them should have been enough to sustain an army of 18 million men. Even allowing for the fact that the Wehrmacht lived liked 'kings in France', there was clearly money to spare. The precise uses to which this gigantic flow of funds was put were opaque, even to the Wehrmacht.[69] But it is clear that much of the money was used for further German imports and that in excess of 1 billion Reichsmarks were used to pay for the purchase of raw materials and consumer goods on the black market.[70] In any case, the totals paid towards occupation costs were so large that they clearly exceeded even the large deficits piling up in the clearing accounts.

Since the demands for occupation costs were enormous, the Germans helpfully suggested to France, their most important victim, that they would be willing to take payment in the shares of French companies, at a somewhat reduced rate. If pushed to the limit this would certainly have provided a mechanism for a wholesale transfer of capital, but the French resisted the invitation, at least with regard to French firms. What they did reluctantly agree to sell were French interests in Eastern and South-eastern Europe.[71] Since the late nineteenth century French capital had bankrolled the industrial development of much of Eastern Europe. Famously, a large part of this investment had been lost in the aftermath of the Russian Revolution. But in the inter-war years French bankers retained important though largely loss-making interests in Polish heavy industry, in Yugoslavia and Romania. By the end of 1941 these shares were transferred to Germany in lieu of reparations. Most important from the German point of view was the substantial French stake in the Romanian oil industry, which formed the basis for Germany's newly founded 'oil multinational', the Kontinentale Oel AG.[72] Also of vital strategic significance were the French interests in the Mines de Bor in Yugoslavia, Europe's largest copper mine. Since 1939 the French interest had been used to artificially restrict Yugoslav copper deliveries to Germany. Now the mine was transferred completely to German control. In all three cases, however, it was not private German interests that were the principal beneficiaries. The real driving force of German corporate imperialism in the 1940s were entities such as the Reichswerke Hermann

Table 10. Like 'kings in France'

Million RM (per quarter)	Occupation levy on France	Addition to French clearing surplus
III/1940	249	
IV/1940	1,510	43
I/1941	1,208	76
II/1941	1,295	146
III/1941	1,331	262
IV/1941	1,253	327
I/1942	1,657	409
II/1942	1,812	336
III/1942	2,209	408
IV/1942	2,194	555
I/1943	2,645	769
II/1943	2,240	908
III/1943	2,418	845
IV/1943	2,495	793
Overall total	24,516	5,877

Source: A. S. Milward, *The New Order and the French Economy* (Oxford, 1984), 279

Goering, or Kontinentale Oel, hybrids that included private industrial interests, but which were dominated by party men operating under the protection of Hermann Goering.[73]

I V

Germany's victory over France gave it a remarkable position of power on the Continent of Europe. However, it was clear that its long-term plans all depended on the final outcome of the war. In the full flush of victory in the last days of May 1940, the Wilhelmstrasse made its sketches of the future *Grossraum* on the assumption that the British Empire would soon come to terms. And in the weeks following the

French collapse, Hitler clearly did hope that Britain would react to the loss of its major continental ally by accepting Germany's offer of an Imperial partnership. Britain would retain its Empire in return for its acceptance of German domination of the European continent, allowing Hitler finally to realize the blueprint of *Mein Kampf*. However, even without Churchill's decisive leadership, there was little prospect of the British cabinet ever accepting such an agreement. In the hope of American backing, London by the end of May 1940 had already decided to reject any offer of a negotiated peace.[74] Britain would continue to resist German domination of Europe and act as a rallying point for anti-Nazi forces across the Continent. And the signs from Washington, certainly as seen through German eyes, were ominous. Roosevelt had launched America on its own all-out rearmament programme and on 19 July, in announcing his candidacy for a third term, he re-emphasized his unrelenting hostility to Germany. For Germany's embattled embassy in Washington the situation was clear: 'As an exponent of Jewry . . . Roosevelt wants England to go on fighting and to prolong the war . . . until the armaments effort of the United States is fully in gear . . .' 'Never before has Roosevelt's responsibility for the outbreak and prolongation of the war been more obvious.'[75] Roosevelt's latest pronouncements merely confirmed his role as an agent of the anti-German world Jewish conspiracy.[76]

Faced with this obstacle, Hitler chose once more to resume the offensive. On 12 July he ordered the wholesale redirection of the German armaments effort towards the navy and the Luftwaffe, the weapons required to subdue Britain.[77] Word went out to Walther Funk, the skittish head of the civilian economic administration, that any talk of an imminent end to the war and a rapid return to the conditions of a peacetime economy was premature. By August, this was reinforced by the instruction to the Wehrmacht to prepare itself for an attack on the Soviet Union. Along with the expansion of the navy and the air force, the army was now to be reinforced as well. And it was under the pressure of intensified rearmament that Goering issued his Decree of 26 August 1940 demanding an intensified exploitation of the occupied territories: 'It is a political necessity in order to fulfil orders placed for the further conduct of the war that the capacity and raw materials of the occupied Western territories should be employed in a planned way and to do as much as possible to support German armaments production and to increase war potential.'[78]

As the euphoric summer months wore into the autumn, the world's most sophisticated barometers of public opinion, the Gallup polling organization in the United States and the Gestapo in Germany, registered inverse movements in the public mood. By September the Gestapo was reporting a growing impatience amongst the German public whose great hope had been that victory on the Continent would translate into an imminent end to the war with Britain. By October optimistic impatience was giving way all over Germany to uncertainty, resignation and increasing indifference.[79] Conversely, in the United States, Gallup opinion pollsters registered a dramatic rebound between June and August 1940 in public confidence in ultimate British victory.[80] Whereas in the immediate aftermath of the defeat of France, Americans had been evenly divided on the likely outcome of the war, by the autumn those expecting an eventual British victory again outnumbered those expecting German success, by a margin of three to one. Despite the Wehrmacht's triumph in France, British recalcitrance exposed the fundamental problem of German strategy. Hitler had unleashed a war with Britain without a coherent plan as to how to defeat that country.[81] The superiority of the German army was unquestionable. But how could it be brought to bear? This was the question that haunted German strategy over the next twelve months.

I 2

Britain and America: Hitler's
Strategic Dilemma

In July 1940, in a desperate bid to unhitch the Soviet Union from its pact with Germany, Churchill sent Stafford Cripps, his new ambassador in Moscow, to a meeting with the Soviet dictator. To Cripps, Stalin explained with chilling clarity the logic that had motivated his agreement with Hitler eleven months earlier. The Soviet aim had been to upset the balance of power in Europe and in this the Hitler–Stalin pact had succeeded brilliantly. When Cripps replied that the Soviet alliance with Hitler had in fact destroyed any kind of balance in Europe and that the entire Continent was now threatened by German hegemony, Stalin snapped back: 'I am not so naive as to believe the German assurances that they have no desire for hegemony, but what I am convinced of is the physical impossibility of such hegemony, since Germany lacks the necessary seapower.'[1] Stalin was surely right.[2] Germany's victories in the West had shaken the structure of European power to its foundations, but any talk of German hegemony was premature. As desperate as the British situation clearly was in the summer of 1940, the Third Reich had neither finished the war nor won it.

Far-sighted observers on all sides had sought to avoid a major war in the 1930s, precisely because they could see no way that any of the European powers could benefit from such a conflict. The most likely outcome was a bloody impasse, which could result only in common ruin. They had been wrong about the nature of the land battle. The defeat of France in a matter of weeks was a devastating surprise. But by the autumn of 1940 the war had nevertheless reached a point of stalemate. Britain and Germany faced each other, with neither side having the weapons necessary to force a decision. For Britain, the situation was clearly ruinous. If it was to survive as a great power it had no option but to continue fighting. To do so, however, required Britain to throw itself on the mercy of the United States.[3] Germany's situation was clearly far more comfortable. But once Roosevelt was safely re-elected in November 1940 and the Anglo-American alliance began to take on concrete form, the Third Reich too faced an acute strategic dilemma.[4] In the short term neither Britain nor America posed a direct military threat. But in the medium term, their enormous economic potential made them enemies that had to be taken extremely seriously.

I

To launch an invasion of Britain, Germany needed control of the Channel by air and sea. Despite the euphoria that followed the victory parades of July 1940, these basic preconditions for the defeat of Britain were never met.[5] At no point in the war did Germany assemble the naval or aerial forces necessary to dominate the British Isles though this was not for lack of trying. The task was simply beyond Germany's industrial resources. The deficiency was most extreme with regard to the navy. In September 1939 the gulf between British and German naval power had been enough to cast Admiral Raeder into a suicidal mood. After the losses incurred in the course of the Norwegian campaign, the situation was even worse. To secure the iron ore of Sweden, the German navy paid an exorbitant price.[6] On the first day of operation Weser-Uebung, the Oslo garrison ignominiously dispatched Germany's newest heavy cruiser, the *Bluecher*, with an ancient coastal battery bought second-hand from Krupp. Then the Royal Navy sank the entire fleet of ten modern destroyers that had delivered the German landing party to the Narvik fjords. Finally, Raeder sent two more heavy cruisers into Norwegian waters, the *Gneisenau* and the *Scharnhorst*, only for them to be disabled by British torpedoes. Coming on top of the scuttling of the *Graf Spee*, these losses were crippling. By June 1940, as the German army romped across France, the German surface navy had been eliminated as a significant factor in the conflict. When the time came to consider the possibility of a cross-Channel invasion, all Admiral Raeder could offer by way of protection was one heavy cruiser, two light cruisers and four modern destroyers. By comparison, the British Home Fleet alone mustered 5 battleships, 11 cruisers and a rapid reaction force of no less than 30 destroyers based within easy reach of the invasion beaches, and this was only a fraction of British naval power.[7] Even during the most anxious months of the summer of 1940, the Admiralty kept at least half of the fleet in Gibraltar, ready for offensive operations against the Italians, rather than defence against the improbable contingency of a German invasion.

In the summer of 1940, Admiral Raeder and the Kriegsmarine did step up their planning for the construction of a new generation of giant battleships.[8] But these would take years to come to fruition and, given Britain's overwhelming initial advantage, they were a distraction from the real contest. As should have been obvious from the start, Germany's only hope of mounting a direct challenge to the supremacy of the Royal Navy was to embark systematically on the design and construction of what British naval strategists referred to as a 'freak' fleet.[9] Apart from submarines, a crucial component of such an unconventional force would have been a significant number of super-fast cruisers, designed specifically to distract and to disperse the Royal Navy's lumbering battle groups. Given that U-boat technology had failed to advance significantly since World War I, success with submarines alone was never thought probable. By 1940 the chance to concentrate on the construction of battlecruisers had been squandered. At the same time, however, the conquest of the North Sea and Atlantic coastline transformed the operational possibilities of the German navy. The question has therefore to be asked: why did Germany not commit itself in the summer of 1940 to an all-out U-boat campaign?[10] Churchill certainly regarded the 'Wolf-packs' preying on the trans-Atlantic supply lines as the most serious threat to Britain's survival. In Berlin, the case for the U-boats was consistently argued by Admiral Karl Doenitz, the commander of the German submarines and a fanatical National Socialist.

At the start of the war, Britain disposed of no less than 18 million tons of domestically owned shipping. It had the option of leasing or chartering many millions more. British shipyards were capable of turning out more than a million new tons every year. More could be ordered in the United States. To achieve decisive success against this formidable volume of shipping, Doenitz calculated that his crews would need to sink at least 600,000 tons per month for a period of at least a year. To 'force England to its knees' Germany would need at least 300 U-boats sufficient to ensure that 100 were operational in the North Atlantic at any one time. But this, like every other strategic option, was a question of resources and timing. The German navy started the war with just 57 U-boats, of which 32 were capable of operating in the Atlantic. After the cancellation of the Z Plan in early September, the navy did its best to adjust to the new realities. On 10 October 1939 Raeder presented Hitler with a plan to construct 658 U-boats, enough, allowing for losses, to reach Doenitz's target by the end of 1942. The cost of each U-boat was tiny when compared to the cost of a single battleship – between 2 and 4 million Reichsmarks per boat, as compared to over 200 million for a battleship of the *Bismarck* class.[11] But to build hundreds of submarines was not a minor undertaking. Apart from the initial outlay of billions of Reichsmarks, U-boats were disproportionately demanding of raw materials, particularly copper and rubber, both of which were in extremely short supply in the first winter of the war.[12] Furthermore, the concrete infrastructure required by such a large U-boat fleet was an extremely daunting proposition. In advance of the attack on France, the Reich could not afford a long-term programme of this kind. Priority had to be given to the immediate needs of the army and the Luftwaffe. For lack of labour and raw materials, only 20 U-boats were produced between September 1939 and June 1940. Given the steady rate of U-boat losses, the number of boats actually available in the Atlantic fell by the summer of 1940 to only 25. By March 1940, this tiny force had managed to sink almost 680,000 tons of British shipping.[13] But this was no more than a small dent in Britain's fleet.

In July 1940 Hitler did briefly assign highest priority in the German armaments effort to the U-boat programme.[14] Tens of thousands of tons of steel were reallocated from the army's ammunition production to U-boat building. Production targets were raised to 25 U-boats per month. But, the naval bonanza did not last. By the autumn of 1940, the priority had again reverted to the army and actual U-boat deliveries between June 1940 and March 1941 came to only 72, of which the majority were needed for training. The number of U-boats operating in the Atlantic continued to fall, reaching a low point of only 22 in February 1941.[15] With growing experience and good luck this fleet did terrible damage, sinking over 2 million tons of British shipping between June 1940 and March 1941. In the spring of 1941, before the United States began to intervene decisively in the naval war, it did briefly seem as though British supply lines might be severed. However, thanks to Enigma decrypts, aggressive new convoy tactics and the growing involvement of the Americans, the balance soon swung back against the U-boats. By the summer of 1941 losses of British shipping were safely below 100,000 tons per month. This was nowhere near enough to achieve a rapid result. And ultimately it was the time-factor that told most decisively against the U-boat strategy.[16] In the optimistic summer months of 1940, Doenitz estimated that, with a full fleet of U-boats, he might be able to complete the isolation of Britain by the autumn of 1941.[17] It would then take many more months to starve the British out. This was not what Hitler needed. He was looking to decide the war on a much shorter timescale. Germany's strategic dilemma in the summer of 1940 was not merely how to defeat Britain. The problem was how to neutralize Britain before America could intervene decisively on its side. Unleashing the U-boats against the Anglo-American umbilical cord was certainly the most direct approach to this problem. But it was not quick-acting and it was the strategy that bore the highest risk of bringing down upon Germany the full weight of American power.

To achieve a rapid victory over Britain without further exacerbating tension with the United States, Hitler looked to the Luftwaffe. In Churchill's high-flown rhetoric, the clash between the Luftwaffe and the Royal Air Force in August and September 1940 was made to appear as a decisive turning point of the war.[18] But in retrospect it seems an extremely one-sided affair. Even before Adlertag, 13 August, the official beginning of the German air offensive, the Luftwaffe had suffered serious attrition.[19] As we have seen, the operation in France had cost the Luftwaffe almost 30 per cent of its initial strength. And fighter losses continued at a high rate throughout the summer. The aircraft could be replaced, the pilots could not. The initial impact of the German aerial onslaught on Britain was severe. In the last days of August, RAF fighter command was stretched dangerously thin. But the Luftwaffe lacked the equipment with which to deliver a fatal blow. Nor can this be blamed on any peculiar failing of German planning or preparation. To do the job, the Luftwaffe would have needed a much larger and more powerful fleet of bombers and plenty of long-range fighter escorts. As the great daylight battles on 15 August and 15 September 1940 proved, the Luftwaffe's existing escort fighters were hopelessly inadequate to the task. Of the force dispatched from Norway on 15 August, the Luftwaffe lost 20 per cent. For effective nighttime bombing, judging by the experience of RAF Bomber Command, Goering would have needed a huge fleet of heavy bombers. In 1938 the Reich Air Ministry had asked for a fleet of 500 He 177s, for completion by 1941–2.[20] But there were technical problems with Heinkel's design. And even if these had been resolved, 500 by 1941–2 was too little, too late. Much has been made of the disparity in German and British aircraft production during the critical months of the Battle of Britain. In the second half of 1940, desperate efforts on the part of the British enabled them to produce twice as many fighters as the Germans, which was no doubt reassuring in giving the RAF an extra margin of security.[21] But this was hardly decisive to the outcome of the battle. The fundamental point was simple: in 1940 neither Britain nor Germany had developed the technology nor had they mobilized the resources necessary to provide the kind of smothering air superiority that would make a cross-Channel invasion into a viable proposition.

By September 1940, Hitler thus faced a real strategic dilemma. The German army had proved itself devastatingly effective, but both the navy and the Luftwaffe had failed. Against Britain, Germany's one decisive weapon could not be brought to bear. The British, of course, were in a far more serious position. The army was without weapons. The Royal Navy and Royal Air Force were largely restricted to defensive duties. But nevertheless, Britain continued to pose a threat to the Third Reich. The Royal Navy blockade continued to impose painful restrictions on Germany's continental *Grossraum*.[22] To strike at Germany itself, the British in the autumn of 1940 embarked on the enormous task of building an air fleet of heavy bombers with which Churchill hoped to 'pulverize the entire industry and scientific structure on which the war effort and economic life of the enemy depend . . .'.[23] To achieve this outcome, the RAF estimated that it would need a front-line strength of at least 4,000 medium and heavy bombers, four times the number that Hitler had been able to launch against Britain in 1940.[24] There was no thought in 1940 of any imminent British return to Europe. Contrary to later legend, D-Day was not on Churchill's mind. But Italy's declaration of war in June 1940 did at least allow the land armies of the British Empire to be directed against the 'soft underbelly' of the Axis. By the end of January 1941 British Imperial forces had defeated the Italian colonial army in North Africa and were poised to seize control of the entire southern coastline of the Mediterranean.[25] A month later they completed the destruction of the Italian Empire in East Africa. Ethiopia was liberated from the genocidal regime imposed on it by the Fascist conquest of 1936–8. In April 1941 decisive German intervention tilted the balance back towards the Axis with Erwin Rommel taking charge of a combined German and Italian force based on Tripoli. In addition, the Wehrmacht drove the British out of Greece and took Crete with dramatic parachute landings. But in strategic terms these Axis triumphs were less significant than Britain's success between May and July 1941 in putting down the German-sponsored insurgency in Iraq and seizing Syria from Vichy forces. In military terms these encounters may have been relatively minor. But they ensured that the African possessions of Italy, France and Belgium would not be combined into a single Axis empire and consolidated Britain's grip on the vital Suez Canal zone. With Britain entrenched on both sides of the Indian Ocean, a blocking position was established between Germany's European empire and Japan in the East. This in turn enabled President Roosevelt to declare the approaches to the Suez Canal no longer a war zone, removing the legal obstacles that prevented American shipping from making direct deliveries to the forces of the British Empire in Egypt.

No one, of course, imagined that these gains promised imminent victory. But Britain had decisively affirmed its determination to continue the fight. And for Hitler this posed a fundamental strategic problem. For, as long as Britain remained in the war, the United States had a means through which to project its awesome industrial power against Nazi Germany.

II

In the summer of 1940 this might seem a distant prospect. The spotlight was on the German armies parading down the Champs-Elysées. However, viewed from the perspective of the early twenty-first century, the German triumphs of 1940 seem less significant than the decisions that they precipitated in Washington. Alarmed by Germany's bid to overturn the balance of power in Europe, the Roosevelt administration, backed by a bi-partisan majority in Congress, took urgent steps to transform the United States into the pre-eminent military superpower that it remains today. The sequence of events was rapid. On 16 May 1940, three days after Kleist's Panzer Group A had broken through on the river Maas, President Roosevelt put before Congress the proposal to construct the world's largest military-industrial complex, a manufacturing base capable of supplying the United States with no less than 50,000 aircraft per year.[26] Roosevelt picked this number out of the air and it was unclear how it would be put into practice. But he made his point. The Luftwaffe and the RAF, even in their wildest moments, had never conceived of aircraft production on this scale. 'Fifty thousand per year' was less a planning target than a statement of American industrial supremacy. Only a few weeks later, Congress approved the Two Oceans Navy Expansion Act, which laid the foundations for the vast carrier-fleets with which the United States still projects force into every corner of the globe. There followed over the summer the unprecedented introduction of a peacetime draft, designed to raise a trained force of 1.4 million men.[27] By 1941, America, a nation still at peace, was producing almost as much weaponry as either Germany or Britain and was doing so whilst at the same time enjoying the first sustained increase in civilian consumption since the late 1920s.[28]

What was ominous from the German point of view was that this enormous accumulation of force was ultimately directed across the Atlantic, in support of Britain and its war against Hitler.[29] Britain's willingness to go on resisting Germany depended critically on the assumption that the United States would provide it with massive material aid. At first, of course, Britain would have to pay. Britain, unlike Germany, was not bankrupt. In 1939 it was still a large international creditor with foreign assets estimated at c. $5 billion (15–20 billion Reichsmarks), enough to match an entire year of German armaments output with purchases from abroad. But to defeat Germany, Britain would clearly need far more.[30] The premise of British strategy was therefore, as Churchill put it to Roosevelt, that Britain would pay for as much as it could, but that 'when we can pay no more you will give us the stuff all the same'. Perhaps not surprisingly, Roosevelt did not reply to this bold statement of British dependence. The tortured politics of World War I war debts were still fresh in the memory.[31] Britain was to be driven to the point of financial exhaustion before Congress opened the floodgates of lend-lease in the spring of 1941. London, therefore, had every reason to be nervous. But Churchill's gamble was clearly based on a fundamentally correct strategic assessment. Roosevelt had had his heart set on a major American contribution to the air effort against Germany since at least November 1938.[32] By the autumn of 1940 it was not hard to convince a large majority of Americans that they had a stake in Britain's survival. Following his triumphant re-election in November Roosevelt openly committed America to providing Britain with 'all support short of war'. The British would do the fighting, but the Americans would provide them with 'the means to do the job'.

Whatever the political difficulties of the Anglo-American alliance, the total volume of foreign resources that Britain was able to draw on during the emergency of 1940 and 1941 was remarkable, a fact that is too often ignored in comparisons of the relative rate of German and British mobilization in the early phases of World War II.[33] For all Churchill's rhetoric of blood, sweat and tears, Britain never matched Germany in its mobilization of domestic resources.[34] What allowed Britain to dramatically close the gap on German armaments production in the early years of the war was the readiness with which it could draw on the Empire and the United States. In 1940, imports from abroad, whether paid for in cash or through loans, accounted for no less than one-third of the British war effort. By contrast, though Germany now controlled all of Western Europe, it faced considerable difficulties in mobilizing the conquered territories for the purposes of the war. In explaining Germany's ability to defeat France in May 1940, the macroeconomic aggregates may not help us very much.[35] But what they certainly do help us to understand is why Britain went on fighting, denying Hitler the chance to turn his stunning Blitzkrieg victory into a conclusive and victorious end to the war.[36]

In the desperate summer of 1940 the denuded British army was re-equipped with a hoard of 1918-vintage rifles, machine guns and field guns from American stores. In August, Britain's convoy strength was bolstered by the negotiation of the famous 'destroyers for bases deal'.[37] The United States provided 50 World War I destroyers in exchange for naval bases in Newfoundland, the Caribbean and the British Atlantic islands. But what is less widely appreciated is the extent to which Anglo-American joint planning had already begun to go beyond these emergency measures. As early as the summer of 1940 the British and Americans were moving towards a concerted strategy to defeat Germany in the air war, by means of a completely unprecedented expansion in the production of aircraft and aero-engines.[38] Given the wider uncertainties that surrounded the Anglo-American relationship at this early stage, these talks were shrouded in secrecy and limited to technical issues. But they bore abundant fruit. The evidence from the record of aircraft production is inescapable. The dramatic surge in American aircraft output from the last quarter of 1941 onwards, which tipped the balance decisively against the Luftwaffe, cannot be explained except by reference to an expansion in factory capacity that must have begun at the latest by the autumn of 1940, well before the announcement of lend-lease, let alone Pearl Harbor.[39] And this focus on the air war was no accident. As we have seen, the aircraft industry was at the very heart of the modern military-industrial complex. It was no coincidence either that in Nazi-dominated Europe it was the Luftwaffe which took the lead in seeking ways to mobilize the economies of occupied Europe.[40] But though the logic impelling both sides was the same, the contrast in the scale of their possibilities was quite remarkable.

France was pivotal to both sides. As Europe's third largest industrial economy, France had a substantial aircraft and aero-engine industry, potentially capable of producing thousands of aircraft. But in 1939 French strategy, like that of Britain, had depended on multiplying its own capacity by procuring large numbers of aircraft in the United States. When France fell in June 1940, Germany inherited France's aircraft factories. Britain inherited France's orders in the United States. Combined with the contracts Britain itself had placed since the start of the war, London by the end of June 1940 was expecting delivery from the United States of no less than 10,800 aircraft and 13,000 aero-engines over the next eighteen months.[41] This was in addition to Britain's own production of 15,000 military aircraft. At the same time, the British Ministry of Aircraft Production was negotiating with the Americans to order many thousands more. By way of comparison, total German aircraft production in 1940 came to only 10,826 aircraft and in 1941 it expanded to only 12,000, a disappointing increase which we shall discuss in greater detail below. In addition, there was America's own gigantic rearmament programme, which tilted the balance even further against Germany. In fact, so large were the combined demands of the British and American programmes that they stretched even America's industrial resources. But the United States did not respond by seeking to restrict British purchases; quite the contrary. On 23 July 1940 British procurement agents in Washington were invited to a clandestine meeting with American industrial planners, from which emerged a scheme to

Table 11. Friends when you need them: domestic and external resource mobilization in Britain and Germany

	Britain				Germany			
	% of net national production mobilized for war	of which: Externally provided	of which: Domestic	% external contribution to war effort	% of net national production mobilized for war	of which: Externally provided	of which: Domestic	% external contribution to war effort
1938	7	5	2	71	17	-1	18	-6
1939	16	8	8	50	25	1	24	4
1940	48	17	31	35	44	8	36	18
1941	55	14	41	25	56	12	44	21
1942	54	11	43	20	69	17	52	25
1943	57	10	47	18	76	16	60	21
1944	56	9	47	16				
1945	47	11	36	23				

Source: M. Harrison, 'Resource Mobilization for World War II', *Economic History Review* (1988), 184.

expand the capacity of the United States aircraft industry so that it would be able to deliver no less than 72,000 aircraft per annum, guaranteeing a supply to the British of 3,000 planes per month, three times the current German output.[42] As it turned out, Britain never received aircraft at this rate and never had to face the question of how to pay for them. But the expansion of the American industry set in motion in 1940 was real enough. In 1940 the United States produced 6,019 military aircraft, of which Britain received 2,006 and the French 557.[43] In 1941 the United States produced 19,433 military aircraft, more than either Britain or Germany, of which the British share came to 5,012.[44] In 1942 the number of military aircraft produced in the United States rocketed to almost 48,000, just shy of Roosevelt's target. Britain received only 7,775. But this hardly mattered since the United States was now in the war. By 1943, America had surpassed the 'utopian' target of 72,000 aircraft, with a staggering production figure of 85,898 aircraft. Even more were to come in 1944. It may seem anachronistic to refer to these production figures in a discussion of the summer of 1940, but this is precisely the point. Though the mobilization of the American economy after Pearl Harbor is the stuff of legend, it did not start in December 1941. The foundation of the Allies' overwhelming aerial superiority was laid as early as the summer of 1940, in direct response to Germany's victory over France. Whether the bombers would be flown by British or American pilots remained to be decided, as did the embarrassing question of finance, but the bombers were coming in any event.

III

Hitler's dismissive views about the degeneracy of American society are well documented, but so is the clear awareness in Berlin of the threat posed by America's industrial potential and the need to counter it with decisive action.[45] Nor was America merely a material threat. Roosevelt, as we have seen, had been pictured since January 1939 as the arch-enemy, the most dangerous exponent of the world Jewish conspiracy. Anti-Semitism suffused every aspect of the German strategic assessment. The first line of the report from the Washington embassy on lend-lease, received by the Foreign Ministry, the Wehrmacht high command, the army and the Air Ministry, stated bluntly: 'The Lend-Lease Act currently before Congress . . . stems from the pen of leading Jewish confidants of the President. It is intended to give him the possibility of pursuing without limitation his policy of influencing the war through all means "short of war". With the passage of the law the Jewish world-view will therefore have firmly asserted itself in the United States.' It then went on to itemize the huge deliveries that could now be expected by 'England, China and other vassals'.[46]

As we have seen, American industrial assistance for France and Britain had been very much on Hitler's mind in the first months of the war. In March 1940 Fritz Todt had highlighted Hitler's concern about 'USA-potential'. And this was reiterated fifteen months later by General Thomas in a retrospective review: 'A victorious end to the war was to be achieved at all costs in 1940, above all to negate American assistance for the Western powers, the acceleration of which . . . was already then part of our calculations.'[47] Britain's continuing resistance raised the stakes. On 21 July, in the wake of America's rearmament decisions, Hitler instructed the Wehrmacht high command 'to consider seriously the Russian and American question'.[48] In public speeches Hitler rubbished America, but in the light of popular fears about American industrial might this is hardly surprising. The euphoria surrounding victory over France was in large part due to the fact that this appeared to make impossible an American intervention in the war.[49] Local offices of the Gestapo were unanimous in reporting a popular preoccupation with all things American: aid for Britain, the prospects for Roosevelt's re-election and the likely entry of America into the war.[50] To manage this anxiety Goebbels adopted a cautious strategy of news management.[51] A complete news blackout was imposed in relation to the destroyer deal, which behind closed doors in Berlin was regarded as a decisive break in American neutrality.[52] Nor were there to be any news reports of America's rearmament effort. The public needed reassurance, as did foreign diplomats who visited Berlin in the autumn of 1940.[53] Hitler did not deny that America was now underwriting the British war effort. But he believed that Germany had some time. Following Roosevelt's re-election he remarked to the Hungarian premier that American shipments to Britain would not get fully under way before the winter of 1941–2 and this was also the view taken by the German navy.[54] This, as it turned out, was a fairly accurate assessment and it had clear implications for German strategy. On 17 December 1940, the day on which Roosevelt introduced lend-lease to the world's media, Hitler formulated his strategic outlook in direct response to the American threat. To the leaders of the OKW he expressed the view that 'all continental European problems' had to be resolved in the coming year, because in 1942 the United States would be in a position to intervene decisively in the war.[55]

For obvious reasons, the Germans followed the Anglo-American air programme particularly attentively. In the autumn the Wehrmacht assumed that aircraft deliveries to Britain were already running at the rate of roughly 300 per month.[56] This was not yet overwhelming, but given that German output barely exceeded 1,000 planes per month it was already important in tilting the balance in Britain's favour. The real threat, as the Germans fully understood, was that the trans-Atlantic flow would soon increase dramatically both in quantity and quality. The long-term potential of American industry was brought to the Air Ministry's attention by a variety of industrialists.[57] And all the evidence suggests that Goering's officials responded. Indeed, the signs are that over the winter of 1940–41 the Luftwaffe leadership was focusing as much attention on the industrial prerequisites for the coming air war with Britain and America as it was on the imminent invasion of the Soviet Union. As we shall see in the next chapter, from the autumn of 1940 onwards huge investments began to be made in capacity expansion. And it was above all the threat of American deliveries that motivated the Reich Air Ministry to undertake a serious effort to enrol the conquered territories of Western Europe as a manufacturing base.[58] But whilst Britain was being encouraged by the Americans to consider orders running into many tens of thousands of aircraft, the possibilities open to Germany in occupied Western Europe were far more modest. The initial contract to be placed in France was for between 2,500 and 3,000 aircraft, with deliveries to 'peak' at 60 aircraft per month, one-fiftieth of the figure being discussed in Washington.[59] And even this modest proposal was stalled for months by French hesitation and the German insistence that they should be given a controlling stake in France's state-owned aircraft factories. At the end of January 1941 Goering's patience finally snapped. He harangued the German negotiating team in highly revealing language: 'You must understand that for us ... [the Luftwaffe production programme in France] it is a matter of vital necessity and that it is absolutely impossible for us to wait. England is doing all she can to put at her disposal an entire continent . . . We have to do the same thing as far as our means permit.'[60]

On 12 February 1941 the Luftwaffe finally got its deal. France agreed to produce 3,000 aircraft under licence as well as 13,500 aero-engines. So anxious was the Reich Air Ministry to get production started, that it abandoned its demand for ownership of the French factories. But a highly significant sticking point remained. To make the aircraft, France would need aluminium and, though France had bauxite and smelting capacity, it lacked the coal necessary to generate electricity. The French calculated that to meet the German demands they would need a delivery of 120,000 tons of coal per month. Germany could promise only 4,000 tons.[61] A few weeks later, on the other side of the Atlantic, the long-awaited Lend-Lease Act passed through its final stages. On 11 March 1941 Congress made an immediate appropriation of $8.3 billion for British war supplies. At between 25 and 33 billion Reichsmarks, depending on exchange rates, this was equivalent to two years of German armaments output. Two billion dollars alone were earmarked for an immediate order of 11,800 military aircraft, doubling the number of planes that Britain already had under contract. At the same moment, the combined total of all Wehrmacht orders in occupied Europe came to 3 billion Reichsmarks, or roughly $750 million.[62] By the end of 1941, whereas Britain had taken delivery of 5,012 complete aircraft from the United States, Germany had received a grand total of 78 aircraft from France and the Netherlands.[63] In 1942, with the bulk of United States output being retained for its own use and British deliveries restricted to 7,775 planes, the Luftwaffe received 743 aircraft from the occupied Western territories. In total, during the entire war, the Luftwaffe, the Wehrmacht's most adventurous sub-contractor, took delivery of only 2,517 aircraft from France and 947 from Holland. The Luftwaffe soon despaired of contracting out entire aircraft to the occupied territories. Labour productivity in the French aircraft factories was so low that it took four times as many workers to produce a German aircraft in France as it did to produce the same plane in Germany. Not surprisingly, in light of these figures, the main contribution made by the occupied territories directly towards armaments production for the Reich was the conscription of millions of foreign workers for labour in Germany.

IV

The territories that Germany had conquered in 1940, though they provided substantial booty and a crucial source of labour did not bear comparison with the abundance provided to Britain by America.[64] The aerial arms race was the distinctive Anglo-American contribution to the war and it played directly to America's dominance in manufacturing. But though the disparity in aircraft deliveries was extreme it was not untypical. A similarly vast gulf was also evident in relation to energy supplies, the most basic driver of modern urban and industrial society. Whereas the Anglo-American alliance was energy rich, Germany and its Western European *Grossraum* were starved of food, coal and oil.

The disparity with respect to oil was most serious. Between 1940 and 1943 the mobility of Germany's army, navy and air force, not to mention its domestic economy, depended on annual imports of 1.5 million tons of oil, mainly from Romania.[65] In addition, German synthetic fuel factories, at huge expense, produced a flow of petrol that rose from 4 million tons in 1940 to a maximum of 6.5 million tons in 1943. Seizing the fuel stocks of France as booty in no way resolved this fundamental dependency. In fact, the victories of 1940 had the reverse effect. They added a number of heavy oil consumers to Germany's own fuel deficit. From its annual fuel flow of at most 8.9 million tons, Germany now had to supply not only its own needs, but those of the rest of Western Europe as well. Before the war, the French economy had consumed at least 5.4 million tons per annum, at a per capita rate 60 per cent higher than Germany's.[66] The effect of the German occupation was to throw France back into an era before motorization. From the summer of 1940 France was reduced to a mere 8 per cent of its pre-war supply of petrol. In an economy adjusted to a high level of oil consumption the effects were dramatic. To give just one example, thousands of litres of milk went to waste in the French countryside every day, because no petrol was available to ensure regular collections. Of more immediate concern to the military planners in Berlin were the Italian armed forces, which depended entirely on fuel diverted from Germany and Romania. By February 1941, the Italian navy was threatening to halt its operations in the Mediterranean altogether unless Germany supplied at least 250,000 tons of fuel.[67] And the problems were by no means confined to the Reich's satellites. Germany itself coped only by dint of extreme economy. In late May 1941, General Adolf von Schell, the man responsible for the motor vehicle industry, seriously suggested that in light of the chronic shortage of oil it would be advisable to carry out a partial 'demotorization' of the Wehrmacht.[68] It is commonly remarked that the Luftwaffe suffered later in the war because of the inadequate training of its pilots, due in large part to the shortage of air fuel.[69] But in 1941 the petrol shortage was already so severe that the Wehrmacht was licensing its soldiers to drive heavy trucks with less than 15 kilometres of on-road experience, a measure which was blamed for the appalling attrition of motor vehicles during the Russian campaign.[70] Shortages made themselves felt across the German economy. So tight were fuel rations that in November 1941 Opel was forced to shut down production at its Brandenburg plant, Germany's largest truck factory, because it lacked the petrol necessary to check the fuel pumps of vehicles coming off the assembly line. A special allocation of 104 cubic metres of fuel had to be arranged by the Wehrmacht's economic office so as to ensure that there were no further interruptions.[71]

The contrast to the Anglo-American combination could hardly have been more stark. Britain produced barely 1 million tons of synthetic fuel per annum. But it made up for this by importing oil at a phenomenal rate. In 1942, despite the fierce naval battles raging in the Atlantic, Britain managed to import 10.2 million tons. This was five times the amount received by Germany from Romania, at a time when the Wehrmacht had an army of more than 3 million men locked in intense combat on the Eastern Front. In 1944, in preparation for Normandy, shipments of oil to Britain peaked at more than 20 million tons, nine times the maximum figure ever imported by Germany during the war.[72] In January 1941, when Germany is sometimes described as being 'glutted' with oil, stocks came to barely more than 2 million tons. In London, alarm bells went off whenever stocks fell below 7 million tons. So great was the disparity that the British Ministry of Economic Warfare, charged with assessing Germany's economic situation, had difficulty believing its highly accurate estimates of German oil stocks. To the British it seemed implausible that Hitler could possibly have embarked on the war with such a small margin of fuel security, an incredulity shared by both the Soviets and the Americans, who agreed in overestimating Germany's oil stocks by at least 100 per cent.[73]

For oil, the problem was one of absolute scarcity. In the case of coal, on which the Western European economies relied for 80 per cent of their energy inputs, the problem was one of relative shortage. Prior to the war many countries in Europe had imported substantial quantities of coal from Britain. Those entirely dependent on imported energy included Sweden, Norway, Denmark, Switzerland and Italy, all of which were key trading partners of Hitler's Germany. The biggest and most important item, however, were the 30 million tons of coal that France needed to import to supply 40 per cent of its annual requirement. To counterbalance these deficits, Germany controlled huge coal reserves in Silesia, the Ruhr, Belgium and northern France.[74] Setting total demand against total supply, the net deficit of the core countries of the German *Grossraum* amounted to only 11 million tons, no more than a few per cent of overall consumption. On paper, therefore, it was possible to construct a viable coal distribution for Europe.[75] To have achieved this balance, however, would have required a quite heroic effort of production, organization and logistics. Tens of millions of tons of material would have needed to have been redirected around the rail networks of Europe. France would have needed either to have substantially increased the output of its coalfields, or to have substantially reduced its national consumption. As the foremost historian of the European coal industry has put it: 'With extreme care, superb organization, and unqualified technical cooperation the coal deficit in western Europe *could* have been overcome.'[76] It is hardly surprising that it was not.

In reality, German-controlled Western Europe in 1940 and 1941 found itself facing a growing problem of both coal production and coal transport. The difficulties were worst in the occupied territories. As we have seen, to prevent a repeat of the disastrous rail crisis of the winter of 1939–40, the German occupation forces took their pick from amongst the rolling-stock of France, Belgium and the Netherlands. By the autumn of 1940 this had raised the stock of trucks available to the German economy, not including the needs of the Wehrmacht, to 800,000 wagons, compared to only 650,000 in 1938.[77] In the occupied territories, however, the effects were disastrous, most notably in northern France, where the movement of coal from pithead to the cities was regularly interrupted. The coal famine itself could only have been alleviated if Germany had been able to raise production in the main French, Belgian and Dutch coalfields. France was not only Europe's largest importer of

Table 12. The precarious coal balance of the *Grossraum*

	Production (000 tons 1937)	Imports (–) / exports (+)	% Imported (–) / exported (+)
Net Importers:			
France	44,657	−29,263	−40
Italy	1,229	−12,933	−91
Sweden	460	−9,719	−95
Denmark	0	−6,278	−100
Belgium-Luxembourg	29,859	−4,234	−12
Switzerland	0	−3,509	−100
Austria	1,851	−3,450	−65
Norway	780	−2,735	−78
Totals	78,836	−72,121	−48
Net Exporters:			
Germany	230,690	45,733	20
Poland	36,222	11,291	31
Czechoslovakia	27,564	2,734	10
Netherlands	14,368	1,268	9
Totals	308,844	61,026	20
Overall balance	387,680	−11,095	−3

Source: C. Lewis, *Nazi Europe and World Trade* (Washington, 1941), 116

coal. Behind Germany and Britain it was also Europe's third largest producer. But production in France was not increasing; on the contrary. Output slumped by 18 per cent in 1940, never to recover. Productivity per worker in the French mines fell inexorably. Furthermore, in the summer of 1941 the German occupation authorities had to contend with a major strike wave in the Belgian and northern French coalfields. There was no mystery as to the cause. In the first winter of the occupation there were miners' wives in front of city halls across Wallonia waving empty potato sacks in silent protest.[78] Well-informed German sources estimated that if food rations could be increased this would permit a 10–15 per cent increase in Belgian production.[79] But this ran up against another fundamental constraint on the European economy. As we shall see, Europe was not only short of coal and oil, it was short of food as well. And the shortage of coal in turn had a debilitating effect on heavy industry. As the total quantity of coal available to French industry fell to only half its pre-war level, the production of steel in the Lorraine and northern France plunged.[80]

At first Germany itself was protected from the worst effects of the coal squeeze. The Reich authorities managed to avoid a repeat of the spectacular supply crisis of the previous winter. However, by the beginning of 1941 there could be no doubt that the German coal mines were in trouble as well. In the first instance the problems were political. By early 1941 a heated stand-off had developed between the powerful regional syndicates of the coal producers and Reich Coal Commissioner Paul Walter, the man appointed by Goering in 1939 to provide political leadership to the industry.[81] Walter was a party hack from Robert Ley's German Labour Front, who was mistrusted by the industry. In 1940 he managed to add further to the antagonism by proposing a major reorganization of the coal trade that would have stripped the producers of control over coal distribution.[82] By January 1941 rumours were circulating that Walter was planning to impose on the coal industry a system of market organization (*Marktordnung*) like that prevailing in agriculture. Walter also indulged in an ill-considered bout of anti-capitalist rhetoric assailing the unjustified profits earned by the coal merchants at the expense of the coal miners, the new darlings of the Nazi community of labour. What Walter misjudged, however, was the dramatic shift in the politics of the coal industry brought about by the rise of the Reichswerke Hermann Goering, headed by Paul Pleiger. Pleiger, of course, was a party man with impeccable credentials. But through a combination of Aryanization deals in Czechoslovakia and annexation in formerly Polish Silesia, Pleiger had also established himself as one of the Reich's leading coal producers.[83] And he had no truck with Walter's ill-timed anti-capitalism. By February 1941, with Pleiger in the lead, the industry was in open mutiny against the commissioner. Walter was removed and the syndicates were swiftly incorporated into a new national coal organization (the Reichsvereinigung Kohle), headed by Pleiger. The association incorporated the pre-existing structure of the cartels and bound them directly to the Reich Ministry of Economic Affairs, where Pleiger's close friend Hans Kehrl now dictated industrial policy. After having hired a team of brilliant industrial statisticians from Germany's leading Institute of Economic Research, Pleiger's coal association established a system of production management that was to be a model for the reorganization of heavy industry in 1942.[84]

No amount of reorganization, however, could disguise the industry's production problems. In late 1940 the German steel industry commissioned the leading engineer Hermann Winkhaus to report on the feasible maximum of steel output in the German-controlled areas. This, everyone realized, was a critical variable in determining the economic future of Hitler's empire. It would constrain all industrial projects whether in war or peace. The Winkhaus report concluded that maximum current capacity in the German-controlled zone was in the order of 46 million tons per annum, of which 17.5 million would come from the Ruhr. Whether or not Germany could come close to this figure would depend on the supply of ores. But having opened up Germany's domestic orefields and conquered those of France, this was no longer the rate limiting factor. The real issue was coking coal. Germany could not come close to realizing the full potential for steel production unless coal output in Germany, Belgium and the Netherlands could be increased by 15 million tons.[85] Since 1939, however, rather than increasing, coal output in Germany had been stagnant. Production in the Saar border region had been badly affected by the fighting in the West. Upper Silesia, the only German coalfield to show any real dynamism, was badly affected in 1941 by the redeployment of the Wehrmacht to the eastern frontier. The Ruhr, which accounted for just under 70 per cent of Germany's annual output of coal and virtually all its production of coke, had reached its peak in 1939 at just over 130 million tons per annum. In 1941 Ruhr production was in decline, falling by 2 million tons per month between March and August.[86] And the cause of the problems was obvious.[87] Though since the 1920s Germany had led Europe in mechanization, coal mining was still a highly labour intensive industry, which suffered chronic problems of recruitment. Like agriculture, coal mining, as a notoriously dirty, dangerous and underpaid occupation, was at a severe disadvantage in the competition for young male labour. Unlike in the case of agriculture, however, the Nazi regime was determined to redress this balance. In the autumn of 1940 Robert Ley announced a radical new German Labour Front programme to reorder the entire blue-collar wage system, so that skilled miners would

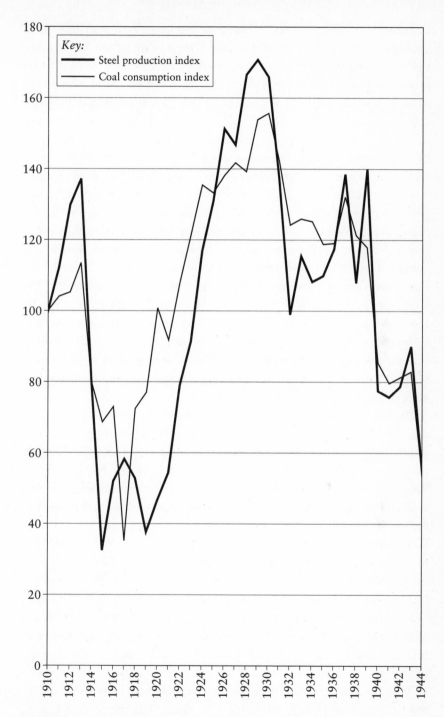

Figure 16. The coal and steel nexus: France 1910–1944 (1910 = 100)

command premium wages.[88] The coal industry, however, had more immediate problems. Even though the German labour market authorities had seen to it that the mining industry suffered no net loss of workers at the start of the war, the Wehrmacht draft had taken the best young men. The result was a steady decline in per capita productivity. In due course, the industry could make up for this with further investment. But in the short term Pleiger needed emergency measures. As of the spring of 1941, Sunday shifts became a normal feature of life on the Ruhr, allowing the men not even a day to recover from their gruelling working week. To restore the quality of the workforce, the Wehrmacht was persuaded to return as many trained mine workers as possible to the mines. As the Wehrmacht office pointed out with remarkable frankness, this concession was necessary above all for political reasons. If there was another coal crisis like that in the first winter of the war, it was vital that it was not the Wehrmacht that was blamed for the disaster.[89] But increasingly the industry resorted to drafting foreign conscripts. By May of 1941 there were already close to 70,000 foreign workers in German mines, thousands of Poles, tens of thousands of French prisoners of war, and many thousands of Silesians drafted under Goering's conscription decree of 1938.[90] In this, too, Pleiger and the coal industry were forerunners of the 'Speer system'.

Drafting conscript workers was one thing. But unless they were adequately fed they were useless. There was no industry in the 1940s in which the correlation between labour productivity and calorific input was more direct than in mining.[91] But after 1939 the food supply in Western Europe was no less constrained than the supply of coal.[92] As was true of Germany, the high-intensity dairy farms of France, the Netherlands and Denmark were dependent on imported animal feed. Grain imports in the late 1930s had run at the rate of more than 7 million tons per annum mostly from Argentina and Canada. These sources of supply were closed off by the British blockade. In addition Western Europe had imported more than 700,000 tons of oil seed.[93] Of course, France was a major producer of grain in its own right. But French grain yields depended, as they did in Germany, on large quantities of nitrogen-based fertilizer, which could be supplied only at the expense of the production of explosives. And like German agriculture, the farms of Western Europe depended on huge herds of draught animals and on the daily labour of millions of farm workers. The removal of horses, manpower, fertilizer and animal feed that followed the outbreak of war set off a disastrous chain reaction in the delicate ecology of European peasant farming. By the summer of 1940, Germany was facing a Europe-wide agricultural crisis.[94] Danish farmers began systematically to cull their swine herds and poultry flocks. Dutch yields steadily deteriorated in line with the fall in fertilizer supplies. Most dramatic of all was the situation in France, where the grain harvest in 1940 was less than half what it had been in 1938.[95] In Germany itself, 1940 brought a noticeable fall in grain yields and this was compounded by the poor harvest in Yugoslavia and Hungary, which were amongst the Reich's main suppliers.[96] In 1940 German grain imports from Yugoslavia and Hungary fell by almost 3 million tons, a shortfall offset only by a dramatic increase in deliveries from Romania.

The rations set for the German population at the outbreak of the war had been relatively generous. But they could be sustained in 1940–41 only by making severe inroads into the large stocks accumulated since 1936. The Reichsnaehrstand started the war with a reserve of 8.8 million tons of grain, almost enough to provide bread for the German population for an entire year.[97] In the first year of the war, these were reduced by only 1.3 million tons. But the shortfall in the European harvest of 1940–41 confirmed Herbert Backe's worst fears. Unless Germany could find additional sources for millions of tons of grain, it would soon need to make serious cuts to food rations, starting with a mass slaughter of its livestock herd, which would permanently reduce the available supply of protein and fat. And the situation in the urban centres of the occupied territories was, of course, far worse than in Germany. By 1941 there were already signs of mounting discontent due to the inadequate food supply. In Belgium and France, the official ration allocated to 'normal consumers' of as little as 1,300 calories per day, was an open invitation to resort to the black market. Daily allocations in Norway and the Czech Protectorate hovered around 1,600 calories.[98]

In 1938 the Western European countries now dominated by Germany had been a formidable economic force, with a combined GDP greater than that of Britain. The combined effect of the British blockade and the German occupation was to reduce them to a shadow of their former selves.[99] Whilst output in both Germany and Britain increased substantially over the course of the war and whilst output in the United States rocketed, Germany's European empire was a basket case. Despite the voracious demands of the German war effort, no Western European country occupied in 1940 experienced any economic growth over the next five years. In the two smallest territories, Denmark and Norway, output precariously held steady. But this mattered little when compared to the situation in the far larger economies of Belgium, the Netherlands and above all France, where economic activity collapsed in 1940, never to recover.

V

Despite the extraordinary extent of the Wehrmacht's victories, the space under Germany's control in the autumn of 1940 was not, therefore, the self-sufficient *Lebensraum* of which Hitler had dreamed. Nor did Western Europe provide a promising platform from which to fight the long war of attrition that Britain and its backers in the United States were clearly determined to force on Germany. In economic terms, the Wehrmacht's victories in 1940 did not release Germany from the dependence on the Soviet Union into which it had entered a year earlier.[100] In fact, in the short term the only way to sustain Germany's Western European *Grossraum* at anything like its pre-war level of economic activity was to secure a vast increase in fuel and raw material deliveries from the Soviet Union.[101] Only the Ukraine produced the net agricultural surpluses necessary to support the densely packed animal populations of Western Europe. Only in the Soviet Union were there the coal, iron and metal ores needed to sustain the military-industrial complex. Only in the Caucasus was there the oil necessary to make Europe independent of overseas supply. Only with access to these resources could Germany face a long war against Britain and America with any confidence. By the winter of 1940–41, Roosevelt had settled the terms on which the United States would provide Britain the 'stuff' it need to continue the war. For Hitler and Stalin, the question remained to be answered.[102]

Hitler certainly had the option to continue the war with Stalin as his ally, rather than as a mortal enemy.[103] The Nazi–Soviet pact was still in effect in the summer of 1940, and after Germany's stunning defeat of France the Soviet Union had no intention of cancelling the arrangement. For a brief period between July and October 1940, this gave rise, particularly in the Reich Foreign Ministry, to the hope that Germany might counter the emerging Anglo-American coalition with the formation of its own 'continental bloc', an eastward extension of the Western European *Grossraum* that was being discussed so excitedly over the summer of 1940.[104] A step in this direction seemed to be the Tripartite Pact signed between Japan, Italy and Germany on 27 September 1940. In the first instance this was intended to revive the nightmare of British strategy, forcing the Royal Navy to choose between the Mediterranean and Singapore. But the Tripartite Pact also committed the parties to mutual assistance in case they were attacked by a power not presently involved in the war. Since relations with the Soviet Union were explicitly excluded from the terms of the agreement, this was clearly directed against the United States. But if the Tripartite alliance was intended as a deterrent, it had the opposite effect. In Washington it was seen as confirming the aggressive intentions of the Axis powers and it served only to reinforce Roosevelt's growing commitment to Britain, as the key bastion both against Germany in Europe and Japan in Asia.[105] As Foreign Minister Ribbentrop clearly realized, the only thing that would really have turned the tables on the Anglo-American alliance would have been an extension of the Tripartite Pact to include the Soviet Union, creating a truly formidable Eurasian alliance, stretching from the Atlantic to the Pacific. This, however, would have required a reconciliation of the Japanese–Soviet antagonism, which in the summer of 1939 had spilled into open fighting in Manchuria. The Japanese leadership was perennially split on this issue. But the possibility of a rapid thrust to the south to take control of Dutch, French and British colonial possessions, combined with the increasingly aggressive stance pursued by the United States towards Japan, strengthened the case for a rapprochement with the Soviet Union.[106] The Soviet Union, for its part, faced with Germany's unexpected triumph in the West, was only too keen to pacify its eastern frontier. So in April 1941, Japanese Foreign Minister Matsuoka Yosuke was welcomed in Moscow to sign a five-year neutrality treaty with the Soviet Union. In Berlin, meanwhile, the advocates of the continental bloc strategy were harbouring wide-ranging fantasies of empire. The Eurasian axis of the anti-British alliance was to be complemented by a new African empire, based on the gigantic Belgian possessions in the mineral-rich Congo. In the autumn of 1940 there was intense competition in Berlin for future positions in the new German colonial administration. And the African vision of the German Foreign Ministry also included the grotesque proposal to 'evacuate' the entire Jewish population of Poland as well as of German-occupied Western Europe to the French colony of Madagascar.[107] The Jews would thus be safely eliminated as a 'contaminating' influence in European affairs. Hundreds of thousands would certainly die in transit. Those that survived could be held hostage against the event that Wall Street Jewry tried to push Roosevelt into a declaration of open war.

But, though the continental bloc could certainly satisfy both 'ideological' and 'pragmatic' criteria, the advocates of a long-term alliance with the Soviet Union were never in a majority in Berlin and this too was as much for pragmatic as for ideological reasons. In the long term a genuine alliance would have involved an unacceptable degree of German dependence on the Soviets. As General Halder noted in his diary in December 1940: 'Every weakness in the position of the Axis brings a push by the Russians. They cannot prescribe the rules for transactions, but they utilize every opportunity to weaken the Axis position.'[108] In a Eurasian continental bloc, it would be the central power, the Soviet Union, not Japan or Germany, that would ultimately occupy the dominant position. The Third Reich had no intention of slipping into the kind of humbling dependence that Britain now occupied in relation to the United States, mortgaging its assets and selling its secrets, simply to sustain the war effort. That this was the direction in which Germany might be headed was evident already in the spring of 1940. Just prior to the German offensive in the West, Moscow demanded as part payment for its raw material deliveries the construction of two chemicals plants in the Soviet Union, one for coal hydrogenation (synthetic fuel), the other to embody IG Farben's revolutionary Buna process (synthetic rubber).[109] The Soviet Union was to have full access to both the blueprints and the complex instrumentation necessary to monitor the high-pressure reactions. Not surprisingly, IG Farben balked and with the support of the German military the deal was blocked. But the fact that the Soviets could even make such demands indicates the seriousness of the German dilemma. The hugely increased volume of trade needed to sustain Germany's blockaded *Grossraum* was bound to give the Soviet Union ever-increasing leverage.

By the autumn of 1940, Germany's dependence on deliveries of raw materials, fuel and food from the Soviet Union was creating a positively schizophrenic situation. In trade negotiations, German machine tools were one of the means of settlement prized most highly by the Soviets. Such exports, however, were in direct conflict with the preparations of Germany's own armed forces for the invasion of the Soviet Union. Astonishingly, rather than interrupting the Soviet deliveries to prioritize the Luftwaffe, Goering in early October 1940 ordered that, at least until 11 May 1941, deliveries to the Soviet Union, and thus to the Red Army, should have equal priority with the demands of the Wehrmacht.[110] Even in the immediate prelude to operation Barbarossa, Germany could not afford to do without Soviet deliveries of oil, grain and alloy metals.

The willingness to engage in such bizarre compromises reflected the increasing concern in Berlin over the precarious situation of Germany's raw material supplies.[111] As the military-economic office of the Wehrmacht concluded at the end of October 1940: 'Current favourable raw material situation (improved by stocks captured in enemy territory) will, in case of prolonged war and after consumption of existing stocks, re-emerge as bottleneck. From summer 1941 this is to be expected in case of fuel oil as well as industrial fats and oils.'[112] And Germany's dependence was made even more acute by the poor harvest of 1940. When Soviet Foreign Minister Molotov made a three-day visit to Berlin in November 1940, one of the first items on the German agenda was an urgent request to double the import of grain from the Soviet Union, from the current level of 1 million tons per annum.[113] By the end of 1940, the grain stocks were preoccupying even the military leadership. With regard to the food situation, General Halder noted anxiously in his diary: 'We will swindle our way through 1941.'[114] Thereafter, the situation was unforeseeable. In the event, unexpected salvation arrived in early January 1941 when the Soviets more than doubled their deliveries, even agreeing to dip into their national grain reserve to meet the German demands.[115] Ironically, however, this Soviet effort to 'buy off' the Germans had the opposite effect. Their ability to make such substantial concessions at such short notice appears only to have encouraged Hitler in his belief that the conquest of the Ukraine was the obvious next step in his campaign of aggression.

In fact, even before the unsuccessful outcome of the Battle of Britain, Hitler appears to have convinced himself that the military conquest of the Soviet Union in 1941 was the key to ultimate victory in the war as a whole. At the Berghof on 31 July 1940, in conference with the military leadership, Hitler emphasized that the Soviet Union would have to be knocked out of the war, if Britain was to be brought to heel and America's support neutralized.[116] 'Britain's hope lies in Russia and the United States. If Russia drops out of the picture, America, too, is lost for Britain, because elimination of Russia would tremendously increase Japan's power in the Far East.' Russia, according to Hitler, was the 'Far Eastern sword of Britain and the United States', a spearhead pointed at Japan.[117] Attacking and decisively defeating the Soviet Union in 1941 would rob Britain of its 'dagger on the mainland' and unleash Japan. If Britain did choose to continue the war and if Japanese aggression provoked American entry, complete control of the Eurasian landmass would at least secure for Germany the resources it needed for a true transatlantic confrontation. As Hitler put in on 9 January 1941, after the conquest of *Lebensraum* in the East, Germany would be ready for a 'war against continents'.[118] Indeed, he seems to have rated the economic potential of such an empire greater than that of Britain and America combined. And it was this vision of a combined Japanese-German war on Britain and America to which he returned six months later, during the euphoric early weeks of July 1941, when he proposed to the Japanese ambassador an offensive alliance against the United States.[119]

Meanwhile, what Hitler needed was for the United States to stay out of the war until the Soviet Union was defeated. And it was surely no coincidence that on 30 January 1941, two years after he had issued his first public threat about the fate of European Jewry, Hitler chose to do so again.[120] As we have seen, over the winter of 1940–41 Berlin was increasingly preoccupied with the menacing pace of American rearmament and on 30 January 1941, unlike on the same occasion in January 1939, Hitler issued his threat directly to the United States, warning America to abstain from any European intervention. Significantly, however, he redated his earlier pronouncement from 30 January 1939 to 1 September, the day of the German assault on Poland. In Hitler's mind the threat of world war, the Americans and the Jews were inextricably intertwined. The real pressures of the global arms race and the imaginary horrors of Hitler's ideological world-view came together in operation Barbarossa, in a synthesis of extraordinary ambition and violence.[121]

With hindsight it is hard to avoid the conclusion that after the defeat of France Germany would have done better to adopt a defensive posture, consolidating its position in Western Europe, attacking British positions in the Mediterranean and forcing the British and the Americans to bomb their way onto the Continent. Given that the Red Army ultimately proved to be the nemesis of the Wehrmacht, this is hard to deny. But what is too often ignored in such counterfactual arguments is the growing awareness in Berlin that, even after the occupation of Western Europe, Germany did not have the upper hand in a long war against Britain and America. The chronic shortage of oil, the debility of the European coal mines and the fragility of the food chain, made it seem unlikely that Germany would in fact be able to 'consolidate' its conquests of 1940 without falling into excessive dependence on the Soviet Union. Even if this were possible, the combined manufacturing capacity of Britain and America vastly exceeded the industrial capacity currently under German control and this, in turn, spelled disaster in a protracted air war. The German army, on the other hand, had proved its ability to achieve decisive victory against what were thought to be the strongest armies in Europe. When we bear this range of factors in mind it is easier to appreciate why a defensive strategy seemed like a second-best in the autumn of 1940. After the defeat of France, the dream of a gigantic land empire seemed within reach, and, given the industrial strength looming on the other side of the Atlantic, there was no time to waste.

PART III

World War

13

Preparing for Two Wars at Once

On 31 July 1940, within weeks of victory over France, Hitler ordered the Wehrmacht to begin preparing for a campaign to destroy the Soviet Union. By early 1941 the decision was irrevocable. Thanks to the complexity of the action and continued difficulties of access to archival material in the former Soviet Union, our knowledge of the fighting on the Eastern Front is still far from complete. But what is indisputable is that it was on the Eastern Front that the Third Reich was bled dry and that it was the Red Army that was chiefly responsible for destroying the Wehrmacht. By issuing the order for the attack on the Soviet Union, Hitler thus ushered in his own destruction.

Was this outcome inevitable? For some the question remains open.[1] John Kenneth Galbraith, the celebrity economist who conducted the after-the-battle assessment for the US Army Air Force, put the case bluntly in an article published in *Fortune* magazine in 1945: 'The simple fact is that Germany should never have lost the war . . .'[2] According to Galbraith, the Wehrmacht's invasion of the Soviet Union ended in disaster only because the Nazi dictatorship failed to mobilize the German economy sufficiently to supply the German army with the equipment it needed for victory. According to Galbraith, this under-mobilization was due to a mixture of overconfidence and incompetence compounded by a chronic lack of political will. As a result, the German home front was never asked to make the kinds of sacrifice that were taken for granted by its opponents. And for Galbraith the implications were far-reaching. German defeat was 'conclusive testimony to the inherent inefficiencies of dictatorship and the inherent efficiencies of freedom'.[3] Galbraith's assessment was not original. He derived it from interrogations of Albert Speer and his staff, who strongly reinforced his voluntarist reading. Before 1942, according to Speer's chief statistician, Hitler's regime chose to operate a 'peacetime economy at war'.[4] Speer, who was widely credited for rousing the German war economy from its slumbers, suggested that if he had been placed in charge two years earlier, the Wehrmacht could have invaded the Soviet Union with twice as much weaponry.[5] Hans Kehrl, the Nazi enthusiast who by 1943 had become Speer's chief of staff, took the same highly critical view. It was the indolence and disorganization of the war effort in 1940 and 1941 that cost Germany the war.[6] And this kind of argument has continued to influence the mainstream of historical writing about the Third Reich.[7]

The aim of this chapter is to suggest an alternative interpretation. If we wish to understand what the Germans were doing in advance of operation Barbarossa, what we must concentrate on is Germany's strategic situation. As we argued in earlier chapters, despite the fantastic victory over France this was far from simple. The defeat of France had not won the war for Germany. Britain had not been defeated. From the spring of 1941 onwards Britain could count on massive support from the United States and, given the economic vulnerability of Germany's new empire, the strategic outlook of the Third Reich was set to deteriorate from 1942 onwards. In this situation, the conquest of the Soviet Union, even though it was an immense undertaking and even though it satisfied deep imperatives of Nazi ideology, could not be viewed in isolation. It was a means to the end of consolidating Germany's position for the ultimate confrontation with the Western powers. And this in turn explains why the German war effort could not be geared exclusively towards defeating the Red Army or indeed towards the immediate production of armaments. In line with their confident expectation of a speedy and decisive victory, the Third Reich calibrated its attack on the Soviet Union so that as many resources as possible could be freed at the earliest possible opportunity for the ongoing struggle with Britain and its backers in the United States.[8] In this sense, it was in anticipation of Barbarossa that Nazi Germany really did adopt a fully fledged Blitzkrieg strategy, a synthesis of campaign plan, military technology and industrial armaments programme, all premised on the assumption of lightning battlefield success. No such grand synthesis had been conceivable prior to the campaign in France, because the effects that could be achieved by combining modern technology with classical maxims of operational warfare came as a surprise even to the German leadership. It was only after the defeat of France that the possibility of decisive battlefield success within the space of a few months began to be taken for granted as an integral component of Hitler's war strategy. And it was only then that armaments policy could be systematically organized on this assumption.

To avoid misunderstandings, it is important to emphasize that the purpose of adopting this Blitzkrieg strategy in the autumn of 1940 was not to spare the home front. As we have seen, the idea that the German home front was 'under-mobilized' in the first months of the war is really nothing more than a myth. The native labour force was at full stretch, so much so that the regime was forced to import hundreds of thousands of racially undesirable Poles to sustain agricultural production. The manufacture of industrial consumer goods – clothing, furniture and domestic equipment of all kinds – had already been severely curtailed and, despite the euphoria of the summer of 1940, this decision was never reversed. Not that the German leadership were uninterested in the state of civilian morale. In the autumn of 1940 Hitler made a number of dramatic announcements about the benefits that would follow Germany's ultimate victory. Most notably, these included a luxurious housing programme costed optimistically at 63 billion Reichsmarks and a programme of similar dimensions for the modernization of German agriculture.[9] These, however, were post-war projects and this meant, even on optimistic assumptions about Barbarossa, that they could be begun at the earliest in 1942. In the mean time Hitler's priorities as far as the German population was concerned were quite specific: securing the food supply and protecting Germany against aerial attack. And as the war was conceived by Hitler and the military, there was no contradiction between these objectives and the need to further expand the prosecution of the war. On the contrary, the strongest arguments for rushing to conquer the Soviet Union in 1941 were precisely the growing shortage of grain and the need to knock Britain out of the war before it could pose a serious air threat. The significance of the Blitzkrieg strategy adopted in 1940–41 was not that it allowed the overall level of mobilization to be kept to a minimum, but that it allowed the German war effort to be split into two parts. The factories producing for the army directed their efforts towards providing the equipment for a swift, motorized Blitzkrieg against the Soviet Union. Meanwhile, the rest of the German military-industrial complex began to gird itself for the aerial confrontation with Britain and America.

Since this strategy involved the balancing of a variety of competing objectives, it was bound to produce distributional conflict between the various interested parties within the Nazi state. It is possible therefore to tell the history of the second year of the war as an intricate narrative of bureaucratic in-fighting.[10] Once the ammunition crisis of 1940 had passed, Fritz Todt's bid to assume complete control of the armaments effort faltered. An uneasy stand-off developed between Todt, the OKW's military-economic office under General Thomas and the procurement offices of the three armed forces. This power struggle was further compli-cated by Goering's dual position as head of the air force and head of the Four Year Plan, and by the occasional interventions of Walther Funk, the head of the civilian economic administration. All sides in this multi-sided bureaucratic battle hurled allegations of incompetence and inefficiency. The archival paper trail thus appears to confirm the statistical indicators produced later in the war by the Speer Ministry, which appear to demon-strate the inefficiency and under-mobilization of the German war econ-omy in 1940 and 1941. But if we are interested in the real outcomes of the armaments effort, the bureaucratic battles in Berlin are a distraction. The politics of the German war effort may have been messy, but the record of industrial production between June 1940 and June 1941 in fact bears the unmistakable imprint of strategic design. Armaments production and economic policy were linked to a strategic war plan and when the data are analysed carefully, the evidence suggests that this strategy was successful in producing a very substantial further mobiliz-ation of the German economy. That this was not enough to defeat the Soviet Union is another matter.

I

The German army's requirements for Barbarossa – Ruestungsprogramm B – were agreed within a fortnight of Hitler's order to prepare for an attack on the Soviet Union. As of August 1940, this programme was to dictate the output of the German armaments economy for the next eight months.[11] So eager have historians been to demonstrate the incompet-ence and lassitude of the Nazi regime in this decisive period that we are in danger of losing sight of the considerable effort that *was* made in advance of Barbarossa. The attack launched by the Wehrmacht on

22 June 1941 was the largest single military operation in recorded history.[12] A force numbering no less than 3,050,000 men was involved in the assault, organized into three gigantic Army Groups operating simultaneously on three fronts, over a front line in excess of 1,000 kilometres. Barbarossa can legitimately claim to be the end point of a European tradition of operational warfare that stretches back at least to the eighteenth century. In preparation for this immense campaign the Third Reich was not idle. The army was expanded between May 1940 and June 1941 from 143 to 180 divisions.[13] Of course, not all of the new divisions could be used in Russia. Significant forces had to be diverted to the defence of Germany's new empire in the West. The occupation of Yugoslavia and Greece in the spring of 1941 and the campaigns in North Africa added further distractions. On the other hand, the military booty of 1940 was more than enough to equip the Wehrmacht divisions stationed in the quieter zones of Hitler's empire.

What Ruestungsprogramm B aimed to provide was a significant increase in Germany's offensive firepower. And, in contrast to the preparations for the attack on France, the German army's production priorities were now squarely focused on the requirements of armoured warfare. After their astonishing success in France, tanks were never far from Hitler's mind. Even during the first weeks of July 1940, when he was seriously contemplating a large-scale reduction in army strength, Hitler excluded the 'schnellen Truppen' (Blitz troops) from these cuts.[14] Instead, between the summer of 1940 and the summer of 1941 the number of Panzer divisions was doubled, from 10 to 20. It is possible to downplay this expansion by pointing to the fact that the number of tanks did not increase in proportion to the number of divisions. But, as we have already established, the total number of vehicles is meaningless as a guide to the effective fighting strength of the Panzer divisions. What mattered was not the total number of tanks, but the number of combat-worthy medium tanks – Mark IIIs, IVs and Czech-made 36- and 38-ton tanks. If we focus on this group, German tank strength doubled between May 1940 and June 1941, exactly in proportion to the number of tank divisions.[15] There was also a proportional increase in half-tracks, which provided the mobility for 10 divisions of motorized infantry, whose performance was key to the success of the Blitzkrieg. Tanks could fire and move, but they could not hold ground unless they were backed up by fast-moving infantry.

The tank production drive of 1940–41 is also significant because it created one of the most durable organizational structures of the German war economy. With a clear eye for the main chance, Fritz Todt seized the initiative in the bureaucratic battle in the summer of 1940, by attaching a new Main Committee for Tanks to his Ministry for Ammunition and Weapons.[16] The basic ingredients for this Committee's success were clear enough. The tank programme was adequately provided with raw materials, labour and manufacturing capacity. Todt's system of enrolling the manufacturers in the allocation of production contracts had already proved its effectiveness as a mobilizing device. The Main Committee was chaired between 1940 and 1943 by Dr Walter Rohland, the energetic chief of the Deutsche Edelstahlwerke Krefeld, one of the leading suppliers of armoured plate. Rohland's authority rested in turn on his status as a board member of the giant Vereinigte Stahlwerke and as the favourite of Albert Voegler, unarguably the most powerful individual in German heavy industry. It was with Voegler's blessing that Rohland succeeded Ernst Poensgen in 1943 as chief of the entire Vereinigte Stahlwerke complex. Rohland had been a party member since 1933, but the real political muscle on the Main Committee was provided by Karl Otto Saur, Fritz Todt's pugnacious deputy. Saur, who oversaw tank production uninterruptedly between the summer of 1940 and the end of the war, earned himself a well-justified reputation as one of the war economy's most fanatical slave-drivers. The combination of industrial and political authority provided by Rohland and Saur energized the existing members of the tank cartel as well as enrolling new capacity. By 1941, the Mark III medium tank, which was now replacing the Mark II as the mainstay of the Panzer divisions, was being produced by no less than four different factories – MAN in Nuremberg, MIAG in Brunswick and the Alkett and Daimler-Benz facilities in Berlin.[17] Spreading production across so many factories was not calculated to achieve optimal economies of scale, but it was a quick way of expanding capacity. It minimized disputes between producers and by dispersing production it was to make the German tank industry remarkably insensitive to aerial bombardment.

Nor were the preparations for Barbarossa confined to the expansion in the tank force. The programme also assumed a substantial increase in the firepower of the infantry divisions with increases in the number of light field howitzers and the complete replacement of World War I vintage machine guns, still widely used in May 1940, with the modern MG 34.[18] Significantly, the programme also specified large-scale upgrades to Germany's anti-aircraft defences, with particularly high targets set for 8.8 and 10.5 centimetre calibre guns, weapons that competed directly with the artillery requirements of the army. As can be seen from Appendix Table A4, the targets of Ruestungsprogramm B were largely met. Compared to May 1940, the Wehrmacht by the summer of 1941 was increased not only in terms of total manpower, but also firepower.

During the designated period of Ruestungsprogramm B, October 1940 to April 1941, the year-on-year increase in the output of weapons and military vehicles was 54 per cent, for aircraft the figure was 40 per cent, the production of U-boats more than tripled.[19] What has tended to obscure this considerable growth in the production of weaponry is the simultaneous decline in the production of ammunition, which, as we have seen, had been Hitler's number one priority in the first nine months of the war. This shift in emphasis is the defining feature of the German armaments effort between the summer of 1940 and the spring of 1942. And we can better appreciate its significance if we remind ourselves that by July 1940 ammunition accounted for no less than 36 per cent of total armaments production. By the summer of 1941 its share had fallen to less than 20 per cent. Inevitably, this sudden downgrading of ammunition in the priority list must have caused some confusion and a degree of wastage, especially in the heavy engineering sector where artillery shells were made. For the third time, after 1937 and 1939, German industry had tooled up for an ammunition production drive only to find its orders suddenly cancelled. However, given the huge stocks of ammunition accumulated by the summer of 1940, it would have been absurd to continue production at the rates commanded by Hitler six months earlier. By September 1940, the German army had stockpiled no less than 21.9 million 10.5 centimetre howitzer rounds, each of which embodied more than 30 kilos of steel and 3 kilos of precious copper.[20] For the majority of calibres, there was enough in hand to cover more than twelve months of heavy fighting. Though it did not look good in the armaments statistics, halting the overproduction of ammunition was clearly a first priority of rational armaments strategy.[21]

Given the huge ammunition stocks accumulated by the summer of 1940, steel could be reallocated away from the immediate production of armaments without reducing the effective striking power of the German army. Between the second quarter of 1940 and the second quarter of 1941, the army's steel ration was cut by more than a third, whilst its striking power increased by roughly the same percentage.[22] The steel released from the army was not reallocated towards civilian consumption. In the second half of 1940, the reduction in the army's steel supply was almost exactly matched by the increased allocation to exports (see Appendix, Table A3). Even after the outbreak of the war, therefore, the requirements of the balance of payments continued to compete with armaments production as one of the chief economic preoccupations of the Nazi regime. As we have seen, Germany was doing its best in 1940 to engineer a massive trade deficit. However, in the twelve months after October 1940 German exports rose by 25 per cent from the trough they had reached in the first summer of the war. This flow of goods was crucial to maintaining Germany's relations with its Allies, including the Soviet Union, Hungary and Romania, but also with important neutrals such as Spain and Sweden. Indeed, as we have seen, one of the main advocates of wartime exports was the military-economic office of the Wehrmacht, not because it wanted to favour the 'civilian economy', but because it viewed continued trade as indispensable to Germany's survival in a long war.

Another clue to interpreting German military-economic strategy in anticipation of Barbarossa can be found in the management of the labour force.[23] As in the case of steel, this was arranged so as to allow the army to complete its programme, whilst at the same time releasing resources for other uses. What certainly did not happen was any reduction in the overall level of mobilization. In the immediate aftermath of the defeat of France, German industry had been promised a 'victory dividend' in the form of a large reduction in the front-line strength of the army. This decision, however, was reversed within weeks, following Hitler's order to prepare for an attack on the Soviet Union. After dipping briefly from a strength of 5.767 million in June 1940, the Wehrmacht began to grow again in the autumn of 1940, reaching a total of 7.3 million men by the following summer. Teenaged cohorts provided roughly 660,000 men per annum. But a large part of this increase was attributable to a further extension of the draft to men previously exempted on grounds of their importance to the war economy. Compared to May 1940, the workforce census of May 1941 counted an additional 1.4 million workers as having been called up for military service. By the summer of 1941, the population of German men between the ages of 16 and 56 had been divided into three unequal groups: 7.388 million were under arms and another 2.12 million teenagers between the ages of 16 and 19 were undergoing military training; 3.6 million men of all ages had been disqualified as unfit for military service, largely on medical grounds; the rest, totalling 5.516 million, were those exempted as indispensable to the war economy (*Unab-koemmlich*).[24] By the summer of 1941, the Wehrmacht was already scraping the manpower barrel. Due to the small number of children born during World War I, Germany had no option but to send virtually all its young men into battle.[25] Of those aged between 20 and 30, who were physically fit for military service, 85 per cent were already in the Wehrmacht in the summer of 1941. Only 640,000 men in this prime age group were granted exemptions on grounds of their importance to the war economy. Those who had been exempted on economic grounds were overwhelmingly over the age of 30. But it was on this population of middle-aged family men, the backbone of the armaments industries, that any future recruitment would have to draw.[26] Barbarossa was a Blitzkrieg campaign also in this sense. The best available manpower was fully committed to the initial assault. There was little or nothing in reserve.

To square the circle over the winter of 1940–41, an elaborate system was devised for releasing experienced soldiers back to German industry, whilst the Wehrmacht trained the maximum number of new recruits. Under the so-called 'armaments holiday scheme' the battle-tested veterans were to manufacture the weapons that they and their comrades would use in the Soviet Union the following summer. By implication, however, the industrial effort to complete Ruestungsprogramm B by April 1941 was time-limited.[27] Once the Ostheer (the German Army in the East) began to build to its maximum strength ready for the actual invasion of the Soviet Union, German industry would be stripped of some of its most valuable workers and industrial output was bound to suffer. After the 'armaments holiday' of the winter, the German economy would take a 'war holiday'. This, of course, was on the assumption that the Barbarossa campaign would be brief. Hitler promised his soldiers that they would be back at their workbenches by the end of August.[28] As late as the last weeks of October 1941, the Wehrmacht was still planning for the imminent dissolution of one-third of the army's strength and the redirection of hundreds of thousands of soldiers to the production of weapons for war against Britain and the United States.[29]

What we would like to know, of course, is how efficiently German industry used the limited quantity of labour that was at its disposal in 1940 and 1941. Given the very bold claims that have been made about the character of the German industrial war effort, it is perhaps worth reminding ourselves that before the war it was accepted that German manufacturing was easily on a par with Great Britain and second only to the United States in terms of productive efficiency. Nevertheless, an entire narrative of 'inefficiency, egotism and incompetence' has been built on a set of rather rough data which appear to show a catastrophic collapse in labour productivity in the first years of the war.[30] This result is obtained by comparing statistics for the number of people working for the Wehrmacht between 1939 and 1941 with the most widely cited indicator of armaments production. According to these sources, whereas the Wehrmacht workforce doubled, armaments production increased by only 70 per cent between 1939 and 1941. Indeed, in the case of the Luftwaffe it has been claimed that an increase in workforce of 50 per cent between 1939 and 1941 raised output by only 15 per cent.[31] Both comparisons, if they were true, would imply a disastrous fall in output per worker. But in fact these claims should carry a severe health warning. The statistics on which they are based are extremely deficient and do not withstand closer inspection.

Figure 17 shows a new calculation of the monthly index of armaments production plotted against a revised estimate of the armaments workforce.[32] Despite monthly fluctuations, the general movement of the series is parallel, suggesting no collapse in productivity. There may have been some underperformance in the later months of 1941. But this is hardly surprising given the disruption caused by the mobilization for Barbarossa. The transport system was again in disarray and whilst the overall number of Wehrmacht workers continued to increase, production was disrupted by the drafting of key personnel. There are serious problems in going beyond this kind of broad-brush statement, because of the difficulty of obtaining truly comparable measures for both production and the workforce in the armaments sector. In the case of the army and navy there was almost certainly no deterioration in labour productivity, because as we have seen the output of army equipment and naval vessels grew quite dramatically between 1940 and 1941, whereas the labour

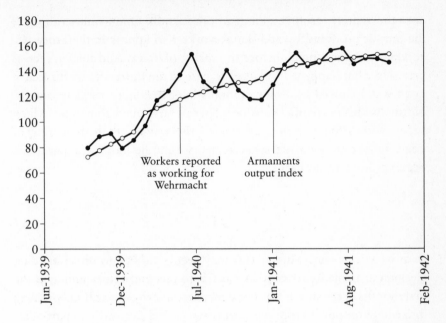

Figure 17. Labour input and armaments output (1st quarter 1940 = 100)

force in the army plants expanded by only 20 per cent and in the navy's case by as little as 7 per cent.[33] Any shortfall due to the reduction in ammunition production must be described as the outcome of deliberate policy rather than inefficiency. The most likely suspect for a productivity decline in the run-up to Barbarossa is the Luftwaffe, where most of the increase in the official 'Wehrmacht' labour force was recorded between 1940 and 1941. The official figures for Luftwaffe employment, which are inflated by an uncertain margin, do show a 40 per cent increase in the Luftwaffe workforce between the spring of 1940 and the autumn of 1941.[34] When compared to figures for aircraft output, this would imply stagnation in labour productivity in 1941 but certainly no collapse. As will be discussed below, there were specific technical factors impeding aircraft production in Germany in 1940–41. And this sector, too, suffered from the disruption caused by Barbarossa. More importantly, however, hasty comparisons of output and employment in 1941 take no account of the fact that aircraft production takes time – at least six months from raw material to finished aircraft. It is hardly surprising, therefore, that the large increase in the Luftwaffe workforce in 1941 did not immediately result in a surge in production. One would not expect the output produced by additional workers to appear in the Luftwaffe acceptance figures much before the spring of 1942. And this, in fact, is precisely what happened. A large increase in the Luftwaffe workforce in 1941 was followed six to nine months later by a huge surge in output. Normally this is credited to Albert Speer's 'armaments miracle', which began with a major reorganization of the war effort in the spring of 1942. In fact, the evidence suggests that we should look to preparations begun at least a year earlier.[35]

II

In any case, as surprising as this may seem, the key to understanding German armaments strategy in 1941 is to recognize that, unlike in the first months of the war, it was not directed primarily towards maximizing immediate output.[36] From the start of 1941, the Luftwaffe in particular was focusing its attention as much on the continuation of the war against Britain and the United States as it was on Barbarossa. Hitler himself set the tone with his address to the commanders-in-chief at Berchtesgaden on 9 January 1941. Treating the defeat of the Soviet Union as a foregone conclusion, Hitler sketched a future of boundless possibilities, in which Germany would wage a 'battle of the continents', by which he clearly meant a war with the United States.[37] To secure this future of global power, German armaments strategy in 1941 needed to be directed as much towards investment in future capacity as towards current production. In the prelude to Barbarossa, therefore, the army, the Four Year Plan and the Luftwaffe all engaged in substantial investment drives. Coming on top of the expansion programmes set in motion in 1938 and the more targeted investment triggered by the Fuehrer's ammunition programme of early 1940, the result was an investment boom, the like of which had never before been seen by German industry.[38]

As far as the German army was concerned, the chief priorities were tanks and explosives. Despite the enormous scale of operation Barbarossa, the German army shared the view that the ultimate military enemies of the Third Reich were Britain and the United States. Furthermore, the army anticipated that after victory in the East it would struggle to assert itself against the rival claims of the Luftwaffe and the navy. As an alternative to the air and naval war, the army's staff therefore devised a variety of operations through which it might strike at the British Empire in Western Asia. Once the Soviet Union had been defeated, powerful armoured columns would be launched into the Middle East and northern India from bases in Libya, Anatolia and the Caucasus. To deliver this death blow, the Generals dreamed of a vast fleet of 36 Panzer divisions, 15,000 strong.[39] An internal planning document produced by the army in May 1941 called for the production of almost 40,000 tanks and 130,000 half-tracks over the next three years.[40] These schemes for a Eurasian war on a scale not seen since Alexander the Great have generally been dismissed as little more than thought-experiments. In fact, however, tank production by the end of the war comfortably exceeded the quantities specified in the army's Mesopotamian fantasy.[41] And this increase in production was only possible because the army's post-Barbarossa planning did not remain on paper.[42] In 1941 hundreds of millions of Reichsmarks were invested in the tank industry. In Kassel, Henschel & Sohn added almost a hundred thousand square metres of new floor space. A gigantic new plant, the Nibelungen works, was opened at Sankt Valentin, Austria, and two new factories – Vomag at Plauen and the Maschinenfabrik Niedersachsen – were converted to tank production.[43] The year 1941 also saw an important shift in technological terms. Germany finally abandoned large-scale production of obsolete light tanks and concentrated all available energies on the medium tank designs that were to see the Wehrmacht through to the summer of 1943. Furthermore, the decision was taken to accelerate the development of two new heavy tanks, specifically intended to counter the remarkable T-34 and KV-1 vehicles that caused so much trouble to the German forces in Russia. Like that of the Luftwaffe, the future of the German tank force was decided, not in 1942 or 1943, but in the summer and autumn of 1941.

The tank programme was only one of a number of major investment programmes undertaken by the army. Funding for these came from the MONTAN GmbH, the army's investment holding.[44] The balance sheet of the MONTAN provides an extraordinary insight into the expansion of the German military-industrial complex in the first years of the war. It clearly highlights the immense capital requirements, particularly of the chemicals side of the armaments complex. Driven upwards by the Schnellplan of 1938 and Hitler's demands of early 1940, explosives

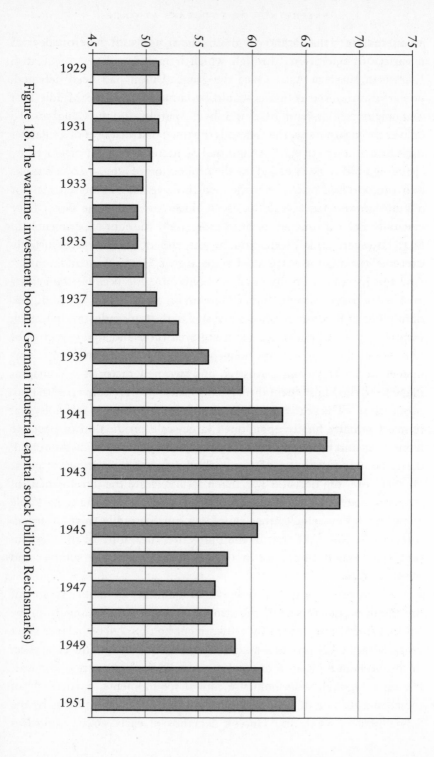

Figure 18. The wartime investment boom: German industrial capital stock (billion Reichsmarks)

accounted for 70–80 per cent of the army's investment in industrial capacity during the war.

Chemistry was the common denominator of much of Germany's wartime investment boom. As we have seen, by the winter of 1940–41 there were mounting concerns about the long-term raw material situation. Chief amongst Germany's problems were its inadequate supplies of rubber and oil. Both problems had been alleviated by the stocks captured in the summer of 1940, but neither had been solved. Assuming that the full force of the Wehrmacht was back in action from the spring, the military-economic staff predicted serious shortages of both oil and rubber by the second half of 1941. One possible remedy was a renewed effort to expand synthetic fuel capacity, another was the conquest of the Caucasus. In 1941 and 1942 the Third Reich pursued both.

Over the winter of 1940–41 Carl Krauch, now acting both as chairman of IG Farben's supervisory board and as chemicals supremo in the Four Year Plan, moved once again to the centre of the German war effort.[45] As General Thomas later noted, Krauch took the question of 'USA-competition' very seriously.[46] His first priority, therefore, was to increase dramatically the production of air fuel. The second priority was rubber. In November 1940 Krauch instructed IG Farben to expand its three existing Buna plants and to build a fourth facility in the newly acquired Polish territories, sufficiently far to the east to be safe from the threat of British bombers. In February 1941 he set fuel expansion targets that aimed to raise Germany's production from 4.3 million tons expected in 1941 to more than 6 million tons by 1943.[47] The longer-term goal, first envisioned in 1938, was to achieve production of more than 10 million tons of oil by 1945.

It was at the very end of 1940 that Carl Krauch and IG Farben began to concentrate their attention on the small Upper Silesian town of Auschwitz.[48] Situated on level ground, close to the coalfields of Cracow and central Upper Silesia, boasting both an ample supply of water and excellent railway connections, Auschwitz was the ideal site for a large chemicals complex. It was first identified by Krauch's staff as a site for one of the new generation of hydrogenation plants, to be built by an IG licensee. But in December 1940 IG Farben itself scouted the site for its top-priority rubber plant and by February 1941 they had arranged with the SS for the transfer of an industrial terrain measuring 8 by 3 kilometres, just to the east of Auschwitz. At this point, the small

Table 13. The balance sheet of the MONTAN GmbH, 1938–1943: industrial investment by the German army

Million RM	Assets on 31 March 1938	Assets added in year ending:					Assets on 31 March 1943
		1938/9	1939/40	1940/41	1941/2	1942/3	
Tools	3.9	1.9	0.6	0.5	1.7	0.3	8.9
Weapons, vehicles, tanks	61.3	48.7	72.6	106.8	124.8	81.0	495.2
Cartridges	77.3	9.9	9.8	9.1	4.9	7.9	118.9
Shells	13.5	1.6	1.8	3.1	-17.5	74.2	76.7
Fuses	18.3	2.2	-0.5	0.2	-0.1	4.2	24.3
Explosives and chemicals	139.0	237.9	387.4	852.1	911.3	347.1	2,874.8
Housing	2.5	12.3	30.3	75.9	68.0	78.7	267.7
Manufacturing assets only	313.3	302.2	471.7	971.8	1,025.1	514.7	3,598.8
All assets	315.8	314.5	502.0	1,047.7	1,093.1	593.4	3,866.5

Source: B. Hopmann, *Von der MONTAN zur Industrieverwaltungsgesellschaft (IVG) 1916–1951* (Stuttgart, 1996), 120

prison camp occupied by the SS in Auschwitz did not figure prominently in Himmler's planning, but in due course Krauch, IG and the SS were all to dramatically scale up their ambitions. In industrial terms, Auschwitz came to be conceived not simply as a Buna factory, but as a complex state-of-the-art chemicals facility, suitable for the production of Buna, methanol, carbide and iso-octane, the crucial additive for the Luftwaffe's air fuel. The final budget for the Auschwitz plant was 776 million Reichsmarks, making it the largest single investment in the entire portfolio of the Four Year Plan. At least 610 million Reichsmarks were actually spent by the end of the war.[49] In terms of sheer scale, the chemicals plant dwarfed the expanding extermination centre that the SS established just a mile to the west. Nor was Auschwitz an isolated investment. IG Farben's decision to build the fourth rubber plant at Auschwitz-Monowitz (Dwory) incorporated it into a triangle of huge chemicals projects in eastern Upper Silesia. The other nodes were Heydebreck, also built by IG Farben for the production of iso-octane air fuel, and a second synthetic fuel plant built at Blechhammer by the firm that was originally to be awarded the Auschwitz site. Altogether, the Upper Silesian chemicals complex must have consumed in the order of 1.3 billion Reichsmarks, or roughly 13 billion euros in modern money.

It is commonplace to dismiss these projects as nothing more than 'investment ruins' (*Investitionsruinen*), exercises in murderous futility that bore no practical relation to the German war effort.[50] Since all three chemicals facilities in Silesia were built at least in part by concentration camp labour, this impulse is more than understandable. The construction of IG Farben's plant at Monowitz claimed the lives of at least 30,000 inmates.[51] In light of such horror, it is easier to think of Auschwitz as a place of pure negativity, of destruction pure and simple.[52] Unfortunately, however, the reality is more complicated and disturbing. It is true, as is commonly remarked, that IG Auschwitz never produced any rubber. But by 1942 it was no longer simply a Buna facility. Under severe pressure from the Berlin authorities to justify their huge investment, IG's managers at Auschwitz decided in the summer of 1942 to start up methanol production at the earliest possible opportunity.[53] Methanol was a vital ingredient of war production, both for aircraft fuel and as one of the basic ingredients in the manufacture of explosives.[54] The first tanker load of methanol to leave Auschwitz-Monowitz in October 1943 was the occasion of a major celebration, to which IG not surprisingly invited Camp Commandant Rudolf Hoess. By 1944 Speer's Armaments Ministry expected Auschwitz to account for one-tenth of the total supply of methanol. Heydebreck was scheduled for twice that much. When British and American bombers started doing serious damage to IG Farben's plant at Leuna in 1944, the Silesian complex stood ready. According to the United States Strategic Bombing Survey, Auschwitz and Heydebreck 'came to the rescue' of the German war effort in 1944.[55] By the end of 1944 Auschwitz was responsible for 15 per cent of Germany's methanol production and, in acknowledgement of the plant's success, Dr Johann Giesen, the man responsible for the Auschwitz fuel programme, was nominated by Speer's Armaments Ministry to take charge of the methanol sector across the Reich. Though it is certainly true that the expenditure of resources in Silesia was out of all proportion to the net benefit received, this was a question of timing, not inherent logic. The chief beneficiaries of Krauch's huge investment programme turned out to be the Soviets, who dismantled much of the high-pressure apparatus, and the Poles, who inherited the buildings and electricity generators. By the 1950s, the renamed facility at Auschwitz-Oswiecim was the hub of coal-based chemistry in the Silesian region. The plant also survived the fall of Communism and is today the third-largest producer of synthetic rubber in Europe, with capacity equal to roughly 5 per cent of global consumption. As of 2003, at least two of the world's leading tyre manufacturers source their rubber from the plant at Oswiecim, the foundations for which were laid in 1941, when Carl Krauch received his largest-ever allocation of steel. According to the records of the Four Year Plan, no less than 2.5 billion Reichsmarks were channelled into Krauch's chemicals projects in 1940 and 1941.[56]

The only rivals to the chemicals industry as recipients of wartime investment were the Luftwaffe industries. In 1940–41 it was the Luftwaffe, not the army, that was at the crux of Germany's strategic dilemma. The army would fight the Soviet Union. The navy would fight the British. The Luftwaffe was the only arm that faced the full demands of a two-front war. It was also the Luftwaffe that would be the first to face the terrifying industrial might of the United States. It was in the air war that the Germans really feared the American contribution to the Allied war effort. Roosevelt's announcement in May 1940 that he wanted to see American industry turning out at least 3,000 aircraft per month and reaching a final production level of 50,000 sent shock waves through the Reich Air Ministry. The mythology surrounding American mass-production, and particularly its phenomenal success in mass-producing internal combustion engines, was daunting to say the least. Though it was William S. Knudsen of General Motors who was leading the discussions with the British, the question in Berlin was: 'What will Ford do?' ('*Was macht Ford?*'). Given Henry Ford's isolationist proclivities, the company in fact hestitated. But by September 1940 ground had been broken on a state-of-the-art aero-engine plant at River Rouge, and by the spring of 1941 construction was under way at Willow Run, where Ford was to construct its famous factory for the mass-production of B24 heavy bombers.[57] Willow Run did not enter production until much later in the war. But the noises from America were worrying enough for the industrialist Fritz Siebel, an acquaintance of Hermann Goering's, to appeal for an urgent increase in German aircraft production.[58]

In 1940 and 1941, however, the fundamental problem was less one of quantity than of quality. If there was one thing that the Battle of Britain had made clear, it was the shortcomings of the Luftwaffe's development programme. The aircraft that were already in production had proved themselves unable to achieve a decisive victory over the Royal Air Force. The Junkers 88 medium bomber was far from being the war-winning universal combat aircraft that had been sold to Goering in 1938. A battlefield report commissioned from squadrons stationed on the Channel coast recorded that the aircrew were 'not afraid of the enemy, but were afraid of the Junker 88'.[59] It was slow, it lacked effective defensive armament and for strategic bombing its payload was hopelessly inadequate. With upgraded engines, both the older-generation medium bombers, the He 111 and the Do 17, proved capable of outperforming the Ju 88, their designated successor. And this was no mere technicality. The Luftwaffe's entire industrial plan since 1938 had been built around the primacy of the Ju 88, the Junkers corporation and Heinrich Koppenberg, its CEO. To call into question the qualities of the Ju 88 was to call into question the entire basis of Luftwaffe development over the previous three years, as well as hundreds of millions of Reichsmarks of investment.

The Luftwaffe's other main aircraft, the Messerschmitt Bf 109 was an excellent short-range fighter-interceptor, but it had been in operation since the Spanish Civil War and it could be kept competitive only by repeated upgrading. Over the winter of 1940–41 the difficulties of getting the Bf 109 E, or 'Emil', into production accounted for a large part of the sharp dip in aircraft production that caused great embarrassment to the Luftwaffe. And it was clear that in the foreseeable future it too would need to be replaced. The Focke Wulf FW 190, which was nearing combat readiness in early 1941, offered a substantial advance in performance. But Focke Wulf's management lacked the political clout of Willy Messerschmitt, and the BMW radial engine around which the plane had been designed was proving extremely troublesome. Messerschmitt's other mainstay, the Me 110 heavy fighter was one of the real casualties of the Battle of Britain. Intended as a long-range escort for Germany's bombers, it had been hopelessly outclassed by the fighters of the RAF. According to Ernst Udet's plans, the Me 110 was soon to be replaced by the much improved Me 210. However, this aircraft was turning into one of the great development disasters of the war.[60] The same could also be said of Heinkel's long-range strategic bomber, the four-engined He 177. The future of the Luftwaffe as a strategic weapon, and Heinkel's future as a major aircraft developer, depended on the performance of this plane. A dedicated factory annexe had been built at Heinkel's state-funded plant in Oranienburg, laid out specifically to enable the large-scale employment of concentration camp labour, a major new experiment for the armaments industries.[61] However, thanks largely to its absurd specifications, which called for dive-bombing capability, the He 177 was a disaster. Its wings were prone to falling off and its peculiar back-to-back engine configuration resulted in frequent self-combustion.[62]

In light of these technical difficulties, it is hardly surprising that the Reich Air Ministry in early 1941 found it hard to come up with a coherent long-range production plan. The Luftwaffe urgently needed a new generation of aircraft and this seemed all the more important given the worrying news about the American plans for mass-production. Germany's only hope, it seemed, was to counter quantity with quality. As the Luftwaffe chief of staff put it, in far from optimistic tones, in September 1941: 'If there is any way for the German air force to achieve a decisive victory over the American-British aerial enemy, then it can only be the qualitative superiority of its armaments.'[63] Since new models that were already scheduled for series production were proving troublesome, the leading development firms, Junkers, Heinkel and Messerschmitt, plunged into a new wave of designs – the Ju 288 to replace the

Ju 88, the Me 209 to replace the Me 109 – in the hope of gaining a decisive advantage in the next major round of procurement. Meanwhile, the second-tier manufacturers who produced aircraft under licence, had every incentive to hedge their bets by avoiding over-commitment to any particular design or aircraft component. The result of this competitive process was a profusion of prototypes and innovations, but not the optimal exploitation of economies of scale. What this should not obscure, however, is the process of acceleration that was already beginning to take hold of German air force planning in the last months of 1940, in direct response to the Anglo-American air threat. At the heart of this acceleration were Carl Krauch's enormous new schemes for the production of synthetic rubber and air fuel. But in 1940 and 1941 Krauch's entrepreneurship was multiplied by the no less energetic activity of Heinrich Koppenberg of Junkers. To meet the threat of American mass-production, Koppenberg set in motion an enormous expansion, both in the output of aluminium and, a no less significant new investment, in the production of aero-engines. In this respect as well, the foundations for an increase in aircraft production were laid well before the results began to make themselves felt in 1942.

In 1940, thanks to the huge expansion undertaken by the Wehrmacht, Germany was the world's leader in aluminium production, with annual output of 300,000 tons. In the autumn of 1940, however, officials in the Reich Air Ministry and the Four Year Plan were alarmed by the news that the United States was planning to raise its production to 450,000 tons by 1942.[64] To counter this threat, the Reich embarked on a gigantic European scheme, to be centred on Norway. As a result of its natural endowment with mineral wealth and abundant hydroelectricity, Norway in the inter-war period had become a hub for European ore mining and metal smelting. The industry was largely foreign-owned and thus susceptible to immediate German penetration. For Heinrich Koppenberg, it was an opportunity to realize his Fordist vision of a fully integrated aircraft conglomerate, producing everything from the raw material to the finished product.[65] Eager to forestall any move by the established German aluminium producers, Koppenberg descended on Norway even before the fighting was over. By the end of the year, he had established a German-owned aluminium syndicate whose aim was to quadruple Norwegian production from 45,900 tons to at least 200,000 tons by 1944. This gigantic programme was costed initially at

300–400 million Reichsmarks and it was to be a truly pan-European affair. Bauxite and other raw materials were to be transported to Norway from France, Croatia and Greece. Norway would do the smelting. Then the raw aluminium would be shipped south for processing at Junkers' plants in central Germany. By the summer of 1941, as the Luftwaffe scaled up its aircraft production plans, Koppenberg adjusted the scale of the aluminium programme accordingly. By June he was discussing with Goering a scheme to raise production within the German *Grossraum* to no less than 1 million tons, costed at 1.5 billion Reichsmarks.

Koppenberg was also the driving force behind the proposal to build a gigantic new aero-engine factory.[66] The idea of an 'American-style' factory for the mass-production of aero-engines had been discussed in Berlin at least since 1938. But in the autumn of 1940 it took on a new urgency. In November 1940 Koppenberg reported to one of Ernst Heinkel's representatives in Berlin that the Americans were planning to build a new motorworks with a capacity of 1,000 motors per month.[67] According to Koppenberg, the 'only way' to meet this challenge was for Germany also to build a new plant of similar dimensions, capable of reaping the full benefits of mass-production. In November 1940 Koppenberg had the Junkers engineering office draw up a plan for a thousand-engine plant to supply the engine needs of the Ju 288. By May 1941 Junkers was lobbying for an allocation of no less than 685 million Reichsmarks to build the Flugmotorenwerke Ostmark (FMO) safely beyond the reach of Allied bombers, in Austria. In practice, the FMO was to become one of the truly disastrous investments of the Third Reich.[68] After two changes of management, the 'thousand-engine plant' reached its maximum output in 1944 at the very modest rate of only 198 engines per month.

The travails of the FMO, however, should not distract from the real expansion in aero-engine capacity that was set in motion in the autumn of 1940.[69] Most of the investment flowed, not into green-field sites, but into existing aero-engine and airframe plants, such as Daimler-Benz's plant at Genshagen, which provided a precise counterpoint to the FMO debacle. In September 1940, at the same time as Koppenberg was conceiving his grandiose white elephant, Daimler-Benz agreed to raise the capacity of its main aero-engine facility from 350 engines per month to 800, at a comparatively modest capital cost of only 50 million Reichsmarks. In the summer of 1941, the target was raised to 1,200 engines per month, now requiring an investment of 170 million Reichsmarks. In practice, the rate of return at Genshagen turned out to be even better than this. With an investment of only 98 million Reichsmarks, Daimler by the second quarter of 1944 reached an output of no less than 1,200 engines per month.[70] And Daimler's expansion was compounded by investments at the other plants producing its DB 605 engine under licence. Without this investment, initiated in 1940–41, the enormous increase in the production of Me 109 fighters later in the war would simply not have been possible. In total, it is claimed that the Luftwaffe industries sank 5.18 billion Reichsmarks into expansion between September 1939 and January 1942, a figure so large as to seem implausible.[71] We can say with more certainty that between December 1940 and March 1941 the Reich Air Ministry authorized investments totalling 762.8 million Reichsmarks, of which 533.4 million were directed into the aero-engine industry.

The floodgates in Luftwaffe planning finally opened in the summer of 1941 with the completion of the army's Barbarossa programme and the long-awaited decision to shift priority to the air war. In June 1941 the Air Ministry proposed a doubling of output to 20,000 aircraft per year over the following three years.[72] To implement this expansion, Goering's staff came to an agreement with Fritz Todt to carry out the reallocation of resources from the army to the Luftwaffe in a 'consensual fashion'. Todt himself was to oversee the identification of spare capacity and to ensure continuity of employment for army contractors.[73] Days after the invasion of the Soviet Union, the Luftwaffe revealed the full urgency and ambition of its new plans. At a meeting with representatives of the OKW, State Secretary Milch announced that, as of 1 May 1941, German intelligence believed that combined British and American output had exceeded that of Germany and Italy. The United States alone was turning out 2,800 high-performance aero-engines per month. On current trends, Anglo-American output would be twice that of the Axis by the end of 1942. 'There is not a minute to lose . . .', Milch declared. By the summer of 1942 Germany needed to increase its production of aircraft by 150 per cent, to roughly 3,000 planes per month.[74] The precise target set by Milch was new, but not the basic thrust of his comments. As we have seen, the expansion in productive capacity had already begun in the autumn of 1940. Milch's new target of 3,000 aircraft per month, however, required a further scaling up. Since earlier in the year Krauch had been envisioning a medium-term increase in the production of air fuel from 1 to 1.5 million tons. Now he raised his target to no less than 3 million tons. Given the cost of the hydrogenation process, it was unrealistic to assume that this could be produced from German coal. Hydrogenation was simply too expensive. Krauch's promise therefore hinged on the assumption that the Wehrmacht would conquer the Caucasus in the next few months and that Germany by 1942 would be importing Russian oil at the rate of at least one million tons per annum.[75] Here was the perverse logic of Barbarossa in a nutshell. The conquest of the oilfields of the Caucasus, 2,000 kilometres deep in the Soviet Union, was not treated as the awesome military-industrial undertaking that it was. It was inserted as a precondition into another gargantuan industrial plan designed to allow the Luftwaffe to fight an air war, not against the Soviet Union, but against the looming air fleet of Britain and the United States.

III

However optimistic the Wehrmacht may have been in the assessment of its own capacities, the sheer size of the task facing them in the Soviet Union could not be denied. Most fundamentally, the Germans were grossly outnumbered. Even allowing for the unreliability of Stalinist statistics, the population of the Soviet Union cannot have been less than 170 million in 1941. The population of Germany was less than half that: 83.76 million people in 1939.[76] Though the German army that invaded the Soviet Union probably outnumbered the Red Army troops stationed in the western sectors, the Germans had already conscripted virtually all their prime manpower. By contrast, the Red Army could call up millions of reservists. From the outset, therefore, it was clear that the Wehrmacht must not be sucked into a battle of attrition. And this imbalance of manpower was compounded by the enormous expanse of Soviet territory and the sheer impassability of the terrain. If the Red Army were able to withdraw in good order this would present Germany with insuperable problems. If on the other hand the coherence of the Soviet force could be broken, then the difficulty of maintaining communications would hamper their efforts to restore coherence no less than it impeded the German advance.[77] Everything depended on deciding the battle, as in France, in the first weeks of the campaign. This was the assumption on which Barbarossa was premised.[78] A massive central thrust towards Moscow, accompanied by flanking encirclements of the Soviet forces trapped in the north and south, would allow the Red Army to be broken on the Dnieper–Dvina river line within 500 kilometres of the Polish-German border. The Dnieper–Dvina river line was critical because beyond that point logistical constraints on the German army were binding.[79] These limitations on Germany's new style of 'Blitzkrieg' had not been obvious in 1940, because the depth of operations required by Manstein's encircling blow (*Sichelschnitt*) had never exceeded a few hundred kilometres. The entire operation could therefore be supplied by trucks shuttling back and forth from the German border. On the basis of their experience in France, the Wehrmacht's logistical staff calculated that the efficient total range for trucks was 600 kilometres, giving an operational depth of 300. Beyond that point the trucks themselves used up so much of the fuel they were carrying that they became inefficient as a means of transport. Given the vast distances encountered in the Soviet Union, an operational depth of 300 kilometres was absurdly restrictive. To extend the range of the logistical system, the Wehrmacht therefore split its motor pool into two segments. One set of trucks would move forward with the Panzer units and would ferry fuel and ammunition from intermediate dumps that would be resupplied by the main fleet operating from the borders of the General Government. By this expedient, it was hoped that the initial logistical range could be extended to 500 kilometres. By happy chance, this coincided exactly with the Dnieper–Dvina line. Halder, the army's chief of staff, was clearly aware of the fundamental importance of this constraint. In his diary at the end of January 1941 he noted that the success of Barbarossa depended on speed. 'Speed! No stops! Do not wait for railway! Do everything with motor vehicles.' There must be 'no hold ups', 'that alone guarantees victory'.[80]

If serious fighting were to extend beyond this initial phase of the assault, it was clear from the outset that the Wehrmacht's problems would progressively multiply. If the Red Army escaped destruction on the Dnieper–Dvina river line, the Wehrmacht would not be able to engage in hot pursuit, because it would first need to replenish its supply bases closer to the front line. After that, all operations would ultimately depend on the capacity of the Soviet railway system and the speed with which the Wehrmacht could build up forward supply bases to support a second 500 kilometre advance. The problems the Germans encountered in adapting Russia's narrow-gauge railway lines are well known. To make matters worse, the retreating Red Army became extremely proficient at evacuating rolling stock and sabotaging bridges, tracks and other railway installations. However, the problems were more fundamental than this and were evident already at the planning stage. The existing Russian rail infrastructure, even if it had been captured intact, was insufficient to support the German army. As a rule of thumb, German logistical experts liked to assign at least one high-capacity railway line to each army-sized unit. But for the ten armies with which they invaded the Soviet Union, the Wehrmacht was able to assign only three main railway lines, one for each army group.[81] And the situation for Army Group Centre, where the bulk of the German forces were to be concentrated, was particularly bad. From the outset, therefore, the German army had to assume that not all units would be equally well supplied. Critical stores were to be reserved above all for the main strike force of 33 tank and motorized infantry divisions. If the battle extended much beyond the first months of the attack, the fighting power of the rest of the German army would dwindle rapidly.

Fundamentally, the Wehrmacht was a 'poor army'.[82] The fast-striking motorized element of the German army in 1941 consisted of only 33 divisions out of 130. Three-quarters of the German army continued to rely on more traditional means of traction: foot and horse. The German army in 1941 invaded the Soviet Union with somewhere between 600,000 and 750,000 horses.[83] The horses were not for riding. They were for moving guns, ammunition and supplies. Weeks prior to the invasion, 15,000 Panje carts were issued to the infantry units that would trail behind the fast-moving Panzers. The vast majority of Germany's soldiers marched into Russia, as they had into France, on foot. Of course, things would have been better if Germany had had three times as many tanks and trucks. But to imagine a fully motorized Wehrmacht, poised for an attack on the Soviet Union, is a fantasy of the Cold War, not a realistic vision of the possibilities in 1941. To be more specific, it is an American fantasy. The Anglo-American invasion force of 1944 was the only military force in World War II to fully conform to the modern model of a motorized army. The German army was not poor in motor transport because it had neglected to prepare properly. It was poor because of the incomplete industrial and economic development of Germany itself. Most German freight transport in the 1940s was accomplished by rail. For short distances, the horse was still essential in both town and countryside. Of course, the German motor vehicle industry might have been coaxed into producing more trucks. But the basic constraint on the use of motor vehicles in wartime Europe was not the supply of vehicles, but the chronic shortage of fuel and rubber. As we have seen, the fuel shortage by the end of 1941 was expected to be so severe that the Wehrmacht was seriously considering demotorization as a way of reducing its dependence on scarce oil.[84]

Everything therefore depended on the assumption that the Red Army would crack under the impact of the first decisive blow. It was hoped that, like the French, the Soviet forces would disintegrate, allowing them to be finished off in a series of encirclement battles. In the second phase of the operation, the German army would advance towards Moscow against disorganized opposition, precipitating the political collapse of Stalin's regime. In World War I it had taken almost four years for the combined forces of Austria and Imperial Germany to bring about the final disintegration of the Tsarist army. The assumption was clearly that the Communist regime was weaker and that the initial blow struck by the Wehrmacht would be far more dramatic. The racist assumptions built into this axiom of German planning are obvious. It was not, however, devoid of all rationality. Expressed most succinctly in terms of per capita GDP, there was a major developmental difference between Germany and the Soviet Union. According to the best modern estimates, German per capita GDP was two and a half times that in the Soviet Union in 1940. On this basis there was good reason to think that the huge quantitative advantage apparently enjoyed by the Red Army would turn out to be illusory. The far greater organizational capacity of the Wehrmacht, the superior quality of its equipment and the greater training of its soldiers would carry the day. After all, this was the army that had defeated the combined forces of France, the British Expeditionary Force, Belgium and the Netherlands in six weeks. By launching its army against the Soviet Union, rather than prosecuting a direct air and sea assault on Britain and its backers in the United States, the Third Reich was not making an irrational strategic choice.[85] It was deploying its best weapon against what still appeared to be the 'weakest link in the chain'.

Not that the Germans were oblivious to the modernization of the Soviet Union since World War I. As the Wehrmacht's own economic staff well knew, Stalin's Five Year Plans had substantially transformed the geography of the Soviet economy. According to credible Western estimates we now believe that Stalin's regime increased total industrial output by 2.6 times between 1928 and 1940, and armaments output grew by vastly more.[86] In their haste to industrialize, the Soviet planners had placed a large amount of investment in Western economic zones vulnerable to the German onslaught.[87] But as the planners in Berlin fully understood, the First Five Year Plan of 1928–32 had established a new Soviet industrial base, safely to the east of the Urals, which had the capacity to sustain a self-sufficient population of at least 40 million people.[88] Even if an invader managed to overrun a large part of the western Soviet Union, war production could continue at new industrial centres, such as the gigantic engineering works at Sverdlovsk. Overall, Soviet industrial capacity was clearly very substantial. In 1939 the German steel association put the Soviet Union well ahead of Great Britain, in third place behind the United States and Germany, with an annual output of 18 million tons of steel, compared to Germany's 23.3 million tons.[89] And on paper at least the Red Army was a formidable force. Throughout the spring of 1941 Franz Halder recorded Hitler's ruminations about the Soviets' immense stocks of tanks and aircraft.[90] Hitler knew that the Soviets had modern aircraft and 'mammoth' tanks with enormous guns. But he comforted himself with the fact that most of the Red Army's equipment was obsolete. On the assumption that the Wehrmacht would be able to achieve a massed concentration at strategic points he was happy to predict that the Soviets would 'crumple under the massive impact of our tanks and planes'.

No one, however, could deny the sheer vastness of the Soviet Union, and this alone made Barbarossa into a daunting proposition. Beneath the thick layer of hubris and optimism that surrounded the planning for Barbarossa, there were those in Berlin who expressed severe misgivings from the start. The doubts, interestingly, were of two kinds. There were at least some officers who questioned the feasibility of the operation itself. Significantly these included Field Marshal Fedor von Bock, commander of Army Group Centre, to whom fell the awesome task of crushing the main body of the Red Army en route to Moscow. By the end of January 1941, Bock was so concerned about the scale of the mission assigned to his army group that he forced Halder, the chief of army staff, to concede that there was a distinct possibility that the

Red Army might escape beyond the Dnieper–Dvina line.[91] What would happen in this eventuality was the key question. One of the earliest war games done to test the Barbarossa plan concluded that unless both the destruction of the Red Army and the capture of Moscow could be accomplished within a matter of months, Germany would face a 'long-drawn-out war, beyond the capacity of the German armed forces to wage'.[92] Generalmajor Marcks, the officer commissioned to prepare the first draft for the plan of attack, also prepared a wide-ranging strategic assessment of the campaign, in which he considered the possibility that the Red Army might be able to prolong the battle beyond the autumn of 1941. Then, Marcks conceded, Germany would need to prepare itself for a war on two fronts against a coalition consisting of the Soviet Union and the British Empire, backed by the economic potential of the United States. Faced with this unappealing prospect Marcks consoled himself with the belief that if Germany could take possession of the grain lands of the Ukraine and secure complete control of the Baltic, it would have little to fear from the overwhelming economic might of its enemies.[93]

It is at this key point, however, that the real fragility of Barbarossa becomes apparent. Following the same logic as Marcks, Hitler consistently prioritized the need to secure the industrial and economic resources of the western Soviet Union at the earliest possible opportunity.[94] For this purpose he envisioned the possibility that large elements of Bock's Army Group Centre might have to be diverted both north to secure the Baltic coastline and south into the Ukraine. Only after these essential economic objectives were achieved would the main body of the German army turn eastwards towards Moscow. This was the priority inscribed in Hitler's Weisung Nr 21, which reached final draft on 17 December 1940. Prioritizing economic objectives, however, was seriously at odds with the plan of the campaign as envisioned by Halder. For Halder, the priority of Moscow was absolute. Only by concentrating all forces on this objective, he believed, could the Red Army be brought to battle and decisively defeated. So fundamental an issue was this for Halder that Hitler's decision to water down the priority of Moscow caused him to question the rationale of the entire campaign. On 28 January 1941, Halder noted in his diary: 'Barbarossa: purpose not clear. We do not hurt the English. Our economic base is not significantly improved. Risk in West should not be underestimated. It is possible that Italy might collapse after the loss of her colonies, and we get a southern front in

Spain, Italy, and Greece. If we are then tied up in Russia, a bad situation will be made worse.'[95] As in the autumn of 1939, therefore, Hitler and Halder were fundamentally at odds. As in 1939–40, Germany's entire future was at stake. But unlike in 1939, Halder did not force the issue to the point of near mutiny. After the spectacular success of the French campaign, the army high command could no longer assert absolute authority in military matters. Hitler could claim at least as much credit for the victory in France, and Halder knew it. He may also have believed that, once battle was joined with the Red Army, his version of the campaign would prevail. Above all, however, everyone agreed in hoping that the main work of destruction could be done on the Dnieper–Dvina river line.

Another latent disagreement is revealed by Halder's comment that the conquest of the Soviet Union would not 'significantly improve' Germany's 'economic base'. This is remarkable because it flies in the face of Hitler's fundamental assumption about the profits to be gained from conquest, particularly of the Ukraine. Until the middle of February 1941, however, it was Halder's pessimistic assessment that reflected the mainstream view in Berlin. The army's military-geographic study of the Soviet Union, finished on 10 August 1940, expected much from the conquest of the Ukraine, but it ruled out any consideration of the Caucasus oilfields as being beyond the immediate reach of even the Panzer divisions. It also emphasized the considerable Soviet industrial potential beyond the German reach in the Urals.[96] In October, a staffer at the Moscow embassy, Gebhardt von Walther, forwarded an even more pessimistic assessment to Halder. This warned against expecting any immediate Soviet collapse following a German attack and played down the benefits to be expected from the Ukraine. The territory was even more overpopulated and impoverished that it had been when it fell into German hands in 1917, and it had been a disappointment then.[97] In January 1941, both the military-economic staff of the Wehrmacht and the offices of the Four Year Plan were hard at work on negative assessments. On 22 January 1941 General Thomas's staff pointed out that an invasion would interrupt deliveries of alloy metals such as manganese, for which the Soviet Union was currently Germany's only source of supply.[98] Furthermore, any major offensive would accelerate the depletion of Germany's already inadequate stocks of fuel and rubber.[99] Similar conclusions had been reached by the offices of the Four Year Plan. The only significant exception was State Secretary Backe of the Agriculture Ministry, who had long been an advocate of expansion towards the east. What precisely Backe said to Hitler in January 1941 was not clear even to insiders such as General Thomas. As one OKW memo put it: 'It is said that State Secretary Backe has informed the Fuehrer that possession of the Ukraine would relieve us of any economic worry. Actually what Backe is supposed to have said is that if any territory could help us, it was the Ukraine. Only the Ukraine was a [grain] surplus region, European Russia as a whole was not.'[100] As we shall see, this distinction was soon to take on an ominous significance. In any case, in the light of reports he was receiving about Hitler's own view of the campaign, General Thomas engineered an abrupt about-turn in the view taken by his staff.[101]

On 22 January 1941 Thomas had informed his boss, Keitel, that he was planning to submit a report urging caution with regard to the military-economic benefits of the invasion.[102] Now he reversed direction. As it became clear that Hitler was justifying Barbarossa first and foremost as a campaign of economic conquest, Thomas began systematically working towards the Fuehrer. He instructed his staff to collaborate closely with Backe in formulating plans for the agricultural exploitation of the Soviet Union, a decision that was vindicated in the second week of February by the Fuehrer's initial response to staff papers on possible shortages of fuel and rubber. The Fuehrer let it be known that he would not be swayed in his strategic judgement by such short-term concerns. In 1940, too, he had been warned of the impending exhaustion of Germany's stocks and his high-risk strategy had been triumphantly vindicated. The attack on the Soviet Union, with the Ukraine as its immediate objective, would go ahead regardless. Responding to this lead, Thomas submitted a report to Hitler on 20 February that was completely unprecedented in its optimism. The OKW now claimed that in its first thrust the Wehrmacht would be able to seize control of at least 70 per cent of the Soviet Union's industrial potential. This would render long-term resistance by the Red Army hopeless. And the profits of occupation would be huge. Together with Backe, Thomas's staff had worked out a plan to 'free up' at least 4 million tons of grain from the Ukraine. And Thomas went further than any previous analyst in insisting that the conquest of the Caucasus was a natural complement to the occupation of the Ukraine. In fact, without the conquest of the Caucasus the Ukraine would be of little value, since Germany would need a huge fleet of tractors and trucks to bring in the harvest, for which the fuel could only come from the Soviet Union itself. Astonishingly, Thomas made no comment on the logistical and operational considerations involved in extending Germany's invasion 2,000 kilometres to the east.[103]

Surveying this remarkable collection of rationalizations three things, at least, are clear. First of all, Hitler's authority was too great, following the success in France, for anyone to mount a serious challenge to his decision to invade the Soviet Union. Halder backed away from an open clash. General Thomas did an about-face to conform to Hitler's point of view. Beneath the veneer of consensus, however, it is clear that there were deep divisions both about the design of the operation and its strategic rationale. As late as the spring of 1941, the Foreign Ministry was still opposing the coming war, preferring to continue the alliance with the Soviet Union against the British Empire.[104] But even more powerful than the Fuehrer myth in silencing debate was the common faith in the Wehrmacht. If the Red Army could indeed be destroyed in the first weeks of the campaign, west of the Dnieper–Dvina river line, then, as in 1940, the worries that preceded the attack would soon be forgotten. There would be no need for arguments about the relative priorities of economic as opposed to purely military objectives. The resources of the western Soviet Union would be shackled to the German war effort and the Third Reich would finally be able to impose its will on the entire continent of Europe. But this assumption of immediate military success was also the central weakness of all the Wehrmacht's planning. If the shock of the initial assault did not destroy Stalin's regime, it was already evident in February 1941 that the Third Reich would find itself facing a strategic disaster.

14

The Grand Strategy of Racial War

The last four chapters have focused on disentangling the complex military-economic considerations that motivated Hitler and his regime between 1939 and 1941. Once we appreciate the scale of the international escalation that Hitler had set in motion in 1938, reaching its climax in the summer of 1940 with the dramatic rearmament decisions of the United States, it is possible to reconstruct an intelligible and consistent strategic logic behind Hitler's actions. Though by the late 1930s Nazi Germany was by far the most highly mobilized society in Western Europe, it was a European economy of modest resources. By the summer of 1939 the limits of Germany's peacetime capacity for mobilization were fully apparent. The combined economic potential of the European powers arrayed against Germany was daunting enough. Once the United States was added to the equation, the disparity was completely overwhelming. From 1938 onwards the alignment of the United States with the Western powers was taken for granted in Berlin. From 1939 onwards it was assumed that America would soon be making a decisive contribution to the armaments effort arrayed against Germany. If Hitler was to realize his dream of fundamentally overturning the global balance of power, he had to strike fast and hard and he had, at all costs, to retain the initiative. This was the consistent if perhaps 'mad' logic that impelled first his decision to risk a general war over Poland in September 1939, then his decision to press home the attack on France regardless of risk and shortly thereafter to prepare for an assault on the Soviet Union. In the light of the threat posed by the British and American armaments effort, in the light of the frailties of the blockaded European economy and in the light of the apparent invincibility of the German army, there was every reason to press onwards as quickly as possible.

Insisting on this strategic logic, however, is not in any way meant to obscure the Manichaean racial ideology that provided the animating force of Hitler's government. For Hitler, 'conventional strategy' was inseparably intertwined with racial ideology. Strategy for Hitler was the grand strategy of race struggle. If it is true that Hitler's decision to drive against the Soviet Union as early as 1941 was motivated by a strategic calculation centred on the war in the West, this does not make the attack on the Soviet Union any less 'ideological'. As we have seen, for Hitler and the Nazi leadership 1938 had marked a fundamental shift. As it was understood in Berlin, the war in the West had been forced on Germany by the world Jewish conspiracy pulling the strings in London and Washington.[1] From the Sudeten crisis onwards, this perverse hidden linkage came to be personified by Roosevelt on the one hand and by Churchill, the arch-opponent of appeasement, on the other. And as we have seen, this conspiratorial interpretation was maintained consistently throughout 1940 and 1941. Documents captured in the Foreign Ministries in Warsaw and Paris only served to confirm the view that Hitler's decision to start the war in 1939 had pre-empted a vicious British and American plot to encircle and strangle Germany. The identification of Roosevelt with the 'world Jewish conspiracy' was unrelenting. Seen in this light, the question of whether Hitler was motivated to attack the Soviet Union primarily by the need to knock Britain out of the war, thereby forestalling American intervention, or by his pursuit of his long-held ideological vision of racial struggle, is based on a false alternative. The conquest of *Lebensraum* in the East had of course always been Hitler's central strategic objective. The threat posed by the Anglo-American alliance, masterminded by world Jewry, simply made this more urgent and more necessary than ever.

There can be no doubt, however, that in its execution, if not in its rationale, Barbarossa did mark a fundamental departure. On 22 June 1941 the Third Reich launched not only the most massive campaign in military history, it also unleashed an equally unprecedented campaign of genocidal violence. The concentrated focus on the destruction of the Jewish population has come to be seen as the truly defining aspect of this campaign. However, in Eastern Europe, the epicentre of the Holocaust, the Judaeocide was not an isolated act of murder. The German invasion of the Soviet Union is far better understood as the last great land-grab in the long and bloody history of European colonialism.[2]

Destroying the Jewish population was the first step towards rooting out the Bolshevik state. What was to follow was a gigantic campaign of land clearance and colonization, which also involved the 'clearance' of the vast majority of the Slav population and the settlement of millions of hectares of eastern *Lebensraum* with German colonists. Complementing this long-term programme of demographic engineering was a short-term strategy of exploitation, motivated by the 'practical' need to secure the food balance of the German *Grossraum*. The attainment of this entirely 'pragmatic' objective required nothing less than the murder, by organized famine, of the entire urban population of the western Soviet Union. As Hans Frank and Herbert Backe had already demonstrated in the General Government in the spring of 1940, Hitler and his regime were determined that in this world war, it would not be the Germans who were starved into defeat.

I

From the moment that Germany invaded Poland in September 1939, the genocidal impulses of Nazi ideology towards both the Jews and the Slavs had taken on concrete form in an extraordinary programme of population displacement and colonial settlement.[3] The architects of this programme were Heinrich Himmler and his technical staffs in the Reichssicherheitshauptamt (RSHA) and the offices of the Reichskommissar fuer die Festigung deutschen Volkstums (RKF). The practical success of this early programme was limited. But it was crucial in establishing the close connection in SS thinking between the removal of the Jews and the wider project of racial reorganization and Germanic settlement.

As we have seen, the idea of colonial settlement in the East had long been central to radical German nationalism. In 1939 this was compounded by two more immediate impulses. The incorporation of a large part of Polish territory into the Reich faced Germany with the question of what to do with millions of new, non-German inhabitants. On the other hand, agreements reached with the Soviet Union and Italy in September and October 1939 meant that Germany had to accommodate the 'return' to the Reich of hundreds of thousands of ethnic Germans from the Baltic and South Tyrol. To make room for this influx, the SS prepared to remove both the entire Jewish population and the vast majority of the Polish inhabitants from the Polish territory now annexed to the Reich.[4] One early version of the Generalplan specified the goal of deporting 1 million Jews and 3.4 million Poles.[5] The only native inhabitants who were to remain were the small minority judged fit for incorporation into the German racial community, plus an ample supply of forced labour. This proved wildly over-ambitious. In early 1940 Himmler and Heydrich hoped to drive 600,000 people out of the newly annexed territory and into the General Government. To do so, however, would have produced chaos. By April 1940 'only' 261,517 people had been displaced, half Jews, half Polish peasants. By the end of 1940 the total had risen to 305,000. Instead of removing the Jews, the German administrators resorted to concentrating them in large urban ghettos, the largest at Łódź. Millions of Poles, meanwhile, were conscripted for work in Germany or for forced labour on formerly Polish soil. By the end of 1940, 180,000 ethnic Germans had been settled on Polish farms, a process accompanied by brutal evictions and much publicity. However, the numerical imbalance remained frustrating. By January 1941 more than 530,000 ethnic Germans had been repatriated to the Reich, having left behind farms and other property in their original homeland valued at no less than 3.315 billion Reichsmarks.[6] But instead of taking over prime agricultural settlements, the majority of the returnees found themselves languishing in SS-run transit camps.

This practical failure, however, did not deflate the enthusiasm of Heydrich and the SS. As of September 1940, the process of racial sifting began in earnest with the introduction of the *Volksliste*. Of 8.53 million Poles within Germany's borders, only 1 million were deemed worthy of inclusion in this list. They were ranked into four classes according to the speed with which the SS 'racial scientists' believed that they could be assimilated into the German fold. The fate of the 7 million other Poles was left uncertain. Their legal status was reduced to that of 'dependants of the Reich with limited domestic rights' (*Schutzangehoe-rige des deutschen Reiches mit beschraenkten Inlaenderrechten*). By the end of 1940 the Reich Agriculture Ministry reported that the majority of Polish peasants in the new German territories were refusing to plant their fields for the new season, because they did not expect to be in possession of their farms come harvest time.[7] Given what Heydrich had in mind, this was only realistic. In January 1941 Heydrich had initiated a new round of planning, both for a 'final solution' to the Jewish problem, which in 1941 was still predominantly a Polish-Jewish problem, and for a massive displacement of native Poles. His most immediate objective was to find homes for the repatriated ethnic Germans by displacing 770,000 Poles into the General Government at the earliest possible opportunity. This, however, ran foul of conditions in the General Government and the transport needs of the German army in advance of Barbarossa. Instead of the 250,000 people that Heydrich had hoped to move by May 1941, the SS in fact managed to displace only 25,000.

These, however, were merely short-term difficulties. The news of Germany's impending attack on the Soviet Union unleashed euphoria amongst the SS staffs. The Soviet Union offered the chance to solve the problems of territory and population on a scale unimaginable in the confines of Poland. Unwanted bodies could be swallowed up in the wastelands of the East, huge tracts could be allocated for German settlement. Here finally was the stage on which to resolve the problems of population and space in a truly radical fashion. On 30 January 1941 Hitler repeated to the ecstatic crowds in the Sportpalast the threat he had made two years earlier.[8] In a speech directed above all towards asserting the futility of Britain's continued war against Germany, Hitler ended by restating his 'prophecy' that 'if Jewry were to plunge the world into war, the role of Jewry would be finished in Europe'. Unlike in 1939, this was no longer a conditional threat. It was a firm intention. The agitation of America against Germany was after all an established fact. Whether or not Germany was involved in an open world war, it was fighting a global coalition and would soon face the full flood of lend-lease. Hitler could therefore assert with some confidence: 'The coming months and year will prove that I prophesied rightly in this case too.' A few weeks earlier Heydrich had received his first order to prepare for a truly comprehensive solution for the European Jewish problem.[9] Jews from all over Europe, from the Reich and from Poland would be sent to their deaths on marshy construction sites in the desolated territory of the East stripped bare by the German occupying forces. In March the Wehrmacht and the SS drafted guidelines calling for the liquidation of all elements who could be dangerous to German authority in the newly conquered territories, a category that Goering defined for Heydrich as including the 'GPU-organization, the political commissars, Jews, etc.'[10] By 6 June this had been formalized by the army high command as the notorious

Commissar Order, which called for indiscriminate and immediate execution of all political representatives of the Soviet state. Those left behind by the Wehrmacht would be dealt with by the Einsatzgruppen – 3,000 police and SS men who since the second half of May had been undergoing ideological training at the Border Police School at Pretzsch near Leipzig. Though they were to direct themselves against the organs of the Soviet state in the first instance, Heydrich in his frequent meetings with the Einsatzgruppen leaders reiterated the role of Jewry in instigating Bolshevism and demanded with ominous redundancy the liquidation of all Jews in the service of the party and state.[11] Within days of the invasion the balance between these three categories was to shift dramatically.

Meanwhile, the impending attack on the Soviet Union also energized the broader programme of racial rearrangement that had been initiated in Poland. In the middle of June 1941 German planning offices began to consider the possibility of removing, not only the Polish population of the German annexed territories, but the population of the General Government as well.[12] They began, in other words, to consider a genocide against the entire Polish population. On 21 June 1941 Himmler instructed the staff of the RKF to prepare an outline plan for the demographic reorganization of the entire Eastern territory that was expected to fall under German control.[13] A few weeks earlier Himmler had requested additional funds to establish an independent construction administration of the SS. Over the following twelve months the evolution of policy towards the Jews and the development of long-term planning for the settlement of Eastern Europe were pushed forward in constant interchange between the offices of the RSHA, the RKF and the SS economic adminstration.[14] The first sketch of the so-called Generalplan Ost was finished in a matter of weeks by the RKF's settlement expert, Professor Konrad Meyer. It was presented to Himmler as early as 15 July 1941. In the autumn the order was given to construct a number of base camps in Poland from which slave-labour columns would begin the enormous construction programme called for by Meyer's Generalplan. Meanwhile, Reinhard Heydrich's RSHA worked both on the outline plan for the Final Solution and a second draft of the Generalplan. A general statement on the outline of the Final Solution, to embrace not only the millions of Jews living in Poland and the Soviet Union but also the far smaller communities of Western Europe, was ready by December 1941.[15] The meeting had to be postponed until

January, but when the Secretaries of State met at Wannsee in January 1942, Heydrich's proposal received no criticism. By contrast, the second rough draft of the Generalplan Ost, which addressed itself not to the Jewish minority but to the far larger non-Jewish populations of Poland and the Soviet Union, was subject to such fierce attacks from within the Reich's administration that the task of preparing the plan was transferred back from the RSHA to Professor Meyer of the RKF.[16] Meyer completed his final draft in May 1942 and after consultation with Hitler, it was approved by Himmler in July 1942 as the outline for future SS settlement activity in the East.[17] It provides what is effectively a blueprint for the kind of social order that the SS leadership hoped to create in Eastern Europe.

The first and most fundamental assumption of all SS territorial planning from 1939 onwards was the assumption that the integration of Eastern European territory as German *Lebensraum* required the removal of the vast majority of the native population. Meyer's Generalplan did not speak specifically of the Jews, but their removal was clearly taken for granted. Only in Poland and the Ukraine did the Jews constitute a minority large enough for their removal to significantly alter the population balance. Meyer addressed himself primarily to the majority Slav population. For Poland he foresaw the removal of 80–85 per cent of the native population. This was to be followed by the expulsion of 64 per cent of the population of the Ukraine and 75 per cent of the White Russian population.[18] The Russian territory around Leningrad was to be completely depopulated. The various drafts of the Generalplan differed in their estimates as to the actual numbers involved, but the lowest figure was 31 million displaced people, not including the Jewish minority. More realistic estimates, which allowed for the natural rate of population increase over the period in which the programme would be implemented, put the number of victims at closer to 45 million people.[19] There was still no absolute clarity about the final destination of the displaced populations. But what cannot have been in doubt is that the process of 'evacuation' would involve mass death on an epic scale. Only those capable of work were of any interest to the Germans. By the end of 1942 the talk was of the possible 'physical annihilation' of entire populations, not only the Jewish minority, but the Poles and Ukrainians as well.[20] Any moral consideration had long ago been set aside. The question was one of practicalities.

The genocidal implications of the Generalplan Ost were clearly revealed by a 'trial run' organized in the summer of 1942. On 18–19 July 1942, at the same time as Himmler communicated the definitive order for the killing of the Jews in the General Government, he also issued instructions to Odilo Globocnic to carry out an experimental 'evacuation' of the entire Polish population of the Zamość region.[21] This was intended as the first step towards widening the process of Germanization beyond the borders of the Reich. After completing the 'evacuation' of the entire Jewish population, Odilo Globocnic began a second round of *Selektionen*, which split the Polish population into four groups, by age, sex and political dangerousness. Men and women capable of work were divided into two segregated groups, exactly as Heydrich had demanded for the Jews at the Wannsee meeting. Polish children were separated from their families and allocated at random to men and women over the age of 60. These ill-matched 'family groups' were then dispatched to so-called 'retirement villages', which were in fact the settlements left vacant by the gassing of their Jewish inhabitants. The fourth group of Poles, those judged most dangerous by the German authorities, were dispatched directly to Auschwitz and Majdanek, where they were executed or worked to death.[22] In practice, the Zamość evacuation was not a success. The efforts by the SS to round up the inhabitants met with intense armed resistance and required the mobilization of thousands of German police, troops and auxiliaries. Tens of thousands of Poles escaped into the forests.[23] By the summer of 1943, Globocnic was forced to abandon the experiment. Compared to the outright murder of the Jewish population of the General Government, the Zamość experiment was small in scale. However, it was highly significant in indicating the full extent of the Third Reich's genocidal ambition. The Generalplan Ost set a timetable for the extinction of the entire population of Eastern Europe. It should be taken no less seriously than the programme outlined by Heydrich at the Wannsee conference.

Given the scale of the horror that the SS was contemplating, it may seem grotesque to consider the 'constructive' plan they had in mind for the territory vacated by the tens of millions of people they were planning to murder and uproot. However, it is necessary to do so if we are to understand the way in which the perpetrators rationalized their programme of murder and the meaning that they gave to the concept of *Lebensraum*. Into the enormous space cleared by the Generalplan Ost, Himmler and his staff foresaw, over a period of twenty to thirty years,

1. German negotiators: Gustav Stresemann (*left*) with the German ambassador in the Hague, Count Zech, during the Young Plan negotiations, August 1929.

2. German poverty: the one-room apartment of an unemployed miner, April 1931.

3. Propaganda: Hitler enthusiastically starts work on the first autobahn, September 1933. In fact, the programme contributed little to work creation.

4. The new Reichsbank: Hitler and Hjalmar Schacht, May 1934.

5. The agrarian elite: Walter Darre in the centre, Herbert Backe, who succeeded him in 1942, far left. Note the black SS uniforms.

6. The first display of Germany's new tanks at the Nuremberg party rally, September 1935. Four years later many Panzer units still relied on these diminutive training vehicles.

7. Goering savouring the aroma of synthetic fuel, August 1939.

8. Rural labour shortage: women and Hitler Youth harvest potatoes, October 1938.

9. 'A terrible waste of foreign exchange': broken plate glass windows after Kristallnacht, 9 November 1938.

Bauchredner Baruch —

— hielt eine Neujahrsansprache

10. January 1939, anti-Semitic anti-Americanism: Bernard Baruch ventriloquizes Roosevelt's State of the Union address.

11. Hitler challenges America and world Jewry: address to the Reichstag, 30 January 1939.

12. Lifeline: Soviet deliveries of oil to Germany under the Hitler–Stalin pact,
August 1940.

13. German soldiers with one of the much-feared French heavy tanks (Char 2 C),
May–June 1940.

14 and 15. (*above*) A Ju 88 loading bombs for an attack on Britain, October 1940. Compare this small aircraft with the Avro Lancaster heavy bomber (*below*), a true weapon of strategic air war, used by the RAF from 1943.

16. Plunder in the West: Wehrmacht meat requisitioning in France, 1940.

17. Hunger in the East: meat market in Lublin ghetto, November 1940.

18. 'Reconstruction and Planning in the East', March 1941: an exhibition attended by
Heinrich Himmler (*pointing*), Hess (*next to Himmler*), Fritz Todt (*in suit*) and
Reinhard Heydrich (*second from right, partly concealed*).

19. Condemned to starve: Soviet prisoners, July–August 1941.

20. The road to Moscow: Operation Typhoon bogs down, October 1941.

21. The war turns: some of the first Germans taken prisoner by the Soviet counter-offensive at Moscow, 7 December 1941.

22. Rallying the home front with armaments propaganda: 'mass-production' of tanks as shown in German newsreels, May 1942.

23. Stabilizing the home front: Reich harvest festival, October 1942, Herbert Backe (*left*), Goering (*centre*), Goebbels (*right*). Goering is about to announce increased food rations paid for by occupied territories.

24. Saukel's recruits: Ukrainian women prior to departure for Germany, August 1942.

25. Speer and his staff during the 'sub-components crisis', June 1943: Karl Otto Saur (*far left*), Wilhelm Zangen (*back to camera*), Walther Schieber (*speaking*), Albert Speer.

26. Speer and his colleagues during a rare moment of relaxation, December 1943: (*from left*) Walther 'Panzer' Rohland, Speer, Erhard Milch with cigar (Luftwaffe), Wilhelm Werner (aero-engines).

27. Inspecting IG Farben's Auschwitz building site: Heinrich Himmler (*second from left*), foreman, Max Faust (site manager) and Rudolf Hoess (*far right*), July 1942.

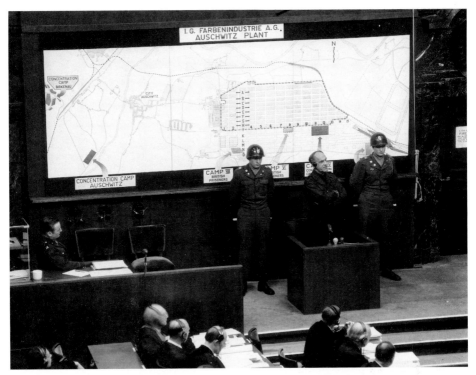

28. Prosecution exhibit in IG Farben trial 1946, showing relative size of IG Farben synthetic rubber plant (*right*) and death camp (*left*).

29. Keeping the faith: after his convalescence, Albert Speer rallies armaments workers, May 1944.

30. Speer lectures on the 'armaments miracle', June 1944.

31. A leap into the future? Mass-producing V2 ballistic missiles in the Mittelbau.

the settlement of at least 10 million Germans. The ethnic boundary of the German race was to be forced 1,000 kilometres to the east.[24] The SS planners involved in these discussions were only too aware that by conjuring up images of the Teutonic knights they were in danger of appearing outlandishly archaic. In their self-understanding, however, they were anything but. Not that Konrad Meyer and his staffers distanced themselves from the tradition of German settlement in the East. But to understand this as an archaic attachment was to miss the point. As one official in Frank's General Government explained, the Third Reich was resuming a historic mission of modernization. 'In reality the Masters of the German Order and above all the leaders of the settlement [Lokatoren], who built up and settled the villages and farms on a commercial basis, were ... anything but Romantics. They were cool calculators and stemmed in considerable numbers from the commercial classes.'[25] Nor was the project impractical or 'merely ideological' in its intent. The East would offer a prosperous future for the hard-pressed German peasantry. For Konrad Meyer, the architect of the Generalplan Ost, it was the chance of a new beginning beyond the overcrowded confines of the Reich. As he put it in a programmatic article:

The land folk of tomorrow will be a different people from that of yesterday ... For our rural population the dawning of this new age means a fundamental change of character ... The choice between traditional or progressive, primitive or modern, can only be resolved in favour of a healthy, communally conscious idea of progress and performance. This implies a clear decision in favour of struggle as opposed to those ... who see the salvation of the peasantry in the protection of a nature reserve. There can be no return to the 'good old days'. It is therefore best to give up complaining about the fact that the 'old peasantry' is gone and to affirm the new peasantry of the Third Reich and to fight for it.[26]

The vision that inspired the German colonial project in the East had more in common with the American ideology of the frontier than it did with the Middle Ages. In the autumn of 1941 Hitler returned repeatedly to the American example in discussing Germany's future in the East. The Volga, he declared, would be Germany's Mississippi. And the bloody conquest of the American West provided Germany with the historical warrant it needed to justify the clearance of the Slav population. 'Here in the East a similar process will repeat itself for a second time as in the conquest of America.' A 'superior' settler population would displace an 'inferior' native population opening the way towards a new era of economic possibility. 'Europe – and not America – will be the land of unlimited possibilities.'[27]

The Generalplan Ost envisioned, not a return to the past, but a new and expansive phase of German economic development. It belongs in the company of the German Labour Front's enormous housing programme announced in the autumn of 1940 and the pre-war Volkswagen scheme. In the East, a new abundance of natural resources would be combined with German know-how and capital to enable a dramatic increase in the standard of living. The most succinct expression of this ambition was population density. In the initial planning for Poland this was set at 100 people per square kilometre. Once the territory of the Soviet Union was incorporated into the Generalplan Ost, the target was reduced to 80 people per square kilometre. This target was significantly lower than the density in Germany in 1939, at 133 people per square kilometre. But it was higher than that prevailing in France at the time.[28] Nor were the agronomists working for the SS under any illusion about the standard of living that could be expected in a society consisting entirely of peasant farmers. Instead, Meyer's ideal was the population structure of Bavaria or Hanover, which in the 1930s sustained an uncluttered balance of agriculture, industry and services.[29] The Generalplan projected an agricultural share in the workforce of no more than one-third, with a similar share employed in industry, crafts, commerce and public services. Placed in relation to the long-run development of the German occupational structure, the SS vision involved turning the clock back not to the Middle Ages, but to 1900.

In light of the problems in the Reich, achieving the correct distribution of land was clearly a key question in Germany's colonization in the East. The majority of German settlers would be provided with self-sufficient homesteads (known as Hufen), of at least 20 hectares. As we have seen, farms of 20–30 hectares were the mainstay of the Erbhoefe in the Reich. In those areas where the quality of land required farms of more than 30 hectares, the family farm was not a viable unit. These territories would be given over to larger estates run by veterans of the SS, employing gangs of Slavs as farmhands. The initial planning for Poland provided that two-thirds of the land was to be divided between 150,000 Hufen, each supporting a German peasant family. One-third of the land was to be given over to 12,000 large Wehrbauernhoefe, to be reserved for SS

Table 14. Proposed population distribution
Generalplan Ost

% of population reliant on	The SS ideal (Hanover and Bavaria)	Reich average 1933
Agriculture	35	21
Crafts	35	39
Industry and commerce	15	17
Public services	7	8
Other	8	15

Source: C. Madajczyk (ed.), *Vom Generalplan Ost zum Generalsiedlungsplan* (Munich, 1994), 3–14, doc. 1

officers. The goal of complete Germanization, however, would never be achieved if German farmers were forced to rely on native Slavs to do the bulk of the fieldwork. So land was also allocated to provide allotments for a substantial population of German farm labourers.

The settlement in the East was directly coupled with the efforts of the RNS to bring about the wholesale rationalization of agriculture within Germany, announced by Darré at the end of 1940.[30] In the words of an early planning document, it was assumed that 'the constructive effort in the East will ... permit the final reconstruction of the areas of partible inheritance in the old Reich. From Wuerttemberg and Baden alone 100,000 peasant and craftsmen families will be made available.'[31] From the summer of 1940 onwards teams of experts from the Reichsnaehrstand, under the direction of the ubiquitous Professor Meyer, undertook a comprehensive inventory of rural Germany.[32] In painstaking local enquiries they evaluated a sample of 4,500 German villages with a combined population of 5 million inhabitants. In every village, every farm was graded according to its viability. In future no farm would be acceptable in Germany that did not yield a money income of at least 3,000 Reichsmarks per annum, placing the farming family comfortably above the median point in the national income distribution. In practice this meant that farms would need to have a minimum size of 18 hectares, in some regions closer to 30. In areas of partible inheritance such as the Rhineland, upwards of 30 per cent of all farms were designated for consolidation or liquidation. If it had been possible to disregard local sensibilities altogether, the rate of consolidation would have been closer to 50 per cent. And Meyer's teams graded not only the farms but also the farming population. Hard-working farmers who lacked land were to be assisted by the consolidation of smaller holdings taken from part-time farmers or less adequate cultivators. Young families of good German stock would be encouraged to take up the opportunities for settlement in the East. The final version of the Generalplan completed by Meyer in 1942 called for no less than 220,000 families to be drawn from the overpopulated rural areas of the Reich. In addition, the SS hoped to be able to attract 220,000 young couples starting life in agriculture and at least 2 million colonists from the urban areas of Germany.[33]

But the agrarian planners did not merely intend to seize land and redistribute population. The goal of creating a 'high-intensity' (*hochintensiven*) *Lebensraum* could only be achieved by substantial investment.[34] An enormous flow of German capital would have to follow the German settlers into the East. The farms would need to be well equipped with livestock and machinery. But most important of all was the need to improve the transport infrastructure. Modern agriculture could not prosper without links to the towns and the cities. Meyer's initial costing for the Generalplan Ost came to 40 billion Reichsmarks, which was soon inflated, on Himmler's insistence, to 67 billion Reichsmarks.[35] This was as much as Germany had spent on rearmament between 1930 and 1939. It was more than the combined total of all investment in the German economy between 1933 and 1938. It was approximately two-thirds of Germany's GDP in 1941.[36] Half a million marks was to be sunk into every square kilometre of Germany's vast new Eastern empire. Assuming the territory was populated at the density of 80 persons per square kilometre, this implied an investment of 6,250 Reichsmarks per inhabitant. Here too there is no trace of backward-looking nostalgia. On the plans endorsed by both Himmler and Hitler, land remediation and agriculture would claim only 36 per cent of Germany's investment in the East. The rest was earmarked for investments in transport infrastructure, industry and urban settlement.[37] And this was only the state-directed element in Eastern economic development. Huge sums were expected to flow from private industry. The Reich, it was hoped, would provide at least 15.67 billion Reichsmarks from the national budget; 4.29 billion would come from a special fund at the disposal of Heinrich Himmler as RKF; German local government was expected to provide 3.04 billion. These public funds would be concentrated above all on forestry, infrastructure, road building and agricultural amelioration. The Reichsbahn was expected to contribute at least 1.5 billion towards expanding the railway infrastructure. Finally, in excess of 20 billion was expected to be raised on more or less commercial terms for industrial and urban development. If the Generalplan Ost had ever been carried out, it would have involved a massive reallocation of German national capital towards the east.[38]

It was through the issue of costing and the consequent decision to rely heavily on forced labour that the Generalplan was linked directly to the Final Solution.[39] As Himmler put it to a meeting of senior SS leaders in the summer of 1942:

If we do not fill our camps with slaves – in this room I mean to say things very firmly and very clearly – with worker slaves, who will build our cities, our villages, our farms without regard to any losses, then even after years of war we will not have enough money to be able to equip the settlements in such a manner that real Germanic people can live there and take root in the first generation.[40]

Planners such as Konrad Meyer and the SS building chief Hans Kammler expressed themselves in less drastic language, but their intent was no less clear.[41] The total labour demands of the Generalplan Ost were estimated to be in the order of 400,000–800,000 for the first phase. At a minimum, the number of forced labourers was set at 175,000 – 'Jews, Poles and Soviet prisoners of war'.[42] On average, Meyer estimated, employing slave labour would reduce the cost of construction by 40 per cent in cash terms. Half of this saving, however, would be offset by the cost of maintaining the workforce with food and clothing, a debit item that Meyer added almost as an afterthought.

For the future of the SS concentration camp system, these figures had important implications.[43] In the first half of 1941 the population of the camps numbered no more than 60,000. Clearly there needed to be a dramatic expansion. To provide for the needs of the Generalplan, the SS building staff on 27 September 1941 ordered the construction of two new camps, each to house 50,000 inmates. One was to be sited in the Lublin-Majdanek. The other was to be built at Birkenau, a hamlet

Table 15. Proposed investment priorities of Generalplan Ost (spring 1942 version)

	billion of Reichsmarks invested	of which:	% of total	Purpose:
Landscape amelioration:	3.3		7	
Forestry		0.6		11,000 square kilometres to be afforested
Landscape restructuring		0.6		Protective hedging and afforestation of agricultural area
Technical land improvement		2.2		20,000 square kilometres of agricultural land need proper drainage
Agriculture:	13.5		30	
Agricultural reconstruction		8.6		Complete reconstruction of agriculture in most of Poland
Rural crafts		0.8		40,000 small-scale crafts and other businesses required by population
Rural industry		0.4		Large-scale food processing, lumber industry, etc.
Rural cultural facilities		1.0		Community centres, schools, Hitler Youth centres, welfare centres, Kindergarten, sports facilities
Other rural housing		0.9		For farming population and for teachers, doctors, civil servants, workers
Village infrastructure		1.8		Local infrastructure: roads, tracks, local electricity and telephone connections

Transport and infrastructure:	7.8	17	
Road building	1.2		Aim is to reach the density of roads of East Prussia
Autobahn building	1.0		Two north–south and two east–west routes
Railway construction	1.5		Narrow-gauge system to be built up to connect agriculture to trunk lines
Waterways	2.6		Flood regulation and navigation on Weichsel and Warthe
Electricity supply	1.5		Electrification to be raised to level of East Prussia
Industrial	5.2	11	650,000 industrial jobs at c. 8,000 Reichsmarks investment per job
Urban:	15.4	34	
Urban housing	9.0		1 million large apartments for urban population of 4.3 million
Urban cultural facilities	2.0		Minimum provision with educational facilities, cultural facilities and hospitals, the rest to be built with own funds
Urban crafts	0.8		45,000 craft and other businesses for needs of population
Urban utilities	3.6		Local infrastructure plus gas, sewerage and local transport facilities
Equipment for construction	0.5	1	
Total	45.7	100	

Source: C. Madajczyk (ed.), *Vom Generalplan Ost zum Generalsiedlungsplan* (Munich, 1994), 91–123, doc. 23

adjacent to the existing concentration camp at Auschwitz.[44] By the end of the year the SS had raised its targets to envision camp populations of 125,000 at Majdanek and 150,000 at Auschwitz. Both facilities were originally intended to house Soviet prisoners of war, but for reasons that will soon become apparent the vast majority of the billets at Auschwitz ended up being occupied by Jews. In any case, the instrumentalization of the concentration camps as a source of forced labour was well under way in the last week of January 1942 when Himmler wrote to the SS office in charge of camp administration to inform them:

Since Russian prisoners of war can no longer be expected in the near future, I intend to send to the camps a large number of Jews and Jewesses who are being emigrated [sic] out of Germany. Please get ready to receive in the concentration camps in the next four weeks 100,000 male Jews and up to 50,000 Jewish women. Major economic tasks will be addressed to the concentration camps in the coming weeks.[45]

A week earlier, Heydrich had hosted the meeting at the Wannsee conference centre, at which a key group of civil servants was inducted into the SS vision of the Final Solution. At the Wannsee meeting Heydrich referred neither to gassing nor shooting as means of disposing of the Jewish populations of Poland or Western Europe. Instead, he proposed that they should be evacuated eastwards in giant construction columns: 'Under suitable command, Jews are now to be deployed for labour in the East as part of the final solution. In large labour columns, under separation of the sexes, Jews capable of labour are to be led, building roads, into the territory, in the process of which, without doubt, a large part will drop out due to natural wastage.'[46] As we have seen, Meyer's Generalplan Ost had specified new roads as the first requirement; 1.2 billion Reichsmarks had been earmarked for their construction.

II

The full extent of the SS's genocidal ambition is staggering and for obvious reasons it has held the historical centre stage. However, what is less widely appreciated is that the Wehrmacht entered the Soviet Union intent upon not one, but two programmes of mass murder.[47] Whereas the Final Solution and the Generalplan Ost were secrets closely guarded by the SS, for fear, amongst other things, of antagonizing the local population, the second programme, which openly envisioned the killing of tens of millions of people within the first twelve months of the German occupation, was agreed between the Wehrmacht, all the key civilian Ministries and the Nazi political leadership as early as the spring of 1941. Nor can the so-called 'Hunger Plan' be described as secret. It was referred to in official instructions issued to thousands of subordinates. And, perhaps most importantly, no effort was made to hide the wider rationale of the individual acts of brutality that the programme required. On the contrary, all German soldiers and occupation administrators in Soviet territory were enjoined to understand and to commit themselves to its strategic logic. This genocidal plan commanded such wide-ranging support because it concerned a practical issue, the importance of which, following Germany's experience in World War I, was obvious to all: the need to secure the food supply of the German population, if necessary at the expense of the population of the Soviet Union.

As we have discussed, the 'bread basket of the Ukraine' played a key role in all the various military-economic assessments of the Barbarossa campaign prepared over the winter of 1940–41. For Hitler, it was *the* key priority, to be achieved prior to any other military consideration, the importance of which was only reinforced by the alarming decline in the German grain stocks. By December 1940 the entire military and political leadership of the Third Reich was convinced that this was the last year in which they could approach the food question with any confidence. Nor was this simply a German problem. All of the Western European territories which had fallen under German domination in 1940 had substantial net grain deficits.

Unless additional sources of feed grain could be secured, the only solution was a mass slaughter of Europe's animal herds reminiscent of the famous 'pig massacre' of 1916. Given the isolation imposed on the European continent by the British blockade, only the Ukraine could provide Western Europe with the millions of tons of grain it needed to sustain its animal populations. Not surprisingly, therefore, when Hitler gave the definitive order in early December 1940 to begin preparing for an attack on the Soviet Union, State Secretary Herbert Backe in the Agriculture Ministry reacted with alacrity.

For Backe this was a moment of considerable personal significance. Ever since the 1920s he had been fixated on the conquest of Russian territory as the ultimate solution to the problems of the 'people without space' (*Volk ohne Raum*).[48] Now the first requirement was that Germany's Army in the East – numbering 3 million men and 600,000 horses – should be fed from the territory of the Soviet Union. As Backe well understood, however, the Ukraine was not the limitless granary of imperialist cliché. The Ukraine, in fact, produced only a small net surplus of grain for export outside the Soviet Union. This was due, on the one hand, to the backwardness of Russian agronomy and on the other hand to the extraordinarily rapid growth in the Soviet urban population. Since 1928 Stalin had stamped an urban civilization of 30 million inhabitants out of the ground. The food for this vast new urban proletariat came from the Ukraine. To conventional economic analysts in Berlin this implied that even if the Ukraine were successfully conquered, Germany could expect little immediate benefit.[49] It would, after all, take years before productivity could be substantially increased. Herbert Backe, however, drew radically different conclusions. To enable the grain surplus of the Ukraine to be directed immediately towards German needs, it was necessary simply to cut the Soviet cities out of the food chain. After ten years of Stalinist urbanization, the urban population of the western Soviet Union was now to be starved to death.

That such a scheme should come from the pen of Herbert Backe can come as no surprise. He was a doctrinaire racial ideologue, a long-time associate of Walther Darré and a personal friend of Reinhard Heydrich. As we have seen, he had already demonstrated his willingness to use food as a means of genocide in Poland in the first year of the war. What is perhaps more surprising is the alacrity with which Backe's breathtaking suggestion was taken up by the rest of the Ministerial bureaucracy in Berlin, above all by the chief economic expert of the Oberkommando Wehrmacht (OKW), General Thomas. At times, as we have seen, Thomas had toyed with opposition to Hitler's war. But at heart, the General was a ruthless pragmatist. Germany's future as a great power was Thomas's only real concern. The *raison d'être* of his office in the OKW was to prevent the kind of domestic crisis that had crippled the German war effort in World War I. Thomas was fully apprised of the precariousness of Germany's food situation and saw no reason to quibble with Backe's calculations. Furthermore, Hitler's mind was clearly made up on the issue. He had set his heart on the Ukraine. And to clinch the argument, Thomas also had specifically military reasons for supporting Backe's proposal. In early 1941, the German army was increasingly concerned with the logistical preparations for Barbarossa. The map exercises conducted by the quartermaster's staff revealed a glaring discrepancy between the supply needs of the German army and the limited railway capacity running eastward into the Soviet Union. Even under the most optimistic assumptions it was hard to see how sufficient food, fuel and ammunition could be pushed through this bottleneck. If, on the other hand, the Wehrmacht could satisfy its demand for food and animal fodder from local sources, then this would allow all available transport capacity to be concentrated on the Wehrmacht's chief priorities – fuel and ammunition.

On 2 May 1941 the State Secretaries representing all the major Ministerial agencies met in conference with General Thomas to draft plans for the occupation. The result is one of the most extraordinary bureaucratic records in the history of the Nazi regime. In far more unvarnished language than was ever used in relation to the Jewish question, all of the major agencies of the German state agreed to a programme of mass murder, which dwarfed that which Heydrich was to propose to the Wannsee meeting nine months later. According to General Thomas's secretariat the meeting concluded as follows:

1.) The war can only be continued, if the entire Wehrmacht is fed from Russia in the third year of the war.
2.) If we take what we need out of the country, there can be no doubt that many millions of people will die of starvation.
3.) The most important issues are the recovery and removal of oil seeds, oil cake and only then the removal of grain.[50]

The minute did not specify the number of millions that the Germans intended to starve. However, Backe's imprint on the discussion is unmistakable.[51] Backe himself put the figure for the 'surplus population' of the Soviet Union at between 20 and 30 million, and over the following months these numbers established themselves as a common reference point. In mid-June, a week before the invasion of the Soviet Union, Himmler addressed SS Gruppenfuehrer on the forthcoming 'race war' (Volkstumskampf). It would, he opined, be a fight to the death in the course of which 'through military actions and the food problems 20 to 30 million Slavs and Jews will die'.[52] In November, Goering boasted to Count Ciano, the Italian Foreign Minister, that the starvation of

20–30 million Soviet citizens was an essential element of Germany's occupation policy. Following Backe's thinking to the letter, the guidelines issued by the OKW for the management of agriculture in the occupied Eastern territories – the so-called 'Green Book' – called for all of the industrial and urban centres of western Russia, including the wooded region between Moscow and Leningrad, to be cut off from their food sources.[53] As a result, the German occupation authorities were instructed to prepare themselves for a human catastrophe on an unprecedented scale. 'Many tens of millions of people in this area will become surplus to requirements and will die or will be forced to emigrate to Siberia.'[54] In case the occupying authorities should be moved to alleviate the situation, the guidelines reaffirmed the essential connection between mass starvation and the continuation of the German war effort:

Efforts to save the population from death by starvation by drawing on the surplus of the black earth regions can only be at the expense of the food supply to Europe. They diminish the staying power of Germany in the war and the resistance of Germany and Europe to the blockade. There must be absolute clarity about this . . . A claim by the [local] population on the German administration . . . is rejected right from the start.

III

After months of talk, on 22 June 1941 the invasion of the Soviet Union began. Never, before or since, has battle been joined with such ferocity by so many men, on such an extended battlefront. As the German spearheads plunged deep into the western Soviet Union, immediately behind the line of the Wehrmacht's advance the Einsatzgruppen of the SS began their work of murder. In total, the four Einsatzgruppen (A Baltic, B Belorussia and central Russia, C Ukraine, D Romania and the Crimea) numbered only 3,000–3,200 men. But the SS rapidly gathered around them tens of thousands of local militia.[55] In addition, from the autumn of 1941 the Einsatzgruppen were reinforced by fresh contingents of German personnel – Waffen SS and numerous battalions of armed German police. The rate at which the Einsatzgruppen killed depended on the speed at which 'their' Army Group advanced and the density of Jewish population that they encountered. Einsatzgruppe A was certainly the most devastating. It was responsible for the destruction of the great Jewish communities of Lithuania and Latvia, starting on 25–6 June with a horrific pogrom at Kaunas. By the spring of 1942, Einsatzgruppe A had claimed more than 270,000 victims, the overwhelming majority of whom were Jewish, more than half the total killed by all four Einsatzgruppen. Like the other SS teams, Einsatzgruppe A murdered by hand, using rifles, pistols and machine guns. Local helpers sometimes resorted to clubs and pickaxes. Amongst a defenceless and largely docile population this was enough to wreak havoc. The Judaeocide thus rapidly took on an awful and concrete reality. Indeed, so intense was this experience that it set in motion a learning process, which by the end of 1941 was leading to the first experiments with gas vans, a method considered more adequate to the humanity of the perpetrators. However, the vans never caught on. They were improvised and slow-working contraptions and were subject to the same limitations encountered by the rest of the Wehrmacht's motorized transport in Russia. As a means of killing, asphyxiation by carbon monoxide was simply too slow. Whilst experiments began in Poland with more efficient stationary gassing facilities, execution by hand remained the favoured practice in the Soviet Union even in the second sweeps in 1942, which claimed the lives of at least another 360,000 Jews in the Ukraine and Belorussia. In Galicia, where it is estimated that as many as 500,000 Jews were killed in the course of the German occupation, shooting and gassing were combined, as Heydrich had intended, with 'destruction through labour' (*Vernichtung durch Arbeit*).[56] The opportunity for the latter was provided by the construction of a major strategic highway necessary to secure the supply lines for Army Group South.

By contrast with the immediacy of the Einsatzgruppen, Backe's Hunger Plan had a more abstract quality. The German authorities seem to have imagined that millionfold starvation could be induced simply by requisitioning all available grain and 'shutting off' the cities. In practice, this vision of mass starvation as a result of systematic inaction turned out to be naive.[57] The Soviet population did not wait to be starved. The only large groups that it proved possible to kill simply by not feeding them were recognizable minorities within the urban population and people confined in captivity: in other words, the urban Jewish population and Soviet prisoners of war. Immediately after the arrival of the German troops, those Jews who were not executed by the Einsatzgruppen were banned from food markets or from dealing directly with farmers. They were also banned from purchasing the scarcer forms of food such as eggs, butter, milk, meat or fruit. In Belorussia within the sector of Army Group Centre, the 'ration' allocated to Jewish inhabitants of Minsk and other cities was no more than 420 calories per day.[58] In most places less was available. Over the winter of 1941–2, tens of thousands of Jewish men, women and children succumbed to hunger and hunger-related illnesses.

But it was the Soviet prisoners of war from whom the Hunger Plan exacted the heaviest toll.[59] In the first phase of Barbarossa no less than 3.3 million Red Army soldiers fell into the hands of the German army. The Wehrmacht could not claim that it lacked experience in dealing with prisoners of war. On the Western Front it had coped quite adequately with 2 million men taken in the space of only two months. But in advance of the Barbarossa campaign an order was given to exempt Soviet prisoners from the normally accepted standards of the Geneva Convention. Special guidelines were laid down for the isolation and execution of those judged to be politically dangerous. The prisoners were to be separated into distinct ethnic categories. No adequate preparations were made for housing them over the winter months. In so far as any thought was given to the matter, the assumption seems to have been that they would dig mud dugouts. Special rations were prescribed providing far less nutrition than for any other category of prisoner. Even well-managed prisoner-of-war camps are not healthy places. Many Red Army soldiers were in a poor condition when they were captured. Many were wounded or suffering from shock and exhaustion. Many had not eaten for days. To add to their misery they were forced to march out of the combat zone in treks stretching over hundreds of kilometres. Given normal mortality rates, one would have expected tens of thousands of deaths. But the statistics leave no doubt that, aside from this 'normal attrition', the Wehrmacht was systematically starving its prisoners to death. By the end of December 1941, according to the Wehrmacht's own records, the prisoner count had reached 3.35 million.[60] Of these, only 1.1 million were still alive and only 400,000 were in sufficiently good physical state to be capable of work. Of the 2.25 million that had died, at least 600,000 had been shot, falling victim to the Kommissarbefehl, which gave the German army and the SS Einsatzgruppen the licence to execute any Soviet citizens thought to be politically dangerous.

The rest died of 'natural' causes. Six hundred thousand died between December 1941 and February 1942 alone. If the clock had been stopped in early 1942, this programme of mass murder would have stood as the greatest single crime committed by Hitler's regime.

Destroying the urban population of occupied Russia turned out to be far more difficult. To have completely shut off Minsk, Kiev or Kharkov from their agricultural hinterland would have required a security operation of very substantial proportions.[61] With severe fighting continuing on all fronts, the Wehrmacht lacked the necessary manpower. Furthermore, harassed occupation officials could see no logic in unnecessarily antagonizing the civilian population by implementing an immediate programme of genocide. It was necessary to make at least a show of feeding the population. Though the Germans always avoided any talk of official rations, for fear that this would imply a degree of entitlement, food did begin to be distributed. The result was a messy compromise, recorded with astonishing sangfroid by one local Wehrmacht administrator:

In the last months for the first time and then ever more frequently there has been mention of the civilian food supply in the course of the working day. That the Russians are still here too, we never really considered. No, that is not quite right. Following the official instructions we were . . . not supposed to consider them. But the war has taken a different turn . . . Under these circumstances we cannot afford not to consider the population in food terms. But where are we supposed to get anything from?[62]

This question was never satisfactorily answered. The urban population of western Russia survived by resort to the black market and increasingly by abandoning the cities, returning to live with family members who were still resident in the countryside. The Wehrmacht for its part did its best to feed itself from the land. Within weeks of the invasion, the principal task of large parts of the German army was the requisitioning of food.[63] The troops plundered huge quantities of grain, livestock and dairy produce. Nevertheless, the German armies were not able to sustain themselves at the levels they expected. Especially in Belorussia, where the bulk of German forces were concentrated, local sources proved inadequate in every respect. Large quantities of extra food had to be shipped eastwards from Germany.[64] But given the inadequacy of the transport infrastructure even this was not enough. Army

Group Centre never suffered hunger to compare with that which haunted the Soviet forces opposing them. But during the winter of 1941–2, with the transport system in disarray, many German soldiers did go without rations for days and sometimes weeks on end.[65]

Fundamentally, however, the Hunger Plan was never implemented in its full horror, because the German zone of occupation never included the two largest urban concentrations of the Soviet Union, Moscow and Leningrad. Though they were key targets in the planning of Barbarossa, the Wehrmacht never captured either city. Indirectly, however, this did fulfil the objective of the Hunger Plan. The front line severed millions of Soviet citizens from their main sources of food, thereby freeing the Ukrainian harvest for German use. The Soviets were forced to feed their war effort from what little remained of Soviet agriculture. The result, behind the Soviet lines, was ever-present hunger and in many cases, outright starvation, a situation exemplified most dramatically by the besieged city of Leningrad.[66] The German and Finnish pincers closed around Leningrad in early October 1941. Two and a half million civilians and soldiers were trapped in a giant encirclement. Uncertain about the situation of the Soviet defenders, the German 18th Army, which had responsibility for the siege, began canvassing options for dealing with the population.[67] The army's staff proposed three possibilities: encircle the city and 'starve the lot' (*alles verhungert*); evacuate the civilians westwards into the German zone of occupation; or arrange for their evacuation behind Soviet lines. The memo presented no decision, but set out the advantages and disadvantages of each option. Starving the population of Leningrad to death would eliminate a large number of Communists and would relieve the Germans of the burden of feeding millions of people. The only real disadvantage was propagandistic. The foreign media would have a field day. In addition, the 18th Army feared the psychological impact on its soldiers of watching at close quarters as 4 million civilians starved to death. Evacuating the civilian population westwards, into the German-controlled rear areas, would deprive the Allies of their 'horror story'. But it would force the Germans to find food for 4 million extra people and there could be no illusions on that score: 'A large part of the people coming out of Petersburg will starve in any case.' This too would upset the troops. Finally, there was the possibility of arranging with the Soviets for them to accept the evacuees. This would have propaganda advantages, but the Wehrmacht was concerned that the exodus from Leningrad might degenerate into a public relations disaster. Tens of thousands of civilians would clearly die en route to the Soviet lines. The one option that was never even considered was the possibility of feeding the Soviet population from German stores. By December 1941 Leningrad was in the grip of a severe famine. Over the Christmas period and into January 1942 men, women and children died at the rate of nearly 4,000 per day.[68] According to the best available evidence, 653,000 Leningraders died in the first eleven months of the siege.[69] By 1944 hunger and hunger-related disease may have claimed as many as 700,000 lives.

15

December 1941: Turning Point

In the six months between June and December 1941 the history of the Third Reich reached its climactic turning point. This was the moment at which Hitler and his regime seemed to have within their grasp the full realization of their ideological vision. But with the winter came strategic catastrophe. In attacking the Soviet Union in June 1941, Hitler had gambled that the Wehrmacht could sustain a war on two fronts, so long as the Red Army could be destroyed by the end of the year. As he put it to Mussolini in an early morning missive on 22 June: 'Whatever may come now, Duce, our situation cannot become worse as a result of this step; it can only improve.'[1] As was to become apparent by November 1941, this was to hope in vain. The German programme of depopulation and colonization had barely even begun before the Red Army's counter-offensive outside Moscow revealed the threadbare military resources that underpinned Hitler's imperial ambition. In the first two weeks of December 1941, precisely at the moment that Reinhard Heydrich had planned to introduce the Reich's Ministries to his plans for the Final Solution of the 'European Jewish problem', the conditions for the full realization of that awful objective were torn from underneath the Third Reich. It was the frustration of Barbarossa as a military project that determined that the victims of the Holocaust numbered almost 6 million, not the 11.3 million enumerated by Heydrich. Even before it had fully unfolded its murderous aspect, the Third Reich's effort to destroy the Soviet Union, to create a lasting empire in the East and to completely overturn the balance of global power had come undone.

I

As we have seen, the success of Barbarossa turned on the ability of the Wehrmacht to paralyse and destroy the Red Army on the Dnieper–Dvina river line, within 500 kilometres of the border. To describe this as optimistic is an understatement. In this respect as well, Barbarossa qualifies as the last great example of a colonial land-grab: an extraordinarily presumptuous attempt by a medium-sized European state to impose its murderous will on a supposedly less-developed people of vastly greater number. Fundamentally, the Germans assumed that the Soviet leadership was so weak and incompetent that it would be incapable of using its superior manpower and considerable military equipment to suck them into a war of attrition. The huge gains made in the first weeks of the campaign seemed initially to vindicate this arrogance. On 3 July, army chief of staff Franz Halder famously concluded that the battle had been won.[2] The bulk of the Red Army had been eliminated 'this side of the Dvina and Dnieper'. Finishing off the campaign in the East would demand the Wehrmacht's attention as a mopping-up operation, but it was time for the German leadership to turn its mind towards future operations against the umbilicus of the British Empire, the land route between the Nile and the Euphrates.

Only a few weeks later, this bubble had burst. By the end of July 1941, all three German army groups had reached the feasible limit of their supply system and had halted their advance. The Red Army, though it had suffered devastating casualties, had not been destroyed.[3] It was still fighting and inflicting serious losses. The situation was at its most critical in the central segment of the front line around Smolensk.[4] In the last days of July, by driving his tanks to the very limit of their endurance Heinz Guderian completed yet another gigantic encirclement and seized control of the 'land bridge' between the upper reaches of the rivers Dvina and Dnieper. Moscow was now less than 400 kilometres away. But, in pulling off this spectacular coup, Guderian outran his supply lines and left the main bulk of Army Group Centre trailing hundreds of kilometres to the west. Faced with savage Soviet counterattacks, Guderian's overstretched units were forced to dig in and to defend the outer perimeter of their encirclement.[5] Sensing that a critical moment had arrived, the Red Army hurled no less than seventeen armies against

Army Group Centre, six of them concentrated against Guderian.[6] Though the cost in blood was terrible, the unrelenting Soviet counterattacks achieved their intended effect. As Field Marshal Bock, Commander-in-Chief of Army Group Centre, noted in his diary, 'How a new operation is to start from this position with the slowly falling combat value of the troops, who are attacked again and again, I don't quite know yet.'[7] A few days later Bock noted: 'If the Russians do not collapse somewhere soon, then it will be very difficult before the winter to hit them so hard as to eliminate them.'[8]

It would be September at the very earliest before Army Group Centre could resume an attack towards Moscow.[9] This was precisely the kind of hold-up against which Halder had warned so emphatically in his early assessment of the Barbarossa campaign plan. In early 1941 he had written that only uninterrupted speed, preventing the Red Army from regrouping, guaranteed success. Now, with the forward advance halted all along the line, Halder was forced to conclude that the German invasion of the Soviet Union had been based on a fundamental misapprehension. In early August his diary contains the following telling admission:

On the fronts not involved in the offensive movement reigns the quiet of exhaustion. What we are now doing is the last desperate attempt to prevent our front line from becoming frozen in positional warfare . . . Our last reserves have been committed. Any regrouping now is merely a shifting of forces on the baseline within individual army group sectors . . . In the entire situation it is becoming ever more apparent that the Russian colossus, which had prepared itself for war with all the uninhibitedness that is characteristic of totalitarian states, has been underestimated by us. This is true whether one considers organizational as well as economic forces, the transport system, but above all with regard to purely military capability. At the start of the war we reckoned with about 200 enemy divisions. Now we have already counted 360. These divisions are certainly not armed and equipped in our sense, in many cases they have tactically inadequate leadership. But they are there. And when a dozen have been smashed, then the Russian puts up another dozen.[10]

In fact, Halder continued to underestimate the scale of the challenge facing the Wehrmacht in Russia. By the end of 1941 the Red Army had fielded not 360 divisions, but a total of 600.[11]

As Halder now acknowledged, if there was any power in the 1930s and 1940s that exemplified the Fascist slogan of the 'triumph of will' over material circumstances it was not Nazi Germany, or Fascist Italy, but Stalin's Marxist dictatorship. Not only did the Soviet regime not crack like its Tsarist predecessor, it proved capable of absorbing casualties vastly greater than those suffered by any other combatant. And despite its relative economic backwardness, it proved capable during the emergency of 1941–2 of mobilizing a greater share of national economic resources.[12] Rather than succumbing to its supposed lack of sophistication, the Soviet Union punched several classes above its weight. In large part this was an effect of terroristic coercion. But Stalin's political power was inextricably tied up with the real achievement of Soviet industrialization, of which the excellent weaponry of the Red Army was the most dramatic expression.[13] In France in 1940 the Wehrmacht had found ways of defeating France's lumbering Char Bs. To the thousands of agile, heavily armoured T-34s that now began to pour off the Soviet production lines, the Germans had no answer.

Hitler succumbed to doubt even before his generals. As early as the end of July he began to consider the possibility that the Red Army might not be destroyed in 1941. On his instruction, Wehrmacht high command issued a strategic directive openly acknowledging this possibility.[14] Indeed, Hitler's moment of strategic realism appears to have gone further than this. When Goebbels visited the Hauptquartier in Rastenburg on 18 August 1941, he was shocked to find his Fuehrer talking of a negotiated peace with Stalin.[15] For Hitler, furthermore, the possibility of a stalemate in the East had immediate operational implications. Ever since the first staff studies of Barbarossa, Hitler and the Wehrmacht high command had assumed that, if the initial assault failed to destroy the Red Army, strategic economic considerations would take priority. If Germany was to face a long war on two fronts it was essential to secure full control of the grain and raw materials of the Ukraine, as well as complete command of the Baltic, without which Germany could not guarantee its deliveries of iron ore from Scandinavia.

There was certainly cause for strategic concern in the late summer of 1941.[16] Following the announcement of lend-lease, the Anglo-American alliance showed every sign of further consolidation. In July the United States occupied Iceland to further extend its coverage of the Atlantic shipping lanes.[17] Shooting encounters between the German and American navy were occurring on a monthly basis. Like the Luftwaffe, the

German navy watched the dramatic expansion in American production with mounting concern. Unless it could soon begin an all-out attack on the Atlantic shipping lanes and begin in earnest the process of starving the British out, the huge capacity of America's dockyards would be in a position to negate any losses that the U-boats might inflict.[18] On 14 August 1941 the United States sealed its irrevocable commitment to the British war effort with the announcement of the Atlantic Charter. Churchill had hoped for an American declaration of war. Roosevelt could not go so far. But in Berlin, the outbreak of open war with the United States was now considered only a matter of time. And Hitler was no longer thinking in the long term.[19] From the summer of 1941 onwards he spoke of war with the United States as being merely a matter of months away, ideally to begin after the successful conclusion of the Eastern operation. Everything, however, depended on the Japanese.[20] The U-boats could sink American shipping in the Atlantic. But Japan with its powerful and modern navy was Germany's only hope of countering the might of the American fleet. For the same reason, Japan was also Germany's best hope of striking directly against the British Empire. In July 1941 Hitler had offered Japan an offensive alliance against the Americans, if they would also enter the war against Britain. The Japanese bided their time. But these strategic considerations made it all the more imperative to secure the key economic objectives in the Soviet Union.

In August 1941 the fragile consensus that had underpinned the preparations for Barbarossa broke down. As we have seen, Halder had always regarded the southern thrust into the grain lands of the Ukraine as a diversion from the real objective, the destruction of the Red Army in front of Moscow. Despite the fierce ongoing fighting at Smolensk, Halder still wanted to concentrate all available forces in the central sector for the earliest possible assault towards the Soviet capital.[21] During the crucial weeks in August 1941, however, he was unable to mobilize full support either from Army Group Centre, or from Brauchitsch, Commander-in-Chief of the army. After a series of rather half-hearted confrontations, Hitler got his way. Rather than preparing for an offensive towards Moscow, which could at the earliest have been launched in mid-September, Hitler on 21 August swung the main Panzer force of Army Group Centre southwards in a gigantic right hook. This manoeuvre was to produce what was arguably the greatest single German victory in the Eastern war. In three weeks of savage fighting,

Kiev was encircled, 665,000 men were taken prisoner and the road was opened for the complete conquest of the heavy industrial zone of the Donetz. With the encirclement of Leningrad also completed in early September, the excitement of victory pushed the disagreements of August into the background.[22] It now seemed that there would after all be time to complete all the objectives for Barbarossa in a single year. On 6 September, Army Group Centre was ordered to begin planning for a direct thrust towards the Soviet capital defended by what were assumed to be the last remnants of the Red Army.[23]

The weeks surrounding the launching of this operation, code-named Taifun, were a key moment in the progressive radicalization of the Nazi regime. To Goebbels, Hitler opined that the Wehrmacht would soon be advancing towards Stalingrad and the Don. Britain, finally, would have no option but to come to terms. Prime Minister Churchill would be removed from power. The British Empire would be left intact, but 'England . . . has no future in Europe'.[24] The Eurasian landmass would be reserved for Germany, providing it with the resources it needed to make itself into a truly global power. In his address to the troops of Army Group Centre on 2 October, Hitler made no secret of what was at stake. He linked the battle for Moscow directly to the racial struggle. Germany was now at war both with capitalistic Britain and Bolshevik Russia. Superficially different, the two economic systems were in fact fundamentally alike. Bolshevism was no better than the worst kind of capitalism. It was a creator of poverty and destitution and 'the bearers of this system', 'in both cases', were 'the same: Jews and only Jews!' The assault on Moscow was to deliver a 'deadly thrust' against this arch-enemy of the German people.[25]

Whether or not it was in October 1941 that Hitler took the definitive decision for the immediate murder of the entire Jewish population of Europe, remains unclear.[26] What is beyond doubt is that the euphoria surrounding the German victory in the Ukraine and the success of the first weeks of Taifun coincided with a sharp escalation in anti-Semitic policy and rhetoric. On 15 October the long-awaited evacuation of the German and Austrian Jewish populations finally began. In the woods outside Łódź, Eichmann inspected what was soon to become an experimental gassing facility. On 17 October, in front of Armaments Minister Fritz Todt and Gauleiter Fritz Sauckel, Hitler presented a veritable panorama of the future of the conquered East. The Slav inhabitants were to be treated like 'Red Indians' (*Indianer*). Those that were useful would be retained. The population of the cities was to be starved to death. All destructive Jewish elements were to be exterminated immediately. Hitler on this occasion did not speak of gassing and he restricted his immediate threats to 'destructive Jews'. But, in the light of the killing already done by the Einsatzgruppen, in light of the millionfold starvation of Soviet prisoners of war and the projected death toll of the Hunger Plan, it is not easy to see what significance should be attached to such distinctions. Whether or not Heydrich had already devised a concrete and specific plan for the destruction of the comparatively small Jewish populations of Western Europe, the Third Reich was already committed to a programme of millionfold murder that aimed at nothing less than the demographic reconstruction of Eastern Europe.

At first Taifun satisfied every expectation. The Wehrmacht inflicted terrible wounds. Six Soviet armies were engulfed in the double encirclement at Vyazma and Bryansk. Six hundred thousand prisoners of war trudged westwards to die behind German lines.[27] In the second week of October 1941, Stalin's regime came close to breaking point.[28] Following rumours that the Communist leadership was fleeing the city, the population of Moscow briefly panicked. Order, however, was soon restored. Stalin stayed in the capital and General Georgi Zhukov managed to reconstruct one more defensive line. On 7 November the Red Army celebrated the anniversary of the Bolshevik Revolution with a defiant Red Square parade. Meanwhile, the logistical constraints that hobbled the Wehrmacht reimposed themselves. Even during the build-up to Taifun, the concentration of all Germany's offensive strength on one army group had created huge transport bottlenecks. In September and October the supply dumps in Gomel, Roslawl, Smolensk and Witebsk were lucky on any given day to receive even two-thirds of the stores needed to maintain Taifun at full strength.[29] And though the Red Army suffered terribly, the Wehrmacht also paid a heavy price. By mid-October, 4th Panzer division had been reduced to only 38 vehicles after a devastating encounter with the T-34s of the 1st Guards Rifle Corps.[30] The Panzers were no longer invincible. The Wehrmacht's luck was running out. Within two weeks of the opening of Taifun 10th Panzer division had lost 140 of its 200 tanks. The pride of the division, Lieutenant Walter Rubarth, who with a squad of men had single-handedly forced the Maas river crossing on 13 May 1940, was killed on

26 October 1941 in the bitter fighting for the Minsk–Moscow motor-way. Lieutenant Heinrich Hanbauer, who had followed Rubarth on that heroic day on the Maas, had died on the Beresina bridge four months earlier.[31] And as if to drive home the contrast to the heroic mood of May 1940, on 8 October the autumn rains began. Within days the entire central sector of the German army was turned into an impassable quagmire. By the end of October, Army Group Centre was halted 100 kilometres short of Moscow.

II

Throughout the autumn the scale of the Wehrmacht's victories was enough to paper over the mounting dissonances in Germany's strategic position. In the third week of August 1941 Keitel, as chief of the OKW, chaired a meeting to coordinate the armaments plans of the three Wehrmacht branches on the explicit assumption that the land war was effectively over. Resources could therefore be shifted away from the army towards the Luftwaffe to meet the growing menace of the Anglo-American airfleet.[32] Ironically, the determination of the German army to finish the war by the end of 1941 helped only to reinforce this illusion. Despite the ongoing fighting, the army procurement offices raised little or no protest about the imminent shift in priorities. By October, how-ever, as Taifun ground to its first, muddy climax, the German war economy began to come apart at the seams.

The fuel situation, as long predicted by the Wehrmacht military-economic office, was rapidly approaching a critical point. By early 1942, it would not be the Russian mud but the exhaustion of Germany's petrol supplies that would ensure the 'complete paralysis of the army'.[33] In the event, by dipping into the Wehrmacht's operational fuel reserve and by throttling consumption, the army retained its mobility.[34] The navy was not so fortunate. In November 1941 the fuel oil situation of both the Italian and German navies was described by the Wehrmacht as 'catastrophic'.[35] In May 1941 the Royal Navy had sunk the battleship *Bismarck* as it made a futile bid to escape into the Atlantic shipping lanes. By the autumn the rest of Germany's surface fleet was confined to harbour, not only by the British but also by the chronic lack of fuel.[36] To meet the minimum fuel requirements of the navy and the merchant fleet of roughly 90,000 tons of heavy oil per month, Germany disposed of monthly production of only 52,000 tons plus stocks of only 220,000 tons.[37] An Atlantic operation by Germany's capital ships would double consumption and threaten the imminent paralysis of all Axis shipping. As the Wehrmacht's military-economic office concluded: 'It follows from this that we simply cannot wage war simultaneously with all three branches of the Wehrmacht.'[38]

And it was not only the military who were worried. The pressures imposed by the Barbarossa armaments programme and the Luftwaffe's huge new schemes were threatening to destabilize the precarious fiscal and monetary balance of the entire German economy. On 17 September 1941 the Reichsbank's economics department concluded that the situation of the German currency could be summarized in two succinct statements: the supply of consumer goods had halved; the volume of money in circulation had doubled.[39] The result was a severe disparity between demand and supply and growing inflationary pressure.[40] What particularly concerned the Reichsbank was the dramatic acceleration in the rate of money expansion that had occurred since April 1941. Between April and August, currency in circulation had increased by 10.9 per cent, three and a half times faster than in the same period in 1940. At the same time sales of government debt to banks had declined in relative terms. Though the Reichsbank did not doubt the willingness of the population to accept a severe reduction in the civilian standard of living, there were signs of increasing resort to the black market. Amongst those with access to scarce commodities, such as farmers, craftsmen and small shopkeepers, barter trade was becoming the norm.[41] At the current rate of monetary expansion, the price and wage controls in force since the mid-1930s would soon be overwhelmed; Germany would then face a disastrous slide into inflation, with collapsing productivity and civil unrest, just as in the early 1920s.[42] 'If one only had to reckon with a short war,' the Reichsbank went on, 'one could *in extremis* accept even such a development.' But a short war now seemed 'improbable', since there were still 'three major military tasks [Soviet Russia, Mediterranean, England] that will take much time to resolve'. In the light of Germany's strategic situation, the Reichsbank could not afford to be idle. Urgent 'countermeasures' (*Gegenmassnahmen*) were necessary, including a vigorous assault on the black market and a new propaganda drive to encourage popular saving.[43] The Reichsbank also proposed a compulsory wartime savings scheme and a major increase in taxes to 'cream off' excessive purchasing power. To minimize military expenditure it demanded a 'drastic reduction in the prices paid for armaments'.

Over the following months the Reich authorities made a determined effort to restore Germany's fiscal balance. As has often been remarked,[44] the Third Reich did not resort to a major increase in personal income tax to finance the war. But, given the modest standard of living and the high per capita tax burden even before the war, this is hardly surprising. What the Reich did instead was to encourage saving and to raise taxes on profits and higher incomes.[45] In mid-1941, the standard rate of corporation tax was raised from 40 to 50 per cent and then, as of January 1942, to 55 per cent. Revenue from this source rose by 1.5 billion Reichsmarks in 1941–2 and by a further 1.8 billion Reichsmarks in 1942–3.[46] More important was the mortgaging of future revenues from the Hauszinssteuer, a measure first proposed by the Reich Finance Ministry in December 1941. As we have seen, this tax had been introduced by the Weimar Republic in the 1920s to finance public housing construction. It generally brought in about 850 million Reichsmarks per annum. To combat the wartime fiscal emergency, the Finance Ministry originally proposed a prepayment of four years' worth of tax. But on the insistence of the Prussian Finance Ministry and others this was raised to a one-off prepayment of ten years of tax.[47] At least 4.5 billion Reichsmarks came out of liquid bank accounts and cash reserves of property owners; the rest was raised in the form of new mortgages. In total in 1942, this one-off measure brought in 8 billion Reichsmarks. Together with an increase in contributions from the occupied territories, it was enough to raise the share of Reich expenditure covered by tax revenues in 1942 to more than 54 per cent, despite a sharp increase in spending. The inflationary spiral was halted, at least for the time being.

Not surprisingly, however, it was the suggestion of a major cut in armaments prices that caused the most furore. Since the rationalization drive following the Sudeten crisis in the autumn of 1938, the pricing of public contracts had been regulated by the so-called LSOe system. Though this was far from optimal it was not, as has sometimes been suggested, a licence for gross inefficiency.[48] Under the LSOe, prices were set on the basis of estimated costs, plus a rate of profit, normally 5 per cent, calculated not as a percentage of these costs, but on the capital employed. Once agreed, the prices were fixed and if unit costs fell below the estimate, the profit, at least initially, accrued to the producers. There was, therefore, a clear incentive for cost-cutting and efficiency. And the evidence suggests that armaments contractors took advantage. Despite the fact that the Wehrmacht price control agencies boasted of squeezing armaments prices by an average of 18 per cent in the first two years of the war, it is also generally agreed that this was a high point for corporate profitability.[49] Indeed, by the end of 1940 profits earned under LSOe contracts had become so excessive that Reich price commissioner, Gauleiter Josef Wagner, began to demand drastic action.[50] Wilhelm Zangen, the head of the Reich Group for industry, managed to deflect this initial attack.[51] But in the autumn of 1941, as anxiety amounted about an inflationary crisis, the price commissioner abruptly adopted a more confrontational stance. In light of the Reich's swelling debt and ballooning military expenditure, the agreed system of profit clawback was insufficient, as were the ad hoc price reductions being conceded by industry. To counter the fiscal emergency, Gauleiter Wagner proposed retrospectively to reduce the permissible profit rates for 1940–41 by 20 per cent. And the excess profit rules were to be applied retroactively to the entire 1939–40 tax year. Furthermore, all depreciation allowances on plant that could not be made good during the war were to be transferred to the Reich. In future, rather than providing individualized prices for each government contractor, as under LSOe, firms would be required to meet a standard price, set at the level of costs achieved by a 'good firm', minus 10 per cent.[52] In total, the price commissioner hoped that this package of measures would bring in at least 2 billion Reichsmarks.[53] The response from industry, not surprisingly, was one of outraged indignation. Zangen and his deputy Stahl threatened to resign. Their industrial constituency could have no confidence in them, if the question of profit clawback 'was handled 100 per cent differently than had been agreed in many months of meetings with the price commissioner'. The drastic new proposals would undermine the basis on which 'industry had been working and managing its affairs' for the last year.[54] In the event, it was not Zangen and Stahl who resigned but price commissioner Wagner, apparently as a result of an unrelated intrigue by the SS.[55] But the incident is nevertheless indicative of the tensions building up within the German war economy. In the autumn of 1941, even the relatively harmonious relationship between German industry and the armaments authorities – the political foundation of the war effort since Todt's appointment in the spring of 1940 – was under threat.

An even more pressing challenge, however, was posed by the increasingly debilitated condition of Germany's heavy industry. As usual, the problems circled around coal and steel. By the late spring of 1941, stocks of coal in Germany were virtually non-existent and output was well short of requirement. At a meeting of the Four Year Plan at the end of June, General Hanneken reported that the German *Grossraum* faced an overall coal deficit of roughly 40 million tons. This reflected both the lagging production of the pits and the ever-increasing demands of German industry.[56] As a result, the occupied territories were being supplied at a rate of only 60 per cent of requirement.[57] Within Germany, the steel industry was having its coal consumption throttled by 15 per cent and there was the threat that this might soon be increased to 25 per cent.[58] Even the producers of electricity and gas could no longer be exempt. Cutting the coal allocated to households was not an option, since to ensure the continuity of industrial supplies in the first half of 1941, inadequate preparations had been made for laying in the necessary household stocks for the coming winter.[59] Unless a serious effort was made over the coming months to ensure adequate stockpiling there would be a public relations disaster on the home front. To make room for these essential transports, there was even talk of a drastic 40 per cent reduction in the supply to all non-essential industrial customers. As Hanneken put it to Thomas of the OKW: 'The moment has come at which the Fuehrer himself must decide what should be done in the raw material field over the winter.'[60] The shortages were such as to render absurd the gigantic chemicals expansion schemes that Krauch had set out only a few weeks earlier. To provide the raw materials and power for Krauch's fuel hydrogenation and Buna targets, Germany's coal production would have had to have been raised by a further 30 million tons, on top of the existing deficit of 35–40 million tons.[61]

In the end it was not Hitler but Keitel of Wehrmacht high command who intervened. At a series of meetings between 14 and 16 August 1941, he attempted to force the three branches of the Wehrmacht to tailor their armaments programmes to fit the constraints imposed by the coal shortage. Instead of monthly steel production of 2 million tons Germany would have to make do with only 1.65 million tons.[62] Combined with the obvious limitations of German metalworking capacity, this meant

that the Wehrmacht's overall allocation would have to be sharply curtailed to prevent any further acceleration of the already severe 'steel
inflation'. The physical counterpart to the monetary overhang that so
concerned the Reichsbank was an accumulated total of 12 million tons
of steel entitlements, equivalent to roughly six months of production,
unmatched by any corresponding steel output. Within weeks of
announcing the gigantic Goering programme, the Luftwaffe was forced
by Keitel to settle for the extraordinarily modest objective of simply
replacing the aircraft destroyed on the Eastern Front over the last two
months. In the foreseeable future there was neither the steel nor the
labour to complete the huge synthetic fuel and rubber plants that would
be necessary to supply the gigantic air fleet envisioned a few months
earlier. And whereas the Luftwaffe was merely frustrated in its programme of expansion, the army faced truly devastating cuts. On
25 October 1941 the army's steel ration was set at a miserly 173,000
monthly tons, a level not seen since before the May crisis in 1938.[63] This
drastic shift was fully in line with German armaments strategy since the
autumn of 1940 – shifting resources to the Luftwaffe and navy as soon
as the battle in the East was won. But it was starkly at odds with the
reality facing the Wehrmacht in Russia. As Taifun exhausted itself on
the Smolensk highway, the German generals began finally to adjust to
the realization that the Red Army would not be defeated in 1941.
Faced with drastic cuts to its steel ration, the army procurement office
panicked.[64] Without extra steel, it saw no possibility of resupplying the
Ostheer to continue the war in 1942. And the army was not bluffing. As
we have seen, the production of ammunition had been deliberately run
down in 1940 and 1941. After months of intense fighting, stocks of shells
and bullets had fallen to dangerously low levels.[65] If the Wehrmacht was
to continue active operations in 1942, it desperately needed to replenish
its stocks. Not only that, given the startling superiority of much of the
Red Army's weaponry, the Wehrmacht needed an entire new generation
of tanks and infantry weapons.

What the Third Reich was facing in October 1941 was not another
bout of inter-service bickering. What it faced was the bankruptcy of its
entire war fighting strategy. Nevertheless, it suited Keitel to blame the
army for the derailment. He denounced the army's new steel demands as
an 'unconscionable blackmail' (unerhoerte Erpressung) and immediately
took steps to involve Hitler. Hitler for his part was in no mood for

arguments about raw materials. As Thomas's office noted: 'He refuses to believe that there are not enough raw materials. After all, he has conquered all of Europe. The armed forces must be given what they demand.'[66] Only two days after the OKW had announced the reallocation of steel away from the army, Hitler decreed that the Wehrmacht should ignore the raw material rationing system altogether.[67] Rather than follow through on the decision to shift priorities towards the Luftwaffe, each branch of the armed forces was free until the end of the year to order as much material as it liked. With everything hanging on Army Group Centre's agonizing progress towards Moscow, any pretence of strategic coherence in the organization of Germany's armaments effort was simply abandoned.[68] In fact, in light of the exhaustion both of the workforce and of coal supplies, the Wehrmacht's military-economic office looked forward to the upcoming holiday season with unconcealed relief. In late November General Thomas's office recommended that the German armaments economy should shut down for an extended holiday between 24 December and 1 January 1942 enabling it to conserve both coal and manpower.[69]

Whilst the German war economy thus reached a total impasse, the tattered remnants of the Panzer divisions fought their way to within sight of Moscow.[70] But, as logistical calculations in early November had predicted, they were far too weak to force a decision. The Ostheer (German Army in the East) had once more reached the limit of its transport capacity. It was impossible to sustain a major offensive against fierce Soviet opposition, at a distance of almost 500 kilometres from the forward supply dumps around Smolensk. The Ostheer was now in grave danger. No preparations had been made for active operations in the winter. Cold-weather stores had been provided only for a scaled-down occupation force and even these had not been brought forward because of the need to prioritize the transport of fuel and ammunition. Army Group Centre, where the bulk of German forces were concentrated, was completely exposed. In its drive on Moscow it had left no time to prepare adequate shelter and defensive positions for its troops. The front-line units were exhausted by months of non-stop fighting and more than a thousand kilometres of advance. With temperatures falling in early December 1941 to as low as -25 degrees Fahrenheit, frostbite was claiming tens of thousands of casualties.

Fully aware of the Wehrmacht's impending exhaustion, the Red Army had been husbanding all possible resources for a massive counter-stroke. Informed by their excellent intelligence sources that the Japanese definitely intended to honour the Neutrality Pact of April 1941, the Soviets moved a significant number of first-line troops from Siberia and the Manchurian border to Moscow to form the 1st Shock Army, the 10th and 20th Armies.[71] In total, by early December 1941 Zhukov's Western Front controlled an offensive force of 1.1 million men, 7,652 guns and mortars, 774 tanks and 1,370 aircraft. Given the huge losses sustained since June, there was no margin of numerical superiority, but the Red Army had the initiative and achieved total surprise.[72] For the first time in the war the tables were turned on the German army. The offensive began to the north of Moscow on 5 December. Within days, Army Group Centre was knocked to its knees. The war diary of Panzer Group Three reported a dramatic state of collapse: 'Discipline is breaking down. More and more soldiers are heading west on foot without weapons, leading a calf on a rope or pulling a sled loaded with potatoes. The road is under constant air attack. Those killed by bombs are no longer being buried. All the hangers-on (cargo troops, Luftwaffe, supply train) are pouring back to the rear in full flight.'[73] Field Marshal Fedor von Bock was so overwhelmed that he had to be relieved of his command. By the end of 1941 he had been followed by the Commander-in-Chief of the army, Brauchitsch, General Guderian and the Commanders-in-Chief of both Army Groups North and South.

From the Baltic to the Black Sea, the Wehrmacht lost 380,000 soldiers in two months of intense fighting; 150,000 killed, wounded or missing in action, the rest from illness and frostbite.[74] In the first days of January 1942, in the judgement of the most competent military analysts, the position of Army Group Centre was untenable.[75] German 4th Army, whose Panzers had spearheaded the thrust towards Moscow, was threatened with encirclement on both its southern and northern flanks. If Army Group Centre had been broken, the entire Ostheer would have been forced, at the very least, into a far-reaching withdrawal. Moscow 1941 might well have become a disaster for the Wehrmacht even greater than it was to suffer at Stalingrad twelve months later. Tragically, however, it was precisely this sense of impending victory that led Stalin to overreach. Believing that he was in a position to win the war, on 7 January 1942 he ordered the Red Army onto the offensive along the entire 1,500 kilometre front line.[76] The losses that the Red Army inflicted in its winter campaign were severe. In February and March 1942, the Germans suffered another 190,000 battlefield casualties as well as losing 150,000 men to illness and frostbite. Altogether, the winter crisis claimed more than 700,000 fighting men. It was not until April 1942 that reinforcements to the Ostheer exceeded monthly losses, enabling the Wehrmacht to rebuild.[77] But, in retrospect, Stalin's failure to concentrate all his forces against the weakest point in the German line was a terrible mistake, enabling the Army Group Centre to stabilize its position at a distance of 100–150 kilometres from Moscow. By March 1942, with the Germans still lodged deep in the Soviet Union, the Eastern Front relapsed into relative calm.

III

It is commonly said that the Wehrmacht 'failed' to take Moscow. But this does no justice to the immensity of the shock delivered by the Red Army in the winter of 1941–2. Army Group Centre, the pride of the German army, had suffered a shattering battlefield defeat. The reverse in Germany's strategic position was even more catastrophic. In choosing to widen the war in 1941, Hitler had gambled on the Wehrmacht's ability to conquer the Soviet Union before America entered the conflict. He had thus hoped to place Britain in an impossible position. But when the Wehrmacht appeared to be on the point of defeating the Soviet Union, the immediate effect was to drive Roosevelt and Churchill ever closer together. The Atlantic Charter of August 1941 cemented the United States as the centrepiece of the anti-Nazi coalition. In Berlin, the Charter was read as tantamount to a declaration of war. The United States navy was now actively engaged in hunting down German U-boats in mid-Atlantic. And the British and Americans were further intensifying their joint armaments effort. By October, a joint planning committee had begun to work on a programme described simply as 'the requirements of victory'. When the figures were totalled up in the first week of December 1941, this programme called for the expenditure of no less than $150 billion (in excess of 500 billion Reichsmarks) over the next two years alone.[78] This was more than the Third Reich was to spend on armaments in the entire war and the United States had not yet even actively entered the conflict.

Hitler, of course, continued to comfort himself and his entourage with bluster about the inferiority of the mongrelized Americans. But far more powerful in Berlin was the fatalistic sense that hostilities between Germany and America were inevitable.[79] It was understood that electoral considerations and the fine balance of opinion in Congress continued to moderate Roosevelt's hostility. And the British, whose entire war fighting strategy depended on the United States, were repeatedly frustrated in their hope of an American declaration of war.[80] But, given the seemingly inexorable progression from the summer of 1940, when the United States first began to provide Britain with active military assistance via the announcement of lend-lease in December 1940, to the more or less open engagement of the United States navy in the Atlantic battle, everything seemed to point towards war. The obvious interest of the British in engaging the Americans, the obvious interest of American business in the booming armaments economy, and Roosevelt's open hostility to Germany were all rational elements in this assessment. But, as we have seen, this was compounded, at least since 1938, by a powerful strain of anti-Semitic conspiracy theory. The idea that Roosevelt was acting as an agent of 'international Jewry' in fomenting an all-embracing anti-Nazi coalition had been a staple of Hitler's thinking at least since the violent American response to Kristallnacht. And it was to his speech of January 1939, with its prophecy of doom, that Hitler returned once more in the latter half of 1941. He made the connection explicitly in August 1941. He did so again in late October after the deportation of German Jewry had begun.[81] On 12 August, as Roosevelt and Churchill met in Placentia Bay, Newfoundland, Hitler could hardly have been more explicit. To the Spanish ambassador he declared: 'The main guilty parties in this war . . . are the Americans, Roosevelt with his freemasons, Jews and the entirety of Jewish Bolshevism. The result of this war against Bolshevism must be the great unity of Europe. The Americans are the greatest scoundrels . . . America will pay a bitter price.'[82] And the same theme recurred two weeks later during Mussolini's visit to Hitler's headquarters in the Ukraine, when the Fuehrer regaled his captive audience with a 'detailed analysis of the Jewish clique surrounding Roosevelt and exploiting the American people'.[83]

Given these dark forces at work behind the scenes, the question was not whether Germany would have to face the awesome industrial might of the United States but how soon and on what terms. In this calculation, as had been clear since the autumn of 1940 at the latest, the crucial consideration was Japan. Ribbentrop, for one, favoured enlisting the Japanese as allies against Russia. But for Hitler this was secondary. Even after the failure of Taifun, Hitler remained convinced that the Wehrmacht could win the battle against the Red Army alone. Though the full extent of the Moscow debacle did not become apparent until late December, Hitler retained this confidence even in 1942. The failure of the Ostheer in the winter of 1941 was principally a failure of leadership that Hitler would now personally put right. Indeed, Hitler seems to have regarded the battle on the Eastern Front as a test of the entire German nation. As he put it at the end of January 1942: 'If the German people is not ready to fully commit itself to the struggle for its survival, that's fine: then it should disappear!'[84] The question in relation to Japan, as it had been since 1938, was whether the Japanese were willing to undertake offensive operations against the British and American positions in Asia and the Pacific. The logic of pre-emption that we have traced through Hitler's actions since the summer of 1939 continued to hold, even after the frustration of Barbarossa. If Japan were ready to throw its considerable military weight into the scales against Britain and America that would buy enough time for the Wehrmacht to destroy the Red Army, consolidating Hitler's grip on the European continent. Given Hitler's assumption that war with America was inevitable in any case, the essential thing was simply to finish the war in the East in 1942.

The real nightmare of German strategy was the possibility that Japan might come to terms with the United States, leaving Germany to fight Britain and America alone. To forestall this possibility, Hitler had offered to declare war on the United States in conjunction with Japan already in the spring of 1941.[85] But at the time the Japanese had refused to commit themselves and instead entered into a last round of negotiations with America, which in August culminated in the suggestion of a summit meeting between Roosevelt and Prime Minister Fumimaro Konoe. It was not until October and the fall of the Konoe government that Berlin could feel sure that the Japanese–American discussions were going nowhere.[86] When in November 1941 Tokyo began to signal that Japan was about to commit itself against the West, it was the cause of relief, bordering on euphoria in Berlin.[87] Finally, Hitler and Ribbentrop had the chance to complete the global strategic alliance they had been hoping for since 1938. And they did not hesitate. Without prior knowledge of the Japanese timetable for a surprise attack on Pearl Harbor, Hitler pledged himself to following Japan in a declaration of war on the United States. The appropriately revised version of the Tripartite Pact was completed on 11 December, just in time for Germany's declaration of war on America.

The political and ideological implications of this dramatic turn of events were spelled out by Hitler to the Reichsleiter and Gauleiters of the Nazi party at an audience in his private rooms in Berlin on 12 December. According to Goebbels, the gist of his remarks was as follows: 'Concerning the Jewish question, the Fuehrer is determined to make a clean sweep. He prophesied to the Jews that if they were once again to cause a world war, the result would be their own destruction. That was no figure of speech. The world war is here, the destruction of the Jews must be the inevitable consequence.'[88] The Einsatzgruppen, of course, were by this point fully engaged and in the last week of November they claimed their first German-Jewish victims. On 25 and 29 November in Kaunas, units from Einsatzgruppe A shot 5,000 men, women and children recently arrived from Berlin, Breslau, Munich, Frankfurt and Vienna. Heydrich clearly felt it was time to explain the full extent of the project to the rest of the civil service and to firmly establish the leading role of the SS in the execution of the Final Solution. A meeting with representatives of the Reich Ministries was scheduled for 9 December, only to be cancelled at the last moment because of the dramatic turn of military events. But the intention to destroy the entire Jewish population of Europe was now firmly established. What remained unclear was how this was to be done. As Hans Frank explained to his subordinates on 16 December. 'These 3.5 million Jews [in the General Government] we cannot shoot. We cannot poison them. But we will nevertheless make interventions that in some way lead to an exterminatory success in particular in connection with large measures to be discussed at the Reich-level. The General Government must become just as "Jewfree" as the Reich.'[89] What precisely those 'large measures' were remains unclear. But when he addressed the civil servants in Wannsee on 20 January 1942 the suggestion that Heydrich made was that they should be worked to death on the transport infrastructure of the Generalplan Ost.[90]

Given the firmness of his ideological framework and his fatalistic willingness to gamble, Hitler was not unnerved by the global constellation of December 1941. The alliance of Britain and the Soviet Union backed by the United States was the strategic nightmare with which General Ludwig Beck had tried to scare him in 1937. But since then he had marched from triumph to triumph. The Wehrmacht had eliminated France and driven Britain off the Continent. The Red Army was severely weakened, if not destroyed. Germany did now face the United States as a combatant, but, unlike the Kaiser in 1917, Hitler had Japan as a firm military ally.[91] Even if the Japanese were eventually to succumb to the United States they had at least committed themselves by the Treaty of 11 December not to seek a separate peace. As we have seen, Hitler since 1939 had repeatedly and emphatically stressed the time-factor. His decision to declare war on the United States in December 1941 was one more calculated gamble against time.[92] And there were those in the German military leadership who shared Hitler's optimistic outlook.[93] The relief clearly felt by both the Wehrmacht high command and the German navy in the wake of Pearl Harbor confirms retrospectively the strategic anxieties that we highlighted as the driving force behind Hitler's decision to launch the assault on the Soviet Union twelve months earlier. As we have seen, in December 1940 Hitler had justified the urgency of Barbarossa precisely by pointing to the risk that, unless Germany acted fast, the strategic initiative might pass to Britain and America in 1942. Barbarossa had failed, but now, in a strategic assessment of 14 December 1941, the Wehrmacht credited the dramatic Japanese offensive with robbing the Western Allies of their chance. In its worst-case assessment, the Wehrmacht would still have to face the possibility that Britain and America would pursue a strategy of 'Germany first'. In that case, Germany would have to deal with a full-scale invasion attempt in 1943. But, as the experts of the German navy emphasized, an all-exclusive focus on the European theatre was most unlikely. The fall of Hong Kong and Singapore over the winter of 1941–2 demonstrated that Britain and America could ill afford to neglect the war in Asia. Within weeks, Japan had dealt a shattering blow to the British Empire. For the foreseeable future, the Western powers would be spread across the entire globe. For Hitler, meanwhile, the chief priority continued to be the Soviet Union. As he had done since the summer of 1940, he continued to regard the successful elimination of the Soviet Union as the essential precondition for a global war against Britain and America. Well into the early summer of 1942 Hitler speculated that the blows inflicted by the Japanese, combined with fresh German successes against the Red Army, would be enough to split asunder the unnatural alliance between Britain and America. As events in Asia were demonstrating only too clearly, Britain was in imminent danger of losing its Empire. Only America stood to profit from continuing the struggle. Once the Red Army was knocked out by Germany's second effort, the British people would surely realize the folly of their government. Churchill would be removed and Britain would throw in its lot with Germany. And it was this continuing hope of an imminent British collapse that made Hitler deaf to any signals of a compromise peace from Moscow. On the other hand, if Britain did remain in the war, then the conquest of the Caucasus at least offered Germany the hope of going over to the strategic defensive from a position of strength.

Hitler's sense of urgency was strongly reinforced by the uniformly pessimistic analysis provided by the men responsible for Germany's war economy. As the failure of Barbarossa sank in, the mood amongst those most closely acquainted with the economic parameters of the war was bleak. Ernst Udet, chief of the Luftwaffe procurement organization, had already shot himself on 17 November 1941.[94] In part this can be blamed on an intrigue by Secretary of State Erhard Milch, who was determined to oust Udet from control of aircraft procurement. But it was not office politics that drove Ernst Udet to kill himself. Since the previous autumn, he had repeatedly sought to alert Hitler and Goering to the danger posed by the Anglo-American air programme. By 1942, the Air Ministry knew, the Luftwaffe would be fighting against massively adverse odds, even ignoring the Eastern Front. Ernst Udet certainly had ample reason to seek a desperate escape. Nor would he be the last member of the Luftwaffe leadership to do so. General Thomas of the OKW, who had vacillated over the rationale of Barbarossa from the start, drafted a despairing memo on the futility of Germany's position as early as the summer of 1941.[95] In late December he hosted a meeting of supply officers who provided a depressing *tour d'horizon* of the Ostheer's situation. Thomas's summary was characteristically self-justifying: 'The setback was predetermined by supply problems. General staff has foreseen these and repeatedly pointed them out. Its warnings, however, have not been taken seriously by the leadership.'[96] By the New Year, Thomas's mood had darkened further. On 2 January 1942 he had a discussion with Field Marshal Keitel concerning the situation of Germany's fuel supplies and their implications for operations in the coming year. Even Keitel was worried 'that the Ostheer will not get back up by the summer and then that there will be no petrol'.[97] Thomas was more preoccupied with his place in history: 'We must now present a completely clear picture since some day somebody will be held responsible.'[98]

Even an ardent Nazi such as Fritz Todt, Reich Minister for Armaments, was under no illusions about Germany's situation. According to both Walter Rohland, head of the Main Committee for tank production, and Hans Kehrl, Todt had harboured serious reservations about the Russian campaign from an early date.[99] In November 1941, as Army Group Centre fought its way towards Moscow, Todt dispatched Rohland and a team of armaments industrialists to the very front of the German advance, to visit General Guderian at his headquarters in Orel. They returned deeply depressed. By contrast with the Soviet forces whose men and equipment were obviously well adapted to fighting in extreme conditions, the Wehrmacht was freezing to death. For leading representatives of German industrialism, the picture presented by the Ostheer in November 1941 was deeply shocking. As Rohland reported: 'Our troops were far too lightly dressed, in some cases wrapped in blankets! An assorted picture of frozen-up cars abandoned at the side of the road, with Panje carts drawn by Russian ponies doing their best to provide inadequate supplies. The tanks could not be employed; if the motors and gearboxes still worked, the weapons failed due to freezing up.'[100] On his return, Rohland immediately scheduled a meeting in the Ruhr with Albert Voegler, chairman of the supervisory board of the Vestag, and Borbet of the Bochumer Verein. On 28 November they confronted Todt in a conference that ended, according to Rohland, with the conclusion that 'the war against Russia cannot be won!' The next day, Todt and Rohland met with Hitler at Fuehrer headquarters in the presence of Army Supreme Commander Brauchitsch. Rohland recounted his experiences in Russia and combined them with his intimate knowledge of British and American industry to paint an apocalyptic picture. Once the United States entered the conflict, there would be no way of winning the war. Todt then drove home the point by insisting: 'This war can no longer be won by military means.' Hitler listened calmly before asking 'How then shall I end the war?' To which Todt replied with the obvious conclusion: 'It can only be ended politically.' As we have seen, Hitler had already discussed this possibility with Goebbels in August

1941. But now, with negotiations already under way with Japan, he had other ideas.

Nor was the meeting between Hitler, Todt and Rohland the only discussion of a possible peace at Fuehrer headquarters in November 1941. On 24 November, as the drive on Moscow was approaching its end, Halder noted the despairing mood of General Friedrich Fromm, commander of the reserve army and director of the army's armaments effort: 'Fromm gives an overall picture of our arms production. Declining output! He thinks of the necessity to make peace!'[101] Six weeks later, when it seemed as though the Soviet counter-offensive might rip the heart out of the German line, Fromm seriously considered stripping all of the home army training units of their expert instructors so as to be able to provide a final draft of fifteen first-class infantry divisions.[102] This would have helped to restore the situation of Army Group Centre, but it would also have halted the training of any new recruits. Fromm, therefore, decided to hold off until 'Germany's final moment of peril' (*Deutschlands letzte Not*). But the fact that Fromm was considering such extremities is indicative. On 20 January 1942 Hitler and Goebbels conferred anxiously about the defeatism spreading throughout the high command, the army and the economic administration. Most recently, Minister for Economic Affairs Walther Funk had disgraced himself at Goering's birthday party, where he had declaimed morosely about the 'misfortune that had broken over the nation'.[103] For Borbet of the Bochumer Verein, one of the first men in whom Rohland had confided, the calamity was too much. In January 1942, he followed Udet's example and shot himself.[104] To cover up the embarrassment, a state funeral was hastily arranged, attended by all the dignitaries of German industry.

Clearly, neither Todt nor Fromm was under any illusion about Germany's situation. But whether Germany was to fight on or to negotiate, it needed to do so from a position of strength. And this depended on rebuilding the fighting power of the Wehrmacht for a second great effort in the East in 1942. At the height of the Third Reich's first military crisis Todt did his best to rally Germany's leading industrialists around the war effort. The existing system of regional and national armaments committees was reorganized into a structure of five Main Committees: the three existing committees for ammunition, weapons and tanks and two new committees, one for engineering, the other for general Wehrmacht equipment. Todt also formed a new Ministerial advisory Committee to include representatives both from 'his' industries and the Luftwaffe.[105] On 7 February 1942, after the first plenary session of the new Committees, Todt left Berlin for a further round of meetings with Hitler in Rastenburg.[106] There is no surviving record of the final conversation between Todt and his Fuehrer. Testimony from those who were present in Rastenburg suggests that it did not go well. It is possible that Todt reminded Hitler of their conversation the previous November and that this provoked an outburst from Hitler, but this is an unsubstantiated claim. In any case, after a brief night's sleep, Todt boarded his plane to return to Berlin. As his aircraft took off, it veered to the left as if to make an emergency landing. Seconds later it exploded in mid-air. When Rohland heard the news he was immediately convinced that Todt had been assassinated by the SS and he stuck to this version of events long after 1945. The evidence does not support this view. But, whatever the true circumstances of Todt's death, the fact that such suspicions were crowding in upon a man as level-headed as Walter Rohland is evidence of the acute sense of crisis pervading the leadership of the Third Reich. It is no less indicative that as Todt's replacement Hitler chose, not an insider to the war effort, but a man of unquestionable personal loyalty, in the form of Albert Speer.

Whilst Speer established himself in his new office, General Fromm, who retained responsibility for the army's manpower and armaments, was desperate that Hitler should face military realities.[107] Given the terrible damage suffered by the Wehrmacht in 1941, and the absence of substantial manpower reserves, Fromm saw only two options. Hitler could spread the available men across the entire Ostheer. This would add strength to the German lines, but it would not be sufficient to restore the offensive capacity of any of the army groups. The Ostheer would have to reconcile itself to waiting for the Soviet summer offensive. Alternatively, Fromm proposed that Army Groups North and Centre should be left in their 'burnt-out' (*ausgebrannt*) condition and all available reserves concentrated on Army Group South, preparing it for the push towards the oil of the Caucasus.[108] There was now no argument that economics had to take priority. Oil was all-important. Nor did Hitler need convincing. Neither Fromm nor Hitler, however, any longer expected to win the war with a single blow. The most that Germany could hope for was to eliminate the threat posed by the Red Army and to consolidate the raw-material base necessary for a long war against

Britain and the United States. According to Albert Speer, Fromm in fact was already convinced that only a miracle weapon could save Germany from defeat.[109] What Fromm had in mind was the extraordinary work of a group of physicists who theorized that the energy contained in the elementary particles of matter might provide both a boundless source of power and a potentially war-winning explosive device. Fromm, as the head of the German army weapons office, was fully apprised of the project's potential, but considered it long-term.[110] The army's time-horizons were now shorter and Fromm thus looked to transfer the project to the civilian sector. After months of organizational argument, in the summer of 1942 the physicists made a major presentation to an audience including Albert Speer. All present were impressed with the extraordinary potential of the scheme, but, when pressed, Werner Heisenberg and his colleagues confirmed Fromm's view that an atomic bomb was a long-term proposition. The project would come to fruition in two or three years' time at the earliest and would require a huge investment. Given Germany's situation in 1941 that made it an irrel-evance. What the leadership of the Third Reich was looking for was a decisive success on the Eastern Front in the coming summer.

With hindsight it is clear that the decision made by Speer and his colleagues was essentially correct. Even working with virtually limitless resources, the Americans did not manage to complete a viable atomic weapon in time for it to be used against Germany. But the eagerness with which the Western Allies seized on the atomic bomb at precisely the same moment that it was deprioritized in Germany is yet more evidence of the gulf that separated the industrial and technical resources of the two sides.[111] Informed by his chief scientific adviser in September 1941 that the atomic bomb programme had a chance of success some-where between one in ten and one in two, Churchill did not hesitate to instruct the British scientists to accelerate the programme to top speed. Wreaking havoc on the German home front was the essence of Britain's strategy and the atomic bomb was clearly the ideal weapon for that job. On 7 May 1942 the British cabinet formally agreed that RAF Bomber Command was to destroy fifty-eight of Germany's largest towns and cities, 'dehousing' at least 22 million people.[112] In line with the expansive goals of the Victory Programme, the Americans took the decision to accelerate what became the Manhattan Project even before the Japanese struck at Pearl Harbor. At the very least, the possibility that Germany might be working on a similar device required insurance, a kind of strategic calculation, which the Third Reich was never able to afford.

IV

The narrative segues in this and the previous chapters – from Germany's genocidal imperialism, via the defeat of Army Group Centre, to the atomic bomb – may at first seem bewildering. But they reflect the shocking 'contemporaneity of the uncontemporaneous' (*Gleichzeitigkeit des Ungleichzeitigen*) which characterizes this crucial turning point in world history. The point is not that Germany's imperialism in Eastern Europe represented a regression into atavistic barbarism. The Nazi programme of genocide was certainly barbaric. But, as we have seen, it was tied to an ambitious project of colonial settlement and violent modernization. The point is not that Nazi racism was atavistic. The point is that it was anachronistic. The concrete manifestions of German imperialism in 1941 – the tiny tanks dwarfed embarrassingly by their Soviet counterparts, the bedraggled army of horses and Panje wagons, the primitive brutality of the Einsatzgruppen, the fumbling attempts to construct asphyxiation chambers – all appear grotesquely crude, by comparison with the cutting-edge physics and high-tech engineering that were opening the door to the nuclear era in the deserts of New Mexico. Barbarossa was a belated and perverse outgrowth of a European tradition of colonial conquest and settlement, a tradition that was not yet fully aware of its own obsolescence. The ignorant condescension shown by all sides, not just by the Germans, but by the British and Americans as well, towards the fighting power of the Red Army is indicative of this. But, as the Wehrmacht found to its cost, the Soviet Union was not an object that could be operated on in the manner of Edwardian imperialism. What Germany encountered in Soviet Russia in 1941 was not 'Slavic primitivism', but the first and most dramatic example of a successful developmental dictatorship, and what was revealed in the Wehrmacht's floundering advance towards Moscow was not the backwardness of Russia, but Germany's own partial modernization.

By the 1940s, the nineteenth-century map of economic and military power, centred on the established states of Western Europe, no longer existed. This was the most basic fallacy underpinning the effort by the

Third Reich to create an empire in the East. America's emergence as an economic superpower on the one hand and the explosive development of the Soviet Union on the other had fundamentally altered the balance of global power. Hitler was not oblivious to this shift. An awareness of the stakes involved runs clearly through both *Mein Kampf* and his 'Second Book'. The same theme was reiterated in his strategic assessments of the 1930s and early 1940s. The conquest of *Lebensraum* in the East was not, after all, the end point of the historical trajectory on which Hitler had embarked. The conquest of natural resources and territory to match those of North America was the precondition for a true programme of 'modernization', both for German society and the German military. It was through the achievement of *Lebensraum* on an American scale that the Third Reich hoped to achieve both the standard of affluence and the encompassing reach of global power already attained by Britain and the United States. As events between June and December 1941 made clear, Nazi Germany lacked both the time and the resources to take this first step.

16

Labour, Food and Genocide

Following the military crisis of 1941–2, manpower was the over-whelming preoccupation of the German war economy. In its vain effort to match the Red Army, backed by a population twice the size of Germany's, the Third Reich engaged in a war of attrition unlike that experienced by any of the Western powers. Figure 19 shows the most concentrated index of this haemorrhage. In the three years between June 1941 and May 1944, the average rate of loss for the Wehrmacht was almost 60,000 men killed every month on the Eastern Front. In the last twelve months of the war, the blood-letting reached truly extraordinary proportions.[1]

The way in which the Third Reich responded to this catastrophic drain of manpower was to become one of the defining features of Hitler's regime. As we have seen, the Wehrmacht had already reached the bottom of the manpower barrel at the time of Barbarossa. By the autumn of 1941 there were virtually no men in their twenties who had not already been conscripted. Fresh cohorts of teenagers provided the Wehrmacht with less than a million fresh recruits in 1942, enough only to replace the losses inflicted by the Red Army. To achieve any kind of expansion, the recruiters needed to draw on middle-aged German men previously exempted from the draft, including large numbers of armaments workers. In the first half of 1942 the Wehrmacht draft included at least 200,000 men taken from the armaments factories.[2] At a time when Germany desperately needed to increase its armaments output, this was a disaster.[3]

One obvious solution was a further mobilization of German women. It has become a commonplace to compare the mobilization of Germany's female labour force in World War II unfavourably to that of Britain. This, however, ignores the obvious. As we have seen, German women

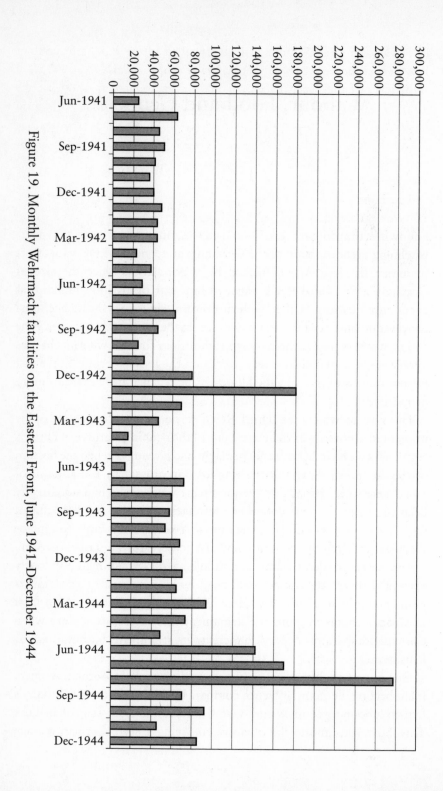

Figure 19. Monthly Wehrmacht fatalities on the Eastern Front, June 1941–December 1944

in 1939 were already more actively engaged in the labour force than Britain's women were to be even at the end of the war. When the chief statistician of the Reich Labour Ministry investigated the issue in the autumn of 1943, using data that were very unfavourable to Germany, he arrived at the conclusion that the share of women in war work was 25.4 per cent in the United States, 33.1 per cent in Britain and 34 per cent in Germany.[4] Another comparative study in the spring of 1944 arrived at the same conclusion. Though British regulations appeared to conscript a wider age range, Germany's level of mobilization actually exceeded that of Britain.[5] The expert administrators also rejected any unfavourable comparisons with World War I. At the height of the battles at Verdun and on the Somme, German women's labour market participation rate had been 45.3 per cent, somewhat less than the participation rate of their daughters twenty-five years later. Of course, even more might have been squeezed out of the German female population. But one should not exaggerate the extent of the 'slack'. The 'Total War' registration drive of 1943, covering all women between the ages of 16 and 45, yielded only 1.5 million potential workers of whom at least 700,000 required part-time positions.[6] This was frustrating, but in 1944 the Reich plenipotentiary for labour claimed that even with the 'powers of Stalin' he would be able to mobilize no more than 1 million additional women.[7] And Hans Kehrl, one of the most draconian advocates of total mobilization, never hoped for more than 700,000 additional female workers.[8] These are not the kind of figures which could have made much of a difference. Germany needed not hundreds of thousands but millions of additional workers. And the only places from which to recruit in such numbers were the countries of occupied Europe.

On National Heroes Day, 21 March 1942, Hitler appointed Gauleiter Fritz Sauckel to the new position of general plenipotentiary for labour mobilization (GBA). In many ways this could be seen as a counterpoint to Hitler's choice to replace Fritz Todt with Albert Speer a few weeks earlier. Whereas the new Armaments Minister was the handsome, urbane technocrat, Gauleiter Sauckel was a stocky, moustached representative of the populist, 'socialist' wing of the Nazi party, the very archetype of the deracinated petty bourgeois.[9] In the sound recordings of the Nuremberg trial one can still hear the distinctive traces of Sauckel's plebeian origins in his heavy Franconian accent and stilted delivery. Nor was this a populist affectation. Born 1894, the son of a post office clerk and a seamstress, Sauckel's family could not even afford for him to complete secondary school. After an early period of adventure as a merchant sailor in the Scandinavian trade, Sauckel returned to Germany from French captivity in 1919 determined to resume his education. To pay his way he took a temporary job as a lathe operator in one of the great ball-bearing factories in Schweinfurt. By 1923, he had finally abandoned his hopes of a university degree, married the daughter of a foreman, joined the Nazi party and committed himself to a lifetime of populist political activism. Sauckel was certainly an *Alter Kaempfer*. He was credited at Nuremberg with a party membership number as low as 1,395, placing him in the innermost core of Hitler's movement. From 1927 he was the regional boss of Thuringia, making his Gau into one of the true bastions of National Socialism. And after 1933 Sauckel remained true to his origins, a strong advocate of the left line of Nazi ideology, combining vivid anti-Semitism with deep suspicion of liberal capitalism and a florid commitment to the welfare of 'ordinary' German men and women. The Gauleiter also retained a keen eye for a populist public relations stunt, joining one of the first U-boats to be sent against the Royal Navy as a stowaway.

Such buffoonery, however, should not lead one to misjudge Sauckel. The simple contrast between Sauckel the plebeian radical and Speer the cool technocrat is doubly misleading. As will be argued in the next chapter, it radically underestimates the political role played by Albert Speer. And it also seriously underestimates Sauckel. He was more than just a Hitler loyalist. As Gauleiter in Thuringia he presided after 1933 over one of the key regional hubs of the German military-industrial complex.[10] Situated in the heart of Germany, Thuringia was at the extreme range of Allied bombers. The town of Jena was home to Carl Zeiss, one of the Wehrmacht's most indispensable suppliers. Suhl and Zella Mehlis were two of the oldest centres of gun-making in Germany. Rheinmetall, the Reich's leading armourer after Krupp, maintained a large plant at Soemmerda. And Sauckel himself carried out the early Aryanization of Simsons & Co., one of Germany's largest makers of pistols, rifles and machine guns. In 1935 Simsons was incorporated into the Wilhelm Gustloff Stiftung, Sauckel's personal armaments holding, which by the early 1940s had an annual turnover of several hundred million Reichsmarks. Displaying a keen eye for the economic potential of Himmler's carceral complex, Sauckel made sure that the largest of the second generation of concentration camps was sited at Buchenwald, just outside the state capital of Weimar. It was no coincidence, finally, that the underground manufacturing facilities both for the world's first jet fighters and the world's first ballistic missile were sited in Thuringia. To say that Fritz Sauckel was no novice in the industrial politics of the Third Reich is an understatement.

Charged by Hitler in March 1942 with special responsibility for foreign labour recruitment, Gauleiter Sauckel set in motion one of the largest coercive labour programmes the world has ever seen.[11] In the spring of 1941, Germany already employed 1.2 million prisoners of war, mainly Frenchmen, and 1.3 million 'civilian' workers, mainly Poles, accounting for 8.4 per cent of the workforce. Over the course of 1941, the number of civilian foreign workers increased by a further million, mainly from Poland. As we have seen, it was the demands of the Reich Ministry of Food and Agriculture that had set this programme in motion. And it was not until the debacle at Moscow that the needs of industry began to drive Germany's import of foreign workers. Sauckel responded by mobilizing literally millions of workers from all over Europe. The arrivals were mainly young men and women. More than half the females drafted in Eastern Europe were teenagers between 12 and 22 years old.[12] They were drawn from the occupied territory of the Soviet Union – the Baltic Republics, Belorussia, the Ukraine and to a lesser extent from Russia itself. Poland was Sauckel's most intensive area of recruitment. But he also plied his brutal trade in the Czech Protectorate, France, Belgium, the Netherlands and Italy. Between January 1942 and the end of June 1943 the GBA delivered 2.8 million new foreign workers to Germany: the workforce of a great factory – 34,000-strong – every week, for seventy-eight weeks. By the summer of 1943 the total foreign workforce had increased to 6.5 million, of whom 4.95 million were civilians rather than prisoners of war. After the summer of 1943 the pace slowed somewhat, but Sauckel continued to bring in workers. By February 1944 the total of foreign civilians and prisoners of war had risen to 7.356 million. By the autumn of 1944 it had reached a maximum of 7.907 million. At this point, foreign workers accounted for more than 20 per cent of the German workforce. Of the armaments workers of the Third Reich, more than a third were foreign. In the plants of the Reichswerke Hermann Goering and the Luftwaffe, the foreign share routinely exceeded 40 per cent.[13] On individual production lines the percentage could be even higher. As State Secretary Milch boasted in June 1943, the Stuka Ju 87 was being '80 per cent manufactured by Russians'.[14]

Since the Nuremberg tribunal introduced the term 'slave labour' into the discussion, Sauckel and his programme have been variously described as 'millennial' and 'Pharaonic'.[15] Such terms certainly capture the increasingly brutal means to which Sauckel resorted in recruiting 'his' workers. But such anachronistic language also tends to obscure the fact that Germany's programme of foreign labour conformed to the most elementary principles of classical economics. Labour had been desperately scarce in Germany since 1939. Per capita productivity was far higher in Germany than anywhere else in continental Europe. It made sense, therefore, for a 'rational economic dictator' to redeploy the workers of Europe so as to concentrate them in the factories of the Reich. The fact that Sauckel, with his woolly National Socialist rhetoric, did not conform to the ideal type of the technocrat should not obscure the basic rationality that underpinned his efforts. Of course, coercive recruitment had costly 'side effects' in the territories that Germany occupied. Later in the war, this was to persuade Albert Speer to favour increased trade in goods with France, rather than a last-ditch effort to extract millions of additional workers.[16] However, the logic of this 'European strategy' was political, not economic. Speer wanted to stabilize relations with Germany's western neighbour and he also wanted to unseat Sauckel.[17] In economic terms, given the desperate shortage of labour in Germany and the ever-increasing productivity gap between Germany and the collapsing economy of France, the case for concentrating as many workers as possible within the Reich remained strong. Significantly, no one in Berlin, even in 1944, ever questioned the necessity of continuing to press-gang Polish or Soviet workers. As fresh recruitment from Western Europe ground to a halt in the second half of 1943, it continued with unabated brutality in the East.[18] Between October 1943 and the summer of 1944 the retreating German armies in the East evacuated more than 400,000 people from the combat zone for work in Germany.[19]

In the most basic sense, therefore, the Third Reich's immediate response to the winter crisis of 1941–2 was 'rational'. Germany was short of labour. By any Western standard, there was no way of increasing the mobilization of the native labour force. So Gauleiter Sauckel and his staff sallied forth and brought literally millions of additional foreign workers to Germany. The result was that, by the final stages of the war, the Third Reich was a society playing host to at least as many foreigners as the 'multi-cultural' Germany of today. Because of the overwhelming emphasis on recruiting young workers, the representation of foreigners in the workplace – both in industry and agriculture – was far greater than it has ever been, before or since. Prior to 1942, foreign workers were most in evidence in the countryside. But after Sauckel's gigantic recruitment drives, huge crowds of men and women drawn from all over the Nazi Empire populated Berlin, Hamburg, Cologne, Munich and every other industrial city in Germany. Camps and hostels for foreign workers studded every city and town. To take just one example, Munich, the Bavarian capital, was home to at least 120 prisoner of war camps, 286 barracks camps and hostels for civilian foreigners, 7 branch facilities of concentration camps and 2 labour re-education facilities, as well as a brothel for foreign workers.[20] Total Lager capacity was in excess of 80,000 beds. By far the largest employer of foreign workers in Munich was BMW, which was one of the Luftwaffe's main suppliers of aero-engines. In September 1944, in its Munich plants alone, BMW employed more than 16,600 foreign workers, housed in eleven dedicated facilities, including a prisoner of war camp and a particularly notorious subsidiary of Dachau concentration camp, in the suburban town of Allach.[21]

I

In approaching this huge phenomenon of forced migration one should not forget that supposedly liberal societies throughout the last century and a half have often responded in a paradoxical fashion to the migration flows unleashed by rapid economic change. To this day, virtually all the rich countries in the world pursue profoundly contradictory immigration regimes and their politicians struggle to give anything resembling rational leadership on issues of migration, asylum and race relations. The Third Reich was the very antithesis of a liberal society. As we have seen, only months before Sauckel embarked on his foreign labour programme Nazi Germany had instigated multiple programmes of mass murder of a quite unprecedented scale and ferocity. Furthermore, we know that from its very inception in the spring of 1940 the foreign labour programme had been cross-cut by savage lines of racial discrimination. This continued after 1942, even when foreign labour procurement was a top priority. The result was a series of ghastly contradictions. On the one hand, Gauleiter Sauckel made strenuous efforts to mobilize millions of workers for employment in the Reich. At the same time, the SS and the Wehrmacht were deliberately murdering millions of people, who could just as well have served as workers for the German war economy. In relation to the cardinal problem of manpower, it is hard to avoid the impression that the Third Reich faced an unresolvable contradiction between its genocidal racial ideology and the practical imperatives of production.

This contradiction first made itself drastically evident in relation to the millions of Soviet prisoners captured in the first months of the Barbarossa campaign. As we have seen, the Wehrmacht initially set about starving entire armies of prime manpower. And yet, as early as November 1941, given the impasse on the Eastern Front, Hitler had taken the decision that Soviet prisoners of war were to be employed, not only in the rear areas, but in Germany itself.[22] Hundreds of thousands of men were shipped to Germany over the following months, but the mistreatment continued, resulting in mass deaths in prisoner of war camps in Germany itself, and a continuing wastage of labour power.[23] Even before Sauckel was appointed, the OKW's military-economic office and the Reich Group for industry had complained to the Food Ministry that it was simply pointless to import hundreds of thousands of workers only for them to succumb to malnutrition.[24] In early March the Mitteldeutsche Motorenwerke, a contractor for the Air Ministry, felt forced to spell out the difference between employing Eastern workers as construction labourers and employing them in the manufacture of aeroengines: 'If in the case of road building in the East we employ 2,000 Russians, and as a result of inadequate food supplies we lose a few hundred Russians per quarter, the missing labourers can simply be replaced by new Russians.' By contrast, 'In the manufacturing processes of an armaments plant it is simply not possible suddenly to exchange a man, who has been operating a special piece of machinery, with another worker.'[25]

In a somewhat less extreme form, the same paradoxical treatment was also meted out to the civilian Ostarbeiter recruited to Germany in ever-increasing numbers in 1942. In part this was attributable to the sheer success of Sauckel's recruitment drive, which overwhelmed Germany's local authorities. In the summer of 1942 literally thousands of new workers were arriving in the major industrial centres every day. It was impossible to organize either adequate housing or rations. Conditions varied between cities and between employers, but in many cases, perhaps particularly in heavy industrial areas, the situation was awful. In December 1942 a commission of inquiry by the Ostministerium and Wistab Ost visited Ostarbeiterlager across the Ruhr and reported in shocked tones. As just one example, they singled out the camp operated by the Bochumer Verein, a member of the Vestag trust, where they witnessed a 'picture of desolation and immiseration' which would 'never be extinguished'.[26] Coming from 'unsentimental' bureaucrats with ample experience of the East, these were strong words. And they were confirmed by the behaviour of Ostarbeiter themselves. For generations, the Anglo-American public has been regaled with stories of daring escapes by British and American airmen and soldiers. However, from 1942 onwards they were vastly outnumbered by absconding Soviet prisoners of war and Ostarbeiter. Between April and July 1942 the number of Soviet absconders increased from 2,059 to 22,603. In August 1942 the Gestapo estimated that it would have to deal with a further 30,000 escapes in the coming months. Of the 42,714 foreign workers who were reported as having absconded between April and July 1942, the Gestapo claimed to have recaptured 34,457.[27] But given these numbers it was clearly impractical to continue with conventional police methods. In September 1942 the chief of the Gestapo himself, SS Gruppenfuehrer Heinrich Mueller, took personal charge of the effort to control the population of Eastern workers. Instead of pursuing tens of thousands of individual cases, he instituted a new and comprehensive system of police cordons on all major roads, railway stations and in town centres across the country.[28]

By the autumn of 1942, given the conditions in the camps, tens of thousands of half-dead Ostarbeiter had to be shipped back eastwards under nightmarish conditions. In September one transport was described in apocalyptic terms: 'There were dead passengers on the returning train. Women on that train gave birth to children that were tossed from the open window during the journey, while people sick with tuberculosis and venereal disease rode in the same coach. The dying lay in freight cars without straw, and one of the dead was ... thrown onto the embankment.'[29] Obviously, this account is suffused with a sense of biblical exaggeration. However, a number of reports confirm the claim that the emaciated corpses of Ostarbeiter were dumped on German railway embankments,[30] not to mention the fact that trainloads of Eastern workers were routinely abandoned in railway yards for hours on end, in full view of regular German passengers, without any form of sanitation. By word of mouth and through letters home, rumours soon spread about the treatment that Ostarbeiter could expect in Germany. Not surprisingly, by September 1942 the managers of foreign labour camps in the Ukraine were reporting 'Transportangstpsychosen'. By the end of the summer, the flow of voluntary recruits had come to a complete halt, which in turn precipitated an extreme escalation of violence on the part of Sauckel's recruiting agents.[31]

Horrific as all of this clearly was, it pales by comparison with the even more shocking contradiction engendered by Germany's expanding campaign of Judaeocide. The manpower crisis unleashed by the defeat at Moscow was followed within months by the murderous peak of the Holocaust in the second half of 1942. As we have seen, the executions by the Einsatzgruppen in Soviet territory had already begun in June 1941 and mass murders by firing squad continued in the occupied territory of the Soviet Union right up to the final German evacuation in 1944. But the Judaeocide reached its peak in 1942, with the decision to liquidate the Jewish population of pre-war Poland, numbering well over 2 million people. Hundreds of thousands were shot or worked to death, or died of starvation and disease in the ghettos. But the main means of killing the bulk of the Jewish population of Poland were three dedicated killing centres, Treblinka, Sobibor and Chelmno, as well as the gas chamber complex at the concentration camp at Auschwitz. Whilst the first three were shut down in 1943, Auschwitz continued, to become the final destination for hundreds of thousands of Jews from across Western Europe in 1942 and 1943 and Hungary in 1944.

Even assuming that the Jews were to be used only for the most menial forms of work the Holocaust involved a catastrophic destruction of labour power. Applying the Germans' own conservative standards, the Holocaust must have claimed the lives of at least 2.4 million potential workers. Adding this to Nazism's other acts of mass murder after January 1942, we arrive at an astonishing total. Of the 1.65 million inmates of concentration camps employed at one time or another in the German economy – referring here to camps not involved in the extermination phase of the Final Solution – no more than 475,000 survived the war.[32] This implies the death of at least 1.1 million workers, at least 800,000 of whom do not also number amongst the victims of the Holocaust. Of the 1.95 million Soviet prisoners of war who are thought to have been employed in Germany after November 1941, less than half survived the war. As many as a million Soviet prisoners may, therefore, have died after they were designated as potential contributors to the German war effort. This is in addition to the 2 million who had starved to death over the winter of 1941–2. Of the 2.775 million Soviet civilians who were recorded as working in Germany between 1941 and 1945, it is estimated that at least 170,000 died during their time in the Reich. This is almost certainly an underestimate, since it takes no account of the number of 'worn-out' workers repatriated to an uncertain fate in the Eastern territories. Most ominously, it neglects the gap in the German statistics between those who were deported from the Eastern territories and those who were registered as workers in the Reich. This gap numbers in the hundreds of thousands. There are similar questions surrounding the figures for Polish workers, of whom at least 130,000 died during their stay in Germany. Amongst the 'Western workers', the group that suffered most were the Italian soldiers interned by the Germans after the Italian surrender in the autumn of 1943. Of these unfortunates, no less than 32,000 were starved and worked to death over the winter of 1943–4. Totalling these deaths amongst various categories of forced labour after January 1942, we arrive at a figure of perhaps 2.4 million for the non-Jewish-worker victims of the Nazi regime. Added to the figure of at least 2.4 million potential Jewish workers we arrive at a total of at least 4.8 million workers murdered by the Third Reich after it confronted the military crisis of 1941–2, closer to 7 million if we include the Soviet prisoners of war killed in 1941.

II

One could conclude from these staggering numbers that the Third Reich was simply a regime for which economic concerns were of secondary importance. In the last instance, the primacy of the political was absolute. The murder of millions of racial enemies, regardless of their potential usefulness to Germany's war economy, is incontrovertible proof of this.

Clearly, it would be absurd entirely to deny the force of this argument. However, over the last three decades, historians have accumulated a mass of evidence that suggests a far more nuanced picture. One model for thinking about this problem is that of a compromise between the more and less ideological elements of the Nazi regime.[33] If one accepts that the Judaeocide was an ideological end in itself, indeed an obsessive fixation of the Nazi leadership, then it is even possible to see the forced labour programme and the genocide less as contradictions than as complementary. Gauleiter Sauckel's success in recruiting millions of workers from across Eastern and Western Europe made the Jews appear dispensable.[34] Only in Poland and the Ukraine did the Jews account for more than a small minority of the population. Everywhere else they could be murdered without seriously reducing the overall workforce at Germany's disposal.[35] Furthermore, this process of extermination had an autonomous bureaucratic logic because it was carried forward on the independent initiative and authority of the SS, above all the RSHA, with backing from Hitler and Himmler at the very top. This interpretation is further reinforced by archival evidence from the middle ranks of the occupation bureaucracy in Eastern Europe. This shows local officials of the SS arguing for the murder of skilled Jewish workers, against the interests of the Wehrmacht and other agencies employing them on war work, of which the most famous example was Oskar Schindler in the General Government.[36] In these documents, the SS present themselves as a committed minority forcing the programme of Judaeocide down the throats of an uncomprehending military administration.[37] As we shall see, Himmler himself liked to indulge in this kind of rhetoric in relation to the liquidation of the Polish ghettos in 1942 and 1943. Viewed in this way, the Holocaust can be made to appear as a concession extracted from the pragmatic mainstream of the German state administration by the ideologically committed leadership of the SS. It was a concession to ideology, made possible by Sauckel's success in recruiting non-Jewish labour from all over Europe. Jewish workers could be dispensed with, since there always appeared to be other workers to replace them.

In fact, however, despite the rhetoric espoused by Himmler, the SS were not oblivious to economic concerns in their killing of the Jewish population. The practice of 'Selektion' was a ubiquitous first step in virtually every massacre.[38] The population was divided into those incapable and those capable of work. This meant that once initial inhibitions were overcome, it was women, children and old people that tended to be killed first, particularly in 1942, the high point of the Judaeocide. In dealing with the large Jewish communities of the Ukraine or Galicia, the SS returned on several occasions to the same location or township, progressively reducing the Jewish population to an 'indispensable core'. In many cases this productive remnant was then transported to a central ghetto location for further exploitation, before the ghetto itself was finally liquidated in 1943 or even as late as 1944. In Poland, the practice was first applied at the end of 1941, in the so-called Warthegau, one of the provinces newly annexed to Germany. Those judged incapable of work in the Warthegau were amongst the first to be killed by gassing at the experimental facility at Chelmno. Those that were still capable of exploitation were concentrated in the Łódź (Litzmannstadt) ghetto, which continued as a centre of war production until early 1944. This established a template which was applied to the 'clearance' of the Jewish population of the General Government, a population estimated at the Wannsee conference to include no less than 2.28 million people. Here, too, 'Selektion' was the first principle of the operation. In the Lublin district, presided over by Odilo Globocnik, the Jewish council was instructed in early 1942 to issue identity cards and to draw up lists of all Jews 'that do not work productively'.[39] According to an entry in Goebbels's diary in the spring of 1942, the assumption was that '60 per cent will have to be liquidated, whereas only 40 per cent can still be employed as labour'.[40]

The fate initially intended for the group selected for labour seems to have been that outlined by Heydrich at the Wannsee conference. They were to be separated by sex and were to be worked to death on the far-flung building sites of the Generalplan Ost. At least until the autumn of 1942, the Generalplan was very much a live proposition. On 16 July

1942 Himmler visited his masseur and confidant Felix Kersten in an enthusiastic mood. His elation was due to a meeting a few days earlier, at which he had presented Hitler with the final version of the Generalplan, complete with maps and architectural plans for German peasant villages. With his armies roaring towards the Caucasus in the Wehrmacht's last great summer offensive, Hitler was again convinced that the war in the East would soon be won. As Himmler reported it: 'The Fuehrer not only listened to me, he even refrained from constant interruptions, as is his usual habit . . . today he went so far as to approve of my proposals, asking questions and drawing my attention to important details . . .' 'This is the happiest day of my life,' Himmler proclaimed. 'Everything I have been considering and planning on a small scale can now be realized. I shall set to at once on a large scale . . .'[41]

The crucial point here is that Himmler's conception of Jewish labour was always very specific. It was closely tied up with the Pharaonic construction plans of the Generalplan Ost and involved columns of slave labourers working under close SS guard, hundreds if not thousands of kilometres to the east of the Reich. By contrast, Himmler consistently opposed the employment of Jews in manufacturing, particularly in war industries. These were the kinds of jobs that should be filled as soon as possible by other forms of foreign labour. It was not until Stalingrad, when the prospect of immediate German settlement in the East finally passed out of sight, that Himmler lost all interest in retaining any Jewish labour at all. By this point, however, the only Jews left alive in Poland were those employed in factories working for the Germans, concentrated in a handful of large labour camps and ghettos. It involved no shift in position on the part of Himmler for him to insist on their liquidation in the course of 1943.[42]

The transports of Jews from Western and South-eastern Europe destined above all for Auschwitz were subject to the same basic procedure.[43] Often the transports were 'preselected' at their origin as a group either destined for employment or for immediate extermination. Alternatively, the SS carried out the Selektion on arrival at the railway yard in Auschwitz. At a conservative estimate, 1.1 million Jews were deported to Auschwitz between 1941 and 1945. Of these 900,000 were killed immediately; 200,000 were retained for forced labour. Of course, Selektion for labour was only a stay of execution. But for those who escaped immediate gassing, the process of killing was in some cases protracted

over a number of months, or even years. And despite its central importance as an extermination facility, Auschwitz never lost its original
identity as a labour camp. Apart from the 200,000 Jews selected for
labour, the Camp Kommandatur also managed a steady flow of non-
Jewish inmates, including a total of 140,000 Poles, approximately
20,000 gypsies from various countries, more than 10,000 Soviet prisoners of war, and more than 10,000 prisoners of other nationalities. In
total, 400,000 people were at one time or other registered as inmates in
the records of the Auschwitz Stammlager, half of them Jewish. Conditions, particularly for the Jews, were appalling, so that the majority
of these inmates died in a matter of months. In addition, tens of thousands of inmates were shuffled around the concentration camp system,
as needs dictated. Auschwitz itself reached its maximum strength in the
autumn of 1943, when the camp complex contained 90,000 inmates.
At any one time, between 50 and 60 per cent of these were judged fit
enough for work. This workforce was never employed on the far-flung
building sites of the Generalplan, as had been the intention when the
camp was expanded in 1941. But the majority of work done by the
inmates was nevertheless connected in one way or another to the programme of Germanization in the East, starting at Auschwitz itself. The
camp's inmates helped to construct IG Farben's prestige chemicals facility at Auschwitz-Monowitz, as well as many other industrial facilities
dotted around eastern Silesia.[44] They were thus laying the foundations
for a Silesian industrial complex to rival the Ruhr. But the majority of
the inmates worked on the camp itself, which was no less a bastion of
German settlement in the East than the much larger industrial facilities
that sprang up around it. By 1942 the SS architects had drawn up plans
for a permanent slave labour complex at Auschwitz-Birkenau counting
no less than 600 buildings. More than 300 of these were completed by
the end of the war. In addition, thousands of inmates worked on the
4,000-hectare estate that Himmler had carved out of the surrounding
Polish countryside, which was intended to be the leading centre for
agronomical research in the German East.[45] To sustain the economy of
the camp, the SS operated a variety of small-scale industrial plants,
including a Portland cement works, a quarry, a slaughterhouse, a dairy
and a camp bakery. Only in the final stages of the war did these various
SS projects recede into the background in favour of immediate war
production. In this mode, the coupling of labour and destruction at

Auschwitz reached its high point in the summer of 1944, when the Jews of Hungary became the last great population to be sucked into the maelstrom of destruction.[46] Whilst the gas chambers worked at full capacity to kill hundreds of thousands of Hungarian Jews judged unfit for work, tens of thousands of young men and women were selected for dispatch across Germany to the highest-priority armaments factories of the Reich.

In the case of the Holocaust, ideological imperatives were clearly paramount, but subject to pragmatic compromise as circumstances demanded. Conversely, one can describe Sauckel's forced labour programme as a compromise between ideology and pragmatic necessity with the signs reversed. The demands of the war economy were paramount, but they had to be reconciled with the requirements of ideology. As we have seen, when Germany invaded Poland in 1939 the intention had not been to equip Germany's farms with an army of Polish workers. Himmler as chief of police reluctantly agreed to Backe's demands, but only on strict conditions. It was clear to all involved that these conditions were counterproductive in the sense that they made voluntary recruitment virtually impossible and reduced the productivity of workers when they were in Germany. However, the creation of a racially pure society was a project in which Hitler's regime had invested too much for it to be simply abandoned. It is possible, with this in mind, to attribute the early disasters of the Ostarbeiter programme in 1942 to the slow unravelling of this contradiction between ideology and pragmatic necessity.[47] Sauckel, for one, seems to have had every intention of ensuring that 'his' workers, once they were in Germany, were treated well enough for them to make a productive contribution to the war effort.[48] Furthermore, the foreign labour programme was to serve an ideological purpose in spreading the word throughout Europe of the benefits brought to ordinary working people by the National Socialist revolution. Old habits, however, died hard. The administrators of the foreign labour camps were often negligent and arbitrary in their distribution of food. The rations allocated by the Reich Food Ministry were rarely distributed at the correct levels. There are several well-documented cases of corruption in which food intended for Sauckel's workers found its way onto the black market. Routine, grass-roots racism amongst the German population expressed itself in persistent rumours of favouritism being shown to civilian foreigners. The Italians, whose rations included a larger proportion of fruit and vegetables, in keeping with their accustomed diet, were singled out for particular criticism. The tenets of racial dogmatism, both from above and below, made it difficult to fashion a rational foreign labour programme. Nevertheless, it is clear that by the autumn of 1942 German industry was beginning to search systematically for answers to its new problems of labour management. How were the various grades of foreign workers to be treated? What sanctions were permitted to enforce performance? How far were foremen and managers permitted to go in seeking to extract the maximum performance from their foreign workers?

The question of corporal punishment particularly exercised German management. Was it permissible for firms to authorize the beating of recalcitrant workers? Sauckel as GBA insisted that corporal punishment was tantamount to common assault and should be treated as such in the courts.[49] Foreign workers should be subject to the strictest discipline, but responsibility was to lie with the police, courts and SS, who could make use of labour re-education camps and concentration camps as powerful deterrents.[50] Such procedures, however, were long-winded and often meant that the employer 'lost' the worker concerned.[51] In many cases it clearly seemed more efficient to settle the matter there and then in the workplace. After all, casual physical violence was by no means unknown in German industry and this was particularly the case in coal mining, where questions concerning the proper employment of Ostarbeiter were at their most acute. As we have seen, the shortage of coal and coal miners was a central preoccupation of the German war effort from the spring of 1941 onwards. Providing miners for Paul Pleiger's hard-pressed pits was amongst Sauckel's top priorities.[52] But unless these workers could be fed and disciplined they would be useless to the German war effort. As a result, Pleiger supported Sauckel in pleading for increased food allocations. Without extra calories, protein and fat, Pleiger simply could not get the coal so desperately needed by German heavy industry.[53] At the same time, however, Pleiger also advocated the systematic use of coercive force. In early October 1942 Pleiger, together with Robert Ley of the DAF, chaired a working meeting of mine managers from the Ruhr in the luxurious surroundings of the Kaiserhof hotel in Essen. As head of the DAF, Ley was jointly responsible with Sauckel for overseeing the foreign workforce. The key item on the agenda of the Kaiserhof session was the question of 'how to treat the

Russians'.[54] A remarkable verbatim report of the meeting kept by a Krupp manager gives a startling insight, not only into the brutal practices of the foreign labour programme. It also reveals the terrifying fears that crowded in upon the leaders of German industry, whenever they paused to contemplate the wider situation of the Third Reich. Robert Ley, as usual, was drunk. And when Ley was drunk he was prone to speaking his mind: 'The coal must be got, whatever happens. If not with you, gentlemen, then against you.' If the Ruhr failed, so would the entire armaments effort and in the autumn of Stalingrad that would spell disaster. 'After us there is nothing, everything will be over . . . Germany will be destroyed. Everybody will be slaughtered, murdered, burned and destroyed. We have, after all, burned all bridges behind us, deliberately, we have. We have practically solved the Jewish question in Germany. That alone is something so awesome.' With so much at stake there was no room for compassion or civility. No degree of coercion was too much and Ley expected the mine managers to back up their foremen in meting out the necessary discipline. As Ley put it: 'When a Russian pig has to be beaten', it would be the ordinary German worker who would have to do it. 'You won't be doing it and I won't.' To make sure the mine managers got the message, Pleiger added with characteristic cynicism: 'Below ground it is dark and Berlin is a long way away.' Clearly, Ley and Pleiger expected Germany's coal miners to ignore Sauckel's sanctimonious injunctions. If Ostarbeiter did not work, they were to be beaten. But if employers did prefer a more formal mode of discipline, Heinrich Himmler's police could always be counted upon. Pleiger referred enthusiastically to the results achieved by the 'small but perfectly formed concentration camp' that he used to discipline his workforce at the Reichswerke.[55]

At precisely the same time as the Kaiserhof meeting, the mining industry in Upper Silesia began experimenting with a new system, which turned food itself into the main means of discipline. Bonuses of various kinds were widely used by German employers. But Guenther Falkenhahn, the Generaldirektor of the Plessschen Werke, a mine that supplied IG Farben's Silesian chemicals complex, took bonuses to a new, existential level. Under a system he dubbed *Leistungsernaehrung*, or 'performance feeding', he divided his Ostarbeiter into three classes. Only those achieving an adequate, average performance would receive the normal ration. Those underperforming would have deductions made from their rations. These deductions would then serve as bonuses for the above-average performers.[56] The system was designed to manage scarcity. It implied no overall increase in the food ration. It simply rewarded the strong at the expense of the weak. The key idea was to concentrate the available food on those workers who were providing the best return per unit of calories. For the Ostarbeiter it implied a form of triage. Those falling below the norm were threatened by a fatal spiral of malnutrition and underperformance. Falkenhahn doubled as the chairman of the Reich coal organization in Upper Silesia and with his encouragement the system of performance feeding was soon adopted as best practice throughout the region. By 1943 it was getting national recognition. In his end-of-year message Albert Speer personally recommended the system.[57] By the end of 1944 'performance feeding' had been promulgated by order of the Armaments Ministry as standard practice in the employment of Ostarbeiter.[58]

The most extraordinary version of this emerging compromise between ideology and pragmatism, was the practice of 'destruction through labour' (*Vernichtung durch Arbeit*). The concentration camps of the SS, as opposed to the extermination facilities set up in 1942, had inmate populations, some of whom had been employed on the industrial projects of the SS since the late 1930s.[59] In 1942, given the manpower crisis facing the Reich, Himmler enthusiastically advocated expanding the use of concentration camp labour. At the time, however, the overall inmate population was too small for their exploitation to make a significant contribution to the war effort. From 1942 onwards the SS therefore engaged in a conscious policy of expanding the concentration camp population and legitimizing these institutions in terms of the services they provided to the war effort. The agency responsible was the SS office for economic administration under Oswald Pohl, which had oversight over those concentration camps not exclusively concerned with the Final Solution, most notably Dachau, Mauthausen, Sachsenhausen, Buchenwald, Majdanek, Stutthof and Auschwitz.[60] Under Pohl's direction the concentration camp population rocketed. A significant fraction of the new inmates were Jewish, men and women who had been singled out, for one reason or another, for a fate other than immediate execution. But the majority of the concentration camp inmates were political prisoners from Germany, Soviet prisoners who had escaped or otherwise come to the attention of the Gestapo, or Ostarbeiter who were being disciplined by the SS. Some unfortunates were simply recruited as foreign workers and handed over to the SS to bolster their workforce.

The first camp to farm out its inmates on a large scale was Auschwitz, which, apart from the IG building site at Monowitz, also provided labour to heavy industrial projects throughout Silesia. It was followed by Oranienburg, which contracted to supply Heinkel with 800 inmates in September 1942, and Ravensbrueck, which provided female workers to Siemens. Before long Mauthausen had struck up a relationship with Steyr Daimler Puch. Sachsenhausen serviced the Daimler-Benz plant at Genshagen. Dachau was in business with BMW. Other notable partners of the SS included the Reichswerke Hermann Goering, the VW plant in Fallersleben, the Akkumulatorenfabrik AG in Hanover and Henschel's Rax subsidiary in Vienna.[61] Up to the end of 1943, the aircraft industry was certainly the chief industrial employer of inmate labour, with Heinkel, Messerschmitt and BMW leading the way.[62] But in the later stages of the war it is hard to think of any major new armaments facility that was not constructed on the presumption that concentration camp labour would be used. On 23 February 1944 Albert Speer wrote personally to his 'dear party comrade Himmler' to request that every effort should be made to provide inmate labour to the armaments factories.[63] And Himmler did not hold back. By the end of 1944, it is estimated, Himmler's camps provided the German war effort with at least 500,000 workers, or roughly 5 per cent of the industrial workforce; 140,000 were employed in constructing giant underground factories under SS control, 130,000 worked for the Organisation Todt, which was responsible for construction in the occupied territories, and 230,000 were hired out to private industry.[64]

In all of the concentration camps, productive labour was coupled with a regime of ill-treatment, overwork and starvation that resulted in mass death. This took place under the eyes of German managers and workers, not to mention the civilian population at large, who often lived as neighbours of the branch camps such as BMW's Allach. Viewed in the large, working inmates to death was of course only marginally less irrational than murdering them outright. Here, however, it is crucial to distinguish between logics operating at the macro and the micro level and to consider the time-factor. Whereas the incarceration of more and more potential workers in murderous concentration camps was clearly irrational from the point of view of the overall war effort, from the point of view of the individual employer the concentration camps were often a godsend. Even in 1944, Himmler was still able to provide new workers. Though these people were quickly worn out, the advantage of the SS was precisely that they were able to offer their industrial clients an apparently limitless flow of new inmates. Here too, Selektion was the crucial term.[65] So long as the SS supervisors carried out regular inspections, weeded out those workers whose productivity had fallen below acceptable levels and replaced them with fresh inmates, the employer had little to complain about. This process of continuous selection and replacement was the essence of the concentration camp labour system. A concentration camp labour force was not a stock but a flow. The SS did not undertake to supply firms with particular individuals, but with a particular unit of labour power. It was the SS, not the employer, who were responsible for maintaining the flow. In some cases, however, it clearly did seem rational for employers to make at least some effort to stabilize their inmate labour force. At Auschwitz, IG Farben negotiated with the SS to provide food supplements as premiums.[66] On the other hand, when punishment was necessary, IG's site management made clear that they preferred beatings to take place behind the barbed wire of the concentration camp.[67] They did not question the SS's right to treat their inmates in any way they wished, but they found that 'the exceedingly unpleasant scenes that occur on the construction site' because of the floggings were 'beginning to have a demoralizing effect on the free workers [Poles], as well as on the Germans'. Within the camps themselves there was a parallel process of adjustment to the new priority of wartime labour. The essence of camp life, as it had developed since 1933, was to mete out a regime of punitive treatment and malnutrition calculated to break the will of the inmates and, in the majority of cases, to result in a slow and agonizing death. By 1942, mortality in the camps was so staggeringly high that the SS economic administration found itself unable to meet the targets for the slave population set by Himmler. If the concentration camps really were to serve as an important reservoir of labour the rate of attrition would clearly have to be lowered. To do so the economic administration of the SS took practical steps.[68] The medical establishment of the camps was instructed to take seriously its responsibility for maintaining inmate productivity. Most importantly, from the winter of 1942–3 onwards the economic administration of the SS ordered that food rations for the inmates should be increased.

Following the IG example, brutal punishment was increasingly combined with bonuses of food or cigarettes calculated to stimulate productivity. As a result, in 1943 mortality declined significantly throughout the system.

Who exactly benefited most from the employment of concentration camp labour, the most barbarous aspect of Germany's foreign labour programme, is a matter of some contention.[69] It is clear that in industrial manufacturing the balance between the costs of inmate labour, as specified by the 'fees' paid to the SS, and the productivity of average inmate workers was very favourable to the employer. In construction, where the majority of inmate labour was consumed, the balance was less good. Here everything depended on the rate at which the workforce was replenished with new inmates. Perversely, in low-skilled occupations, employers actually had an incentive to accelerate the rate of Selektion. Whether or not these arrangements were more or less favourable than employing German workers depended on the precise balance between the relative productivity of the inmates, the fees paid to the SS, the additional overheads involved in employing inmate labour and the price for the job granted by the official procurement agency. This last variable is the true unknown in the economics of forced labour, both for concentration camp inmates and other categories of workers.[70] For the vast majority of firms who were allocated foreign labour and, in particular, concentration camp labour, the Reich was not only the supplier of labour. It was also the ultimate customer. Public procurement officials had no interest in leaving their contractors with 'unnecessary' profits that had been earned by employing cheap labour supplied at the expense of the Reich. But the complex set of connections between labour costs, productivity and prices is fully documented in only a handful of cases, one of which was the Loibl tunnel, which connects Carinthia in Austria with Slovenia.[71] Detailed cost accounts compiled by Universale Hoch und Tiefbau AG, a prime contractor that employed a multi-national workforce of 800 inmates from the Mauthausen concentration camp, show that their productivity was on average 40 per cent lower than that of German labour. Nevertheless, even allowing for the full cost of remunerating the SS, providing extra security personnel, replacing those workers who were too weak to work and providing bonuses, the concentration camp inmates were still more profitable to employ than non-inmate labour. The contractor, however, was not permitted to retain all

Table 16. The economics of slave labour

	SS rental fee for appropriately skilled inmate labour, RM	Normal German pay rates, RM	Productivity at which concentration camp labour is cost neutral, as % of German productivity norm assuming unadjusted contract prices	Actual productivity of concentration camp labour, as % of German productivity norm	Concentration camp labour more or less profitable than normal German labour assuming unadjusted contract prices?
Metalworking Industry:					
Skilled	0.545	1.21	45	40–60	Y
Semi-skilled	0.364	1.011	36	40–60	Y
Labourer	0.364	0.795	46	30–50	?
Female worker	0.364	0.582	63	60+	Y
Electrical engineering:					
Female worker	0.364	0.629	58	60+	Y
Construction:					
Carpenter, concrete specialist	0.545	0.969	56	28–38	N
Bricklayer	0.545	0.929	59	28–38	N
Road worker	0.364	0.684	53	28–38	N

Source: M. Spoerer, 'Profitierten Unternehmen von KZ-Arbeit?', HZ 268 (1999)

of this surplus profit. To allow for the services provided by the SS prisoners, the Reich claimed an automatic reduction in the contract price, finely calculated at 3.515 per cent.

Clearly, ways were found to reconcile the murderous ideological impulses of the regime with a rational system of exploitation that was functional from the point of view of the individual employer, if not for the war economy as a whole. This 'learning process' began in 1940, intensified following the shock of the winter crisis of 1941–2 and finished amongst the ruins of the German home front in the autumn and winter of 1944. The most severe contradictions arose because the invasion of the Soviet Union in June 1941 had unleashed Nazi ideology as a rampant force, only for the military crisis at Moscow to force an abrupt and completely unanticipated shift in priorities. Over the follow-ing three years the resulting contradictions were progressively resolved in favour of the priority of the war effort. The Holocaust began in June 1941, accelerated into 1942 and reached its completion, except for the Hungarian Jewry, by the end of 1943. In 1942 the simultaneous intensification of foreign labour recruitment and the unresolved tension between ideology and pragmatism resulted in chaos and murderous confusion in the prisoner of war and Ostarbeiter camps. But by 1943 the most counterproductive mistreatment of the Ostarbeiter had run its course. Those that survived were put to work with increasing effective-ness. Mortality, especially amongst Soviet prisoners, continued to be high. However, for civilian Ostarbeiter the statistics suggest that by the autumn of 1943 the situation was broadly speaking 'under control'. In July and August 1943, two months for which we have precise statistics, there were 'only' 2,300 deaths out of a total population of 1.6 million civilian Ostarbeiter in Germany.[72] This was twice the rate of mortality in the German population and a third higher than would have been expected amongst a similar group in the Soviet Union in the 1930s. But this category of foreign workers was certainly no longer suffering 'mass attrition'. Sauckel, as GBA, the employers and the SS had arrived at a compromise, which satisfied the essential demands of all sides.

Ultimately, it is productivity that must serve as the yardstick of the forced labour programme. In this regard the evidence clearly supports the story of adjustment and compromise just described. The unsatisfac-tory conditions prevailing in the first chaotic phase of the Ostarbeiter programme were well illustrated by the situation at Krupp's home plant, the Gusstahlfabrik at Essen, in the autumn of 1942.[73] In the space of only a few months in the summer of that year, Krupp became a gigantic employer of foreign labour. The Gusstahlfabrik's foreign contingent, which in January 1942 had stood at only 2,861, increased in a single year by more than nine times. By the end of the year, almost 25,000 foreign workers were employed in the Essen steelworks. Not surprisingly, management had difficulty in coping with this extraordinary transformation in their workforce and the immediate impact on productivity was severe. A snapshot in November 1942 suggested that Krupp's largest group of foreign workers, French civilians, underperformed their German counterparts by between 15 and 30 per cent. French prisoners of war and Eastern European women performed similarly.[74] However, male workers from Eastern Europe averaged only 57 per cent of their German counterparts and for Soviet prisoners the figure was even worse, at 42 per cent. When one considered the special taxes levied on employers of foreign labour, the pay owed to the workers and the cost of housing and feeding them, it was clear that foreign workers were considerably more expensive to employ than Krupp's German workers. This is a relative statement. It does not mean that employing foreign workers was unprofitable. However, it does suggest that Krupp would have had good reason to prefer employing Germans, if it had had the opportunity to do so. Krupp (and this is certainly true for most other German businesses) employed foreign workers because there was no alternative. It did so, not because they were particularly profitable, but because they were the only labour available and because employing them was a precondition for continuing production. After 1942 employing foreign labour was simply the entry ticket to the war economy.

All subsequent investigations of the performance of Germany's foreign workers suggested a considerable improvement in productivity relative to 1942.[75] Eight months after the Krupp study, French workers were generally credited with 80–90 per cent of German norms. Eastern women came close to matching their German counterparts. All studies of male Ostarbeiter performance also showed increases in productivity. The performance range was wide, 60–80 in one study, 80–100 in another, but in no case did it fall below 60 per cent of the German level. Only the performance of concentration camp inmates, and Russian prisoners of war employed in construction, remained at 50 per cent of the German level or less. There is little reason to doubt, therefore, that as the foreign labour population expanded in size, their average level of productivity improved, certainly when compared to the disastrous levels of 1942. German managers were finding ways to make the foreign labour system pay.

III

Given the strength of evidence accumulated in support of the 'compromise' interpretation, there can be little doubt that it captures essential features of Nazi policy. Obviously, ideology was decisive in the last instance, especially in relation to the Judaeocide. There could be no other reason for killing one group with such awful thoroughness. The assumption of a racial struggle was an unalterable given in the Nazi worldview. On the other hand, it is also clear that, as the war ground on, sustaining the war effort increasingly came to override every other preoccupation of Hitler's regime. The result was a certain segmentation of policy, in which the SS was permitted to pursue the ideological imperative of exterminating the Jewish population. At the same time the treatment of the foreign labour force, the concentration camp population and at least a small remnant of the Jewish population was progressively 'economized' to take account of the needs of the war economy. This is a powerful interpretative framework, as far as it goes. Its key weakness, however, is the fact that it considers only two contradictory imperatives: the ideological imperative for mass murder and the productive requirement for more labour. By reducing the 'economic imperative' to the question of labour, what is obscured is the no less important question of food. We are thus led to ignore what in 1941 had been an independent and powerful 'economic' imperative for mass murder.[76]

Let us remind ourselves: in the first weeks of 1941, the Reich Ministry of Food and the Wehrmacht military-economic staff had agreed on the Hunger Plan, a scheme which called for the deliberate starvation of no less than 30 million inhabitants of the Soviet Union. This explicit commitment to mass murder was made official policy, months before the SS began to formulate a concrete and specific plan for the extermination of the Jewish population of Europe. Food cut across the contradiction between economics and ideology, between the need for labour and the imperative for genocide. It provided the Third Reich with a starkly economic incentive for murder on a scale larger even than the Holocaust. Furthermore, the problem of food supply was at the heart of the entire crisis of the foreign labour programme in 1942. It was for want of food that the Soviet prisoners of war, the concentration camp inmates and the other Ostarbeiter died in such dreadful numbers even after they were supposed to be deployed for the purposes of the war effort. It was the improvement in the food supply to these workers after the autumn of 1942 that was largely responsible for the stabilization of their situation and the improvement in productivity.[77] It is for more reasons, therefore, than narrative consistency that we must return to the Hunger Plan, which bulked so large in previous chapters. When we place it alongside the ideological impulse for mass murder and the pragmatic needs of the war economy, many of the contradictions that appear to characterize Nazi policy, above all in 1942, resolve themselves into a ghastly pattern of coherence.

The military crisis of the winter of 1941–2 frustrated Herbert Backe's immediate aim of bringing about a massive rearrangement of the food balance in the Eastern territories. But at the same time it confirmed his deepest anxiety. Backe had not been bluffing in 1941. In light of the extension of the war into the indefinite future, Germany was facing a severe food problem.[78] The German grain harvest in both 1940 and 1941 had been well below average and imports from the occupied territories had not made up the difference.[79] For lack of feed the swine herd had been reduced by 25 per cent since the start of the war, triggering a cut in meat rations as of June 1941.[80] Bread rations had only been sustained by making severe inroads into grain stocks. By the end of 1941, these were nearing exhaustion. When the order to ship large numbers of Eastern workers to Germany for work was first given by Goering in November 1941, Backe protested vigorously.[81] The 400,000 Soviet prisoners of war already in Germany were more than he could provide for. Goering had spoken casually of feeding the Eastern workers on cats and horse-meat.[82] Backe had consulted the statistics and reported glumly that there were not enough cats to provide a ration for the Eastern workers and horse-meat was already being used to supplement the rations of the German population.[83] If the Russians were to be given meat, they would have to be supplied at the expense of the German population. The official ration that was settled on for Soviet prisoners and Ostarbeiter in December 1941 was clearly inadequate for men intended for hard labour. It consisted of a weekly allocation of 16.5 kilos of turnips, 2.6 kilos of 'bread' (made up of 65 per cent red rye, 25 per cent sugar beet waste and 10 per cent straw or leaves), 3 kilos of potatoes, 250 grams of horse- or other scrap meat, 130 grams of fat and 150 grams of Naehrmittel (yeast), 70 grams of sugar and two and a third litres of skimmed milk. The appalling quality of the bread caused serious damage to the digestive tract and resulted in chronic malnutrition. The vegetables had to be cooked for hours before they were palatable, robbing them of most of their nutritional content. Though this was a diet that was, relatively speaking, high in carbohydrates, providing a nominal daily total of 2,500 calories, it was grossly deficient in the fat and protein necessary to sustain hard physical labour. It was certainly not enough to restore half-starved Soviet prisoners to good health. To make matters worse, in the vast majority of camps nothing like this official ration was ever delivered to the inmates.

The Wehrmacht, which had been Backe's co-author of the Hunger Plan, drew radical conclusions. Only days after Sauckel's appointment, at a time when the GBA was still drawing up his plans for mass recruitment, the Wehrmacht's military-economic office spelled out to him the basic equation between calories and labour power:

The concepts of normal labour, heavy labour and extra heavy labour have to be regarded in objective terms, independent of racial consideration, as a through-put of calories and muscular effort. It is illusory to believe that one can achieve the same performance from 200 inadequately fed people as with 100 properly fed workers. On the contrary: the 100 well-fed workers produce far more and their employment is far more rational. By contrast, the minimum rations distributed simply to keep people alive, since they are not matched by any equivalent performance, must be regarded from the point of view of the national war economy as a pure loss, which is further increased by the transport costs and administration [involved in recruiting them].[84]

Here it was not the 'anti-economic' logic of anti-Semitism but the ruthlessly materialistic logic of the Hunger Plan that was counterposed to Sauckel's programme of forced recruitment. The Hunger Plan had arrived at the conclusion that millions of people needed to be killed, starting not from the principles of the racial struggle, but from the food balance. The Wehrmacht now spelled out the same logic in relation to the workforce. The problem was that of achieving the most efficient balance between calories and muscular effort. If they could not be properly fed, the millions of foreign workers who were being imported would add little to Germany's effective labour power. Indeed, in maintaining large numbers of foreign workers in a vegetative state, Germany was burdening itself with a whole new population of 'useless eaters' ('*unnuetze Esser*'). It would be far better to return to the radical logic of the Hunger Plan. If there was not enough food to maintain everyone at an optimal level of efficiency, it would be far better to concentrate those rations that were available on a smaller group of productive workers. What the 'national war economy' certainly could not afford was to allocate food to foreign workers simply to keep them alive.

Backe, for his part, was clearly not oblivious to these arguments. In its comments, the OKW was merely extending the logic of the Hunger Plan, which Backe himself had devised. But Backe was in an impossible position. The Fuehrer had demanded more workers. Gauleiter Sauckel was dedicated to delivering them. Hitler and Sauckel now demanded that the workers be fed, which was clearly a necessity if they were to be productive. And yet, given the level of grain stocks, Backe was unable to meet this demand. What was called for was a reduction in consumption, not additional provisions for millions of new workers. The seriousness of the situation became apparent to the wider public in the spring of 1942 when the Food Ministry announced cuts to the food rations of the German population. Given the regime's mortal fear of damaging morale, the ration cuts of April 1942 are incontrovertible evidence that the food crisis was real. Lowering the rations was a political step of the first order, which Backe would never have suggested if the situation had not absolutely required it.[85] The Wehrmacht had prepared the way in 1942, by decreeing a ration cut for the fighting troops. When the reduction in the civilian ration was announced it produced a response which justified every anxiety on the part of the Nazi leadership. On 23 March 1942 the SD reported that news of the impending cut was causing extreme disquiet amongst German civilians. It was, reported the SD's informants, 'devastating' like 'virtually no other event during the war'.[86] Studies by nutritional experts added to the leadership's concerns. The reduced ration prevailing since the start of the war had had a serious impact on the population's reserves of body fat. The tendency of factory workers doing heavy manual labour to gain weight in middle age had been completely negated. This was cause for alarm, because the fat reserves in the bodies of the labour force had acted as a buffer in the first years of the war. It was now to be expected that any further reduction in the ration would result in a precipitate decline in performance, particularly in industries such as mining.[87]

Against this backdrop, there was no hope of pushing through any improvement in the rations for Sauckel's newly arrived Ostarbeiter. It was true, of course, that the most disadvantaged Ostarbeiter and Soviet prisoners numbered altogether just over a million in the spring of 1942 and that a substantial improvement in their rations would have required only a very modest further cut in the food supplied to the German population. But given the mood both in the Food Ministry and in the population at large, any such redistribution was out of the question. The public demanded that if the German ration was to be reduced, the foreign workers should fare even worse. Backe responded to these conflicting demands as best he could. On the one hand he introduced a new higher ration category for Ostarbeiter doing heavy work.[88] At the same time he cut the ration for the lowest category of 'normal' Ostarbeiter to well below the standard German level. In addition, Ostarbeiter were excluded altogether from access to the most sought after items such as eggs. In any case, none of the rations set in April 1942 were sufficient to secure the labour power of the Eastern workers. Whilst Sauckel's office vainly issued memorandums calling for adequate treatment of the Ostarbeiter, hundreds of thousands of underfed and underclothed workers arrived from the Eastern territories, to find themselves penned in barbed wire encampments and facing a diet of slow starvation. One armaments firm reported in the spring of 1942 that it had almost daily cases of 'Ukrainians who are willing to work, collapsing unconscious at their machines'.[89] It is characteristic of the state of mind in Germany at the time that the firm felt it necessary to point out that its complaint had nothing to do with sentimental humanitarianism. They requested more food for their workers, 'only for the purpose of getting the greatest possible performance out of Ukrainian workers who are undoubtedly diligent and usable'. In the summer of 1942 the Daimler-Benz plant at Untertuerkheim reported in a similar spirit to its regional food office. Its consignment of Russians was refusing to work for lack of food. The ringleaders of the mutiny had been dispatched to a concentration camp. But to complement these sanctions they needed an increase in rations, to maintain both morale and the physical strength of the workforce. The management asked specifically for larger quantities of carbohydrates, even if this came at the expense of a further reduction in quality.[90] By the end of the summer Sauckel himself was deeply frustrated. He had risen to the challenge of recruiting hundreds of thousands of workers for Germany, but their productive potential was being wasted by the utterly inadequate diet allocated to them by the Reich Food Ministry. At a meeting with DAF officials in early September, Sauckel stamped his foot. The Fuehrer himself had made clear that it was completely unacceptable for anybody to be starving on the territory of Germany, when the Wehrmacht had full control of the Ukraine. If the rations of both Germans and Ostarbeiter were not immediately increased there would be 'a scandal of the greatest proportions'. And Sauckel would stop at nothing: 'He would find ways and means to make use of the Ukrainian grain and cattle, even if he had to set up all the Jews of Europe as a human conveyor belt to move packing cases out of the Ukraine.'[91]

The threat of the concentration camp, physical intimidation and 'performance feeding' all offered micro-solutions to the crisis of the foreign labour programme in 1942. But, if Sauckel's recruits were to be used efficiently, there clearly needed to be an improvement in the overall situation of the food supply. If the ration cuts of spring 1942 were sustained, or even repeated in the autumn as some feared, there would be a chronic and irreversible decline in the productivity of both German and foreign workers and an increasingly serious problem of public order. Everything depended on reversing the decline in Germany's food stocks and the political leadership of the Nazi regime was fully aware of this imperative. The food crisis of 1942 precipitated a restructuring at the top of the Third Reich, which is crucial to understanding the history of the Nazi war economy. As we have already noted, it is a commonplace to contrast the appointment of the 'technocratic' Albert Speer with the choice of Gauleiter Sauckel as GBA. What this false contrast obscures is the no less significant shift in the Ministry of Food and Agriculture.[92] Following the disastrous ration cut of April 1942, Hitler took the highly unusual step of retiring Walther Darré, one of his longest-serving Ministers, and promoting Herbert Backe from State Secretary to the position of acting Minister. Since 1936, Backe had served as the representative of agriculture in the Four Year Plan. He was therefore well connected with Goering and his staff. As a senior member of the SS and a close friend of Reinhard Heydrich, he also had excellent connections to Himmler. The evidence suggests that from April 1942 onwards Backe spearheaded a coalition of some of the most radical elements in the Nazi regime, dedicated to securing the German food supply at any price. In this coalition, Herbert Backe and Heinrich Himmler provided the executive energy, but they enjoyed the full backing of both Goering and Hitler himself.

The essence of Backe's strategy was a return to the principles of the Hunger Plan. Unlike in 1941, however, the Hunger Plan was now to be directly coupled to the programme of racial genocide and above all to its centrepiece, the murder of the Jews of Poland. By the end of May 1942 Backe had met both with Hitler and General Governor Frank and had agreed that food was to be redistributed on a massive scale. As of 1942, all food deliveries from the Reich to the Wehrmacht in the field were to cease. Germany's armies were to feed themselves from the territories they occupied, without regard to the consequences for the local population.[93] Entire groups were to be excluded from the food supply, most notably the Jews. As Goebbels noted in his diary, the new regime would be based on the principle that before Germany starved 'it would be the turn of a number of other peoples'. This slogan, which was commonly attributed to Hitler, was to be repeated almost verbatim throughout 1942. The main sources of additional food deliveries follow-ing the harvest of 1942 were to be the Ukraine and France. However, it was in the General Government that the interlinking of food policy and genocide was most clear-cut.

As we have seen, after the occupation of autumn 1939 the most fertile regions of Poland had been annexed to Germany, leaving the General Government as an agricultural deficit territory. In the first year of the German occupation, Backe and Governor General Frank had agreed on food imports from the Reich that were sufficient to give food to those Poles working for the Germans. The majority of the Polish population were left to fend for themselves. The result was an epidemic of malnutri-tion and outright starvation, particularly amongst the Jewish population confined in the ghettos. Faced with Germany's food shortage in 1942, Backe went much further. He now demanded that the Governor General should reverse the flow. Rather than receive food supplements from Germany, the General Government was to make sizeable food deliveries.

In the critical weeks between May and August 1942, in which the murder of the Jews of Poland accelerated to its most awful intensity, Backe and Himmler combined to exercise massive pressure on the administrators of the General Government to reduce the food consumption of their territory. And in these negotiations, Backe predicated his demands specifically on the elimination of the Polish Jews from the food chain. On 23 June 1942, two months before the harvest, Backe confronted the administrators of the General Government for the first time with the Reich's new demands. When the local officials protested that the existing Polish rations were too low and that it would be impossible to raise the necessary supplies, Backe replied: 'In the General Government there are currently still 3.5 million Jews. Poland is to be sanitized within the coming year.'[94] Eliminating the Jews would not only reduce the number of people that needed feeding; it would also remove a large element of the black market, which was crucial to the survival of the ghettos. Only if they controlled every step in the marketing of grain would the Germans be able to secure the vastly increased share of the grain supply that Backe demanded. After his initial round of meetings in Poland, Backe confirmed the new plans with Hitler and Goering on 4 and 5 July 1942. A few days later Hitler and Himmler conferred – the meeting that left Himmler in a state of euphoria and precipitated his fateful summer tour of Silesia and the General Government. After visiting Auschwitz and designating it as the killing centre for the Jews of Western Europe, Himmler on 18–19 July issued not one, but three orders to Globocnik and Krueger in Lublin. All Jews in Poland not needed for work were to be killed by the end of the year. The settlement programme in the General Government was to begin with the clearance of the Lublin–Zamość region. Finally, Himmler conveyed a draconian set of instructions concerning the harvest, which was now only weeks away. In the General Government, the hunt for grain was to be pursued with complete ruthlessness. For the entire month of August, the city of Warsaw was to be sealed off from its agricultural hinterland. Peasants who failed to meet their delivery quotas were to be summarily shot.[95] Copies of this latter order, which was treated as highly sensitive by the General Government administration, went to Backe, Goering and Gauleiter Sauckel. Himmler and Backe were sending a signal to their colleagues in Berlin that there was now to be a serious effort to resolve the conjoined problems of food and labour.

This was confirmed explicitly in late July 1942, first at the eleventh session of the Zentrale Planung on 22 July, at which Backe and Sauckel's problems were addressed under a single agenda item, and then in separate meetings involving first Speer and Backe and then Backe, Goering and Sauckel, from which Sauckel emerged with a promise that the rations of both German and foreign workers would soon be increased.[96] Backe and Goering had now raised their demands on the General Government from 100,000–150,000 tons, the amount discussed in June, to the extraordinary figure of 500,000 tons. The political appeal of this new agenda was so irresistible that Goering heaved himself back into action. On 5 August 1942, in the presence of Speer, he chaired a stressful meeting with the Gauleiter at which they gave vent to the festering resentment in the German population.[97] The next day, Goering announced the full scope of Backe's new food programme to representatives from all over the occupied territories. There was going to be, Goering announced, a fundamental rearrangement of the food supply in Europe: the Third Reich controlled

regions ... such as we never had during the last world war, and yet I have to give a bread ration to the German people which can no longer be justified. I have had foreign workers brought to Germany from all regions, and these foreign workers, regardless of where they come from, declared that they had better food at home than here in Germany ... The Fuehrer repeatedly said, and I repeat after him: if any one has to go hungry, it shall not be the Germans, but other peoples ... In every one of the occupied territories, I see the people fed to bursting and among our own people there is starvation.

It was time to return to the spirit of the Hunger Plan, of which Goering had been an enthusiastic advocate. In the first difficult winter in the Soviet Union, concessions had had to be made to public order. Now, with the summer offensive going well, Goering wanted a reassertion of the basic priorities. 'God knows, you are not sent out there [to the occupied territories] to work for the welfare of the people in your charge, but to get the utmost out of them, so that the German people can live.' Goering then passed on the delivery quotas he had discussed the previous day with Backe.

I have here before me reports on what you are expected to deliver ... it makes no difference to me in this connection if you say that your people will starve. Let them do so, as long as no German collapses from hunger. If you had been present when the Gauleiter spoke here, you would understand my boundless anger over the fact that we conquered such enormous territories through the valour of our troops, and yet our people have almost been forced down to the miserable rations of the First World War . . . I am interested only in those people in the occupied regions who work in armaments and food production. They must receive just enough to enable them to continue working.[98]

Feeding them any more would simply encourage resistance. In the manuscript minutes of Goering's meeting of 6 August there is one crucial page missing, a page on which Goering clearly referred to the fate of the Jews, connecting it directly to the food supply issue. This page has disappeared. It is not preserved even in the original copy of the document unearthed in the Moscow Special Archive in the early 1990s. One may infer that it was excised even before it fell into Soviet hands. All that remains is the following tell-tale line delivered by the Reichskommissar for the Ostland, Hinrich Lohse, apparently in response to a question by Goering: 'I can respond to that as well. Only a small fraction of the Jews are still alive; many thousands are gone.'

The demands formulated by Backe and Goering to resolve the food crisis of 1942 were completely unprecedented and at first caused heated debate amongst the administrators in the occupied territories. According to Goering's secretary Paul Koerner, the German military commander in France thought Goering's quotas so outrageous that he refused to pass them on to the authorities in Paris.[99] However, certainly in relation to the General Government, Backe refused to back down. For occupied Poland, the implications were drastic. Given the expected harvest and the new level of German demands, Frank expected that at least 3 million Poles who lived in the cities but did not work directly for the Germans would have to be cut off from the bread ration as of 1 March 1943. The resulting mass starvation would obviously have serious implications for public order, but Frank responded by reiterating Hitler's slogan: 'These consequences must be accepted, because before the German population starves in any way, others must . . . pay.'[100] The first group to do so would be the Jews. Whereas the Polish ration was to be cut off in March 1943, the feeding of 1.2 million Jews was to cease immediately. As of the autumn of 1942, only 300,000 Jews classified as workers would receive any official food allocation. If some of the 1.2 million 'condemned to starve' did manage to obtain food through the black market, then the General Government administration 'hoped' that this would lead to an 'acceleration of anti-Jewish measures'. Frank and his colleagues need not have worried. In the autumn of 1942 Treblinka, Chelmno and Belzec were operating at full speed. By the end of 1942, 300,000 was the number of Polish Jews remaining alive.

By the end of August 1942 this extraordinary series of measures spread a palpable mood of relief throughout Berlin. Backe, Himmler and Goering had staved off a disastrous downward spiral in the food supply. With the harvest operation in full swing, Backe had concluding discussions with Hitler, Himmler and Goering on 24–6 August. On 6 September Himmler reported to Goering on the progress of the harvest in the General Government. Two days later Backe thanked Himmler for the assistance provided by the SS in securing grain both in the General Government and the Ukraine. In the second half of August, with Warsaw under a 'lock-down' and the population of the ghetto being shipped to Treblinka, Joseph Goebbels, in his capacity as Gauleiter of Berlin, made a personal visit to the General Government to secure an increased supply of vegetables for the population of the German capital. In his opening speech for the winter charity drive at the end of September 1942, Hitler made a particular point of stressing the importance of the Ukraine for Germany's food supply.[101] Goebbels for his part coined a new propaganda line. Germany, he declared, was 'digesting' the 'occupied territories'. A few days later, at the annual harvest festival, Goering triumphantly announced the imminent restoration of rations in Germany.[102] As of 19 October, the food rations for both Germans and foreigners working in Germany was substantially increased, an improvement 'paid for' by the excellent yield of the German harvest and by a huge increase in food supplies to the Third Reich from the occupied territories. Total European deliveries of grain doubled from 2 million tons per annum, to more than 5 million tons in the harvest year 1942–3. There was also a huge increase in the delivery of potatoes and fats. Comparing 1940–41 and 1942–3, the total deliveries of grain, meat and fat provided by France and the occupied territory of the Soviet Union increased from 3.5 million tons to 8.78 million tons (measured in grain equivalents).[103] In 1942–3 occupied Europe supplied Germany with more than a fifth of its grain, a quarter of its fats and almost 30 per cent of its meat.[104] Most of these provisions never crossed the German border. The food went directly to the Wehrmacht. Of those deliveries that did enter the Reich, the General Government supplied an astonishing 51 per cent of German rye imports, 66 per cent of oats and 52 per cent of German potato imports. This was directly at the expense of the local population. Thanks to a remarkably good harvest in the General Government, rations were not cut off completely as Frank had anticipated in August 1942. But they remained at pitiful levels until after the harvest of 1943. By that time, all but a tiny remnant of the Jewish population was dead.

The upshot of this train of argument is that the grand contradiction between economics and ideology with which we started this chapter needs to be revised in a number of ways. Not only was the contradiction between the labour requirements of the war economy and the genocidal impulses of the regime 'softened' by a process of compromise and functional specialization, but the overriding need to improve the food situation actually created a perverse functional connection between the extermination of the Jewish population of the General Government and the improvement in food rations that was necessary to sustain the labour force working in the mines and factories of the Reich. The underlying logic of the modified Hunger Plan was still blind to race, as the comment by the OKW in early 1942 made clear. It was simply a matter of calories and muscle power. It is also clear that if the harvest of the General Government had not been as good as it turned out to be in 1942, then millions of non-Jewish Poles would have been condemned to starve the following spring. However, in the summer of 1942 it was the concerted extermination of Polish Jewry that provided the most immediate and fail-safe means of freeing up food for delivery to Germany.

IV

In response to the crisis on the Eastern Front, the organization of the German war effort in the spring of 1942 underwent three crucial shifts. Two of these have been examined in this chapter: the emergence of the Backe–Himmler–Goering axis on the food question, and Gauleiter Sauckel's appointment in the spring of 1942 as GBA.[105] The third, the appointment of Hitler's personal favourite Albert Speer to replace Fritz Todt as Reich Armaments Minister, will be the subject of the next chapter. All three of these shifts happened between February and April 1942 and they amounted to a decisive consolidation of the grip held by the inner circle of the Nazi leadership over the German war effort. This, in turn, casts the aftermath of the Moscow crisis in a rather different light to that in which it is commonly portrayed. Not only was Albert Speer, the head of the new armaments drive, an eminently political actor in his own right, as will be argued in what follows, but the preconditions for his 'armaments miracle' were created by some of the most ruthless exponents of Nazi ideology: Gauleiter Sauckel as the impresario of the labour programme, and Herbert Backe and Heinrich Himmler as the fixers of the food crisis. This politicization of the Third Reich's war effort is not surprising when we bear in mind the devastating blows to Germany's military prospects in the first weeks of December 1941. But it is important to emphasize it, since it belies the juxtaposition between ideological commitment and practical effectiveness that continues to underpin much historical writing about the Third Reich. Stereotypes about incompetence, ideological obsession and bureaucratic infighting continue to haunt the literature to such a degree that it is at times hard to understand how the Third Reich was able to continue the war for as long as it did, unless, of course, one posits that the war economy, after the crisis at Moscow, was separated from the rest of the regime and placed under the leadership of 'unpolitical' businessmen and techno-crats. In fact, the opposite was true. Following the frustration of its Blitzkrieg strategy in the autumn of 1941, the leadership of the Third Reich proved capable of yet another act of innovative, strategic improvis-ation. From the spring of 1942 onwards, the new leaders of the German war economy combined an expansive effort at industrial mobilization with some of the most destructive components of Nazism's ideology, to fashion a radical new synthesis of total war. This was not a strategy that promised Nazi Germany any real chance of victory. In this sense, the turning point in December 1941 was final and decisive. But it did allow the regime to survive for a remarkable three and a half years, despite the overwhelming material superiority of its enemies. It allowed the SS to complete a large part of the mission that Heydrich had out-lined at Wannsee and it also ensured that the Third Reich, unlike the Wilhelmine Empire, Fascist Italy or Imperial Japan, went down fighting, taking with it millions of its enemies. The key to this awful resilience of the Third Reich lay precisely in the alliance formed in the aftermath of Moscow between some of the most brutal exponents of Nazi ideology and the key powerholders in the German economy. The essential arbiter of this concord between political clout and industrial muscle was Albert Speer.

17

Albert Speer: 'Miracle Man'

Albert Speer, Armaments Minister of the Third Reich from 1942 to 1945, saved his neck at Nuremberg with a carefully calculated mixture of confession, contrition and denial, capped in his final address to the court with a bizarre burst of cod philosophy concerning the dangers of technology in modern life.[1] After he was released from Spandau jail in 1966 this same cocktail was to make his memoirs and his prison journal into global best-sellers. Indeed, the public preoccupation with Speer continues to this day, making him the subject of biographies, television documentaries and stage plays.[2] There are two main strands to the mythology of Albert Speer. The first is the suggestion that Speer was 'unpolitical'. In one version of this myth Speer is presented as an artistic soul, an architect, who was pushed reluctantly to take on wider responsibilities. This was a self-image that Speer shared with Hitler.[3] A less romantic rendition casts Speer as an 'unpolitical technician', a man given the task of resurrecting the German war effort, who did his job without asking questions about the wider purpose of his work or the wider activities of the regime that he served. This version of the 'unpolitical Speer' was solidly founded on the second pillar of the Speer myth, the myth of the so-called 'armaments miracle'. This refers to the remarkable upsurge in the armaments output apparently presided over by Speer after February 1942, an upsurge that was widely credited with keeping Germany in the war (see Appendix, Table A6). On the assumption that Nazi ideology and technocratic efficiency were mutually exclusive, Speer's triumphant production record was enough in itself to put distance between him and other less appetizing defendants in the dock at Nuremberg. Speer was simply too intelligent, too good at his job, to be compared to primitive anti-Semites such as Julius Streicher, or self-seeking ogres like Hermann Goering.

Yet Speer's claim to have been an unpolitical actor was always self-evidently absurd. Speer (1905–81) applied to join the Nazi party in early 1931, in the first flush of Hitler's electoral success, but at a time when the party was still far from the mainstream of German political life. From the first May Day celebration of 1933 onwards, Speer was personally responsible for crafting the dramatic public image of the regime. The annual rallies at Nuremberg, the gigantic harvest festivals of the RNS and the 1936 Olympics were all his creations. Speer built his entire career on his contacts within the Nazi party and above all his close personal relationship with Hitler, a trump card that he played for all it was worth. Speer manoeuvred his way through the office politics of the Third Reich with skill and ruthlessness.[4] He was closely allied both with Fritz Todt and, through Erhard Milch, with Goering's Air Ministry. From the late 1930s onwards he also enjoyed a cooperative working relationship with Heinrich Himmler and the SS. After the outbreak of the war, Speer accumulated a wide portfolio of projects, including the entire construction programme of the Luftwaffe as well as a number of major building sites in the occupied Eastern territories. When Fritz Todt was killed in his mysterious accident, Speer was not perhaps his most obvious successor. But neither was he a rank outsider. He was clearly one of the few men that Hitler really trusted and Speer's enormous influence after 1942 depended above all on that fact.

For our purposes, however, the more fundamental point concerns the second element of the Speer myth: Speer's role in relation to the armaments economy. Rather than seeing the performance of the German war economy as a warrant for Speer's status as an unpolitical technician, the point to be stressed here is the eminently political function that Speer's 'armaments miracle' performed for Hitler's regime. Of all Albert Speer's contributions to Nazi propaganda, the 'armaments miracle' was by far the most important. From his first days in his new job, Speer displayed a clear consciousness of the symbolic importance of the armaments effort. He did not simply produce more weapons. He made them tell a story. The dramatic statistics of production were intended to demonstrate to the German people that the war could still be won, by the efforts of the German worker united with the heroism of the soldiers on the front line. The solipsistic rhetoric of production records served to silence the wider questions that had crowded in upon the German leadership during the winter crisis of 1941–2. As we have seen, at that point, all the men most closely associated with the organization of the German war effort had come to the conclusion that the war could no longer be won. General Fromm, General Thomas and Fritz Todt all agreed that the rational thing for the German leadership to do, in the light of the debacle at Moscow, was to search for a 'political' solution. And this was the truly vital sense in which Speer was 'unpolitical'. He shut down the train of reasoning that moved from a rational assessment of Germany's war capacity, via a comparison with the military potential of its enemies, to 'political' suggestions about the need for an end to the war. By elevating Germany's armaments production and by ensuring that this story was told as a miraculous story of rebirth, Speer enabled the Nazi regime to continue the war, not only in practical terms, by providing the Wehrmacht with more equipment, but also in political terms, by expounding a propaganda story of limitless possibility. The armaments miracle was one more instance of the Triumph of the Will. The genius of Nazi leadership combined with the iron determination of the German people would overcome any adversity.

Within months of taking office, Speer put a new and determinedly optimistic face on the armaments effort.[5] In discussion with Hitler he devised an orchestrated propaganda display stressing the new dynamism of the war economy and its intimate connection to the Wehrmacht, an image to be transmitted to the entire nation in a series of newsreels.[6] As Speer put it to journalists in June 1943, he was determined not to repeat the mistake made in 1917, when the Kaiser's regime had allowed the German public to slip into a defeatist mood by failing to keep them properly informed about the remarkable performance of German indus-try.[7] For the first time, in April 1942 the newsreels began to give extended attention to the home front, including a clip showing tank construction in a giant assembly hall, which attracted much public comment. The audience was impressed by the fact that 'the German tanks appeared more powerful and compact' than the Soviet models shown later in the film. 'The "magnificent mass-production" was reassuring and had raised hopes of decisive success in the forthcoming battles.'[8] A few weeks later the home front was surprised by a dramatic public ceremony in Berlin in honour of 'Germany's most productive armaments worker' – foreman Franz Hahne of the Alkett (Rheinmetall) tank plant in Berlin – who on 20 May 1942 was awarded the coveted Ritterkreuz zum Kriegsverdienst-kreuz (War merit cross).[9] The medal was pinned to Hahne's chest by the well-known war hero, Corporal Krohn.[10] Attending the celebrations were Goering, Speer, Erhard Milch of the Air Ministry, Keitel of the Wehrmacht, Generals Fromm and Leeb from the army and Secretary of State Backe. It was an impressive display of the new dispensation in the German war economy. Simultaneously with the Berlin ceremony, 1,000 Kriegsverdienstkreuze, second class, were awarded in factories throughout Germany. The newsreels then showed foreman Hahne parading past an honour guard of soldiers, sailors, airmen and Waffen-SS, whilst the voice-over intoned: 'The best soldiers with the best weapons will defeat the enemy.' Later the same week the population was treated to the first weekly newsreel devoted entirely to armaments production, a sequence of previously secret images from the armaments factories, which Goebbels thought to be 'overwhelmingly powerful', 'reassuring' to the home front and daunting for Germany's enemies.[11]

By the autumn of 1942 Speer had established a regular liaison committee with the Goebbels Ministry devoted specifically to 'armaments propaganda'.[12] Its slogan was simple: 'The best weapons bring victory.' Amongst the weapons to be given the full propaganda treatment was Germany's new machine gun the MG 42, which was credited by the armaments propagandists with the phenomenal rate of fire of 3,000 rounds per minute.[13] In 1943 Speer sought to maintain his public relations momentum, first with the bombastic rhetoric of the Adolf Hitler Panzer Programme, launched in the immediate aftermath of Stalingrad, then on 13 May with a 'general report' to Hitler on the triumphs of armaments production, an occasion which was capped by the award to Speer of the 'Dr Todt Ring'.[14] Then on 5 June 1943 Speer addressed a mass rally of 10,000 armaments workers at the Sportspalast in Berlin at which, for the first time, all the major industrialists and managers of the war effort were decorated for their services to the German nation.[15] Speer showered his audience with spectacular statistics, claiming a sixfold increase in ammunition production and a fourfold increase in artillery production since 1941. The production of anti-tank guns had quadrupled and the delivery of tanks in May 1943 was according to Speer 12.5 times greater than on average in 1941. But insiders noted that Speer gave no absolute figures.[16] He made no mention of the fact that his indices were calculated with reference to well-chosen periods in 1941 when production had been particularly low, and he ignored altogether the fact that Germany's production records were entirely eclipsed by the overwhelming mass of material being thrown against Germany by its enemies.

To insist on the ideological function of Speer's 'armaments miracle' is, of course, by no means to imply that it was 'mere' illusion. At least until the summer of 1944, the statistical rhetoric was not fraudulent. Armaments output did go up. Indeed, the peculiar importance of the Speer story to the propaganda machine lay precisely in the fact that this was one aspect of the news that the regime could still control. Whereas Goebbels was becoming painfully aware of the difficulty of managing bad military news, the German armaments effort at least until the spring of 1943 developed largely without interference by the Allies. This was one arena in which the well-practised techniques of stage management could still be counted upon. Records could be broken and spectacular new weapons presented promptly for the Fuehrer's birthday. Every tank, every aeroplane that came out of the factories reiterated the same solipsistic point: as long as Germany could keep on producing weapons of such excellence at an ever-increasing rate, its fate could surely not be sealed.

The increase in armaments output was real enough. But given the highly political function of the 'armaments miracle' the historical record of the Speer Ministry must be approached with a very wary eye. Too many historians have been far too uncritical in their acceptance of Speer's rhetoric of rationalization, efficiency and productivism.[17] A cold-eyed examination of the statistics suggests that the increases achieved after February 1942 were far less exceptional than is commonly believed. The sudden upsurge in German armaments production was far from miraculous. It was due to perfectly natural causes: reorganization and rationalization efforts begun long before Speer acceded to power; the ruthless mobilization of factors of production; the coming on stream of investments made earlier in the war; and a deliberate sacrifice of quality for an immediate increase in quantity. And this critique is more than mere nit-picking. It goes to the very heart of Speer's ideological vision of the war economy, as a limitless flow of output released by energetic leadership and technological genius. The basic point is simple. The Speer miracle was not unconstrained. The German war economy after 1942 was limited by the same fundamental trade-offs that had restricted it since the first years of the war. And by the summer of 1943, these constraints, combined with the first systematic attack against

German industry by Allied bombers, brought Speer's 'miracle' to a complete halt. This abrupt interruption of the armaments boom in the summer of 1943 and its crucial political implications have hitherto been underrated.[18] Not only did armaments output stagnate, but Speer's most basic assumption was revealed as an illusion. For all their efforts, Speer and his collaborators could do nothing to alter Germany's strategic predicament. In July 1943, the solipsistic bubble of Speer's armaments propaganda was pricked by a succession of military disasters so dramatic that the prospect of defeat could no longer be hidden from the German population. And it was at that moment of crisis that Speer showed his true colours. Unwavering in his loyalty to the Fuehrer, Albert Speer did not shrink from resorting to the most extreme means of coercion, if they were required for a further round of sacrificial mobilization.

I

In so far as there was a strategic rationale to the German armaments effort after December 1941 – beyond the struggle for mere survival – it was focused on Speer's first year in office, February 1942 to early 1943. The narrowness of this window of opportunity is important to emphasize, since it contradicts the usual treatment of the 'Speer era' as a single chronological unit, an undifferentiated expanse of rising armaments production and success.[19] The emphasis on this initial phase of Speer's Ministry, however, follows directly from Hitler's desperate gamble in November and December 1941. As we have seen, the central objective, following the declaration of war on the United States in December 1941, was to complete the defeat of the Red Army by the winter of 1942–3 and to do so by means of a determined drive towards the Caucasus. This would bring the Soviet Union to its knees and dramatically shift the balance of power throughout Western Asia. With both the Ukraine and the Caucasus in its possession, Germany would have the food, raw materials and oil needed to continue the war against Britain and the United States. Combined with a successful offensive by the Afrika Korps it would pose a mortal threat to Britain's position in the Middle East. The overriding priority therefore was to rebuild the offensive capacity of the Ostheer for this second great offensive with all available resources concentrated on Army Group South.[20]

The time-factor in this strategic calculation was all-important. America's entry into the war might not be fatal, provided Germany could finish the war in the East in the next year. As Speer himself explained to his closest colleagues, it was of vital importance that the Wehrmacht should be given the extra margin of offensive strength it needed to decide the war in the East over the winter of 1942–3. Otherwise the war would degenerate into a 'war of duration', allowing the full weight of the Anglo-American coalition to make itself felt. If not in 1943 then certainly by 1944 Germany would find itself facing what Speer would only describe as 'a different situation'.[21] Even amongst those who kept the faith, it was clear that Germany could only retain the initiative if the Wehrmacht struck a truly shattering blow against the Soviet Union in the next twelve months. The campaigning season of 1942 was therefore the last period in the history of the Third Reich in which the armaments effort was impelled by a strategic rationale with some degree of plausibility. And despite the crisis of confidence following the defeat at Moscow in December 1941, it was this element of plausibility that ensured that the German war effort in 1942 was still sustained by a widely based consensus that embraced both the economic elite and the majority of the workforce.[22] And Speer certainly needed all the help he could get.

When he was appointed Armaments Minister in February 1942 Speer's sphere was no more extensive than that of Fritz Todt. Speer did not control the entirety of the armaments economy, let alone the rest of the industrial economy. His immediate authority extended only to the equipment needs of the army. Only in the field of ammunition did Speer have overarching responsibility for all three services. Until the summer of 1943, his writ extended to about 45 per cent of the armaments effort, consuming perhaps one-sixth of industrial output.[23] As we have seen, the procurement bureaucrats of the army had already seen their sphere of responsibility substantially curtailed by Todt's appointment in 1940. The chief victim of Speer's rise to power in 1942 was the military-economic office of the Wehrmacht, headed by General Thomas, which was broken up and stripped of any pretension to overarching leadership in the war economy.[24] Both the navy and the Luftwaffe, however, retained their autonomous procurement authorities. The navy was not incorporated into Speer's sphere of control until June 1943. The Luftwaffe, which by itself accounted for 35–40 per cent of the entire armaments effort, retained its autonomous industrial organization until the spring of 1944, and in this sphere it was Erhard Milch not Albert Speer who called the shots. Given this distribution of responsibility, the German war effort after February 1942 can only be properly understood as a partnership between Milch and Speer.[25] Of the increase in armaments output that was attained between February 1942 and the summer of 1943, only half was attributable to 'Speer's' sectors. Forty per cent was due to the increase in Luftwaffe production. The rest was attributable to the navy and chemicals organization of the Four Year Plan.

The practical and political focus of this alliance was the Zentrale Planung, the central planning committee, which was without doubt the most significant organizational innovation that followed Speer's appointment.[26] The Zentrale Planung was not an appendage of Speer's Armaments Ministry, but an overarching body, presided over jointly by Speer, Milch (representing the Luftwaffe) and Paul Koerner, secretary to Hermann Goering. The meetings were also frequently attended by Hans Kehrl of the Reich Ministry for Economic Affairs, Gauleiter Sauckel, as special plenipotentiary for labour issues, and Herbert Backe of the Food Ministry. In addition, the business of the Zentrale Planung also required the frequent attendance of both Pleiger, as head of the coal industry, and key representatives from the steel industry. It was Speer's chairmanship of the Zentrale Planung that gave him a genuine claim to overarching authority. In practice, however, what transpired in the Zentrale Planung was a collective effort, dominated by Speer and Milch who between them controlled 90 per cent of the armaments economy. Milch attended virtually every session and spoke as the absolute authority in his sector.[27] The significant difference between Speer and Milch was political, not functional. Speer's unrivalled access to Hitler made him the chief conduit through which the Fuehrer's priorities were transmitted down the chain of command.

Since 1936 there had been numerous efforts to create a central governing authority for the German armaments effort, all of them in various ways centred around the figure of Goering. Even in 1942, Speer's official title was as Goering's special plenipotentiary for armaments and the Zentrale Planung met formally with Goering's blessing. Given this history, the real significance of the Zentrale Planung was the fact that it did actually meet on a regular basis, thus establishing a true institutional legitimacy, as well as increasingly formalized proceedings and a proper order of business. In total, between 27 April 1942 and the end of the war, the Zentrale Planung met sixty-two times. Fifty-two of these meetings took place in the first twenty months of its existence between April 1942 and the end of 1943, roughly one session every ten days, thus establishing the Zentrale Planung as the true war cabinet of the German economy.

Whereas the Zentrale Planung was responsible for organizing the supply of raw materials, the production of armaments in Speer's sector was overseen before and after February 1942 by the system of Committees set up by Fritz Todt in the aftermath of the 'ammunition crisis' of 1940.[28] Responsibility for the Committees within the Armaments Ministry lay with the so-called Technisches Amt. Head of the Amt was Karl Otto Saur. Any idea that the Speer Ministry was a haven of 'unideological efficiency' is rendered absurd by the central position occupied within it by Saur. Saur (1902–66) was the living embodiment of the 'political engineer'. A former employee of the Thyssen steel firm, Saur had joined the party in the 1920s. By the late 1930s he had risen within the National Socialist league of German technicians to become Fritz Todt's deputy. After Todt's death, Saur rapidly developed a close working relationship with Speer. And he continued in his role as the Rottweiler of the Armaments Ministry until the very last days of the war. By that time Saur was notorious throughout German industry as a blunt-talking and intemperate bully, who was by no means averse to physical violence. On at least one occasion during a plant visit Saur personally assaulted a group of recalcitrant workers.[29] Speer for his part made no secret of his admiration, indeed his fondness for Saur. And it was altogether fitting that, following his disillusionment with Speer in April 1945, Hitler in his last will and testament named Saur as his successor as Armaments Minister.

Saur's Committees were both key organizing devices for armaments production and key points of political connection between the Reich authorities and German industry. After Walter Rohland reported back from his apocalyptic tour of the Eastern Front at the end of November 1941, the mood in the boardrooms of the Ruhr was bleak. There can be no doubt that the crisis shook the confidence of even the most loyal business leaders in Nazi Germany. For some, such as Walter Borbet of the Bochumer Verein, the shock of Germany's first defeat was too much. Borbet, once one of the most enthusiastic advocates of rearmament, was found dead in his office on 4 January 1942. The majority of German industrial leaders, however, rallied around the regime as never before. In 1939 the German elite had been divided, but the Wehrmacht's spectacular early successes had gone a long way towards healing these rifts. The mood of euphoria and limitless possibility following the defeat of France created an identification with Hitler and his regime that was more complete than at any point before or afterwards.[30] Unlike the attack on France in May 1940, which was expected with fearful trepidation, the invasion of the Soviet Union was eagerly anticipated. From the autumn of 1940 onwards the impending assault was an open secret in Berlin. General Thomas's Wehrmacht office was in regular meetings with leading German corporations with experience in the Soviet Union. IG Farben, Siemens and AEG all contributed their expertise. Discussions even went as far as the allocation of Soviet plants to particular German firms.[31] And once the invasion began, the involvement of German business with the occupation authorities only intensified.

Added to this imperialist euphoria was the financial bonanza of the first years of the war. The industrial boom over which the Nazi regime had presided since 1933 continued unabated into the 1940s. The war-related industries were swamped with orders, investment in machinery and plant accelerated to record levels and from the summer of 1940 onwards there was a significant recovery in lucrative export orders. Certainly, businesses did not appreciate the bureaucracy of the war economy, the price controls, the wrangling over raw materials, the difficulty of getting hold of skilled labour. But in 1940, with domestic demand booming, profits rocketed to quite unprecedented levels.[32] And it was surely indicative of the balance of influence in Hitler's regime that the two party men who dared to challenge the business interest most directly – Paul Walter in coal and Josef Wagner as commissioner for price control – were both unceremoniously dumped in the course of 1941. Furthermore, though the winter crisis of 1941–2 was clearly a profound shock to German society, the unexpected recovery of the Red Army also meant that the war was now a matter of life and death. Defeat would mean not only national humiliation and the destruction of Hitler's regime. The awful spectre of Stalinism now loomed over Germany and no group had more to fear from a Soviet victory than the leaders of German business.

The organizational expression of this intensified alliance between the regime and German business was the extension of Todt's system of industrial organizations, which took place between December 1941 and May 1942. Already in early December Todt had announced the reorganization of his Committee structure. Alongside the existing Main Committees for Ammunition, Weapons, Tanks and Electronic Equipment, he set up a Main Committee for General Wehrmacht Equipment (Allgemeines Wehrmachtsgeraet). This had the important function of gathering together the thousands of Wehrmacht suppliers not immediately involved in the production of armaments. To head this 'general' Committee, the obvious man was Wilhelm Zangen (1891–1971). Chair of the Reich Group for industry since 1938, Zangen was a ruthless careerist, who as CEO of Mannesmann had carved out a considerable industrial empire on the back of a series of opportunistic Aryanization transactions. Assured of Zangen's full backing, Todt addressed the rest of the German industrial leadership at the Council of the Reich Group for industry on 13 January 1942, and between 4 and 6 February 1942 chaired a three-day conference with all the leading armaments producers.[33] In the weeks following Todt's death, Speer sustained his organizational momentum by adding two new Main Committees, one for locomotives, to address the shortage crippling the Reichsbahn, the other for ship-building. For the Luftwaffe, Erhard Milch had already initiated a parallel reorganization of his sphere of activity in the autumn of 1941.[34]

In the field of final assembly, Speer thus added little to the basic structure of industrial organizations put in place by Todt and Milch. His original initiative, perhaps suggested to him by Albert Voegler of the Vereinigte Stahlwerke, was to establish a new set of organizations to manage the supply of raw materials, semi-finished products and subcomponents, known as 'Rings'.[35] There were five Main Rings – for iron and steel production, iron and steel processing, nonferrous metals, engineering components and electrotechnical equipment. The chairmen of the Rings, predictably enough, were chosen from amongst the largest industrial suppliers, including Siemens and the Reichswerke Hermann Goering. But the man Speer appointed to oversee the entire structure was, like Saur, a political animal. Walther Schieber (1896–1960) was a veteran of Nazi industrial policy who had paid his dues in private industry.[36] In the 1930s he had been a successful plant manager for IG Farben and an activist in the Thuringian Nazi party, with close links to

Gauleiter Sauckel. In 1935 Schieber left IG Farben to take control of the Thuringian staple fibre plant newly established by Hans Kehrl. Through this involvement, Schieber became closely associated with Kehrl, who from 1938 onwards was the leading Nazi enforcer in the Reich Ministry for Economic Affairs. In 1939 Schieber was appointed Gau economic adviser in Thuringia and the following year he moved to Berlin to serve Fritz Todt as his chief adviser for chemical issues. Schieber also cultivated close links with the SS, holding the honorary rank of SS Brigadefuehrer and participating regularly in the meetings of the Freundeskreis Heinrich Himmler, a group of businessmen particularly closely associated with the regime. After Todt's death it was only logical that Schieber, like Saur, should play a key role in Speer's Ministry, as head of the Ruestungslieferungsamt (office for armaments supplies). To further consolidate relations between the Ministry and the business community, Schieber was appointed to act as Zangen's deputy at the Reich Group for industry.[37]

In total, at the end of 1942, the telephone book of the Speer Ministry listed 249 Committees and Subcommittees, Rings and Sub-Rings.[38] Obviously, an organization as ramified as this defies simple categorization. Speer's own slogan was 'Selbstverantwortung', the 'self-responsibility' of industry. The Reich Armaments Ministry would set the targets, leaving responsibility for meeting them to German industry. And on closer inspection, the chairmen of Speer's Committees and Rings appear to have been a carefully weighted cross-section of the German industrial establishment. Of the list of the top one hundred industrial firms in 1938 there was not one that did not hold the chairmanship of at least one of Speer's Subcommittees or Rings, and the number of chairmanships allocated to each company corresponded predictably to the hierarchy of size and political importance. The Vestag, Germany's leading heavy industrial conglomerate, held at least twelve chairmanships either directly or through its subsidiaries. This put it on a par with Paul Pleiger's Reichswerke. Siemens was well represented with Dr Friedrich Lueschen occupying a pivotal position as chair both of the Main Committee for Communications Equipment and the Main Ring for Electrical Subcomponents. In total, Siemens held eight chairmanships. Krupp, AEG, Mannesmann, Rheinmetall, Flick, GHH were all involved. IG Farben held only four chairmanships, but this was hardly surprising given the products covered by the Committee system and the role played

by Carl Krauch in the Four Year Plan. With the chairman of its supervisory board overseeing the planning of the entire chemical war effort,
there was little need for IG to dirty its hands with further Committee
work. Zeiss and Zeiss-Ikon oversaw three Subcommittees for precision
optics. Bosch was responsible for fuel injection, and its Blaupunkt subsidiary oversaw electro-acoustic equipment. The Vereinigte Deutsche
Metallwerke (dominated by the Metallgesellschaft) were responsible for
nonferrous components for the aircraft industry. But as well as including
Germany's largest industrial corporations, an important feature of
Speer's system was its enrolment of dozens of smaller suppliers of sub-
components and parts. Apart from the members of the top one hundred,
there were seventy other firms that chaired one or more Subcommittee
or Ring: Bauer & Schaurte for screws and fastenings; Mahle for pistons;
Kugelfischer for roller bearings; Koch & Sterzel for electrical transformers; Klein, Schanzlin & Becker for valves; Karl Schmidt of Neckar-
sulm for vehicle components; Behr for radiators; Warnecke & Boehm
for specialist aircraft paint; Roehm & Haas for Plexiglas canopies. Sixty
years later, these same firms – household names in engineering circles
– still form the backbone of Germany's high-quality manufacturing
industry.[39]

There were of course many points of conflict and contention within
this complex structure of cooperation between Hitler's regime and leading elements of German industry, some of which we shall return to
below. However, if there was one issue that had the potential to sour
relations more generally, it was the question of pricing, profits and taxes.
As we have seen, this had been a matter of debate since late 1940. In
November 1941, in the context of mounting concern about inflation, a
serious conflict appears to have erupted between price commissioner
Gauleiter Wagner and the Reich Group for industry, which at one point
provoked Wilhelm Zangen into talk of resignation. Over the coming
months these differences were ironed out, in a compromise that was
highly characteristic of the Speer era.[40] Though the initiative predated
his arrival at centre stage by many months, Speer presented the resulting
reform of the public pricing system as a key element in his armaments
miracle. In Speer's account, the public procurement system that was in
operation up to November 1941 was an aberrant outgrowth of state
bureaucracy that positively encouraged inefficiency by granting firms a
profit mark-up proportional to their cost-base. The higher a firm's costs,

the larger its profits.[41] From 1942 onwards, Speer claimed, this system was swept aside and replaced by what is usually referred to as a 'fixed price system'. All producers were asked to match a single standard price. Any profits they made by reducing costs below this standard price were theirs to keep. At a stroke of a pen, a gross inducement to inefficiency was thus abolished and German industry was set on course to efficiency and rationalization.

Though this story-line was rhetorically compelling and has continued to attract historians, it was in fact a travesty of the real course of events.[42] As we have seen, authorized profits under the existing guidelines were not in fact calculated as a percentage of costs, but as a percentage of capital employed.[43] And the cost accounting guidelines were certainly strict.[44] From the point of view of the new rationalization agenda, the essential flaw of the pre-Speer system was not that it allowed producers to inflate costs and prices as they liked. Nor was it devoid of incentives to efficiency. Once a price had been agreed, it was fixed and contractors thus had every incentive to cut costs.[45] In the early years of the war, it was precisely the question of how to claw back the resulting 'excess profits' that was the source of controversy between the Reich Group for industry, the Reich price commissioner and the fiscal authorities. The real flaw in the system from the point of view of the rationalization agenda was that it did not set a single, standard price for all producers to aim towards. This, too, was not mere incompetence on the part of the authorities. The system was designed to ensure that the state could issue contracts to the widest possible range of new armaments producers, even if they could not meet the performance standards of the established and experienced suppliers. In this sense, it was a system well suited to the early phases of wartime mobilization, when new producers needed to be enrolled en masse in unfamiliar lines of production, whilst at the same time controlling the profits earned by the more experienced incumbent firms. Where the system clearly did sacrifice efficiency was in failing to require the less efficient producers to meet the prevailing 'best practice price'. Furthermore, the tailor-made contracts required repeated and intrusive investigations by military auditors, who not surprisingly chose to concentrate their attention on the larger firms, making the system unpopular with the more influential members of the Reich Group for industry.

In November 1941, as part of the discussion of fiscal consolidation, the decision was taken to adopt a new system of standard prices. These were to be based on the costs of a 'good-to-average' producer, calculated according to the existing rules. Initially, this measure was proposed as part of a fiscal consolidation package designed to curb corporate profits and reduce state expenditure, thus helping to prick the inflationary bubble. In the name of rationalization, the standard prices were subject to a general 10 per cent deduction. Furthermore, a serious clawback was threatened in relation to profits earned in 1940 and 1941. But after Gauleiter Wagner's departure and his replacement by the Austrian banker Hans Fischboeck, the tone softened markedly.[46] Certainly there were no more threats of resignation from Zangen and his colleagues. The new standard price system was accompanied by a cast-iron promise from Speer that those who met the price would be exempt from any further official inspections and would be free to retain a large part of the profits they earned by beating the standard costing. Responsibility for dealing with excess profit shifted from the price commissioner to the Finance Ministry, and the excess profit guidelines issued at the end of March 1942 certainly did little to dampen industrial enthusiasm. Only profits more than 50 per cent higher than those earned in 1938 were subject to excess profit tax, giving an in-built advantage to those firms who had already profited from rearmament before the war.[47] And Albert Speer made clear that he would accept no interference in his sphere of activity by the meddling 'bureaucrats' of the Finance Ministry and the price commissioner. Paragraph 14 of the excess profit guidelines allowed those firms that agreed to accept the new standard prices set by the Armaments Ministry to claim back a substantial share of their excess profit payments.[48] For Speer, wider concerns about spiralling state expenditure and inflation were irrelevant. All that mattered was the enthusiastic cooperation of German business in his drive to maximize production.

II

These measures of reorganization were accompanied by a rhetoric of reform and rationalization that promised to resolve the problems of the German war effort by producing more for less. This ideological trope, however, always competed in the vocabulary of the German war effort with a no less determined emphasis on radical mobilization. In this respect, Speer was to a large degree the beneficiary of wider efforts to rally and stabilize the regime.

Though Speer deliberately prevented the Reich's fiscal authorities from making a major raid on corporate profits in 1942, the success of his Ministry was in no small part due to the continuing stability of the Reichsmark. This in turn depended in large part on the one-off fiscal exactions levied particularly on property owners in 1942. A major contribution to the Reich's revenue was also of course made by the occupied territories. Together, the increases in domestic and external revenue were enough to stem the threat of inflation for at least another eighteen months. Even more vital to sustaining the German war effort were the increased supplies of both food and labour obtained from the occupied territories in 1942–3. The 280,000 workers drained from the armaments factories in the twelve months that followed the Moscow crisis were more than offset by an influx of 970,000 foreign workers provided by Sauckel. And the prime beneficiaries were in Speer's sector.[49] Whereas the overall increase in the armaments workforce in 1942 came to only 15 per cent, in Speer's sector of army production the increase was in excess of 30 per cent. Of the increase of 513,000 workers that could be attributed specifically to one of the three branches of the Wehrmacht, Speer's area of responsibility claimed no less than 420,000.[50] Speer's top-priority programmes were lavishly provided. The tank workforce in 1942 increased by almost 60 per cent and by an even larger percentage in 1943. In the case of locomotive building, one of Speer's most widely touted success stories, the dramatic increase in annual production, from 1,918 locomotives in 1941 to 5,343 in 1943, was underpinned by a 90 per cent increase in the workforce in 1942 alone.[51] All of this was the exact reverse of the pattern in 1941, when the prime beneficiaries of labour mobilization had been the Luftwaffe and the navy.[52]

For cash, food and labour Speer could rely on others. His own particular contribution to resource mobilization was in the sphere of raw materials. Though the Zentrale Planung was clearly a major organizational innovation, the subject matter of its meetings was achingly familiar. The overriding preoccupation was steel. Thirty of sixty-two meetings were addressed directly to this issue.[53] In addition, eleven sessions were devoted to coal, which was important above all because the supply of coal determined the quantity of steel that could be produced.

Another eight sessions dealt with issues connected to the labour supply in which the coal mines had first priority. Even in apparently unrelated fields such as the chemicals programme, the issue at stake was steel. Chemicals were an unavoidable issue for the Zentrale Planung because the entire war machine would grind to a halt without fuel. Nitrogen, furthermore, was the key ingredient both for explosives and fertilizer. However, the Zentrale Planung had a claim to control over Carl Krauch and his chemicals, because Krauch's gigantic factories needed substantial allocations of steel. The conclusion is inescapable: whoever was in charge of the armaments economy and however they organized their authority, steel remained at the heart of German armaments politics, before and after February 1942.

Steel was indispensable for all armaments production outside the Luftwaffe. Even the Luftwaffe needed steel for bombs, anti-aircraft guns and airfield installations. But, as we have seen repeatedly since 1937, within the Wehrmacht's steel budget the great swing variable was the quantity of steel allocated to ammunition. The easiest way to relieve pressure on German heavy industry was to cut back ammunition production, releasing steel for other uses. This had been done in 1937, in the summer of 1939 and again in the summer of 1940. In 1942, faced with the prospect of a long and bloody war in Russia, this was no longer an option. In the months following the Moscow crisis, Hitler returned to the obsession that had gripped him in the first months of the war.[54] The 'armaments programme 1942' announced on 10 January, a month before Speer took office, called for the creation of new stocks of ammunition sufficient to cover six months at the heavy rates of consumption experienced in 1941. These targets were specified with the summer offensive in mind. But Hitler also now had to secure himself against the prospect of a long war on two fronts. At the end of March, the OKW noted, 'Fuehrer has ordered Speer to run up ammunition production on a really big scale, so that two-front trench war can be fought for years'.[55] Nor can one fault the logic of concentrating on ammunition first. Due to its sheer size, the ammunition programme conditioned all the choices that followed. Ammunition did not receive the same attention in Speer's armaments propaganda as more glamorous items such as tanks.[56] Ammunition belonged rather to the visual repertoire of World War I than to the 'Blitzkrieg' campaigns of Hitler's war. But shells, bombs and bullets in fact accounted for 50 per cent of the total increase in armaments production in the first eight months of Speer's tenure.[57] Even in the middle of 1943, at the end of the first phase of the armaments miracle, ammunition accounted for half the increase achieved within Speer's personal sphere of responsibility. A proper sense of proportion is conveyed if we consider the relative scope of the three Main Armaments Committees overseen by Speer's Ministry. In the autumn of 1943, 450,000 workers were employed in ammunition production, compared with 160,000 making tanks and 210,000 making weapons.[58] In terms of steel, ammunition's dominance was even more pronounced. In the last quarter of 1942 it hogged more than half the army's total allocation of steel, as compared to 15 per cent each going to tanks and weapons.[59] Ammunition's political ramifications were no less significant. As in 1939–40, meeting Hitler's huge new ammunition demands required an immediate and wrenching reallocation of raw materials the impact of which could only be softened in the medium term by a substantial increase in the output of steel.

The scale of the shift was dramatic. In the last quarter of 1941, in line with the priorities of armaments planning set before Barbarossa, the German army out of its measly ration of 185,000 tons of steel had proposed to allocate only 25,000 tons to ammunition. Now Hitler demanded that the ammunition programme should be established with a regular monthly quota of no less than 350,000 tons of steel, an increase by a factor of 14.[60] Even before Speer took office, the army's overall steel ration had been doubled to more than 350,000 tons per month in the first quarter of 1942. This was 'paid for' in part by cuts to the Luftwaffe's expansion plans and sharp reductions in the production of bombs and anti-aircraft shells. The navy's ration was also cut. But this was not enough to make room for the army's new needs. In 1942 large quantities of steel were still being allocated to the investment programmes begun in 1940 and 1941, and significant quantities of steel were still going to export orders. The immediate effect of the crisis on the Eastern Front and the sudden need to give top priority to the army was therefore to exacerbate the 'steel inflation' that had already been causing increasing concern in the autumn of 1941. Significantly more steel entitlements were issued than there were quantities of actual steel. So large was the discrepancy that it threatened to disorganize the entire war effort. Steel producers overloaded with orders, all of which were backed by official steel entitlements, were free to pick and choose the grades of steel they produced. High-priority programmes were forced to wait for months before their requirements were met. Meanwhile, hundreds of thousands of tons of steel went to waste because they were delivered after the armaments programmes for which they were intended had been cancelled.

The first task of Speer's new administration was to get to grips with this 'ration inflation'. As we have seen, the crisis of the coal sector in 1941 had led to the formation in March 1941 of the Reich coal organization (RVK) under Paul Pleiger, which managed both the production and distribution of coal. In the spring of 1942, the Reich Ministry for Economic Affairs began to push for the formation of a similar organization for the steel industry. This finally came to fruition on 1 June 1942, in the form of the Reichsvereinigung Eisen (RVE).[61] What the Reich Ministry seems initially to have had in mind was an industrial dictatorship headed by a single individual, a 'steel tsar'. What actually emerged was a classic compromise between the key interest groups in the German steel industry, bartered between Speer and Albert Voegler, who as chairman of the Vestag supervisory board was still the dominant figure in the German steel industry.[62] Instead of the unworkable idea of a steel dictator, who would have been bound to attract hostility from one or more of the major steel regions, the RVE was run by a chairman flanked by a powerful presidium, in which all of the major steel interests were represented. Initially, Speer suggested to Hitler that Voegler himself should chair the RVE, but, as Speer noted, 'He [Hitler] considers my suggestion of Voegler acceptable, but believes that Roechling would do the job even better. Leaves the decision to us.'[63] Speer of course took the hint. Hermann Roechling was certainly one of the regime's most prominent industrial collaborators, but he was no advocate of a state dictatorship over industry. Amongst the active industrialists of World War II, Roechling was one of the senior exponents with a record stretching back to the annexationist debates of World War I. Throughout his long career, Roechling's overriding preoccupation was the expansion of German control over the Lorraine and its adjoining areas.[64] But, despite his prominence and excellent connections to the Nazi party, he had not been favoured in the final distribution of French assets in January 1941, losing out to Flick and the Reichswerke Hermann Goering. By 1942 Roechling was so antipathetic to the Reichswerke that he willingly cooperated with Ruhr interests to hold at bay any further extension of Pleiger's interests.[65]

Pleiger for his part, was so suspicious of the heavy industrial establishment that he refused even to join the RVE's presidium.

Ten days after his appointment Roechling spelled out to an assembly of leading steel industrialists precisely what was at stake.[66] The steel industry had to be raised to a new peak of performance. On their success hung both the future of the German war effort and the 'future of the private economy'. The battles raging on the Eastern Front left no doubt about the seriousness of the situation. The performance of Soviet industry, as Roechling frankly acknowledged, had been nothing short of miraculous. Even in besieged Leningrad fresh tanks continued to roll off the production lines. Despite the destruction of no less than 20,000 Soviet combat aircraft, the Red Air Force was still throwing new planes into combat. How had the Soviet Union managed to build and sustain engineering capacity of such robust quality and quantity? The battle on the Eastern Front was a true battle of the systems. It was not Roechling's place to speculate about the military outcome of the war. But the question as far as the economy was concerned was clear-cut. 'To justify the existence of the private economy we must achieve extraordinary performance . . . If we . . . should not succeed, people are probably going to try other means.' And, Roechling continued, 'In the end what this is about is whether or not the private economy can produce the necessary results . . . or whether other forms of organization are needed.' This, surely, is the best characterization of the Speer system, certainly in its first eighteen months. What emerged in the aftermath of the winter crisis of 1941 was an alliance between Hitler's regime and the leading elements of German industrial capitalism, to secure their common survival in the life and death struggle with Stalinism.[67]

Two basic challenges faced the steel industry: to increase production and to reorganize the rationing system. The job of reorganization was given to a committee of steel industrialists, headed by the ubiquitous Voegler.[68] Voegler, in turn, entrusted the technical details to Hans Kehrl of the RWM. Kehrl was no steel expert. But he had consolidated his reputation as one of the toughest practitioners of Nazi economic policy by imposing a tightly disciplined rationing system on the textiles sector. Replacing regular currency with coupons, he had drastically curtailed household demand for clothing. He had also been instrumental, in cooperation with his friend Paul Pleiger, in the reorganization of the coal industry. Kehrl now applied the same principles to the management of the steel economy, with a system that was presented to the Zentrale Planung on 15 May 1942.[69] The enormous backlog of steel orders was to be cancelled. To ensure that there was no further inflation, rations would in the future be issued only up to 90 per cent of total steel production, leaving a reserve of 10 per cent for top priority contracts. Rolling mills, for their part, would be required to take on no more orders than they were able to supply within a reasonable time period.[70] Then in the third quarter of 1942 the overall quantity of steel rations was slashed to bring it into line with actual production. The total military allocation was cut by 7 per cent, with the navy being the main casualty. The army's allocation continued to increase. By contrast, the total allocation for non-armaments purposes was cut by almost a quarter, the brunt being borne by the export sector. This provoked protests, not only from the civilian economic administration but also from Wehrmacht high command, which was seriously concerned about the impact on Germany's allies, most notably Italy. However, as the battle for Stalingrad reached its dreadful climax, Speer had little difficulty in insisting on the absolute priority of the army.

This took care of steel allocation. But the more fundamental problem, clearly, was the inadequate production of steel. As we have seen, in the late summer and autumn of 1941 the German war effort was haunted by the fear of a severe setback to steel output as a result of the difficulties in coal supply. By juggling steel types and supplementing with high-quality foreign iron ore and scrap, the steel firms in fact managed to maintain production at a relatively high level, at least until the last quarter of 1941.[71] But after that output began to fall sharply, bottoming out in early 1942, when the supply of coal was severely disrupted by a renewed crisis of the German railway system, this time precipitated by the strain of covering thousands of extra kilometres of track in the Soviet Union. Having rearranged the system for allocating steel and adjusted allocations to bring them into line with actual output, Roechling's overriding priority was to raise steel production. As early as the end of June 1942, Speer and Hitler had agreed that Germany would need to raise monthly production by at least 600,000 tons by the end of the year.[72] As Roechling presented it to the steel industry in the summer of 1942, the immediate goal was to match Hitler and Speer's demands by raising output from its current level of roughly 31 million tons per annum to at least 36 million tons.[73] In the longer term, Roechling could see virtually no limit to the demand for this basic commodity. In years to come he could foresee European production of in excess of 85 million tons, greater than the United States at its peak. The problem, however, was coal. To meet Hitler and Speer's target, the steel industrialists claimed to need at least 400,000 extra tons of coking coal per month, as well as more skilled labour and a large quantity of scrap metal for smelting. On this point, however, there seemed no possibility of reconciling the demands of Roechling and his colleagues with the production forecasts provided by Paul Pleiger and the Reich coal association.

On this rocky terrain of heavy industrial politics, the entire 'Speer system' very nearly came to grief in the autumn of 1942. So critical was the issue that it was taken to an extended meeting with Hitler on 11 August 1942. Apart from Speer, the meeting was attended by Hans Kehrl (RWM), Sauckel as the plenipotentiary for labour, Pleiger for coal and the three-man leadership team of the steel industry, Roechling, Rohland and Alfried Krupp, the heir to the Krupp throne. Initially, Pleiger stuck to his guns, pronouncing himself unable to deliver the necessary coke. As we have seen, coal was in critically short supply throughout the German Empire. Pleiger was struggling to raise output from Germany's ageing pits. Productivity in Belgium and northern France was falling fast. Norway and Sweden badly needed to rebuild their stocks if they were to avoid disaster in the coming winter months, on top of which Pleiger also had to consider the German electricity grid and Krauch's synthetic chemicals plants. Civilian morale was already suffering under shortages of household coal. Speer's suggestion that British coal rationing was even more severe than that in Germany was immediately refuted by RVK statistics. Pleiger could see no way of meeting the demands of the steel industry, unless Sauckel could give him tens of thousands of experienced miners from the Ukraine and Poland. At this point Gauleiter Sauckel stepped in to assure Hitler that he was perfectly capable of supplying the labour that Pleiger demanded. Hitler concurred. 'If this question could not be resolved on a voluntary basis, he would agree to any coercive measure, and this applied to the Western occupied territories as well, not only in the East.'[74] However, given his experience with the malnourished and demoralized Eastern workers, Pleiger was not reassured. As we have seen, productivity in the mines had been falling since the outbreak of the war and the half-starved Eastern workers were no substitute for prime German manpower.

At this point, however, Hitler suddenly silenced any further debate by announcing: 'Herr Pleiger, if, due to the shortage of coking coal the output of the steel industry cannot be raised as planned, then the war is lost.' As we have seen, Hitler was under no illusions about the narrowness of Germany's window of strategic opportunity, but rarely did he set out Germany's predicament with this kind of brutal clarity. After a moment of stunned silence, Pleiger was left with no alternative but to reply: 'My Fuehrer, I will do everything humanly possible to achieve the goal.'[75] Somehow, the iron determination of National Socialist leadership would triumph over the natural limitations of Europe's coal seams. We have already seen how the brutal consequences of this imperative were spelled out by Pleiger and Ley for the rest of the coal fraternity at the drunken Kaiserhof meeting in Essen in October 1942. If necessary, the foreign labour force would be worked to death. As Ley had put it, 'after us there is nothing, everything will be over ... Germany will be destroyed. Everybody will be slaughtered, murdered, burned and destroyed.'[76] Nevertheless, in August 1942, in the more sober surroundings of the Fuehrerhauptquartier, Pleiger insisted on putting on record his 'deep reservations' about the feasibility of the steel plan.[77]

Inevitably, the agreement struck on 11 August was not the end of the steel saga. By October 1942 it was clear that Pleiger would not be able to meet the targets forced on him at the August meeting. When this broke into the open at the meeting of the Zentrale Planung on 23 October, Speer found himself facing a crisis of his entire 'system'.[78] To meet its expansion targets, the steel industry claimed to need 2.12 million tons of coal per month. In October 1942 it had received only 1.4 million tons and Pleiger now proposed to slash this to 925,000 tons. This would imply a 40 per cent cut in iron production, with disastrous consequences for the entire armaments programme. Without adequate workers, Pleiger could not dig coal. Sauckel had not delivered the 120,000 men he had promised. The pits were short of 107,417 miners. A further 9,000 were needed by the railway system serving the mines. To make matters worse, the Ruhr was suffering an epidemic of absenteeism, with some shifts reporting up to 60 per cent sick.[79] What now threatened the German economy was a chain reaction like those that had caused such disruption during the winters of 1939–40 and 1941–2.[80] Inadequate coal supplies would lead to power cuts and bottlenecks radiating across the economy. For Speer, a failure to resolve the problems of coal and steel would be a political disaster. As he put it to the Zentrale Planung, it would be 'a conclusion that would do severe damage to the theory which I generally advocate, namely that we get furthest by relying on the self-responsibility of industry'.[81] The implied threat was obvious. Pleiger's inability to meet his delivery targets 'entailed such grave consequences as to make it impossible for anybody in Zentrale Planung to accept responsibility: such matters could only be dealt with by the Reichsmarschall [Goering] and the Fuehrer.' As Roechling had predicted, failure to meet the demands of the war effort would jeopardize the cooperative relationship between the Armaments Ministry and industry that had provided the foundation of the German war economy since 1940.

In a desperate effort to avert a calamity, the last days of October 1942 were filled with intense meetings between Schieber, Kehrl and representatives of the steel and coal associations. These were interspersed with periodic plenary sessions of the Zentrale Planung at which Speer harangued Pleiger and Rohland and reminded them of their broken promise to the Fuehrer. In the event, all the parties had too much invested in 'Speer's system' for it to be allowed to fail. The necessary coal was 'squeezed out' by imposing a 10 per cent cut on domestic consumers, which meant that the German per capita allocation was now 15 per cent lower than that in Britain.[82] In addition, Pleiger introduced tough new regulations under which the coal mines belonging to the largest steel firms were required to pool their output with the supply available for general distribution. Those steel producers who economized on coal use were rewarded by being allowed to retain a greater share of their 'own' coal. Rather than collapsing, as the RVE had feared, steel output rose in the first quarter of 1943 to a wartime record of 2.1 million tons per month in the pre-war territory of Germany. For the German *Grossraum* as a whole, the monthly average in early 1943 was 2.7 million tons. On the crest of this heavy industrial boom, Speer delivered the 'armaments miracle'. By February 1943 the combined armaments index exceeded twice the level it had reached when Speer took over. The driving force of this spectacular increase, however, was anything but miraculous. To reiterate, in so far as Speer was responsible, the most important factor was ammunition. And the increased production of ammunition was not primarily an effect of rationalization or reorganization. It was a direct result of a hugely increased allocation of steel.[83] From September 1939 to the end of 1943, there is a near-perfect

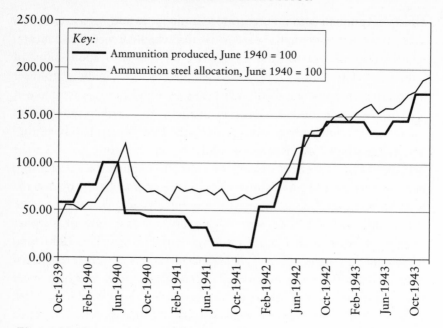

Figure 20. Ammunition production and steel allocated to ammunition

correlation between the allocation of steel to ammunition production and the quantity of ammunition produced.[84] When plenty of steel was allocated, ammunition production was buoyant. When the steel supply was restricted, so was the production of ammunition, and this relationship holds both before and after February 1942. To the extent that there was a major surge in labour productivity within the remit of the Speer Ministry, the indicator usually used to measure rationalization success, this in fact confirms the rate-limiting role of steel. Without enough raw material, neither labour nor the available industrial plant could be used efficiently.

III

Under closer inspection, therefore, it is clear that increased mobilization of money, labour and raw materials was fundamentally important in allowing Speer to dramatically raise production. At the same time, however, it is undeniable that this was compounded by the beneficial effects of rationalization. Furthermore, rationalization was clearly a key term in the self-understanding of those responsible for the German war economy after the winter crisis of 1941–2. No other concept so neatly encapsulated the central theme of Speer's armaments propaganda: the possibility of achieving vastly higher output without any additional input of either labour or material. Given the overwhelming industrial coalition now arrayed against the Third Reich, it was on the power of this voluntarist idea that the future of the German war effort depended. The timing could hardly be more indicative. Rationalization as a slogan of government policy came to the fore in the midst of the crisis on the Eastern Front in the autumn of 1941. At that moment, as Hitler's war ran aground in the snowy outskirts of Moscow, Nazi Germany needed nothing more urgently than a magic bullet. On 3 December 1941 Hitler even went so far as to issue a decree making rationalization into a top priority for the German war effort.[85] The fact that the ordinary business of production engineers had been turned into a political issue of this magnitude should suggest the caution with which this topic should be approached. The simple story spun by Speer, that the German war economy up to 1941 was an inefficient sink for labour and raw materials and that it was only after December 1941, by means of the Fuehrer's decree and Speer's inspired leadership, that it was awakened to the need for efficiency, is clearly a myth. As we have already seen, the statistics usually invoked to support this description of the pre-Speer era simply do not stand up to detailed scrutiny. Conversely, Speer's success in increasing armaments output dramatically in his sector was due largely to a surge in ammunition output, best explained not by rationalization but by a dramatic mobilization of raw materials.

Where rationalization clearly did play a crucial role was not in Speer's sector but in the sphere of Erhard Milch and the Air Ministry. Between early 1942 and early 1943 the monthly output of aircraft more than doubled. But unlike in the army's sector this increase in output took place with a much smaller increase in the labour force and no increase whatsoever in the allocation of raw aluminium. This certainly suggests very considerable efficiency gains. At the same time, a close inspection of the Luftwaffe's production record also reveals the ambiguous complexity of the rationalization concept in Nazi industrial politics.[86]

As the leading new industry of metalworking in the 1930s, the aircraft-industrial complex of the Third Reich had been haunted from its inception by 'American' visions of rationalization and mass-production. As we have seen, the most bullish exponent of this ideology of mass-production was Heinrich Koppenberg, the man installed as CEO of Junkers in 1933. Koppenberg's effort to construct a 'Fordist' aircraft firm had centred on the search for maximum scale of production and maximum vertical integration. The Ju 88 was sold to the Air Ministry in 1938 as an aircraft specifically conceived for mass-production. In 1940, in direct response to the American threat, Koppenberg followed this up with his grandiose plans for a 1,000-engine aero-engine plant and a huge aluminium complex to be centred on Norway. Given the titanic production figures being touted by the British and Americans and the general infatuation with Fordism in inter-war Europe, such visions had an irresistible and recurring appeal. They followed naturally in the giant footsteps left by Pleiger's Salzgitter steel complex and Porsche's no less gargantuan VW plant at Fallersleben.

Though risks of failure were correspondingly huge, as exemplified by white elephants such as the failed '1,000-engine plant' in Austria, the drive for scale was not mere illusion. As we have seen, Daimler-Benz's aero-engine plant at Genshagen was successfully expanded to a capacity in excess of 1,000 engines per month at very reasonable cost. There were other success stories, too, such as the tank complex near Linz.[87] The advantages of concentrating production on a handful of gigantic factories were real. The ability of both the United States and the Soviet Union to operate truly enormous production facilities, out of the range of enemy bombers, clearly contributed to the productivity advantage that they enjoyed over both Germany and Britain.[88] Though on a smaller scale, the production records both of Milch's Air Ministry and Speer's Armaments Ministry would not have been possible but for the investment programmes that had been initiated in the autumn of 1940 and continued well into 1943.

By the same token, however, the agglomeration of resources in the pursuit of 'efficiency' and 'scale' was also one of the principal drivers of internecine industrial competition, entirely incompatible with the efficient management of the overall war effort. After almost a decade of experience with the ruthless egotism of Germany's aircraft producers, Erhard Milch in the Air Ministry was all too aware of this. In advance of the Luftwaffe's great expansion programme of the summer of 1941, Milch therefore initiated a series of changes to the governance of the aircraft industry that were to prove crucial to his later efforts at rationalization.[89] In May 1941, ten months before Speer took office, Milch set up the industrial council of the Air Ministry (Industrierat), in which the aircraft procurement plans of the Ministry were subject to a process of peer review. As a quasi-parliamentary body, it acted as a powerful check on the effort of individual firms to exert undue influence on the Ministry. Then, in a spectacular series of corporate coups, he cut major producers down to size. Junkers and BMW were the first to be subjected to the new regime. After a series of disasters in the development of radial engines, BMW was placed under the supervision of William Werner, an efficiency expert recruited from the car maker Auto-Union.[90] At Junkers, Koppenberg was unceremoniously shunted into retirement. Junkers itself was subject to a tight new regime of financial oversight. At Messerschmitt, Milch exploited Willy Messerschmitt's embarrassment over the failure of the Me 210 (about which we shall have more to say below) to remove him from managerial control. To further curb corporate autonomy, Milch ended the easygoing financial arrangements under which manufacturers received advance payment for their deliveries to the Air Ministry. At Heinkel, this produced a financial crisis, which Milch used to restructure the management and to push Ernst Heinkel into a purely developmental role. All three major aircraft developers – Junkers, Messerschmitt and Heinkel – were thus brought under direct Ministerial control.

It was only after he had decisively re-established the authority of the Air Ministry that Milch began to promote an agenda of rationalization, in the sense of optimizing manufacturing efficiency. For airframes, aero-engines and aircraft equipment, Milch established a system of Rings, later renamed to match Todt and Speer's Main Committees. Karl Frydag, chief engineer from the Henschel corporation, headed the Airframe Ring. William Werner ran the Aero-engine Ring. Hans Heyne of AEG-Telefunken oversaw the aircraft equipment industry.[91] They too were advocates of 'American-style' mass-production. Werner had worked at Chrysler, Heyne was a protégé of General Electric. But unlike the empire builders of the 1930s, theirs was the mantra of 'more for less'. Werner, in particular, introduced himself in 1941 with a series of devastating reports on the antediluvian metalworking practices commonplace in aero-engine production.[92] He was particularly incensed by the wastage of raw materials resulting from the application of traditional metal-cutting techniques. As he put it in a much-quoted report, the German aero-engine industry was producing more waste chips, by weight, than engines.[93]

There can be little doubt, of course, that Werner was right. But his aggressive rhetoric of reform and improvement must be seen in context. What Werner was voicing was the critique developed since the early 1930s by advocates of new, state-of-the-art technologies, which replaced traditional metal-cutting tools, such as lathes, with grinding, casting, stamping and pressing, all of which were far more economical in their use of both materials and labour. Frydag at Henschel was a world leader in this field.[94] But to take the rationalizing rhetoric of men like Werner and Frydag at face value and infer that the Luftwaffe industries suffered before November 1941 from a peculiar level of inefficiency would be naive. A high degree of wastage in metalworking was completely normal in the 1920s and 1930s, both in Germany and the United States.[95] Furthermore, it would be misleading to counterpose the agenda of Werner, Frydag and Co. as 'rational' rationalization to the 'fantastic' schemes previously touted by the likes of Koppenberg and Ernst Heinkel. In the crisis-stricken politics of the Nazi regime in the autumn of 1941, one rhetoric of rationalization in fact substituted for the other. Werner's critique of existing production practice could have been made with equal force of virtually any factory in Germany – or anywhere else in the world for that matter – at any time since the early 1930s. Indeed, Werner had been making his case to the Air Ministry for at least two years before he was finally taken up at the national level by Fritz Todt.[96] His critique was brought to the fore only in October 1941, precisely at the moment at which it became apparent that there was neither manpower nor materials to realize the enormous expansion plans that Milch and Goering had embarked upon so confidently only a few months earlier. In this sense, it was the Luftwaffe that gave birth to the 'rhetorical fix' that was generalized by Hitler's rationalization decree of 3 December to the entire armaments economy: minute attention to the production process would unlock virtually limitless output and enable Germany to transcend all resource constraints. The hard-headed Werner, of course, had promised something far more modest. He had spoken about the possibility of raising output by perhaps 40 per cent.

Furthermore, as was obvious to all involved, mass-production of extremely complex machinery such as aircraft came at a price.[97] Production had to be restricted to a limited number of models and these had to be 'frozen' for a sufficiently long period of time for the factories to gain significant economies of scale. There was therefore an inescapable trade-off between quantity and quality. Since Germany could not hope to compete directly with America's volume of output, this was not a trade-off to strike easily. As we have seen, in 1941 Udet had held off from committing more resources to the mass-production of existing models, precisely because he hoped that new aircraft under development, most notably the Me 210 and He 177, would offer a significant advance in technology. By the end of the year, with Udet dead, Milch found himself facing two humbling development disasters. One must be careful not to read too much into these problems. To conclude that they reflected some deep-seated structural weakness in the German military-industrial complex is wide of the mark.[98] After all, Germany was already well advanced in developing a new generation of jet-engined planes that were at the cutting edge of aeronautical engineering. The development problems encountered with the Me 210 combat aircraft were due to a high stakes gamble in which the Luftwaffe had engaged in the late 1930s.[99] Rather than going through the normal four-year development cycle from prototype to series production, the Air Ministry had attempted to leap ahead in the air race by shortening the timeline to three years. This involved the deliberate risk of rushing into series production aircraft that were not yet fully tested. In the case of the Ju 88, the gamble did not backfire. Though the Ju 88 was not the miracle weapon that Goering had been promised, it was certainly a serviceable aircraft. And neither the Me 210 heavy fighter nor even Heinkel's ill-fated He 177 was a true dud. By 1943 both had emerged as viable combat aircraft. What both aircraft needed was more time in development and a more reasonable design specification. In early 1942, however, this was little consolation to Erhard Milch. Hundreds of dangerously unstable Me 210s were coming off the production lines at Messerschmitt's Regensburg and Augsburg facilities. Even more half-finished planes were piling up in the assembly halls, and parts for another 800 aircraft were already in stock. Milch had no option but to cut his losses and cancel the entire programme. Instead, in a desperate bid to match quantity with quality Milch decided to concentrate all available capacity on the mass-production of those models that had been tried and tested in the first years of the war.[100]

The new focus on mass-production certainly produced results. By the summer of 1943, aircraft production was more than double the level in the winter of 1941–2. The gap that had opened up between Britain and Germany was substantially reduced. For the first time, the German aircraft industry was able to achieve substantial economies of scale. The resources pumped into the Luftwaffe in 1940–41 were now concentrated in mass assembly. The available machine tools were set up in an efficient manner to produce long series of identical aircraft. There was nothing miraculous about this process, however. Ever since the 1920s, when full metal aircraft had first been introduced, German aircraft engineers had estimated that costs would decline in a geometric progression, as the scale of production increased.[101] They had even calculated a formula describing these so-called learning-curve effects in algebraic terms. And experience in the 1940s proved that these predictions were remarkably accurate. Costs plunged as each factory concentrated on 'its' standard model. Germany continued to manufacture in somewhat smaller batches than did the Americans. But what is striking about the production record after 1942 is not how far apart but how close per capita productivity became. Whereas in most manufacturing industry the United States enjoyed an advantage over Germany of at least 2:1, the differential in airframes in 1942 and 1943 was no more than 50 per cent.[102]

But the price that Germany paid for this quantitative expansion in output was a high one: the increasing technological obsolescence of the Luftwaffe's armoury. As early as October 1941 a commission of front-line airmen, charged by the air staff with evaluating the Luftwaffe's development programme, had expressed horrified disbelief at Milch's demand for a large increase in the production of Heinkel 111s.[103] The Luftwaffe had first tested this medium bomber in February 1934, when Goering's air force was still in its clandestine phase. At the time the He 111 had been an advanced aircraft and had benefited from continuous upgrading. But in the autumn of 1941 Luftwaffe commanders considered it unsuitable for use over Britain, even under cover of night. As it turned out, the He 111, along with the Luftwaffe's other twin-engined aircraft such as the Me 110 and 210/410, gained a new lease on life after 1942 in a defensive role, as night fighters in the battle against the RAF. Since RAF Bomber Command flew its missions without fighter escorts, the task of night interception put little premium on absolute speed or

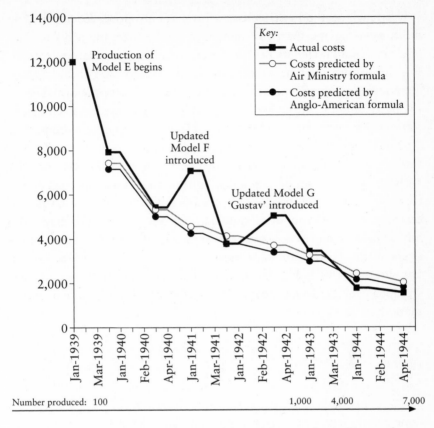

Figure 21. Learning to make Me 109s at Messerschmitt-Regensburg
(hours per plane)

manoeuvrability. To track down and destroy the slow-moving bomber
streams, what the German crews needed were bulky electronics and
heavy guns which could be easily accommodated in the twin-engined
bombers of 1930s vintage. It was not until the US Army Air Force began
escorted daylight bombing raids in the second half of 1943, directly
challenging the Luftwaffe's fighter forces, that the true costs of Milch's
development decision began to make themselves felt. The mainstay of
the Luftwaffe's daytime defensive strength were Me 109s. Of the huge
increases in aircraft output achieved by Milch after 1942, these fighters
accounted for by far the largest share. When it was first combat-tested
in the Spanish Civil War in 1937, Messerschmitt's 109 had been state
of the art. Five years later, due to deficiencies in its aerodynamic design,

it was reaching the limit of its performance envelope. Equipped with bulky new engines, the 1943 version of the Me 109, the Me 109 G or 'Gustav', could match its British, American and Soviet rivals in straight-line speed, but only by sacrificing combat agility. According to one American ace who flew all the major combat aircraft of World War II, the poor handling of the Me 109 G made it 'unacceptable as a fighter', 'obsolete' from the start, 'a hopeless collection of lumps' and 'bumps'.[104] At combat speed, it required four seconds to turn into a 45-degree roll. For an aircraft flying at 500 kilometres per hour, this was absurdly sluggish. In low-altitude dogfights, Spitfire and Mustang pilots found that they could often provoke their hapless German counterparts into crashing into the ground, so slow was the Me 109 G to recover from any violent manoeuvre. Between 1942 and the end of 1944 Milch oversaw the production of almost 24,000 of these inferior aircraft. For thousands of Luftwaffe fliers who squeezed themselves into their cramped cockpits Milch's mass-produced Messerschmitts became little more than death traps.[105]

IV

The brief period between the spring and the autumn of 1942 was Speer's honeymoon. It was the perfect moment to launch the propaganda of the armaments miracle. Rising output coincided with the last phase of the war in which the Axis powers could dictate the pace and intensity of the fighting.[106] Up to the summer of 1942, it seemed as though Hitler's greatest gamble, his alliance with Japan against the United States, might actually pay off. In early 1942 the Japanese swept unchecked into Burma, Malaya, Indonesia and the Philippines dealing a death blow, if not to America, then at least to the British Empire in Asia. In the Atlantic the U-boats were wreaking havoc amongst unprotected American shipping. In North Africa, Rommel made extraordinary progress against inept opposition, taking Tobruk on 21 June 1942 and advancing rapidly towards Egypt. With Britain stumbling from one disaster to the next, it seemed that Hitler might still realize his fondest dream. Churchill faced a motion of no confidence in the Commons.[107] Perhaps the British might yet be driven out of the war. Meanwhile, the Ostheer appeared to have recovered from its shock of the winter.[108]

In May 1942 the Wehrmacht swatted aside a botched Soviet offensive towards Kharkov, yielding a haul of almost a quarter of a million prisoners. A few weeks later, General Manstein took a further 150,000 prisoners in the Crimea. The German army that began the great southern offensive on 28 June was weaker in every respect than that which had invaded the Soviet Union a year earlier. But, at first, Army Group South made astonishing progress. Stalin had deployed his remaining reserves, not in the South but in defence of Moscow. For the Russian units facing the main thrust of the German attack the overriding priority was to avoid any further encirclement. By the last week of July 1942 1st Panzer Army had stormed Rostov and the southern sector of the Soviet line was showing signs of disintegration. Buoyed by these early successes, Hitler split Army Group South into two prongs. The weaker northern flank drove due east towards Stalingrad on the Volga. The main force headed south-east towards the oil of the Caucasus. On 9 August an advance guard of mountain troops reaching Maikop, the closest of the Caucasian oilfields. The oil installations were so thoroughly sabotaged that the Germans decided that they would have to drill new wells. For this purpose, huge consignments of heavy drilling gear were laboriously hauled over the mountain passes. The German foothold was tenuous, and it remained unclear how the Germans would ship large quantities of oil out of the Caucasus even if they were able to hold their position. But the psychological boost of actually having reached the fabled oilfields was enormous. Even Baku now seemed within reach. On 30 August 1942, 3rd Panzer division seized a bridgehead over the Terek river, the last major natural obstacle en route to Grosny and the railway line south towards the Caspian.[109]

In public, at least, the Third Reich returned to its familiar tone of bravado. In July Hitler moved his headquarters to the Ukraine to be closer to the action and on 23 July he issued Directive No. 45, which announced that 'in a campaign of little more than three weeks, the broad goals set for the southern flank of the Eastern Front . . . have been essentially achieved. Only weak enemy forces . . . have succeeded in escaping envelopment . . .'[110] It again seemed as though the Soviet Union might be on the point of collapse. Given the disappointment of the previous winter and spring, the German public was initially somewhat suspicious.[111] However, by the end of July 1942 the Gestapo was reporting a wave of optimism, which Goebbels and Goering did their best to fan into a fever of excitement. The focus was now squarely on the plunder to be had in the Ukraine. And as we have seen, a renewed and ruthless effort was being made to ensure that Germany did actually receive increased food deliveries from the occupied territories. The summer of 1942 was to be the last great season for projects of Eastern settlement and racial empire. Whilst the oil troops laboured in Maikop, Kontinental Oel, Germany's freshly minted oil major, hatched plans to take control of British oil assets in Egypt.[112] In Russia, the Einsatzgruppen were well into the second phase of their ghastly programme of murder. Between 17 and 19 July Heinrich Himmler visited Auschwitz and the General Government to transmit his fateful instructions from Berlin. The shock of December 1941 was fading into the background. Having broken the Red Army and conquered the southern Soviet Union, the Nazi regime would no longer have to face a major threat in the East. It would need only to defend its continental empire against Britain and America. As in the previous year, Hitler even speculated about the possibility of releasing hundreds of thousands of skilled German workers from the army to concentrate on the production needs of the Luftwaffe and the navy.[113]

But despite this wave of optimism, the anxieties first unleashed by the winter crisis of 1941–2 were never completely silenced. As we have seen, the coal–steel balance on which the continuation of Speer's armaments miracle depended had already become critical in August. The terms in which Hitler threatened Pleiger on 11 August were in stark contrast to the optimism being doled out so thickly by Goering and Goebbels. For Hans Kehrl, who had not been privy to the desperate conversations of the previous winter, Hitler's open talk of the possibility of defeat was profoundly disconcerting.[114] A few weeks earlier Hitler had stunned another audience by announcing that unless the oil wells of the Caucasus were taken by the end of the year that too would mean the end of the war.[115] Ever more, it was the looming battle with the Western powers that was preoccupying Hitler.[116] By August, Churchill had ridden out the disasters of the first half of the year and Hitler was afraid that, in the event of a sudden Soviet collapse, the British and Americans would attempt an immediate, improvised landing in France or Norway. So seriously did he take this possibility that he ordered the redeployment of several high quality SS divisions from the Eastern Front to the West. In addition, on 13 August 1942 he set in motion the accelerated construction of the monstrous Atlantikwall, his Maginot Line on the sea.

Hitler knew that if he wanted to permanently cripple the anti-Nazi coalition he had only a few more months to finish the war in the East. But as in 1941 this begged the question: was the Red Army actually defeated? General Halder, chief of army staff, was already convinced by the end of July that the Ostheer was too weak to be able to force the Red Army to a decisive defeat. On 23 July, the day that Rostov was taken and Hitler announced the achievement of the major objectives of the southern operation, Halder confided to his diary that the 'chronic tendency to underrate enemy capabilities is gradually assuming grotesque proportions and develops into a positive danger'.[117] Halder's gloom was confirmed only days later by a violent Soviet counter-attack directed towards Rzhev at the heart of Army Group Centre.[118] As Fromm had already spelled out in February 1942, the Ostheer was running out of manpower. Since starting its offensive, Army Group South had suffered 280,000 losses, of which only half had been replaced. All told, Halder expected a deficit of 750,000 soldiers by November 1942, more than the entire cohort of teenagers to be expected by the end of the year.[119] And the situation was made even worse at the end of August, when the Soviet Northern Front launched a massive attempt to break the encirclement of Leningrad.[120] Army Group North did manage to seal off the Soviet penetration and eventually to destroy the attacking Soviet force. But it did so at the cost of at least 26,000 casualties, negating any hope Hitler might have had of crushing the Soviet defences in the city.[121] At the end of September 1942 General Fromm, as chief of the army's armaments supply, submitted a memorandum to Hitler demanding a negotiated end to the war as the only way of saving Germany from disaster. Fromm had a close working relationship with Speer, who was fully informed of Fromm's views. But Speer remained silent. Hitler was in no mood for defeatism. By the end of September he had replaced Halder as chief of staff and Fromm was well on his way to political oblivion.[122]

As the bitter resistance of the Red Army prolonged the war in the East into its second year, the odds against the Wehrmacht lengthened. As compared to the autumn of 1941, when the Germans and their allies had at times enjoyed substantial numerical superiority over the Red Army, by the autumn of 1942 the correlation of forces favoured the Soviets by a margin that tended towards 2 to 1.[123] Given the horrendous casualties suffered by the Soviets up to the autumn of 1942, this was as much a testament to the extraordinary mobilizing capacity of Stalin's regime as a reflection of the underlying demographic balance. Even more remarkable, however, was the fact that, at key points in the line, the Soviets were able to back their superiority in manpower with a similar preponderance of guns, tanks and aircraft. The fact was that despite the optimistic newsreel propaganda, Speer and Milch were losing the battle of the factories. Even leaving aside the British and Americans, who produced under far more favourable circumstances, Germany was being outdone by the embattled Soviet Union. If there was a true 'armaments miracle' in 1942 it occurred, not in Germany, but in the armaments factories in the Urals. Despite having suffered territorial losses and disruption that resulted in a 25 per cent fall in total national product, the Soviet Union in 1942 managed to out-produce Germany in virtually every category of weapons. The margin for small arms and artillery was 3:1. For tanks it was a staggering 4:1, a differential compounded by the superior quality of the T34 tank. Even in combat aircraft the margin was 2:1.[124] It was this industrial superiority, contrary to every expectation, that allowed the Red Army, first to absorb the Wehrmacht's second great onslaught and then in November 1942 to launch a whole series of devastating counterattacks. It would be quite wrong, of course, to attribute the successes of the Red Army after the summer of 1942 entirely to brute force. By the autumn of 1942 the Red Army leadership was developing a capacity for operational planning to match that of all but the very best on the German side. On the other hand, it is also undeniable that the triumphs of Zhukov and his colleagues would have been impossible but for the excellent military material supplied by Russia's factories.

To avoid misunderstandings, this is emphatically a story of Soviet success not German failure. In the third full year of the war there was little difference between the level of German and British armaments production. Two economies which in 1936 had had industrial sectors of roughly equal size were now producing roughly similar levels of armaments output.[125] Britain of course benefited from the abundance of lend-lease, whereas Germany had to make do with far more meagre pickings in occupied Europe. Alongside armaments, Germany in 1942 also produced a far larger volume of investment goods than Britain, an advantage that would pay off by 1944 in substantially higher armaments output. The exceptional performer was the Soviet Union, which in 1942 produced twice as many infantry weapons, as many artillery pieces and almost as many combat aircraft and tanks as the United States, the undisputed manufacturing champion of the world. The Soviet miracle was not due to Western assistance. Lend-lease did not begin to affect the balance on the Eastern Front until 1943. The best single explanation for this remarkable triumph was the extraordinary concentration of Soviet production on a limited number of weapons produced in a hand- • ful of giant factories, permitting the fullest possible realization of economies of mass-production.[126] But what is also clear is that the production miracle came at the expense of enormous sacrifice on the Soviet home front, where hundreds of thousands if not millions of people starved to death for the sake of the war effort.[127] With farm labour cut to the bone, to permit the maximum concentration of manpower on the Red Army and on armaments production, only those who worked received adequate rations. By the same token, the extraordinary pitch of mobilization achieved by the Soviet Union in 1942 and early 1943 was not sustainable. By 1944 Germany had clawed back the Soviet advantage in every category. By then, however, it no longer mattered. As Albert Speer and Erhard Milch well knew, 1942 was the pivotal year in the war. If the Third Reich was to have any chance of survival, they needed to give Army Group South the necessary equipment to inflict a crippling defeat on the Red Army. And thanks to the extraordinary efforts of the Soviet Union, they failed.

18

No Room for Doubt

Though the exhaustion of the German Army in the East could no longer be ignored by the autumn of 1942, the material superiority of Hitler's enemies first made itself overwhelmingly felt, not on the Eastern Front, but in North Africa.[1] And the moment at which the balance shifted can be timed very precisely. On 21 June 1942 Rommel's tiny Afrika Korps humiliated the much larger British 8th Army at Tobruk. In immediate response, President Roosevelt dispatched the first of a series of emergency convoys to Egypt, loaded with 400 American tanks and self-propelled artillery. Once they arrived in Suez the Afrika Korps, whose tank strength rarely exceeded 250 vehicles, would be hopelessly outnumbered. After the first bloody confrontation at El Alamein at the end of July 1942, Rommel knew that he had no more than a few weeks in which to achieve a decisive success against the Commonwealth forces blocking the route to the Suez Canal. By 6 September, thanks to dogged Commonwealth resistance, massive British air superiority and a chronic shortage of petrol, Rommel's last offensive had ground inconclusively to a halt at Alam el Halfa. The first Sherman tanks arrived in Egypt in the first days of September. By 11 September their number had risen to more than 300. General Montgomery could begin his counter-offensive confident of overwhelming numerical superiority. On the night of 23–4 October, at the second battle of El Alamein, the 8th Army attacked with a fleet of almost 1,000 tanks, at least half of which were American-built and equipped with powerful 75 millimetre guns. By contrast, Rommel had only 123 up-to-date Mark IIIs and Mark IVs; the rest of his strength were obsolete light tanks. Montgomery's force of 200,000 men was made up of troops from Britain, South Africa, New Zealand, Australia and India. Rommel and his Italian allies could muster barely 100,000. Despite the heavy losses suffered by the Commonwealth forces, the outcome was never in doubt. By 4 November the Afrika Korps began a three-week retreat that did not halt until 26 November on the Marsa el Brega position almost 400 kilometres west along the Libyan coastline. By then the Western Allies had already delivered a second formidable demonstration of their strategic reach.[2] On 8 November 1942 a fleet of almost 700 vessels, accompanied by no less than 5 battleships, 7 aircraft carriers and 14 cruisers, landed 63,000 men and 430 tanks simultaneously on three beachheads in Morocco and Algeria. Thirty-five thousand men under General Patton had been projected straight across the Atlantic from Chesapeake Bay. The rest had steamed down to Africa from the Firth of Clyde.

On the Eastern Front, the summer campaign was following the pattern already established in 1941.[3] The huge expanse of Soviet territory and the fierce resistance of the Red Army stretched the Germans to the limit. For three bitter months Zhukov pinned the 6th Army in the ruins of Stalingrad, tempting Hitler to commit more and more armour and infantry.[4] The Soviets in the mean time, under cover of deception and maximum secrecy, concentrated fresh reserves on the flanks, along the Don and the lower course of the Volga. This time, unlike in December 1941, the Red Army had the weight of numbers firmly on its side. Along the entire Southern Front, the Soviet advantage was probably in the order of two to one. But more important was the fact that the Red Army had now perfected the principle of concentration that the Germans had put to such good use early in the war. On the crucial South-western Front, from which the Red Army was to launch the first arm of the Stalingrad encirclement, 12 full-strength assault divisions with hundreds of tanks and more than 170,000 troops were massed along a sector of only 22 kilometres.[5] When the storm broke on 19 November the Romanian 3rd Army and an understrength German Panzer corps were simply torn apart. It was, a German officer later wrote, 'a picture of horror. Whipped by the fear of the Soviet tanks, [German] trucks, command vehicles, motorbikes, horsemen and horse-carts raced westwards, crashed, got stuck, turned over, blocked the road. In the midst of all this, pedestrians thrust, pushed, pressed and rolled their way through. Whoever tripped and fell to the ground did not get back on their feet. They were trampled, run over and flattened.'[6] On 20 November the full intent of the Soviet offensive became clear when to the south of Stalingrad the Soviet 51st Army blasted its way through the weak

Romanian screening forces and raced north-west towards the Don. By 23 November the Soviet pincers had linked up, encircling the German 6th Army, as well as the remnants of the 4th Panzer Army and Romanian 3rd and 4th armies. The last survivors surrendered on 2 February 1943, after a ten-week siege, for the loss of 250,000 Wehrmacht soldiers as well as uncounted numbers of Italians, Romanians and Soviet auxiliaries. Two weeks earlier, the Soviet counterattack had forced the abandonment of the German foothold in the Caucasus. By the middle of February 1943, the ragged Ostheer had been forced back to the positions from which it had started its offensive the previous June. At this point, the battlefield superiority of the German army was still sufficient to halt the slide. Rommel in North Africa and Manstein in the Ukraine were able for a time at least to stabilize the situation and to halt the Allied offensives. However, the lull was only short lived. As the Eastern Front lapsed into exhausted calm, the British and Americans renewed their attrition of the Afrika Korps in Tunisia, completing their inevitable victory on 13 May 1943. 'Tunisgrad' cost Germany another 290,000 men.

Things were going no better in the naval war.[7] Having redeployed in the spring of 1942 from the Atlantic coast to Norwegian waters, the German surface fleet quietly ended its war in December 1942.[8] There was insufficient fuel to sustain long-range operations. There were no aircraft carriers to provide air cover. Germany could well do without the propaganda disaster of losing a capital ship. Far more important, however, was the fate of the U-boats. In the spring of 1943 they were still doing terrible damage to Allied merchant shipping. Between 16 and 20 March 1943 convoys HX 229 and SC 122, totalling 100 ships, fought the biggest single convoy battle of the war with three packs of 40 U-boats. The Allies lost 21 vessels rated at 140,842 tons. Dozens of U-boats were badly damaged, but only one was sunk. It was, declared Admiral Doenitz, the greatest victory of the U-boat arm. But such successes could not disguise the increasingly one-sided nature of the battle. Of the seventeen major convoys crossing the Atlantic in mid-March 1943, the U-boats intercepted only three. Though total U-boat sinkings in March 1943 came to almost 650,000 tons, this was not enough to seriously threaten the trans-Atlantic supply line. Losses of Allied shipping ran at in excess of 500,000 tons per month throughout 1942 and early 1943, but were more than made up by the enormous production of America's dockyards, which were now capable of turning out more than a million tons of shipping per month. From August 1942 onwards, under constant U-boat attack, Allied shipping capacity was expanding not contracting. Meanwhile, U-boat losses were rising alarmingly. Guided by the decrypts of the U-boats' radio communications, deploying new sonar equipment and complete air supremacy, the British and American navies broke the submarine menace. By May 1943, Admiral Doenitz was losing U-boats and crews at the rate of one per day. With a fifth of his Atlantic fleet sunk in a single month, Doenitz gave the order on 24 May 1943 for the wolf-packs to withdraw. Unable to sustain a battle of attrition against the overwhelming industrial and technological superiority of its enemies, the weakest branch of the German armed forces had been knocked out of the war.

I

The response by Hitler and Speer to the disasters of early 1943 was predictable: a heightened mobilization drive and a crescendo of 'armaments propaganda'.[9] The soldiers of the 6th Army would not die in vain.[10] The slow-motion destruction of the last hopeless pockets of resistance in Stalingrad had given the rest of the German Southern Front the chance to withdraw in reasonably good order to a position not much different from that which they had occupied in June 1942. Germany still controlled most of the Ukraine and the coal and iron ore of the Donetz. For three months, Hitler ordered all the output of Speer's Ministry to be directed exclusively to the Eastern Front.[11] On 13 January 1943, Keitel, Hans Lammers and Martin Bormann installed themselves as a triumvirate with the mission to oversee the total mobilization of the German population for war work. Every last man and woman in the country was to be registered by the labour exchanges and assessed for the contribution they might make to the war effort. All businesses in the civilian sector were to be subject to ruthless investigation. Those that were not strictly essential to the war effort were to be closed down. Armaments output in the first months of 1943 was expanding rapidly on a broad front. By the end of May 1943 it was almost 120 per cent higher than when Speer took over. Half of this increase was accounted for by the Luftwaffe, the rest by Speer's sector, in which ammunition, artillery and infantry weapons continued to dominate. But 'progress on a broad front' was not the rallying cry that Speer and Hitler needed in the desperate winter of 1942–3. They needed a 'big story' with which to re-energize the home front. The answer was the Adolf Hitler Panzer Programme, announced to enormous fanfare on 22 January 1943.[12]

Tanks were, of course, nothing new for the German armaments effort and Speer clearly appreciated their symbolic importance from the outset. Within days of taking office he had made an extended visit to the tank-proving grounds at Sankt Johann and Kummersdorf where he was photographed at the helm of the latest vehicles.[13] As we have seen, the tank committee had drastically scaled up its production programme as early as the summer of 1941. The new models – the Panther and the Tiger – had been eagerly anticipated since the summer of 1942. Gigantic new production centres were under construction, most notably the Nibelungenwerk at Sankt Valentin near Linz. In early September 1942, Speer agreed with Rohland, the chair of the Main Committee for Tanks, on a new production target of 1,400 vehicles per month by the spring of 1944, made up of 600 Panthers, 50 Tigers, 150 light tanks and a mixture of 600 assault guns and self-propelled artillery.[14] Under the impact of the Stalingrad disaster, Hitler took the impulsive decision to double this figure. By the end of 1944, he now expected 900 tanks and no less than 2,000 assault guns per month. The decree empowering Speer to carry out the Adolf Hitler Panzer Programme was couched, not in the technocratic language of rationalization, but in the drastic rhetoric of Total War. Achieving an 'immediate increase in tank production' was 'of such decisive importance for the outcome of the war, that all civilian and military agencies are to support this production drive with all available resources under the direction of the Reich Ministry of Armaments and Ammunition'.[15] Tank production was to be 'amply and generously' provided with labour, raw materials, energy and machines, 'even if this meant that other important programmes of the armaments economy were temporarily disadvantaged'. Workers in tank firms were to be exempt from call-ups and all those drafted by the Wehrmacht since 18 December 1942 were to be returned to their factories. Anyone failing to cooperate in the Adolf Hitler Panzer Programme would find themselves in front of the dreaded Volksgerichtshof. The decree was coupled with a major patriotic appeal to the tank workforce delivered at the Alkett-Rheinmetall tank plant in Berlin by Speer and Goebbels.[16] Tank factories were authorized to go over to a seventy-two-hour working week. Henschel's Tiger tank plant in Kassel worked around the clock in two twelve-hour shifts from the autumn of 1942. Some Stakhanovites, caught up in the enthusiasm of the Fuehrer's programme, apparently volunteered to work back-to-back twenty-four-hour stints.[17] By way of compensation, the heroes of National Socialist labour were provided with extra food, vitamin pills and special rations of clothing. Speer singled them out for decorations. An entire Tyrolese holiday resort was reserved for the use of their families.[18] In the newsreels, Speer was shown shaking hands with tank workers and their children, alongside General Guderian, the new tank supremo.

There can be no doubt that the Wehrmacht needed more tanks. By the last week of January 1943, the Ostheer had been battered to the point where it had only 495 Panzers on its books, not all of which were in working order.[19] Nor can there be any argument with the effectiveness of the Adolf Hitler Panzer Programme. The number of tanks produced in May 1943 was more than twice the number produced in the autumn of 1942. Measured by weight, the introduction of the new heavier models meant that total production increased by as much as 160 per cent. However, the extraordinary propagandistic emphasis given to the Adolf Hitler Programme and the extraordinary powers granted to Speer to implement it, were out of all proportion to the significance of the tank in the overall war effort. Even at the height of the Adolf Hitler Programme, the share of tanks in total armaments production did not exceed 7 per cent. Meanwhile, other sectors were severely disadvantaged, both in practical and symbolic terms.[20] Speer's tank propaganda had its intended effect in focusing every German industrialist on the new top priority. Even if other programmes had high-priority rankings they found it hard to get the attention of key sub-contractors. The Luftwaffe, in particular, found it virtually impossible to get prompt delivery of crankshafts for aero-engines, given the priority now enjoyed by the Maybach tank engine factory. The Adolf Hitler Programme also hogged more than its fair share of freight capacity, holding up critical deliveries. So overwhelming was the furore created by the Programme, that the Luftwaffe resorted to the absurd expedient of applying 'Panzer priority' to aircraft orders, a privilege first granted by the Zentrale Planung in April 1943. And despite these handicaps, it was Milch's aircraft production, not Speer's tank programme, that was chiefly responsible for the continuing upsurge in armaments output in the first half of 1943.

In May 1943 Milch matched Speer's tank triumph with an even more dramatic record of his own: the production of 2,200 combat aircraft in a single month. This was in every respect a more significant achievement than Speer's heralded production of 1,270 tanks. For Karl Frydag, who, as senior engineer at Henschel, oversaw both the production of the Tiger tank *and* the Main Committee for Airframes, there was no comparison: 'Tank production and Luftwaffe production are always being compared to each other. They cannot be compared; tank production is dirt, when set against the Luftwaffe.'[21] In light of the armaments statistics, it is hard to disagree. In terms of value produced or resources consumed, the production of combat aircraft was at least five times more important than the output of tanks.

The Adolf Hitler Panzer Programme maintained the propagandistic excitement surrounding Speer's Armaments Ministry in the first half of 1943.[22] However, what would determine the future of armaments production was the supply of steel. Driving their workers and plants to breaking point, the steel mills managed to raise output in March 1943 to in excess of 2.7 million tons, sufficient to 'fund' a record Wehrmacht allocation of more than 1.4 million monthly tons in the first quarter of 1943.[23] Following the temporary stabilization of the Eastern Front in early April 1943, Speer and Hitler optimistically discussed the possibility of raising steel output by a further 1 million tons, enabling the extraordinary increases in armaments output to be continued into another year.[24] In late May 1943, as the Ostheer readied itself for its last great effort to stabilize the Eastern Front by means of an attack against the Soviet salient at Kursk, the Reich steel association presented detailed estimates of what might be possible, if Germany could retain control of the manganese deposits of the Ukraine. On the assumption that Field Marshal Manstein could hold Krivoj Rog, the RVE predicted that it could reach 3 million monthly tons of steel by October 1944, rising to 3.25 million tons in April of 1945.[25] On this basis, Speer expected armaments output to go on increasing, at the spectacular rate achieved in his first year of office, for at least another year.

In the spring of 1943, however, the German war economy itself was sucked directly into the fighting. As we have seen, the threat of Anglo-American bombing had bulked large in German strategic thinking at least since 1940. But until early 1943 it proved remarkably easy to counter. The Royal Air Force simply did not have enough heavy bombers to do sustained damage to the German home front, nor did it have the technology necessary to guide them to their targets. The heavy air raids on Luebeck (28/29 March 1942), Rostock (23/24 April 1942) and the 'thousand-bomber raids' on Cologne (30/31 May 1942) and Essen (1 June 1942) gave some indication of what was in store, but they did not develop into a sustained campaign of aerial destruction.[26] It was not until March 1943 that RAF Bomber Command had the planes with which to mount a prolonged attack on the heart of German heavy industry, or the technology with which to guide them to their targets. The 'Battle of the Ruhr' began on 5 March with an attack on the industrial city of Essen, the home of Krupp.[27] Between 8.58 p.m. and 9.36 p.m., following the invisible beam of the OBOE electronic guidance system, 362 bombers hit the main target with a combination of incendiaries and high explosives leaving a trail of blazing destruction.[28] This time the RAF not only attacked in force but returned repeatedly over a period of five months, dropping a total of 34,000 tons of bombs. The sequence of heavy attacks was relentless and interspersed by daily harassing raids by small forces of light Mosquito bombers. Heavy attacks were delivered against every major node of the Ruhr conurbation: Essen (5 March, 12/13 March, 3/4 April, 30 April, 27 May, 25 July), Duisburg (26/27 March, 8/9 April, 26/27 April, 12/13 May), Bochum (13/14 May, 12 June), Krefeld (21 June), Duesseldorf (25 May, 11 June) and Dortmund (4 May, 23 May), Barmen-Wuppertal (29 May), Muelheim (22 June), Elberfeld-Wuppertal (24 June), Gelsenkirchen (25 June, 9 July), Cologne (16 June, 28 June, 3 July, 8 July). To increase the misery, on 16 May specially adapted bombs destroyed the dams on the Moehne and Eder rivers, inundating the surrounding countryside and cutting off the water supply. The bombers killed thousands of people and did heavy damage to the urban fabric. Above all, however, they struck against the most vital node in the German industrial economy, precisely at the moment that Hitler, Speer and the RVE were hoping to energize armaments production with a fresh surge in steel production.

Reading contemporary sources, there can be no doubt that the Battle of the Ruhr marked a turning point in the history of the German war economy, which has been grossly underestimated by post-war accounts.[29] As Speer himself acknowledged, the RAF was hitting the right target.[30] The Ruhr was not only Europe's most important producer of coking coal and steel, it was also a crucial source of intermediate components of all kinds. Disrupting production in the Ruhr had the capacity to halt assembly lines across Germany. When the first of the heavy raids struck Krupp in Essen, Speer immediately travelled to the Ruhr with a view to learning general lessons in disaster management.[31] He was forced to return in May, June and July to energize the emergency response and to rally the workforce with well-advertised displays of personal bravery.[32] The Ruhr was raised from the status of the home front to that of a war zone. Speer established a special emergency staff with absolute authority over the local economy and made plans for the total evacuation of the non-essential population. The remaining workforce was to be organized along para-military lines, uniformed and housed in camp accommodation so that they could be redeployed at a moment's notice to whichever plants were still operational.[33] But all Speer could do was to limit the damage. He could not stop the bombers or prevent them from seriously disrupting the German war effort. Following the onset of heavy air raids in the first quarter of 1943, steel production fell by 200,000 tons. Having anticipated an increase in total steel production to more than 2.8 million tons per month and allocated steel accordingly, the Zentrale Planung now faced a shortfall of almost 400,000 tons. All the painstaking effort that had gone into reorganizing the rationing system was negated by the ability of the British to disrupt production more or less at will. In light of the steel shortage, Hitler and Speer had no option but to implement an immediate cut to the ammunition programme.[34] After more than doubling in 1942, ammunition production in 1943 increased by only 20 per cent.[35] And it was not just ammunition that was hit. In the summer of 1943, the disruption in the Ruhr manifested itself across the German economy in a so-called 'Zulieferungskrise' (sub-components crisis). All manner of parts, castings and forgings were suddenly in short supply.[36] And this affected not only heavy industry directly, but the entire armaments complex. Most significantly, the shortage of key components brought the rapid increase in Luftwaffe production to an abrupt halt. Between July 1943 and March 1944 there was no further increase in the monthly output of aircraft. For the armaments effort as a whole, the period of stagnation lasted throughout the second half of 1943. As Speer himself acknowledged, Allied bombing had negated all plans for a further increase in production.[37] Bomber Command had stopped Speer's armaments miracle in its tracks.

Worse was to come. The mood of relative calm that had prevailed in the spring and early summer of 1943 depended above all on the temporary stabilization of the Eastern Front. But it was clear to both sides that this lull could not last. It was only a matter of time before the Red Army resumed its bloody efforts to expel the German invaders. In an attempt to anticipate and disrupt the Soviet summer offensive, the Germans after weeks of delay launched their own offensive on 5 July against the Kursk salient. The resulting confrontation was one of the largest land battles in history.[38] But in retrospect it seems like an exercise in perverse futility. In 1941, the Wehrmacht had attacked the Soviet Union on three fronts simultaneously, on a line stretching more than 1,000 kilometres from end to end. In 1942, Hitler had been forced to confine himself to the Southern Front using only one Army Group. In 1943, operation Zitadelle was directed against a single salient, at the junction of two Army Groups.[39] Rather than a climactic turning point, the battle at Kursk turned out to be a pointer to the hopelessness of Germany's situation. To ward off the German attack and prepare for their own counter-stroke, the Soviets had massed 1.3 million men in the Central and Voronezh fronts. Another 573,000 were held in reserve. By contrast, even after stripping their reserves the Germans could offer up only 777,000 men. The efforts of the Adolf Hitler Panzer Programme had certainly served to improve the quality of the German tank force. Two hundred of the new Panthers and 146 Tigers had been especially assembled to lead the assault. In addition, the Panzer divisions were now increasingly equipped with new versions of the Mark IV, with a powerful 75 millimetre gun. The Soviets by contrast were still relying on the first generation of T-34s. The problem for the German Panzer divisions was no longer quality, but quantity. Having concentrated 70 per cent of its entire tank force on the Eastern Front at Kursk, the Wehrmacht could field 2,451 tanks and assault guns, as opposed to a Soviet strength of 5,128 vehicles. The Luftwaffe was at a similar disadvantage in the air. And in artillery the odds against the Germans stretched to more than 4 to 1. Most importantly, the Germans had forfeited any element of surprise, a key element in their success both in 1941 and 1942.[40] Thanks to excellent intelligence, the Soviet defences were so well prepared that the German army was not even able to achieve a substantial initial penetration. For the first time since the beginning of the war, a German offensive failed at its earliest stage. After

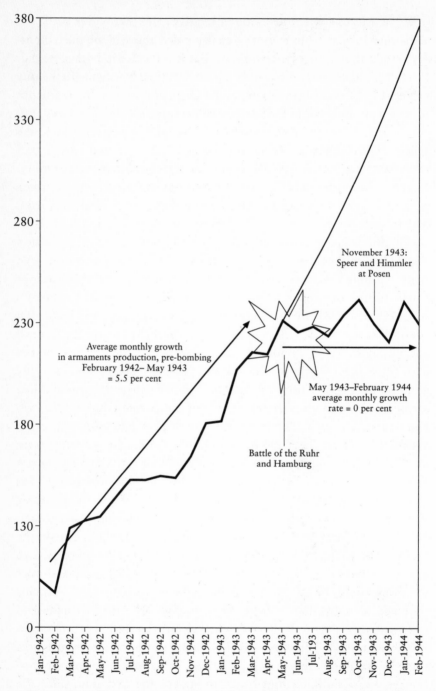

Figure 22. The armaments miracle halted: two years of armaments
production under Speer (January–February 1942 = 100)

suffering 50,000 casualties in a fortnight of fighting and after a vast expenditure of material, the last German offensive on the Eastern Front was called off. The Wehrmacht was given no chance to recover. It was the Red Army alone that now dictated the pace of events. Even before the Germans had halted their attack, the Red Army had gone over to the offensive in the central section of the front line.[41] In August they began a second massive assault against Army Group South, driving it back to the Dnieper. The Soviet Union was now significantly assisted, for the first time, by deliveries of aid from the United States. Hundreds of thousands of American cargo trucks and half-tracks motorized the Red Army's logistical train, enabling it to maintain a relentless pace of advance throughout 1943 and 1944.[42]

Only three days after the Germans launched their assault at Kursk, the British and Americans landed on Sicily.[43] Inexcusably, the Allies allowed the Germans to evacuate their garrison, permitting them to mount a vigorous defence of the Italian mainland without having to divert substantial forces from the Eastern Front. But the political repercussions of the invasion were dramatic. On 25 July 1943 the Italian army deposed Mussolini, sending shock waves throughout international public opinion. The days of the fascist dictators were now clearly numbered. That same night the RAF launched one last attack on Essen, combined with a probing raid against Hamburg. Three days later the British bombers returned and incinerated Germany's second city in an apocalyptic firestorm the like of which the world had never seen.[44] No fire had ever reached the intensity of heat generated in the eastern districts of Hamburg early in the morning of Wednesday, 28 July. Glass melted. Human bodies were mummified. Forty thousand people suffocated or were burned alive. In a matter of days, the British and American air forces destroyed a quarter of a million homes and reduced a large part of the central city to a mountain of 43 million cubic metres of rubble. Nine hundred thousand people were driven to flight. Panic and disorder spread throughout the surrounding towns and rural areas. It appeared to be the vindication of all the hopes that Churchill and the rest of the British leadership had for so long invested in strategic bombing. RAF Bomber Command was finally developing into a truly war-winning weapon.

II

In fact, it was to take nearly two more years to finish off the Third Reich. In Italy, the fighting was prolonged until the very end of the war. The bloodletting on the Eastern Front did not reach its nightmarish climax until the first weeks of 1945. The RAF was to try night after night, but in 1943 it managed to ignite only one more firestorm, in Kassel on 22 October.[45] That killed 6,000 people, a slightly higher percentage of the population even than in Hamburg. Eight thousand people were blinded by the effects of smoke and heat; 123,800, or 62 per cent of the population, were 'dehoused'. Production of Tiger tanks and heavy 8.8 centimetre anti-tank guns was set back for months. After that, however, the RAF was distracted by the fruitless effort to repeat in Berlin what had been achieved in Hamburg.[46] Though the attraction of Berlin as a target was obvious, it was a far larger objective than any of the Ruhr cities and it was at the very limit of RAF range. Furthermore, in industrial terms Berlin was nowhere near as promising a target as the Ruhr. Not that Berlin was not an important centre of armaments production. But Berlin was pre-eminently a centre of manufacturing, by contrast with the Ruhr, which was Germany's chief supplier of the most basic inputs of coal and steel.[47] Shutting down the Ruhr and the transport links that connected it to the rest of Germany had the potential to disrupt production throughout the entire country. The repeated raids on the Ruhr in 1943 had exacted a terrible toll from RAF Bomber Command. Nearly 4,000 crew were killed or taken prisoner, and 640 bombers were shot down or crashed. Terrible as this attrition was, however, thanks to the mounting output of the British aircraft factories, the RAF's bomber strength actually increased between February and August 1943.[48] The Ruhr was the choke point and in 1943 it was within the RAF's grip. The failure to maintain that hold and to tighten it was a tragic operational error. The ongoing disaster that Speer and his cohorts clearly expected in the summer of 1943 was put off for another year.

With hindsight, therefore, it is clear that the Third Reich was not yet finished. But the impact on contemporaries of the events of July 1943 cannot be exaggerated. Even the most rabid adherents of the Third Reich could hardly deny that the 'end was nigh'. Hans Kehrl faced this reality, on the first night of Hamburg's devastation, when he was woken by a telephone call from his close associate Gauleiter Karl Kaufmann, who begged him to accelerate the delivery of several trainloads of quicklime, which would be needed for the rapid disposal of tens of thousands of corpses.[49] After Kehrl rushed to the Ministry and was informed of the dimensions of the disaster, he suffered a temporary collapse. For the first time in years, this obsessive workaholic was forced to return home where he spent hours roaming around his garden in a daze. Not surprisingly, as the news from Hamburg leaked, the Gestapo picked up reports of shock and dismay from across the country. Mussolini's sudden removal added to the panic. The SD noted that party members were no longer wearing their party badges in public and people were avoiding the Hitler salute wherever possible.[50] Speer found that even party audiences no longer responded to his boasts about the triumphs of the armaments miracle.[51] Amongst senior industrial leaders, the SD reported, there was no longer anyone who believed in the possibility of a German victory.[52] To admit as much in public, however, was extremely dangerous.

The Nazi leadership reacted to the crisis of morale with a determined escalation of violence.[53] On 24 August 1943 Heinrich Himmler, Reichsfuehrer of the SS, took over the Interior Ministry. By the end of the year the regional bosses of the Nazi party, the Gauleiter, had been formally instituted as the overseeing authority of local government. The party and the state were increasingly fused and it was the party that set the tone. The politicization of the judiciary, which had taken on ever more aggressive forms since the beginning of the war, was intensified. By 1943 the courts were issuing death penalties against Germans for defeatism and sabotage at the rate of a hundred a week. Even prominent businessmen were no longer immune. Indeed, Heinrich Himmler and the Gestapo made a point of singling out bourgeois defeatists for especially aggressive reprisals. In the autumn of 1943 two senior branch managers of the Deutsche Bank were arrested and executed for making defeatist remarks.[54] A designated board member of the electricity giant RWE suffered the same fate, despite the intervention of Albert Voegler.[55] In this drive to impose discipline on the German home front, Himmler could count on the full support of Albert Speer. As the crisis of the Third Reich deepened, Speer moved closer than ever before to the absolute centre of power. In so doing he made himself into one of the foremost advocates of radicalization and used his authority ruthlessly to silence debate about the wider rationale of the war effort.

Speer, of course, was not blind to the seriousness of Germany's situation. When the Zentrale Planung met on 29 July 1943 Hamburg was still burning and Speer could not avoid drawing drastic conclusions:

Only if the enemy air attacks can be stopped will it be possible to think of an increase in production. If, however, the air attacks continue on the same scale as hitherto, they [the Zentrale Planung] would, within twelve weeks, be automatically relieved of a lot of questions that they were now discussing ... A greater output of fighter aircraft is the only means of preventing everything being smashed up, otherwise they might as well put a bullet through their heads.[56]

There were some members of the German leadership who took this literally. On 18 August 1943, Hans Jeschonnek, the Luftwaffe chief of staff, the man most immediately responsible for the conduct of the German air war, shot himself.[57] Erhard Milch completely lost his composure, proclaiming to an audience of Gauleiter, Ministers and senior civil servants: 'We have lost the war! Definitely lost it.' Hitler was forced to dispatch Goebbels to administer what they referred to as a 'shot of cement'.[58] Speer, for his part, refused to countenance any defeatism. The crisis of the summer of 1943 provided him with an opportunity to expand the reach of his Ministry and to mobilize more resources for the war effort.[59] Hitherto, the civilian Ministry of Economic Affairs had retained responsibility for raw materials and rights of supervision of those firms that were not under the control of the Wehrmacht. Speer's aim was to mobilize hundreds of thousands of extra workers for the war effort, by conducting a thorough 'comb-out' of this civilian sector.

On the day before the attack on Hamburg, Speer held a meeting with Hans Kehrl, who by now was the leading man at the civilian Economics Ministry, to discuss the terms of the merger. Kehrl was a ruthless Nazi. However, he was also well informed and independent minded. From his years of experience in Nazi industrial politics, he was one of the keenest critics of Speer's armaments propaganda. Kehrl had seen the Four Year Plan come and go. He had no time for Speer's loose talk of armaments miracles, or for his managerial style of 'organized improvisation'.[60] As the man most closely involved in the technicalities of raw material rationing, Kehrl was all too familiar with the real constraints that limited Germany's military potential. When Speer made his imperious demand that Kehrl and his entire department should subordinate themselves to the Reich Armaments Ministry, Kehrl responded by asking him for an explanation as to the wider strategic purpose of the German war effort.[61] Speer responded with shocked indignation. 'It was completely outlandish', he declared, 'to imagine that after returning from the Fuehrer headquarters the Minister would report ... on the political situation, let alone about the content of his discussions with the Fuehrer.'[62] Kehrl thereupon asked to be allowed to resign from the Ministry, only to be informed a few days later that failure to comply with Speer's design would be construed as tantamount to desertion.[63] Over the following months, Kehrl and his raw-materials staff were duly merged into the Armaments Ministry, where Kehrl also took responsibility for setting up the Planning Office (Planungsamt), the expert think tank that went a long way towards rationalizing the discussions of the Zentrale Planung.

Nor did Speer limit himself to the verbal intimidation of his colleagues. Since the armaments miracle was the basis of his authority and since propaganda and persuasion were clearly no longer enough to secure its continuation, Speer resorted to the full repressive apparatus of the Nazi regime. From the summer of 1943 onwards, in the hope of restarting the expansion in armaments production, Speer moved into an ever closer alliance with Heinrich Himmler. At the end of July 1943 Speer agreed that plant security operations in the armaments industry should be overseen by the SS.[64] And on 5 October 1943 Speer signed a formal memorandum of cooperation with Himmler, which authorized the informant network of the SD to carry out checks on civilian production throughout German industry.[65] To celebrate the arrangement, Speer made a speech to an audience of one hundred leading Gestapo officers. The next day Speer and Himmler made a show of their new partnership at the annual gathering of the Gauleiter at the town hall conference centre in Posen, the capital of the Warthegau.[66] The programme of speeches on 6 October 1943 was extremely heavy. Apart from Speer and Himmler, there were appearances by Admiral Doenitz, who had recently taken control of the navy, and Erhard Milch, as well as three key members of Speer's staff. The massed appearance by these key figures in the armaments effort was clearly no accident. It was calculated to make the regional leaders of the Nazi party aware of a new axis of power within the leadership of the Third Reich.

Speer's speech, which he delivered immediately before lunch, was drastic in tone and reflected Germany's critical military situation.[67] The purpose of his address Speer announced to the Gauleiter was 'to remove from you in future any excuse that you did not know what we were dealing with . . . I receive again and again proposals from the respective Gauleiter which point to a misunderstanding of the present situation. I would ask you, now, in this hour, to be clear about this, that only the sharpest measures can ameliorate the situation for us.' Speer reminded his audience of his triumphant address to the Sportspalast only a few months earlier, at which he had promised increases in armaments production of 15–20 per cent per month. The RAF's sustained attack on the Ruhr had put paid to that. 'Since the beginning of the air attacks,' Speer explained, 'we have, it is sure, had a slow rise in production but only about 3 to 5 per cent monthly. That is absolutely insufficient.'[68] In fact, Speer was over-optimistic. The monthly index of armaments showed no consistent increase whatsoever in the second half of 1943. Speer also acknowledged that Germany had fallen behind in terms of the quality of its weapons:

We have lived through times in army equipment when our tanks were inferior to those of the Russians . . . The Luftwaffe in the course of the last two years has quite indubitably suffered from an absolute inferiority, a technical inferiority to the weapons of the enemy. And you can see from this example what it means to be able to procure the quantity and to be qualitatively inferior. This is quite insupportable in our situation.

The hope for the coming months was that Germany would soon be able to match the quality of its enemy's weapons, thanks to the breakthroughs of its scientists and engineers. What Germany now needed was to compound its technological advances with a renewed surge in the quantity of production. And Speer hammered home his message:

It is not only possible, it is necessary. It is urgently necessary because we are no longer in the happy position as we were after the French campaign [summer 1940] when we could determine what the enemy had to do, but today the enemy dictates to us with his production what we have to do. And if we do not follow this dictation by the enemy then, in the long run, the front cannot hold.

What Speer demanded was that the Gauleiter should assist him in mobilizing the last reserves of the civilian economy. No cooperation could be expected from the industrialists in the consumer goods industries. 'The business groups are, in their present constellation, mainly the representatives of the large firms,' Speer said. 'Now when the large firms in these consumer industries are to be eliminated, one lie after another is sent to me. Everything I am told is a lie, whether it comes from the printing industry, paper production or from the textile industry, from beginning to end nothing but lies and deceptions.' Furthermore, they enjoyed political protection, because scarce consumer durables such as refrigerators and radios made excellent bribes. To put an end to this scandalous situation, Speer announced that he was appointing 'hell hounds' from the armaments sector to hunt down all unnecessary civilian production. And Speer did not hesitate to invoke the ultimate deterrent:

I have asked the Reichsfuehrer SS Himmler to place the SD at my disposal for the tracing of these types of products and we have made an arrangement with the SD that the latter has access to all the armaments firms and that it can institute there the necessary enquiries ... I am ready to bear the risks that are bound up with these closures. I am ready to answer all charges, which will come from the most varied places.

And he asked the Gauleiter 'to note one thing: there can and will no longer be any room for the former manner in which individual Gaue exempted themselves from closure programmes. It is not possible that one Gau rides a sharp race and the other Gau on the other side does exactly the reverse.' Speer gave the Gauleiter a fortnight to implement his closure programme. After that, he would impose the closures from Berlin, '. . . and I can assure you that I am quite prepared in this case to assert the Reich's authority at all costs. I have spoken to Reichsfuehrer SS Himmler and I shall now deal with Gaue that do not execute these measures accordingly.'

Speer concluded with a rallying cry:

If we carry out these measures with the necessary brutality and if you give me your support in the matter, then I am absolutely convinced that we shall be able to force through the advantage, which we have undoubtedly achieved in the quality of armaments, in quantity as well, in order to withstand the enemy and then to defeat him finally.

Having lost his own brother at Stalingrad, Speer was under no illusions about the nature of this struggle. But he did not hesitate to espouse the most brutal logic of attrition:

It must be us who have the last divisions. Particularly in the fight against Russia it will be decisive to be the one who can throw reserves into the field to the very end. I have no anxiety that we shall be able to supply the equipment ... we are in a position to do it if we are given the necessary support.

Not for a minute did Speer allow the possibility that this was not a battle that Germany could win. Against all the evidence to the contrary, he insisted that the German home front still had the will to continue and that success was simply a matter of leadership.

Our homeland itself, the German people, wants to help us and will help us. It is prepared to bring the necessary sacrifices. It has been waiting long enough for the moment that this serious conception takes the upper hand. It is up to us, to us alone, the leadership of the German Reich, whether we can gain prevalence for this will of the people.

What happened after Speer's threatening appeal is a matter of debate.[69] Speer claimed to his dying day that he took lunch in Posen and then left, in the company of Walter Rohland, to attend an evening session with Hitler. Apart from self-serving affidavits supplied long after the event by Walter Rohland and the manager of the Posen conference centre, there is little to support this version of events. It is far more likely that Speer was still in the Posen conference hall late in the afternoon, when Heinrich Himmler rose to make his address to the Gauleiter. The full text of Himmler's speech on 6 October has not survived.[70] However, the excerpts we have suggest that it was nearly identical to an address he had given two days earlier at the same venue to key leaders of the Waffen SS. The greater part of both speeches was taken up by a rambling discussion of the military situation on the Eastern Front, as one would expect from the Commander-in-Chief of the Waffen SS. Himmler also spent some time discussing the employment of Russian labour, a faint echo of the grandiose plans of 1941 and 1942. Both speeches, however, also contain a short but extraordinary section in which Himmler drew his audience into full complicity in the Judaeocide. By 1943, it would be naive to imagine that the Final Solution was news to an audience of Gauleiter. All of them had been at least indirectly involved in its execution. A number of them were leading perpetrators. Rather than revealing a secret, the purpose of Himmler's address was precisely to puncture the complacency that surrounded commonplace discussion of the 'Final Solution' and to spell out to the party comrades what it meant to have actually accomplished the deed. Like Speer, Himmler wanted to rob the Gauleiter of 'any excuse':

You all accept happily the obvious fact that there are no more Jews in your province. All Germans, with very few exceptions, realize perfectly well that we couldn't have lasted through the bombs and the stresses of the fourth, perhaps in the future the fifth and even sixth year of the war, if this destructive pestilence were still present within our body politic. The brief sentence 'The Jews must be exterminated' is easy to pronounce, but the demands on those who have to put it into practice are the hardest and most difficult in the world . . . I ask that you only listen but never speak of what I am saying to you here today. We, you see, were faced with the question, 'What to do about the women and children?' . . . The hard decision had to be taken to have this people disappear from the face of the earth. For the organization which had to carry out this order, it was the most difficult one we were ever given . . . I consider it my duty to speak to you, who are the highest dignitaries of the party, of our political order, the Fuehrer's political instrument, for once quite openly about this question . . . to tell you how it was.

By the end of this year, the matter of the Jews will have been dealt with in the countries under our occupation . . . You will not doubt that the economic aspect presented many great difficulties, above all in the clearing of ghettos: in Warsaw we fought street battles for four weeks . . . Because that ghetto produced fur coats and textiles, we were prevented from taking it over when it would have been easy: we were told we were interfering with essential production. 'Halt!' they called. 'This is war production!'

Of course this has nothing to do with party comrade Speer: it wasn't *your doing* [italics JAT]. It is precisely this kind of so-called war production enterprise, which party comrade Speer and I will clean out together over the next weeks. We will do this just as unsentimentally as all things must be done in this fifth year of the war: unsentimentally but from the bottom of our hearts, for Germany . . .

And with this I want to finish about the matter of the Jews. You are now informed, and you will keep the knowledge to yourselves. Later, perhaps, we can consider whether the German people should be told about this. But I think it is better that we – we together – carry for our people the responsibility . . . responsibility for an achievement, not just an idea . . . and then take the secret with us to our graves . . .

In the 1970s Speer claimed to have no memory of the afternoon sessions on 6 October 1943. He even had the effrontery to suggest that

Himmler had addressed him personally at this critical point in the speech because the Reichsfuehrer SS was short-sighted, was not wearing his glasses and was, therefore, unaware that Speer had left the hall. In fact, it is far more likely that Speer, Milch and other key figures in the armaments effort sat through the entire address. In any case, it is grossly implausible to suggest that they were not acquainted by the autumn of 1943 with the atrocities that were being committed against Jews all over Europe and on the Eastern Front in general. Nobody could make visits to the Ukraine or the General Government after 1941, let alone oversee the operation of factories there, without being aware of the mass murders that were going on. To give just one example, in the autumn of 1942, in a report to Erhard Milch, Ernst Heinkel, one of Germany's leading aircraft manufacturers, observed casually that it was virtually impossible to start up aircraft production in Poland, due to the disorganization being caused by the 'extirpation of the Jews', a remark which apparently required no further comment.[71] As we have seen, Paul Pleiger and Robert Ley had discussed the 'final solution of the Jewish question' with leading coal industrialists in the autumn of 1942.[72] Speer, furthermore, had been fully informed of the decision to reallocate the European food supply in 1942. When in 1944 the SS undertook the evacuation of hundreds of thousands of Hungarian Jews to Auschwitz, of which only a minority were designated for work, the movement of this huge number of people caused not even a ripple of consternation in the Armaments Ministry.[73] No one could possibly have imagined that the camp at Auschwitz was intended to accommodate these people alive. At the very minimum, it would have required a major allocation of food, a measure which was never even discussed. The truth is that mass murder was not something that required any particular comment amongst men who were familiar with the realities of the General Government and the Eastern territories. Of course, no one liked to dwell on the gory details, or to be personally involved in the murders. But the enormity of the crimes that had been committed against the Jews, the Soviet prisoners of war and the civilian population of Eastern Europe was an open secret.

In any case, what concerns us here is not the question of personal knowledge and guilt, but the extraordinary equation that Himmler created in his speech, the equation between the clearing of the Warsaw ghetto and the 'combing-out' of Germany's consumer industries. Himmler appealed to the Gauleiter to approach the painful sacrifices required by wartime mobilization with the same kind of radical enthusiasm which they took for granted in relation to the Jewish question. Both were tasks that were essential to the survival of the Nazi regime. Both were tasks that had to be accomplished with a complete lack of sentimentality. Everyone in the room shared responsibility for both. Whether or not Speer was still present, Himmler clearly wanted his audience to believe that he was. Speer had repeatedly invoked Himmler in his speech. Himmler was returning the gesture. The idea that Speer or Milch would have wanted to distance themselves from anything that the Reichsfuehrer SS had to say, would surely have struck their audience as absurd. The entire purpose of Himmler and Speer's joint appearance in Posen was to highlight the complementarity between Speer's expanded authority over the civilian economy and Himmler's new role as Reich Minister of the Interior. As we have seen, by the end of the year, the Gauleiter were to be formally coopted into this relationship, by being given political oversight over the local civilian administration in addition to their role as regional Reichsverteidigungskommissare (regional defence commissioners).[74] The purpose of the Posen meeting was to unite the regional Nazi leadership around the new axis formed by Speer and Himmler in Berlin. The common ground was the shared commitment to a last-ditch defence of Hitler's regime, a struggle motivated, at least in part, by their shared responsibility for a campaign of mass murder on a barely imaginable scale.

III

The one glimmer of hope that Speer offered his audience at Posen was the prospect that Germany would soon be able to reverse the technological deficit that it had accumulated since the start of the war.[75] As Germany's military situation grew more hopeless, the promise of technological miracles began to play an ever more important role in the politics of the Nazi war effort. In 1942 and early 1943, Hitler had placed great hopes in the new generation of Panzers. But at Kursk, neither the Panther nor the Tiger had proved decisive.[76] In fact, Hitler was so disillusioned with the Panther that he seriously considered dismantling the surviving vehicles, so as to use their high velocity guns in static anti-tank defences. This pattern of exaggerated expectation followed by devastating disillusionment was to become typical of German weapons development after the winter crisis of 1941–2. And some have been tempted to interpret this cycle as a symptom of deep dysfunction and irrationality, in particular as indicative of the regime's inability to form wide-ranging networks between military and civilian expertise.[77] This, however, is surely to over-dramatize.[78] After all, it can hardly be claimed that the German weapon developments programme was significantly less productive than that, say, of Great Britain. The source of the problems lay, not in the peculiar irrationality of the 'Nazi social system', but in the hopeless situation in which Germany found itself. The desperate need for a technical fix resulted both in exaggerated hopes being placed in individual weapons systems and in accelerated high-risk development programmes that were made even more unpredictable by the ever-pressing constraints of manpower and materials. The Me 210, the Panther and Tiger tanks, the V1 and V2 rockets, the variety of jet and rocket aircraft, the Mark XXI U-boat, were all promising weapons. By the end of the conflict, the Panther, which had been such a disappointment at Kursk, had developed into a combat vehicle that was the envy of the Western powers and the model for post-war Main Battle Tank development.[79] Its early teething problems, like those of the other miracle weapons, resulted from the fact that it was rushed into combat and mass-production without adequate testing. Furthermore, like all its cousins, it was powerless to affect Germany's hopeless strategic situation and thus bound to disappoint.

As an illustration of the predicament of the German war effort in the later stages of World War II, it is tempting to use the much-hailed Mark XXI U-boat, which exemplifies both the increasing unreality of German armaments propaganda and the increasingly authoritarian style of the Speer Ministry.[80] In 1942 ship-building had illustrated relations between the Speer Ministry and German industry at their most cordial. Though naval procurement initially remained outside Speer's remit, Fritz Todt had discussed setting up a Main Committee as early as the autumn of 1941. He had been enthusiastically seconded in this by Rudolf Blohm, who as the owner of the Blohm & Voss yard in Hamburg was by far the most prominent ship-builder in the country. Blohm was a reactionary capitalist in the Roechling mould and like Roechling he was one of Hitler's favourites. As chair of the Main Committee from the spring of 1942, Blohm worked closely with Ernst Cords, a representative of

Krupp's Germaniawerft, to push through a major reorganization in the production of the standard Mark VII C submarine.[81] Long-series production was encouraged in the established dockyards and as much work as was feasible was contracted out to inland steel construction firms. Given the situation in the Battle of the Atlantic, however, the efforts of Blohm and Cords were not enough to save the U-boat campaign. Though the number of U-boats available for operations in the Atlantic rose from 85 in May 1942 to more than 200 a year later, the Mark VII C submarines that formed the bulk of the German fleet were increasingly outclassed by the airpower and electronic technology deployed by the British and American navies. By the end of May 1943, Doenitz was forced to abandon the battle in the main shipping lanes of the Atlantic.

As a direct result of this defeat, Doenitz, who had been appointed Commander-in-Chief of the navy in early 1943, turned to Speer, in the hope that he might be able to bring about an 'armaments miracle' for the navy.[82] In exchange for subordinating the dockyards directly to the authority of the Armaments Ministry, Doenitz hoped that Speer would secure the manpower and materials needed to mass-produce a new generation of technologically advanced submarines. The hopes of the German navy rested on the revolutionary Mark XXI U-boat, arguably the world's first true submarine. Prior to the advent of the XXI, the submarines of the German and other navies were designed to spend most of their time above water, where they could use diesel engines to maintain a reasonable cruising speed. U-boats only submerged and switched to their much less powerful electric engines when they were in direct contact with the enemy. The XXI by contrast was designed specifically to maximize underwater speed and endurance. Its streamlined form and high-powered batteries enabled it to reach maximum underwater speeds of 17 knots, enabling it to outrun British and American sonar systems. And it could cruise underwater for days at a time, needing to spend no more than three out of every twenty-four hours close enough to the surface for its diesel engines to suck air through a snorkel attachment. The problem, as with all Germany's wonder weapons, was the time required to develop the excellent XXI design into a fully functional weapon that was suitable for bulk production. In the spring of 1943 the German navy estimated that even with an accelerated development programme, the soonest they could reckon with the first Mark XXI U-boats was November 1944. Series production could not begin before March 1945. This spelled disaster. Having lost the battle in the Atlantic, Admiral Doenitz could not afford to allow the Allies a breathing space of two entire years.

For Speer, by contrast, the problem was not one of objective constraints, but of mind-set. He was convinced that the sluggish rate of U-boat production was not the result of inadequate resourcing or shortages of skilled labour. It was the product of a conservative procurement culture, in which naval bureaucrats and 'traditional' manufacturers colluded to produce U-boats on a piece-by-piece basis, with little concern for efficiency. For men such as as Blohm, Speer believed, the 'old system of ship-building' had become 'almost a form of Weltanschauung'.[83] The alternative, predictably enough, was American. In the spring and early summer of 1943 newspapers around the world were reporting the record-breaking successes of the Kaiser shipyards in turning out tramp steamers, so-called Liberty ships, from prefabricated sections.[84] This, Speer decided, was the system that Germany needed for its Mark XXI U-boat. Since the ship-building traditionalists could not be expected to carry out this revolution, it would, following the Speer formula, have to be imposed by an 'outsider'. As his man for U-boat production Speer chose Otto Merker. Merker was a perfect poster boy for the 'Speer system'.[85] In his early forties, equipped with a curriculum vitae that included considerable time in tank development at the MAN works, Merker had joined Kloeckner-Humboldt-Deutz AG in 1937 to run their Magirus engineering works, a leading producer of firefighting equipment. In a period of only six years he had managed to more than triple turnover. He came to Speer's attention as the energetic director of the special committee for fire engines, a role that had headline-grabbing potential given the nightly incendiary attacks by the Royal Air Force. Whereas for Speer, Merker's lack of experience in ship-building was a positive recommendation, for Rudolf Blohm, the patriarch of German ship-building, to be displaced by a man like Merker was an extraordinary insult.[86] In an unusual and highly symbolic move, Blohm refused to retire voluntarily from his positions, either as chair of the Main Committee or the Business Group, forcing Speer to sack him. The real conflict, however, was not about Blohm's personal authority, but about the future of German U-boat construction. What led Blohm and most of his colleagues into conflict with Speer was the firmly held belief that Merker was jeopardizing the war effort by imposing a system of mass-production that was quite unsuitable to the situation of the German dockyards in 1943.

Merker's system for the mass-production of the Mark XXI U-boats proposed that U-boat production should be split into three stages. In the first stage, the hull, which had to be manufactured out of heavy sheet metal, was divided into eight sections, each of which was assigned to a group of inland steel construction firms, firms such as the MAN subsidiary at Gustavsburg, one of Germany's leading constructors of steel bridges.[87] In the second stage of the process, the huge steel cross-sections were delivered by special freight cars to dockyards, where they were fitted with all the necessary internal equipment and machinery. Finally, these prefabricated sections were transported, again by rail, to three dedicated assembly yards: Blohm & Voss in Hamburg, Deschimag in Bremen (purchased by Krupp in 1941), and Schichau in the East. Merker touted his system as providing three key advantages. It would mobilize a large slice of new capacity outside the traditional ship-building sector, by making use of inland construction firms. The dry docks themselves, which up to now had been the major bottleneck, would be occupied for the minimum amount of time required to assemble each boat from the completed segments. Finally, it was hoped that by subdividing the process of U-boat building, the manufacturers at each step in the chain would be able to achieve significant scale economies. From the rolling of the steel plate to the delivery of the vessel, Merker promised that construction of each U-boat would take no more than 175 days. The first Mark XXI U-boat was scheduled for delivery in mid-April 1944, with mass-production to follow immediately. By the end of the summer 1944, the navy was promised a fleet of at least 30 revolutionary new submarines with 30 more coming off the production line every month.

Following the Adolf Hitler Panzer Programme, Merker's triumphant transformation of the U-boat industry was to be the next big success story for the Speer Ministry. It had all the important elements of the Speer storyline: conservative military bureaucrats and industrialists overcome by thrusting young managers (Merker), backed by the full authority and energy of Albert Speer, yielding the triumphant introduction of a radical new weapons system, capable of turning the course of the war against all the odds.[88] Speer's public relations machine made sure that the first Mark XXI U-boat was launched at Schichau promptly in time for Hitler's birthday on 19 April 1944. On 12 May 1944, shortly after his recuperation from the serious illness that had debilitated him since January, Speer appeared before the Hamburg dockworkers to hail their achievements: 'We are really experiencing a miracle. Not one of us would have believed it after the first attacks and the heavy attack on Hamburg. Then we said to ourselves: if this goes on for another few months, we are done for.' In fact, they had pulled themselves out from under the ruins and now things looked 'really not that bad'. The U-boat crews, Speer proclaimed, were the best of the best. Once they had the 'the right boat under their arses, they would be off'.[89] The Mark XXI U-boat was to be one of the key weapons in the battle for the 'final victory' (*Endsieg*). And Speer stuck to this script three months later, in August 1944, in what had become his annual speech to the Gauleiter at Posen.[90] Returning to his promise of the previous year, Speer boasted that despite Allied bombing the output of U-boat tonnage would have tripled by the end of the year.

In fact, however, there was no part of the German war effort in which the gulf between armaments propaganda and reality was more extreme. The 'hidebound' traditionalists of the dockyards were proved right on every point. Merker's attempt to rush the untested Mark XXI model into mass-production was an expensive fiasco.[91] The U-boat presented for Hitler's birthday in Danzig was a hastily thrown together mock-up, which leaked so badly that it had to be towed back into dry dock as soon as the crowds had dispersed. Of the 80 Mark XXI U-boats delivered by the end of 1944, not one was fit for operations. By the end of January 1945 only four of Speer's miraculous U-boats were ready for action. Only two ever went to sea in anger. Neither scored a single success against Allied shipping. Captured Mark XXI U-boats provided the template for much of the world's submarine industry in the 1950s, but they had no practical impact on the war whatsoever.

In part, the disappointment of the XXI programme was due to the familiar problems of pushing a a revolutionary new design straight from the drawing board into mass-production, without extensive testing. Not surprisingly, it soon became clear that the new boats required extensive debugging. The steering system, most importantly, needed a substantial redesign. But, added to this, the programme was hampered by the dogmatic insistence of the Speer Ministry on its sectional construction concept. The U-boat construction experts at Blohm & Voss had doubted from the start whether inexperienced, inland construction firms with limited naval experience would be capable of delivering U-boat sections with sufficient accuracy for them to be assembled into pressure-tight submarine hulls. They were right. In the hull sections delivered to the assembly yards, there were deviations of up to 3 centimetres. There were persistent leaks both around the transmission and the snorkel. Imprecision in the assembly of the complex steering system led to repeated rudder jammings. Most seriously, and most predictably, when the prefabricated sections of the outer hull were subject to extreme pressure, unevenness in the welding resulted in potentially lethal fractures. The sections could be trusted only after extensive testing and fixing. Altogether, the U-boats, which had taken 175 days to manufacture, required another 120 days of repairs before they could be passed fit for action. Merker's system, furthermore, required an elaborate administrative apparatus to oversee the flow of sections and sub-assemblies across the three stages. This was not ready in time. Indeed, in 1944 there was not even a full set of drawings and jigs available for the sub-contractors, meaning that measurements had to be taken from the first submarines being assembled in the dry docks in Hamburg and Bremen. As a result, the final assemblers were never supplied with the smooth flow of prefabricated sections on which Merker's system depended. Instead, they found themselves having to divert large quantities of labour to tasks which would normally have been put out to sub-contractors. In the short term at least, the well-practised and wide-ranging sub-contracting arrangements already in place for the Mark VII C model yielded far better results than Merker's radical sectional concept. Evolution rather than revolution would almost certainly have brought greater real gains.

It is indicative of the attitude of the Speer Ministry in the last eighteen months of the war that it responded to these well-documented problems, not by reconsidering its plans, but by ever more dictatorial coercion.[92] As Karl Otto Saur put it: 'The path is chosen and will be followed with iron-hard resolution.'[93] The result was escalating tension between the Ministry and the shipyards. By May 1944, as the fiasco of the Mark XXI unfolded, Merker and Rudolf Blohm were reduced to accusing one another of self-interested conservatism and incompetence. A month later Merker made personal threats against Blohm, announcing that to rescue the programme he would act 'without consideration of person or status . . . and if there [was] no alternative, also with the necessary hardness'.[94]

By August 1944, Rudolf's brother Walther Blohm recorded in his diary that Merker had accused Blohm to his face of sabotage, an extraordinary allegation given Blohm's track record. Walther Blohm in turn attributed Merker's remarks to his desperate need to hide 'the complete failure of his system and his own performance'. In the autumn of 1944, allegations of this kind could have serious consequences. In early October an allied bombing raid destroyed six aircraft on the runway at Blohm & Voss's aircraft affiliate. In retribution, Walther Blohm was hauled in front of a court martial and was sentenced to six months' imprisonment for failing to take adequate air raid precautions. The Blohm family was able to use its contacts in the Gauleitung and in Berlin to get the judgement revoked. However, the incident was indicative of the tension that pervaded every level of the German war effort by the end of 1944. More significantly from the point of view of the dockyard, Merker and Speer's mistrust was such that they took the extraordinary step of removing Rudolf Blohm from control of his own yard, appointing a so-called Werksbeauftragten who was responsible directly to the Ministry. In practice, Speer's commissar was a trusted director of the firm, and Rudolf Blohm seems to have remained very much in charge. But the symbolic degradation of one of the regime's most loyal industrial supporters could hardly have been more drastic.[95] At the Deschimag yard in Bremen, which had been owned by Krupp since the end of 1941, the Speer Ministry went even further.[96] Like Blohm, Deschimag's Generaldirektor Franz Stapelfeldt had repeatedly criticized Merker's sectional scheme and like Blohm he had found it impossible to meet the Ministry's exaggerated targets. After months of increasingly acrimonious exchanges, Stapelfeldt was arrested by the Gestapo on 3 October and held hostage until the spring of 1945, forcing Krupp to appoint a new director more to the liking of the Speer Ministry.

IV

However, to let the fiasco of the Mark XXI U-boat programme and the tension with the dockyards stand for the industrial politics of the Speer Ministry in the later stages of the war would be misleading.[97] Not that the other miracle programmes of 1943–5 were significantly more successful in affecting the outcome of the war. But it is hard to think of any other industry in which relations between the regime and German business deteriorated as badly as they did in ship-building. The rocket programme and the jet aircraft programme, by contrast, exhibit an ever closer alliance between Albert Speer's armaments industry, Heinrich Himmler's slave labour system and Germany's leading industrial firms.

Like the Mark XXI U-boat, the sudden acceleration of the V2 rocket programme in 1943 was clearly a power play by Albert Speer, and the V2 too was a response to failure. In this case, the German leadership was searching for a means to respond offensively to British and American bombing. The Luftwaffe had failed to develop its own heavy bomber and even if the He 177 had been a more successful design, German industry lacked the resources to sustain the kind of huge airfleets now being deployed by Britain and the United States. Wernher von Braun's A4 (V2) rocket, by contrast, promised to give Germany a means of attack against which there was no effective defence. It was, however, a huge technological gamble, and, from the start, it was unclear whether Germany would ever be able to produce enough of the rockets to deliver a truly decisive blow against Britain. Hitler, when the rocket first began to be seriously discussed in the summer of 1942, showed good judgement in dismissing it as a fanciful project.[98] However, the A4 rocket, as an army scheme, fell squarely within Speer's field of responsibility and he therefore had every interest in promoting it as a means of outflanking the Luftwaffe. Characteristically, the decision to go for large-scale production of the rockets was taken in January 1943 as the disasters of Stalingrad and North Africa unfolded. As a sign of his seriousness, Speer ordered the creation of a Special Committee for the rocket headed by Gerhard Degenkolb, the hero of the crash locomotive production programme in 1942.[99] The decision to proceed to mass-production was confirmed in March after successful test-firing. Finally, in July 1943 Hitler gave the project top priority with the so-called A4 Erlass. This gave Speer the right to requisition resources even from the Luftwaffe. In this sense it was the ideal successor to the Adolf Hitler Panzer Programme, which in the aftermath of the Kursk debacle had lost much of its lustre. Along with the U-boat project, the V2 was the top priority programme that Speer needed in the desperate summer of 1943 to maintain the expansive momentum of his bureaucratic empire. And it certainly took on impressive dimensions. In the last years of the war, the A4 programme was to emerge as the biggest single armaments project of the Nazi regime, costed at 2 billion Reichsmarks; a huge bill for a weapon that could do no more than inflict random devastation on the suburbs of London and Antwerp.

It was also typical of Speer that he chose to stake his Ministry's reputation on 'miracle programmes' that were offensive in nature. Both the U-boat and rocket programmes appealed to the propagandistic need for vengeance. But, by the same token, they were also irrelevant to Germany's strategic situation. What Germany needed after 1942 were not means of offence, but defence. In this respect, the Luftwaffe's jet aircraft programme was far more promising. The Me 262, the world's first operational jet fighter, was a truly extraordinary technological achievement. The fact that in 1945, in the most difficult of circumstances, Germany was capable of producing hundreds of these aircraft should give the lie to any claims about the inherent weaknesses in the German 'technological system'. In the list of dei ex machina with which Hitler might have changed the course of the war, it is amongst the most commonly cited.[100] But it is also one of the weapons most surrounded by self-serving post-war mythology. After the war, Ernst Heinkel, Willy Messerschmitt and the chief of Germany's fighter forces Adolf Galland colluded in the construction of a highly one-sided account of the Me 262's history, designed to celebrate the genius of German technology, whilst at the same time demonstrating the incompetence of the Nazi leadership. In their account, popularized in best-selling biographies and television interviews, it was the meddling of Hitler, Goering and Milch that robbed Galland and his valiant fighter pilots of a weapon with which they might have protected Germany against the merciless onslaught of the bombers. This was a myth that appealed to numerous themes in post-war German political culture: regret at the chance of a victory wasted, the consolation provided by the supposed superiority of 'German technology', the self-righteous commemoration of the horror of Allied bombing. But contrary to legend, all the evidence, in fact, suggests that the Reich Air Ministry seized the opportunity of jet power with every possible speed. What prevented the Me 262 from exercising a decisive influence on the air war was not incompetence and conservatism, but the debilitating material limitations of the German war economy.

As soon as Heinkel tested the first jet-powered prototype in August 1939, both Messerschmitt and Heinkel immediately began developing combat aircraft. Indeed, so actively were these options pursued that they cast a pall of technological uncertainty over the entire piston-engined development programme in the early 1940s. The first designs for the Me 262 were brought to Hitler's attention in the summer of 1942 and he immediately gave it his enthusiastic backing.[101] By the end of May 1943, after further testing, the Air Ministry committed itself definitively to pushing the aircraft into mass-production and began to exert severe pressure on Messerschmitt to devote all its resources to the project. If there was any obstacle to accelerated production at this point, it came from Messerschmitt. After the war Willy Messerschmitt and Ernst Heinkel liked to suggest to their audience that the Me 262 was 'ready' in 1943, or even in 1942. But this is grossly misleading. In any aircraft development programme, the step from prototype to series production is preceded by literally thousands of hours of testing.[102] This is then followed by experimental series production. Only after completing this indispensable learning process is it safe to invest heavily in mass-production facilities. In 1943 Messerschmitt was still recovering from the disaster it had experienced with the over-hasty series production of the Me 210. Instead of forcing the Me 262 into mass-production, Messerschmitt therefore offered the Air Ministry an entire portfolio of designs, including a conventional piston-engined replacement for the Me 109 fighter.[103] Indeed, Messerschmitt intrigued with Speer throughout 1943 to obstruct Milch's efforts to concentrate all available resources on the mass-production of the jet.[104] The main technical problems, in any case, concerned not the airframe but the engines, the truly revolutionary element of the design. Even if prototypes were being successfully tested, the world's first operational jet engine was still far from ready for mass-production. Given the enormous technological obstacles that had to be overcome, not only in mass-producing an entirely new kind of propulsion system, but doing so whilst economizing on high-performance alloy metals, this is hardly surprising.[105] Despite the extraordinary pace of the development work the Junkers-Jumo jet engine was not ready even for limited series production before the summer of 1944.

In the effort to get Speer's rockets and Milch's jet fighters into mass-production, a brutal cooperation emerged between German industry, the Armaments Ministries and the SS.[106] Immediately following the RAF's highly successful bombing raids on the Peenemuende rocket facility on 18 August 1943, Speer raised the issue of transferring production of the A4 to underground tunnels. To carry out this Herculean construction task, Speer and Hitler quickly agreed that the SS, with its captive workforce of concentration camp inmates, was the obvious contractor. Within days Speer and Saur had settled the terms with Himmler. A suitable underground location was provided by a huge fuel storage facility in Thuringia and the entire project was put on an independent footing with the foundation of the Mittelwerke GmbH. Its board was to consist of General Hans Kammler, the SS construction chief, and two key figures from the Speer apparatus – Degenkolb, of locomotive fame, and Karl Maria Hettlage, Speer's chief financial expert on secondment from the Commerzbank. The actual operation of the plant was overseen by other veterans of the armaments miracle, including Albin Sawatzki, who had been responsible for Tiger tank production at Henschel during the heady days of the Adolf Hitler Panzer Programme. The initial contract was for 12,000 V2 rockets, to a total value of 750 million Reichsmarks.[107] By the end of the month, Kammler had a detachment of concentration camp inmates from Buchenwald at work on the new facility. By the end of the year his slave labour workforce had swollen to such an extent that the 'Dora' concentration camp was spun off as a separate operation.[108]

With the A4 decree in hand, Speer thus secured a temporary advantage over the Air Ministry. But Milch was not far behind. He too had excellent connections with the SS. Since 1942 it had been the Luftwaffe that had led the way in the employment of concentration camp labour in armaments production.[109] Both Heinkel and Messerschmitt were particularly enterpreneurial in this respect. When Milch ordered BMW and Junkers to begin preparations for the mass-production of jet engines at the end of August 1943, he did so on the assumption that they would deploy labour from the Dachau and Oranienburg concentration camps.[110] By the end of 1943 it was agreed that Kammler's tunnels would house production lines for both the V2 and Milch's Me 262 jet plane. After the war, Speer was asked to explain the three-way working relationship between the SS, the Air Ministry and the Armaments Ministry by a trial judge investigating the Dora concentration camp. Pointing out the fact that Kammler had been simultaneously working for Himmler, Goering and Speer, the judge suggested 'this must surely have led to collisions', only for Speer to snap back '. . . or to cooperation . . .

we tried everything to arrive at close cooperation'.[111] Coming from Speer, who was later to construct an entire interpretation of the Third Reich around his supposed life-and-death struggle with the SS, this was a highly significant admission.[112]

In a construction effort that combined ruthless brutality and speed, Hans Kammler got the Mittelbau tunnel complex into production by the end of the year.[113] To honour this remarkable feat, Speer and his staff visited the site on 10 December.[114] What they saw left a deep impression. In the dock at Nuremberg, Speer denied ever having seen the true conditions in a concentration camp. But in his memoirs he no longer hid from the horror that he had witnessed at the Mittelbau. To meet the timetable set by Speer's Armaments Ministry, Kammler had sacrificed the lives of his inmate workforce.[115] No time had been wasted in building housing. The labourers slept on site, inside the tunnels, seeing daylight at most once a week, deprived of access to clean water and sanitation.[116] They died in their thousands.[117] To encourage those still alive, Kammler strung recalcitrants from the rafters. Speer and his staff saw a factory littered with corpses. Speer later claimed that this tour of inspection caused many of his staff real distress. His office diary records in less emotive terms that the exertions of the Mittelbau project required some members of the Ministry to take an extra period of leave.[118] Whatever the truth of the matter, it did not dent Speer's commitment to his alliance with Himmler and his admiration for the slave-driver in chief. A week after his inspection of Dora, Speer wrote to Kammler congratulating him effusively on his remarkable feat, 'in transforming the underground installation in Niedersachsenwerfen (Mittelbau) from its raw condition two months ago into a factory, which has no equal in Europe and which is unsurpassed even when measured against American standards. I take this opportunity to express my appreciation for this really unique achievement and to ask you also in future to support Herr Degenkolb in this wonderful way.'[119]

On 1 January 1944 Degenkolb and Sawatzki delivered the first three rockets, all of which suffered from serious production defects.[120] By the end of January, production had risen to 56 units and it topped 400 per month in May. There were still problems with production quality, which resulted in disastrous misfires both on the launching pads and in mid-air, and output was well short of the ambitious target of 1,000 per month. By the summer of 1944 there were also pressing questions about the strategic rationale of the entire programme, which resulted in priority shifting several times between the V2, the smaller and cheaper V1 'doodle bug' and the Me 262 jet plane. But despite all this, under Kammler's personal supervision, the first Mittelwerke rocket was successfully launched against London on 8 September 1944 and in that month production rose above 600 units, a level that was sustained until February 1945.[121] One could hardly ask for more telling testimony to the ambiguities of rationalization discourse in the Third Reich. Other than the atomic bomb, the nightmarish tunnel complex in Thuringia produced the two most futuristic weapons of World War II. The factory itself was clearly regarded as a triumph of the American logic of large scale.[122] And it was built in record time by the ruthless but highly effective application of slave labour. Though the top secret project could not be made into the object of armaments propaganda, it was a perfect continuation of Speer's 'armaments miracle'. Above all, it was a triumphant vindication of the new alliance between the two strong men of Hitler's regime – Albert Speer and Heinrich Himmler.

19
Disintegration

Doom did not descend on the Third Reich with a single blow. It struck at irregular intervals and shifted from one theatre to another. In between, there were moments of relief during which Speer, Goebbels and the rest did their best to rekindle the flame of fanatical belief. July 1943 had seen a nightmarish coincidence of setbacks on every front: in the air war, in Italy and at Kursk. In the East, the six months that followed brought a seemingly endless retreat. Nevertheless, by frantic manoeuvring, Army Group South somehow managed to end 1943 still in control of the vital iron and metal ore deposits of the Ukraine.[1] This kept alive the hopes of the German war economy, at least for a few more months. Even in Italy, Mussolini's demise did not spell immediate calamity. Making best use of the impassable terrain and Allied caution, a modest Wehrmacht contingent of 20 divisions was able to stop the British 8th Army well short of Rome and to contain the under-strength American landing at Anzio.[2] Meanwhile, as the autumn wore on, the nightmare of Hamburg lifted. Instead of concentrating on industrial targets in western Germany, RAF bomber command exhausted itself in the perverse attempt to 'win the war' by wrecking Berlin.[3] There were nights when British aim was good and terrible damage was done to the 'big city'. On 22 November 1943 Harris's bombers killed 3,500 people, left 400,000 homeless and scored direct hits on the administrative centre of German government, including the offices of Speer's Ministry and army procurement.[4] But over many months, thanks to constant evolution of tactics and technology, the German night fighters were able to keep the upper hand.[5] By the end of 1943 the Allied bombers were still not winning the war. For a few precious weeks the leadership of Nazi Germany recovered its breath. The sense of powerlessness and defeat receded into the background. Speer even attempted to lift the mood with a series of conferences about post-war reconstruction.[6] At OKW, Alfred Jodl optimistically discussed the protective buffer provided to Germany by the gigantic territory of the Soviet Union. No enemy thrust in 1944 could be immediately fatal. The chief vulnerability were the oilfields of Romania, Germany's one source of imported petrol.[7]

Nor was this lost on the Soviets. On Christmas Eve 1943 they set about breaking the bloody stalemate in the South. Pounding attacks on the Zhitomir–Kiev axis threatened to turn the northern wing of German Army Group South. But still the Germans clung to the ore mines in Nikopol and Krivoi Rog. Only in February was their grip finally broken and the Wehrmacht driven back once and for all from the Dnieper bend.[8] Army Group South's front line, though intact, was now suspended dangerously between Ternopol and the Black Sea, with no natural defensive position of any kind. Again, the Red Army took full advantage. On 4 March 3rd Guards Tank Army sliced due south from Ternopol unhinging the entire German position in the Ukraine. Pressured all along the front line, struggling to keep a grip on their Romanian allies, the Germans reeled backwards first across the Bug and then the Dniester. And even on that last, vital river line they were unable to prevent the Red Army from seizing bridgeheads, the launching pads for the next thrust into Romania.[9] When that came, as Jodl had acknowledged, it would strike a fatal blow to the German war effort. The more immediate threat, however, in the first months of 1944, was the imminent defeat of the Luftwaffe. In early 1944, the US Army Air Force dramatically turned the tables in the daytime battle by introducing a new generation of long-range escort fighters with performance substantially greater than Milch's outdated Messerschmitts. Literally thousands of Mustang P51s equipped with disposable fuel tanks now accompanied the bombers deep into Germany and picked off the Luftwaffe's interceptors before they even got close to the bomber streams. 'Big Week' – 20–25 February 1944 – is commonly regarded as the critical turning point in the air war.[10] On six consecutive days, thousands of American bombers were hurled against all the major aircraft factories in Germany. The Luftwaffe was not destroyed in a single week. However, the US Army Air Force gave notice that the Germans would now face an utterly unsustainable rate of attrition. In February the Luftwaffe lost one-third of its fighters and a fifth of its crews. In March, it lost more than half its fighter aircraft. In April 43 per cent were shot down and in May and June the loss rate hovered around 50 per cent. Over the first five months of 1944 the Luftwaffe's entire complement of fighter pilots was either killed or disabled. A few German aces survived long enough to notch up extraordinary tallies but the working life of the average Luftwaffe pilot was now measured in weeks.[11]

I

Faced with the imminent extinction of the German air force, the Reich Air Ministry followed the navy in offering to throw in its lot with Speer's Armaments Ministry. The result was the formation of the so-called Jaegerstab (Fighter Staff). Nominally, the Jaegerstab was headed by Albert Speer. But in the first weeks of 1944, exhausted by overwork, Speer suffered a physical collapse. Until early May, he was removed from day-to-day business in Berlin. Having 'surrendered' the independence of the Air Ministry, Erhard Milch therefore remained effectively in control of Luftwaffe production at least until the summer.[12] Now, however, he was able to call on the brutal energies of Karl Otto Saur, a squad of senior officials from Speer's Ministry, and the particular expertise of SS General Kammler. Equipped with undisputed priority in the entire armaments effort, empowered to take any measures necessary to raise production, the Jaegerstab successfully revived the 'armaments miracle'. Measured in terms of airframe weight, aircraft output doubled between February and July 1944. The increase in the number of aircraft produced was even more spectacular – from 1,323 in February 1944 to 3,538 aircraft by September, of which almost 2,900 were fighters.

It was this sudden and late burst in aircraft production to which the Speer Ministry owes its legendary reputation. As things stood in January 1944, German armaments output after two years of Speer's leadership was 'only' 130 per cent higher than it had been when he took office.[13] Since the traumatic events of July 1943, there had been no sustained progress whatsoever. Suddenly in February 1944 the armaments output index, which was now being calculated on a regular basis by Hans Kehrl's planning office, shot upwards, by almost 50 per cent in only five months. Relative to an index of 100 when Speer took office, the armaments index which stood at 230 in February 1944 rose to a record level of 330 in July 1944. Two-thirds of this increase was attributable to the last-minute triumphs of the Jaegerstab. And Speer and Saur were clearly well aware of the importance of this remarkable late surge to the reputation of their Ministry. It formed the ideal concluding chapter in the propaganda narrative of the armaments miracle. One by one the Armaments Ministry had taken in hand the key elements of the German war effort: first the army and the Reichsbahn, then the Panzer programme, then the U-boat programme, followed by the miracle of the Mittelbau and the V2. Now Speer and his men would bring salvation to the Luftwaffe. And their secret of success was always the same, 'rationalization' combined with the 'self-responsibility of industry'.

Inexplicably, the Allied interrogators who began picking over the ruins of the German war economy in 1945 took this story at face value, choosing to make Karl Otto Saur, of all people, into one of their chief sources of information on the German war effort.[14] In fact, as was true of the U-boat programme and the Adolf Hitler Panzer Programme before it, the Saur–Speer version of the Jaegerstab's history should be approached with extreme caution. What is indisputable is that the Jaegerstab brought a new measure of coercive violence to the armaments economy and that this extended across the board to German management, to the German workforce, but most of all to the various grades of foreign labour employed in Luftwaffe production.[15] Milch was charged with crimes against humanity in this connection before the Nuremberg tribunal. How Saur escaped the dock is hard to fathom. In the case of the Jaegerstab, the system of 'industrial self-responsibility' touted first by Todt and then by Speer quite definitely mutated into dictatorship uninhibited by any rule of law or code of civilization. After the first wave of American bombers struck at the end of February 1944, Saur and Milch toured all the aircraft factories in a special train, code-named Hubertus, from which they dispensed summary justice to plant managers they considered to have failed in their duties.[16] At Regensburg they court-martialled two German contractors for allegedly holding up the reconstruction of the Messerschmitt plant by demanding reasonable accommodation for their German workers.[17] On 25 March Erhard Milch addressed an audience of air force engineers and chief quartermasters and introduced them to the work of the staff in the most drastic terms:

Please go wherever you are going and knock down everybody who blocks your way! We cover up everything here. We do not ask whether he [sic] is allowed to or whether he is not allowed to. For us, there is nothing but this one task. We are fanatics in this sphere ... No order exists which could prevent me from fulfilling this task. Nor shall I ever be given such an order ... do not let anything deter you, and get your people to the point that no one deters them ... Gentlemen, I know, not every subordinate can say: For me, the law no longer exists ...

Such weaker souls needed 'someone who covers up for him ... If ... you keep in touch [with the Jaegerstab] and immediately clarify difficult points so that something can be done, then we are willing to accept responsibility, whether this is the law or not.' Germany's survival dictated a system completely unfettered by anything other than the priority of production. With the Luftwaffe losing half its planes every month, Milch could see

only two possibilities for me and for Germany: either we succeed and thereby save Germany, or we continue these slipshod methods and get the fate that we deserve. I prefer to ... [be] ... doing something that is against the rules but that is right and sensible and be called to account for it and, if you like, hanged, rather than be hanged because Papa Stalin is here in Berlin, or the Englishman. I have no desire for that ... We are in the fifth year of war. I repeat: the decision will come within the next six weeks![18]

The first key to increased production was clearly an increased work-rate. Across the aircraft and aero-engine facilities, a seventy-two-hour week was the norm from the spring of 1944 onwards. On the model of the Adolf Hitler Programme this gruelling pace of work was sustained by supplying favoured employees with extra rations of food, sweets, cigarettes and spirits, pullovers, warm underwear, socks and even special allocations of vitamin pills.[19] These bonuses, however, were reserved in large measure for the German workforce and the very best performing foreigners. For the rest, Milch and Saur offered only the most severe discipline. Foreign workers, Milch complained,

run away. They do not keep to any contract. There are difficulties with Frenchmen, Italians, Dutch. The prisoners of war are ... unruly and fresh. These people are also supposed to be carrying on sabotage. These elements cannot be made more efficient *by small means. They are just not handled strictly enough.* If a decent foreman would sock one of those unruly guys because the fellow won't work, then the situation would soon change. *International law cannot be observed here.* I have asserted myself very strongly, and with the help of Saur

I have very strongly represented the point of view that the prisoners, with the exception of the English and the Americans, *should be taken away from the military authorities*. Soldiers are not in a position, as experience has shown, to cope with these fellows. I shall take very strict measures here and shall put such a prisoner of war before my court martial. If he has committed sabotage or refused to work, I will have him hanged, right in his own factory. I am convinced that that will not be without effect. (*Italics in original.*)

The methods of Kammler's Mittelbau were thus extended to the entire Luftwaffe sector.[20]

This increasingly draconian attitude to labour discipline reached its limit in the drive to mobilize the reserves of concentration camp labour. A fortnight after the establishment of the Jaegerstab Himmler wrote to Milch to inform him that the Luftwaffe was currently employing 36,000 concentration camp inmates in its factories and that he hoped to raise this in the near future to 90,000.[21] As an example of a productive collaboration, Himmler cited the case of Messerschmitt's fighter plant at Regensburg, which had entered into a sub-contracting deal with the Flossenbuerg concentration camp. Instead of working in the notorious quarry, the inmates at Flossenbuerg were now producing aerodynamic engine cowlings and radiator covers for Me 109s. In February Regensburg also started drawing parts of the fuselage from the Mauthausen camp. By the summer of 1944, it is estimated, 35 per cent of the output credited to Messerschmitt's Regensburg factory was, in fact, due to its SS sub-contractors.[22] Whilst they were contributing in this fashion to the production records of the Speer Ministry, Flossenbuerg and its Aussenlager consumed the lives of at least 20,000 people, in addition to the many thousands more who died at Mauthausen.[23]

Though concentration camp inmates had become increasingly ubiquitous in armaments production, up to the spring of 1944 Jewish inmates, the lowest category in the Nazi racial hierarchy, had been debarred from such employment. The Jaegerstab broke even this ideological taboo. To ensure that it played its part in the defence against the Red Army, Hungary was militarily occupied by the Wehrmacht on 19 March 1944. Within weeks, the possibility of employing hundreds of thousands of Hungarian Jews for war work was being excitedly discussed in the Fuehrer headquarters.[24] The first priority for the allocation of Jewish labour were Kammler's gigantic underground building sites, but given the emergency facing the Luftwaffe the possibility of employing Jews in aircraft factories was no longer ruled out. Eichmann began the deportation of Hungarian Jewry, at the rate of 12,000–14,000 per day, in mid-May. According to the familiar principle of 'Selektion', the majority would be gassed. However, at least a third were expected to be suitable for forced labour in the Reich. Auschwitz was to serve as the 'collecting camp' for the incoming transports. Those chosen for work were to be allocated directly to Sauckel, the Todt construction organization, or other high-priority employers, such as the Jaegerstab.[25] It is estimated that of the 509,000 Jews eventually deported from Hungary, more than 120,000 survived the war as forced labourers.[26] In the Jaegerstab, the employment of Hungarian Jews was discussed first on 26 May 1944, the first meeting attended by the rejuvenated Albert Speer. The Jaegerstab was anxious to know what number of Jews they could expect and heard a report from an official who was clearly in regular contact with Auschwitz. With Eichmann's transport operation eleven days old, the news from the camp was not good. From the first arrivals, the Armaments Ministry had been offered only 'children, women, and old men with whom very little can be done'. The best male labour, it seems, was being retained in Hungary, digging tank traps for the Wehrmacht. The minute concluded laconically that: 'Unless the next transports bring men of an age fit for work, the whole action will not have much success.'[27] At this stage in the war nobody can really have been in any doubt about the fate of those Jews who were not considered fit for employment. But that did not concern Speer or the Jaegerstab. A month later the flow of human material was improving and the Jaegerstab was pleased to learn that Auschwitz was now ready to make good on its promises. In particular, the SS were hoping to deliver '13,000 Hungarian Jewesses in batches of 500. Thus the smaller firms, too, will be in a position to employ these concentration camp Jewesses better.'[28]

But coercive labour discipline and the mobilization of tens of thousands of concentration camp inmates can only go so far in explaining the remarkable increase in aircraft production in the first half of 1944. And Karl Otto Saur, when he was explaining the triumphs of the Jaegerstab to his credulous interrogators from the Bombing Survey, not surprisingly focused on other issues. According to his version of events, the key to the Jaegerstab's success was the 'total revolution' which it brought about in aircraft production, a 'singular' intervention, with 'decisive effects'.[29] Prior to 1944, Saur claimed, aircraft production had been feather-bedded. It was only the decisive action of the Speer Ministry that forced the industry to focus all its attention on maximizing output. In making these claims, however, Saur was doing little more than reciting the standard propaganda line. The suggestion that Luftwaffe producers, who since 1941 had been under the thumb of men like Karl Frydag (airframes) and William Werner (power plants), had much to learn about rationalization from Karl Otto Saur is implausible, to say the least. And not surprisingly, perhaps, the officials of the Reich Air Ministry took a rather more jaundiced view of the hype surrounding the Jaegerstab's achievements. Perplexed by the production records being claimed by Saur, the Air Ministry in the summer of 1944 undertook a close analysis of the sudden miraculous increase in production that had taken place since Speer's men had taken over. As their report makes clear, it is not only the criminal immorality of the Jaegerstab that deserves critical scrutiny.[30]

For one thing, Saur's story took no account of the inevitable time lags in aircraft production. Even the simplest fighter took six months to produce, from raw material to finished machine. Since the Jaegerstab itself came into existence in February of 1944, the measures it had taken and the resources it had mobilized could not show their full effects before August 1944. A large part of the increase in production up to July 1944 could only be explained in terms of measures taken prior to the formation of the Jaegerstab. Most importantly, the Air Ministry in the course of 1943 had extracted 317,000 workers from Sauckel for the Luftwaffe industries, in addition to 243,000 workers obtained on its own initiative. Amongst this number the Air Ministry claimed 'credit' for the extra 100,000 concentration camp inmates supplied by the SS in 1943 and 1944. The Ministry had also set in motion the expansion in aero-engine production, without which the huge surge in aircraft output in 1944 would not have been possible. What rankled most of all, however, was the inconsistent attitude of the Speer Ministry. The essence of Saur's story was that it was only the 'lightning-fast response' of Speer and his staff that had saved the Luftwaffe from immediate disaster in February 1944.[31] But this ignored the fact that in the early autumn of 1943, in the immediate aftermath of Hamburg, the Air Ministry had drafted its own plan to bolster Germany's fighter defences.[32] The draft version of the so-called Reichsverteidigungsprogramm (Luftwaffe programme 224) had called for monthly production by July 1944 of no less than 5,390 aircraft, of which two-thirds were to be fighters. A key part of this programme was to be a sharp reduction in the production of older models, in favour of the accelerated mass-production of the Me 262 jet fighter. But rather than assisting Milch in the implementation of this crucial production drive, Speer had conspired with Willy Messerschmitt to unseat the priority of the Me 262. Meanwhile, Saur and his 'rationalization experts' declared the production targets to be unachievable.[33] The autumn was filled with acrimonious meetings, in which Speer launched a dramatic personal attack on William Werner, the same man who two years earlier had been universally acclaimed as the leading expert on mass-production, the same man to whom Speer in 1943 had personally entrusted overall responsibility for the production of motors, even over the protests of Maybach, the established monopolist in the tank sector.[34] It was only in February 1944, once control over aircraft production had passed to the Speer Ministry, that everything suddenly changed. Not only did Speer's Jaegerstab take credit for the resources accumulated by the Air Ministry in 1943. Saur and his cohorts were also free to adopt a programme in the summer of 1944 (programme 226) that was virtually identical to the 'impracticable' Air Ministry proposal of nine months earlier.

Though the Air Ministry obviously had its own axe to grind, the Jaegerstab's claims on behalf of the 'Speer system' clearly do need to be regarded with scepticism. The Air Ministry had prepared the way for the dramatic discontinuity in aircraft production in early 1944 with its initiatives in the second half of 1943. By contrast with the rhetoric of violent urgency that accompanied the actions of the Jaegerstab in 1944, they had received little or no assistance in this effort from Saur and Speer. Only when Milch surrendered and agreed to share control of the Luftwaffe sector was Speer willing to allow aircraft production to benefit from the full authority of the Reich's Armaments Ministry and the practical benefits that conferred. Even in 1944 there were no miracles of rationalization. Contrary to Saur's assertions, aircraft production clearly did not levitate. Though the confusion of 1944 makes a precise accounting impossible, it is clear that the unlimited powers of the Jaegerstab enabled it to back up the increased production of Me 109s and FW 190 fighters with an unprecedented quantity of raw materials, labour, food and transport capacity. In fact, Speer himself confirmed this interpretation in an unguarded comment to journalists in June 1944. To explain the extraordinarily robust rebound in aircraft production, he commented: 'I have to add . . . that here an alteration in the system has taken place on the quiet, in that from February we have, as we have done in the other industries, brought in capacities from the armour and Panzer industries into the aircraft industry. This is the reason, in my opinion, for the speedy recovery.'[35] As the confidential diary of the Speer Ministry frankly admitted, the uncanny robustness in tank production in 1943, in the face of sustained Allied bombing, had depended on Speer's ability to support the Main Committee with extra rations of steel, drawn from 'secret sources' known neither to Kehrl nor the Zentrale Planung. Now the Jaegerstab benefited from the same slush funds. As the Air Ministry had suspected, it was Speer's jealously guarded control over key resources and his ability to confer 'Panzer priority' that was the truly decisive factor.[36]

II

Whoever ultimately deserved the credit, the Jaegerstab formed the springboard in the summer of 1944 for yet another round of armaments propaganda in the service of one last radicalization of the war effort. Returning from his prolonged convalescence, Albert Speer pushed himself vigorously back into the limelight as the saviour of the Nazi regime. The propaganda of the armaments miracle resumed in early May 1944 with Speer's speech to dockyard workers in which he hailed their achievement in bringing into mass-production the new generation of Mark XXI U-boats. He conveniently skated over the fact that none of these vessels would set to sea until early the next year and that none of them would be ready for combat until April 1945. On 9 June, immediately following the Allied landings in Normandy, Speer rallied the forces of the Ruhr with a lecture entitled simply 'The Miracle of Armaments' (Das Wunder der Ruestung).[37] What is clear from the text of the speech, and his subsequent remarks to a handpicked press conference, is that Speer now felt obliged to defend the system of 'self-responsibility' that was so central to the entire mythology of his regime. The system was coming under fire, both from the ranks of industry and from inside the Ministry. Radicals such as Hans Kehrl wanted to turn the increasingly shambolic system of Committees, Rings and emergency staffs into a permanent, streamlined structure of state direction, backed up by a concerted fiscal consolidation.[38] At the same time, however, Speer was facing a groundswell of opinion from business against the increasingly brutal interventions of his Ministry.[39] Faced with these opposing tendencies, Speer played his strongest card: his unrivalled relationship with the Fuehrer. The Speer–Hitler relationship had gone through turbulent times since October 1943, but in May 1944 Speer had resumed his intimacy with the Fuehrer. Though Hitler's health was failing badly and he was increasingly unwilling to speak in public, he agreed to make a major appearance on Speer's behalf. On 24–5 June, in Linz, under tight military security, Speer organized a conference for all the key figures in the armaments economy, 300 in all.[40] The audience were treated to a packed lecture programme. Speer's own address lasted for three hours, copiously illustrated with slides and graphs, depicting the triumphs of the Reich Armaments Ministry and the achievement of his key collaborators – Saur, Degenkolb, Schieber *et al*. It was a presentation designed to vindicate the embattled system of 'self-responsibility' and to demonstrate its indispensable importance to the war effort. The evenings were taken up with an uplifting programme of classical music, including Bruckner, chamber music on period instruments and an appearance by Herbert von Karajan.[41] For a select group of delegates, the high point came on 26 June with a visit to the Plattenhof at Berchtesgaden, at which they were privileged to hear what was to be Hitler's last public speech, a speech that Speer effectively wrote. As his script, Speer had provided Hitler with a restatement of the message that the Armaments Ministry had been peddling for the last two months. The 'self-responsibility of industry' was the key to success. The achievements so far were miraculous. Defeatism was unjustified. But to prevail, Germany needed one last effort. If German industry failed to meet the demands of the war, the consequences would be catastrophic. Speer clearly wanted to emphasize this point in particular. No mercy was to be expected, even from the Western Allies. Speer's notes for Hitler were emphatic: 'Should the war be lost! . . . merciless extirpation of German industry, to eliminate competition in world markets. The enemy has concrete economic plans, which confirm this.'[42] To stave off this awful prospect, virtually any sacrifice could be justified. The brutal methods of the Jaegerstab would have to be put up with. But, once victory had been achieved,

German business could look forward to a return of entrepreneurial freedom. As Speer–Hitler put it: 'When this war is decided by our victory, then the private initiative of German business will experience its greatest moment!' Hitler promised German business 'perhaps its greatest flourishing of all time'.[43] In the midst of ever more violent coercion, Speer persuaded Hitler to put on record his belief in 'the further development of humanity through the promotion of private initiative, in which alone I see the precondition for all real progress'.

Amidst the horror of 1944, it is hard to imagine how tired such phrases must have sounded. In his memoirs Hans Kehrl recalled the shock of seeing the deterioration in Hitler, who now appeared a sick and aged man.[44] This disillusionment, however, was far from universal. Walter Rohland, now the CEO of the Vereinigte Stahlwerke and still one of Speer's chief supporters in heavy industry, had been one of the parties most keen to have Hitler make a public statement in favour of entrepreneurial initiative. A few days after the event, Rohland wrote to Speer to congratulate him on the 'armaments conference, which went really marvellously well'.[45]

If Hitler appeared distracted, he had good reason. On 6 June the British and Americans had finally made their landings in France.[46] Predictably, the smothering Allied air superiority prevented the Wehrmacht from responding quickly enough to drive the invaders back into the sea. On D-Day the entire Luftwaffe in the West managed only 275 sorties, as compared with 14,000 flown by Allied aircraft.[47] Three weeks later, the British were pulverizing Caen and the Americans were threatening to encircle tens of thousands of German troops in Brittany. This battle in the West, however, was small-scale and slow-moving by comparison with the epic drama unfolding in the East.[48] On 22 June, on the third anniversary of the German assault on the Soviet Union, the Red Army unleashed operation Bagration against the Wehrmacht's Army Group Centre.[49] Compounding the numerical and qualitative superiority of their equipment, with superior intelligence and the logistical support provided by American trucks and half-tracks, Marshals Zhukov and Vasilevsky pulled off what is widely regarded as the 'most impressive ground operation of the war'.[50] Within days of the attack three entire German armies were destroyed. By 4 July Soviet forces had liberated Minsk and were well on their way towards the Polish border. On 11 July the Wehrmacht reported that Army Group Centre had lost 28 divisions and 300,000 men. By the end of the battle for Belorussia that figure had risen to 450,000.[51] Huge columns of German prisoners paraded forlornly through the wide Moscow avenues. On 24 July the troops of Marshal Konstantin Rokossovskii's left-flank armies liberated the first major concentration camp, Majdanek near Lublin. Four days later, after an advance of almost 600 kilometres in six weeks, the Red Army was finally fought to a standstill within earshot of the Warsaw suburbs. After three years of savage fighting the Wehrmacht had been driven back to its starting line in June 1941.

Meanwhile, the Allied air forces were finally concentrating their strength against Germany's synthetic fuel plants.[52] Verbatim minutes of meetings on 22–3 May suggest that following the first round of attacks, even Speer momentarily lost his cool.[53] However, the Third Reich's unstoppable Armaments Minister soon regained his momentum. The final agony of the German war effort would be the moment at which his power reached its fullest extent.[54] In June 1944, in the run-up to the Linz conference, he forced Goering to acknowledge the logical consequence of the formation of the Jaegerstab. With effect from 1 August 1944, the Luftwaffe's entire industrial complex was placed directly under the control of Speer's Super-Ministry. For the first time in the history of the Third Reich, the whole armaments effort was formally concentrated under one single authority. And this was not enough. The military emergency demanded that literally every facet of German society should be put at the service of the war effort. On 12 July Speer wrote to Hitler demanding that, alongside his expanded powers over the armaments economy, Joseph Goebbels should be placed in charge of mobilizing the home front and Heinrich Himmler should be given responsibility for the army's reserve formations. Only the ruthless determination of National Socialist leadership could see Germany through. Even at this late stage, Speer refused to concede defeat. In his report to Hitler he stressed that 'with the new, technically superior weapons, aircraft, U-boats and with the deployment of the A4 [rocket] and with the increase in production of tanks and assault guns we will in the next three to four months overcome the apex of the crisis, which, as yet, still lies ahead . . .'.[55] Goebbels's appointment as Reich plenipotentiary for total war followed on 18 July.[56] Himmler's promotion came two days later.[57] In the days prior to 20 July, Speer thus allied himself firmly with the two men who were to prove themselves to be the key pillars of the Nazi regime in the desperate hours following the attempt on Hitler's life. At the moment that the bomb went off in Hitler's bunker, Speer was with Goebbels and remained with him throughout the following hours. Nor, despite the mendacious obfuscation in Speer's memoirs, can there be any doubt where his sympathies lay.[58] Four days after the failure of the coup attempt, whilst the SS were rounding up thousands of suspects, Speer hailed Himmler and Goebbels's new appointments in enthusiastic tones. Speer told his staff that these were the men to ensure that Total War was no longer a matter 'for discussion, but a fact'.[59] At the beginning of August 1944, on the occasion of the absorption of the Luftwaffe sector into his Ministry, Speer struck the same tone to the newly formed Armaments Staff, an organization modelled on the now defunct Jaeger-stab. Speer spoke about the 'select' few, who were now in charge of the Reich, 'at the head of which, under our Fuehrer, stand men like Himmler and Goebbels'.[60] Given Germany's military situation, the task of the Armaments Staff was, Speer stressed, as much psychological as practical. Apart from continuing to raise armaments output, their chief mission was to spread a spirit of 'optimism and calm'. They were to hold together to the last, as a 'sworn community' born out of years of common labour in the armaments effort.[61]

Speer's own efforts to promote optimism reached their high point a few days later at Posen, where, as in 1943, he and Himmler addressed the Gauleiter. Speer's talk consisted of the usual concoction of impressive sounding armaments statistics, but on this occasion he went one step further. To ensure that the figures for July 1944 really were the highest on record, Speer added the prospective output for the first week of August to the July totals.[62] Speer had succumbed to the final temptation of the 'big lie'. He was no longer simply dramatizing, heightening and manipulating reality. He was engaged in a conscious act of deception. For the coming months, Speer promised the Gauleiter further huge increases in the production of all key weapons and calibres of ammunition. The next day, Hitler affirmed Speer's central position in his post-conference address to the Gauleiter at the Fuehrer headquarters, making a special point of emphasizing the achievements of Speer's Ministry over the last year. Despite Speer's unreal optimism, however, the German war effort was past its peak. From July onwards armaments production fell. From early 1945 it plunged. Production did not decline at the same speed for all types of armaments. Weapons and tanks reached their highest level only in the last months of 1944. Ammunition peaked in September. But aircraft production, the most complex component of the military industrial system and the industry that had been targeted most heavily by Allied bombing, collapsed precipitously from the summer of 1944 onwards.

Since this effectively marked the end of the arms race that has been one of the driving forces in our narrative since at least the late 1930s, it is worth pausing to take stock.[63] Predictably, in the light of what has already been said, the disparity in total output between Germany and its enemies was stark. On the back of the triumphs of the Jaegerstab, Germany in 1944 managed to produce a total of 34,100 combat aircraft. By contrast, the combined output of its major opponents – Britain, the Soviet Union and the United States – came to 127,300 of which the United States accounted for 71,400, a margin of superiority of 3.7 to 1.[64] In tanks the disparity was similarly large: 18,300 produced in Germany as opposed to 54,100 by the Allies, with the Soviet Union in this category accounting for 29,000 of the Allied total. The ratios for artillery, rifles and machine guns were somewhat less unfavourable to Germany, varying between 2.1 and 2.7 to 1 against. But 1944 was the peak year for German production, whereas in these categories the output of its enemies reached its maximum in 1943. In short, nothing that Albert Speer and his colleagues had done since 1942 had made any difference to the Wehrmacht's fundamental predicament. But though on the one hand the triumphalism that surrounds the Speer Ministry clearly needs to be taken with more than a pinch of salt, there is no reason, on the other hand, to talk in terms of failure. Once Germany had engaged both Britain and the Soviet Union and once the United States threw its weight fully into the scales, the odds against the Third Reich were bound to be overwhelming. In 1941, before the German invasion of the Soviet Union but also before the American economy hit full stride, the combined GDP of Britain, the Soviet Union and the United States exceeded that of Germany by a factor of 4.36 to 1. Similarly, in the 1930s the combined steel output of Britain, the Soviet Union and the United States had been almost exactly four times greater than that of Germany and that at a time when American industry was well short of its productive peak.[65] By 1944 the ratio of steel output, even if we add the output of Belgium, France and Poland to the German side, was 4.5 to 1 against Germany. What Germany faced by 1944 was simply the crushing material superiority that German strategists had always feared.

Germany's conquests early in the war certainly did something to offset this disadvantage. A further mobilization of 'foreign capacity', notably in France, was one of the trump cards with which Speer sought to rally the German war effort in the autumn of 1943.[66] Between 17 and 19 September 1943 Speer and Kehrl hosted French Minister of Production Jean Bichelonne in Berlin to discuss the possibility of a major increase in the outsourcing of production to France. Given the state of the French economy, however, this was a last-ditch effort of little practical significance. Over the entire period from 1939–45, the occupied territories were undeniably important to the German war effort. Above all, they provided labour, food and raw materials. They also provided a gigantic territorial cushion without which the Wehrmacht could never have prolonged the end of the war until 1945. What they could not do, however, was to offset the overwhelming industrial advantage imparted to Germany's European enemies by the involvement of the United States. We have seen how derisory was Luftwaffe outsourcing early in the occupation of the Western territories. The situation did not improve significantly later in the war. In 1943, the last full year of occupation, the combined deliveries to Germany of military equipment from France, Belgium, the Netherlands, the General Government, Denmark, Norway and Serbia amounted to only 9.3 per cent of total armaments production.[67] Only in ship-building, communications equipment and motor vehicles did the occupied territories make a notable contribution to the combat equipment of the Wehrmacht. In absolute terms, in 1943 all deliveries to the Wehrmacht from occupied Europe came to 4.6 billion Reichsmarks.[68] By contrast, out of American munitions production in 1943 valued at $54.4 billion (c. 150 billion Reichsmarks), Britain received deliveries valued at $6.7 billion (c. 20 billion Reichsmarks).[69] Even on very favourable assumptions about exchange rates, the ratio in the external supply of munitions to the two European powers cannot have been less than 4:1 against Germany. Given the desperately poor productivity in the occupied territories, the foreign labour programme was clearly by far the most important contribution that occupied Europe made to Germany's armaments effort. By 1944, one in three workers in Wehrmacht armaments production was a foreigner.[70]

Table 17. Axis and Allied armaments production, 1942–1944, in relation to economic potential

000s:	Rifles	Machine pistols	Machine guns	Guns	Mortars	Tanks	Combat aircraft	Major naval vessels	1990 PPP $:		000 tons:	
									1941 GDP	1944 GDP	Steel production 1939	Steel production 1944
United States	10,714	1,685	2,291	512	61.6	86	153.1	6,755	1,094	1,499	55,731	81,321
Britain	2,052	3,682	610	317	65.3	20.7	61.6	651	344	346	13,716	12,337
Soviet Union	9,935	5,501	1,254	380	306.5	77.5	84.8	55	359	495	18,796	16,350
Total, Allies	22,701	10,868	4,155	1,209	433.4	184.2	299.5	7,461	1,797	2,340	88,243	110,008
Germany	6,501	695	889	262	66.0	35.2	65.0	703	412	437	21,528	24,218
Italy			83	7	11.3	2.0	8.9	218	144	137	2,283	1,025
Japan	1,959	3	341	126	4.3	2.4	40.7	438	196	189	6,693	6,366
Total Axis	8,460	698	1,313	395	81.6	39.6	114.6	1,359	752	763	30,504	31,609
Allies/Axis	2.7	15.6	3.2	3.1	5.3	4.7	2.6	5.5	2.4	3.1	2.9	3.5
Allies/ Germany	3.5	15.6	4.7	4.6	6.6	5.2	4.6	10.6	4.4	5.4	4.1	4.5

Sources: *Statistisches Handbuch*, 292. M. Harrison (ed.), *The Economics of World War II* (Cambridge, 1998), 17

III

By the last years of the war, the devastating blows delivered by the Allies were rocking the German war economy to its foundations. However, to assign sole responsibility for Germany's final collapse to such 'external shocks' would again be to collude with Speer's mythic narrative. In fact, by 1944 what could no longer be obscured was that the German war economy was disintegrating from within. Barring truly drastic counter-measures, it was clear by the summer of 1944 that Germany would soon face an inflation no less severe than that which had dissolved the structure of the Wilhelmine state between 1914 and 1923. And this points to one more blind spot in the heroic narrative of the Speer Ministry. Up to the summer of 1944 it would hardly be unfair to say that the Reich Ministry had been oblivious to money as an essential instrument of macroeconomic management. As we have seen, in the interests of maximizing armaments production, Speer in 1942 had opposed the efforts of the price commissioner and Finance Ministry to cream off excess profits. The Armaments Ministry's entire system of economic management had been based on extending and perfecting a mechanism of physical controls over German industry. By 1944, how-ever, the problem of inflation was catching up with Speer. Money could no longer be ignored, even by the most fervent advocates of direct physical control.

In July 1944 Hans Kehrl's planning office compiled a memorandum on 'Purchasing Power, Prices and War Finance', which began in dramatic terms: 'The German economy', Kehrl's office declared, 'is threatening to fall into an anarchy, against which even an extended and improved system of economic controls [Wirtschaftslenkung] will struggle in vain.'[71] From top to bottom the erosion of the value of money was robbing economic actors of their incentive to comply with the demands of the regime, as well as their basic standards of economic calculation. Germany was on the slippery slope from a state-directed economy, in which private economic actors responded of their own free will to incentives provided by the central authorities, to a full-blown state economy (Staatswirtschaft), in which economic action was motivated only by 'coercion or idealism' (Zwang oder Idealismus). And as Kehrl's memo pointed out, even the 'totally planned economy of Soviet Russia' had learned the importance of retaining a stable monetary standard as a foundation for accounting and statistical measurement.

The inflation threatening Germany was the direct result of the huge strain being placed on the economy by the war effort. As all the major combatants found, the financial consequences of the war could be managed, if the burden was not excessive and if government authority was sufficient to levy taxes and ensure the smooth functioning of rationing and price controls.[72] In addition, borrowing from savers, on the financial markets or from banks, provided a crucial source of relief, though this of course depended on maintaining public confidence in the war effort. The inflation that threatened to destabilize the German war effort was indicative of the fact that by 1944 these crucial thresholds had been breached. Not surprisingly, the process of disintegration began on the periphery of the Nazi Empire and it was worst in the Balkans.[73] By the middle of 1942, the price level in Greece had already increased by more than 340 per cent.[74] In Romania, a crucial source both of grain and oil, prices had doubled by the autumn of 1942. In Bulgaria and Hungary they had increased by at least 70 per cent. There was similarly rapid inflation in France and Belgium, though they preferred not to publish official price statistics. By 1943 all of Nazi-occupied Western Europe was clearly in the grips of an inflationary wave that brought with it an increasing disorganization and collapse in production. By 1943 Greek national output was half what it had been before the war. Less cruel in its effects but more significant in economic terms was the progressive disintegration of the French economy, where output by 1943 was down by a third on its pre-war level. There was no mystery as to the cause of this monetary collapse. In the French case, German demands may have accounted by 1943 for as much as 50 per cent of national income, a burden impossible to finance either through taxation or sound long-term borrowing.[75]

As we have seen, as a result of enormous military spending the German economy had been suffering from substantial excess demand at least since 1938. But until 1943 the symptoms of inflationary dysfunction were relatively well controlled. The silent system of war finance instituted in the autumn of 1939 worked well. The tax increases of 1941–2, combined with the ever greater contributions from the occupied territories, permitted the Reich Finance Ministry to finance 54 per cent of expenditure in 1942 and 44 per cent in 1943 out of revenue.[76] In

1942 tax revenues were so buoyant that the Reich was actually able to reduce its dependence on borrowing relative to 1941. Until 1943, furthermore, the flow of household savings was sufficient for at least 17 per cent of total public expenditure to be financed through safe long-term borrowing. This still left between 28 and 33 per cent of expenditure in the budget years 1941, 1942 and 1943 to be covered by short-term borrowing, but the Reichsbank was able to stow away most of this 'floating debt' in the money market. Meanwhile, officially sanctioned prices remained fixed and a strict wartime code confined legitimate barter to trades between households. Black marketeering was sanctioned outside Germany, but not within the Reich. Goebbels exploited the winter crisis of 1941–2 to launch a major publicity campaign against illegal market activity, which helped to reinforce public hostility towards profiteers. On one optimistic estimate, the black market accounted for only 2 per cent of consumption expenditure in the early years of the war.[77] Despite the disastrous setback on the Eastern Front and the huge mobilization of both domestic and foreign resources in which Speer and his colleagues engaged, the stability of the economic order was broadly preserved. Indeed, we should go further than this. Without the largely unacknowledged success of the Reich's monetary and fiscal authorities in preserving the overall economic balance until the summer of 1943, the triumphs of the Armaments Ministry would have been harder if not impossible to achieve. As Kehrl's planning office belatedly acknowledged, if inflation had been allowed to run riot, a far greater degree of coercion would have been required to mobilize resources for military production. The functioning monetary system was a crucial lubricant for the armaments miracle.

From the early summer of 1943 onwards, however, the fragile equilibrium of Germany's war finances progressively collapsed. Speer's last round of armaments mobilization made demands on the German economy that were increasingly unsustainable. In 1943, according to the best available estimates, domestically financed war expenditure accounted for 60 per cent of German net national product, a higher proportion than in any of the other combatants.[78] In 1944 mobilization further intensified. Civilian consumption and investment were compressed yet again, as Wehrmacht expenditure continued to increase. In the fifth year of the war, between September 1943 and the end of August 1944 the Wehrmacht consumed the staggering sum of 99.4 billion Reichsmarks, more than total national income in the late 1930s. By contrast, tax revenues both from Germany and the occupied territories stagnated at the high point reached in 1942 and, even more worryingly, Germany's financial institutions were reaching the limit of their ability to absorb state debt. The Gestapo could repress overt expressions of defeatism. But they could not directly control the day-to-day financial decisions of the German population. Already in the aftermath of Stalingrad, Gestapo informants reported an ever greater willingness to resort to the black market.[79] As households came to rely ever more on such illegal sources there was a corresponding decline in their willingness to inform on them. As in World War I, the war made criminals out of ordinary, law-abiding householders. Over the course of the war, more than a hundred thousand prosecutions for breach of the war-economy regulations were brought before the courts. According to one independent estimate, the black market by the end of the war accounted for at least 10 per cent of household consumption. As cash increasingly flooded into illegal channels, the system for recycling excess purchasing power broke down. Precisely at the moment in the early summer of 1943 when Speer's armaments miracle first ground to a halt, savings deposits fell sharply for the first time since the early months of the war.[80] By the summer of 1944 a total monetary collapse was under way. The sale of long-term investment products such as life insurance had fallen off sharply already in the spring and large cash withdrawals were reported from banks across the country. The financial institutions, for their part, increasingly turned away from either long- or short-term government bonds, forcing the Reichsbank to absorb ever larger quantities of government paper into its accounts. Cash in circulation ballooned. Between September 1944 and the end of April 1945 the volume of banknotes expanded by more than 80 per cent.[81] Germany now faced the imminent threat of hyperinflation. This in turn undermined the functioning of the 'real economy'. Given that there were fewer and fewer consumer goods to buy in the shops, and given the near inevitability that unspent savings would be wiped out by a post-war inflation, the money wages paid to workers became increasingly meaningless. It was this which forced the resort to material incentives such as extra rations of food, cigarettes or clothing. And it was this also which accelerated the spiral of coercive violence. As positive incentives failed, threats and police sanctions inevitably followed. Firms could have little interest in piling up profits in bank accounts which would soon evaporate once the post-war inflation cut loose. Instead, they did everything they could to sink their funds into stocks of raw materials, new buildings, capital equipment and the shares of other companies, all of which would retain their value regardless of the dislocation of the monetary system. As far as possible, they also began to export capital from Germany, to safe havens in Sweden, Switzerland and Portugal.[82] From the point of view of the Speer Ministry, however, this 'drive to substance' ('*Drang zur Substanz*') was deeply dysfunctional. It ran directly contrary to the desire of the planners to cut down on the hoarding of stocks and to prevent firms from placing orders for new plant that could not possibly make any contribution to the immediate war effort. By 1944, every Reichsmark invested in new machine tools or new buildings distracted resources away from the immediate production of armaments.[83]

It was only, therefore, in the summer of 1944 that the Speer Ministry was finally forced to consider the wider economic consequences of its relentless production drive. Up to this point it had been happy to see both producers and workers well rewarded in financial terms for their ever greater contribution to war production. It was only when the disintegration of the monetary system began to render these microeconomic incentives ineffective that the Armaments Ministry finally began to consider the bigger picture. To remedy the situation, the planning office in the first instance called for further controls, tighter allocation of raw materials and ever more intrusive regulation of company behaviour and employment practices.[84] However, as the memorandum of July 1944 acknowledged, this endless search for perfection in the planning mechanism was doomed to frustration unless it was combined with an equally determined effort to restore the functioning of the monetary system. Kehrl's staff thus called for a sharp increase in taxes on consumer expenditure and a system of forced saving whereby armaments contractors and workers would be paid a fraction of their income, not in cash, but in the form of government bonds, which would be redeemable only after the war was over.

As we have seen, the idea of creaming off the profits earned in the armaments sector had been discussed repeatedly since the start of the war, but not until the summer of 1944 did it finally gain the backing of the managers of the armaments effort. In 1943 the Finance Ministry had proposed a set of measures that would have raised an additional

8 billion Reichsmarks per annum.[85] However, the dangers involved in any large increase in taxation were apparent from the experience in the summer of 1942, when the German banking system was swept by rumours that the Reich was about to impose a punitive tax on savings. The savings banks, a crucial link in the conveyor belt of 'silent financing', were unsettled by a series of panic withdrawals. Unsurprisingly, the proposed package of tax increases was vetoed by Hitler and the party authorities in early 1943, and the Academy for German Law, which had provided the main forum for academic discussion of the Reich's fiscal problems, shut down the relevant committee.[86] On 22 September 1944 Hitler again vetoed any further discussion of major tax increases. In February 1945, as the money supply surged out of control, the Finance Ministry made one last desperate appeal to siphon off at least 25 billion Reichsmarks.[87] As the Third Reich collapsed, a bewildered and out-of-touch Fuehrer was finally persuaded to put his signature to a tax decree. He did so, however, on the condition that the tax increases should come into force only after the end of the war.

Much could be made of this unwillingness on the part of the Third Reich to impose the full cost of the war on the *Volksgenossen*. It could be read as a symptom of the regime's deep-seated 'populism'. But the irony, of course, was that the decision not to tax did not imply that the real burdens of the war were not imposed on the German population. Whether or not they were directly appropriated by the state, an increasing share of the wages and social benefits paid out during the war could not be spent, or could only be spent on black-market purchases at exorbitant prices. In this sense, it would be naive to infer from the failure to impose draconian war taxes that the Third Reich was not willing to impose the full cost of the war on its citizens.[88] Whatever happened to money incomes, rationing and the restriction in the production of consumer goods, combined with the impact of British and American bombing, were severely reducing the real standard of living of the German population. Choosing not to match this real reduction with equivalent taxes on money incomes was at best ambiguous in its effects. It may have left some people feeling richer on account of the funds accumulating in savings accounts or in war bonds. But these were promises of future purchasing power that depended for their real value on the success of the Reich's authorities in maintaining the value of the Reichsmark. Meanwhile, the inflationary danger posed by this pent-up purchasing power necessitated ever more stringent controls, which arguably had even greater political costs. When Kehrl's planning office advocated taxation in the summer of 1944, it did so not as an act of 'rigour', but as a means of avoiding the disastrous inefficiencies that would result from an inflationary collapse of the currency. Taxation, in so far as it helped to ward off inflation, would in fact have provided the best defence of the minimal version of economic freedom that the Third Reich still provided for its citizens. It might have been politically uncomfortable in the short term, but from the point of view of the regime itself, let alone the population at large, a stable monetary order was clearly preferable either to hyperinflationary anarchy or total state control.

IV

In the event, the political leadership of the Third Reich never had to face the full consequences of its own fiscal inaction. By the autumn of 1944, despite the halting advance of the British and American armies and the awful casualties still being exacted from the Red Army, the final defeat of the Wehrmacht was clearly only a matter of months away. What was unclear in the last months of the war was whether it would be the Wehrmacht or the German war economy that collapsed first. The losses of territory suffered from the beginning of 1944 signed the death warrant of the war economy. The evacuation of the Ukrainian ore mines in February 1944 restricted German steel production to a time-horizon of eighteen months at most.[89] The supply of oil from Romania – an absolute precondition for the continuation of large-scale mobile warfare – was cut off by April 1944. These losses put a time limit on German survival. But they did not by themselves imply immediate collapse. In a typically bullish assessment prepared for Hitler in the first week of September 1944, Speer reckoned that German stocks of raw materials were sufficient to allow production to continue, even if Germany was forced to retreat altogether from the Balkans, Western Europe, northern Italy and halfway across Hungary.[90] It was not territorial losses that paralysed the German economy but the onset of a campaign of aerial bombardment, of completely unprecedented intensity.[91]

In the first half of 1944 the British and American air forces had been distracted by the preparations for the invasion of Normandy. The Allies left nothing to chance. To protect the beachheads from rapid German counterattack they methodically pulverized the entire French transport system. The only significant diversions from this tactical bombing were a series of devastating attacks on Germany's fuel hydrogenation plants. Once Normandy was secured, the bombers were finally free to turn their full attention to Germany, and they did so with dreadful intensity. It had taken four long and painful years since the fateful decisions in the summer of 1940 to construct the Anglo-American air weapon. But the war-winning airfleet was now ready. In March 1943, at the start of the strategic bombing campaign, the British and Americans had disposed of 1,000 aircraft with a combined bomb-lifting capacity of 4,000 tons.[92] By February 1944, in time for the all-out offensive of Big Week, the combined force had swollen to 3,000 bombers and was increasing rapidly to reach 5,250 by July 1944, the level at which it stabilized for the rest of the war. Five times as many aircraft as in 1943 were now capable of delivering a staggering 20,000 tons of bombs in a single lift. And from June 1944 onwards this fearful weapon was turned relentlessly against the Reich. Between June and October 1944 the British and Americans rained down on Germany no less than half a million tons of bombs, more than in the entire war up to that point. Over the next six months they dropped a further 545,000 tons. Berlin and the Ruhr were visited with raids of unprecedented intensity. The 8th US Army Air Force hit Berlin on 3 February 1945 with a force of 1,000 heavy bombers, a raid which claimed 2,893 lives. But it was not just the big cities that were now being targeted. Dozens of smaller towns were laid waste by fire and explosives: Darmstadt on 12 September 1944 (8,400 dead), Freiburg on 27/28 November (2,000 dead), Heilbronn on 4 December (7,000 dead), Nuremberg on 2 January 1945 (1,790 dead) and again on 20 and 21 February, Magdeburg on 16 January 1945 (4,000 dead), Dresden on 13/14 February (35,000 dead), Wuerzburg on 16/17 February (5,000 dead), Pforzheim on 23/24 February (17,000 dead) and Swinemünde on 12 March (5,000 dead). The RAF's last major night-time raid was against Potsdam on 14/15 April 1945, a sortie by 500 bombers which killed at least 3,500 people and incinerated the historical records of the Prussian army.[93]

In a general sense, this destruction clearly contributed to the dislocation of the German home front. It also clearly satisfied a heartfelt desire for revenge. The heaviest month of bombing in the entire war was

March 1945, with a total payload of 133,329 tons, at a time when such raids could have no conceivable impact, even in accelerating the end of the fighting. Not that the devastating bombardment did not have serious economic effects. Factories were obliterated, burned out, buried in mountains of rubble, or paralysed for lack of raw materials and power. But the correlation between the area bombing of Germany's cities and the collapse of its war production was loose, at best. There was probably no single plant to which the Allies devoted more attention than Krupp's Gusstahlfabrik in Essen, the ultimate symbol of German industrial militarism.[94] By the end of the war, the Gusstahlfabrik had been targeted no less than twenty-five times. In 1943 it was repeatedly bombed as part of the 'Battle of the Ruhr'. But steel production was not definitively ended until 23–5 October 1944, when Essen was attacked by a total of 1,200 planes. They ended the Gusstahlfabrik's contribution to the German war effort by destroying its electrical power supply. The heaviest attack of all, however, came on 11 March 1945, by which time the bombers were doing little more than ploughing a field of rubble. The wanton destruction of German cities could disrupt production, but it could not bring it to a complete standstill. The way in which the bombers achieved that effect was by severing the rail links and waterways between the Ruhr and the rest of Germany.

The disaster began at the end of September with an attack by RAF Bomber Command which drained the Dortmund–Ems canal.[95] The giant marshalling yard at Hamm was hit repeatedly in September and October, reducing its capacity by 75 per cent. The Rhine was blocked on 14 October by the destruction of the Cologne–Muelheim bridge. Between 14 and 18 October rail shipments of coal from the Ruhr were halted completely, and the disruption in the reverse direction was even more severe. In early October only one of fifty ore trains was making it into the Ruhr. For lack of iron ore, steel production in the Ruhr by January 1945 was down by 66 per cent relative to the previous year. Though Allied bombing strategy actually shifted in November and December away from the absolute prioritization of transport targets, the sheer weight of tonnage dropped was sufficient to bring about near total collapse. Between November 1944 and January 1945 the British and American air forces delivered no less than 102,796 tons against transport targets, mainly railway marshalling yards. On 11 November Speer reported to Hitler that the Ruhr was effectively sealed off from the rest of the Reich.[96] The shortfall in hard coal deliveries from the Ruhr between August 1944 and January 1945 was a massive 36.5 million tons, at least six weeks of normal consumption. In December 1944 Germany faced the first of three consecutive winters without adequate supplies of coal. Not until 1948 were reliable connections restored between the Ruhr mines and the urban centres of Germany. For a mid-twentieth-century European society this spelled imminent paralysis. Already in January 1945 the impact of the coal famine was making itself severely felt. Upstream from the Ruhr in the southern industrial hub of Mannheim–Ludwigshafen, coal shortages accounted for an 80 per cent fall in production at Brown, Boveri and Cie, one of the Reich's principal producers of electrical transformers. Opel in Ruesselsheim and BMW in Munich were both closed in early 1945 for lack of coal. By the spring contemporaries were noting that the Rhine was running clean for the first time in generations. There were no factories left in operation to pollute it.[97]

At this point, the Armaments Ministry was defeated. The bombers were unstoppable. The collapse of industrial production in Germany was only a matter of time. But in the autumn of 1944 the war went through the last of the periods of stagnation, which were so essential to the ability of Hitler's regime to rally itself and to convince itself time and time again that all was not lost. In September 1944 the Allied advance across France came to a halt on the borders of the Reich. There followed months of grinding defensive battles, in which progress was agonizingly slow and the superior fighting skill of the Wehrmacht showed itself to remarkable effect. In the East, the Red Army halted outside Warsaw. For the following months, fighting on the Eastern Front was largely confined to the flanks. German Army Group North was cut off and trapped against the Baltic coastline. In the South, after the Red Army took Romania on the run, its progress through Hungary was far less swift. At the end of November the Wehrmacht still clung to Budapest. A year of unmitigated military disaster thus ended, as Alfred Jodl had predicted, with the frontiers of the Reich intact. And on 16 December, Speer's mobilization of the tank industry permitted Hitler to indulge in the last great surprise of the war: the Ardennes offensive.[98] In an absurd attempt to repeat the success of May 1940, 1,800 tanks, each fuelled with one load of petrol, plunged through the Belgian hills towards the Meuse and the gigantic Allied petrol dumps at Antwerp.[99]

On Christmas Eve 1944 they reached the river crossings at Dinant that had marked the turning point four years earlier. This time, however, they penetrated no further. Though outnumbered, the American units caught in the initial assault fought a dogged rearguard action, giving Eisenhower time to respond. As soon as the winter clouds lifted, Allied air superiority reimposed itself and reinforcements were rushed in. It was, as Patton put it, 'a clear cold Christmas, lovely weather for killing Germans'.[100] In practice, however, it took the Allies until the end of January 1945 to reverse the gains made by the Wehrmacht's last futile offensive. At Fuehrer headquarters, spirits were still not broken.[101] Speer reassured Goebbels that, despite the loss of all the occupied territories, armaments production could continue for at least another year. The loss of Upper Silesia to the Red Army at the end of January 1945, the first major zone of German industry to fall to the enemy, forced Speer to revise this estimate. But he was determined, as he put it to Goebbels, to 'do what could be done'. Indeed, he requested from Hitler one final expansion of his administrative powers, taking control of the entire transport system of the Reich, so as to ensure that the priority of the military and the armaments industries were defended against the clamour of terror-stricken civilians fleeing the Red Army.

In early March, Speer made a final visit to the Ruhr to inspect the work being done by his most important collaborators in German industry, Albert Voegler and Walter Rohland, who now headed an emergency staff charged with sustaining armaments production in the Ruhr.[102] Under the impression of that visit, Speer wrote a report, which he forwarded to Hitler on 15 March. In this memorandum, Speer famously argued that, rather than engage in a wholesale policy of scorched earth, the Wehrmacht should take measures to paralyse German industry in the West rather than destroying it permanently. This at least would provide the German population with the minimal means for survival. What has recently emerged from the archives is a second memorandum, which Speer submitted to Hitler three days later, in which he advocated a completely different strategy for the territories still under German control. Speer may have opposed the wanton destruction of industry in the West. But on 15 March the Wehrmacht was still holding defensible positions on the eastern banks of the Rhine. At the same time, the Red Army was halted on the Weichsel. This inner zone of Germany, between the Rhine and the Weichsel, Speer proposed to defend to the last man.

This was not an economically viable unit and Speer accepted that 'economic collapse' was now inevitable. But he still believed that armaments production could be continued for a period of eight weeks. Every available soldier was to be massed along the river banks for one last slaughter. Even now, Speer did not relinquish the hope that Germany had some power to influence the outcome of the war. 'A dogged defence of the current front line for a few weeks', he wrote, 'may yet demand respect from the enemy and may yet be able to influence the end of the war in a positive direction.'

Nobody should underestimate the consequences of this kind of thinking on the part of the political leadership of the Third Reich. World War II in Europe did not end with a whimper. The final battles of the war were the most bloody in the entire conflict. Setting aside the casualties suffered by the Soviets, the Americans, the British and their Commonwealth allies, the losses suffered by the Wehrmacht were horrendous enough. The defeats of 1944 had cost the Germans 1.8 million men killed.[103] In the first five months of 1945, whilst Speer was encouraging his Fuehrer to one last show of resistance, 1.4 million German soldiers met their deaths, 450,000 in January alone. Nor does this include the tens of thousands of civilians who fell victim to Allied bombing. To describe the destruction of Germany in 1945 in the language of the Holocaust is both obscene and inaccurate.[104] This was a war, not a massacre of the innocents. It may have felt like slaughter to those on the receiving end, but this was an effect of the means used, not the ends intended. The Western Allies broke no law of war that had not been breached by the Wehrmacht a hundred times over. The Red Army behaved barbarically in the territories it occupied, but the Soviets did not perpetrate a genocide. Nazi Germany had challenged three of the greatest industrial powers on earth. It had taken them five long years to bring their industrial might fully to bear. But now their war machines were fully assembled and in the first five months of 1945 they cut their way into the territory of Germany with truly horrendous effects. The Allies waged war with a volume of firepower unlike that ever used in any previous conflict. The results were nightmarish and would have been even worse but for the fact that the policy of 'Germany first' meant that the Nazi regime was destroyed before the atomic bomb was ready for use.

Less than a week after Speer wrote his counsel of sacrificial destruction, the flimsy German defences on the Rhine were breached. The

Armaments Minister returned to Berlin for a last business meeting with Hitler on 29/30 March.[105] There is no authentic record of this encounter, only the mocking commentary of Goebbels's diary and Speer's unreliable memoirs. It seems that Hitler extracted from Speer the promise that he would do everything 'to raise resistance to its utmost limit'. And Speer was not able to persuade Hitler to withdraw his order to scorch the earth ahead of the invaders. Goebbels reported simply Speer has 'given in'. Both Speer and Hitler chose to preserve their relationship until the very end. Speer objected to Hitler's Nero order, but not to his face. It was only after his final conference with the Fuehrer that Speer issued detailed instructions for the execution of the evacuation order, effectively countermanding Hitler's intention. Local authorities were permitted to paralyse German industrial facilities and render bridges unusable without blowing them up. It was action at the local level that now mattered. As the German state disintegrated, so did the national economy. Regions, firms and individuals were reduced to desperate strategies of survival. In the Ruhr, Albert Voegler and Walter Rohland argued inconclusively with the local military commanders about the demolition of one of the most important bridges across the Ruhr. They agreed that though the bridge should be made impassable, power, water and gas lines would be left intact. In the end, what had survived the bombing was saved by the arrival of the American forces. Back at headquarters in the capital, Herbert Backe, who had once planned the food supply for all of Europe, was now principally concerned with filling the granaries of Berlin, in the hope that urban life could be sustained at least until the next harvest was brought in. Hans Kehrl continued to work feverishly at plans.[106] He collaborated with Backe on an emergency production programme for agricultural equipment, on the assumption that farming and food would be Germany's chief preoccupations in the years to come. He also prepared a programme to ensure a minimal supply of clothing to the German population after the collapse. By this point, however, the personal safety of his family was an unavoidable issue. With the help of Hellmuth Roehnert, the CEO of Rheinmetall, Kehrl dispatched his wife and young daughter westwards to the testing grounds in the Lueneburger Heide, safely out of reach of the vengeful Red Army. Large parts of Kehrl's former office, the Ministry of Economic Affairs, were dispatched to the Thuringian countryside in a double-decker bus, stuffed with papers, cash and gold. Meanwhile, Rolf Wagenfuehr, the chief statistician in Speer's Ministries, busied himself with an impressive collection of statistics, which to this day provide us with the most influential account of the German war effort.[107] No veil of silence was to be drawn over the armaments miracle. As the ghastly reality of the Nazi war economy was finally being liquidated, the writing of its history had already begun.

20

The End

The jaws of defeat finally closed on the Third Reich in the last week of April 1945. Just before midday on 25 April advanced patrols of the US 1st Army's 69th infantry division and the Soviet 1st Ukrainian Army linked up on the banks of the Elbe at the small Saxon town of Strehla amidst the gruesome wreckage of a German refugee trek. The banks of the river, where Lieutenant Albert Kotzebue's GIs embraced their Soviet counterparts, were littered with the dismembered corpses of dozens of old men, women and children. Three days earlier they had fallen victim to retreating Wehrmacht soldiers, who had been so desperate to escape capture by the Red Army that they had blown up the makeshift pontoon bridge whilst hundreds of civilians were still streaming across it. As many as four hundred may have drowned or been blown to pieces by the twin detonations.

Not surprisingly, the official occasion for the world-defining Soviet–American encounter was shifted 45 kilometres downstream to the town of Torgau, where contact was made later the same afternoon. The official photograph on Torgau's broken-backed bridge was staged the following day. Contrived though it may have been, the handshake was highly significant. Along the course of the Elbe, Torgau lay midway between the burned-out baroque splendour of Dresden and the cradle of Lutheran Europe at Wittenberg. A few miles further to the north was Dessau, home not only to the Junkers bomber factories but also to the seminal early twentieth-century modernism of the Bauhaus. In Germany there was no more symbolic terrain on which to enact the epochal shift in the global balance of power from old Europe to the new powers of the United States and the Soviet Union.

From an economic point of view, Torgau was the logical outcome of two truly dramatic developments that defined the early twentieth century. The first and most obvious was the emergence of the United States as the dominant force in the world economy. The second, which did not become apparent until the 1930s, was the astonishing transformation of the Russian Empire wrought by the Bolshevik dictatorship. As the linking up of American and Soviet infantrymen deep in the heart of Central Europe confirmed, the history of the Continent in the first half of the twentieth century, the history of Germany and the history of Hitler's regime cannot be understood but in relation to these twin developments in the United States and the Soviet Union. Certainly, this is the backdrop against which this particular account of the rise and fall of the Nazi economy has been set.

Hitler never ceased to hark back to the revolutions that swept Europe in 1917–18. Anti-Communism was an unwavering element in his politics, tightly interwoven with a particularly toxic form of conspiratorial anti-Semitism. But anti-Communism was generic on the German right, as were projects of Eastern expansionism. Furthermore, though the Soviet Union remained a looming presence in European affairs, it turned inwards from the late 1920s onwards and in the 1930s tended to be belittled as a factor in European power politics. To identify the peculiarity and motivating dynamic of Hitler's regime, it therefore seemed more illuminating in the early chapters of this book to focus on the relations between the Third Reich and the Western powers.

The rise of the United States confronted Germany, as it did Britain and France, with a choice. With Stresemann as Foreign Minister, the Weimar Republic responded with remarkable flexibility and realism to the new situation. As we have shown, the Weimar Republic premised its entire security strategy on the economic power of the United States, both as a guarantor of its security and as a lever through which to pressure Britain and France into revision of the Treaty of Versailles. And as we have seen, this strategic choice continued to define the policy of the last respectable government of the Weimar Republic up to the summer of 1932. Not until the final spasm of the Great Depression in 1932–3 and the collapse of American hegemony in Europe was the path really open for Hitler's brand of aggressively unilateralist nationalism.

In one of his final conversations with Martin Bormann, in February 1945, Hitler remarked: 'An unfortunate historical accident fated it that my seizure of power should coincide with the moment at which the chosen one of world Jewry, Roosevelt, should have taken the helm in the White House ... Everything is ruined by the Jew, who has settled upon the United States as his most powerful bastion.'[1] What weighed on Hitler's mind, in the last months of the war, was the pivotal role played by Roosevelt in frustrating his project of Continental conquest. In 1933, however, the role of the United States was the reverse. As Hitler came to power and Roosevelt took office, the American economy was racked by a last, devastating banking crisis. Washington's decision to unfasten the dollar from gold, taken without regard to its international ramifications, destroyed what little chance there was of assembling a combined international front to contain Hitler's regime before it had consolidated its grip on Germany. The coincidence of Hitler's seizure of power with America's temporary retreat from global affairs – a retreat that left Europe orphaned as it had not been since World War I – was of incalculable importance.

Though he disagreed profoundly with Stresemann's strategy in relation to the United States, Hitler was by no means oblivious to the changed world of the 1920s. In his 'Second Book', written in 1928, Hitler posed the central strategic questions with startling clarity: how was Germany, as a European state, to react to the 'threatened global hegemony of North America'? How could it forestall America's seemingly inevitable economic and military dominance? How was Germany's political leadership to respond to the material aspirations awakened in its population by the example of American affluence? These are undeniably modern questions. Indeed, they are with us still. Hitler's answers, however, were explosive. The solution was not to ally Germany with the United States, or to adopt American modes of life and production. Any such attempt at 'Americanization' was bound to end in frustration and disaster. Behind America, after all, stood the malevolent force of world Jewry, cloaked in the garb of liberalism, capitalism and democracy. The only adequate response to the American challenge was to create a *Lebensraum* for the German people sufficient to match that provided by the continent of the United States. Space on this scale was only available in the East and it could be attained only through conquest. There seems no reason to doubt that this mission of conquest was the sustaining ambition of Hitler's regime. For Hitler, a war of conquest was not one policy option amongst others. Either the German race struggled for *Lebensraum* or its racial enemies would condemn it to extinction.

Mounting such a challenge required a diplomatic strategy and a major military effort, both of which were ultimately founded on economics. The enormous effort of national mobilization must be the central focus of any account of the economic history of Hitler's regime. By comparison with the military-industrial complex, the various civilian work creation measures set in motion between June and December 1933, the domestic social policy initiatives and abortive projects of mass-consumption that followed, were nothing more than interim measures, which could attain their real significance only after a successful campaign of conquest. In any case, it would be a mistake to assume that the remilitarization of German society was something imposed from the top down, with the majority of Germans preferring butter to guns. For many millions, the reconstruction of the Wehrmacht was clearly the most successful aspect of the regime's domestic policy and the collective mass-consumption of weaponry was a more than sufficient substitute for private affluence.

As should be evident from the first half of this book, rearmament was the overriding and determining force impelling economic policy from the earliest stage. Everything else was sacrificed to it. In the six years between January 1933 and the autumn of the Munich crisis, Hitler's regime raised the share of national output going to the military from less than 1 to almost 20 per cent. Never before had national production been redistributed on this scale or with such speed by a capitalist state in peacetime. This extraordinary effort at redistribution was certainly eased by the simultaneous growth in German output. Putting to work 6 million unemployed provided for the needs of the Wehrmacht, whilst allowing consumption and civilian investment to be increased as well. But it is easy to forget, given its wealth today, that Germany in the 1930s was a generation away from affluence and that the majority of the population subsisted on a very modest standard of living. Rearmament came at a serious cost and this was made even more pressing by the often crippling constraints imposed by Germany's balance of payments. Already in 1934 the interests of both consumer goods industries and farmers were being sacrificed to rearmament. From 1935 in many German cities, butter and meat were surreptitiously rationed. From 1938 onwards, with military spending reaching wartime levels, the trade-off between consumption and armaments became truly severe. That Hitler's regime was able to impose this redistribution of resources betokens not inefficiency and disorganization, but a system that was highly effective in pursuit of its central objectives. Furthermore, it should lead us to question any interpretation of Hitler's regime based on the assumption that it lacked solid internal foundations. To reiterate, the Third Reich shifted more resources in peacetime into military uses than any other capitalist regime in history. And this advantage in terms of domestic resource mobilization continued to hold throughout the ensuing world war.

So far-reaching were the regime's interventions in the German economy – starting with exchange controls and ending with the rationing of all key raw materials and the forced conscription of civilian workers in peacetime – that one is tempted to make comparisons with Stalin's Soviet Union. Such a comparison is certainly suggestive in pointing to the kind of synthesis between militarization and domestic social and economic restructuring that might have been necessary to fulfil Hitler's ambitions. Since the emergence of the United States as a world power in the early twentieth century, only Soviet-style militarism has been able to mount a credible and sustained challenge to its hegemony. And judged against Stalin's regime, one might indeed describe Hitler's state as a 'weak dictatorship'. As we have seen, this was the conclusion reached by well-informed observers such as General Franz Halder in the autumn of Barbarossa's failure in 1941. Most notably, in comparison with the Soviet Union, the Third Reich shrank from a dramatic rationalization of the most backward sectors of its society, peasant agriculture and the craft sector, a measure which might have 'freed' millions of additional workers. But given what we now know about the Generalplan Ost and the comprehensive agrarian restructuring that it was supposed to initiate, it seems that this was a matter of timing. The comprehensive restructuring of German society was simply postponed until after the conquest of *Lebensraum* in the East. If one must therefore concede that the Nazi party, unlike the cadres of Soviet Communism, was not a battle-hardened weapon of class war, by Western European standards it can hardly be faulted for its lack of redistributional energy. Never before, in peacetime, had a sophisticated capitalist economy been redirected so purposefully.

Setting aside the Stalinist counterfactual, one might equally well ask the opposite question. How was the Third Reich able to push its control over the German economy as far as it did? Why did Germany's business lobby tolerate this dramatic intrusion of state power after 1933? Only a decade earlier, 'big business' had after all played an important part in frustrating the reforming ambitions of the early Weimar Republic. The answer given here consists basically of four elements. First and foremost, one must emphasize the damage done to the independent power of the business lobby by the Great Depression. Even if they had been predisposed to do so, Germany's big businessmen were in no position to put up a serious fight in 1933. Secondly, though the Nazi autarchic turn was certainly at odds with the international agenda of the German business lobby, the domestic authoritarianism of Hitler's coalition was much to their liking, as were the healthy profits that rolled in from the mid-1930s. Thirdly, though there clearly was a dramatic assertion of state power over business after 1933, naked coercion was applied only selectively and in many spheres the regime was only too willing to harness the independent initiative of businessmen, managers and technicians. Finally, given the highly uneven structure of ownership and organization in the German economy and the lack of unity between competing capitalist interests, a series of well-chosen tactical alliances were all that was needed to push vital parts of industry and commerce in the direction desired by the regime.

Once we bear in mind the constraints under which it operated it is, therefore, hard to escape the conclusion that the Third Reich was an extremely effective mobilizing regime. Furthermore, it is clear that this mobilization was from the outset directed towards the resurrection of Germany as a military power and in some general sense towards the achievement of Hitler's goals of conquest. But if one asks whether this economic mobilization was part of a coherent strategic synthesis, if one asks whether diplomacy, military planning and economic mobilization were united after 1933 in a coherent war plan, the answer delivered by this book is negative. In this respect we still struggle to unpick the effect of hindsight. We know, after all, that up to the frustration of Barbarossa in the autumn of 1941, Hitler's armies carried all before them. It seems hard to imagine that this remarkable military preponderance was not the result of long-term preparation. But the vertiginous conclusion suggested by recent military history is that this was indeed the case. Germany started the war in September 1939 with no substantial material or technical superiority over the better-established military powers of the West. It was only the fatal interlocking of Allied and German operational planning that led to the defeat of France in a few short weeks in May and June 1940. And it was this in turn that unleashed the Wehrmacht for its rampage through Southern and Eastern Europe in 1941, which was finally and predictably brought to a halt by the enormous expanse of the Soviet Union and the dogged though ill-directed resistance of the Red Army. The central chapters of this book are devoted to unlocking the puzzles that are implied by these compelling findings of battlefield historians. If the huge rearmament drive of the 1930s and the annexation of Austria and Czechoslovakia were not enough to give Germany a substantial material advantage over its enemies, if their immediate effect was to drive Britain and France into abandoning their pacificism in favour of an aggressive strategy of containment and to force both Washington and Moscow to reconsider their positions in Europe, why did Hitler go to war in September 1939?

Faced with this question, some historians choose to argue that Hitler simply miscalculated. He did not intend to precipitate a general European war, they insist. After his experience at Munich in 1938 he expected Britain and France to stand aside in Eastern Europe. It was not Hitler, but the Western powers who chose to turn Poland into a *casus belli*. That argumentative option is rejected here since it does not accord with the diplomatic evidence of the last days leading up to the war. In August 1939, as in September 1938, Hitler was confronted with the near certainty that Britain and France would declare war. On the former occasion he had pulled back. In 1939 he chose not to. Why he plunged forward rather than pulling back is explained in this book through a novel synthesis of three distinct elements.

The first point to emphasize is that Hitler knew by the summer of 1939 that his effort to develop a long-term programme of preparation for a war with the Western powers had failed. This, indeed, is one of the key findings of this book. Though, in 1938, Hitler's regime did attempt to respond to the growing resistance of the Western powers by embarking on a gigantic programme for 'full spectrum' rearmament and though Hitler and Ribbentrop did attempt to create a global alliance with the reach to match the emerging Western coalition, this attempt was frustrated. By the summer of 1939, German efforts to unite Italy and Japan into a triple threat against the British had manifestly failed. Furthermore, as this book shows for the first time in full detail, the German armaments economy in the summer of 1939 was being seriously squeezed by the persistent problems of the balance of payments. This is not to say that the Third Reich was facing an economic crisis. The combination of controls put in place in the course of the 1930s was undeniably effective in preventing the recurrence of a general crisis of the kind that had come close to destabilizing Hitler's regime in 1934. But in 1939 the precarious situation of the German balance of payments permitted no further acceleration of the armaments effort. Since Britain, France, the United States and the Soviet Union were all accelerating their rearmament at precisely this moment, Hitler found himself facing a sharp deterioration in the balance of forces at a date far earlier than he had expected.

Adding to the pressure for immediate action was the dramatic shift in the global diplomatic constellation. Through his breakneck aggression in 1938 and early 1939 Hitler had dismantled the French security cordon in Central Europe that had hinged on Czechoslovakia. However, after the occupation of Prague in the spring of 1939 the diplomatic fronts were hardened by the British and French guarantees to Poland and Romania. Everything now depended on the behaviour of the two flanking powers, the United States and the Soviet Union. In the summer of 1939 Stalin's decision to opt for a strategy based on fomenting inter-capitalist war tilted the balance in favour of Germany. The Nazi–Soviet pact guaranteed Germany against a second front in the East, and protected it against the worst effects of the much feared Anglo-French blockade. One can therefore construct a compelling economic-strategic rationale for Hitler's decision to go to war in September 1939. Given Germany's deteriorating economic position and the unexpectedly favourable shift in the diplomatic balance, Hitler had nothing further to gain by waiting. And as we have seen, Hitler spelled out this logic in virtually these words to anyone who would listen after September 1939.

But to confine ourselves to these rational elements of strategy would be to miss the crucial third ingredient in Hitler's decision-making process. To argue in terms of a strategic window of opportunity begs the question of why Hitler believed that war with the Western powers was inevitable. Why did he feel compelled to seize the opportunity, to gamble the future of his entire regime on a war with Britain and France, at a moment when Germany enjoyed, at most, only a slender military advantage? To explain this decision we must invoke ideology. This might seem paradoxical in light of the fact that Hitler was departing so flagrantly from the programme outlined in *Mein Kampf*. In that book, dictated in a prison cell in Landsberg fifteen years earlier, Hitler had called for an Anglo-German alliance against the Judaeo-Bolshevik threat. In 1939 he went to war with fronts reversed: in alliance with Stalin against Britain. This, however, is simplistic. The key to Hitler's ideology was not a particular diplomatic schema, but his obsessive fixation on racial struggle and in particular the antagonism between Aryans and Jews. In the Four Year Plan memorandum of 1936, the emphasis had still been on the Judaeo-Bolshevik conspiracy. Two years later, as foreign policy and armaments policy were directed ever more clearly against the West, there is a striking parallel in the shifting focus of the regime's anti-Semitic rhetoric. From 1938 onwards, in Hitler's public utterances, the Jewish question in its wider sense was emphatically a Western and above all an American question. As was shown in Chapters 8 and 9, from the Évian conference onwards and with ever greater intensity after Kristallnacht, President Roosevelt was identified as the chief agent of a worldwide Jewish conspiracy bent on the destruction of National Socialist Germany. It was no coincidence that Hitler's famous threat of annihilation of 30 January 1939 came as a direct response to Roosevelt's State of the Union address. The United States, as everyone understood, was the key to deciding the balance of the arms race. If Britain and France could count firmly on American aid, their position would be well nigh unassailable. But the position of the United States was precariously balanced. Whilst Roosevelt led the rhetorical assault against Hitler and encouraged Britain, France and Poland in their resistance to Nazi expansionism, isolationist currents in the United States were still strong. Hitler and the rest of the Nazi leadership could not help but interpret this complex situation through the dark haze of Manichaean anti-Semitism. For them, it was obvious that it was Jewish elements in Washington, London and Paris, bent implacably on the destruction of Nazi Germany, that were tightening the international encirclement. And it was this paranoid sense of menace that precipitated Hitler's decision to launch his strike against Poland and then against the Western coalition that continued to stand obstinately in his way.

It is perhaps not surprising that this factor was not emphasized in the speeches that Hitler made to the military leadership between May and August 1939 – certainly not in the notes taken by the military men who attended. But after the fact Hitler made no secret of its importance. Most emphatically in their conversations with the Italian leadership in the spring of 1940, both Hitler and Ribbentrop stressed the role of world Jewry in forcing the pace of events in 1939. And what is more, this peculiar combination of strategic and economic factors, overarched by Hitler's abiding anti-Semitic obsession, is capable not only of accounting for Hitler's decision to go to war. It can also make sense of his subsequent willingness to escalate the conflict to an ever larger scale. The decision to risk a general European war over Poland, the decision in the summer of 1940, after having defeated France but not having defeated Britain, to begin immediate preparations for an attack on the Soviet Union and finally in November–December 1941 the decision to support Japan in its aggression against the United States, all followed the same pattern. Faced with the coalition of enemies that had first shown itself in 1938, orchestrated, as Hitler believed, by the 'chosen one of world Jewry', he knew that time was not on his side. The combined economic might of the Western powers, added after June 1941 to that of the Soviet Union, was overwhelming. If he was ever to secure the *Lebensraum* that Germany needed for true strategic freedom, Hitler needed to strike hard and fast.

In relation to the early years of World War II, there are four points of novelty to emphasize as conclusions of this book.

The anti-Western turn in Nazi anti-Semitism, which we have identified as an important theme of 1938–9, continued unabated throughout 1940 and 1941. Having precipitated the war by backing Britain and France in their guarantee for Poland, Roosevelt was now prolonging the war by backing Churchill in his refusal to surrender, a constellation which in Berlin could be explained only by reference to the malevolent role of Jews in both Washington and London. This in turn implies that as far as motivation is concerned any hard and fast distinction between the wars in the West and the East must be softened if not abandoned altogether. Though in their modes of execution the wars were drastically different, to think of them as motivated in fundamentally different ways is mistaken. The war in the West against Churchill and Roosevelt was no less an ideological war than the war for *Lebensraum* in the East. And though the primary motivation for invading the Soviet Union in 1941, as opposed to a later date, was to force the pace of events in the West, by driving Britain into submission before America could intervene, this too must be seen as part of the larger war against world Jewry. To counterpose this 'strategic rationale' to Hitler's long-held ideological vision of a war of conquest in the East is to pose a false alternative.

Since 1938 Hitler had seen himself as locked in a global confrontation with world Jewry. Linking the campaign in the East to the war in the West, therefore, in no way diminishes its ideological content.

Having cleared aside that possible source of misunderstanding, the second point to make is that there was a compelling economic case for Hitler's decision to widen the war in 1941. The astonishing defeat of France in the early summer of 1940 had promised to change everything. But in fact the Wehrmacht's spectacular victory did not resolve Hitler's fundamental strategic dilemma. The German navy and air force were too weak to force Britain to the negotiating table. The competitive logic of the arms race continued to apply in 1940 and 1941. Rather than surrender to Hitler's will, Britain proved willing to go to the point of national bankruptcy before being rescued by lend-lease. And thanks to its comparatively abundant foreign reserves and American assistance it could mobilize a far larger percentage of foreign resources than Germany at this critical point in the war. In Berlin, by contrast, once the euphoria of victory had worn off, a considerable disillusionment set in over the economic viability of Germany's new *Grossraum*. Conquering most of Western Europe added a drastic shortage of oil, nagging difficulties in coal supply and a serious shortage of animal feed to Germany's already severe deficiencies. The populations of Western Europe were a vital asset, as was their industrial capacity, but, given the constraints imposed by the British blockade, it was far from clear that these resources could be effectively mobilized. Unless Germany could secure access to the grain surpluses and oil of the Soviet Union, and organize a sustained increase in coal production, continental Europe was threatened with a prolonged decline in output, productivity and living standards. Added to which, Roosevelt had launched his own spectacular rearmament programme within days of Germany's breakthrough at Sedan. The strategic pressure on Hitler to pre-empt decisive American intervention in the war can only really be appreciated if we do full justice to the scale of the Anglo-American effort from as early as the summer of 1940. In this respect, the truly vast discrepancy between Anglo-American aircraft procurement and Germany's relatively insignificant outsourcing to France and the Netherlands is very telling. It was an imbalance that was not lost on Goering and the German Air Ministry.

Giving due weight to the trans-Atlantic arms race in German calculations in 1940–41 also helps us to explain another conundrum which has continued to preoccupy students of the Nazi regime and which seriously influences the way in which we write its history. Contrary to the claims of some authors, the Ostheer of 1941 was considerably more powerful than that which invaded France. But it is equally undeniable that it was a force carefully calibrated on the assumption that the Red Army could be destroyed in a short campaign. German planning provided for no margin of error. Even on a charitable reading, therefore, the Barbarossa campaign was surrounded by enormous risks. It appears irrational and foolhardy when this evidence of minimal mobilization is combined with the most widely cited industrial statistics, which appear to show stagnation in armaments output and a catastrophic collapse in labour productivity between 1940 and 1941. In the light of this data, it would seem that complacency and inefficiency following the victory over France, combined with racist condescension towards the Soviets, prevented the Wehrmacht from maximizing its chances in what was clearly the decisive campaign of the war. If this were true, this moment of 'failure' should clearly stand at the centre of our entire interpretation of Hitler's regime. However, once we consider the wider strategic situation and combine this with critical scrutiny of the economic evidence, a very different picture emerges. The idea that armaments production in Germany lagged in 1940–41 and that there was a dramatic collapse in productivity is in large part a statistical illusion. Furthermore, a narrow focus on armaments production ignores what was one of the most distinctive features of the early German war effort, a huge wave of investment that continued almost uninterruptedly between 1939 and 1942. When we give this its due weight, we realize something crucial. Thanks to America's backing for Britain, Germany continued to be locked into the logic of the trans-Atlantic arms race, even whilst it was girding itself for Barbarossa. Germany's industrial resources could never be fully concentrated on the Soviet Union, because at the same time enormous preparations needed to be set in train for the coming air war with Britain and America. It was after the stupendous German military victories in France, therefore, that Hitler adopted what can justifiably be described as a Blitzkrieg strategy, a coordinated strategy in which both armament production and strategic planning were premised on the assumption of swift and decisive battlefield victory over the Red Army. Its purpose, however, was not to cushion the civilian population. Its purpose was to allow Germany to fight two wars at once.

One might in fact say that the Third Reich in the spring of 1941 was preparing itself not for two wars, but for three wars: one against the Red Army, one against the British and Americans and a third against the civilian population of Eastern Europe, beginning with the Jews. And here too 'pragmatic economic' motives and genocidal ideology were inseparably intertwined. On the one hand the SS programmes of genocidal population clearance, to begin with the Jews, were embedded in the Generalplan Ost in an extraordinary vision of agricultural and industrial colonization. Conversely, in the Hunger Plan agreed by the Ministries in the spring of 1941 the most straightforward pragmatic calculation of the food supply was combined with assumptions of racial hierarchy to produce a plan for mass murder, which dwarfed even the Wannsee programme.

This global Blitzkrieg, this grand strategy of racial war, turned out, however, to be a strategy not of victory but of defeat. Already at Smolensk in July–August 1941 Barbarossa ran aground. Meanwhile America was ever more firmly committed to providing aid both to Britain and the Soviet Union. Faced with the ever greater certainty of having to fight a two- or even three-front war, the extraordinary strategic synthesis that the Third Reich had concocted over the previous twelve months fell apart. By December Hitler, true to his conspiratorial logic, had declared war on the United States in alliance with the Japanese. Convinced that open war with the United States was, in any case, only a matter of months away, he seized on the strategic diversion provided by the Japanese offensive in the Pacific. It was to his verbal exchanges of January 1939 with Roosevelt that Hitler repeatedly returned in the autumn of 1941 as he was mulling over both the ultimate shape of the Final Solution and the possibility of a strategic escape from the two-front war in which the Third Reich now found itself.

By any reasonable estimation, Hitler's declaration of war on the United States sealed the fate of Germany. The economic and military forces arrayed against the Third Reich by early 1942 were overwhelming. As we have shown, this fatalistic view was shared by all those most closely involved with the management of the German war effort up to the Moscow crisis. Udet of the Luftwaffe, Fromm of the army, Thomas of the Wehrmacht high command, Todt in the Armaments Ministry, Canaris in intelligence, Rohland and his colleagues in the Ruhr, all came to the same conclusion. All these men had thrown in their lot with

Hitler's regime. But they were not ignorant of the basic trends of early twentieth-century history. They were as convinced as the vast majority of their contemporaries of the pivotal importance of the United States economy. None of them doubted that once American industrial capacity was mobilized – and they were fully aware of the measures that had already been taken in 1940 and 1941 – Germany's situation would be worse than that of 1918. To have thought anything else would have been to fly in the face of contemporary common sense, well reflected in the anxieties of the general public that were faithfully recorded by Gestapo informants. The full extent of America's production triumphs after 1942 came as a surprise even to the Americans. But the basic script had already been written in 1917–18 and in the endless retelling of the Fordist narrative throughout the 1920s and 1930s. And the fact was, of course, that the pessimism of the leading German experts did not even give full weight to the extraordinary industrial and military staying power of the Soviet Union that in fact turned out to be the Wehrmacht's main problem in 1942 and 1943.

This pessimism, however, should throw stark light on the group of individuals who took charge of the German war effort in the aftermath of the Moscow crisis. There has never been any argument about the motivations of men such as Herbert Backe, the orchestrator of the Hunger Plan, or Gauleiter Fritz Sauckel with his pan-European press-gangs. Nor should there be any further argument about Albert Speer. These men were not unpolitical agents of technocratic efficiency. They were the Hitler loyalists willing to do their bit for the Third Reich to the bitter end. They were the men on whom Hitler could rely even in the last months of the war. And they would literally stop at nothing to continue the fight. Speer's 'armaments miracle' relied on resources mobilized by every facet of the Nazi state. The Reichsbank, the Ministry of Economic Affairs and the Finance Ministry played an important but largely unacknowledged role in preserving the stability of the German currency, at least until the beginning of 1944. German industry rallied all its energies in a desperate effort to prevail against the Soviet Union. But these seemingly innocuous components of the German war effort were multiply interconnected with the sinister nexus of political power organized around the questions of labour and food by Gauleiter Sauckel, State Secretary Herbert Backe, Hermann Goering and Heinrich Himmler. Through their combined efforts, in 1942 millions of extra workers were mobilized for German industry and the food balance of Europe was drastically redistributed so as to secure the calories and protein necessary to fuel Albert Speer's armaments miracle. As we showed in Chapter 16, in the summer of 1942 even the wholesale gassing of the Jews of Poland was made to serve a functional purpose in this radicalized form of Total War. And from the summer of 1943 onwards Speer came to rely ever more heavily on a coercive partnership with Heinrich Himmler and the SS.

The emphasis on rationalization in the management of the German war effort that emerged from the crisis of 1941 was certainly new. And after Speer's appointment German armaments output did increase. However, to treat this as the apolitical expression of Speer's technocratic abilities is to miss the point. The entire purpose of the 'armaments miracle' was political. Loudly trumpeted by the new line in 'armaments propaganda', it served to answer the fundamental doubt that increasingly beset the German war effort. The essential message of the rationalization campaign was that Germany's obvious material inferiority need not be fatal. With the proper application of will-power and energetic youthful improvisation, more could be produced for less. And, as the Wehrmacht had so often demonstrated, there was no limit to what German soldiers could achieve, provided only that they had the necessary weapons.

The point is not of course to dismiss entirely the increase in armaments production achieved by Speer and Milch. It was real enough. But no less real was its strategic failure. The essence of Hitler's gamble in December 1941 was timing. After the declaration of war on the United States the need to achieve a decisive success against the Red Army was more pressing than ever. In this crucial respect Speer's Armaments Ministry failed. In 1942, in the first full flush of the 'armaments miracle', Germany was considerably outproduced by the extraordinary mobilization of the Soviet economy. This Soviet effort was unsustainable. By 1944 Germany had caught up with and overtaken the Soviet Union. But as both the Soviets and the Germans knew, the summer, autumn and winter battles of 1942–3 were the key to deciding the war on the Eastern Front. And in this crucial period it was the Soviet factories that prevailed. This window of opportunity was so important because during most of 1942 Britain and America's offensive operations against the Third Reich were marginal in their impact. As of the autumn of 1942 this was no longer the case. The weight of British and American material made itself felt

first in North Africa and the Mediterranean, then in the defeat of the
German U-boats and, as of the spring of 1943, in sustained aerial
bombardment. Combined with the elimination of Mussolini in July
1943, the opening of a significant 'second front' had a truly dramatic
effect. For six months in 1943 the disruption caused by British and
American bombing halted Speer's armaments miracle in its tracks. The
German home front was rocked by a serious crisis of morale. By July
1943 the war was obviously lost.

The final, famous acceleration of German armaments production in
1944, on which the reputation of Speer's Armaments Ministry largely
rests, took place amidst a maelstrom of apocalyptic violence that consumed the lives of millions of people and laid waste to a large part of
the Continent. First in the Mittelbau and then in the brutal practices of
the Jaegerstab, the murderous violence of the SS police state was
imported directly into the war economy. Tens of thousands of out-of-
date fighters were squeezed out of Germany's factories in the first half of
1944 by mobilizing all available labour and materials, applying virtually
limitless powers of repression and exploiting every possibility for economies of scale. In the summer of 1944, Speer and the Jaegerstab maintained a telephone hotline to the ramp at Auschwitz, where SS guards
were processing the Jews of Hungary, the last great population to be
fed to the gas chambers. It was in the dank, deathly gloom of Hans
Kammler's underground factories that the Third Reich made its final
futile bid to match the Americans in mass-production.

Hitler had prophesied that if Germany did not prevail against its
enemies, it would face a national catastrophe unlike anything in modern
history. From 1942 onwards he and his collaborators, Albert Speer chief
amongst them, steered Germany directly towards this outcome. Even
now, the damage inflicted by Hitler's regime and by his futile war is
almost unbearable to contemplate. Decades after the event, the memory
of the harm done – to the population of Europe, to the physical fabric
of daily life, to the very idea of European civilization – is still enough to
inspire feelings of despair, rage and resentment, and not only on the
part of Germany's victims. Here is not the place to attempt a review of
this horror. But since economic historians have ways of making disasters,
such as that which Germany brought down upon itself in 1945, disappear from the long-run trajectory of economic growth, it is worth
lingering a little on this scene.

The destruction and human misery in Germany in 1945 is barely describable in its scale.[2] As the Third Reich collapsed, quite apart from the millionfold murder that Germany had committed across Europe, more than one-third of the boys born to German families between 1915 and 1924 were either dead or missing. Amongst those born between 1920 and 1925 losses amounted to 40 per cent. The rest of the German population was subject to uprooting and displacement on a truly epic scale. Whilst the 11 million Wehrmacht men who had survived the war in uniform were herded into makeshift prisoner of war camps administered by the occupying forces, a similar number of 9–10 million non-German displaced persons enjoyed an unwonted degree of freedom, whilst they waited to be repatriated to their homes in Eastern and Western Europe. At the same time 9 million German evacuees streamed back towards their devastated cities. Meanwhile, to the east there was an extraordinary human avalanche, as 14.16 million ethnic Germans were driven systematically out of their homes in Eastern and Central Europe by the embittered Slav population. Of this spectacular exodus at least 1.71 million would die en route. The country to which they 'returned' presented a scene of devastation and poverty that defies description. Large parts of Germany had been reduced to 'a rubble-strewn wasteland in which the living often envied the dead'.[3] At least 3.8 million out of a stock of 19 million apartments had been destroyed. In the cities hit hardest by the bombing, losses in housing stock ran to 50 per cent.[4] Huddled in overcrowded and half-ruined apartments, the German population, which until the autumn of 1944 had been reasonably well fed, now starved and froze.

Unlike the Germans during their reign over Europe, the Allies did what was necessary to keep the German population alive. But they did so with reservations. As General Lucius D. Clay, Eisenhower's deputy, put it in June 1945: 'Conditions are going to be extremely difficult in Germany this winter and there will be much cold and hunger. Some cold and hunger will be necessary to make the German people realize the consequences of a war which they caused.'[5] Nevertheless, Clay also insisted that 'this type of suffering should not extend to the point where it results in mass starvation and sickness'.[6] Joint Chiefs of Staffs Directive 1067, the basic instructions issued to the occupying forces in 1945, specified that food should be provided to Germany sufficient only to prevent 'disease and unrest'. Until 1948, however, the food supply in all four zones of occupation fell well short of what was required. As a direct result of decisions taken by Speer and the Zentrale Planung in 1943 and 1944, the nitrogen fertilizer needed by German farms had been directed instead to the production of explosives and ammunition. Yields were drastically down. To make matters worse, Germany's richest grain surplus area east of the Oder–Neisse was awarded to the Poles at the Potsdam agreement. Supplies were brought in from across the Atlantic, but by the early summer of 1946 rations in many parts of urban Germany were below 1,000 calories per day. Despite the flourishing black market, the evidence of serious malnutrition was unmistakable. Mortality increased as did the incidence of hunger-related diseases. Infection rates for diphtheria, typhoid and tuberculosis in the British and American zones doubled. The birth weight of babies fell drastically. Even the most intrepid statisticians hesitate to plumb the depths to which Germany had fallen by the end of 1945. Money had long since ceased to function in any ordinary sense of the word. One estimate for 1946 puts German per capita GDP at just over $2,200, a figure not seen since the 1880s, one-tenth the level that Germans enjoy today. And this certainly exaggerates the actual level of economic activity in the second half of 1945. Coal production, the lifeline of modern urban society, was down by 80 per cent, and the coal that was available could not be distributed, given the ruination of the railway system.

Nor should we underestimate the intensity of hatred felt towards Germany by its neighbours and former enemies. If it is true that Germans after 1945 were forced to swallow at least some of their sense of victimhood, it is no less true that Germany's former enemies thought it better to forget the sense of rage that clearly motivated much of Allied policy in the immediate aftermath of the war. In 1945 along the Dutch-German border, American GIs passed signs that read: 'Here Ends the Civilized World'.[7] It is one of the most persistent myths in post-war history that the Allies learned the lesson from World War I not to extract reparations from Germany. In fact, both halves of Germany paid substantially higher reparations after 1945 than the Weimar Republic ever did. Not surprisingly, the Soviets were most determined in their pursuit of compensation. What was to become the German Democratic Republic suffered the dismantling of at least 30 per cent of its industrial capital stock and paid occupation costs and reparations to the Soviet Union which even in 1953 still totalled almost 13 per cent of its national income.[8] The Federal Republic for its part was more leniently treated. But it too made payments between 1953 and 1992 totalling in excess of 90 billion Deutschmarks. And it was not merely physical capital that was dismantled. In the Soviet zone, tens of thousands of suspect members of the Nazi party were rounded up for interrogation and summary trials. Many thousands were executed. The Western powers, not surprisingly, adopted more legalistic procedures. Roughly 200,000 Nazi suspects were arrested and detained in internment camps, including many leaders of German big business. Of 5,153 individuals accused of major war crimes, 668 were condemned to death by military tribunals. In addition, in the first burst of enthusiasm, the Western Allies dismissed almost half the civil servants in their zones and required millions to register for denazification. Though this process ultimately degenerated into a cynical farce, in its early stages it was perceived by the German population as a threatening intervention in the structure of social life. Viewed in conjunction with the high-profile trials at Nuremberg, it was one more sign of Germany's pariah status.

The initial post-war period thus went a long way towards confirming Hitler's apocalyptic view of politics. Germany had ceased to exist as a political entity, as a military force or an economic unit. The terrible irony, however, is that in the years that followed it was not Hitler's logic but Stresemann's that prevailed. In 1919, with his eye on the Bolshevik threat in the East, Stresemann had predicted that the time would soon come when Germany would again be needed. After World War II, with the Red Army in Vienna and Berlin, it took barely two years for the same insight to impose itself in Washington and London. To stave off collapse and a surge in support for the Communist party, reconstruction began already over the winter of 1946–7. In the 1920s Stresemann had gambled that the German economy was so integral to the wider economy of Europe that it would be in the interest of none of the victor powers to see it permanently crippled. In 1947 American Secretary of State General George Marshall made his famous offer of aid to Europe dependent on the inclusion of Germany. At first this was hard for France to swallow. France's national programme of economic reconstruction after 1945 was premised on the assumption that it would be France not Germany that controlled the resources of the Ruhr. But within three years of Marshall's announcement, it was the French, as they had done in 1929, who came forward with proposals for European integration based this time around a European Coal and Steel Community and a European Defence Community. To complete the bitter irony, Konrad Adenauer, who as the Chancellor of the Federal Republic between 1949 and 1963 was to steer West Germany towards its position at the heart both of the European Community and NATO, was in fact two years older than Gustav Stresemann, who had been only 51 at the time of his death in 1929.[9]

A functioning parliamentary system, an alliance with America and closer European economic integration were all goals to which Stresemann clearly aspired. But in the 1920s Weimar politics had still been animated and ultimately destabilized by the idea that Germany would one day re-emerge as a great power in the classic eighteenth- and nineteenth-century sense. What precisely this meant was already questionable in the aftermath of World War I and its demonstration of the futility of war as a means of great power politics. But 'freedom of action' in international relations was clearly still constitutive of full sovereignty, for Stresemann as much as for most other Europeans. After the horror of Nazism and World War II, democratization, the Western alliance and closer European integration were all back to the fore. The apocalyptic temptation of militarism was largely exorcized from Europe. Its dying embers flared up only occasionally in the rearguard actions of empire. But with it also went any aspiration to the 'freedom' once implied by great power status. As early as the autumn of 1943, after the Battle of Kursk, the United States had realized that the dominant power in Europe for the foreseeable future would be the Soviet Union, not Britain, let alone France. At first Roosevelt's administration hoped to adjust to this new reality in cooperation with the Soviets. Together the two superpowers would rule both Europe and the world, under which circumstances it might have been possible to 'do without Germany'. But by 1947 that option was clearly off the table. First West Germany and then East Germany were resurrected as independent states. Their subsequent economic recovery along with that of the rest of Europe was one of the true miracles of the twentieth century. The success in creating a democratic polity in West Germany was also remarkable. So free, in fact, did West Germany seem of the tensions that had plagued the Weimar Republic, that some were even tempted to suppose that the curative fire of National Socialism had been necessary to drive out the German demons. What this ignores, however, is that German democracy after

1945 was not as anyone had imagined it in the 1920s. It existed within a strange and truncated form of statehood and much the same might be said for most, if not all, of the former 'great powers' of Europe. Through the middle of Germany's territory ran the new battle lines of the Cold War. Huge forces of occupation were massed on either side, non-European forces – American on one side, Soviet on the other. The threat of nuclear annihilation hung over everyone. And though West Germany certainly had a functioning democracy, the scope of political debate was also incomparably more restricted than it had been in the 1920s. The most explosive issues of Weimar politics – the question of territorial integrity and the question of military parity – were removed, it seemed, for ever from the political agenda. The economic miracle was the abiding preoccupation of the West German Republic, as it was for the rest of Europe. The drama of twenty-five years of unprecedented economic growth moved 'politics', in the classic sense, to the sidelines. Even the remarkable project of European integration resolved itself into an endless process of bartering over milk quotas and national rebates. The catastrophe of the Third Reich had not brought about the extinction of Germany, but what it had done was to draw the curtain on the classic era of European politics. Sixty years later, what else there might be to politics in Europe beyond the tiresome squabbles of discontented affluence remains an open question.

Appendix:
Supplementary Data

Table A1. The current account: Germany's dependence on foreign resources

	Current account (1)	Balance of trade (2)	Balance of trade in services, interest, dividends and reparations (3)
1913	939	−673	1,612
1924	−1,664	−1,816	152
1925	−3,045	−2,444	−601
1926	−39	793	−832
1927	−4,244	−2,960	−1,284
1928	−3,192	−1,311	−1,881
1929	−2,469	−44	−2,425
1930	−610	1,558	−2,168
1931	1,040	2,778	−1,738
1932	257	1,052	−795
1933	132	666	−534
1934	−534	−373	−161
1935	−107	−8	−99
1936	615	544	71
1937	259	437	−178
1938	−566	−319	−247
1939	53	376	−323
1940	−1,012	−72	−940
1941	−3,331	39	−3,370

Note: Column (1) is the sum of (2) and (3). A positive entry on the current account implies that Germany was accumulating claims on foreign economies. Conversely, a negative entry implies German borrowing from abroad, or other unrequited acquisitions of foreign exchange or gold, e.g. taking control of Austrian gold reserves or imposing occupation payments not described as reparations.

Sources: W. G. Hoffmann, *Das Wachstum der deutschen Wirtschaft* (Berlin, 1965), 816–28; A. Ritschl, 'Die deutsche Zahlungsbilanz 1936–1941', *VfZ* 39 (1991), 123

Table A2. Production of key raw material inputs, Germany pre-1938 territory

	Production in 000 tons:						Production relative to 1929:						
	Coal (anthracite)	Raw steel	Electrically smelted steel	Aluminium	Fuel hydration, oil drilling and benzol	Zellwolle and artificial silk	Total industrial production	Coal (anthracite)	Raw steel	Electrically smelted steel	Aluminium	Fuel hydration, oil drilling and benzol	Zellwolle and artificial silk
1929	163,441	16,246	131	34	499	28	100	100	100	100	100	100	100
1930	142,695	11,538	95	32	546	29	83	87	71	73	94	109	104
1931	118,634	8,292	83	31	575	31	66	73	51	63	91	115	111
1932	104,731	5,764	71	24	535	28	58	64	35	54	69	107	100
1933	109,905	7,612	120	18	584	33	67	67	47	91	54	117	118
1934	124,891	11,916	172	37	690	46	83	76	73	131	109	138	164
1935	143,013	16,446	260	71	994	62	97	88	101	198	208	199	221
1936	158,407	19,216	380	97	1,294	88	107	97	118	289	285	259	314
1937	184,489	19,849	526	128	1,621	156	119	113	122	401	374	325	557

1938	186,186	22,656	697	166	1,928	220	132	114	139	531	486	386	786
1939	187,956	22,508	914	200	2,344	280	140	115	139	697	585	470	1,000
1940	184,354	19,141	992	211	3,318	317	135	113	118	756	620	665	1,132
1941	186,531	20,836	1,163	234	3,946	383	138	114	128	886	686	791	1,368
1942	187,920	20,480	1,276	264	4,649	411	140	115	126	973	774	932	1,468
1943	190,482	20,758	528	250	5,149	411	157	117	128	402	733	1,032	1,468
1944	166,059	18,318	1,512	244	4,018	389	154	102	113	1,152	716	805	1,389

Sources: *Statistisches Handbuch von Deutschland; Statistisches Jahrbuch fuer das Deutsche Reich* (various); R. Wagenfuehr, *Die deutsche Industrie im Kriege* (Berlin, 1954)

Table A3. Steel production and allocation, 1937–1944 (000 monthly tons)

| | Production: | | Allocations to: | | | | | | |
	Steel production, pre-war Germany	Steel production Grossraum	Total allocation	Wehrmacht total/direct armaments	Army	Four Year Plan OKW	Export	Pre-1938, steel available for other purposes	Grossraum steel available for other purposes
1937/II	1,531			300	146	120	505	606	
1937/III	1,580			235	146	120			
1937/IV	1,638			268	146	105			
1938/I	1,881			302	146	145			
1938/II	1,891			325	146	100	398	1068	
1938/III	1,994			658	387	140	398	798	
1938/IV	2,011			593	387				
1939/I	2,090			525	210				
1939/II	2,026			628	210				
1939/III	1,976			575	215				
1939/IV	1,819			859	306	206	173	581	
1940/I	1,678		1,835	924	342	247	200	307	
1940/II	1,736		1,884	880	445	252	200	404	

1940/III		1,820	1,885	900	305	225	258	437	
1940/IV		1,916	2,204	1,017	350	242	330	327	
1941/I	2,298	1,922	2,258	1,000	290	287	364	271	647
1941/II	2,374	1,970	2,375	1,040	270	304	451	175	579
1941/III	2,378	1,970	2,519	1,120	227	355	455	40	448
1941/IV	2,362	1,961	2,309	1,032	180	322	403		605
1942/I	2,141	1,786	2,644	1,153	349	388	418		182
1942/II	2,283	1,857	2,777	1,073	350	371	418		421
1942/III	2,473	1,975	2,217	994	400	294	270		915
1942/IV	2,684	2,141	2,611	1,253					
1943/I	2,687		2,654	1,414					
1943/II	2,511		2,896	1,475					
1943/III	2,517		2,431	1,298					
1943/IV	2,486		2,374	1,269					
1944/I	2,573		2,562	1,338					
1944/II	2,496		2,600	1,363					
1944/III	2,236		2,328	1,246					
1944/IV	1,314		2,054	1,179					

Note: Rations before 1938 are adjusted downwards to allow for the fact that rations after 1938 are counted in finished steel weight which is generally lower than the raw steel measure used in the first months of rationing.

Sources: USSBS, *The Effects of Strategic Bombing*, 250–51; R. Wagenfuehr, *Die deutsche Industrie im Kriege* (Berlin, 1954), 168; M. Geyer, 'Ruestungsbeschleunigung und Inflation', *MGM* 30 (1981), 163; Mueller, in *DRZW* 5/2. 555

Table A4. Armaments position of the Wehrmacht

	Numbers of weapons:				% Increase:				
	October 1939	May 1940	June 1941	January 1942	May 1940 over October 1939	June 1941 over May 1940	January 1942 over June 1941	Firepower per man, May 1940 over October 1939	Firepower per man, June 1941 over May 1940
Rifles K 98	2,569,300	3,228,500	4,372,800	4,717,500	25.7	35.4	7.9	7.1	13.8
MP 38 and 40	5,711	27,800	166,700	205,450	386.8	499.6	23.2	315.0	403.9
MGs	103,300	150,400	203,250	206,500	45.6	35.1	1.6	24.1	13.6
2 centimetre Flak 30	895	1,487	2,153	2,690	66.1	44.8	24.9	41.6	21.7
3.7 centimetre Pak	10,560	14,257	15,522	13,348	35.0	8.9	-14.0	15.1	-8.5
Light mortar	5,062	9,957	16,129	15,579	96.7	62.0	-3.4	67.7	36.1
Heavy mortar	3,959	7,091	11,767	11,719	79.1	65.9	-0.4	52.7	39.4
10 centimetre Nebelwerfer	179	288	1,112	953	60.9	286.1	-14.3	37.2	224.5
Light Infantry Gun 18	2,931	3,365	4,176	4,022	14.8	24.1	-3.7	-2.1	4.3
Heavy Infantry Gun 33	367	491	867	866	33.8	76.6	-0.1	14.1	48.4
L. Howitzer 16 u. 18	4,919	5,538	7,076	6,772	12.6	27.8	-4.3	-4.0	7.4
H. Howitzer	2,434	2,383	2,867	2,746	-2.1	20.3	-4.2	-16.5	1.1

Heavy artillery 21–42 centimetre	47	163	442	548	246.8	171.2	24.0	195.7	127.9
Infantry ammunition, million rounds	6,665	8,459	9,774	7,176	26.9	15.5	–26.6	8.2	–2.9
Pz. U. Pak shells, million rounds	36	77	79	69	115.4	2.0	–11.7	83.6	–14.3
Artillery shells, million rounds	29	57	90	64	94.7	58.2	–29.7	66.0	32.9
PzKampfW I	1,305	1,266	966	817	–3.0	–23.7	–15.4	–17.3	–35.9
PzKampfW II	991	1,110	1,159	996	12.0	4.4	–14.1	–4.5	–12.3
PzKampfW III	151	785	1,440	1,866	419.9	83.4	29.6	343.2	54.2
PzKampfW IV	143	290	572	511	102.8	97.2	–10.7	72.9	65.7
PzKampfW 38 t	122	238	754	434	95.1	216.8	–42.4	66.3	166.2
Total light tank	2,296	2,376	2,125	1,813	3.5	–10.6	–14.7	–11.8	–24.8
Total medium tank	416	1,313	2,766	2,811	215.6	110.7	1.6	169.1	77.0
Half-tracks	5,200	7,997	15,642	19,129	53.8	95.6	22.3	31.1	64.4
Wehrmacht strength	4,556,000	5,766,448	7,309,000	7,648,000	26.6	26.8		4.6	
Army numbers	3,706,000	4,347,000	5,200,000	5,428,000	17.3	19.6		4.4	

Sources: Kroener, in DRZW 5/1. 731, 826, 834, 959; Mueller, in DRZW 5/1. 554–5

Table A5. Germany's grain supply, 1932–1944 (million tons)

	1932–3	1933–4	1934–5	1935–6	1936–7	1937–8	1938–9
Grain harvest	22.8	24.3	20.3	21.0	20.9	21.1	24.9
Net imports	0.4	-0.4	1.1	0.0	1.2	1.6	1.6
Stocks at start of year	1.0	2.0	3.1	3.4	1.7	2.0	3.2
Available quantity	25.1	27.0	24.8	22.8	24.1	25.8	33.1
Seed and loss	2.5	2.5	2.4	2.4	2.4	2.3	2.5
Domestic consumption	19.8	20.3	18.8	20.4	19.5	19.1	20.7
Stocks at end of year	2.0	3.1	3.4	1.7	2.0	3.2	6.6

	1938–9	1939–40	1940–41	1941–2	1942–3	1943–4
Grain harvest	29.6	27.5	24.0	23.6	22.7	23.9
Net imports	2.5	2.1	2.2	3.0	5.1	4.6
Stocks at start of year	4.8	8.8	7.5	3.1	1.8	2.5
Available quantity	36.9	38.4	33.7	29.7	29.6	31.0
Seed and loss	3.0	3.0	2.9	3.0	2.9	2.9
Domestic consumption	25.1	27.9	27.7	24.9	24.2	25.0
Stocks at end of year	8.8	7.5	3.1	1.8	2.5	3.1

Sources: A. Hanau and R. Plate, *Die deutsche landwirtschaftliche Preis- und Marktpolitik im Zweiten Weltkrieg* (Stuttgart, 1975), 49; *Statistisches Handbuch von Deutschland*, 489–90; *Statistisches Jahrbuch fuer das Deutsche Reich 1937*, 367

Table A6. The armaments production index of the Speer Ministry

	Armaments index	Weapons	Tanks	Vehicles	Aircraft	Ships and submarines	Ammunition	Powder	Explosives
1941	97	106	81	n/a	97	110	102	96	103
1942	133	137	130	120	133	142	166	129	132
1943	216	234	330	138	216	182	247	200	191
1944	277	348	536	110	277	157	306	212	226
January 1942	103	98	93	108	112	90	98	103	101
February 1942	97	102	107	93	88	111	102	97	99
March 1942	129	111	80	129	151	109	115	111	123
April 1942	133	122	129	123	135	162	124	108	125
May 1942	135	150	152	125	133	113	144	116	141
June 1942	144	125	122	137	131	165	173	129	149
July 1942	153	148	122	131	145	113	177	132	138
August 1942	153	135	134	123	140	136	201	134	122
September 1942	155	149	131	105	142	133	202	160	131
October 1942	154	150	144	116	133	134	209	151	147
November 1942	165	155	146	109	134	202	222	148	153
December 1942	181	195	199	135	155	187	229	153	150
January 1943	182	169	154	128	172	190	215	168	176
February 1943	207	185	169	132	227	164	230	184	169
March 1943	216	216	210	168	205	233	239	185	200
April 1943	215	212	289	145	216	185	229	194	169
May 1943	232	235	465	144	211	207	245	205	191

Table A6. The armaments production index of the Speer Ministry – *continued*

	Armaments index	Weapons	Tanks	Vehicles	Aircraft	Ships and submarines	Ammunition	Powder	Explosives
June 1943	226	238	340	161	233	208	230	200	199
July 1943	229	238	367	146	236	163	238	214	192
August 1943	224	240	328	129	228	158	245	200	189
September 1943	234	260	495	128	222	191	259	201	194
October 1943	242	269	454	133	237	171	265	216	206
November 1943	231	264	364	122	216	168	282	219	211
December 1943	222	280	415	116	186	140	288	208	198
January 1944	241	274	438	142	232	140	281	204	208
February 1944	231	284	460	122	186	170	303	219	234
March 1944	270	301	498	133	262	153	314	226	163
April 1944	274	320	527	121	285	127	302	230	254
May 1944	285	337	567	126	295	152	301	242	276
June 1944	297	361	580	133	321	107	307	223	276
July 1944	322	384	589	117	367	139	319	209	267
August 1944	297	382	558	116	308	141	323	224	182
September 1944	301	377	527	84	310	184	335	219	175
October 1944	273	372	516	79	255	217	321	205	205
November 1944	268	375	571	78	274	124	307	173	201
December 1944	263	408	598	63	224	233	263	166	178
January 1945	227	284	557	60	231	164	226	162	128

Source: R. Wagenfuehr, *Die deutsche Industrie im Kriege* (Berlin, 1954), 180–81

Notes

In the Notes, the most frequently cited secondary works are abbreviated as follows:

Domarus	M. Domarus (ed.), *Adolf Hitler: Reden und Proklamationen, 1932–1945* (Munich, 1965), 2 vols.
DRZW	*Das deutsche Reich und der Zweite Weltkrieg* (Stuttgart, 1979–), 9 vols.
Eichholtz	D. Eichholtz, *Geschichte der deutschen Kriegswirtschaft 1939–1945* (Berlin, 1969–96), 3 vols.
Halder Diary	C. Burdick and H.-A. Jacobsen (eds.), *The Halder War Diary 1939–1942* (London, 1988)
Weinberg, *Foreign Policy I*	G. L. Weinberg, *The Foreign Policy of Hitler's Germany: Diplomatic Revolution in Europe, 1933–1936* (Chicago, 1970)
Weinberg, *Foreign Policy II*	G. L. Weinberg, *The Foreign Policy of Hitler's Germany: Starting World War II, 1937–1939* (Chicago, 1980)

The major collections of published sources referred to are abbreviated as follows:

ADAP	*Akten zur deutschen auswaertigen Politik*, ser. D. (Baden-Baden, 1950–57)
DGFP	*Documents on German Foreign Policy*, ser D. (London, 1962–4)
IMT	International Military Tribunal, *Trial of the Major War Criminals before the International Military Tribunal, Nuremberg 14 November 1945–1 October 1946* (Nuremberg, 1949), 42 vols.
Meldungen	H. Boberach (ed.), *Meldungen aus dem Reich 1938–1945: Die geheimen Lageberichte des Sicherheitsdienstes der SS* (Herrsching, 1984), 17 vols.

Archival references are abbreviated as follows:

BAH	Bundesarchiv Hoppegarten Branch
BAL	Bundesarchiv Lichterfelde Branch
BAMA	Bundesarchiv Militaerarchiv Freiburg
MA	Moscow Archives
NA	National Archive Washington
PRO	Public Record Office (National Archive, UK)

Other abbreviations used:

GG	*Geschichte und Gesellschaft*
HWJ	*History Workshop Journal*
HZ	*Historische Zeitschrift*
IfK	Institut fuer Konjunkturforschung
IWM	Imperial War Museum
JbW	*Jahrbuch fuer Wirtschaftsgeschichte*
MGM	*Militaergeschichtliche Mitteilungen*
VfZ	Vierteljahreshefte fuer *Zeitgeschichte*
VWSG	*Vierteljahresschrift fuer Wirtschafts- und Sozialgeschichte*
VzK	*Vierteljahreshefte zur Konjunkturforschung*

Preface

1 K. Marx, '18th Brumaire of Louis Napoleon', in K. Marx and F. Engels, *Selected Works in Two Volumes* (Moscow, 1958), I. 247.
2 M. Burleigh, *The Third Reich: A New History* (London, 2000).
3 B. Wegner, 'Hitler, der Zweite Weltkrieg und die Choreographie des Untergangs', *Geschichte und Gesellschaft*, 26 (2000), 493–518.

1 Introduction

1 For reflections on this polarity, see M. Geyer, 'The Stigma of Violence, Nationalism, and War in Twentieth-Century Germany', *German Studies Review*, 15 (1992), 75–110, and K. H. Jarausch and M. Geyer, *Shattered Past: Reconstructing German Histories* (Princeton, 2003).
2 H. James, *A German Identity 1770–1990* (London, 1989), 177–89.
3 For summaries, see P. Krueger, *Die Aussenpolitik der Republik von Weimar* (Darmstadt, 1985) and G. Niedhart, *Die Aussenpolitik der Weimarer Republik* (Munich, 1999). For ideological continuities W. D. Smith, *The Ideological Origins of Nazi Imperialism* (Oxford, 1986).
4 G. Feldman, *The Great Disorder: Politics, Economics and Society in the German Inflation, 1914–1924* (Oxford, 1993).
5 For a useful review of the current state of Stresemann studies, see K. H. Pohl, 'Gustav Stresemann: New Literature', *German Historical Institute London: Bulletin*, 26/1 (2004), 35–62.
6 J. Wright, *Gustav Stresemann* (Oxford, 2002), 420.
7 I. Kershaw, *Hitler, 1889–1936: Hubris* (London, 1998), 240–42.
8 G. Weinberg (ed.), *Hitlers Zweites Buch: Ein Dokument aus dem Jahr 1928* (Stuttgart, 1961) (henceforth *Zweites Buch*).
9 M. Berg, *Gustav Stresemann und die Vereinigten Staaten von Amerika: Weltwirtschaftliche Verflechtung und Revisionspolitik 1907–1929* (Baden-Baden, 1990), 19–21.
10 Wright, *Stresemann*, 8–58.
11 For the theme of Americanism in early twentieth-century Germany, see A. Luedtke, I. Marssolek and A. von Saldern (eds.), *Amerikanisierung: Traum und Alptraum im Deutschland des 20. Jahrhunderts* (Stuttgart, 1996).
12 Berg, *Stresemann*, 43.
13 Ibid., 98.
14 *Zweites Buch*, 23.
15 Wright, *Stresemann*, 373–83 and 412–13.
16 S. A. Schuker, *The End of French Financial Predominance in Europe: The Financial Crisis of 1924 and the Adoption of the Dawes Plan* (Chapel Hill, NC, 1976), 180–86.

F. Costigliola, *Awkward Dominion: American Political, Economic and Cultural Relations with Europe, 1919–1933* (Ithaca, NY, 1984), 111–27.

17 J. Y Case and E. N. Case, *Owen D. Young and American Enterprise* (Boston, 1982), 272–335.

18 G. Hardach, *Weltmarktorientierung und relative Stagnation* (Berlin, 1976), 34–5. H. O. Schoetz, *Der Kampf um die Mark 1923/24* (Berlin, 1987). At 4.20 Reichsmarks to the dollar the Reichsmark like the pound sterling after 1925 was substantially overvalued.

19 W. C. McNeil, *American Money and the Weimar Republic* (New York, 1986). For a more precise chronology, see M. Wala, *Weimar und Amerika: Botschafter Friedrich von Prittwitz und Gaffron* (Stuttgart, 2001), 110–22. For a nicely illustrated history of the bonds, see H.-G. Glasemann, *Deutschlands Auslandsanleihen 1924–1945* (Wiesbaden, 1993).

20 Nicely illustrated in H. G. Moulton and L. Pasvolsky, *War Debts and World Prosperity* (New York, 1932).

21 W. G. Pullen, *World War Debts and United States Foreign Policy 1919–1929* (New York, 1987).

22 H. James, *The Reichsbank and Public Finance in Germany 1924–1933* (Frankfurt, 1985), 19–56.

23 A. Ritschl, *Deutschlands Krise und Konjunktur 1924–1934* (Berlin, 2002), 120–27.

24 W. Link, *Die amerikanische Stabilisierungspolitik in Deutschland 1921–1932* (Duesseldorf, 1970), 411–21. Costigliola, *Awkward Dominion*, 196–210.

25 For a recent summary, Kershaw, *Hitler: Hubris*, 1–69.

26 For the importance of this idea, see A. Ritschl, 'Die NS-Wirtschaftsideologie – Modernisierungsprogramm oder reaktionaere Utopie?', in M. Prinz and R. Zitelmann (eds.), *Nationalsozialismus und Modernisierung* (Darmstadt, 1991), 48–70.

27 *Zweites Buch*, 46–69.

28 For an outline of the specifics of his Eastern European strategy, see Weinberg, *Foreign Policy I*, 14–20.

29 On the Karl May–Hitler link, see the controversial article of K. Mann, 'Cowboy Mentor of the Fuehrer', *Living Age*, 359 (1940), 217–22. For an effort to rescue May from Hitler, B. Linkemeyer, *Was hat Hitler mit Karl May zu tun?* (Abstadt, 1987). On May in the context of German literary imaginings of America, see J. L. Sammons, *Ideology, Mimesis, Fantasy* (Chapel Hill, NC, 1998), 229–45. For May's popularity and the genre of adventure fiction, see R. Frigge, *Das erwartbare Abenteuer: Massenrezeption und literarisches Interesse am Beispiel der Reiserzaehlungen von Karl May* (Bonn, 1984), 150–58.

30 For this and the following, see the subtle discussion in P. Gassert, *Amerika im Dritten Reich* (Stuttgart, 1997), 35–6 and 87–103, which supersedes all previous work on Hitler and America.

31 *Zweites Buch*, 58.

32 Ibid., 123.

33 Ibid., 123–4.

34 Ibid., 127–8.

35 Ibid., 130.

36 For an analysis of Hitler's historical understanding, see F.-L. Kroll, *Utopie als Ideologie: Geschichtsdenken und politisches Handeln im Dritten Reich* (Paderborn, 1998). Kroll gives insufficient weight to Hitler's apocalyptic world-view.

37 *Zweites Buch*, 71.

38 L. E. Jones, *German Liberalism and the Dissolution of the Weimar Party System, 1918–1933* (Chapel Hill, NC, 1988), 301–5.

39 After almost two decades of productive revisionism, it is surely time to return our focus squarely to the consequences of America's flawed hegemony in the 1920s, as classically outlined by C. P. Kindleberger, *The World in Depression, 1929–1939* (Berkeley, 1986) and elaborated by Link, *Stabilisierungspolitik*, and Costigliola, *Awkward Dominion*. The

immediate agent of trouble, of course, was the German nationalist backlash, which in turn produced a 'failure of cooperation' on the part of the French. Nor did the British help matters. But, given the all too obvious fragility of European relations, the exogenous causal factor was the failure of American policy to do what could have been done.

40 Case and Case, *Owen D. Young*, 434–54.

41 Costigliola, *Awkward Dominion*, 206–15.

42 P. Heyde, *Das Ende der Reparationen: Deutschland, Frankreich und der Youngplan 1929–1932* (Paderborn, 1998), 65–9. It was almost equally unsatisfying to London. See R. W. D. Boyce, *British Capitalism at the Crossroads 1919–1932* (Cambridge, 1987), 186–216.

43 For an evaluation of the relative importance of interest rates and the Young Plan effect, see Ritschl, *Krise und Konjunktur*, 107–41.

44 E. E. Schattschneider, *Politics, Pressures and the Tariff* (New York, 1935). In broader historical overview, the significance of Smoot–Hawley was to return American tariffs to the highest levels that had prevailed before 1914. See A. E. Eckes, *Opening America's Markets* (Chapel Hill, NC, 1995), 106–9. Emphasizing the uncertainty rather than the absolute level of the new tariff, see H. James, *The End of Globalization: Lessons from the Great Depression* (Cambridge, Mass., 2001), 29.

45 Krueger, *Aussenpolitik*, 498–9, Wright, *Stresemann*, 475–6.

46 For the general public disillusionment with the United States in the late 1920s and early 1930s, see Gassert, *Amerika*, 78–86.

47 The best short account is H. James, 'Hjalmar Schacht', in R. Smelser, E. Syring and R. Zitelmann (eds.), *Die Braune Elite* (Darmstadt, 1993), II. 206–18. Excellent also N. Muehlen, *Der Zauberer: Leben und Anleihen des Dr Hjalmar Horace Greeley Schacht* (Zurich, 2nd edn., 1938).

48 Feldman, *Great Disorder*, 792–6 and 821–3.

49 Schoetz, *Kampf um die Mark*, and Feldman, *Great Disorder*, 827–35.

50 Johann Houwink ten Cate, 'Hjalmar Schacht als Reparationspolitiker (1926–1930)', *Vierteljahrschrift fuer Sozial- und Wirtschaftsgeschichte*, 74 (1987), 186–228.

51 Berg, *Stresemann*, 380–87.

52 Hardarch, *Weltmarktorientierung*, 110–11.

53 H. A. Winkler, *Weimar 1918–1933* (Munich, 1993), 364–80.

54 J. von Kruedener (ed.), *Economic Crisis and Political Collapse: The Weimar Republic 1924–1933* (Oxford, 1990) and I. Kershaw (ed.), *Weimar: Why Did German Democracy Fail?* (London, 1990). The last in the line of proto-Keynesian and Keynesian critiques is R. Meister, *Die Grosse Depression: Zwangslagen und Handlungsspielraeume der Wirtschafts- und Finanzpolitik in Deutschland 1929–1932* (Regensburg, 1991).

55 For the original German statement of this point, see K. Borchardt, 'Zwangslage und Handlungsspielraeume in der grossen Weltwirtschaftskrise der fruehen dreissiger Jahre', in K. Borchardt, *Wachstum, Krisen, Handlungsspielraeume der Wirtschaftspolitik* (Goettingen, 1982), 165–82. For its international complement, see B. Eichengreen, *Golden Fetters: The Gold Standard and the Great Depression, 1919–1939* (Oxford, 1992), 230–46.

56 Opinions differ as to whether the international capital market was absolutely closed to Germany following the Young Plan; compare Ritschl, *Krise und Konjunktur*, 105–20 and T. Ferguson and P. Temin, 'Made in Germany: The German Currency Crisis of July 1931', *Research in Economic History*, 21 (2003), 1–53. The squeeze was certainly sufficient to necessitate major domestic adjustment.

57 Hardarch, *Weltmarktorientierung*, 120–21.

58 Wala, *Weimar und Amerika*, 158–66.

59 Krueger, *Aussenpolitik*, 507–51.

60 For Schacht's dismissive view of France, see Cate, 'Hjalmar Schacht'.

61 In complete agreement with Ferguson and Temin, 'Made in Germany'.

62 Winkler, *Weimar*, 404–14.

63 The point first made by Hardach, *Weltmarktorientierung*, 126–31 and reinforced by Ferguson and Temin, 'Made in Germany'.

64 As Winkler says, Bruening could have celebrated the Hoover moratorium as a triumph of German foreign policy; Winkler, *Weimar*, 415.

65 Costigliola, *Awkward Dominion*, 235–8. On American policy in Berlin between December 1930 and July 1931, see B. V. Burke, *Ambassador Frederic Sackett and the Collapse of the Weimar Republic, 1930–1933* (Cambridge, 1994), 113–44.

66 Ritschl, *Krise und Konjunktur*, 150–51 and Wala, *Weimar und Amerika*, 169–79.

67 Heyde, *Das Ende*, 200–24.

68 G. D. Feldman in L. Gall, G. D. Feldman, H. James, C.-L. Holtfrerich and H. E. Buschgen, *The Deutsche Bank 1870–1995* (London, 1995), 240–76.

69 Hardach, *Weltmarktorientierung*, 139.

70 Heyde, *Das Ende*, 255–64. As Ritschl, *Krise und Konjunktur*, 154–6, points out, this too prioritized the interests of American short-term creditors.

71 *The Economist*, 26 September 1931, 547–8.

72 *Der Deutsche Volkswirt*, 1 April 1932, 869 and 875.

73 J. Schiemann, *Die deutsche Waehrung in der Weltwirtschaftskrise 1929–1933* (Berne, 1980), 166–292, Heyde, *Das Ende*, 280–96 and K. Borchardt, 'Zur Frage der waehrungspolitischen Optionen Deutschlands in der Weltwirtschaftskrise', in Borchardt, *Wachstum, Krisen, Handlungsspielraeume*, 206–24.

74 For contemporary comment, see *The Economist*, 3 October 1931, 613.

75 Schiemann, *Die deutsche Waehrung*, 188, 207–14.

76 For the American role in pushing Germany towards exchange controls, see Ritschl, *Krise und Konjunktur*, 153–4. France similarly opposed any such move; Schiemann, *Die deutsche Waehrung*, 195–200.

77 H. Mommsen. 'Heinrich Bruening as Chancellor', in H. Mommsen, *From Weimar to Auschwitz* (Cambridge, 1991), 119–40.

78 Winkler, *Weimar*, 435–7.

79 *The Economist*, 12 December 1931, 1115.

80 S. Gillmann and H. Mommsen (eds.), *Politische Schriften und Briefe Carl Friedrich Goerdelers* (Munich, 2003), 179–83, 214–32, 240–47.

81 A. Reckendrees, *Das 'Stahltrust-Projekt'* (Munich, 2000), 471–507.

82 G. D. Feldman 'From Crisis to Work Creation: Government Policies and Economic Actors in the Great Depression', in J. Kocka, H.-J. Puhle and K. Tenfelde (eds.), *Von der Arbeiterbewegung zum modernen Sozialstaat* (Munich, 1994), 703–18.

83 October 1931 was also the moment at which the right wing of the DVP, Stresemann's former party, forced a breach with Bruening; Winkler, *Weimar*, 430–32.

84 On the applause for Hitler and Schacht, see G. Schulz (ed.), *Politik und Wirtschaft in der Krise 1930–1932* (Duesseldorf, 1980), doc. 341, Blank to Reusch, 12 October 1931, II. 1039–43. On the sensation caused by Schacht's speech, see the reports on 11 and 12 October 1931 in *Schulthess' Europaeischer Geschichtskalender* (Munich, 1932), 224–9.

85 Gustav Stolper's *Der Deutsche Volkswirt* continued to rally the forces of liberalism; see for instance Wilhelm Roepke's review of Ferdinand Fried's recent publications in *Der Deutsche Volkswirt*, 6 January 1933, 437–8.

86 James, *The End of Globalization*, 187–99.

87 E. Teichert, *Autarkie und Grossraumwirtschaft in Deutschland 1930–1939* (Munich, 1984).

88 See for example the remarkable elision in the title of D. P. Silverman, *Hitler's Economy: Nazi Work Creation Programs, 1933–1936* (Cambridge, 1998).

89 Most notably perhaps in the genealogy of German Keynesianism offered by the five volumes of G. Bombach *et al.* (eds.), *Der Keynesianismus* (1976–84). For a remarkable recent instance of the genre by no less a personage than the economics correspondent of the BBC, see J. Peter and M. Stewart, *Apocalypse 2000: Economic Breakdown and the Suicide of Democracy 1989–2000* (London, 1987).

90 For Schacht's warning to Hitler in August 1932 to avoid any overly specific commitments on economic policy, see IMT, *Nazi Conspiracy and Aggression* (Washington, 1946–7), II, EC-456, 513–14.

91 On the interconnections between the three conferences, see M. Geyer, *Aufruestung oder Sicherheit: Die Reichswehr in der Krise der Machtpolitik 1924–1936* (Wiesbaden, 1980), 236–44, Costigliola, *Awkward Dominion*, 218–61 and P. Clavin, *The Failure of Economic Diplomacy: Britain, Germany, France and the United States, 1931–36* (New York, 1996).

92 For an effective summary see H. Sirois, *Zwischen Illusion und Krieg: Deutschland und die USA 1933–1941* (Paderborn, 2000), 51–9.

93 M. Geyer, 'Etudes in Political History: Reichswehr, NSDAP, and the Seizure of Power', in Peter D. Stachura (ed.), *The Nazi Machtergreifung* (London, 1983), 101–23, and M. Geyer, 'Militaer, Ruestung und Aussenpolitik: Aspekte militaerischer Revisionspolitik in der Zwischenkriegszeit', in Manfred Funke (ed.), *Hitler, Deutschland und die Maechte* (Duesseldorf, 1976), 239–68.

94 M. Geyer, 'Das Zweite Ruestungsprogramm (1930–1934)', *MGM* 17 (1975), 125–72.

95 On military support for ailing firms, see E. W. Hansen, *Reichswehr und Industrie* (Boppard, 1978), 179–85.

96 Heyde, *Das Ende*, 408–55 and Clavin, *Failure*, 30–59.

97 C. R. S. Harris, *Germany's Foreign Indebtedness* (Oxford, 1935), 110.

98 This also had been the clear message of the Layton report on Germany's situation in August 1931; see Winkler, *Weimar*, 420.

99 The result, rather than a principled decision for low tariffs, was a bruising stalemate between agricultural and industrial exporting that could only be resolved by a series of embarrassing short-term expedients which did, however, keep tariffs low at least until 1929; see R. M. Spaulding, *Osthandel und Ostpolitik: German Foreign Trade Policies in Eastern Europe from Bismarck to Adenauer* (Providence, RI, 1997), 123–37. D. Stegmann, 'Deutsche Zoll- und Handelspolitik 1924/5–1929', in H. Mommsen, D. Petzina and D. Weisbrod (eds.), *Industrielles System und politische Entwicklung in der Weimarer Republik* (Duesseldorf, 1977), II. 499–513.

100 Clavin, *Failure*, 61–80.

101 S. Dengg, *Deutschlands Austritt aus dem Voelkerbund und Schachts Neuer Plan* (Frankfurt, 1986), 386–7 and R. Neebe, *Grossindustrie, Staat und NSDAP 1930–1933* (Goettingen, 1981), 122–6.

102 Kershaw, *Hitler: Hubris*, 414.

103 For the development of German protectionism in a European context, see M. Tracy, *Government and Agriculture in Western Europe 1880–1988* (Hemel Hempstead, 1989).

104 W. Pyta, *Dorfgemeinschaft und Parteipolitik 1918–1933* (Duesseldorf, 1996), 203–33.

105 See W. A. Boelcke, *Deutschland als Welthandelsmacht 1930–1945* (Stuttgart, 1994), 17–20.

106 A point not lost on advocates of industrial protection in sectors like textiles but resisted by the Minister for Economic Affairs; see K. Wiegmann, *Textilindustrie und Staat in Westfalen 1914–1933* (Stuttgart, 1993), 220–22.

107 D. Petzina, *Die Verantwortung des Staates fuer die Wirtschaft* (Essen, 2000), 10–45.

108 This hiatus is glossed over in Spaulding, *Osthandel*, 222–33.

109 Apart from trade issues, the main concern of the Reichslandbund was to stall any effort to break up the eastern great estates and open them up to peasant settlement. See S. Merkenich, *Gruene Front gegen Weimar: Reichs-Landbund und agrarischer Lobbyismus 1918–1933* (Duesseldorf, 1998), 300–19.

110 Winkler, *Weimar*, 509–12.

111 T. Stolper, *Ein Leben in Brennpunkten unserer Zeit* (Vienna, 1967), 309–10.

112 For international comment, see *The Economist*, 17 September 1932, 493. For a review of the contemporary literature, see C. Buchheim, 'Die Erholung von der Weltwirtschaftskrise 1932/33 in Deutschland', *Jahrbuch fuer Wirtschaftsgeschichte*, 1 (2003), 13–26.

113 *Der Deutsche Volkswirt*, 8 July 1932, 1340.

114 Reichskreditgesellschaft, *Germany's Economic Situation at the Turn of 1932/1933* (Berlin, 1933).

115 For a critique of the institute's continued pessimism, see *Der Deutsche Volkswirt*, 9 December 1932, 291.

116 *The Economist*, 24 December 1932, 1185–6.

117 Perpetuated, in the face of all evidence, by W. Abelshauser, 'Kriegswirtschaft und Wirtschaftswunder: Deutschlands wirtschaftliche Mobilisierung fuer den Zweiten Weltkrieg und die Folgen fuer die Nachkriegszeit', *VfZ* 47 (1999), 505–6.

118 H. A Turner, *Hitler's Thirty Days to Power: January 1933* (New York, 1996), 1–2.

119 G. Jasper, *Die Gescheiterte Zaehmung: Wege zur Machtergreifung Hitlers, 1930–1934* (Frankfurt, 1986).

120 e.g. Abelshauser, 'Kriegswirtschaft und Wirtschaftswunder'.

2 'Every Worker his Work'

1 H. Hoehne, *Zeit der Illusionen* (Duesseldorf, 1991), 51.

2 Domarus, I. 191–4.

3 Domarus, I. 193.

4 Domarus, I. 198.

5 K. J. Mueller, *Armee und Drittes Reich 1933–1939* (Paderborn, 1989), 263.

6 BAL R43II 536, 20, minutes of meeting of work creation committee, 9 February 1933.

7 D. Petzina, 'Hauptprobleme der deutschen Wirtschaftspolitik 1932/33', in Petzina, *Die Verantwortung des Staates fuer die Wirtschaft* (Essen, 2000), 90–124.

8 B. Wulff, *Arbeitslosigkeit und Arbeitsbeschaffungsmassnahmen in Hamburg 1933–1939: Eine Untersuchung zur Nationalsozialistischen Wirtschafts- und Sozialpolitik* (Frankfurt, 1987), 36–48.

9 R. J. Evans, *The Coming of the Third Reich* (London, 2003), 309–90.

10 D. P. Silverman, *Hitler's Economy: Nazi Work Creation Programs, 1933–1936* (Cambridge, 1998), 63–4.

11 In the Reichstag discussions of 9–10 May 1932 at which Gregor Strasser first introduced the Nazis' work creation scheme, Reinhardt spoke first, setting the stage for the former's dramatic announcement. See *Verhandlungen des Reichstages, Stenographische Berichte* (1932), 61st Sitzung, 9 May 1932, 2491–4. Even after his resignation from the party Reinhardt continued his advocacy of the Strasserite line; see *Der Deutsche Volkswirt*, 23 December 1932, 356.

12 K. Gossweiler, *Die Roehm Affaere: Hintergruende – Zusammenhaenge – Auswirkungen* (Cologne, 1983), 342.

13 C. P. Kindleberger, *The World in Depression, 1929–1939* (Berkeley, 1986), 195–201 and B. Eichengreen, *Golden Fetters: The Gold Standard and the Great Depression, 1919–1939* (Oxford, 1992), 317–47.

14 P. Clavin, *The Failure of Economic Diplomacy: Britain, Germany, France and the United States, 1931–36* (New York, 1996), 83–8.

15 See his speech to the Reichsbank assembly, 7 April 1933. Hitler reiterated his commitment to avoid currency experiments, see Domarus, I. 233.

16 H. James, *The German Slump* (Oxford, 1986), 403.

17 Wulff, *Arbeitslosigkeit*, 41 and 49–62.

18 For summaries of the German debate see H. Janssen, *Nationaloekonomie und Nationalsozialismus: Die deutsche Volkswirtschaftslehre in den dreissiger Jahren* (Marburg, 1998) and W. Grotkopp, *Die grosse Krise: Lehren aus der Ueberwindung der Wirtschaftskrise 1929–32* (Duesseldorf, 1954).

19 See the discussion of the financing mechanism in K. Schiller, *Arbeitsbeschaffung und Finanzordnung in Deutschland* (Berlin, 1936).

20 H.-J. Kwon, *Deutsche Arbeitsbeschaffungs und Konjunkturpolitik in der Weltwirt-*

schaftskrise: Die 'Deutsche Gesellschaft fuer oeffentliche Arbeiten AG (Oeffa)' als Instru-
ment der Konjunkturpolitik von 1930 bis 1937 (Osnabrueck, 1997).

21 Silverman, *Hitler's Economy*, 69–146.

22 Of the national river regulation and land amelioration fund of 100 million Reichsmarks, Prussia received an allocation of 60 million Reichsmarks of which East Prussia received a third. See Silverman, *Hitler's Economy*, 75.

23 For Schacht's scathing characterization of work creation spending, see Wulff, *Arbeitslosigkeit*, 60–66.

24 Ibid., 60.

25 R. Stammer (ed.), *Reichsautobahnen: Pyramiden des Dritten Reiches* (Marburg, 1982).

26 The emphasis placed on motorization as a major engine of German economic recovery by R. J. Overy, *War and Economy in the Third Reich* (Oxford, 1994), 68–89, is not supported by the evidence.

27 K. H. Ludwig, *Technik und Ingenieure im Dritten Reich* (Duesseldorf, 1974), 303–44.

28 F. W. Seidler, *Fritz Todt: Baumeister des Dritten Reiches* (Frankfurt, 1986), 97–102.

29 Silverman, *Hitler's Economy*, 160.

30 BAL R43II 537, 55–69.

31 Wulff, *Arbeitslosigkeit*, 65–7.

32 W. S. Allen, *The Nazi Seizure of Power: The Experience of a Single German Town 1930–1935* (Chicago, 1965), 192–208 and 258–71.

33 Wulff, *Arbeitslosigkeit*, 170–71.

34 S. Dengg, *Deutschlands Austritt aus dem Voelkerbund und Schachts Neuer Plan* (Frankfurt, 1986).

35 See the preliminary discussion of the pros and cons by the Reichsbank in BAL R2501 6439, 165–208.

36 Contemporary estimates in *VzK* 8 January 1934, 175.

37 Quoted in N. Forbes, *Doing Business with the Nazis* (London, 2000), 99.

38 See the estimate of Germany's likely capital account balance for March–December 1933, prepared by the Reichsbank on 15 March 1933, in BAL R2501 6440, 48–51.

39 See the discussion of the Reichsbank's position in BAL R2501 6440 and 6505.

40 H.-J. Schroeder, *Deutschland und die Vereinigten Staaten 1933–1939* (Wiesbaden, 1970), 78.

41 For accounts of the visit, see G. Weinberg, 'Schachts Besuch in den USA im Jahre 1933', *VfZ* 11 (1963), 166–80 and A. O. Offner, *American Appeasement: United States Foreign Policy and Germany, 1933–1938* (Cambridge, Mass., 1969), 28–9.

42 Suspicions confirmed by internal Reichsbank statistics BAL R2501 6440, 127.

43 B. J. Wendt, *Economic Appeasement: Handel und Finanz in der britischen Deutschland-Politik 1933–1939* (Duesseldorf, 1971), 131–40 and Forbes, *Doing Business*, 69.

44 Clavin, *Failure*, 108.

45 Ibid., 89–165. Though shedding new light on the British role, Clavin surely goes too far in downplaying American responsibility for the failure of the Conference. For an illuminating review of French responses to the Conference, see C. Maddison, 'French Inter-war Monetary Policy' (EUI thesis, 1997), 276–304.

46 For the debilitating impact of these divisions on Hull's efforts to secure an Anglo-American trade deal in 1933 which would have posed a major challenge to Schacht's intended strategy, see P. Clavin, 'Shaping the Lessons of History: Britain and the Rhetoric of American Trade Policy, 1930–1960', in A. Marrison (ed.), *Free Trade and its Reception 1815–1960* (London, 1998), 287–307, and M. A. Butler, *Cautious Visionary: Cordell Hull and Trade Reform, 1933–1937* (Kent, Ohio, 1998), 15–45. And America was divided not only on economic issues. Congress also undermined the administration's efforts to take a lead on disarmament. See Offner, *American Appeasement*, 35–41.

47 P. J. Hearden, *Roosevelt Confronts Hitler: America's Entry into World War II* (Dekalb, Ill., 1987), 33.

48 The argument for this dating is made in M. Geyer, 'Das Zweite Ruestungsprogramm

(1930–1934)', *MGM* 17 (1975), 134. The scale of the 35 billion Reichsmark programme is documented in a report republished in M. Geyer, 'Ruestungsbeschleunigung und Inflation: Zur Inflationsdenkschaft des Oberkommandos der Weltmacht vom November 1938', *MGM* 30 (1981), 121–86, which dates the programme to the spring of 1934. Though the coincidence would be less neat if we follow that dating, it would make no substantial difference to the argument made here.

49 E. L. Homze, *Arming the Luftwaffe* (Lincoln, Nebr., 1976), 258.

50 M. Geyer, *Aufruestung oder Sicherheit: Die Reichswehr in der Krise der Machtpolitik 1924–1926* (Wiesbaden, 1980) 348.

51 W. Feldenkirchen, *Siemens 1919–1945* (Munich, 1995), 497–8 and W. Abelshauser, in L. Gall (ed.), *Krupp im 20. Jahrhundert* (Berlin, 2002), 273.

52 L. Budrass, *Flugzeugindustrie und Luftruestung in Deutschland* (Duesseldorf, 1998), 317–18.

53 Somewhat surprisingly, Schroeder, *Deutschland und die Vereinigten Staaten*, 29–92 and 121–67 gives little space to the consequences of Germany's default, focusing instead on trade. Weinberg gives ample space to default but fails to set it against the 1920s backdrop; see Weinberg, *Foreign Policy I*, 133–45. For a better balanced summary, see H. Sirois, *Zwischen Illusion und Krieg: Deutschland und die USA 1933–1941* (Paderborn, 2000), 51–9.

54 Domarus, I. 269–78.

55 See Weinberg, *Foreign Policy I*, 89–93, 111–14.

56 Dengg, *Deutschlands Austritt*, 278–306.

57 P. Bernard and H. Dubief, *The Decline of the Third Republic 1914–1938* (Cambridge, 1988), 219–28.

58 B. R. Kroener, *'Der starke Mann im Heimatkriegsgebiet': Generaloberst Friedrich Fromm. Eine Biographie* (Paderborn, 2005), 219–21.

59 H. Pophanken, *Gruendung und Ausbau der 'Weser'-Flugzeugbau GmbH 1933 bis 1939* (Bremen, 2000), 25, 30, Homze, *Arming*, 46–62 and Budrass, *Flugzeugindustrie*, 293–335.

60 *Das deutsche Reich und der Zweite Weltkrieg* (henceforth *DRZW*) (Frankfurt, 1989), 1. 487–8 and W. Deist, *The Wehrmacht and German Rearmament* (London, 1981), 28–31.

61 W. A. Boelcke, *Deutschland als Welthandelsmacht, 1930–1945* (Stuttgart, 1994), 23–6.

62 This fear was first expressed in a Reichsbank memo drafted on 28 March 1933, BAL R2501 6439, 165–208. It was reiterated in all further discussion. See the useful summary in R2501 6604, 375–404.

63 Wendt, *Economic Appeasement*, 162–9 and Forbes, *Doing Business*, 74–82.

64 J. Duelffer, *Weimar, Hitler und die Marine: Reichspolitik und Flottenbau, 1920–1939* (Duesseldorf, 1973), 251–3. J. Duelffer, *Handbuch zur deutschen Militaergeschichte 1648–1939*, VIII (Munich, 1977), 453–5. *DRZW* 1. 540–46.

65 Britain, France and the United States already had good intelligence about German rearmament at the time of the World Economic Conference in 1933; see Clavin, *Failure*, 182.

66 Weinberg, *Foreign Policy I*, 169–72.

67 This Nazi song celebrating the national community of labour and Hitler's heroic leadership can be downloaded as an audio file from at least one site on the web. It is also available in CD format.

68 BAL R3101 9930, 602.

69 P. Schulz, *Nicht die Zeit, um auszuruhen: Dokumente und Bilder zur Geschichte der hannoverschen Arbeiterbewegung* (Hanover, 1990), 469–70.

70 BAL 43II 537, 99.

71 Silverman, *Hitler's Economy*, 82–4.

72 BAL 43I 537, 161.

73 See the summary of their concerns in BAL 43I 537, 208.

74 Wulff, *Arbeitslosigkeit*, 125.

75 Based on figures from A. Ritschl, 'Deficit Spending in the Nazi Recovery, 1933–1938: A Critical Reassessment', Working Paper No. 68, Institute for Empirical Research in Economics, University of Zurich (December 2000), table 5.

76 Silverman, *Hitler's Economy*, 253–4.

77 J. A. Tooze, *Statistics and the German State 1900–1945: The Making of Modern Economic Knowledge* (Cambridge, 2001).

78 See H. A. Turner, *Hitler's Thirty Days to Power: January 1933* (New York, 1996), 1–2.

79 James, *German Slump*, C. Buchheim and R. Garside (eds.), *After the Slump: Industry and Politics in 1930s Britain and Germany* (Frankfurt, 2000), A. Ritschl, *Deutschlands Krise und Konjunktur 1924–1934* (Berlin, 2002), all agree on this counterfactual.

80 For this reason also I see no reason to engage in an extended discussion of multiplier effects. As was already well understood by contemporaries, Hitler's economic recovery was anything but Keynesian; see C. Bresciani Turroni, 'The "Multiplier" in Practice: Some Results of Recent German Experience', *Review of Economic Statistics*, 20 (1938), 76–88.

81 The difficulty of estimating consumption expenditure is the main source of differences in the interpretation of the recovery between Ritschl, *Krise und Konjunktur* and studies based on data taken from W. G. Hoffmann, *Das Wachstum der deutschen Wirtschaft* (Heidelberg, 1965), 617–705. Here I am relying on the figures from Ritschl. These show consumption falling in the first half of 1933 and rising only in the second half of the year, followed by stagnation in 1934.

82 Gossweiler, *Die Roehm Affaere*, 342–7; confirmed by BAL R2501 6510 and R3101 9932.

83 Due to a misinterpretation of the data, H. James, 'Innovation and Conservatism in Economic Recovery: The Alleged "Nazi Recovery" of the 1930s', in T. Childers and J. Caplan (eds.), *Reevaluating the Third Reich* (New York, 1993), 114–38, goes too far in dismissing the fiscal policy boost provided in 1933 and 1934. R. L. Cohn, 'Fiscal Policy in Germany during the Great Depression', *Explorations in Economic History*, 29 (1992), 318–42 is closer to the mark.

84 Ritschl's reassessment of the public accounts and the GDP figures renders untenable those interpretations of the Nazi economic recovery which attribute priority within government spending to civilian work creation rather than rearmament. The most notable instances of this genre are R. Overy, *The Nazi Economic Recovery 1932–1938* (Cambridge, 1996) and C. W. Guillebaud, *The Economic Recovery of Germany: From 1933 to the Incorporation of Austria in March 1938* (London, 1939). What remains open to question is the importance of government policy to the recovery, not the priority within policy of rearmament.

85 Ritschl, *Krise und Konjunktur*, appendix C.2.

86 This is the very stern test of causality applied by Ritschl, 'Deficit Spending'.

87 M. Geyer, 'Zum Einfluss der Nationalsozialistische Ruestungspolitik auf das Ruhrgebiet', *Rheinische Vierteljahresblaetter*, 45 (1981), 255.

3 Breaking Away

1 The following pages are based on I. Kershaw, *Hitler 1889–1936: Hubris* (London, 1998), 499–519 and K. J. Mueller, *Armee und Drittes Reich 1933–1939* (Paderborn, 1989), 62–70.

2 The text of the agreement is in Mueller, *Armee und Drittes Reich*, 192–5.

3 Weinberg, *Foreign Policy I*, 87–107.

4 See the extraordinarily vivid first-hand accounts of the atmosphere along the Italian-Austrian-Yugoslav border in July and August 1934 by Gareth Jones for the *Western Mail* and *South Wales News*.

5 G. Morsch, *Arbeit und Brot: Studien zur Lage, Stimmung, Einstellung und Verhalten der deutschen Arbeiterschaft, 1933–1936/37* (Frankfurt, 1993), 184.

6 Due to the acute shortage of foreign exchange, the economic situation was far closer to

one of uncontrollable crisis than the tensions of the late 1930s stressed by Tim Mason; see J. Caplan (ed.), *Nazism, Fascism and the Working Class: Essays by Tim Mason* (Cambridge, 1995).

7 *Schulthess Europaeischer Geschichtskalender* (Munich, 1934), 19 April 1934, 108. On the significance of this seeming technical infringement on liberty see the perceptive comments in F. Hayek, *Road to Serfdom* (London, 1944), 66–9. Its import has finally been widely recognized through the literature on the economic persecution of the Jews.

8 *Die Deutsche Volkswirtschaft*, 10 (1934), 289–91.

9 *Die Deutsche Volkswirtschaft*, 14 (1934), 420.

10 *Schulthess 1934*, 131, report of Goebbels speech, 11 May 1934.

11 Wilhelm Keppler (1882–1960) was born into an industrial family in North Baden that produced photographic gelatin under licence from Eastman Kodak in the United States. An active Nazi since 1927, Keppler was influential in 1931–2 in gathering a small coterie of businessmen around the Nazi party. Crucially, Keppler was acquainted with the banker Kurt von Schroeder, who hosted the key meeting between Hitler and Papen in January 1933; H. A. Turner, *German Big Business and the Rise of Hitler* (Oxford, 1985), 192, 238–46, 314–16. Keppler's role after 1933 has tended to be downplayed, but in fact he continued to play a pivotal role in Nazi industrial politics throughout the 1930s.

12 S. Dengg, *Deutschlands Austritt aus den Voelkerbund und Schachts Neuer Plan* (Frankfurt, 1986), 362–79 and D. Doering, *Deutsche Aussenwirtschaftspolitik 1933–35* (Berlin, 1969). For a more narrowly economic analysis, see M. Ebi, *Export um jeden Preis: Die deutsche Exportfoerderung von 1932–1938* (Stuttgart, 2004).

13 The drama of the crisis is conveyed most clearly in the literature on Anglo-German relations: see B. J. Wendt, *Economic Appeasement: Handel und Finanz in der britischen Deutschland-Politik 1933–1939* (Duesseldorf, 1971), 180–219 and Forbes, *Doing Business*, 90–92. See also the impatient commentary in *The Economist*, 23 June 1934, 1378–9.

14 'Die Preise hoch, Kartelle fest geschlossen/das Kapital marschiert mit leisem Schritt/die Boersianer sind Parteigenossen/und fuer das Kapital sorgt nun Herr Schmitt.' Quoted in N. Muehlen, *Der Zauberer: Leben und Anleihen des Dr Hjalmar Horace Greeley Schacht* (Zurich, 2nd edn., 1938), 159.

15 G. D. Feldman, *Allianz and the German Insurance Business, 1933–1945* (Cambridge, 2001), 101–2.

16 Muehlen, *Der Zauberer*, 162.

17 IfK, Supplement to *Weekly Report*, 11 April 1934; ibid., 25 April 1934, 73–4.

18 For an account of the situation of Saxony, a classic export region, see M. C. Schneider, 'Die Wirtschaftsentwicklung', in C. Vollnhals (ed.), *Sachsen in der NS-Zeit* (Leipzig, 2002), 72–84.

19 Ebi, *Export*, 62–92.

20 See the review of obstacles to German exports in *Wirtschaftsdienst*, 29 (20 July 1934), 990–93. The traditional nineteenth-century form of trade protection, the tariff, raised the price of imports through a tax but left it up to consumers to decide how much of the more expensive foreign goods they wanted to purchase. The quota systems of the 1930s imposed direct regulations on the actual quantities imported from particular countries.

21 For concerns about the clearing system and the view that it was forced on Germany by its creditors, see Reichsbank memos and speeches in BAL R2501 6602, 489–98 and R2501 6604, 375–404.

22 A. Barkai, *From Boycott to Annihilation: The Economic Struggle of German Jews* (Hanover, 1989), 13–53.

23 In chronological order, see BAL R2501 6440, 102–19, R2501 6601, 331–42, R2501 6602, 150–73.

24 P. Longerich, *Politik der Vernichtung: Eine Gesamtdarstellung der nationalsozialistischen Judenfolgung* (Munich, 1998), 46–56.

25 See BAL R2501 6444, 198.

26 F. Bajohr, *'Aryanisation' in Hamburg: The Economic Exclusion of Jews and the Confiscation of their Property in Nazi Germany* (Oxford, 2002), 121. The figure was raised from 20 to 60 per cent. By 1936 the discount was to rise to 80 per cent and in 1938 to 90 per cent.

27 Longerich, *Politik*, 125.

28 *Schulthess 1934*, 11 May 1934, 131.

29 BAL R2501 6423, 29–36.

30 BAL R2501 6603, 2–15.

31 *Konjunkturstatistisches Handbuch*, 121.

32 The best description of this and other subsidy systems is Ebi, *Export*, 32–61.

33 The essential point made with the requisite force, ibid., 91–2.

34 *The Economist*, 2 June 1934, 1186 and 23 June 1934, 1378–9.

35 A. O. Offner, *American Appeasement: United States Foreign Policy and Germany, 1933–1938* (Cambridge, Mass., 1969), 78–9.

36 K. Gossweiler, *Die Roehm Affaere: Hintergruende – Zusammenhaenge – Auswirkungen* (Cologne, 1983), 71–5, 339–49.

37 See the discussion in BAL R2501 6510 and R3101 9932.

38 H. Kehrl, *Krisenmanager im Dritten Reich* (Duesseldorf, 1973), 58.

39 For Schmitt's 1945 version of the Obersalzberg meeting, see Feldman, *Allianz*, 101. As Feldman points out, Schmitt was concerned after the war to avoid presenting Schacht in too unfavourable a light.

40 For the deliberate nature of these steps, see BAL R2501 6601, 396–438.

41 For this and the following see Ebi, *Export*, 93–116 and Doering, *Deutsche Aussenwirtschaftspolitik*, 222–46.

42 See, for instance, the line taken by *Die Deutsche Volkswirtschaft*, 4 (1933), 100.

43 For critiques by the Reichsbank of the Hansa Bund's proposal to hitch the Reichsmark to sterling for foreign trade purposes, see BAL R2501 6601, 188–94, 202–19, 242–52. The Reichsbank was alarmed by the considerable publicity for the Hansa Bund scheme.

44 *Wirtschaftsdienst*, 7, 16 December 1934, 216; 8, 23 February 1934, 252–3; 17, 27 April 1934, 563–4, 559–63.

45 *The Economist*, 12 May 1934, 1025.

46 *Wirtschaftsdienst*, 19, 11 May 1934, 641. A few weeks later a parallel debate about devaluation began in France, sparked by a speech by Paul Reynaud in the Chamber of Deputies on 28 June 1934; see C. Maddison, 'French Inter-war Monetary Policy' (EUI thesis, 1997), 99–433.

47 This contract provided an asymmetric cover against fluctuations in the value of the Reichsmark. In case the Reichsmark devalued, customers were to pay for their rubber in gold at the rate of one Reichsmark per 1/2790 kg of fine gold; *Die Deutsche Volkswirtschaft*, 24 (1934), 739–40.

48 *Wirtschaftsdienst*, 21, 25 May 1934, 699–701.

49 W. A. Boelcke, *Die deutsche Wirtschaft 1930–1945* (Duesseldorf, 1982), 53, 64, 75, 87.

50 For a Reichsbank critique, see BAL R2501 6601, 396–438. For support for the scheme from within the Ministry, see BAL R2501 6603, 16–32 and for party support, see BAL R2501 6603, 33–47.

51 Dengg, *Deutschlands Austritt*, 396–7 and Ebi, *Export*, 110–17.

52 The incident is recorded in Kehrl, *Krisenmanager*, 58.

53 A. Ritschl, 'Nazi Economic Imperialism and the Exploitation of the Small', *Economic History Review*, 54 (2001), 324–45.

54 See the clear-headed assessment by the Reichsbank during the crisis of January 1934, BAL R2501 6601, 287–92.

55 In its report of 24 April 1933, in BAL R2501 6439, 242–3, the Reichsbank even speculated that the United States might find itself supporting Germany against the selfish claims of European creditors with whom Germany ran trade surpluses.

56 BAL R2501 6603, 1–22.

57 Wendt, *Economic Appeasement*, 220–88.

58 See the remarkable account in N. Forbes, *Doing Business with the Nazis* (London, 2000), 97–115.

59 See the excited assessment by a senior Reichsbank economist in BAL R2501 6604, 375–404.

60 Royal Institute of International Affairs, *The Problem of International Investment* (London, 1937), 304–9.

61 Offner, *American Appeasement*, 93–106; H. Sirois, *Zwischen Illusion und Krieg: Deutschland und die USA 1933–1941* (Paderborn, 2000), 88–99.

62 M. A. Butler, *Cautious Visionary: Cordell Hull and Trade Reform, 1933–1937* (Kent, Ohio, 1998), 82–120; A. E. Eckes, *Opening America's Markets* (Chapel Hill, NC, 1995), 140–57. For a typically iconoclastic analysis, see S. A. Schuker, *American 'Reparations' to Germany 1919–1933: Implications for the Third-World Debt Crisis* (Princeton, 1988), 102–3.

63 Quoted in H. J. Schroeder, *Die USA und Deutschland 1918–1975* (Munich, 1978), 123.

64 D. A. Irwin, 'From Smoot–Hawley to Reciprocal Trade Agreements: Changing the Course of US Trade Policy in the 1930s', NBER Working Paper Series, 5895 (1997), 28.

65 Brazil fired warning shots in December 1934 over a proposed cotton barter deal with Germany; see P. J. Hearden, *Roosevelt Confronts Hitler: America's Entry into World War II* (Dekalb, Ill., 1987), 43–5.

66 The Anglo-German Payments Agreement did not prevent a very severe reduction in German imports from the British Empire, either. In real terms, German imports from Britain fell 30 per cent between 1928 and 1938. W. Graevell, *Der Aussenhandel in der Nationalwirtschaft* (Stuttgart, 1937), 85.

67 In an early assessment of 29 May 1934, the Reichsbank estimated that approximately 900 million Reichsmarks, or one-fifth of German imports, could be shifted to suppliers with which it currently had trade surpluses. See BAL R2501 6601, 396–438.

68 Guido Radio von Radiis, *Die deutsche Aussenhandelspolitik unter dem Einfluss der Devisenbewirtschaftung von 1931 bis 1938* (Zurich, 1938), 122–5, 130–32.

69 The point Schacht was making was actually against American trade policy. But it applied with equal force to his own trade policy; quoted by Schroeder, *Die USA und Deutschland*, 122.

70 See the remarkably illuminating account of Brazil's position in S. E. Hilton, *Brazil and the Great Powers, 1930–1939* (Austin, Tex., 1975).

71 W. Feilchenfeld, D. Michaelis and L. Pinner, *Haavara-Transfer nach Palaestina und Einwanderung deutscher Juden 1933–1939* (Tuebingen, 1972).

72 See the papers in BAL R2501 6441, 6002 and 6003; Ebi, *Export*, 118–48 and Dengg, *Deutschlands Austritt*, 402–5.

73 Hitler also closely followed the Anglo-German discussions in the autumn of 1934 and gave his personal approval to the Payments Agreement; see Wendt, *Economic Appeasement*, 276.

74 *Schulthess 1934*, 26 August 1934, 221–6.

75 *Konjunkturstatistisches Handbuch*, 52 and 92.

76 BAL R2501 6602, 320–22.

77 This and the following from BAL R2501 6603, 1–22.

78 BAL R2501 6603, 33–47.

79 Ebi, *Export*, 159–91. Impressive statistics on the scale of the levy and its distribution between industries are contained in BAL R2 31.034.

80 Firms were required to pay 0.4 per cent on the first 15 million Reichsmarks of domestic sales, 0.6 per cent on the next 15 million, 1 per cent on the next 15 million, rising by 0.4 per cent for every additional 15 million Reichsmarks of domestic turnover. See P. Hayes, *Industry and Ideology: IG Farben in the Nazi Era* (Cambridge, 1987), 152.

81 The chemical giant, IG Farben, perhaps not surprisingly, paid the highest export levy, which varied in its case between 5 and 9 per cent. Its total bill for 1935–6 came to 50–60

million Reichsmarks. The net burden was smaller because IG Farben as a champion exporter was also one of the largest recipients of the new subsidy.

82 Benson Ford Research Center, Acc. 732, box 435.

83 See BAL R13I 618, 85 for the response offered to the steel industry.

84 BAL R2501 6447, 152–5.

85 The most significant exception to this rule was Gottfried Dierig, co-owner of Christian Dierig AG, the dominant textile firm in Germany, who served as chair of the Reich Group for industry between December 1936 and October 1938; see R. Eckert, 'Die Leiter und Geschaeftsfuehrer der Reichsgruppe Industrie', I, *Jahrbuch fuer Wirtschaftsgeschichte*, 4 (1979), 264.

86 For an in-depth survey, see G. Hoeschle, *Die deutsche Textilindustrie zwischen 1933 und 1939: Staatsinterventionismus und oekonomische Rationalitaet* (Stuttgart, 2004).

87 As noted succinctly in I. Kershaw, *The 'Hitler Myth'* (Oxford, 1987), 62–78 and documented in painstaking detail in Morsch, *Arbeit und Brot*.

88 Baden was less hard hit by the Depression but recovered more slowly than the rest of Germany; see R. Peter, *Ruestungspolitik in Baden: Kriegswirtschaft und Arbeitseinsatz in einer Grenzregion im Zweiten Weltkrieg* (Munich, 1995), 79–95.

89 Morsch, *Arbeit und Brot*, 188.

90 Ibid., 170.

91 Ibid., 178–9.

92 Ibid., 157.

4 Partners: The Regime and German Business

1 This and the following quotations are from IMT, *Nazi Conspiracy and Aggression* (Washington, 1946–7), VI. 1080–85, H. A. Turner, *German Big Business and the Rise of Hitler* (Oxford, 1985), 329–32 and P. Hayes, *Industry and Ideology: IG Farben in the Nazi Era* (Cambridge, 1987), 82–7.

2 Weinberg suggests that the lack of references to foreign conquests may simply be due to the fact that Hitler did not want to repeat some of the more aggressive suggestions he had made at the Duesseldorf industrial club a year earlier; Weinberg, *Foreign Policy I*, 28.

3 The list forms part of IMT, *Nazi Conspiracy and Aggression*, VII, NI-391, 565–8.

4 A huge literature, well summarized in H. U. Wehler, *Deutsche Gesellschaftsgeschichte* (Munich, 2003), IV. 664–90 and 721–31.

5 See P. Suess, *'Ist Hitler nicht ein famoser Kerl?': Graetz. Eine Familie und ihr Unternehmen vom Kaiserreich bis zur Bundesrepublik* (Paderborn, 2003), 115. The quote, 'Isn't Hitler a fabulous guy?', is from Erich Graetz, the owner and manager of a medium-sized producer of gas lamps and consumer electronics.

6 T. Mason, 'Zur Entstehung des Gesetzes zur Ordnung der nationalen Arbeit vom 20. Januar 1934', in H. Mommsen, D. Petzina and D. Weisbrod (eds.), *Industrielles System and politische Entwicklung in der Weimarer Republik* (Duesseldorf, 1977), I. 322–51. See also M. Frese, *Betriebspolitik im Dritten Reich: DAF, Unternehmer und Staatsbuerokratie in der westdeutschen Grossindustrie 1933–1939* (Paderborn, 1991), 93–113.

7 B. Weisbrod, *Schwerindustrie in der Weimarer Republik* (Wuppertal, 1978), 495–6. For the self-stylization of German industrial elites, see S. Unger, 'Die Wirtschaftselite als Persoenlichkeit', in V. R. Berghahn, S. Unger and D. Ziegler (eds.), *Die deutsche Wirtschaftselite im 20. Jahrhundert* (Bochum, 2003), 295–316.

8 M. Schneider, *Unterm Hakenkreuz: Arbeiter und Arbeiterbewegung 1933 bis 1939* (Bonn, 1999), 290–300. R. Hachtmann, *Industriearbeit im 'Dritten Reich'* (Goettingen, 1989), 92–112.

9 See the articles by C. Buchheim and B. Eichengreen in C. Buchheim *et al.* (eds.), *Zerrissene Zwischenkriegszeit: Wirtschaftshistorische Beitraege* (Baden-Baden, 1994), 97–122 and 177–204. It should also be noted, however, that unlike in other countries real product wages did not actually rise in Germany during the Depression.

10 W. Buehrer, 'Zum Wandel der wirtschafts- und sozialpolitischen Zukunftsvorstellungen in der deutschen Industrie zwischen Weltwirtschaftskrise und Wirtschaftswunder', in M. Prinz and M. Frese, *Politische Zaesur und gesellschaftlicher Wandel im 20. Jahrhundert* (Paderborn, 1996), 81–104; W. Zollitsch, *Arbeiter zwischen Weltwirtschaftskrise und Nationalsozialismus* (Goettingen, 1990).

11 For Krupp's position, see W. Abelshauser, 'Gustav Krupp und die Gleichschaltung des Reichsverbandes der Deutschen Industrie, 1933–1934', *Zeitschrift fuer Unternehmensgeschichte*, 47 (2002), 3–26.

12 This is the consistent theme running through all the Reichsverband's publications up to the early 1930s: *Stellung der deutschen Industrie in der Weltwirtschaft* (Berlin, 1922); *Deutsche Wirtschafts- und Finanzpolitik* (Berlin, 1925), 20–21 and 53–7; *Aufstieg oder Niedergang?* (Berlin, 1929), 15 and 41–2; H. Kraemer, *Europaeische Handelspolitik* (Berlin, 1930).

13 See R. Frommelt, *Paneuropa oder Mitteleuropa: Einigungsbestrebungen im Kalkuel deutscher Wirtschaft und Politik 1925–1933* (Stuttgart, 1977). On the 'European' outlook of leading German steel industrialists, see G. Mollin, *Montankonzerne und 'Drittes Reich'* (Goettingen, 1988), 55–7.

14 See the discussion of the formation of the steel cartel in K. H. Pohl, *Weimars Wirtschaft und die Aussenpolitik der Republik 1924–1926: Vom Dawes-Plan zum Internationalen Eisenpakt* (Duesseldorf, 1979).

15 G. Kuemmel, *Transnationale Wirtschaftskooperation und der Nationalstaat: Deutsch-amerikanische Unternehmensbeziehungen in den dreissiger Jahren* (Stuttgart, 1995).

16 On the complexities of the relationship, see Pohl, *Weimars Wirtschaft*.

17 G. Feldman, *The Great Disorder: Politics, Economics and Society in the German Inflation, 1914–1924* (Oxford, 1993), 498–504, 720–80.

18 For the nationalist clique within industry, see A. Meyhoff, *Blohm & Voss im 'Dritten Reich'* (Hamburg, 2001), 44–51.

19 For the Dawes decision, see M. Berg, *Gustav Stresemann und die Vereinigten Staaten von Amerika: Weltwirtschaftliche Verflechtung und Revisionspolitik 1907–1929* (Baden-Baden, 1990), 187–217. For the Young Plan, see R. Neebe, *Grossindustrie, Staat und NSDAP 1930–1933* (Goettingen, 1981), 53–7. For industrial support of anti-Hugenbergers within the DNVP, see L. E. Jones, *German Liberalism and the Dissolution of the Weimar Party System, 1918–1933* (Chapel Hill, NC, 1988), 352–5.

20 E. W. Hansen, *Reichswehr und Industrie* (Boppard, 1978). Predictably, Blohm, Borsig and their DNVP friends were enthusiastic participants.

21 M. Gruebler, *Die Spitzenverbaende der Wirtschaft und das erste Kabinett Bruening* (Duesseldorf, 1982).

22 C. Kopper, *Zwischen Marktwirtschaft und Dirigismus: Bankenpolitik im 'Dritten Reich' 1933–1939* (Bonn, 1995), 51–67.

23 On FAVAG, see G. D. Feldman, *Allianz and the German Insurance Business, 1933–1945* (Cambridge, 2001), 17–26. On HANOMAG, see P. Schulz, *Nicht die Zeit, um auszuruhen: Dokumente und Bilder zur Geschichte der hannoverschen Arbeiterbewegung* (Hanover, 1990), 306–37. On Schultheiss, see M. Fiedler, 'Netzwerke des Vertrauens', in D. Ziegler (ed.), *Grossbuerger und Unternehmer* (Goettingen, 2000), 96–106.

24 W. Feldenkirchen, *Siemens 1919–1945* (Munich, 1995), 127–8.

25 A. Reckendrees, *Das 'Stahltrust-Projekt'* (Munich, 2000), 471–506.

26 In early January 1933 the Thyssen–Schacht–Papen–Hitler axis had little support, even on the right wing of industrial politics, with the Ruhr grouping of Reusch–Krupp–Voegler favouring a DNVP-led government without Hugenberg and with the SA having been detached from the rest of the Nazi party. See Neebe, *Grossindustrie*, 142–52. On Schacht's inability to rally a wide base of industrial support in December 1932, see Feldenkirchen, *Siemens*, 437–8.

27 Already in October 1931 senior industrialists were conspicuous by their absence from the Harzburg meeting. See G. Schulz (ed.), *Politik und Wirtschaft in der Krise 1930–1932* (Duesseldorf, 1980), doc. 342, 13 October 1931, Gilsa to Reusch, II. 1043–4.

28 Feldenkirchen, *Siemens*, 212 and 557 and Abelshauser, 'Gustav Krupp'.

29 Neebe, *Grossindustrie*, 122–7.

30 G. D. Feldman, 'The Economic Origins and Dimensions of European Fascism', in H. James and J. Tanner (eds.), *Enterprise in the Period of Fascism in Europe* (Aldershot, 2002), 6–8.

31 In parallel to his underestimate of the fiscal policy boost administered in 1933, H. James, 'Innovation and Conservatism in Economic Recovery: The Alleged "Nazi Recovery" of the 1930s', in T. Childers and J. Caplan (eds.), *Reevaluating the Third Reich* (New York, 1993), also underestimates the changes within the system of import control and export promotion between 1931 and 1935.

32 For an excellent account which makes clear the highly politicized nature of the system and Schacht's role in imposing it, see Meyhoff, *Blohm & Voss*, 88–107. For the political background, see A. Barkai, *Das Wirtschaftssystem des Nationalsozialismus* (Frankfurt, 1988), 110–31. For an organizational summary, see I. Esenwein-Rothe, *Die Wirtschafts-verbaende von 1933 bis 1945* (Berlin, 1965).

33 R. Eckert, 'Die Leiter und Geschaeftsfuehrer der Reichsgruppe Industrie', I and II, *Jahrbuch fuer Wirtschaftsgeschichte*, 4 (1979).

34 J. A. Tooze, *Statistics and the German State 1900–1945: The Making of Modern Economic Knowledge* (Cambridge, 2001), 177–214.

35 On the intermingling of business interests and the state administration in the foreign trade system, see W. A. Boelcke, *Die deutsche Wirtschaft 1930–1945* (Duesseldorf, 1982), 88–107.

36 Meyhoff, *Blohm & Voss*, 104–5.

37 *Konjunkturstatistisches Handbuch* (Berlin, 1935), 107.

38 On Goerdeler, see S. Gillmann and H. Mommsen (eds.), *Politische Schriften und Briefe Carl Friedrich Goerdelers* (Munich, 2003). Gestapo reports confirmed the positive popular response to the creation of the post of price commissioner; G. Morsch, *Arbeit und Brot: Studien zur Lage, Stimmung, Einstellung und Verhalten der deutschen Arbeiterschaft, 1933–1936/37* (Frankfurt, 1993), 197.

39 The best discussions are still A. Schweitzer, *Big Business in the Third Reich* (Bloomington, Ind., 1964), 184–96 and 265–87, and F. Neumann, *Behemoth: The Structure and Practice of National Socialism 1933–1944* (New York, 1944), 261–73. See also R. Puppo, *Die wirtschaftsrechtliche Gesetzgebung im Dritten Reich* (Konstanz, 1989).

40 See the commentary in *Der Deutsche Volkswirt*, 20 November 1936, 359.

41 The breakthrough work is M. Spoerer, *Von Scheingewinn zum Ruestungsboom: Die Eigenkapitalrentabilitaet der deutschen Industrieaktiengesellschaften 1925–1941* (Stuttgart, 1996).

42 *Die Deutsche Volkswirtschaft*, 10, 1 April 1934.

43 S. Lurie, *Private Investment in a Controlled Economy* (New York, 1947), 122–47; W. A. Boelcke, *Die Kosten von Hitlers Krieg: Kriegsfinanzierung und finanzielles Kriegserbe in Deutschland 1933–1948* (Paderborn, 1985), 36–50.

44 Kopper, *Zwischen Marktwirtschaft und Dirigismus*, 86–125.

45 A point, first made by Barkai, *Das Wirtschaftssystem*, 195–204, that has become a recurring theme in H. James, *The Deutsche Bank and the Nazi Economic War against the Jews* (Cambridge, 2001), 285–91, H. James, 'Banks and the Era of Totalitarianism', in James and Tanner, *Enterprise in the Period of Fascism*, 14–25 and H. James, *The Nazi Dictatorship and the Deutsche Bank* (Cambridge, 2004), 22–37.

46 On this crucial sector we have only the little-noticed study of B. Hopmann, *Von der MONTAN zur Industrieverwaltungsgesellschaft (IVG) 1916–1951* (Stuttgart, 1996).

47 Somewhat surprisingly, the 'Mannesmann connection', despite its obvious importance, has barely featured in James's many studies of the Deutsche Bank. For the classic conspiratorial interpretation, see OMGUS, *Ermittlungen gegen die Deutsche Bank* (Noerdlingen, 1985), 103–11, 150–52.

48 D. Schweer and W. Thieme (eds.), *'Der glaeserne Riese' RWE: Ein Konzern wird transparent* (Essen, 1998).

49 Ibid., 82. Generally on HOCHTIEF, see M. Pohl and B. Siekmann, *HOCHTIEF and its History* (Munich, 2001). Today, HOCHTIEF, one of the world's largest construction companies, is majority-owned by RWE.

50 For an excellent 'muckraking' account, see W. Zaengl, *Deutschlands Strom: Die Politik der Elektrifizierung von 1866 bis heute* (Frankfurt, 1989).

51 J. O. Kehrberg, *Die Entwicklung des Elektrizitaetsrechts in Deutschland: Der Weg zum Energiewirtschaftsgesetz von 1935* (Frankfurt, 1997) and B. Stier, *Staat und Strom: Die politische Steuerung des Elektrizitaetssystems in Deutschland 1890–1950* (Ubstadt-Weihler, 1999), 442–70.

52 For examples of how this operated to the advantage of the large generators, see Zaengl, *Deutschlands Strom*, 182–3.

53 Tooze, *Statistics*, 40–102.

54 Testimony reproduced with a complete lack of critical distance in Boelcke, *Die deutsche Wirtschaft*, 88–9.

55 The concentration of power in the nation-state emerges as the only common denominator of 'National Socialist' also in G. Ambrosius, 'Was war eigentliche "nationalsozialistisch" an den Regulierungsansaetzen der dreissiger Jahre?', in W. Abelshauser, J.-O. Hesse and W. Plumpe (eds.), *Wirtschaftsordnung, Staat und Unternehmen: Neue Forschungen zur Wirtschaftsgeschichte des Nationalsozialismus* (Essen, 2003), 41–60.

56 For a contemporary discussion of the balance of payments problem by the prestigious Verein fuer Sozialpolitik, see R. Meerwarth *et al.*, *Problem der deutschen Zahlungsbilanz* (Munich, 1924). For a critical review of contemporary theories, see C.-L. Holtfrerich, *Die deutsche Inflation 1914–1923* (Berlin, 1980), 154–71.

57 This historicist view was strongly pushed by the Institut fuer Konjunkturforschung in all its publications and summarized by E. Wagemann in *Zwischenbilanz der Krisenpolitik* (Berlin, 1935).

58 The downplaying of business agency in relation to the regime is one of the dangers involved in an over-hasty incorporation of Tim Mason's statement of the 'primacy of the political' into the business history literature of the Third Reich. For the original statement, see J. Caplan (ed.), *Nazism, Fascism and the Working Class: Essays by Tim Mason* (Cambridge, 1995), 53–76.

59 For a statistical outline, see R. Krengel, *Anlagevermoegen, Produktion und Beschaeftigung der Industrie im Gebiete der Bundesrepublik von 1924 bis 1956* (Berlin, 1958) and J. A. Tooze, " 'Punktuelle Modernisierung": Die Akkumulation von Werkzeugmaschinen im "Dritten Reich" ', *Jahrbuch fuer Wirtschaftsgeschichte*, 1 (2003), 79–98.

60 See the tradition of muckraking literature on IG that runs from J. Borkin and C. A. Welsh, *Germany's Master Plan: The Story of Industrial Offensive* (London, 1943), via J. E. Dubois, *Generals in Grey Suits* (London, 1953) to J. Borkin, *The Crime and Punishment of IG Farben* (London, 1979).

61 The best book on IG, indeed the best book on business in the Third Reich, is Hayes, *Industry and Ideology*. In the same vein, see the R. G. Stokes contribution to W. Abelshauser *et al.*, *BASF: The History of a Company* (Cambridge, 2004), 206–361. More problematic is G. Plumpe, *Die IG Farbenindustrie AG* (Berlin, 1990).

62 For an account, see J. A. Johnson in Abelshauser *et al.*, *BASF*, 151–76; Hayes, *Industry and Ideology*, 1–19.

63 J. Radkau, *Technik in Deutschland* (Frankfurt, 1989), 263–8.

64 Johnson in Abelshauser *et al.*, *BASF*, 204, and Stokes, ibid., 222–33.

65 D. Yergin, *The Prize: The Epic Quest for Oil, Money and Power* (New York, 1991), 207–52.

66 Britain's ICI, which had also embarked on a fuel hydrogenation programme in the 1920s, also pressured the British government for protection; see Plumpe, *Die IG Farbenindustrie*, 265–79.

67 We owe this basic insight above all to Mollin, *Montankonzerne*, 64–7. For contemporary comment on the new coal–chemistry axis, see *Der Deutsche Volkswirt*, 3 June 1932, 1185–7.

68 Plumpe, *Die IG Farbenindustrie*, 272. Gottfried Feder, author of the Nazi party's manifesto, was parachuted into the RWM for a brief stint as Secretary of State; he was soon to be sidelined by Schacht.

69 For the following, see T. Buetow and F. Bindernagel, *Ein KZ in der Nachbarschaft: Das Magdeburger Aussenlager der Brabag und der 'Freundeskreis Himmler'* (Cologne, 2003), 9–68, and W. Birkenfeld, *Der synthetische Treibstoff 1933–1945* (Goettingen, 1964), 35–48.

70 Carl Krauch (1887–1968) joined BASF in Ludwigshafen in 1912 as a Ph.D. chemist. As a result of his excellent performance in the synthetic nitrogen effort during World War I, he was rapidly promoted, first as technical director in Ludwigshafen, then as general manager of the Ammoniakwerk Merseburg (Leuna). He joined the IG Farben board in 1925 as a deputy director. His promotion to a full member of the board in 1934 corresponded to his pivotal role in managing the company's relations with the emerging Nazi dictatorship. He appears to have been closely associated with Albert Voegler. Disappointment at not being selected as chairman of the board of IG when Carl Bosch retired in the spring of 1935 may account for Krauch's increasing commitment to the autarchic programmes of the regime rather than strictly company business. Hayes, *Industry and Ideology*, 156–8.

71 Reckendrees, *Das 'Stahltrust-Projekt'* and A. Chandler, *Scale and Scope: The Dynamics of Industrial Capitalism* (Cambridge, Mass., 1990), 550–58.

72 J. R. Gillingham, *Industry and Politics in the Third Reich: Ruhr Coal, Hitler and Europe* (London, 1985).

73 Remarkably, we still lack a comprehensive treatment of heavy industry in the Third Reich. The best guide is Mollin, *Montankonzerne*.

74 Abelshauser, 'Gustav Krupp'.

75 On Paul Reusch, the best recent work is C. Rauh-Kuehne, 'Zwischen "verantwortlichem Wirkungskreis" und "haeuslichem Glanz": Zur Innenansicht wirtschaftsbuerglicher Familien im 20. Jahrhundert', in Ziegler (ed.), *Grossbuerger und Unternehmer*, 215–48. Otherwise we must still rely on E. Maschke, *Es entsteht ein Konzern: Paul Reusch und die GHH* (Tuebingen, 1969).

76 See Turner, *German Big Business*, 145–8 and 264–5 and most recently E. O. Eglau, *Fritz Thyssen* (Berlin, 2003).

77 W. Abelshauser, in L. Gall (ed.), *Krupp im 20. Jahrhundert* (Berlin, 2002), 328–33. The statistics reproduced by Abelshauser refer only to the Gusstahlfabrik in Essen, whose product portfolio was more diversified than that of Krupp-Gruson.

78 Ibid., 344–7, stresses the lack of profitability and small scale of activities at Germania even in the late 1930s. For a more appropriate stress on the importance of the yard for German U-boat history and in particular for the development of U-VII, see E. Roessler, *Die deutschen U-Boote und ihre Werften* (Koblenz, 1990), 38–90 and E. Roessler, *Geschichte des deutschen U-Bootbaus* (Augsburg, 1996), I. 162–70.

79 Again, we have no reliable biography. For a hagiography, see G. von Klass, *Albert Voegler* (Tuebingen, 1957). Voegler's centrality to German business politics has recently been confirmed by the quantitative network analysis of Martin Fiedler. In a sample of the board members of Germany's 354 largest public companies in 1927 and 1938 consisting of between 3,000 and 4,000 people, Voegler was the eighth most 'central' figure in 1927 and by far the best connected in 1938. Added to which, Voegler was one of only two people to appear in the list in both 1927 and 1938. The other was Emil Georg von Strauss of Deutsche Bank-Daimler Benz who was eleventh in 1927 and eighth in 1938. See M. Fiedler and B. Lorentz, in Berghahn, Unger and Ziegler (eds), *Die deutsche Wirtschaftselite*, 51–74.

80 Neebe, *Grossindustrie*, 189–91.

81 M. Pohl, *VIAG* (Munich, 1998), 112–13; Kopper, *Zwischen Marktwirtschaft und Dirigismus*, 89.

82 Eckert, 'Die Leiter und Geschaeftsfuehrer', II.

83 Mollin, *Montankonzerne*, 40–42.

84 W. Weber, 'Walter Borbet (1881–1942)', in W. Weber (ed.), *Ingenieure im Ruhrgebiet* (Muenster, 1999), 224–56, and G. H. Seebold, *Ein Stahlkonzern im Dritten Reich: Der Bochumer Verein 1927–1945* (Wuppertal, 1981), 239–45.

85 W. Rohland, *Bewegte Zeiten: Erinnerungen eines Eisenhuettenmannes* (Stuttgart, 1978).

86 Schulz, *Nicht die Zeit, um auszuruhern*, 480–82 and Seebold, *Ein Stahlkonzern*, 74–7.

87 For Rohland's summary of the state of the art, see Rohland, 'Die Entwicklung des Lichtbogen-Elektrostahlofens zum Grossraumofen und seine metallurgische Anwendung', *Stahl und Eisen*, 61 (1941), 1–12. Rohland was critical of the so-called Duplex process preferred by Borbet.

88 This is the key finding of Reckendrees, *Das 'Stahltrust-Projekt'*.

89 F. Sommer and H. Pollack, *Elektrostahlerzeugung* (Duesseldorf, 1950), 10–14 and E. Ploeckinger and O. Etterich, *Electric Furnace Steel Production* (Chichester, 1985), 4–7.

90 A point established in monumental style by L. Budrass. *Flugzeugindustrie und Luftruestung in Deutschland* (Duesseldorf, 1998). See also E. L. Homze, *Arming the Luftwaffe* (Lincoln, Nebr., 1976). The following section, unless otherwise indicated, is based on these works.

91 M. Fiedler, 'Die hundert groessten Unternehmen in Deutschland – nach der Zahl ihrer Beschaeftigten – 1907, 1938, 1973, 1995', *Zeitschrift fuer Unternehmensgeschichte*, 44 (1999), 32–66 and 'Nachtrag', ibid., 235–42. For an annotated list of the top 100 firms, see www.hist.cam.ac.uk/academic_staff/further_details/tooze.html

92 Rheinmetall was the only other industrial firm of any size with an equivalent dependence on the Wehrmacht and even at Rheinmetall in 1938 weapons accounted for only 57 per cent of turnover. See Imperial War Museum (henceforth IWM), FD 717/46, box 248, Rheinmetall reports.

93 Budrass, *Flugzeugindustrie*, 321–33.

94 Ibid., 326–8.

95 H. Pophanken, *Gruendung und Ausbau der 'Weser'-Flugzeugbau GmbH 1933 bis 1939* (Bremen, 2000), 34–5.

96 Feldenkirchen, *Siemens*, 380–82.

97 Hayes, *Industry and Ideology*, 139–42 and Kuemmel, *Transnationale Wirtschaftskooperation*, 168.

98 Pohl, *VIAG*, 165–72.

99 The standard reference is now G. Hoeschle, *Die deutsche Textilindustrie zwischen 1933 und 1939: Staatsinterventionismus und oekonomische Rationalitaet* (Stuttgart, 2004). But see also J. Scherner, 'Zwischen Staat und Markt: Die deutsche halbsynthetische Chemiefaserindustrie in den 1930er Jahren', *VWSG* 89 (2002), 427–48.

100 Both viscose-rayon and staple fibre are produced from plant cellulose using the same chemical techniques. Viscose-rayon is produced as continuous threads ready for weaving on specialized machinery, eliminating the need for spinning. Staple fibres are cheaper to produce, but due to their short length must be spun like wool or cotton to form threads, which can then be worked up on standard weaving or knitting frames. For a richly illustrated introduction see VGF, *Die Kunstfaser: Wie werden Kunstseide und Zellwolle hergestellt und verarbeitet?* (Stuttgart, 1938).

101 On Kehrl, see H. Kehrl, *Krisenmanager im Dritten Reich* (Duesseldorf, 1973), 87–92 and R.-D. Mueller, *Der Manager der Kriegswirtschaft: Hans Kehrl* (Essen, 1999).

102 S. Reich, 'Corporate Social Responsibility', in F. R. Nicosia and J. Huener (eds.), *Business and Industry in Nazi Germany* (Berghahn, 2004), 115–17.

103 For Ford's troubled history of investment, see S. Reich, *The Fruits of Fascism: Postwar Posterity in Historical Perspective* (Ithaca, NY, 1990).

104 N. Forbes, *Doing Business with the Nazis* (London, 2000), 133–65.

105 Kuemmel, *Transnationale Wirtschaftskooperation*, 232.
106 Ibid., 191.

5 *Volksgemeinschaft* on a Budget

1 Credit for alerting us to this aspect of Hitler's thought is owed to R. Zitelmann, *Hitler: Selbstverstaendnis eines Revolutionaers* (Stuttgart, 1987).
2 For this and the following, see W. Koenig, 'Das Scheitern einer nationalsozialistischen Konsumgesellschaft', *Zeitschrift fuer Unternehmensgeschichte*, 48 (2003), 152–3.
3 C. Clark, 'Internationaler Vergleich der Volkseinkommen', *Weltwirtschaftliches Archiv*, 47 (1938), 51–76, followed by his defining work, *The Conditions of Economic Progress* (London, 1940).
4 The importance of Clark's analysis was clearly appreciated in Germany as is betokened by the quasi-official response it received from a representative of the Reich Statistical Office. See P. Jostock, 'Wieweit sind Volkseinkommen international vergleichbar?', *Weltwirtschaftliches Archiv*, 49 (1939), 241–73, and P. Jostock, *Die Berechnung des Volkseinkommens und ihr Erkenntniswert* (Stuttgart, 1941).
5 See A. Maddison, *The World Economy: A Millennial Perspective* (Paris, 2001). The unit of comparison in which these accounting exercises are conducted is the so-called Geary-Khamis dollar of 1990.
6 For a needlessly polemical discussion of the 'imposition' of the American standard of living on Europe, see V. de Grazia, *Irresistible Empire: America's Advance through Twentieth-Century Europe* (Cambridge, Mass., 2005). See also W. Koenig, *Geschichte der Konsumgesellschaft* (Stuttgart, 2000), 108–22.
7 For the following, see the literature surveyed in S. L. Engermann and R. E. Gallman, *The Cambridge Economic History of the United States*, vol. III (Cambridge, 2000), 829–45.
8 H. Ford, *My Life and Work* (London, 1923), was translated into German immediately, as was H. Ford, *The International Jew* (Leipzig, 1922).
9 T. von Freyberg, *Industrielle Rationalisierung in der Weimarer Republik* (Frankfurt, 1989) and T. Siegel and T. von Freyberg, *Industrielle Rationalisierung unter dem Nationalsozialismus* (Frankfurt, 1991). For the diffusion of innovative modes of machine-tool use in German industry in the inter-war period, see J. A. Tooze, ' "Punktuelle Modernisierung": Die Akkumulation von Werkzeugmaschinen in "Dritten Reich" ', *Jahrbuch fuer Wirtschaftsgeschichte*, 1 (2003).
10 A. Chandler, *Scale and Scope: The Dynamics of Industrial Capitalism* (Cambridge, Mass., 1990), 393–502.
11 Hohner, for instance, which in 1929 manufactured almost 22 million harmonicas, exporting them to virtually every country in the world. See H. Berghoff, *Zwischen Kleinstadt und Weltmarkt: Hohner und die Harmonika 1857–1961* (Paderborn, 1997), 391.
12 J. H. Morrow, *German Air Power in World War I* (Lincoln, Nebr., 1982) and L. Budrass, *Flugzeugindustrie und Luftruestung in Deutschland* (Duesseldorf, 1998), 21–66. Engermann and Gallman, *Cambridge Economic History of the US*, III. 839.
13 L. Rostas, 'Industrial Production, Productivity and Distribution in Britain, Germany and the United States', *Economic Journal*, 53 (1943), 39–54.
14 For the Anglo-German comparison from the British point of view, see S. Broadberry, *The Productivity Race: British Manufacturing in International Perspective, 1850–1990* (Cambridge, 1997).
15 In 1936 per capita value added in agriculture in Reichsmarks of 1913 came to 1,200 Reichsmarks, as opposed to non-agricultural per capita productivity of 2,400 Reichsmarks; figures from W. G. Hoffmann, *Das Wachstum der deutschen Wirtschaft* (Heidelberg, 1965), 205–6 and 454.
16 See K. Helfferich, *Deutschlands Volkswohlstand 1888–1913* (3rd edn., Berlin, 1914).
17 See the controversy surrounding contemporary estimates of national investment discussed

in J. A. Tooze, *Statistics and the German State 1900–1945: The Making of Modern Economic Knowledge* (Cambridge, 2001), 172.

18 The recurring theme in A. Zischka's hugely popular books on raw materials, including *Der Kampf um die Weltmacht Baumwolle* (Leipzig, 1935), *Wissenschaft bricht Monopole* (Leipzig, 1936, total sales 616,000), *Brot fuer Zwei Milliarden Menschen* (Leipzig, 1938), *Oelkrieg* (Leipzig, 1939) and *Englands Buendnisse* (Leipzig, 1940). Zischka's total sales pre-1945 numbered in the millions.

19 Figures are for 1939 from SRA, *Statistisches Jahrbuch fuer das Deusche Reich (1941/42)* (Berlin, 1942), 382. See the detailed discussion in R. Hachtmann, *Industriearbeit im 'Dritten Reich'* (Goettingen, 1989).

20 For this and the following, see G. Thost, 'Das Einkommen der Arbeiter, Angestellte und Beamten', *Die Deutsche Volkswirtschaft*, 20 (1939), 776–80.

21 SRA, *Statistisches Jahrbuch fuer das Deutsche Reich*, 377–80.

22 Ibid., 448. According to Clark, *Conditions*, 69, Americans spent virtually the same amount of money as Germans on food, but this accounted for only 21.5 per cent of their incomes. The contrast between Germany and Britain was less stark, but nevertheless significant. By comparison with Germany, British households spent only 30 per cent of their incomes on food.

23 For a vivid and well-illustrated account of everyday life in inter-war Germany, see G. Kaehler (ed.), *Geschichte des Wohnens* (Stuttgart, 1996), IV.

24 ILO, *An International Enquiry into Costs of Living: A Comparative Study of Workers' Living Costs in Detroit (USA) and Fourteen European Cities* (2nd rev. edn., Geneva, 1931), 33–45.

25 For a contemporary economic history written from this liberal point of view, see G. Stolper, *German Economy: 1870–1940. Issues and Trends* (New York, 1940).

26 See C. S. Maier, 'Society as Factory', in his *In Search of Stability: Explorations in Historical Political Economy* (Cambridge, 1987), 19–69 and M. Nolan, *Visions of Modernity: American Business and the Modernization of Germany* (Oxford, 1994).

27 A. Luedtke, 'The "Honour of Labour" ', in D. F. Crew (ed.), *Nazism and German Society 1933–1945* (London, 1994), 67–109.

28 J. Gillingham, 'The "Deproletarianization" of German Society: Vocational Training in the Third Reich', *Journal of Social History*, 19 (1986), 423–32.

29 On the collapse of faith in liberal economic progress, see for instance the Austrian émigré and future management guru P. F. Drucker, *The End of Economic Man* (New York, 1939).

30 For the following, see A. Ritschl, 'Die NS-Wirtschaftsideologie – Modernisierungsprogramm oder reaktionaere Utopie?', in M. Prinz and R. Zitelmann (eds.), *Nationalsozialismus und Modernisierung* (Darmstadt, 1991), 48–70.

31 R. Luxemburg, *The Accumulation of Capital* (1913).

32 See the Malthusian lecture that Keynes delivered to the Eugenics Society in 1937, reprinted in *Population and Development Review*, 4 (1978), 517–23, and A. Hansen's Presidential Address to the American Economic Association in 1938, reprinted in *Population and Development Review*, 30 (2004), 329–42.

33 See Hitler's remarks to the Berlin car show in 1934, Domarus, I. 369–71, 7 March 1934.

34 W. Koenig, *Volkswagen, Volksempfaenger, Volksgemeinschaft: 'Volksprodukte' im Dritten Reich. Vom Scheitern einer nationalsozialistischen Konsumgesellschaft* (Paderborn, 2004).

35 As ibid., 243–57.

36 IfK, *Weekly Report*, 22 August 1935.

37 Koenig, *Volkswagen*, 25–99.

38 This eased the cash flow problems but added substantially to the cost of the equipment, since it implied an interest rate of almost 14 per cent. See the copy at the excellent website www.ve301.de.

39 IfK, *Weekly Report*, 11 August 1938, 61–4.

40 Koenig, *Volkswagen*, 145 and the entries for Seibt, Bruckern & Stark, Lumophon and Owin in www.radiomuseum.org/dsp_hersteller_detail.cfm.

41 Three years later, thanks to huge sales of the cheap DKE receivers, Germany had drawn level with Britain. See Koenig, *Volkswagen*, 84.

42 This comparison was of course biased by the overvaluation of the German exchange rate but nevertheless reflected the overwhelming advantage of American producers. Ibid., 80–81.

43 See the equation between cars and aeroplanes with which Hitler began his speech to the international motor exhibition in Berlin, 11 February 1933, Domarus, I. 208.

44 R. Flik, *Von Ford lernen? Automobilbau und Motorisierung in Deutschland bis 1933* (Cologne, 2001).

45 Since the population of Berlin actually declined between 1933 and 2002 from 4.23 million to only 3.38 million, the density of cars in relation to population has actually increased by a factor of 30.

46 Domarus, I. 209.

47 'Die steuerliche Belastung der Kraftfahrzeuge im In- und Ausland', *Vierteljahrshefte zur Statistik des Deutschen Reichs*, 42 (1933), 136–46.

48 IfK, *Haltungskosten von Personenkraftfahrzeugen* (Jena, 1938), 42–3, 68.

49 Assuming a fuel consumption of 8.5 litres per 100 km, daily earnings of 5 Reichsmarks and a fuel price of 39 Pfennigs per litre.

50 Flik, *Von Ford lernen*, 78.

51 Ibid., 131–241.

52 For the contemporary phenomenon that was Ruesselsheim, see the photo-reportage by H. Hauser, *Am laufenden Band* (Frankfurt, 1936) and *Im Kraftfeld von Ruesselsheim* (Munich, 1942), both with images by P. Wolf, the latter including an unprecedented range of colour photographs.

53 The following pages, unless otherwise stated, are based on H. Mommsen and M. Grieger, *Das Volkswagenwerk und seine Arbeiter im Dritten Reich* (Duesseldorf, 1996), 53–226.

54 Domarus, I. 577–8.

55 Mommsen and Grieger, *Das Volkswagenwerk*, 129.

56 M. Fuehrer, *Mieter, Hausbesitzer, Staat und Wohnungsmarkt: Wohnungsmangel und Wohnungszwangswirtschaft in Deutschland 1914–1960* (Stuttgart, 1995), 27–46. For one well-documented calculation, see IfK, Supplement to *Weekly Report*, 22 April 1936, which suggested that there were 750,000 households with sufficient funds to be able to afford a small housing unit if it were available and another 750,000 who needed housing but lacked the necessary income.

57 G. Schulz, 'Die Diskussion ueber Grundlinien einer Nachkriegssozialpolitik im Nationalsozialismus', in M. Prinz and M. Frese (eds.), *Politische Zaesur und gesellschaftlicher Wandel im 20. Jahrhundert* (Paderborn, 1996), 111.

58 For the situation at the end of the 1920s, see Deutsche Bau- und Bodenbank AG, *Die Entwicklung der deutschen Bauwirtschaft im ersten Halbjahr 1929* (Berlin, n.d.), 20–21.

59 Kaehler (ed.), *Geschichte des Wohnens*, table 12, 720.

60 T. Harlander, *Zwischen Heimstaette und Wohnmaschine: Wohnungsbau und Wohnungspolitik in der Zeit des Nationalsozialismus* (Basle, 1995), 30–53.

61 F. Luetge, *Wohnungswirtschaft* (Jena, 1940), 199–206.

62 Harlander, *Zwischen Heimstaette und Wohnmaschine*, 60.

63 K. C. Fuehrer, 'Das NS Regime und die "Idealform des deutschen Wohnungsbaues"', *VWSG* 89 (2002), 141–66.

64 Fuehrer, *Mieter*, 230–50 and Harlander, *Zwischen Heimstaette und Wohnmaschine*, 97–100.

65 A construction company involved in housing construction found that, of its own employees, 18 per cent paid rents of more than 30 Reichsmarks, 37 per cent paid between 20 and 30 Reichsmarks and 45 per cent paid less than 20 Reichsmarks. See BAH R131,

594, Niederschrift ueber die Sitzung des Beirates der Industrieabteilung der Wirtschafts-kammer Duesseldorf, 14 October 1940.

66 Koenig, *Volkswagen*, 115–24.

67 Harlander, *Zwischen Heimstaette und Wohnmaschine*, 198–206.

68 On the discussion of rationalization in the construction industry in the late 1930s, see Luetge, *Wohnungswirtschaft*, 107–12.

69 *Zweites Buch*, 144.

70 There is in fact consistent evidence pointing to widespread popular support for Hitler's *Lebensraum* vision. See B. Stoever, *Volksgemeinschaft im Dritten Reich: Die Konsens-bereitschaft der Deutschen aus der Sicht sozialistischer Exilberichte* (Duesseldorf, 1993), 236–7.

71 W. Landhoff, *Die grossen Militaerparaden des dritten Reiches* (Kiel, 2002).

72 See the image of crowds viewing a detachment of Mark I tanks at the Bueckeberg, probably in 1935, in W. J. Spielberger, *Die Panzerkampfwagen I und II* (Stuttgart, 3rd edn., 1991), 41.

73 Stoever, *Volksgemeinschaft*, 180–82, who also notes the popularity of the remilitariz-ation of the Rhineland.

74 Ibid., 139, with examples from Dornier, Messerschmitt, Heinkel and MAN.

75 To avoid confusion, the tank in question, the Tiger, was not in production until 1943 and the actual cost price to the Wehrmacht of the Tiger was 300,000 Reichsmarks, including a full complement of ammunition for its 8.8 cm gun. The language is nevertheless extremely telling. W. J. Spielberger, *Tiger and King Tiger Tanks* (Sparkford, 1987), 104, 220–21.

76 A. Luedtke, 'Ikonen des Fortschrittes', in A. Luedtke, I. Marssolek and A. von Saldern (eds.), *Amerikanisierung: Traum und Alptraum im Deutschland des 20. Jahrhunderts* (Stuttgart, 1996), 199–210. For a nuanced account of the evolution of Wehrmacht propa-ganda, see E.-M. Unger, *Illustrierte als Mittel zur Kriegsvorbereitung in Deutschland 1933 bis 1939* (Cologne, 1984), 137–270.

77 K. Moeser, 'World War I and the Creation of Desire for Automobiles in Germany', in S. Strasser, C. McGovern and M. Judt, *Getting and Spending: European and American Consumer Societies in the Twentieth Century* (Cambridge, 1998), 195–222.

78 P. Fritzsche, *A Nation of Fliers: German Aviation and the Popular Imagination* (Cam-bridge, Mass., 1992), 185–219.

6 Saving the Peasants

1 J. C. Weaver, *The Great Land Rush and the Making of the Modern World, 1650–1900* (Montreal, 2003) and A. W. Crosby, *Ecological Imperialism: The Biological Expansion of Europe, 900–1900* (Cambridge, 1986).

2 For contemporary reflections, see D. Goodman and M. Watts (eds.), *Globalising Food: Agrarian Questions and Global Restructuring* (London, 1997).

3 For a vivid contemporary account, see H. H. Tiltman, *Peasant Europe* (London, 1934).

4 For an account that stresses the dualism of the German economy in the inter-war period, see B. Lutz, *Der kurze Traum immerwaehrender Prosperitaet* (Frankfurt, 1989).

5 For the case of miners, see M. Prinz and H. Hanke, ' "Man weiss nicht, was noch kommt": Zum Wandel wirtschaftlicher Zukunftsvorstellungen seit dem Ersten Weltkrieg im Spiegel bergmaennischen Wohnens', in M. Prinz and M. Frese (eds.), *Politische Zaesuren und gesellschaftlicher Wandel im 20. Jahrhundert* (Paderborn, 1996), 35–58.

6 See Bessel's comments in M. Fulbrook (ed.), *German History since 1800* (London, 1997), 251.

7 L. Wiethaler, *Lust und Plage der alten Bauernarbeit* (Mirskofen, 1983).

8 A. Hitler, *Mein Kampf* (Boston, 1947), 4–5.

9 A. Offer, *The First World War: An Agrarian Interpretation* (Oxford, 1989).

10 C. P. Vincent, *The Politics of Hunger: The Allied Blockade of Germany, 1915–1919* (Athens, Ohio, 1985), 124–51.

11 A. Luedtke, 'Hunger in der Grossen Depression: Hungerfahrungen und Hungerpolitik am Ende der Weimarer Republik', *Archiv fuer Sozialgeschichte*, 27 (1987), 145–76.

12 R. W. Davies, M. Harrison and S. G. Wheatcroft, *The Economic Transformation of the Soviet Union, 1913–1945* (Cambridge, 1994), 62–4.

13 G. Corni and H. Gies, *Brot, Butter, Kanonen: Die Ernaehrungswirtschaft in Deutschland unter der Diktatur Hitlers* (Berlin, 1997), 43–62.

14 For the following, see G. Corni and H. Gies, *Blut und Boden: Rassenideologie und Agrarpolitik im Staat Hitlers* (Idstein, 1994), 17–24.

15 R. W. Darré, *Das Bauerntum als Lebensquell der Nordischen Rasse* (1928).

16 F.-L. Kroll, *Utopie als Ideologie: Geschichtsdenken und politisches Handeln im Dritten Reich* (Paderborn, 1998), R. Breitman, *The Architect of Genocide: Himmler and the Final Solution* (London, 1991) and P. Padfield, *Himmler Reichsfuehrer SS* (London, 1990).

17 U. Mai, *'Rasse und Raum': Agrarpolitik, Sozial- und Raumplanung im NS-Staat* (Paderborn, 2002), 113–54.

18 In this sense, Darré fits neatly within the characterization of fascism provided by R. Griffin, *The Nature of Fascism* (London, 1991).

19 Corni and Gies, *Blut und Boden*, 68.

20 See the naive characterization of Backe in J. K. Galbraith, 'Germany was Badly Run', *Fortune* (December 1945), 177.

21 For a brief Backe biography, see J. Lehmann, 'Technokrat und Agrarideologe', in R. Smelser, E. Syring and R. Zitelmann (eds.), *Die Braune Elite: 22 biographische Skizzen* (Darmstadt, 1993), II. 1–12.

22 The following portrait of Backe's ideological vision is based on H. Backe, *Das Ende des Liberalismus in der Wirtschaft* (Berlin, 1938) and H. Backe, *Um die Nahrungsfreiheit Europas: Weltwirtschaft oder Grossraum* (Leipzig, 1942). The latter was almost certainly ghosted, but clearly reflects Backe's self-understanding.

23 Speech to Reichsrat, 2 February 1933, Domarus, I. 237.

24 Backe, *Um die Nahrungsfreiheit*, 15, an argument that eerily foreshadows the critique of liberal imperialism offered by M. Davies, *Late Victorian Holocausts* (London, 2001).

25 H. Backe, 'Grundsaetze einer lebensgesetzlichen Agrarpolitik', *Deutsche Agrarpolitik*, 3 (September 1932), 164–77.

26 M. Sering (ed.), *Die agrarischen Umwaelzungen im ausserrussischen Osteuropa* (Berlin, 1930).

27 F. Wunderlich, *Farm Labor in Germany 1810–1945* (Princeton, 1961), 14–17.

28 See the account books in A. Muenzinger, *Der Arbeitsertrag der baeuerlichen Familienwirtschaft*, I and II (Berlin, 1929).

29 On the emergence of 20 hectares as the ideal of Nazi agricultural planning, see Mai, *'Rasse und Raum'*, 155–88.

30 According to contemporary agronomists, on smaller, high-intensity farms one full-time man was required for every 2–2.5 hectares. See E. Laur, *Landwirtschaftliche Betriebslehre fuer baeuerliche Verhaeltnisse* (Aarau, 1927), 191.

31 G. Corni, *Hitler and the Peasants: Agrarian Policy of the Third Reich, 1930–1939* (Oxford, 1990), 4–5, 222 and Mai, *'Rasse und Raum'*, 16–47.

32 Hitler, *Mein Kampf*, 133–43.

33 Ibid., 654.

34 IMT II. 332–4.

35 See the version issued to German authorities in the occupied Soviet Union in 1941, H. Backe, *Die russische Getreidewirtschaft als Grundlage der Land- und Volkswirtschaft Russlands* (Berlin, 1941).

36 Ibid., 168.

37 Corni, *Hitler and the Peasants*, 28.

38 For the following, see the excellent website maintained by Bernhard Gelderblom, www.gelderblom-hameln.de/

39 Domarus, I. 304–5, 1 October 1933.

40 F. Grundmann, *Agrarpolitik im Dritten Reich: Anspruch und Wirklichkeit des Reichs-erbhofgesetzes* (Frankfurt, 1979) and Mai, *'Rasse und Raum'*, 48–58.

41 Corni and Gies, *Blut und Boden*, 33–7.

42 B. Herlemann, *'Der Bauer klebt am Hergebrachten': Bauerlicher Verhaltensweisen unterm NS auf dem Gebiet des heutigen Landes Niedersachsen* (Hanover, 1993), 105–6.

43 See W. G. Hoffmann, *Das Wachstum der deutschen Wirtschaft* (Heidelberg, 1965), 225–6.

44 Herlemann, *Der Bauer*, 93–4.

45 Corni and Gies, *Brot, Butter, Kanonen*, 75–396 and A. Barkai, *Das Wirtschaftssystem des Nationalsozialismus* (Frankfurt, 1988), 131–49.

46 Backe, 'Grundsaetze', 175.

47 K. Meyer, *Gefuege und Ordnung der deutschen Landwirtschaft* (Berlin, 1939), 636–78.

48 Corni and Gies, *Brot, Butter, Kanonen*, 101–21. For the first of a series of reports on the RNS and other party agencies by the Reichsbank, see BAL R2501 6506, 114–22.

49 According to an analysis prepared for Hitler by Darré, the administrative costs of the RNS market management organization came to only 30 million Reichsmarks compared to a total turnover of 30 billion Reichsmarks, and given the profits earned through the sale of imported animal feedstuffs the organization more than paid for itself. See Corni and Gies, *Brot, Butter, Kanonen*, 164.

50 Data from Hoffmann, *Das Wachstum*, 454–5 and subsidiary tables.

51 F. Fried, *Die Zukunft des Aussenhandels* (Jena, 1934).

52 Corni and Gies, *Brot, Butter, Kanonen*, 269.

53 Corni, *Hitler and the Peasants*, 160–61.

54 Freemasons ranked second only to Jews in the demonology of Heinrich Himmler and the SS.

55 E. Woermann, *Die Veredlungswirtschaft* (Berlin, 1933). Woermann was one of the leading agronomical advisers to the RNS.

56 Hoffmann, *Das Wachstum*, 528.

57 Corni, *Hitler and the Peasants*, 159.

58 Grundmann, *Agrarpolitik*, 121.

59 Unfortunately, Corni and Gies continue this habit in *Brot, Butter, Kanonen*, 309–15. For a more balanced summary, see M. Kutz, 'Kriegserfahrung und Kriegsvorbereitung: Die agrarwirtschaftliche Vorbereitung des Zweiten Weltkrieges … II. Teil', *Zeitschrift fuer Agrargeschichte und Agrarsoziologie*, 32 (1984), 135–64, and one of the last great works of East German economic history, R. Berthold (ed.), *Produktivkraefte in Deutschland 1917/18 bis 1945* (Berlin, 1988), 224–83.

60 H. von der Decken, *Entwicklung der Selbstversorgung Deutschlands mit landwirt-schaftlichen Erzeugnissen* (Berlin, 1938), 13.

61 H. von der Decken und H. Liebe, 'Die Ernaehrungswirtschaft Deutschlands im Weltkrieg und heute', *Vierteljahrshefte zur Wirtschaftforschung*, 1 (1940/41), 5–28.

62 On animal feed, see IfK, *Weekly Report*, 30 May 1934, 20–21, 93–94. On the grain market see IfK, Supplement to *Weekly Report*, 7 November 1934. A. Hanau and R. Plate, *Die deutsche landwirtschaftliche Preis- und Marktpolitik im Zweiten Weltkrieg* (Stuttgart, 1975), 82.

63 Von der Decken, *Entwicklung*, 92–3. The discussion of the feed question in Corni and Gies, *Brot, Butter, Kanonen*, 267–8 and 309–310 is misleading since it focuses only on one type of feed – feed grain – and uses 1933 as its standard of comparison, a year of bumper harvest in which Germany needed to import virtually no grain. As Decken's data show, the sustained reduction in feed imports was far more impressive than Corni and Gies admit.

64 Hanau and Plate, *Preis- und Marktpolitik*, 41–2.

65 For a summary of the measures taken to cope with the grain shortfall in 1936, see BAL R43II 31, 155–64.

66 See the predictably critical report by the Reichsbank, BAL R2501 6799, 107, 20 October 1936.

67 Contrary to Corni and Gies, *Brot, Butter, Kanonen*, 274 and Corni, *Hitler and the Peasants*, 165–7.

68 *Statistisches Handbuch von Deutschland* (Munich, 1949), 489–90 and Hanau and Plate, *Preis- und Marktpolitik*, 49. By failing to consider stock-building, Corni and Gies misinterpret the import of 2.5 million tons of grain in 1938/9 as a sign of 'shortage'. See Corni and Gies, *Brot, Butter, Kanonen*, 314.

69 For a convincing rebuttal of exaggerated reports of crisis in the British media, see IfK, Supplement to *Weekly Report*, 10 February 1937.

70 This has led some authors to describe the peasantry, if not exactly as victims of Nazism, then at least as a group that was neglected by the regime. See H. James, *The German Slump* (Oxford, 1986), 357 and A. von Saldern, *Mittelstand im 'Dritten Reich'* (Frankfurt, 1979), 125–6.

71 Herlemann, *Der Bauer*, 145.

72 Ibid., 147–50.

73 *Statistisches Handbuch von Deutschland*, 607.

74 N. R. Reagin, 'Marktordnung and Autarkic Housekeeping: Housewives and Private Consumption under the Four-Year Plan, 1936–1939', *German History*, 19 (2001), 162–84.

75 Paradoxically, the Communist land reform created not large cooperatives, or even viable 20-hectare farms, but a mass of smallholdings of between 5 and 10 hectares. See A. Bauerkaemper, 'Antinomien der Modernisierung: Die Bodenreform in Mecklenburg 1945', in Prinz and Frese, *Politische Zaesuren*, 361–87.

76 For a striking example, see A. Muenzinger, 'Aussiedlung als letztes Mittel der Erhaltung des Bauerntums', *Berichte ueber die Landwirtschaft*, 23 (1938), 205–45. See also Mai, 'Rasse und Raum', 69–74. W. Pyta, 'Menschenoekonomie: Das Ineinandergreifen von laendlicher Sozialraumgestaltung und rassenbiologischer Bevoelkerungspolitik im NS-Staat', *HZ* 273 (2001), 31–94.

77 IfK, *Weekly Report*, 10 August 1939, 198.

78 Ironically, one of the frankest admissions of the true goals of the nationalist programme of conquest came not from Hitler or the Nazis but from the arch-agrarian Hugenberg, at the World Economic Conference in 1933 (see Chapter 2), and this was not lost on Stalin. See J. V. Stalin, 'Report to the 17th Party Congress, January 1934', in J. V. Stalin, *Problems of Leninism* (Peking, 1976), 690–92.

79 The following is based on A. D'Onofrio, 'Rassenzucht und Lebensraum: Zwei Grundlagen im Blut- und Boden-Gedanken von Richard Walther Darré', *Zeitschrift fuer Geschichtswissenschaft*, 49 (2001), 141–57.

7 1936: Four Years to War

1 For a global survey, see Z. Steiner, *The Triumph of the Dark: European International History, 1933–1939* (Oxford, 2006). For Germany, the best survey remains Weinberg, *Foreign Policy I*, 239–356.

2 A. W. Schatz, 'The Anglo-American Trade Agreement and Cordell Hull's Search for Peace 1936–1938', *Journal of American History*, 57 (1970), 87.

3 For the British position, see F. McDonough, *Neville Chamberlain, Appeasement and the British Road to War* (Manchester, 1998), R. A. C. Parker, *Chamberlain and Appeasement: British Policy and the Coming of the Second World War* (New York, 1993) and G. Schmidt, *The Politics and Economics of Appeasement: British Foreign Policy in the 1930s* (New York, 1986).

4 For France, see R. Frankenstein, *Le Prix du réarmement français 1935–1939* (Paris, 1982), 65–81. For Britain, Parker, *Chamberlain and Appeasement*, 272–82.

5 For a short summary, see P. Clavin, *The Great Depression in Europe, 1929–1939* (Basingstoke, 2000), 186–97.

6 A. O. Offner, *American Appeasement: United States Foreign Policy and Germany, 1933–1938* (Cambridge, Mass., 1969), 171–82.

7 P. Gassert, *Amerika im Dritten Reich* (Stuttgart, 1997), 190–94.

8 D. Ades *et al.*, *Art and Power: Europe under the Dictators 1930–1945* (London, 1996), 58–118.

9 On the ambiguities of 1930s 'normality', see U. Herbert 'Die guten und die schlechten Zeiten', in L. Niethammer (ed.), *'Die Jahre weiss man nicht, wo man die heute hinsetzten soll': Faschismuserfahrungen im Ruhrgebiet* (Berlin, 1983), 67–96.

10 For a sample, see the reports of the Social Democrats in exile on widespread fears of war in early 1936, *Deutschland Berichte*, 3 (1936), 300–14; 4 (1936), 460–78; 6 (1936), 675–80; 8 (1936), 963–8; 9 (1936), 1097–104.

11 IfK, *Weekly Report*, 6 May 1936.

12 See the brilliant analysis in S. Friedlaender, *Nazi Germany and the Jews* (London, 1997), I. 177–89.

13 An important reference is still provided by the contributions of H.-E. Volkmann and W. Deist to *DRZW*1, 211–640, which first appeared in 1979. For an up-to-date summary, which, however, is unconvincing on a number of key points, see K. H. Roth, 'Von der Ruestungskonjunktur zum Raubkrieg', in W. Roehr, B. Berlekamp and K. H. Roth, *Der Krieg vor dem Krieg: Politik und Oekonomik der 'friedlichen' Aggression Deutschlands 1938/1939* (Hamburg, 2001), 29–97.

14 For a brilliant short survey, see M. Geyer, *Deutsche Ruestungspolitik 1860–1980* (Frankfurt, 1984).

15 The following is based on data from the appendices of A. Ritschl, *Deutschlands Krise und Konjunktur 1924–1934* (Berlin, 2002), and 'Deficit Spending in the Nazi Recovery, 1933–1938: A Critical Reassessment', Working Paper No. 68, Institute of Empirical Research in Economics, University of Zurich (December 2000).

16 N. Muehlen, *Der Zauberer: Leben und Anleihen des Dr Hjalmar Horace Greeley Schacht* (Zurich, 2nd edn., 1938), 166. The display was captured in Leni Riefenstahl's short documentary, *Tag der Freiheit* (1935).

17 As in R. Overy, *The Nazi Economic Recovery 1932–1938* (Cambridge, 1996), 44–5.

18 H. Sirois, *Zwischen Illusion und Krieg: Deutschland und die USA 1933–1941* (Paderborn, 2000), 74.

19 The theme of W. Deist, *The Wehrmacht and German Rearmament* (London, 1981), now amplified in B. R. Kroener, *'Der starke Mann im Heimatkriegsgebiet': Generaloberst Friedrich Fromm. Eine Biographie* (Paderborn, 2005), 232–8.

20 Kroener, *Fromm*, 242–7.

21 K.-H. Voelker, *Die deutsche Luftwaffe 1933–1939: Aufbau, Fuehrung und Ruestung der Luftwaffe sowie die Entwicklung der deutschen Luftkriegstheorie* (Stuttgart, 1967), 98.

22 E. L. Homze, *Arming the Luftwaffe* (Lincoln, Nebr., 1976), 149.

23 The Reichsbank agonized over how to finance totals of more than 6 billion Reichsmarks. BAL R2501 6627, Denkschrift 21 November 1935, 224–7.

24 M. Geyer, *Aufruestung oder Sicherheit: Die Reichswehr in der Krise der Machtpolitik 1924–1936* (Wiesbaden, 1980), 446.

25 IMT XXXVI. 292, Schacht to Blomberg, 24 December 1935.

26 James, 'Innovation and Conservatism in Economic Recovery: The Alleged "Nazi Recovery" of the 1930s', in I. Childers and J. Caplan (eds.), *Reevaluating the Third Reich* (New York, 1993), 130.

27 For the severity of the squeeze in textiles in 1936, see G. Hoeschle, *Die deutsche Textilindustrie zwischen 1933 und 1939: Staatsinterventionismus und oekonomische Rationalitaet* (Stuttgart, 2004), 74–106.

28 The process of negotiation is documented in BAH R131 605 and BAL R131 447, 141–5. The authorities were initially supportive but backed away from the idea in May.

29 For growing military interest in synthetic rubber, see IMT VII, NI-4713, 778–84.

30 M. Riedel, *Eisen und Kohle fuer das Dritte Reich: Paul Pleigers Stellung in der NS-Wirtschaft* (Goettingen, 1973), 66–8.

31 A. Kube, *Pour le Mérite und Hakenkreuz: Hermann Goering im Dritten Reich* (Munich, 1986), 140–46, R. J. Overy, *Goering* (London, 1984), 39–47, D. Petzina, *Autarkiepolitik im Dritten Reich* (Stuttgart, 1968), 30–48.

32 For the meetings in May and June, see BAL R26I 36, 1–48.

33 Riedel, *Eisen und Kohle*, 86.

34 Deist, *Wehrmacht*, 45.

35 The key documents are contained in BAMA RH15/70. See also K. J. Mueller, *Armee und Drittes Reich 1933–1939* (Paderborn, 1989), doc. 136–140, pp. 296–308. For the background, see Kroener, *Fromm*, 254–61. See also Deist, *Wehrmacht*, 36–53.

36 For the details of Fromm's plan, see BAMA RH15/70, 110–47.

37 On the standard vehicle complements, see B. Mueller-Hillebrand, *Das Heer 1933–1945* (Darmstadt, 1954), I. 71. For a valuable introduction to the evolution of Panzer division organization, see the website http://www.achtungpanzer.com/ maintained by George Parada.

38 On French tank production, see Frankenstein, *Le Prix*, 228, 311.

39 Mueller-Hillebrand, *Das Heer*, I. 71 and R. L. DiNardo, *Mechanized Juggernaut or Military Anachronism? Horses and the German Army of World War II* (New York, 1991).

40 In the spring of 1938, 74 per cent of Germany's artillery, including a majority of its heavy artillery, was horse-drawn. See F. Hahn, *Waffen und Geheimwaffen des deutschen Heeres 1933–1945* (Bonn, 3rd edn., 1998), I. 15.

41 BAL R2501 6608, 2–15 contains a memorandum from mid-August 1936 in which the Reichsbank contemplated the introduction of rationing for clothing, in case of a sudden shortage of hard currency imports.

42 P. Longerich, *Politik der Vernichtung: Eine Gesamtdarstellung der nationalsozialistischen Judenverfolgung* (Munich, 1998), 119.

43 BAL R2501 6446, 13–19.

44 Riedel, *Eisen und Kohle*, 88–9.

45 The following is based on the contents of Moscow Special Archive (henceforth MA) 700 VJP 1/2. On Goerdeler, see S. Gillmann and H. Mommsen (eds.), *Politische Schriften und Briefe Carl Friedrich Goerdelers* (Munich, 2003), 267–9 and 411–64.

46 Offner, *American Appeasement*, 146–53 and G. Kuemmel, *Transnationale Wirtschaftskooperation und der Nationalstaat: Deutsch-amerikanische Unternehmensbeziehungen in der dreissiger Jahren* (Stuttgart, 1995), 89.

47 In striking contrast to the conflict between the United States and Germany was the growing engagement between the United States and the British Empire. Canada and the United States had concluded a reciprocal trading agreement in 1935. See I. M. Drummond and N. Hillmer, *Negotiating Freer Trade: The UK and the US, Canada and the Trade Agreements of 1938* (Waterloo, Ont., 1989), 39–45.

48 K. Mouré, *Managing the Franc Poincaré: Economic Understanding and Political Constraint in French Monetary Policy, 1928–1936* (Cambridge, 1991), 191–273. Highlighting the drama of this break, with gold standard orthodoxy, Margairaz speaks of a 'véritable mutation mentale et culturelle pour l'État.' See M. Margairaz, *L'État, les finances et l'économie: Histoire d'une conversion, 1932–1952* (Paris, 1991), I. 263.

49 Drummond and Hillmer, *Negotiating Freer Trade*, 35.

50 Goerdeler referred to the 'grandiose Moeglichkeit'. The best discussion of Goerdeler's memorandum is still G. Ritter, *Carl Goerdeler und die deutsche Widerstandsbewegung* (Stuttgart, 1954), 76–9.

51 MA VJP 700 1/2, 82, Goerdeler to Staatsrat Neumann, 2 September 1936, 12.

52 On economic ideas in oppositional circles, see E. Mueller, *Widerstand und Wirtschaftsordnung* (Frankfurt, 1988), 49–69.

53 On Buecher's position, see P. Hayes, *Industry and Ideology: IG Farben in the Nazi Era* (Cambridge, 1987), 130–31. J. Scholtyseck, *Robert Bosch und der liberale Widerstand gegen Hitler 1933 bis 1945* (Munich, 1999), 183–224.

54 On Goerdeler's opposition to 'Waehrungsexperimente' in 1934, see Ritter, *Carl Goerdeler*, 68–70 and Gillmann and Mommsen, *Politische Schriften*, August 1934 report, 361.

55 See the clippings from a variety of European newspapers in the spring of 1936 in BAL R2501 2629.

56 Mouré, *Managing*, 238–9. C. Maddison, 'French Inter-war Monetary Policy' (EUI thesis, 1997), 436–545.

57 For the popular rumour mill on devaluation, see SOPADE, *Deutschland Berichte*, 3 June 1936, 706–10.

58 BAL R2501 6424, 290–327 ('Die deutsche Waehrung im Falle einer Abwertung des Goldblocs').

59 BAL R2501 6424, 327.

60 November 1935, BAL R2501 6516, 119–34 and R2501 6627, 224–7; December 1935, R2501 6517, 31–5; February 1936, R2501 6627, 228–38; culminating in May 1936, R2501 6517, 314–19 and 294–303. The last of these suggests a general démarche by the Reichsbank leadership, of the kind attempted in January 1939.

61 Petzina, *Autarkiepolitik*, 47.

62 MA VJP 700 1/2.

63 W. Treue, 'Hitlers Denkschrift zum Vierjahresplan 1936', *VfZ* 3 (1955), 184–210.

64 IMT XXVII, 1301-PS, 153–4.

65 *DRZW* 1. 525.

66 IMT XXXVI, 416-EC, 488–91.

67 Friedlaender, *Nazi Germany*, I. 183–4.

68 Kube, *Pour le Mérite*, 160–61. Kube uses the evidence of this discontent to claim that the Four Year Plan was a non-party institution. This is clearly to exaggerate the nature of the differences.

69 Muehlen, *Der Zauberer*, 187. See also the report by US Ambassador Dodd in http://www.fdrlibrary.marist.edu/psf/box32/t300i07.html, Dodd to Moore, 31 August 1936.

70 Credit for unearthing this nugget goes to Harold James who spotted the false transcription of the word 'abwerten' as 'abwarten' in the widely used edition of Goebbels's diary. James, 'Innovation', 130.

71 Kube, *Pour le Mérite*, 158–60. Goering announced his strategy to a Ministerial Council meeting 21 October 1936, BAL RO26IV, 4 fol. 1, 16–17.

72 Homze, *Arming*, 149.

73 BAMA RH15/148, 2–4.

74 BAMA RH15/70, 80.

75 IMT VII, NI-051, Prosecution exhibit 421 Goering's speech at the 'Preussenhaus' 17 December 1936, 815–17.

76 L. Budrass, *Flugzeugindustrie und Luftruestung in Deutschland* (Duesseldorf, 1998), 480–81.

77 For contending views on the nature of the Four Year Plan organization, see Petzina, *Autarkiepolitik*, 58–9, Kube, *Pour le Mérite*, 160–61, G. Mollin, *Montankonzerne und 'Drittes Reich'* (Goettingen, 1988), 60–61, W. A. Boelcke, *Die deutsche Wirtschaft 1930–1945* (Duesseldorf, 1982), 178–92, Overy, *Goering*, 58–60 and Budrass, *Flugzeugindustrie*, 471–2.

78 H. Kehrl, *Krisenmanager im Dritten Reich* (Duesseldorf, 1973), 101.

79 Petzina, *Autarkiepolitik*, 81–2.

80 Kehrl, *Krisenmanager*, 87–96.

81 Petzina, *Autarkiepolitik*, 83–4.

82 J. Streb, 'Technologiepolitik im Zweiten Weltkrieg: Die staatliche Foerderung der Synthesekautschukproduktion im deutsch-amerikanischen Vergleich', *VfZ* 50 (2002), 367–97 and G. Plumpe, *Die IG Farbenindustrie AG* (Berlin, 1990), 356–78.

83 On Krauch's role, the most reliable guide is still Hayes, *Industry and Ideology*, 156–8.

84 Born in 1884, a lawyer by training, Schnitzler had joined the managerial board of IG in 1926 and chaired its traditional dye business. As such he was more internationally minded than some of his counterparts from the synthetics side of the company.

85 IG Farben Case VII, NI-5196, 1503–17.

86 By January 1937 German stocks of iron ore were sufficient to cover only one month's production. See BAH R13I 619, 132.

87 These figures from BAH R13I 408, 105–8.

88 For the pressure on scrap and other iron prices, see BAH R13I 605, 34–41.

89 A draft in BAL R26IV 4, 69–84.

90 For resulting action by the Stahlwerks-Verband, BAH R13I 459, 107–10.

91 To date the only reliable study is the unpublished dissertation by T. Sarholz, 'Die Auswirkungen der Kontingentierung von Eisen und Stahl auf die Aufruestung der Wehrmacht von 1936 bis 1939' (Darmstadt, 1983), which focuses on the impact on the Wehrmacht.

92 See the protest in BAMA RH15/148, 10–15.

93 BAMA RH15/148, 139–47.

94 Sarholz, 'Auswirkungen', 225 and Kroener, *Fromm*, 306–12.

95 Sarholz, 'Auswirkungen', 232.

96 BAMA RH15/148, 66–7, 75–85.

97 BAMA RL3/2477 and Homze, *Arming*, 153. The immediate squeeze was applied to the Luftwaffe through spending cuts, but this was coupled with a corresponding reduction in raw material allocations, see Sarholz, 'Auswirkungen', 219–36.

98 Homze, *Arming*, 145.

99 See the figures in BAMA RL3/2617.

100 BAL R2 31.034. See discussion in steel industry circles, BAH R13I 619, 71–2. M. Ebi, *Export um jeden Preis: Die deutsche Exportfoerderung von 1932–1938* (Stuttgart, 2004), 192–222. Though Ebi provides an excellent technical account of the operation of the system, he completely ignores both the strategic decision to prioritize exports in the allocation of steel and the wider political context, both domestic and international, in which the system operated.

101 S. Newton, *Profits of Peace: The Political Economy of Anglo-German Appeasement* (Oxford, 1996), 60–63.

102 On Schacht's contacts with France and Britain in 1937, see Weinberg, *Foreign Policy II*, 67–94.

103 IMT XXXVI, EC 286, 282–91. See Appendix, Table A3.

104 BAH R13I 619, 107–9.

105 Petzina, *Autarkiepolitik*, 111.

106 Riedel, *Eisen und Kohle*, 62–154 and Mollin, *Montankonzerne*, 70–76.

107 BAH R13I 597, 176–222.

108 Riedel, *Eisen und Kohle*, 101–226.

109 IMT XII, Pleiger testimony, 630–48.

110 Apart from his engagement with Goering and Pleiger, Brassert was also involved between 1936 and 1938 in a controversial Japanese project to develop supplies of iron ore from the Koolan Island ore fields in Yampi Sound, Western Australia. See 'Documents of Australian Foreign Policy, 1937–1938', 1, available online at http://www.info.dfat.gov.au/info/historical/HisDocs.nsf/.

111 C. R. S. Harris, *Germany's Foreign Indebtedness* (New York, 1978), 117 and A. Reckendrees, *Das 'Stahltrust-Projekt'* (Munich, 2000), 255.

112 Riedel, *Eisen und Kohle*, 172.

113 BAH R13I 597, 106–17.

114 Flick received his copy at 13.49 on 24 August 1937. See BAL R8122 7, 19.

115 BAL R8122 7, Flick, 11–14.

116 For two different interpretations of Zangen's cynical behaviour, see BAL R8122 7, 51–2 and BAH R13I 597, 64–9.

117 BAH R13I 597, 106–17.

118 R. J. Overy, *War and Economy in the Third Reich* (Oxford, 1994), 144–74, and *Goering*, 111–18. A. Meyer, *Hitlers Holding: Die Reichswerke Hermann Goering* (Munich, 1999).

119 For a complete listing of its various holdings, see BAL R2Anh84, 94–113.

120 On the dismemberment of the Petschek coal empire, see Mollin, *Montankonzerne*, 184–7 and H. James, *The Deutsche Bank and the Nazi Economic War against the Jews* (Cambridge, 2001), 100–104. On the seizure of Czech and Silesian assets, see W. Roehr, 'Zur Rolle der Schwerindustrie im annektierten polnischen Oberschlesien fuer die Kriegswirtschaft Deutschlands von 1939 bis 1949', *Jahrbuch fuer Wirtschaftsgeschichte*, 4 (1991), 9–58. For the Reichswerke's expansion into other heavy industrial areas, see H. Radant, 'Die Vitkovicer Berg- und Eisenhuetten-Gewerkschaft als Organisationszentrum der Reichswerke AG "Hermann Goering" fuer die Beherrschung der Eisen- und Stahlwirtschaft suedosteuropaeischer Laender', *Jahrbuch fuer Wirtschaftsgeschichte*, 3 (1973), 17–41.

121 BAMA RH15/148, 170–73.

122 Sarholz, 'Auswirkungen', 237.

123 BAMA RH15/149, 40. Sarholz, 'Auswirkungen', 246.

124 BAMA RH15/149, 36–8.

125 BAMA RH15/149, 57–62. Sarholz, 'Auswirkungen', 253.

126 IMT XXV, 386-PS, 402–13.

127 Weinberg, *Foreign Policy II*, 18–51. Weinberg's stress on a 'Blitzkrieg conception' supposedly espoused by Hitler in November 1937 hardly seems warranted by the text of the Hossbach memorandum.

128 BAMA RH15/149, 84–97.

129 Sarholz, 'Auswirkungen', 257–9.

130 This vital decision, which has been hitherto overlooked in the literature, is recorded in BAH R13I 472, 204, confirmed by BAH R13I 606, 178–86 and BAL R8122, 347, 25 February 1938 and 3 March 1938.

131 BAMA RH15/150, 12–13, significant because it dates to 24 February 1938, a number of weeks prior to the escalation of tension following the Anschluss.

132 The first to highlight this key point was Geyer, *Deutsche Ruestungspolitik*, 146–7.

133 BAMA RH15/149, 106–13.

134 A point most clearly articulated by M. Knox, 'Conquest, Foreign and Domestic, in Fascist Italy and Nazi Germany', *Journal of Modern History*, 56 (1984), 1–57.

135 M. Broszat, *Der Staat Hitlers* (Munich, 1969), 363–75.

136 I. Kershaw, *Hitler 1936–1945: Nemesis* (London, 2000), 51–60.

137 Boelcke, *Die deutsche Wirtschaft*, 182.

138 Ibid., 183.

139 In Kershaw's monumental biography, the essential issue of steel merits not even a single index entry. See Kershaw, *Hitler: Nemesis*.

8 Into the Danger Zone

1 IG Farben Case VII, 1538–9, document NI-14507.

2 Weinberg, *Foreign Policy II*. On the decision-making process, see G. C. B. Waldenegg, 'Hitler, Goering, Mussolini und der "Anschluss" Oesterreichs an das Deutsche Reich', *VfZ* 51 (2003), 147–82.

3 Not, as has been implausibly suggested by K. H. Roth, on the economic pressures within Germany. For both Roth's view and a persuasive critique, see W. Roehr, B. Berlekamp and K. H. Roth (eds.), *Der Krieg vor dem Krieg: Politik und Oekonomik der 'friedlichen' Aggression Deutschlands 1938/1939* (Hamburg, 2001).

4 For the following, see IfK, *Weekly Report*, 11, 16 March 1938, 4 April 1938 and 14 December 1938.

5 G. Mollin, *Montankonzerne und 'Drittes Reich'* (Goettingen, 1988), 115–24.
6 See the assessment by VJP officials in BAL R26IV 5, 166–170 and RO26IV, 4 fol. 1, 56–64.
7 R. Banken, 'Die deutsche Goldreserven und Devisenpolitik 1933–1939', *JbW* 1 (2003), 49–78.
8 IfK, *Weekly Report*, 11, 29 June 1938, 193–6.
9 M. Ebi, *Export um jeden Preis: Die deutsche Exportfoerderung von 1932–1938* (Stuttgart, 2004) 223–37.
10 BAL RO26IV, 4 fol. 1, 39–44.
11 See the analysis in IfK, *Weekly Report*, 11, 4 April 1938, 118.
12 D. E. Kaiser, *Economic Diplomacy and the Origins of the Second World War: Germany Britain, France and Eastern Europe, 1930–1939* (Princeton, 1980), 244.
13 For the May panic and the subsequent anti-British turn, see J. Henke, *England in Hitlers politischem Kalkuel 1935–1939* (Boppard, 1972), 150–62.
14 Conscious of this risk, the British government did its best to calm press comment. See R. A. C. Parker, *Chamberlain and Appeasement: British Policy and the Coming of the Second World War* (New York, 1993), 149.
15 R. Overy, 'Germany and the Munich Crisis', *Diplomacy and Statecraft*, 10 (1999), 191–215. K. J. Mueller, *Armee und Drittes Reich 1933–1939* (Paderborn, 1989), doc. 152, 333–5. K. J. Mueller, *General Ludwig Beck: Studien und Dokumente zur politisch-militaerischen Vorstellungswelt und Taetigkeit des Generalstabschefs des deutschen Heeres 1933–1938* (Boppard, 1980), 512–20. Since he ignores the evidence from the armaments economy, S. Kley, *Hitler, Ribbentrop und die Entfesselung des Zweiten Weltkrieges* (Paderborn, 1996), 59–62, underestimates the importance of the announcement on 28 May 1938.
16 For the importance of 1938 in bringing into the open Hitler's antagonism towards the West, see Weinberg, *Foreign Policy II*, 355 and 465–6. W. Michalka, *Ribbentrop und die deutsche Weltpolitik 1933–1940* (Munich, 1980), 228–9.
17 For German assessments, see the essays in F. Knipping and K. J. Mueller (eds.), *Machtbewusstsein in Deutschland am Vorabend des Zweiten Weltkrieges* (Paderborn, 1984).
18 For a brilliant analysis of the self-confidence of British naval planning, see J. A. Maiolo, *The Royal Navy and Nazi Germany, 1933–1939: A Study in Appeasement and the Origins of the Second World War* (Basingstoke, 1998), especially 111–20.
19 T. C. Imlay, *Facing the Second World War: Strategy, Politics and Economics in Britain and France 1938–1940* (Oxford, 2003).
20 For a contemporary analysis of international naval spending and ship-building see IfK, *Weekly Report*, 20 July 1938. According to the report, Germany had one-tenth the tonnage of modern warships available to Britain. Data published in the summer of 1939, IfK, *Weekly Report*, 12 July 1939 showed that even after giving top priority to the Kriegsmarine in early 1939, German naval spending exceeded that budgeted by Britain by no more than 5 per cent.
21 H. Sirois, *Zwischen Illusion und Krieg: Deutschland und die USA 1933–1941* (Paderborn, 2000), 159.
22 M. M. Postan, *British War Production* (London, 1952), 14–23. C. Peden, *British Rearmament and the Treasury: 1932–1939* (Edinburgh, 1979), 128–34. S. Ritchie, *Industry and Air Power: The Expansion of British Aircraft Production 1935–1941* (London, 1997).
23 R. Frankenstein, *Le Prix du réarmament français 1935–1939* (Paris, 1982), 88–92, 195–7. H. Chapman, *State Capitalism and Working-Class Radicalism in the French Aircraft Industry* (Berkeley, 1991), 149–74.
24 See the instructions for a dramatic increase in army procurement, BAMA RH15/150, 80.
25 Compare BAMA RH15/150, 56–7 with 86–9.
26 L. Budrass, *Flugzeugindustrie und Luftruestung in Deutschland* (Duesseldorf, 1998), 536–56.

27 J. Duelffer, *Handbuch zur deutschen Militaergeschichte 1648–1939*, VII (Munich, 1978), 475 and J. Duelffer, *Weimar, Hitler und die Marine: Reichspolitik und Flottenbau, 1920–1939* (Duesseldorf, 1973), 468–9.

28 W. Birkenfeld, *Der synthetische Treibstoff 1933–1945* (Goettingen, 1964), 112–25. D. Petzina, *Autarkiepolitik im Dritten Reich* (Stuttgart, 1968), 116–30. P. Hayes, *Industry and Ideology: IG Farben in the Nazi Era* (Cambridge, 1987), 206–11. G. Plumpe, *Die IG Farbenindustrie AG* (Berlin, 1990), 722–40.

29 Ambros, born in 1901, had made a spectacular career as IG's leading expert for synthetic rubber and as one of Krauch's close collaborators. By the late 1930s he was a member of the managerial board and chair of IG's Buna commission.

30 A summary of the various plans is provided by IMT VII. 874–909. A helpful but needlessly polemical overview is Plumpe, *Die IG Farbenindustrie*, 722–34.

31 Shortly afterwards, Goering used a similar title to indicate the joint priority of the Ju 88 and the chemicals plans, appointing Koppenberg to the position of Sonderbevollmaechtigte des Generalfeldmarschalls Goerings fuer die Herstellung der Ju 88. See L. Budrass, 'Unternehmer im Nationalsozialismus: Der "Sonderbevollmaechtigte des Generalfeldmarschalls Goering fuer die Herstellung der Ju 88" ', in W. Plumpe and C. Kleinschmidt (eds.), *Unternehmen zwischen Markt- und Macht* (Essen, 1992), 74–89.

32 T. Sarholz, 'Die Auswirkungen der Kontingentierung von Eisen und Stahl auf die Aufruestung der Wehrmacht von 1936 bis 1939' (thesis, Darmstadt, 1983), 310.

33 For the financial pressure on the Air Ministry in early 1938, see E. L. Homze, *Arming the Luftwaffe* (Lincoln, Nebr., 1976), 155–6. For the anxieties in the Reichsbank, see the reports in BAL 2501 6520.

34 W. A. Boelcke, *Die Kosten von Hitlers Krieg: Kriegsfinanzierung und finanzielles Kriegserbe in Deutschland 1933–1948* (Paderborn, 1985), 33.

35 BAMA RH15/150, 108.

36 M. Geyer, 'Ruestungsbeschleunigung und Inflation', *MGM* 30 (1981), 145.

37 See the price adjusted figures in A. Ritschl, *Deutschlands Krise und Konjunktur 1924–1934* (Berlin, 2002), table B.8.

38 Geyer, 'Ruestungsbeschleunigung', 163. See Appendix, Table A3.

39 For this deliberate acceleration, see BAH R13I 606, 178–86, 151–69, 111–20, 66–75, 51–3, R13I 692, 105–20 and BAL R8122, 347.

40 Sarholz, 'Auswirkungen', 309 and B. R. Kroener, *'Der starke Mann im Heimatkriegsgebiet': Generaloberst Friedrich Fromm. Eine Biographie* (Paderborn, 2005), 314–15.

41 For this and the following quotes, see IMT XXXVIII. 376–400, R-140.

42 For Goering's realization in the spring of 1938 that the United States must be considered an enemy of National Socialism, see A. O. Offner, *American Appeasement: United States Foreign Policy and Germany, 1933–1938* (Cambridge, Mass., 1969), 242–3.

43 See the highly competent discussion in Gerold von Minden, *Wirtschaftsfuehrung im Grossdeutschen Reich* (Berlin, 1939). Minden was adviser to Funk as Generalbevollmaechtigter fuer die Wirtschaft.

44 BAL R3102 2700.

45 J. A. Tooze, *Statistics and the German State 1900–1945: The Making of Modern Economic Knowledge* (Cambridge, 2001), 177–245.

46 See the charts and statistical estimates in BAL R3102 3154.

47 Most recently, G. Aly, *Hitlers Volksstaat* (Frankfurt, 2005).

48 This at least was an *idée fixe* within the Reich's bureaucracy. See the discussion of relative financing capacity in May 1938 in BAL R2501 6639, 292–307, the public justification offered in R2501 6521, 1–17 and the comprehensive comparison of tax rates in R2501 6652, which showed German taxes on wages and salaries to be higher than anywhere in North-western Europe. Taxes on capital were higher than everywhere except France for most categories of firm.

49 The sense of urgency that motivated this decision is well conveyed in *Der Deutsche Volkswirt*, 12, 5 August 1938, 45.

50 IMT XII. 503–9, NG-5328, circulars from Krosigk, 5 July 1938.

51 See the estimates of funding capacity, BAL R2501 6639, 339–41, 347–64.

52 Deutsche Bau- und Bodenbank, *Die Entwicklung der deutschen Bauwirtschaft im Jahre 1938* (Berlin, 1939), 6–7, 28–9.

53 T. Harlander, *Zwischen Heimstaette und Wohnmaschine: Wohnungsbau und Wohnungspolitik in der Zeit des Nationalsozialismus* (Basle, 1995), 139–40.

54 A. C. Mierzejewski, *The Most Valuable Asset of the Reich: A History of the German National Railway*, II: *1933–1945* (Chapel Hill, NC, 2000), 67–9.

55 Ibid., 54–6.

56 *Deutschland Berichte*, 5, 5 November 1938, 1221.

57 'The Difficulties of Germany's Railways', *The Economist*, 3 June 1939, 544.

58 A brief minute is contained in BAL R2501 6520.

59 From the end of December 1937 onwards the Reichsbank began its own surveys of wage and price inflation independently of the official indices published by the Reich Statistical Office. BAL R2501 6581, 353–91.

60 IfK, Supplement to *Weekly Report*, 26 January 1938, 'The Limits of the Labour Supply'.

61 T. Mason, *Arbeiterklasse und Volksgemeinschaft* (Opladen, 1975), doc. 144, Schreiben des RAM 14 July 1938, 836.

62 Ibid., 898.

63 This is the repetitive refrain in the documents gathered ibid., 601–979.

64 H. Kahrs, 'Die ordnende Hand der Arbeitsaemter: Zur deutschen Arbeitsverwaltung 1933 bis 1939', in W. Gruner *et al.*, *Arbeitsmarkt und Sondererlass: Menschenverwertung, Rassenpolitik und Arbeitsamt* (Berlin, 1990), 9–61.

65 R. von Valta, 'Das Arbeitsbuch in der Statistik', *Allgemeines Statistisches Archiv*, 27 (1937–8), 263–73.

66 Mason, *Arbeiterklasse*, 251.

67 The Wehrmacht and the labour administration had agreed on the need for this decree three weeks earlier. See BAMA RH15/150, 109–10.

68 Mason, *Arbeiterklasse*, 127, 735–43.

69 G. Corni and H. Gies, *Blut und Boden: Rassenideologie und Agrarpolitik im Staat Hitlers* (Idstein, 1994), 168.

70 See the secret Reichsbank report in BAL R2501 6581, 353–72.

71 For an analysis of Landflucht by the Reich Statistical Office, see P. Bramstedt, 'Lohngefaelle und Landflucht', *Die Deutsche Volkswirtschaft*, 8 (1939), 285–90.

72 G. Corni, *Hitler and the Peasants: Agrarian Policy of the Third Reich, 1930–1939* (Oxford, 1990), 220.

73 A. Schuermann, 'Niedersachsen', in K. Meyer and K. Thiede (eds.), *Die laendliche Arbeitsverfassung im Westen und Sueden des Reiches: Beitraege zur Landfluchtfrage* (Heidelberg, 1941), 31.

74 D. Muenkel, ' "Du, deutsche Landfrau bist verantwortlich!" Bauer and Baeuerin im NS', *Archiv fuer Sozialgeschichte*, 38 (1998), 141–64; B. Herlemann, '*Der Bauer klebt an Hergebrachten*': Bauerlicher Verhaltensweisen unterm NS auf dem Gebiet des heutigen Landes Niedersachsen (Hanover, 1993), 169–71; S. Jacobeit, 'Zum Alltag der Baeuerinnen in Klein- und Mittelbetrieben waehrend der Zeit des deutschen Faschismus 1933 bis 1939', *JbW* 1 (1982), 7–30.

75 Schuermann, 'Niedersachsen', 35.

76 Corni and Gies, *Blut und Boden*, 167–9.

77 Ibid., 56 and 171–82.

78 Mueller, *Beck*, 493–6 and 521–8. Geyer, 'Ruestungsbeschleunigung', 136.

79 Geyer, 'Ruestungsbeschleunigung', 154.

80 Mason, *Arbeiterklasse*, doc. 150, 866.

81 For data on employment and construction on the Westwall, see IWM EDS, Mi. 14/351.

82 W. Bauer and P. Dehen, 'Landwirtschaft und Volkseinkommen', *Vierteljahrshefte zur Wirtschaftsforschung*, 13 (1938–9), 411–32. H. L. Fensch, 'Die Unterbewertung der

Landarbeit in den verschiedenen Betriebsgruppen der deutschen Landwirtschaft', *Berichte ueber die Landwirtschaft*, NS 28/2 (1942), 169–224.

83 Corni and Gies, *Blut und Boden*, 171–85.

84 Taking figures for employment and constant price value added from W. G. Hoffmann, *Das Wachstum der deutschen Wirtschaft* (Heidelberg, 1965), 205–6 and 454, per capita value added in agriculture in 1936 came to 1,200 Reichsmarks as opposed to non-agricultural per capita productivity of 2,400 Reichsmarks.

85 A point made quite clearly by Reichskommissar fuer Preisbildung J. Wagner in 'Preispolitik und Landwirtschaft', *Die Deutsche Volkswirtschaft*, 1 (1939), 15–17. See also the sceptical comments in 'Landwirtschaft und Volkseinkommen', *Die Deutsche Volkswirtschaft*, 32 (1939), 1163–4.

86 A. S. Milward, 'The Reichsmark Bloc and the International Economy', in G. Hirschfeld and L. Kettenacker (eds.), *Der 'Fuehrerstaat': Mythos und Realitaet* (Stuttgart, 1981), 377–428.

87 See reports in BAL R2501 6591, 24–66 and R2501 6522.

88 BAL R2501 6591, 39.

89 Darré's speech to the 6th Bauerntag in Goslar, 27 November 1938, W. Darré, *Aufbruch des Bauerntums: Reichsbauerntagreden 1933 bis 1938* (Berlin 1942), 115 and 119.

90 Contrary to Corni, who describes Darré's appeal as 'irrational'. See Corni, *Hitler and the Peasants*, 220.

91 Ibid., 258.

92 G. Ritter, *Carl Goerdeler und die deutsche Widerstandsbewegung* (Stuttgart, 1954), and S. Gillmann and H. Mommsen (eds.), *Politische Schriften und Briefe Carl Friedrich Goerdelers* (Munich, 2003). R. A. Blasius, *Fuer Grossdeutschland – gegen den grossen Krieg: Ernst von Weizsaecker in den Krisen um die Tschechoslowakei und Polen* (Cologne, 1981). U. von Hassel, *Die Hassel-Tagebuecher 1938–1944: Aufzeichnungen vom andern Deutschlands* (Berlin, 1989).

93 A. Kube, *Pour le Mérite und Hakenkreuz: Hermann Goering im Dritten Reich* (Munich, 1986), 363–4 and R. J. Overy, *Goering* (London, 1984), 80–81.

94 See the documents collected in Mueller, *Armee*, 309–57.

95 Mueller, *Beck*, 504 and 523.

96 W. Murray, *The Change in the European Balance of Power, 1938–1939* (Princeton, 1984), 245–53. K.-H. Voelker, *Die deutsche Luftwaffe, 1933–1939: Aufbau, Fuehrung und Ruestung der Luftwaffe sowie die Entwicklung der Luftkriegstheorie* (Stuttgart, 1967), 160.

97 Mueller, *Beck*, 527.

98 Ibid., 299–304.

99 B.-J. Wendt, *Grossdeutschland: Aussenpolitik und Kriegsvorbereitung des Hitler-Regimes* (Munich, 1987), 150–52. Weinberg, *Foreign Policy II*, 378–464.

100 D. Reynolds, *From Munich to Pearl Harbor: Roosevelt's America and the Origins of the Second World War* (Chicago, 2001), 40.

101 Mueller, *Beck*, 561.

102 Ibid., 559.

103 Blasius, *Fuer Grossdeutschland*, 44

104 All of the following quotation is from IMT XII. 419, 509–14, RFM to Hitler 1 September 1938.

105 A point ignored by Overy, who claims that the 'conservative opposition' tended to exaggerate the seriousness of Germany's economic difficulties. See R. J. Overy, *War and Economy in the Third Reich* (Oxford, 1994), 208–12.

106 See the Reichsbank's analysis in BAL R2501 6549 and IfK, *Weekly Report*, 11, 7 September 1938, 'Der Kursrueckschlag am Aktienmarkt', 251–4.

107 All of the following is from IMT XII. 419, 511–12, RFM to Hitler 1 September 1938.

108 The hostility of America had been made clear at least since October 1937 and Roosevelt's quarantine speech. It intensified during 1938. See Sirois, *Zwischen Illusion*, 105–10, 117–28.

109 For a recent evaluation of the military 'resistance' in 1938, see *DRZW* 9/1, 751–6.

110 K. J. Mueller, *Das Heer und Hitler: Armee und nationalsozialistisches Regime 1933–1940* (Stuttgart, 1969), 361.

111 For the crisis from the British point of view, see Parker, *Chamberlain and Appeasement*, 174–81.

112 I. Kershaw, *Hitler 1936–1945: Nemesis* (London, 2000), 113–25.

113 For the following, see P. Longerich, *Politik der Vernichtung: Eine Gesamtdarstellung der nationalsozialistischen Judenverfolgung* (Munich, 1998), 153–225.

114 BAL R2501 6446, 128–31.

115 For a clear-headed contemporary description, see *ADAP* D V doc. 575, Reichsstelle fuer Devisenbewirtschaftung an das Auswaertiges Amt, 7 December 1937, 650–53.

116 F. Bajohr, '*Aryanisation' in Hamburg: The Economic Exclusion of Jews and the Confiscation of their Property in Nazi Germany* (Oxford, 2002), deserves credit for having highlighted the significance of this administrative harassment. What we still lack, however, is a clear sense of the degree of discrimination suffered by Jews within a generally oppressive system of controls.

117 Longerich, *Politik*, 181.

118 Quoted in H. Safrian, *Eichmann und seine Gehilfen* (Frankfurt, 1995), 29.

119 Quoted in A. Barkai, *From Boycott to Annihilation: The Economic Struggle of German Jews* (Hanover, 1989), 129. As Bajohr points out, Barkai dramatically overstates the degree of Aryanization that had taken place before 1938 through his incautious use of the census statistics for the number of Jewish businesses in 1933. See Bajohr, '*Aryanisation*', 108.

120 H. James, *The Deutsche Bank and the Nazi Economic War against the Jews* (Cambridge, 2001).

121 W. Moenninghoff, *Enteignung der Juden: Wunder der Wirtschaft Erbe der Deutschen* (Hamburg, 2001), 91–106.

122 On this at least one can fully agree with Aly, *Hitlers Volksstaat*.

123 Barkai, *Boycott*, 118–19 and Longerich, *Politik*, 161.

124 Longerich, *Politik*, 192.

125 For the wave of arrests in Frankfurt, see M. Kingreen (ed.), '*Nach der Kristallnacht': Juedisches Leben und antijuedische Politik in Frankfurt am Main 1938–1945* (Frankfurt, 1999), 19–90.

126 Mason, *Arbeiterklasse*, 908–33, Goering to 1st meeting of Reichsverteidigungsrat, 18 November 1938, 915–16.

127 Aly, *Hitlers Volksstaat*, 60–66.

128 IMT XII, document 1412-PS, Goering decree issued in Reichsgesetzblatt 1938 I, 1579, 12 November 1938. Longerich, *Politik*, 212.

129 Ibid., 213.

130 Aly, *Hitlers Volksstaat*, 54–6.

131 A point first made by G. Aly and S. Heim, *Vordenker der Vernichtung: Auschwitz und die deutschen Plaene fuer eine neue europaeische Ordnung* (Hamburg, 1991), 22–49.

132 Figures from BAL R2Anh78, 213–29, Archiv des ehem. RFM, 'Massnahmen gegen die juedische Bevoelkerung und ihre Einrichtungen seit 1933', 20 February 1949.

133 According to the *Statistisches Handbuch*, 555, total Reich revenue from tax and customs in 1938–9 came to 18.2 billion Reichsmarks. The basis on which Aly (*Hitlers Volksstaat*, 62) arrives at the much higher estimate of 9 per cent is obscure. But it would appear that he attributes the entire revenue from the wealth levy to a single year, 1938, whereas in fact it was spread over three fiscal years. It may be significant in this connection that in the pages in which he deals with this issue, Aly cites material from BAL R2Anh, but not the detailed study quoted above.

134 For the following, see R. Weingarten, *Die Hilfeleistung der westlichen Welt bei der Endloesung der deutschen Judenfrage* (Frankfurt, 1981) and T. Sjoeberg, *The Powers and the Persecuted* (Lund, 1991).

135 For the following, see the documents in *ADAP* D V, 753–91, Weingarten, *Die Hilfe-leistung*, 97–147, Sjoeberg, *The Powers*, 44–58, C. Browning, *The Final Solution and the German Foreign Office* (New York, 1978), 17–19, and S. Friedlaender, *Nazi Germany and the Jews* (London, 1997), I. 311–16.

136 Longerich, *Politik*, 211.

137 By January 1939 Schacht and Rublee were discussing a less ambitious version of the scheme more akin to the Haavara agreement. BAL R2501 6641, 44–56.

138 For figures, see H. A. Strauss, 'Jewish Emigration from Germany – Nazi Policies and Jewish Responses', I and II, *Leo Baeck Institute Year Book*, 25 (1980), 313–62 and 26 (1981), 343–410, and W. Rosenstock, 'Jewish Emigration from Germany', *Leo Baeck Institute Year Book*, 1 (1956), 373–90.

139 Safrian, *Eichmann*, 23–67.

140 For the following, see Friedlaender, *Nazi Germany*, I. 308–16.

141 IMT XXXVIII. 140-R, 377.

142 Weinberg, *Foreign Policy II*, 517–22.

143 D. C. Watt, *How War Came: The Immediate Origins of the Second World War, 1938–1939* (London, 1989), 91.

144 The best-known statement is G. L. Weinberg, 'Hitler's Image of the United States', *American Historical Review*, 69 (1964), 1006–21.

145 Weinberg's view of the irrelevance of the United States to Hitler's calculations has been comprehensively challenged by a succession of works, of which the most notable are S. Friedlaender, *Prelude to Downfall: Hitler and the United States 1939–1941* (London, 1967), A. Hillgruber, *Hitlers Strategie* (Frankfurt, 1965), 192–206, A. Hillgruber, 'Hitler und die USA', in D. Junker (ed.), *Deutschland und die USA 1890–1985* (Heidelberg, 1986), 27–41, D. Junker, *Kampf um die Weltmacht: Die USA und das Dritte Reich 1933–1945* (Duesseldorf, 1988), P. Gassert, *Amerika im Dritten Reich* (Stuttgart, 1997), and Sirois, *Zwischen Illusion*.

146 For students of American–German relations, the new importance of the 'Jewish question' is dramatically obvious in 1938–9. See Gassert, *Amerika*, 199–209 and 257–61, and Sirois, *Zwischen Illusion*, 126–35. By contrast, this refocusing of the Jewish question on the West, which parallels the redirection of foreign policy since 1938, has gone largely unremarked in the Holocaust literature. Friedlaender is the exception in noting that 'the Western democracies and the United States in particular were temporarily taking the place of Bolshevik Russia as the seat of international Jewish power' (*Nazi Germany*, 311). But he does not explore the wider ramifications of this shift. Even more emphatic in the minds of the SS leadership was the identification of Roosevelt with freemasonry. See *Meldungen* II, Jahreslagebericht 1938, 8–20.

147 On the early prominence of anti-Semitic themes, see Gassert, *Amerika*, 199–209. By focusing on the single issue of emigration, Friedlaender underplays the impact of Kristallnacht on both British and American relations with Germany; Friedlaender, *Nazi Germany*, 298–302.

148 S. Casey, *Cautious Crusade: Franklin D. Roosevelt, American Public Opinion and the War against Nazi Germany* (Oxford, 2001), 20.

149 *Documents of German Foreign Policy* (henceforth *DGFP*), series D IV, 639–640.

150 Reynolds, *From Munich*, 50–54.

151 For remarkable cartoon images, see *Deutschland-Berichte*, 6 (1939), 145–9.

152 *ADAP* D V doc. 664, 782. On the long-standing anti-Semitism of the German Foreign Office, see Browning, *The Final Solution*, 11–22. On the increasing influence of the SS on the German Foreign Office after 1938, see H.-J. Doescher, *Das Auswaertige Amt im Dritten Reich: Diplomatie im Schatten der 'Endloesung'* (Berlin, 1986).

153 Domarus, II. 1053.

9 1939: Nothing to Gain by Waiting

1 For this and the following, BAL R2501 6521, 291–305.
2 BAL R2501 6521, 119–26, Entwurf 15 October 1938.
3 BAL R2501 6521, 291–305, Teilentwurf 3 October 1938, 295.
4 For this estimate, see M. Geyer, 'Zum Einfluss der nationalsozialistischen Ruestungspolitik auf das Ruhrgebiet', *Rheinische Vierteljahresblaetter*, 45 (1981), 255.
5 U. von Hassel, *Die Hassel-Tagebuecher 1938–1944: Aufzeichnungen vom andern Deutschlands* (Berlin, 1989), 51.
6 G. Thomas, *Geschichte der deutschen Wehr- und Ruestungswirtschaft* (Boppard, 1966), 509.
7 IMT XII. 515–18, 1301-PS, minutes of Conference in Reich Air Ministry, 14 October 1938, 515. See also the instruction to the Four Year Plan in BAL R26IV 5, 180–85, 31st Generalrat meeting, 14 October 1938.
8 For the army, see BAMA RH15/150 212, 228–30. IMT XXVII. 164–6, 1301-PS, Report dated 27 October 1938. Total Wehrmacht demands came to 1.08 million tons per month as compared to output of only 1.8 million tons.
9 L. Budrass, *Flugzeugindustrie und Luftruestung in Deutschland* (Duesseldorf, 1998), 557–75.
10 See the procurement plan in BAMA RL3 2199, 20 October 1938.
11 J. Duelffer, *Weimar, Hitler und die Marine: Reichspolitik und Flottenbau, 1920–1939* (Duesseldorf, 1973), 471–512. Duelffer, *Handbuch zur deutschen Militaergeschichte 1648–1939* (Munich, 1977), VIII. 482–4. IMT, TMWC doc. 854-D.
12 BAL R2501 6639, 371.
13 Thomas, *Geschichte*, 1–3.
14 The best summary of Thomas's activities is B. A. Carroll, *Design for Total War: Arms and Economics in the Third Reich* (The Hague, 1968).
15 M. Geyer, 'Ruestungsbeschleunigung und Inflation', *MGM* 30 (1981), 127–9.
16 For the general background, ibid. For material provided by the Reichsbank to Thomas's office, see BAL R2501 6446, 201–5. IMT, *Nazi Conspiracy and Aggression* (Washington, 1946–7), VI. 267–70, 3575-PS, and T. Mason, *Arbeiterklasse und Volksgemeinschaft* (Opladen, 1975), 907–33.
17 Budrass, *Flugzeugindustrie*, 515–75.
18 On this scheme, see G. Aly and K. H. Roth, *Die restlose Erfassung* (Berlin, 1984), 44–52.
19 See the discussions of the state of the railway system in BAL RO26IV 4 fol. 1, 10, Sitzung des kleinen Generalrats, 13 October 1938; R26IV 5, 32. Sitzung des Generalrats, 28 October 1938.
20 An idea that was popular in the Reichsbank. See BAL R2501 6641, 27–36, memo on 3 November 1938.
21 Mason, *Arbeiterklasse*, 932.
22 H. Mommsen and M. Grieger, *Das Volkswagenwerk und seine Arbeiter im Dritten Reich* (Duesseldorf, 1996), 333–4.
23 F. W. Seidler, *Fritz Todt: Baumeister des Dritten Reiches* (Frankfurt, 1986), 212. See also Deutsche Bau- und Bodenbank, *Die Entwicklung der deutschen Bauwirtschaft im Jahre 1938* (Berlin, 1939), 6–13, which estimated that public construction accounted for 80 per cent of all building activity in 1938.
24 A. Meyhoff, *Blohm & Voss im 'Dritten Reich'* (Hamburg, 2001), 234–43.
25 M. Geyer, 'Ruestungsbeschleunigung und Inflation', *MGM* 30 (1981), 181.
26 I agree on this point with R. Overy, 'Reply', *Past and Present*, 122 (1989), 222–40. But, as will become clear below, this strategy collapsed almost as soon as it was formulated.
27 On Germany's anti-Western line post-Munich, see Weinberg, *Foreign Policy II*, 465–534, J. Henke, *England in Hitlers politischen Kalkuel 1935–1939* (Boppard, 1972), 162–221, S. Kley, *Hitler, Ribbentrop und die Entfesselung des Zweiten Weltkrieges* (Paderborn, 1996), 147–258 and W. Michalka, *Ribbentrop und die deutsche Weltpolitik 1933–1940* (Munich, 1980), 239–94.

28 The key document is the Wehrmacht memo for Ribbentrop on German-Italian military negotiations, 30 November 1938, no. 411, *DGFP* D IV, 529–32.

29 The American figure is far higher only if we add in the US Navy Air Force and the aircraft operated by the Marine Corps. Total American air strength in both combat and non-combat planes in all theatres exceeded 90,000 aircraft at the end of 1944. See J. Ellis, *The World War II Databook* (London, 1993), 231–43.

30 E. L. Homze, *Arming the Luftwaffe* (Lincoln, Nebr., 1976), 223.

31 Budrass, *Flugzeugindustrie*, 558–63.

32 BAMA RL3 2199, 324–8.

33 See P. W. Zieb, *Logistik Probleme der Kriegsmarine* (Neckargemuend, 1961), 105–6 and W. Meier-Doernberg, *Die Oelsversorgung der Kriegsmarine 1935 bis 1945* (Freiburg, 1973), 29–31.

34 BAL R2501 6549, 73.

35 H. James was the first to highlight the significance of the following episode in his contribution to L. Gall et al., *The Deutsche Bank 1870–1995* (London, 1995), 289–91.

36 IMT, *Nazi Conspiracy and Aggression*, VII, EC 369, 426.

37 The exchange from which the following paragraphs and its quotes are taken is recorded in BAL R3 003847, 189–93.

38 Hassel, *Hassel-Tagebuecher*, 81.

39 This and the following from IMT, *Nazi Conspiracy and Aggression*, VII, EC-369, 427–32.

40 IMT XXXV, D-855, 597.

41 Based on a figure of 16 billion for the army, from T. Sarholz, 'Die Auswirkungen der Kontingentierung von Eisen und Stahl auf die Aufruestung der Wehrmacht von 1936 bis 1939' (Darmstadt, thesis, 1983), 412 and figures for Luftwaffe from Homze, *Arming*, 228.

42 See the unpublished budget figures in Institut fuer Zeitgeschichte, Da 03.03, Reichshaushalt 1939.

43 G. Albrecht, 'Der neue Finanzplan', *Finanzarchiv*, 7 (1940), 147–51. IfK, Supplement to *Weekly Report*, 20 April 1939.

44 W. A. Boelcke, *Die Kosten von Hitlers Krieg: Kriegsfinanzierung und finanzielles Kriegserbe in Deutschland 1933–1948* (Paderborn, 1985), 21.

45 Hassel, *Hassel-Tagebuecher*, 87.

46 As predicted by the Reichsbank, BAL R2501 6641, 126–57.

47 Three billion, plus 2.7 billion in short-term bills issued by the Wehrmacht during the height of the Czech crisis which only came up for payment in the next tax year. Institut fuer Zeitgeschichte, Da 03.03, Reichshaushalt 1939.

48 BAL R2501 6646, 425–6.

49 BAL R26IV 5, 181, my emphasis.

50 BAL R2501 6446, 419–24.

51 As R. Banken, 'Die deutsche Goldreserven und Devisenpolitik 1933–1939', *JbW* 1 (2003), 49–78, has shown, this was not strictly speaking true. The Reichsbank throughout the late 1930s maintained a hidden last-ditch gold reserve of between 370 and 550 million Reichsmarks, enough to finance about one month of imports. What Banken does not appreciate is that the accumulation of this reserve depended not only on the acquisition of new foreign exchange from the sale of German private assets and foreign plunder, but also on the concerted programme of balance of payments management discussed in this and previous chapters. Rearmament was not absolutely paramount, as he supposes, but constantly weighed up against the need to export. Germany's foreign exchange accounts therefore are an ex post variable, and Banken's attempt to infer the pressures acting on policy-makers from this data is bound to be misleading, since what policy-makers actually responded to were ex ante anticipations of future disaster. The fact that the Reichsbank managed to retain at least a minimal foreign exchange reserve does not imply that there was not the potential for crisis, it simply shows that their strategy of crisis management

was effective. For a position which is closer to that taken here, see A. Ritschl, 'Die deutsche Zahlungsbilanz 1936–1941 und das Problem des Devisenmangels vor Kriegsbeginn', *VfZ* 39 (1991), 103–23.

52 IMT, *Nazi Conspiracy and Aggression*, VII, EC-369, 430. The credit in question is the credit extended in the period between the delivery and payment for goods.

53 On the balance of trade, see W. Graevell, 'Stoerungen im Aussenhandel', *Die Deutsche Volkswirtschaft*, 1 (1939), 43–50.

54 BAL R26IV 5, 180–81.

55 Boelcke, *Kosten*, 59 and Geyer, 'Ruestungsbeschleunigung', 144.

56 See the discussion of the mammoth, two-and-half-hour speech in Domarus, II. 1047–67.

57 Domarus II. 1053.

58 Sarholz, 'Auswirkungen', 351. IMT, *Nazi Conspiracy and Aggression*, III. 868, 1301-PS.

59 BAMA RH15/151, 5–6.

60 BAMA RH15/151, 44–8.

61 BAMA RH15/151, 61–3.

62 Sarholz, 'Auswirkungen', 427–8.

63 BAMA RH15/152, 37.

64 BAMA RH15/151, 197 suggests 91,000 in ammunition. RH15/152, 5 estimates 100,000 apparently in weapons.

65 It is to an early article by Richard Overy that we owe the first thorough analysis of this phenomenon. See R. Overy, 'The German Pre-war Aircraft Production Plans', *English Historical Review*, 90 (1975), 778–97. Overy, however, treats this retreat as an idiosyncrasy of Luftwaffe planning rather than symptomatic of broader problems in the armaments economy.

66 BAMA RL3 2630 LC 7, 21 July 1939, Aktennotiz.

67 Budrass, *Flugzeugindustrie*, 585–7. See also RL3 2630 GL, 24 July 1939, Protokoll.

68 Weinberg, *Foreign Policy II*, 535–602.

69 For Hitler's mounting frustration, see D. C. Watt, *How War Came: The Immediate Origins of the Second World War 1938–1939* (London, 1989), 190.

70 See the view of 'third parties' such as Turkey and Romania described ibid., 284–5.

71 A. W. Schatz, 'The Anglo-American Trade Agreement and Cordell Hull's Search for Peace 1936–1938', *Journal of American History*, 57 (1970), 85–103.

72 H. J. Schroeder, 'Machtpolitik und Oekonomie: Zur nationalsozialistischen Aussenpolitik im Jahre 1938', in F. Knipping and K.-J. Mueller (eds.), *Machtbewusstsein in Deutschland am Vorabend des Zweiten Weltkrieges* (Paderborn, 1984), 221.

73 C. A. Macdonald, *The United States, Britain and Appeasement 1936–1939* (London, 1981), 114.

74 D. Reynolds, *From Munich to Pearl Harbor: Roosevelt's America and the Origins of the Second World War* (Chicago, 2001), 42–8 and C. Macdonald, 'Deterrent Diplomacy: Roosevelt and the Containment of Germany, 1938–1940', in R. Boyce and E. M. Robertson (eds.), *Paths to War: New Essays on the Origins of the Second World War* (New York, 1989), 297–329.

75 J. M. Haight, *American Aid to France 1938–1940* (New York, 1970), 18–102.

76 As Weinberg concedes, 'The alignments of the future were already becoming apparent, at least in outline.' Weinberg, *Foreign Policy II*, 521. As far as Hitler was concerned it was surely more than an 'outline'.

77 *DGFP* D VI No. 14, 14. It was estimated that it would cut German exports to the United States from 200 million to 115 million Reichsmarks, jeopardizing Germany's access to American cotton. *DGFP* D VI No. 130, 159–60. Sirois, *Zwischen Illusion*, 162–9.

78 See the incoherence of his strategic assessment at the address to commanders-in-chief, 23 May 1939, IMT XXXVII, doc. O79-L, 546–56.

79 Watt, *How War Came*, 190–92.

80 IMT VII, EC 282, 944–56.

81 *DGFP* D VI No. 78, 91–6.

82 See the graphic account by Goering's representative Wohlthat that confirms the importance of military pressure by Hungary, Germany's ally. *DGFP* D VI No. 131, 160–66.

83 Watt, *How War Came*, 271–312 emphasizes British and French success. By contrast, Weinberg, *Foreign Policy II*, 584–92 credits Germany with a qualified success in securing at least its most basic economic interests.

84 See the alarm in Berlin at rumours of a Turkish shift into the Franco-British camp. *DGFP* D VI No. 59, 68.

85 D. E. Kaiser, *Economic Diplomacy and the Origins of the Second World War: Germany, Britain, France and Eastern Europe, 1930–1939* (Princeton, 1980), 269–71.

86 Ibid., 278.

87 IMT XXXVI, doc. EC 028, 113.

88 Agreeing with Carroll, *Design*, 104 and Weinberg, *Foreign Policy II*, 28.

89 G. Schreiber, 'Das strategische Lagebild von Luftwaffe und Kriegsmarine im Jahre 1938', in Knipping and Mueller, *Machtbewusstsein*, 188. This, it should be stressed, was a relative statement. None of the European air forces at this point, including the Luftwaffe, had anything like the strength that was required to fight a sustained campaign of strategic bombing. This too was the subject of Luftwaffe staff reports later in the year. See Homze, *Arming*, 243–5.

90 IMT, *Nazi Conspiracy and Aggression*, IV. 4–6, Conference Goering–Ciano 15 April 1939, 1874-PS. And Hitler confirmed the assessment of the air balance in 1939 eleven months later in an interview with Mussolini: 'Last autumn, Germany's air superiority was very considerable. Even so, Germany had feared that this superiority would in part be lost through the much-publicized construction programmes in England and France, and the deliveries from America.' Hitler–Mussolini conversation, 18 March 1940. *DGFP* D IX No. 1, 1–16, doc. 1.

91 B. R. Kroener, *'Der starke Mann im Heimatkriegsgebiet': Generaloberst Friedrich Fromm. Eine Biographie* (Paderborn, 2005), 317–22. Early drafts, BAMA RH15/151, 162–72.

92 IWM EDS, box 71, 71433.

93 BAMA RH15/152, 46.

94 BAMA RH15/152, 174–9. Sarholz, 'Auswirkungen', 436.

95 IWM EDS, Mi. 14/521, 71527.

96 The following revealing exchange is in IWM EDS, box 71, 71534 and 71535.

97 *DGFP* D VI No. 52, 57–62. He immediately qualified this with respect to the navy.

98 C. Hartmann and S. Slutsch, 'Franz Halder und die Kriegsvorbereitungen im Fruehjahr 1939', *VfZ* 45 (1997), 467–95.

99 Kroener, in *DRZW* 5/1. 711. By contrast, in September 1938 the Wehrmacht had been able to commit only 37 divisions against the Czechs, of which 3 were armoured.

100 W. Murray, *The Change in the European Balance of Power, 1938–1939* (Princeton, 1984), 348–50.

101 Amplifying and reinforcing the view taken by J. Duelffer, 'Der Beginn des Krieges 1939: Hitler, die innere Krise und das Maechtesystem', *GG* 2 (1976), 443–70 and B.-J. Wendt, 'Durch das "strategische Fenster" in den Zweiten Weltkrieg', in W Backes, E. Jesse and R. Zitelmann (eds.), *Die Schatten der Vergangenheit: Impulse zur Historisierung des Nationalsozialismus* (Berlin, 1990), 344–79.

102 For different versions of this speech, see K. J. Mueller, *Das Heer und Hitler: Armee und nationalsozialistisches Regime 1933–1940* (Stuttgart, 1969), 409–11; B.-J. Wendt, *Grossdeutschland: Aussenpolitik und Kriegsvorbereitung des Hitler-Regimes* (Munich, 1987), 163; *DRZW* 1. 842; Kaiser, *Economic Diplomacy*, 281.

103 A. Speer, *Inside the Third Reich* (London, 1970), 236.

104 *ADAP* D VIII, doc. 663, Hitler to Duce, 8 March 1940, 687 (my italics).

105 The view taken by A. Hillgruber, *Die Zerstoerung Europas: Beitraege zur Weltkriegs-epoche 1914 bis 1945* (Frankfurt, 1988), 212.

106 Reynolds, *From Munich*, 49–50.

107 Watt, *How War Came*, 268.

108 Haight, *American Aid*, 124–31.

109 The importance of the time factor was emphasized throughout German strategic debates in 1939. See *DGFP* D VI No. 107, 129–35.

110 R. A. C. Parker, *Chamberlain and Appeasement: British Policy and the Coming of the Second World War* (New York, 1993), 227–31.

111 G. Roberts, 'The Alliance that Failed: Moscow and the Triple Alliance Negotiations, 1939', *European History Quarterly* (1996), 383–414.

112 See the navy's dire forecast of relative fleet strengths, dated 15 June 1939, in J. Maiolo, *The Royal Navy and Nazi Germany, 1933–1939: A Study in Appeasement and the Origins of the Second World War* (Basingstoke, 1998), 183.

113 For a penetrating account of the shift in Stalin's position over the course of 1939, see S. Pons, *Stalin and the Inevitable War, 1936–1941* (London, 2002). For a later dating of the shift in the Soviet position, see G. Roberts, 'The Soviet Decision for a Pact with Nazi Germany', *Soviet Studies*, 44 (1992), 57–78, criticized by J. Haslam, 'Soviet-German Relations and the Origins of the Second World War: The Jury Is Still Out', *Journal of Modern History*, 69 (1997), 785–97.

114 The key point in Pons's reinterpretation. See *DGFP* D VI No. 112, 138–40.

115 *DGFP* D VI No. 441, 589–93.

116 *DGFP* D VI No. 424, 558–9 and No. 446, 597–8.

117 For Germany's growing disenchantment with Japan and Japan's growing preoccupation with its war in China, see *DGFP* D VI No. 447, 599–600, No. 457, 614–15, No. 538, 737–40, No. 548, 750–51, No. 597, 821–2, No. 619, 858–60. By early July it seemed evident that no deal would be struck with Japan committing it to war with Britain and France in case of a European conflict. Weinberg, *Foreign Policy II*, 601–27.

118 *DGFP* D VI No. 459, 617–20.

119 In conversation with Mussolini, Goering suggested that the naval balance would be favourable at the earliest in 1942–3. *DGFP* D VI No. 21, 258–63.

120 *DGFP* D VI No. 607, 834–6.

121 F. Thyssen, *I Paid Hitler* (London, 1941), 52–7. G. Mollin, *Montankonzerne und 'Drittes Reich'* (Goettingen, 1988), 124–8.

122 On the evolution in Hitler's views towards the acceptance of the calculated risk of a war in the West, see J. Henke, *England*, 235–302.

123 Hillgruber rightly stresses the fundamental significance of this statement delivered to C. J. Buckhardt on 11 August 1939 in emphasizing the deliberate way in which Hitler steered towards a confrontation with the Western powers. See Hillgruber, *Zerstoerung*, 208.

124 *DRZW* 4. 142.

125 The RWM described the deliveries of grain, oil and phosphates as 'vital' (*lebenswichtig*), *DRZW* 4. 147.

126 H. Schwendemann, *Die wirtschaftliche Zusammenarbeit zwischen dem Deutschen Reich und der Sowjetunion von 1939 bis 1941: Alternative zu Hitlers Ostprogramm?* (Berlin, 1993), 373.

127 E. Wagner (ed.), *Der Generalquartiermeister: Briefe und Tagebuchaufzeichnungen des Generalquartiermeisters des Heeres General der Artillerie Eduard Wagner* (Munich, 1963), 106.

128 As Weinberg, *Foreign Policy II*, 629, notes; see also pp. 638–46. The British declaration of war on 3 September was a disappointment but no surprise.

129 One of the points strongly made in Kley, *Hitler, Ribbentrop*, 258–320. The incomprehension of the army is well documented in Kroener, *Fromm*, 342–50.

130 In contrast to R. Overy, 'Hitler's War Plans and the German Economy', in Boyce and Robertson, *Paths to War*, 96–127. See also I. Kershaw, *Hitler 1936–1945: Nemesis* (London, 2000), 155–80.

131 On this key point we must take our leave of the thesis advanced in various forms by T. Mason, *Nazism, Fascism and the Working Class* (Cambridge, 1995), 33–52, 104–30, 295–322.

132 Taking up a formulation offered by Budrass, *Flugzeugindustrie*, 574.

133 See Weinberg, *Foreign Policy II*, 654. See also the perceptive comments by J. A. Maiolo, 'Armaments Competition', in R. Boyce and J. A. Maiolo (eds.), *The Origins of World War Two: The Debate Continues* (Basingstoke, 2003), 286–307.

134 J. Gooch, 'Fascist Italy', in Boyce and Maiolo, *The Origins of World War Two*, 45–8. See also B. R. Sullivan, 'Italy's Path from Non-alignment to Non-belligerency to War, 1937–1940', in N. Wylie (ed.), *European Neutrals and Non-belligerents During the Second World War* (Cambridge, 2002), 119–49.

135 For Stalin's confidence in the Soviet position in the autumn of 1939, see Pons, *Stalin*, 186–7.

136 Kaiser, *Economic Diplomacy*, 239.

137 Cited in G. L. Weinberg, *A World at Arms: A Global History of World War II* (Cambridge, 1994), 164.

138 See the remarkable description in E. R. May, *Strange Victory: Hitler's Conquest of France* (New York, 2000), 195–212.

139 As Hitler put it to Goering, he was playing '*va banque*'; Hillgruber, *Zerstoerung*, 212. The famous phrase refers to a high stakes gamble in baccarat in which a player wagers a sum equivalent to that held by the banker.

140 For his continuing adherence to this interpretation of Anglo-American relations, see S. Friedlaender, *Prelude to Downfall: Hitler and the United States 1939–1941* (London, 1967), 90.

141 See T. Jersak, in *DRZW* 9/1, 295–6.

142 An interpretation reinforced in the minds of anti-Semitic conspiracy theorists by diplomatic documents seized in Warsaw in 1939. These appeared to provide clear evidence of America's role in instigating Polish resistance to Germany and provided grist to the Nazi conspiracy theory. See *ADAP* D VIII, doc. 665, Ribbentrop–Mussolini meeting, 10 March 1940, 696. See also Friedlaender, *Prelude*, 73–7.

143 On the drift in German expectations about the timing of American aid, see P. Gassert, *Amerika im Dritten Reich* (Stuttgart, 1997), 269.

144 The threat of total annihilation implied by *Vernichtungswillen* was invoked by Ribbentrop in conversation with Mussolini on 10 March 1940 and was clearly implied by Hitler's written message quoted above. See *ADAP* D VIII, doc. 665, 696. The term *Vernichtungskrieg* was also used by the German representative in Washington in a report to Berlin of 17 May 1939. See H. Sirois, *Zwischen Illusion und Krieg: Deutschland und die USA 1933–1941* (Paderborn, 2000), 184.

10 Going for Broke: The First Winter of War

1 The title of this chapter is chosen in appreciative imitation of I. Kershaw, *Hitler 1936–1945: Nemesis* (London, 2000), 181–242.

2 For accounts of these events and copies of tables like those Thomas presented, see IWM EDS, al 1492 and BAMA RW19/205, 120–43.

3 G. Thomas, *Geschichte der deutschen Wehr- und Ruestungswirtschaft* (Boppard, 1966), 509–10.

4 G. Wagner (ed.), *Lagevortraege des Oberbefehlhabers der Kriegsmarine vor Hitler 1939–1945* (Munich, 1972), 20–21.

5 K.-H. Voelker, *Die deutsche Luftwaffe, 1933–1939: Aufbau, Fuehrung und Ruestung der Luftwaffe sowie die Entwicklung der deutschen Luftkriegstheorie* (Stuttgart, 1967), 159–62 and E. L. Homze, *Arming the Luftwaffe* (Lincoln, Nebr., 1976), 240–47.

6 C. Hartmann and S. Slutsch, 'Franz Halder und die Kriegsvorbereitungen im Fruehjahr 1939', *VfZ* 45 (1997), 467–95.

7 *Time*, 34 (25 September 1939), 13.

8 *Meldungen*, 9 October 1939, 331.

9 Ibid., 18 October 1939, 364, 20 October 1939, 372.

10 Ibid., 23 October 1939, 382. 'Vater Chamberlain, der du bist in London, vertilgt werde dein Name, dein Reich verschwinde . . .' There was also a topical version of 'Tannenbaum'.
11 Ibid., 25 October 1939, 390.
12 *Halder Diary*, 27 September 1939, 62 and A. Hillgruber, *Die Zerstoerung Europas: Beitraege zur Weltkriegsepoche 1914 bis 1945* (Frankfurt, 1988), 210.
13 Ibid., 211.
14 The passage, with my italics, is taken from a speech to the Wehrmacht leadership on 23 November 1939. Weinberg, in his well-known essay 'Hitler's Image of the United States', distorts the meaning by tearing the first sentence out of context and omitting the crucial qualifier 'yet' from his translation. Oddly, in the next essay in his collection Weinberg corrects the misleading translation, but never comments on the difference. See G. L. Weinberg, *World in the Balance: Behind the Scenes of World War II* (London, 1981), 63, 81. For more persuasive accounts see S. Friedlaender, *Prelude to Downfall: Hitler and the United States 1939–1941* (London, 1967), 86–7 and H. Sirois, *Zwischen Illusion und Krieg: Deutschland und die USA 1933–1941* (Paderborn, 2000), 189–209.
15 Thomas, *Geschichte*, 170–78.
16 F. Hahn, *Waffen und Geheimwaffen des deutschen Heeres 1933–1945* (Bonn, 3rd edn., 1998), II. 198–9.
17 *Halder Diary*, 24 September 1940, 61. For the response, see Kroener, in *DRZW* 5/2. 819–24 and W. Murray, 'The German Response to Victory in Poland: A Case Study in Professionalism', *Armed Forces and Society*, 7 (1981), 285–98.
18 Hahn, *Waffen*, II. 194–6.
19 K.-H. Frieser, *Blitzkrieg-Legende: Der Westfeldzug 1940* (Munich, 1996), 71–7.
20 For the ensuing dispute with Hitler, see *Halder Diary*, 27 September 1939–24 November 1939, 61–82.
21 E. R. May, *Strange Victory: Hitler's Conquest of France* (New York, 2000), 215–26 and Kershaw, *Hitler: Nemesis*, 233–79.
22 E. Wagner (ed.), *Der Generalquartiermeister: Briefe und Tagebuchaufzeichnungen des Generalquartiermeisters des Heeres General der Artillerie Eduard Wagner* (Munich, 1963), 147.
23 G. Engel, *Heeresadjutant bei Hitler 1938–1943: Aufzeichnungen des Majors Engel*, ed. Hildgard von Kotze (Stuttgart, 1974), 66–7. Kershaw, *Hitler: Nemesis*, 270.
24 See Hillgruber, *Zerstoerung*, 215.
25 The seminal description of the early German war effort as 'a peacelike war economy' is R. Wagenfuehr, *Die deutsche Industrie im Kriege* (Berlin, 1954), 25. For a powerful critique see R. J. Overy, *War and Economy in the Third Reich* (Oxford, 1994), 233–314. For a primarily political and organizational discussion, see Mueller, in *DRZW* 5/1. 349–90.
26 J. M. Haight, *American Aid to France 1938–1940* (New York, 1970), 132–88.
27 *DRZW* 1. 427.
28 Friedlaender, *Prelude*, 83–4.
29 Haight, *American Aid*, 189–231. H. D. Hall, *North American Supply* (London, 1955), 117–68.
30 Medlicott's official history of the blockade, which begins on a famously downbeat note – 'too much . . . was expected of the blockade' – in fact cites little or no evidence from the German side and shows no appreciation of the severity of the Reich's import problem. W. N. Medlicott, *The Economic Blockade* (London, 1952), I. 411.
31 See successive issues of SRA, *Monatlicher Nachweisueber den Auswaertigen Handel*, 1939–44.
32 BAMA RW19/172, 23 October 1939.
33 W. Murray, *Luftwaffe* (London, 1985), 62–3.
34 Though committed to a narrative of organizational chaos, R. D. Mueller finds little evidence for a setback to civilian production. See Mueller, in *DRZW* 5/1. 380. In the armaments sector, the Wehrmacht was pleased to report that there was no shock; BAMA

RH15/159, 330–33. Wagenfuehr's discussion of the so-called 'war shock' or 'Kriegsstoss' consists of political sniping rather than substantive analysis. See Wagenfuehr, *Die deutsche Industrie*, 24–8.

35 In successive versions this thesis became more emphatic. Klein put the argument rather cautiously: 'Hitler was less able to subordinate the various private interests . . . than has been commonly assumed'; B. H. Klein, *Germany's Economic Preparations for War* (Cambridge, Mass., 1959), 25. Six years later Milward was more emphatic: 'The files of the office of the Berlin President of Police were well stocked with fearful anticipations of the political unrest that would be caused by the negligible hardships of Germany's capital investment programme.' Blitzkrieg was attractive because it allowed Hitler not to restrict consumption; A. S. Milward, *The German Economy at War* (London, 1965), 12. Finally, Mason in 1966 stated: 'The domestic–political function of the Blitzkrieg plans resided in their promise of bringing the war to a swift and successful conclusion without demanding any undue sacrifices of the German people'; T. Mason, *Nazism, Fascism and the Working Class* (Cambridge, 1995), 69.

36 Mueller, in *DRZW* 5/1. 375–83.

37 See Goering's attack on Funk in BAMA RH15/159, 275–9.

38 Mueller, in *DRZW* 5/1. 410–15.

39 BAMA RW19/205, 125.

40 Mueller, in *DRZW* 5/1. 384.

41 NA T77 339 Wi/IF 5.2151, Stellungnahme fuer Chef des WFA, 18 October 1939.

42 See Hanneken's report to VJP in early January 1940, IWM EDS, al 1905 ex Wi. If. 5. 405.

43 For Thomas's conviction that the battle in the West would be a *Materialschlacht*, see his comments on likely transport requirements in BAMA RW19/172, 27.

44 NA T77 339 Wi/IF 5.2151, undated memo from Wi Rue Amt files, probably early 1940.

45 Weinberg, *Foreign Policy II*, 19–20 offers a succinct version of this Hitlerine critique. Oddly, however, Weinberg places it in 1937, whereas Hitler only actually confronted Thomas's position directly in 1939–40.

46 Regardless also of long-term prospects. In the autumn of 1939 he refused to grant the top priority demanded by the army and Albert Speer for the Peenemuende rocket programme, on the grounds that it could have no impact on the war before 1941 at the earliest. See BAMA RH15/153, 123–5.

47 IWM EDS, al 1571, Chef Wi Rue Amt Aktennotiz, 4 December 1939. See the earlier note by Thomas along similar lines IMT, *Nazi Conspiracy and Aggression* (Washington, 1946–7), VII, EC-615, 603.

48 IWM EDS, al 1571, Inspekteurbesprechung, 24 March 1940.

49 See the résumé in BAMA RW19/172 OKW, 23 October 1939.

50 On the shock to the dockyards, see A. Meyhoff, *Blohm & Voss im 'Dritten Reich'* (Hamburg, 2001), 243–53.

51 E. Roessler, *Geschichte des deutschen U-Bootbaus* (Augsburg, 1996), I. 192–208.

52 L. Budrass, *Flugzeugindustrie und Luftruestung in Deutschland* (Duesseldorf, 1998), 587–90.

53 H. Strachan, *The First World War* (Oxford, 2001), I. 993–1048.

54 As became clear at his first armaments conference of the war in October 1939, BAMA RH15/159, 330–33.

55 E. Leeb, *Aus der Ruestung des Dritten Reiches (Das Heereswaffenamt 1938–1945)* (Berlin, 1958).

56 See the comments on the damage done to the army's reputation amongst industrialists already in 1937, BAMA RH15/149, 3–22.

57 BAMA RH15/159, 330–33.

58 BAMA RW19/205, 129 and Mueller, in *DRZW* 5/1. 425–6.

59 BAMA RW19/173, 246–59. As the army experts pointed out, the quality of ammunition had improved dramatically since World War I, both in terms of range and explosive

impact. Reaching World War I levels of production would only be possible at the expense of a return to cast-iron shells filled with ersatz explosives.

60 BAMA RW19/164, 3–10, OKW Tagebuch. For details, see BAMA RH15/160, Waffenamt 10 January 1940.

61 For expressions of incredulity from army procurement, see BAMA RH15/160, 264. On this truly ubiquitous but unsung weapon, see Hahn, *Waffen*, 146–61. Over the course of the war a significant fraction of German heavy industry was occupied with the production of 17,000 light howitzers and the 110 million shells they fired.

62 The account most indebted to Thomas is Mueller, in *DRZW* 5/1. 349–426, who focuses on the 'polycentric' politics of the German war effort. Though writing from a different perspective, Overy also stresses inefficiency as a result of organizational failure in the early war years. See Overy, *War and Economy*, 313 and 343–56.

63 The following is based on a recalculated monthly index of armaments production, details of which are available from the author's website and J. A. Tooze, 'Arming the Reich: Armaments Production in Hitler's Germany' (forthcoming), available from the author's website.

64 See BAMA RL3 2630, Beschaffungslage, December 1939.

65 Goering initiated the campaign against the army procurement office already at the end of November. See BAMA RH15/159, Vortragsnotiz, 29 November 1939.

66 A point made emphatically by the army procurement staff in answer to their critics. See BAMA RH15/153, 128–30 and RH15/159, 248–50, but ignored by Wagenfuehr, Mueller and Overy.

67 IWM, M14/328, Niederschrift ueber Rue In Besprechung, 8/9 January 1940, 2–3.

68 First anxious discussions of the transport problem were held in November 1939. See BAMA RW19/172, 22–30 and BAH R131 607, 81–6.

69 *Statistisches Handbuch von Deutschland* (Munich, 1949), 349–51.

70 A. C. Mierzejewski, *The Most Valuable Assest of the Reich: A History of the German National Railway*, II: *1933–1945* (Chapel Hill, NC, 2000), 57–93.

71 *Meldungen*, III: 27 December 1939, 606. Remarkably, in 1939 railway accidents across Germany claimed the lives of 1,920 people (not including suicides) and left 4,523 injured. Both figures were 100 per cent higher than in 1937. See SRA, *Statistisches Jahrbuch fuer das Deutsche Reich (1941/42)* (Berlin, 1942), 242.

72 *Meldungen*, III: 17 January 1940, 652, 29 January 1940, 705–6.

73 IWM FD717/46, box 248 255 ff., Rheinmetall Informationsbericht, 1939. For the impact of the coal shortage on morale in Berlin and elsewhere, see *Meldungen*, III: 8 January 1940, 622–4, 26 January 1940, 686–7.

74 BAMA RW19/263, OKW Report, 2 April 1940, 6–13.

75 IWM EDS, al 1571, 16 February 1940, Besprechung.

76 *Halder Diary*, 27 January 1940, 173–4.

77 BAMA RH15/160, 254–69.

78 This and Keitel's response quoted below are in IWM EDS, al 1492.

79 BAMA RH15/151, 104–5.

80 IWM. Mi. 14 328, Rue In Besprechung, 8/9 January 1940.

81 IWM EDS, al 1492, Aktennotiz Vortrag bei Keitel, 27 January 1940.

82 By contrast, Mueller, though he fully understands the political nature of the 'ammunition crisis', falls in uncritically with contemporary attacks on the 'military bureaucrats' and regards every step towards Todt's appointment as a step towards greater efficiency. See Mueller, in *DRZW* 5/1. 423, 453–66.

83 IWM EDS al 1492, Chef OKW to the Oberbefehlhaber des Heeres 2 March 1940.

84 BAMA RW19/164, diary entry 4 March 1940, 65–6. Mueller in *DRZW* 5/1. 462–78. K. H. Ludwig, *Technik und Ingenieure im Dritten Reich* (Duesseldorf, 1974), 344–60.

85 D. Eichholtz, *Anatomie des Krieges: Neue Dokumente ueber die Rolle des deutschen Monopolkapitals bei der Vorbereitung und Durchfuehrung des Zweiten Weltkrieges* (Berlin, 1969), 243–58.

86 Eichholtz, I. 121–32.

87 Over the following days he also met with Albert Voegler of Vestag, Helmuth Roehnert of Rheinmetall and Erich Tgahrt the CEO of Hoesch AG.

88 The industry associations also supplied him with lists of candidates for his committees. See BAH R131 657, 51, 53–9.

89 See Todt's instructions to the RgI in BAMA RW19/263.

90 W. Weber, 'Walter Borbet (1881–1942)', in W. Weber (ed.), *Ingenieure im Ruhrgebiet* (Muenster, 1999), 252–3.

91 Domarus, II. 1540–59.

92 Mueller, in *DRZW* 5/1. 467.

93 Herbst, *Das nationalsozialistische Deutschland 1933–1945* (Frankfurt, 1996), 304, cites quarterly production figures for ammunition in 1939–40, but draws the wrong conclusion.

94 IWM 14/328, January 1940, Rue In Besprechung, 8/9 January 1940.

95 On the operation of the arrangement from the industrialists' point of view, see BAH R131 593, Niederschrift, 15 March 1940. Mueller, in *DRZW* 5/1. 448. Mueller dismisses this arrangement, because the Rue In was too selective in the firms it actually chose to involve, which is odd since Mueller also accuses the military of a lack of discrimination in their procurement practices.

96 As Budrass points out, the concrete model of contracting that was mentioned in 1940 was the Junkers model of the Luftwaffe. Budrass, *Flugzeugindustrie*, 654–5.

97 The first historian to make this crucial point against the prevailing consensus was Overy. See Overy, *War and Economy*, 259–314.

98 For their plebiscitary character, see G. Aly, *Hitlers Volksstaat* (Frankfurt, 2005), 334–9.

99 These figures for net additions are from *Statistisches Handbuch*, 340–41.

100 See the assessment in BAL R2501 7006, 321–4.

101 Eichholtz, III. 703–8.

102 BAL R2501 6557, 505–6.

103 Mueller, in *DRZW* 5/1. 396–405. G. Corni and H. Gies, *Brot, Butter, Kanonen: Die Ernaehrungswirtschaft in Deutschland unter der Diktatur Hitlers* (Berlin, 1997), 555–75. H. Kehrl, *Krisenmanager im Dritten Reich* (Duesseldorf, 1973), 178–84.

104 The Reichsbank and the SRA estimated that even for low-income working-class households the reduction in expenditure would be in the order of 12 per cent as a direct result of rationing. BAL 2501 6610, 391–6. For higher income households the effect would be far larger.

105 BAH R13I 607, 113–27, 81–6.

106 This was already a larger share than had been allocated to armaments during the Hindenburg programme in 1917. See BAL R2501 7006, 83–90. It was also larger than the share of steel allocated to war purposes in Britain at the same time. See W. P. Howlett, 'The Competition Between the Supply Departments and the Allocation of Scarce Resources in the Second World War' (Cambridge, Ph.D. thesis, 1988), 65.

107 *Meldungen*, III: 8 December 1939, 552. See the list of restricted items in BAH R13I 677.

108 BAMA RW19/164, 28–9. In BAMA RW19/173, 58, Hanneken described it simply as 'irresponsible'. See the astonished reaction by representatives of the Flick corporation recorded in BAL R8122 58, Notiz fuer Herrn Flick 13 February 1940. See also the completely unsustainable allocations of nonferrous metals in BAMA RW19/173, 121 and 139–41.

109 IWM EDS, al 1571, Chef Wi Rue Amt, 30 January 1940. He reiterated the same point to a larger group on 9 February 1940, BAMA RW19/173, 114–17.

110 The key sources are Kroener, in *DRZW* 5/1 and 5/2.

111 A key point made both by Overy, *War and Economy*, 291–303 and T. Siegel, *Leistung und Lohn in der nationalsozialistischen 'Ordnung der Arbeit'* (Opladen, 1989), 161–73.

112 See data on regional employment patterns in SRA, *Statistisches Jahrbuch fuer das Deutsche Reich*, 54–65.

113 Kroener, in *DRZW* 5/1. 819–29.

114 On the types of manpower preferred by the Luftwaffe, see Voelker, *Luftwaffe*, 115–25.

115 Budrass, *Flugzeugindustrie*, 767–8.

116 Mueller, in *DRZW* 5/1. 401.

117 On the shortage of potatoes, the staple of German nutrition, in early 1940, see *Meldungen*, 15 January 1940, 648–9, 31 January 1940, 714–15, 14 February 1940, 756.

118 U. Herbert, *Hitler's Foreign Workers: Enforced Foreign Labour in Germany under the Third Reich* (Cambridge, 1997), 61–94. C. Madajczyk, *Die Okkupationspolitik Nazideutschlands in Polen 1939–1945* (Berlin, 1987), 216–32.

119 Russian–Polish tensions were arguably even more severe. On the system of repression established in the Polish territories seized by Stalin in the autumn of 1939, see B. Musial, *'Konterrevolutionaere Elemente sind zu erschiessen': Die Brutalisierung des deutsch-sowjetischen Krieges im Sommer 1941* (Munich, 2000), 25–97.

120 G. Aly, *'Endloesung': Voelkerverschiebung und der Mord an den europaeischen Juden* (Frankfurt, 1995) and G. Aly and S. Heim, *Vordenker der Vernichtung: Auschwitz und die deutschen Plaene fuer eine neue europaeische Ordnung* (Hamburg, 1991).

121 M. Spoerer, *Zwangsarbeit unter dem Hakenkreuz* (Stuttgart, 2001), 45. No more than a few hundred survived the war.

122 H. Frank, *Das Diensttagebuch des deutschen Generalgouverneurs in Polen 1939–1945*, ed. W. Praeg and W. Jacobmeyer (Stuttgart, 1975), 176–7, meeting on labour question, 21 April 1940.

123 IMT, *Nazi Conspiracy and Aggression*, VIII, NG-1408, 328.

124 IMT XII, NID-15581, 8th Meeting of General Council, 17 April 1940, 959–60.

125 See comments in Frank, *Das Diensttagebuch*, 148–9, 200–201. To avoid misunderstandings, these comments refer to the spring and summer of 1940, when the bulk of the Wehrmacht was in the West, and to the thinly occupied General Government, not the territories of Poland annexed to Germany. Earlier in the occupation, between September and December 1939, the SS had already slaughtered 43,000 Gentiles and 7,000 Jewish Poles in their effort to 'liquidate' the 'Polish leadership'. See A. B. Rossino, *Hitler Strikes Poland: Blitzkrieg, Ideology and Atrocity* (Lawrence, Kan., 2003).

126 The euphemism preferred by Frank was a 'programme of pacification' (*Befriedungsprogramm*). See Frank, *Das Diensttagebuch*, 202–3.

127 On 30 May 1940 Frank reassured his officials that he had a direct authorization from Hitler to carry out these killings, see Frank, *Das Diensttagebuch*, 211–12.

128 Ibid., 88–9.

129 Ibid., 188–9.

130 IWM Mi. 14/328, Niederschrift . . . 8/9 January 1940, 68–72.

11 Victory in the West – *Sieg im Westen*

1 For the following I am hugely indebted to K.-H. Frieser, *Blitzkrieg-Legende: Der Westfeldzug 1940:* (Munich, 1996).

2 In the largest eastern pocket at Kiev in the summer of 1941, Germany bagged 665,000 Soviet prisoners. At Stalingrad the Germans themselves lost 'only' 110,000 prisoners of war.

3 I. Kershaw, *Hitler 1936–1945: Nemesis* (London, 2000), 297–300. *Meldungen*, 6 June 1940, 1218; 17 June 1940, 1261; 20 June 1940, 1274–5, 1284.

4 See for instance the line taken in M. Harrison (ed.), *The Economics of World War II* (Cambridge, 1998), 1–2.

5 For the genesis of this idea, see Frieser, *Blitzkrieg-Legende*, 5–12.

6 The classic exposition of this thesis is A. S. Milward, *War, Economy and Society 1939–1945* (Harmondsworth, 1977), 23–30. It was based on Milward, *The German Economy at War* (London, 1965) and B. H. Klein, *Germany's Economic Preparations for War* (Cambridge, Mass., 1959), which in turn owed much to United States Strategic Bombing

Survey, *The Effects of Strategic Bombing on the German War Economy* (Washington, 1945).

7 R. H. S. Stolfi, 'Equipment for Victory in France in 1940', *History*, 55 (1970), 1–20, amplified on basis of Frieser, *Blitzkrieg-Legende*, 33–65.

8 J. M. Haight, *American Aid to France 1938–1940* (New York, 1970), 139, 238–50. In one spectacular encounter in early November 1939, nine newly arrived American P-36s tangled with 27 Me 109s and shot down nine for no loss.

9 H. A. Jacobsen, *Fall Gelb: Der Kampf um den deutschen Operationsplan zur Westoffensive 1940* (Wiesbaden, 1957), Frieser, *Blitzkrieg-Legende*, 66–116 and E. R. May, *Strange Victory: Hitler's Conquest of France* (New York, 2000), 215–26.

10 M. Geyer, 'Restorative Elites, German Society and the Nazi Pursuit of War', in R. Bessel (ed.), *Fascist Italy and Nazi Germany: Comparisons and Contrasts* (Cambridge, 1996), 139–44.

11 D. Bourgeois, *Das Geschaeft mit Hitlerdeutschland: Schweizer Wirtschaft und Drittes Reich* (Zurich, 2000), 165, my italics.

12 *Sieg im Westen. Ein Film des Oberkommando des Heeres* (Berlin, 1940, distributed by International Historic Films Chicago, 1985).

13 K.-H. Frieser, *Ardennen, Sedan: Militaerhistorischer Fuehrer durch eine europaeische Schicksalslandschaft* (Frankfurt, 2000).

14 *DRZW* 9/1. 511.

15 W. Murray, 'The German Response to Victory in Poland: A Case Study in Professionalism', *Armed Forces and Society*, 7 (1981), 285–98, and R. A. Doughty, *The Breaking Point: Sedan and the Fall of France, 1940* (Hamden, Conn., 1990).

16 The question asked in R. Overy, *Why the Allies Won* (London, 1995).

17 On the abiding emphasis on the offensive, see G. P. Gross, 'Das Dogma der Beweglichkeit', in B. Thoss and H.-E. Volkmann (eds.), *Erster Weltkrieg: Zweiter Weltkrieg* (Paderborn, 2002), 143–66.

18 The Mark I was armed only with machine guns. The Mark II carried a 20 millimetre cannon. Both could be penetrated by even the lightest anti-tank guns. W. J. Spielberger, *Die Panzerkampfwagen I und II* (Stuttgart, 3rd edn., 1991).

19 *DRZW* 5/1. 554.

20 On the rare occasions in May 1940 that Panzer forces did meet well-prepared French defensive positions, they did not come off well, proving vulnerable to the French superiority in field artillery. See J. A. Gunsburg, 'The Battle of Gembloux, 14–15 May 1940: The "Blitzkrieg" Checked', *Journal of Military History*, 64 (2000), 97–140.

21 For the epic fight put up by a handful of Char Bs in the battle for Stonne on 15 and 16 May, see Frieser, *Blitzkrieg-Legende*, 259–65.

22 For the following, see ibid., 105–6 and 415.

23 W. Murray, *Luftwaffe* (London, 1985), 69–78.

24 This figure is inflated by 170 transports lost in the airborne assaults, but is nevertheless extraordinarily high. See Frieser, *Blitzkrieg-Legende*, 428.

25 Ibid., 117–35.

26 For the use of Pervitin in the elite 1st Panzer division, see ibid., 136. For a far-out discussion of drugs in the Third Reich, see W. Pieper (ed.), *Nazis on Speed: Drogen im 3. Reich* (Loherbach, n.d.), 114–54.

27 W. Murray, *The Change in the European Balance of Power, 1938–1939* (Princeton, 1984), 361.

28 See the excellent summary in D. Reynolds, '1940: Fulcrum of the Twentieth Century?', *International Affairs*, 66 (1990), 325–50.

29 *DRZW* 2. 189–234. G. L. Weinberg, *A World at Arms: A Global History of World War II* (Cambridge, 1994), 77–8 and 113–21.

30 J.-J. Jaeger, *Die wirtschaftliche Abhaengigkeit des Dritten Reiches vom Ausland: Dargestellt am Beispiel der Stahlindustrie* (Berlin, 1969), 133.

31 P. Marguerat, *Le IIIe Reich et le pétrole roumain, 1938–1940* (Leiden, 1977).

32 W. N. Medlicott, *The Economic Blockade* (London, 1952), I. 250–59.

33 See the extreme concern expressed IWM EDS, al 1057, 1058.

34 BAMA RW19/173, 37–8.

35 A. Hillgruber, *Hitlers Strategie* (Frankfurt, 1965), 126–44, C. Leitz, *Nazi Germany and Neutral Europe During the Second World War* (Manchester, 2000), N. Wylie (ed.), *European Neutrals and Non-belligerents During the Second World War* (Cambridge, 2002).

36 C. Leitz, *Economic Relations between Nazi Germany and Franco's Spain, 1936–1945* (Oxford, 1996), 131–5. With reference to our later argument, Leitz also notes the rapidity with which the Spanish posture shifted back against Germany by the autumn of 1940.

37 N. Wylie, *Britain, Switzerland and the Second World War* (Oxford, 2003).

38 Bourgeois, *Das Geschaeft*, 64.

39 P. Hug, *Schweizer Ruestungsindustrie und Kriegsmaterialhandel zur Zeit des Nationalsozialismus* (Zurich, 2002).

40 The first to apply up to date macroeconomic statistics to the economic history of World War II was Harrison, *The Economics of World War II*.

41 *DRZW* 5/1. 216–25.

42 A. S. Milward, *The New Order and the French Economy* (Oxford, 1984), 81. In this context, 'booty' refers to goods confiscated from French citizens or institutions.

43 F. Hahn, *Waffen und Geheimwaffen des deutschen Heeres 1933–1945* (Bonn, 3rd edn., 1998), II. 205.

44 Ibid., 178–9.

45 J. Freymond, *Le IIIe Reich et la réorganisation économique de l'Europe 1940–1942* (Leiden, 1974). Milward, *The New Order*. *DRZW* 5/1. 210–64. R. Opitz (ed.), *Europastrategien des deutschen Kapitals 1900–1945* (Bonn, 1994). R. J. Overy, G. Otto and J. Houwink ten Cate, *Die 'Neuordnung' Europas: NS-Wirtschaftspolitik in den besetzten Gebieten* (Berlin, 1997).

46 R. Frommelt, *Paneuropa oder Mitteleuropa: Einigungsbestrebungen im Kalkuel deutscher Wirtschaft und Politik 1925–1933* (Stuttgart, 1977), E. Teichert, *Autarkie und Grossraumwirtschaft in Deutschland 1930–1939* (Munich, 1984) and V. R. Berghahn, *Quest for Economic Empire: European Strategies of German Big Business in the Twentieth Century* (Oxford, 1996).

47 Particularly interesting in this respect is M. Buggeln, 'Waehrungsplaene fuer den europaeischen Grossraum', in *Europaeische Integration: Deutsche Hegemonialpolitik gegenueber Westeuropa 1920–1960* (Goettingen, 2002), 41–76.

48 See the comments of Schlotterer of the RWM to the RgI, recorded in BAL R8122 125, 7.

49 Buggeln, 'Waehrungsplaene', 63. In March 1940 the Reichsbank Economics Department proposed a 50 per cent devaluation to follow a successful end to the war. See BAL R2501 6433, 369–83.

50 Reichsbank estimates of the degree of Reichsmark overvaluation versus the European currencies as of June 1940 are in BAL R2501 6612, 491–503.

51 Born 1906, the son of a Wuerttemberg master baker, Schlotterer joined the NSDAP as early as 1923 as an enthusiastic young apprentice banker. He later graduated in business science and completed a doctoral thesis on Marxian economics. During the Machtergreifung he became an influential figure in Hamburg politics and a driving force in early Aryanization measures, before moving in 1935 to the RWM. From 1938 onwards he was the key figure in the Ministry's trade policy. After the war he made a profitable career in the international steel trade, retiring to Duesseldorf where he died in 1989. Buggeln, 'Waehrungsplaene', 51.

52 Ibid., 61. It is worth noting that only a few months later Schlotterer gave a speech to the same audience in which he backed away from the draconian rhetoric of the summer of 1940 and emphasized cooperation rather than domination. See BAL R8122 125, 1–32.

53 H. Berger and A. Ritschl, 'Die Rekonstruktion der Arbeitsteilung in Europa: Eine neue

Sicht des Marshallplans in Deutschland 1947–1951', *VfZ* 45 (1995), 495. They also make the point that a crucial part of post-war American policy in Europe was to ensure that these debts were effectively cancelled. Marshall aid was given to Germany in the form of a credit that had priority over all other German debts. So long as the United States refused to demand repayment, Germany's wartime clearing creditors were denied the possibility of reclaiming the money that was owed to them, thus enabling West Germany to emerge as a credit-worthy trading partner free of wartime obligations.

54 Figures on export volumes relative to 1938 from A. Maddison, *Dynamic Forces of Capitalist Development* (Oxford, 1991), 316–19.

55 Milward, *The New Order*, 283.

56 Whereas the overall volume of German exports in 1942 was 25 per cent below the 1937 level, exports of both raw materials and semi-finished goods had fully recovered, raising their share in German export trade from 22 to 32 per cent. See *Statistisches Handbuch von Deutschland* (Munich, 1949), 394–5.

57 P. Hayes, *Industry and Ideology: IG Farben in the Nazi Era* (Cambridge, 1987), 278–90. IMT VII. 1446–58, translation of docs. NI-6840 and NI-11252, Farben memo 7 August 1940.

58 As agreed with the Reich in the summer of 1940, the final settlement of ownership issues was postponed until after the war. See BAH R13I 607, 22–4.

59 G. Mollin, *Montankonzerne und 'Drittes Reich'* (Goettingen, 1988), 220–51.

60 The *Final Report of the Second World War Assets Contact Group* (Amsterdam, 2000) puts the total of assets plundered from Dutch Jews at 1 billion gulden, or roughly 1.3 to 1.5 billion Reichsmarks, of which roughly 300 million gulden may have been business assets.

61 Thomson's, like AEG of Germany, had long been a business partner of General Electric of the United States and it was AEG that was assigned control of the French firm. See H. Homburg, 'Wirtschaftliche Dimensionen der deutschen Besatzungsherrschaft in Frankreich 1940–1944: Das Beispiel der elektrotechnischen Industrie', in W. Abelshauser, J.-O. Hesse and W. Plumpe (eds.), *Wirtschaftsordnung, Staat und Unternehmen: Neue Forschungen zur Wirtschaftsgeschichte des Nationalsozialismus* (Essen, 2003), 181–204.

62 R. Bohn, *Reichskommissariat Norwegen: 'Nationalsozialistische Neuordnung' und Kriegswirtschaft* (Munich, 2000), 296–301.

63 For a discussion of Germany's limited penetration in Holland, see G. Aalders, 'Three Ways of German Economic Penetration in the Netherlands: Cloaking, Capital Interlocking and "Aryanization" ', in Overy, Otto and Cate (eds.), *Die 'Neuordnung' Europas*, 273–98 and L. Nestler (ed.), *Europa unterm Hakenkreuz: Die faschistische Okkupationspolitik in Belgien, Luxemburg und den Niederlanden (1940–1945)* (Berlin, 1990), 160.

64 Mollin, *Montankonzerne*, 245–9.

65 Document 124 in Opitz, *Europastrategien*, 794–9. This, of course, is an aggregate argument. Even if a country is running a large current account deficit it will be possible for individual firms to make acquisitions abroad. They will not be able to do so in the aggregate, however, unless alternative sources of finance are available.

66 See the discussion of the clearing problem in the second half of 1943 in BAL R2501 6448, 6449.

67 See the Franco-German negotiations recorded in IMT XIII. 767–89.

68 On Wehrmacht construction in Norway, see Bohn, *Reichskommissariat*, 355–76.

69 See the extraordinary exchanges documenting the confusion of the German civilian and military authorities in 1942–3 in IMT, *Nazi Conspiracy and Aggression* (Washington, 1946–7), IV, 1741-PS, 228.

70 IMT XII, NG-4526, extracts from Wiehl's report, 26 November 1942, 813–15.

71 Milward, *The New Order*, 97–100.

72 On the acquisition of the French oil interests in Romania, see Eichholtz, I. 238 and Milward, *The New Order*, 96–8. For a discussion of Kontinentale Oel, emphasizing its wider ambitions in the Middle East, see T. Kockel, 'Eine Quelle zur Vor- und Gruendungs-

geschichte der Kontinentale Oel AG aus dem Jahr 1940', *Jahrbuch fuer Wirtschaftsgeschichte*, 1 (2003), 175–208.

73 R. J. Overy, *War and Economy in the Third Reich* (Oxford, 1994), 144–74 and 315–42.

74 D. Reynolds, 'Churchill and the British "Decision" to Fight on in 1940: Right Policy, Wrong Reasons', in R. Langhorne (ed.), *Diplomacy and Intelligence during the Second World War* (Cambridge, 1985), 147–67, and D. Reynolds, *The Creation of the Anglo-American Alliance 1937–41: A Study in Competitive Cooperation* (London, 1981), 88–108.

75 *ADAP* D X doc. 195, Boetticher and Thomsen to AA, 20 July 1940, 209–10 and doc. 199, Dieckhoff memo, 21 July 1940, 213–14.

76 A role confirmed, according to the German Foreign Ministry, by the embassy material captured in Warsaw. See *ADAP* D X, doc. 252, Dieckhoff memo, 29 June 1940, 287–96.

77 BAMA RW19/164, and the retrospective account in IWM EDS al 1492, Chef Wi Rue Amt, 20 August 1940, Aktennotiz.

78 Milward, *The New Order*, 65.

79 Between August and October 1940 the Gestapo registered a dramatic deterioration in public confidence. See *Meldungen*, V. 1424–689. Once the disappointment of a second winter of war had been overcome, confidence bounced back in December, see *Meldungen* VI. 1808–77.

80 S. Casey, *Cautious Crusade: Franklin D. Roosevelt, American Public Opinion, and the War Against Nazi Germany* (Oxford, 2001), 26.

81 L. Gruchmann, *Der Zweite Weltkrieg* (Munich, 2nd edn., 1971), 77.

12 Britain and America: Hitler's Strategic Dilemma

1 Quoted in German in A. Hillgruber, *Die Zerstoerung Europas: Beitraege zur Weltkriegsepoche 1914 bis 1945* (Frankfurt, 1988), 342. See also S. Pons, *Stalin and the Inevitable War, 1936–1941* (London, 2002), 202–3.

2 Ironically, General Franco took a similar position when pressed by Germany to enter the war in January 1941. See I. Kershaw, *Hitler 1936–1945: Nemesis* (London, 2000), 330.

3 D. Reynolds, '1940: Fulcrum of the Twentieth Century?', *International Affairs*, 66 (1990), 325–50.

4 My interpretation in this section of the book owes an enormous debt to Andreas Hillgruber's monumental Habilschrift, *Hitlers Strategie* (Frankfurt, 1965). One of the most unfortunate side effects of the infamous German historians' controversy (Historikerstreit) was the way in which it overshadowed the immense contribution that Professor Hillgruber made to our understanding of the Third Reich. I am delighted to find myself in agreement with Goetz Aly in acknowledging this debt. See the 'Afterword' to Aly, *'Endloesung: Voelkerverschiebung und der Mord an den europaeischen Juden* (Frankfurt, 1995), 448.

5 *DRZW* 2. 368–74.

6 M. Salewski, *Die deutsche Seekriesgsleitung 1935–1945* (Frankfurt, 1970), I. 175–207. *DRZW* 2. 224. The strategic implications are spelled out in G. L. Weinberg, *A World at Arms: A Global History of World War II* (Cambridge, 1994), 117–18.

7 Hillgruber, *Hitlers Strategie*, 168 and 79–80.

8 Weinberg, *World at Arms*, 175–82.

9 J. A. Maiolo, *The Royal Navy and Nazi Germany, 1933–1939: A Study in Appeasement and the Origins of the Second World War* (Basingstoke, 1998), 66–74.

10 The following is based on *DRZW* 2. 182–5 and 345–8.

11 A. Meyhoff, *Blohm & Vass im 'Dritten Reich'* (Hamburg, 2001), 139–49 quotes 196.8 million Reichsmarks for the *Bismarck* and U-boat prices of between 4.3 million and 2.4 million Reichsmarks per piece. E. Roessler, *Geschichte des deutschen U-Bootsbaus* (Augsburg, 1996) 170 and 218, gives U-boat prices of between 7.5 million Reichsmarks for small runs of larger U-boat and 2 million for a standard mass-produced U VII C at the end of 1943.

12 The U-boat programme would have required a tripling in the navy's allocation of rubber. See Salewski, *Die deutsche Seekriegsleitung*, I. 131.

13 For a short summary of the Atlantic battle, see W. Murray and A. R. Millett, *A War to be Won: Fighting the Second World War* (Cambridge, Mass., 2000), 234–61.

14 Mueller in *DRZW* 5/1. 502–22. A sign of the urgency is the fact that this shift was already being envisioned on 23 May 1940, only two weeks into the French offensive. See BAMA RW19/164, 88.

15 *DRZW* 6. 313–36.

16 Hillgruber, *Hitlers Strategie*, 159–62.

17 A more realistic timetable for producing and bringing into service the larger U-boat fleet was two years. See W. Rahn, 'Strategische Optionen', in B. Thoss and H.-E. Volkmann (eds.), *Erster Weltkrieg: Zweiter Weltkrieg* (Paderborn, 2002), 235. Naval planning in October 1939, which called for U-boat output to rise to as many as 29.3 U-boats per month and assumed losses of only 10 per cent per month, implied that the target would not be reached until the end of 1943. See A. Niestle, 'Wechselwirkung', in Thoss and Volkmann, *Erster Weltkrieg*, 249. In fact, due to strong output and lower than expected losses, Doenitz reached a total strength of 346 U-boats already in August 1942, but was able to deploy a far smaller fraction than expected in the Atlantic.

18 D. Reynolds, *In Command of History: Churchill Fighting and Writing the Second World War* (London, 2004), 184–9.

19 A key point we owe to W. Murray, *Luftwaffe* (London, 1985), 69–107.

20 L. Budrass, *Flugzeugindustrie und Luftruestung in Deutschland* (Duesseldorf, 1998), 557–62 and R. J. Overy, 'From "Uralbomber" to "Amerikabomber": The Luftwaffe and Strategic Bombing', *Journal of Strategic Studies*, 1 (1978), 154–78.

21 See the figures for single-and twin-engined aircraft in British Bombing Survey Unit, *The Strategic Air War Against Germany 1939–1945* (London, 1998), 100.

22 With remarkable accuracy, the British Ministry of Economic Warfare predicted that 'during the second half of 1941 the raw materials blockade might be expected to have serious effects' on the German and Italian economies. It was not believed. W. N. Medlicott, *The Economic Blockade* (London, 1952), I. 415–21.

23 Reynolds, *In Command*, 175.

24 M. M. Postan, *British War Production* (London, 1952), 123–6.

25 Weinberg, *World at Arms*, 205–34.

26 I. B. Holley, *Buying Aircraft: Materiel Procurement for the Army Air Forces* (Washington, 1964), 209–28.

27 H. C. Thomson and L. Mayo, *The Ordnance Department: Procurement and Supply* (Washington, 1960), 24–5.

28 Opinions differ as to what happened to American consumption once the United States entered the war, but there is no argument that in 1940 and 1941 rearmament was good for the American standard of living. H. Rockoff, 'The United States', in M. Harrison (ed.), *The Economics of World War II* (Cambridge, 1998), 91.

29 For the response in Berlin to Roosevelt's rearmament addresses, see S. Friedlaender, *Prelude to Downfall: Hitler and the United States 1939–1941* (London, 1967), 94–7.

30 H. D. Hall, *North American Supply* (London, 1955), 128–9.

31 P. Clavin, *The Great Depression in Europe* (Basingstoke, 2000), 154–7.

32 Roosevelt's preoccupation with aircraft deliveries is brought out clearly by D. Reynolds, *From Munich to Pearl Harbor: Roosevelt's America and the Origins of the Second World War* (Chicago, 2001), 43–6.

33 External assistance is mentioned neither by B. H. Klein, *Germany's Economic Preparations for War* (Cambridge, Mass., 1959), 96–101, nor Mueller, in *DRZW* 5/1. 523–6.

34 M. Harrison, 'Resource Mobilization for World War II', *Economic History Review* (1988), 184.

35 The point made forcefully in Harrison, *The Economics of World War II*, 1–8.

36 See the contemporary assessment in G. Crowther, *Ways and Means of War* (Oxford, 1940). Though rose-tinted for morale-boosting purposes, Crowther's strategic assessment was solidly founded on an understanding of Britain's macroeconomic advantages.

37 Hall, *North American Supply*, 131–45.

38 Ibid., 146–203. In his standard account of the making of the Anglo-American alliance, Reynolds underestimates the longer-term industrial significance of these aircraft talks. See D. Reynolds, *The Creation of the Anglo-American Alliance 1937–41: A Study in Competitive Cooperation* (London, 1981), 108–32. Writing from the German perspective, Friedlaender, *Prelude*, 121, comes closer to giving them the emphasis they deserve.

39 Between the last quarter of 1940 and the last quarter of 1941 the output of combat aircraft in the United States tripled to over 600 units per month. By the third quarter of 1942 it had doubled again to 1,200 per month. Since it took at least twelve months to contract for and build a functioning aircraft factory and six months, at the very least, from raw material to finished aircraft, this expansion must have been initiated in the summer of 1940. Figures from British Bombing Survey Unit, *The Strategic Air War*, 100.

40 R. Overy, 'The Luftwaffe and the European Economy 1939–1945', *MGM* 2 (1979), 55–78.

41 Hall, *North American Supply*, 146–55.

42 Ibid., 170.

43 H. D. Hall and C. C. Wrigley, *Studies of Overseas Supply* (London, 1956), 30. Hall, *North American Supply*, 133.

44 Ibid., 217–18, 265.

45 A point which is fundamental to Hillgruber, *Hitlers Strategie*, 192–397. By contrast, Weinberg has consistently, but unconvincingly, argued that Hitler and the German leadership ignored or underrated Anglo-American economic power. See G. L. Weinberg, *World in the Balance: Behind the Scenes of World War II* (London, 1981), 53–95 and Weinberg, *World at Arms*, 170–86.

46 *ADAP* D XII, doc. 88, 132–4.

47 BAMA RW19/473, 171, Memo drafted in June 1941, months before American entry into the war.

48 *DRZW* 4. 28.

49 *Meldungen*, IV: 10 June 1940, 1236; 13 June 1940, 1249; 17 June 1940, 1262.

50 For anxieties and attitudes in the five months prior to Roosevelt's re-election see *Meldungen*, V: 25 July 1940, 1415; 29 July 1940, 1424; 12 August 1940, 1460; 22 August 1940, 1492; 9 September 1940, 1550; 30 September 1940, 1620; 14 October 1940, 1665; 17 October 1940, 1677; 24 October 1940, 1700; 31 October 1940, 1719; 7 November 1940, 1739; 11 November 1940, 1751–2.

51 P. Gassert, *Amerika im Dritten Reich* (Stuttgart, 1997), 281–8.

52 Friedlaender, *Prelude*, 121–6.

53 Ibid., 160–63.

54 A. Hillgruber, *Staatsmaenner und Diplomaten bei Hitler* (Frankfurt, 1967), I. 344–5. A week earlier he also urged the Spanish to join the war in the hope of forestalling American action; ibid., 329.

55 *DRZW* 4. 58. P. Schramm (ed.), *Kriegstagebuch des Oberkommandos der Wehrmacht* (Frankfurt, 1961), I. 996. See also *Halder Diary*, 18 January 1941, 311.

56 Friedlaender, *Prelude*, 163.

57 Including Koppenberg of Junkers, William Werner of Auto Union and Fritz Siebel, a personal acquaintance of Goering and Udet's. On Siebel, see Mueller, in *DRZW* 5/1. 527–8. As Budrass points out, there is in fact no good evidence for the often repeated assertion that Hitler pooh-poohed Siebel's warnings. Budrass, *Flugzeugindustrie*, 707–8. IWM, Milch Papers, vol. 56, 2926–33.

58 For the French perspective, see H. Chapman, *State Capitalism and Working Class Radicalism in the French Aircraft Industry* (Berkeley, 1991), 237–55.

59 A. S. Milward, *The New Order and the French Economy* (Oxford, 1984), 84.

60 Ibid., 84, directly contradicting Goering's derogatory bluster about American military potential, cited in Weinberg, *World in the Balance*, 84.

61 Milward, *The New Order*, 85.

62 BAMA RW19/177, 7.

63 All figures from Overy, 'The Luftwaffe and the European Economy'.

64 The Germans themselves drew a dispiriting comparison between what Japan was doing for them and what the United States was doing for Britain. See Weinberg, *World in the Balance*, 87.

65 W. Birkenfeld, *Der synthetische Treibstoff 1933–1945* (Goettingen, 1964), 219–20.

66 Calculated on basis of oil consumption estimates, ibid., 218, and Milward, *New Order*, 262.

67 BAMA RW19/164, 127, a threat repeated in even more drastic tones in November 1941: RW19/166, 5.

68 BAMA RW19/165, 347.

69 Murray, *Luftwaffe*, 337–8.

70 BAMA RW19/166, 211.

71 BAMA RW19/166, 19.

72 Central Statistical Office, *Fighting with Figures* (London, 1951), 99. In reading these tables, those used to German conditions must take care to avoid confusing weekly British figures with German monthly returns.

73 Medlicott, *The Economic Blockade* I. 51–2.

74 On Polish coal resources, see W. Roehr, 'Zur Rolle der Schwerindustrie im annektierten polnischen Oberschlesien fuer die Kriegswirtschaft Deutschlands von 1939 bis 1949', *Jahrbuch fuer Wirtschaftsgeschichte*, 4 (1991), 9–58.

75 See the estimate of 97 per cent self-sufficiency quoted uncritically in *DRZW* 5/1. 211.

76 For this and the following see J. R. Gillingham, *Industry and Politics in the Third Reich: Ruhr Coal, Hitler and Europe* (London, 1985), 152; his italics. Much the same could be said for other critical European industries, such as nitrogen, where the notional level of self-sufficiency was 85 per cent but actual production in the autumn of 1940 due to transport difficulties covered 50 per cent of requirement. See BAMA RW/19/164, 99.

77 See BAH R13I 594, 110.

78 Gillingham, *Industry and Politics*, 153.

79 See the discussion in the Wg Eisen 6 June 1941, BAH R13I 595, 244.

80 A linkage acknowledged by the Wehrmacht for Lothringen in BAMA RW19/205, 2–21. They also reported coal supply problems in the East. By the summer of 1941 the Wg Eisen estimated the coal shortfall in France at 50 per cent and Belgium at 40 per cent. See BAH R13I 595, 245.

81 See the frank summary of the situation in BAMA RW19/164, 172.

82 See the dossier of material documenting the industry's grievances in BAH R10VIII, 2.

83 G. Mollin, *Montankonzerne und 'Drittes Reich'* (Goettingen, 1988), 180–83.

84 H. Kehrl, *Krisenmanager im Dritten Reich* (Duesseldorf, 1973), 260–63.

85 BAH R13I 621, 27–9.

86 U. Herbert, *Hitler's Foreign Workers: Enforced Foreign Labour in Germany under the Third Reich* (Cambridge, 1997), 143.

87 See Pleiger's explanation to Thomas of the OKW, BAMA RW19/165, 68–9.

88 This in turn seems to have triggered the argument between Walter and the industry, since Walter was seen as Ley's stooge and the new proposals involved a huge increase in the coal industry's wage bill, which Walter hoped to recoup by squeezing the coal trade.

89 BAMA RW19/165, 75–6.

90 See Herbert, *Hitler's Foreign Workers*, 88–9, 96.

91 For the entire war period there was an 84 per cent correlation between the nutritional content of miners' diet and their coal-cutting performance. W. F. Werner, *Bleib Uebrig! Deutsche Arbeiter in der nationalsozialistischen Kriegswirtschaft* (Duesseldorf, 1983), 300–302.

92 B. Martin and A. S. Milward (eds.), *Agriculture and Food Supply in the Second World War* (Ostfildern, 1985) and K. Brandt, *Management of Agriculture and Food in the German-occupied and Other Areas of Fortress Europe* (Stanford, Calif., 1953).

93 C. Lewis, *Nazi Europe and World Trade* (Washington, 1941), 18–22 and 25–31. Germany's own net import of grain came to 4.116 million tons in 1937 and its import of fats to 604,000 tons.

94 Brandt, *Management of Agriculture and Food in the German-occupied and Other Areas of Fortress Europe*, 518–19. In Spain, the situation over the winter of 1940–41 approached famine conditions and the inability of Germany to guarantee sufficient grain supplies was a major factor in persuading Franco not to declare on the German side. See E. Hernandes-Sandoica and E. Moradiellos, 'Spain and the Second World War, 1939–1945', in N. Wylie (ed.), *European Neutrals and Non-belligerents During the Second World War* (Cambridge, 2002), 241–59. For the famine in Greece, see M. Mazower, *Inside Hitler's Greece* (New Haven, 1993), 23–52.

95 P. Barral, 'Agriculture and Food Supply in France', in Martin and Milward, *Agriculture and Food Supply*, 89.

96 SRA, *Statistisches Jahrbuch fuer das Deutsche Reich (1941/42)* (Berlin, 1942), 295 and 42–3*.

97 A. Hanau and R. Plate, *Die deutsche landwirtschaftliche Preis- und Marktpolitik im Zweiten Weltkrieg* (Stuttgart, 1975), 49.

98 H.-E. Volkmann, *Oekonomie und Expansion: Grundzuege der NS-Wirtschaftspolitik* (Munich, 2003), 393.

99 Note the stark difference in Harrison, *The Economics of World War II*, 7–10, between table 1.2 which counts 'Axis gains' by 1942 in terms of GDP in 1938, and table 1.3 which shows France's actual wartime GDP.

100 *DRZW* 4. 150–51.

101 In the long run there were of course ample opportunities for the development of the Western European economic bloc. See for instance H. von der Decken, 'Die Intensivierung der europaeischen Landwirtschaft', *Vierteljahrshefte zur Wirtschaftsforschung*, NF 2/3 (1940–41), 94–119. But these were irrelevant within the time parameters set by the war.

102 Though I follow Weinberg in stressing the symmetry of this relationship, one must insist that the balance was hugely favourable to Britain. See Weinberg, *World in the Balance*, 84.

103 The central thesis of H. Schwendemann, *Die wirtschaftliche Zusammenarbeit zwischen dem Deutschen Reich und der Sowjetunion von 1939 bis 1941: Alternative zu Hitlers Ostprogramm?* (Berlin, 1993).

104 Hillgruber, *Hitlers Strategie*, 241–5, 317–20.

105 Reynolds, *From Munich*, 89–92.

106 Hillgruber, *Hitlers Strategie*, 409–19.

107 C. R. Browning, *The Path to Genocide: Essays on Launching the Final Solution* (Cambridge, 1992), 18–19. C. R. Browning, *The Origins of the Final Solution: The Evolution of Nazi Jewish Policy. September 1939-March 1942* (Lincoln, Nebr., 2004), 81–8.

108 *Halder Diary*, 5 December 1940, 294.

109 *DRZW* 4. 151–2.

110 BAMA RW19/164, 114. *DRZW* 4. 204. The Germans also took seriously Soviet complaints in May 1941 about shortfalls in coal deliveries, BAMA RW19/165, 69.

111 For worries about rubber in October 1940, see BAMA RW19/164, 80–85.

112 BAMA RW19/164, 117.

113 *DRZW* 4. 204–5.

114 *Halder Diary*, 23 December 1940, 308. *DRZW* 5. 200.

115 *DRZW* 4. 207 and *Halder Diary*, 291.

116 *DRZW* 4. 38–41.

117 *Halder Diary*, 31 July 1940, 244 and Hillgruber, *Zerstoerung*, 192.

118 *DRZW* 4. 159.

119 Hillgruber, *Zerstoerung*, 193–4. As Weinberg points out, 'having tried to turn the Japanese against the Western powers since 1938' Hitler was 'happy to give the pact the broadest and most aggressive interpretation'; Weinberg, *World in the Balance*, 86.

120 Kershaw, *Hitler: Nemesis*, 349–53.

121 Jersak's most recent effort to separate strategic and ideological motivations from 'concrete economic and food policy interests' seems highly artificial. Hitler's strategy was ideologically tinged and his strategic calculations had consistently revolved, since *Mein Kampf* and his 'Second Book', around 'concrete' issues of food and raw material supply and industrial capacity. See T. Jersak's contribution to *DRZW* 9/1. 284–5.

13 Preparing for Two Wars at Once

1 For the views of military historians, see A. J. Levine, 'Was World War II a Near-run Thing?', *Journal of Strategic Studies*, 8 (1985), 51–7.

2 J. K. Galbraith, 'Germany was Badly Run', *Fortune* (December 1945), 200. For a vigorous critique, see P. Hayes, 'Polycracy and Policy in the Third Reich: The Case of the Economy', in T. Childers and J. Caplan (eds.), *Reevaluating the Third Reich* (New York, 1993), 190–210.

3 Galbraith, 'Germany', 200.

4 R. Wagenfuehr, *Die deutsche Industrie im Kriege* (Berlin, 1954), 25. For a critical analysis of Wagenfuehr's flawed statistics, see J. A. Tooze, 'No Room for Miracles', *GG*, 31 (2005), 439–64.

5 A. Speer, *Inside the Third Reich* (London, 1970), 250–65, and W. Bleyer, 'Der geheime Bericht ueber die Ruestung des faschistischen Deutschlands vom 27. Januar 1945', *Jahrbuch fuer Wirtschaftsgeschichte* (1969), 347–68.

6 See H. Kehrl, 'Kriegswirtschaft und Ruestungsindustrie', in *Bilanz des Zweiten Weltkrieges. Erkenntnisse und Verpflichtungen fuer die Zukunft* (Oldenbourg, 1953), 272–7. For Kehrl's association with the revisionist far right, see his article 'Zum Untergang des Dritten Reiches', *Historische Tatsachen*, 8 (Vlotho, 1981), published by the Verlag fuer Volkstum und Zeitgeschichtsforschung.

7 R. J. Overy, *Goering* (London, 1984), 138 summarizes the period 1940–41 as an 'era of egotism and incompetence', a period in which Germany squandered its chance to win the war. By contrast with many others, Overy is commendably frank in his willingness to couple this kind of judgement with open counterfactual speculation about the possibility of alternative outcomes to the war. By contrast, the history of World War II produced by the Militaergeschichtliches Forschungsamt speaks of Germany 'squandering its armaments advantage' in 1940 and 1941, but is less willing to engage in overt counterfactual argument. *DRZW* 5/1. 486–522.

8 S. Friedlaender, *Prelude to Downfall: Hitler and the United States 1939–1941* (London, 1967), 158 points out that orders to Thomas of the OKW to prepare for a long war followed only days after Roosevelt's re-election on 6 November 1940.

9 M. L. Recker, *Nationalsozialistische Sozialpolitik im Zweiten Weltkrieg* (Munich, 1985), 128–54, and G. Corni and H. Gies, *Blut und Boden: Rassenideologie und Agrarpolitik im Staat Hitlers* (Idstein, 1994), 61.

10 An approach exemplified at its painstaking best by Mueller, in *DRZW* 5/1.

11 See the summary of the situation in September 1940 in BAMA RW19/205, 22–39.

12 A point sometimes lost in more academic accounts but brought out with dramatic force in A. Clark, *Barbarossa: The Russian-German Conflict 1941–1945* (London, 1965), 44–57.

13 Mueller, in *DRZW* 5/1. 513.

14 As explained by Todt in BAMA RW19/164, 100.

15 Data in Mueller, in *DRZW* 5/1. 554–5. On the centrality of the Mark III to tank planning, see *Halder Diary*, 5 December 1940, 297.

16 For the following, see H. H. Knittel, *Panzerfertigung im Zweiten Weltkrieg: Industrieproduktion fuer die deutsche Wehrmacht* (Herford, 1988), 30–44.

17 On this important technical transition, W. J. Spielberger, *Die Panzer-Kampfwagen I und II* (Stuttgart, 3rd edn., 1991), and W. J. Spielberger and F. Wiener, *Die deutschen Panzerkampfwagen III und IV mit ihren Abarten 1935–1945* (Munich, 1968).

18 In September 1939 only 84,078 of the Wehrmacht's total of 126,800 machine guns were of modern MG 34 type. See F. Hahn, *Waffen und Geheimwaffen des deutschen Heeres 1933–1945* (Bonn, 3rd edn., 1998), I. 56–61.

19 For details, see J. A. Tooze, 'Arming the Reich: Armaments Production in Hitler's Germany' (forthcoming), available from the author's website. See also Eichholtz, II. 7–9 and 36–40.

20 BAMA RH8I 1012, 202.

21 The importance of ammunition production is often overlooked in unfavourable comparisons of the early mobilization of the German and British economies. The comparative tables in M. Harrison (ed.), *Economics of World War II* (Cambridge, 1998), 15–16, ignore ammunition altogether. In fact, Germany outproduced Britain by a factor of 4 to 1 in artillery shells in 1940 and 2 to 1 in 1941. B. H. Klein, *Germany's Economic Preparations for War* (Cambridge, Mass., 1959), 98.

22 For steel allocation figures, see Mueller, in *DRZW* 5/2. 555.

23 For the following, see the contributions by Kroener to *DRZW* 5/1 and 5/2. The only criticism one can make of Kroener is that his account of labour policy is not correlated sufficiently with the simultaneous decisions about raw materials.

24 These data from Kroener, in *DRZW* 5/2. 854–5.

25 Kroener, in *DRZW* 5/1. 883.

26 Kroener, in *DRZW* 5/1. 959.

27 See the final report dated 16 May 1941, BAMA RW19/294, 6–20. As is clear from his angry reaction to the discrepancy between actual output and maximum capacity as of May, Hitler did not fully understand this. See BAMA RW19/165, 55 and 61.

28 BAMA RW19/164, 192.

29 Kroener, in *DRZW* 5/1. 868–9.

30 For a critical re-examination, see Tooze, 'No Room for Miracles'.

31 R. J. Overy, *War and Economy in the Third Reich* (Oxford, 1994), 346. In fact, in light of the production data cited by Overy himself in his Ph.D. dissertation, this is clearly a misstatement. See R. J. Overy, 'German Aircraft Production 1939–1942: A Study in German War Economy' (Cambridge, Ph.D. 1978), 151. The data in the later publication should be taken as referring to 1941 alone. Over the entire period between 1939 and 1941 both employment and output roughly doubled.

32 Sources in Tooze, 'Arming the Reich'.

33 See the figures for army, navy and Luftwaffe labour forces in Kroener, in *DRZW* 5/1. 788, and PRO FO 1078/138.

34 Thanks to Lutz Budrass for supplying employment data for the Luftwaffe between 1939 and 1943.

35 Setting aside the unconvincing claims about productivity, this is the essential message of Overy, 'German Aircraft Production', 53.

36 This was made explicit by Keitel on 20 May 1941 in discussion of the post-Barbarossa armaments programme. See BAMA RW19/165, 55.

37 *DRZW* 4. 159.

38 R. Krengel, *Anlagevermoegen, Produktion und Beschaeftigung der Industrie im Gebiete der Bundesrepublik von 1924 bis 1956* (Berlin, 1958).

39 Knittel, *Panzerfertigung*, 49. These figures would imply a tank strength per division similar to that prevailing in the spring of 1940 before the 'dilution' preceding Barbarossa.

40 *DRZW* 4. 221.

41 The fantastic aspect of these plans lay not in the monthly production figures but in the idea of operating with a tank force of 15,000 vehicles. The vast majority of the Panzers produced after May 1941 were destroyed in combat within months of leaving the factory. At the high point of its tank strength in 1944 the Wehrmacht disposed of less than 9,700

fighting vehicles, of which half were relatively cheap assault guns, see Mueller, in *DRZW* 5/2. 654.

42 Knittel, *Panzerfertigung*, 49. As in the case of the Luftwaffe discussed above, the point at issue is the importance of decisions taken prior to February 1942.

43 USSBS, *Tank Industry Report* (Washington, 1945), 6–7.

44 B. Hopmann, *Von der MONTAN zur Industrieverwaltungsgesellschaft (IVG) 1916–1951* (Stuttgart, 1996), a book whose title gives no indication of the vital importance of its subject matter.

45 See Goering's decision on priorities, 3 February 1941, BAMA RW19/164, 129.

46 BAMA RW19/166, 233, as is also borne out by Krauch's comment in the spring of 1939.

47 W. Birkenfeld, *Der synthetische Treibstoff 1933–1945* (Goettingen, 1964), 164.

48 On this hotly contested topic see P. Hayes, *Industry and Ideology: IG Farben in the Nazi Era* (Cambridge, 1987), 347–68, G. Plumpe, *Die IG Farbenindustrie AG* (Berlin, 1990), 378–90, R. J. van Pelt and D. Dwork, *Auschwitz: 1270 to the Present* (New Haven, 1996), 197–235, P. Hayes and H. Deichmann, 'Standort Auschwitz: Eine Kontroverse', 1999, 11 (1996), 79–101, F. Schmaltz and K. H. Roth, 'Neue Dokumente zur Vorgeschichte des IG Farben-Werks Auschwitz-Monowitz', 1999, 13 (1998), 100–16 and B. C. Wagner, *IG Auschwitz: Zwangsarbeit und Vernichtung von Haeftlingen des Lagers Monowitz 1941–1945* (Munich, 2000).

49 Hayes, *Industry and Ideology*, 351, and Plumpe, *Die IG Farbenindustrie*, 389.

50 See H. Mommsen, *Mythen der Modernisierung: Zur Entwicklung der Ruestungsindustrie im Dritten Reich* (Essen, 1999).

51 Wagner, *IG Auschwitz*, 7, 10, 287.

52 As Sybille Steinbacher has pointed out, the camp and industrial site were the foundation of a thriving experiment in urban Germanization in Eastern Silesia. See S. Steinbacher, *'Musterstadt' Auschwitz: Germanisierungspolitik und Judenmord in Ostoberschlesien* (Munich, 2000).

53 See the comments made by Himmler during his visit to IG's building site on 18 July 1942. IMT, IG Farben Case VIII, NI 14551, 477–8.

54 The role of the IG Farben manager Johann Giesen, who was later employed in the Swiss chemicals industry, in the development of methanol production at Auschwitz has been highlighted by Lukas Straumann in his contribution to the OnlineReports.che website, 'Das dunkelste Kapitel in Christoph Blochers Ems Chemie'. See also J. R. White, 'Target Auschwitz: Historical and Hypothetical German Responses to Allied Attack', *Holocaust and Genocide Studies*, 16 (2002), 54–76.

55 USSBS, *Over-all Report (European War)* (Washington, 1945), 51.

56 D. Petzina, *Autarkiepolitik in Dritten Reich* (Stuttgart, 1968), 183.

57 For a detailed account of Ford's wartime production, see the in-house history in Benson Ford Research Center, Acc. 435.

58 L. Budrass, *Flugzeugindustrie und Luftruestung in Deutschland* (Duesseldorf, 1998), 707–11.

59 Ibid., 636.

60 On the Me 110 and its ill-fated successor, see H. J. Ebert, J. B. Kaiser, K. Peters, *Willy Messerschmitt* (Bonn, 1992), 150–75, P. Schmoll, *Die Messerschmittwerke im Zweiten Weltkrieg* (Regensburg, 1998), 56–60 and A. van Ishoven, *Messerschmitt: Aircraft Designer* (London, 1975), 149–65.

61 K. Orth, *Das System der nationalsozialistischen Konzentrationslager* (Hamburg, 1999), 175–9, Budrass, *Flugzeugindustrie*, 775–87.

62 M. Griehl and J. Dressel, *Heinkel He 177, 277, 274* (Shrewsbury, 1998). Fires were caused by hydraulic fluid leaking on to the hot exhaust. See H.-J. Braun, 'Krieg der Ingenieure?', in B. Thoss and H.-E. Volkmann (eds.), *Erster Weltkrieg: Zweiter Weltkrieg* (Paderborn, 2002), 208.

63 R. Schabel, *Die Illusion der Wunderwaffen: Duesenflugzeuge und Flugabwehrraketen in der Ruestungspolitik des Dritten Reiches* (Munich, 1994), 177.

64 P. Bohn, *Reichskommisariat Norwegen: 'Nationalsozialistische Neuordnung' und Kriegs-wirtschaft* (Munich, 2000), 395. Interestingly, the United States was unhesitatingly identified as an enemy power.

65 Budrass, *Flugzeugindustrie*, 602–18.

66 Ibid., 645–9.

67 This may well have been Ford's facility for the mass-production of Pratt and Whitney radial engines at River Rouge. Benson Ford Research Center, Acc. 435, box 5.

68 N. Gregor, *Daimler-Benz in the Third Reich* (New Haven, 1998), 128–31.

69 Ibid., 84–100.

70 Ibid., 118, 125–6.

71 Budrass, *Flugzeugindustrie*, 648 and 659.

72 Ibid., 715–16.

73 Eichholtz, II. 13–19. Budrass, *Flugzeugindustrie*, 718.

74 See the text of Milch's presentation to the OKW military economic office of 26 June 1941 in G. Thomas, *Geschichte der deutschen Wehr- und Ruestungswirtschaft* (Boppard, 1966), 448–51. It is probably this presentation which triggered Thomas's highly pessimistic reflections dated 'end of June', BAMA RW19/473, 167–76, in which he spoke of 'the effective entry into the war of the United States on the side of England'.

75 Birkenfeld, *Der synthetische Treibstoff*, 164, Budrass, *Flugzeugindustrie*, 718, and Eichholtz, II. 13–18. The German navy in November 1941 made the same assumption, demanding the occupation of Maikop by December 1941 so as to enable oil production to begin by the spring of 1942. See W. Meier-Doernberg, *Die Oelversorgung der Kriegsmarine 1935 bis 1945* (Freiburg, 1973), 59.

76 Harrison, *The Economics of World War II*, 7–8.

77 *Halder Diary*, 5 December 1940, 297.

78 *DRZW* 4. 271–94.

79 K. A. F. Schueler, *Logistik im Russlandfeldzug* (Frankfurt, 1987).

80 *Halder Diary*, 28 January 1941.

81 Schueler, *Logistik*, 190–91, 198–9.

82 For a brilliant overview, see M. van Creveld, *Supplying War: Logistics from Wallenstein to Patton* (Cambridge, 1977), 142–201.

83 R. L. DiNardo, *Mechanized Juggernaut or Military Anachronism? Horses and the German Army of World War II* (New York, 1991), 35–54.

84 R. Goralski and R. W. Freeburg, *Oil & War* (New York, 1987), 348.

85 For emphasizing this point I am particularly grateful to M. Harrison.

86 See Davies, 'Industry', in R. W. Davies, M. Harrison and S. G. Wheatcroft, *The Economic Transformation of the Soviet Union, 1913–1945* (Cambridge, 1999), 150.

87 M. Harrison, 'Soviet Industrialization and the Test of War', *HWJ* 29 (1990), 65–84.

88 *DRZW* 4. 272–3.

89 Figures refer to 1938. See *Statistisches Jahrbuch fuer die Eisen- und Stahlindustrie* (Duesseldorf, 1939), 204.

90 *Halder Diary*, 17 February 1941, 320, and 30 March 1941, 345.

91 *DRZW* 4. 59.

92 W. Goerlitz, *Paulus and Stalingrad* (London, 1963), 107.

93 *DRZW* 4. 278–9.

94 *DRZW* 4. 288–94.

95 *Halder Diary*, 28 January 1941, 313–14.

96 *DRZW* 4. 272–3.

97 *DRZW* 4. 158–9.

98 BAMA RW19/164 106, 119.

99 BAMA RW19/164 108, 115.

100 BAMA RW19/164, 126. See also the calculations done by the Reichsnaehrstand about a 10 per cent reduction in Soviet food consumption, RW19/164, 150.

101 For a devastating indictment of Thomas's volte-face, see *DRZW* 4. 170–71.

102 BAMA RW19/164, 108.

103 Ironically, once the campaign started Thomas was again beset by profound doubts. See BAMA RW19/473, 167–76.

104 See von Weizaecker in *DRZW* 4. 185 and *DGFP*, D XII, 661–2, doc. 419.

14 The Grand Strategy of Racial War

1 P. Burrin, *Hitler and the Jews: The Genesis of the Holocaust* (London, 1994), 84–5.

2 For a review of relevant comparative literature, see J. Zimmerer, 'Holocaust und Kolonialismus', *Zeitschrift fuer Geschichtswissenschaft*, 51 (2003), 1098–119. As Zimmerer points out, the key difference between 1941 and nineteenth-century colonialism is the prominent role of the state.

3 We owe this fundamental insight above all to C. Madajczyk, *Die Okkupationspolitik Nazideutschlands in Polen 1939–1945* (Berlin, 1987), of which the first Polish edition appeared in 1970, followed by G. Aly and S. Heim, *Vordenker der Vernichtung: Auschwitz und die deutsche Plaene fuer eine neue europaeische Ordnung* (Hamburg, 1991) and G. Aly, *'Endloesung': Voelkerverschiebung und der Mord an den europaeischen Juden* (Frankfurt, 1995).

4 Aly, *'Endloesung'*, 59–138.

5 C. Madajczyk (ed.), *Vom Generalplan Ost zum Generalsiedlungsplan* (Munich, 1994), 3–14, doc. 1.

6 Aly, *'Endloesung'*, 163–206. Over the course of the war the DUT property firm was to handle 5–6 billion Reichsmarks worth of assets. See IMT XII. 599–643. Chair of its supervisory board was Wilhelm Keppler.

7 Aly, *'Endloesung'*, 210.

8 I. Kershaw, *Hitler 1936–1945: Nemesis* (London, 2000), 348–53.

9 P. Longerich, *Politik der Vernichtung: Eine Gesamtdarstellung der nationalsozialistischen Judenfolgung* (Munich, 1998), 287–91. Aly, *'Endloesung'*, 268–79.

10 Kershaw, *Hitler: Nemesis*, 354.

11 On the ghastly massacres of 'counter-revolutionary elements' perpetrated by the retreating NKVD in occupied Polish territories, which further reinforced this connection in the minds both of the Germans and the local non-Jewish population, see B. Musial, *'Konterrevolutionaere Elemente sind zu erschiessen': Die Brutalisierung des deutschsowjetischen Krieges im Sommer 1941* (Munich, 2000), 98–297.

12 Aly, *'Endloesung'*, 290. D. Pohl, *Von der 'Judenpolitik' zum Judenmord: Der Distrikt Lublin des Generalgouvernements 1939–1944* (Frankfurt, 1993), 89, 95–7. Hitler apparently gave an order for the removal of the entire Polish population in March 1941. J. E. Schulte, *Zwangsarbeit und Vernichtung: Das Wirtschaftsimperium der SS* (Paderborn, 2001), 248.

13 Madajczyk, *Vom Generalplan Ost*, 14–15, doc. 2, Prof. Dr Konrad Meyer to Himmler, 15 July 1941. See also I. Heinemann, *'Rasse, Siedlung, deutsches Blut': Das Rasse- und Siedlungshauptamt der SS und die rassenpolitische Neuordnung Europas* (Goettingen, 2003), 359–76.

14 For a novel stress on the importance of the economic and construction administration, see Schulte, *Zwangsarbeit*, 239–79.

15 For a statistical picture of the expanding scope of the Final Solution between June 1940 and the end of 1941, see Aly, *'Endloesung'*, 303.

16 Madajczyk, *Vom Generalplan Ost*, 50–81, doc. 16, Stellungnahme und Gedanken von Dr Erhard Wetzel zum Generalplan Ost.

17 Ibid., 91–130, doc. 23, Denkschrift Generalplan Ost rechtliche wirtschaftliche und raeumliche Grundlagen des Ostaufbaus, June 1942.

18 Ibid., 265, doc. 74, notes taken by Hermann Krummey, 1–2 February 1943.

19 C. R. Browning, *The Origins of the Final Solution: The Evolution of Nazi Jewish Policy. September 1939–March 1942* (Lincoln, Nebr., 2004), 241, points out that the May

1942 version of the Generalplan includes a passage which moderates the demand for the immediate and total evacuation of the local population. This however is ambiguous, referring simply to the need to gain support of the local population and the need to move them to collective farms, which indicates that it was a concession that applied to former Soviet territory not Poland. That the complete *Eindeutschung* of the General Government, Estland and Lettland should be achieved within twenty years was emphatically restated by Himmler a few weeks later. See Madajczyk, *Vom Generalplan Ost*, 133–4, doc. 27.

20 M. Roessler and S. Schleiermacher, *Der 'Generalplan Ost': Hauptlinie der nationalsozialistischen Planungs- und Vernichtungspolitik* (Berlin, 1993), 48–52, doc. 2, Referat Dr Ehlich, 10–11 December 1942.

21 See the documents in C. Madajczyk, *Zamojszczyzna – Sonderlaboratorium SS* (Warsaw, 1977), I. 49–140, Madajczyk, *Die Okkupationspolitik*, 424–7, Heinemann, *'Rasse'*, 376–415, and Pohl, *Von der 'Judenpolitik'*, 113–57.

22 Madajczyk, *Sonderlaboratorium*, 155–7, 175–6.

23 For a harrowing personal account of the chaotic situation in the Zamość region by a Polish doctor and antiquarian, see Z. Klukowski, *Diary from the Years of Occupation 1939–1944* (Urbana, Ill., 1993).

24 See the maps in Roessler and Schleiermacher, *Der 'Generalplan Ost'*, 62–6.

25 Madajczyk, *Vom Generalplan Ost*, 389, Anlage 2.

26 K. Meyer 'Neues Landvolk', in K. Meyer, *Landvolk im Werden* (Berlin, 1942), 21. See also the discussion in W. Pyta, 'Das Dorf im Fadenkreuz der Politik', in D. Muenkel (ed.), *Der lange Abschied vom Agrarland* (Goettingen, 2000), 209–26.

27 Kershaw, *Hitler: Nemesis*, 434.

28 In 1939 France had a population density of 75.1 per square kilometre as opposed to 133.5 in Germany, 194.6 for the United Kingdom and 283.3 for Belgium. See SRA, *Statistisches Jahrbuch fuer das Deutsche Reich (1941/42)* (Berlin, 1942), 7*.

29 Madajczyk, *Vom Generalplan Ost*, 3–14, doc. 1 Planungsgrundlagen, April–May 1940.

30 In organizational terms Meyer was to form the linchpin between the Agricultural Ministry and SS as Reichskommissar, see Madajczyk, *Vom Generalplan Ost*, 132–3, doc. 26.

31 Ibid., 12, doc. 1.

32 W. Pyta, 'Menschenoekonomie: Das Ineinandergreifen von laendlicher Sozialraumgestaltung und rassenbiologischer Bevoelkerungspolitik im NS-Staat', *HZ* 273 (2001), 31–94.

33 Madajczyk, *Vom Generalplan Ost*, 127, doc. 23.

34 Ibid., 48, doc. 14.

35 Ibid., 91–123, doc. 23. In so-called Geary-Khamis dollars of 1990, this was $172 billion and $288.1 billion respectively. To translate Reichsmarks of the inter-war period into dollars of 1990, multiply the Reichsmark figure by a factor of 4.3. This figure is arrived at by dividing the contemporary estimate of GDP in 1937 Reichsmarks of 73.757 billion Reichsmarks, into Maddison's estimate of German GDP in 1937 as $317.7 billion of 1990.

36 On this basis, the scale of the Generalplan in 'modern terms' is even more huge. A proposal to spend two-thirds of German GDP in 2001 on a single investment project would be a proposal to spend in the order of a trillion 1990 dollars.

37 Madajczyk, *Vom Generalplan Ost*, 88, doc. 21.

38 Ibid., 109, doc. 23.

39 Schulte, *Zwangsarbeit*, 332–64.

40 J. E. Schulte, 'Vom Arbeits- zum Vernichtungslager: Die Entstehungsgeschichte von Auschwitz-Birkenau 1941/42', *VfZ* 50 (2002), 48.

41 Dr Hans Kammler, born in 1901, studied at the Technische Hochschule Danzig and Munich, taking his Ph.D. in November 1932 after years of practical work in local building administration. He joined the party in March 1932, the SS in May 1933 and the Reichsernaehrungsministerium in 1933. He moved to the Air Ministry in June 1936 and joined SS administration as a full-time official, with the rank of SS Standartenfuehrer, in August 1940. He was to become the leading slave-driver of the SS.

42 Exactly the same groups, though in a different order, were named by Kammler in early February. See Schulte, *Zwangsarbeit*, 346.

43 For a good summary of the transformation of the concentration camp system in 1941–2, see K. Orth, *Das System der nationalsozialistischen Konzentrationslager* (Hamburg, 1999), 141–68. See also J. Tuchel, 'Dimensionen des Terrors: Funktionen der Konzentrationslager in Deutschland 1933–1945', in D. Dahlmann and G. Hirschfeld (eds.). *Lager, Zwangsarbeit, Vertreibung und Deportation: Dimensionen der Massenverbrechen in der Sowjetunion und in Deutschland 1933 bis 1945* (Essen, 1999), 371–89.

44 R.-J. van Pelt, 'A Site in Search of a Mission', in Y. Gutman and M. Berenbaum (eds.), *Anatomy of the Auschwitz Death Camp* (Bloomington, Ind., 1994), 93–156, and Schulte, 'Vom Arbeits- zum Vernichtungslager'. By October the target for Auschwitz had been raised to 100,000 inmates.

45 Longerich, *Politik*, 480.

46 I see no reason to treat this proposal as a euphemistic cover for a secret programme of executions whether by shooting or gas and in this respect I follow Longerich, *Politik*, 466–82, Kershaw, *Hitler: Nemesis*, 491–3, and H. Mommsen, *Auschwitz 17. Juli 1942* (Munich, 2002), 160–63. By contrast, both Aly, *'Endloesung'*, 362, and Browning, *The Origins*, 411–12, insist that a decision for immediate, execution-style killing had already been taken and that Heydrich was speaking in code.

47 We owe our awareness of this remarkable fact first to R.-D. Mueller's contribution to *DRZW* 4. 184–93, originally published in 1982, and more recently to work by Aly and Heim, *Vordenker der Vernichtung*, 365–93, C. Gerlach, *Kalkulierte Morde: Die deutsche Wirtschafts- und Vernichtungspolitik in Weissrussland 1941 bis 1944* (Hamburg, 1999) and C. Gerlach, *Krieg, Ernaehrung, Voelkermord: Deutsche Vernichtungspolitik im Zweiten Weltkrieg* (Zurich, 2nd edn., 2001).

48 This had been the subject of Backe's failed Ph.D. dissertation, 'Die Russische Getreidewirtschaft als Grundlage der Land- und Volkswirtschaft Russlands' (1925–6), which in 1941 was issued as confidential background information for the occupation authorities in the Soviet Union.

49 See the Reichsbank's pessimistic report of June 1941, BAL R2501 7007, 233–56.

50 IMT XXXI. 84.

51 For the following, see Gerlach, *Kalkulierte Morde*, 46–59.

52 Browning, *The Origins*, 240.

53 The position was reiterated in the autumn of 1941. See IMT XIII. 855–63, NI-440.

54 Wirtschaftspolitische Richtlinien, 23 May 1941, in IMT XXXVI. 141.

55 H. Krausnick, *Die Truppe des Weltanschauungskrieges: Die Einsatzgruppen der Sicherheitspolizei und des SD, 1938–1942* (Stuttgart, 1981) and P. Klein (ed.), *Die Einsatzgruppen in der besetzten Sowjetunion, 1941/42* (Berlin, 1997).

56 T. Sandkuehler, 'Judenpolitik und Judenmord im Distrikt Galizien, 1941–1942', in U. Herbert (ed.), *Nationalsozialistische Vernichtungspolitik 1939–1945: Neue Forschungen und Kontroversen* (Frankfurt, 1998), 122–47.

57 Gerlach, *Kalkulierte Morde*, 265–318.

58 Ibid., 668–74.

59 See the extraordinary, path-breaking study by C. Streit, *Keine Kameraden: Die Wehrmacht und die sowjetischen Kriegsgefangenen 1941–1945* (Stuttgart, 1978), followed by A. Streim, *Behandlung sowjetischer Kriegsgefangenen im 'Fall Barbarossa'* (Heidelberg, 1981).

60 Streit, *Keine Kameraden*, 128–37.

61 See for instance Goering's appeal for more security divisions to prevent the population for 'gypsying around' and consuming what food was available. BAL R26IV 51, 18 September 1941.

62 KTB WiKdo Bobruisk, January 1942, quoted in Gerlach, *Kalkulierte Morde*, 277.

63 Ibid., 255.

64 Supplementary deliveries for six months, plus the creation of a two-month reserve, were

agreed in late November 1941, but only on condition that Wehrmacht rations were reduced. BAMA RW19/166, 25, 36.
65 BAMA RW19/166, 665.
66 J. Barber and A. R. Dzeniskevich (eds.), *Life and Death in Besieged Leningrad* (Basingstoke, 2005), and H. E. Salisbury, *The 900 Days: The Siege of Leningrad* (London, 1969).
67 For the following, see Madajczyk, *Vom Generalplan Ost*, 440–42, Anlage 8, and G. Hass, 'Leben, Sterben und Ueberleben im belagerten Leningrad (1941–1944)', *Zeitschrift fuer Geschichtswissenschaft*, 50 (2002), 1080–98.
68 D. M. Glantz, *The Siege of Leningrad, 1941–1944* (Staplehurst, 2001), 75–81.
69 N. Cherepina, 'Assessing the Scale of the Famine and Death', in Barber and Dzeniskevich (eds.), *Life and Death*, 28–71.

15 December 1941: Turning Point

1 *DGFP* D XII, 1066–9.
2 *Halder Diary*, 3 July 1941, 446–7.
3 Ibid., 26 July 1941, 486–7.
4 On the crucial significance of the Smolensk battle, see A. Hillgruber, 'Die Bedeutung der Schlacht von Smolensk', in A. Hillgruber, *Die Zerstoerung Europas: Beitraege zur Weltkriegsepoche 1914 bis 1945* (Frankfurt, 1988), 296–312.
5 *Halder Diary*, 20 July 1941, 482, 22 July 1941, 483, 26 July 1941, 485, 30 July 1941, 489, 3 August 1941, 494.
6 W. Murray and A. R. Millett, *A War to be Won: Fighting the Second World War* (Cambridge, Mass., 2000), 128. D. M. Glantz and J. M. House, *When Titans Clashed: How the Red Army Stopped Hitler* (Lawrence, Kan., 1995), 58–61.
7 Quoted in Hillgruber, 'Smolensk', 30 and K. A. F. Schueler, *Logistik im Russlandfeldzug* (Frankfurt, 1987), 359.
8 Quoted in K. Reinhardt, *Moscow – the Turning Point: The Failure of Hitler's Strategy in the Winter of 1941–1942* (Oxford, 1992), 47.
9 The idea that there was a lost opportunity for Army Group Centre to have advanced directly towards Moscow in August 1941, advocated principally by Franz Halder both during and after the war, ignores the logistical constraints that prevented any kind of significant attack before mid-September 1941. See M. van Creveld, *Supplying War: Logistics from Wallenstein to Patton* (Cambridge, 1977), 16–174, and Schueler, *Logistik*, 368–84.
10 *Halder Diary*, 12 August 1941, 505–6.
11 Glantz and House, *When Titans*, 68.
12 M. Harrison, 'Resource Mobilization for World War II', *Economic History Review* (1988), 184.
13 A symbiosis brilliantly described in S. Kotkin, *Magnetic Mountain: Stalinism as Civilization* (Berkeley, 1997).
14 Reinhardt, *Moscow*, 39, and I. Kershaw, *Hitler 1936–1945: Nemesis* (London, 2000), 417.
15 Ibid., 412.
16 *DRZW* 9/1. 304–9.
17 For the following, see P. Herde, 'Japan, Deutschland und die Vereinigten Staaten', and J. Rohwer, 'Die USA und die Schlacht im Atlantik 1941', in Rohwer and E. Jaeckel (eds.), *Kriegswende Dezember 1941* (Koblenz, 1984), 36–54 and 81–103.
18 W. Rahn, 'Strategische Optionen', in B. Thoss and H.-E. Volkmann (eds.), *Erster Weltkrieg: Zweiter Weltkrieg* (Paderborn, 2002), 237.
19 Hillgruber, 'Hitler und die USA', in *Zerstoerung*, 195.
20 Kershaw, *Hitler: Nemesis*, 442–4.
21 *Halder Diary*, 21 July 1941 to 24 August 1941, 482–516.
22 Kershaw, *Hitler: Nemesis*, 415–16.

23 Reinhardt, *Moscow*, 57–60.
24 Kershaw, *Hitler: Nemesis*, 416.
25 Schueler, *Logistik*, 400. Kershaw, *Hitler: Nemesis*, 431.
26 As argued by C. R. Browning, *The Origins of the Final Solution: The Evolution of Nazi Jewish Policy. September 1939–March 1942* (Lincoln, Nebr., 2004), 370–73. For a contrasting thesis, which places Hitler's decision to prepare for wholesale murder in August, but insists on the fact that timing and method of killing was left open, see Jersak in *DRZW* 9/1. 304–5.
27 Murray and Millett, *War to be Won*, 131–3. Glantz and House, *When Titans*, 78–81.
28 J. Barber and M. Harrison, *The Soviet Home Front, 1941–1945: A Social and Economic History of the USSR in World War II* (London, 1991), 64.
29 Schueler, *Logistik*, 403.
30 Glantz and House, *When Titans*, 80–81.
31 As K. H. Frieser, *Blitzkrieg-Legende: Der Westfeldzug 1940* (Munich, 1996), 208–11, makes clear, but for their heroics the attack on Sedan might well have stalled.
32 See the discussion chaired by Keitel on 18 August 1941, BAMA RW19/177, 222–34.
33 BAMA RW19/165, 297, OKW Wi Rue Amt note, 24 October 1941.
34 BAMA RW19/166, 71.
35 BAMA RW19/166, 2. See also W. Meier-Doernberg, *Die Oelversorgung der Kriegsmarine 1935 bis 1945* (Freiburg, 1973), 59–63.
36 It was not just fuel that was in short supply. The constant pressure to repair the bomb- and torpedo-damage suffered by the big ships during their brief and largely futile sorties was blocking valuable dockyard space and limiting U-boat construction. See Rahn, 'Strategische Optionen', in Thoss and Volkmann (eds.), *Erster Weltkrieg*, 236.
37 BAMA RW19/177, 135–8.
38 BAMA RW19/166, 5–6.
39 BAL R2501/7007, 266–9.
40 A later report by the Reichsbank estimated that the price of scarce civilian goods had risen by 60 per cent, despite official controls. See BAL R2501/7007, 330–38.
41 BAL R2501/7007, 268.
42 BAL R2501/7007, 332.
43 L. Herbst, *Der Totale Krieg und die Ordnung der Wirtschaft: Die Kriegswirtschaft im Spannungsfeld von Politik, Ideologie und Propaganda 1939–1945* (Stuttgart, 1982), 190.
44 Most recently, G. Aly, *Hitlers Volksstaat* (Frankfurt, 2005).
45 For the new savings scheme known as Eisernes Sparen, see the advertising suggestions in BAL R2501/7007, 341, 102, and M. L. Recker, *Nationalsozialistische Sozialpolitik im Zweiten Weltkrieg* (Munich, 1985), 194–206.
46 Aly, *Hitlers Volksstaat*, 78.
47 For contradictory accounts, see ibid., 79–81 and M. Fuehrer, *Mieter, Hausbesitzer, Staat und Wohnungsmarkt: Wohnungsmangel und Wohnungszwangswirtschaft in Deutschland 1914–1960* (Stuttgart, 1995), 228–30.
48 For an excellent recent account correcting earlier confusions in the literature, see C. Rauh-Kuehne, 'Hitlers Hehler? Unternehmerprofite und Zwangsarbeiterloehne', *HZ* 275 (2002), 1–55.
49 G. Thomas, *Geschichte der deutschen Wehr- und Ruestungswirtschaft* (Boppard, 1966), 137.
50 As explained in Zangen's speech to the RgI, 19 December 1940, BAH R131/594, 50–59. See also the sceptical Reichsbank commentary on a complacent report by the OKW price control agency, BAL 2501/7007, 409–11.
51 Manoeuvring documented in BAL R8122/336 and 337, plus R131 599.
52 See the explanation of the course of negotiations in BAL R2501/7008, 94–8.
53 BAL R2501/7007, 412–13.
54 BAL R8122/338, Notiz, 8 November 1941.
55 According to the widely accepted version of events, Wagner was removed on account of

his excessive attachment to Catholicism. But, as Rauh-Kuehne, 'Hitlers Hehler', 25–6, points out, the possible connection to his dispute with the Reich Group for industry has so far not been explored.

56 The balance between demand and supply factors is nicely elucidated in an address by Dr Regul of the Reichsvereinigung Kohle, BAH R131/595, 168–9.

57 BAMA RW19/177, 165.

58 BAH R131/652, 9.

59 This key point is made in BAMA RW19/177, 9–10.

60 BAMA RW19/165, 169–70, Wi Rue Amt Stab, 28 July 1941.

61 BAMA RW19/165, 131.

62 See Conference, 18 August 1941, BAMA RW19/177, 226.

63 BAMA RW19/177, 269–73. Even more extreme was the redistribution of copper, of which the army was allocated only 800 tons, as compared to 3,300 for the navy and 4,000 tons allocated to the Luftwaffe.

64 B. R. Kroener, 'Der starke Mann im Heimatkriegsgebiet': Generaloberst Friedrich Fromm. Eine Biographie (Paderborn, 2005), 417–21.

65 See the comments on mortar rounds and other ammunition in BAMA RW19/166, 141.

66 BAMA RW19/165, 554.

67 Mueller, in DRZW 5/1. 610.

68 As noted by the OKW's Wi Rue Amt Stab, 22 November 1941, BAMA RW19/166, 28.

69 See BAMA RW19/166, 35.

70 Reinhardt, Moscow, 222–8, 243–8, and Schueler, Logistik, 404.

71 Ibid., 279–83.

72 J. Erickson, The Road to Stalingrad: Stalin's War with Germany (London, 1975), 269–73.

73 E. F. Ziemke and M. E. Bauer, Moscow to Stalingrad: Decision in the East (New York, 1988), 77.

74 Koerner, in DRZW 5/1. 885.

75 Reinhardt, Moscow, 326.

76 Erickson, The Road to Stalingrad, 297–342.

77 DRZW 6. 780–81.

78 H. D. Hall, North American Supply (London, 1955), 328–35.

79 On the crucial importance of this idea to rationalizing Hitler's policy, see S. Friedlaender, Prelude to Downfall: Hitler and the United States 1939–1941 (London, 1967), 307–14.

80 D. Reynolds, The Creation of the Anglo-American Alliance 1937–41: A Study in Competitive Cooperation (London, 1981), 213–30.

81 Browning, The Origins, 318.

82 Meeting between Hitler and the Spanish ambassador, 12 August 1941, quoted in A. Hillgruber (ed.), Staatsmaenner und Diplomaten bei Hitler (Frankfurt, 1967), I, doc. 86, 624.

83 Hitler–Mussolini, 25 August 1941, DGFP D XIII, 383–8, doc. 242, 387. Friedlaender, Prelude, 266–9.

84 Hitler Monologe, 239, cited Wegner, in DRZW 6. 114. See also Reinhardt, Moscow, 376, and Kroener, in DRZW 5/1. 965–6.

85 Kershaw Hitler: Nemesis, 364.

86 Friedlaender, Prelude, 270–85.

87 Kershaw, Hitler: Nemesis, 442–6.

88 Browning, The Origins, 407.

89 H. Frank, Das Diensttagebuch des deutschen Generalgouverneurs in Polen 1939–1945 (Stuttgart, 1975), 458. Longerich, Politik, 468.

90 See the comments in the previous chapter on the contested interpretation of this meeting.

91 E. Jaeckel, 'Die deutsche Kriegserklaerung an die Vereinigten Staaten von 1941', in F. J. Kroneck and T. Oppermann (eds.), Im Dienste Deutschlands und des Rechtes (Baden-Baden, 1981), 117–37.

92 *DRZW* 6. 110–12.

93 *DRZW* 6. 97–127.

94 L. Budrass, *Flugzeugindustrie und Luftruestung in Deutschland* (Duesseldorf, 1998), 724.

95 BAMA RW19/473, Thomas memo, end June 1941.

96 BAMA RW19/166, 79.

97 BAMA RW19/166, 87.

98 BAMA RW19/166, 676.

99 W. Rohland, *Bewegte Zeiten: Erinnerungen eines Eisenhuettenmannes* (Stuttgart, 1978), 75, and H. Kehrl, *Krisenmanager im Dritten Reich* (Duesseldort, 1973), 217–18. See also K. H. Ludwig, *Technik und Ingenieure im Dritten Reich* (Duesseldorf, 1974), 386–93, 401–3. Ludwig is clearly apologetic in his reference to Todt as a 'resister'. However, the critique of Speer that follows is vital.

100 For this and the following, Rohland, *Bewegte Zeiten*, 77–8.

101 *Halder Diary*, 564. Kroener, *Fromm*, 409–17.

102 Kroener, in *DRZW* 5/1. 921–2.

103 E. Froehlich (ed.), *Die Tagebuecher von Joseph Goebbels* (Munich, 1994), II/3, 20 January 1942, 154–5.

104 W. Weber, 'Walter Borbet (1881–1942)', in Weber (ed.), *Ingenieure im Ruhrgebiet* (Muenster, 1999), 253–6.

105 See the instructions in BAH R13I 658, 108.

106 Rohland, *Bewegte Zeiten*, 79–81.

107 Mueller, in *DRZW* 5/1. 668 and Koerner, in *DRZW* 5/1. 920–21.

108 Mueller, in *DRZW* 5/1. 667–8, and Kroener, *Fromm*, 427–31.

109 A. Speer, *Inside the Third Reich* (London, 1970), 314, a belief on Fromm's part only reinforced by conversations with head of the Abwehr Canaris, see Kroener, *Fromm*, 437–45 and 482–92.

110 As is made clear in M. Walker, *German National Socialism and the Quest for Nuclear Power 1939–1949* (Cambridge, 1989), 46–80, the issue of timing was crucial to German decision-making in relation to the bomb.

111 R. Rhodes, *The Making of the Atomic Bomb* (London, 1986), 394–407.

112 *DRZW* 6. 509–10.

16 Labour, Food and Genocide

1 R. Overmans, *Deutsche militaerische Verluste im Zweiten Weltkrieg* (Munich, 1999), 238–9. data. Since these figures record only fatal casualties, they seriously understate Germany's actual losses due to injury, illness and capture.

2 Kroener, in *DRZW* 5/2. 792.

3 See the anxiety of the OKW's military-economic office, BAMA RW19/166, 115.

4 W. Naasner, *Neue Machtzentren in der deutschen Kriegswirtschaft 1942–1945* (Boppard, 1994), 88.

5 IWM FD 3354/45, 196 ZP 54th Session.

6 Eichholtz, II. 230–32.

7 Naasner, *Neue Machtzentren*, 68–9.

8 See the contemporary charts reproduced without comment in H. H. Knittel, *Panzerfertigung in Zweiten Weltkrieg: Industrieproduktion fuer die deutsche Wehrmacht* (Herford, 1988), 126.

9 P. W. Becker, 'Fritz Sauckel', in R. Smelser, E. Syring and R. Zitelmann (eds.), *Die Braune Elite: 22 biographische Skizzen* (Darmstadt, 1993), I. 236–45.

10 J. John, 'Ruestungswirtschaftlicher Strukturwandel und NS Regionalpolitik', in D. Heiden and G. Mai (eds.), *Nationalsozialismus in Thueringen* (Weimar, 1995), 213–45.

11 The best surveys are U. Herbert, *Hitler's Foreign Workers: Enforced Foreign Labour in Germany under the Third Reich* (Cambridge, 1997), M. Spoerer, *Zwangsarbeit unter*

dem Hakenkreuz (Stuttgart, 2001) and E. L. Homze, *Foreign Labor in Nazi Germany* (Princeton, 1967).

12 Spoerer, *Zwangsarbeit*, 223.

13 G. Wysocki, *Arbeit fuer den Krieg* (Brunswick, 1992), 67–75, and L. Budrass, *Flugzeugindustrie und Luftruestung in Deutschland* (Duesseldorf, 1998), 799.

14 Ibid., 771.

15 A. S. Milward, *The New Order and the French Economy* (Oxford, 1984), 149. Pharaonic is the word used by Justice Jackson at the IMT.

16 For Hans Kehrl's self serving account of this conflict, see Kehrl, *Krisenmanager in Dritten Reich* (Duesseldorf, 1973), 341–52. For academic accounts, see Milward, *The New Order*, 147–80 and Kroener, in *DRZW* 5/2. 896–916.

17 Mueller, in *DRZW* 5/2. 379. In the autumn of 1942 Speer had supported Sauckel against the German military authorities in France precisely on the grounds that French workers were better employed in German factories. See BAL R3/1736, 26 October 1942, 83.

18 Successive Sauckel-Aktionen in France yielded 240,000 men in June–December 1942, 250,000 in January–April 1943, 106,000 in May–October 1943 and only 36,000–50,000 between January and June 1944. See R. Frankenstein, 'Die deutschen Arbeitskraefteaushebungen in Frankreich', in W. Dlugoborski, *Zweiter Weltkrieg und sozialer Wandel* (Goettingen, 1981), 211–23.

19 R. D. Mueller. 'Die Rekrutierung sowjetischer Zwangsarbeiter', in U. Herbert (ed.), *Europa und der 'Reichseinsatz'* (Essen, 1991), 236.

20 A. Heusler, *Auslaendereinsatz: Zwangsarbeit fuer die Muenchener Kriegswirtschaft* (Munich 1996), 32–41.

21 H. Moennich, *The BMW Story: A Company in its Time* (London, 1991), 283–4.

22 Herbert, *Hitler's Foreign Workers*, 143–50.

23 At the Stalag XB Sandbostel, which housed both Soviet and Western prisoners, 35,000 Soviet prisoners may have died over the winter of 1941–2 and a further 3,600–3,700 in each subsequent year of the war. See W. Borgsen and K. Volland, *Stalag XB Sandbostel* (Bremen, 1991), 22–3 and 252. A study of Camp 326 in the Senne region of Westphalia gives 65,000 as a plausible estimate of the number of Soviet prisoners who died there. See K. Hueser and R. Otto, *Das Stammlager 326 (V/K) Senne 1941–1945* (Bielefeld, 1992), 190. Lower but no less horrific figures may emerge from the meticulous examination of the sources proposed by R. Keller and R. Otto, 'Das Massensterben der sowjetischen Kriegsgefangenene und die Wehrmachtbuerokratie', *MGM* 57 (1998), 149–80. It must be emphasized, too, that these figures refer to Soviet prisoners who made it to Germany and do not reflect the even higher mortality rates immediately behind the front line in the East.

24 Eichholtz, II. 215–16.

25 Spoerer, *Zwangsarbeit*, 131.

26 Eichholtz, II. 26.

27 Ibid., 289.

28 Ibid., 290.

29 IMT XXV. 161–4.

30 IMT XXV, doc. 054-PS, 100–10.

31 A vicious spiral of which Albert Speer was fully apprised. See BAL R3/1736, 1 September 1942, 68.

32 Spoerer, *Zwangsarbeit*, 229.

33 'Compromise' is the central theme of Herbert's work. For examples of his use of the term, see Herbert, *Hitler's Foreign Workers*, 64, 93–4, 134–5, 143. However, as Naasner points out, this term tends to exaggerate the conflict of interest between Sauckel as the provider of the labour and the SS as the providers of discipline. Naasner prefers to speak of an 'ideological-pragmatic synthesis', which if it were not so clumsy would have much to recommend it; Naasner, *Neue Machtzentren*, 111.

34 This is the argument advanced by U. Herbert, 'Arbeit und Vernichtung', in D. Diner

(ed.), *Ist der Nationalsozialismus Geschichte?* (Frankfurt, 1987), 198–236, and U. Herbert, 'Labour and Extermination: Economic Interest and the Primacy of Weltanschauung in National Socialism', *Past and Present*, 138 (1993), 144–95.

35 On the decision to deport German Jewish workers in 1941, see W. Gruner, 'Der "Geschlossene Arbeitseinsatz" ', in M. Kingreen (ed.), *'Nach der Kristallnacht': Juedisches Leben und antijuedische Politik in Frankfurt am Main 1938–1945* (Frankfurt, 1999), 259–88.

36 On the attitude of the General Government administration in the summer of 1942, including Ruestungsinspektor Schindler, who still regarded the Jews as an indispensable workforce, see Hauptabteilungsleiter meeting in Cracow in H. Frank, *Das Diensttagebuch des deutschen Generalgouverneurs in Polen 1939–1945* (Stuttgart, 1975), 22 June 1942, 515–17.

37 A typical example is reproduced in J. Noakes and G. Pridham, *Nazism* (Exeter, 1988), III. 821, 1098.

38 See P. Longerich, *Politik der Vernichtung* (Munich, 1998), 476.

39 On the evolution of policy towards Polish Jewish labour between February and July 1942, see D. E. Pohl, *Von der 'Judenpolitik' zum Judenmord: Der Distrikt Lublin des Generalgovernements 1939–1944* (Frankfurt, 1993), 110–29.

40 E. Froehlich (ed.), *Die Tagebuecher von Joseph Goebbels* (Munich, 1994), II/3. 561, entry for 27 March 1942. It should be noted that, under normal circumstances, roughly 50–60 per cent of a population is economically active. The figure for 40 per cent thus implies the intention to make use of the vast majority of economically active Jews.

41 F. Kersten, *The Kersten Memoirs 1940–1945* (London, 1956), 132–40. Since this source chimes well with other material on the Generalplan, I follow R. J. van Pelt and D. Dwork, *Auschwitz: 1270 to the Present* (New Haven, 1996), 307–15, in taking it seriously.

42 For Himmler's reluctant acceptance of Jewish factory labour in the General Government in 1942 and their subsequent liquidation, see Pohl, *Von der 'Judenpolitik'*, 157–67, and E. Georg, *Die wirtschaftlichen Unternehmungen der SS* (Stuttgart, 1963), 90–99.

43 The following is based on F. Piper, 'Die Ausbeutung der Arbeit der Haeftlinge', in W. Dlugoborski and F. Piper, *Auschwitz 1940–1945: Studien zur geschichte des Konzentrations- und Vernichtungslagers Auschwitz* (Oswięcim, 1999), II. 83–167.

44 B. C. Wagner, *IG Auschwitz: Zwangsarbeit und Vernichtung von Haeftlingen des Lagers Monowitz 1941–1945* (Munich, 2000).

45 S. Heim, *Kalorien, Kautschuk, Karrieren: Pflanzenzuechtung und landwirtschaftliche Forschung in Kaiser-Wilhelm Instituten 1933–1945* (Goettingen, 2003), 172–93.

46 C. Gerlach and G. Aly, *Das letzte Kapitel: Der Mord an den ungarischen Juden* (Stuttgart, 2002).

47 The narrative that drives Herbert, *Hitler's Foreign Workers*, 137–252.

48 Ibid., 176–82. As Sauckel hastened to emphasize, this was for entirely 'unsentimental' reasons.

49 See the expressions from frustration from IG Auschwitz at the restrictiveness of Sauckel's attitude, IMT VIII. 490–91, NI-14532 IG, Auschwitz weekly report 80 and 81, 30 November–13 December 1942.

50 On the re-education camps (*Arbeitserziehungslager*), see G. Lotfi, *KZ der Gestapo: Arbeitserziehungslager im Dritten Reich* (Stuttgart, 2000).

51 See the comments from IG Farben's building site at Auschwitz in IG Farben Case VIII, 490–91.

52 For an overview of sources, see H. Menne and M. Farrenkopf, *Zwangsarbeit im Ruhrbergbau waehrend des Zweiten Weltkrieges: Spezialinventar der Quellen in nordrhein-westfaelischen Archiven* (Bochum, 2004). As this book went to press there appeared the massive documentation, H.-C. Seidel and K. Tenfelde, *Zwangsarbeit im Bergwerk: Der Arbeitseinsatz im Kohlenbergbau des deutschen Reiches und der besetzten Gebiete im Ersten und Zweiten Weltkrieg* (Essen, 2005).

53 See the comments in W. A. Boelcke, *Deutschlands Ruestung im Zweiten Weltkrieg: Hitlers Konferenzen mit Albert Speer 1942–1945* (Frankfurt, 1969), 172.

54 All of the following is from W. Abelshauser, in L. Gall (ed.), *Krupp im 20. Jahrhundert* (Berlin, 2002), 412.

55 Ibid., 412.

56 Eichholtz, II. 277.

57 Ibid., III. 248.

58 N. Gregor, *Daimler-Benz in the Third Reich* (New Haven, 1998), 191, and Spoerer, *Zwangsarbeit*, 129–30.

59 T. Allen, *The Business of Genocide* (Chapel Hill, NC, 2002), 1–77, H. Kaienburg, *Die Wirtschaft der SS* (Berlin, 2003), 114–138, and J. E. Schulte, *Zwangsarbeit und Vernichtung: Das Wirtschaftsimperium der SS* (Paderborn, 2001), 103–25.

60 Ibid.

61 Kaienburg, *Die Wirtschaft der SS*, 434–5. Schulte, *Zwangsarbeit*, 392–4.

62 Budrass, *Flugzeugindustrie*, 775.

63 Schulte, *Zwangsarbeit*, 398.

64 Herbert, *Europa*, 14. For slightly different figures, see Schulte, *Zwangsarbeit*, 401.

65 J.-C. Wagner, 'Noch einmal: Arbeit und Vernichtung', in N. Frei, S. Steinbacher and B. C. Wagner (eds.), *Ausbeutung, Vernichtung, Oeffentlichkeit* (Munich, 2000), 11–41.

66 Wagner, *IG Auschwitz*, 129–33.

67 IMT VIII. 392–3, NI-14543, weekly report on Auschwitz building programme, 9 August 1941, 393. With time, the IG construction site management began to take a more relaxed attitude towards corporal punishment on and off site. See Wagner, *IG Auschwitz*, 230–38.

68 The process of 'Oekonomisierung' was first traced in the pioneering work by F. Pingel, *Haeftlinge unter SS-Herrschaft* (Hamburg, 1978).

69 M. Spoerer, 'Profitierten Unternehmen von KZ-Arbeit', *HZ* 268 (1999), 61–95.

70 C. Rauh-Kuehne, 'Hitlers Hehler? Unternehmerprofite und Zwangsarbeiterloehne', *HZ* 275 (2002).

71 See the internet memorial, http://loibl-memorial.uni-klu.ac.at/. Still in heavy use sixty years later, the Loibl tunnel was rated the most dangerous in Europe in 2002 and has been undergoing dramatic reconstruction since November 2002 in preparation for Slovenia's EC accession.

72 Spoerer, *Zwangsarbeit*, 227–8.

73 See the path-breaking account in Herbert, *Hitler's Foreign Workers*, 205–38, to which little is added by Abelshauser, in Gall (ed.), *Krupp*, 400–17.

74 Herbert, *Hitler's Foreign Workers*, 300.

75 Naasner, *Neue Machtzentren*, 155–6, and Herbert, *Hitler's Foreign Workers*, 305.

76 Though he does not formulate it explicitly, as we have here, as a reply to Herbert's position on foreign labour we owe this key insight above all to Christian Gerlach. See Gerlach, *Kalkulierte Morde: Die deutsche Wirtschafts- und Vernichtungspolitik in Weissrussland 1941 bis 1944* (Hamburg, 1999) and *Krieg, Ernaehrung, Voelkermord: Deutsche Vernichtungspolitik im Zweiten Weltkrieg* (Zurich, 2nd edn., 2001).

77 For foreign labour and food, see Herbert, *Hitler's Foreign Workers*, 182–3 and 288–95, and Naasner, *Neue Machtzentren*, 129–62. For the concentration camp system, see Naasner, *Neue Machtzentren*, 274–8 and Pingel, *Haeftlinge unter SS-Herrschaft*, 130–38.

78 See the frank report dated 11 March 1942, BAL R161V 51, 81–73. See also Appendix, Table A5.

79 On the disappointing deliveries from the Soviet Union and Romania, see BAMA RW19/166, 14 and 17, respectively.

80 BAMA RW19/473, 177–9 and RW19/177, 19. The intention of Hitler's orders was to reverse this cut over the coming winter on the basis of meat taken from the Soviet Union, RW19/177, 164.

81 See his immediate response in BAMA RW19/165, 310.

82 IMT XXVII, doc. 1206–PS, 67.

83 IMT XXXIX, 177–USSR, 446–8. Handwritten notes on this report by Koerner,

Goering's Secretary of State, suggest the pressure that Backe was under: 'Please double-check the situation since State Secretary Backe seems to be losing his nerve.'

84 Eichholtz, II. 216.

85 See the extended justification offered in the report dated 11 March 1942, BAL R16IV 51, 81–73. Interestingly, this does not yet contain the suggestion for a major reallocation at the expense of the occupied territories.

86 *Meldungen*, IX: 23 March 1942, 3504–5. The announcement was preceded by weeks of speculation and followed by months of disgruntlement. See *Meldungen*, X: 30 March 1942, 3543; 2 April 1942, 3566; 9 April 1942, 3595; 16 July 1942, 3951. As was noted in *Meldungen*, X: 13 April 1942, 3614, the announcement of death sentences against black marketeers did something to life the mood. See also G. Corni and H. Gies, *Brot, Butter, Kanonen: Die Ernaehrungswirtschaft in Deutschland unter der Diktatur Hitlers* (Berlin, 1997), 562–4, and Herbert, *Hitler's Foreign Workers*, 189.

87 BAL R3102 (R24), 55. W. F. Werner, *Bleib Uebrig! Deutsche Arbeiter in der national-sozialistischen Kriegswirtschaft* (Duesseldorf, 1983), 300–302.

88 Eichholtz, II. 216. Herbert, *Hitler's Foreign Workers*, 173, fails to distinguish between normal and heavy labour rations.

89 Eichholtz, II. 215.

90 Gregor, *Daimler-Benz*, 186.

91 IMT XXV, doc. 025-PS, 86–7. Naasner, *Neue Machtzentren*, 105.

92 The significance of Backe's appointment was downplayed specifically on Goebbels's insistence. See Froehlich (ed.), *Die Tagebuecher von Joseph Goebbels*, II/4. 327–8, entry for 21 May 1942. For a rather cursory treatment, see Corni and Gies, *Brot, Butter, Kanonen*, 416–19. Gerlach is the first to note its real significance. See Gerlach, *Krieg, Ernaehrung, Voelkermord*, 192–7.

93 See the OKW order of 29 August 1942, IMT XXXIX, 175–USSR.

94 Quoted in Gerlach, *Krieg, Ernaehrung, Voelkermord*, 175.

95 Frank, *Das Diensttagebuch*, 522.

96 See Zentrale Planung minutes, BAL R10III 81, 2–4. For Speer and Backe's meeting on 27 July 1942, see BAL R3/1736, 58. This should be considered as one more link in the chain of evidence that connects Albert Speer to the Holocaust.

97 For Speer's presence, see BAL R3/1736, 5 August 1942, 60.

98 IMT XXXIX, 170-USSR, 384–412.

99 IMT XIII. 838–40.

100 Frank, *Das Diensttagebuch*, Regierungssitzung, 24 August 1942, 549.

101 Domarus, II. 1913–24.

102 Herbert, *Hitler's Foreign Workers*, 192.

103 This huge increase offset a smaller decline in deliveries from Denmark and South-eastern Europe. K. Brandt, *Management of Agriculture and Food in the German-occupied and Other Areas of Fortress Europe* (Stanford, Calif., 1953), 614.

104 Ibid., 610.

105 By implication, I am down-grading Himmler's decision of early 1942 to involve the concentration camps more closely in the war economy, which features as the third pillar in Naasner's excellent account. See Naasner, *Neue Machtzentren*, 197–429. The SS did eventually become an important factor in the war economy, but only from the second half of 1943. In 1942 they were far less significant than the Backe–Himmler–Goering axis on food, first highlighted by Gerlach.

17 Albert Speer: 'Miracle Man'

1 On Speer at Nuremberg, see M. Schmidt, *Albert Speer: The End of a Myth* (London, 1984), 145–68, G. Sereny, *Albert Speer: His Battle with Truth* (London, 1995), 563–96, D. van der Vat, *The Good Nazi: The Life and Lies of Albert Speer* (Boston, 1997), 239–82, and J. C. Fest, *Speer: Eine Biographie* (Berlin, 1999), 383–416.

2 He has been the subject of a five-hour made-for-television film, *Inside the Third Reich* (1982), directed by Marvin J. Chomsky, and at least two stage plays, one by E. Vilar (Almeida, 1999) and one by David Edgar, *Albert Speer* (Royal National Theatre, 2000). Most recently he was the subject of a four-part television documentary, *Speer und er*, by Heinrich Breloer (2005).

3 See Speer's remarks to the Gauleiter Tagung of 24 February 1942, BAL R26IV 51, 441–8 and to his architect colleagues on 2 March 1942, BAL R3/1736, Chronik, 17. See also Speer's insistence on the difference between architects and engineers discussed in K. H. Ludwig, *Technik und Ingenieure im Dritten Reich* (Duesseldorf, 1974), 412.

4 For the differences between Todt and Speer, see ibid., 405–8.

5 See Speer's remarks to the press, BAL R3/1736, Chronik 9 April 1942, 25.

6 W. A. Boelcke, *Deutschlands Ruestung im Zweiten Weltkrieg: Hitlers Konferenzen mit Albert Speer 1942–1945* (Frankfurt, 1969), 6/7 May 1942, 109.

7 BAL R3/1737, Chronik June 1943, 79. Goebbels, too, noted the contrast to 1917. See E. Froehlich (ed.), *Die Tagebuecher von Joseph Goebbels* (Munich, 1994), II/4, 9 May 1942, 263.

8 *Meldungen*, X: 23 April 1942, 3665; see also 14 May 1942, 3734.

9 *Meldungen*, X: 28 May 1942, 3753–4. Picture in Fest, *Speer*, 190.

10 BAL R3/1736, Chronik 20 May 1942, 42. Boelcke, *Deutschlands Ruestung*, 117.

11 Speer, Goebbels and Hitler personally vetted the film. See BAL R3/1736, 21 May 1942, 43, and Froehlich (ed.), *Die Tagebuecher von Joseph Goebbels*, 23 May 1942, 345. It apparently worked better on male rather than on female audience members. See *Meldungen*, X: 4 June 1942, 3791–2. Over the following months armaments propaganda became a regular feature of the newsreels. See the excited response to images of the giant Thor mortar with which the Wehrmacht reduced the defences of Sevastopol, *Meldungen*, X: 9 July 1942, 3929.

12 Boelcke, *Deutschlands Ruestung*, 184. BAL R3/1736, 2 November 1942, 85.

13 Ludwig, *Technik*, 439. Its actual sustainable rate of fire was closer to 500 rounds.

14 BAL R3/1737, Chronik 13 May 1943, 59–63.

15 BAL R3/1737, 5 June 1943, 74–7.

16 See the sceptical remarks recorded by the SS-SD in *Meldungen*, XIV: 10 June 1943, 5341–2, and H. Kehrl, *Krisenmanager im Dritten Reich* (Duesseldorf, 1973), 298.

17 See the devastating review of R. D. Mueller's contribution to *DRZW* 5/2 by L. Budrass, http://hsozkult.geschichte.hu-berlin.de/rezensionen/id=169.

18 Only Sereny has reason to take special note of Speer's relative silence about 1943, see Sereny, *Albert Speer*, 370–71.

19 Paradoxically, in the two best studies of the Speer Ministry very little space is given to 1942. G. Janssen, *Das Ministerium Speer: Deutschlands Ruestung im Krieg* (Frankfurt, 1968) allocates only a dozen pages to the armaments programme of 1942. Even in the excellent second and third volumes of Eichholtz's history, 1942 is given short shrift when compared to the hundreds of pages devoted to 1943 and 1944–5.

20 See Mueller, in *DRZW* 5/1. 668, Kroener, in *DRZW* 5/1. 920–21.

21 Speer to 21st meeting of the Zentrale Planung, 30 October 1942, BAL R3/1697, 5. On Speer's understanding of the narrow window of strategic opportunity, see Ludwig, *Technik*, 424–5.

22 As opposed to Abelshauser, who speaks of a 'dictatorship' of the '6,000 most dynamic, loyal and assertive managers, technicians and engineers' over private industry. See W. Abelshauser, 'Modernisierung oder institutionelle Revolution', in Abelshauser, J. -O. Hesse and W. Plumpe (eds.), *Wirtschaftsordnung, Staat und Unternehmen: Neue Forschungen zur Wirtschaftsgeschichte des Nationalsozialismus* (Essen, 2003), 27.

23 Calculated on basis of the statistics in R. Wagenfuehr, *Die deutsche Industrie im Kriege* (Berlin, 1954), 12 and 180.

24 As highlighted by Mueller, in *DRZW* 5/2. 281–98.

25 Hence the scepticism towards Speer mythology evident in L. Budrass, *Flugzeugindustrie und Luftruestung in Deutschland* (Duesseldorf, 1998), 865–6 and 891–2.

26 For its official inauguration, see BAL R3/1562, 3–4.

27 Unfortunately, the best source on Milch is still D. Irving, *The Rise and Fall of the Luftwaffe: The Life of Luftwaffe Marshal Erhard Milch* (London, 1973).

28 For this line of continuity, see Ludwig, *Technik*, 415–19.

29 W. Abelshauser, in L. Gall (ed.), *Krupp im 20. Jahrhundert* (Berlin, 2002), 392.

30 L. Herbst, 'Der Krieg und die Unternehmensstrategie deutscher Industrie-Konzerne in der Zwischenkriegszeit', in M. Broszat and K. Schwabe (eds.), *Die deutschen Eliten und der Weg in der Zweiten Weltkrieg* (Munich, 1989), 134–5.

31 *DRZW* 4. 177–84.

32 M. Spoerer, *Vom Scheingewinn zum Ruestungsboom: Die Eigenkapitalrentabilitaet der deutschen Industrieaktiengesellschaften 1925–1941* (Stuttgart, 1996), 147.

33 Eichholtz, II. 54.

34 Budrass, *Flugzeugindustrie*, 713–14. Originally known as Rings (for airframes, aero-engines and aircraft equipment), these were later renamed Committees to create at least the appearance of a unified structure.

35 For Voegler's role, see BAH R13I/599, 53–4.

36 Kehrl, *Krisenmanager*, 89–90, 200, 212–14. For his Thuringian background, see D. Heiden (ed.), *Nationalsozialismus in Thueringen* (Weimar, 1995), 230.

37 See Zangen's explanation of this somewhat surprising development to members, BAH R13I/621, 2–4.

38 For a complete listing, see the Speer Ministry phone book contained in PRO FO 935/137.

39 A brief Google excursion reveals that every one of these entries in the Speer phone book is still active. With the exception of Koch & Sterzel, which was located in the GDR, they are all world-leaders in their fields.

40 The following is based above all on C. Rauh-Kuehne, 'Hitlers Hehler? Unternehmenprofite und Zwangsarbeiterloehne', *HZ* 275 (2002).

41 BAL R26IV/51, 444–5.

42 W. A. Boelcke, *Die Kosten von Hitlers Krieg: Kriegsfinanzierung und finanzielles Kriegserbe in Deutschland 1933–1948* (Paderborn, 1985), 44–6, amongst others, follows Speer. The real course of events is more accurately described in the justificatory statement issued by Wehrmacht price control, 1 April 1942, BAL R8122 364.

43 For a clear description, see S. Lurie, *Private Investment in a Controlled Economy* (New York, 1947), 163–82, and Rauh-Kuehne, 'Hitlers Hehler?', 11–15.

44 See the discussion in BAMA RW19/173, 260–65, between OKW and industrial representatives on 30 November 1939, at which it was commonly agreed that strict application of LSOe guidelines would in fact lead to losses for many firms because they failed to cover overheads fully.

45 The same was also true of Luftwaffe contracts, which were also issued on a fixed price basis from as early as March 1937. See L. Budrass, J. Scherner and J. Streb, 'Demystifying the German "Armaments Miracle" during World War II' (forthcoming).

46 As a meeting of steel industrialists heard on 16 March 1942, the situation with regard to the profits question was now 'vollstaendig veraendert', completely changed. BAH R13I 621, 7.

47 H. J. Weyres, *Die deutsche Ruestungswirtschaft von 1942 bis zum Ende des Kriegs* (Munich, 1975), 189.

48 Eichholtz, III. 700.

49 On 19 March Speer asked Hitler to ensure that the army rather than the Luftwaffe was prioritized in new allocations of labour. Boelcke, *Deutschlands Ruestung*, 76.

50 For this data, see the Beschaeftigungsmeldung records in PRO FO 1078/137 and 1078/138.

51 For the labour figures, see IMT XXVII, 1739-PS, 597. For the locomotive workforce

they refer only to 1942. For the surge in locomotive production, see Mueller, in *DRZW* 5/2. 462.

52 Speer clearly appreciated the efforts of Sauckel and his staff. For the delivery of the two-millionth Russian worker, they were rewarded with tickets to the Berlin Opera. See BAL R3/1736, 21 August 1942, 65.

53 Eichholtz, II. 83.

54 Boelcke, *Deutschlands Ruestung*, 83.

55 BAMA RW19/166, 829.

56 A neglect which clearly had practical consequences in the allocation of labour and other resources, as was belatedly acknowledged by the Speer Chronik in the summer of 1944. See BAL R3/1739, May 1944, 102–3.

57 Calculated on the basis of the data in Wagenfuehr, *Die deutsche Industrie*, 180–81; see Appendix, Table A6.

58 Eichholtz, II. 171.

59 BAMA RH8v. 1025 and Mueller, in *DRZW* 5/2. 554.

60 Boelcke, *Deutschlands Ruestung*, 122. See Appendix, Table A3.

61 BAH R10III/32, 31–4.

62 See the explanation given by Hanneken on 1 May 1942, BAH R10III/32, 15–21.

63 Boelcke, *Deutschlands Ruestung*, 106. This hardly amounts to the 'Hitler veto' claimed by G. Mollin, *Montankonzerne und 'Drittes Reich'* (Goettingen, 1988), 305.

64 Roechling's manifesto of 31 August 1914 is reprinted in R. Opitz (ed.), *Europastrategien des deutschen Kapitals 1900–1945* (Bonn, 1994), 211–12.

65 For the bitterness between Pleiger and Roechling, see the correspondence in BAH R10VIII/20, 19–21.

66 BAH R10III/31, 1–6. Significantly, Mollin, *Montankonzerne*, 136, in his effort to demonstrate that the RVE was a dictatorial organization quotes only selectively from this crucial speech.

67 Perhaps not surprisingly, by the end of 1942 the regime's most hawkish elements had come to the conclusion that the RVE was nowhere near dictatorial enough. Hans Kehrl in particular concluded that the RVE had done little or nothing to modify the peacetime production patterns of German heavy industry. Inexplicably, Mollin, who insists in the most simplistic terms that the RVE constituted a subordination of heavy industry to the dictates of the 'command economy', starts his book with a quotation from precisely this report. See Mollin, *Montankonzerne*, 15–16. Speer himself noted that the RVE was distinctive amongst the armaments organizations in that its leadership consisted of leading CEOs rather than younger technical staff, see BAL R3/1740, August 1944, 208.

68 Weyres, *Ruestungswirtschaft*, 179. The full membership of his committee was Voegler, Hellmuth Roehnert (of Rheinmetall), Arthur Tix (a long-standing Speer collaborator), Karl Hettlage (Speer's finance expert from the Kommerzbank) and Alfred Stellwaag (a steel veteran of World War I who had also collaborated with Todt). See Eichholtz, II. 84–5.

69 Kehrl, *Krisenmanager*, 257–9.

70 Weyres, *Ruestungswirtschaft*, 179–80. The system was subsequently improved by a rationalization of the number of agencies entitled to issue iron cheques and by regular checking by RWM and Speer Ministry staff. See IWM FD 3353/45, 15th session of Zentrale Planung on 20 October 1942.

71 BAH R13I/668, 75–9.

72 Boelcke, *Deutschlands Ruestung*, 148–9.

73 Weyres, *Ruestungswirtschaft*, 52. Eichholtz, II. 363.

74 Boelcke, *Deutschlands Ruestung*, 171.

75 Kehrl, *Krisenmanager*, 278.

76 Abelshauser, in Gall (ed.), *Krupp*, 412.

77 According to the quasi-official minute in Boelcke, *Deutschlands Ruestung*, 172.

78 Minutes of 16th meeting of Zentrale Planung in IMT XIII. 987–99.

79 Eichholtz, II. 252.

80 BAL R3/1692, 23 October 1942, 16th meeting of the Zentrale Planung, Milch remarks.

81 BAL R3/1699 ZP 23, 3 November 1942.

82 BAL R3/1694, 3.

83 Speer himself was in no doubt about this simple connection. See his retrospective remarks to the Ammunition Committee in August 1944, BAL R3/1740, 202.

84 The much-cited table in United States Strategic Bombing Survey, *The Effects of Strategic Bombing on the German War Economy* (Washington, 1945), 180, which shows a strong correlation only up to the end of 1942, is misleading, since it relates ammunition output, not to primary steel input, but to the intermediate output of steel components.

85 BAH R131/658, 99–104, and Mueller, in *DRZW* 5/1. 612–20.

86 For what follows, see the outstanding account in Budrass, *Flugzeugindustrie*, 705–66.

87 N. Gregor, *Daimler-Benz in the Third Reich* (New Haven, 1998), 115–26, and H. H. Knittel, *Panzerfertigung im Zweiten Weltkrieg: Industrieproduktion fuer die deutsche Wehrmacht* (Herford, 1988), 52–3, 95–9.

88 R. Overy, *Why the Allies Won* (London, 1995), 180–207, is good on the Soviet Union and the United States but exaggerates the German difficulties.

89 For the following, see Budrass, *Flugzeugindustrie*, 706–15.

90 Born in 1883 in New York, William Werner rose through the ranks of the German engineering industry, before spending a number of years at Chrysler in Detroit studying American mass-production techniques. After returning to Germany in 1929 he was made technical director first of Horch and then in 1933 of the Auto-Union merger.

91 Born in 1900, Hans Heyne worked in the United States in the 1920s and early 1930s, before returning to Germany on the strength of a recommendation from General Electric to take a position at AEG. He rose rapidly through the ranks and became a board member of AEG in 1942.

92 PRO FO 178, Werner on BMW.

93 Budrass, *Flugzeugindustrie*, 641, 710–11. Mueller, in *DRZW* 5/1. 602.

94 Budrass, *Flugzeugindustrie*, 417–22.

95 See the very similar criticisms made by Ford production experts when they muscled their way into the production of Pratt and Whitney radial aircraft engines in late 1940s. Benson Ford Research Center, Acc. 435, box 5.

96 Budrass, *Flugzeugindustrie*, 641.

97 Milch had already explained the basic programme to the OKW on 22 October 1941 with explicit emphasis on mass-production, as described by Werner, and on reduced number of models, on the assumption that German fighters would remain up to date for the foreseeable future. See BAMA RW19/177, 280–86.

98 For an excellent critique, see R. Schabel, *Die Illusion der Wunderwaffen: Duesenflugzeuge und Flugabwehrraketen in der Ruestungspolitik des Dritten Reiches* (Munich, 1994), 115–23.

99 H. J. Ebert, J. B. Kaiser and K. Peters, *Willy Messerschmitt* (Bonn, 1992), 150–75, P. Schmoll, *Die Messerschmittwerke in Zweiten Weltkrieg* (Regensburg, 1998), 60–64 and A. van Ishoven, *Messerschmitt: Aircraft Designer* (London, 1975), 149–65.

100 Budrass, *Flugzeugindustrie*, 738–41.

101 Ibid., 844–6.

102 R. Overy, *The Air War 1939–1945* (London, 1980), 168. In 1944, as American production hit full stride, the differential rose to 2:1.

103 Budrass, *Flugzeugindustrie*, 739.

104 Col. 'Kit' Carson, 'The Best of the Breed', *Airpower* (1976), 6, 4.

105 On the tactics and deception devices used to keep the Me 109 G competitive, see J. Scutts, *Messerschmitt Bf 109: The Operational Record* (Shrewsbury, 1996), 91–102.

106 G. L. Weinberg, *A World at Arms: A Global History of World War II* (Cambridge, 1994), 310–56.

107 K. Jeffreys, *The Churchill Coalition and Wartime Politics, 1940–1945* (Manchester, 1991), 85–111.

108 *DRZW* 6. 761–886.

109 *DRZW* 6. 932–51.

110 H. R. Trevor-Roper (ed.), *Hitler's War Directives 1939–1945* (London, 1966), 193–7.

111 L. Herbst, *Der Totale Krieg und die Ordnung der Wirtschaft: Die Kriegswirtschaft im Spannungsfeld von Politik, Ideologie und Propaganda 1939–1945* (Stuttgart, 1982), 191–4.

112 Eichholtz, II. 409.

113 Kroener, in *DRZW* 5/2, 793.

114 Kehrl, *Krisenmanager*, 278.

115 Eichholtz, II. 484. For the severity of the oil problems in late 1942, see *DRZW* 6. 945–6.

116 *DRZW* 6. 891–8.

117 *Halder Diary*, 646.

118 Weinberg, *World at Arms*, 427 and *Halder Diary*, 649–50, 653–4, 657 and 660–61. Army Group Centre's attempt to respond with an offensive of its own became bogged down within days.

119 Kroener, in *DRZW* 5/2. 797.

120 D. M. Glantz, *The Siege of Leningrad, 1941–1944* (Staplehurst, 2001), 97–107.

121 *DRZW* 6. 903–6.

122 B. R. Kroener, '*Der Starke Mann in Heimatkriegsgebiet': Generaloberst Friedrich Fromm. Eine Biographie* (Paderborn, 2005), 457–71.

123 D. M. Glantz and J. M. House, *When Titans Clashed: How the Red Army Stopped Hitler* (Lawrence, Kan., 1995), 301–3.

124 M. Harrison (ed.), *The Economics of World War II* (Cambridge, 1998), 15–16.

125 See the commonly cited figures in R. Goldsmith, 'The Powers of Victory: Munitions Output in World War II', *Military Affairs*, 10 (1946), 69–80.

126 Virtually everything we know about the Soviet economy at war we owe to the extraordinary pioneering work of Mark Harrison. See M. Harrison, *Soviet Planning in Peace and War, 1938–1945* (Cambridge, 1985), J. Barber and Harrison, *The Soviet Home Front, 1941–1945: A Social and Economic History of the USSR in World War II* (London, 1991), M. Harrison, *Accounting for War: Soviet Production, Employment and the Defence Burden, 1940–1945* (Cambridge, 1996) and J. Barber and M. Harrison, *The Soviet Defence-Industry Complex from Stalin to Khrushchev* (Basingstoke, 2000), 99–117.

127 Barber and Harrison, *The Soviet Home Front*, 77–90.

18 No Room for Doubt

1 *DRZW* 6. 630–709. W. Murray and A. R. Millett, *A War to be Won: Fighting the Second World War* (Cambridge, Mass., 2000), 271. J. Ellis, *Brute Force: Allied Strategy and Tactics in the Second World War* (London, 1990), 253–88.

2 *DRZW* 6. 710–39.

3 *DRZW* 6. 962–1063.

4 A. Beevor, *Stalingrad* (London, 1998).

5 *DRZW* 6. 1000.

6 *DRZW* 6. 1022.

7 *DRZW* 6. 298–321 and 347–69.

8 *Fuehrer Conferences on Naval Affairs 1939–1945* (Trowbridge, 1990), 306–8.

9 On Speer's discussions with Goebbels and Goering concerning Ruestungspropaganda, see BAL R3/1737, March 1943, 34.

10 W. Wette and G. R. Ueberschaer (eds.), *Stalingrad* (Frankfurt, 1992), 43–60.

11 Mueller, in *DRZW* 5/2. 649 and Eichholtz, II. 123.

12 Eichholtz, II. 121, 262, and Mueller, in *DRZW* 5/2. 572.

13 BAL R3/1736, February 1942, 15–16.

14 W. A. Boelcke, *Deutschlands Ruestung im Zweiten Weltkrieg: Hitlers Konferenzen mit*

Albert Speer 1942–1945 (Frankfurt, 1969), 179; Mueller, in *DRZW* 5/2. 569–71 and H. J. Weyres, *Die deutsche Ruestungswirtschaft von 1942 bis zum Ende des Kriegs* (Munich, 1975), 78.

15 Eichholtz, II. 12.

16 BAL R3/1737, 3 February 1943, 17.

17 T. Vollmer and R. Kulla, *Panzer aus Kassel: Die Ruestungsproduktionen der Firmen Henschel und Wegmann* (Kassel, 1994), 18–19.

18 Mueller, in *DRZW* 5/2. 572.

19 W. Murray, *Luftwaffe* (London, 1985), 221.

20 PRO FO 1078/142, Ueber die Gruende der erhoehten Lieferungen, 15–22.

21 L. Budrass, *Flugzeugindustrie und Luftruestung in Deutschland* (Duesseldorf, 1998), 866.

22 Remarkably, Speer was still harking back to the triumphs of the tank programme in May 1944, when he challenged the dockyards to outdo the tank industry. See BAL R3/1739, 85.

23 R. Wagenfuehr, *Die deutsche Industrie im Kriege* (Berlin, 1954), 168–9.

24 Weyres, *Ruestungswirtschaft*, 124.

25 Eichholtz, II, 28 May 1943, 365.

26 *DRZW* 6. 513–20.

27 A. W. Cooper, *The Air Battle of the Ruhr: RAF Offensive March to July 1943* (Shrewsbury, 1992).

28 It was not until the Duesseldorf raid in June that the RAF perfected the technique of sequential bombing, using high explosives to remove roofs so as to allow incendiary bombs to penetrate the interior of buildings. R. Neilland, *The Bomber War: Arthur Harris and the Allied Bomber Offensive 1939–1945* (London, 2001), 219.

29 For lack of sustained attention to contemporary evidence from inside the German war economy rather than the post-war accounts, the entire literature to date underestimates the importance of the Ruhr battle. For the first dismissive account see United States Strategic Bombing Survey, *The Effects of Strategic Bombing on the German War Economy* (Washington, 1945), 104–5. In *DRZW* 7. 16–21, Horst Boog speaks casually of a loss of output of 4–6 weeks from the Ruhr, as though this were an insignificant dent to an armaments effort that had previously been expanding at a rate of 7–8 per cent per month. The methodology adopted by the British Bombing Survey in assessing bomb damage seems almost calculated to minimize the impact, see British Bombing Survey Unit, *The Strategic Air War Against Germany 1939–1945* (London, 1998), 88–97.

30 BAL R3/1737, 23 June 1943, 96. This was so alarming to Speer that he immediately attempted to assert his influence over the Luftwaffe's targeting.

31 BAL R3/1737, 18 March 1943, 34.

32 See the vivid account in BAL R3/1738, 11 June 1943, 83–5.

33 Mueller, in *DRZW* 5/2, 357 and Eichholtz, II. 143.

34 Hitler–Speer discussion of 13–15 May 1943. Weyres, *Ruestungswirtschaft*, 144. Eichholtz, II. 233.

35 For the anxieties surrounding the stalling of the ammunition programme, see BAL R3/1738, Chronik, second half 1943, 126.

36 For the direct connection between the Battle of the Ruhr, shortfalls in steel supply and the Zulieferungskrise, see BAL R3/1737, 10 June 1943, meeting at Ruhrstahl, 83; IWM FD 3353/45, vol. 180, 29 July 1943, 44th meeting Zentrale Planung; BAL R3/1738, 15 September 1943, 145.

37 See his speech to Gauleiter in Berlin, 21 June 1943, Mueller, in *DRZW* 5/2. 357.

38 The following is based on the powerful revisionist account by N. Zetterling and A. Frankson, *Kursk 1943: A Statistical Analysis* (London, 2000), which has the endorsement of M. Glantz.

39 Jodl of the OKW instructed propaganda to refer to the German attack as a counter-offensive to disguise the dramatic reduction in the scale of Germany's offensive possibilities.

See E. F. Ziemke, *Stalingrad to Berlin: The German Defeat in the East* (Washington, 1968), 130.

40 For the force ratios, see D. M. Glantz and J. M. House, *When Titans Clashed: How the Red Army Stopped Hitler* (Lawrence, Kan., 1995), 165, and O. Groehler, *Geschichte des Luftkrieges 1910 bis 1980* (East Berlin, 1981), 364.

41 D. M. Glantz and J. M. House, *The Battle of Kursk* (Shepperton, 1999), 227–54.

42 Glantz and House, *When Titans*, 150.

43 G. L. Weinberg, *A World at Arms: A Global History of World War II* (Cambridge, 1994), 593–601.

44 M. Middlebrook, *The Battle of Hamburg: The Firestorm Raid* (Harmondsworth, 1983).

45 *DRZW* 7. 42.

46 M. Middlebrook, *The Berlin Raids: RAF Bomber Command Winter 1943–1944* (Harmondsworth, 1988), 6–9, makes clear the fascination that Berlin exercised on both Churchill and Harris. *DRZW* 7. 75–87.

47 For an oustanding account of the Ruhr's importance, see A. C. Mierzejewski, *The Collapse of the German War Economy, 1944–1945* (Chapel Hill, NC, 1988).

48 Murray, *Luftwaffe*, 235.

49 H. Kehrl, *Krisenmanager im Dritten Reich* (Duesseldorf, 1973), 299–301.

50 L. Herbst, *Der Totale Krieg und die Ordnung der Wirtschaft: Die Kriegswirtschaft im Spannungsfeld von Politik, Ideologie und Propaganda 1939–1945* (Stuttgart, 1982), 232.

51 See the comments on a speech Speer gave on 24 September 1943 to Reichsredner of the party organized by Goebbels in the Kroll opera house, BAL R3/1738, 150.

52 Eichholtz, II. 145.

53 On the mobilization of the party, see *DRZW* 9/1. 160–68.

54 H. James, *The Deutsche Bank and the Nazi Economic War against the Jews* (Cambridge, 2001), 350.

55 D. Schweer and W. Thieme (eds.), *'Der Glaeserne Riese' RWE: Ein Konzern wird transparent* (Essen, 1998), 139–40.

56 IWM FD 3353/45, vol. 180, 44th meeting Zentrale Planung, 29 July 1943.

57 *DRZW* 7. 230–33.

58 *DRZW* 7. 40.

59 Mueller, in *DRZW* 5/2. 331–51.

60 Kehrl, *Krisenmanager*, 297.

61 Mueller, *Kehrl*, 98–101.

62 BAL R3/1737, 27 July 1943, 113–14.

63 Kehrl, *Krisenmanager*, 310.

64 Eichholtz, II. 173.

65 Mueller, in *DRZW* 5/2. 340.

66 Eichholtz, II. 174 and Mueller, in *DRZW* 5/2. 341.

67 English translation of the full text of the speech in NA T73 192.

68 Eichholtz II. 175.

69 G. Sereny, *Albert Speer: His Battle with Truth* (London, 1995), 388–401.

70 For the following, see B. F. Smith and A. F. Peterson, *Heinrich Himmler Geheimreden 1933 bis 1945 und andere Ansprachen* (Frankfurt, 1974), 169–70.

71 Budrass, *Flugzeugindustrie*, 784. Nor can there be any doubt that Heinkel was talking about the Holocaust itself. The word he used was 'Ausrottung' and the factory he was referring to was located in the Lublin, Cracow and Lemberg triangle, at the very epicentre of the Judaeocide.

72 W. Abelhauser, in L. Gall (ed.), *Krupp im 20. Jahrhundert* (Berlin, 2002), 413.

73 Sereny, *Albert Speer*, 420–21, and Chapter 19 below.

74 For the increased role of the party in the armaments effort, see *DRZW* 9/1. 168–76.

75 K. H. Ludwig, *Technik und Ingenieure im Dritten Reich* (Duesseldorf, 1974), 444–51.

76 Boelcke, *Deutschlands Ruestung*, 292.

77 R. J. Overy. *The Air War 1939–1945* (London 1980), 2–4, 209–11.

78 Following R. Schabel, *Die Illusion der Wunderwaffen: Duesenflugzeuge und Flug-abwehrraketen in der Ruestungspolitik des Dritten Reiches* (Munich, 1994).

79 W. J. Spielberger, *Panther and its Variants* (Hereford, 1993).

80 E. Roessler, *U-Boottyp XXI* (Bonn, 6th edn., 2002) and A. Meyhoff, *Blohm & Voss im 'Dritten Reich'* (Hamburg, 2001), 327–491, G. Schulze-Wegener, *Die deutsche Kriegs-marine-Ruestung 1942–1945* (Hamburg, 1997), 129–46.

81 E. Roessler, *Geschichte des deutschen U-Bootsbaus* (Augsburg, 1996), 213–21.

82 Mueller, in *DRZW* 5/2. 373.

83 Meyhoff, *Blohm & Voss*, 409.

84 Speer's eye may have been caught by a report in *Time Magazine* in July 1943, which credited Californian Shipbuilding Corporation in Los Angeles with the staggering output of 19 ships in April and 20 in June. See 'Every 36 Hours', *Time*, 42 (12 July 1943), 2.

85 See the jubilant tone of the Ministerial chronicle in reporting his early clashes with the 'traditional' ship-builders, BAL R3/1737, 24 July 1943, 112.

86 Meyhoff, *Blohm & Voss*, 405–14.

87 G. Neliba, *MAN Werk Gustavsburg bei Mainz: 100 Jahre zivile und militaerische Produktion (1860–1960)* (Frankfurt, 2002), 3–110.

88 The template for this storyline was provided by the earlier efforts of Gerhard Degenkolb, another of Speer's poster boys, to reorganize locomotive production. See the critical discussion in A. B. Gottwaldt, *Deutsche Kriegslokomotiven 1939–1945* (Stuttgart, 1973) and A. B. Gottwaldt, *Deutsche Eisenbahnen im Zweiten Weltkrieg* (Stuttgart, 1985).

89 BAL R3/1739, 12 May 1944, 85–7, and Mueller, in *DRZW* 5/2. 610.

90 Mueller, in *DRZW* 5/2. 551 and Eichholtz, III. 56.

91 For unanimously sceptical views, see Meyhoff, *Blohm & Voss*, 462–78, Schulze-Wegener, *Kriegsmarine-Ruestung*, 147, Roessler, *U-Boottyp XXI*, 50–55.

92 As Speer admitted to Saur, he was not unaware of the practical problems of the pro-gramme but blamed them on the resistance of the dockyards and his own failure to give Merker enough backing. Mueller, in *DRZW* 5/2. 376.

93 The Speer Chronik in early 1944 celebrated the 'iron determination' with which Merker faced all obstacles. BAL R3/1739, 8.

94 Meyhoff, *Blohm & Voss*, 475.

95 The deliberate nature of this campaign of intimidation is clear from BAL R3/1739, 28 June 1944, 133–5. For Speer's personal involvement, see Mueller, in *DRZW* 5/2. 376. And the symbolism was further driven home by Speers conferral on Merker of the coveted Ritterkreuz zum Kriegsverdienstkreuz in August 1944. See BAL R3/1740, 207.

96 Abelshauser, in Gall (ed.), *Krupp*, 349–53.

97 As in the case of W. Abelshauser, 'Modernisierung oder institutionelle Revolution', in Abelshauser, J.-O. Hesse and W. Plumpe (eds.), *Wirtschaftsordnung Staat und Unter-nehmen: Neue Forschungen zur Wirtschaftsgeschichte des Nationalsozialismus* (Essen, 2003), which appears to derive a general characterization of the Speer system from Krupp's experience after 1943.

98 Boelcke, *Deutschlands Ruestung*, 137.

99 M. J. Neufeld, *The Rocket and the Reich: Peenemuende and the Coming of the Ballistic Missile Era* (Cambridge, Mass., 1995), 169–75, 190–95.

100 For a brilliant critical dissection, see Schabel, *Die Illusion*, 28–31.

101 Boelcke, *Deutschlands Ruestung*, 23 June 1943, 138.

102 Schabel, *Die Illusion*, 117–19.

103 On the 209 and 309, see H. J. Ebert, J. B. Kaiser and K. Peters, *Willy Messerschmitt* (Bonn, 1992), 137–50.

104 Budrass, *Flugzeugindustrie*, 858–67 and Boelcke, *Deutschlands Ruestung*, 294–5.

105 Specifically, the all important rotor blades in the Junkers jet engine were manufactured out of a new Krupp alloy known as Tinidur, which though it economized on nickel was so brittle that the rotors had a lifespan of only 25–30 hours. Schabel, *Die Illusion*, 234. For similar problems with other Luftwaffe engines, see H.-J. Braun, 'Krieg der Ingenieure?',

in B. Thoss and H.-E. Volkmann (eds.), *Erster Weltkrieg: Zweiter Weltkrieg* (Paderborn, 2002), 208–9.

106 F. Freund, *Arbeitslager Zement: Das Konzentrationslager Ebensee und die Racketenrue-stung* (Vienna, 1989), 37–9.

107 M. Bornemann, *Geheimprojekt Mittelbau: Die Geschichte der deutschen V-Waffen-Werke* (Munich, 1971), 53. The standard price per unit, once production reached 5,000 units, was to be 50,000 Reichsmarks per rocket.

108 J. C. Wagner, 'Das Aussenlagersystem des KL Mittelbau-Dora', in U. Herbert, K. Orth and C. Dieckmann (eds.), *Die nationalsozialistischen Konzentrationslager* (Frankfurt, 2002), II. 707–29.

109 Messerschmitt became active in this respect as early as October 1942. Budrass, *Flugzeug-industrie*, 798.

110 Schabel, *Die Illusion*, 183, and H. Moennich, *The BMW Story: A Company in its Time* (London, 1991), 282–3.

111 Eichholtz, III. 74.

112 A. Speer, *The Slave State* (London, 1981).

113 Neufeld, *Rocket*, 197–213, and T. Allen, *The Business of Genocide* (Chapel Hill, NC, 2002), 208–31.

114 Sereny, *Albert Speer*, 403–7 and A. Speer, *Inside the Third Reich* (London, 1970), 499–501.

115 J.-C. Wagner, 'Noch einmal: Arbeit und Vernichtung', in N. Frei, S. Steinbacher and B. C. Wagner (eds.), *Ausbeutung, Vernichtung, Oeffentlichkeit* (Munich, 2000).

116 Even the Chronik acknowledges that Speer was informed in January 1944 about the terrible health conditions, and in the light of their impact on performance he agreed to increase medical provision. BAL R3/1739, 13 January 1944, 8.

117 Bornemann, *Geheimprojekt*, 65–7, states that, of 17,500 prisoners provided to the Mittelbau up to April 1944, 2,937 had died by the end of March 1944, and a further 2,000 had been removed as too ill to work. At the end of 1943 Kammler's work squads had the highest death rate in the entire concentration camp system. See E. Schulte, *Zwangs-arbeit und Vernichtung: Das Wirtschaftsimperium der SS* (Paderborn, 2001), 407.

118 BAL R3/1738, 10 December 1943, 205.

119 Eichholtz, III. 75 and Freund, *Zement*, 57.

120 Bornemann, *Geheimprojekt*, 103–10.

121 It seems odd in the light of these figures that Neufeld, *Rocket*, 174, describes Degenkolb's proposal in early 1943 to reach production of 600 rockets per month by September 1944 as 'absurd' and as evidence for the fact that Degenkolb 'failed to understand that a missile was much more complex than a locomotive'. Nor is it, in fact, obvious why a mass-produced ballistic missile is a more complex technological artefact than a mass-produced locomotive. Relative prices suggest rather the opposite: the standard price for a V2 was 50,000 Reichs-marks as opposed to a minimum of 100,000 Reichsmarks for a stripped-down Series 52 Kriegslok. Nor was there any significant difference in terms of construction times – 12,000–17,000 hours were required for a locomotive, 12,950 hours for a V2 rocket. See Gottwaldt, *Kriegslokomotiven*, 38 and 66, and Bornemann, *Geheimprojekt*, 114.

122 Massive 'American' scale was a hallmark of the entire underground factory programme. See Saur's final report to Hitler in the summer of 1944, Mueller, in *DRZW* 5/2, 361.

19 Disintegration

1 For Hitler's determination to hold the Donetz region, see W. A. Boelcke, *Deutschlands Ruestung im Zweiten Weltkrieg: Hitlers Konferenzen mit Albert Speer 1942–1945* (Frank-furt, 1969), 288 and Manstein's account in E. von Manstein, *Lost Victories* (Chicago, 1958), 450–512.

2 J. Ellis, *Brute Force: Allied Strategy and Tactics in the Second World War* (London, 1990), 306–42.

3 M. Middlebrook, *The Berlin Raids: RAF Bomber Command Winter 1943–1944* (Harmondsworth, 1988).

4 BAL R3/1738, 190–92. Speer could not resist even this opportunity for grandstanding at the expense of the military. Shunting aside the procurement officers, he took personal charge of the rescue effort. Echoing Goebbels's notorious headline 'the march is easier without baggage', Speer even expressed relief that so much burdensome paperwork had been destroyed. Hans Kehrl, who had a more realistic appreciation of what went into running the war economy, was incensed. See H. Kehrl, *Krisenmanager im Dritten Reich* (Duesseldorf, 1973), 326–30.

5 *DRZW* 7. 75–87 and 272–81.

6 Mueller, in *DRZW* 5/2. 379.

7 IMT XXXVII, doc. 1 172, 662.

8 E. F. Ziemke, *Stalingrad to Berlin: The German Defeat in the East* (Washington, 1968), 218–47.

9 Ibid., 272–95.

10 W. Murray, *Luftwaffe* (London, 1985), 319–20 and *DRZW* 7. 87–111, 261–72.

11 Judged against the Allied standard of 5 kills, no less than 5,000 Luftwaffe pilots qualified as aces. As compared to the leading Allied score of 65 kills, compiled by the Russian Ivan Kohzedub, there were 82 German pilots with 100 or more victories and 7 men with more than 200 kills, including Eric Hartmann with a staggering 352. see J. Scutts, *Messerschmitt Bf 109: The Operational Record* (Shrewsbury, 1999), 132. For the other end of the spectrum, see Murray, *Luftwaffe*, 338.

12 As the Speer Chronik noted, the Jaegerstab until Speer's return on 26 May 1944 was based 'too heavily' on the Air Ministry. See BAL R3/1739, 26 May 1944, 93.

13 An obvious but too often overlooked fact, duly noted by Boelcke in his introduction to *Deutschlands Ruestung*, 12.

14 See the highly favourable comments on Saur as a potential source in PRO FO 935/161, Saur FD 3250/45, USSBS team 86 Record. Abelshauser too notes the horrible irony of Saur's appearance at the post-war industrialists' trials, not as a defendant charged with crimes against humanity, but as a witness for the prosecution. See W. Abelshauser, in L. Gall (ed.), *Krupp im 20. Jahrhundert* (Berlin, 2002), 470.

15 T. Allen, *The Business of Genocide* (Chapel Hill, NC, 2002), 232–9.

16 For an account of the train which provided a conference centre and accommodation for 60–80 men, see BAL R3/1740, August 1944, 205.

17 P. Schmoll, *Die Messerschmittwerke im Zweiten Weltkrieg* (Regensburg, 1998), 144.

18 Milch Case, II. 527, NOKW-017 54.

19 Eichholtz, III. 23.

20 After an outbreak of indiscipline in the Erla Messerschmitt factory, in the spring of 1944, Kammler recommended to the Jaegerstab the practice of hanging 20 or 30 choice troublemakers. 'Since they were strung up, everything has got back to normal.' O. Groehler, *Geschichte des Luftkrieges 1910 bis 1980* (East Berlin, 1981), 415. The German clearly implies that they were left hanging as an example to their colleagues.

21 IMT, *Nazi Conspiracy and Aggression* (Washington, 1946–7), IV, 1584–III*-PS, 118–24.

22 Schmoll, *Messerschmittwerke*, 7, 186–7. Conversely, the Luftwaffe was by far the largest employer of Flossenburg labour, accounting for 50 per cent of the 34,000 slaves it provided to the war effort. The next largest employers were the ammunition producers with 17.5 per cent; 12 per cent of the inmate-labour worked on tanks. See K. Orth, *Das System der nationalsozialistischen Konzentrationslager* (Hamburg, 1999), 239.

23 On Flossenbuerg and Mauthausen's labour contracting, see H. Brenner, 'Der Arbeitseinsatz der KZ-Haeftlinge in den Aussenlagern des KZ-Flossenburg', and B. Perz, 'Der Arbeitseinsatz im KZ-Mauthausen', in U. Herbert, K. Orth and C. Dieckmann (eds.), *Die nationalsozialistischen Konzentrationslager* (Frankfurt, 2002), II. 682–706 and 533–57.

24 C. Gerlach and G. Aly, *Das letzte Kapitel: Der Mord an den ungarischen Juden* (Stuttgart, 2002), 163–71.

25 Eichholtz, III. 239.

26 Orth gives the somewhat different figures of 458,000 deportations to Auschwitz from Hungary and 350,000 gassings. See Orth, *Das System*, 256–7.

27 Milch Case, II. 555. Jaegerstab conference, 26 May 1944, NOKW-336.

28 Milch Case II. 557–8, Jaegerstab conference, 27 June 1944, NOKW-359. This same group is also referred to in the Speer Chronik though they are not identified as Jews, see BAL R3/1739, June 1944, 137.

29 PRO FO 935/161, Saur, FD 3250/45, minutes of interview with Herr Saur, 7 June 1945, 26.

30 PRO FO 1078/142, Ueber die Gruende der erhoehten Lieferungen.

31 PRO FO 935/161, Saur, FD 3250/45, USSBS team 86 R, 4.

32 In October 1943 Milch even boasted that German production in 1944 would soon overtake that of the United States. See *DRZW* 7. 237.

33 The same conclusion is reached by L. Budrass, *Flugzeugindustrie und Luftruestung in Deutschland* (Duesseldorf, 1998), 867–8.

34 See the carping remarks in BAL R3/1738, 128–9, 136, 145, 186. For Speer's celebration of Werner only a year earlier, see R3/1736, 7 August 1942, 61, and for his insistence on Werner's authority over Maybach, see R3/1737, 3 March 1943, 30–31, and 18 April 1943, 46.

35 See remarks to press conference in NA T73 192.

36 See BAL R3/1738, 2 December 1943, 201.

37 Mueller, in *DRZW* 5/2. 550 and Eichholtz, III. 44.

38 L. Herbst, *Der Totale Krieg und die Ordnung der Wirtschaft: Die Kriegswirtschaft im Spannungsfeld von Politik, Ideologie und Propaganda 1939–1945* (Stuttgart, 1982), 339, 436–7; Eichholtz, III. 43. The Speer Chronik is full of critical comments on Kehrl's overly bureaucratic tendencies. See in particular BAL R3/1738, 17 December 1943, 207.

39 Already in January Speer had discussed with the Gestapo-SD the measures necessary to protect his collaborators against unwarranted criticism. See BAL R3/1739, 14. He also enforced an agreement between Kehrl on the one hand, and Hayler and Ohlendorf, the SS men who now controlled the Ministry of Economic Affairs, on the need for a 'positive attitude towards the system of Selbstverantwortung'. BAL R3/1739, 20.

40 Herbst, *Totale Krieg*, 334. Eichholtz, III. 47–8. Mueller, in *DRZW* 5/2. 351–2. NA T73 192, 448 FD 3353/45, 90.

41 BAL R3/1739, 23 June 1944, 130.

42 Herbst, *Totale Krieg*, 334.

43 Eichholtz, III. 48.

44 H. Kehrl, *Krisenmanager im Dritten Reich* (Duesseldorf, 1973), 395–7.

45 Eichholtz, III. 48.

46 *DRZW* 7. 536–56.

47 Murray, *Luftwaffe*, 374.

48 For Hitler's preoccupation with the Eastern Front at this juncture, see H. Heiber (ed.), *Hitlers Lagebesprechungen: Die Protokollfragmente seiner militaerischen Konferenzen 1942–1945* (Stuttgart, 1962), 583–621. See also the remarks on behalf of the Speer Ministry on the extreme seriousness of the situation, BAL R3/1740, 9 July 1944, 156–7.

49 Ziemke, *Stalingrad to Berlin*, 313–32; J. Erickson, *The Road to Berlin* (London, 1983), 215–46; D. M. Glantz and J. M. House, *When Titans Clashed: How the Red Army Stopped Hitler* (Lawrence, Kan., 1995), 195–215.

50 W. Murray and A. R. Millett, *A War to be Won: Fighting the Second World War* (Cambridge, Mass., 2000), 450. For details, see D. M. Glantz and H. S. Orenstein (eds.), *Belorussia 1944: The Soviet General Staff Study* (London, 2001). According to one estimate, the Soviet Union received 125,000 American-made trucks in 1944 and 150,000 after January 1945. A typical Soviet Howitzer regiment in the spring of 1944 relied for its mobility on 7 Soviet 1.5-ton trucks, 35 American-made 2.5-ton vehicles and a jeep. See W. S. Dunn, *Soviet Blitzkrieg* (London, 2000), 76–7.

51 Glantz and House, *When Titans*, 214.

52 Eichholtz, III. 37, and Murray, *Luftwaffe*, 367.

53 Eichholtz, III. 33.

54 G. Janssen, *Das Ministerium Speer: Deutschlands Ruestung im Krieg* (Frankfurt, 1968), 265–82.

55 Eichholtz III. 112.

56 Eichholtz, III. 50.

57 Mueller, in *DRZW*, 2. 346–7, 570, W. Naasner, *Neue Machtzentren in der deutschen Kriegswirtschaft 1942–1945* (Boppard, 1994), 77–8.

58 Compare A. Speer, *Inside the Third Reich* (London, 1970), 507–31, with the contemporaneous account of Speer's activities in BAL R3/1740, 20–21 July 1944, 168–9.

59 Eichholtz, III. 53.

60 Mueller, in *DRZW* 5/2. 402–3.

61 Ibid., 402. The Speer Chronik notes the wave of enthusiasm that swept the war administration in the aftermath of the bomb plot. See BAL R3/1740, 27 July 1944, 171. By September 1944 Speer resorted to issuing special green ties to those colleagues who demonstrated particularly robust optimism. See BAL R3/1740, 19 September 1944, 258.

62 Mueller, in *DRZW* 5/2. 551.

63 See the fascinating discussion of the seriously inaccurate contemporary estimates in Eichholtz, III. 95–113. The following is based instead on M. Harrison (ed.), *The Economics of World War II* (Cambridge, 1998), 10–17.

64 Aircraft was the one area in which Japanese production made a really significant difference to the balance, with Japanese production running at 21,000 aircraft in 1944. However, the figures given here understate the Axis disadvantage since they record numbers of aircraft rather than airframe weight or the value of planes produced. British and American production included large numbers of extremely expensive heavy bombers, for which neither Japan nor Germany had any counterpart.

65 *Statistisches Handbuch von Deutschland* (Munich, 1949), 292.

66 Kehrl, *Krisenmanager*, 316–18. Mueller, in *DRZW* 5/2. 365–9.

67 Eichholtz, II. 508.

68 These figures clearly include equipment other than armaments. *DRZW* 5/2. 187.

69 R. G. D. Allen, 'Mutual Assistance between the US and the British Empire, 1941–1945', *Journal of the Royal Statistical Society* (1946), 243–77, and Special Combined Committee of Combined Production and Resources Board, *The Impact of the War on Civilian Consumption in the United Kingdom, the United States and Canada* (London 1945), 8–9.

70 Assuming that their average productivity was 70 per cent of their German colleagues and assuming that labour's share in overall output (as opposed to the share attributable to German capital) was 70 per cent, foreign labour's contribution to German armaments output can be estimated roughly at 15 per cent.

71 Two drafts are in IWM FD 3038/49, Sc. 395, 145–53 and 154–8 respectively. The quotes come from the second document. See also Herbst, *Totale Krieg*, 420–21.

72 On the global experience with inflation during World War II, see A. J. Brown, *Great Inflation, 1939–1951* (London, 1955), and A. S. Milward, *War, Economy and Society 1939–1945* (Harmondsworth, 1977), 105–9.

73 W. A. Boelcke, *Die Kosten von Hitlers Krieg: Kriegsfinanzierung und finanzielles Kriegserbe in Deutschland 1933–1948* (Paderborn, 1985), 112.

74 The following is from BAL R 2501 6452, Reichsbank report, 31 August 1942. On the Greek economy under occupation, see G. Etmektsoglou, 'Changes in the Civilian Economy as a Factor in the Radicalization of Popular Opposition in Greece, 1941–1944', in R. J. Overy, G. Otto and J. Houwink ten Cate, *Die 'Neuordnung' Europas: NS-Wirtschaftspolitik in den besetzten Gebieten* (Berlin, 1997), 193–240, and M. Mazower, *Inside Hitler's Greece* (New Haven, 1993), 53–72.

75 A. S. Milward, *The New Order and the French Economy* (Oxford, 1984), 136–7 and

273. Clearly, these demands for food, consumer goods, industrial supplies and construction services went far beyond the armaments deliveries discussed above.

76 Data from *Statistisches Handbuch von Deutschland*, 555, and similar results in Boelcke, *Kosten*, 83–114.

77 W. A., Boelcke, *Die deutsche Wirtschaft 1930–1945* (Duesseldorf, 1982), 344.

78 M. Harrison, 'Resource Mobilization for World War II', *Economic History Review* (1988), 184.

79 M. Brackmann, *Vom Totalen Krieg zum Wirtschaftswunder: Die Vorgeschichte der westdeutschen Waehrungsreform 1948* (Essen, 1993), 69–74.

80 G. Aly, *Hitlers Volksstaat* (Frankfurt, 2005), 334–9.

81 Boelcke, *Kosten*, 106–7.

82 Eichholtz, III. 567–71.

83 On Kehrl's frustration at his inability to control investment, see Herbst, *Totale Krieg*, 405.

84 IWM FD 3038/49, Sc. 395, 145–53 and 154–8.

85 Brackmann, *Vom Totalen Krieg*, 71. M. L. Recker, *Nationalsozialistische Sozialpolitik im Zweiten Weltkrieg* (Munich, 1989), 217–33.

86 Ibid., 47.

87 Herbst, *Totale Krieg*, 419.

88 This is one of the serious misreadings that undermine the central thesis of Aly, *Hitlers Volksstaat*.

89 Mueller, in *DRZW* 5/2, 432.

90 Eichholtz, III. 54–5.

91 For an excellent account, see A. C. Mierzejewski, *The Collapse of the German War Economy, 1944–1945* (Chapel Hill, NC, 1988).

92 British Bombing Survey Unit, *The Strategic Air War Against Germany 1939–1945* (London, 1998), 41.

93 *DRZW* 9/1. 443–57.

94 Abelshauser, in Gall (ed.), *Krupp*, 437.

95 Mierzejewski, *The Collapse*, 103–76.

96 Eichholtz, III. 65.

97 J. F. Trent, 'Food Shortages in Germany and Europe 1945–1948', in G. Bischof and S. E. Ambrose (eds.) *Eisenhower and the German POWs* (Baton Rouge, La., 1992), 104.

98 *DRZW* 7. 619–34.

99 Ellis, *Brute Force*, 421.

100 Murray and Millett, *War to be Won*, 470.

101 See Heiber (ed.), *Hitlers Lagebesprechungen*, 724–80.

102 All quotes in what follows from H. Schwendemann, 'Lebenslaeufer ueber verbrannte Erde', *Frankfurter Allgemeine Zeitung*, 26 April 2000, and H. Schwendemann, 'Drastic Measures to Defend the Reich at the Oder and the Rhine . . . A Forgotten Memorandum of Albert Speer of 18 March 1945', *Journal of Contemporary History*, 38 (2003), 597–614. The English translation of the document in this article paints Speer in an even worse light than the German original reproduced in the *FAZ*.

103 For the following, see R. Overmans, *Deutsche militaerische Verluste im Zweiten Weltkrieg* (Munich, 1999).

104 The central flaw of Joerg Friedrich's otherwise powerful book, *Der Brand: Deutschland im Bombenkrieg 1940–1945* (Munich, 2002).

105 For what follows, Eichholtz, III. 663–9.

106 Kehrl, *Krisenmanager*, 419–34.

107 For one copy of Wagenfuehr's report, see IWM FD 3057/49, FIAT Report 1312, later published as *Die deutsche Industrie im Kriege* (Berlin, 1954).

20 The End

1 *Hitlers politisches Testament* (Hamburg, 1981), 103.
2 A useful summary is provided by H.-U. Wehler, *Deutsche Gesellschaftsgeschichte* (Munich, 2nd edn., 2003), IV. 941–54.
3 M. R. Marrus, *Unwanted: European Refugees in the Twentieth Century* (New York, 1985), 324.
4 G. W. Harmsson, *Reparation, Sozialprodukt, Lebensstandard: Versuch einer Wirtschafts-bilanz* (Bremen, 1948), 57.
5 J. E. Smith (ed.), *The Papers of General Lucius D. Clay* (Bloomington, Ind., 1974), I. 24.
6 Ibid., I. 41.
7 G. Bischof and S. E. Ambrose (eds.), *Eisenhower and the German POWs* (Baton Rouge, La., 1992), 17.
8 R. Karlsch, *Allein bezahlt? Die Reparationsleistungen der SBZ/DDR 1945–1953* (Berlin, 1993), 234.
9 J. Wright, *Gustav Stresemann*, Oxford, 2002, 515.

Index

Credits

Chart 1   *Statistisches Jahrbuch f.d. Deutsche Reich*, various editions.

Chart 2   IfK, *Konjunkturstatistisches Handbuch 1936* (Berlin, 1935), 135.

Chart 3   IfK, *Konjunkturstatistisches Handbuch 1936* (Berlin, 1935), 91, 93.

Chart 4   *Statistisches Jahrbuch f.d. Deutsche Reich*, various editions.

Chart 5   IfK, *Konjunkturstatistisches Handbuch 1936* (Berlin, 1935), 52–59.

Chart 6   M. Spoerer, *Von Scheingewinn zum Ruestungsboom* (Stuttgart, 1996), 147.

Chart 7   Ritschl & Spoerer, 'Das Bruttosozialprodukt', *JBW* (1997/2), 27–54.

Chart 8   *Statistisches Jahrbuch f.d. Deutsche Reich*, various editions and *Statistisches Handbuch von Deutschland*.

Chart 9   BAL R 3102 3154.

Chart 10   BAMA RL3/2617, IWM EDS 71.

Chart 11   IWM Eds Mi. 14/521, Box 71.